Lecture Notes in Computer Science 10593

Commenced Publication in 1973
Founding and Former Series Editors:
Gerhard Goos, Juris Hartmanis, and Jan van Leeuwen

More information about this series at http://www.springer.com/series/7407

Lecture Notes in Computer Science   10593

Commenced Publication in 1973
Founding and Former Series Editors:
Gerhard Goos, Juris Hartmanis, and Jan van Leeuwen

More information about this series at http://www.springer.com/series/7407

Yuhui Shi · Kay Chen Tan
Mengjie Zhang · Ke Tang
Xiaodong Li · Qingfu Zhang
Ying Tan · Martin Middendorf
Yaochu Jin (Eds.)

Simulated Evolution and Learning

11th International Conference, SEAL 2017
Shenzhen, China, November 10–13, 2017
Proceedings

 Springer

Editors

Yuhui Shi
Southern University of Science
  and Technology
Shenzhen
China

Kay Chen Tan
City University of Hong Kong
Hong Kong, Kowloon
Hong Kong

Mengjie Zhang
Victoria University of Wellington
Wellington, Wellington
New Zealand

Ke Tang
Southern University of Science
  and Technology
Shenzhen
China

Xiaodong Li
RMIT University
Melbourne, VIC
Australia

Qingfu Zhang
City University of Hong Kong
Kowloon Tong
Hong Kong

Ying Tan
Peking University
Beijing
China

Martin Middendorf
University of Leipzig
Leipzig
Germany

Yaochu Jin
University of Surrey
Guildford, Surrey
UK

ISSN 0302-9743   ISSN 1611-3349 (electronic)
Lecture Notes in Computer Science
ISBN 978-3-319-68758-2   ISBN 978-3-319-68759-9 (eBook)
https://doi.org/10.1007/978-3-319-68759-9

Library of Congress Control Number: 2017956129

LNCS Sublibrary: SL1 – Theoretical Computer Science and General Issues

Printed on acid-free paper

This Springer imprint is published by Springer Nature
The registered company is Springer International Publishing AG
The registered company address is: Gewerbestrasse 11, 6330 Cham, Switzerland

Preface

This LNCS volume contains papers presented at SEAL 2017, the 11th International Conference on Simulated Evolution and Learning, held during November 10–13, 2017, in Shenzhen, China. SEAL is a prestigious international conference series in evolutionary computation and learning. This biennial event was first held in Seoul, Korea, in 1996, and then in Canberra, Australia (1998), Nagoya, Japan (2000), Singapore (2002), Busan, Korea (2004), Hefei, China (2006), Melbourne, Australia (2008), Kanpur, India (2010), Hanoi, Vietnam (2012), and Dunedin, New Zealand (2014). The Steering Committee decided to change the conference year from even to old years from 2017 to avoid clashing with WCCI.

We received 145 paper submissions from nearly 30 countries. After a rigorous peer-review process involving at least three reviewers for each paper, the best 40 papers were selected to be presented at the conference as oral presentations (acceptance rate of 27.6%) and an additional 45 papers as poster presentations.

The papers included in this volume cover a wide range of topics in simulated evolution and learning. The accepted papers have been classified into the following main categories: (a) evolutionary optimization, (b) evolutionary multi-objective optimization, (c) evolutionary machine learning, (d) theoretical developments, (e) feature reduction and dimensionality reduction, (f) dynamic and uncertain environments, (g) real-world applications, (h) adaptive systems, and (i) swarm intelligence.

The conference featured seven distinguished keynote speakers: Professors Kenneth De Jong, Sanaz Mostaghim, Yew Soon Ong, Philip C.L. Chen, Jun Wang, Hisao Ishibuchi, and Yiu-ming Cheung. The seven keynotes covered the state-of-the-art research topics in simulated evolution and learning such as co-evolution, multi-objective and many-objective optimiztaion, neuro-evolution, broad and deep learning, transfer learning, and multitask optimization. In addition, SEAL 2017 also featured an Editor-in-Chief Forum, including the current and past Editor-in-Chiefs of the prestigious journals such as *IEEE Transactions on Evolutionary Computation* (Prof. Xin Yao and Prof. Kay Chen Tan); *IEEE Transactions on Cybernetics* (Prof. Jun Wang); *IEEE Transactions on Systems, Man, and Cybernetics: Systems* (Prof. Philip C.L. Chen); *IEEE Transactions on Emergent Topics in Computational Intelligence* (Prof. Yew Soon Ong); and *IEEE Computational Intelligence Magazine* (Prof. Hisao Ishibuchi). We were very fortunate to have such internationally renowned research leaders giving talks at SEAL 2017, given their busy schedules. Their presence at the conference was yet another indicator of the importance of the SEAL conference series on the international research map.

SEAL 2017 also included the opening of the Shenzhen Key Lab for Computational Intelligence, with a number of distinguished professors including fellows (academicians) from the Chinese Academy of Sciences. The first SUSTech-VUW Joint Workshop on Evolutionary Optimization and Learning was also held at the conference, with the key people in this field from Southern University of Science and Technology

(SUSTech) and Victoria University of Wellington (VUW). SEAL 2017 also included five tutorials delivered by Prof. Kenneth De Jong, Prof. Xiaodong Li, Prof. Mengjie Zhang, Prof. Jing Liu, and Prof. Mustafa Misir, which were free to all conference participants. These five tutorials covered some of the hottest topics in evolutionary computation and learning and their applications such as unified evolutionary computation, evolutionary large-scale global optimization, genetic programming and evolutionary deep learning, evolutionary complex and social networks, and online–offline algorithm selection. They provided an excellent start to the four-day conference.

The success of a conference depends on its authors, reviewers, participants, and Organizing Committees. SEAL 2017 was no exception. We are very grateful to all the authors for their paper submissions and to all the reviewers for their outstanding effort in refereeing the papers within a tight schedule. We relied heavily upon a team of volunteers to keep SEAL 2017 running smoothly and efficiently. They were the true heroes working behind the scene. We are most grateful to all the student volunteers for their great efforts and contributions.

We would also like to thank our sponsors for providing all the support to SEAL 2017, including the Department of Computer Science and Engineering, Southern University of Science and Technology (China), School of Engineering and Computer Science and Evolutionary Computation Research Group, Victoria University of Wellington (New Zealand), City University of Hong Kong (China), RMIT University (Australia), Springer, and EasyChair. Particular thanks should go to Southern University of Science and Technology (China), who provided significant financial support to the conference.

November 2017   Yuhui Shi
                                                                                                        Kay Chen Tan
                                                                                                        Mengjie Zhang
                                                                                                                Ke Tang
                                                                                                        Xiaodong Li

Organization

The 11th International Conference on Simulated Evolution and Learning (SEAL 2017) was organised and hosted by Southern University of Science and Technology, Shenzhen, China.

SEAL 2017 Conference Committee

Honorary Chairs

Russell C. Eberhart, USA
Xin Yao, China

General Chairs

Yuhui Shi, China
Kay Chen Tan, Hong Kong

Programme Chairs

Mengjie Zhang, New Zealand
Ke Tang, China

Technical Co-chairs

Xiaodong Li, Australia
Qingfu Zhang, Hong Kong
Ying Tan, China
Martin Middendorf, Germany
Yaochu Jin, UK

Advisory Committee Chairs

Hussein Abbass, Australia
Kalyanmoy Deb, USA
Zbigniew Michalewicz, Australia
Lipo Wang, Singapore
Carlos A. Coello Coello, Mexico
Hisao Ishibuchi, Japan and China
Jong-Hwan Kim, South Korea

Local Organizing Chairs

Zexuan Zhu, China
Guangming Lin, China
Xuefeng Zhang, China

Special Sessions Chairs

Ben Niu, China
Cara MacNish, Australia

Tutorial Chairs

Han Huang, China
Frank Neumann, Australia

Publicity Chairs

Yew-Soon Ong, Singapore
Lam Thu Bui, Vietnam
Carmelo Bastos Filho, Brazil
Shi Cheng, China
Vasile Palade, UK
Bing Xue, New Zealand
Hemant Singh, Australia
Hisashi Handa, Japan
Sung-Bae Cho, South Korea
Bob Reynolds, USA

SEAL 2017 Keynotes

Co-evolutionary Algorithms: Theory and Practice
Kenneth De Jong
Multi-Objective Optimiztaion and Decision Making in Dynamic Environments
Sanaz Mostaghim
Why Restrict to One Task or Problem? From Transfer to Multitask Optimization
Yew Soon Ong
Evolutionary Many-Objective Optimization and Performance Evaluation
Hisao Ishibuchi
Neurodynamic Approaches to Distributed, Global, and Multi-objective Optimization
Jun Wang
Broad Learning System: An Effective and Efficient Incremental Learning System Without the Need for Deep Architecture
C.L. Philip Chen
On Learning from Imbalanced Data for Classification
Yiu-ming Cheung

SEAL 2017 Tutorials

Evolutionary Computation: A Unified Approach
Kenneth De Jong
Evolutionary Large-Scale Global Optimization: An Introduction
Xiaodong Li
Genetic Programming: Recent Developments and Applications
Mengjie Zhang
Evolutionary Computation and Complex Networks
Jing Liu
Algorithm Selection Online + Offline Techniques
Mustafa Misir

Sponsoring Institutions

Department of Computer Science and Engineering, Southern University of Science and Technology, China
School of Engineering and Computer Science and Evolutionary Computation Research Group, Victoria University of Wellington, New Zealand
Department of Computer Science, City University of Hong Kong, Hong Kong
Evolutionary Computation and Machine Learning Group (ECML), School of Science (Computer Science and Software Engineering), RMIT University, Australia

Acknowledgements

We would like to thank particularly Southern University of Science and Technology, China for their financial support.

Program Committee

Hussein Abbass	UNSW-Canberra, Australia
Nadia Abd-Alsabour	Cairo University, Egypt
Hernán Aguirre	Shinshu University, Japan
Youhei Akimoto	Shinshu University, Japan
Harith Al-Sahaf	Victoria University of Wellington, New Zealand
Luigi Barone	University of Western Australia, Australia
Urvesh Bhowan	IBM Ireland, Ireland
Will Browne	Victoria University of Wellington, New Zealand
Lam Thu Bui	Le Quy Don Technical University, Vietnam
Stefano Cagnoni	University of Parma, Italy
Jinhai Cai	University of South Australia, Australia
Xinye Cai	Nanjing University of Aeronautics and Astronautics, China
Zhenjiang Cai	Agricultural University of Hebei, China
Gang Chen	Victoria University of Wellington, New Zealand
Qi Chen	Victoria University of Wellington, New Zealand
Wei-Neng Chen	Sun Yat-Sen University, China
Ying-Ping Chen	National Chiao Tung University, Taiwan
Yu Chen	Wuhan University of Technology, China
Long Cheng	Institute of Automation, Chinese Academy of Sciences, China
Ran Cheng	University of Surrey, UK
Shi Cheng	Shaanxi Normal University, China
Kazuhisa Chiba	The University of Electro-Communications, Japan
Raymond Chiong	The University of Newcastle, Australia
Sung-Bae Cho	Yonsei University, South Korea
Siang Yew Chong	University of Nottingham, Malaysia
Vic Ciesielski	RMIT University, Australia
Carlos A. Coello Coello	CINVESTAV-IPN, Mexico
Kalyanmoy Deb	Michigan State University, USA
Hepu Deng	RMIT University, Australia
Grant Dick	University of Otago, New Zealand
Haibin Duan	Beihang University, China
Daryl Essam	University of New South Wales, Australia
Zhun Fan	Shantou University, China
Wei Fang	Jiangnan University, China
Liang Feng	Chongqing University, China
Xiang Feng	East China University of Science and Technology, China
Carmelo Bastos Filho	University of Pernambuco, Brazil
Wenlong Fu	Victoria University of Wellington, New Zealand
Marcus Gallagher	University of Queensland, Australia
Shangce Gao	University of Toyama, Japan
Yang Gao	Nanjing University, China

Wenyin Gong	China University of Geosciences, China
Richard Green	The University of Canterbury, New Zealand
Steven Gustafson	MAANA Inc., USA
Toshiharu Hatanaka	Osaka University, Japan
Jinsong He	University of Science and Technology of China, China
Jun He	Aberystwyth University, UK
Tim Hendtlass	Swinburne University of Technology, China
Wei-Chiang Hong	Oriental Institute of Technology, India
Zeng-Guang Hou	Institute of Automation, Chinese Academy of Sciences, China
Han Huang	South China University of Technology, China
Muhammad Iqbal	Victoria University of Wellington, New Zealand
Hisao Ishibuchi	Osaka Prefecture University, China
David Jackson	University of Liverpool, UK
Xiuyi Jia	Nanjing University of Science and Technology, China
Zhaohong Jia	Anhui University, China
He Jiang	Dalian University of Technology, China
Min Jiang	Xiamen University, China
Licheng Jiao	Xidian University, China
Yaochu Jin	University of Surrey, UK
Mark Johnston	University of Worcester, UK
Junfeng Chen	Hohai University, China
Zhou Kang	Wuhan Polytechnic University, China
Liangjun Ke	Xi'an Jiaotong University, China
Michael Kirley	The University of Melbourne, Australia
Mario Koeppen	Kyushu Institute of Technology, Japan
Yun Sing Koh	University of Auckland, New Zealand
Krzysztof Krawiec	Poznan University of Technology, Poland
Albert Y.S. Lam	The University of Hong Kong, China
Ivan Lee	University of South Australia, Australia
Per Kristian Lehre	University of Birmingham, UK
Andrew Lensen	Victoria University of Wellington, New Zealand
Bin Li	University of Science and Technology of China, China
Bingdong Li	University of Science and Technology of China, China
Jinlong Li	University of Science and Technology of China, China
Miqing Li	University of Birmingham, UK
Tianrui Li	Southwest Jiaotong University, China
Xiaodong Li	RMIT University, Australia
Jing Liang	Zhengzhou University, China
Qiuzhen Lin	Shenzhen University, China
Ying Lin	Sun Yat-sen University, China
Cong Liu	University of Shanghai for Science and Technology, China
Jialin Liu	Queen Mary University of London, UK
Jing Liu	Xidian University, China
Qunfeng Liu	Dongguan University of Technology, China

Wenjian Luo	University of Science and Technology of China, China
Hui Ma	Victoria University of Wellington, New Zealand
Lianbo Ma	Northeastern University, China
Syahaheim Marzukhi	National Defence University Malaysia, Malaysia
Michael Mayo	University of Waikato, New Zealand
Yi Mei	Victoria University of Wellington, New Zealand
Kathryn Merrick	University of New South Wales, Australia
Seyedali Mirjalili	Griffith University, Australia
Irene Moser	Swinburne University of Technology, Australia
Gul Muhammad Khan	University of York, UK
Syed Saud Naqvi	Victoria University of Wellington, New Zealand
Kourosh Neshatian	University of Canterbury, New Zealand
Frank Neumann	The University of Adelaide, Australia
Hoai Bach Nguyen	Victoria University of Wellington, New Zealand
Su Nguyen	Victoria University of Wellington, New Zealand
Yew-Soon Ong	Nanyang Technological University, Singapore
Vasile Palade	Coventry University, UK
Xingguang Peng	Northwestern Polytechnical University, China
Yiming Peng	Victoria University of Wellington, New Zealand
Chao Qian	University of Science and Technology of China, China
Kai Qin	Swinburne University of Technology, Australia
Rong Qu	University of Nottingham, UK
Juan Rada-Vilela	FuzzyLite Limited, New Zealand
Marcus Randall	Bond University, Australia
Tapabrata Ray	University of New South Wales, Australia
Ramesh Rayudu	Victoria University of Wellington, New Zealand
Zhilei Ren	Dalian University of Technology, China
Patricia Riddle	University of Auckland, New Zealand
Ramon Sagarna	Nanyang Technological University, Singapore
Hiroyuki Sato	The University of Electro-Communications, Japan
Mahdi Setayesh	Victoria University of Wellington, New Zealand
Lin Shang	Nanjing University, China
Ronghua Shang	Xidian University, China
Yuhui Shi	Southern University of Science and Technology, China
Shinichi Shirakawa	Yokohama National University, Japan
Hemant Singh	University of New South Wales, Australia
Andy Song	RMIT University, Australia
Chaoli Sun	University of Surrey, UK
Yifei Sun	Shaanxi Normal University, China
Yu Sun	University of Science and Technology of China, China
Kay Chen Tan	City University of Hong Kong, China
Ke Tang	Southern University of Science and Technology, China
Yiming Tang	Hefei University of Technology, China
Chuan-Kang Ting	National Chung Cheng University, Taiwan
Binh Tran	Victoria University of Wellington, New Zealand

Krzysztof Trojanowski	Cardinal Stefan Wyszyński University in Warsaw, Poland
Markus Wagner	The University of Adelaide, Australia
Feng Wang	Wuhan University, China
Handing Wang	University of Surrey, China
Lipo Wang	Nanyang Technological University, Singapore
Rui Wang	National University of Defense Technology, China
Xianpeng Wang	Northeastern University, China
Yong Wang	Central South University, China
Yuping Wang	Xidian University, China
Peter Whigham	University of Otago, New Zealand
John Woodward	University of Stirling, UK
Jason Xie	Oracle NZ, New Zealand
Jian Xiong	National University of Defense Technology, China
Xin Xu	Wuhan University of Science and Technology, China
Bing Xue	Victoria University of Wellington, New Zealand
Sun Yanan	Sichuan University, China
Ming Yang	Nanjing Normal University, China
Peng Yang	University of Science and Technology of China, China
Shengxiang Yang	De Montfort University, UK
Yubin Yang	Nanjing University, China
Lean Yu	Academy of Mathematics and Systems Sciences, Chinese Academy of Sciences, China
Tina Yu	Memorial University of Newfoundland, Canada
Yang Yu	Nanjing University, China
Bo Yuan	Southern University of Science and Technology, China
Defu Zhang	Xiamen University, China
Mengjie Zhang	Victoria University of Wellington, New Zealand
Qingfu Zhang	City University of Hong Kong, China
Shichao Zhang	Guangxi Normal University, China
Sihai Zhang	University of Science and Technology of China, China
Xingyi Zhang	Anhui University, China
Zizhen Zhang	Sun Yat-sen University, China
Dongbin Zhao	Institute of Automation, Chinese Academy of Sciences, China
Zhaopin Su	Hefei University of Technology, China
Cui Zhihua	Complex System and Computational Intelligence Laboratory
Aimin Zhou	East China Normal University, China
Xiaofeng Zhu	Guangxi Normal University, China
Zexuan Zhu	Shenzhen University, China
Xingquan Zuo	Beijing University of Posts and Telecommunications, China
Shinya Watanabe	Muroran Institute of Technology, Japan

Additional Reviewers

Ameca-Alducin, Maria-Yaneli
Bingbing, Jiang
Binh, Huynh Thi Thanh
Hong, Wei-Chiang
Jin, Di
Lin, Zhi Yi
Lou, Yang
Lu, Xiaofen
Ma, Xiaoliang
Peng, Hu
Sawczuk Da Silva, Alexandre
Song, Hui
Suksonghong, Karoon
Tang, Xu

Tian, Ye
Tran, Cao Truong
Turky, Ayad
Wang, Shanfeng
Weiyan, Zhang
Witt, Carsten
Wu, Kai
Wu, Zujian
Xue, Xingsi
Yu, Xiang
Zhang, Boyu
Zhen, Liangli
Zhou, Xiaohan

Contents

Evolutionary Optimisation

Maximum Likelihood Estimation Based on Random Subspace EDA:
Application to Extrasolar Planet Detection 3
    Bin Liu and Ke-Jia Chen

Evolutionary Game Network Reconstruction by Memetic Algorithm
with $l_{1/2}$ Regularization 15
    Kai Wu and Jing Liu

A Simple Brain Storm Optimization Algorithm via Visualizing
Confidence Intervals 27
    YingYing Cao, Wei Chen, Shi Cheng, Yifei Sun, Qunfeng Liu, Yun Li,
    and Yuhui Shi

Simulated Annealing with a Time-Slot Heuristic for Ready-Mix
Concrete Delivery 39
    Muhammad Sulaman, Xinye Cai, Mustafa Mısır, and Zhun Fan

A Sequential Learnable Evolutionary Algorithm with a Novel Knowledge
Base Generation Method 51
    Yang Lou and Shiu Yin Yuen

Using Parallel Strategies to Speed up Pareto Local Search 62
    Jialong Shi, Qingfu Zhang, Bilel Derbel, Arnaud Liefooghe,
    and Sébastien Verel

Differential Evolution Based Hyper-heuristic for the Flexible Job Shop
Scheduling Problem with Fuzzy Processing Time 75
    Jian Lin, Dike Luo, Xiaodong Li, Kaizhou Gao, and Yanan Liu

ACO-iRBA: A Hybrid Approach to TSPN
with Overlapping Neighborhoods 87
    Yuanlong Qin and Bo Yuan

An Evolutionary Algorithm with a New Coding Scheme for Multi-objective
Portfolio Optimization 97
    Yi Chen, Aimin Zhou, Rongfang Zhou, Peng He, Yong Zhao,
    and Lihua Dong

Exact Approaches for the Travelling Thief Problem. 110
    Junhua Wu, Markus Wagner, Sergey Polyakovskiy, and Frank Neumann

On the Use of Dynamic Reference Points in HypE   122
   Jingda Deng, Qingfu Zhang, and Hui Li

Multi-Factorial Evolutionary Algorithm Based on M2M Decomposition.   134
   Jiajie Mo, Zhun Fan, Wenji Li, Yi Fang, Yugen You, and Xinye Cai

An Efficient Local Search Algorithm for Minimum Weighted Vertex Cover
on Massive Graphs   145
   Yuanjie Li, Shaowei Cai, and Wenying Hou

Interactive Genetic Algorithm with Group Intelligence Articulated
Possibilistic Condition Preference Model   158
   Xiaoyan Sun, Lixia Zhu, Lin Bao, Lian Liu, and Xin Nie

GP-Based Approach to Comprehensive Quality-Aware Automated
Semantic Web Service Composition   170
   Chen Wang, Hui Ma, Aaron Chen, and Sven Hartmann

Matrix Factorization Based Benchmark Set Analysis:
A Case Study on HyFlex   184
   Mustafa Mısır

Learning to Describe Collective Search Behavior of Evolutionary
Algorithms in Solution Space   196
   Lei Liu, Chengshan Pang, Weiming Liu, and Bin Li

Evolutionary Multiobjective Optimisation

A Hierarchical Decomposition-Based Evolutionary
Many-Objective Algorithm.   211
   Fangqing Gu and Hai-Lin Liu

Adjusting Parallel Coordinates for Investigating Multi-objective Search   224
   Liangli Zhen, Miqing Li, Ran Cheng, Dezhong Peng, and Xin Yao

An Elite Archive-Based MOEA/D Algorithm   236
   Qingling Zhu, Qiuzhen Lin, and Jianyong Chen

A Constraint Partitioning Method Based on Minimax Strategy
for Constrained Multiobjective Optimization Problems.   248
   Xueqiang Li, Shen Fu, and Han Huang

A Fast Objective Reduction Algorithm Based on Dominance Structure
for Many Objective Optimization   260
   Fangqing Gu, Hai-Lin Liu, and Yiu-ming Cheung

A Memetic Algorithm Based on Decomposition and Extended Search
for Multi-Objective Capacitated Arc Routing Problem   272
   Ronghua Shang, Yijing Yuan, Bingqi Du, and Licheng Jiao

Improvement of Reference Points for Decomposition Based Multi-objective
Evolutionary Algorithms   284
   Hemant Kumar Singh and Xin Yao

Multi-Objective Evolutionary Optimization for Autonomous
Intersection Management   297
   Kazi Shah Nawaz Ripon, Jostein Solaas, and Håkon Dissen

Study of an Adaptive Control of Aggregate Functions in MOEA/D   309
   Shinya Watanabe and Takanori Sato

Use of Inverted Triangular Weight Vectors in Decomposition-
Based Many-Objective Algorithms   321
   Ken Doi, Ryo Imada, Yusuke Nojima, and Hisao Ishibuchi

Surrogate Model Assisted Multi-objective Differential Evolution Algorithm
for Performance Optimization at Software Architecture Level*   334
   Du Xin, Ni Youcong, Wu Xiaobin, Ye Peng, and Xin Yao

Normalized Ranking Based Particle Swarm Optimizer for Many
Objective Optimization   347
   Shi Cheng, Xiujuan Lei, Junfeng Chen, Jiqiang Feng, and Yuhui Shi

Evolutionary Machine Learning

A Study on Pre-training Deep Neural Networks Using Particle
Swarm Optimisation   361
   Angus Kenny and Xiaodong Li

Simple Linkage Identification Using Genetic Clustering   373
   Kei Ohnishi and Chang Wook Ahn

Learning of Sparse Fuzzy Cognitive Maps Using Evolutionary Algorithm
with Lasso Initialization   385
   Kai Wu and Jing Liu

A Bayesian Restarting Approach to Algorithm Selection   397
   Yaodong He, Shiu Yin Yuen, and Yang Lou

Evolutionary Learning Based Iterated Local Search for Google Machine
Reassignment Problems   409
   Ayad Turky, Nasser R. Sabar, Abdul Sattar, and Andy Song

Geometric Semantic Genetic Programming with Perpendicular Crossover
and Random Segment Mutation for Symbolic Regression.   422
  Qi Chen, Mengjie Zhang, and Bing Xue

Constrained Dimensionally Aware Genetic Programming for Evolving
Interpretable Dispatching Rules in Dynamic Job Shop Scheduling.   435
  Yi Mei, Su Nguyen, and Mengjie Zhang

Visualisation and Optimisation of Learning Classifier Systems for Multiple
Domain Learning   448
  Yi Liu, Bing Xue, and Will N. Browne

Adaptive Memetic Algorithm Based Evolutionary Multi-tasking
Single-Objective Optimization   462
  Qunjian Chen, Xiaoliang Ma, Yiwen Sun, and Zexuan Zhu

Effective Policy Gradient Search for Reinforcement Learning Through
NEAT Based Feature Extraction   473
  Yiming Peng, Gang Chen, Mengjie Zhang, and Yi Mei

Generalized Hybrid Evolutionary Algorithm Framework with a Mutation
Operator Requiring no Adaptation.   486
  Yong Wee Foo, Cindy Goh, Lipton Chan, Lin Li, and Yun Li

A Multitree Genetic Programming Representation for Automatically
Evolving Texture Image Descriptors   499
  Harith Al-Sahaf, Bing Xue, and Mengjie Zhang

Theoretical Developments

Running-Time Analysis of Particle Swarm Optimization with a Single
Particle Based on Average Gain   515
  Wu Hongyue, Huang Han, Yang Shuling, and Zhang Yushan

Evolutionary Computation Theory for Remote Sensing Image Clustering:
A Survey.   528
  Yuting Wan, Yanfei Zhong, Ailong Ma, and Liangpei Zhang

Feature Selection and Dimensionality Reduction

New Representations in Genetic Programming for Feature Construction
in k-Means Clustering   543
  Andrew Lensen, Bing Xue, and Mengjie Zhang

Transductive Transfer Learning in Genetic Programming
for Document Classification   556
  Wenlong Fu, Bing Xue, Mengjie Zhang, and Xiaoying Gao

Automatic Feature Construction for Network Intrusion Detection   569
Binh Tran, Stjepan Picek, and Bing Xue

A Feature Subset Evaluation Method Based
on Multi-objective Optimization   581
Mengmeng Li, Zhigang Shang, and Caitong Yue

A Hybrid GA-GP Method for Feature Reduction in Classification.   591
Hoai Bach Nguyen, Bing Xue, and Peter Andreae

Kernel Construction and Feature Subset Selection in Support
Vector Machines.   605
Shinichi Yamada and Kourosh Neshatian

KW-Race and Fast KW-Race: Racing-Based Frameworks for Tuning
Parameters of Evolutionary Algorithms on Black-Box
Optimization Problems.   617
Mang Wang, Xin Tong, and Bin Li

Dynamic and Uncertain Environments

A Probabilistic Learning Algorithm for the Shortest Path Problem.   631
Yiya Diao, Changhe Li, Yebin Ma, Junchen Wang, and Xingang Zhou

A First-Order Difference Model-Based Evolutionary Dynamic
Multiobjective Optimization   644
Leilei Cao, Lihong Xu, Erik D. Goodman, and Hui Li

A Construction Graph-Based Evolutionary Algorithm for Traveling
Salesman Problem.   656
Gang Li, Zhi feng Hao, Hang Wei, and Han Huang

Real-world Applications

Bi-objective Water Cycle Algorithm for Solving Remanufacturing
Rescheduling Problem   671
Kaizhou Gao, Peiyong Duan, Rong Su, and Junqing Li

A New Method for Constructing Ensemble Classifier in Privacy-Preserving
Distributed Environment   684
Yan Shao, Zhanjun Li, and Ming Li

Greedy Based Pareto Local Search for Bi-objective Robust Airport Gate
Assignment Problem   694
*Wenxue Sun, Xinye Cai, Chao Xia, Muhammad Sulaman, Mustafa Mısır,
and Zhun Fan*

Multi-neighbourhood Great Deluge for Google Machine
Reassignment Problem.   706
  Ayad Turky, Nasser R. Sabar, Abdul Sattar, and Andy Song

Evolutionary Optimization of Airport Security Inspection Allocation   716
  Zheng-Jie Fan and Yu-Jun Zheng

Evolving Directional Changes Trading Strategies with a New
Event-Based Indicator   727
  Michael Kampouridis, Adesola Adegboye, and Colin Johnson

Constrained Differential Evolution for Cost and Energy Efficiency
Optimization in 5G Wireless Networks   739
  Rawaa Dawoud AL-Dabbagh and Ahmed Jasim Jabur

Evolutionary Computation to Determine Product Builds in Open
Pit Mining   751
  Adam Ghandar

An Evolutionary Vulnerability Detection Method for HFSWR Ship
Tracking Algorithm.   763
  Pengju Zhang, Kun Wang, Ling Zhang, Zexiao Xie, and Liqin Zhou

Genetic Programming for Lifetime Maximization in Wireless Sensor
Networks with a Mobile Sink.   774
  Ying Li, Zhixing Huang, Jinghui Zhong, and Liang Feng

Unsupervised Change Detection for Remote Sensing Images Based on
Principal Component Analysis and Differential Evolution.   786
  Mi Song, Yanfei Zhong, Ailong Ma, and Liangpei Zhang

Parallel Particle Swarm Optimization for Community Detection in
Large-Scale Networks   797
  Shanfeng Wang, Maoguo Gong, Yue Wu, and Xiaolei Qin

Multi-objective Memetic Algorithm Based on Three-Dimensional
Request Prediction for Dynamic Pickup-and-Delivery Problem
with Time Windows   810
  Yanming Yang, Xiaoliang Ma, Yiwen Sun, and Zexuan Zhu

Optimization of Spectrum-Energy Efficiency in Heterogeneous
Communication Network   821
  Fangqing Gu, Ziquan Liu, Yiu-ming Cheung, and Hai-Lin Liu

Large Scale WSN Deployment Based on an Improved Cooperative
Co-evolution PSO with Global Differential Grouping   833
  Yazhen Zhang and Wei Fang

Adaptive Systems

Learning Fuzzy Cognitive Maps Using a Genetic Algorithm with
Decision-Making Trial and Evaluation   845
  Xumiao Zou and Jing Liu

Dynamic and Adaptive Threshold for DNN Compression from Scratch   858
  Chunhui Jiang, Guiying Li, and Chao Qian

Cooperative Design of Two Level Fuzzy Logic Controllers for Medium
Access Control in Wireless Body Area Networks   870
  Seyed Mohammad Nekooei, Gang Chen, and Ramesh Rayudu

Statistical Analysis of Social Coding in GitHub Hypernetwork   883
  Li Kuang, Feng Wang, Heng Zhang, and Yuanxiang Li

Swarm Intelligence

Sparse Restricted Boltzmann Machine Based
on Multiobjective Optimization   899
  Yangyang Li, Xiaoyu Bai, Xiaoxu Liang, and Licheng Jiao

A Knee Point Driven Particle Swarm Optimization Algorithm
for Sparse Reconstruction   911
  Caitong Yue, Jing Liang, Boyang Qu, Hui Song, Guang Li,
  and Yuhong Han

Multivariant Optimization Algorithm with Bimodal-Gauss   920
  Baolei Li, Jing Liang, Caitong Yue, and Boyang Qu

Enhanced Comprehensive Learning Particle Swarm Optimization with
Exemplar Evolution   929
  Xiang Yu, Yunan Liu, Xiangsheng Feng, and Genhua Chen

Recommending PSO Variants Using Meta-Learning Framework
for Global Optimization   939
  Xianghua Chu, Fulin Cai, Jiansheng Chen, and Li Li

Augmented Brain Storm Optimization with Mutation Strategies   949
  Xianghua Chu, Jiansheng Chen, Fulin Cai, Chen Chen, and Ben Niu

A New Precedence-Based Ant Colony Optimization
for Permutation Problems   960
  Marco Baioletti, Alfredo Milani, and Valentino Santucci

A General Swarm Intelligence Model for Continuous
Function Optimization   972
  Satoru Iwasaki, Heng Xiao, Toshiharu Hatanaka, and Takeshi Uchitane

A Hybrid Particle Swarm Optimization for High-Dimensional
Dynamic Optimization.   981
    Wenjian Luo, Bin Yang, Chenyang Bu, and Xin Lin

Visualizing the Search Dynamics in a High-Dimensional Space
for a Particle Swarm Optimizer.   994
    Qiqi Duan, Chang Shao, Xiaodong Li, and Yuhui Shi

Particle Swarm Optimization with Winning Score Assignment for
Multi-objective Portfolio Optimization   1003
    Karoon Suksonghong and Kittipong Boonlong

Conservatism and Adventurism in Particle Swarm
Optimization Algorithm.   1016
    Guangzhi Xu, Rui Li, Xinchao Zhao, and Xingquan Zuo

A Competitive Social Spider Optimization with Learning Strategy for PID
Controller Optimization   1026
    Zhaolin Lai, Xiang Feng, and Huiqun Yu

Author Index   1039

Evolutionary Optimisation

Maximum Likelihood Estimation Based on Random Subspace EDA: Application to Extrasolar Planet Detection

Bin Liu[1(✉)] and Ke-Jia Chen[2]

[1] School of Computer Science, Nanjing University of Posts and Telecommunications,
Nanjing 210023, Jiangsu, China
bins@ieee.org
[2] Jiangsu Key Laboratory of Big Data Security and Intelligent Processing,
Nanjing 210023, Jiangsu, China

Abstract. This paper addresses maximum likelihood (ML) estimation based model fitting in the context of extrasolar planet detection. This problem is featured by the following properties: (1) the candidate models under consideration are highly nonlinear; (2) the likelihood surface has a huge number of peaks; (3) the parameter space ranges in size from a few to dozens of dimensions. These properties make the ML search a very challenging problem, as it lacks any analytical or gradient based searching solution to explore the parameter space. A population based searching method, called estimation of distribution algorithm (EDA), is adopted to explore the model parameter space starting from a batch of random locations. EDA is featured by its ability to reveal and utilize problem structures. This property is desirable for characterizing the detections. However, it is well recognized that EDAs can not scale well to large scale problems, as it consists of iterative random sampling and model fitting procedures, which results in the well-known dilemma *curse of dimensionality*. A novel mechanism to perform EDAs in interactive random subspaces spanned by correlated variables is proposed and the hope is to alleviate the *curse of dimensionality* for EDAs by performing the operations of sampling and model fitting in lower dimensional subspaces. The effectiveness of the proposed algorithm is verified via both benchmark numerical studies and real data analysis.

Keywords: Estimation of distribution · Extrasolar planet detection · Maximum likelihood estimation · Nonlinear model · Optimization · Random subspace

1 Introduction

This paper presents an evolutionary computation based maximum likelihood (ML) estimation method for multivariate highly nonlinear time series models. This work is motivated by a challenging signal detection task, which aims to

© Springer International Publishing AG 2017
Y. Shi et al. (Eds.): SEAL 2017, LNCS 10593, pp. 3–14, 2017.
https://doi.org/10.1007/978-3-319-68759-9_1

detect extrasolar planets (exoplanets) based on observations collected by astronomical instruments such as NASA's Kepler space telescope [1]. The terminology "exoplanets" denotes planets outside our solar system. The goal of exoplanet science is to answer the scientific quest whether we are alone or whether there are other planets that might support life in the universe [1–3]. Exoplanet science has become a booming field in astrophysics since 1992 when the first detection of an exoplanet was confirmed [4]. In this paper, we focus on the radial velocity (RV) method of exoplanet detection [3,5,6]. This method has become one of the most productive techniques for detecting exoplanets so far.

Signal processing (SP) plays an important part in exoplanet detection, which contributes to improve the signal-to-noise ratio of the observations, detect signals of potential planets and so forth. Current SP techniques fall short of meeting the fundamental requirement for the future of this field. For example, the ML based periodogram method was developed to deal with correlated noise in RV time series [7], while, it is just limited to detect one signal. Many planetary systems are found to contain more than one planet, which means the RV time series should exhibit more than one signal. The Bayesian simulation techniques have been applied to explore the parameter space of a global RV model using Markov Chain Monte Carlo (MCMC) or adaptive importance sampling methods [3,6,8], while such methods require very large computational overhead to guarantee a satisfactory performance in parameter estimation and signal detection.

The objective of this paper is to propose a computationally efficient method to address the problem of exoplanet detection based on ML fitting of complex RV models. This problem is featured by the following properties: (1) the candidate models under consideration are highly nonlinear; (2) the likelihood surface has a huge number of peaks; (3) the parameter space ranges in size from a few to dozens of dimensions. This problem lacks any analytical or gradient based searching solution to explore the parameter space. The proposed approach is based on an evolutionary computation method called estimation of distribution algorithm (EDA) [9–11]. A novel mechanism is proposed to perform EDAs in a series of random subspaces spanned by correlated variables. The basic idea is that, since the dimension of each subspace will be smaller than that of the full parameter space, the number of occurrences of sample-starved model fitting will decrease and then the *curse of dimensionality* is hoped to be alleviated. A benchmark numerical study and a real data analysis are used to demonstrate the effectiveness of the new algorithm.

2   RV Models and the ML Based Model Fitting

In this section, we present the RV time series models and then introduce the ML parameter fitting problem in the context of exoplanet detection.

2.1   RV Models

A succinct introduction of the RV models is presented here. For more details, readers are referred to [6]. We use $\mathcal{M}_j$, $j = 0, 1, \ldots, J$, to denote the j-planet model, corresponding to the hypothesis that there is (are) j planet(s) in the extrasolar system under consideration. In the 0-planet model $\mathcal{M}_0$, the ith element of the RV data v_i is modeled to be Gaussian distributed as follows

$$v_i \mid \mathcal{M}_0 \sim \mathcal{N}\left(C, \sigma_i^2 + s^2\right), \tag{1}$$

where C and $\sigma_i^2 + s^2$ are its mean and variance, respectively. Here C denotes constant center-of-mass velocity of the star relative to earth and s denotes the square root of the "stellar jitter", which represents the random fluctuations in a star's luminosity or fluctuations stemming from other systematic sources, e.g., starspots. The additional variance component σ_i^2 is a calculated error of v_i due to the observation procedure.

In the 1-planet model $\mathcal{M}_1$, v_i is modeled as follows

$$v_i \mid \mathcal{M}_1 \sim \mathcal{N}\left(C + \Delta V(t_i \mid \phi_1), \sigma_i^2 + s^2\right), \tag{2}$$

where $\Delta V(t_i \mid \phi)$ is the velocity shift caused by the presence of the planet. Such velocity shift is a family of curves parameterized by a 5-dimensional vector $\phi \triangleq (K, P, e, \omega, \mu_0)$ defined as follows

$$\Delta V(t \mid \phi) = K[\cos(\omega + T(t)) + e\cos(\omega)], \tag{3}$$

where $T(t)$ is the "true anomaly at time t" given by

$$T(t) - 2\arctan\left[\tan\left(\frac{E(t)}{2}\right)\sqrt{\frac{1+e}{1-e}}\right], \tag{4}$$

and $E(t)$ is called the "eccentric anomaly at time t", which is the solution to a transcendental equation

$$E(t) - e\sin(E(t)) = \mathrm{mod}\left(\frac{2\pi}{P}t + \mu_0, 2\pi\right). \tag{5}$$

In the above expressions, K denotes the velocity semi-amplitude, P the orbital period, c the eccentricity ($0 \le e \le 1$), ω the argument of periastron ($0 \le \omega \le 2\pi$), and μ_0 the mean anomaly at time $t = 0$, ($0 \le \mu_0 \le 2\pi$). The parameters C, K and s have the same unit as velocity; the velocity semi-amplitude K is usually restricted to be non-negative to avoid identification problems; C may be positive or negative. The eccentricity parameter e, $0 \le e < 1$, is unitless, with $e = 0$ corresponding to a circular orbit, and larger e means more eccentric orbits. Periastron is the point at which the planet is closest to the star and the argument of periastron ω measures the angle at which we observe the elliptical orbit. The mean anomaly μ_0 is an angular distance of a planet from periastron.

More generally, a j-planet model ($j \ge 1$) represents the expected velocity by $C + \Delta V(t_i \mid \phi_1, \ldots, \phi_j)$, in which the overall velocity shift ΔV takes the form of the summation of velocity shifts of each individual planet, i.e.,

$$\Delta V(t_i \mid \phi_1, \ldots, \phi_j) = \sum_{a=1}^{j} \Delta V(t_i \mid \phi_a). \tag{6}$$

Therefore the parameter dimension of a j-planet model is $2 + 5j$. So the more planets covered by the model, the higher dimensional it is. Moreover, the RV models $\mathcal{M}_1, \mathcal{M}_2, \ldots$ are highly nonlinear due to the velocity shift item $\triangle V$ included in these models.

2.2   ML Parameter Estimation of RV Models

Here we treat exoplanet detection as a problem of model selection, which means, given a set of RV observations $\mathbf{v} \triangleq (v_1, \ldots, v_n)$, how to select from the candidate models $\{\mathcal{M}_0, \mathcal{M}_1, \ldots, \mathcal{M}_j\}$ the one that fits the data best in terms of Bayesian criterion. A full Bayesian solution needs to calculate the marginal likelihood of each candidate model, which involves large scale stochastic integrations over the whole parameter space of the candidate models [3,6]. It is computationally expensive to solve such stochastic integrations. Here we resort to the Bayesian information criterion (BIC) to evaluate the fitness of the candidate models to the data. A Bayesian argument for adopting BIC was presented in [12]. We use θ_i and Θ_i to denote the parameters of $\mathcal{M}_i$ and the corresponding value space, respectively. The BIC metric of $\mathcal{M}_i$ is defined as

$$\mathrm{BIC}_i = -2 \cdot \ln \hat{L}_i + k_i \cdot \ln(n) \tag{7}$$

where k_i is the number of free parameters to be estimated for $\mathcal{M}_i$, $\hat{L}_i$ is the maximal likelihood function value associated with $\mathcal{M}_i$, i.e., $\hat{L}_i = p(\mathbf{v}|\hat{\theta}_i, \mathcal{M}_i)$, where $\hat{\theta}_i$ are the parameter values that maximize the likelihood function, namely

$$\hat{\theta}_i = \arg\max_{\theta \in \Theta_i}\ p(\mathbf{v}|\theta, \mathcal{M}_i). \tag{8}$$

Given a finite set of models, the model with the lowest BIC value is preferred, according to the BIC criterion. Since the second item on the right-hand side of Eq. (7) is a constant given the model, calculation of BIC_i then translates to how to solve the maximization problem defined in Eq. (8).

3   General EDA Procedure

To address an optimization problem such as that defined in Eq. (8), a general EDA procedure typically works with a population of candidate solutions defined over the full parameter space. The initial population is generated according to the uniform distribution over all admissible solutions. The fitness function gives a numerical ranking for each solution. Here the likelihood function $p(\mathbf{v}|\theta, \mathcal{M}_i)$ plays the role of a fitness function. A subset of the most promising solutions is selected by the *selection* operator. A commonly used selection operator selects a certain proportion, e.g., the best 50% of solutions. A probabilistic model is then constructed to estimate the probability distribution of the selected solutions. Given the above model, the algorithm generates new solutions by sampling the distribution defined by the model. The new population of solutions replaces the old population and then the modeling and sampling procedure is repeated until some termination criteria are met. The main scheme for an iteration of the EDA method is summarized as follows: starting from a population of solutions P,

– Select a population of promising solutions S from P;
– Build a probabilistic model M from S;
– Sample new candidate solutions Q based on M;
– Replace the old population with the new population, namely set P to be Q.

For more details about the EDA algorithm, readers are referred to [11]. As an iterative sampling and modeling procedure, the general EDA method suffers from the well-known dilemma *curse of dimensionality*. Specifically speaking, with the increase in the dimension of the solution space, the volume of the space increases so fast that the available data points used for constructing the model become sparse, making the resulting model not qualified for guiding the searching process to find better solutions.

4   Random Subspace EDA (RS-EDA)

In this section, we propose a new EDA algorithm, namely RS-EDA. The idea is to partition the original multivariate parameter space into a series of random subspaces, and then perform EDAs in these subspaces, rather than the full parameter space, with the hope to alleviate the *curse of dimensionality* for EDA type methods. Figure 1 shows one iteration of the RS-EDA method, wherein d denotes the dimension of θ. The iteration ends when the estimate of the global optimal solution keeps unchanged for a fixed number of iterations. Taking the maximization problem as an instance, we describe in what follows the details of the four operators included in Fig. 1.

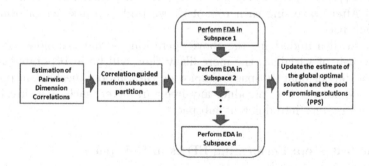

Fig. 1. A conceptual scheme for one iteration of RS-EDA

4.1   The 1st Step: Estimation of Variable Correlations

This step corresponds to the leftmost box in Fig. 1. The purpose is to provide a rough estimate on correlations among the variables (or dimensions) of θ. Such estimation is made based on a pool of promising solutions (PPS), given by the previous one iteration of the RS-EDA. If it is currently in the first iteration, we initialize the PPS based on available prior knowledge on the variable correlations. If there is no such prior knowledge, we just draw a number of random samples uniformly from the solution space and then initialize the PPS via an operation of truncation selection. Specifically, we preserve the fittest 20% of the sample for use and throw away the others. The data in PPS is formulated by an $a \times d$ matrix, where a denotes the number of samples in PPS. The operation of correlation estimation returns the sample linear partial correlation coefficients between pairs of variables in PPS, controlling for the remaining variables in PPS. We use MATLAB's built-in function "partialcorr" to perform the above operation. The output of this function is a symmetric $d \times d$ matrix C, whose (i, j)-th entry is the sample linear partial correlation corresponding to the ith and jth columns of the PPS matrix.

4.2   The 2nd Step: Random Subspace Partition

This step corresponds to the second box in Fig. 1. The purpose is to partition the whole parameter space into subspaces based on the correlation matrix C given by the 1st step. This 2nd step consists of a series of procedures performed on each row of C. Take the procedures corresponding to C_i, the ith row of C, for example. We first sort the elements of C_i, namely $\{C_{i,1}, \ldots, C_{i,d}\}$, according to their values from large to small. This procedure outputs $\{C_{i,j1}, \ldots, C_{i,jd}\}$, where $\{j1, \ldots, jd\}$ is a rearrangement of $\{1, \ldots, d\}$ with $C_{i,jm} \geq C_{i,jn}$ as long as $m < n$. Let $S = \sum_{m=1}^{d} C_{i,jm}$ and then set $C_{i,jm} = C_{i,jm}/S$ for each m in $\{1, \ldots, d\}$. Now we have $\sum_{m=1}^{d} C_{i,jm} = 1$. Then we set $C'_{i,m} = \sum_{k=1}^{m} C_{i,jk}$ for $m = 1, \ldots, d$, draw a random number r from a uniform distribution between 0 and 1, find the minimum index m from $\{1, \ldots, d\}$ that satisfies $C'_{i,m} \geq r$, and finally return the indexes $\{j1, \ldots, jm\}$, which we use to constitute the coordinates of the ith subspace. After traversing each row of C, we build up a series of overlapped random subspaces.

The basic idea underlying the above operations is that the more correlation between a pair of variables, the more likely they will be incorporated into the same lower dimensional subspace. Employing the random mechanism presented above, we do not need to introduce any free parameter, such as a threshold, to cluster the variables into different subspaces.

4.3   The 3rd Step: Performing EDAs in Subspaces

This step corresponds to the elliptical box in Fig. 1. Now we focus on a specific subspace and present the EDA operations endowed with it. Assume that the current estimate of the global optimal solution takes value at $\hat{\theta} = (\hat{\theta}_1, \ldots, \hat{\theta}_d)$ and the subspace under consideration is associated with variables $(\theta_{j1}, \ldots, \theta_{jm})$. We use a Gaussian model to fit the PPS data mapped to this subspace. Specifically, we calculate the empirical mean and sample covariance of this Gaussian model based on the PPS data mapped to the dimensions $\{j1,\ldots,jm\}$. Then we draw $R \times m$ new samples from this Gaussian distribution, where R is a constant prescribed beforehand. As the dimensions of all the exoplanet models of our concern are less than 100, we select $R = 100$ in our experiments, which is big enough to prevent from sample-starved model fitting in the follow-up EDA operations. We assign these newly generated samples' values to the corresponding variables $\{j1,\ldots,jm\}$ of $\hat{\theta}$ and keep the other variables unchanged. Then we get a set of full dimensional samples. We calculate the fitness values of these samples, based on which we select 20% fittest samples for use in updating the Gaussian model. During the above process, once better solutions are found, we shall update the estimate of the global optimal solution and the PPS accordingly to guarantee that the PPS maintains the fittest samples that have been found so far. Then we iterate the model fitting, sampling and selection procedure until the estimate of the global optimal solution keeps unchanged in the most recent continuous five iterations. We regard this phenomenon as an indication of algorithm convergence.

4.4 The 4th Step: Updating the Estimate of the Global Optimum and the PPS

This step occupies the rightmost box in Fig. 1 for ease of presentation, while, in practice, it is totally interactive with the 3rd step presented above. Once better solutions have been found in an EDA procedure included in the 3rd step, the estimate of the global optimal solution and the PPS will be updated accordingly. In this way, the PPS always keeps a set of the fittest solutions. The EDA procedure of the next subspace will be performed based on the most recent estimate of the global optimal solution and the most recently updated PPS. After carrying out the EDA procedures of all subspaces, the finally outputted PPS will then act as the input for the 1st step in the next iteration.

5   Numerical Study with Benchmark Function

To test the potential of our idea and the ability of our algorithm to improve the scalability of EDAs to search a near-optimal solution in large-scale problem settings, we tested it based on a benchmark function listed in the suite of benchmark test functions released by a special session on real-parameter optimization of the 2013 Congress on Evolutionary Computation [13]. We selected the Rotated Schaffers F7 (RSF7) function, which is multimodal, nonseparable, asymmetrical, and has a huge number of the local optimum. It is defined as follows [13]

$$f(\theta) = \left(\frac{1}{d-1} \sum_{i=1}^{d-1} \left(\sqrt{z_i} + \sqrt{z_i} \sin^2 \left(50 z_i^{0.2} \right) \right) \right)^2 - 800 \qquad (9)$$

where $z_i = \sqrt{y_i^2 + y_{i+1}^2}$ for $i = 1, \ldots, d$, $y = \Lambda_d^{10} M_2 T_{asy}^{0.5}(M_1(\theta - o))$. In the above expressions, o is the shifted global optimum, Λ_d^α denotes a d dimensional diagonal matrix, the ith diagonal element of which is $\alpha^{\frac{i-1}{2(d-1)}}$, $i = 1, 2, \ldots, d$. $T_{asy}^\beta(x)$ is an operator that transforms x_i to be $x_i^{1+\beta\frac{i-1}{d-1}\sqrt{x_i}}$ for $x_i > 0$, $i = 1, 2, \ldots, d$. M_1 and M_2 are orthogonal matrices whose entries are standard normally distributed. More details about this function can be found in [13].

The RSF7 function is designed for minimization tasks. We consider maximizing the function $g(\theta) = -f(\theta)$ in order to mimic the ML estimation problem. The maximum function value of $g(\theta)$ is 800, which is the target for the algorithm to search. The first instance we considered was a low dimensional case, in which d was set at 5. We initialized the PPS of RS-EDA using $N = 20000$ random samples and we allowed a fixed budget of 10^6 function evaluations. We compared RS-EDA with other three leading evolutionary computation methods, namely the Trelea type vectorized Particle Swarm Optimization (PSO) algorithm [14], the Covariance Matrix Adaptation Evolution Strategy (CMAES) method [15] and a classical EDA method termed EMNA$_{global}$ [16]. The difference between EMNA$_{global}$ and our method is that the former always employs a full-dimensional multivariate Gaussian distribution model, while the latter performs EDA operations in subspaces. The population size of EMNA$_{global}$ is set at $N = 20000$. The population size of the PSO is set at 1000. The CMAES method of [15] was included in our comparison because it is developed to handle high dimensional problems and it currently represents the gold-standard for comparisons in new EDA research. We used the Matlab implementation available from the authors with the diagonal option, default parameter settings and random initialization [17]. We ran all these baseline methods with a maximum number of, i.e., 10^6, function evaluations, the same as for the RS-EDA method. We ran each method for 50 times and calculated the mean of its estimate on the maximal function value. Figure 2 gives a visual summary of the results obtained in comparison. It

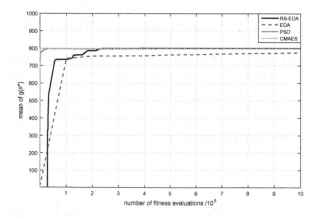

Fig. 2. Algorithm comparison in a maximization task using a 5-dimensional benchmark function $g(\theta)$

is shown that the proposed RS-EDA method finds the global optimum with a slower convergence speed than PSO and CMAES and a faster convergence speed than EDA.

We then focused on a higher dimensional instance with d set at 20. Compared with the first instance, the population size of each method involved increased by 10 times. The maximum function evaluations allowed for each method is 5×10^6. Figure 3 shows the summary of the results corresponding to 50 independent runs of each method. The result of the EDA method totally diverged, so it is not included in Fig. 3. We see that the RS-EDA beats all the other methods. Combining the two instances for a joint analysis, we see a potential of the proposed idea of random subspace in improving the scalability of EDAs in dealing with higher dimensional problems. However, it is worthy of further investigation.

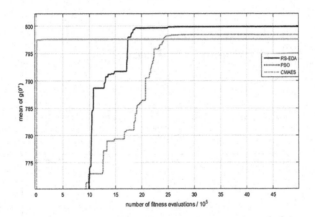

Fig. 3. Algorithm comparison in a maximization task using a 20-dimensional benchmark function $g(\theta)$

6   Analysis of Real Exoplanet Data

We applied the proposed RS-EDA method to analyze a real data set released in [18]. This data set was claimed by the astronomers to have two planets [18]. An adaptive annealed importance sampling (AAIS) method was developed in [6], which calculates out the probabilities of the hypothetical models based on the given RV measurements.

We fit the data based on $\mathcal{M}_1$ and $\mathcal{M}_2$, respectively. For each model, we apply RS-EDA to estimate the ML model parameters. The search space is constrained by the value ranges of the model parameters as listed in Table 1. These ranges are provided by the astronomers based on their experiences [6]. Figure 4 shows the fitting results based on $\mathcal{M}_1$ and $\mathcal{M}_2$, respectively. The calculated logarithm of MLs and BIC metrics associated with $\mathcal{M}_1$ and $\mathcal{M}_2$ are listed in Table 2. Both the visual fitting result and the quantitative comparison of the BIC metrics suggest that $\mathcal{M}_2$ holds. This result is consistent with that reported in [6,18].

Table 1. Parameter value ranges of RV models

$P_{\min}$	1 day	$P_{\max}$	$1,000$ years
$K_{\min}$	$1\,\mathrm{m/s}$	$K_{\max}$	$2128\,\mathrm{m/s}$
C_{min}	$-2128\,\mathrm{m/s}$	C_{max}	$2128\,\mathrm{m/s}$
$s_{\min}$	$1\,\mathrm{m/s}$	$s_{\max}$	$2128\,\mathrm{m/s}$

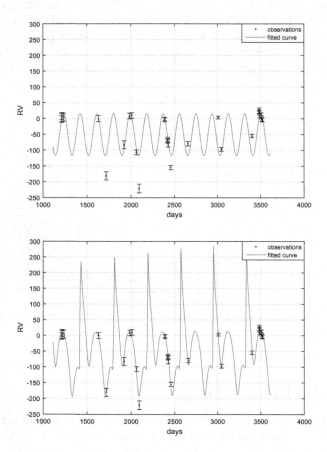

Fig. 4. Measured RV data released in [18] and two ML fits to the data based on $\mathcal{M}_1$ (the top panel) and $\mathcal{M}_2$ (the bottom panel), respectively. The ML solution is provided by the proposed RS-EDA method.

Table 2. The calculated BIC metrics of $\mathcal{M}_1$ and $\mathcal{M}_2$

	$\ln(\mathrm{ML})$	BIC
One planet model : $\mathcal{M}_1$	-148.4024	320.6132
Two planet model : $\mathcal{M}_2$	-111.5458	263.9060

7 Concluding Remarks

In this paper, we proposed an RS-EDA algorithm in the context of exoplanet detection based on ML estimation. The most important feature of the RS-EDA method lies in the proposed operation of constructing random subspaces and then endowing the routine sampling and model fitting operations of EDAs into the lower dimensional parameter spaces, with the hope to alleviate the *curse of dimensionality* for EDA type methods. The effectiveness of the proposed method was demonstrated by numerical studies and real data analysis. The results show a potential of the proposed technique in dealing with complex nonlinear models with multimodal likelihood functions and in solving high dimensional optimization tasks. The scalability of the proposed method and new approaches for constructing random subspaces are both worthy of further investigations.

Acknowledgement. This work was partly supported by the National Natural Science Foundation (NSF) of China under grant No. 61571238, China Postdoctoral Science Foundation under grant Nos. 2015M580455 and 2016T90483, the Six Talents Peak Foundation of Jiangsu Province under grant No. XYDXXJS-CXTD-006 and the Scientific and Technological Support Project (Society) of Jiangsu Province under grant No. BE2016776.

References

1. Lissauer, J.J., Dawson, R.I., Tremaine, S.: Advances in exoplanet science from Kepler. Nature **513**(7518), 336–344 (2014)
2. Borucki, W.J., Koch, D., Basri, G., Batalha, N., Brown, T., Caldwell, D., Caldwell, J., Christensen-Dalsgaard, J., Cochran, W.D., DeVore, E., et al.: Kepler planet-detection mission: introduction and first results. Science **327**(5968), 977–980 (2010)
3. Loredo, T.J., Berger, J.O., Chernoff, D.F., Clyde, M.A., Liu, B.: Bayesian methods for analysis and adaptive scheduling of exoplanet observations. Stat. Methodol. **9**(1), 101–114 (2012)
4. Wolszczan, A., Frail, D.A.: A planetary system around the millisecond pulsar PSR 1257+ 12. Nature **355**(6356), 145–147 (1992)
5. Desort, M., Lagrange, A.-M., Galland, F., Udry, S., Mayor, M.: Search for exoplanets with the radial-velocity technique: quantitative diagnostics of stellar activity. Astron. Astrophys. **473**(3), 983–993 (2007)
6. Liu, B.: Adaptive annealed importance sampling for multimodal posterior exploration and model selection with application to extrasolar planet detection. Astrophys. J. Suppl. Ser. **213**(14), 1–16 (2014)
7. Baluev, R.V.: PlanetPack: a radial-velocity time-series analysis tool facilitating exoplanets detection, characterization, and dynamical simulations. Astron. Comput. **2**, 18–26 (2013)
8. Brewer, B.J., Donovan, C.P.: Fast Bayesian inference for exoplanet discovery in radial velocity data. Mon. Not. R. Astron. Soc. **448**(4), 3206–3214 (2015)
9. Zhang, Q., Muhlenbein, H.: On the convergence of a class of estimation of distribution algorithms. IEEE Trans. Evol. Comput. **8**(2), 127–136 (2004)
10. Pelikan, M., Goldberg, D.E., Lobo, F.G.: A survey of optimization by building and using probabilistic models. Comput. Optim. Appl. **21**(1), 5–20 (2002)

11. Hauschild, M., Pelikan, M.: An introduction and survey of estimation of distribution algorithms. Swarm Evol. Comput. **1**(3), 111–128 (2011)
12. Schwarz, G.: Estimating the dimension of a model. Ann. Stat. **6**(2), 461–464 (1978)
13. Liang, J., Qu, B., Suganthan, P., Hernández-Díaz, A.G.: Problem definitions and evaluation criteria for the CEC 2013 special session on real-parameter optimization. Technical report, Computational Intelligence Lab, Zhengzhou University, Zhengzhou, China and Nanyang Technological University, Singapore (2013)
14. Trelea, I.C.: The particle swarm optimization algorithm: convergence analysis and parameter selection. Inf. Process. Lett. **85**(6), 317–325 (2003)
15. Ros, R., Hansen, N.: A simple modification in CMA-ES achieving linear time and space complexity. In: Rudolph, G., Jansen, T., Beume, N., Lucas, S., Poloni, C. (eds.) PPSN 2008. LNCS, vol. 5199, pp. 296–305. Springer, Heidelberg (2008). doi:10.1007/978-3-540-87700-4_30
16. Larranaga, P., Lozano, J.A.: Estimation of Distribution Algorithms: A New Tool for Evolutionary Computation. Kluwer Academic Publishers, Dordrecht (2002)
17. Hansen, N.: CMA-ES source code. https://www.lri.fr/~hansen/cmaes_inmatlab.html
18. Tinney, C.G., Butler, R.P., Marcy, G.W., Jones, H.R., Laughlin, G., Carter, B.D., Bailey, J.A., O'Toole, S.: The 2:1 resonant exoplanetary system orbiting HD73526. Astrophys. J. **647**(1), 594–599 (2006)

Evolutionary Game Network Reconstruction by Memetic Algorithm with $l_{1/2}$ Regularization

Kai Wu and Jing Liu[(⊠)]

Key Laboratory of Intelligent Perception and Image Understanding of Ministry
of Education, Xidian University, Xi'an 710071, China
kaiwu@stu.xidian.edu.cn, neouma@163.com

Abstract. Evolutionary Game (EG) theory is effective approach to understand
and analyze the widespread cooperative behaviors among individuals. Reconstructing EG networks is fundamental to understand and control its collective
dynamics. Most existing approaches extend this problem to the l_1-regularization
optimization problem, leading to suboptimal solutions. In this paper, a memetic
algorithm (MA) is proposed to address this network reconstruction problem with
$l_{1/2}$ regularization. The problem-specific initialization operator and local search
operator are integrated into MA to accelerate the convergence. We apply the
method to evolutionary games taking place in synthetic and real networks,
finding that our approach has competitive performance to eight state-of-the-art
methods in terms of effectiveness and efficiency.

Keywords: Compressed sensing · Network reconstruction · Memetic
algorithm · Evolutionary games · Sparse reconstruction

1 Introduction

An important class of collective dynamics is evolutionary games (EG) [8–10] in the
human society. For example, through game theory, economists can analyze how people
make choices about money. For the criminal gang, the police need to master the
relationships between the members, namely, agent-to-agent networks. However, in the
real life, it is difficult to directly access to this network, and maybe only the payoff and
strategy of its members are available. Therefore, our goal is to reconstruct the
agent-to-agent networks from these available information, namely, profit sequences.

There have been recent efforts in addressing EG network reconstruction problem
which is converted into a sparse signal reconstruction problem that can be solved by
exploiting l_1-minimization algorithms, such as the LASSO [1] and compressed sensing
(CS) [2]. This problem also is solved by multiobjective evolutionary algorithm with l_1
regularization [29]. However, the l_1 regularization may generate inconsistent selections
when coping with variable selection and often introduces extra bias in estimation. As a
further modification, the $l_{1/2}$ regularization [11, 12] is naturally assured. Moreover, $l_{1/2}$
regularization can assuredly generate more sparse solutions than l_1 regularization.

The $l_{1/2}$ regularization is nonconvex, nonsmooth, and non-Lipschitz optimization
problem. In general, it is different to solve. In this paper, we develop a memetic algorithm (MA) to cope with EG network reconstruction problem with $l_{1/2}$ regularization,

© Springer International Publishing AG 2017
Y. Shi et al. (Eds.): SEAL 2017, LNCS 10593, pp. 15–26, 2017.
https://doi.org/10.1007/978-3-319-68759-9_2

termed as MAEGNet. MAs [4] are hybrids of global search procedures and local search procedures [5, 6]. They can explore better solutions around the best solution found so far. The proposed algorithm combines a genetic algorithm as the global search method and an iterative shrinkage-thresholding (IST) strategy [7] as the local search procedure. To achieve greater chance to increase the speed of convergence toward the optimal solutions, we employ a problem-specific initialization operator [29] for MA. To validate the performance of MAEGNet, EG models [8, 9] taking place on different model-based networks are used. The experimental results show that MAEGNet is able to effectively reconstruct EG networks. The systematic comparison with existing algorithms shows that MAEGNet matches or exceeds the other algorithms.

The remainder of this paper is organized as follows. Section 2 introduces the EG models and the network reconstruction problem. Section 3 gives an introduction to MAEGNet. Section 4 presents experimental data, and compares the performance of MAEGNet against eight state-of-the-art methods. Section 5 concludes the work in this paper.

2 Network Reconstruction Model

Evolutionary games (EG) model a common type of interactions in various complex, networked, natural and social systems. In an evolutionary game, at any time, one agent can select a certain strategy, such as cooperation or defection. The payoffs of the two agents in a game have four possibilities. For example, in the prisoner's-dilemma game (PDG) [10], the agents get rewards R or Pu if both choose to cooperate or defect, respectively. In the remaining two cases the defector's and cooperator's payoff are Te (temptation to defect) and S (sucker's payoff), respectively. The ranking of $Te > R > Pu > S$ and $2R > Te + S$ still holds. We use the same setting as in [8], $R = 1$, $Pu = S = 0$, and $Te = b$, where $b \in (1, 2)$ that keeps the essentials of the Prisoners' dilemma. At each round, all agents play game with their neighbors and then obtain payoffs. For agent i, its payoff is

$$Y_i = \sum_{j \in \Gamma_i} S_i^T P S_j \tag{1}$$

where S_i and S_j denote the strategies of agents i and j at the time and the sum is over the neighbor-connection set Γ_i of i. After a round of game, an agent updates its strategy using the Fermi rule [11] which can maximize its payoff at the next round. Fermi rule is defined as follows

$$W(S_i \leftarrow S_j) = \frac{1}{1 + \exp[(Y_i - Y_j)/\kappa]} \tag{2}$$

where κ characterizes the stochastic uncertainties introduced to permit irrational choices. We use the same setting as in [29], b is set to 1.2, and $\kappa = 0.1$.

We assume that only the profit sequences of all agents and their strategies in each round are available. The key to reconstruct agent-to-agent networks lies in the relationships between agents' payoffs and strategies. The interactions among agents in the network can be characterized by an $N \times N$ adjacency matrix X with elements $x_{ij} = 1$ if agents i and j are connected, and $x_{ij} = 0$ otherwise. The payoff of agent i can be expressed by

$$Y_i(t) = \sum_{\substack{j=1 \\ i \neq j}}^{N} x_{ij} S_i^T(t) PS_j(t) \tag{3}$$

where x_{ij} $(j = 1, 2, \ldots, N)$ represents a possible connection between agent i agent j; $x_{ij} S_i^T(t) PS_j(t)$ $(l = 1, 2, \ldots, N)$ stands for the possible payoff of agent i from the game with agent j; and $t = 1, 2, \ldots, m$ is the number of rounds that all agents play the game with their neighbors. Equation (3) can be simplified as $Y_i = A_i \times X_i$, where

$$Y_i = (Y_i(1), Y_i(2), \cdots, Y_i(m))^T \tag{4}$$

$$X_i = (x_{i1}, \cdots, x_{i,i-1}, x_{i,i+1}, \cdots x_{iN})^T \tag{5}$$

$$A_i = \begin{pmatrix} D_{i1}(1) & \cdots & D_{i,i-1}(1) & D_{i,i+1}(1) & \cdots & D_{iN}(1) \\ D_{i1}(2) & \cdots & D_{i,i-1}(1) & D_{i,i+1}(2) & \cdots & D_{iN}(2) \\ \vdots & \vdots & \vdots & \vdots & \vdots & \vdots \\ D_{i1}(m) & \cdots & D_{i,i-1}(m) & D_{i,i+1}(m) & \cdots & D_{iN}(m) \end{pmatrix} \tag{6}$$

where $D_{x,y}(t) = S_x^T(t) PS_y(t)$. Y_i can be obtained directly from the payoff data and A_i can be calculated from the strategy data.

Our goal is to reconstruct X_i from Y_i and A_i. To solve this network reconstruction problem, the following tradeoff form is developed:

$$\min_{X_i} \left(\frac{1}{2} \|A_i X_i - Y_i\|_2^2 + \lambda \|X_i\|_{1/2}^{1/2} \right) \tag{7}$$

where λ is a constant that controls the tradeoff between the reconstruction error and the sparseness of network. Being different from L_0 and L_1 regularization of R^N, $L_{1/2}$ can assuredly generate sparser solutions than L_1 regularization [11, 12]. Thus, in this paper, we optimize (7) using MA and can obtain the solution X_i. In a similar fashion, the neighbor-connection vectors of all other agents can be predicted, yielding the network adjacency matrix $X = (X_1, X_2, \cdots, X_N)$.

3 MAEGNet

To solve Eq. (7), we employ the proposed problem-specific memetic algorithm, termed as MAEGNet. The whole framework of MAEGNet is shown in Algorithm 1. For each agent, the steps from line 3 to line 13 are implemented. In line 3, the data for Eq. (7) are assigned. In lines 3 to 12, MA is employed to dealing with the problem (Eq. (7)). In line 4, MAEGNet completes the population initialization task according to Sect. 3.1. In line 5, the individual with the minimum fitness is selected as the best individual. Inline 7, MAEGNet uses the tournament selection method to select *pool* parental individuals for mating. Then in line 8, the BLX-α crossover [13] and the non-uniform mutation operation [14] are employed on the chosen parental individuals $P^t_{Selection}$. In line 9, MAEGNet performs IST local search for P^t_{GO}. In line 10, the current population is refreshed by taking the best *pop* individuals from $P^t_{Local} \cup P^t$. In line 11, we update the best individual and λ. When stopping criterion satisfies, MA stops and outputs $X^{temp}_i \leftarrow P^{t+1}_{best}$ (line 12). When $i > N$, MAEGNet stops and outputs X.

3.1 Initialization Operator for MA

In this paper, we employ a new initialization operator to initialize population [29]. The L_1-minimization algorithm LASSO [3] solves the following problem:

$$\min_{X_i} \left(\frac{1}{2} \|A_i X_i - Y_i\|^2_2 + \lambda \|X_i\|_1 \right) \tag{8}$$

In LASSO, different choices for λ in the above equation may result in different optimal solutions. Moreover, we will obtain a set of solutions by using LASSO with different value of λ. Then, we briefly present this operator as follows. In order to generate *pop* individuals, we need to set *pop* different value of $\lambda_i \in [0.00001, 10]$ randomly, $i = 1, 2, 3, \ldots, pop$, and then solve Eq. (8) using the LASSO to generate *pop* solutions.

3.2 Shrinkage-Thresholding Local Search

Iterative shrinkage-thresholding algorithm (ISTA) [7] is one of L_1-minimization algorithms for solving linear inverse problem Eq. (8). Basically, we can use the following equation to update the next individual.

$$X^{k+1}_i = \Xi_\alpha \big(g(X^k_i) \big) \tag{9}$$

where $\alpha = \lambda/L$ and $\Xi_\alpha : R^n \rightarrow R^n$ is the shrinkage operator defined by:

$$\Xi_\alpha(x) = \text{sgn}(x)(|x| - \alpha)_+ \tag{10}$$

and $g(X^t_i)$ stands for

$$g(X^t_i) = X^t_i - \frac{1}{c} \nabla f(X^t_i) \tag{11}$$

Algorithm 1 Framework of MAEGNet

Input:
maximum generation: *maxgen*;
population size: *pop*;
mating pool size: *pool*;
tournament size: *tour*;
crossoverprobability: *pc*;
mutation probability: *pm*;
balance factor in Eq. (7): λ;
beta: β;
lambda bars: λ_{bar};
thepayoff data: Y;
the strategy data: A;

Output:
Agent-to-agent network X.

1:      Agent $i \leftarrow 1$;
2:      **while** ($i < N$) **do**
3:          Obtain Y_i from the payoff data and calculate A_i from the strategy data;
4:          Population initialization: $P^0 = \left\{ P_1^0, P_2^0, \cdots, P_{pop}^0 \right\}^T$;
5:          Obtain the individualwith the minimum fitness: $P_{best}^0 = P_i^0$; Generation $t \leftarrow 0$;
6:          **while** ($t < maxgen$) **do**
7:              Select parental chromosomes: $P_{Selection}^t = Selection\left(P^t, pool, tour \right)$;
8:              Perform genetic operators on: $P_{GO}^t = GeneticOperation\left(P_{Selection}^t, pc, pm \right)$;
9:              Perform local search: $P_{Local}^t = LocalSerach\left(P_{GO}^t, \lambda, A_i, Y_i \right)$;
10:             Update population: $P^{t+1} = UpdatePopulation\left(P_{Local}^t, P^t \right)$;
11:             Update the best individual P_{best}^{t+1} and $\lambda \leftarrow max\ (\beta\lambda, \lambda_{bar})$; $t \leftarrow t+1$;
12:         **end while**
13:     $X_i \leftarrow P_{best}^{t+1}$; $i \leftarrow i+1$;
14:     **end while**

---

where $f(X_i) = \|A_i X_i - Y_i\|_2^2$ and the parameter c is chosen by optimizing the so-called Barizilai-Borwein equation:

$$c = \frac{\left(X_i^k - X_i^{k-1}\right)^T \left(\nabla f\left(X_i^k\right) - \nabla f\left(X_i^{k-1}\right)\right)}{\left(X_i^k - X_i^{k-1}\right)^T \left(X_i^k - X_i^{k-1}\right)} \tag{12}$$

To obtain better solutions efficiently, we employ a shrinkage-thresholding strategy improved from ISTA to refine the individuals of P_{GO}. In this paper, the regularizing coefficient λ is generated by a decreasing sequence of $\{\lambda_k\}$. To obtain X_i^k and X_i^{k-1}, we first sort P_{GO} and split P_{GO} into two equal subsets $\{P_{GOL}, P_{GOR}\}$, where P_{GOL} is better than P_{GOR}. We then calculate c and obtain X_i^{k+1} using Eq. (9).

4   Experiments

Our experiments fall into three parts. Section 4.1 introduces performance measures to evaluate the performance of MAEGNet and parameters settings for MAEGNet. Section 4.2 compares the performance of MAEGNet against eight state-of-the-art methods on synthetic networks. Section 4.3 shows the experiments on six real social networks.

4.1   Experimental Setup

To quantify the performance of our reconstruction method, two standard measurement indices are introduced, namely, the area under the receiver operating characteristic curve (AUROC) and the area under the precision-recall curve (AUPR) [16].

In practice, the learned x_{ij} is real number. Thus, a cut-off CO can be used to distinguish the relationship between node i and node j. in this paper, we set $CO = 0.2$. If nodes i and j are connected, $x_{ij} \geq CO$; otherwise, $x_{ij} < CO$.

Numerical simulation of EG is described as follows. Initially, a fraction of agents is set to choose the strategy of cooperation and the remaining agents are set to choose the strategy of defection. Nodal states are updated in parallel. For agent i of degree $\langle k \rangle$, at round t, the payoff of this agent is calculated using Eq. (2). To maximize the payoff of agent i, its strategy is updated using Eq. (3). A Monte Carlo round t is referred to the situation where all the states at $t + 1$ have been updated according to their states at t.

For MAEGNet, we have chosen a reasonable set of values and have not made any effort in finding the best parameter settings. We leave this task for a future work. The parameters of MAEGNet are showed in Table 1. Six real social networks are employed, including football [30], polbooks [31], dolphin [32], ZK [33], lesmis [15], neuralnet [17].

Table 1.   The parameter settings of MAEGNet.

Parameter	Meaning	Value
maxgen	The maximum generation	1000
pop	Population size	100
pm	Mutation rate	0.2
pool	Size of the mating pool	50
tour	Tournament size	2
pc	Crossover rate	0.5
β	Beta	0.98

4.2   Analysis of MAEGNet on Synthetic Networks

In this section, we study the effect of the parameters, such as $\langle k \rangle$, on MAEGNet. We simulate evolutionary games on different model-based networks, including Erdős-Rényi random networks (ER) [17], Barabási-Albert scale-free networks (BA) [18], Newman-Watts small-world networks (NW) [19], and Watts-Strogatz small-world networks (WS) [20]. The experiments are conducted on network size $N = 100$. $\langle k \rangle = 18$. Note that we can obtain common conclusion for other values of N and $\langle k \rangle$. N_M is the total data length M divided by network size N. Here, N_M is increased from 0.2 to 0.8 in steps of 0.1. Rewriting probability of small-world networks is 0.3. Each data point is obtained by averaging over 30 independent runs. The performance of MAEGNet is compared with those of LASSO [1], OMP [21], basis pursuit (BP) [22], homotopy method [23, 24], fast iterative soft-thresholding algorithm (FISTA) [25], LARS [26], primal augmented lagrangian methods (PALM) [27], and L1LS [28] in terms of AUROC and AUPR, which are reported in Figs. 1 and 2, respectively. In order to fairly compare with other methods, we set $\lambda = (100, 10, 1, 0.1, 0.01, 0.001, 0.0001, 0.00001)$. For all algorithm, we select the best results in terms of AUPR and AUROC. For these methods, we have identical parameter settings as

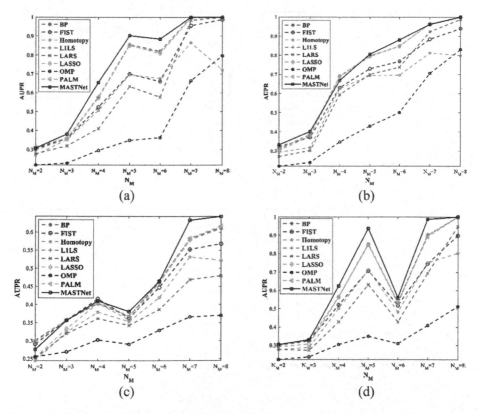

Fig. 1. AUPR as a function of the relative data length N_M of time series for (a) ER networks, (b) BA networks, (c) NW networks, and (d) WS networks. Here, $\langle k \rangle = 18$.

suggested in the original codes. The code of these methods can be obtained from https://people.eecs.berkeley.edu/~yang/software/l1benchmark/ or http://sparselab.stanford.edu/.

The results demonstrate that the length of data sequences has an important effect on the performance of MAEGNet, even for small value of N_M, most links can be identified, as reflected by the high values of AUPR and AUROC. As seen, in terms of average AUPR and AUROC, MAEGNet almost outperforms all the others. Note that there are the curves descending rapidly for WS networks in terms of AUPR and AUROC. The reason is that the average degree $\langle k \rangle$ of WS networks with a certain value of N_M become greater than the general. Furthermore, the experimental results show that although MAEGNet cannot perform better than all methods in some cases, it just performs slightly worse than the best performer.

4.3   Application to Real-World Networks

We also test MAEGNet on several empirical networks. The experiments are conducted on EG dynamic with six real-world networks. Here, N_M is increased from 0.3 to 0.6 in

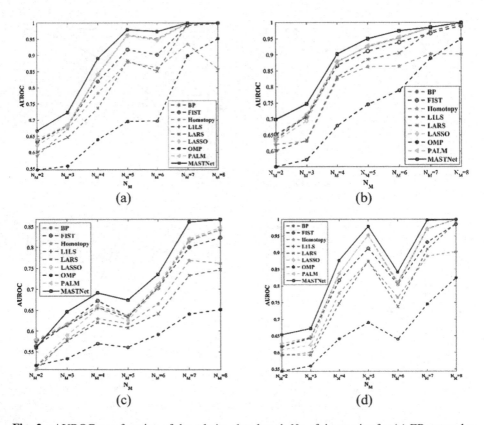

Fig. 2. AUROC as a function of the relative data length N_M of time series for (a) ER networks, (b) BA networks, (c) NW networks, and (d) WS networks. Here, $\langle k \rangle = 18$.

steps of 0.1. Each data point is obtained by averaging over 30 independent realizations. The parameters of these approaches are similar to Sect. 4.2. The results are reported in Tables 2 and 3.

As seen, on the cases with $N_M \geq 0.4$, the performance of MAEGNet matches or exceeds that of the remaining methods in terms of AUPR and AUROC. On the football dataset with $N_M = 0.3$, AUPR of MAEGNet outperforms that of LARS, LASSO and OMP, but is worse than that of BP, FIST, L1LS, and PALM. On this case, AUROC of MAEGNet has a similar performance to AUPR of MAEGNet. On the neuralnet dataset with $N_M = 0.3$, AUPR of MAEGNet outperforms that of FIST, LARS, LASSO and OMP, but is worse than that of BP, L1LS, LASSO, and PALM. On the ZK dataset with $N_M = 0.3$, AUROC of MAEGNet outperforms that of LARS, LASSO and OMP, but is worse than that of BP, FIST, L1LS, and PALM. On each of polbooks, dolphin, ZK, and lesmis datasets, AUPR of MAEGNet performs better than the remaining methods. On each of polbooks, dolphin, lesmis, and neuralnet datasets, the performance of MAEGNet performs better than the remaining methods in terms of AUROC.

Table 2. The comparison of MAEGNet against other methods in terms of AUPR.

N_M	Dataset	BP	FIST	L1LS	LARS	LASSO	OMP	PALM	MAEGNet
0.3	football	**0.239**	0.234	**0.240**	0.170	0.187	0.139	0.238	0.223
	polbooks	0.681	0.617	0.682	0.551	0.659	0.204	0.679	**0.723**
	dolphin	0.885	0.770	0.890	0.767	0.881	0.358	0.882	**0.902**
	ZK	0.825	0.809	0.825	0.808	0.789	0.719	0.825	**0.830**
	lesmis	0.607	0.492	0.609	0.405	0.531	0.273	0.605	**0.620**
	neuralnet	**0.218**	0.192	**0.216**	0.132	0.207	0.072	0.210	0.201
0.4	football	0.492	0.449	0.491	0.351	0.476	0.194	0.495	**0.546**
	polbooks	0.746	0.672	0.747	0.631	0.748	0.301	0.740	**0.778**
	dolphin	**1.000**	0.982	**1.000**	**1.000**	**1.000**	0.824	**1.000**	**1.000**
	ZK	**1.000**	0.987	**1.000**	**1.000**	0.973	0.841	**1.000**	**1.000**
	lesmis	0.922	0.827	0.919	0.817	0.860	0.512	0.922	**0.979**
	neuralnet	0.306	0.228	0.303	0.185	0.304	0.110	0.295	**0.354**
0.5	football	0.656	0.543	0.654	0.436	0.654	0.212	0.644	**0.764**
	polbooks	0.967	0.865	0.970	0.872	0.976	0.510	0.965	**0.984**
	dolphin	**0.976**	**0.976**	**0.976**	**0.976**	**0.976**	**0.976**	**0.976**	**0.976**
	ZK	**1.000**	0.987	**1.000**	**1.000**	**1.000**	**1.000**	**1.000**	**1.000**
	lesmis	**0.998**	0.901	**0.998**	0.958	**0.999**	0.634	**0.998**	0.997
	neuralnet	0.393	0.339	0.390	0.215	0.367	0.150	0.374	**0.429**
0.6	football	0.977	0.867	0.976	0.878	0.982	0.454	0.974	**1.000**
	polbooks	0.961	0.862	0.961	0.900	0.960	0.497	0.954	**0.996**
	dolphin	**0.973**	0.967	**0.973**	**0.973**	0.971	0.947	**0.973**	**0.973**
	ZK	**1.000**	**1.000**	**1.000**	**1.000**	**1.000**	**1.000**	**1.000**	**1.000**
	lesmis	**0.997**	0.953	0.995	0.982	0.988	0.884	**0.996**	0.995
	neuralnet	0.565	0.479	0.567	0.351	0.555	0.212	0.548	**0.619**

Table 3. The comparison of MAEGNet against other methods in terms of AUROC.

N_M	Dataset	BP	FIST	L1LS	LARS	LASSO	OMP	PALM	MAEGNet
0.3	football	0.660	0.658	0.660	0.593	0.610	0.562	**0.666**	0.658
	polbooks	0.899	0.887	0.899	0.851	0.890	0.652	0.903	**0.935**
	dolphin	**0.960**	0.937	**0.960**	0.930	0.951	0.784	**0.961**	**0.960**
	ZK	**0.984**	0.952	**0.984**	0.922	0.914	0.901	**0.984**	0.940
	lesmis	0.897	0.855	0.897	0.792	0.848	0.700	0.897	**0.908**
	neuralnet	0.702	0.688	0.702	0.661	0.698	0.583	0.705	**0.749**
0.4	football	0.826	0.807	0.825	0.756	0.818	0.632	0.834	**0.864**
	polbooks	0.937	0.923	0.938	0.907	0.939	0.740	0.938	**0.958**
	dolphin	**1.000**	**0.999**	**1.000**	**1.000**	**1.000**	0.971	**1.000**	**1.000**
	ZK	**1.000**	0.991	**1.000**	**1.000**	0.992	0.969	**1.000**	**1.000**
	lesmis	0.980	0.952	0.978	0.954	0.968	0.860	0.980	**0.998**
	neuralnet	0.779	0.768	0.780	0.730	0.780	0.634	0.781	**0.828**
0.5	football	0.903	0.870	0.902	0.826	0.901	0.662	0.904	**0.944**
	polbooks	0.994	0.976	0.995	0.973	0.995	0.855	0.995	**0.998**
	dolphin	**0.984**	**0.984**	**0.984**	**0.984**	**0.984**	**0.984**	**0.984**	**0.984**
	ZK	**1.000**	0.999	**1.000**	**1.000**	**1.000**	**1.000**	**1.000**	**1.000**
	lesmis	**1.000**	0.983	**1.000**	0.992	0.996	0.974	**1.000**	**1.000**
	neuralnet	0.828	0.807	0.828	0.773	0.822	0.673	0.830	**0.869**
0.6	football	0.994	0.976	0.994	0.977	0.996	0.842	0.993	**1.000**
	polbooks	0.992	0.967	0.992	0.975	0.992	0.860	0.992	**0.999**
	dolphin	**0.983**	**0.982**	**0.983**	**0.983**	0.981	0.979	**0.983**	**0.983**
	ZK	**1.000**	**1.000**	**1.000**	**1.000**	**1.000**	**1.000**	**1.000**	**1.000**
	lesmis	**0.999**	0.994	**0.999**	0.992	0.996	0.974	**1.000**	**1.000**
	neuralnet	0.896	0.875	0.896	0.852	0.894	0.729	0.897	**0.925**

5 Conclusions

In this paper, we have developed an efficient MA to reconstruct EG networks from profit sequences. It is noteworthy that the proposed approach is quite flexible and not limited to the networked systems discussed here, such as gene regulatory networks, transportation networks, and communications networks. Being different from l_1 minimization methods, we solve EG network reconstruction problem with $l_{1/2}$ regularization. Then, a problem-specific memetic algorithm incorporated both LASSO initialization and shrinkage-thresholding local search has been proposed to optimize this problem. The experiments on synthetic and real networks illustrate that the proposed MAEGNet achieve good performance in terms of accuracy.

Acknowledgements. This work is partially supported by the Outstanding Young Scholar Program of National Natural Science Foundation of China (NSFC) under Grant 61522311, the Overseas, Hong Kong & Macao Scholars Collaborated Research Program of NSFC under Grant 61528205, and the Key Program of Fundamental Research Project of Natural Science of Shaanxi Province, China under Grant 2017JZ017.

References

1. Han, X., Shen, Z., Wang, W.X., Di, Z.: Robust reconstruction of complex networks from sparse data. Phys. Rev. Lett. **114**, 028701 (2015)
2. Wang, W.X., Lai, Y.C., Grebogi, C., Ye, J.: Network reconstruction based on evolutionary-game data via compressive sensing. Phys. Rev. X **1**, 021021 (2011)
3. Tibshirani, R.: Regression shrinkage and selection via the lasso. J. R. Stat. Soc. Ser. B (Methodol.) **58**, 267–288 (1996)
4. Moscato, P.: On evolution, search, optimization, genetic algorithms and martialarts: towards memetic algorithms. Caltech Concurrent Computation Program, C3P Rep., 826 (1989)
5. Chen, X., Ong, Y.S., Lim, M.H., Tan, K.C.: A multi-facet survey on memetic computation. IEEE Trans. Evol. Comput. **15**(5), 591–607 (2011)
6. Ong, Y.S., Lim, M.H., Chen, X.: Research frontier-memetic computation–past, present & future. IEEE Comput. Intell. Mag. **5**(2), 24–31 (2010)
7. Herrity, K.K., Gilbert, A.C., Tropp, J.A.: Sparse approximation via iterative thresholding. In: Proceedings of IEEE International Conference on Acoustics, Speech, and Signal Processing, pp. 624–627 (2006)
8. Nowak, M.A., May, R.M.: Evolutionary games and spatial chaos. Nature **359**, 826–829 (1992)
9. Szabó, G., Fath, G.: Evolutionary games on graphs. Phys. Rep. **446**, 97–216 (2007)
10. Szabó, G., Tőke, C.: Evolutionary prisoner's dilemma game on a square lattice. Phys. Rev. E **58**, 69 (1998)
11. Xu, Z.B., Guo, H., Wang, Y., Zhang, H.: Representative of $L_{1/2}$ regularization among L_q $(0 < q < 1)$ regularizations: an experimental study based on phase diagram. Acta Automatica Sinica **38**(7), 1225–1228 (2012)
12. Xu, Z.B., Chang, X., Xu, F., Zhang, H.: $L_{1/2}$ regularization: a thresholding representation theory and a fast solver. IEEE Trans. Neural Netw. Learn. Syst. **23**(7), 1013–1027 (2012)
13. Eshellman, L.J.: Real-coded genetic algorithms and interval-schemata. Found. Genetic Algorithms **2**, 187–202 (1993)
14. Neubauer, A.: A theoretical analysis of the non-uniform mutation operator for the modified genetic algorithm. In: Proceedings of the IEEE Congress on Evolutionary Computation, pp. 93–96 (1997)
15. Knuth, D.E.: The Stanford Graph Base: A Platform for Combinatorial Computing. Addison-Wesley, Reading (1993)
16. Grau, J., Grosse, I., Keilwagen, J.: PRROC: computing and visualizing precision-recall and receiver operating characteristic curves in R. Bioinformatics **31**(15), 2595–2597 (2015)
17. Watts, D.J., Strogatz, S.H.: Collective dynamics of 'small-world' networks. Nature **393**, 440–442 (1998)
18. Erdős, P., Rényi, A.: On random graphs. Publicationes Mathematicae Debrecen **6**, 290–297 (1959)
19. Barabási, A.L., Albert, R.: Emergence of scaling in random networks. Science **286**(5439), 509–512 (1999)
20. Newman, M.E., Watts, D.J.: Renormalization group analysis of the small-world network model. Phys. Lett. A **263**(4), 341–346 (1999)
21. Davis, G., Mallat, S., Avellaneda, M.: Adaptive greedy approximations. Constr. Approx. **13**(1), 57–98 (1997)
22. Chen, S.S., Donoho, D.L., Saunders, M.A.: Atomic decomposition by basis pursuit. SIAM Rev. **43**(1), 129–159 (2001)

23. Donoho, D.L., Tsaig, Y.: Fast solution of l1 norm minimization problems when the solution may be sparse. IEEE Trans. Inf. Theory **54**(11), 4789–4812 (2008)
24. Malioutov, D.M., Cetin, M., Willsky, A.S.: Homotopy continuation for sparse signal representation. In: Proceedings of IEEE International Conference on Acoustics, Speech, and Signal Processing, pp. 733–736 (2005)
25. Beck, A., Teboulle, M.: A fast iterative shrinkage-thresholding algorithm for linear inverse problems. SIAM J. Imaging Sci. **2**(1), 183–202 (2009)
26. Efron, B., Hastie, T., Johnstone, I., Tibshirani, R.: Least angle regression. Ann. Stat. **32**(2), 407–499 (2004)
27. Bertsekas, D.: Constrained Optimization and Lagrange Multiplier Methods. Athena Scientific, Belmont (1982)
28. Kim, S., Koh, K., Lustig, M., Boyd, S., Gorinevsky, D.: An interior-pointmethod for large-scale l1-regularized least squares. IEEE J. Sel. Topics Sig. Process. **1**(4), 606–617 (2007)
29. Wu, K., Liu, J., Wang, S.: Reconstructing networks from profit sequences in evolutionary games via a multiobjective optimization approach with lasso initialization. Sci. Rep. **6**, 37771 (2016)
30. Newman, M.E.: Finding community structure in networks using the eigenvectors of matrices. Phys. Rev. E **74**, 036104 (2006)
31. Krebs, V.: http://www.orgnet.com/divided.html
32. Lusseau, D., Schneider, K., Boisseau, O.J., Haase, P., Slooten, E., Dawson, S.M.: The bottlenose dolphin community of doubtful sound features a large proportion of long-lasting associations. Behav. Ecol. Sociobiol. **54**(4), 396–405 (2003)
33. Zachary, W.W.: An information flow model for conflict and fission in small groups. J. Anthropol. Res. **33**, 452–473 (1977)

A Simple Brain Storm Optimization Algorithm via Visualizing Confidence Intervals

YingYing Cao[1], Wei Chen[1], Shi Cheng[2], Yifei Sun[3,4], Qunfeng Liu[1(✉)], Yun Li[1(✉)], and Yuhui Shi[5]

[1] School of Computer Science and Network Security,
Dongguan University of Technology, Dongguan, China
{liuqf,liy}@dgut.edu.cn
[2] School of Computer Science, Shaanxi Normal University, Xi'an, China
[3] Key Laboratory of Modern Teaching Technology,
Ministry of Education, Xi'an, China
[4] School of Physics and Information Technology,
Shaanxi Normal University, Xi'an, China
[5] Department of Computer Science and Engineering,
Southern University of Science and Technology, Shenzhen, China

Abstract. Visualizing confidence intervals method developed recently for benchmarking stochastic optimization algorithm is adopted in this paper to benchmark and study the brain storm optimization algorithm in depth. Through analyzing numerical effects of different components of brain storm optimization, a simplified brain storm optimization algorithm is developed. It is tested and shown to perform better than the original brain storm optimization algorithm in the objective space.

Keywords: Brain storm optimization · Visualizing confidence intervals · Benchmarking · Swarm intelligence · Evolutionary computation

1 Introduction

Having been utilized for innovative problem solving, brainstorming is now modeled to form the brain storm optimization (BSO) algorithm [11,12]. Since then, it has become a promising swarm intelligence algorithm, and has attracted more and more research both theory and practice [2,4,5,13–15].

An important progress of BSO is to transform operations in the solution space to operations in the objective space [14]. The resultant new version of BSO is easier in implementation, and lower in computational cost on "clustering" [14]. In this paper, we refer BSO to BSO in the objective space, unless otherwise stated.

In the BSO algorithm, there often contains three components which are "disruption", "generating new individuals", and "population updating". In the disruption stage, some individual will be disrupted randomly. In the new individuals

© Springer International Publishing AG 2017
Y. Shi et al. (Eds.): SEAL 2017, LNCS 10593, pp. 27–38, 2017.
https://doi.org/10.1007/978-3-319-68759-9_3

generating stage, a new population will be generated. The old population will be updated through evaluating the new population at the population updating stage.

In this paper, our goal is to investigate how different components affect the numerical performance of BSO via the visualing confidence intervals (VCI) method. The VCI method can be regarded as an extension of data profile technique [8] and performance profile technique [3] for evaluating algorithms in mathematical programming. Through adopting confidence intervals to replace stochastic tests, the VCI method is a distribution-free benchmarking method and is convenient for large set of benchmark functions [7]. In other words, we adopt the VCI method to evaluate the different components of the BSO algorithm and try to improve it in this paper.

The remainder of this paper is organized as follows. In Sect. 2, the BSO algorithm, especially its main components, is reviewed briefly. Then a simplified BSO algorithm is developed. The VCI method is reviewed in Sect. 3 and is adopted in Sect. 4 to benchmark different components of the BSO and compare BSO with SimBSO. Finally, conclusions are drawn in Sect. 5.

2 Brain Storm Optimization

2.1 Brain Storm Optimization in the Objective Space

The brain storm optimization (BSO) algorithm in objective space was proposed in 2015 [14]. The procedure is listed in Algorithm 1.

Algorithm 1. Brain Storm Optimization (BSO).

---

1 Initialization: generate the initial population randomly;
2 **while** *stopping conditions do not hold* **do**
3   **Disruption**: select an individual from the population randomly, and change its value in a randomly selected dimension;
4   **for** *each individual in the population* **do**
5   **Categorization and selection**: select one or two individuals from the best 20% individuals or the worst 80% individuals to generate a child;
6   Generate a new child by add a white noise to the child's each dimension;
7   Record the new child if it is better than the current individual;
8   **Update**: update the whole population;

In the BSO algorithm, the initialized population is often randomly generated. In the main loop of the algorithm, three components including "disruption (Line 3 in Algorithm 1)", "generating new individuals (Line 5–6 in Algorithm 1)" and "population updating (Line 8 in Algorithm 1)" will be executed. In "disruption" stage, one individual is selected randomly from the population, and its value in one random dimension will be replaced by a random number. It is helpful when diversity is critical for the algorithm to solve problems [12], and it is often done with a small probability. The "disruption" strategy could avoid the premature convergence, and help individuals 'jump out' of the local optima.

The most important component of BSO is to generate new individuals. Firstly, all individual is categorized into two classes according to their fitness values: the best 20% of individuals is classified as "elitists" and the rest 80% is classified as "normals". Then for each given individual, one or two individuals are selected randomly from "elitists" or "normals" and combined linearly. The resulted "child" is then be used to generate a new individual by adding different white noises in its different dimensions. The variances of these white noises are controlled by the following step-size function

$$\xi(t) = \mathrm{logsig}\left(\frac{0.5 \times T - t}{c}\right) \times \mathrm{rand}(t), \tag{1}$$

where logsig() is a logarithmic sigmoid function, T and t are the maximum and current number of iterations, respectively, c is a coefficient to change logsig() function's slope, and rand() return a random value between 0 and 1.

The "population updating" strategy is utilized to keep good solutions. The new individual generated in the above stage will be recorded if its fitness value is better than the current given individual. But the current individual will not be replaced until all new individuals are generated and evaluated (see Algorithm 1). In other words, new individuals are all generated from the old population in BSO, and the whole population will be updated for generating individuals at the next iteration [14].

2.2   Simplified BSO

Not all components are necessary in optimization. A simplified BSO (SimBSO) algorithm is proposed. In SimBSO, the disruption operation is abandoned. The reason is that the white noise (see Line 6 in Algorithm 1) possesses similar function as the disruption operation, and therefore, it may not be necessary for BSO. The categorization operation is also abandoned in SimBSO. There are two reasons for us to do so. Firstly, the new strategy supports brainstorming better in proposing free ideas. In SimBSO, new individuals (new ideas) are not necessary to be generated from two clusters (elitists and normals). Secondly, the new

---

Algorithm 2. Simplified Brain Storm Optimization (SimBSO).

---

1 Initialization: generate the initial population randomly;
2 **while** *stopping conditions do not hold* **do**
3   **for** *each individual in the population* **do**
4   Select three individuals from the population randomly, and generate a child by combining them linearly;
5   Generate a new child by add a white noise to the child's each dimension;
6   Update the current individual if the new child is better;

---

strategy eliminates the need to set parameters for category (e.g., the 20% best individuals are regarded as elitists).

The procedure of SimBSO algorithm is listed in Algorithm 2, where the population is updated timely. We will test if the BSO can be improved by simplifying it. Before reporting our experiments results, we present the VCI method which is necessary for our experimental data analysis.

3   The VCI Method

The VCI method is developed for analyzing the experimental data gathered when testing (especially stochastic) optimization algorithms, and it is proposed to replace the traditional statistic test based methods with the VCI method [7]. Through visualizing confidence intervals of the best objective function values found as computational cost increasing, the VCI method is shown to be convenient for benchmarking stochastic global optimization algorithms, especially when the set of benchmark functions or the number of algorithms is large [7].

Suppose there is a set $\mathbb{S}$ of optimization solvers needed to be compared numerically, and a set $\mathbb{P}$ of benchmark problems is selected. Then given any budget of function evaluations μ_f, run each solver $s \in \mathbb{S}$ on each problem $p \in \mathbb{P}$ for n_r times, and record the found best function values. After all tests finished, a 4-D matrix H with size $\mu_f \times n_r \times n_p \times n_s$ is obtained, where the 4-tuple element $H(k, r, j, i)$ denotes the found best function value during k function evaluations at the r-th run when test the i-th solver on the j-th problem.

Then matrix H is used to generate a sample mean matrix $\overline{H}$, sample variance matrix S_H^2, confidence upper bound matrix H_{upper} and confidence lower bound matrix H_{lower} for each algorithm $i = 1, ..., n_s$ on each problem $j = 1, ..., n_p$ with $k = 1, ..., \mu_f$ function evaluations according to the following equations [7].

$$\overline{H}(k, j, i) = \frac{1}{n_r} \sum_{r=1}^{n_r} H(k, r, j, i), \tag{2}$$

$$S_H^2(k, j, i) = \frac{1}{n_r - 1} \sum_{r=1}^{n_r} \left[H(k, r, j, i) - \overline{H}(k, j, i) \right]^2, \tag{3}$$

$$H_{upper}(k, j, i) = \overline{H}(k, j, i) + \frac{2S_H(k, j, i)}{\sqrt{n_r}}, \tag{4}$$

$$H_{lower}(k, j, i) = \overline{H}(k, j, i) - \frac{2S_H(k, j, i)}{\sqrt{n_r}}. \tag{5}$$

In [7], the popular data profile method [8] is adopted to analyze $\overline{H}, H_{upper}$ and H_{lower} statistically. The data profile is defined for any solver $s \in \mathbb{S}$ as the following cumulative distribution function

$$d_s(\kappa) = \frac{1}{|\mathbb{P}|} \text{size} \left\{ p \in \mathbb{P} : \frac{t_{p,s}}{D_p + 1} \leq \kappa \right\} \tag{6}$$

where $|\mathbb{P}|$ denotes the number of test problems, D_p is the dimension of the problem p, and size$\{\}$ returns the size of a set. In (6), $t_{p,s}$ is the number of function evaluations needed for solver s to find a position x such that the convergence condition

$$f(x_0) - f(x) \geq (1 - \tau)(f(x_0) - f_L) \tag{7}$$

holds, where x_0 is the starting point, $\tau > 0$ is a tolerance and f_L is the smallest objective function value obtained by any solver within μ_f of function evaluations. $t_{p.s} = \infty$ if the condition (7) does not satisfy after μ_f function evaluations.

Specifically, the data profile method is used to analyze $\overline{H}$ firstly. From the generated data profiles, a winner solver can be determined in the sense of best average performance. Then the data profile method is used to analyze H_{upper} and H_{lower} — the winner solver's H_{upper} and the other solvers' H_{lower}. The purpose is to confirm that the winner solver performs the best in the sense of the worst deviation.

In summary, the VCI method possesses several advantages than the traditional methods (e.g., statistic test based methods), and is convenient to present results on large set of benchmark functions. Therefore, in next section, we adopt the VCI method to analyze experimental data when benchmarking different versions of BSOs on some large sets of benchmark functions.

4   Benchmarking for Improving BSO via the VCI Method

The VCI method [7] is adopted to benchmark BSO with or without the following components:

- Disruption
- Categorization
- Timely updating of population.

Specifically, the BSO algorithm [14] is compared with the following modifications:

- BSO-1: BSO without disruption;
- BSO-2: BSO with timely updating of population, i.e., updating each individual in the population if the generated new individual is better.
- BSO-3: BSO without categorization. New individual is generated as follows: select an individual randomly from the whole population, and then add a different white noise to different dimension, just like in the BSO.
- BSO-4: BSO without categorization. New individual is generated as follow: select two individuals randomly from the whole population, combine them linearly, and then add a different white noise to different dimension.

Through comparing the performance of the BSO with its modifications, our purpose is to find out how the above components affect BSO's performance.

In this paper, the Hedar test set [6] is adopted to test BSO and its modifications. Table 1 shows the function names, dimensions, Characteristic, search regions and their minimal function values. There are 7 unimodal functions and 28 multimodal functions in Hedar test set. Since some functions have variant dimensions, there are 16 unimodal problems and 52 multimodal problems in total. See Table 1 for more details.

In our experiments, 50 independent runs are executed for each problem, and all algorithms stops only when 20,000 function evaluations are consumed on each problem in the Hedar test set.

4.1 BSO Without Disruption

Firstly, we compare the BSO with BSO-1 by the VCI method. The left subfigure of Fig. 1 shows the resulted data profiles from comparing their average performance.

From the left subfigure of Fig. 1 we can see that BSO-1 performs almost the same as BSO. Specifically, both BSO and BSO-1 can solve almost the same proportion of problems as computational cost increasing, and finally they solved about 75% problems. Since the average performances of both BSO and BSO-1 are very similar, and it is unnecessary to compare their confidence bounds.

Therefore, we can conclude that the disruption in BSO does not affect its numerical performance significantly, at least on the Hedar test set.

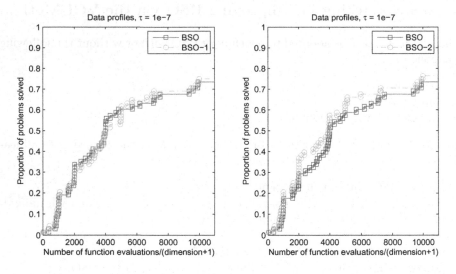

Fig. 1. Data profiles resulted from comparing BSO's average with BSO-1's (left subfigure) or BSO-2's (right subfigure) by the VCI method.

4.2 BSO with Updating Population

The right subfigure of Fig. 1 shows the data profiles resulted from comparing BSO with BSO-2 by the VCI method. From the subfigure we can see that BSO-2

Table 1. Information about the Hedar test set.

Function	Dimension n	Characteristic	Search region	Minimal function value
Beale	2	Unimodal	$[-4.5, 4.5]^2$	0
Matyas	2	Unimodal	$[-8, 12.5]^2$	0
Sphere	2, 5, 10, 20	Unimodal	$[-4.1, 6.4]^n$	0
Sum squares	2, 5, 10, 20	Unimodal	$[-8, 12.5]^n$	0
Trid	6	Unimodal	$[-36, 36]^6$	-50
Trid	10	Unimodal	$[-100, 100]^{10}$	-200
Zakharov	2, 5, 10, 20	Unimodal	$[-5, 10]^n$	0
Ackley	2, 5, 10, 20	Multimodal	$[-15, 30]^n$	0
Bohachevsky 1	2	Multimodal	$[-80, 125]^2$	0
Bohachevsky 2	2	Multimodal	$[-80, 125]^2$	0
Bohachevsky 3	2	Multimodal	$[-80, 125]^2$	0
Booth	2	Multimodal	$[-100, 100]^2$	0
Branin	2	Multimodal	$[-5, 10] * [0, 15]$	0.397887357729739
Colville	4	Multimodal	$[-10, 10]^4$	0
Dixson Price	2, 5, 10, 20	Multimodal	$[-10, 10]^n$	0
Easom	2	Multimodal	$[-100, 100]^2$	-1
Goldstein and price	2	Multimodal	$[-2, 2]^2$	3
Griewank	2, 5, 10, 20	Multimodal	$[-480, 750]^n$	0
Hartman 3	3	Multimodal	$[0, 1]^3$	-3.86278214782076
Hartman 6	6	Multimodal	$[0, 1]^6$	-3.32236801141551
Hump	2	Multimodal	$[-5, 5]^2$	0
Levy	2, 5, 10, 20	Multimodal	$[-10, 10]^n$	0
Michalewics	2	Multimodal	$[0, \pi]^2$	-1.80130341008983
Michalewics	5	Multimodal	$[0, \pi]^5$	-4.687658179
Michalewics	10	Multimodal	$[0, \pi]^{10}$	-9.66015
Perm	4	Multimodal	$[-4, 4]^4$	0
Powell	4, 12, 24, 48	Multimodal	$[-4, 5]^n$	0
Power sum	4	Multimodal	$[0, 4]^4$	0
Rastrigin	2, 5, 10, 20	Multimodal	$[-4.1, 6.4]^n$	0
Rosenbrock	2, 5, 10, 20	Multimodal	$[-5, 10]^n$	0
Schwefel	2, 5, 10, 20	Multimodal	$[-500, 500]^n$	0
Shekel 5	4	Multimodal	$[0, 10]^4$	-10.1531996790582
Shekel 7	4	Multimodal	$[0, 10]^4$	-10.4029405668187
Schkel 10	4	Multimodal	$[0, 10]^4$	-10.5364098166920
Shubert	2	Multimodal	$[-10, 10]^2$	-186.730908831024

performs slightly better than the BSO. Specifically, for any given computational cost, BSO-2 can solve more problems than BSO, and when $\kappa > 2000$, BSO-2 solves about 1%–4% problems more than BSO. Finally, BSO-2 solves about 76% problems, 3% more than BSO.

Since the average performances of both BSO and BSO-2 are similar, and it is unnecessary to compare their confidence bounds, too. These results imply that updating the population timely is better than updating it at the end of each iteration, at least on the Hedar test set.

4.3   BSO Without Categorization

In this subsection, we compare BSO with BSO-3 and BSO-4. BSO-3 and BSO-4 are two examples of BSO without categorization, and the only difference between them is that they select one or two "father individuals" from the whole population to generate a child. On the contrary, in BSO, the "father individuals" are selected from both the elites and the normals, respectively.

Figure 2 shows the resulted data profiles when comparing BSO's average with BSO-3's (left subfigure) or BSO-4's (right subfigure). Significant performance differences are observed from these subfigures. For instance, BSO-3 performs much (about 45% performance difference) worse than BSO, while BSO-4 performs much (about 21% performance difference) better than BSO.

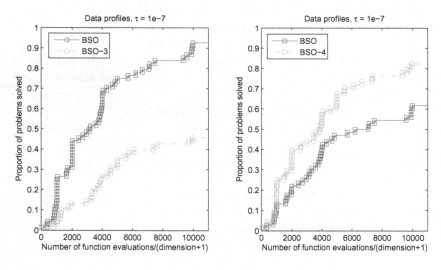

Fig. 2. Data profiles resulted from comparing the BSO's average with BSO-3's (left subfigure) or BSO-4's (right subfigure) by the VCI method.

Then confidence bounds of BSO, BSO-3 and BSO-4 are taken into account to verify whether the performance differences are significant in statistic sense. Figure 3 shows the resulted data profiles. From the left subfigure in Fig. 3 we see that BSO's confidence upper bound "performs" similarly to BSO-3's confidence lower bound. Combined with the left subfigure in Fig. 2, it implies that BSO actually performs better than BSO-3. On the other hand, BSO-4's confidence upper bound "performs" worse than BSO's confidence lower bound. Therefore,

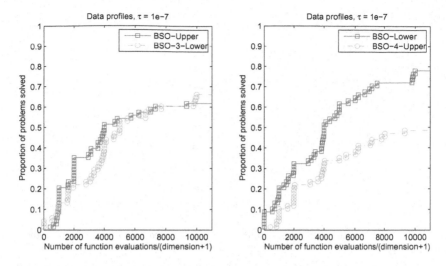

Fig. 3. Data profiles resulted from comparing BSO and BSO-3 (left subfigure) or BSO-4 (right subfigure) by the VCI method. BSO's confidence upper bounds and BSO-3's confidence lower bounds are compared in the left subfigure, while BSO's confidence lower bounds and BSO-4's confidence upper bounds are compared in the right subfigure.

combining with the right subfigure in Fig. 2, we can not say that BSO-4 performs significantly better than BSO.

These results indicate that the categorization in BSO is necessary if only one "father individual" is selected to generate a child, however it is unnecessary if two "father individuals" are selected. In order to understand what will happen when more than two "father individuals" are selected, we have tested algorithms which are similar as BSO-4 while three or more "father individuals" are selected. The results show that three "father individuals" is even better than BSO-4 in sense of average performance, however, four "father individuals" becomes worse than BSO-4.

4.4 Improving BSO with Simplification

Based on the abover numerical results, we found that the "disruption" may not necessary for BSO; and the "categorization" may not necessary if we select two or three "father individuals" to generate a child; moreover, updating the population timely is better. These support the simplifications in SimBSO (see Algorithm 2). In order to verify whether putting all these simplifications together still work, we then compare SimBSO and BSO on the Hedar and the CEC2017 test set [1].

Figure 4 shows the resulted data profiles on the Hedar test set. The average performances are considered in the left subfigure, while the confidence bounds are taken into account in the right subfigure. From Fig. 4 we can see that the SimBSO performs much better (about 32% performance difference) than BSO

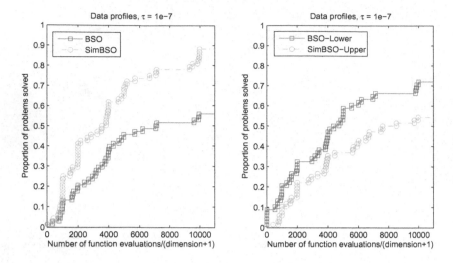

Fig. 4. Numerical comparison between BSO and SimBSO on the Hedar test set.

in the sense of average performance, although the SimBSO's confidence upper bounds "performs" worse than BSO's confidence lower bounds.

Figure 5 shows the average performances on the CEC2017 test set, where all benchmark functions with 2-D and 10-D are tested, and 100,000 function evaluations are consumed. The left subfigure shows the data profiles on 30 problems with the lowest dimension (18 2-D problems and 12 10-D problems), and the

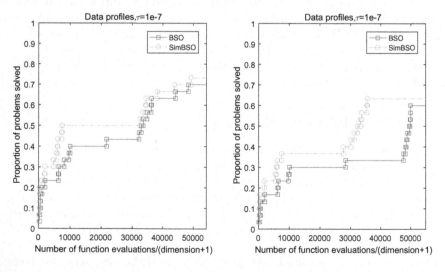

Fig. 5. Numerical comparison between BSO and SimBSO on the CEC2017 test set. 30 problems with the lowest dimension are tested in the left subfigure, and 30 10-D problems are tested in the right subfigure.

right subfigure shows the data profiles on 30 10-D problems. From Fig. 5, we can see that SimBSO performs better than BSO on both cases. Specifically, in the left subfigure, SimBSO solves about 74% problems, 4% better than BSO. In the right subfigure, SimBSO solves 64% problems, and about 4% better than BSO.

From the above numerical results, we conclude that SimBSO performs better than BSO on both the Hedar test set and the CEC2017 test set. In a word, through simplifying the BSO algorithm, the SimBSO becomes not only simplified but also more efficient, at least in the sense of average performance.

5   Conclusions and Future Work

Through benchmarking different components of the BSO algorithm via the VCI method, a simplified BSO (SimBSO) is developed. The SimBSO is tested and shown to be more efficient than BSO. Since SimBSO possesses simpler structure than BSO, it may be more suitable for extendability, e.g., co-evolution [9,10], and easier for theoretical analysis. Moreover, it seems that SimBSO has close relationship with the genetic algorithm. It is valuable to research further on these topics in the future.

The success of BSO's simplification implies that the VCI method is helpful in improving a stochastic optimization algorithm by providing sufficient experimental results. We hope it can be used to improving other evolutionary algorithms.

Acknowledgement. This work was supported in part by the National Natural Science Foundation of China (No. 11271069), in part by Natural Science Foundation of Guangdong Province, China (No. 2015A030313648), in part by Natural Science Basic Research Plan in Shaanxi Province, China (No. 2017JQ6070), and in part by the Fundamental Research Funds for the Central University (Nos. GK201703062, GK201603014).

References

1. Awad, N.H., Ali, M.Z., Liang, J.J., Qu, B.Y., Suganthan, P.N.: Problem definitions and evaluation criteria for the CEC 2017 special session and competition on single objective bound constrained real-parameter numerical optimization. Nanyang Technological University, Singapore, Technical report (2016)
2. Cheng, S., Qin, Q., Chen, J., Shi, Y.: Brain storm optimization algorithm: a review. Artif. Intell. Rev. **46**(4), 445–458 (2016)
3. Dolan, E.D., Moré, J.: Benchmarking optimization software with performance profiles. Math. Program. **91**, 201–213 (2002)
4. Duan, H., Li, S., Shi, Y.: Predator-prey brain storm optimization for dc brushless motor. IEEE Trans. Magn. **49**(10), 5336–5340 (2013)
5. Guo, X., Wu, Y., Xie, L.: Modified brain storm optimization algorithm for multimodal optimization. In: Tan, Y., Shi, Y., Coello, C.A.C. (eds.) ICSI 2014. LNCS, vol. 8795, pp. 340–351. Springer, Cham (2014). doi:10.1007/978-3-319-11897-0_40
6. Hedar, A.R.: Global optimization test problems. http://www-optima.amp.i.kyoto-u.ac.jp/member/student/hedar/Hedar_files/TestGO.htm

7. Liu, Q., Chen, W.N., Deng, J.D., Gu, T., Zhang, H., Yu, Z., Zhang, J.: Benchmarking stochastic algorithms for global optimization problems byvisualizing confidence intervals. IEEE Trans. Cybern. 1–14 (2017). doi:10.1109/TCYB.2017.2659659
8. Moré, J., Wild, S.: Benchmarking derivative-free optimization algorithms. SIAM J. Optim. **20**, 172–191 (2009)
9. Peng, X., Liu, K., Jin, Y.: A dynamic optimization approach to the design of cooperative co-evolutionary algorithms. Knowl.-Based Syst. **109**, 174–186 (2016)
10. Peng, X., Wu, Y.: Large-scale cooperative co-evolution using niching based multimodal optimization and adaptive fast clustering. Swarm Evol. Comput. (2017). doi:10.1016/j.swevo.2017.03.001
11. Shi, Y.: Brain storm optimization algorithm. In: Tan, Y., Shi, Y., Chai, Y., Wang, G. (eds.) ICSI 2011. LNCS, vol. 6728, pp. 303–309. Springer, Heidelberg (2011). doi:10.1007/978-3-642-21515-5_36
12. Shi, Y.: An optimization algorithm based on brainstorming process. Int. J. Swarm Intell. Res. (IJSIR) **2**(4), 35–62 (2011)
13. Shi, Y.: Developmental swarm intelligence: developmental learning perspective of swarm intelligence algorithms. Int. J. Swarm Intell. Res. (IJSIR) **5**(1), 36–54 (2014)
14. Shi, Y.: Brain storm optimization algorithm in objective space. In: Proceedings of 2015 IEEE Congress on Evolutionary Computation, (CEC 2015), Sendai, Japan, pp. 1227–1234. IEEE (2015)
15. Zhan, Z.H., Chen, W.N., Lin, Y., Gong, Y.J., Li, Y.L., Zhang, J.: Parameter investigation in brain storm optimization. In: 2013 IEEE Symposium on Swarm Intelligence (SIS), pp. 103–110, April 2013

Simulated Annealing with a Time-Slot Heuristic for Ready-Mix Concrete Delivery

Muhammad Sulaman[1], Xinye Cai[1(✉)], Mustafa Mısır[1], and Zhun Fan[2]

[1] College of Computer Science and Technology,
Nanjing University of Aeronautics and Astronautics, Nanjing, China
sulman0909@gmail.com, {xinye,mmisir}@nuaa.edu.cn
[2] School of Engineering, Shantou University, Guangdong, China
zfan@stu.edu.cn

Abstract. The concrete delivery problem (CDP) is an NP-hard, real world combinatorial optimization problem. The CDP involves tightly interrelated routing and scheduling constraints that have to be satisfied by considering the tradeoff between production and distribution costs. Various exact and heuristic methods have been developed to address the CDP. However, due to the limitation of the exact methods for dealing with such a complex problem, (meta-)heuristics have been more popular. For this purpose, the present study proposes a hybrid algorithm combining simulated annealing (SA) with a time-slot heuristic (TH) for tackling the CDP. The TH is applied for generating new solutions through perturbation while simulated annealing is utilized to decide on whether to accept these solutions. The proposed algorithm, i.e. SA-TH, is compared to an existing CDP heuristic on a diverse set of CDP benchmarks. The computational results conducted through a series of experiments validate the efficiency and success of SA-TH.

Keywords: Ready-mix concrete delivery · Vehicle routing · Scheduling

1 Introduction

The concrete delivery problem (CDP) [1] is concerned with the distribution of ready-mixed concrete to the requested construction sites. The CDP, as an NP-hard problem, consists of various constraints from the Vehicle Routing Problem with time windows (VRPTW) [2], and Vehicle Scheduling Problem with time Windows (VSPTW) [3]. The CPD involves additional constraints, which make it even more challenging. To name a few, because of the perishable nature, concrete must be delivered within a certain amount of time otherwise it would be hardened and even destroy the barrel maintaining concrete. Vehicle must be dispatched with the full capacity of concrete otherwise it would increase the rate of hardening. This property prevents the vehicle for delivering the concrete to more than one construction centers. It is necessary to bound the time between consecutive deliveries to the same customer as the concrete could partially harden before the arrival of next delivery. The concrete must be delivered within the

© Springer International Publishing AG 2017
Y. Shi et al. (Eds.): SEAL 2017, LNCS 10593, pp. 39–50, 2017.
https://doi.org/10.1007/978-3-319-68759-9_4

requested duration otherwise it may affect the construction process. All these constraints result in a highly complex routing and scheduling problem related to supply chain, logistics and just in time production.

In addition to these constraints, the concrete delivery process is affected by various factors. For instance, the processing time of concrete delivery vehicles varies with the size of a vehicle and type of processing activities. Different size of vehicles have different processing times which could affect the dispatching interval at production centers. As another factor, the number of deliveries depends on the requested amount of concrete from same customer. The demand usually exceeds the capacity of a single vehicle thus orders need to be divided into partial deliveries.

The CDP has been widely addressed directly by human effort, requiring to decide on the complete delivery plan by hand. This ineffective strategy has been taken over by different exact and heuristic methods, at least in academia. In the literature, because of the challenging characteristics of the CDP, the majority of the existing studies focuses on simple, unrealistic CDPs or encounter with scalability issues. The present paper proposes a hybrid algorithm combining simulated annealing [4] with a time-slot heuristic (SA-TH) for the CDP. SA-TH is designed in a way that it can solve the CDP instances with varying sizes in reasonable time. An empirical comparison provided against a recent CDP heuristic revealed its capabilities both in terms of solution quality and speed.

The remainder of the paper is organized as follows. Section 2 is dedicated to the related research on the production and distribution of ready-mix concrete. Section 3 presents the CDP. The proposed algorithm is described in Sect. 4. Section 5 provides the experimental results and their analysis. Finally, Sect. 6 provides a summary and discussion together with the follow-up research questions to be investigated.

2   Background

The concrete delivery problem (CDP) has been targeted both with exact approaches and (meta-)heuristic techniques. Regarding the exact methods, different mathematical models were proposed. In [5], a network model integrating the concrete production scheduling and vehicle dispatching and a solution method incorporating the mathematical programming solver for CDP is presented. This model obtained a good performance over the existing system but only one site CDP was considered. A general mixed integer programming model along with a local search was introduced in [6]. This model involves a set of constraints for guaranteeing that some customers receive the concrete only from a subset of production centers. In [1], several solution approaches including a number of constructive heuristics, a local search approach, mixed-integer and constraint programming models were studied. As in the other studies, the exact approaches failed to overcome more realistic, comparatively larger CDP instances.

Besides the exact methods, a number of evolutionary and (meta-)heuristic approaches were studied. A software package integrating the Discrete Event Simulation (DES) with evolutionary methods was proposed in [7]. The recent versions of their package are included with different heuristic solvers including Particle Swarm Optimization (PSO) [8] and Genetic Algorithm (GA) [9]. In [10], an integrated scheduling model was solved, where sequences are the chromosomes which consist of construction centers, delivery orders and vehicles IDs. Although good quality results were reached, the CDP was with a single production center and one mixer vehicle. In [11], a model based bee colony optimization (BCO) algorithm was developed and the results are compared with tabu search and GA. Another bee algorithm [12] was developed for solving single production center to multiple sized customers. Moreover, in [12], only 3–9 vehicles were considered.

In [13], a mathematical model of the considered supply chain as a cost minimization problem is presented. In the subsequent step, a scheduling algorithm combining a GA with a set of heuristics was introduced. The customers demands are assigned to the production centers, and all the deliveries are carried out by homogenous vehicles. To find the minimum cost route, a Column Generation (CG) algorithm for large scale concrete delivery problem was developed in [14]. Pricing was divided into to a subproblem as a minimum-cost multi-commodity flow problem. For solving this subproblem, an efficient network simplex method was used while considering the homogeneous fleet of vehicles. Most recently, an integer programming model assisted by the heuristics was developed by [15]. In their model, only one delivery was allowed to satisfy a customer and a vehicle are permitted to visit more than one customers. A planning horizon was defined and the vehicle can be used only once within the planning horizon.

In [16,17], the scheduling was focused at the production centers. In [16], fix time was considered for each vehicle irrespective of its location whereas only one production center was considered in [17]. Furthermore, only homogeneous fleet of trucks are considered for all customers which simplifies the implementation of their algorithms. In addition, the CDP without time windows is considered and no synchronization for scheduling the deliveries at construction centers is imposed. In [18], a traditional selection hyper-heuristic was developed.

3   The Concrete Delivery Problem

We considered the same CDP model as in [1]. In [1], two well known models for two capacitated vehicle routing problem (CVRP) with time windows and split deliveries, and the Parallel Machine Scheduling Problem (PMSP) with Time Windows and Maximum Time Lags are combined by overcoming the limitation of single vehicle constraint for same customer. The parameters and notations used to define the model are given in Table 1.

The CDP model assumes that each vehicle is dispatched from a source depot. At the end of the day, after performing delivery tasks between production and construction centers, all vehicles return to a sink depot. An integer variable is used to compute the upper bound on deliveries that a vehicle can perform for customer i can be calculated as given below.

Table 1. Parameters defining the CDP

Parameter	Description
P	Set of concrete production sites
C	Set of customers
$0, n+1$	Resp. the start and end depots of the delivery vehicles
V	$V = P \cup C \cup \{0\} \cup \{n+1\}$
K	Set of vehicles
q_i	Requested amount of concrete by customer $i \in C$
q_k	Capacity of vehicle $k \in K$
p_k	Time required to empty the vehicle $k \in K$
a_i, b_i	Time window during which the amount of concrete may be delivered to customer i
t_{ij}	Time to travel from i to j, $i, j \in V$
γ	Maximum time lag between consecutive deliveries for the same customer

$$n(i) = \lceil q_i / min_{k \in K}(q_k) \rceil \tag{1}$$

The routing problem can be modeled by a directed weighted graph G(V,A). Although, routing problem can be solved by computing upper bound on deliveries, but tackling the scheduling constraints altogether with routing ones are difficult. Two solutions can be considered for this issue: first, the deliveries to a particular customer are enumerated; second, the distinct deliveries performed by a single truck are enumerated. The first solution is considered in assignment-based formulation as given in [19] for scheduling problem.

c_i^j is used to denote a visit where delivery i is assigned for customer j. For each delivery $u \in C^i$, $[a_u, b_u]$ is associated initializing the time window for each corresponding customer $i \in C$ such that $[a_u, b_u] = [a_i, b_i]$ for all deliveries $i \in Cu \in C_i$. Lastly, D is the combination of all deliveries $D = \bigcup_{i \in C} C_i$.

Let $G(V, A)$ be a directed weighted graph, consisting of vertex set $V = \{0\} \cup D \cup \{n+1\}$, the ark set is defined as follows:

- The source depot has outgoing edges whereas the sink depot has incoming edges from other vertices.
- A delivery node c_h^i has a directed edge to a delivery node c_j^i if $h < j, i \in C, h, j \in C_i$.
- There is a directed edge from c_u^i to $c_v^j, i \neq j$, except if c_v^j needs to be schedule before c_u^i.

The arc set costs are defined as follows.

- $c_{0,c_j^i} = min_{p \in P} t_{0,p} + t_{p,i}$ for all $c_j^i \in D$.
- $c_{c_u^i, c_v^j} = min_{p \in P} t_{i,p} + t_{p,j}$ for all $c_u^i, c_v^j \in D, cu^i \neq c_v^j$.
- $c_{c_j^i, n+1} = t_{i,n+1}$.
- $c_{0,n+1} = 0$.

The objective, in our case, is to maximize the amount of delivered concrete to the satisfied customers as in Eq. (2).

$$max. \sum_{i \in C} q_i y_i \qquad (2)$$

where q_i is requested amount of concrete by customer $i \in C$ and y is a binary variable which denotes whether it is delivered.

4   Simulated Annealing with a Time-Slot Heuristic

To solve the concrete delivery problem, simulated annealing with a time-slot heuristic (SA-TH) is proposed. Algorithm 1 illustrates the SA approach [20] we used. Our SA implementation accommodates an exponential cooling schedule depending on the remaining execution time, T_r. It doesn't require an initial temperature to be specified yet the total time budget, T_d, should be provided. The search is being performed by our Time-slot Heuristic (TH), $TimeSlotHeuristic$, as the neighborhood operator of SA, in the form of single-point search [21]. At each iteration, TH is being applied to the current solution, S_c, for generating a new solution, S_w, through perturbation. Then, it has been decided to whether to accept the new solution, so to replace S_c with S_w. If S_w is better than or equal to S_c in terms of their objective values, S_w is being used as the new current solution. Additionally, as the key feature of SA, S_w is being accepted even though it is a worsening solution if the probability condition (on line 10) is true. Accepting worse quality solutions is practical for preventing to get stuck at local optima during a search. In the meantime, the overall best solution, S_b, is being maintained.

Algorithm 1. Simulated Annealing with Time-slot Heuristic (SA-TH)

Input: Vehicles: K, Permutation of Customers: π, Total Running Time T_t
Output: A feasible solution: S_b

1   $S_w = intializeSolution(K, \pi)$;
2   $S_c = S_w$; $T_r = T_t$; **while** $T_r > 0$ **do**
3      $improved = false$;
4      $S_w = TimeSlotHeuristic(K, C, S_c)$;
5   **if** $f(S_w) \geq f(S_c)$ **then**
6         $improved = true$;
7   **end**
8   **else if** $exp[-(f(S_c) - f(S_w)/(T_r/T_t)] > rand(0, 1)$ **then**
9         $improved = true$;
10   **end**
11   **if** $improved = true$ **then**
12         $S_c = S_w$;
13   **if** $f(S_b) > f(S_c)$ **then**
14            $S_b = S_c$;
15   **end**
16   **end**
17      $S_w = S_c$;
18 **end**
19 **return** S_b;

4.1   Time-Slot Heuristic

Our time-slot heuristic (TH) is designed in such a way that the weaknesses of the best fit constructive heuristic [1] which was used to solve the CDP, are avoided. The best fit heuristic generates a CDP solution from scratch due to its constructive nature. The construction process is carried out depending on the permutation of the customers. A good permutation is determined based on requested amount of concrete and the time windows for the concrete orders. One of the main drawbacks of this heuristic is that a new delivery is assigned to a vehicle to a time slot strictly after its latest assigned delivery. Thus, large time gaps can be present in the resulting schedules due to ignoring the intermediate available time slots. For instance, if a delivery at 3:00 pm is assigned to a vehicle as its first delivery, any delivery before 3:00 pm won't be assigned to this vehicle even though it is free before that time. To overcome this limitation, TH looks for a slot between existing visits to schedule the remaining deliveries. The TH first removes all the deliveries of a randomly selected satisfied customer from the solution at hand to find a new solution. Then, it searches for a time slot in the current vehicles' schedule for the unsatisfied customers. Next, a vehicle is selected depending on the earliest availability and minimum waste. Finally, all the unsatisfied customers are removed.

Algorithm 2 illustrates how TH works in detail. Initially, a satisfied customer C_s is selected from the solution S (line 1). Then, all deliveries of the chosen customer are removed (line 2). After that, all the unsatisfied customers are extracted and shuffled, respectively (line 3 $\rightarrow$ 4). Next, TH checks all the unsatisfied customers one-by-one (line 8 $\rightarrow$ 41). A nearest position of a delivery d in the schedule of a particular vehicle S_k, where a new delivery is to be added (line 15 $\rightarrow$ 20). If a vehicle has no assigned delivery, then the new delivery will be the first visit in the schedule S_k, and the start time for corresponding delivery will be computed accordingly. Otherwise, the feasibility of a new delivery will be computed by checking the constraints, as in Algorithm 3. In Algorithm 3, it is ensured that the start and end time of a new delivery do not overlap with the exiting deliveries (line 2). The end time of a new delivery is guaranteed to be earlier than the start time of the next delivery (line 5). For clarity, procedures used in Algorithm 2 are defined as follows:

- $selectAllUnsatisfiedCustomers(S)$: returns a set of all unsatisfied customers in solution S.
- $ShuffleCustomers(\pi)$: returns new a permutation of unsatisfied customers after shuffling them.
- $satisfied(S, c)$: this procedure returns if the total demand of customer c is delivered in solution S.
- $CalculateStartTimeForVisit(S, k, c_d, i)$: returns the possible start time after computing the driving time from customer of ith delivery to the customer of c_d in kth schedule.
- $wasteOfVisit(S, k, c_d)$: computes and returns the amount of waste $0 \leq waste \leq q_k$ introduced by vehicle $k \in K$.

- $startOfPreviousVisit(S, c, t)$: compute the start time of previous delivery to customer c. Value t is returned if it is the first visit to the customer c.
- $scheduleDelivery(S, BestVehicle, c_d)$: delivery c_d is scheduled in S by using vehicle $BestVehicle$ if all constraints for corresponding delivery are satisfied.
- $applyChaining(S, c)$: if a vehicle is available but it's possible start time for customer c is not same as required time then this procedure tries to shifts the visits of c to a later point in time by taking the maximum time lag γ and deadline b_k into account.
- $clean(S)$: if no more visit can be added to the schedule, all the deliveries to unsatisfied customers are removed to clean the solution S.

5   Experimental Results

In this section, a number of experiments is conducted to compare the performance of our hybrid algorithm, i.e. Simulated Annealing with a Time-slot Heuristic (SA-TH), with the SD heuristic proposed in [1]. 3 datasets [22] of dataset A, dataset B and dataset Large are considered for the experiments. dataset A is consisted of 10–20 customers with 2–5 vehicles, dataset B is consisted of 20–50 customers with 6–20 vehicles whereas the dataset Large is consisted of 100–200 customers with 20–50 vehicles. To asses the quality of the solutions, the upper bounds for the A and B datasets are computed as in [1]. For the Large dataset, the todal demand is considered upper bound.

Since SD is deterministic, it is run only once on each CDP instance. Due to the stochastic nature of SA-TH, it is applied 30 times to each instance. The total execution time for each instance is set no more than the time taken by the SD heuristic for all the instances.

The difference between the SD heuristic and SA-TH in term of time and objective vales is visualized in Figs. 1 and 2. SA-TH found 3 new optimal solutions in terms of average and 6 in term of best objective values on dataset A with compared to SD heuristic. No big difference is observed between the worst values obtained by SA-TH and best values obtained by the SD heuristic. On the other hand, on most of instances, SA-TH obtained the best objective values with significant difference. SA-TH performs better than the SD heuristic on 26 out of 32 instances on average and 28 out of 32 in terms of best objective values. Whereas SD performs better only on 6 out of 32 instances with respect to the average objective values obtained by SA-TH. Overall, the SA-TH outperforms SD in terms of both solution quality and speed.

For the dataset B, SA-TH performed better than the SD heuristic on 61 our of 128 in term of average values and 69 out of 128 in term of best objective values whereas the SD heuristic performed better than SA-TH only on 26 instances. For rest of the instances, both algorithms performed equally by generating optimal solutions or same objective values. A significant difference between the objective obtained by both algorithms can be observed on most of the instances. The SA-TH performed better than SD on 57 out of 78 instances in term of average and 65 out of 78 in term of best objective values.

Algorithm 2. $TimeSlotHeuristic(K, \pi, S)$

Input: K, π, S
Output: A solution: S

1 c_s = Randomly select a satisfied Customer from π;
2 $S = S \setminus C_s$; Remove all deliveries of c_s from S;
3 $\pi = selectAllUnsatisfiedCustomers(S)$;
4 $\pi = ShuffleCustomers(\pi)$;
5 **foreach** $c \in \pi$ **do**
6       $found = true$;
7   **while** $found > 0$ & $- satisfied(S, c)$ **do**
8           $found = false$;
9   c_d : Current delivery for customer C
10          $minStartTime = MaxVal$;
11          $minWaste = MaxVal$;
12          $BestVehicle = -1$;
13          $i = -1$;
14   **foreach** $k \in K$ **do**
15   **foreach** $d \in S_k$ **do**
16   **if** $c_d.start - d.start < 0$ **then**
17                      $break$;
18   **end**
19                  $i + +$;
20   **end**
21              $start = CalculateStartTimeForVisit(S, k, c_d, i)$;
22              $slotFound = findSlotInK(S_k, start, i)$;
23   **if** $slotFound = true$ **then**
24                  $waste = wasteOfVisit(S, k, c_d)$;
25                  $prevStart = startOfPreviousVisit(S, c, start)$;
26   **if** $start \leq prevStart + \gamma$ & $start + p_k \leq b_c$ **then**
27                      $found = true$; $newBest = false$;
28   **if** $start = minStartTime$ & $waste < minWaste$ **then**
29                          $newBest = true$;
30   **else if** $start = minStartTime$ & $waste = minWaste$ & $q_k > q_{bestK}$
                     then
31                          $newBest = true$;
32   **if** $newBest$ **then**
33                          $minStartTime = start$;
34                          $minWaste = waste$;
35                          $BestVehicle = k$;
36   **end**
37   **end**
38   **end**
39   **end**
40   **if** $found$ **then**
41              $ScheduleDelivery(S, BestVehicle, c_d)$;
42   **end**
43   **else**
44              $applyChaining(S, c)$;
45
46   **end**
47 **end**
48 $clean(S)$;
49 **return** S;

For SA-TH, we set different time limits (no more than 5 min) on dataset large. For the instances with 100 customers, the same time is allocated as consumed by the SD heuristic. The SD heuristic could perform better only on 8 out 48 instances with slightly better solutions than SA-TH whereas the SA-TH performed better than SD on 38 out of 48 instances. The experimental results demonstrate that SD is unable to deal with the large problems. The order of the

---

Algorithm 3. $findSlotInK(S_k, start, i)$

Input: S_k:Vehicle Schedule, $start$: Possible Start Time, i: index of a delivery in S_k
Output: true/false:

1 $i = 0$;
2 **if** $(start - S_k[i].end) \geq 0 \| (S_k[i].start - start + q_k) \geq 0$ **then**
3 | $return false$;
4 **end**
5 **if** $(start + q_k + drivingTime) > S_k[i + 1].startTime$ **then**
6 | $return false$;
7 **end**
8 $return true$;

---

customers in customer permutation becomes less effective especially for large scale problems. This is mainly due to the fact that the order of the customers are based on the criteria of customer deadline, demand and release time of concrete. In large scale problems, this criteria may be similar for many customers which causes the inefficiency of the heuristic. Furthermore, at each iteration of the SD, a new solution is constructed for varying customer permutations from scratch and all shifts and moves in customers permutation is considered which is computationally expensive. Besides that, the total required time to run SD increases exponentially with the number of customers. SA-TH finds the good solutions in relatively little time (Table 2).

The experimental summary on all datasets is provided in the Table 3. A significant difference between the performance of both algorithms can be observed. The SA-TH outperformed SD 16.9% on dataset A and 5.4% on dataset B in term of average gap. For dataset large, the SA-TH obtained 27.5% whereas the SD obtained 35.3% average gap. The average time consumed by the SD heuristic on large dataset is 47.3 min, whereas the SA-TH consumed only 3.9 min.

Table 2. Datasets Kinable [22]

	Set-A	Set-B	Set-Large
Instances	64	128	48
Customers	10–20	20–50	100–200
Customer demand	10–75	20–50	10–75
Time windows	$q_i \times [1.1,2,1]$	$q_i \times [1.1,2,1]$	$q_i \times [1.1,2,1]$
Maximum time lags	5	5	5
Vehicles	2–5	6–20	20–50
Capacity	10–25	10–25	10–25
Vehicles classes	2–3	3	3
Processing time	$p_k = q_k$	$p_k = q_k$	$p_k = q_k$
Stations	1–4	1–4	1–4
Production centers	1–25	1–25	1–25
Construction centers	1–30	1–30	1–30

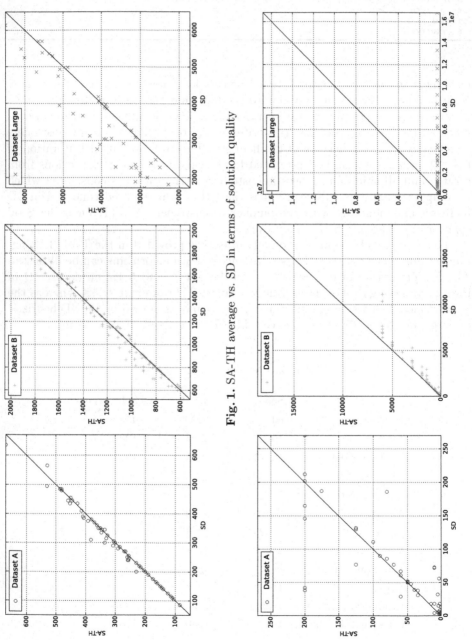

Fig. 1. SA-TH average vs. SD in terms of solution quality

Fig. 2. SA-TH average vs. SD in terms of runtime

Table 3. Summary

Algorithm	Dataset A		Dataset B		Dataset large	
	AVG gap (%)	Time (ms)	AVG gap (%)	Time (ms)	AVG Gap (%)	Time (ms)
SD-heuristic	8.9	48	16.5	1840	35.3	2835946
SA-TH	7.4	47	15.6	1428	27.5	232137

6 Conclusion

Ready-mix concrete suppliers have been looking for a practical solution for maximizing the number of satisfied customers. We introduced a hybrid algorithm combining simulated annealing with a new time-slot heuristic (SA-TH) designed for the concrete delivery problem (CDP). The time-slot heuristic tries to search the time slot in each vehicle schedule for scheduling the visits for each customer one by one. Then, a best vehicle in terms of availability and minimum waste is selected for the corresponding visit. After searching time slots in the complete schedule, the TH returns the solution to SA, where SA compares the resulting solution with previously archived solutions for tracking the best solution. Publicly available datasets are considered to compare and validate the performance of SA-TH. The proposed algorithm is compared with a steepest descent (SD) heuristic used to solved the CDP. The experimental results indicated that SA-TH outperforms SD both in terms of speed and solution quality. Besides that SD has scalability issues for relatively large CDP instances due to its design while SA-TH's speed and quality performance becomes more apparent.

Acknowledgment. This work was supported in part by the National Natural Science Foundation of China (NSFC) under grant 61300159, by the Natural Science Foundation of Jiangsu Province of China under grant BK20130808 and by China Postdoctoral Science Foundation under grant 2015M571751. The authors thank J. Kinable, T. Wauters and G. Vanden Berghe, for providing their CDP source code.

References

1. Kinable, J., Wauters, T., Berghe, G.V.: The concrete delivery problem. Comput. Oper. Res. **48**, 53–68 (2014)
2. Kallehauge, B., Larsen, J., Madsen, O.B., Solomon, M.M.: Vehicle routing problem with time windows. In: Desaulniers, G., Desrosiers, J., Solomon, M.M. (eds.) Column Generation, pp. 67–98. Springer, Boston (2005). doi:10.1007/0-387-25486-2_3
3. Frizzell, P.W., Giffin, J.W.: The split delivery vehicle scheduling problem with time windows and grid network distances. Comput. Oper. Res. **22**(6), 655–667 (1995)
4. Aarts, E., Korst, J., Michiels, W.: Simulated annealing. In: Burke, E., Kendall, G. (eds.) Search Methodologies, pp. 265–285. Springer, Boston (2014). doi:10.1007/978-1-4614-6940-7_10
5. Yan, S., Lai, W., Chen, M.: Production scheduling and truck dispatching of ready mixed concrete. Transp. Res. Part E: Logist. Transp. Rev. **44**(1), 164–179 (2008)

6. Asbach, L., Dorndorf, U., Pesch, E.: Analysis, modeling and solution of the concrete delivery problem. Eur. J. Oper. Res. **193**(3), 820–835 (2009)
7. Lu, M.: HKCONSIM: a simulation platform for planning and optimizing concrete plant operations in Hong Kong. In: Proceedings of International Conference on Innovation and Sustainable Development of Civil Engineering in the 21st Century, Beijing, China, pp. 278–283 (2002)
8. Lu, M., Wu, D., Zhang, J.: A particle swarm optimization-based approach to tackling simulation optimization of stochastic, large-scale and complex systems. In: Yeung, D.S., Liu, Z.-Q., Wang, X.-Z., Yan, H. (eds.) ICMLC 2005. LNCS, vol. 3930, pp. 528–537. Springer, Heidelberg (2006). doi:10.1007/11739685_55
9. Lu, M., Lam, H.C.: Optimized concrete delivery scheduling using combined simulation and genetic algorithms. In: Proceedings of the 37th Conference on Winter Simulation, Winter Simulation Conference, pp. 2572–2580 (2005)
10. Liu, Z., Zhang, Y., Li, M.: Integrated scheduling of ready-mixed concrete production and delivery. Autom. Constr. **48**, 31–43 (2014)
11. Lin, P.C., Wang, J., Huang, S.H., Wang, Y.T.: Dispatching ready mixed concrete trucks under demand postponement and weight limit regulation. Autom. Constr. **19**(6), 798–807 (2010)
12. Mayteekrieangkrai, N., Wongthatsanekorn, W.: Optimized ready mixed concrete truck scheduling for uncertain factors using bee algorithm. Songklanakarin J. Sci. Technol. **37**(2), 221–230 (2015)
13. Naso, D., Surico, M., Turchiano, B., Kaymak, U.: Genetic algorithms for supply-chain scheduling: a case study in the distribution of ready-mixed concrete. Eur. J. Oper. Res. **177**(3), 2069–2099 (2007)
14. Maghrebi, M., Periaraj, V., Waller, S.T., Sammut, C.: Column generation-based approach for solving large-scale ready mixed concrete delivery dispatching problems. Comput.-Aided Civil Infrastruct. Eng. **31**(2), 145–159 (2016)
15. Devapriya, P., Ferrell, W., Geismar, N.: Integrated production and distribution scheduling with a perishable product. Eur. J. Oper. Res. **259**(3), 906–916 (2017)
16. Silva, C., Faria, J., Abrantes, P., Sousa, J., Surico, M., Naso, D.: Concrete delivery using a combination of GA and ACO. In: 44th IEEE Conference on Decision and Control, 2005 and 2005 European Control Conference, CDC-ECC 2005, pp. 7633–7638. IEEE (2005)
17. Yan, S., Lai, W.: An optimal scheduling model for ready mixed concrete supply with overtime considerations. Autom. Constr. **16**(6), 734–744 (2007)
18. Misir, M., Vancroonenburg, W., Verbeeck, K., Berghe, G.V.: A selection hyper-heuristic for scheduling deliveries of ready-mixed concrete. In: Proceedings of the Metaheuristics International Conference (MIC), Udine, Italy, pp. 289–298 (2011)
19. Berghman, L., Leus, R., Spieksma, F.C.: Optimal solutions for a dock assignment problem with trailer transportation. Ann. Oper. Res. **213**, 1–23 (2014)
20. Bilgin, B., Demeester, P., Misir, M., Vancroonenburg, W., Vanden Berghe, G.: One hyper-heuristic approach to two timetabling problems in health care. J. Heuristics **18**(3), 401–434 (2012)
21. Salomon, R.: Evolutionary algorithms and gradient search: similarities and differences. IEEE Trans. Evol. Comput. **2**(2), 45–55 (1998)
22. Kinable, J.: (2013). https://sites.google.com/site/cdplib

A Sequential Learnable Evolutionary Algorithm with a Novel Knowledge Base Generation Method

Yang Lou[(✉)] and Shiu Yin Yuen[(✉)]

Department of Electronic Engineering,
City University of Hong Kong, Hong Kong SAR, China
felix.lou@my.cityu.edu.hk, kelviny.ee@cityu.edu.hk

Abstract. Sequential learnable evolutionary algorithm (SLEA) provides an algorithm selection framework for solving the black box continuous design optimization problems. An algorithm pool consists of set of established algorithms. A knowledge base is trained offline. SLEA uses the algorithm-problem features to select the best algorithm from the algorithm pool. Given a problem, the default algorithm is run for the initial round. After that, an algorithm-problem feature is collected and used to map to the most similar problem in the knowledge base. Then the best algorithm for solving the problem is used in the second round. This process iterates until n rounds have been made. It is revealed that the algorithm-problem feature is a good problem identifier, thus SLEA performs well on the known problems that have been encountered. However, the performance on those unknown problems is limited if the knowledge base is biased. In this paper, we propose a modified SLEA, which performs the training process using a novel method. A relatively unbiased knowledge base is formed. Experimental results show that the modified SLEA maintains the performance of SLEA on solving the CEC 2013 test suite, while it performs better than SLEA on solving a set of randomly generated max-set of Gaussian test problems.

Keywords: Evolutionary algorithm · Algorithm selection · Black box design optimization problem · Algorithm-problem feature

1 Introduction

Many important engineering problems are black box continuous design optimization problems [1–5]. A black box design problem is defined as follows: A design space Ω contains the set of feasible design solutions. Let $x \in \Omega$ be a feasible solution. Then $x = (x_1, \ldots, x_D)$ is a D-dimensional vector, where each component variable x_j ($j = 1, \ldots, D$) is in general a continuous variable. There is a cost function $f : \Omega \to \mathbb{R}$, where $\mathbb{R}$ is the set of real number. The objective is to find the best design $x^* \in \Omega$ which is the global minimum. Without loss of generality, we consider the problems of minimizing the design cost. When the problem is a black box problem, no problem knowledge is known a priori. The derivative of f is not available, so gradient based descent methods are also inapplicable or have to be estimated. An algorithm is sought after which can find as good a solution as possible. A solution $(x, f(x))$ is good if $f(x) - f(x^*)$ is small.

© Springer International Publishing AG 2017
Y. Shi et al. (Eds.): SEAL 2017, LNCS 10593, pp. 51–61, 2017.
https://doi.org/10.1007/978-3-319-68759-9_5

For a design optimization problem, only one good design is needed, which is different from repetitive optimization problems [6]. Therefore, for solving a design optimization problem, an algorithm is usually run n rounds, each time with T evaluations. Then the best result out of n rounds is taken as the final solution. This practice enables the algorithm to minimize the risk of being trapped in a local optimal design.

Sequential learnable evolutionary algorithm (SLEA) [7] provides an algorithm selection technique for solving the black box continuous design optimization problems. SLEA uses algorithm-problem features to select the best algorithm to run from the algorithm pool. An algorithm-problem feature is defined as a feature which is specific to an algorithm. SLEA is trained offline. Given a problem, the default algorithm is run. After the initial round, an algorithm-problem feature is collected and used to map to the most similar problem. Then the best algorithm for solving the problem is used in the second round. This process iterates until n rounds have been made. Experimental results reveal that the algorithm-problem feature is a good problem identifier [7].

Algorithm selection in SLEA is made based on the training knowledge. During the training process, some algorithms are eliminated because they do not win the first place on any of the employed training problems. However, the eliminated algorithms may perform well on other problems. To address this issue, we refine the training problems in SLEA, such that no algorithm will be eliminated, while each algorithm wins the first place on its favorable problem instance. Thus, a modified SLEA with a novel knowledge base generation method is proposed in this paper. Comparing with SLEA, the modified SLEA has the following features: (1) It is trained on a more balanced set of problems, thus has an unbiased knowledge base; (2) the modified SLEA uses random selection on the initial algorithm to run, while in SLEA the overall best performing EA is employed for the initial round. The modified SLEA is trained as follows: A set of established algorithms are employed. For each algorithm, a favorable (uniquely easy) problem instance is found or intentionally generated as its training problem. Thus, each algorithm wins on its favorable problem. The training process forms an unbiased knowledge base. No algorithm in the pool is eliminated after training. The training problems are collected to intentionally form a uniform problem space, such that under this circumstance, no algorithm outperforms other algorithms [8]. Accordingly, there is not an overall best performing EA trained in the modified SLEA, which eliminates bias towards a particular algorithm. This is a good characteristic as the problem to be solved by the modified SLEA is unknown.

Algorithm selection has recently gained increasing attention. It is an active research topic in combinatorial search such as propositional satisfiability, constraint satisfaction, quantified Boolean formulae, combinatorial optimization and scheduling [9], but little work on algorithm selection has been done within the field of evolutionary computation on black box continuous optimization. Explorative landscape analysis (ELA) methods extract landscape features such as number of local optima, basins of attraction, etc. [11, 12], and is used as features for algorithm selection. ELA methods consume extra function evaluations. The methods can be expensive if sufficient and accurate information is required [10]. Recently a low-budget ELA method is proposed in [11] to address this problem. However, a judicious selection of features using the training problems is needed. A survey of other related works can be found in [7]. Our work is different from previous works in the sense that it addresses the problem on what knowledge should be acquired and retained in the knowledge base for algorithm selection.

The rest of this paper is organized as follows: Sect. 2 recaps the SLEA in [7], and Sect. 3 introduces the modified SLEA. Section 4 reports experimental results. Section 5 concludes the paper.

2   Sequential Learnable Evolutionary Algorithm

This section is a recap of SLEA. For full details, please refer to [7].

Figure 1 shows the framework of SLEA. The training process forms the learnable knowledge base. The algorithm suggestion system collects the algorithm-problem feature after the previously suggested algorithm is run. The collected feature is then compared with the information in the knowledge base. Before the allowed maximum computational budget is used up, the algorithm suggestion system continuously suggests an algorithm for the next round to run.

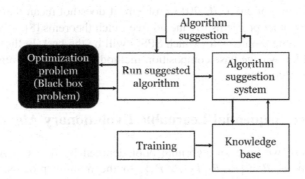

Fig. 1. Flowchart of sequential learnable evolutionary algorithm framework.

Let p_x be the current black box problem being solved. The algorithm suggestion (or algorithm selection) in SLEA works in three steps described as follows:

1. Collecting the algorithm-problem feature: The entire converging process (i.e., from initialization till the stopping criteria is met) in the last round on solving p_x is collected, which is used as the algorithm-problem feature F.
2. Identifying the most similar problem: By comparing F with the stored information in the knowledge base, the algorithm suggesting system tries to map the current problem p_x to a known problem p_i in the knowledge base, such that p_i and p_x have the most similar algorithm-problem feature.
3. Suggesting the best algorithm: In the knowledge base, the known problems are well-studied. The best algorithm for each known problem has been learnt in advance, i.e., in the training process. Suppose a_j is the best algorithm for solving the known problem p_i, then a_j is recommended for solving the unknown problem p_x for the next round to run.

SLEA is trained offline. The training data are stored in the knowledge base. The knowledge base in SLEA contains two main parts: (1) the algorithm-problem features for all known problems, and (2) the problem-to-best-algorithm mapping table, which indicates the best algorithm for each known problem. In [7], five algorithms are employed to form the algorithm pool. They are artificial bee colony (ABC) [12], covariance matrix adaptation evolution strategy (CMA-ES) [13], composite differential evolution (CoDE) [14], the 2011 standard particle swarm optimization (SPSO) [15], and self-adaptive differential evolution (SaDE) [16]. The CEC 2013 benchmark test suite [17] (with 28 benchmark problems) is employed as the training problems. Each algorithm runs on each benchmark problem a number of times. The algorithm-problem features are collected by recording the entire converging process, and the problem-to-best-algorithm mapping table is generated by recording the best algorithm for each benchmark problem.

Selecting the winner of problem instances is a recently proposed strategy to form a portfolio [7, 18], but this strategy may be limited by the training problem set. For example, in [7], SPSO is automatically eliminated after training since it does not win the first place on any problem of the CEC 2013 test suite. On the other hand, although SPSO is not a winner of any CEC 2013 problem, it does not mean that SPSO cannot win when solving other problems. By the no free lunch theorems [8], it is highly likely that there exists some problems for which SPSO will be the best. In the following, we propose a novel knowledge base composition method which aims to remove this bias against any such algorithm.

3 A Modified Sequential Learnable Evolutionary Algorithm

In SLEA, suppose we have an algorithm pool denoted by $A = \{A_1, A_2, A_3\}$, and a training problem set $P = \{P_1, P_2, P_3, P_4, P_5\}$. In the training process, algorithm A_1 wins the first place on problems P_1, P_2, and P_3, while algorithm A_2 wins on problems P_4 and P_5. Thus, algorithm A_3 is eliminated and the portfolio is formed as $A_{SL} = \{A_1, A_2\}$.

When the testing problems are identical to the training set, there is no doubt that A_{SL} is good enough and there is no need for A. However, suppose there is an unknown problem P_6, on which algorithm A_3 outperforms A_1 and A_2, it is now impossible for A_{SL} to outperform the single algorithm A_3 on problem P_6.

The modified SLEA follows the SLEA framework shown in Fig. 1, but with a better training process to address the problem mentioned above. In the modified SLEA, suppose we have an algorithm pool denoted by $A = \{A_1, A_2, A_3\}$, and a training problem set $P = \{P_1, P_2, P_3, P_4, P_5\}$. After an initial training process as in the original SLEA, $A_{SL} = \{A_1, A_2\}$ is formed. Later, the eliminated algorithm A_3 is picked up, and a favorable (uniquely easy) problem instance (denoted by P_{A3}) for A_3 is intentionally searched from another problem set, or generated by evolving on tunable benchmark generators [19–21]. The modified training result is $A'_{SL} = \{A_1, A_2, A_3\}$ and $P' = \{P_1, P_2, P_3, P_4, P_5, P_{A3}\}$. Therefore, the knowledge base is enriched: (1) the eliminated algorithm is added back to the SLEA portfolio; and (2) the intentionally searched or generated instances are added as training problems.

4 Experimental Study

In this section, we compare the modified SLEA with SLEA on two different benchmark suites. We employ four algorithms, namely ABC, CMA-ES, CoDE, and SPSO. Comparing with [7], SaDE is not included because both SaDE and CoDE are differential evolution (DE) [22] variants. The CEC 2013 suite and the max-set of Gaussian (MSG) generator [19] are employed for training and testing of SLEA. The details of parameter settings are: The problem dimension is set to $D = 10$ for both the CEC and MSG problems. The maximum number of evaluations for an algorithm on solving a problem is set to $T = 3 \times 10^5$. The number of multiple restarts in both SLEA and the modified SLEA is set $n = 3$.

Details of the CEC 2013 problem suite can be found in [17], which consist of 28 problems (denoted as CEC-F1 to CEC-F28). The search range of MSG instances is set to be the same as the CEC 2013 problems (i.e., $[-100, 100]^D$). Each MSG problem instance has five randomly distributed local optima, among which the global optimum has the global minimum value which is -100. To reduce the randomness on evaluating algorithm performance, all the results are averaged from 30 independent runs.

Table 1 shows the training results of SLEA and the modified SLEA. Since the performance of SLEA on known problems has been revealed in [7], we focus on testing SLEA and the modified SLEA on unknown problems. In our experiment, problems CEC-F2, CEC-F9 and CEC-F21 are employed for training, while the other 25 problems are used for testing. Problems CEC-F2, CEC-F9 and CEC-F21 are employed because CMA-ES wins the first place on solving CEC-F2, CoDE wins on solving CEC-F9, and ABC wins on solving CEC-F21.

Table 1. Training results of SLEA and the modified SLEA

	SLEA	modified SLEA
ABC	CEC-F21	CEC-F21
CMA-ES	CEC-F2	CEC-F2
CoDE	CEC-F9	CEC-F9
SPSO	N/A	MSG-SPSO

Since SPSO does not win for any problem in the CEC 2013 suite, it is eliminated in SLEA. Thus, the trained SLEA algorithm set is $A_{SLEA} = \{\text{ABC, CMA-ES, CoDE}\}$, where ABC, CMA-ES and CoDE are the winners for problems CEC-F21, CEC-F2 and CEC-F9 respectively. In contrast, for training the modified SLEA, an intentionally generated problem instance MSG-SPSO (an MSG problem instance that is uniquely easy for SPSO) is added, and thus it comes out that $A'_{SLEA} = \{\text{ABC, CMA-ES,}$ $CoDE, SPSO\}$. MSG-SPSO is generated using an evolutionary algorithm (i.e., DE) in the tunable Gaussian landscape space. The tunable parameters of MSG are regarded as the chromosomes in DE. By maximizing the algorithm performance difference between SPSO and the other three algorithms, a novel problem instance (i.e., MSG-SPSO) is generated. SPSO wins the first place on solving MSG-SPSO.

When running SLEA, if an encountered unknown problem is identified as the most similar to, for example, problem CEC-F21, then ABC is selected for the next round to run. However, SLEA cannot identify a problem that is similar to MSG-SPSO due to lack of such knowledge. However, the modified SLEA can add such complementary knowledge, not only for SPSO, but for any other algorithm which cannot win and get a position in SLEA.

In SLEA, CMA-ES (the overall best performing algorithm in A_{SLEA}) is used as the initial algorithm to run [7], while in the modified SLEA, the initial algorithm is uniformly-randomly selected from A'_{SLEA}. Since we set the number of multiple restarts as $n = 3$, it means there are two chances (excluding the initial round) for SLEA to identify the problem and select a proper algorithm to run. The best result obtained among three rounds is collected as the final result.

Table 2 shows the results of SLEA and the modified SLEA on solving the CEC 2013 suite. Problems CEC-F2, CEC-F9 and CEC-F21 are excluded in the testing set as they have been used for training.

Table 2. Experimental results on the CEC 2013 test suite

	SLEA	Modified SLEA		SLEA	Modified SLEA
CEC-F1	−1400	−1400	CEC-F16	200.1413	200.2428
CEC-F3	−1200	−1200	CEC-F17	309.0275	310.0884
CEC-F4	−1100	−1100	CEC-F18	419.959	420.6585
CEC-F5	−1000	−1000	CEC-F19	500.1026	500.1295
CEC-F6	−899.848	−899.922	CEC-F20	603.0131	602.3059
CEC-F7	−793.942	−795.791	CEC-F22	1043.734	942.5849
CEC-F8	−679.811	−679.839	CEC-F23	1531.231	1355.735
CEC-F10	−499.991	−499.988	CEC-F24	1146.942	1149.898
CEC-F11	−398.74	−398.773	CEC-F25	1263.433	1258.135
CEC-F12	−290.489	−289.875	CEC-F26	1323.508	1315.353
CEC-F13	−183.583	−184.823	CEC-F27	1634.835	1630.986
CEC-F14	111.9729	146.0375	CEC-F28	1505.922	1524.239
CEC-F15	572.9286	544.4738			

A neck to neck comparison of SLEA and the modified SLEA is made. Table 3 shows the ranks of the results. The average rank of the modified SLEA (1.44) is marginally better than SLEA (1.56). This means that after adding back SPSO into the SLEA algorithm set, the overall performance on the CEC 2013 suite is maintained. Although SPSO is recognized as the overall worst performing algorithm on the CEC 2013 suite [7], it does not mean SPSO performs bad on each single run. The contribution of SPSO to the modified SLEA is investigated in Figs. 2 and 3 (attached at the end of the paper).

Figure 2 shows the number of contributing runs of SPSO (in 30 independent runs) on solving the CEC 2013 problems. A contributing run of SPSO is defined when the result obtained by SPSO is the best out of the three rounds. For example, ABC is

Table 3. Rank table of experimental results on the CEC 2013 test suite

	SLEA	Modified SLEA		SLEA	Modified SLEA
CEC-F1	1.5	1.5	CEC-F16	1	2
CEC-F3	1.5	1.5	CEC-F17	1	2
CEC-F4	1.5	1.5	CEC-F18	1	2
CEC-F5	1.5	1.5	CEC-F19	1	2
CEC-F6	2	1	CEC-F20	2	1
CEC-F7	2	1	CEC-F22	2	1
CEC-F8	2	1	CEC-F23	2	1
CEC-F10	1	2	CEC-F24	1	2
CEC-F11	2	1	CEC-F25	2	1
CEC-F12	1	2	CEC-F26	2	1
CEC-F13	2	1	CEC-F27	2	1
CEC-F14	1	2	CEC-F28	1	2
CEC-F15	2	1	Avg. rank	1.56	1.44

randomly selected in the beginning, and it returns a result f_{ABC}. Then CMA-EA is run and returns f_{CMA-ES}. In the third round SPSO is selected and returns f_{SPSO}. The result obtained by SLEA is collected as $f_{SLEA} = \min\{f_{ABC}, f_{CMA-ES}, f_{SPSO}\}$. If $f_{SLEA} = f_{SPSO}$, then it is counted as a contributing run of SPSO. Otherwise, if SPSO is not selected or SPSO does not perform the best in the three rounds, it is not counted as a contributing run. The sum of contributing runs of SPSO is 71, which is the sum value of all the bars in Fig. 2.

As can be seen from Fig. 2, SPSO contributes more than 8 times (out of 30 times) on solving problems CEC-F1, CEC-F15, CEC-F20 and CEC-F23. It is also shown in Table 3 that the modified SLEA (with SPSO) wins on solving problems CEC-F15, CEC-F20 and CEC-F23, while receiving a draw on CEC-F1, comparing with the original SLEA (without SPSO).

Figure 3 shows the number of contributing runs of SPSO on solving the MSG problem instances. SPSO contributes more frequently in this case. Meanwhile, the modified SLEA recommends SPSO more frequently.

Tables 4 and 5 show the results and rank table of SLEA vs. the modified SLEA on solving 12 randomly generated MSG problem instances. Note that MSG-SPSO is intentionally generated to be favorable for SPSO, while problems MSG-F1 to MSG-F12 are uniformly-randomly generated in the Gaussian landscape problem space. The only similarity between MSG-PSO and these 12 instances is that all these instances are with five local optima, but the shapes, distributions, and the basins of attraction are different. Thus, MSG-F1 to MSG-F12 are unknown problems for both SLEA and the modified SLEA.

The ranks in Table 5 indicate that the modified SLEA outperforms SLEA. SLEA outperforms the modified SLEA only on two problem instances (MSG-F6 and MSG-F7), while the modified SLEA outperforms SLEA on five problems. The comparison ranks shown in Tables 3 and 5 show the effectiveness of adding SPSO back to SLEA.

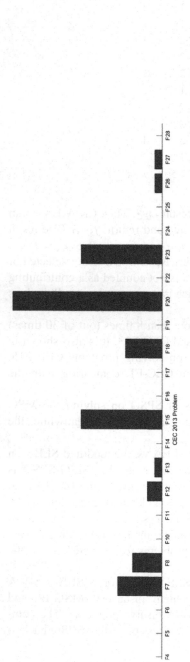

Fig. 2. Number of contributing runs of SPSO in 30 independent runs on solving the test problems in the CEC 2013 suite

Fig. 3. Number of contributing runs of SPSO in 30 independent runs on solving the randomly generated MSG test problems

Table 4. Experimental results on 12 randomly generated MSG problem instances

	SLEA	Modified SLEA		SLEA	Modified SLEA
MSG-F1	−93.3737	−100	MSG-F7	−99.1639	−98.5366
MSG-F2	−96.6955	−100	MSG-F8	−100	−100
MSG-F3	−100	−100	MSG-F9	−100	−100
MSG-F4	−96.6847	−100	MSG-F10	−96.6667	−100
MSG-F5	−99.8578	−99.9287	MSG-F11	−100	−100
MSG-F6	−99.9645	−99.9407	MSG-F12	−100	−100

Table 5. Rank table of experimental results on 12 randomly generated MSG problem instances

	SLEA	Modified SLEA		SLEA	Modified SLEA
MSG-F1	2	1	MSG-F7	1	2
MSG-F2	2	1	MSG-F8	1.5	1.5
MSG-F3	1.5	1.5	MSG-F9	1.5	1.5
MSG-F4	2	1	MSG-F10	2	1
MSG-F5	2	1	MSG-F11	1.5	1.5
MSG-F6	1	2	MSG-F12	1.5	1.5
			Avg. rank	1.63	1.38

Table 6 gives the statistics on computational budget allocation (number of evaluations) of SLEA and the modified SLEA. The initial round is not counted, since SLEA uses a default algorithm (i.e., CMA-ES) while the modified SLEA uses a randomly selected algorithm. Neither SLEA nor the modified SLEA performs algorithm selection in the initial round. For the CEC 2013 suite, there are 25 testing problems, two times to restart, and on each problem 30 independent runs. Thus, there are $25 \times 2 \times 30 = 1500$ times for (modified) SLEA to perform algorithm selection. As for the MSG problems, there are $12 \times 2 \times 30 = 720$ algorithm selections.

Table 6. The total number of algorithm selections in the experimental studies

	SLEA on CEC13	Modified SLEA on CEC13	SLEA on MSG	Modified SLEA on MSG
ABC	568	504	467	248
CMA-ES	769	700	234	27
CoDE	163	100	19	20
SPSO	0	196	0	425
Total eval.	1500	1500	720	720

The modified SLEA suggests SPSO 196 times out of 1500 times (13.07%) on solving the CEC 2013 problems. Among the 196 recommendations on SPSO, there are

71 contributing runs of SPSO (36.22%). Thus, in the modified SLEA, SPSO is neither banned nor frequently suggested, but reasonably suggested.

5 Conclusion

In this paper, a modified version of sequential learnable evolutionary algorithm (SLEA) is proposed. SLEA provides an algorithm selection framework for solving the black box continuous design optimization problems. Algorithm selection in SLEA is based on a knowledge base which is trained offline. It uses an algorithm-problem feature to select the best algorithm to run from the algorithm pool. Given a problem, the default algorithm is run. After the initial round, the algorithm-problem feature is collected and used to map to the most similar problem in the knowledge base. Then the best algorithm for solving the problem is used in the second round and so on.

SLEA performs well on the known problems that have been encountered. However, the performance on unknown problems is limited due to the biased knowledge base. In the modified SLEA, the training process is improved. A relatively unbiased knowledge base is formed, which extends the suitability of SLEA on solving unknown problems. Experimental results show that the modified SLEA maintains the performance of SLEA on solving the CEC 2013 test suite, while it performs better than SLEA on solving a set of randomly generated max-set of Gaussian test problems.

Acknowledgement. The work described in this paper was supported by a grant from the Research Grants Council of the Hong Kong Special Administrative Region, China [Project No. CityU 125313]. Yang Lou acknowledge the Institutional Postgraduate Studentship and the Institutional Research Tuition Grant from City University of Hong Kong.

References

1. Roy, R., Hinduja, S., Teti, R.: Recent advances in engineering design optimisation: challenges and future trends. CIRP Ann. Technol. **57**, 697–715 (2008)
2. Zhang, X., Zhang, X., Yuen, S.Y., Ho, S.L., Fu, W.N.: An improved artificial bee colony algorithm for optimal design of electromagnetic devices. IEEE Trans. Magn. **49**, 4811–4816 (2013)
3. Zhang, X., Fong, K.F., Yuen, S.Y.: A novel artificial bee colony algorithm for HVAC optimization problems. HVAC R Res. **19**, 715–731 (2013)
4. Fong, K.F., Lee, C.K., Chow, C.K., Yuen, S.Y.: Simulation-optimization of solar-thermal refrigeration systems for office use in subtropical Hong Kong. Energy **36**, 6298–6307 (2011)
5. Fong, K.F., Yuen, S.Y., Chow, C.K., Leung, S.W.: Energy management and design of centralized air-conditioning systems through the non-revisiting strategy for heuristic optimization methods. Appl. Energy **87**, 3494–3506 (2010)
6. Eiben, A.E., Smith, J.E.: Introduction to Evolutionary Computing, vol. 53. Springer, Heidelberg (2003)
7. Yuen, S.Y., Zhang, X., Lou, Y.: Sequential learnable evolutionary algorithm: a research program. In: IEEE International Conference on Systems, Man, and Cybernetics, SMC, pp. 2841–2848 (2015)

8. Wolpert, D.H., Macready, W.G.: No free lunch theorems for optimization. IEEE Trans. Evol. Comput. **1**, 67–82 (1997)
9. Kotthoff, L.: Algorithm selection for combinatorial search problems: a survey. In: Bessiere, C., De Raedt, L., Kotthoff, L., Nijssen, S., O'Sullivan, B., Pedreschi, D. (eds.) Data Mining and Constraint Programming. LNCS, vol. 10101, pp. 149–190. Springer, Cham (2016). doi:10.1007/978-3-319-50137-6_7
10. Muñoz, M.A., Sun, Y., Kirley, M., Halgamuge, S.K.: Algorithm selection for black-box continuous optimization problems: a survey on methods and challenges. Inf. Sci. **317**, 224–245 (2015)
11. Kerschke, P., Preuss, M., Wessing, S., Trautmann, H.: Low-budget exploratory landscape analysis on multiple peaks models. In: Genetic and Evolutionary Computation Conference, GECCO, pp. 229–236 (2016)
12. Karaboga, D., Basturk, B.: A powerful and efficient algorithm for numerical function optimization: artificial bee colony (ABC) algorithm. J. Glob. Optim. **39**, 459–471 (2007)
13. Loshchilov, I.: CMA-ES with restarts for solving CEC 2013 benchmark problems. In: IEEE Congress on Evolutionary Computation, CEC, pp. 369–376 (2013)
14. Wang, Y., Cai, Z., Zhang, Q.: Differential evolution with composite trial vector generation strategies and control parameters. IEEE Trans. Evol. Comput. **15**, 55–66 (2011)
15. Zambrano-Bigiarini, M., Clerc, M., Rojas, R.: Standard particle swarm optimisation 2011 at CEC-2013: a baseline for future PSO improvements. In: IEEE Congress on Evolutionary Computation, CEC, pp. 2337–2344 (2013)
16. Qin, A.K., Huang, V.L., Suganthan, P.N.: Differential evolution algorithm with strategy adaptation for global numerical optimization. IEEE Trans. Evol. Comput. **13**, 398–417 (2009)
17. Liang, J.J., Qu, B.Y., Suganthan, P.N., Hernández-Díaz, A.G.: Problem definitions and evaluation criteria for the CEC 2013 special session on real-parameter optimization. Technical report 201212, Zhengzhou China; Singapore; CEC 2013 (2013)
18. Muñoz, M.A., Kirley, M.: ICARUS: Identification of complementary algorithms by uncovered sets. In: IEEE Congress of Evolutionary Computation, CEC, pp. 2427–2432 (2016)
19. Gallagher, M., Yuan, B.: A general-purpose tunable landscape generator. IEEE Trans. Evol. Comput. **10**, 590–603 (2006)
20. Hemert, J.I.Van: Evolving combinatorial problem instances that are difficult to solve. Evol. Comput. **14**, 433–462 (2006)
21. Langdon, W.B., Poli, R.: Evolving problems to learn about particle swarm optimisers and other search algorithms. IEEE Trans. Evol. Comput. **11**, 561–578 (2007)
22. Storn, R., Price, K.: Differential evolution – a simple and efficient heuristic for global optimization over continuous spaces. J. Glob. Optim. **11**, 341–359 (1997)

Using Parallel Strategies to Speed up Pareto Local Search

Jialong Shi[1,2]($\boxtimes$), Qingfu Zhang[1,2], Bilel Derbel[3,4], Arnaud Liefooghe[3,4], and Sébastien Verel[5]

[1] Department of Computer Science, City University of Hong Kong,
Hong Kong, Hong Kong
jlshi2-c@my.cityu.edu.hk, qingfu.zhang@cityu.edu.hk
[2] The City University of Hong Kong Shenzhen Research Institute,
Shenzhen, China
[3] CNRS, Centrale Lille, UMR 9189 – CRIStAL, University of Lille,
59000 Lille, France
{bilel.derbel,arnaud.liefooghe}@univ-lille1.fr
[4] Dolphin, Inria Lille – Nord Europe, 59000 Lille, France
[5] LISIC, University Littoral Côte d'Opale, 62100 Calais, France
verel@lisic.univ-littoral.fr

Abstract. Pareto Local Search (PLS) is a basic building block in many state-of-the-art multiobjective combinatorial optimization algorithms. However, the basic PLS requires a long time to find high-quality solutions. In this paper, we propose and investigate several parallel strategies to speed up PLS. These strategies are based on a parallel multi-search framework. In our experiments, we investigate the performances of different parallel variants of PLS on the multiobjective unconstrained binary quadratic programming problem. Each PLS variant is a combination of the proposed parallel strategies. The experimental results show that the proposed approaches can significantly speed up PLS while maintaining about the same solution quality. In addition, we introduce a new way to visualize the search process of PLS on two-objective problems, which is helpful to understand the behaviors of PLS algorithms.

Keywords: Multiobjective combinatorial optimization · Pareto local search · Parallel metaheuristics · Unconstrained binary quadratic programming

1 Introduction

Pareto Local Search (PLS) [14] is an important building block in many state-of-the-art multiobjective combinatorial optimization algorithms. PLS naturally stops after reaching a Pareto local optimum set [15]. However, it is well known that the convergence speed of the basic PLS is low. Several strategies have been proposed [3,4,6,8] in order to overcome this issue. However, those strategies are inherently sequential, i.e. only a single computing unit is considered. With the increasing popularity of multi-core computers, parallel algorithms have attracted

© Springer International Publishing AG 2017
Y. Shi et al. (Eds.): SEAL 2017, LNCS 10593, pp. 62–74, 2017.
https://doi.org/10.1007/978-3-319-68759-9_6

a lot of research interest in the optimization community since they constitute both a highly valuable alternative when tackling computing tasks, and an opportunity to design highly effective solving methodologies. In this paper, we propose and investigate a flexible parallel algorithm framework offering several alternative speed-up PLS strategies. In our framework, multiple PLS processes are executed in parallel and their results are combined at the end of the search process to provide a Pareto set approximation. More specifically, we focus on four components of the PLS procedure. For each component, we define two alternative strategies, one alternative corresponds to the basic PLS procedure while the other alternative is a proposed speed-up strategy. Consequently, we end-up with 12 parallel PLS variants, each one being a unique combination of the considered strategies with respect to the PLS components. The performances of the so-obtained parallel variants are studied on the multiobjective Unconstrained Binary Quadratic Programming (mUBQP) problem with two objectives. Our experimental results show that the proposed parallel strategies significantly speed up the convergence of PLS while maintaining approximately the same approximation quality. Additionally, we introduce a diagram to visualize the PLS process on two-objective problems that we term as "*trajectory tree*". By referring to the shape of the trajectory tree, we are able to visualize the behavior of PLS, hence providing both a friendly and insightful tool to understand what makes a PLS variant efficient.

The paper is organized as follows. In Sect. 2, we introduce the related concepts of multiobjective combinatorial optimization and the basic PLS procedure. In Sect. 3, we present the mUBQP and the details about the proposed parallel strategies. In Sect. 4, we provide an experimental analysis of the proposed approaches. In Sect. 5, we conclude the paper.

2 Pareto Local Search

A multiobjective optimization problem (MOP) is defined as follows:

$$\begin{array}{ll} \text{maximize} & F(x) = (f_1(x), \ldots, f_m(x)) \\ \text{subject to} & x \in \Omega \end{array} \tag{1}$$

where Ω is a set of feasible solutions in the decision space. When Ω is a discrete set, we face a Multiobjective Combinatorial Optimization Problem (MCOP). Many MCOPs are challenging because of their NP-hardness and their intractability [5]. This is the case of the mUBQP problem considered in the paper [9].

Definition 1 (Pareto dominance). An objective vector $u = (u_1, \ldots, u_m)$ is said to *dominate* an objective vector $v = (v_1, \ldots, v_m)$, if and only if $u_k \geqslant v_k$ $\forall k \in \{1, \ldots, m\} \ \wedge \ \exists k \in \{1, \ldots, m\}$ such that $u_k > v_k$. We denote it as $u \succ v$.

Definition 2 (Pareto optimal solution). A feasible solution $x^\star \in \Omega$ is called a *Pareto optimal solution*, if and only if $\nexists y \in \Omega$ such that $F(y) \succ F(x^\star)$.

Definition 3 (Pareto set). The set of all Pareto optimal solutions is called the *Pareto Set* (PS), denoted as $PS = \{x \in \Omega \mid \nexists y \in \Omega, F(y) \succ F(x)\}$.

Due to the conflicting nature between the different objectives, the PS, which represents the best trade-off solutions, constitutes a highly valuable information to the decision maker. In order to approximate the PS, a number of metaheuristics have be proposed in the past [3,6,7,13], and many of them actually use PLS as a core building block.

PLS can be seen as a natural extension of single-objective local search methods. Starting from an initial set of non-dominated solutions, PLS approaches the PS by exploring the neighborhood of solutions in its archive. The basic version of PLS iteratively inserts new non-dominated solutions contained within the archive, and removes dominated solutions from this archive. Algorithm 1 shows the pseudocode of the basic PLS. In practice, the basic PLS procedure shown in Algorithm 1 requires a long time to converge to a good approximation of the PS. Several speed-up strategies have been proposed in recent years [3,4,6,8], but they are in the scope of sequential algorithms. In this paper, we discuss some possible speed-up strategies of PLS in a parallel algorithm framework.

Algorithm 1. Pareto Local Search (standard sequential version)

input: An initial set of non-dominated solutions A_0
$\forall x \in A_0$, set explored$(x) \leftarrow$ FALSE
$A \leftarrow A_0$
while $A_0 \neq \emptyset$ **do**
    $x \leftarrow$ a randomly selected solution from A_0 *// selection step*
    for each x' in the neighborhood of x **do**   *// neighborhood exploration*
        if x' is not dominated by any solution in A **then**   *// acceptance criterion*
            explored$(x') \leftarrow$ FALSE
            $A \leftarrow$ Update(A, x')
        end if
    end for
    explored$(x) \leftarrow$ TRUE
    $A_0 \leftarrow \{x \in A \mid$ explored$(x) =$ FALSE$\}$
end while
return A

---

3   Parallel Speed-up Strategies

Before discussing the speed-up strategies of PLS in a parallel multi-search framework, let us first introduce the mUBQP problem considered as a benchmark and visualize how PLS is actually operating in the objective space.

3.1   The mUBQP Problem

The multiobjective Unconstrained Binary Quadratic Programming (mUBQP) problem can be formalized as follows.

$$\text{maximize} \quad f_k(x) = x'Q_k x = \sum_{i=1}^{n}\sum_{j=1}^{n} q_{ij}^{k} x_i x_j, \ k = 1, \ldots, m$$

$$\text{subject to} \qquad\qquad x \in \{0,1\}^n$$

where $F = (f_1, \ldots, f_m)$ is an objective function vector with $m \geqslant 2$, $Q_k = [q_{ij}^k]$ is a $n \times n$ matrix for the kth objective, and x is a vector of n binary (0–1) variables. In this paper, the neighborhood structure is taken as the 1-bit-flip, which is directly related to a Hamming distance of 1. In this paper, we only consider mUBQP instances from [9] with $m = 2$ objectives. Notice that PLS has been shown to provide a high-quality Pareto set approximation for those instances, and is actually a core building block of the state-of-the-art [10].

3.2 Trajectory Tree

In order to better understand the behaviors of PLS in the objective space, we here introduce a diagram called *"trajectory tree"*. Let's consider a step of PLS where a solution x from the archive is selected to be explored. Then each time a neighboring solution x' is accepted to be inserted into the archive, the diagram maps x with x' in the objective space by drawing an edge connecting them. In the trajectory tree example of Fig. 1(a), we can read that from an initial solution x_0, three neighboring solutions $\{x_1, x_2, x_3\}$ were actually included into the archive. Then, at the next step, x_2 is selected to be explored and three of its neighbors $\{x_4, x_5, x_6\}$ are included to the archive. Note that the trajectory tree records the entire history of PLS, hence the solutions that are removed from the archive based on Pareto dominance will actually *not* be removed from the trajectory tree (e.g. x_0, x_1, x_2 and x_3 in Fig. 1(a)). A real case of the PLS trajectory is given in Fig. 1(b), where a standard PLS process starts from a randomly-generated solution and stops naturally into a Pareto local optimum set. In Fig. 1(b) the two-objective mUBQP instance has $n = 100$ variables with a correlation coefficient between both objectives of $\rho = 0$.

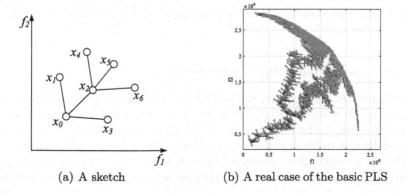

(a) A sketch   (b) A real case of the basic PLS

Fig. 1. Using trajectory tree to visualize PLS process.

3.3   Designed Methodology and Rationale

In this paper we aim at speeding up the standard PLS by running L parallel PLS processes. The core design principle behind of our framework is inspired by the concept of decomposition in the objective space. In fact, let us consider L weight vectors $\{\lambda^\ell \mid \ell = 1, \ldots, L\}$, where $\lambda^\ell = (\lambda_1^\ell, \ldots, \lambda_m^\ell)$ is defined such that $\sum_{k=1}^m \lambda_k^\ell = 1$ and $\lambda_k^\ell \geqslant 0$ for all $k \in \{1, \ldots, m\}$. The standard (sequential) PLS workflow is then carefully modified in order to map the parallel PLS processes to the weight vectors. More concretely, we manage to independently guide the ℓth PLS process on the basis of the ℓth weight vector λ^ℓ, hence our framework maintains ℓ archives that are updated independently in parallel. After all PLS processes terminate, we merge their respective archives (maintained locally and in parallel) and remove dominated solutions in order to obtain a Pareto set approximation. In addition, we remark from Fig. 1(b) that there can be many branches in the middle phase of the PLS trajectory tree, which makes the tree be in a shape of a triangle "$\triangledown$". However, having too many branches in the middle phase might be unnecessary and could actually be a waste of computing effort. We hence argue that reducing the number of branches in the middle phase of PLS is a key ingredient to speed-up the search. Roughly speaking, in our framework, we try to convert the "$\triangledown$"-shape trajectory tree to multiple parallel "T"-shape trajectory trees as illustrated in Fig. 2. For this purpose, we propose to review the main PLS components accordingly, which is described in detail in the next section.

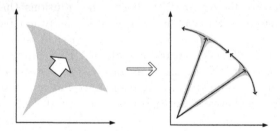

Fig. 2. Parallel speed-up framework: replacing one "$\triangledown$"-tree by multiple "T"-trees.

3.4   Alternative Algorithm Components

As depicted in Algorithm 1, sequential PLS has three main problem-independent components: the *selection step*, the *acceptance criterion* and the *neighborhood exploration*. In [4,8], the design of these components was shown to be crucially important for the anytime performance of sequential PLS. In this paper, we similarly discuss possible alternatives for these components, however our proposed alternatives are designed specifically with respect to the target parallel multi-search framework. For this reason, we also involve an additional component in our discussion: the *boundary setting*.

Alternatives for Selection Step. In this step, PLS selects a solution from the current archive to explore its neighborhood. The basic strategy is to randomly select a solution from the archive, which we denote as $\langle RND \rangle$. Since each PLS process now has a weight vector λ^ℓ, the other alternative that we consider is to select the solution that has the highest weighted-sum function value, i.e., $f_{ws}(x) = \sum_{k=1}^{m} \lambda_k^\ell f_k(x)$, which we denote as $\langle HWF \rangle$.

Alternatives for Acceptance Criterion. The basic version of PLS accepts any non-dominated solution to be included into the archive, and we denote this strategy as $\langle \nprec \rangle$. We propose the following alternative strategy denoted $\langle w_> \nprec \rangle$: if a neighboring solution that has a higher f_{ws}-value than the highest f_{ws}-value from the archive is found, only such neighboring solutions are accepted, and if no such neighboring solution can be found, the acceptance criterion switches to accepting solutions that are non-dominated.

Alternatives for Neighborhood Exploration. In the basic version of PLS, all neighboring solutions are evaluated. This can be seen as an extension of the *best-improving* rule in single-objective local search, hence we denote this strategy as $\langle \star \rangle$ [8]. The alternative could correspond to the *first-improving* rule in single-objective local search: if a neighboring solution that satisfies the acceptance criterion is found, the neighborhood exploration stops immediately and the current solution is marked as explored. In addition, after all solutions from the archive have been marked as explored using the first-improving rule, all solutions will be marked as unexplored and be explored again using the best-improving rule. We denote this alternative strategy as $\langle 1\star \rangle$. Note here that, if the $\langle w_> \nprec \rangle$ acceptance criterion is used, the $\langle 1\star \rangle$ strategy changes to: if a neighboring solution is accepted because it has an even higher f_{ws}-value than the archive's highest f_{ws}-value, the neighborhood exploration stops immediately, otherwise the neighborhood exploration continues, and after all solutions in the archive have been marked as explored using the first-improving rule, all solutions will be marked as unexplored and be explored again using the best-improving rule.

Alternatives for Boundary Setting. We notice that the parallel PLS processes are expected to approach the Pareto front from different directions in the objective space when different weight vectors are used in the selection/acceptance step. We additionally manage to set boundaries between different PLS processes to avoid wasting computing resource. We denote the original unbounded alternative as $\langle UB \rangle$, and the bounded alternative as $\langle B \rangle$. More precisely, in the bounded alternative $\langle B \rangle$, the boundaries are defined as the middle lines between adjacent weight vectors, as shown in Fig. 3. At the early stage of PLS, the space between the boundaries are relatively narrow, hence it is very likely that all solutions in the archive are outside the boundary. To prevent premature termination, we define the alternative $\langle B \rangle$ as: the neighboring solutions outside the boundary will not be accepted, except when the archive is empty or all solutions in the archive are outside the boundary.

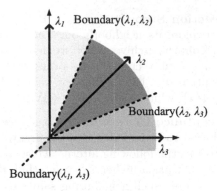

Fig. 3. Defining boundaries for 3 weight vectors.

By combining the aforementioned alternatives, we can design different parallel PLS variants. For instance, a basic parallel PLS, which executes multiple basic PLS processes in parallel, is obtained by the combination $\langle \text{RND}, \not\prec, \star, \text{UB} \rangle$.

3.5 Related Works and Positioning

Liefooghe et al. [8] decompose the PLS procedure into several problem-independent components and investigate the performance of the PLS variants obtained using different alternative strategies. A similar methodology can be found in the work of Dubois-Lacoste et al. [4], which intends to improve the anytime performance of PLS. Our proposal differs from those works in the sense that we aim to speed up PLS in a *parallel multi-search framework*. We decompose the original problem by assigning different weight vectors to the parallel PLS processes, and previous works do not consider such an alternative in the setting of PLS components.

The concept of decomposition in our parallel framework is inspired by the widely-used MOEA/D framework [16], in which the original multiobjective problem is decomposed into a number of scalarized single-objective sub-problems and the algorithm tries to solve them in a cooperative manner. Derbel et al. [2] investigate the hybridization of single-objective local search move strategies within the MOEA/D framework. Besides, the multiobjective memetic algorithm based on decomposition (MOMAD) proposed by Ke et al. [7] is one of the state-of-the-art algorithms for MCOPs. At each iteration of MOMAD, a PLS procedure and multiple scalarized single-objective local search procedures are conducted. Liu et al. [11] propose the MOEA/D-M2M algorithm, which decomposes the original problem into a number of sub-problems by setting weight vectors in the objective space. In MOEA/D-M2M, each sub-problem corresponds to a sub-population and all sub-populations evolve in a collaborative way. MOEA/D-M2M is similar to the NSGA-II variant proposed by Branke et al. [1], in which the problem decomposition is based on cone separation.

Other works intend to enhance PLS by using a higher-level control framework. Lust and Teghem [13] propose the Two-Phase Pareto Local Search (2PPLS) algorithm which starts PLS from the high-quality solutions generated by heuristic methods. Lust and Jaszkiewicz [12] speed up 2PPLS on the multiobjective traveling salesman problem by using TSP-specific heuristic rules. Geiger [6] presents the Pareto Iterated Local Search (PILS) in which a variable neighborhood search framework is applied to PLS. Drugan and Thierens [3] discuss different neighborhood exploration strategies and restart strategies for PLS. At last, for the mUBQP problem, Liefooghe et al. [9,10] conduct an experimental analysis on the characteristics of small-size instances and the performances of some metaheuristics, including PLS, on larger instances.

4   Experimental Analysis

4.1   Pilot Experiment

To visualize the change of trajectory tree when different alternatives are used, we execute five parallel PLS variants on a $\{m = 2, n = 100, \rho = 0\}$ mUBQP instance. In each execution, $L = 3$ PLS processes start from the same initial solution, which is randomly generated. Figure 4 shows the trajectory trees of those five parallel PLS variants in sequence: $\langle \text{RND}, \not{\prec}, \star, \text{UB} \rangle$, $\langle \text{HWF}, \not{\prec}, \star, \text{UB} \rangle$, $\langle \text{HWF}, w_>\ \not{\prec}, \star, \text{UB} \rangle$, $\langle \text{HWF}, w_>\ \not{\prec}, 1\star, \text{UB} \rangle$ and $\langle \text{HWF}, w_>\ \not{\prec}, 1\star, \text{B} \rangle$. In this sequence, we alter one component of the algorithm at a time.

Figure 4(a) shows the trajectory trees of the basic parallel PLS $\langle \text{RND}, \not{\prec}, \star, \text{UB} \rangle$, which simply runs multiple basic PLS processes in parallel. Figure 4(b) shows the trajectory trees of $\langle \text{HWF}, \not{\prec}, \star, \text{UB} \rangle$. By comparing Fig. 4(a) and (b), we can see that after changing the selection step from $\langle \text{RND} \rangle$ (i.e. random) to $\langle \text{HWF} \rangle$ (i.e. based on the weighted-sum function), different PLS processes are navigated to different direction in the objective space. Then, as shown in Fig. 4(c), after changing the acceptance criterion from $\langle \not{\prec} \rangle$ (non-dominance) to $\langle w_>\ \not{\prec} \rangle$ (higher weighted-sum function value and non-domination), the number of branches in each trajectory tree decreases. From Fig. 4(d) we can see that, after changing the neighborhood exploration strategy from $\langle \star \rangle$ (best-improvement) to $\langle 1\star \rangle$ (first-improvement and best-improvement), the branch number in each trajectory tree is further reduced. Actually, in Fig. 4(d) the search trajectory of each PLS process is a single-line trajectory in the middle phase of the search. In the last variant, we set boundaries between different PLS processes, and we can see from Fig. 4(e) that the overlaps between different PLS processes are reduced. Notice that Fig. 4(e) perfectly presents the parallel multi-search framework we aim to achieve, as previously sketched in Fig. 2.

4.2   Performance Comparison

In this section, we investigate 12 different Parallel PLS (PPLS) variants. The different variants' strategies are summarized in Fig. 5. Among the variants, PPLS-1 is the basic variant $\langle \text{RND}, \not{\prec}, \star, \text{UB} \rangle$ as illustrated in Fig. 4(a) and PPLS-12 is the

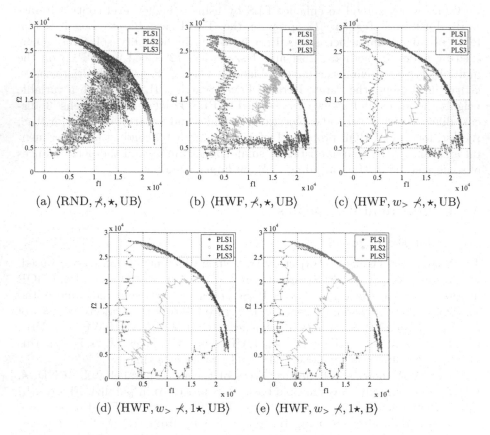

(a) $\langle \text{RND}, \not\lt, \star, \text{UB} \rangle$ (b) $\langle \text{HWF}, \not\lt, \star, \text{UB} \rangle$ (c) $\langle \text{HWF}, w_> \not\lt, \star, \text{UB} \rangle$

(d) $\langle \text{HWF}, w_> \not\lt, 1\star, \text{UB} \rangle$ (e) $\langle \text{HWF}, w_> \not\lt, 1\star, \text{B} \rangle$

Fig. 4. Trajectory trees of different parallel PLS variants.

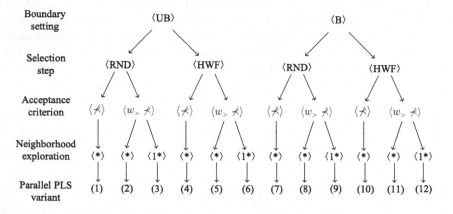

Fig. 5. The 12 investigated parallel PLS variants.

Table 1. Experimental results of the 12 PPLS variants.

n	ρ	PPLS-1	PPLS-2	PPLS-3	PPLS-4	PPLS-5	PPLS-6	PPLS-7	PPLS-8	PPLS-9	PPLS-10	PPLS-11	PPLS-12
		Average hypervolume ($\times 10^9$)											
200	−0.5	7.948	7.948	**7.949**	**7.949**	**7.949**	7.948	7.938	7.939	7.942	7.942	7.943	7.943
	0.0	4.008	4.008	4.008	**4.009**	**4.009**	4.008	4.000	4.006	4.006	4.005	4.005	4.000
	0.5	1.296	1.295	1.299	**1.300**	**1.300**	**1.300**	1.294	1.295	1.297	1.297	1.295	1.296
300	−0.5	28.55	28.56	28.57	28.57	28.57	**28.58**	28.52	28.52	28.56	28.56	28.56	28.52
	0.0	14.44	14.45	**14.46**	14.45	14.45	14.45	14.40	14.39	14.42	14.42	14.42	14.42
	0.5	3.753	3.752	**3.755**	3.750	3.750	3.751	3.739	3.738	3.741	3.736	3.734	3.738
500	−0.5	124.47	124.46	**124.50**	**124.50**	124.49	124.48	124.24	124.23	124.35	124.4	124.41	124.39
	0.0	62.74	62.74	**62.79**	62.78	62.77	62.77	62.43	62.44	62.48	62.54	62.51	62.49
	0.5	15.38	15.38	15.40	**15.41**	15.40	15.40	15.32	15.33	15.37	15.32	15.31	15.31
		Average runtime (s)											
200	−0.5	1310.41	1371.06	1194.99	547.25	546.30	516.81	219.53	356.07	48.00	22.91	21.10	**19.56**
	0.0	9.91	10.98	10.87	7.21	7.04	7.27	2.50	2.98	0.43	0.22	**0.20**	**0.20**
	0.5	73.52	86.51	85.54	38.59	38.17	39.23	20.31	26.08	3.18	1.69	1.75	**1.59**
300	−0.5	122.89	130.12	109.57	52.95	53.79	49.30	88.46	97.65	77.81	36.84	39.57	**35.39**
	0.0	1.29	1.20	1.18	0.61	0.54	0.59	1.00	0.96	0.80	0.45	0.46	**0.42**
	0.5	10.77	10.81	10.50	4.84	4.71	4.32	6.55	7.00	5.41	2.97	2.99	**2.81**
500	−0.5	3193.27	3350.61	2592.14	2013.39	1935.30	1574.11	363.24	554.65	210.56	**147.73**	171.51	151.51
	0.0	43.89	49.51	44.88	22.53	23.01	23.13	4.07	5.65	3.36	2.32	2.36	**2.21**
	0.5	287.82	326.62	275.87	125.07	122.76	118.43	30.49	62.49	12.50	7.93	7.62	**7.59**

ultimate variant $\langle \mathrm{HWF}, w_>, \not\prec, 1\star, \mathrm{B}\rangle$ as illustrated in Fig. 4(a). We consider 9 standard mUBQP instances by setting $m = 2$, density $= 0.8$, $n = \{200, 300, 500\}$ and $\rho = \{0.0, 0.5, -0.5\}$. On each instance, 20 runs of each PPLS variant are performed. In each run, $L = 6$ parallel processes start from the same randomly-generated solution and terminate naturally. The algorithms are implemented in GNU C++ with the -O2 compilation option. The computing platform is two 6-core 2.00 GHz Intel Xeon E5-2620 CPUs (24 Logical Processors) under CentOS 6.4. Table 1 shows the obtained results. We use the *hypervolume* metric [17] to measure the quality of the Pareto set approximations obtained by each variant, and we also record the runtime of each variant. Note here that the runtime of PPLS equals to the runtime of its slowest PLS process. In Table 1 the best metric values are marked by bold font.

From Table 1, we can see that the difference of hypervolume-values between different variants is relative small, which means that all variants get approximately the same solution quality. In general the variants without boundaries (i.e. PPLS-1,···, PPLS-6) achieve slightly higher hypervolume values than the variants with boundaries (i.e. PPLS-7,···,PPLS-12). It is because, when there is no boundary, the overlaps between the PLS processes increase the chance to find better solutions. On the contrary, the runtime difference between different variants is relatively large. We can see that the variants with boundaries are significantly faster than the variants without boundaries. It is because, within the bounded strategy, each PLS process only needs to search in a limited region of the objective space. Among all variants, PPLS-3 and PPLS-4, i.e. $\langle \mathrm{RND}, w_>, \not\prec, 1\star, \mathrm{UB}\rangle$ and $\langle \mathrm{HWF}, \not\prec, \star, \mathrm{UB}\rangle$, get the highest hypervolume in most cases. Compared to the basic variant PPLS-1, PPLS-3 does not show an obvious speedup, while PPLS-4 does. Indeed, on most instances PPLS-4 reaches a higher hypervolume with a much smaller runtime than PPLS-1. Among all variants, PPLS-12, i.e. $\langle \text{HWF}, w_>\not\prec, 1\star, \text{B}\rangle$, is the one with the overall smallest runtime. At last, Fig. 6 reports the boxplots of hypervolume and runtime of the PPLS variants on the three instances with $n = 500$ variables. We can see that the proposed parallel strategies can speed up the basic PLS with a relatively

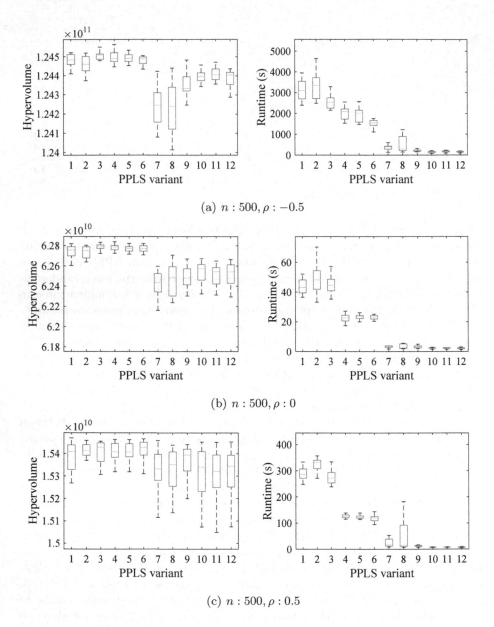

(a) $n : 500, \rho : -0.5$

(b) $n : 500, \rho : 0$

(c) $n : 500, \rho : 0.5$

Fig. 6. Experimental results on three mUBQP instances with $n = 500$.

small loss in terms of approximation quality. In particular, while the obtained hypervolume decreases slightly when using the bounded strategy (for $\rho < 0$, i.e. conflicting objectives), the gap with the unbounded strategy in terms of runtime is consistently much more impressive.

5 Conclusions

In this paper, several speed-up strategies for PLS have been investigated. Compared to the existing works, our strategies are proposed in a parallel multi-search framework. In addition, we propose a diagram called trajectory tree to visualize the search process of PLS. In our experiments, we test the performance of 12 different parallel PLS variants on nine mUBQP instances with two objectives. Each variant is a unique combination of the proposed parallel strategies. The experimental results show that, compared against the basic parallel PLS variant, some variants can get a better solution quality with a shorter runtime, and some variants can significantly speed up PLS while maintaining approximately the same solution quality. In the future, we plan to investigate the performance of the proposed approaches on multiobjective combinatorial problems with different characteristics and to investigate the scalability of the parallel PLS variants.

Acknowledgments. The work described in this paper was supported by the National Science Foundation of China under Grant 61473241, and a grant from ANR/RCC Joint Research Scheme sponsored by the Research Grants Council of the Hong Kong Special Administrative Region, China (Project No. A-CityU101/16), and France National Research Agency (ANR-16-CE23-0013-01).

References

1. Branke, J., Schmeck, H., Deb, K., Reddy, S.M.: Parallelizing multi-objective evolutionary algorithms: cone separation. In: IEEE Congress on Evolutionary Computation. vol. 2, pp. 1952–1957. IEEE (2004)
2. Derbel, B., Liefooghe, A., Zhang, Q., Aguirre, H., Tanaka, K.: Multi-objective local search based on decomposition. In: Handl, J., Hart, E., Lewis, P.R., López-Ibáñez, M., Ochoa, G., Paechter, B. (eds.) PPSN 2016. LNCS, vol. 9921, pp. 431–441. Springer, Cham (2016). doi:10.1007/978-3-319-45823-6_40
3. Drugan, M.M., Thierens, D.: Stochastic Pareto local search: Pareto neighbourhood exploration and perturbation strategies. J. Heuristics **18**(5), 727–766 (2012)
4. Dubois-Lacoste, J., López-Ibáñez, M., Stützle, T.: Anytime pareto local search. Eur. J. Oper. Res. **243**(2), 369–385 (2015)
5. Ehrgott, M.: Multicriteria Optimization. Springer, Heidelberg (2006)
6. Geiger, M.J.: Decision support for multi-objective flow shop scheduling by the Pareto iterated local search methodology. Comput. Ind. Eng. **61**(3), 805–812 (2011)
7. Ke, L., Zhang, Q., Battiti, R.: Hybridization of decomposition and local search for multiobjective optimization. IEEE Trans. Cybern. **44**(10), 1808–1820 (2014)
8. Liefooghe, A., Humeau, J., Mesmoudi, S., Jourdan, L., Talbi, E.G.: On dominance-based multiobjective local search: design, implementation and experimental analysis on scheduling and traveling salesman problems. J. Heuristics **18**(2), 317–352 (2012)

9. Liefooghe, A., Verel, S., Hao, J.K.: A hybrid metaheuristic for multiobjective unconstrained binary quadratic programming. Appl. Soft Comput. **16**, 10–19 (2014)
10. Liefooghe, A., Verel, S., Paquete, L., Hao, J.K.: Experiments on local search for bi-objective unconstrained binary quadratic programming. In: 8th International Conference on Evolutionary Multi-Criterion Optimization, vol. 9018, pp. 171–186 (2015)
11. Liu, H.L., Gu, F., Zhang, Q.: Decomposition of a multiobjective optimization problem into a number of simple multiobjective subproblems. IEEE Trans. Evol. Comput. **18**(3), 450–455 (2014)
12. Lust, T., Jaszkiewicz, A.: Speed-up techniques for solving large-scale biobjective TSP. Comput. Oper. Res. **37**(3), 521–533 (2010)
13. Lust, T., Teghem, J.: Two-phase Pareto local search for the biobjective traveling salesman problem. J. Heuristics **16**(3), 475–510 (2010)
14. Paquete, L., Chiarandini, M., Stützle, T.: Pareto local optimum sets in the biobjective traveling salesman problem an experimental study. In: Gandibleux, X., Sevaux, M., Sörensen, K., T'kindt, V. (eds.) Metaheuristics for Multiobjective Optimisation. LNE, vol. 535, pp. 177–199. Springer, Heidelberg (2004). doi:10.1007/978-3-642-17144-4_7
15. Paquete, L., Schiavinotto, T., Stützle, T.: On local optima in multiobjective combinatorial optimization problems. Ann. Oper. Res. **156**(1), 83–97 (2007)
16. Zhang, Q., Li, H.: MOEA/D: a multiobjective evolutionary algorithm based on decomposition. IEEE Trans. Evol. Comput. **11**(6), 712–731 (2007)
17. Zitzler, E., Thiele, L., Laumanns, M., Fonseca, C.M., Da Fonseca, V.G.: Performance assessment of multiobjective optimizers: an analysis and review. IEEE Trans. Evol. Comput. **7**(2), 117–132 (2003)

Differential Evolution Based Hyper-heuristic for the Flexible Job-Shop Scheduling Problem with Fuzzy Processing Time

Jian Lin[1(✉)], Dike Luo[1], Xiaodong Li[2], Kaizhou Gao[3],
and Yanan Liu[1]

[1] School of Information, Zhejiang University of Finance and Economics,
Hangzhou 310018, China
linjian1001@126.com
[2] School of Science (Computer Science and IT), RMIT University,
Melbourne, VIC 3001, Australia
[3] School of Computer, Liaocheng University, Liaocheng 252059, China

Abstract. In this paper, a differential evolution based hyper-heuristic (DEHH) algorithm is proposed to solve the flexible job-shop scheduling problem with fuzzy processing time (FJSPF). In the DEHH scheme, five simple and effective heuristic rules are designed to construct a set of low-level heuristics, and differential evolution is employed as the high-level strategy to manipulate the low-level heuristics to operate on the solution domain. Additionally, an efficient hybrid machine assignment scheme is proposed to decode a solution to a feasible schedule. The effectiveness of the DEHH is evaluated on two typical benchmark sets and the computational results indicate the superiority of the proposed hyper-heuristic scheme over the state-of-the-art algorithms.

Keywords: Differential evolution · Hyper-heuristic · Flexible job-shop scheduling · Fuzzy processing time · Solution decoding

1 Introduction

The flexible job-shop scheduling problem (FJSP) widely exists in modern manufacturing systems and industrial processes, such as automobile assembly, chemical processes, and intelligent transport systems [1]. Compared with the regular job-shop scheduling problem, FJSP is more complicated to solve since an operation can be processed on multiple machines. There exist two sub-problems in FJSP: assignment of machines to operations and sequencing of the operations on the assigned machines.

FJSP has been extensively studied in recent years and many approaches have been proposed. A tabu search (TS) algorithm was presented by Logendran and Sonthinen [2] for scheduling a flexible manufacturing system. An integer linear programming method was developed by Gomes et al. [3] for solving the FJSP which considers the parallel machines, limited intermediate buffers and negligible set-up effects. A two-phase TS algorithm was proposed by Saidi-Mehrabad and Fattahi [4] to solve FJSP with sequence-dependent setups. The genetic algorithm (GA) was firstly applied to solve

© Springer International Publishing AG 2017
Y. Shi et al. (Eds.): SEAL 2017, LNCS 10593, pp. 75–86, 2017.
https://doi.org/10.1007/978-3-319-68759-9_7

FJSP in [5]. Thereafter, three typical versions of GAs were also presented in [6–8]. Moreover, a knowledge-based variable neighborhood search was proposed by Karimi et al. [9], a hybrid differential evolution was presented by Yuan and Xu [10], a disjunctive graph model-based ant colony optimization algorithm was developed by Rossi [11], an efficient constructive procedure-based heuristic was proposed by Ziaee [12] to obtain high-quality schedules quickly. However, fixed processing time or due-date is the common assumption in these studies. In the real world, the manufacturing process will be impacted by many emergencies, such as the maintenance activities, machine breakdowns, rush job, etc. Therefore, the processing time of an operation cannot be obtained in advance precisely. To handle this issue, the processing time and due-date using fuzzy values are frequently adopted in practical situations [13].

By considering the processing time with fuzzy values, FJSP with fuzzy processing time (FJSPF) resemble more closely to the production reality. Up to now, meta-heuristics are the common approaches to solve the FJSPF [14, 15]. Two efficient GAs, namely decomposition-integration genetic algorithm [16] and co-evolutionary genetic algorithm [17], were proposed by Lei [16]. More recently, a hybrid artificial bee colony (HABC) algorithm [18], an estimation of distribution algorithm (EDA) [19], a teaching-learning-based optimization (TLBO) algorithm [20] and a hybrid biogeography-based optimization (HBBO) [21] were presented to solve the FJSPF. However, meta-heuristics that performs well on a particular problem may yield very poor solutions for new problems, or even for new instances of the same problem. As a recent trend in search and optimization, hyper-heuristic is emerged as a new search methodology that controls a set of heuristics to provide near-optimal solutions for various problems. Instead of searching directly in the solution domain, hyper-heuristics operate in the heuristic domain to find an optimal sequence of heuristics that can find the best solution.

During the past few years, there is a growing literature in the field of hyper-heuristics. In particular, meta-heuristics have been used to construct hyper-heuristic schemes. For example, a particle swarm optimization based hyper-heuristic approach was proposed by Koulinas et al. [22], evolutionary hyper-heuristics were presented by Sanz et al. [23], and Gascón-Moreno et al. [24], a harmony search based hyper-heuristic was developed by Anwar et al. [25], a backtracking search based hyper-heuristic was developed by Lin et al. [26], and a bacterial foraging based hyper-heuristic was designed by Rajni and Chana [27]. Recently, hyper-heuristics have been proposed for treating well-known scheduling problems such as the flow shop scheduling problem [28] and the job shop scheduling problem [29]. However, to the best of our knowledge, there is no hyper-heuristic approach has been applied to address the FJSPF.

This paper aims at employing an effective differential evolution based hyper-heuristic (DEHH) to handle the FJSPF with makespan criterion. In the DEHH, differential evolution [30] is used as the high-level strategy, which manages a set of low-level heuristics rather than directly on solutions. Experiments and comparisons are carried out on a typical FJSPF benchmark set to show the effectiveness of the proposed hyper-heuristic scheme.

The rest of the paper is organized as follows. In Sect. 2, the problem is briefly introduced. In Sect. 3, the framework of the DEHH scheme is described. The computational results on benchmark instances as well as comparison to some state-of-the-art algorithms are conducted in Sect. 4. Finally, a conclusion is drawn in Sect. 5.

2 Problem Description

The FJSPF can be stated as follows: There are n jobs $J = \{J_1, J_2, \cdots, J_n\}$ to be processed on m machines $M = \{M_1, M_2, \cdots, M_m\}$. Each job J_i contains n_i operations $\{O_{i,1}, O_{i,2}, \cdots, O_{i,n_i}\}$. The processing time of the $O_{i,j}$ on machine M_k can be denoted as a triangular fuzzy number (TFN) $p_{i,j,k} = (p_{i,j,k}^1, p_{i,j,k}^2, p_{i,j,k}^3)$, where $p_{i,j,k}^1$, $p_{i,j,k}^2$ and $p_{i,j,k}^3$ are the best, probable and worst processing times, respectively. Correspondingly, the fuzzy makespan of $O_{i,j}$ is denoted as a TFN $C_{i,j} = (C_{i,j}^1, C_{i,j}^2, C_{i,j}^3)$. The definitions of certain fuzzy number operations are detailed in [21, 31]. In the FJSPF, the following assumptions are applied:

(1) Each machine can process only one operation at a time.
(2) Each operation can be processed by only one machine at a time.
(3) Preemption is not allowed once an operation is started.
(4) The transfer times between different machines are included in the processing time.

The objective of FJSPF [16] is to determine both the assignment of machines and the sequence of operations on all the machines, with the aim of minimizing the fuzzy makespan, $C_{\max} = \max\limits_{i=1,2,\cdots,n} C_{i,m}$.

3 Differential Evolution Based Hyper-heuristic Algorithm

3.1 Differential Evolution (DE)

DE [30] is a very popular population-based meta-heuristic, which includes three operations: mutation, crossover and selection. As one of the most widely-used mutation schemes [32], DE/target-to-best/1 strategy as in Eq. (1) is adopted here. After this, the crossover operator is carried out to generate the trial vector u_i as in Eq. (2).

$$v_i = x_i + F \times (x_{\text{best}} - x_i) + F \times (x_{r_1} - x_{r_2}), \quad r_1 \neq r_2 \neq i \tag{1}$$

$$u_{ij} = \begin{cases} v_{ij}, & \text{if } rand(0,1) \leq CR \text{ or } j = j_n, \\ x_{ij}, & \text{otherwise.} \end{cases} \quad i = 1,2,\cdots,N_P; j = 1,2,\cdots,D \tag{2}$$

where v_i is the mutant vector of the ith individual, and x_{r_1} and x_{r_2} are two individuals randomly selected from the current population; F is the mutation factor; CR is the crossover rate, and j_n is a randomly generated integer in [1, N]. After crossover, a greedy selection is performed as follows:

$$x_i^{g+1} = \begin{cases} x_i^g, & \text{if } f(x_i^g) \leq f(u_i^g) \\ u_i^g, & \text{if } f(x_i^g) > f(u_i^g) \end{cases} \tag{3}$$

where x_i^g and x_i^{g+1} denote the ith individual in the current generation and the next generation, respectively. u_i^g denotes the ith new individual in gth iteration.

3.2 Solution Encoding and Decoding Schemes

In DEHH, each individual is represented by a sequence of low-level heuristics, and is associated with a solution of FJSPF. The low-level heuristics in an individual are applied to operate on the solution domain which is composed of a set of operation sequences. Additionally, a hybrid decoding scheme integrating with the earliest completion machine (ECM) rule [21] and the left-shift scheme [33] is proposed to find a machine which can process an operation with the earliest fuzzy completion time. The pseudo-code of the proposed decoding scheme is depicted in Fig. 1.

Procedure hybrid decoding scheme (π)
  For each machine m
    $\gamma_m = 0$;
    $\Lambda^m(\gamma_m) = \Phi$;
  Next for
  For $t = 1$ to n
    Compute the completion time for $\pi(t)$ by using the left-shift scheme;
    Find the machine m that can process $\pi(t)$ with the earliest completion time;
    $\gamma_m = \gamma_m + 1$;
    $\Lambda^m(\gamma_m) = \pi(t)$;
  Next for
End procedure

Fig. 1. Pseudo-code of the proposed hybrid decoding scheme.

3.3 Low-Level Heuristics

It is widely accepted that the design of the low-level heuristics is important for the efficiently of the hyper-heuristic approach [22]. In the proposed hyper-heuristic scheme, five easy-to-implement heuristic rules, denoted as LLH1, LLH2 through LLH5, are designed to construct the set of low-level heuristics, which are detailed as follows:

(1) LLH1 (Swap): Randomly select two different operations O_a and O_b from the processing sequence and then swap them.
(2) LLH2 (Forward-insert): Randomly choose two different operations O_a and O_b $(b > a)$ from the sequence and then insert O_b before O_a.
(3) LLH3 (Backward-insert): Randomly choose two different operations O_a and O_b $(b > a)$ from the sequence and then insert O_a before O_b.
(4) LLH4 (Inverse): Inverse the subsequence $\{O_a, O_{a+1}, \cdots, O_b\}$ between two randomly chosen positions a and b in the sequence.
(5) LLH5 (Adjacent-swap): Randomly choose one position a from the sequence, and swap it with the next position of the sequence. Especially, if the chosen position a is the last position of the sequence, swap it with the first position of the sequence.

To improve the local search ability of the designed heuristic rules, simulated annealing is embedded into the low-level heuristics of LLH1 to LLH5. The pseudo-code of the improved version of LLHi ($i = 1, 2, \cdots, 5$) is shown in Fig. 2.

Procedure Improved_LLHi (ω)

Set an initial temperature T_0;

$\pi = \omega$;

Generate a permutation π' from π using the LLHi;

While $T_0 < T_f$

    Get a solution π'' from π' using the LLHi;

    If $\Delta = C_{\max}(\pi'') - C_{\max}(\pi') < 0$ **then**

        $\pi' = \pi''$;

        $T_0 = \xi T_0$;

    End if

End while

If $C_{\max}(\pi') < C_{\max}(\omega)$ **then**

    $\omega = \pi'$;

End if

End procedure

Fig. 2. The pseudo-code of the improved low-level heuristic.

3.4 Framework of the DEHH

In this section, the framework of the DE based hyper-heuristic (DEHH) algorithm is presented, and the main procedure is described. In the DEHH, each individual is a sequence of low-level heuristics as mentioned in Sect. 3.3, and is associated with a solution. An individual can be evaluated by applying the low-level heuristics to the solution domain. The general framework of DEHH scheme is presented in Fig. 3.

In the DEHH, DE is employed as a high-level strategy to manipulate the low-level heuristics on the heuristic domain. By introducing the domain barrier, the low-level heuristics in the solution domain could be separated from the high level strategy. For a problem instance, each low-level heuristic search the solution domain directly, modify the current solution and find a new one, which is further evaluated with the objective function. As for the high-level strategy in the DEHH scheme, the DE searches the solution domain indirectly, using the low-level heuristics, aims to find an optimal heuristic generating the best solution for the FJSPF. The main procedure of the DEHH is shown in Fig. 4, and can be described as follows:

(1) The initial population is generated randomly in the way that each heuristic appears once in each individual, so the dimension of the heuristic domain equals to the number of low-level heuristics.

(2) The output of the trial vector as in Eq. (2) is a set of real values. We get an integer for each trial vector u_i with Eq. (4).

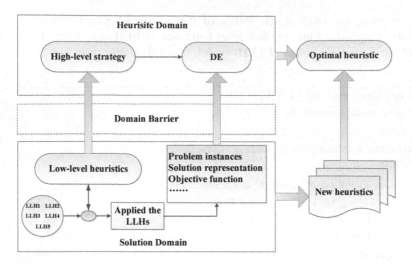

Fig. 3. The framework of DEHH scheme.

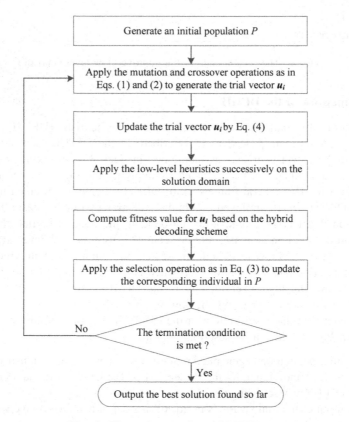

Fig. 4. The main procedure of DEHH.

$$u_{ij} = \begin{cases} 1, & \text{if } u_{ij} < 1 \\ L_n, & \text{if } u_{ij} > L_n \\ [u_{ij}] & \text{otherwise} \end{cases} \quad (4)$$

where L_n is the number of the available low-level heuristics, $[u_{ij}]$ is the rounding operation for each u_{ij}.

(3) As the order of appearance in u_i, the low-level heuristics are applied to the solution domain to achieve a better solution. Each individual is evaluated based on the best solution obtained by the sequence of low-level heuristics, and the hybrid decoding scheme is used to generate a feasible schedule.

4 Computational Results and Discussion

To validate the effectiveness of the proposed DEHH algorithm in solving the FJSPF, five instances given by Lei [16, 17], with the size from 10 jobs, 10 machines and 40 operations, to 15 jobs, 10 machines and 80 operations, are used in our experiments. Five existing state-of-the-art algorithms for the FJSPF including HBBO [21], TLBO [20], EDA [19], HABC [18] and CGA [17] are employed for comparison with the DEHH. To make a fair comparison, several critical parameters in the DEHH are set to the same values as in the literature [21], such as the population size of 200, the maximum generations of 500 and the maximum evaluation number of 100,000. Among the compared algorithms, the maximum evaluation number performed by the EDA and the CGA are 150,000, while the DEHH and the HBBO are 100,000, which means that fewer evaluations are conducted in the DEHH for solving the FJSPF. The DEHH is implemented in C++ and performed on a core i5-4210U processor with 2.40 GHz and 4 GB RAM.

Table 1. Computational results of various algorithms on the Lei instances.

Instance	Algorithm	Average value	Best value	Worst value
Case 1	DEHH	**(18.5, 26.8, 35.4)**	**(20, 26, 34)**	**(20, 27, 35)**
	HBBO	(20.8, 28.0, 37.2)	(21, 28, 37)	(19, 28, 39)
	TLBO	(20.3, 29.9, 40.9)	(19, 28, 39)	(21, 32, 42)
	EDA	(20.3, 30.5, 41.6)	(20, 28, 40)	(22, 32, 43)
	HABC	(21.0, 32.0, 43.6)	(19, 30, 43)	(23, 33, 46)
	CGA	(23.1, 33.1, 43.4)	(21, 29, 41)	(25, 37, 47)
Case 2	DEHH	**(28.4, 39.9, 52.5)**	**(27, 39, 54)**	**(32, 39, 54)**
	HBBO	(30.0, 45.0, 58.0)	(30, 45, 58)	(30, 45, 58)
	TLBO	(32.6, 46.4, 58.5)	(30, 45, 58)	(36, 49, 63)
	EDA	(33.7, 46.9, 57.9)	(32, 46, 57)	(34, 48, 58)
	HABC	(33.0, 47.8, 62.2)	(33, 46, 58)	(36, 48, 65)
	CGA	(35.0, 47.1, 60.6)	(32, 47, 57)	(38, 49, 64)

(continued)

Table 1. (*continued*)

Instance	Algorithm	Average value	Best value	Worst value
Case 3	DEHH	**(29.6, 42.4, 55.2)**	**(30, 42, 54)**	**(29, 43, 55)**
	HBBO	(30.2, 43.8, 58.1)	(30, 42, 60)	(31, 45, 57)
	TLBO	(31.5, 46.7, 62.2)	(30, 45, 60)	(33, 50, 70)
	EDA	(32.8, 47.2, 62.9)	(31, 46, 60)	(34, 49, 66)
	HABC	(33.9, 50.8, 67.3)	(33, 47, 64)	(36, 54, 70)
	CGA	(36.4, 50.8, 66.0)	(34, 47, 63)	(38, 53, 71)
Case 4	DEHH	**(21.7, 32.7, 46.5)**	**(21, 33, 45)**	**(23, 33, 47)**
	HBBO	(22.8, 34.0, 47.9)	(24, 33, 47)	(23, 35, 48)
	TLBO	(24.9, 36.5, 50.8)	(21, 36, 50)	(26, 40, 57)
	EDA	(24.8, 37.2, 51.9)	(21, 36, 50)	(24, 39, 57)
	HABC	(25.5, 40.0, 56.3)	(23, 38, 53)	(25, 44, 59)
	CGA	(27.4, 40.4, 55.0)	(26, 37, 51)	(29, 42, 59)
Case 5	DEHH	**(34.8, 52.6, 73.0)**	**(35, 52, 69)**	**(36, 53, 74)**
	HBBO	(37.2, 54.0, 74.3)	(36, 54, 70)	(37, 55, 75)
	TLBO	(36.1, 57.5, 78.2)	(36, 55, 72)	(37, 61, 82)
	EDA	(38.6, 56.9, 78.3)	(36, 55, 73)	(40, 60, 81)
	HABC	–	–	–
	CGA	(47.0, 65.4, 86.0)	(42, 62, 82)	(49, 70, 91)

Note: The bold values mean better results.

For each instance, DEHH is run 30 times independently, and the obtained makespan values are represented as the triangular fuzzy numbers (TFNs). The computational results of the average, the best and the worst makespan values are listed in Table 1, where the results of the compared algorithms are quoted directly from the literature [21]. From Table 1, it can be seen that DEHH exhibits much better performance when solving the benchmark instances. The average, the best and the worst values obtained by the DEHH are clearly better than those by the other algorithms. In particular, new best solutions can be found by DEHH for all instances. The Gantt chart of the new best solution obtained by the DEHH for case 5, the most complicated instance in the set, is shown in Fig. 5.

In addition, a pair-wise t-test [34] at 95% confidence level is conducted on the average values of the compared algorithms, and the results are listed in Table 2, where, SD is the standard deviation and SEM is the standard error of mean. It can be drawn from the table that the performance of the DEHH is significantly better than the other algorithms. Moreover, the average CPU times employed by the compared algorithms over 30 runs are listed in Table 3. It can be observed from the table that DEHH spends much less CPU time than the other algorithms except HBBO. The main reason is that, DEHH generates a feasible schedule by using a hybrid decoding scheme based on the ECM rule and the left-shift scheme, while only the former rule is used in HBBO to decode a solution. However, the computational efficiency of the DEHH is acceptable and the CPU time does not increase greatly as the problem size increases.

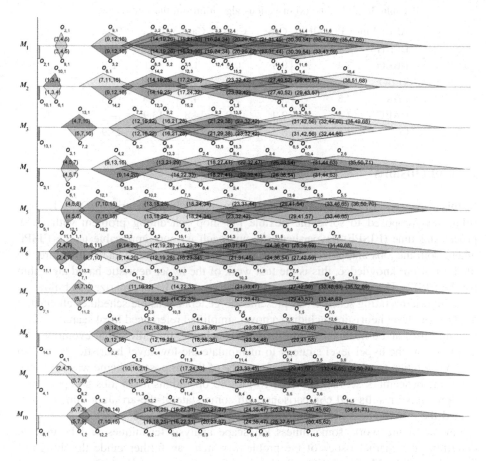

Fig. 5. The best solution obtained by the DEHH for Case 5.

Table 2. Pair-wise t-test of various algorithms on small-sized instances.

Algorithm	Mean	SD	SEM	t	Significance
DEHH vs. HBBO	−2.085	1.261	0.564	−3.698	0.021
DEHH vs. TLBO	−4.280	0.927	0.414	−10.327	0.000
DEHH vs. EDA	−4.790	0.897	0.401	−11.939	0.000
DEHH vs. HABC	−7.038	1.283	0.641	−10.971	0.002
DEHH vs. CGA	−8.455	2.510	1.122	−7.534	0.002

Table 3. CPU time (s) of various algorithms on the Lei instances.

Algorithm	CPU (GHz)	Case 1	Case 2	Case 3	Case 4	Case 5
DEHH	2.4	1.3	1.3	2.3	2.3	3.7
HBBO	2.4	0.8	0.8	1.1	1.1	2.9
TLBO	3.4	2.9	2.9	4.0	4.1	9.6
EDA	2.3	3.7	3.6	4.9	4.6	9.8
HABC	2.8	9.9	10.9	14.8	13.9	–
CGA	1.7	8.3	8.3	10.7	10.8	23.9

5   Conclusions

In this paper, an effective differential evolution based hyper-heuristic (DEHH) algorithm was proposed to solve the flexible job-shop scheduling problem with fuzzy processing time (FJSPF). Hyper-heuristic approach is more applicable to the FJSPF where both the jobs and processing time are highly diverse and dynamic in nature. To the best of our knowledge, this is the first work of the hyper heuristic-based algorithm for the FJSPF. The main contributions of this work could be summarized as follows: a novel hybrid decoding scheme was presented to generate feasible schedules efficiently; a set of low-level heuristics including a novel simplified referenced local search method was designed and embedded within the DEHH scheme; the differential evolution was employed as the hyper-level strategy to manipulate the low-level heuristics to find an optimal solution for the FJSPF; the performance of the proposed scheme was evaluated using the benchmark set ranging from 10 jobs 40 operations to 15 jobs 80 operations. Computational results and comparisons with some state-of-the-art algorithms demonstrated the effectiveness of the proposed hyper-heuristic scheme.

In our future work, some fitness landscape analysis techniques will be used to determine the characteristics of the problem, which can further guide the design of hyper-heuristics. Moreover, it will also be interesting to apply the hyper-heuristic scheme for solving other realistic scheduling problems.

Acknowledgment. This research is part of a project supported by the Zhejiang Provincial Natural Science Foundation of China (Grant nos. LQ15F030002 and LY15F020014), the National Natural Science Foundation of China (Grant nos. 61503331, 71671160 and 61603169), the National Undergraduate Training Programs for Innovation and Entrepreneurship (201611482012) and the Zhejiang Key Laboratory of Solid State Drive and Data Security (Grant No. 2015E10003).

References

1. Wang, L., Zhou, G., Xu, Y., Wang, S.Y., Liu, M.: An effective artificial bee colony algorithm for the flexible job-shop scheduling problem. Int. J. Adv. Manuf. Technol. **60**, 303–315 (2012)
2. Logendran, R., Sonthinen, A.: A Tabu search-based approach for scheduling job-shop type flexible manufacturing systems. J. Oper. Res. Soc. **48**, 264–277 (1997)

3. Gomes, M.C., Barbosa-Povoa, A.P., Novais, A.Q.: Optimal scheduling for flexible job shop operation. Int. J. Prod. Res. **43**, 2323–2353 (2005)
4. Saidi-Mehrabad, M., Fattahi, P.: Flexible job shop scheduling with tabu search algorithms. Int. J. Adv. Manuf. Technol. **32**, 563–570 (2007)
5. Chen, H.X., Ihlow, J., Lehmann, C.: A genetic algorithm for flexible job-shop scheduling. In: 1999 IEEE International Conference on Robotics and Automation, Detroit, MI, USA, pp. 1120–1125. IEEE (1999)
6. Pezzella, F., Morganti, G., Ciaschetti, G.: A genetic algorithm for the flexible job-shop scheduling problem. Comput. Oper. Res. **35**, 3202–3212 (2008)
7. Gutierrez, C., Garcia-Magarino, I.: Modular design of a hybrid genetic algorithm for a flexible job-shop scheduling problem. Knowl.-Based Syst. **24**, 102–112 (2011)
8. Gholami, M., Zandieh, M.: Integrating simulation and genetic algorithm to schedule a dynamic flexible job shop. J. Intell. Manuf. **20**, 481–498 (2009)
9. Karimi, H., Rahmati, S.H.A., Zandieh, M.: An efficient knowledge-based algorithm for the flexible job shop scheduling problem. Knowl.-Based Syst. **36**, 236–244 (2012)
10. Yuan, Y., Xu, H.: Flexible job shop scheduling using hybrid differential evolution algorithms. Comput. Ind. Eng. **65**, 246–260 (2013)
11. Rossi, A.: Flexible job shop scheduling with sequence-dependent setup and transportation times by ant colony with reinforced pheromone relationships. Int. J. Prod. Econ. **153**, 253–267 (2014)
12. Ziaee, M.: A heuristic algorithm for solving flexible job shop scheduling problem. Int. J. Adv. Manuf. Technol. **71**, 519–528 (2014)
13. Sakawa, M., Kubota, R.: Fuzzy programming for multiobjective job shop scheduling with fuzzy processing time and fuzzy duedate through genetic algorithms. Eur. J. Oper. Res. **120**, 393–407 (2000)
14. Gao, K.Z., Suganthan, P.N., Pan, Q.K., Tasgetiren, M.F.: An effective discrete harmony search algorithm for flexible job shop scheduling problem with fuzzy processing time. Int. J. Prod. Res. **53**, 5896–5911 (2015)
15. Gao, K.Z., Suganthan, P.N., Pan, Q.K., Chua, T.J., Chong, C.S., Cai, T.X.: An improved artificial bee colony algorithm for flexible job-shop scheduling problem with fuzzy processing time. Expert Syst. Appl. **65**, 52–67 (2016)
16. Lei, D.M.: A genetic algorithm for flexible job shop scheduling with fuzzy processing time. Int. J. Prod. Res. **48**, 2995–3013 (2010)
17. Lei, D.M.: Co-evolutionary genetic algorithm for fuzzy flexible job shop scheduling. Appl. Soft Comput. **12**, 2237–2245 (2012)
18. Wang, L., Zhou, G., Xu, Y., Liu, M.: A hybrid artificial bee colony algorithm for the fuzzy flexible job-shop scheduling problem. Int. J. Prod. Res. **51**, 3593–3608 (2013)
19. Wang, S., Wang, L., Xu, Y., Liu, M.: An effective estimation of distribution algorithm for the flexible job-shop scheduling problem with fuzzy processing time. Int. J. Prod. Res. **51**, 3778–3793 (2013)
20. Xu, Y., Wang, L., Wang, S.Y., Liu, M.: An effective teaching-learning-based optimization algorithm for the flexible job-shop scheduling problem with fuzzy processing time. Neurocomputing **148**, 260–268 (2015)
21. Lin, J.: A hybrid biogeography-based optimization for the fuzzy flexible job-shop scheduling problem. Knowl.-Based Syst. **78**, 59–74 (2015)
22. Koulinas, G., Kotsikas, L., Anagnostopoulos, K.: A particle swarm optimization based hyper-heuristic algorithm for the classic resource constrained project scheduling problem. Inf. Sci. **277**, 680–693 (2014)

23. Salcedo-Sanz, S., Matías-Román, J.M., Jiménez-Fernández, S., Portilla-Figueras, A., Cuadra, L.: An evolutionary-based hyper-heuristic approach for the Jawbreaker puzzle. Applied Intelligence **40**, 404–414 (2014)
24. Gascón-Moreno, J., Salcedo-Sanz, S., Saavedra-Moreno, B., Carro-Calvo, L., Portilla-Figueras, A.: An evolutionary-based hyper-heuristic approach for optimal construction of group method of data handling networks. Inf. Sci. **247**, 94–108 (2013)
25. Anwar, K., Khader, A.T., Al-Betar, M.A., Awadallah, M.A.: Harmony search-based hyper-heuristic for examination timetabling. In: 2013 IEEE 9th International Colloquium on Signal Processing and its Applications, Kuala Lumpur, Malaysia, pp. 176–181. IEEE (2013)
26. Lin, J., Wang, Z.-J., Li, X.: A backtracking search hyper-heuristic for the distributed assembly flow-shop scheduling problem. Swarm Evol. Comput. **36**, 124–135 (2017)
27. Rajni, Chana, I.: Bacterial foraging based hyper-heuristic for resource scheduling in grid computing. Future Gener. Comput. Syst. **29**, 751–762 (2014)
28. Ouelhadj, D., Petrovic, S.: A cooperative hyper-heuristic search framework. J. Heuristics **16**, 835–857 (2010)
29. Hart, E., Sim, K.: A hyper-heuristic ensemble method for static job-shop scheduling. Evol. Comput. **24**, 609–635 (2016)
30. Storn, R., Price, K.: Differential evolution–a simple and efficient heuristic for global optimization over continuous spaces. J. Global Optim. **11**, 341–359 (1997)
31. Bortolan, G., Degani, R.: A review of some methods for ranking fuzzy subsets. Fuzzy Sets Syst. **15**, 1–19 (1985)
32. Das, S., Suganthan, P.N.: Differential evolution: a survey of the state-of-the-art. IEEE Trans. Evol. Comput. **15**, 4–31 (2011)
33. Gao, J., Sun, L.Y., Gen, M.: A hybrid genetic and variable neighborhood descent algorithm for flexible job shop scheduling problems. Comput. Oper. Res. **35**, 2892–2907 (2008)
34. Boussaid, I., Chatterjee, A., Siarry, P., Ahmed-Nacer, M.: Biogeography-based optimization for constrained optimization problems. Comput. Oper. Res. **39**, 3293–3304 (2012)

ACO-iRBA: A Hybrid Approach to TSPN with Overlapping Neighborhoods

Yuanlong Qin and Bo Yuan$^{(\boxtimes)}$

Intelligent Computing Lab, Division of Informatics,
Graduate School at Shenzhen, Tsinghua University,
Shenzhen 518055, People's Republic of China
956441594@qq.com, yuanb@sz.tsinghua.edu.cn

Abstract. The traveling salesman problem with neighborhoods (TSPN) is a generalization of TSP and can be regarded as a combination of TSP and TPP (Touring Polygons Problem). In this paper, we propose a hybrid TSPN solution named ACO-iRBA in which the TSP and TPP tasks are tackled simultaneously by ACO (Ant Colony Optimization) and iRBA, an improved version of RBA (Rubber Band Algorithm), respectively. A major feature of ACO-iRBA is that it can properly handle situations where the neighborhoods are heavily overlapped. Experiment results on benchmark problems composed of random ellipses show that ACO-iRBA can solve TSPN instances with up to 70 regions effectively and generally produce higher quality solutions than a recent heuristic method CIH.

Keywords: TSP · TPP · TSPN · Hybrid · iRBA

1 Introduction

TSP with neighborhoods (TSPN), introduced by Arkin and Hassin [1], is a generalization of TSP. The scenario of TSPN can be explained as follows: a salesman wants to meet a group of potential buyers; each buyer specifies a connected region in the plane (neighborhood) within which he/she is willing to meet the salesman; the salesman needs to schedule a tour with the shortest length that visits all buyers and finally returns to the initial departure point [2, 3].

Since TSPN is a generalization of TSP, TSPN is also an NP-hard problem. Traditionally, there are mainly two ways to solve TSPN problems. The first one is to convert TSPN to group TSP (GTSP) by sampling some points in each region and replace neighborhoods with the corresponding points [4–6]. However, it has two drawbacks: (i) the search space can increase significantly if too many points are sampled from each region; (ii) using GTSP to approximate TSPN will inevitably bring in errors and may not obtain satisfactory results.

Another approach relies on the divide-and-conquer strategy. For example, each region can be reduced to a single point as the representative and TSPN is transformed into two sub-problems: TSP and touring polygons problem (TPP) [7]. In practice, a TSP solver is applied on the set of representatives to acquire a visiting sequence. Then, this sequence of regions is used as the input of the TPP solver, which searches for an optimal visiting point for each region. However, it is usually not known how to choose

© Springer International Publishing AG 2017
Y. Shi et al. (Eds.): SEAL 2017, LNCS 10593, pp. 87–96, 2017.
https://doi.org/10.1007/978-3-319-68759-9_8

the proper representatives and consequently the sequence obtained by the TSP solver may not be a good sequence for TPP/TSPN, leading to sub-optimal solutions.

Recently, Gentilini et al. [8] formulated TSPN as a non-convex mixed-integer nonlinear programming (MINLP) problem, which is efficient only for TSPN with a small number of regions. Alatartsev et al. [9] proposed a heuristic TSPN method named Constricting Insertion Heuristic (CIH), which splits TSPN into TSP and TPP and solves them simultaneously. Their experiments show that high quality solutions can be obtained within a short period of time for problems with more than 100 regions.

As to TPP, the rubber band algorithm (RBA) by Bülow and Klette [10] is aimed at finding minimum-length polygonal curves in cube-curves in 3D spaces. Variations of this algorithm have been used to solve various Euclidean shortest path (ESP) problems, such as touring polygons, parts cutting, safari and the watchman route.

In this paper, we first modify RBA to make it suitable for cases with overlapping regions and then propose a hybrid algorithm ACO-iRBA to solve TSPN with overlapping neighborhoods effectively. The proposed algorithm splits TSPN into TSP and TPP, which are solved in parallel rather than step by step. Section 2 introduces the related techniques and the details of ACO-iRBA are presented in Sect. 3. The experiments investigating the effectiveness of iRBA compared with RBA and the performance of ACO-iRBA compared with CIH on 18 TSPN benchmark instances are given in Sect. 4. This paper is concluded in Sect. 5 with some directions for future work.

2 Related Work

2.1 RBA

Algorithm 1   RBA for a sequence of pairwise disjoint simple polygons
Input: Sequence of n pairwise disjoint areas $A = (A_1, ..., A_n)$, accuracy ε
Output: Tour $T = (p_1, ..., p_n)$
1.   Construct a feasible sequence $T = (p_1, ..., p_n)$ so that $p_i \in A_i$
2.   Let $L_0 = \infty$. Calculate $L_1 = \sum_{i=1}^n d(p_i, p_{i+1})$ where $p_{n+1} = p_1$.
3.   **while** $L_0 - L_1 \geq \varepsilon$ **do**
4.   **for** $i = 1, 2, \cdots, n$ **do**
5.   Find $p_i' \in \partial A_i$, such that $d(p_{i-1}, p_i') + d(p_i', p_{i+1}) =$
$min\ (d(p_{i-1}, p_i) + d(p_i, p_{i+1})), p_i \in \partial A_i$
6. $p_i \leftarrow p_i'$
7.   **end**
8.   Let $L_0 = L_1$ and calculate $L_1 = \sum_{i=1}^n d(p_i, p_{i+1})$
9.   **end**
10. **return** T;

The basic version of TPP is to find a shortest path, which starts at p and then visits the polygons according to the given order, and finally ends at q (p, q are two points that do not belong to any polygons). There are many algorithms for solving TPP or its variants [11–14] and it is a NP-hard problem except in some special cases [11].

Pan et al. [12] proposed an effective TPP algorithm based on RBA. RBA features linear time complexity and can handle large scale problems efficiently. The general structure of RBA is shown as Algorithm 1 where ∂A_i is the frontier of polygon A_i and $d(p_i, p_{i+1})$ is the distance between p_i and p_{i+1}.

The basic idea of RBA is to construct a feasible tour $T = (p_1, \ldots, p_n)$ by randomly allocating one point inside each region with $p_i \in A_i$ and iteratively improving it. In each iteration, in order to find a better point $p_i' \in \partial A_i$, the adjacent points p_{i-1} and p_{i+1} of p_i are fixed, so that the distance $d(p_{i-1}, p_i') + d(p_i', p_{i+1})$ can be minimized (Fig. 1). For example, if the region is a disk, we can find p_i' by performing a binary search on the radian values within $[0, 2\pi]$. RBA stops when a maximum number of iterations are performed or the desired accuracy threshold ε is reached.

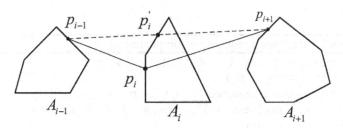

Fig. 1. An illustration of Step 5 in Algorithm 1 where point p_i is replaced by a new point p_i'

2.2 TSP-TPP

The TSP-TPP strategy solves TSPN in two steps: (i) construct a TSP Tour based on representative points $(p_1, \ldots, p_n)$; (ii) search for a set of n meeting/visiting points based on the sequence produced in the previous step. Suppose π^{TSP} is the permutation of representative points in the optimal TSP tour, whereas π^{TSPN} is the permutation of regions in the optimal TSPN tour. The key idea is to use π^{TSP} in place of the unknown π^{TSPN} in the search process for the optimal meeting points.

The validity of the TSP-TPP strategy is established on the assumption that when the sizes of regions are small enough with respect to the distances among them, π^{TSP} is likely to be identical to π^{TSPN}. Yuan et al. [7] investigated TSPN with pairwise disjoint disks and the results show that the TSP-TPP strategy works well in practice. However, Fig. 2 gives a counterexample with $\pi^{TSP} = (1, 2, 3, 4, 5)$ and $\pi^{TSPN} = (1, 3, 2, 4, 5)$, which is more likely to happen when regions are close to each other or even overlapped.

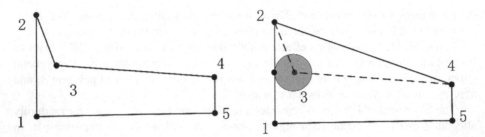

Fig. 2. A case where π^{TSP}(left) is different from π^{TSPN}(right) when point 3 is replaced by a disk. The TSPN tour (right) is also shorter than the TSP tour (left).

3   Methodology

3.1   iRBA

Algorithm 2   iRBA for a sequence of simple polygons

Input: Sequence of n areas A $= (A_1, ..., A_n)$, accuracy ε
Output: Tour $T = (p_1, ..., p_n)$
1.   Construct a feasible sequence $T = (p_1, ..., p_n)$ so that $p_i \in A_i$
2.   Let $L_0 = \infty$. Calculate $L_1 = \sum_{i=1}^{n} d(p_i, p_{i+1})$ where $p_{n+1} = p_1$.
3.   **while** $L_0 - L_1 \geq \varepsilon$ **do**
4.   **for** $i = 1,2, \cdots, n$ **do**
5.   **if** $is\_in(A_i, p_{i-1})$ && $is\_in(A_i, p_{i+1})$==True
6. $p'_i = (p_{i-1} + p_{i+1})/2$
7.   **else**
8.   Find $p'_i \in \partial A_i$, such that $d(p_{i-1}, p'_i) + d(p'_i, p_{i+1})=$
                     $min\ (d(p_{i-1}, p_i) + d(p_i, p_{i+1})), p_i \in \partial A_i$
9.   **end**
10. $p_i \leftarrow p'_i$
11.   **end**
12.   Let $L_0 = L_1$ and calculate $L_1 = \sum_{i=1}^{n} d(p_i, p_{i+1})$
13. **end**
14. **return** T;

[#]The function $is\_in(A_i, p_j)$ is to judge whether point p_j is within region A_i.

RBA works well for TPP in non-overlapping cases. However, the regions in TSPN may be significantly overlapped, resulting in unsatisfactory performance. In Fig. 3, p_{i-1} and p_{i+1}, the two adjacent points of p_i, are both located within region A_i. Since RBA only checks the candidate points on the frontier of region A_i, it cannot correctly identify the optimal point located inside A_i.

So, we propose iRBA by modifying the original RBA to solve the above issue. iRBA works by checking whether the two adjacent points of p_i are both inside region A_i before searching for the new point p'_i. If so, iRBA simply takes the midpoint between

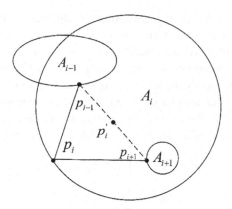

Fig. 3. A case where the optimal point p_i' is within A_i rather than on the frontier of A_i

p_{i-1} and p_{i+1} as p_i', that is, $p_i' = (p_{i-1} + p_{i+1})/2$. The implementation details of iRBA are shown in Algorithm 2.

3.2 ACO-iRBA

Although it is tempting to identify the sequence of regions by solving a TSP problem in the first place and fix it during the subsequent TPP phase, there is no guarantee that this TSP sequence is optimal for the corresponding TSPN, as shown in Sect. 2.2.

In this paper, we propose a hybrid algorithm that combines evolutionary algorithms (EAs) for the TSP phase and dedicated heuristic methods for the TPP phase. The main idea is to evolve a population of individuals representing candidate sequences for TSPN and apply a TPP solver on each individual. The tour length obtained by the TPP solver is returned as the fitness value of the specific individual, which is the key information that drives the evolution. In this way, the TSP phase and the TPP phase are optimized simultaneously, making it possible to achieve better solutions.

There are many TSP algorithms in the domain of EAs [15–18]. We adopt ant colony optimization (ACO) largely due to two concerns:

 (i) ACO is purposefully designed to solve path planning problems;
 (ii) ACO is a metaheuristic algorithm with great flexibility and can be potentially applied to different problems.

The basic version of ACO [17] was used in our work, as our current focus is to demonstrate the feasibility of the proposed hybrid strategy while leaving in-depth refinement as future work.

In ACO, the migration probability (i.e., ant k moves from city i to city j) when constructing a route is defined as follows:

$$p_{ij}^k = \frac{\tau_{ij}^\alpha \eta_{ij}^\beta}{\sum_s \tau_{is}^\alpha \eta_{is}^\beta} \quad s \in allowed_k \tag{1}$$

where $allowed_k = C - tabu_k$ is the collection of alternative cities for ant k ($tabu_k$ represents the cities that ant k has visited and C is the collection of total cities). η_{ij} is a heuristic function, which is the inverse of the distance between cities i and j ($\eta_{ij} = 1/d_{ij}$). β is a parameter that weights the importance of heuristic information, and the larger β is, the more greedy the rule is. τ_{ij} is the amount of pheromone trail on edge e_{ij}, and α is a parameter that weights the importance of the accumulated pheromone: the larger its value, the tighter the cooperation among the population.

Once the travel of ants is finished, τ_{ij} is updated according to the following rules:

$$\tau_{ij}(n+1) = (1 - \rho)\tau_{ij}(n) + \Delta\tau_{ij} \tag{2}$$

$$\Delta\tau_{ij} = \sum_{k=1}^{m} \Delta\tau_{ij}^k \tag{3}$$

where $\rho(0 \leq \rho \leq 1)$ is the pheromone volatilization coefficient and $\Delta\tau_{ij}^k$ is the pheromone that ant k leaves on the edge e_{ij}. Dorigo and Gambardella [16] presented three rules of $\Delta\tau_{ij}^k$ among which the Ant Cycle System is widely used:

$$\Delta\tau_{ij}^k = \begin{cases} \frac{Q}{L_k}, & \text{if ant } k \text{ has passed } e_{ij} \text{ in this cycle} \\ 0, & else \end{cases} \tag{4}$$

where Q is a constant that can be simply set to 1 and L_k is the route length of ant k in this cycle. Note that we use the TPP length T_k returned by iRBA as L_k, which means that iRBA is applied to every sequence s_k to get T_k (i.e., $T_k = iRBA(s_k)$) with region centers selected as the initial points.

4 Experiments

The following experimental studies were conducted on a PC with Intel Core i7-3770 CPU at 3.4 GHz with 8 GB RAM and all algorithms were implemented in Matlab 2014a. In the first part of experiments, we compared iRBA with RBA on randomly generated synthetic problems with overlapping regions. In the second part of experiments, we compared ACO-iRBA with CIH on 18 benchmark problems.

4.1 Experiment on iRBA

Each problem consisted of a set of ellipses in a 4×4 rectangle with random radius values and locations. Therefore, the overlap rate is expected to grow with the number of ellipses. We selected the centers as initial points to get the best TSP sequence, and then used this sequence as the input for RBA and iRBA. The results are given in Fig. 4.

In Fig. 4, ρ is an index used to measure the relative improvement of iRBA: $\rho = (RBA - iRBA)/RBA$. The greater ρ is, the better the relative performance of iRBA. The horizontal axis represents the number of regions in each problem, ranging from 5 to 25. To account for randomness, 20 instances were generated for each case and the average ρ values and error bars are plotted. It is clear that there is a positive

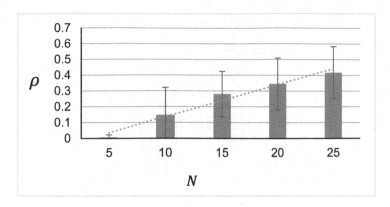

Fig. 4. The effectiveness of path reduction by iRBA compared to RBA

correlation between ρ and N, which means that the benefit of iRBA over RBA is more significant when regions are heavily overlapped. The results on one of the instances are shown in Fig. 5.

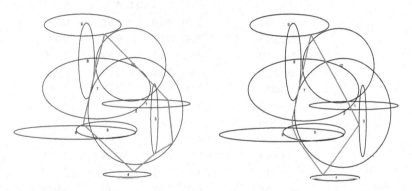

Fig. 5. The comparison of routes found for an instance ($N = 10$) by RBA (left, length = 5.05) and iRBA (right, length = 4.47)

4.2 Experiment on ACO-iRBA

In order to evaluate the performance of ACO-iRBA, we chose the 18 test instances developed by Gentilini et al. [8]. For example, the instance labeled "30_1_5" is an instance with 30 ellipses and the radius of one axis is stretched by one to five times, in comparison to another axis. Alatartsev et al. [9] gives a detailed description on how to construct the instances and the best known values of instances are also available [19].

In our experiment, the number of ants m was 200 and the number of iterations N was 100. Other parameter values were: $\alpha = 1$, $\beta = 5$, $Q = 1$, $\varepsilon = 0.2$. Figure 6 shows a TSPN tour for instance "30_1_10", and all results over 30 trials are given in Table 1.

In Table 1, the performance is measured by the relative distance to the best known result with optimal value 0. For example, 2% means that the length of the TSPN tour is

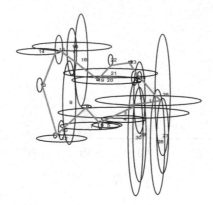

Fig. 6. The TSPN route for instance "30_1_10" with length 307.895

Table 1. The performance of ACO-iRBA on TSPN instances with 20 to 70 ellipses

No.	Instance	Best known value	CIH	ACO-iRBA		
			(%)	Best (%)	Avg. (%)	Std
1	20_1_1	318.904	2.39	**0.00**	0.02	0.338
2	20_1_5	312.915	3.30	**0.00**	0.01	0.607
3	20_1_10	252.350	0.00	0.17	2.57	1.420
4	30_1_1	383.578	1.44	**0.06**	0.14	0.864
5	30_1_5	316.854	0.00	1.47	2.47	2.384
6	30_1_10	306.637	0.00	0.34	0.74	1.017
7	40_1_1	416.556	3.58	**2.06**	2.76	1.327
8	40_1_5	366.637	0.53	1.08	1.89	3.474
9	40_1_10	311.714	0.00	8.44	9.30	4.391
10	50_1_1	438.215	3.10	**1.97**	2.50	2.242
11	50_1_5	435.158	6.97	**2.67**	3.40	0.943
12	50_1_10	391.303	2.44	6.71	8.65	4.147
13	60_1_1	559.042	8.87	**1.66**	1.89	2.431
14	60_1_5	550.121	2.93	**1.64**	2.25	4.379
15	60_1_10	482.289	7.85	**5.31**	5.84	1.540
16	70_1_1	599.819	5.74	**2.93**	3.91	2.224
17	70_1_5	564.303	7.60	**4.13**	5.58	7.580
18	70_1_10	447.452	9.28	**6.56**	9.05	5.788
Avg.			3.67	**2.57**	3.51	

2% longer than the best known shortest tour. On 12 out of the 18 test instances, the best tours found by ACO-iRBA over 30 trials were better than those found by CIH. On average, the best tours found by ACO-iRBA were only 2.57% longer than the best known shortest tours, compared to 3.67% of CIH.

Moreover, there is a clear tendency that when the number of ellipses was larger, the advantage of ACO-iRBA over CIH was also more consistent. Furthermore, Fig. 7 shows the convergence pattern of ACO-iRBA averaged over 30 trials on problems with different numbers of ellipses. The vertical axis shows the ratio between the best tour length at the 100th iteration and that at the current iteration, showing that in most cases our algorithm features quick convergence speed.

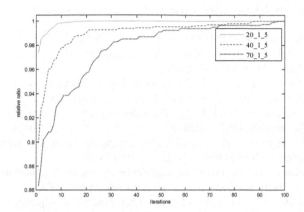

Fig. 7. The convergence of ACO-iRBA with different numbers of eclipses. The vertical axis shows the relative performance compared to the final value at the 100th iteration.

5 Conclusion

This paper presented a hybrid algorithm ACO-iRBA to solve the challenging TSPN problems, which is purposefully targeted at cases with significantly overlapping neighborhoods. In order to solve TSPN, we divided TSPN into two sub-problems: TSP and TPP and solved them simultaneously, avoiding the potential drawbacks of solving them in separate stages. The proposed iRBA is an extension of RBA and suits for touring a sequence of overlapping regions. Note that, as the TSP solver, ACO can be conveniently replaced by other EA-based TSP algorithms that take the tour lengths produced by iRBA as inputs, bringing high flexibility to the proposed method. Experimental studies on 18 standard test instances confirmed that ACO-iRBA worked reasonably well in most cases compared to CIH, which is one of the latest heuristic methods for TSPN, especially when the space was densely populated by ellipses. As to future work, we will generalize our algorithm to situations where the regions are represented by irregular shapes, instead of circles or ellipses.

References

1. Arkin, E.M., Hassin, R.: Approximation algorithms for the geometric covering salesman problem. Discrete Appl. Math. **55**(3), 197–218 (1994)

2. Dumitrescu, A., Mitchell, J. S.: Approximation algorithms for TSP with neighborhoods in the plane. In: Proceedings of the Twelfth Annual ACM-SIAM Symposium on Discrete Algorithms, pp. 38–46. Society for Industrial and Applied Mathematics (2001)
3. de Berg, M., Gudmundsson, J., Katz, M.J., Levcopoulos, C., Overmars, M.H., van der Stappen, A.F.: TSP with neighborhoods of varying size. J. Algorithms 57(1), 22–36 (2005)
4. Jang, D.S., Chae, H.J., Choi, H.L.: Optimal control-based UAV path planning with dynamically-constrained TSP with neighborhoods. arXiv preprint arXiv:1612.06008 (2016)
5. Isaacs, J.T., Klein, D.J., Hespanha, J.P.: Algorithms for the traveling salesman problem with neighborhoods involving a Dubins vehicle. In: American Control Conference, pp. 1704–1709 (2011)
6. Wang, W., Shi, H.S., Wu, D.J., Huang, P.Y., Gao, B.J., Wu, F.P., Xu, D., Chen, X.J.: VD-PSO: an efficient mobile sink routing algorithm in wireless sensor networks. Peer-to-Peer Netw. Appl. 10, 1–10 (2016)
7. Yuan, B., Orlowska, M., Sadiq, S.: On the optimal robot routing problem in wireless sensor networks. IEEE Trans. Knowl. Data Eng. 19(9), 1252–1261 (2007)
8. Gentilini, I., Margot, F., Shimada, K.: The travelling salesman problem with neighbourhoods: MINLP solution. Optim. Methods Softw. 28(2), 364–378 (2013)
9. Alatartsev, S., Augustine, M., Ortmeier, F.: Constricting insertion heuristic for traveling salesman problem with neighborhoods. In: ICAPS (2013)
10. Klette, R., Bülow, T.: Critical edges in simple cube-curves. In: 9th International Conference on Discrete Geometry for Computer Imagery, pp. 467–478 (2000)
11. Dror, M., Efrat, A., Lubiw, A., Mitchell, J.S.: Touring a sequence of polygons. In: Proceedings of the Thirty-Fifth Annual ACM Symposium on Theory of Computing, pp. 473–482 (2003)
12. Pan, X., Li, F., Klette, R.: Approximate shortest path algorithms for sequences of pairwise disjoint simple polygons. Department of Computer Science, University of Auckland, pp. 175–178 (2010)
13. Li, F., Klette, R.: Rubberband algorithms for solving various 2D or 3D shortest path problems. In: Computing: Theory and Applications, pp. 9–19. IEEE Press (2007)
14. Ahadi, A., Mozafari, A., Zarei, A.: Touring a sequence of disjoint polygons: complexity and extension. Theoret. Comput. Sci. 556, 45–54 (2014)
15. Grefenstette, J., Gopal, R., Rosmaita, B., Van Gucht, D.: Genetic algorithms for the traveling salesman problem. In: Proceedings of the First International Conference on Genetic Algorithms and Their Applications, pp. 160–165 (1986)
16. Dorigo, M., Gambardella, L.M.: Ant colonies for the travelling salesman problem. Biosystems 43(2), 73–81 (1997)
17. Wang, K.P., Huang, L., Zhou, C.G., Pang, W.: Particle swarm optimization for traveling salesman problem. In: 2003 International Conference on Machine Learning and Cybernetics, pp. 1583–1585 (2003)
18. Wong, L.P., Low, M.Y. H., Chong, C.S.: A bee colony optimization algorithm for traveling salesman problem. In: AICMS 2008 Second Asia International Conference on Modeling and Simulation, pp. 818–823 (2008)
19. Alatartsev, S., Mersheeva, V., Augustine, M., Ortmeier, F.: On optimizing a sequence of robotic tasks. In: 2013 IEEE/RSJ International Conference Intelligent Robots and Systems (IROS), pp. 217–223 (2013)

An Evolutionary Algorithm with a New Coding Scheme for Multi-objective Portfolio Optimization

Yi Chen[1], Aimin Zhou[1(⊠)], Rongfang Zhou[2], Peng He[2], Yong Zhao[2], and Lihua Dong[2]

[1] Shanghai Key Laboratory of Multidimensional Information Processing, Department of Computer Science and Technology, East China Normal University, 3663 North Zhongshan Road, Shanghai, China
amzhou@ecnu.edu.cn
[2] Shanghai Clearing House, 2 East Beijing Road, Shanghai, China

Abstract. A portfolio optimization problem involves optimal allocation of finite capital to a series of assets to achieve an acceptable trade-off between profit and risk in a given investment period. In the paper, the extended Markowitz's mean-variance portfolio optimization model is studied. A major challenge with this model is that it contains both discrete and continuous decision variables, which represent the assignment and allocation of assets respectively. To deal with this hard problem, this paper proposes an evolutionary algorithm with a new coding scheme that converts discrete variables into continuous ones. By this way, the mixed variables can be handled, and some of the constraints are naturally satisfied. The new approach is empirically studied and the experiment results indicate its efficiency.

Keywords: Multi-objective portfolio · Constraints handling · Mixed variables

1 Introduction

Portfolio selection problem [4, 11] is a well-known and well-studied financial problem and appeals to allocate limited money among a finite number of different assets, such as stocks, bonds, and derivatives in order to achieve higher reward and lower risk. Markowitz's mean-variance model [10] assumes that future market of the assets can be validly reflected by the historical market assets. The mean-variance (MV) model, which is a mixed integer quadratic program, appeals to make a trade-off between profit and risk and selects *efficient* portfolios afterwards [5,6]. The compromise between profit and risk forms a curve including the best collections. It is called *efficient frontier* or *Pareto-optimal front*.

However, the classic MV model assumes a perfect market where some constraints in practice are disregarded. In the paper, the following four practical

© Springer International Publishing AG 2017
Y. Shi et al. (Eds.): SEAL 2017, LNCS 10593, pp. 97–109, 2017.
https://doi.org/10.1007/978-3-319-68759-9_9

constraints [8] are investegated: (i) *cardinality constraint:* It limits the number of assets in portfolio. The management of too many assets makes it too hard to monitor, and the management of too less assets makes it lose degree of diversification. (ii) *floor and ceiling constraints:* They specify the minimum and maximum limits on the proportion of each asset in portfolio. An investor prefers to avoid numerous administrative costs for very small holdings and excessive risks for great quantity holdings. (iii) *pre-assignment constraint:* It considers the investor's subjective preference. In practice, investors wish some specific assets to be held with fixed or determined proportion intuitively. (iv) *round lot constraint:* It requires the number of any asset in the portfolio to be exact multiple of the normal trading lots. Some similar extended Markowitz's mean-variance portfolio optimization models have been studied intensively [3,8,16,18].

In this paper, we focus on the constraints proposed above and implement a monolithic solver based on evolutionary algorithm that tackles the mixed variables at one time. In general, researchers tend to study the portfolio problem with step-by-step solvers, which separate the problem into two subproblem as assignment and allocation of assets. Obviously, the step-by-step solvers may lead to several troubles such as error propagation, which occurs when the assignment of assets is not appropriate, and neglect of correlation between assignment and allocation.

To address the problem with the step-by-step solvers, a new coding scheme is proposed and combined with random keys [1]. This coding scheme is integrated into Multi-objective Evolutionary Algorithm Based on Decomposition (MOEA/D) [19] to solve the multi-objective portfolio problems. Although there are some work that applies evolutionary algorithms in portfolio problems [9,12,14], these algorithms can hardly deal with mixed variables in a uniform encoding. In this paper, we adopt the random-key genetic algorithm [1], which is extensively used for maintaining uniformity of encoding. The new approach is compared with a state-of-the-art step-by-step algorithm [18] and a basic step-by-step random key based method. The experimental results demonstrate that the proposed algorithm is highly efficient in terms of inverted generational distance (IGD) [14] and percentage deviation (PD) [3], which are the widely used metrics in portfolio optimization.

The rest of the paper is structured as follows. In Sect. 2, the formulation of multi-objective portfolio optimization problem is described. In Sect. 3, the algorithm framework is presented. In Sect. 4, the paper discusses the analysis of simulation results. Finally, Sect. 5 concludes the paper and outlines some future works.

2   Multi-objective Portfolio Optimization Problem

The classic MV model of portfolio optimization is a bi-objective optimization problem that compromises risk and return [2]. The objective in this work is to find a set of *efficient* portfolios that satisfy four real-world constraints, i.e., cardinality, quantity, pre-assignment and round lot simultaneously. Mathematically, the problem [8] can be formulated as follows:

$$min \quad f_1 = \sum_{i=1}^{N} \sum_{j=1}^{N} w_i w_j \sigma_{ij}, \tag{1}$$

$$max \quad f_2 = \sum_{i=1}^{N} w_i \mu_i, \tag{2}$$

$$subject \quad to \quad \sum_{i=1}^{N} w_i = 1, \qquad 0 \leq w_i \leq 1, \tag{3}$$

$$\sum_{i=1}^{N} s_i = K, \tag{4}$$

$$w_i = y_i * v_i \qquad i = 1, ..., N, \quad y_i \in \mathbb{Z}_+, \tag{5}$$

$$\epsilon_i s_i \leq w_i \leq \delta_i s_i, \qquad i = 1, ..., N, \tag{6}$$

$$z_i \leq s_i, \qquad i = 1, ..., N, \tag{7}$$

$$s_i, z_i \in \{0, 1\}, \qquad i = 1, ..., N. \tag{8}$$

where N is the number of available assets, w_i is the proportion of asset i ($i = 1,...,N$), μ_i is the expected return of asset i, σ_{ij} is the covariance between assets i and j ($i = 1,...,N$; $j = 1,...,N$), $\sigma_{ij} = \rho_{ij} dev_i dev_j$ where ρ_{ij} is the correlation between assets i and j, dev_i and dev_j are the deviations of assets i and j. Equation (4) is the cardinality constraint where K is the number of assets held. Equation (5) defines the round lot constraint where v_i is the minimum lots. Equation (6) defines the proportion of asset i as w_i which lie in $[\epsilon_i, \delta_i]$, ϵ_i, δ_i is the floor and ceiling constraints. If s_i is one, it suggests asset i is chosen, otherwise asset i is not invested and w_i equals to zero. Equation (7) defines the pre-assignment constraint where z_i implies asset i is pre-assignment if z_i is one. Equation (8) is the discrete constraint, it restricts the s_i and z_i to be zero or one.

3 Algorithm Framework

In this section we present the details of the our new approach, including a new coding scheme, a repair process and the MOEA/D framework. The whole algorithm is given in Algorithm 1.

3.1 New Coding Scheme

In general, a meta-heuristic algorithm such as evolutionary algorithm (EA) or genetic algorithm (GA) tend to solve problems directly in an actual solution space (see Fig. 1(a)). In contrast, the random keys strategy prefers to sample random numbers from some space, typically $[0, 1]^n$. Points in the random keys space are mapped to points in an actual solution space (see Fig. 1(b)). The

---

Algorithm 1. Algorithm Framework

1: **INITIALIZATION**:
2: Randomly sample initial population P from $[0, 1]^n$.
3: **DECODE**:
4: Multi-dimensional mapping (see Sect. 3.1) and repair (see Sect. 3.2).
5: **while** *stopping criterion not met* **do**
6:    **GENERATE**:
7:    MOEA/D (see Sect. 3.3).
8:    **DECODE**:
9:    Multi-dimensional mapping and repair.
10: **end while**

---

new coding scheme is different from the strategy mentioned above. Points in the surrogate space are mapped to points in multiple actual solution space (see Fig. 1(c)). The proposed coding scheme is called multi-dimensional mapping and based on the assumption that the degree of "preference" of asset implies degree of significance. Under the assumption more allocation in the assets with higher degree of "preference" will result in a better solution than the algorithm which neglects of the correlation between assignment and allocation of assets.

The main advantages of monolithic solver based on multi-dimensional mapping can be outlined as follows:

1. The error propagation is avoided, which may lead to a better result, with respect to step-by-step solver, at the end.
2. The result of the algorithm may converge quicker and better, when take the correlation between assignment and allocation in consideration.

Specifically, the new coding scheme maps the population vector P to vectors S and W (see Algorithm 2). The two vectors of size N are used to define a portfolio p: a binary vector s_i (i = 1,...,N) indicating whether asset i is included in the portfolio, and a positive decimal vector w_i (i = 1,...,N) denoting the proportion of the capital invested in the asset i.

The random keys strategy is applied as the representation of population. At each generation, the decoding function is employed once, but discrete and continuous variables are generated all at the same time.

Firstly, the population is sorted in a descending order with the value p_i, setting the p_{pre} temporarily to one to ensure the asset pre-assigned is held in portfolio.

$$index = sort(K, population)$$

Secondly, specifying s_i to one corresponding to the first K index in sorted population.

$$s_i = \begin{cases} 1, & \textbf{if } i \in index \\ 0, & \text{otherwise} \end{cases}$$

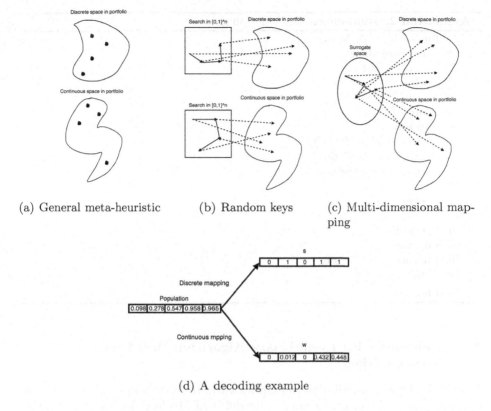

(a) General meta-heuristic   (b) Random keys   (c) Multi-dimensional mapping

(d) A decoding example

Fig. 1. Three different representations and an example

Thirdly, fixing the value of w_i. The formulation following satisfies the Eq. 3 naturally which implies the constraint of allocation (continuous variables) is removed. An example is given in Fig. 1(d).

$$w_i = \frac{s_i p_i}{\sum_{i=1}^{N} s_i p_i}$$

3.2 Repair Process

Finally, new candidate portfolio is modified [15] if the quantity and round lot constraint are violated as follows:

1. All weights that are smaller than the value of $((\epsilon_i \bmod v_i + 1) * v_i)$ are adjusted by setting $w_i = ((\epsilon_i \bmod v_i + 1) * v_i)$.
2. The weight are then adjusted to the nearest round lot level by setting $w_i = w_i - (w_i \bmod v_i)$.
3. The remaining amount of capital is added to the largest w_i.

Algorithm 2. Multi-dimensional mapping

1: **for** each $i \in [1, N]$ **do**
2:   **if** i=pre **then**
3:     $p_i^{temp} = 1$
4:   **else**
5:     $p_i^{temp} = p_i$
6:   **end if**
7: **end for**
8: $index = sort(K, P^{temp})$
9: **for** each $i \in [1, N]$ **do**
10:   **if** $i \in index$ **then**
11:     $s_i = 1$
12:   **else**
13:     $s_i = 0$
14:   **end if**
15: **end for**
16: **for** each $i \in [1, N]$ **do**
17:   $w_i = \frac{s_i p_i}{\sum_{i=1}^{N} s_i p_i}$
18: **end for**

3.3 Multi-objective Evolutionary Algorithm Based on Decomposition

MOEA/D [19] is a generic algorithm framework. It decomposes a multi-objective optimization problem into a number of different single objective optimization subproblems (or simple multi-objective optimization subproblems) and then uses a population-based method to optimize these subproblems simultaneously. Many algorithms in portfolio problems are based on decomposition of the objective [5–7,13], while this paper combines the proposed coding scheme with MOEA/D. To obtain a set of different Pareto optimal solutions to approximate the PF, MOEA/D solves a set of single objective optimization subproblems with different weight vectors simultaneously. MOEA/D defines neighborhood relations among these subproblems based on the distances between their weight vectors. Each subproblem is optimized in MOEA/D by using information mainly from its neighboring subproblems. In principle, MOEA/D can use any decomposition approach for defining their subproblems. In this paper, the Tchebycheff technique is adopted as follow:

$$g^{te}(x|\lambda^j, z^*) = \max_{1 \leq i \leq m} \{\lambda_i^j |f_i(x) - z_i^*|\}.$$

where $\lambda = (\lambda_1, ..., \lambda_m)$ is a weight vector, i.e., $\lambda_i \geq 0$ for all $i = 1, ..., m$ and $\sum_{i=1}^{m} \lambda_i = 1$. $z^* = (z_1^*, ..., z_m^*)$ is a reference point, i.e., $z_i^* = \min\{f_i(x)|x \in \Omega\}$, Ω is the decision space, for each $i = 1, ..., m$.

4   Experiment Studies

In this section, the test problems and performance metrics used for evaluating the proposed multi-dimensional mapping algorithm (MDM) are introduced. The monolithic solver based on proposed algorithm is compared with a state-of-the-art step-by-step algorithm [18] and a basic step-by-step random keys [1] in terms of two different performance metrics.

4.1   Algorithm Settings

In this section, a series of experiments are performed. Five test problems based on well-known major market indices for the portfolio optimization problems from the publicly available OR-library [3] is used to evaluate the performance of the algorithms. As for MOEA/D, the population size is 100, the neighbor size is 100, the termination condition is 1000 iterations, the decomposition method is Tchebycheff approach, crossover method and mutation method are based on basic differential evolutionary algorithm (DE) [17]. In addition, all the experiments are implemented with cardinality $K = 10$, floor $\epsilon = 0.01$, ceiling $\delta = 1.0$, pre-assignment $z_{30} = 1$ and round lot $\upsilon = 0.008$. The details of these benchmark indices about the origin, name, and number of assets are as follows: (i) *HongKong, Hang Seng*, 31; (ii) *Germany, DAX* 100, 85; (iii) *UK, FTSE* 100, 89; (iv) *US, S&P* 100, 98; and (v) *Japan, Nikkei*, 225. Meanwhile, the five datasets are built from weekly price data from March 1992 to September 1997, and all the data of experiments is collected after 10 runs.

In this study, two universally known performance metrics are utilized, inverted generational distance (IGD) [14] and percentage deviation (PD) [3]. The IGD considers proximity, diversity and distribution of a multi-objective algorithm and is adopted extensively, and the percentage deviation is frequently applied in portfolio problem.

The inverted generational distance uses the true Pareto front as a reference and measures the distance of each of its elements from the true Pareto front to the non-dominated front obtained by an algorithm. It is mathematically defined as:

$$IGD = \frac{\sum_{i=1}^{Q} d_i}{Q}$$

where Q is the number of solutions in the true Pareto front. The true Pareto fronts for the highly constrained multi-objective portfolio problems are unknown. Hence, the best known unconstrained efficient frontiers (UCEFs) [3] are implemented in this work as the true Pareto front reference set, and all of the UCEFs are available at: http://people.brunel.ac.uk/~mastjjb/jeb/orlib/portinfo.html. This has been widely adopted in the literature. The d_i is the Euclidean distance between each of the solution and the nearest member found in the algorithm.

The metric measures both the diversity and the convergence of acquired *efficient* front. Obviously, the smaller the value is the closer the *efficient* front to the Pareto front is.

Percentage deviation looking in both directions, horizontally and vertically, calculating a percentage deviation in each direction and taking the minimum of these two values as the percentage deviation error measure associated with a portfolio. Details of the percentage deviation calculation can be found in [3].

4.2   Algorithm Comparison

In this section, we have performed a number of experiments, the results of IGD, PD and running time of three algorithms performed on five datasets from OR-library are shown in Fig. 2. The results show that for most of problem instances, except for instance 1, the monolithic solver based on MDM obtains the smallest mean values for IGD and PD. The step-by-step random keys algorithm comes at the second and state-of-the art algorithm comes at the third places. However, the performance of MDM and the other algorithms on instance 1 are incomparable with the performance metrics in this paper, because MDM performs best with PD but worst with IGD. As for CPU time, the step-by-step random keys is the most computationally expensive, although all the algorithms are about the same.

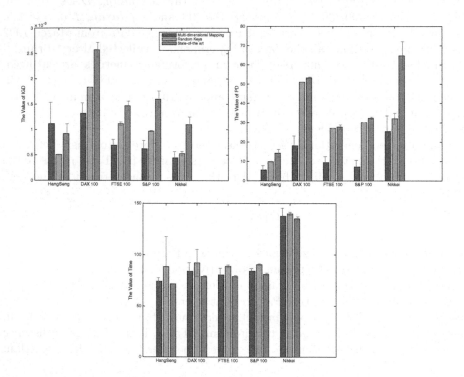

Fig. 2. Effectiveness of three multi-objective evolutionary algorithms

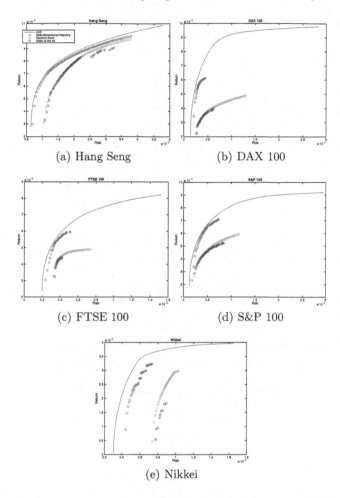

(a) Hang Seng   (b) DAX 100

(c) FTSE 100   (d) S&P 100

(e) Nikkei

Fig. 3. Comparison of convergence of IGD and PD for five datasets.

Figure 3 shows the UCEF and final results of three algorithms. MDM appears the best proximity and diversity. Because of the constraints, none of the final results, except for instance 1, are very close to the UCEF. To gain an intuitive view of the three algorithms over generations, we plot the IGD and PD over generations on the instances in Fig. 4 where the results are averaged over 10 runs. The results confirm that all algorithms considered are able to converge and the monolithic solver based on MDM is able to converge the fastest in all problems. Only in instance 5, the performances of MDM and the step-by-step random keys algorithm are similar. For illustrative purpose, the obtained value for IGD and PD are provided in Tables 1 and 2. At most instances, except for instance 1, MDM obtains the best mean IGD values. And in all of the five instances, MDM

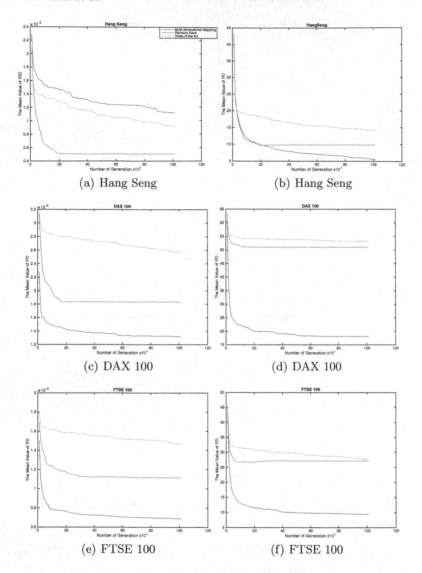

(a) Hang Seng   (b) Hang Seng

(c) DAX 100   (d) DAX 100

(e) FTSE 100   (f) FTSE 100

Fig. 4. Comparison of convergence of IGD and PD for five datasets.

algorithm attains the best PD values. Furthermore, the monolithic solver based on MDM is different from the step-by-step random keys only in the coding scheme of mapping strategy. Hence, the results may demonstrate MDM's effectiveness and efficiency in approximating the *efficient* front in portfolio problems.

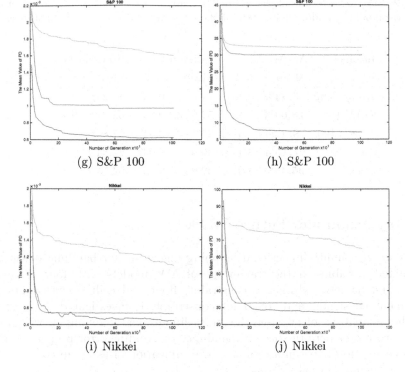

(g) S&P 100   (h) S&P 100

(i) Nikkei   (j) Nikkei

Fig. 4. (*continued*)

Table 1. Statistical results of the IGD metric values of the final populations obtained by multi-mapping, random keys, state-of-the art algorithms on the test instances over 10 runs.

Instance	MDM		Random keys		State-of-the art	
	Mean	Std.	Mean	Std.	Mean	Std.
Hang Seng	1.1132e−03	4.2099e−04	5.0443e−03	6.9464e−06	**9.1739e−04**	1.9380e−04
DAX 100	**1.3167e−03**	2.0606e−04	1.8327e−03	1.8639e−06	2.5716e−03	1.4389e−04
FTS 100	**6.8909e−04**	1.1698e−04	1.1144e−03	3.5567e−05	1.4683e−03	9.1786e−05
S&P 100	**6.2512e−04**	1.6434e−04	9.7286e−04	1.1269e−05	1.6007e−03	1.6249e−04
Nikkei	**4.4604e−04**	1.2466e−04	1.3633e−03	4.2921e−05	1.0975e−03	1.5324e−04

Table 2. Statistical results of the PD metric values of the final populations obtained by multi-mapping, random keys, state-of-the art algorithms on the test instances over 10 runs.

Instance	MDM		Random keys		State-of-the art	
	Mean	Std.	Mean	Std.	Mean	Std.
Hang Seng	**5.54%**	2.25%	9.84%	0.15%	14.23%	1.94%
DAX 100	**18.04%**	5.13%	51.02%	0.05%	52.24%	0.48%
FTSE 100	**9.42%**	3.09%	27.14%	0.04%	27.80%	1.11%
S&P 100	**7.15%**	3.43%	30.04%	0.03%	32.34%	0.52%
Nikkei	**25.44%**	8.07%	32.03%	2.83%	64.73%	7.37%

5   Conclusion and Future Work

In this work, a multi-dimensional mapping algorithm for handling constraints and mixed variables in the framework of MV models with four real-world constraints, namely, cardinality constraint, floor and ceiling constraints pre-assignment constraint and round lot constraint, is investigated. It is proved that the monolithic solver based the multi-dimensional mapping algorithm contributes to better performance on the ability of avoiding error propagation and taking correlation between assignment and allocation of assets in consideration with the random keys algorithm.

For future work, the proposed algorithm can be applied on larger datasets and other mixed-integer problem.

Acknowledgement. This work is supported by the Shanghai Clearing House under the project of 'artificial intelligence methods for complex 0-1 financial optimization', the National Natural Science Foundation of China under Grant No. 61673180, and the Science and Technology Commission of Shanghai Municipality under Grant No. 14DZ2260800.

References

1. Bean, J.C.: Genetic algorithms and random keys for sequencing and optimization. ORSA J. Comput. **6**(2), 154–160 (1994)
2. Bienstock, D.: Computational study of a family of mixed-integer quadratic programming problems. Math. Program. **74**(2), 121–140 (1996)
3. Chang, T.-J., Meade, N., Beasley, J.E., Sharaiha, Y.M.: Heuristics for cardinality constrained portfolio optimisation. Comput. Oper. Res. **27**(13), 1271–1302 (2000)
4. Coello, C.A.C.: Theoretical and numerical constraint-handling techniques used with evolutionary algorithms: a survey of the state of the art. Comput. Methods Appl. Mech. Eng. **191**(11), 1245–1287 (2002)
5. Elton, E.J., Gruber, M.J.: Investments and Portfolio Performance. World Scientific, Singapore (2011)

6. Grinblatt, M., Titman, S., Wermers, R.: Momentum investment strategies, portfolio performance, and herding: a study of mutual fund behavior. Am. Econ. Rev. 1088–1105 (1995)
7. Gulpinar, N., An, L.T.H., Moeini, M.: Robust investment strategies with discrete asset choice constraints using DC programming. Optimization 59(1), 45–62 (2010)
8. Lwin, K., Rong, Q., Kendall, G.: A learning-guided multi-objective evolutionary algorithm for constrained portfolio optimization. Appl. Soft Comput. 24, 757–772 (2014)
9. Mansini, R., Speranza, M.G.: Heuristic algorithms for the portfolio selection problem with minimum transaction lots. Eur. J. Oper. Res. 114(2), 219–233 (1999)
10. Markowitz, H.: Portfolio selection. J. Finance 7(1), 77–91 (1952)
11. Newman, A.M., Weiss, M.: A survey of linear and mixed-integer optimization tutorials. INFORMS Trans. Educ. 14(1), 26–38 (2013)
12. Robič, T., Filipič, B.: DEMO: differential evolution for multiobjective optimization. In: Coello, C.A.C., Hernández Aguirre, A., Zitzler, E. (eds.) EMO 2005. LNCS, vol. 3410, pp. 520–533. Springer, Heidelberg (2005). doi:10.1007/978-3-540-31880-4_36
13. Shaw, D.X., Liu, S., Kopman, L.: Lagrangian relaxation procedure for cardinality-constrained portfolio optimization. Optim. Methods Softw. 23(3), 411–420 (2008)
14. Sierra, M.R., Coello, C.A.C.: Improving PSO-based multi-objective optimization using crowding, mutation and ϵ-dominance. In: Coello, C.A.C., Hernández Aguirre, A., Zitzler, E. (eds.) EMO 2005. LNCS, vol. 3410, pp. 505–519. Springer, Heidelberg (2005). doi:10.1007/978-3-540-31880-4_35
15. Skolpadungket, P., Dahal, K., Harnpornchai, N.: Portfolio optimization using multi-objective genetic algorithms. In: 2007 IEEE Congress on Evolutionary Computation, pp. 516–523. IEEE (2007)
16. Steuer, R.E., Hirschberger, M., Deb, K.: Extracting from the relaxed for large-scale semi-continuous variable nondominated frontiers. J. Glob. Optim. 64(1), 33–48 (2016)
17. Storn, R., Price, K.: Differential evolution-a simple and efficient heuristic for global optimization over continuous spaces. J. Glob. Optim. 11(4), 341–359 (1997)
18. Streichert, F., Ulmer, H., Zell, A.: Evolutionary algorithms and the cardinality constrained portfolio optimization problem. In: Ahr, D., Fahrion, R., Oswald, M., Reinelt, G. (eds.) ORP 2003. Operations Research Proceedings, vol. 2003, pp. 253–260. Springer, Heidelberg (2004). doi:10.1007/978-3-642-17022-5_33
19. Zhang, Q., Li, H.: MOEA/D: a multiobjective evolutionary algorithm based on decomposition. IEEE Trans. Evol. Comput. 11(6), 712–731 (2007)

Exact Approaches for the Travelling Thief Problem

Junhua Wu, Markus Wagner, Sergey Polyakovskiy$^{(\boxtimes)}$, and Frank Neumann

Optimisation and Logistics, School of Computer Science, The University of Adelaide,
Adelaide, SA, Australia
Sergey.Polyakovskiy@edu.au

Abstract. Many evolutionary and constructive heuristic approaches have been introduced in order to solve the Travelling Thief Problem (TTP). However, the accuracy of such approaches is unknown due to their inability to find global optima. In this paper, we propose three exact algorithms and a hybrid approach to the TTP. We compare these with state-of-the-art approaches to gather a comprehensive overview on the accuracy of heuristic methods for solving small TTP instances.

1 Introduction

The travelling thief problem (TTP) [3] is a recent academic problem in which two well-known combinatorial optimisation problems interact, namely the travelling salesperson problem (TSP) and the 0–1 knapsack problem (KP). It reflects the complexity in real-world applications that contain more than one $\mathcal{NP}$-hard problem, which can be commonly observed in the areas of planning, scheduling and routing. For example, delivery problems usually consist of a routing part for the vehicle(s) and a packing part of the goods onto the vehicle(s).

Thus far, many approximate approaches have been introduced for addressing the TTP and most of them are evolutionary or heuristic [17]. Initially, Polyakovskiy, Bonyadi, Wagner, Michalewicz, and Neumann [18] proposed two iterative heuristics, namely the Random Local Search (RLS) and (1+1)-EA, based on a general approach that solves the problem in two steps, one for the TSP and one for the KP. Bonyadi et al. [4] introduced a similar two-phased algorithm named Density-based Heuristic (DH) and a method inspired by co-evolution-based approaches named Co-solver. Mei et al. [11–13] also investigated the interdependency and proposed a cooperative co-evolution based approach similar to Co-solver, and a memetic algorithm called MATLS that attempts to solve the problem as a whole. In 2015, Faulkner et al. [7] outperformed the existing approaches by their new operators and corresponding series of heuristics (named S1–S5 and C1–C6). Recently, Wagner [22] investigated the Max-Min Ant System (MMAS) [21] on the TTP, and El Yafrani and Ahiod [6] proposed a memetic algorithm (MA2B) and a simulated annealing algorithm (CS2SA). The results show that the new algorithms were competitive to the state-of-the-art on a different range of TTP instances. Wagner et al. [23] found in a study involving

Y. Shi et al. (Eds.): SEAL 2017, LNCS 10593, pp. 110–121, 2017.
https://doi.org/10.1007/978-3-319-68759-9_10

21 approximate TTP algorithms that only a small subset of them is actually necessary to form a well-performing algorithm portfolio.

However, due to the lack of exact methods, all of the above-mentioned approximate approaches cannot be evaluated with respect to their accuracy even on small TTP instances. To address this issue, we propose three exact techniques and additional benchmark instances, which help to build a more comprehensive review of the approximate approaches.

In the remainder, we revisit the definition of the TTP in Sect. 2 and introduce our exact approaches in Sect. 3. In Sect. 4, we elaborate on the setup of our experiments and compare our exact and hybrid approaches with the best approximate ones. The conclusions are drawn in Sect. 5.

2   Problem Statement

Given is a set of cities $N = \{1, \ldots, n\}$ and a set of items $M = \{1, \ldots, m\}$. City i, $i = 2, \ldots, n$, contains a set of items $M_i = \{1, \ldots, m_i\}$, $M = \underset{i \in N}{\cup} M_i$. Item k positioned in the city i is characterised by its profit p_{ik} and weight w_{ik}. The thief must visit each of the cities exactly once starting from the first city and return back to it in the end. The distance d_{ij} between any pair of cities $i, j \in N$ is known. Any item may be selected as long as the total weight of collected items does not exceed the capacity C. A renting rate R is to be paid per each time unit taken to complete the tour. v_{max} and v_{min} denote the maximal and minimum speeds of the thief. Assume that there is a binary variable $y_{ik} \in \{0, 1\}$ such that $y_{ik} = 1$ iff item k is chosen in city i. The goal is to find a tour $\Pi = (x_1, \ldots, x_n)$, $x_i \in N$, along with a packing plan $P = (y_{21}, \ldots, y_{nm_n})$ such that their combination $[\Pi, P]$ maximises the reward given in the form of the following objective function.

$$Z([\Pi, P]) = \sum_{i=1}^{n} \sum_{k=1}^{m_i} p_{ik} y_{ik} - R \left(\frac{d_{x_n x_1}}{v_{max} - \nu W_{x_n}} + \sum_{i=1}^{n-1} \frac{d_{x_i x_{i+1}}}{v_{max} - \nu W_{x_i}} \right) \quad (1)$$

where $\nu = (v_{max} - v_{min}) / C$ is a constant value defined by input parameters. The minuend is the sum of all packed items' profits and the subtrahend is the amount that the thief pays for the knapsack's rent equal to the total travelling time along Π multiplied by R. In fact, the actual travel speed along the distance $d_{x_i x_{i+1}}$ depends on the accumulated weight $W_{x_i} = \sum_{j=1}^{i} \sum_{k=1}^{m_j} w_{jk} y_{jk}$ of the items collected in the preceding cities $1, \ldots, i$. This then slows down the thief and has an impact on the overall benefit Z. For a particular graph example, we refer the interested reader to [18].

3   Exact Approaches to the TTP

This section introduces three exact approaches to the TTP. Our first solution is a dynamic program (DP), which adopts the ideas applied to the simplified version of the TTP, the Packing While Travelling problem (PWT). Polyakovskiy and Neumann [17] have recently introduced the PWT, which considers a fixed tour Π and only asks for an optimal packing solution. Neumann et al. [14] show that the problem can be solved in pseudo-polynomial time via dynamic programming taking into account the fact that the weights are integer. Their dynamic programming follows the traditional scheme and sequentially examines all combinations of items and weights so that the optimal packing plan P^* can be selected among all the resulting solutions. The rest of the section first describes the DP and then continues with a branch and bound approach (BnB) and with a constraint programming (CP) technique adopted for the TTP.

3.1   Dynamic Programming

Our DP is based on the Held-Karp algorithm for the TSP [8] augmented by the dynamic programming routine [14] applied to resolve low level PWT subproblems. For a subset of cities $S \subseteq N$ and city $j \in S$, let $A(S, j, w)$ be the maximum reward of the path visiting each city in S exactly once, starting at the home city and ending at j with the total knapsack's weight of w. Obviously, if $|S| > 1$, $A(S, 1, w) = -\infty$ for any $w \in [0, C]$ since the path cannot both start and end at city 1.

Our base case consists of $A(\{1\}, 1, 0) = 0$ and of $A(\{1\}, 1, w) = -\infty$ for $0 < w \leq C$. Our general case for $A(S, j, w)$ is based on $A\left(S \setminus \{j\}, i, w - \overline{W}_j\right)$, which is the path from city 1 to city $i \in S$, plus the reward gained from visiting j right after i. In fact, i must be the best choice:

$$A(S, j, w) = \max_{i \in S : i \neq j} \left\{ A\left(S \setminus \{j\}, i, w - \overline{W}_j\left(S \setminus \{j\}, i\right)\right) + \overline{P}_j\left(S \setminus \{j\}, i\right) - \frac{d_{ij}}{v_{max} - \nu w} \right\}.$$

Here, $\overline{W}_j\left(S \setminus \{j\}, i\right)$ and $\overline{P}_j\left(S \setminus \{j\}, i\right)$ represent the total weight and the total profit of the items chosen in city j. They both result from the best solution of the PWT subproblem, where a subset of items in M_j must be optimally chosen with respect to the set of partial solutions corresponding to $A(S \setminus \{j\}, i, w)$, $w \in [0, C]$. In fact, the sub-problem considers only the items of city j and can be solved via the dynamic programming approach for the PWT [14].

We start computing solutions with all subsets of size $s = 2$ and calculate $A(S, j, w)$ sequentially for all possible knapsack's weights w and subsets $S \subseteq N$ subject to S containing city 1. We iteratively increment s and continue until $s = n$. Finally, we compute the value of an optimal solution for the complete tour as

$$\max_{i \in S : i \neq 1} \left\{ A(N, i, w) - \frac{d_{i1}}{v_{max} - \nu w} \right\}.$$

There are at most $2^n n$ subproblems, and each of them takes the time of $\mathcal{O}(n + mC)$. Therefore, the total running time is $\mathcal{O}(2^n n (n + mC))$. The dynamic programming is also rather expensive in terms of the memory consumption, which reaches $\mathcal{O}(2^n nC)$. In order to speed up computations, let as define an

---

Algorithm 1. Dynamic programming to the TTP

---

set $A(\{1\}, 1, 0) = 0$
for $w = 1$ to C **do**
    set $A(\{1\}, 1, w) = -\infty$
for $s = 2$ to n **do**
    for any $S \subseteq N : |S| = s$, $1 \in S$ **do**
        for $w = 0$ to C **do**
            set $A(S, 1, w) = -\infty$
            for any $j \in S$, $j \neq 1$ **do**
                compute $A(S, j, w) =$
                $$\max_{i \in S : i \neq j} \left\{ A\left(S \setminus \{j\}, i, w - \overline{W}_j\left(S \setminus \{j\}, i\right)\right) + \overline{P}_j\left(S \setminus \{j\}, i\right) - \frac{d_{ij}}{v_{max} - \nu w} \right\}$$
return $\displaystyle\max_{i \in S : i \neq 1} \left\{ A(N, i, w) - \frac{d_{i1}}{v_{max} - \nu w} \right\}$

---

upper bound on the value of a feasible solution that can be derived from the partial solutions corresponding to $A(S \setminus \{j\}, i, w)$, for any $w \in [0, C]$, as follows:

$$E_U(A(S, j, \cdot)) = \max_{0 \leq w \leq W} A(S, j, w) + \sum_{k \in N \setminus S} \sum_{l=1}^{m_k} p_{kl} - R \frac{d_{j1}}{v_{max}}$$

It estimates the maximal profit that the thief may obtain by passing the remaining part of the tour with the maximal speed; that is, generating the minimal possible cost of traveling. Obviously, an optimal solution must not exceed this bound. Therefore, if an incumbent solution $Z([\Pi', P'])$ exists, those partial solutions whose $E_U(A(S, j, w)) < Z([\Pi', P'])$ can be ignored. In practice, we can obtain an incumbent solution in two stages. First, a feasible solution Π' for the TSP part of the problem can be computed by a TSP solver such as Concorde [1] or by the Lin-Kernighan algorithm [10]. Second, the dynamic programming for PWT can be applied to determine the best packing plan P' for Π'.

3.2   Branch and Bound Search

Now, we introduce a branch and bound search for the TTP employing the upper bound E_U defined in Sect. 3.1. Algorithm 2 depicts the pseudocode, where $\Pi_i, i \in \{1, ..., n\}$ denotes a sub-permutation of Π with the cities 1 to i visited, and f_i is the mapping $f : w \mapsto P$ calculated for Π by the dynamic programming for the PWT.

A way to tighten the upper bound E_U is by providing a better estimation of the remaining distance from the current city k to the last city of the tour. Currently, the shortest distance from k to 1, i.e. d_{k1}, is used. The following two ways can improve the estimation: (i) the use of distance d_{f1} from city f to city 1, where f is the farthest unvisited city from 1; (ii) the use of distance $d^* - d_t$, where d^* is the shortest path that can be pre-calculated and d_t is the distance passed so far to achieve city k in the tour Π. These two ideas can be joined together by using the $\max\{d_f, (d^* - d_t)\}$ to enhance the result.

Algorithm 2. Branch and Bound Search for the TTP

1: **procedure** BNB SEARCH
2:     Create an initial solution to gain the benefit *best* and an tour permutation Π
3:     Create an empty mapping M
4:     Set $l = 0$
5:     SEARCH($\Pi, l, M, best$)
6: **function** SEARCH($\Pi, l, M, best$)
7:     **if** $l == n$ **then**
8:         calculate $Z([\Pi, f_n(\cdot)])$ from $Z([\Pi_{n-1}, f_{n-1}(\cdot)])$ in M
9:         **return** $\max\{\max Z([\Pi, f_n(\cdot)]), best\}$
10:    **else**
11:        **for** $i = l + 1$ to n **do**
12:            Swap cities $l + 1$ and i in Π
13:            Set M' = Calculate $Z([\Pi_{l+1}, f_{l+1}(\cdot)])$ from $Z([\Pi_l, f_l(\cdot)])$ in M
14:            **if** $\max E_U([\Pi_{l+1}, f_{l+1}(\cdot)]) > best$ **then**
15:                $best = \max\{best, \text{SEARCH}(\Pi, l + 1, M', best) \}$
16:            Swap cities $l + 1$ and i in Π
17:        **return** $best$

3.3 Constraint Programming

Now, we present our third exact approach adopting the existing state-of-the-art constraint programming (CP) paradigm [9]. Our model employs a simple permutation based representation of the tour which allows the use of the AllDifferent filtering algorithm [2]. Similarly to the Sect. 2, a vector $W = (W_1, \ldots, W_n)$ is used to refer to the total weights accumulated in the cities of tour Π. Specifically, W_i is the weight of the knapsack when the thief departs from city i. The model bases the search on two types of decision variables:

- $\boldsymbol{x}$ denotes the particular positions of the cities in tour Π. Variable x_i takes the value of $j \in N$ to indicate that j is the ith city to be visited. The initial variable domain of x_1 is $D(x_1) = \{1\}$ and it is $D(x_i) = N \setminus \{i\}$ for any subsequently visited city $i = 2, \ldots, n$.
- $\boldsymbol{y}$ signals on the selection of an item in the packing plan P. Variable y_{ik}, $i \in N$, $k \in M_i$, is binary, therefore $D(y_{ik}) = \{0, 1\}$.

Furthermore, an integer-valued vector d is used to express the distance matrix so that its element $n(x_i - 1) + x_{i+1}$ equals the distance $d_{x_i x_{i+1}}$ between two consecutive cities x_i and x_{i+1} in Π.

The model relies on the AllDifferent$[x_1, \ldots, x_n]$ constraint, which ensures that the values of $x_1, \ldots, x_n$ are distinct. It also involves the Element(g, h) expression, which returns the hth variable in the list of variables g. In total, the model (CPTTP) consists of the objective function and constraints as depicted in the Fig. 1. Expression (2) calculates the objective value according to function (1). Constraint (3) verifies that all the cities are assigned to different positions, and thus are visited exactly once. This is a sub-tour elimination constraint. Equation (4) calculates the weight W_i of all the items collected in the cities $1, \ldots, i$. Equation (5) is a capacity constraint.

$$max \sum_{i=1}^{n} \sum_{j=1}^{m_i} p_{ij} y_{ij}$$

$$- R\left(\sum_{i=1}^{n-1} \frac{\text{Element}(d, n(x_i - 1) + x_{i+1})}{v_{max} - \nu\text{Element}(W, x_i)} + \frac{\text{Element}(d, n(x_n - 1) + 1)}{v_{max} - \nu\text{Element}(W, x_n)} \right) \quad (2)$$

$$\text{AllDifferent}[x_1, \ldots, x_n] \quad (3)$$

$$W_i = W_{i-1} + \sum_{j \in M_i} w_{ij} y_{ij}, \quad i \in \{2, \ldots, n\} \quad (4)$$

$$W_n \leq C \quad (5)$$

Fig. 1. Constraint programming model to the TTP

The performance of a CP model depends on its solver; specifically, on the filtering algorithms and on the search strategies it applies. Here, we use IBM ILOG CP OPTIMISER 12.6.2 with its searching algorithm set to the *restart mode*. This mode adopts a general purpose search strategy [19] inspired from integer programming techniques and is based on the concept of the impact of a variable. The impact measures the importance of a variable in reducing the search space. The impacts, which are learned from the observation of the domains' reduction during the search, help the restart mode dramatically improve the performance of the search. Within the search, the cities are assigned to the positions first and then the items are decided on. Therefore, the solver instantiates $x_1, \ldots, x_n$ prior to $y_{21}, \ldots, y_{nm_n}$ variables applying its default selection strategy. Our extensive study shows that such an order gives the best results fast.

4   Computational Experiments

In this section, we first compare the performance of the exact approaches to TTP in order to find the best one for setting the baseline for the subsequent comparison of the approximate approaches. Our experiments run on the CPU cluster of the Phoenix HPC at the University of Adelaide, which contains 3072 Intel(R) Xeon(R) 2.30 GHz CPU cores and 12 TB of memory. We allocate one CPU core and 32 GB of memory to each individual experiment.

4.1   Computational Set up

To run our experiments, we generate an additional set of small-sized instances following the way proposed in [18][1]. We use only a single instance of the original

---

[1] All instances are available online:
http://cs.adelaide.edu.au/~optlog/research/ttp.php.

Table 1. Columns 'n' and 'm' denote the number of cities and the number of items, respectively. Running times are given in seconds for DP, BnB and CP for different numbers of cities and items. '-' denotes the case when an approach failed to achieve an optimal solution in the given time limit.

Instance	n	m	Running time (in seconds)		
			DP	BnB	CP
eil51_n05_m4_uncorr_01	5	4	0.018	0.023	0.222
eil51_n06_m5_uncorr_01	6	5	0.07	0.079	0.24
eil51_n07_m6_uncorr_01	7	6	0.143	0.195	0.497
eil51_n08_m7_uncorr_01	8	7	0.343	0.505	4.594
eil51_n09_m8_uncorr_01	9	8	0.633	1.492	63.838
eil51_n10_m9_uncorr_01	10	9	0.933	5.188	776.55
eil51_n11_m10_uncorr_01	11	10	2.414	23.106	12861.181
eil51_n12_m11_uncorr_01	12	11	3.938	204.786	-
eil51_n13_m12_uncorr_01	13	12	14.217	2007.074	-
eil51_n14_m13_uncorr_01	14	13	13.408	36944.146	-
eil51_n15_m14_uncorr_01	15	14	89.461	-	-
eil51_n16_m15_uncorr_01	16	15	59.526	-	-
eil51_n17_m16_uncorr_01	17	16	134.905	-	-
eil51_n18_m17_uncorr_01	18	17	366.082	-	-
eil51_n19_m18_uncorr_01	19	18	830.18	-	-
eil51_n20_m19_uncorr_01	20	19	2456.873	-	-

TSP library [20] as the starting point for our new subset. It is entitled as eil51 and contains 51 cities. Out of these cities, we select uniformly at random cities that we removed in order to obtain smaller test problems with $n = 5, \ldots, 20$ cities. To set up the knapsack component of the problem, we adopt the approach given in [16] and use the corresponding problem generator available in [15]. As one of the input parameters, the generator asks for the range of coefficients, which we set to 1000. In total, we create knapsack test problems containing $k(n-1)$, $k \in \{1, 5, 10\}$ items and which are characterised by a knapsack capacity category $Q \in \{1, 6, 10\}$. Our experiments focus on *uncorrelated* (uncorr), *uncorrelated with similar weights* (uncorr-s-w), and *multiple strongly correlated* (m-s-corr) types of instances. At the stage of assigning the items of a knapsack instance to the particular cities of a given TSP tour, we sort the items in descending order of their profits and the second city obtains k, $k \in \{1, 5, 10\}$, items of the largest profits, the third city then has the next k items, and so on. All the instances use the "CEIL_2D" for intra-city distances, which means that the Euclidean distances are rounded up to the nearest integer. We set v_{min} and v_{max} to 0.1 and 1.

Tables 1 and 3 illustrate the results of the experiments. The test instances' names should be read as follows. First, eil51 stays for the name of the original TSP problem. The values succeeding n and m denote the actual number of cities and the total number of items, respectively, which are further followed by the generation type of a knapsack problem. Finally, the postfixes 1, 6 and, 10 in the instances' names describe the knapsack's capacity C.

4.2   Comparison of the Exact Approaches

We compare the three exact algorithms by allocating each instance a generous 24-hour time limit. Our aim is to analyse the running time of the approaches influenced by the increasing number of cities. Table 1 shows the running time of the approaches.

4.3   Comparison Between DP and Approximate Approaches

With the exact approaches being introduced, approximate approaches can be evaluated with respect to their accuracy to the optima. In the case of the TTP, most state-of-the-art approximate approaches are evolutionary algorithms and local searches, such as Memetic Algorithm with 2-OPT and Bit-flip (MA2B), Co-solver-based with 2-OPT, and Simulated Annealing (CS2SA) in [6], Co-solver-based with 2-OPT and Bit-flip (CS2B) in [5], and S1, S5, and C5 in [7].

Hybrid Approaches. In addition to existing heuristics, we introduce enhanced approaches of S1 and S5, which are hybrids of the two and that one of dynamic programming for the PWT [14]. The original S1 and S5 work as follows. First, a single TSP tour is computed using the Chained Lin-Kernighan-Heuristic [10], then a fast packing heuristic is applied. S1 performs these two steps only once and only in this order, while S5 repeats S1 until the time budget is exhausted. Our hybrids DP-S1 and DP-S5 are equivalent to these two algorithms, however, they use the exact dynamic programming to the PWT as a packing solver. This provides better results as we can now compute the optimal packing for the sampled TSP tours.

Results. We start by showing a performance summary of 10 algorithms on 432 instances in Table 2. In addition, Table 3 shows detailed results for a subset of the best approaches on a subset of instances. Figure 2 shows the results of the entire comparison. We include trend lines[2] for two selected approaches, which we will explain in the following.

We would like to highlight the following observations:

1. S1 performs badly across a wide range of instances. Its restart variant S5 performs better, however, its lack of a local search becomes apart in its relatively bad performance (compared to other approaches) on small instances.

---

[2] They are fitted polynomials of degree six used only for visualisation purposes.

Table 2. Performance summary of heuristic TTP solvers across all instances for which the optimal result has been obtained. $\#_{opt}$ is the number of times when the average of 10 independent repetitions is equal to the optimum. $\#_{1\%}$ and $\#_{10\%}$ show the number of times the averages are within 1% and 10%.

Gap	MA2B	CS2B	CS2SA	S1	S5	C5	DP-S1	DP-S5
avg	0.3%	15.3%	11.5%	38.9%	15.7%	09.9%	30.1%	3.3%
stdev	2.2%	17.8%	16.7%	29.4%	24.6%	18.8%	20.1%	8.5%
$\#_{opt}$	312	70	117	3	42	193	5	85
$\#_{1\%}$	265	100	132	10	160	193	9	245
$\#_{10\%}$	324	161	206	27	203	240	33	288

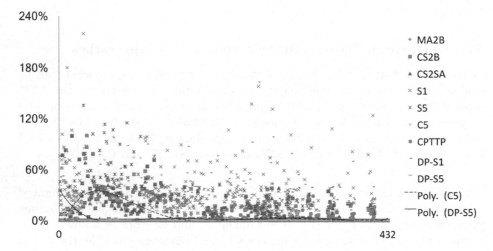

Fig. 2. Showing a gap to an optimal solution when one has been obtained by an exact approach. From left to right: the 432 instances first sorted by the number of cities, then by the total number of items.

2. C5 performs better than both S1 and S5, which is most likely due to its local searches that differentiate it from S1 and S5. Still, we can see a "hump" in its trend line for smaller instances, which flattens out quickly for larger instances.
3. The dynamic programming variants DP-S1 and DP-S5 perform slightly better than S1 and S5, which shows the difference in quality of the packing strategy; however, this is at times balanced out by the faster packing which allows more TSP tours to be sampled. For small instances, DP-S5 lacks a local search on the tours, which is why its gap to the optimum is relatively large, as shown by the respective trend lines.
4. MA2B dominates the field with outstanding performance across all instances, independent of number of cities and number of items. Remarkable is the high reliability with which it reaches a global optimum.

Table 3. Comparison between DP and the approximate approaches running in 10 min limits. Each approximate algorithm runs 10 times for each instance and use the average as the objective Obj. Gap is measured by $\frac{OPT-Obj}{OPT}\%$ and runtime (RT) is in second. The results of C5 and DP-S5 are obtained when they reach the time limit of 10 min per instance. Highlighted in blue are the best approximate results. DP runs out of memory for the instances without results.

Instance	TTP-DP		MA2B			C5		DP-S5	
	OPT	RT	Gap	Std	RT	Gap	Std	Gap	Std
eil51_n05_m4_multiple-strongly-corr_01	619.227	0.02	29.1	12.1	2.71	35.5	1.20e-6	41.3	0.0
eil51_n05_m4_uncorr_01	466.929	0.02	0.0	0.0	3.22	0.0	2.20e-6	0.0	2.20e-6
eil51_n05_m4_uncorr-similar-weights_01	299.281	0.02	0.0	0.0	3.21	7.8	2.40e-6	7.8	1.20e-6
eil51_n05_m20_multiple-strongly-corr_01	773.573	0.08	13.4	0.0	1.44	14.3	0.0	12.8	0.0
eil51_n05_m20_uncorr_01	2144.796	0.07	0.0	0.0	3.35	7.4	0.0	6.6	2.30e-6
eil51_n05_m20_uncorr-similar-weights_01	269.015	0.04	0.0	0.0	3.51	0.0	2.30e-6	0.0	0.0
eil51_n10_m9_multiple-strongly-corr_01	573.897	1.21	0.0	0.0	6.07	0.0	0.0	0.0	0.0
eil51_n10_m9_uncorr_01	1125.715	0.93	0.0	0.0	6.06	0.0	1.30e-6	0.0	1.30e-6
eil51_n10_m9_uncorr-similar-weights_01	753.230	0.86	0.0	0.0	5.87	0.0	0.0	0.0	0.0
eil51_n10_m45_multiple-strongly-corr_01	1091.127	14.89	0.0	0.0	7.99	0.0	0.0	0.0	0.0
eil51_n10_m45_uncorr_01	6009.431	6.39	0.0	0.0	8.6	6.6	2.30e-6	0.0	0.0
eil51_n10_m45_uncorr-similar-weights_01	3009.553	8.87	0.0	0.0	6.78	0.0	2.30e-6	0.0	2.30e-6
eil51_n12_m11_multiple-strongly-corr_01	648.546	4.58	0.0	0.0	6.08	4.6	2.20e-6	4.6	2.20e-6
eil51_n12_m11_uncorr_01	1717.699	3.94	0.0	0.0	7.21	0.0	1.20e-6	0.0	1.20e-6
eil51_n12_m11_uncorr-similar-weights_01	774.107	3.36	0.0	0.0	7.03	0.0	2.30e-6	0.0	2.30e-6
eil51_n12_m55_multiple-strongly-corr_01	1251.780	117.99	0.0	0.0	9.19	0.0	0.0	0.0	0.0
eil51_n12_m55_uncorr_01	8838.012	35.79	0.0	0.0	9.76	0.0	0.0	0.0	0.0
eil51_n12_m55_uncorr-similar-weights_01	3734.895	38.36	12.3	0.0	8.34	12.3	0.0	0.2	0.0
eil51_n15_m14_multiple-strongly-corr_01	547.419	39.82	0.0	0.0	7.87	14.1	1.30e-6	13.3	1.30e-6
eil51_n15_m14_uncorr_01	2392.996	89.46	0.0	0.0	7.28	3.8	0.0	3.8	0.0
eil51_n15_m14_uncorr-similar-weights_01	637.419	16.35	0.0	0.0	6.86	0.0	1.60e-6	0.0	1.60e-6
eil51_n15_m70_multiple-strongly-corr_01	920.372	3984.29	2.1	1.1	12.11	0.0	2.70e-6	0.0	2.70e-6
eil51_n15_m70_uncorr_01	9922.137	740.22	0.0	0.0	9.67	7	1.20e-6	1.9	0
eil51_n15_m70_uncorr-similar-weights_01	4659.623	867.78	0.0	0.0	7.98	0.0	0.0	0.0	0.0
eil51_n16_m15_multiple-strongly-corr_01	794.745	105.5	0.0	0.0	7.7	18.9	1.6e-6	18.9	1.6e-6
eil51_n16_m15_multiple-strongly-corr_10	4498.848	623.4	0.0	0.0	9.1	12.9	0.0	16.6	1.3e-6
eil51_n16_m15_uncorr_01	2490.889	59.5	1.0	0.7	8.4	1.6	2.3e-6	1.6	2.3e-6
eil51_n16_m15_uncorr_10	3601.077	211.5	0.0	0.0	9.0	7.1	1.6e-6	7.1	1.6e-6
eil51_n16_m15_uncorr-similar-weights_01	540.897	36.4	0.0	0.0	8.5	0.0	3.0e-6	0.0	3.0e-6
eil51_n16_m15_uncorr-similar-weights_10	3948.211	245.4	0.0	0.0	8.7	5.8	1.5e-6	13.6	0.0
eil51_n17_m16_multiple-strongly-corr_01	685.565	248.6	0.0	0.0	8.4	0.2	1.5e-6	0.0	1.5e-6
eil51_n17_m16_multiple-strongly-corr_10	3826.098	2190.4	0.0	0.0	9.8	0.0	1.5e-6	0.0	1.5e-6
eil51_n17_m16_uncorr_01	2342.004	134.9	0.0	0.0	8.3	0.0	0.0	0.0	0.0
eil51_n17_m16_uncorr_10	2275.279	554.5	0.0	0.0	9.6	0.0	0.0	0.0	0.0
eil51_n17_m16_uncorr-similar-weights_01	556.851	70.8	0.0	0.0	8.1	0.0	0.0	0.0	0.0
eil51_n17_m16_uncorr-similar-weights_10	2935.961	787.7	0.0	0.0	9.7	0.0	0.0	0.0	0.0
eil51_n18_m17_multiple-strongly-corr_01	834.031	715.7	7.9	0.8	10.2	9.2	0.0	12.9	1.7e-6
eil51_n18_m17_multiple-strongly-corr_10	5531.373	6252.4	0.0	0.0	10.5	0.4	1.5e-6	0.4	1.5e-6
eil51_n18_m17_uncorr_01	2644.491	366.1	0.0	0.0	9.7	0.2	0.0	1.8	0.0
eil51_n18_m17_uncorr_10	3222.603	1462.7	0.0	0.0	10.3	0.0	1.3e-6	0.2	0.0
eil51_n18_m17_uncorr-similar-weights_01	532.906	148.3	0.0	0.0	8.5	0.0	1.3e-6	0.0	1.3e-6
eil51_n18_m17_uncorr-similar-weights_10	4420.438	1929.3	0.0	0.0	9.9	0.0	2.9e-6	0.3	1.8e-6
eil51_n19_m18_multiple-strongly-corr_01	910.229	1771.6	0.0	0.0	9.3	20.1	1.6e-6	20.1	1.6e-6
eil51_n19_m18_multiple-strongly-corr_10	-	-	-	-	10.4	-	-	-	-
eil51_n19_m18_uncorr_01	2604.844	830.2	0.0	0.0	9.7	0.0	0.0	0.0	0.0
eil51_n19_m18_uncorr_10	4048.408	3884.3	0.0	0.0	10.9	0.0	1.4e-6	0.0	1.4e-6
eil51_n19_m18_uncorr-similar-weights_01	472.186	412.3	0.0	0.0	9.2	0.0	1.5e-6	0.0	1.5e-6
eil51_n19_m18_uncorr-similar-weights_10	5573.695	5878.8	0.0	0.0	10.5	0.0	0.0	0.0	0.0
eil51_n20_m19_multiple-strongly-corr_01	518.189	4533.7	0.6	0.6	11.1	14.1	1.4e-6	12.3	0.0
eil51_n20_m19_multiple-strongly-corr_10	-	-	-	-	12.1	-	-	-	-
eil51_n20_m19_uncorr_01	2092.673	2456.9	0.0	0.0	8.7	0.0	0.0	0.0	0.0
eil51_n20_m19_uncorr_10	3044.391	12776.0	0.0	0.0	9.8	0.0	0.0	0.0	0.0
eil51_n20_m19_uncorr-similar-weights_01	451.052	1007.7	0.0	0.0	7.9	0.0	0.0	0.0	0.0
eil51_n20_m19_uncorr-similar-weights_10	4169.799	15075.7	0.0	0.0	9.4	0.0	0.0	0.0	0.0

Interestingly, all approaches seem to have difficulties solving instances with the knapsack configuration multiple-strongly-corr_01 (see Table 3). Compared to the other two knapsack types, TTP-DP takes the longest to solve the strongly correlated ones. Also, these tend to be the only instances for which the heuristics rarely find optimal solutions, if at all.

5   Conclusion

The travelling thief problem (TTP) has attracted significant attention in recent years within the evolutionary computation community. In this paper, we have presented and evaluated exact approaches for the TTP based on dynamic programming, branch and bound, and constraint programming. We have used the exact solutions provided by our DP approach to evaluate the performance of current state-of-the-art TTP solvers. Our investigations show that they are obtaining in most cases (close to) optimal solutions. However, for a small fraction of tested instances we obverse a gap to the optimal solution of more than 10%.

Acknowledgements. This work was supported by the Australian Research councils through grants DP130104395 and DE160100850, and by the supercomputing resources provided by the Phoenix HPC service at the University of Adelaide.

References

1. Applegate, D., Bixby, R., Chvatal, V., Cook, W.: Concorde TSP solver (2006). http://www.math.uwaterloo.ca/tsp/concorde.html
2. Benchimol, P., Van Hoeve, W.-J., Régin, J.-C., Rousseau, L.-M., Rueher, M.: Improved filtering for weighted circuit constraints. Constraints **17**(3), 205–233 (2012). doi:10.1007/s10601-012-9119-x. ISSN 1572-9354
3. Bonyadi, M., Michalewicz, Z., Barone, L.: The travelling thief problem: the first step in the transition from theoretical problems to realistic problems. In: 2013 IEEE Congress on Evolutionary Computation (CEC), pp. 1037–1044 (2013)
4. Bonyadi, M.R., Michalewicz, Z., Przybylek, M.R., Wierzbicki, A.: Socially inspired algorithms for the travelling thief problem. In: Proceedings of the 2014 Annual Conference on Genetic and Evolutionary Computation, GECCO 2014, pp. 421–428. ACM (2014)
5. El Yafrani, M., Ahiod, B.: Cosolver2B: an efficient local search heuristic for the travelling thief problem. In: 2015 IEEE/ACS 12th International Conference of Computer Systems and Applications (AICCSA), pp. 1–5. IEEE (2015)
6. El Yafrani, M., Ahiod, B.: Population-based vs. single-solution heuristics for the travelling thief problem. In: Proceedings of the Genetic and Evolutionary Computation Conference 2016, GECCO 2016, pp. 317–324. ACM (2016)
7. Faulkner, H., Polyakovskiy, S., Schultz, T., Wagner, M.: Approximate approaches to the traveling thief problem. In: Proceedings of the 2015 Annual Conference on Genetic and Evolutionary Computation, GECCO 2015, pp. 385–392. ACM (2015)
8. Held, M., Karp, R.M.: A dynamic programming approach to sequencing problems. In: Proceedings of the 1961 16th ACM National Meeting, ACM 1961, pp. 71.201-71.204. ACM (1961)

9. Hooker, J.N.: Logic, optimization, and constraint programming. INFORMS J. Comput. **14**(4), 295–321 (2002)
10. Lin, S., Kernighan, B.W.: An effective heuristic algorithm for the traveling-salesman problem. Oper. Res. **21**(2), 498–516 (1973)
11. Mei, Y., Li, X., Yao, X.: Improving efficiency of heuristics for the large scale traveling thief problem. In: Dick, G., et al. (eds.) SEAL 2014. LNCS, vol. 8886, pp. 631–643. Springer, Cham (2014). doi:10.1007/978-3-319-13563-2_53. ISBN 978-3-319-13563-2
12. Mei, Y., Li, X., Salim, F., Yao, X.: Heuristic evolution with genetic programming for traveling thief problem. In: 2015 IEEE Congress on Evolutionary Computation (CEC), pp. 2753–2760, May 2015. doi:10.1109/CEC.2015.7257230
13. Mei, Y., Li, X., Yao, X.: On investigation of interdependence between sub-problems of the travelling thief problem. Soft Comput. **20**(1), 157–172 (2016)
14. Neumann, F., Polyakovskiy, S., Skutella, M., Stougie, L., Wu, J.: A Fully Polynomial Time Approximation Scheme for Packing While Traveling. ArXiv e-prints (2017)
15. Pisinger, D.: Advanced Generator for 0–1 Knapsack Problem. http://www.diku.dk/~pisinger/codes.html
16. Pisinger, D.: Where are the hard knapsack problems? Comput. Oper. Res. **32**(9), 2271–2284 (2005). doi:10.1016/j.cor.2004.03.002. ISSN 0305-0548
17. Polyakovskiy, S., Neumann, F.: The packing while traveling problem. Eur. J. Oper. Res. **258**(2), 424–439 (2017)
18. Polyakovskiy, S., Bonyadi, M.R., Wagner, M., Michalewicz, Z., Neumann, F.: A comprehensive benchmark set and heuristics for the traveling thief problem. In: Proceedings of the 2014 Annual Conference on Genetic and Evolutionary Computation, GECCO 2014, pp. 477–484. ACM (2014)
19. Refalo, P.: Impact-based search strategies for constraint programming. In: Wallace, M. (ed.) CP 2004. LNCS, vol. 3258, pp. 557–571. Springer, Heidelberg (2004). doi:10.1007/978-3-540-30201-8_41
20. Reinelt, G.: TSPLIB—a traveling salesman problem library. ORSA J. Comput. **3**(4), 376–384 (1991)
21. Stützle, T., Hoos, H.H.: MAX MIN ant system. Future Gener. Comput. Syst. **16**(8), 889–914 (2000)
22. Wagner, M.: Stealing items more efficiently with ants: a swarm intelligence approach to the travelling thief problem. In: Dorigo, M., Birattari, M., Li, X., López-Ibáñez, M., Ohkura, K., Pinciroli, C., Stützle, T. (eds.) ANTS 2016. LNCS, vol. 9882, pp. 273–281. Springer, Cham (2016). doi:10.1007/978-3-319-44427-7_25
23. Wagner, M., Lindauer, M., Mısır, M., Nallaperuma, S., Hutter, F.: A case study of algorithm selection for the traveling thief problem. J. Heuristics pp. 1–26 (2017)

On the Use of Dynamic Reference Points in HypE

Jingda Deng[1,2]([✉]), Qingfu Zhang[1,2], and Hui Li[3]

[1] Department of Computer Science, City University of Hong Kong,
Hong Kong, Hong Kong
jingddeng2-c@my.cityu.edu.hk, qingfu.zhang@cityu.edu.hk
[2] City University of Hong Kong Shenzhen Research Institute, Shenzhen, China
[3] School of Mathematics and Statistics, Xi'an Jiaotong University, Xi'an, China
lihui10@xjtu.edu.cn

Abstract. In evolutionary multiobjective optimization, hypervolume indicator is one of the most commonly-used performance metrics. To reduce its high computational costs in many objective optimization, Monte Carlo method is used in HypE (Hypervolume Estimation algorithm for multi-objective optimization) for approximating hypervolume values. However, the diversity preservation of HypE can be poor under inappropriate settings of the reference point. In this paper, the influence of the reference point on HypE is discussed and two variants of HypE algorithm with dynamic reference points are proposed to improve the performance of HypE. Our experimental results suggest that the new algorithms outperform HypE with fixed reference points on a set of multiobjective test instances with different shapes of Pareto fronts.

Keywords: Multiobjective optimization · Evolutionary computation · Hypervolume · Reference point

1 Introduction

Many real world applications need to optimize two or more objective functions at the same time. A minimization multiobjective optimization problem (MOP) can be stated as follows:

$$\min F(x) = (f_1(x), f_2(x), \ldots, f_m(x))^T$$
$$s.t. \ x \in X$$

where x is the decision variable, X is the feasible region, $f_i(x), 1 \leq i \leq m$, is the i-th objective function, and F is the objective vector in the objective space R^m.

Trade-offs among different objectives can be expressed by the Pareto optimality. Given $u, v \in R^m$, u dominates v if and only if for each $i \in \{1, \ldots, m\}, u_i \leq v_i$ and there exists an index j such that $u_j < v_j$. A solution is Pareto optimal if and only if it is not dominated by any other solution. The set of all Pareto optimal solutions in the decision space is called Pareto set (PS), and the map of PS in

© Springer International Publishing AG 2017
Y. Shi et al. (Eds.): SEAL 2017, LNCS 10593, pp. 122–133, 2017.
https://doi.org/10.1007/978-3-319-68759-9_11

the objective space is called Pareto front (PF). To find a finite number of representative points in the PF, multiobjective evolutionary algorithms (MOEAs) have attracted many research interests in the past twenty years [5,6].

To measure the quality of the final population generated by algorithms, many performance indicators have been proposed. Performance indicators should assess two aspects of population, i.e., the convergence and diversity. Good convergence means that the distance between the set of all obtained solutions and the PF should be minimized. Good diversity means that all obtained solutions should be well distributed along the PF.

The well-known performance indicator hypervolume [12] of a point set is defined as the volume of the region dominated by the point set and bounded by a reference point. Since hypervolume is consistent with Pareto optimality and only needs one reference point, it has been used for fitness assignment in some MOEAs [2,3]. However, the calculation of hypervolume is expensive when the number of objectives is relatively large [4]. Approximation methods, such as the Monte Carlo method in HypE [2] and an approximation method in [10], can be used to reduce the computational costs.

The setting of the reference point is crucial in hypervolume indicator. Its impacts have been theoretically investigated [1,9]. When applied into algorithms, a reference point too close to the PF will result in incomplete cover of the PF. On the other hand, a reference point too far away from the PF will cause low accuracy in Monte Carlo simulation and mislead algorithms on some MOPs. One approach to reduce the negative impacts of the reference point is to use a dynamic one. In fact, in the early literature about hypervolume [3], the dynamic reference point based on normalization and slight changes in objective values has been considered.

The remainder of this paper is organized as follows. First, the background on diversity preservation in MOEAs and a hypervolume-based algorithm HypE are briefly introduced in Sect. 2. In the following section, we discuss the impacts of the reference point in general hypervolume-based algorithms and particularly in HypE. In Sect. 4, two variants of HypE using dynamic reference points are proposed. Section 5 reports the experimental results. Section 6 concludes the paper.

2   Background

2.1   Diversity Preservation and the Boundary Point

Ideally, the final population of MOEAs should be able to cover the whole PF and have a good distribution along the PF. For this purpose, algorithms need carefully to assign fitness to solutions and rank them for selection during the iterations. Especially, extra attention should be paid on the solutions near the boundary of current population. Taking the well-known fitness assignment method, the crowding distance proposed in NSGA2 [7], as an example, the points in the current non-dominated front with the best value regarding of a certain objective have the highest priorities to survive in next population.

It should be noted that finding the solutions on the boundary of the PF is nontrivial in some cases. In the case of two objectives, the boundary often consists of two extreme points, which are optimal to two objectives separately. In the case of three or more objectives, however, since the PF is usually represented by a manifold with the dimensionality higher than one, it is not always easily described by finite discrete points. Moreover, to precisely determine the boundary of a finite set in high dimensional objective space is also not cheap.

2.2 HypE Algorithm

It has been shown that hypervolume-based algorithms can be effective for obtaining a set of well-distributed non-dominated solutions. However, the calculation of hypervolume suffers from high computational complexity in the high-dimension objective space. One way of dealing with this is to approximate hypervolume values.

HypE algorithm uses Monte Carlo method and shows better performance on many objective optimization problems with up to 50 objectives than some other state-of-the-art algorithms. It also introduced a new selection procedure based on population-based hypervolume contributions. With this procedure HypE generates and eliminates multiple solutions in each iteration. The main loop of HypE is briefly stated in Algorithm 1. Hypervolume contribution approximation is executed in procedure *MatingSelection* in which mating solutions are selected and *EnvironmentalSelection* in which redundant solutions are removed. In each iteration, the former will use Monte Carlo simulation once while the latter will use $(|P| + |Q'| - N)$ times.

Algorithm 1. HypE algorithm

Input: Reference point z^*, population size N, number of sampling points n.
Output: Representative subset P of the PF.

1: Generate N solutions to initialize the population P
2: **while** Termination criterion does not meet **do**
3:     $P' \leftarrow MatingSeletion(P, z^*, N, n)$
4:     $P'' \leftarrow Reproduction(P', N)$
5:     Let $Q := P \cup P''$, $Q' := Non\text{-}dominated(Q)$, $P \leftarrow \emptyset$
6:     **while** $|P| + |Q'| \leq N$ **do**
7:         $P \leftarrow P \cup Q', Q \leftarrow Q \backslash Q'$
8:         $Q' := Non\text{-}dominated(Q)$
9:     **end while**
10:    **if** $|P| < N$ **then**
11:        $Q'' \leftarrow EnvironmentalSelection(Q', z^*, |P| + |Q'| - N, n)$
12:        $P \leftarrow P \cup Q''$
13:    **end if**
14: **end while**

3 Impacts of Reference Point in Hypervolume-Based Algorithms

3.1 General Hypervolume-Based Algorithms

The performance of diversity preservation in hypervolume-based algorithms can be affected by the setting of the reference point.

First of all, if the reference point is set too close to the PF, non-dominated points around the boundary of the PF will have zero or very small hypervolume contributions. Therefore, they are likely to be eliminated from the population. This will result in incomplete cover of the PF.

In [1], the impact of the reference point in the case of bi-objective optimization problems is investigated in depth. It is proved that the boundary points of PF will be included in the population which maximize hypervolume if the tangent line of PF is not parallel to the axis and the components of the reference point are large enough. Let's consider a typical 2-dimensional continuous PF, for example, $f_2 = 1 - f_1$ where $f_1 \in [0,1]$. In this situation, if the reference point is located in the region dominated by $(2,2)^T$, the population maximizing hypervolume will certainly include boundary points $(0,1)^T$ and $(1,0)^T$.

However, using a reference point whose components are too large also has negative impacts. Very recently, the impact of the reference point on hypervolume values in the case of three or more objectives have been studied in [9]. In this work, authors find that for some MOPs with special PF shapes, the population which maximize hypervolume will include more and more boundary points as the components of reference point enlarge.

All above indicate that selecting the reference point is crucial on the performance of hypervolume-based algorithms.

3.2 HypE

In the previous section, we discussed the influence of the setting of reference point in general hypervolume-based algorithms. Furthermore, the influence could be even huger in HypE because the hypervolume is approximated.

Firstly, the reference point determines the upper bound of the sampling space. Since Monte Carlo method uses uniformly distributed samples in the sampling space, the density of samples will decrease exponentially as the components of reference point enlarge, leading to lower accuracy of approximation. Secondly, if the reference point is set too far away from the population, the contributions of boundary points will be overestimated. This is because the hypervolume contributions of the points in the interior part of current population become more difficult to be detected by sparser samples.

To verify above statements, we did some experiments on the selection procedure of HypE in the case of three objectives. Firstly two point sets with triangle and inverted triangle shape are constructed. Then, limited number of points are selected from each point set by environmental selection procedure in HypE with different settings of reference point. For comparison, we also

tested the selection procedure based on exact hypervolume with a reference
point $(2000, 2000, 2000)^T$, which is far away from the point set. The selected
points are plotted in Fig. 1.

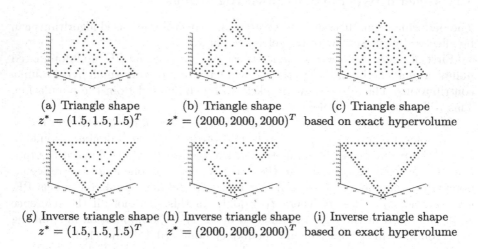

(a) Triangle shape   (b) Triangle shape   (c) Triangle shape
$z^* = (1.5, 1.5, 1.5)^T$ $z^* = (2000, 2000, 2000)^T$ based on exact hypervolume

(g) Inverse triangle shape (h) Inverse triangle shape   (i) Inverse triangle shape
$z^* = (1.5, 1.5, 1.5)^T$ $z^* = (2000, 2000, 2000)^T$ based on exact hypervolume

Fig. 1. Survival points of different shapes from point set after environmental selection
procedure of HypE using different reference point $z^* \in R^3$

As shown in this figure, environmental selection based on approximated
hypervolume tends to preserve more boundary points as the reference point
moves upwards on point sets with triangle and inverted triangle shape (subgraph
(a)(b)(g)(h)). However, the algorithm based on exact hypervolume behaves differently on two different shapes. On the triangle shape, the algorithm performs good even though the components of the reference point are quite large
(subgraph(c)). On the inverted triangle shape, the algorithm tends to preserve
extremely many boundary points (subgraph (i)). The observation in (i) has been
reported and analyzed in [9].

4   Dynamic Reference Point in HypE

According to the discussions in Sect. 3, we believe that an appropriate reference
point should carefully be selected for HypE. It should help algorithm balance
the number of boundary solutions and other solutions in population. Firstly it
should locate above the PF so that boundary points are preserved. At the same
time, it should be close enough to current population so as to keep a high-level
approximation accuracy and not to overestimate the importance of boundary
points.

One simple way to dynamically determine the sampling space for approximation is to use the estimated ideal point z^{ideal} and the nadir point z^{nadir} of

the current population as the lower bound of sampling space and the reference point respectively, where

$$z^{ideal} := (\min_{x \in P} f_1(x), \min_{x \in P} f_2(x), \ldots, \min_{x \in P} f_m(x))^T$$

and

$$z^{nadir} := (\max_{x \in P} f_1(x), \max_{x \in P} f_2(x), \ldots, \max_{x \in P} f_m(x))^T.$$

But this estimation is a little rough. We suggest the following two strategies, aiming at maintaining boundary points more carefully:

1. In Algorithm 1, Monte Carlo method is used in Line 3 and Line 11 based on different point set P and Q'. Therefore z^{ideal} and z^{nadir} should also be differently determined based on each set.
2. The upper bound of sampling space should be a little larger than the nadir point so as to preserve enough boundary points in the next population. As designed in Algorithm 2, the upper bound z^{up} is determined by the input set of points, the ideal point and an addition factor β. Here, β can be a fixed value or adaptively tuned.

Algorithm 2. Upper bound selection for Monte Carlo method
Input: Point set $S = \{s^1, \ldots, s^p\}$, ideal point z^{ideal}, factor $\beta > 1$.
Output: Upper bound $z^{up} \in R^m$
1: Let $b = 0$
2: **for** $k = 1$ to m **do**
3:     $z_k^{up} = \max_{i=1,2,\ldots,p} s_k^i$
4:     $b \leftarrow \max\{b, \beta(z_k^{up} - z_k^{ideal})\}$
5: **end for**
6: $z^{up} \leftarrow z^{ideal} + b(1, 1, \ldots, 1)^T$

The two strategies define a dynamic reference point z^{up} when computing hypervolume values. With the factor β, the algorithm is able to control how many boundary points could survive in selection.

Except for using a pre-determined β in Algorithm 2, we also try the idea to find an appropriate β by adaptively increasing the upper bound in Algorithm 3. In Line 4 of Algorithm 3, those points with the largest value regarding a certain single objective are treated as boundary points. To be honest, this estimation is still rather rough. Line 8–17 use a while loop gradually enlarging β. The loop will terminate when for each objective there exists at least one boundary point able to survive in the environmental selection, that is, the hypervolume contribution ranks no worse than s_{max}. Due to the extra Monte Carlo simulations in the while loop, running time of HypE algorithm with Algorithm 3 could be much larger than original HypE algorithm.

Algorithm 3. Adaptive selection for upper bound

Input: Point set $S = \{s^1, \ldots, s^p\}$, ideal point z^{ideal}, maximal size $s_{max} < p$, number of sampling points n.

Output: Upper bound $z^{up} \in R^m$

1: Let $b = 0$, $flag = 1$
2: **for** $k = 1$ to m **do**
3:     $z_k^{up} := \max_{i=1,2,\ldots,p} s_k^i$
4:     $S_k := \arg\max_{i=1,2,\ldots,p} s_k^i$
5:     $b \leftarrow \max\{b, 1.1(z_k^{up} - z_k^{ideal})\}$
6: **end for**
7: $z^{up} \leftarrow z^{ideal} + b(1, 1, \ldots, 1)^T$
8: **while** $flag$ **do**
9:     $HC := Hypervolume Approximation(S, z^{up}, p, n)$
10:    $SortHC \leftarrow Sort(HC)$, set $flag = 0$
11:    **for** $k = 1$ to m **do**
12:       **if** $\max\{HC(S_k)\} < SortHC(s_{max})$ **then**
13:          $b \leftarrow 1.1b, z^{up} \leftarrow z^{ideal} + b(1, 1, \ldots, 1)^T, flag \leftarrow 1$
14:          **break**
15:       **end if**
16:    **end for**
17: **end while**

5 Numerical Results

5.1 Experiment Settings

Benchmark DTLZ test instances [8] and their inverted version are used for testing algorithms. In [11], an inverted version of DTLZ1, denoted as IDTLZ1, is constructed with an inverted triangle shape of the PF which is similar to the bottom of Fig. 1. In IDTLZ1, each objective value $f_i(x)$ is firstly calculated as in DTLZ1 and then changed as follows:

$$f_i(x) := (1 + g) * 0.5 - f_i(x)$$

In this paper, we follow the above revision and construct inverted version of other DTLZ problems, denoted as IDTLZ2–IDTLZ7. For DTLZ2–DTLZ6, after computing the function value of each objective $f_i(x)$, the following function values are outputted:

$$f_i(x) := (1 + g) - f_i(x)$$

For DTLZ7, the output is changed by:

$$f_i(x) := (1 + g) * m - f_i(x)$$

Five variants of HypE are to be tested. Two of them are HypE with dynamic reference point named HypE-DR1 and HypE-DR2, constructed by Algorithm 2 and 3 in Sect. 4 respectively. The other three variants are HypE using different fixed reference points, HypE(1.5), HypE(5) and HypE(2000). Settings of their reference points are listed in Table 1. These settings are based on the knowledge of the ranges of the PF.

Table 1. Settings of reference points in HypE(1.5), HypE(5) and HypE(2000), $I = (1, 1, 1)^T$

Algorithm	DTLZ1	DTLZ2	DTLZ3	DTLZ4	DTLZ5	DTLZ6	DTLZ7
HypE(1.5)	$0.75I$	$1.5I$	$1.5I$	$1.5I$	$1.5I$	$1.5I$	$10I$
HypE(5)	$5I$	$5I$	$5I$	$5I$	$5I$	$5I$	$15I$
HypE(2000)	$2000I$	$2000I$	$2000I$	$2000I$	$2000I$	$2000I$	$2000I$
Algorithm	IDTLZ1	IDTLZ2	IDTLZ3	IDTLZ4	IDTLZ5	IDTLZ6	IDTLZ7
HypE(1.5)	$0.75I$	$1.5I$	$1.5I$	$1.5I$	$1.5I$	$1.5I$	$4.5I$
HypE(5)	$5I$	$5I$	$5I$	$5I$	$5I$	$5I$	$15I$
HypE(5)	$2000I$	$2000I$	$2000I$	$2000I$	$2000I$	$2000I$	$2000I$

Performance metric is the exact hypervolume with same reference points used in HypE(1.5) in Table 1. Thus, HypE(1.5) uses the most appropriate settings of reference points in the experiments.

5.2 Parameter Settings

1. Population size N is set to be 100;
2. Number of samples n for Monte Carlo method is set to be 10000 for all algorithms as suggested in [2];
3. Maximal number of function evaluations is 50000;
4. All algorithms run 20 times independently;
5. β is set to be 1.5 in HypE-DR1. This setting is similar to HypE(1.5);
6. The maximal number of loops in the procedure of upper bound selection in HypE-DR2 is 5 to balance the computational costs and algorithm performance.

5.3 Experimental Results and Analysis

Hypervolume values of final population and running time of algorithms are listed in Tables 2 and 3. To analyze the effects of dynamic reference point, the upper bound z^{up} used in the last iteration of HypE-DR1 and HypE-DR2 on some typical problems are plotted in box in Fig. 2.

In terms of running time, we have following observations:

1. Running time of HypE(5) and HypE(2000) is much less than HypE(1.5) and HypE with dynamic reference point. It is becuase a reference point far away from the PF makes the loop of the selection procedure in HypE easier to

break out, but that will cause lower accuracy in Monte Carlo simulation. That is why HypE(5) and HypE(2000) have the worst performance on most problems.

2. Running time of HypE-DR1 is quite similar to HypE(1.5). HypE-DR2 is always the slowest one because it needs to select the most appropriate reference point in Algorithm 3.

Table 2. Mean and standard of running time in 20 independent runs on DTLZ and IDTLZ test problems

Instance	HypE-DR1	HypE-DR2	HypE(1.5)	HypE(5)	HypE(2000)
DTLZ1	62.21 (16.51)	92.95 (7.51)	75.54 (5.84)	29.22 (1.23)	25.85 (0.68)
DTLZ2	129.59 (1.64)	187.72 (1.49)	136.49 (1.58)	33.44 (1.65)	34.54 (0.78)
DTLZ3	21.33 (2.47)	29.46 (13.62)	27.98 (5.24)	23.18 (1.70)	20.60 (0.51)
DTLZ4	95.49 (33.92)	155.30 (43.04)	98.16 (34.57)	33.12 (6.62)	29.01 (4.94)
DTLZ5	65.07 (1.62)	92.49 (3.93)	68.50 (1.04)	31.78 (1.14)	23.83 (0.36)
DTLZ6	102.58 (5.32)	136.04 (4.46)	73.81 (4.78)	62.36 (2.72)	29.60 (1.71)
DTLZ7	36.76 (3.69)	55.45 (5.87)	42.58 (3.68)	36.46 (1.58)	27.88 (0.52)
IDTLZ1	78.47 (2.03)	80.79 (2.13)	76.19 (4.12)	33.47 (1.67)	26.17 (1.51)
IDTLZ2	192.10 (2.05)	198.79 (1.88)	199.90 (1.94)	111.23 (0.65)	42.67 (0.87)
IDTLZ3	54.03 (4.20)	65.56 (9.73)	43.93 (8.05)	36.40 (3.30)	21.00 (0.43)
IDTLZ4	203.08 (3.40)	213.22 (2.04)	208.91 (1.70)	110.37 (0.91)	40.61 (3.51)
IDTLZ5	113.14 (7.81)	133.52 (7.16)	154.78 (2.52)	85.76 (5.15)	40.54 (1.23)
IDTLZ6	82.51 (7.34)	124.77 (4.01)	88.64 (14.19)	93.84 (1.81)	25.75 (0.76)
IDTLZ7	114.62 (1.47)	144.40 (1.40)	103.34 (2.25)	68.32 (2.26)	47.90 (2.17)

On DTLZ test problems, HypE-DR2 performs the best on most problems expect DTLZ3, while HypE(1.5) is always the second best one. Following are analysis on these problems:

1. On DTLZ1, 2, 4 and 5, the ranks of algorithms are similar. HypE-DR2 chooses more suitable reference points for its population and obtains better distributions. The components of chosen reference points are a little larger than those used in HypE-DR1 and HypE(1.5).

2. Since DTLZ3 has much difficulty of multimodality in decision space, a stronger convergence of algorithms is required on this problem. As a consequence, in some runs the dynamic reference points used in HypE-DR1 and HypE-DR2 are still far away from the PF at the last iteration. HypE(1.5) runs to the other extreme on DTLZ3. It uses a reference point too close to the PF, so it cannot distinguish solutions dominated by the reference point. Therefore the performance of HypE(1.5) is even worse than HypE(5) on DTLZ3.

Table 3. Mean and standard of hypervolume in 20 independent runs on DTLZ and IDTLZ test problems. The best hypervolume is shown in **bold** and the second best in *Itatic*

Instance	HypE-DR1	HypE-DR2	HypE(1.5)	HypE(5)	HypE(2000)
DTLZ1	0.3909 (0.0094)	**0.3941** (0.0002)	**0.3941** (0.0002)	0.3729 (0.0035)	0.3721 (0.0072)
DTLZ2	2.7812 (0.0015)	**2.7856** (0.0011)	*2.7827* (0.0014)	2.6328 (0.0334)	2.6041 (0.0431)
DTLZ3	2.3320 (0.5644)	2.4061 (0.5954)	*2.4543* (0.8408)	**2.5115** (0.0495)	2.4084 (0.2379)
DTLZ4	2.5519 (0.4269)	**2.6659** (0.2462)	*2.5754* (0.2932)	2.3795 (0.5042)	2.4512 (0.2881)
DTLZ5	2.0313 (0.0007)	**2.0315** (0.0007)	*2.0312* (0.0006)	2.0178 (0.0061)	1.9319 (0.0283)
DTLZ6	*1.8296* (0.0638)	**1.8379** (0.0630)	1.8183 (0.0776)	1.7652 (0.0873)	1.6156 (0.0827)
DTLZ7	706.28 (35.96)	700.07 (57.12)	694.63 (47.96)	**711.66** (26.08)	*708.94* (25.76)
IDTLZ1	**0.2101** (0.0004)	0.2046 (0.0014)	**0.2101** (0.0004)	0.1944 (0.0018)	0.1684 (0.0052)
IDTLZ2	**2.4474** (0.0027)	2.3494 (0.0273)	*2.4452* (0.0030)	2.3806 (0.0093)	1.8258 (0.1372)
IDTLZ3	**2.4279** (0.0111)	2.3316 (0.0419)	2.1934 (0.6417)	*2.3590* (0.0352)	1.8815 (0.5999)
IDTLZ4	**2.4546** (0.0024)	2.4258 (0.0103)	*2.4535* (0.0021)	2.3837 (0.0096)	1.9823 (0.2603)
IDTLZ5	**1.9038** (0.0061)	*1.9034* (0.0064)	1.9029 (0.0063)	1.8914 (0.0060)	1.6936 (0.0877)
IDTLZ6	1.7795 (0.0423)	**1.8350** (0.0226)	0.0000 (0.0000)	*1.8139* (0.0228)	1.2130 (0.1423)
IDTLZ7	*87.723* (0.012)	**87.745** (0.008)	87.691 (0.019)	87.411 (0.080)	86.746 (1.119)

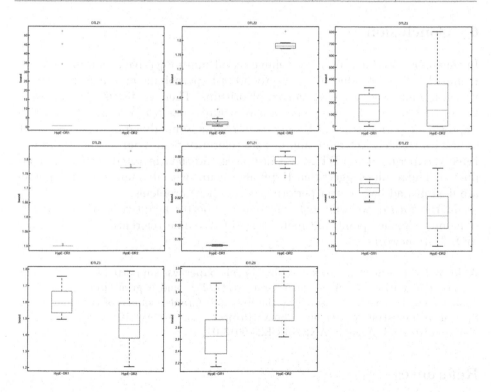

Fig. 2. Upper bounds used in the last iteration by HypE-DR1 and HypE-DR2

3. DTLZ5 and DTLZ6 have degenerated PFs. The performance of HypE algorithms with dynamic reference points is better than HypE(1.5).

On IDTLZ test problems, HypE-DR1 performs the best on most of these problems. Following are analysis on these problems:

1. Dynamic reference points used in HypE-DR1 are similar to those used in HypE(1.5) on IDTLZ1–IDTLZ4, and significantly larger on IDTLZ5–IDTLZ7. Hypervolume values in Table 3 suggest that these selections are more appropriate than HypE(1.5).
2. HypE-DR2 performs not well on IDTLZ1–IDTLZ4. In these problems, there are multiple Pareto optimal solutions with the worst value respect to each single objective. As shown in Fig. 2, on these problems HypE-DR2 tends to select a reference point with smaller components than it should be.
3. It is interesting that HypE(1.5) fails on IDTLZ6. The final population of HypE(1.5) is still far away from the PF so the hypervolume of the population is 0. It is hard for HypE(1.5) to find Pareto optimal solutions of IDTLZ6 whose distance variables are required to very close to 1.

6   Conclusion

In this paper, we focus on hypervolume-based multiobjective evolutionary algorithms. We first introduce the background of hypervolume and diversity preservation in multiobjective evolutionary algorithms. Then we discuss the impact of the setting of the reference point on hypervolume-based algorithms. In order to improve the performance of HypE, we introduce some dynamic reference point strategies which select more appropriate reference points during the iterations. Finally, experiments on DTLZ test instances and their inverted version are conducted. The results suggest that HypE algorithms with dynamic reference points are flexible and have better performance on these problems.

In the future, we will continue to study better adaptive methods for the dynamic reference point and more usage of dynamic reference points in other MOEA frameworks.

Acknowledgment. The work described in this paper was supported by the National Science Foundation of China under Grant 61473241, and a grant from ANR/RCC Joint Research Scheme sponsored by the Research Grants Council of the Hong Kong Special Administrative Region, China (Project No. A-CityU101/16) and France National Research Agency (ANR-16-CE23-0013-01).

References

1. Auger, A., Bader, J., Brockhoff, D., Zitzler, E.: Theory of the hypervolume indicator: optimal μ-distributions and the choice of the reference point. In: FOGA 2009: Proceedings of the Tenth ACM SIGEVO Workshop on Foundations of Genetic Algorithms, pp. 87–102 (2009)

2. Bader, J., Zitzler, E.: HypE: an algorithm for fast hypervolume-based many-objective optimization. Evol. Comput. **19**(1), 45–76 (2011)
3. Beume, N., Naujoks, B., Emmerich, M.: SMS-EMOA: multiobjective selection based on dominated hypervolume. Eur. J. Oper. Res. **181**(3), 1653–1669 (2007)
4. Bringmann, K., Friedrich, T.: Approximating the volume of unions and intersections of high-dimensional geometric objects. In: Hong, S.-H., Nagamochi, H., Fukunaga, T. (eds.) ISAAC 2008. LNCS, vol. 5369, pp. 436–447. Springer, Heidelberg (2008). doi:10.1007/978-3-540-92182-0_40
5. Coello Coello, C.A., Van Veldhuizen, D.A., Lamont, G.B.: Evolutionary Algorithms for Solving Multi-Objective Problems. Springer, Heidelberg (2007)
6. Deb, K.: Multi-objective Optimization Using Evolutionary Algorithms. Wiley, Hoboken (2001)
7. Deb, K., Pratap, A., Agarwal, S., Meyarivan, T.: A fast and elitist multiobjective genetic algorithm: NSGA-II. IEEE Trans. Evol. Comput. **6**(2), 182–197 (2002)
8. Deb, K., Thiele, L., Laumanns, M., Zitzler, E.: Scalable test problems for evolutionary multi-objective optimization. In: Abraham, A., Jain, L., Goldberg, R. (eds.) Evolutionary Multiobjective Optimization, pp. 105–145. Springer, London (2005). doi:10.1007/1-84628-137-7_6
9. Ishibuchi, H., Imada, R., Setoguchi, Y., Nojima, Y.: Hypervolume subset selection for triangular and inverted triangular pareto fronts of three-objective problems. In: Proceedings of the 14th ACM/SIGEVO Workshop on Foundations of Genetic Algorithms, pp. 95–110 (2017)
10. Ishibuchi, H., Tsukamoto, N., Sakane, Y., Nojima, Y.: Hypervolume approximation using achievement scalarizing functions for evolutionary many-objective optimization. In: 2009 IEEE Congress on Evolutionary Computation, pp. 530–537. IEEE (2009)
11. Jain, H., Deb, K.: An evolutionary many-objective optimization algorithm using reference-point-based nondominated sorting approach, Part II: handling constraints and extending to an adaptive approach. IEEE Trans. Evol. Comput. **18**(4), 602–622 (2014)
12. Zitzler, E., Thiele, L.: Multiobjective evolutionary algorithms: a comparative case study and the strength pareto approach. IEEE Trans. Evol. Comput. **3**(4), 257–271 (1999)

Multi-Factorial Evolutionary Algorithm Based on M2M Decomposition

Jiajie Mo[2], Zhun Fan[1,2(✉)], Wenji Li[2], Yi Fang[2], Yugen You[2], and Xinye Cai[3]

[1] Guangdong Provincial Key Laboratory of Digital Signal and Image Processing,
Shantou 515063, China
zfan@stu.edu.cn
[2] Department of Electronic Engineering, Shantou University, Shantou 515063, China
[3] College of Computer Science and Technology,
Nanjing University of Aeronautics and Astronautics, Jiangsu 210016, China

Abstract. This paper proposes a decomposition-based multi-objective multi-factorial evolutionary algorithm (MFEA/D-M2M). The MFEA/D-M2M adopts the M2M approach to decompose multi-objective optimization problems into multiple constrained sub-problems for enhancing the diversity of population and convergence of sub-regions. An machine learning model augmented version is also been implemented, which utilized discriminative models for pre-selecting solutions. Experimental studies on nine multi-factorial optimization (MFO) problem sets are conducted. The experimental results demonstrated that MFEA/D-M2M outperforms the vanilla MFEA on six MFO benchmark problem sets and achieved comparable results on the other three problem sets with partial intersection of global optimal.

Keywords: Multi-factorial optimization · M2M decomposition · Pre-selection

1 Introduction

With the increasing amount of incoming data streams, it is very desirable that the information systems and algorithms are capable of efficient multi-tasking [1]. Evolutionary algorithms (EAs) are population based optimization algorithms that work on Darwinian principles of natural selection or survival of the fittest [2]. The population based search enables multi-objective evolutionary algorithms (MOEAs) to achieve simultaneous convergence toward the entire Pareto Front (PF) for multi-objective optimization problems (MOPs).

Furthermore, recent researches [3–6] show that by exploiting the implicit parallelism offered by a population, a multi-factorial evolutionary algorithm (MFEA) can simultaneously and efficiently solve multiple optimization problems with one single population, where each constitutive problem contributes a unique factor influencing the evolution. Therefore, evolutionary multi-tasking [7–9] is attracting extensive attention as a new paradigm in the field of optimization and evolutionary computation.

© Springer International Publishing AG 2017
Y. Shi et al. (Eds.): SEAL 2017, LNCS 10593, pp. 134–144, 2017.
https://doi.org/10.1007/978-3-319-68759-9_12

In order to enhance the diversity of the population, M2M decomposition approach is augmented with the vanilla MFEA [8]. Furthermore, support vector machines (SVMs) are utilized as pre-selection models for finding promising solutions given only their decision variables.

The rest of this paper is organized as follows. Section 2 describes the preliminaries of vanilla MFEA. Section 3 illustrates the mechanism of combining M2M decomposition with MFEA. Section 4 describes the utilization of SVM for pre-selection. Experimental results and analysis are provided in Sect. 5. Section 6 concludes the paper with a brief discussion of future work.

2   Multi-Factorial Evolutionary Algorithms

Recently, MFEAs [7,8] have been proposed to solve multiple optimization tasks with one population. In MFO, each constitutive task is considered to be contributing a unique factor influencing the evolution of the population.

Without loss of generality, consider the situation where K MOPs to be minimized simultaneously. Denoting the jth task that has M_j objectives as T_j, its D_j dimensional search space as $\mathbf{X}_j \in \mathbb{R}^{D_j}$ and its objective function vector as $\mathbf{F}_j : \mathbf{X}_j \to \mathbb{R}^{M_j}$. The jth MOP in MFO paradigm can be defined as (1).

$$\begin{aligned} \text{minimize} \quad & \mathbf{F}_j(x) = (f_{j,1}(x), \dots, f_{j,M_j}(x))^T \\ \text{subject to} \quad & x \in \mathbb{Y} \end{aligned} \tag{1}$$

where $\mathbb{Y}$ is the unified representation space [5] built on the search spaces $\mathbf{X}_i$, $i \in \{1, 2, \dots, K\}$ of all constitutive MOPs.

A unified search space can be built so that (a) the dimension of the unified search space $D = \max_j(D_j)$, (b) the coding and decoding mapping for different tasks may be different, but all the values of a gene key are mapped into a continuous value in $[0, 1]$ and (c) the coded genotypes of tasks are simply overlapped to form the chromosome. For example, the first D_j genetic key on the chromosome is the corresponding genotype of task T_j.

Given the above settings, the MO-MFO paradigm is introduced for finding a set of multi-factorial optimal solutions, which is defined as (2).

$$\{x_1, x_2, \dots, x_j, \dots, x_K\} = \text{argmin}(\mathbf{F}_1(x), \mathbf{F}_2(x), \dots, \mathbf{F}_j(x), \dots, \mathbf{F}_K(x)) \tag{2}$$

where x_j is a feasible solution in $\mathbf{X}_j$. The composite problem may also be referred to as a K factorial optimization problem.

In order to compare candidate solutions during the evolution of MFEAs, the following properties of a individual p_i, $i \in \{1, 2, \dots, |\mathbf{P}|\}$ in the population $\mathbf{P}$, are defined:

1. Factorial Rank: The factorial rank r_j^i of p_i for task T_j is the index of p_i in the list of population members sorted by non-dominated front (NF) and crowd distance (CD) from NSGA-II [10] with respect to T_j. To be specific, p_2 is preferred over p_1 if any one of the following conditions holds: (a) $NF_2 < NF_1$ or (b) $NF_2 = NF_1$ and $CD_2 > CD_1$.

2. Skill Factor: The skill factor τ_i of p_i is the one task, amongst all other tasks in a K factorial environment, with which the individual is associated. If p_i is evaluated for all tasks, then $\tau_i = \text{argmin}_j(r_j^i)$, $j \in \{1, 2, \ldots, K\}$. Skill factor indicates which task is most preferred by p_i. The solutions in a population can be grouped into different sub-populations named task groups according to their skill factors.

3. Scalar Fitness: The scalar fitness φ_i of p_i is given by $\varphi_i = 1/r_{\tau_i}^i$. φ_i is the inverse of the best ranking index of p_i amongst all tasks, which indicates the best fitness of p_i. Performance comparisons can be performed in a simplistic manner with scalar fitness. An individual p_1 can be considered to dominate another individual p_2 in multifactorial sense simply if $\varphi_1 > \varphi_2$.

The vanilla MFEAs [7,8] are inspired by the bio-cultural models of multifactorial inheritance [11]. Unlike the traditional MOEAs are designed to find a set of Pareto optimal solutions, MFEA are designed to find the a set of global optimal solutions of all constitutive tasks, which means that the trade off between different tasks is not a concern of MFO. Therefore, MFEA splits the population into different task groups according to skill factors of solutions. Solutions in a task group are most suited for the corresponding task. Furthermore, it is possible that the genetic material in a gene pool of a particular task group might be useful for another task. Thus, transfer of genetic materials between tasks may accelerate the overall optimization process.

In the vanilla MFEA, the implicit transfer of genetic material may occur when two parent solutions with different skill factors are selected for reproduction. Then they can have a random matting probability (rmp) to perform SBX crossover [12] and the generated offspring can randomly imitate a skill factor from either parents. These two mechanisms are named as assortative matting and selective imitation [7], respectively.

3   M2M Decomposition Based MFEA

3.1   M2M Decomposition

The M2M decomposition approach is first introduced in MOEA/D-M2M [13]. This approach decomposes a MOP into multiple constrained multi-objective sub-problems by dividing the objective space into multiple sub-regions with direction vectors.

To be more specific, for a MOP with M nonnegative objectives $f_1, \ldots, f_m$, K direction vectors $\lambda^1, \ldots, \lambda^K \in \mathbb{R}_+^M$ was chosen, usually uniformly distributed. Then the objective space R_+^M can be divided into K sub-regions $\Omega^1, \ldots, \Omega^K$, where Ω^k $(k = 1, \ldots, K)$ can be defined as (3).

$$\Omega^k = \{u \in \mathbb{R}_+^M | (a, \lambda^k) \leq (u, \lambda^j), \; \forall j = 1, \ldots, K\} \tag{3}$$

where (u, λ^j) is the acute angle between u and λ^j. In another word, $u \in \Omega^k$ if and only if λ^k has the smallest angle to u amongst all the K direction vectors.

Inspired by the division approach above, the jth constitutive MOP in MFO can be transformed into K constrained multi-objective sub-problems with K uniformly distributed direction vectors $\lambda^1, \ldots, \lambda^K$. The kth sub-problem corresponding to λ^k is defined as (4)

$$\begin{aligned} \text{minimize} \quad & \mathbf{F}_j(x) = (f_{j,1}(x), \ldots, f_{1,M_j}(x))^T \\ \text{subject to} \quad & \mathbf{F}_j(x) \in \Omega_j^k \\ & x \in \mathbb{Y} \end{aligned} \quad (4)$$

where $\mathbb{Y}$ is the aforementioned unified search space. An example of decomposing a objective space of a two objectives optimization problem is provided in Fig. 1.

The pseudocode in Algorithm 1 illustrates the allocation of solutions to sub-problem groups.

Algorithm 1. Solutions Allocation

Input: task group P, direction vectors $\lambda^1, \ldots, \lambda^K$ and size of sub-problem groups S

Output: sub-problem groups $P_1, \ldots, P_K$

    for $j \leftarrow 1$ **to** K **do**

        Initialize P_j with the solutions in P whose objective vectors are in Ω^j.

        if $(|P_j| < S)$ **then** randomly select $S - |P_j|$ solutions from P and add them to P_j.

        else if $(|P_j| > S)$ **then** rank the solutions in P_j using the non-dominated sorting method[10] and remove the $S - |P_j|$ lowest ranked solutions from P_j.

        end if

    end for

    return $P_1, \ldots, P_K$

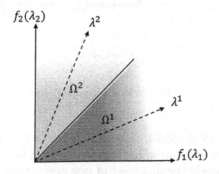

Fig. 1. Direction vectors λ^1, λ^2 divide the objective space into subregions Ω^1, Ω^2

3.2 Constructing Matting Pools

By adopting the M2M decomposition, one can simply decompose constitutive MOPs into different groups of sub-problems, and then solve sub-problems with different sub-populations by MOEAs. However, this approach is not capable of utilizing the most important feature of MFEA, namely genetic transfer, because the individuals in those separated sub-populations or sub-problem groups do not have a chance to reproduce. Prohibiting communication of genetic material between different tasks is undesirable as it constrains exploration and the power of implicit parallelism offered by the entire population [7]. Therefore, a matting pool combining mechanism is needed to ensure genetic transfer in-between different task groups.

In this section, a mechanism of randomly combing sub-problem groups from different task groups to form matting pools is illustrated. To be more specific, K randomly distributed direction vectors are adopted for dividing objective spaces of both constitutive tasks. Note that direction vectors in these two objective spaces might not be the same due to the dimension of spaces might be different. Then K matting pools are generated by randomly combining two sub-problem groups with each sub-problem group randomly picked from different tasks.

4 Pre-selection

When function evaluation is computationally expensive, one may want to spend evaluations wisely use all evaluations on solutions that are promising, which means the solutions have a fair chance of being selected into the next generation.

Inspired by MOEA/D-SVM [14], the support vector machine is adopted as pre-selection model for MFEA/D-M2M. As illustrated in Fig. 2, pre-selection is a procedure that selects unevaluated solutions given their decision variables only. Thus it is possible to select the promising ones for further function evaluation, and discard the rest.

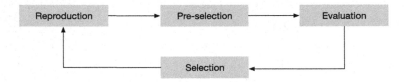

Fig. 2. Pre-selection before actual function evaluation

In order to obtain SVM models that can predict whether or not a solution is promising, the solution set containing solutions of the last generation and their offspring solutions, namely the union set of last generation, are used for training SVM.

Specifically, the decision variable vectors are regarded as feature vectors for representing solutions. And then the solutions in union population are labeled as promising if it survives the last natural selection and labeled as unpromising otherwise. To be more specific, after natural selection takes place, the solutions in current population will be labeled as promising, and solutions in the union set of last generation but not in the current population are labeled as unpromising.

The pseudocode in Algorithm 2 summarizes the MFEA/D-M2M-SVM as follows.

Algorithm 2. MFEA/D-M2M-SVM

Input:

MOPs, A stopping criterion,
K unit direction vectors $\lambda^1, \ldots, \lambda^K$, S the size of sub-problem group,
Genetic operators and their associated parameters.

Output: a set of multi-factorial optimal solutions.

Geneate $|P|$ individuals in $\mathbb{Y}$ to form initial population P.
for every $p_i \in P$ **do** Assign skill factor τ_i and evaluate p_i for task τ_i only.
end for
Compute scalar fitness φ_i for every p_i based on NF and CD
return $P_1, \ldots, P_K$
while(stopping condition is not satisfied) **do**
  Decompose P into subproblem groups with $\lambda^1, \ldots, \lambda^K$. $\to$ Refer **Algorithm 1**.
  for every sub-problem group of task one P_i^{T1} **do** Randomly pick a sub-problem group from task two P_j^{T2} to from a matting pool MP_i.
  for every matting pool population MP_i **do**
  while (offspring number $\leq$ matting pool size)
    Pick two parent solutions with binary tournament selection.
    Generate two offspring solutions with assortative matting.
    if (pre-selection $==$ **true**) **then**
      Use trained SVM model for predicting offsprings, SVM-predict(c).
      while (SVM-predict(c) $==$ unpromising) **do** Regenerate offspring.
      Determine skill factor τ_c and evaluate c with task τ_c only.
    end if
  end for
  Combine current population and offsprings into union.
  Perform non-dominated selection on union population.
  Select $|P|$ fittest solutions in union to form the current population.
  if (trainSVM $==$ **true**) Label solutions in last union population and train SVM model with them.
  return current population P

---

5   Experimental Studies

5.1   Benchmark Problems

The Multi-Objective Multi-Factorial Optimization (MO-MFO) benchmark problem sets [1] are adopted in the experimental studies, which are the same benchmarks used in CEC2017 MFO competition. All the details of these benchmark problem sets can be found in [1,15].

The MO-MFO benchmark contains nine different problem sets. Each problem set contains two constitutive tasks, and each task is a two- or three-objective minimization problem. For more detailed information, readers are referred to [1,15].

The degree of intersection of the global optima: Compete Intersection (CI): the global optimal of two constitutive tasks are identical in the unified search space with respect to all variables. Partial Intersection (PI): the global optimal of the two tasks are identical in the unified search space with respect to a subset of variables only, and are different with respect to the remaining variables. No Intersection (NI): the global optimal of the two tasks are different with respect to all variables.

The similarity of the fitness landscape: High Similarity (HS): problem sets with Spearman's rank correlation coefficient [15] $R_s \geq 0.8$. Medium Similarity (MS): problem sets with $0.8 > R_s > 0.2$. Low Similarity (LS): problem sets with $R_s \leq 0.2$.

Therefore, the nine problem sets in MFO benchmark, are named by their characteristic as follows: CIHS, CIMS, CILS, PIHS, PIMS, PILS, NIHS, NIMS, NILS.

5.2   Experimental Settings

In order to demonstrate the effectiveness of MFEA/D-M2M, several experiments are conducted with comparison of the vanilla MFEA. The experimental settings are as follows:

1. Population size: 200. Number of direction vectors for each task: 10. Size of each sub-problem population: 10.
2. Random mating probability: 0.9.
3. Deferential evolution (DE) crossover probability (CR): 0.9. Deferential evolution crossover factor (F): 0.9.
4. Simulated binary crossover (SBX) probability: 0.9. Distribution index for SBX: 20.
5. Polynomial mutation probability: 1/D (D is the dimensionality of the unified representation space). Distribution index for mutation: 20.
6. The number of function evaluations at every generation: 200. Maximum function evaluation: 200,000.

The deferential evolution crossover is used for problem sets with complete or no intersection of global optimal, and the simulated binary crossover is used for problem sets with partial intersection of global optimal.

5.3 Performance Metric

To compare the performance of the algorithms, a popular metric - inverted generation distance (IGD) [16] is adopted. The definitions of IGD is given by (5).

$$\text{IGD}(A, P^*) = \frac{1}{|P|} \sqrt{\sum_{\mathbf{x} \in P^*} (\min_{\mathbf{y} \in A} d(\mathbf{x}, \mathbf{y}))^2} \tag{5}$$

where A is a set of normalized non-dominated objective vectors that are obtained for a task T_i by the algorithm, P^* is the set of uniformly distributed normalized objective vectors over the PF of T_i, and $d(\mathbf{x}, \mathbf{y})$ is the Euclidean distance between $\mathbf{x}$ and $\mathbf{y}$ in the normalized objective space.

If $|P^*|$ is large enough to represent the PF, the $\text{IGD}(A, P^*)$ can measure both convergence and diversity of A to an extent.

To illustrate the convergence speed of an algorithm, the convergence curve are plotted to describe the trend of IGD values over the number of generations.

5.4 Experimental Results and Discussions

Table 1 summarized the performances of the vanilla MFEA, MFEA/D-M2M and MFEA/D-M2M-SVM on nine benchmark problem sets, in terms of average IGD values over 30 independent runs.

Table 1. Average IGD values of MFEA, MFEA/D-M2M and MFEA/D-M2M-SVM

ProblemSet-Task	MFEA	MFEA/D-M2M	MFEA/D-M2M-SVM
CIHS-T1	4.2878E−04	1.8083E−04	**1.7815E−04**
CIHS-T2	2.7627E−03	**4.9795E−04**	5.1315E−04
CIMS-T1	4.9917E−02	1.9344E−04	**1.8137E−04**
CIMS-T2	8.4888E−03	2.5233E−04	**1.9776E−04**
CILS-T1	2.6345E−04	2.5940E−04	**2.5197E−04**
CILS-T2	1.8532E−04	1.8741E−04	**1.8275E−04**
PIHS-T1	9.9586E−04	1.0479E−03	**9.8242E−04**
PIHS-T2	**3.5382E−02**	6.6400E−02	4.5432E−02
PIMS-T1	**2.9505E−03**	3.4824E−03	4.0440E−03
PIMS-T2	**9.7286E+00**	1.4166E+01	1.3686E+01
PILS-T1	**3.3238E−04**	3.6724E−04	3.5442E−04
PILS-T2	**1.0814E−02**	1.0777E−02	1.1155E−02
NIHS-T1	1.5552E+00	1.4929E+00	**1.4925E+00**
NIHS-T2	4.9591E−04	2.4923E−04	**2.4837E−04**
NIMS-T1	3.3532E−01	**1.5402E−01**	1.5517E−01
NIMS-T2	3.4444E−02	6.9613E−04	**3.0415E−04**
NILS-T1	8.3985E−04	8.9249E−04	**8.6783E−04**
NILS-T2	6.4326E−01	6.4782E−01	**6.4183E−01**

In Table 1, both MFEA/D-M2M and MFEA/D-M2M-SVM have achieve better performances on six problem sets, which are problem sets with complete or no intersection of global optimal. On the other problem sets with partial intersection, the proposed algorithms have achieved comparable result than the vanilla MFEA.

Table 2 shows the h-value (h) and p-value (p) from the T-test of IGD values among MFEA and MFEA/D-M2M-SVM. The significancy level of the T-test is set as 0.05.

Table 2. T-test values of IGD among MFEA and MFEA/D-M2M-SVM

	h	p		h	p		h	p
CIHS-T1	1	1.1633E−13	PIHS-T1	0	7.0901E−01	NIHS-T1	1	8.3695E−16
CIHS-T2	1	9.9410E−21	PIHS-T2	1	4.8330E−04	NIHS-T2	1	9.3051E−14
CIMS-T1	1	2.9975E−04	PIMS-T1	0	7.8677E−02	NIMS-T1	1	1.5667E−03
CIMS-T2	1	2.8867E−03	PIMS-T2	1	3.5863E−05	NIMS-T2	1	9.0970E−03
CILS-T1	0	1.3100E−01	PILS-T1	0	2.8317E−01	NILS-T1	0	1.2037E−01
CILS-T2	1	1.0446E−02	PILS-T2	0	9.4582E−01	NILS-T2	1	2.0513E−21

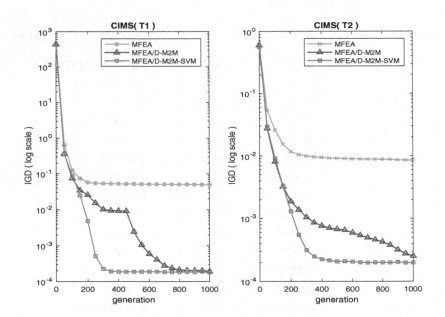

Fig. 3. Convergence curves on CIMS

On problem sets with complete intersection or no intersection of global optimal, such as in Figs. 3 and 4, MFEA/D-M2M and MFEA/D-M2M-SVM achieve better IGD convergence speed and average IGD values than the vanilla MFEA at the end of evolution. Especially in Fig. 3, MFEA/D-M2M-SVM outperforms both MFEA/D-M2M and MFEA in terms of both average IGD value and convergence speed.

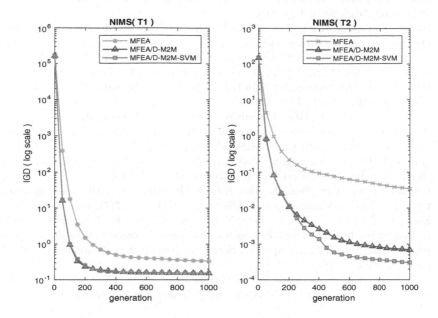

Fig. 4. Convergence curves on NIMS

6   Conclusions

This paper proposes a M2M decomposition based multi-factorial evolutionary algorithm for solving CEC2017 MFO Benchmark problems. The MFEA/D-M2M adopts the M2M approach to decompose multi-objective optimization problems into multiple constrained sub-problems to enhance the diversity of population and convergence of sub-regions. A SVM augmented version is also implemented to improve its performance. The experimental results demonstrate that the proposed algorithms have achieved better performance on both problem sets with complete intersection and no intersection of global optimal, and comparable results on the other three problem sets. The future work includes studying the decomposition approach in MFEAs and solving several real-world optimization problems to further demonstrate the effectiveness of MFEA/D-M2M.

References

1. Yuan, Y., Ong, Y.-S., Feng, L., Qin, A.K., Gupta, A., Da, B., Zhang, Q., Tan, K.C., Jin, Y., Ishibuchi, H.: Evolutionary multitasking for multi-objective continuous optimization: benchmark problems, performance metrics and baseline results. Technical report, Nanyang Technological University (2016)

2. Back, T., Hammel, U., Schwefel, H.-P.: Evolutionary computation: comments on the history and current state. IEEE Trans. Evol. Comput. **1**(1), 3–17 (1997)
3. Gupta, A., Ong, Y.-S., Da, B., Feng, L., Handoko, S.D.: Landscape synergy in evolutionary multitasking. In: 2016 IEEE Congress on Evolutionary Computation (CEC), pp. 3076–3083, July 2016
4. Da, B., Gupta, A., Ong, Y.-S., Feng, L.: Evolutionary multitasking across single and multi-objective formulations for improved problem solving. In: 2016 IEEE Congress on Evolutionary Computation (CEC), pp. 1695–1701. IEEE (2016)
5. Gupta, A., Ong, Y.-S., Da, B., Feng, L., Handoko, S.D.: Landscape synergy in evolutionary multitasking. In: 2016 IEEE Congress on Evolutionary Computation (CEC), pp. 3076–3083. IEEE (2016)
6. Gupta, A., Ong, Y.-S.: Genetic transfer or population diversification? Deciphering the secret ingredients of evolutionary multitask optimization. In: IEEE Symposium Series on Computational Intelligence (SSCI), pp. 1–7 (2016)
7. Gupta, A., Ong, Y.-S., Feng, L.: Multifactorial evolution: toward evolutionary multitasking. IEEE Trans. Evol. Comput. **20**(3), 343–357 (2016)
8. Gupta, A., Ong, Y.-S., Feng, L., Tan, K.C.: Multiobjective multifactorial optimization in evolutionary multitasking. IEEE Trans. Cybern. **47**(7), 1652–1665 (2017)
9. Zhou, L., Feng, L., Zhong, J., Ong, Y.-S., Zhu, Z., Sha, E.: Evolutionary multitasking in combinatorial search spaces: a case study in capacitated vehicle routing problem. In: 2016 IEEE Symposium Series on Computational Intelligence (SSCI), pp. 1–8. IEEE (2016)
10. Deb, K., Pratap, A., Agarwal, S., Meyarivan, T.A.M.T.: A fast and elitist multiobjective genetic algorithm: NSGA-II. IEEE Trans. Evol. Comput. **6**(2), 182–197 (2002)
11. Ong, Y.-S., Gupta, A.: Evolutionary multitasking: a computer science view of cognitive multitasking. Cogn. Comput. **8**(2), 125–142 (2016)
12. Agrawal, R.B., Deb, K., Agrawal, R.B.: Simulated binary crossover for continuous search space. Complex Syst. **9**(2), 115–148 (1995)
13. Liu, H.-L., Gu, F., Zhang, Q.: Decomposition of a multiobjective optimization problem into a number of simple multiobjective subproblems. IEEE Trans. Evol. Comput. **18**(3), 450–455 (2014)
14. Lin, X., Zhang, Q., Kwong, S.: A decomposition based multiobjective evolutionary algorithm with classification. In: 2016 IEEE Congress on Evolutionary Computation (CEC), pp. 3292–3299. IEEE (2016)
15. Da, B., Ong, Y.-S., Feng, L., Qin, A.K., Gupta, A., Zhu, Z., Ting, C.-K., Tang, K., Yao, X.: Evolutionary multitasking for single-objective continuous optimization: benchmark problems, performance metric, and baseline results. Nanyang Technological University, Singapore, Technical report (2016)
16. Van Veldhuizen, D.A., Lamont, G.B.: Multiobjective evolutionary algorithm research: a history and analysis. Technical report, Citeseer (1998)

An Efficient Local Search Algorithm for Minimum Weighted Vertex Cover on Massive Graphs

Yuanjie Li[1,2], Shaowei Cai[1,2(✉)], and Wenying Hou[3]

[1] State Key Laboratory of Computer Science, Institute of Software,
Chinese Academy of Sciences, Beijing, China
{liyj,caisw}@ios.ac.cn
[2] School of Computer and Control Engineering,
University of Chinese Academy of Sciences, Beijing, China
[3] School of Information Technology and Management,
University of International Business and Economics, Beijing, China
houwyvenny@126.com

Abstract. The minimum weighted vertex cover (MWVC) problem is a well known NP-hard problem with various real-world applications. In this paper, we design an efficient algorithm named FastWVC to solve MWVC problem in massive graphs. Two strategies are proposed. One is the *ConstructWVC* procedure, aiming to generate a quality initial vertex cover. The other is a new exchange step for reconstructing a vertex cover. Experiments on 102 instances were conducted to confirm the effectiveness of our algorithm. The results show that the FastWVC algorithm outperforms other algorithms in terms of both solution quality and computational time in most of the instances.

Keywords: Minimum weighted vertex cover · Local search · Massive graph

1 Introduction

The minimum vertex cover (MVC) problem is to find a minimum sized vertex cover in a graph, where a vertex cover is a subset of vertices that contains at least one endpoint of each edge. The minimum weighted vertex cover (MWVC) problem is a generalization of MVC. Each vertex in the MWVC problem has a positive weight and the purpose of the MWVC problem is to find a vertex cover with the minimum weight. The MWVC problem has applications in real-world problems such as network flow, circuit design, transportation and telecommunication.

The MVC problem is NP hard. Moreover, it is NP-hard to approximate MVC within any factors smaller than 1.3606 [7]. Due to the computational intractability of the MVC problem, various heuristic algorithms have been proposed to find approximate solutions within reasonable time. Among them, the most successful ones share the same method called local search, which moves from solution to

© Springer International Publishing AG 2017
Y. Shi et al. (Eds.): SEAL 2017, LNCS 10593, pp. 145–157, 2017.
https://doi.org/10.1007/978-3-319-68759-9_13

solution based on the iterative use of certain criterion until a deemed optimal solution is found or a time bound is elapsed. Typical local search algorithms for MVC include COVER [13], EWLS [3], EWCC [5] and NuMVC [4]. Particularly, NuMVC made a significant improvement on solving the popular DIMACS and BHOSLIB benchmarks. Its main ideas include two-stage exchange step and the forgetting mechanism for edge weighting, as well as the configuration checking strategy. However, all these algorithms are designed for small graphs, and they may fail to perform well on massive graphs. Therefore, some researchers have been working on algorithms that are tailored to massive graphs. The most representative one is FastVC algorithm [2]. It uses a fast heuristic for constructing a vertex cover and a cost-effective heuristic for choosing the vertex. Since the introduction of FastVC, several algorithms have been proposed for solving MVC on large graphs [9,11,12].

Research on MWVC problem is relatively less, which may be due to the fact that MWVC is more complicated than MVC. Most works on MWVC are also focused on heuristic algorithms. In [6], a greedy algorithm was used to find a feasible solution. A population-based iterated greedy algorithm was proposed in [1], which refines a population of solutions at each iteration. Ant colony optimization was also used to get a quality approximate solution [8,15]. In [16], the authors proposed an algorithm which combined genetic algorithms and greedy heuristic. Recently, a tabu algorithm named Multi-Start Iterated Tabu Search algorithm (MS-ITS) [17] achieved state-of-the-art performance on a broad range of benchmarks. As for solving MWVC on massive graphs, a recent algorithm named Diversion Local Search based on Weighted Configuration Checking (DLSWCC) [10] has made a significant improvement and is the best in this direction as far as we know. DLSWCC combines the Weighted Configuration Checking (WCC) strategy with the dynamic scoring strategy.

The direction of solving MWVC on massive graphs calls for more efficient algorithms. Several shortcomings exist in existing algorithms. First, when constructing the initial vertex cover, they either utilize greedy strategy or random strategy to get one initial vertex cover [10,17]. This initial vertex cover may be far from the optimal solution, taking the search process much time to move closer to the final solution. Second, when moving to the next vertex cover in each exchange step, most of them choose to remove just one vertex from the candidate solution and then reconstruct the candidate solution to a vertex cover. However, the number of uncovered edges resulted by removing just one vertex from the candidate solution may be too small, making the search range in the search phase narrow.

To address the shortcomings mentioned above, we propose two strategies. The first one called *ConstructWVC* is an improved version of *ConstructVC* procedure proposed in FastVC [2]. According to it, we construct several vertex covers in the first phase, and then choose the best one, which is then shrunk by removing redundant vertices. The intention of this strategy is to take the advantage of the low complexity of the construction process to get a competitive initial candidate solution.

The second strategy is a new exchange step for reconstructing a vertex cover. In the beginning of each step, C is a vertex cover, and the algorithm moves to a new vertex cover by removing two vertices from C and continuously adding vertices until C becomes a vertex cover again. The first removed vertex is selected based on greedy mechanism and the second is based on a less greedy strategy with tabu mechanism.

Based on these techniques, we develop a new local search algorithm named FastWVC for MWVC. We conducted an extensive experiment study on a large range of benchmarks, covering a variety of fields such as biological networks, collaboration networks, social networks. We compare FastWVC algorithm with state-of-the-art algorithms including MS-ITS and DLSWCC. The results show that FastWVC algorithm outperforms them on more than two thirds of the benchmark graphs.

The reminder of this paper is organized as follows: Sect. 2 presents some preliminaries related with the MWVC problem. Then our proposed FastWVC algorithm is introduced in Sect. 3. Section 4 explains our three main ideas. Detailed description of our FastWVC algorithm is showed in Sect. 5. Section 6 presents the empirical results. Finally, Sect. 7 gives our conclusions and future works.

2   Preliminaries

In this section, we introduce some basic definitions and background knowledge. Then, we also introduce the popular techniques that will be used in our algorithm.

2.1   Basic Definitions

Given an undirected weighted graph $G = (V, E, w)$, V is the vertex set of G, E is the edge set of G, and $w(v) \geqslant 0$ is the weight of vertex v. Each edge $e = (u, v)$ consists of two vertices u and v, we say u and v are the endpoints of edge e. Two vertices are neighbors of each other if they belong to a same edge, and we use $N(v) = \{u \in V | (u, v) \in E\}$ to denote all neighbors of v. A *candidate solution*, denoted as C , is a subset of V, and we say it covers an edge e if it contains at least one endpoint of e. A vertex cover is a special *candidate solution* which covers all $e \in E$. For convenience, we use C^* to denote the current best solution. Further, we use $s_v = \{1, 0\}$ to denote the state of a vertex. If $v \in C$, then $s_v = 1$, otherwise, $s_v = 0$. The number of steps happened since v last changed its state is denoted by $age[v]$.

We use $w(C)$ to denote the total weight of vertices in C, i.e.,

$$w(C) = \sum_{v \in V} s_v \cdot w(v) = \sum_{v \in C} w(v). \tag{1}$$

The MWVC problem is to find a vertex cover C^* such that $w(C^*)$ is minimum.

For local search algorithms adopting edge weighting mechanism, we use a weighting function *edge_w* and each edge $e \in E$ is associated with a positive number $edge\_w(e)$ as its weight. The cost of C denoted by $cost(C)$ means the total weight of edges uncovered by C, which can be formally defined as

$$cost(C) = \sum_{e \in E \text{ and } e \text{ is uncovered by } C} edge\_w(e). \qquad (2)$$

We denote the change on $cost$ caused by changing the state of a vertex v as $dscore(v)$. Formally, we define $dscore$ as

$$dscore = cost(C) - cost(C'), \qquad (3)$$

where C' is the candidate solution after changing the state of v, that is, if $v \in C$, $C' = C \backslash \{v\}$, otherwise $C' = C \cup \{v\}$. Note that $dscore(v) \geqslant 0$ if $v \notin C$ and $dscore(v) \leqslant 0$ when $v \in C$.

In local search algorithms for MWVC, usually a scoring function that considers both vertex weights and the cost is employed. For example, in DLSWCC [10], such a function is defined as follow

$$score(v) = \frac{dscore(v)}{w(v)}. \qquad (4)$$

In this paper, we use two conceptions, namely *gain* and *loss*, which are easier to understand and more clear when explaining the algorithm. They are actually modified versions of *score*, and are used as criteria to choose a vertex to add into or remove from C respectively. Here are the formal definitions:

$$gain(v) = \frac{dscore(v)}{w(v)}. \qquad (5)$$

$$loss(v) = \frac{|dscore(v)|}{w(v)}. \qquad (6)$$

Note that only vertices in $V \backslash C$ have *gain* values and vertices in C have *loss* values.

2.2 Configuration Checking

The Configuration Checking (*CC*) strategy, first proposed in [5], is a strategy aiming to solve the cycling problem. The cycling problem refers to revisiting the same vertices that have been visited recently. It is a main issue for local search algorithms. The *CC* strategy has been successfully applied to local search algorithms for MVC and MWVC, greatly improving the performance of these algorithms. It maintains a boolean array *confChange* for vertices, each vertex $v \in V$ has a configuration value *confChange*[v]. The *confChange* array is maintained by the following rules:

Rule 1: For each $v \in V$, *confChange*[v] is initialized as 1.
Rule 2: When removing v from C, *confChange*[v] is set to 0; for each $u \in N(v)$, *confChange*[u] is set to 1.
Rule 3: When adding v into C, for each $u \in N(v)$, *confChange*[u] is set to 1.

$confChange[v] = 0$ implies the state of $N(v)$ has not changed since v's last removing from C, which indicates the circumstance of v is stable and thus v should not be added back to C, while $confChange[v] = 1$ on the contrary. We adopt this strategy in our algorithm, when adding vertex into C, we only choose from vertices whose $confChange$ values are 1.

A variant of CC strategy is called Weighted Configuration Checking (WCC). We adopt the WCC strategy in our algorithm. It considers the circumstance of a vertex as two parts, one is the state of its neighbors, and the other is the state of its incident edges. Specifically, apart from the three rules above, it adds a new rule:

Rule 4: When updating $edge\_w[e]$, $confChange[u]$ and $confChange[v]$ are set to 1, where u and v are the endpoints of edge e.

2.3 Tabu Search

Tabu search is a meta-heuristic search method that uses memory structures to avoid cycling problem of local search. It prevents the search process from reversing a recent change. Our algorithm uses tabu technique in vertex selection phase by maintaining an array called *tabu list*. If a vertex has just been added into C in the most recent step, it is added into the *tabu list*, and vertices in *tabu list* cannot be considered when choosing vertex to remove from C.

3 Framework

This section describes the general framework of the FastWVC algorithm. Detailed description and analysis will be presented in Sect. 5.

Algorithm 1. FastWVC

Input: An undirected graph $G = (V, E)$, the *cutoff* time
Output: A minimum weighted vertex cover of G
1 **begin**
2     $C \leftarrow ConstructWVC()$;
3     $C^* \leftarrow C$;
4   **while** *elapsed_time* < *cutoff* **do**
5   remove two vertices from C;
6   **while** *there exist edge uncovered by C* **do**
7   add a vertex into C;
8   remove redundant vertices from C;
9   **if** $w(C) < w(C^*)$ **then**
10           $C^* \leftarrow C$;
11   **return** C^*;

At the beginning, an initial vertex cover C is constructed by function $ConstructWVC$. It produces a vertex cover as the initial solution. Then the algorithm repeats the main loop until reaching time limit. In each step, the algorithm firstly removes two vertices, according to two different strategies. After that, the algorithm reconstructs a vertex cover by continuously adding vertices into C until C covers all edges again. Each time a new vertex is added, $confChange$, $tabu$ and edge weights are updated accordingly. Finally, redundant vertices whose $loss$ is 0 are removed from C. If the obtained solution C is better than C^*, C^* is updated to C.

4   Main Ideas

4.1   ConstructWVC

In this section, we introduce the $ConstructWVC$ procedure utilized by the Fast-WVC algorithm to generate an initial vertex cover.

To design a fast vertex cover construction procedure for massive graphs, a procedure called $ConstructVC$ was proposed and used in FastVC [2]. The $ConstructVC$ procedure has an extending phase and a shrinking phase. In the extending phase, it traverses all edges, if the edge being checked is uncovered, the endpoint with a higher degree will be added into C. In the shrinking phase, once it finds a vertex in C, removing which from C will not make C an infeasible solution, it will remove it. The time complexity is confirmed to be $O(m)$, where m is the number of edges.

Based on the idea of $ConstructVC$ procedure, we proposed an extended version named $ConstructWVC$ for MWVC problem, which is outlined below.

The $ConstructWVC$ procedure consists of two phases: a repeated extending phase and a shrinking phase. In the repeated extending phase, a vertex cover is first generated utilizing the same method in the extending phase of $ConstructVC$ (line 3–5). Then, the algorithm utilizes a random strategy to generate vertex covers for max_tries times, each time if the vertex cover generated is better than the current solution, the current solution will be updated accordingly. More specifically, starting with an empty set C' (line 7), while there are uncovered edges in E, the algorithm randomly chooses an uncovered edge e and puts the endpoint of e which has a higher $degree(v)/w(v)$ into C' (line 8–10). If C' is better than C, than updates C to C' (line 11–12). In the shrinking phase, the algorithm removes redundant vertices from C, which is accomplished with the help of an array denoted as $value$, where $value(v)$ measures the number of edges that will change from covered to uncovered after removing v from C. For each $v \in C$, the algorithm removes a vertex v if its $value$ is 0 and then updates $value(u)$ for each $u \in N(v)$ accordingly (line 17–20).

The difference between $ConstructVC$ and $ConstructWVC$ is in the extending phase, where the former constructs one vertex cover as the initial solution but the latter constructs multiple vertex covers and chooses the best one. There are two reasons we make this modification. Firstly, it takes little time to construct more vertex covers. Secondly, the initial solution constructed only once cannot

---

Algorithm 2. ConstructWVC

Input: An undirected graph $G = (V, E)$, max_tries
Output: A weighted vertex cover of G

1 **begin**
2 $\quad$ $C \leftarrow \varnothing$;
3 $\quad$ **foreach** $e \in E$ **do**
4 $\quad\quad$ **if** *both endpoints of e are not in C* **then**
5 $\quad\quad\quad$ put the endpoint with larger $degree(v)/w(v)$ into C;

6 $\quad$ **for** $tries \leftarrow 0$; $tries < max\_tries$; $tries \leftarrow tries + 1$ **do**
7 $\quad\quad$ $C' \leftarrow \varnothing$;
8 $\quad\quad$ **foreach** *uncovered* $e \in E$ *(in a random order)* **do**
9 $\quad\quad\quad$ **if** *both endpoints of e are not in C* **then**
10 $\quad\quad\quad\quad$ put the endpoint with larger $degree(v)/w(v)$ into C';

11 $\quad\quad$ **if** C' *is better than* C **then**
12 $\quad\quad\quad$ $C \leftarrow C'$;

13 $\quad$ $value(v) \leftarrow 0$, for each $v \in C$;
14 $\quad$ **foreach** $e \in E$ **do**
15 $\quad\quad$ **if** *only one endpoint v of e belongs to C* **then**
16 $\quad\quad\quad$ $value(v) \leftarrow value(v) + 1$;

17 $\quad$ **foreach** $v \in C$ **do**
18 $\quad\quad$ **if** $value(v) = 0$ **then**
19 $\quad\quad\quad$ $C \leftarrow C \setminus \{v\}$;
20 $\quad\quad\quad$ $value(u) \leftarrow value(u) + 1$ for each $u \in N(v)$;

21 $\quad$ **return** C;

---

guarantee a good quality. It may be far away from the final solution, taking the search process more time to move closer to the optimal solution. Comparatively, the initial solution constructed by *ConstructWVC* can guarantee a competitive one.

4.2   A New Exchange Step

We propose a new exchange step for our algorithm. In each step, the algorithm tries to seek for another feasible solution by removing two vertices from C and reconstructing C. Different from some of the state-of-the-art algorithms, we remove two vertices from C in this process rather than just one vertex. We choose the first removing vertex greedily and choose the second removing vertex based on a balanced strategy. More specifically, a vertex with the minimum *loss* is firstly removed, making C an infeasible solution. Then one more vertex is selected to removed by the BMS (Best from Multiple Selections) heuristic [2] and the *tabu* mechanism. In detail, the algorithm chooses t (a parameter) vertices from C, and then selects the one not belonging to *tabu list* and with the minimum *loss*. After removing the two vertices, the algorithm continually adds vertices into C until it covers all edges.

Previous local search algorithms for MWVC only removes one vertex from C in each step, and the number of uncovered edges may be limited, especially for sparse graphs such as most massive graphs in real world, making the search range narrower. The purpose we suggest to remove two vertices at each step is to produce more uncovered edges in the removing phase so that more vertices will be considered in the adding phase, making the search range wider and the search process more efficient.

5   The FastWVC Algorithm

In this section, we present the FastWVC algorithm and give a detailed description.

Our algorithm is outlined in Algorithm 3, as described below. The initial solution C is constructed by $ConstructWVC$. The best found solution C^* is initialized as C. $edge\_w(e)$ is set to 1 for each $e \in E$, $confChange(v)$ is set to 1 for each $v \in V$ and then *gain* of vertices in $V \setminus C$ and and *loss* of vertices in C are calculated respectively. Finally, the *tabu list* is set empty.

After the initialization, the algorithm begins a search process of iteratively updating C and C^* until the time bound is elapsed. At the end of each step, if a better solution is found, the best found solution C^* is updated accordingly (lines 23–24).

Each step of the process consists of two phases, one is the vertex removing phase (line 9–15), where C becomes an infeasible solution, and the other is a vertex adding phase (line 16–22), where C is reconstructed to a feasible solution. In the vertex removing phase, the algorithm first removes a vertex from C with the minimum *loss*, note that after this removing, *loss* of vertices are updated accordingly. Next, it removes one more vertex u according to BMS strategy [2], which chooses t (=50 in this work) vertices from C and chooses the one not belonging to *tabu list* and with the minimum *loss*. After each remove, the *confChange* values are updated according to the CC Rules introduced in Sect. 2.

In the vertex adding phase, a loop is executed until C becomes a vertex cover again. In each iteration, the algorithm scans all vertices in $V \setminus C$, chooses a vertex v such that *confChange* is 1 and the *gain* is the largest, breaking ties by preferring the oldest one. Then v is added into C and also *Tabu list*. After that, weights of all uncovered edges are increased by 1. The *confChange* values are updated according to the CC Rules.

Finally, redundant vertices (i.e., those vertices for which *loss* is 0) are removed from C, in a similar way as in $ConstructWVC$, to make C become a minimal vertex cover. If the obtained solution C is better than C^*, update C^* to C.

Algorithm 3. FastWVC

Input: An undirected graph $G = (V, E)$, the *cutoff* time
Output: A minimum weighted vertex cover of G

1 **begin**
2      $C \leftarrow ConstructWVC()$;
3      $C^* \leftarrow C$;
4   for each $e \in E$, $edge\_w(e) \leftarrow 1$;
5   for each $v \in V$, $confChange(v) \leftarrow 1$;
6   calculate *gain* and *loss* of vertices;
7      $tabulist \leftarrow \varnothing$;
8   **while** *elapsed_time* < *cutoff* **do**
9   choose a vertex w with minimum *loss* from C, breaking ties in favor of the oldest one;
10         $C \leftarrow C \setminus \{w\}$;
11         $confChange(w) \leftarrow 0$, $confChange(z) \leftarrow 1$ for each vertex $z \in N(w)$;
12   choose a vertex u with $tabulist[u] = 0$ from C according to *BMS* strategy, breaking ties in favor of the oldest one;
13         $C \leftarrow C \setminus \{u\}$;
14         $confChange(u) \leftarrow 0$, $confChange(z) \leftarrow 1$ for each vertex $z \in N(u)$;
15         $tabulist \leftarrow \varnothing$;
16   **while** *some edge is uncovered by C* **do**
17   choose a vertex v, whose $confChange(v) = 1$, with maximum *gain* from $V \setminus C$, breaking ties in favor of the oldest one;
18             $C \leftarrow C \cup \{v\}$;
19             $tabulist \leftarrow tabulist \cup \{v\}$;
20             $confChange(z) \leftarrow 1$ for each vertex $z \in N(v)$;
21             $w(e) \leftarrow w(e) + 1$ for each uncovered edge e, and for its endpoints (x, y), $confChange(x) \leftarrow 1$ and $confChange(y) \leftarrow 1$;
22   remove redundant vertices from C;
23   **if** $w(C) < w(C^*)$ **then**
24             $C^* \leftarrow C$;
25   **return** C^*;

---

6 Empirical Results

In this section, we present the experimental results. We compare FastWVC with state-of-the-art algorithms, and show that that our algorithm has better performance.

6.1 Benchmark Instances

All the instances we use in our experiments are obtained from Network Data Repository [14], including different types of real-life graphs, which can be categorized into biological networks, collaboration networks, interaction networks, infrastructure networks, massive network data, facebook networks, technological networks, web graphs, scientific networks, retweet networks and recommendation networks. Within all the instances, the number of vertices varies from about 30 to 60 million and the number of edges takes value from about 80 to 100 million. The weight of each vertex is assigned to a value from [20,100] uniformly at random, as with the generation method adopted in testing DLSWCC [10].

6.2 Experimental Protocol

Here we present some preliminaries about our experiments.

Implementation: FastWVC is implemented in C++, the MS-ITS and DLSWCC are implemented in C by their authors. FastWVC has two parameters: the *max_tries* parameter for *ConstructWVC* and the *t* parameter for the *BMS* heuristic when choosing the second removing vertex, and both of them are set to 50, according to our preliminary experiments. Note that both MS-ITS and DLSWCC also have parameters. We compile these solvers by the g++ compiler with the 'O3' option.

Computing Platform: All experiments are run on a 4-way Intel Xeon E7-8850 v2 @ 2.30 GHz CPU with 1 TB RAM server under CentOS 7.2.

Result Reporting Methodology: Each algorithm is executed on each instance 10 times independently within the cutoff time. The cutoff time is set to 1000 s, which means each run will be terminated if 1000 s is reached. We report the following information: the average weight of the solutions found in all runs ("w(avg)"); the minimum weight among the solutions found in all runs ("w(min)"); and the average run-time to find the best found solution over all successful runs ("time"). If an algorithm failed to find a solution for an instance within the cutoff time, we marked it by "*N/A*".

6.3 Comparison with State-of-the-art Algorithms

We compare FastWVC with the most successful algorithms for solving MWVC, including MS-ITS [17] and DLSWCC [10]. The results are shown in Tables 1 and 2.

Although MS-ITS algorithm was effective on three types of instances: SPI, MPI, LPI [17], which means small-scale, middle-scale and large-scale instances, as reported in [10], MS-ITS failed on many massive graphs. Also, since we can only obtain the executable binary but not codes of MS-ITS, we could not set up the cutoff time. So the results for MS-ITS are not under the cutoff time in our experiments. DLSWCC algorithm performs much better than MS-ITS, but also failed to find a solution for some instances within the cutoff time. FastWVC successfully solved all the instances and outperformed the other two algorithms

Table 1. Experiment results on massive graphs.

instance	|V|	|E|	MS-ITS w(avg)	w(min)	time	DLSWCC w(avg)	w(min)	time	FastWVC w(avg)	w(min)	time
bio-celegans	453	2025	13767.0	13767	0.54	13767.0	13767	0.09	13767.0	13767	0.05
bio-diseasome	516	1188	15096.0	15096	0.05	15096.0	15096	0.07	15096.0	15096	0.05
bio-dmela	7393	25569	147949.0	147876	2636.45	147258.8	147210	91.60	147233.7	147228	78.31
bio-yeast	1458	1948	24530.5	24517	16.50	24498.9	24495	1.80	24495.0	24495	0.54
ca-AstroPh	17903	196972	654825.5	654523	7587.39	645016.3	644786	297.96	643111.9	643098	652.19
ca-citeseer	227320	814134	N/A	N/A	N/A	7040764.7	7040526	481.55	7072174.2	7071275	33.05
ca-coauthors-dblp	540486	15245729	N/A	N/A	N/A	N/A	N/A	N/A	27178701.2	27177143	152.45
ca-CondMat	21363	91286	699684.5	699396	15395.41	682003.8	681640	369.07	679193.5	679176	455.49
ca-CSphd	1882	1740	29574.0	29562	8.26	29497.0	29497	4.84	29497.0	29497	1.12
ca-dblp-2010	226413	716460	N/A	N/A	N/A	6632925.4	6632625	351.23	6649380.4	6625143	602.32
ca-dblp-2012	317080	1049866	N/A	N/A	N/A	8980245.9	8979954	819.82	9030774.0	9029616	22.95
ca-Erdos992	6100	7515	26945.0	26945	4.34	26945.0	26945	0.08	26945.0	26945	0.04
ca-GrQc	4158	13422	121718.0	121676	350.75	121613.1	121567	62.36	121564.8	121563	379.93
ca-HepPh	11204	117619	369319.0	369191	4569.85	366828.7	366632	198.17	365496.6	365487	508.27
ca-hollywood-2009	1069126	56306653	N/A	N/A	N/A	N/A	N/A	N/A	49017602.0	49016625	816.33
ca-MathSciNet	332689	820644	N/A	N/A	N/A	7661455.3	7660999	569.05	7730475.5	7729148	73.05
ca-netscience	379	914	11570.0	11570	0.63	11551.0	11551	0.02	11551.0	11551	0.02
ia-email-EU	32430	54397	N/A	N/A	N/A	48447.0	48447	5.09	48447.0	48447	0.42
ia-email-univ	1133	5451	32670.0	32670	35.95	32666.0	32666	0.77	32666.0	32666	0.20
ia-enron-large	33696	180811	N/A	N/A	N/A	695879.5	695527	523.12	692234.1	692227	517.94
ia-enron-only	143	623	4827.0	4827	0.00	4827.0	4827	0.00	4827.0	4827	0.01
ia-fb-messages	1266	6451	32479.5	32476	22.96	32446.0	32446	0.96	32446.0	32446	0.57
ia-infect-dublin	410	2765	16291.0	16291	0.22	16289.0	16289	0.27	16289.0	16289	0.42
ia-infect-hyper	113	2196	5362.0	5362	0.00	5362.0	5362	0.00	5362.0	5362	0.01
ia-reality	6809	7680	4439.0	4439	5.33	4439.0	4439	0.02	4439.0	4439	0.03
ia-wiki-Talk	92117	360767	N/A	N/A	N/A	955588.5	955466	949.84	946170.7	946156	781.54
inf-power	4941	6594	121305.0	121258	443.45	120309.0	120286	75.15	120292.2	120289	142.82
inf-roadNet-CA	1957027	2760388	N/A	N/A	N/A	N/A	N/A	N/A	56947699.5	56922074	1000.00
inf-roadNet-PA	1087562	1541514	N/A	N/A	N/A	N/A	N/A	N/A	31486345.1	31481091	607.65
inf-road-usa	23947347	28854312	N/A	N/A	N/A	N/A	N/A	N/A	668627425.9	668594656	1000.00
rec-amazon	91813	125704	N/A	N/A	N/A	2624500.8	2623301	968.27	2575227.3	2574487	970.41
rt-retweet	96	117	1958.0	1958	0.00	1958.0	1958	0.00	1958.0	1958	0.00
rt-retweet-crawl	1112702	2278852	N/A	N/A	N/A	N/A	N/A	N/A	4734284.0	4732837	981.01
rt-twitter-copen	761	1029	12266.0	12266	1.92	12266.0	12266	0.08	12266.0	12266	0.02
sc-ldoor	952203	20770807	N/A	N/A	N/A	N/A	N/A	N/A	49551537.0	49550246	367.52
sc-msdoor	415863	9378650	N/A	N/A	N/A	N/A	N/A	N/A	22064239.4	22063493	116.37
sc-nasasrb	54870	1311227	N/A	N/A	N/A	2998914.7	2998286	753.58	2985056.9	2984150	931.11
sc-pkustk11	87804	2565054	N/A	N/A	N/A	N/A	N/A	N/A	4878352.1	4876622	918.93
sc-pkustk13	94893	3260967	N/A	N/A	N/A	N/A	N/A	N/A	5192638.6	5191545	956.30
sc-pwtk	217891	5653221	N/A	N/A	N/A	N/A	N/A	N/A	12155895.5	12151340	685.12
sc-shipsec1	140385	1707759	N/A	N/A	N/A	N/A	N/A	N/A	6790277.5	6786381	965.14
sc-shipsec5	179104	2200076	N/A	N/A	N/A	N/A	N/A	N/A	8484227.7	8477677	990.13
soc-BlogCatalog	88784	2093195	N/A	N/A	N/A	N/A	N/A	N/A	1180119.3	1180108	696.51
soc-brightkite	56739	212945	N/A	N/A	N/A	1178546.3	1177737	871.30	1165401.8	1165377	686.92
soc-buzznet	101163	2763066	N/A	N/A	N/A	N/A	N/A	N/A	1739422.9	1739328	812.02
soc-delicious	536108	1365961	N/A	N/A	N/A	N/A	N/A	N/A	4927118.5	4921290	985.50
soc-digg	770799	5907132	N/A	N/A	N/A	N/A	N/A	N/A	5976630.6	5967941	995.70
soc-dolphins	62	159	1835.0	1835	0.00	1835.0	1835	0.00	1835.9	1835	0.00
soc-douban	154908	327162	N/A	N/A	N/A	516117.5	516082	677.40	516082.0	516082	28.15
soc-epinions	26588	100120	N/A	N/A	N/A	542919.8	542653	390.81	538024.7	537998	268.18
soc-flickr	22900	852419	N/A	N/A	N/A	N/A	N/A	N/A	8706624.6	8705430	70.12
soc-flixster	2523386	7918801	N/A	N/A	N/A	N/A	N/A	N/A	5694379.4	5693856	978.16
soc-FourSquare	6621	249959	N/A	N/A	N/A	N/A	N/A	N/A	5282156.1	5281828	884.11
soc-gowalla	9885	506437	N/A	N/A	N/A	4736737.3	4736205	562.84	4703023.1	4682631	987.88
soc-karate	29732	1305757	864.0	864	0.00	864.0	864	0.00	864.0	864	0.00
soc-lastfm	6402	251230	N/A	N/A	N/A	N/A	N/A	N/A	4642613.3	4642497	868.12
soc-livejournal	4033137	27933062	N/A	N/A	N/A	N/A	N/A	N/A	108376264.8	108354007	1000.00
soc-LiveMocha	63392	816886	N/A	N/A	N/A	N/A	N/A	N/A	2462424.1	2462223	930.60
soc-orkut	2997166	106349209	N/A	N/A	N/A	N/A	N/A	N/A	128921417.8	128907034	1000.00
soc-pokec	1632803	22301964	N/A	N/A	N/A	N/A	N/A	N/A	50068176.5	50055454	1000.00
soc-slashdot	41536	1362220	N/A	N/A	N/A	1243175.0	1242765	962.49	1229005.1	1228968	743.47
soc-twitter-follows	11586	568309	N/A	N/A	N/A	138884.0	138884	204.59	138884.0	138884	4.24
soc-wiki-Vote	36364	1590651	22200.0	22192	1.38	22191.0	22191	0.83	22191.4	22191	0.02
soc-youtube	20453	747604	N/A	N/A	N/A	N/A	N/A	N/A	8200371.2	8160145	347.43
soc-youtube-snap	17206	604867	N/A	N/A	N/A	N/A	N/A	N/A	15418150.1	15416414	308.25

on about two thirds of the instances. In general, FastWVC is superior to MS-ITS and DLSWCC algorithms on massive graphs, in terms of both solution quality and computational time.

Table 2. Experiment results on massive graphs (continued).

instance	$|V|$	$|E|$	MS-ITS			DLSWCC			FastWVC		
			w(avg)	w(min)	time	w(avg)	w(min)	time	w(avg)	w(min)	time
socfb-A-anon	3097165	23667394	N/A	N/A	N/A	N/A	N/A	N/A	22291292.3	22236342	997.22
socfb-B-anon	2937612	20959854	N/A	N/A	N/A	N/A	N/A	N/A	17975652.3	17972088	884.16
socfb-Berkeley13	14917	482215	N/A	N/A	N/A	1005984.7	1005551	540.13	1003868.5	1003741	583.51
socfb-CMU	35111	1465654	292932.0	292668	2582.08	290384.3	290311	90.57	290266.2	290217	259.74
socfb-Duke14	30795	1264421	459599.0	459579	5816.58	448232.8	448123	186.93	447911.8	447841	342.78
socfb-Indiana	23831	835946	N/A	N/A	N/A	1369223.1	1368628	953.52	1366024.6	1365785	643.71
socfb-MIT	513969	3190452	271536.0	271482	2502.44	270051.7	269986	87.87	269880.7	269871	486.70
socfb-OR	639014	3214986	N/A	N/A	N/A	2106349.4	2105589	990.54	2084490.4	2084279	858.59
socfb-Penn94	196591	950327	N/A	N/A	N/A	1822006.8	1820549	986.39	1810689.2	1810396	773.28
socfb-Stanford3	34	78	509544.0	509513	16658.55	496945.3	496824	244.68	496657.9	496577	445.02
socfb-Texas84	1191805	4519330	N/A	N/A	N/A	1662664.4	1662115	960.25	1648625.6	1648374	775.23
socfb-uci-uni	58790782	92208195	N/A	N/A	N/A	N/A	N/A	N/A	51473502.1	51468147	906.37
socfb-UCLA	104103	2193083	912087.7	911569	24601.55	886016.5	885721	474.22	884333.8	884262	695.83
socfb-UConn	70068	358647	795207.8	794985	3437.90	774393.3	773807	336.91	773124.3	772903	372.64
socfb-UCSB37	404719	713319	676731.5	676264	14251.28	656378.0	656025	259.92	655418.8	655343	528.06
socfb-UF	889	2914	N/A	N/A	N/A	1604208.2	1603262	996.43	1595017.6	1594572	688.72
socfb-UIllinois	495957	1936748	N/A	N/A	N/A	1408412.3	1407508	951.50	1404889.3	1404688	682.22
socfb-Wisconsin87	1134890	2987624	N/A	N/A	N/A	1076534.7	1076027	539.39	1074010.9	1073751	542.03
tech-as-caida2007	26475	53381	N/A	N/A	N/A	199217.6	198996	235.71	198710.0	198710	257.29
tech-as-skitter	1694616	11094209	N/A	N/A	N/A	N/A	N/A	N/A	29910900.0	29888271	996.07
tech-internet-as	40164	85123	N/A	N/A	N/A	313540.9	313192	375.07	311624.0	311624	184.49
tech-p2p-gnutella	62561	147878	N/A	N/A	N/A	924581.4	924346	795.94	922570.8	922568	327.17
tech-RL-caida	190914	607610	N/A	N/A	N/A	4210338.6	4209563	271.58	4165235.0	4158849	990.57
tech-routers-rf	2113	6632	44546.5	44543	119.02	44499.5	44499	12.73	44496.0	44495	298.75
tech-WHOIS	7476	56943	126748.1	126740	3654.98	126528.5	126499	75.63	126501.1	126496	179.11
web-arabic-2005	163598	1747269	N/A	N/A	N/A	N/A	N/A	N/A	6606173.1	6600438	535.93
web-BerkStan	12305	19500	299224.8	298685	2496.48	289335.7	289132	193.46	288188.5	288172	384.51
web-edu	3031	6474	79244.6	79221	147.78	78828.6	78801	21.75	78749.8	78744	186.19
web-google	1299	2773	27302.0	27302	3.24	27302.0	27302	0.78	27302.0	27302	0.11
web-indochina-2004	11358	47606	403685.4	403612	2439.04	399835.8	399499	164.64	398649.1	398644	441.76
web-it-2004	509338	7178413	N/A	N/A	N/A	N/A	N/A	N/A	23825659.3	23824127	44.39
web-polblogs	643	2280	13129.4	13121	3.68	13107.0	13107	0.03	13107.0	13107	0.01
web-sk-2005	121422	334419	N/A	N/A	N/A	3140551.6	3140399	72.81	3127230.7	3127008	969.52
web-spam	4767	37375	130322.4	130287	1264.10	129958.1	129946	63.30	129952.2	129949	570.21
web-uk-2005	129632	11744049	N/A	N/A	N/A	N/A	N/A	N/A	7563202.4	7563135	246.36
web-webbase-2001	16062	25593	145889.5	145748	2063.89	144166.2	144052	135.15	143927.2	143922	42.46
web-wikipedia2009	1864433	4507315	N/A	N/A	N/A	N/A	N/A	N/A	36465150.1	36460676	675.95

7   Conclusions and Future Work

In this paper, we developed a new local search algorithm for MWVC problem called FastWVC, which works particularly well for massive graphs. A new construction procedure, namely *ConstructWVC*, was proposed to produce a competitive initial candidate solution. A new exchange step was introduced for making the search more effective on massive sparse graphs.

We carried out extensive experiments to compare FastWVC with state-of-the-art algorithms on a board range of benchmarks from real world networks. The results showed that FastWVC performs better on most of the instances. In the future, we would like to further improve the algorithm by low complexity strategies for large graphs.

Acknowledgement. This work is supported by National Natural Science Foundation of China 61502464. Shaowei Cai is also supported by Youth Innovation Promotion Association, Chinese Academy of Sciences.

References

1. Bouamama, S., Blum, C., Boukerram, A.: A population-based iterated greedy algorithm for the minimum weight vertex cover problem. Appl. Soft Comput. **12**, 1632–1639 (2012). Elsevier Science Publishers B. V

2. Cai, S.: Balance between complexity and quality: local search for minimum vertex cover in massive graphs. In: International Conference on Artificial Intelligence, pp. 747–753 (2015)
3. Cai, S., Su, K., Chen, Q.: EWLS: a new local search for minimum vertex cover. In: Twenty-Fourth AAAI Conference on Artificial Intelligence, AAAI 2010, Atlanta, Georgia, USA, July (2010)
4. Cai, S., Su, K., Luo, C., Sattar, A.: NuMVC: an efficient local search algorithm for minimum vertex cover. J. Artif. Intell. Res. **46**(1), 687–716 (2014)
5. Cai, S., Su, K., Sattar, A.: Local search with edge weighting and configuration checking heuristics for minimum vertex cover. Artif. Intell. **175**(9–10), 1672–1696 (2011)
6. Chvatal, V.: A greedy heuristic for the set-covering problem. Math. Oper. Res. **4**(3), 233–235 (1979)
7. Dinur, I., Safra, S.: On the hardness of approximating minimum vertex cover. Ann. Math. **162**(1), 439–485 (2005)
8. Jovanovic, R., Tuba, M.: An ant colony optimization algorithm with improved pheromone correction strategy for the minimum weight vertex cover problem. Appl. Soft Comput. **11**(8), 5360–5366 (2011)
9. Katzmann, M., Komusiewicz, C.: Systematic exploration of larger local search neighborhoods for the minimum vertex cover problem (2017)
10. Li, R., Hu, S., Zhang, H., Yin, M.: An efficient local search framework for the minimum weighted vertex cover problem. Inf. Sci. **372**, 428–445 (2016)
11. Ma, Z., Fan, Y., Su, K., Li, C., Sattar, A.: Local search with noisy strategy for minimum vertex cover in massive graphs. In: Booth, R., Zhang, M.-L. (eds.) PRICAI 2016. LNCS, vol. 9810, pp. 283–294. Springer, Cham (2016). doi:10.1007/978-3-319-42911-3_24
12. Ma, Z., Fan, Y., Su, K., Li, C., Sattar, A.: Random walk in large real-world graphs for finding smaller vertex cover. In: IEEE International Conference on TOOLS with Artificial Intelligence, pp. 686–690 (2016)
13. Richter, S., Helmert, M., Gretton, C.: A stochastic local search approach to vertex cover. In: Hertzberg, J., Beetz, M., Englert, R. (eds.) KI 2007. LNCS (LNAI), vol. 4667, pp. 412–426. Springer, Heidelberg (2007). doi:10.1007/978-3-540-74565-5_31
14. Rossi, R.A., Ahmed, N.K.: The network data repository with interactive graph analytics and visualization. In: Proceedings of the Twenty-Ninth AAAI Conference on Artificial Intelligence (2015). http://networkrepository.com
15. Shyu, S.J., Yin, P.Y., Lin, B.M.T.: An ant colony optimization algorithm for the minimum weight vertex cover problem. Ann. Oper. Res. **131**(1), 283–304 (2004)
16. Singh, A., Gupta, A.K.: A hybrid heuristic for the minimum weight vertex cover problem. Asia-Pac. J. Oper. Res. (APJOR) **23**(2), 273–285 (2011)
17. Zhou, T., Lü, Z., Wang, Y., Ding, J., Peng, B.: Multi-start iterated tabu search for the minimum weight vertex cover problem. J. Comb. Optim. **32**(2), 368–384 (2016)

Interactive Genetic Algorithm with Group Intelligence Articulated Possibilistic Condition Preference Model

Xiaoyan Sun[✉], Lixia Zhu, Lin Bao, Lian Liu, and Xin Nie

School of Information and Electrical Engineering, China University of Mining
and Technology, Xuzhou 221008, Jiangsu, People's Republic of China
xysun78@hotmail.com

Abstract. Interactive evolutionary computation assisted with surrogate models derived from the user's interactions is a feasible method for solving personalized search problems. However, in the initial stage, the estimation of the surrogates is very rough due to fewer interactions, which will mislead the search. Social group intelligence can be of great benefit to solve this problem. Besides, the evaluation uncertainty must be carefully treated. Motivated by this, we here propose an interactive genetic algorithm assisted with possibilistic conditional preference models by articulating group intelligence and the preference uncertainty. The valuable social group is determined according to the given keywords and historical searching of the current user. We respectively construct the possibilistic conditional preference models for the social group and the current user to approximate the corresponding uncertain preferences. We further enhance the current user's preference model by integrating the social one. Thus, the accuracy of the user's preference model is greatly improved, and the fitness estimation from the preference model is more reliable. The proposed algorithm is applied to the personalized search for books and the advantage in exploration is experimentally demonstrated.

Keywords: Interactive genetic algorithm · Social group intelligence · Uncertainty · Personalized search · Possibilistic conditional preference model

1   Introduction

Personalized search is ubiquitous in our daily life. For example, when we retrieve pictures in Google, the search engine will provide and recommend relevant information based on certain sorting criteria. The personalized search is intrinsically a combinatorial optimization when we view the items as the combinations of the attributes. However, the existing work seldom solves the problem using powerful optimization algorithms. It is a new trend of articulating evolutionary algorithms into personalized search. Chawla [1] proposed genetic algorithm based on clustered query sessions to effectively optimize

This work is supported by the National Natural Science Foundation of China with granted number 61473298.

web search. Sun et al. [2] presented interactions based interactive genetic algorithm (IGA) to directly solve the optimization, in which they constructed a conditional preference nets (CP-nets) based on user interactions and applied it to estimate the fitness of items, and then implemented genetic operators to help users quickly find satisfying solutions. These researches show that the combination of personalized search and evolutionary optimization algorithm can greatly improve the efficiency of search.

No matter integrating or not the evolutionary optimization in the personalized search, a user must be involved in the process. Therefore, the uncertainty in the evaluations caused by the user's uncertain preference should not be ignored. Furthermore, there are many researches [3–6] on the Interactive Evolutionary Computations (IECs) for Analyzing Human Characteristics and modeling User Preferences. In our previous work [7], we extracted the evaluation uncertainty according to the behaviour of user interactions and expressed it with a possibilistic conditional preference network (PCP-net). In such an expression, the dependencies of the variables, the user's preference on the variables and the uncertainty are all covered; therefore, we here will also adopt this model as a preference description with evaluation uncertainties.

Even IECs have improved the performance of personalized search, the deficiencies of IECs, e.g., user fatigue, evaluation uncertainties, and small population size, will inevitably limit the effectiveness of the personalized search. The domain knowledge of the personalized search has not been sufficiently explored and applied to enhance the optimization. Specifically, in the initial stage of IECs assisted personalized search, the user preference information is relatively sparse. The social intelligence or group interest on the searched items usually brings high influences on a user's selection, preference or decision. Therefore, exploring and integrating the social intelligence of the personalized search into IECs are of great significance. So we present a social group intelligence assisted IEC to improve the searching performance of personalized search.

The main work and contributions of our paper are as follows. First, based on the search keywords of the current user, the social group who has the similar interest with the current user is recognized. And the possibilistic conditional preference networks for the user and the social group are constructed. Then, the strategy of articulating the social PCP-net to adapt the user's PCP-net is presented. The estimation method for the individual's fitness is presented based on the PCP-net. In the evolutionary process, both the user's and the social group's preference network are updated.

The rest of this paper is organized as follows. Section 2 briefly introduces the framework and notation. Section 3 presents the description of the identification, expression and usage of similar group intelligence. Section 4 provides the implementation of interactive genetic algorithm based on the PCP-net and the estimation strategy of individual fitness. Section 5 illustrates the proposed algorithm in the experimental results. Finally, Sect. 6 summarizes the paper and derives conclusions with the scope of future extension of this work.

2 Framework and Notation

2.1 Framework

The framework of the algorithm shown in Fig. 1 includes three parts: (1) Identification of the group who has the similar preference to the current user. The input keywords and the historical searching of the current user are used to find the valuable social group. (2) Combination the user's possibilistic conditional preference network with the group. Considering the uncertainty of the evaluation and interaction, the preference model of the user's PCP-net is adapted according to the preference model of the group. (3) Interactive evolutionary optimization based on fitness estimation. The individual fitness of the evolutionary population is estimated with the enhanced PCP-net of the current user, and then the evolution is carried out to perform the search.

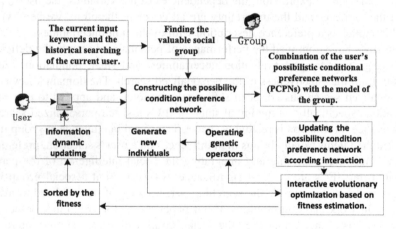

Fig. 1. Framework.

2.2 Notation

In the personalized search, an item is treated as a solution from the viewpoint of optimization. An item to be searched with K attributes (variables) is denoted as $A = \left\{X^1, X^2, \ldots, X^K\right\}$, and the attribute $X^i = \left\{x_1^i, x_2^i, \ldots, x_{K_i}^i\right\}$ with $K_i\psi$ being the total number of possible discrete values. Then, the personalized search is a combinatorial optimization problem and can be expressed as follows.

$$\begin{cases} \max F(X) \\ s.t. X \subset \prod_{i=1}^{K} X^i \end{cases} \tag{1}$$

where the value of $F(X)$ represents the user's preference or evaluation on a solution X, which cannot be explicitly defined.

3   Group Preference Assisted PCP-net for a User

This section has three issues: identification of the group who has similar preference to the current user, the expression of the group's preference with possibilistic conditional preference network, and the articulation of group preference with the current user.

3.1   Identification of the Group with Similar Preference

We here present a novel method to identify users with similar preferences by considering the preference dominances among the attributes of the searched items, which is beneficial to get those users having more similar preferences. We first collect L users as $U_s = \{u_1, u_2, \ldots, u_L\}$ who have evaluated or adopted the items with the similar keywords to the current user. According to all the user's adoptions, we then further get the set $I_t = \{I_1, I_2, \ldots, I_M\}$ of M items preferred by the group user. The preference weight $Fr_j(X^i)$ of the j-th user on the i-th variable is defined as follows.

$$Fr_j\left(X^i\right) = \frac{fr_j(X^i)}{\sum\limits_{i=1}^{K} fr_j(X^i)} \tag{2}$$

where $fr_j(X^i)$ represents the total number of the i-th variable included in all items evaluated by the j-th user. It is nature to accept that the larger value of $Fr_j(X^i)$ is, the j-th user prefers the i-th attribute more since X^i is more frequently concerned by the user. Equation (2) focuses on the involving frequencies of each attribute of the items preferred by the user instead of only items, which not only provides accurate and valuable preference relationships of the directly input keywords but also explore more relative preference dependencies of some other latent attributes. Consequently, the identification of the users with most similar preferences will be more accurate and reliable by using this preference weight of each user.

A directed graph is constructed for each user to explicitly express the preference dependencies of the variables. The preference similarity $Si(u_c, u_j)$ between the j-th user u_j in $U_s = \{u_1, u_2, \ldots, u_L\}$ and the current one u_c is calculated with Eq. (3) by considering the relative preference dominances of the variables.

$$Si\left(u_c, u_j\right) = e^{-\frac{\sum\limits_{i=1}^{k}\left(\left|La_{u_c}\left(x^i\right) - La_{u_j}\left(x^i\right)\right|\right)}{\eta}} \tag{3}$$

where η is a tunable parameter and $La_u(X^i)$ is the layer of the attribute X^i in the directed graph. The larger the $Si(u_c, u_j)$ is, the more similar of the two users are. We select N users from $U_s = \{u_1, u_2, \ldots, u_L\}$ to form the most similar social group $U_s = \{u_1, u_2, \ldots, u_N\}$ when $Si(u_c, u_j) \geq 0.5$.

3.2   PCP-net Based Expression of the Group Preference

We use the PCP-net to express the preference of the group since this model is adopted at quantifying the uncertain preferences of users [7]. We need to calculate the integrated preference weight of the entire group on each variable and the possibilistic preference degrees among the known values of each variable. The integrated preference weight $w_g(X^i)$ of the social group on the variable X^i is obtained from the following Eq. (4) by statistically counting the occurrences of X^i among all items evaluated by all similar users. With this preference weight, we can get the PCP-net for describing the preference dominances among the variables of the group intelligence.

$$w_g\left(X^i\right) = \frac{\sum\limits_{u_1}^{u_N}\sum\limits_{j=1}^{K_i} N_u(x_j^i)}{\sum\limits_{u_1}^{u_N}\sum\limits_{i=1}^{K}\sum\limits_{j=1}^{K_i} N_u(x_j^i)} \tag{4}$$

where $N_u(x_j^i)$ is the occurrence frequency of x_j^i.

The possibilistic preference degree is calculated to get the preference table of PCP-net. Two cases associated with the positions of the variables in the directed graph of the PCP-net are considered.

(1)   A variable is not dominated by others, i.e., no parent nodes in the PCP-net. The preference degree on the corresponding values of such variable is defined in Eq. (5).

$$f_g\left(x_j^i\right) = \frac{\sum\limits_{u1}^{u_N} N_u\left(x_j^i\right)}{\sum\limits_{u1}^{u_N}\sum\limits_{j=1}^{K_i} N_u\left(x_j^i\right)} \tag{5}$$

(2)   The decision variable is dominated by its parent nodes and the preference degree function of the variable values is determined by the values of the associated parent nodes. The group's preference degree $f_g\left(x_j^i \mid p(x_j^i)\right)$ on the j-th value of the variable X^i under the parent $p(X^i)$ is defined as follows.

$$f\left(x_j^i \mid p\left(x_j^i\right)\right) = \frac{\sum\limits_{u1}^{u_N}\sum\limits_{p(x_j^i)} N_u\left(x_j^i \mid p\left(x_j^i\right)\right)}{\sum\limits_{u1}^{u_N}\sum\limits_{j=1}^{K_i} N_u\left(x_j^i\right)} \tag{6}$$

3.3   Preference Model of Current User Served by Group Preference

The group preference is used to improve the accuracy of the preference expression for the current user. The existing study on expressing the preference of a user usually depend only on the very few input keywords and historical information, which merely provides sparse preference dominance among the variables. Then, the associated fitness estimation based on the PCP-net is unreliable. Using the group preference to amend those unknown dependences among the variables in the initial preference model of a user is effective. Furthermore, the preference of the current user may vary along with the search, and the preference model must be updated to precisely track the user's preference. Two main issues will be addressed in this subsection, i.e., the initial construction of the user's preference model & the update of the model by integrating the group preference information. We call the preference model here as group preference assisted PCP-net, shorted as GPCP-net.

Initialization of GPCP-net. According to the user's historical searched information and the current input keywords, the PCP-net including the directed graph and the preference table of the current user is initialized using the methods presented in [7]. The similar groups together with the corresponding preference expression presented in Sect. 3 are carried on for further application. The group's PCP-net is embedded into the current user's by sufficiently keeping the preference of the current user. The integration rule for the directed graph of the GPCP-net is as follows. The existing preference dominance among partial variables of the current user's PCP-net remains unchanged to maintain the current user's preference. The left unknown preference dominance of the current PCP-net is provided according to that in the group's PCP-net. With such operation, the linkage among all the variables in the directed graph of the current user's PCP-net will be greatly improved. For the possibilistic preference table of the GPCP-net, those unknown preference weights on the variable values in the preference table of the current user's PCP-net are directly selected from the preference table of the group's PCP-net.

Update of GPCP-net. The update of a PCP-net consists of two parts, i.e., the directed graph determined by the preference weights and the possibilistic preference table. The preference weights and the preference dominant degree of the variables are recalculated by considering the implemented interactions of the current user. First, the interactions based preference weights on each variable are computed with the method presented in [7].

The group's preference weight on the same variable X^i defined in Eq. (4) is now further integrated with the updated preference weight of the current user to sufficiently guide the evaluation or decision of the user. The integrated preference weight $w(X^i)$ of the current user on the variable X^i is calculated through the following Eq. (7).

$$w(X^i) = tw_c(X^i) + (1 - t)w_g(X^i) \tag{7}$$

where $t \in (0.5, 1]$ is the parameter to keep the pivotal of the current user and $C = \{c_1, c_2, \ldots, c_V\}$ is the set of interactions performed by the user. The linkages of the directed graph will be updated according to the values of $w(X^i)$ as addressed before. Similarly, the possibilistic preference table of the GPCP-net will be updated. For the j-th value of the i-th variable x_j^i, the preference degree $f_c\left(x_j^i\right)$ of the current user is obtained with the method given in [7]. As for other decision variables and their values that not yet appeared, their preference degree is set with a random value α_n, $\alpha_n \in [0, 1)$. The integrated preference table of updated GPCP-net is determined with Eq. (8).

$$f(x_j^i) = kf_c(x_j^i) + (1 - k)f_g(x_j^i) \tag{8}$$

where $k \in (0.5, 1]$ is the parameter to keep the key role of the current user and $f_g(x_j^i)$ is the group's preference degree on the j-th value of the variable X^i.

Update of PCP-net for the Similar Group. According to the current interaction of the user, the preferred attributes or variables can be detected, and accordingly the group with the similar preferences on these attributes will be recollected and updated with the method presented in Sect. 3. For example, the dominant relationship $X^1 \succ X^2 \succ X^3, X^2 \succ X^5$ among the attributes has changed to $X^1 \succ X^2, X^2 \succ X^5 \succ X^4 \succ X^3$ with one interactive iteration, then the similar group will be updated according to the relationship of $X^5 \succ X^4 \succ X^3$.

4 Individual Fitness Estimation and Algorithm Implementation

4.1 Fitness Estimation

The estimation $\hat{F}(X)$ of the preference $F(X)$ on an individual fitness is obtained by using the chain formula, as shown in Eq. (9), taking into account the hierarchical contributions of the attributes and the preference degrees.

$$\hat{F}(X^i) = \prod_{j=1}^{K_i} 2^{(La_u(X^i)-1)} La_u(X^i) f(x_j^i) \tag{9}$$

4.2 Procedure

- Step1. Encoding and setting the values of the parameters;
- Step2. Initializing the population based on the user's input;
- Step3. Collecting the group with similar preference to the current user and getting the corresponding PCP-net as stated in Sect. 3;
- Step4. According to Sect. 3, the GPCP-net is obtained;
- Step5. Estimating the individuals' fitness of the current evolutionary population with (9), and selecting the top M individuals to the user for interaction;
- Step6. If the user finds a satisfactory solution, the algorithm terminates and output the satisfactory solution; otherwise, going to Step7;
- Step7. Performing the update of the GPCP-net and the PCP-net of the group as addressed in Sect. 3;
- Step8. Applying the genetic operators and getting a new population, then going back to Step5.

5   Experiments and Results

We apply the algorithm to the personalized book searching to empirically show its performance. This experiment is based on the classification of psychology books from Douban.com. The detail information of the platform can be found in [7]. There are 14177 books, a total of 537 users, including 3019 similar items. In this system, the attributes of the books are treated as variables and encoded with binary chromosomes. The experimental psychology book attributes are divided into 7 categories, which are expressed with three bits and shown in Table 1. Each category includes some values and total 20 bits are used to represent the values of these attributes and form into individuals, and some examples are given in Table 2. In the experiment, algorithm adopts roulette wheel selection, single point crossover and mutation, the probability of crossover and mutation are respectively 0.6, 0.1. And the population size is 8. Here $\eta = 10$, $t = 0.75$ and $k = 0.8$. Since our algorithm is an improvement of IGA-PCP, therefore, the IGA-PCP is selected as a comparison baseline.

Table 1. Attributes' coding

Attribute	Chromosome
Children	001
Female	010
Personality	011
Cognitive	100
Social	101
Encyclopedia	110
Theory and research	111

Table 2. Books' coding (Individual)

Book	Individual
Children's narrative therapy	00110000000000000000
Successful women psychology	01000010000000000000
Procrastination psychology	11000000000000110000
Psychoanalysis Psychology	11100000000000000100

5.1   Rationality Analyses of Group Preference

Experiments are first conducted to illustrate the rationality of the proposed method of the acquisition and usage of the group preference. To this end, we record the preference weights of the group on seven categories in Fig. 2 to provide the basic information of the group. The preference degree on 24 corresponding values are calculated and shown in Fig. 3. Then the corresponding preference weights and the preference degrees of the integrated GPCP-net are compared with that of PCP-net. The results are illustrated in Figs. 4 and 5.

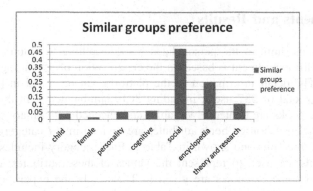

Fig. 2. Similar group preferences

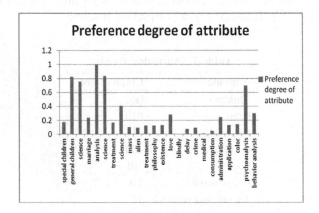

Fig. 3. Preference degree of attribute

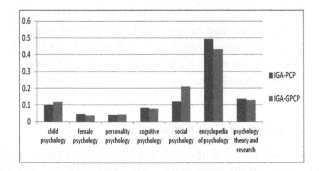

Fig. 4. Relationship of attribute weights

By observing the figures, it can be observed that: (1) the preference dominances on the variables of the current user has only a slight change after integrating the preference information of the group, which indicates that the integrated GPCP-net sufficiently

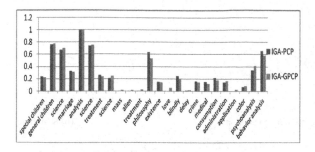

Fig. 5. Attribute values' perfered degree

keeps the preference of the current user even after integrating the similar group's information. (2) The unknown preference linkages among some variable values are amended by the group information, which can greatly improve the accuracy of the PCP-net of the user. Accordingly, the fitness estimation of the individuals based on the GPCP-net will be more accurate and valuable for the evolution.

The fitness of the top 10 individuals of each generation are recorded and averaged, and the results of our algorithm and IGA-PCP are shown in Fig. 6.

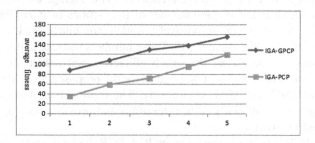

Fig. 6. Change of average fitness

It can be seen from the above figure that the fitness of individuals increases along with the evolutionary operation, which indicates that the two algorithms can effectively track the user preference. On the other hand, the average fitness of the individual only estimated with PCP-net is obviously smaller than that of GPCP-net, which indicates that the GPCP-net is more suitable for the users' preference and gives more reliable guidance of the evolution.

5.2   Comparison with Other Algorithms

The IGA-GPCP is first compared with the IGA-PCP in searching for "psychological treatment for children" since IGA-GPCP is an improvement of IGA-PCP. Each algorithm runs 8 times. The evolutionary generations, the total search time, the number of interactions are compared to show the efficiency of the proposed algorithm, and the ratio of different individuals are recorded to provide the diversity of our algorithm. The results are shown in Fig. 7.

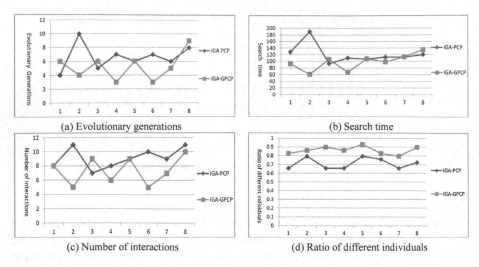

(a) Evolutionary generations   (b) Search time

(c) Number of interactions   (d) Ratio of different individuals

Fig. 7. Experimental results

From the above experimental results, we can see that the IGA-GPCP is more efficient after integrating the group preference. (1) The average evolutionary generations, mean search time and average number of interactions of IGA-GPCP algorithm are 5.25, 97.625 s and 7.375, respectively, which are much smaller than that of IGA-PCP as 6.625, 121.875 s and 9.125. These numbers indicate that the information of similar groups can accelerate the search efficiency and reduce the user fatigue. (2) The average of ratio on different individuals for the proposed IGA-GPCP, as well as the IGA-PCP is 0.862 and 0.711, respectively. The results show that the group preference can improve the diversity of the algorithm and provide more opportunities to find the satisfactory solution.

Our IGA-GPCP is further compared with IGA-PCP, IGA-CP and traditional IGA to show its overall performance in lower user fatigue and higher searching ability. Each algorithm runs 8 times, and the average of evolution generations (AEG), average of search time(AST), average number of interactions(ANI) and average ratio of different individuals (AODI) are shown in Table 3.

Table 3. Experimental results

RESUALS	AEG	AST	ANI	AODI
IGA-GPCP	5.25	97.625	7.375	0.862
IGA-PCP	6.625	121.875	9.125	0.711
IGA-CP	10.25	126.375	13.625	0.626
IGA	12	182.25	16.125	0.634

It can be seen that the algorithm IGA-GPCP can greatly speed up the convergence, improve the algorithm efficiency and reduce user fatigue.

6 Conclusion

In this paper, the user preference is critical for guiding the search direction in the initial search stage of the IECs. However, the initial preference is usually insufficient and fuzzy, which makes IECs difficult to accurately track the search direction. To deal with this problem, we integrate the group preferences to assist the current user to get more valuable information. We propose a method of getting the group preference which is similar to the preference of the current user. Then, we further express the group preference and the user's preference by using the PCP-net. The integration and update of these two models are given in detail. The algorithm is applied to the book search system, and the feasibility and validity of the algorithm are demonstrated. In the evolutionary process, the evolution operators need to be improved according to the user preference, which will be further studied in the future.

References

1. Chawla, S.: Optimization of clustered web search queries using genetic algorithm for effective personalized web search. Innovative Res. Comput. Commun. Eng. **3**, 7343–7352 (2015)
2. Sun, X.Y., Lu, Y.N., Gong, D.W., Zhang, K.K.: Interactive genetic algorithm with CP-nets preference surrogate and application in personalized search. Control Decis. **7**, 1153–1161 (2015)
3. Takagi, H.: Interactive evolutionary computation for analyzing human characteristics. In: Sinčák, P., Hartono, P., Virčíková, M., Vaščák, J., Jakša, R. (eds.) Emergent Trends in Robotics and Intelligent Systems. AISC, vol. 316, pp. 189–195. Springer, Cham (2015). doi:10.1007/978-3-319-10783-7_21
4. Kuzma, M., Andrejková, G.: Interactive evolutionary computation in modelling user preferences. In: Sinčák, P., Hartono, P., Virčíková, M., Vaščák, J., Jakša, R. (eds.) Emergent Trends in Robotics and Intelligent Systems. AISC, vol. 316, pp. 341–350. Springer, Cham (2015). doi:10.1007/978-3-319-10783-7_37
5. Madera, Q., Castillo, O., Garcia-Valdez, M., Mancilla, A.: A method based on interactive evolutionary computation and fuzzy logic for increasing the effectiveness of advertising campaigns. Inf. Sci. **414**, 175–186 (2017)
6. Seyama, T., Munetomo, M.: Development of a multi-player interactive genetic algorithm based 3D modeling system for glasses. In: 2016 IEEE Congress on Evolutionary Computation, CEC 2016, pp. 846–852 (2016)
7. Sun, X.Y., Zhu, L.X., Chen, Y.: Probabilistic conditional preference network assisted interactive genetic algorithm and its application. J. Zhengzhou Univ. Eng. Sci. (2017, to be published)

GP-Based Approach to Comprehensive Quality-Aware Automated Semantic Web Service Composition

Chen Wang[1]($\boxtimes$), Hui Ma[1], Aaron Chen[1], and Sven Hartmann[2]

[1] Victoria University of Wellington, Wellington, New Zealand
chen.wang@ecs.vuw.ac.nz
[2] Clausthal University of Technology, Clausthal-zellerfeld, Germany

Abstract. Comprehensive quality-aware semantic web service composition aims to optimise semantic matchmaking quality and Quality of service (QoS) simultaneously. It is an NP-hard problem due to its huge search space. Therefore, heuristics have to be employed to generate near-optimal solutions. Existing works employ Evolutionary Computation (EC) techniques to solve combinatorial optimisation problems in web service composition. In particular, Genetic Programming (GP) has shown its promise. The tree-based representation utilised in GP is flexible to represent different composition constructs as inner nodes, but the semantic matchmaking information can not be directly obtained from the representation. To overcome this disadvantage, we propose a tree-like representation to directly cope with semantic matchmaking information. Meanwhile, a GP-based approach to comprehensive quality-aware semantic web service composition is proposed with explicit support for our representation. We also design specific genetic operation that effectively maintain the correctness of solutions during the evolutionary process. We conduct experiments to explore the effectiveness and efficiency of our GP-based approach using a benchmark dataset with real-world composition tasks.

1 Introduction

Web services are self-describing software functions that can be deployed, discovered and invoked over the internet. To accommodate complex requirements of service users, web services are loosely coupled to provide a value-added composite service through *web service composition*. These complex requirements include functional and non-functional requirements that ensure interoperability of services and quality of services (QoS) respectively. They also give birth to *semantic web services composition* with resources of web services semantically described for better composing services and *QoS-aware service composition* for finding a near-optimised QoS respectively. Existing works solve composition problems by either a *semi-automated web service composition* approach or a *fully automated web service composition* approach, where a service workflow is pre-defined or automatically generated [13].

© Springer International Publishing AG 2017
Y. Shi et al. (Eds.): SEAL 2017, LNCS 10593, pp. 170–183, 2017.
https://doi.org/10.1007/978-3-319-68759-9_15

In the past a few years, AI planning techniques and Evolutionary Computation (EC) techniques are used to deal with the composition problems. In AI planning, services are considered as actions triggered by one state (i.e., inputs) and resulted in another state (i.e., outputs). Due to the huge search space, efficiency is the main drawback of these approaches [11]. EC techniques are promising to address web service composition problems efficiently for handling large searching spaces using non-deterministic searching strategies [13]. Genetic Algorithms (GA) and Particle Swarm Optimisation (PSO) are popular choices for tackling these NP-hard problems [6,18], but they commonly represent a service composition solution as a vector of integers that must be decoded, adding extra complexity to the service composition process. On other hand, Genetic Programming (GP), unlike the previously discussed techniques, is capable of supporting direct representation as trees. This technique has been utilised to solve fully automated web service composition problems effectively and efficiently [3,9,12,14,20]. Although many works have been conducted to achieve QoS-aware web service composition using GP, most of these works did not recognise the importance of semantic matchmaking quality. Meanwhile, to our best knowledge, none of these GP-based approaches investigate the methods to measure the semantic matchmaking quality on the tree-based representations. It is very challenge to obtain the semantic matchmaking information of a given service, as this information may be distributed across multiple subtrees [14,17,20]. Therefore, we will propose a tree-like representation, where composition constructs could be easily supported, and semantic matchmaking quality could be directly evaluated. The evaluation adopts the comprehensive quality model proposed in our previous paper [19] for jointly evaluating both quality aspects.

The overall goal of this paper is to *develop a GP-based approach to comprehensive quality-aware automated semantic web service composition that jointly optimises both QoS and semantic matchmaking quality.* Particularly, this paper proposes a tree-like representation, and associated genetic operation methods for ensuring the correctness of all evolved individuals. We achieve three objectives in this work:

1. To propose a tree-like representation, which directly copes with semantic matchmaking quality and composition constructs.
2. To propose a GP-based approach, for which we design specific genetic operation methods that maintain the correctness of all evolved individuals during the evolutionary process.
3. To demonstrate the effectiveness of our GP-based approach by comparing it with existing methods, particularly the one presented in [9].

2   Related Work

Web service composition has been approached through various AI planning, EC techniques and hybrid techniques. These works fall into two categories for solution representations: graph-based and tree-based representations. In the first category, AI Planning techniques are used in web service composition to ensure the correctness of the composite services, which are commonly represented as graphs based on a Graphplan algorithm [1]. A combination of Graphplan and Dijkstras algorithm is proposed by [2] to achieve a correct solution with optimised QoS. On the other hand, EC techniques have been utilised to efficiently handle service composition problems. [6] proposes a semi-automated web service composition approach using GA, where a given graph-based abstract workflow is encoded into a genotype. [18] proposes a PSO-based approach, in which a forward graph decoding algorithm is proposed to decode a optimised service queue into a directed acyclic graph (DAG) as a composition solution. A graph-evolutionary approach is introduced in [16] with graph-based genetic operators, which is utilised to evolve graph-based representation. In the approaches discussed above, the graph-based representations are capable of presenting all the matchmaking relationships as edges, but hardly presenting some composition constructs (e.g. loop and choice).

Tree-based representations could be more ideal for practical use, since they can present all composition constructs as inner nodes of trees. However, they could hardly maintain all the edge-related relationships supported by graphs. GP technique is utilised for handling tree-based representations. [14] relies on GP utilising a context-free grammar for population initialisation, and uses a fitness function to penalise invalid individuals throughout evolutionary process. This method is considered to be less efficient as it represents a low rate of fitness convergence. To overcome the disadvantages of [14,20] proposes a GP-based approach employing the standard GP to bypass the low rate of convergence and premature convergence. [9] proposes a hybrid approach combining GP and a greedy algorithm. In particular, a set of DAGs that represent valid solutions are initialised by a random greedy search and transferred into trees using a graph unfolding technique. However, [17] proposes a different transformation algorithm to present composition constructs as the functional nodes of trees. On the whole, all these GP-based approaches [9,14,17,20] consistently ignore the semantic matchmaking quality, and their representations do not preserve semantic matchmaking information and composition constructs simultaneously.

Consequently, to take advantage of the benefits from both graph-based and tree-based representations, we propose a tree-like representation that easily copes with semantic matchmaking quality and supports composition constructs. Meanwhile, a GP-based approach is proposed to support this representation while jointly optimising QoS and semantic matchmaking quality.

3   Preliminaries

Here we extend the concepts from our previous paper [19] to include composition constructs. We consider a *semantic web service* (*service*, for short) as a tuple $S = (I_S, O_S, QoS_S)$ where I_S is a set of service inputs that are consumed by S, O_S is a set of service outputs that are produced by S, and $QoS_S = \{t_S, c_S, r_S, a_S\}$ is a set of non-functional attributes of S. The inputs in

I_S and outputs in O_S are parameters modeled through concepts in a domain-specific ontology $\mathcal{O}$. The attributes t_S, c_S, r_S, a_S refer to the response time, cost, reliability, and availability of service S, respectively. These four QoS attributes are most commonly used [21].

A *service repository* $\mathcal{SR}$ is a finite collection of services supported by a common ontology $\mathcal{O}$. A *service request* (also called *composition task*) over $\mathcal{SR}$ is a tuple $T = (I_T, O_T)$ where I_T is a set of task inputs, and O_T is a set of task outputs. The inputs in I_T and outputs in O_T are parameters described by concepts in the ontology $\mathcal{O}$.

Matchmaking types are often used to describe the level of a match between outputs and inputs [10]. For concepts a, b in $\mathcal{O}$ the *matchmaking* returns *exact* if a and b are equivalent ($a \equiv b$), *plugin* if a is a sub-concept of b ($a \sqsubseteq b$), *subsume* if a is a super-concept of b ($a \sqsupseteq b$), and *fail* if none of previous matchmaking types is returned. In this paper we are only interested in robust compositions where only *exact* and *plugin* matches are considered, see [6]. As argued in [6] *plugin* matches are less preferable than *exact* matches due to the overheads associated with data processing. We suggest to consider the semantic similarity of concepts when comparing different *plugin* matches.

Robust causal link [7] is a link between two matched services S and S', noted as $S \rightarrow S'$, if an output a ($a \in O_S$) of S serves as the input b ($b \in O_{S'}$) of S' satisfying either $a \equiv b$ or $a \sqsubseteq b$. For concepts a, b in $\mathcal{O}$ the *semantic similarity* $sim(a, b)$ is calculated based on the edge counting method in a taxonomy like WorldNet or Ontology [15]. This method has the advantages of simple calculation and good performance [15]. Therefore, the *matchmaking type* and *semantic similarity* of a robust causal link can be defined as follow:

$$type_{link} = \begin{cases} 1 & \text{if } a \equiv b(exact \text{ match}) \\ p & \text{if } a \sqsubseteq b(plugin \text{ match}) \end{cases}, \quad sim_{link} = sim(a, b) = \frac{2N_c}{N_a + N_b} \tag{1}$$

with a suitable parameter $p, 0 < p < 1$, and with N_a, N_b and N_c, which measure the distances from concept a, concept b, and the closest common ancestor c of a and b to the top concept of the ontology $\mathcal{O}$, respectively. However, if more than one pair of matched output and input exist from service S to service S', $type_e$ and sim_e will take on their average values.

The *semantic matchmaking quality* of the service composition can be obtained by aggregating over all robust causal links as follow:

$$MT = \prod_{j=1}^{m} type_{link_j}, \quad SIM = \frac{1}{m} \sum_{j=1}^{m} sim_{link_j} \tag{2}$$

We consider two special atomic services $Start = (\emptyset, I_T, \emptyset)$ and $End = (O_T, \emptyset, \emptyset)$ to account for the input and output of a given composition task T, and add them to $\mathcal{SR}$.

We use formal expressions as in [8] to represent service compositions. We use the constructors $\bullet$, $\|$, $+$ and $*$ to denote sequential composition, parallel composition, choice, and iteration, respectively. The set of *composite service expressions* is the smallest collection $\mathcal{SC}$ that contains all atomic services and that is closed under sequential composition, parallel composition, choice, and iteration. That is, whenever $C_0, C_1, \ldots, C_d$ are in $\mathcal{SC}$ then $\bullet(C_1, \ldots, C_d)$, $\parallel (C_1, \ldots, C_d)$, $+(C_1, \ldots, C_d)$, and $*C_0$ are in $\mathcal{SC}$, too. Let C be a composite service expression. If C denotes an atomic service S then its QoS is given by QoS_S. Otherwise the QoS of C can be obtained inductively as summarized in Table 1. Herein, $p_1, \ldots, p_d$ with $\sum_{k=1}^{d} p_k = 1$ denote the probabilities of the different options of the choice $+$, while ℓ denotes the average number of iterations.

Table 1. QoS calculation for a composite service expression C

$C =$	$r_C =$	$a_C =$	$c_C =$	$t_C =$
$\bullet(C_1, \ldots, C_d)$	$\prod_{k=1}^{d} r_{C_k}$	$\prod_{k=1}^{d} a_{C_k}$	$\sum_{k=1}^{d} c_{C_k}$	$\sum_{k=1}^{d} t_{C_k}$
$\parallel (C_1, \ldots, C_d)$	$\prod_{k=1}^{d} r_{C_k}$	$\prod_{k=1}^{d} a_{C_k}$	$\sum_{k=1}^{d} c_{C_k}$	$MAX\{t_{C_k} \mid k \in \{1, ..., d\}\}$
$+(C_1, \ldots, C_d)$	$\prod_{k=1}^{d} p_k \cdot r_{C_k}$	$\prod_{k=1}^{d} p_k \cdot a_{C_k}$	$\sum_{k=1}^{d} p_k \cdot c_{C_k}$	$\sum_{k=1}^{d} p_k \cdot t_{C_k}$
$*C_0$	$r_{C_0}{}^\ell$	$a_{C_0}{}^\ell$	$\ell \cdot c_{C_0}$	$\ell \cdot t_{C_0}$

When multiple quality criteria are involved in decision making, the fitness of a solution can be defined as a weighted sum of all individual criteria using Eq. (3), assuming the preference of each quality criterion is provided by users.

$$Fitness = w_1 \hat{MT} + w_2 \hat{SIM} + w_3 \hat{A} + w_4 \hat{R} + w_5(1 - \hat{T}) + w_6(1 - \hat{C}) \quad (3)$$

with $\sum_{k=1}^{6} w_k = 1$. We call this objective function the *comprehensive quality model* for service composition. The weights can be adjusted according to users' preferences. $\hat{MT}$, $\hat{SIM}$, $\hat{A}$, $\hat{R}$, $\hat{T}$, and $\hat{C}$ are normalised values calculated within the range from 0 to 1 using Eq. (4). To simplify the presentation we also use the notation $(Q_1, Q_2, Q_3, Q_4, Q_5, Q_6) = (MT, SIM, A, R, T, C)$. Q_1 and Q_2 have minimum value 0 and maximum value 1. The minimum and maximum value of Q_3, Q_4, Q_5, and Q_6 are calculated across all task-related candidates in the service repository $\mathcal{SR}$ using the greedy search in [9,17].

$$\hat{Q}_k = \begin{cases} \frac{Q_k - Q_{k,min}}{Q_{k,max} - Q_{k,min}} & \text{if } k = 1, \ldots, 4 \text{ and } Q_{k,max} - Q_{k,min} \neq 0, \\ \frac{Q_{k,max} - Q_k}{Q_{k,max} - Q_{k,min}} & \text{if } k = 5, 6 \text{ and } Q_{k,max} - Q_{k,min} \neq 0, \\ 1 & \text{otherwise.} \end{cases} \quad (4)$$

To find the best possible solution for a given composition task T, our goal is to maximise the objective function in Eq. (3).

4   Our GP-Based Approach

In this section, we first introduce the tree-like representation that will be used in our approach, and then discuss the differences to the most widely used tree-based representations for GP-based service composition in the literature [3, 17, 20]. Finally, we present our GP-based approach with newly designed genetic operations.

4.1   Tree-Like Representation

Let $\mathcal{G} = (V, E)$ be a DAG representation of a service composition. Let S be a service in $\mathcal{G}$, and let $S_1, \ldots, S_d$ be its successors in $\mathcal{G}$. We define the composite service expression relative to S as follows:

$$C_S = \begin{cases} \bullet(S, \| (C_{S_1}, \ldots, C_{S_d})), & \text{if } d \geq 2, \\ \bullet(S, C_{S_1}), & \text{if } d = 1, \\ S, & \text{if } d = 0, \end{cases} \quad (5)$$

which can be evaluated inductively starting with $Start$ which has no incoming edges in $\mathcal{G}$. The resulting expression C_{Start} is a composite service expression that is equivalent to $\mathcal{G}$.

Example 1. Consider the composition task $T = (\{a, b, e\}, \{i\})$. Figure 1 shows an example of a composition solution. It involves four atomic services $S_1 = (\{a, b\}, \{c, d, j\}, QoS_{S_1})$, $S_2 = (\{c\}, \{f, g\}, QoS_{S_2})$, $S_3 = (\{d\}, \{h\}, QoS_{S_3})$, and $S_4 = (\{f, g, h\}, \{i\}, QoS_{S_4})$. The two special services $Start = (\emptyset, \{a, b, e\}, \emptyset)$ and $End = (\{i\}, \emptyset, \emptyset)$ are defined by the given composition task T. The corresponding service composition expression is $C_{Start} = \bullet(Start, \bullet(S_1, \| (\bullet(S_2, \bullet(S_4, End)), \bullet(S_3, \bullet(S_4, End)))))$.

Formal expressions can be visualized by expression trees. For a composite service expression C let $\mathcal{T}$ denote the corresponding expression tree. Every leaf node in $\mathcal{T}$ is labelled by the corresponding atomic service, while every internal node in $\mathcal{T}$ is labelled by the corresponding composition constructor. For the sake of brevity we only consider $\bullet$ and $\|$ here, but our approach can easily be extended to $+$ and $*$, too. If a subtree of $\mathcal{T}$ (except for End) has an isomorphic copy in $\mathcal{T}$ then we remove it, label its root with a special symbol q, and insert an edge to the root of the copy. As a result we obtain a tree-like representation of a service composition. An example is shown in Fig. 1.

Figure 1 shows for every atomic service S its sets of (least required) inputs $\mathcal{I}_S$ and outputs $\mathcal{O}_S$. Moreover, the set of available inputs $\mathcal{PI}_S$ is shown which is just the union of the input sets of all (direct and indirect) predecessors of S in the DAG. This can be easily generalized to composite service expressions. For a parallel composition $C = \| (C_1, \ldots, C_d)$ we define $\mathcal{I}_C = \cup_{k=1}^d \mathcal{I}_{C_k}$, and $\mathcal{O}_C = \cup_{k=1}^d \mathcal{O}_{C_k}$, and $\mathcal{PI}_C = \cup_{k=1}^d \mathcal{PI}_{C_k}$. For a sequential composition $C = \bullet(S, C')$ we define $\mathcal{I}_C = \mathcal{I}_S \cup (\mathcal{I}_{C'} - \mathcal{O}_S)$, and $\mathcal{O}_C = \mathcal{O}_S \cup \mathcal{O}_{C'}$, and $\mathcal{PI}_C = \mathcal{PI}_S$.

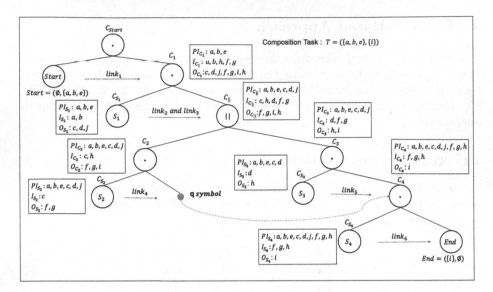

Fig. 1. Example of a tree-like representation

Example 2. Consider the sequential composition $C_4 = \bullet(S_4, End)$ which is shown in the rightmost position in Fig. 1. We obtain $\mathcal{I}_{C_4} = \{f, g, h\}$ which represents the (least required) inputs for this composition, and $\mathcal{O}_{C_4} = \{i\}$ which represents the outputs produced by this composition, and $\mathcal{PI}_{C_4} = \{a, b, e, c, d, j, f, g, h\}$ which represents the union of the input sets of all (direct or indirect) predecessors of S_4 in the DAG (i.e., S_1, S_2 and S_3).

Our representation supports composition constructs that are available in commonly used composition languages, such as BPEL4WS or OWL-S. Note that our representation is different from the most widely used tree-based representations in [3,17,20]. These differences are as follows.

1. *Start* and *End* are included in $\mathcal{T}$, as they are related to measuring the semantic matchmaking qualities regarding I_T and O_T. Symbol q is also included to reduce complexity of presentation structure and transfer information of attributes defined below.
2. $\mathcal{I}_C, \mathcal{O}_C, \mathcal{PI}_C, QoS_C$ are attributes, defined as a tuple $(\mathcal{I}_C, \mathcal{O}_C, \mathcal{PI}_C, QoS_C)$ for any C_S in $\mathcal{T}$. These attributes must be updated after population initialisation and genetic operations described in Sect. 4.2.
3. $\mathcal{T}$ preserves all the semantic matchmaking information, which can be easily used for computing robust casual links.

To compute semantic matchmaking quality, we need to retrieve all the robust causal links on $\mathcal{T}$. This is performed by retrieving robust causal links for every sequential composition $C = \bullet(S, C')$. For example, in Fig. 1, two robust causal links $(link_2 : S_1 \to S_2$ and $link_3 : S_1 \to S_3$) are retrieved from $C_1 = \bullet(S_1, C_{\parallel})$, because outputs $O_{S_1} = \{c, d, j\}$ match inputs $I_{C_{\parallel}} = \{c, h, d, f, g\}$.

4.2   GP-Based Algorithm

Now we present our GP-based approach for service composition, see Algorithm 1. To begin with the algorithm, we generate an initial population P_0, which is then evaluated using our comprehensive quality model. The iterative part of the algorithm comprises lines 3 to 7, which will be repeated until the maximum number of generations is reached or the best solution is found. During each iteration, we use tournament selection to select individuals, on which crossover and/or mutation are performed to evolve the population. These steps correspond to the standard GP steps [4] except for some particularities that will be discussed below.

Algorithm 1. GP-based algorithm for service composition

    Input : T, $\mathcal{SR}$, $\mathcal{O}$
    Output: an optimal composition solution
1: Initialise population P_0 (using a 3-step method);
2: Evaluate each individual in population P_0 (using our comprehensive quality model);
3: **while** *max.populations or max.fitness not yet met* **do**
4:     Select individuals using tournament selection;
5:     Apply crossover and mutation to the selected individuals;
6:     Evaluate each new individual;
7:     Replace the individuals with the worst fitness in the population by the new individuals;
8: Find the individual with the highest fitness in the final population;

Population initialisation. The initial population is created by generating a set of service compositions in the form of DAGs, and then transforming them into their tree-like representations (*the individuals*). The initialisation is performed as follows:

STEP 1. Greedy search is performed to randomly generate a set of DAGs, each representing a (valid) service composition for the given composition task T. For this, a simple forward graph building algorithm is applied starting with the node *Start* and the inputs I_T of the composition task T. Details of this algorithm can be found in [9]. An example of a generated DAG is shown in Fig. 2 with seven robust casual links marked on.

STEP 2. The DAGs can be simplified by removing some redundant edges and service nodes. While this step is not compulsory, it can help to notably reduce the size of the DAG and, consequently, the corresponding tree-like representation.

STEP 3. We transform each DAG into its tree-like representation using an algorithm modified from [17] to satisfy the particular requirements of our proposed approach. For example, Fig. 1 shows an example of a tree-like individual corresponding to the DAG shown in Fig. 2.

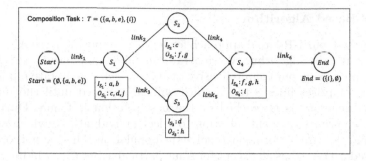

Fig. 2. Example of a DAG used for transferring it into tree-like representation

Crossover and Mutation. During the evolutionary process, the correctness of the representation is maintained by crossover and mutation.

A crossover operation exchanges a subtree of a selected individual (its attributes noted as $C_1(\mathcal{I}_{C_1}, \mathcal{O}_{C_1}, \mathcal{PI}_{C_1}, QoS_{C_1})$) with the subtree of another selected individual (its attributes noted as $C_2(\mathcal{I}_{C_2}, \mathcal{O}_{C_2}, \mathcal{PI}_{C_2}, QoS_{C_2})$) if they represent the same functionality (i.e. $\mathcal{I}_{C_1} = \mathcal{I}_{C_2}$ and $\mathcal{O}_{C_1} = \mathcal{O}_{C_2}$). That is, at the root nodes of both subtrees, there are identical inputs and identical outputs. A crossover operation is performed in two cases: crossover on two functional nodes or on two terminal nodes. We never exchange a functional node with an terminal node, since the two associated subtrees cannot be equivalent in this case. For example, *End* must appear in the subtree associated with any functional node, but not for any selected terminal node (atomic services).

A mutation operation replaces a subtree of the selected individual (its attributes noted as $C_1(\mathcal{I}_{C_1}, \mathcal{O}_{C_1}, \mathcal{PI}_{C_1}, QoS_{C_1})$) with a newly generated subtree satisfying the least required functionality. To do this, a subtree C_1 must be selected from the selected individual, and a new composition task $T = (\{\mathcal{PI}_{C_1}\}, \{\mathcal{O}_{C_1} \cap O_T\})$ or $T' = (\{\mathcal{PI}_{C_1}\}, \{\mathcal{O}_{C_1}\})$ is used to generate a tree in the same way as the 3-step method performed during the population initialisation. We utilise the available inputs and least required outputs for mutation, because it potentially bring more possibilities in generating more varieties of subtrees. The mutation is performed in two cases: mutation on a functional node with T or on a service node with T', two examples shown in Fig. 3(a) and (b). In Fig. 3(a), a functional node $C_{\parallel}$ is selected for mutation, the whole subtree is replaced with the generated subtree excluding its head (i.e., *Start* and its parent node ●). In Fig. 3(b), an atomic service S_1 is selected for mutation, the branch of the selected node (i.e., S_1 and its parent node ●) is replaced with the generated subtree excluding both its head (i.e., *Start* and its parent node ●) and its tail (i.e., *End*).

Note that the set of available nodes considered for crossover and mutation do not include *Start* and *End*, and their parent nodes, because these nodes remain the same for all individuals. In addition, the nodes selected for crossover and mutation must not break the functionality of q symbols. For example, in Fig. 1,

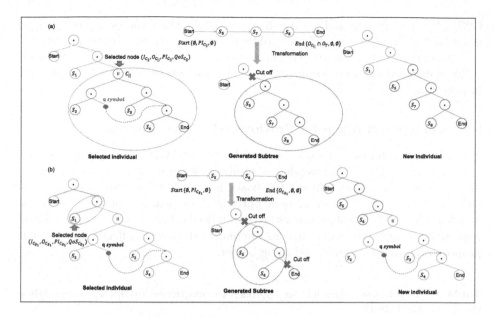

Fig. 3. Examples of two mutations on terminal and functional nodes

both sequential composition C_2 and C_3 are not considered for crossover and mutation as they break the edge of q symbol, but the parallel composition $C_{\parallel}$ can be considered for genetic operations, as it may bring a new fully functional q symbol or a subtree without q symbol involved. The pointed subtree C_4 could also be selected for genetic operations.

5   Experiments

We have conducted experiments to evaluate our proposed approach. For our experiments we have used the benchmark datasets originating from OWLS-TC [5], which have been extended with real-world QoS attributes and five composition tasks [9]. To explore the effectiveness and efficiency of our proposed GP-based approach, we compare it against one recent GP-based approach [9]. For that we have extended the later approach by our proposed comprehensive quality model, so that semantic matchmaking quality can be computed based on the parent-child relationship in the underlying tree representations.

To assure a fair comparison we have used exactly the same parameter settings as in [9]. In particular, the GP population size has been set to 200, the number of generations to 30, the reproduction rate to 0.1, the crossover rate to 0.8, and the mutation rate to 0.1. We have run every experiment with 30 independent repetitions. Without considering any users' true service composition preferences, the weights in fitness function in Eq. (3) have been configured simply to balance semantic matchmaking quality and QoS. Particularly, w_1 and w_2 are both set to

0.25, while w_3, w_4, w_5, and w_6 are all set to 0.125. The parameter p of $type_{link}$ is set to 0.75 (*plugin* match) in accordance with the recommendation in [6].

Our experiments indicate that our method can work consistently well under valid weight settings and parameter p, decided according to users' preferences in practice.

5.1   Comparison Against a Previous GP-Based Approach

Table 2 shows the fitness values obtained by the two GP-based approaches. To compare the results, an independent-samples T-test over 30 runs has been conducted. The results show that our GP-based approach outperforms the previous GP-based approach [9] in finding more optimized composition solutions for Tasks 3 and 4. (Note: the P-values are lower than 0.0001). For Tasks 1, 2 and 5, both approaches achieve the same fitness. Therefore, the overall effectiveness of our proposed approach is considered to be better.

Table 2. Mean fitness values for our approach in comparison to [9] (Note: the higher the fitness the better)

Task	Our GP-based approach	Ma et al. approach [9]
OWL-S TC1	0.923793 ± 0.000000	0.923793 ± 0.000000
OWL-S TC2	0.933026 ± 0.000000	0.933026 ± 0.000000
OWL-S TC3	$0.870251 \pm 0.000000 \uparrow$	0.832306 ± 0.008241
OWL-S TC4	$0.798137 \pm 0.007412 \uparrow$	0.760146 ± 0.005044
OWL-S TC5	0.832998 ± 0.000000	0.832998 ± 0.000000

Table 3 shows the execution times observed for the two GP-based approaches. Again an independent-samples T-test over 30 runs has been conducted. For Tasks 1 and 2 both approaches need about the same time, while for Tasks 3, 4, and 5 our approach needs slightly more time. (Note: the P-values are lower than 0.0001). However, even in the worst case it exceeds [9] by no more than 1 second, which is acceptable for most real-word scenarios. Hence, in terms of efficiency our approach is comparable to [9].

The experiments confirm that there is a trade-off between fitness and execution time in GP-based service composition. It can be argued that our proposed approach achieves a better balance as the computed solutions observe a significantly higher fitness while there is a moderate increase in execution time compared to [9].

5.2   Further Discussion

For Tasks 3 and 4, the optimized composition solutions obtained by the two approaches are shown in Fig. 4(a) and 4(b), respectively. The functional and nonfunctional descriptions of all services involved in these solutions are listed in Fig. 4(c).

Table 3. Mean execution time (in ms) for our approach in comparison to [9] (Note: the shorter the time the better)

Task	Our GP-based approach	Ma et al. approach [9]
OWL-S TC1	7396.366667 ± 772.408168	7310.866667 ± 952.701775
OWL-S TC2	2956.133333 ± 761.350965	3036.966667 ± 777.121101
OWL-S TC3	1057.266667 ± 174.405183	763.800000 ± 221.241232 ↓
OWL-S TC4	4479.466667 ± 519.767172	3068.800000 ± 472.013106 ↓
OWL-S TC5	6276.533333 ± 1075.102328	5030.200000 ± 991.863812 ↓

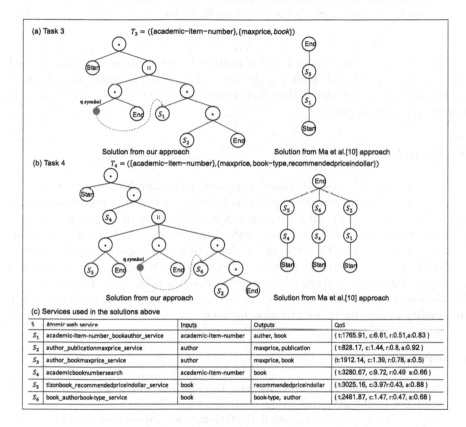

Fig. 4. Example of best solutions using the two GP-based approaches

For Task 3 the composition task is $T_3 = (\{academic\text{-}item\text{-}number\}, \{book, maxprice\})$. The best composition solutions obtained by the two approaches are different, see Fig. 4. Both solutions have the same semantic matchmaking quality as the matchmaking type of all links is *exact* match. However, both solutions differ in their QoSs. This is due to the different services that are involved: S_2 versus S_3. The QoS of S_2 is much better that of S_3. Consequently, the best composition solution obtained by our approach has higher fitness according to our quality model. It is interesting to observe that the best composition solution obtained by our approach for Task 3 can be evolved from the best composition solution in [9] just by a single mutation on S_3 using available inputs.

For $T_4 = (\{academic\text{-}item\text{-}number\}, \{maxprice, book - type, recommended\ price - indollar\})$, the best solutions obtained by the two approaches are also different, see Fig. 4. Note that solution generated by our approach is composed of four atomic services (S_4, S_5, S_6 and S_2) while the solution generated by approach [9] is composed of five atomic services (S_4, S_5, S_6, S_1 and S_2). Both solutions have the same semantic matchmaking quality as the matchmaking type of all links is *exact* match. However, the overall QoS of our approach is better. This is due to the additional S_1 in their approach, which has a significant negative impact on QoS.

We observe from above examples that our approach is able to produce better solutions because our proposed representation keeps available inputs and least required outputs of each node on the tree which unlocks more opportunities for mutation and crossover rather than restricting them to the previously used inputs and outputs only.

6   Conclusion

This work introduces an GP-based approach to comprehensive quality-aware semantic web service composition. In particular, a tree-like representation is proposed to direct cope with the evaluation of semantic matchmaking quality. Meanwhile, crossover and mutation methods are proposed to maintain the correctness of individuals. The experiment shows that our proposed approach could effectively produce better solutions in both semantic matchmaking quality and QoS than the existing approach. Future works can investigate multi-objective EC techniques to produce a set of composition solutions for the situations when the quality preference is not provided by users.

References

1. Blum, A.L., Furst, M.L.: Fast planning through planning graph analysis. Artif. Intell. **90**(1), 281–300 (1997)
2. Feng, Y., Ngan, L.D., Kanagasabai, R.: Dynamic service composition with service-dependent QoS attributes. In: 2013 IEEE 20th International Conference on Web Services (ICWS), pp. 10–17. IEEE (2013)
3. Gupta, I.K., Kumar, J., Rai, P.: Optimization to quality-of-service-driven web service composition using modified genetic algorithm. In: 2015 International Conference on Computer, Communication and Control (IC4), pp. 1–6. IEEE (2015)
4. Koza, J.R.: Genetic Programming: On the Programming of Computers by Means of Natural Selection, vol. 1. MIT press, Cambridge (1992)
5. Küster, U., König-Ries, B., Krug, A.: Opossum-an online portal to collect and share SWS descriptions. In: 2008 IEEE International Conference on Semantic Computing, pp. 480–481. IEEE (2008)

6. Lécué, F.: Optimizing QoS-aware semantic web service composition. In: Bernstein, A., Karger, D.R., Heath, T., Feigenbaum, L., Maynard, D., Motta, E., Thirunarayan, K. (eds.) ISWC 2009. LNCS, vol. 5823, pp. 375–391. Springer, Heidelberg (2009). doi:10.1007/978-3-642-04930-9_24

7. Lécué, F., Delteil, A., Léger, A.: Optimizing causal link based web service composition. In: ECAI. pp. 45–49 (2008)

8. Ma, H., Schewe, K.D., Thalheim, B., Wang, Q.: A formal model for the interoperability of service clouds. SOCA 6(3), 189–205 (2012)

9. Ma, H., Wang, A., Zhang, M.: A hybrid approach using genetic programming and greedy search for QoS-aware web service composition. In: Hameurlain, A., Küng, J., Wagner, R., Decker, H., Lhotska, L., Link, S. (eds.) Transactions on Large-Scale Data- and Knowledge-Centered Systems XVIII. LNCS, vol. 8980, pp. 180–205. Springer, Heidelberg (2015). doi:10.1007/978-3-662-46485-4_7

10. Paolucci, M., Kawamura, T., Payne, T.R., Sycara, K.: Semantic matching of web services capabilities. In: Horrocks, I., Hendler, J. (eds.) ISWC 2002. LNCS, vol. 2342, pp. 333–347. Springer, Heidelberg (2002). doi:10.1007/3-540-48005-6_26

11. Peer, J.: Web Service Composition as AI planning: A Survey. University of St. Gallen, Switzerland (2005)

12. Qi, L., Tang, Y., Dou, W., Chen, J.: Combining local optimization and enumeration for QoS-aware web service composition. In: 2010 International Conference on Web Services (ICWS), pp. 34–41 (2010)

13. Rao, J., Su, X.: A survey of automated web service composition methods. In: Cardoso, J., Sheth, A. (eds.) SWSWPC 2004. LNCS, vol. 3387, pp. 43–54. Springer, Heidelberg (2005). doi:10.1007/978-3-540-30581-1_5

14. Rodriguez-Mier, P., Mucientes, M., Lama, M., Couto, M.I.: Composition of web services through genetic programming. Evol. Intell. 3(3–4), 171–186 (2010)

15. Shet, K., Acharya, U.D., et al.: A new similarity measure for taxonomy based on edge counting (2012). arXiv preprint . arxiv:1211.4709

16. da Silva, A.S., Ma, H., Zhang, M.: GraphEvol: a graph evolution technique for web service composition. In: Chen, Q., Hameurlain, A., Toumani, F., Wagner, R., Decker, H. (eds.) DEXA 2015. LNCS, vol. 9262, pp. 134–142. Springer, Cham (2015). doi:10.1007/978-3-319-22852-5_12

17. da Silva, A.S., Ma, H., Zhang, M.: Genetic programming for QoS-aware web service composition and selection. Soft Comput. 20, 1–17 (2016)

18. da Silva, A.S., Mei, Y., Ma, H., Zhang, M.: Particle swarm optimisation with sequence-like indirect representation for web service composition. In: Chicano, F., Hu, B., García-Sánchez, P. (eds.) EvoCOP 2016. LNCS, vol. 9595, pp. 202–218. Springer, Cham (2016). doi:10.1007/978-3-319-30698-8_14

19. Wang, C., Ma, H., Chen, A., Hartmann, S.: Comprehensive quality-aware automated semantic web service composition. In: Peng, W., Alahakoon, D., Li, X. (eds.) AI 2017. LNCS, vol. 10400, pp. 195–207. Springer, Cham (2017). doi:10.1007/978-3-319-63004-5_16

20. Yu, Y., Ma, H., Zhang, M.: An adaptive genetic programming approach to QoS-aware web services composition. In: 2013 IEEE Congress on Evolutionary Computation, pp. 1740–1747. IEEE (2013)

21. Zeng, L., Benatallah, B., Dumas, M., Kalagnanam, J., Sheng, Q.Z.: Quality driven web services composition. In: Proceedings of the 12th international conference on World Wide Web, pp. 411–421. ACM (2003)

Matrix Factorization Based Benchmark Set Analysis: A Case Study on HyFlex

Mustafa Mısır[✉]

College of Computer Science and Technology,
Nanjing University of Aeronautics and Astronautics, Nanjing, China
mmisir@nuaa.edu.cn

Abstract. The present paper offers an analysis strategy to examine benchmark sets of combinatorial search problems. Experimental analysis has been widely used to compare a set of algorithms on a group of instances from such problem domains. These studies mostly focus on the algorithms' performance rather than the quality of the target benchmark set. In relation to that, the insights about the algorithms' varying performance happen to be highly limited. The goal here is to introduce a benchmark set analysis strategy that can tell the quality of a benchmark set while allowing to retrieve some insights regarding the algorithms' performance. A matrix factorization based strategy is utilized for this purpose. A Hyper-heuristic framework, i.e. HyFlex, involving 6 problem domains is accommodated as the testbed to perform the analysis on.

1 Introduction

Experimental studies are common in research mainly in order to exhibit the superior performance of a new algorithm on a particular problem domain, mostly using a set of well-known, widely-used benchmarks. They are also helpful to present comparative analysis to further understand strengths and weaknesses of multiple algorithms. Although such studies can give useful insights on the behavior of the tested algorithms, they usually lack of characterizing the target problem instances. It might even be the case that the target instances favor a certain type of algorithms. The diversity of the instances plays a critical role in such studies or in experimental algorithm competitions. The diversity level identifies the fairness of a comparison or a competition. Otherwise, an algorithm which performs well on a special type of instances can be considered state-of-the-art if most of the instances is similar to that type. Thus, both for experimental analysis in general and the competitions, a scientific approach should be followed to indicate how fair a benchmark set is.

One way to address this issue is to focus on a set of features characterizing the problem instances. However, if the proper features are not chosen, the resulting analysis can be misleading. Another way would be automatically extracting some features that are expected to be suitable for this purpose. Matrix factorization [1] is a widely studied idea to extract some hidden features, particularly used in he field of collaborative filtering [2]. As its name suggests, matrix factorization

© Springer International Publishing AG 2017
Y. Shi et al. (Eds.): SEAL 2017, LNCS 10593, pp. 184–195, 2017.
https://doi.org/10.1007/978-3-319-68759-9_16

requires a matrix in the first place. In terms of collaborative filtering, a matrix could be a user-item data which is composed of values referring to the preferences of users' on items. Matrix factorization can be used to extract hidden features using this preference matrix both for users and items.

ALORS [3] as an algorithm selection approach [4] borrows the same idea to extract features for the instance-algorithm matrices. Each matrix entry is the performance of an algorithm on a problem instance. Singular Value Decomposition (SVD) [5] was utilized as the matrix factorization method on a performance matrix. It offers an algorithm selection strategy through mapping a set of hand-picked features to those extract features regarding instances.

This study provides an analysis strategy for benchmark sets by using matrix factorization. The analysis is performed on hyper-heuristics across 6 problem domains using HyFlex [6]. Considering the problem-independent nature of hyper-heuristics, the analysis is on all the problems at once. Thus, the proposed approach differentiates from the studies focusing on a single problem domain and utilizing problem specific elements such as instance features. The CHeSC 2011 competition results on HyFlex are additionally reviewed.

The remainder of the paper is presented as follows. Section 2 presents a brief literature on hyper-heuristics and the problem analysis techniques. Section 3 introduces the proposed approach while the computational results are discussed in Sect. 4. The paper is finalized with a summary and the follow-up research path in Sect. 5.

2 Background

2.1 Hyper-heuristics

Hyper-heuristics [7,8] have been successfully applied to various problem domains such as scheduling [9], timetabling [10], routing, cutting & packing [11,12] and decision problems [13]. They have been considered under two types including the *selection* and *generation* hyper-heuristics [14].

The selection hyper-heuristics aim at determining the best possible low-level heuristics to be used while deciding how to act on the resulting solutions by those heuristics. The selection process is handled by a *heuristic selection* mechanism. Incorporating a learning strategy into heuristic selection has been very popular such as case-based reasoning [15], choice function [16], learning automata credit-assignment, dynamic heuristic set and learning classifier systems [17] while rather simple approaches have been also studied such as simple random and greedy [18]. The adaptive operator selection approaches [19] perform a similar task to the heuistic selection and can also be employed in hyper-heuristics [20]. Some of these selection operations are performed *online*, meaning that choosing heuristics while a problem instance is being solved. *Offline* is preferred in others in order to take advantage of prior knowledge. The traditional algorithm selection [4,21] studies also fall into this Offline category. After a selected heuristic is being applied, it is decided whether the resulting partial/complete solution is good enough to accepted. The evaluation operation is performed by a *move acceptance* criterion.

The generation hyper-heuristics are studied to automatically design new heuristics. Genetic programming [22], grammatical evolution [12] and differential evolution [23] have been particularly used for the purpose of generation. The majority of the studies on this type of hyper-heuristics is considered Offline. Hybridisation approaches in particular are proper to perform Online generation.

2.2 Problem Analysis

One way of problem analysis is to consider empirical instance hardness [24–28]. Having some knowledge on instance hardness can help to pick the proper algorithms w.r.t. the instances' hardness levels. Such information can also be utilized to reveal what makes a particular problem instance hard to solve. The outcome can be practical to design or modify a strong algorithm targeting a certain problem/∼ instance. It can also be useful to generate new instances [29–33] that can challenge algorithms or just with particular characteristics.

For understanding instances' comparative hardness or similarities, using a group of hand-picked, descriptive features has been practical. In [34], for example, a group of features for the traveling salesman problem was utilized to analyze the problem instances with the help of algorithm selection. The instances were initially generated such that a certain level of diversity is achieved in terms of the instance hardness. Principal component analysis (PCA) [35] was then used for visualization purposes. As mentioned earlier, in [3], similarly, algorithm selection was used for instance analysis. However, their focus was features extracted from performance data instead of directly relying on the hand-picked features. The extracted features were derived with the help of singular value decomposition (SVD) [5]. Additionally, the Locally Linear Embedding approach [36] was used to quantify the actual contribution of each hand-picked feature to the hardness of the instances depending on the algorithms' performance on those instances.

3   Benchmark Set Analysis

The benchmark set analysis approach, detailed in Algorithm 1, relies on ALORS [3]. ALORS takes a rank matrix $\mathcal{M}_{n \times m}$ where its rows represent m problem instances while its columns refer to n algorithms. Thus, $\mathcal{M}_{i,j}$ indicates the rank performance of algorithm j on instance i. A set of hidden features are extracted from $\mathcal{M}$ using matrix factorization. Matrix factorization basically refers to generating a number of matrices where their multiplication is equal to or approximates to the original matrix. ALORS accommodates singular value decomposition (SVD) as the matrix factorization method.

It essentially produces three matrices. U and V matrices are composed of the latent (hidden) features characterizing the rows and columns of a given matrix. Regarding this paper, U matrix represents instances while V matrix represents algorithms. The third matrix, $\sum$ is a diagonal matrix involving singular values. Singular values can be considered importance metrics of the extracted latent features. Besides that, the singular values are sorted. This means that the first

---

Algorithm 1. Matrix Factorization based Benchmark set Analyzer

---

Input: A performance matrix M, Matrix factorization method θ, Clustering
algorithm Λ, Number of latent features: k
1 **Rank matrix conversion**: $M \rightarrow \mathcal{M}$
2 **Feature extraction**: $\theta(\mathcal{M}_{n \times m}) = \mathrm{U}_{n \times k} \mathrm{V}^{T}{}_{k \times m}$
3 **Instance clustering**: $C = \Lambda(\mathrm{U})$
4 **Feature analysis**: $\Phi : U \rightarrow C$

---

k latent features both for instances and algorithms are more critical or contains more information to represent them than the second latent features. The same situation is valid for the subsequent latent features. Thus, using only the first a few initial features, i.e. dimensionality reduction, can already represent both instances and algorithms rather well. Additionally, it can help to remove the noise in the matrix in case there is. When $k = \max(n, m)$, the multiplication of the SVD's resulting matrices become equal to the original matrix $\mathcal{M}$. Thus, $1 \leq k \leq \max(n, m)$.

The latent features for the instances from U are directly used to examine the instances' diversity and similarity. For this purpose, instances are clustered by using these latent features. k-means clustering [37] is applied to discover different instance groups. The number of clusters is decided w.r.t. the silhouette score [38]. Using the resulting instance clusters, the performance of the constituent algorithms of $\mathcal{M}$ is analyzed. Then, the characteristics of each instance cluster C_i are examined by building a model Φ using random forest [39] classification[1]. The resulting model is used to disclose the contribution of each algorithms' rank to the clusters most by the help of the Gini importance [39].

4   Computational Results

For the analysis, the results of 10 selection hyper-heuristics run reported in [40] are used. Each hyper-heuristic was tested on each instance for 1 h. Considering the stochastic nature of the hyper-heuristics, each instance run was repeated 10 times. Those hyper-heuristics utilize one of the heuristic selection mechanisms between Adaptive Dynamic Heuristic Set (ADHS) and Simple Random (SR). SR is the uniform random selection while ADHS incorporates a learning mechanism. Each of these selection methods is combined with an acceptance criterion among Adaptive Iterated Limited List-based Threshold Accepting (AILLA), Great Deluge (GD), Improving or Equal (IE), Late Acceptance (LATE) and Simulated Annealing (SA). All the acceptance mechanisms except IE can accept worsening solutions. Thus, they are more aggressive in terms of diversification. IE can provide only limited diversification by accepting equal quality solutions. The hyper-heuristics utilized are listed as follows:

---

[1] The scikit-learn library is used with default values.

- ADHS-AILLA, ADHS-GD, ADHS-IE, ADHS-LATE, ADHS-SA
- SR-AILLA, SR-GD, SR-IE, SR-LATE, SR-SA

Each of these hyper-heuristics was run on HyFlex 1.0^2 [6]. As detailed in Table 1, HyFlex contains 68 instances from 6 problem domains. 30 of these instances were used in the first cross-domain heuristic search challenge $(CHeSC)^3$, which will be referred later. To be able to deliver a strong analysis, the best/minimum and average of 10 runs (MIN-AVG) performance are added as two performance metrics for each hyper-heuristic. Thus, $\mathcal{M}$ has $n = 68$ rows and $m = 20$ columns. For SVD, k is set to 5 which means that only the first 5 dimensions are used out of $\max(68, 20) = 20$.

Table 2 presents the detected 7 instance clusters. The cluster C_2 involving 27 instances, about 40% of all the instances, comes as the largest cluster. Referring to the problems contribution to the overall benchmark set, all the TSP and FSP instances except one fall into the same cluster, C_2. Also, 4 BP and 2 NRP instances happen to be in this cluster. This suggest that either TSP or FSP could

Table 1. Problem domains available in HyFlex 1.0 with the CHeSC 2011 instances' indices

Dataset	#Instances	CHeSC 2011
Boolean Satisfiability (MSAT)	12	3, 5, 4, 10, 11
1D Bin Packing (BP)	12	7, 1, 9, 10, 11
Flowshop Scheduling (FSP)	12	1, 8, 3, 10, 11
Personnel Scheduling (NRP)	12	5, 9, 8, 10, 11
Travelling Salesperson (TSP)	10	0, 8, 2, 7, 6
Vehicle Routing (VRP)	10	6, 2, 5, 1, 9

Table 2. Cluster's problem instances (CHeSC 2011 instances are shown in bold)

Cluster# (size)	MSAT	BP	FSP	NRP	TSP	VRP
C_1 (8)	-	6	-	0, 1, **10**	-	**5**, 7, **8, 9**
C_2 (27)	-	**7, 9, 10, 11**	0, **1**, 2, **3**, 4, 5, 7, **8**, 9, **10, 11**	2, **11**	0, 1, **2**, 3, 4, 5, **6, 7, 8**, 9	-
C_3 (7)	1, 2	-	6	6, 7, **8, 9**	-	-
C_4 (4)	-	0, 1, 4, 5	-	-	-	-
C_5 (8)	-	-	-	3, 4, **5**	-	0, **1, 2**, 3, 4
C_6 (4)	-	2, 3, 8	-	-	-	**6**
C_7 (10)	0, **3, 4, 5**, 6, 7, 8, 9, **10, 11**	-	-	-	-	-

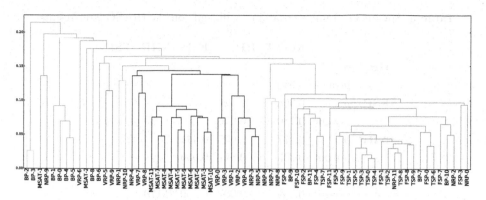

Fig. 1. Hierarchical clustering of the HyFlex instances using the instances' latent features through MIN-AVG data

be switched with a new problem or the problem instances used could be revised for better benchmark diversity. The cluster C_7 also carries an interesting property of having a single problem, i.e. 10 out of 12 SAT instances. As the smallest clusters, C_4 involves only 4 BP instances while C_7 is composed of 3 BP and 1 VRP instances. Rather detailed instance similarity analysis can be performed with the hierarchical clustering as illustrated in Fig. 1. For instance, NRP-11 & TSP-8 and FSP-0 & TSP-6 instances share highly similar characteristics.

In addition to evaluating the complete instance set, the fairness of the CHeSC 2011 competition is examined. For this purpose, the distribution of the instances used in the competition against the clusters are considered. From each cluster, $C_1 \rightarrow C_7$, the proportions of the competition instances are ~38% (3/8), ~56% (15/27), ~29% (2/7), ~25% (1/4), ~38% (3/8), ~25% (1/4) and ~50% (5/10), respectively. Although the instance set is rather small, the selected instances for the competition show reasonable level of diversity. Additionally, the competition results[4] are also taken into account to see whether the clusters found makes sense on the results. It should be noted that the competition results are based on the F1 scoring which gives 10, 8, 6, 5, 4, 3, 2, 1 and 0 from the best to the worst performing hyper-heuristics on each instance. Also, the scores are given based on the average performance of the competing algorithms. Table 3 illustrates both the Spearman's rank correlation coefficients (ρ) and p-values (with 95% confidence) between each problem domain pairs based on the competition. The results indicate there are strong correlations between the following problem pairs: MSAT-VRP, BP-FSP, BP-TSP, FSP-TSP, FSP-VRP and NRP-VRP. Referring to the cluster C_2, the strong similarity between BP, FSP and TSP is also detected on the competition setting. NRP-VRP correlation is also revealed considering that in two clusters, C_1 and C_5, NRP and VRP have instances. Differently, MSAT-VRP pair points out strong correlation even though it was not discovered in the proposed approach. Yet, such a difference possible since

---

[4] http://www.asap.cs.nott.ac.uk/external/chesc2011/results.html.

Table 3. Spearman's rank correlation coefficients on the CHeSC 2011 results

		MSAT	BP	FSP	NRP	TSP
BP	ρ	0.112				
	p-value	0.640				
FSP	ρ	0.368	0.529			
	p-value	0.110	0.016			
NRP	ρ	0.477	−0.037	0.444		
	p-value	0.033	0.877	0.050		
TSP	ρ	0.129	0.582	0.786	0.314	
	p-value	0.589	0.007	0.000	0.178	
VRP	ρ	0.550	0.160	0.552	0.475	0.357
	p-value	0.012	0.502	0.012	0.034	0.122

the presented analysis employs a slightly different performance metric, Rank rather than the Formula 1 scoring. It also uses MIN-AVG data rather than only AVG with the runtime of 1 h instead of 10 min. In the competition, the winning hyper-heuristic, i.e. GIHH, shows near/-best performance on MSAT, BP, FSP, TSP and average performance on NRP, VRP. Considering that the MSAT, BP, FSP, TSP competition instances are from C_2 and $C7$ which are the largest instance clusters, the GIHH's leading performance can be validated also from the clusters. As another example, HAHA performs rather well on MSAT, NRP and VRP yet very poor on BP, FSP and TSP. This shows that HAHA fails to address the instances of C_2 while perform effectively on C_7.

Figure 2 presents the boxplots of the average ranks for each tested hyper-heuristic across all the instances from each cluster. For the cluster C_1, the contribution of heuristic selection is rather limited. Clear performance variations are available for the move acceptance criteria. LATE and AILLA provide the top performance, likely due to their list-based characteristics. Overall, SR-LATE reaches the best average rank performance on the 8 instances of C_1. As the largest instance cluster, C_2 contains 27 instances. Thus, the performance of a hyper-heuristic on C_2 can significantly affect its performance across all the instances. Unlike C_1, C_2 seems to be benefiting from utilizing a learning-based heuristic selection mechanism. In that respect, all the hyper-heuristics incorporating ADHS outperform the hyper-heuristics with SR. Besides that, ADHS-AILLA offers significantly better performance compared to the rest. Referring to the cluster C_3, there is a resemblance to the cluster C_1. Yet, the ranks aren't as robust as in C_1. However, the average quality improves on C_3 for SR-AILLA, SR-IE, ADHS-AILLA and ADHS-IE. Especially improvement over the hyper-heuristics using IE indicates that the instances in C_3 do not require aggressive diversification. The results for C_5 indicate that AILLA as an acceptance criterion is good enough to reach high quality results while ADHS can push its performance even further. Again, IE's poor performance reveals that diversification is

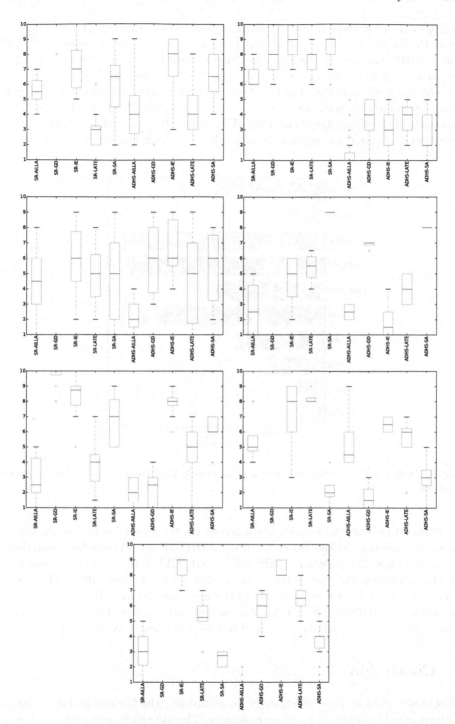

Fig. 2. Average rank boxplots, each plot refers to a cluster (from left to right, top to bottom: the clusters have 8, 27, 7, 4, 8, 4 and 10 instances, respectively)

highly critical for these instances. For C_6, ADHS-GD comes as the best hyper-heuristic for the first time. It should be noted that C_6 is composed of 3 BP and 1 VRP instances as the smallest cluster, with $C4$. In other words, these 4 instances look like rather special case compared to the complete instance set. For C_7, involving only the MSAT instances, there is no clear contribution of one hyper-heuristic sub-mechanism, selection or acceptance. However, the poor performance of the hyper-heuristics with IE denotes that more than limited diversification is required to successfully solve the corresponding MSAT instances.

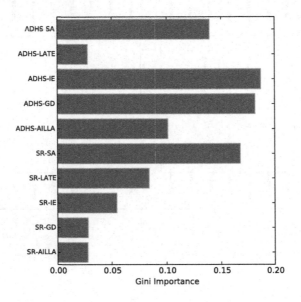

Fig. 3. Importance of each hyper-heuristic's rank performance w.r.t. the instance clusters

Figure 3 presents an importance analysis on the hyper-heuristics' rank performance referring to the latent features. ADHS-IE and ADHS-GD contribute the most to the clusters while ADHS-LATE, SR-AILLA and SR-LATE show limited contribution. This means that if the performance of ADHS-IE or ADHS-GD varies substantially, it is an indicator of the instance diversity. However, the performance of ADHS-LATE, SR-AILLA and SR-LATE give limited information about the instance diversity compared to the other hyper-heuristics tested.

5   Conclusion

This study offers an analysis strategy for examining the fairness and diversity of a given set of benchmark problem instances. The approach performed is practical for any problem where the performance of an algorithm can be quantified, e.g. in terms of solution quality, runtime, success rate etc. It can particularly tell whether a given set of instances is good-enough to evaluate a given algorithm while comparing it against other algorithms tested on the same problem. The analysis approach introduced employs matrix factorization that is applied to a performance data of a suite of algorithms on the instances of a benchmark set. Matrix factorization helps to extract a set of hidden features that can distinguishes the benchmark instances. For experimental analysis, the HyFlex 1.0 hyper-heuristic framework with 6 problem domains is used. Due to the problem-independent nature of hyper-heuristics, the analysis is not just about a single problem but on 6 problems together. The computational results indicated that the proposed idea is able to determine different instance groups, each mainly involving instances from different problem domains. Additionally, it was shown that the existing HyFlex problem instances maintain some level of diversity which could still be further improved. The diversity on HyFlex was also successfully reflected to the 1st cross-domain heuristic search challenge (CHeSC 2011) that was performed a subset of those HyFlex instances.

The study will be extended by using generic instance features, as in [41] , for a deeper analysis. Next, a set of hand-picked problem specific features will be used for each problem so that the existing instance analysis techniques will be incorporated. The hand-picked features will be additionally utilized to perform algorithm selection [4] on hyper-heuristics Also, new problems will be added while providing more instances for each existing problem domain. Finally, the hyper-heuristics from CHeSC 2011 will be integrated in order to make a similar analysis on the algorithms.

References

1. Koren, Y., Bell, R., Volinsky, C., et al.: Matrix factorization techniques for recommender systems. Computer **42**(8), 30–37 (2009)
2. Su, X., Khoshgoftaar, T.M.: A survey of collaborative filtering techniques. Adv. Artif. Intell. **2009**, 4 (2009)
3. Mısır, M., Sebag, M.: Alors: an algorithm recommender system. Artif. Intell. **244**, 291–314 (2017)
4. Rice, J.: The algorithm selection problem. Adv. Comput. **15**, 65–118 (1976)
5. Golub, G.H., Reinsch, C.: Singular value decomposition and least squares solutions. Numer. Math. **14**(5), 403–420 (1970)
6. Ochoa, G., et al.: HyFlex: a benchmark framework for cross-domain heuristic search. In: Hao, J.-K., Middendorf, M. (eds.) EvoCOP 2012. LNCS, vol. 7245, pp. 136–147. Springer, Heidelberg (2012). doi:10.1007/978-3-642-29124-1_12
7. Burke, E.K., Hyde, M., Kendall, G., Ochoa, G., Ozcan, E., Woodward, J.R.: A classification of hyper-heuristic approaches. In: Gendreau, M., Potvin, J.Y. (eds.) Handbook of Metaheuristics. International Series in Operations Research & Management Science, vol. 146, pp. 449–468. Springer, Boston (2010)
8. Burke, E.K., Gendreau, M., Hyde, M., Kendall, G., Ochoa, G., Özcan, E., Qu, R.: Hyper-heuristics: a survey of the state of the art. J. Oper. Res. Soc. **64**(12), 1695–1724 (2013)
9. Chen, S., Li, Z., Yang, B., Rudolph, G.: Quantum-inspired hyper-heuristics for energy-aware scheduling on heterogeneous computing systems. IEEE Trans. Parallel Distrib. Syst. **27**(6), 1796–1810 (2016)

10. Pillay, N.: A review of hyper-heuristics for educational timetabling. Ann. Oper. Res. **239**(1), 3–38 (2016)
11. Terashima-Marin, H., Morán-Saavedra, A., Ross, P.: Forming hyper-heuristics with gas when solving 2D-regular cutting stock problems. In: IEEE Congress on Evolutionary Computation (CEC), vol. 2, pp. 1104–1110. IEEE (2005)
12. Sotelo-Figueroa, M.A., Soberanes, H.J.P., Carpio, J.M., Huacuja, H.J.F., Reyes, L.C., Alcaraz, J.A.S., Espinal, A.: Generating bin packing heuristic through grammatical evolution based on bee swarm optimization. In: Melin, P., Castillo, O., Kacprzyk, J. (eds.) Nature-Inspired Design of Hybrid Intelligent Systems. SCI, vol. 667, pp. 655–671. Springer, Cham (2017). doi:10.1007/978-3-319-47054-2_43
13. Bader-El-Den, M., Poli, R.: Generating SAT local-search heuristics using a GP hyper-heuristic framework. In: Monmarché, N., Talbi, E.-G., Collet, P., Schoenauer, M., Lutton, E. (eds.) EA 2007. LNCS, vol. 4926, pp. 37–49. Springer, Heidelberg (2008). doi:10.1007/978-3-540-79305-2_4
14. Burke, E.K., Hyde, M.R., Kendall, G., Ochoa, G., Ozcan, E., Woodward, J.R.: Exploring hyper-heuristic methodologies with genetic programming. In: Mumford, C.L., Jain, L.C. (eds.) Computational Intelligence. Intelligent Systems Reference Library, vol. 1, pp. 177–201. Springer, Heidelberg (2009)
15. Burke, E.K., MacCarthy, B.L., Petrovic, S., Qu, R.: Knowledge discovery in a hyper-heuristic for course timetabling using case-based reasoning. In: Burke, E., De Causmaecker, P. (eds.) Practice and Theory of Automated Timetabling IV. LNCS, vol. 2740, pp. 276–287. Springer, Heidelberg (2003). doi:10.1007/978-3-540-45157-0_18
16. Maashi, M., Kendall, G., Özcan, E.: Choice function based hyper-heuristics for multi-objective optimization. Appl. Soft Comput. **28**, 312–326 (2015)
17. Marín-Blázquez, J.G., Schulenburg, S.: A hyper-heuristic framework with XCS: learning to create novel problem-solving algorithms constructed from simpler algorithmic ingredients. In: Kovacs, T., Llorà, X., Takadama, K., Lanzi, P.L., Stolzmann, W., Wilson, S.W. (eds.) IWLCS 2003-2005. LNCS, vol. 4399, pp. 193–218. Springer, Heidelberg (2007). doi:10.1007/978-3-540-71231-2_14
18. Cowling, P., Kendall, G., Soubeiga, E.: A hyperheuristic approach to scheduling a sales summit. In: Burke, E., Erben, W. (eds.) PATAT 2000. LNCS, vol. 2079, pp. 176–190. Springer, Heidelberg (2001). doi:10.1007/3-540-44629-X_11
19. Da Costa, L., Fialho, A., Schoenauer, M., Sebag, M.: Adaptive operator selection with dynamic multi-armed bandits. In: Proceedings of Genetic and Evolutionary Computation Conference (GECCO), PP. 913–920. Atlanta, Georgia, USA (2008)
20. Epitropakis, M.G., Caraffini, F., Neri, F., Burke, E.K.: A separability prototype for automatic memes with adaptive operator selection. In: IEEE Symposium on Foundations of Computational Intelligence (FOCI), PP. 70–77. IEEE (2014)
21. Kotthoff, L.: Algorithm selection for combinatorial search problems: a survey. AI Mag. **35**(3), 48–60 (2014)
22. Park, J., Mei, Y., Nguyen, S., Chen, G., Johnston, M., Zhang, M.: Genetic programming based hyper-heuristics for dynamic job shop scheduling: cooperative coevolutionary approaches. In: Heywood, M.I., McDermott, J., Castelli, M., Costa, E., Sim, K. (eds.) EuroGP 2016. LNCS, vol. 9594, pp. 115–132. Springer, Cham (2016). doi:10.1007/978-3-319-30668-1_8
23. Sotelo-Figueroa, M., Soberanes, H., Carpio, J., Fraire Huacuja, H., Reyes, L., Soria Alcaraz, J.: Evolving bin packing heuristic using micro-differential evolution with indirect representation. In: Castillo, O., Melin, P., Kacprzyk, J. (eds.) Recent Advances on Hybrid Intelligent Systems, vol. 451, pp. 349–359. Studies in Computational Intelligence. Springer, Heidelberg (2013)

24. Cheeseman, P., Kanefsky, B., Taylor, W.M.: Where the really hard problems are. In: IJCAI, vol. 91, pp. 331–337 (1991)
25. Jones, T., Forrest, S., et al.: Fitness distance correlation as a measure of problem difficulty for genetic algorithms. ICGA **95**, 184–192 (1995)
26. Ruan, Y., Kautz, H.A., Horvitz, E.: The backdoor key: a path to understanding problem hardness. In: AAAI, vol. 4, pp. 118–123 (2004)
27. Smith-Miles, K., Lopes, L.: Measuring instance difficulty for combinatorial optimization problems. Comput. Oper. Res. **39**(5), 875–889 (2012)
28. Leyton-Brown, K., Hoos, H.H., Hutter, F., Xu, L.: Understanding the empirical hardness of NP-complete problems. Commun. ACM **57**(5), 98–107 (2014)
29. van Hemert, J.I.: Evolving combinatorial problem instances that are difficult to solve. Evol. Comput. **14**(4), 433–462 (2006)
30. Smith-Miles, K., van Hemert, J.I.: Discovering the suitability of optimisation algorithms by learning from evolved instances. Ann. Math. Artif. Intell. **61**(2), 87 (2011)
31. Lopes, L., Smith-Miles, K.: Generating applicable synthetic instances for branch problems. Oper. Res. **61**(3), 563–577 (2013)
32. Smith-Miles, K., Bowly, S.: Generating new test instances by evolving in instance space. Comput. Oper. Res. **63**, 102–113 (2015)
33. Malitsky, Y., Merschformann, M., O'Sullivan, B., Tierney, K.: Structure-preserving instance generation. In: Festa, P., Sellmann, M., Vanschoren, J. (eds.) LION 2016. LNCS, vol. 10079, pp. 123–140. Springer, Cham (2016). doi:10.1007/978-3-319-50349-3_9
34. Smith-Miles, K., Tan, T.T.: Measuring algorithm footprints in instance space. In: IEEE Congress on Evolutionary Computation (CEC), pp. 1–8. IEEE (2012)
35. Jolliffe, I.: Principal Component Analysis. Wiley Online Library, Hoboken (2002)
36. Saul, L.K., Roweis, S.T.: Think globally, fit locally: unsupervised learning of low dimensional manifolds. J. Mach. Learn. Res. **4**, 119–155 (2003)
37. Kaufman, L., Rousseeuw, P.J.: Finding Groups in Data: an Introduction to Cluster Analysis, vol. 344. John Wiley & Sons, Hoboken (2009)
38. Rousseeuw, P.J.: Silhouettes: a graphical aid to the interpretation and validation of cluster analysis. J. Comput. Appl. Math. **20**, 53–65 (1987)
39. Breiman, L.: Random forests. Mach. Learn. **45**(1), 5–32 (2001)
40. Mısır, M.: Intelligent hyper-heuristics: a tool for solving generic optimisation problems. Ph.D. thesis, Department of Computer Science, KU Leuven (2012)
41. Mısır, M., Handoko, S.D., Lau, H.C.: OSCAR: online selection of algorithm portfolios with case study on memetic algorithms. In: Dhaenens, C., Jourdan, L., Marmion, M.-E. (eds.) LION 2015. LNCS, vol. 8994, pp. 59–73. Springer, Cham (2015). doi:10.1007/978-3-319-19084-6_6

Learning to Describe Collective Search Behavior of Evolutionary Algorithms in Solution Space

Lei Liu, Chengshan Pang, Weiming Liu, and Bin Li[✉]

School of Information Science and Technology,
University of Science and Technology of China, Hefei, Anhui, China
binli@ustc.edu.cn

Abstract. Evolutionary algorithms (EAs) are a kind of population-based meta-heuristic optimization methods, which have proven to have superiorities in solving NP-complete and NP-hard optimization problems. But until now, there is lacking in the researches of effective representation method to describe the collective search behavior of the Evolutionary Algorithm, while it is useful for researchers and engineers to understand and compare different EAs better. In the past, most of the theoretical researches cannot directly guide for practical applications. To bridge the gap between theoretical research and practice, we present a generic and reusable framework for learning features to describe collective behavior of EAs in this paper. Firstly, we represent the collective behavior of EAs with a parent-child difference of population distribution encoded by self-organizing map (SOM). Then, we train a Convolutional Neural Network (CNN) to learn problem-invariant features from the samples of EAs' collective behavior. Lastly, experiment results demonstrate that our framework can effectively learn discriminative features representing collective behavior of EAs. In the behavioral feature space stretched by the obtained features, the collective behavior samples of various EAs on various testing problems exhibit obvious aggregations that highly correlated with EAs but very weakly related to testing problems. We believe that the learned features are meaningful in analyzing EAs, i.e. it can be used to measure the similarity of EAs according to their inner behavior in solution space, and further guide in selecting an appropriate combination of sub-algorithm of a hybrid algorithm according to the diversity of candidate sub-algorithm instead of blind.

Keywords: Evolutionary algorithms · Collective behavior · Representation learning · Convolutional neural network · Self-organizing map

1 Introduction

In artificial intelligence, EAs are a kind of stochastic optimization methods. Evolutionary Algorithm (EA) starts with an initial population of solutions, then gradually update them by multiple iterations with the guidance of fitness to obtain optimal solutions. The convergence of EA is usually achieved through iterations, and a set of high dimensional population data is produced in each iteration. So, in the whole

© Springer International Publishing AG 2017
Y. Shi et al. (Eds.): SEAL 2017, LNCS 10593, pp. 196–207, 2017.
https://doi.org/10.1007/978-3-319-68759-9_17

process, a large amount of data is generated. While direct observation and analysis of these data are difficult. Most of the researches mainly focus on the performance of EAs, relatively little attention is paid on the search behavior of EAs. As a result, although EAs have been successfully applied in many domains, there is often full of confusions for users to understand them, let alone to know how the solutions are discovered. Meaningful features can help people understand and compare the behavior of EAs in high-dimensional space, and are useful for people to manipulate EAs in a more reasonable way.

In recent years, a few researchers have dedicated to empirically analyze the collective behavior of EA. In [3], Turkey et al. presented a model that extracts and quantifies features to capture the collective behavior. The proposed model focuses on studying the topological distribution of an algorithm's activity by SOM [1]. It defines two properties called exploitation and exploration behavior, which is an important contribution to investigate the collective search behavior of population-based search algorithms. In [4], the authors defined an indicator of the exploitation behavior of an EA. The above methods are based on the characteristics of manual definition rather than automatic feature learning. In [7], Pang et al. tried to extract discriminative features from the generation-wise collective behavior data of several EAs on fitness landscapes via Slow Feature Analysis (SFA) [14, 15], with purpose to find out whether there exist differences between the searching behavior of different EAs running on the same or different fitness landscapes. It has been shown that the features of one-generation offspring exhibit aggregative and distinguishable nature via unsupervised learning. However, the SFA-based method still has shortcomings: Firstly, when extracting features of a new EA with SFA, all the previous training data must be included, which is computationally expensive. Secondly, it is somehow unnatural to fix the artificially generated parent population and treat its one generation offspring as the samples of EAs' behavior. What we want is a tool that can extract discriminative features of EAs' behavior from the data collected from real runs of the EAs on problems, and after our nets have been well trained, the tool can be used as an off-the-shelf feature extractor that can do feature extraction for any new EAs. To meet this end, a generic and reusable framework is designed and presented in this paper to extract discriminative collective behavior features from data generated by EAs in a real run.

In order to obtain a more natural and reasonable description of EAs' collective behavior, deep representation learning techniques are considered in our research, which has proven to be able to learn features from real running data in many applications [22]. To handle the difficulty of representing population distribution universally, SOM is adopted to map high-dimensional solution space to a 2-dimensional grid, in which the neighborhood relationship between samples (population distributions) is maintained. To overcome the limitation of one-generation offspring, a more general representation of EAs' behavior is designed, that is the variation of arbitrary successive 2 generations represented in SOM-based probability model. The new definition of collective behavior describes better the change in distribution between child-parent populations. The whole framework of the proposed method is illustrated in Fig. 1. Firstly, a number of representative evolutionary algorithms [5], classical evolutionary programming (CEP) [6], differential evolution (DE) [8], evolution strategy (ES) [9] and genetic algorithm (GA) [10], are applied to a number of testing problems of different characteristics, e.g.

single/multiple model, with/without dependence between variables, etc., to get collective data. Then, SOM is adopted to transform the collective data into a uniform representation of population distribution. After that, two data sets, training and testing datasets [19], are prepared for training a Convolutional Neural Network (CNN) [2] as a feature extractor. For CNN training, the task is defined as training a classifier to discriminate various EAs. With this setting, it is possible to learn collective behavior features that are only related to EAs themselves, invariant to various problems under solving.

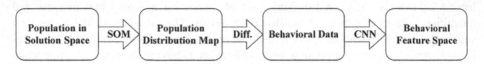

Fig. 1. The schematic of our formulation.

Specifically, in order to promote deeper study in this field, we open our dataset and source code. Our results can be reproduced with the source code and trained models available at https://github.com/liulei13/EAs_analysis.git.

In summary, the main contributions of this paper are listed below:

- A new representation of the collective behavior of EAs based on the difference of SOM-based representation of parent-child population distribution is presented.
- A generic and reusable framework is proposed to learn discriminative features of EAs' collective behavior, empirical studies show that the extracted features are stable with respect to the algorithms.

2 Uniform Representation of Population Distribution of EAs and Definition of Collective Behavior of EA

A universal representation of EAs' collective behavior is an important component for preparing samples for feature learning. Since it is expected that the samples should be taken from real runs of EAs on the testing problems of various characteristics, the representation should be valid to represent the change of population distributions. In this paper, SOM [12, 13] is adopted to build a normalized representation of population distribution. Then, the difference of SOM representations between two successive generations is calculated as the representation of EAs' collective behavior.

The schematic of our formulation is shown in Fig. 1. Firstly, we transfer population in solution space to collective distribution by SOM which can preserve the topological structure of the population in solution space. Then we compute behavioral data in solution space by our definition of the behavior of EAs. Finally, we utilize a trained feature extractor to construct behavioral feature space for different problems. In each feature space, we can easily identify different EAs that only need the previous generations of population data (one generation or ten generations in succession).

2.1   Representing Population Distribution of EAs by SOM

A straightforward way to represent the EAs' population is to chain the individuals sequentially. But such representation suffers from a drawback that it may change when the individuals change their positions in the chain. Since the distribution of the population is what we need really in feature learning, a normalized representation that describes the distribution and will not change with respect to the individual's position in the population. SOM not only can maintain intrinsic neighbor relations but also have strong learning ability and generalization ability, therefore, SOM is adopted in this paper as a normalized representation of population distribution.

SOM [12] is a neural network based on competitive learning, with the ability to map continuous and discrete high-dimensional space V to a two-dimensional or three-dimensional discrete space A. As illustrated in Fig. 2(a), this mapping is a preservative mapping that maintains the original spatial neighborhood.

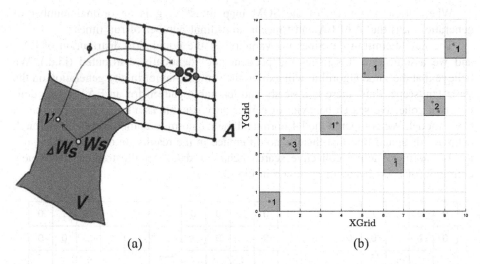

(a)   (b)

Fig. 2. (a) is a description of the high-dimensional space V to low-dimensional space A mapping; (b) is a normalized representation that describes the distribution and will not change with respect to the individual's position in the population.

In Fig. 2(b), we make a more intuitive description of the implementation process and results of SOM. After being trained, a population in the initial 30-dimensional solution space is mapped into a two-dimensional grid, where the hitting times of each node are recorded and used to represent the value of the node. For example, this is a 10×10 SOM grid as showed in Fig. 2(b), and 10 individuals are mapped into the two-dimensional grid. In our work, we adopted 100×100 SOM grid to represent a population of EAs and there are 100 individuals at any generation. Certainly, other sizes of the SOM grid, such as $10 \times 10, 50 \times 50$ and 200×200, are also achievable. It should be noted that the setting of the size of SOM grid is a tradeoff between performance and compute cost.

2.2 Definition of Collective Behavior of EA

In [7], one-generation offspring of EAs from the same initial parental population is regarded as collective search behavior of EAs. It is reasonable because the offspring was obtained by different EAs from the same initial parental population, therefore the offspring contains most differences between EAs. However, this representation is somehow unnatural because, in real applications, it is hard to require all compared algorithms to start from the same parent population all the time. To make the analysis method more appropriate and universal in a real run, a new definition of collective behavior is designed, i.e. the difference of population distributions represented in SOM map in two successive generations of an EA. The formula of the definition for calculation is as follows:

$$\text{Behavior}(g)^{(k,t)} = \left\| SOMmap(g+1)^{(k,t)} - SOMmap(g)^{(k,t)} \right\| \qquad (1)$$

Where $\| \cdot \|$ is a norm of the SOM map in $\mathbb{R}^{p \times p}$, g is an ordinal number of generation, k is the id of EA and t means an ordinal number of run times

The new definition describes the variation of the population distribution of EAs, and we assume that it satisfies independent and identically distributed (i.i.d.). We believe that the same algorithm will exhibit the same behavior in any generation on the same landscape, thus, there is a steady and learnable pattern for an EA. So, the definition of collective search behavior of EAs is very suitable as a training data to train a CNN model. We compared the L1 norm and the L2 norm to compute collective search behavior data, and find that there is no difference in the results. In our dataset, we use the L1 norm to define collective search behavior data. An illustration of our new definition of EAs' behavior is shown in Fig. 3.

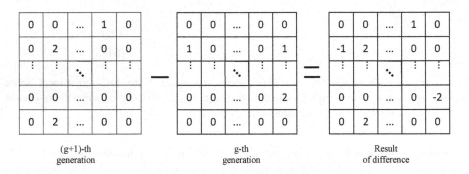

(g+1)-th
generation

g-th
generation

Result
of difference

Fig. 3. An illustration of our new definition of EAs' behavior

3 Learning Discriminative Features of Collective Behavior by CNN

As is known to all, deep convolutional neural networks have recently achieved many successes in visual recognition tasks including image classification [2], object detection [18] and scene parsing [21]. If the training data is sufficient, CNN is capable of learning two-dimensional spatial information. Meanwhile, CNN has the ability to map the high-dimensional nonlinear space into a low-dimensional linear space [20], which is useful to analyze and visualize collective search behavior data of EAs. The method trains an embedder that can transform instances into a feature space.

3.1   Training a CNN as Feature Extractor

It is vital to design a reasonable structure of CNN. We explore different network structures and parameter settings to achieve tradeoffs between performance and speed. Our designed CNN architecture as shown in Fig. 4(b). The flowchart of behavior-to-feature mapping and visualization is shown in Fig. 4(a). Overall, the structure of our CNN contains 2 convolutional layers and 3 fully connected layers.

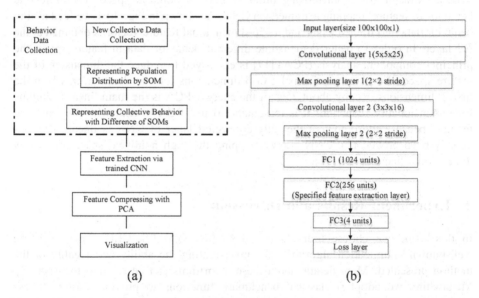

(a)   (b)

Fig. 4. (a) is the flowchart of behavior-to-feature mapping and visualization; (b) is the architecture of the proposed CNN.

In the process of training a CNN, the input layer is input with a $100 \times 100 \times 1$ behavior data. Convolutional layer means the output of the previous layer will be convoluted with filters, where the filter is often 5×5 or 3×3. ReLU is the abbreviation of Rectified Linear Units [16] and follow the convolutional layer, which is an activation function defined as $f(x) = max(0, x)$. Max pooling layer is a form of non-linear down-sampling, which partitions the input data into a set of non-overlapping rectangles and, for each such sub-region, outputs the maximum. In a fully connected layer, neurons have full connections to all activations in the previous layer, as seen in regular Neural Networks. The loss layer specifies how the network training penalizes the deviation between the predicted and true labels and is normally the last layer in the network. Finally, we use Stochastic Gradient Descent (SGD) algorithms to update parameters of convolutional layers and fully connected layers.

In our model, the loss function is the cross-entropy, which can be calculated by:

$$L = - \sum_{i=1}^{S} l_i \log(O_i = 1|W) - \sum_{i=1}^{S} (1 - l_i) \log(O_i = 0|W) \tag{2}$$

where l_i is the label of EAs, We denotes the collection of all network parameters in our model. S denotes the total number of EAs as the training data of our model.

3.2 Behavior-to-Feature Mapping and Visualization

The purpose of this work is not to get a classifier with high accuracy, but to obtain a feature extractor for characterising different EAs in solution space. Therefore, the behavior-to-feature mapping is trained via CNN. As shown in Fig. 4(b), we feed testing behavior data into trained CNN and a 256-dimensional feature vector is obtained at the fc2 layer. In order to better demonstrate different behavior data in feature space, the principal component analysis (PCA) [17] is employed to reduce the dimension of the feature space. We plot the principal 2 or 3 dimensions for visualization, in which the first 2 dimensions occupy about 75% of the energy. PCA is the main linear technique for dimensionality reduction. It is reasonable to use PCA to deal with the extracted features because the output of the fully connected layer of CNN is linear. This has already been proved that CNN allows mapping the high nonlinear space into a low dimensional linear space [20].

4 Experiment Results and Discussion

In this work, we choose four classical EAs (i.e. GA, ES, CEP, DE) which are well-known optimization algorithms for investigating the ability and legality of the method presented. More details about these algorithms can be referred to paper [7]. Meanwhile, we adopt 6 classical benchmark functions to provide various fitness landscapes for investigation, they are: Ackley function [11], the Elliptic function [11], Rastrigin's function [11], Rosenbrock's function [11], Schwefel's problem 1.2 [11], Sphere function [11], which represent different complex problems. In this paper, the dimensionality of all testing functions are set to 30 and the global optimum of each testing function is the minimum value in the solution space for all experiments. More details about the test functions can be referred to paper [7]. Specifically, the main parameters in experiments are given in Table 1.

The sampling process can be merged into the execution of EAs, which makes the method presented in this paper more reasonable and practical. The EAs under analysis were performed on the selected representative testing problems, the successive populations generated at each iteration were adopted as the population samples. To make the experimental research be tractable and comparable, the range of value for each dimension was set from −32 to 32. It is reasonable because the search behavior of algorithms is believed to be independent of the size of the range. In order to obtain the statistical robust features from the random process of EAs' execution, each algorithm

Table 1. The main parameters in experiments.

Parameter	Value
Population size	100
The dimensionality of individual	30
The size of SOM	100×100
The number of EAs	4
The number of test functions	6

was performed 10000 times on each test function. In the article, the proposed method named as the CNN-based method, and will compare it with the SFA-based method [7].

We designed two experiments to verify our idea: (1) Verifying the validity of our behavioral definition on different testing functions with the SFA-based method; (2) Comparing the CNN-based method with the SFA-based method in their behavioral feature space. (3) Analysing multi-generation offspring with the CNN-based method.

In this experiment, we re-implement SFA-based method [7] with two behavioral definitions, which are one-generation offspring defined by the author in the paper [7] and our new behavioral definition. The initial population is randomly sampled in the area $[-32, 32]^{30}$. This is different from the author's area in $[5, 10]^{30}$, as this area does not contain the optimal solution 0, which may easily lead to behavior bias on the behavior of algorithms. The one-generation offspring generated by four algorithms with the same initial population on the same benchmark function are collected as the sample data of collective behavior of EAs, our behavioral data compute the difference between the distribution of the current data and the distribution of the initial population, as illustrated in Fig. 3. There are 2000(offspring populations)$\times$ 4(EAs) = 8000 samples in the input sequence, they is mapped into the 2-D feature space that are extracted via the process presented in Fig. 4(a). Another 8000 new behavioral samples are the distribution of the previous samples subtracting the distribution of the same initial population.

4.1 Verifying the Validity of Our Behavioral Definition on Different Testing Functions with the SFA-Based Method

From Fig. 5, it can be observed that the sample distribution of four algorithms exhibits clear aggregative and discriminative nature in the feature space constructed by slow features. Beyond that, for all the six benchmark functions, the behavior of four EAs exhibits a sort of stable similarity relationship, that is the behavior of CEP, DE and GA are more similar compared to that of ES. The above conclusions are consistent with the authors of the SFA-based method. It must be emphasized that the two definitions yield exactly the same result, so we only draw a set of experimental results in Fig. 5. Why the behavior of the two definitions is surprisingly consistent. This is not difficult to analyze, for a fixed initial population, in the calculation process is equivalent to the same component. The first step of SFA will remove the same component, that is to say, the actual participation in the calculation of the data is exactly the same, although they come from different behavioral definitions. At the same time, it also verifies that the author's behavioral definition has limitations, only a special case of our behavioral definition. In contrast, our behavioral definition is more general and reasonable.

4.2 Comparing of the CNN-Based Method and the SFA-Based Method in Their Behavioral Feature Space

In this experiment, we use the collected behavioral data in 4.1 as testing data. We collected sufficient behavioral data by executing the algorithm under the same conditions for training a feature extractor with CNN, the whole process as described in Sect. 3.1. There are 8000(offspring populations) × 4(EAs)× 6(benchmark functions) = 192 thousand samples. During the training stage of the proposed model, the label of CNN is the class of algorithm. After training, the proposed model achieves a precision over 97%. Meanwhile, it also has fast convergence rate on the test data. To sum up, the fast convergence rate of the model shows that our definition of collective search behavior of EAs is learnable and effective. High accuracy illustrates that our method is appropriate and efficient for extracting discriminative features.

The test data is mapped into the 2-D feature space as illustrated in Fig. 4(a) and the result is shown in Fig. 6. Comparing Fig. 6 with Fig. 5, it can be observed that the distribution of testing samples of EAs exhibits more clear and consistent discrimination on the different test functions than SFA-based method. Beyond that, we find there are stable relative (similar) relationships of four EAs in two different feature space constructed by the SFA-based method and the CNN-based method respectively. The amazing consistency implies that the behavior of different EAs only determined by the inner mechanism of the EA. Another advantage of our method is less computational

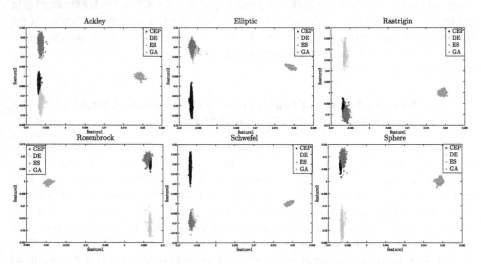

Fig. 5. The distribution of testing samples of 4 EAs on 6 benchmark functions in the behavioral feature space constructed by the SFA-based method.

cost and reusability for new behavior data. The model presented has the capability to

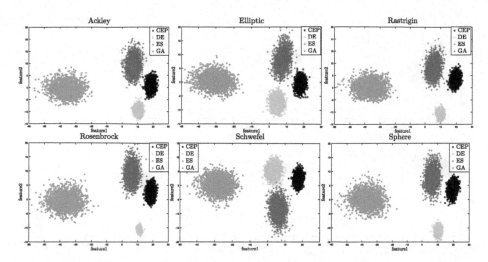

Fig. 6. The distribution of testing samples of 4 EAs on 6 benchmark functions in the behavioral feature space constructed by CNN.

deal with new samples without the need to retrain the system.

4.3 Multi-generation Offspring in Their Behavioral Feature Space Using CNN-Based Method with Our New Definition of Behavior

In this experiment, varying generation number were investigated. Firstly, we collected 1000(run times) × 4(EAs) × 6(benchmark functions) × 5(the number of generations) = 60 thousand samples 80% of which was used as training data and 20% as test data for two specific generation number experiment. Different from the Sect. 4.2, we just fine tuned the training data, then our model achieved precision over 97%, which cost no more than 5 min. It is a big advantage in the calculation of efficiency and reusability without the need for costly re-learning. Therefore, arbitrarily increase in algorithms and test functions is allowed.

In Fig. 7, it can be observed that the distribution of testing samples of EAs also exhibits clearly and steady aggregative and discriminative. Meanwhile, the similarity relationship among 4 EAs is still stable, that is the behavior of CEP, DE and GA are more similar compared to that of ES, which is very weakly related to testing problems. In addition, the experimental results show that our approach allows dealing with multi-generations behavioral data in a real run, which is more close to the nature of the algorithm. Specifically, I have to point out that as the generation number increases, the convergence of the data will become more and more obvious, so we add a scale normalization in the calculation of behavioral data at each generation. The choice of appropriate generation number requires some experience.

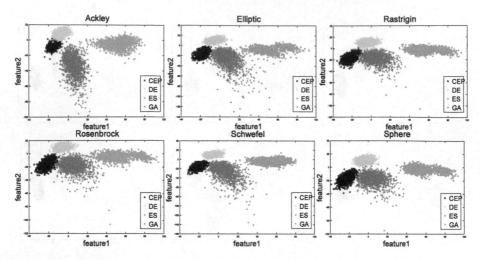

Fig. 7. The distribution of multi-generation offspring samples of 4 EAs on 6 benchmark functions in the behavioral feature space constructed by CNN

5   Conclusions

This paper proposes using a self-organizing map to encode the population distribution of various EAs in the solution space, and a convolutional neural network to extract features which can be used to discriminate the behavior of different algorithms.

Experiment studies are performed with four EAs and six continuous functions, which show that the new definition of EAs' behavior is more accurate and natural, and the CNN-extracted features can more accurately describe the collective search behavior of EAs in the calculation of efficiency, generality, expansibility and reusability than SFA-based method. CNN-derived features are usually difficult to be interpreted, while we can treat it as a black box model in analyzing the behavior of EAs. A very promising application is to calculate the similarity of evolutionary algorithms in the behavioral feature space for algorithm portfolios.

Acknowledgment. The work is supported by the National Natural Science Foundation of China under grand No. 61473271 and No. 61331015.

References

1. Kohonen, T.: The self-organizing map. Neurocomputing **21**, 1–6 (1998)
2. Krizhevsky, A., Sutskever, I., Hinton, G.E.: Imagenet classification with deep convolutional neural networks. In: Advances in Neural Information Processing Systems, pp. 1097–1105 (2012)

3. Turkey, M., Poli, R.: An empirical tool for analysing the collective behaviour of population-based algorithms. In: Di Chio, C., Agapitos, A., Cagnoni, S., Cotta, C., de Vega, F.F., Di Caro, G.A., Drechsler, R., Ekárt, A., Esparcia-Alcázar, A.I., Farooq, M., Langdon, W.B., Merelo-Guervós, J.J., Preuss, M., Richter, H., Silva, S., Simões, A., Squillero, G., Tarantino, E., Tettamanzi, A.G.B., Togelius, J., Urquhart, N., Uyar, A.Ş., Yannakakis, G.N. (eds.) EvoApplications 2012. LNCS, vol. 7248, pp. 103–113. Springer, Heidelberg (2012). doi:10.1007/978-3-642-29178-4_11

4. Turkey, M., Poli, R.: A model for analysing the collective dynamic behaviour and characterising the exploitation of population-based algorithms. Evol. Comput. **22**(1), 159–188 (2014)

5. Collins, T.: The application of software visualization technology to evolutionary computation. In: A case study in genetic algorithms. Dissertation, The Open University (1998)

6. Yao, X., Liu, Y., Lin, G.: Evolutionary programming made faster. IEEE Trans. Evol. Comput. **3**, 82–102 (1999)

7. Pang, C., Wang, M., Liu, W., Li, B.: Learning features for discriminative behavior analysis of evolutionary algorithms via slow feature analysis. In: Proceedings of the 2016 on Genetic and Evolutionary Computation Conference Companion, pp. 1437–1444. ACM, July 2016

8. Storn, R., Price, K.: Differential evolution–a simple and efficient heuristic for global optimization over continuous spaces. J. Global Optim. **11**, 341–359 (1997)

9. Beyer, H.G., Schwefel, H.P.: Evolution strategies–a comprehensive introduction. Nat. Comput. **1**, 3–52 (2002)

10. Goldberg, D.E.: Genetic Algorithms in Search, Optimization, and Machine Learning. Addison-Wesley Publishing Company, Boston (1989)

11. Tang, K., Li, X., Suganthan, P.N., Yang, Z., Weise, T.: Benchmark functions for the CEC 2008 special session and competition on large scale global optimization. Nat. Inspired Comput. Appl. Lab. (2009)

12. Duch, W., Naud, A.: Multidimensional scaling and Kohonen's self-organizing maps. In: Proceedings of 2nd Conference on "Eural Networks and Their Applications", Szczyrk, Poland, pp. 138–143 April 1996

13. Maaten, L.V.D., Hinton, G.: Visualizing data using t-SNE. J. Mach. Learn. Res. **9**, 2579–2605 (2008)

14. Wiskott, L., Sejnowski, T.J.: Slow feature analysis: Unsupervised learning of invariances. Neural Comput. **14**(4), 715–770 (2002)

15. Berkes, P.: Pattern recognition with slow feature analysis. Comput. Neurosci. (2005)

16. Glorot, X., Bordes, A., Bengio, Y.: Deep sparse rectifier neural networks. In: AISTATS, vol. 15, p. 275 April 2011

17. Abdi, H., Williams, L.J.: Principal component analysis. Wiley Interdisc. Rev.: Comput. Stat. **2**, 433–459 (2010)

18. Girshick, R., Donahue, J., Darrell, T., Malik, J.: Rich feature hierarchies for accurate object detection and semantic segmentation. In: Proceedings of the IEEE Conference on Computer Vision and Pattern Recognition, pp. 580–587 (2014)

19. Butail, S., Bollt, E.M., Porfiri, M.: Analysis and classification of collective behavior using generative modeling and nonlinear manifold learning. J. Theor. Biol. **336**, 185–199 (2013)

20. Brahma, P.P., Wu, D., She, Y.: Why deep learning works: a manifold disentanglement perspective. IEEE Trans. Neural Netw. Learn. Syst. **27**(10), 1997–2008 (2016)

21. Farabet, C., Couprie, C., Najman, L., LeCun, Y.: Learning hierarchical features for scene labeling. IEEE Trans. Pattern Anal. Mach. Intell. **35**(8), 1915–1929 (2013)

22. LeCun, Y., Bengio, Y., Hinton, G.: Deep learning. Nature **521**(7553), 436–444 (2015)

Evolutionary Multiobjective Optimisation

A Hierarchical Decomposition-Based Evolutionary Many-Objective Algorithm

Fangqing Gu and Hai-Lin Liu[✉]

Guangdong University of Technology, Guangzhou, Guangdong, China
{fqgu,hlliu}@gdut.edu.cn

Abstract. The evolutionary multiobjective algorithms have been demonstrated the effectiveness in dealing with multiobjective optimization problems. However, when solving the problems with many objectives, i.e., the number of objectives is greater than three, it needs a large population size to maintain population diversity and provide a good approximation to the Pareto front. The dilemma between limited computational resources and the exponentially increasing population size is a big challenge. Thus, we suggest a hierarchical decomposition-based evolutionary algorithm for solving many-objective optimization problems in this paper. Specifically, it constructs a binary tree on a set of large-scale uniform weight vectors. We only compare a candidate solutions with the solutions on the path from root to a leaf node of the tree to assign it into an appropriate node. The proposed algorithm has lower time complexity. Theoretical analysis shows the complexity of the proposed algorithm is $\mathcal{O}(Mlog(\mathbb{N}))$ for dealing with a new candidate solution. Empirical results fully demonstrate the effectiveness and competitiveness of the proposed algorithm.

Keywords: Decomposition · Evolutionary algorithm · Multiobjective optimization · Binary tree

1 Introduction

Without loss of generality, a multi-objective optimization problem can be formulated as follows:

$$\min \ F(\mathbf{x}) = (f_1(\mathbf{x}), f_2(\mathbf{x}), \dots, f_M(\mathbf{x}))^T$$
$$s.t. \ \mathbf{x} \in \Omega, \tag{1}$$

where $\Omega \subset \mathbb{R}^n$ is the decision space and n is the dimension of the decision variable $\mathbf{x} = (x_1, x_2, \dots, x_n)^T$. $F : \Omega \to \mathbb{R}^M$ consists of M real-value objective functions,

This work was supported by the National Natural Science Foundation of China under Grant 61673121, in part by the Projects of Science and Technology of Guangzhou under Grant 201508010008, and in part by the Natural Science Foundation of Guangdong Province under Grant 2017A030310467.

Y. Shi et al. (Eds.): SEAL 2017, LNCS 10593, pp. 211–223, 2017.
https://doi.org/10.1007/978-3-319-68759-9_18

T is the transpose of a matrix, $M \geq 2$ is the number of objectives. The problem with $M \geq 4$ is called as many-objective optimization problems (MaOPs). For simplicity, we assume that all objectives $f_1, \ldots, f_M$ are nonnegative in this paper. Otherwise, we replace f_i by $f_i + \mu$, where μ is a large enough positive number so that $f_i + \mu > 0$ for all i.

A number of evolutionary multiobjective optimization (EMO) algorithms have been developed for finding a set of solutions to approximate the Pareto front (PF) in a single run [2,6,8,17,22] and successfully applied to multiobjective optimization problems. There has been a rapid growth in research on many-objective optimization evolutionary algorithms (MaOEAs) over the past decade. Comprehensive surveys and additional references on MaOEAs can be found in [14]. However, the performance of most well-known EMO algorithms seriously deteriorates over the number of objectives in solving MaOPs [18]. The dominance-based algorithms, such as nondominated sorting genetic algorithm II (NSGA-II) [6] and strength Pareto evolutionary algorithm 2 (SPEA2) [8] use the Pareto-based ranking as the primary selection mechanism and the density-based selection criterion, e.g. crowding distance, as secondary selection mechanism. The Pareto-based methods may fail to converge to the PF since the algorithms lose the selection pressure toward the PF [4,11]. The decomposition-based algorithms decompose an MOP into a series of scalar optimization problems by a set of weight vectors [19]. It has already shown its success in solving MOPs [1]. However, the weight vectors have a great affect on the performance of the algorithms [13]. Generally, a small population size may not be able to well cover the PF and preserve the population diversity for solving MaOPs. However, larger population size leads the algorithm has high computational complexity and the selection pressure is insufficient. The dilemma between limited computational resources and the exponentially increasing population size is a big challenge. It is imperative to accelerate the speed of the algorithm for solving MaOPs.

Considering of this, we present a hierarchical decomposition-based EMO algorithm for MaOPs in this paper. The proposed approach constructs a binary tree on a set of large-scale uniform weight vectors, and each node is associated with a weight vector. For updating a candidate solution, we compare it with the solutions on a path from the root to a leaf of the tree. Specifically, we compared the candidate solution with the solutions in the interior nodes according to the dominance relationship and the distance between the weight vector and the objective vector of the solution, and the solutions in leaf nodes according to the aggregation objectives. In order to investigate the performance of the proposed algorithm, we compared it with six state-of-the-art evolutionary algorithms on two well-known benchmark problems: DTLZ and WFG test suites. The empirical results fully demonstrate the effectiveness and competitiveness of the proposed algorithm.

The remainder of this paper is organized as follows: Sect. 2 gives the detailed description of the proposed hierarchical decomposition-based EMO algorithm. Section 3 gives the algorithm settings, and performance metrics used for the experimental studies, and the empirical results are presented and analyzed in Sect. 3.3. Finally, we draw a conclusion in Sect. 4.

2 The Proposed Hierarchical Decomposition-Based Evolutionary Algorithm

2.1 Framework of the Proposed Algorithm

The framework of the proposed algorithm is described in Algorithm 1. Firstly, we generate $\mathbb{N}$ uniform unit weight vectors $\mathbf{V} = \{\mathbf{v}_1, \ldots, \mathbf{v}_\mathbb{N}\}$, and construct a binary tree on these weight vectors by the method illustrated in Sect. 2.2. And then N solutions are randomly created as the initial population P, and each member in P is used to update the solutions in the tree, the process of which is illustrated in Sect. 2.3. The level of a solution is defined as the level of the node which is associated with this solution in the tree. At each generation, the solutions with smaller value of the level are selected to create offspring, i.e., mating selection, and then the newly generated offspring is used to update the solutions in the tree. The mating selection is illustrated in Sect. 2.4. When the iterative optimization is finished, it outputs all nondominated solutions. In the following paragraphs, the implementation details of each component in the proposed algorithm will be explained step-by-step.

Algorithm 1. General Framework of the Proposed Algorithm

Input :
- A stopping criterion;
- Genetic operators and their associated parameters;
- $\mathbb{N}$: the number of weight vectors;
- N: the size of the mating pool.

Output: The solutions X.

1   Generate $\mathbb{N}$ uniform unit weight vectors $V = \{\mathbf{v}_1, \ldots, \mathbf{v}_\mathbb{N}\}$ and an initial population P with N individuals;

2   $\mathbb{T} \leftarrow$ ConctructTree($\mathbf{V}$);

3   **for** *each* $\mathbf{x}_i \in P$ **do**

4      $\mathbb{T} \leftarrow$ UpdateTree($\mathbb{T}, \mathbf{x}_i$);

5   **end**

6   **while** *termination criterion is not fulfilled* **do**

7      $Q \leftarrow$ MatingSelection($\mathbb{T}, N$);

8   Create an offspring $\mathbf{x}^c$ based on Q;

9      $\mathbb{T} \leftarrow$ UpdateTree($\mathbb{T}, \mathbf{x}^c$);

10   **end**

11   $X \leftarrow$ Output($\mathbb{T}$)

2.2 Hierarchical Decomposition Strategy

The main idea of this paper is to propose a hierarchical decomposition strategy for decomposition-based EMO algorithm. For this purpose, we first construct a binary tree on a set of uniform weight vectors. Each node of the tree is associated with a weight vector.

The weight vector of the root is set to be the center $\mathbf{v}_0 = (\frac{1}{\sqrt{M}}, \frac{1}{\sqrt{M}}, \ldots, \frac{1}{\sqrt{M}})^T$. Let $\mathbf{V} = \{\mathbf{v}_1, \mathbf{v}_2, \ldots, \mathbf{v}_N\}$ in R_+^M be a set of uniform unit weight vectors. These weight vectors are grouped into two cluster by k-medoids algorithm. The weight vectors of the child nodes are set to be the center of each cluster. Each child node corresponds to one center. And then we assign the weight vectors $\mathbf{V}$ excepting the centers into the closest center. That is, for each weight vector $\mathbf{v}_j \in \mathbf{V}$, it is assigned into the child node which is calculated by:

$$k^* = arg \min_i \langle \mathbf{v}_i^c, \mathbf{v}_j \rangle \qquad (2)$$

where $\langle \mathbf{v}_i^c, \mathbf{v}_j \rangle$ is the acute angle between $\mathbf{v}_i^c$ and $\mathbf{v}_j$, and $\mathbf{v}_i^c$ is the center of ith cluster. Afterwards, the assigned weight vectors are used to construct the subtree of the node in a recursive way.

Figure 1 illustrates the constructed binary tree on a set of weight vectors for a 2-dimensional problem. The weight vector of root is $\mathbf{v}_0 = (\frac{1}{\sqrt{2}}, \frac{1}{\sqrt{2}})^T$. The weight vectors $\{\mathbf{v}_1, \ldots, \mathbf{v}_{12}\}$ are divided into 2 clusters by a k-medoids algorithm, and $\mathbf{v}_4$ and $\mathbf{v}_9$ are the centers of clusters. Then the weight vectors of the child nodes of the root are $\mathbf{v}_4$ and $\mathbf{v}_9$. The remaining weight vectors are assigned into these two nodes by (2). The weight vectors assigned into a node are used to construct the subtree of this node. By this way, we can construct the binary tree as shown in Fig. 1. Moreover, the level of the root node is denoted as l_1, and the level of child nodes of root, e.g. $\mathbf{v}_4$ and $\mathbf{v}_9$ as shown in Fig. 1, are l_2, and so on. The

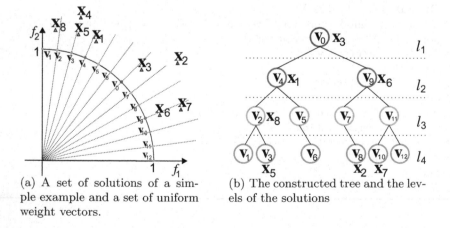

(a) A set of solutions of a simple example and a set of uniform weight vectors.

(b) The constructed tree and the levels of the solutions

Fig. 1. An example of constructed tree and the illustration of the updating procedure.

binary tree showed in Fig. 1 has 4 levels. The level of weight vectors is the same with that of the nodes.

2.3 Updating Strategy of the Solutions in the Tree Based on Dominance and Aggregation Objectives

We suggest a top-down approach based on dominance and aggregation objectives to deal with the candidate solutions one by one. When comparing the candidate solution with the solutions in the interior node, the Pareto relationship works as the primary evaluation mechanism and the distance between the weight vector and the objective vector of the solution as secondary evolution mechanism. This make the proposed algorithm can maintain satisfactory diversity of the population. Whereas the aggregation objective based on the weight vector work as the evaluation criterion for comparing the candidate solution with the solutions in the leaf nodes. It results that the proposed algorithm can have a good convergence ability.

Specifically, Algorithm 2 contains the pseudocode for updating procedure of the solutions in the tree. In the algorithm, $\mathbb{P}$ is a node cursor and initialized with the root of the tree; $\mathbb{P}.\mathbf{v}$ and $\mathbb{P}.\mathbf{x}$ record the weight vector and solution assigned to node $\mathbb{P}$, respectively; $\mathbb{P}.Children$ is the index of the child nodes of $\mathbb{P}$. For a given solution $\mathbf{x}$, it is marked as a nondominated solution at the beginning. We compare it with the solution in the node cursor. If there is no solution corresponds to the node cursor, we directly assign the solution $\mathbf{x}$ into this node (cf. ❸) and no more operation is required; Otherwise, we compare it with the solution in the node cursor. There are three cases of the comparison.

- Case I: If $\mathbf{x}$ dominates the node corresponding solution $\mathbb{P}.\mathbf{x}$, i.e. $\mathbf{x} \prec \mathbb{P}.\mathbf{x}$, then $\mathbb{P}.\mathbf{x}$ is swapped with $\mathbf{x}$ and mark $\mathbf{x}$ as a dominated solution (cf. ❹);
- Case II: If $\mathbf{x}$ is dominated by the node corresponding solution $\mathbb{P}.\mathbf{x}$, i.e. $\mathbb{P}.\mathbf{x} \prec \mathbf{x}$, mark $\mathbf{x}$ as a dominated solution (cf. ❺)
- Case III: If $\mathbf{x}$ and $\mathbb{P}.\mathbf{x}$ are nondominated with each other, this node is associated with the solution which is close to the corresponding weight vector $\mathbb{N}.\mathbf{v}$ by calculating the acute angle between the weight vector and the objective vector (cf. ❻), and $\mathbf{x}$ is associated with the other solution.

Afterwards, the solution $\mathbf{x}$ is transmitted to one child node whose weight vector is closest to the objective vectors of $\mathbf{x}$ (cf. ❼). It can be calculated as:

$$j^* = arg \min_{j \in \mathbb{P}.Children} \langle \mathbb{T}_j.\mathbf{v}, F(\mathbf{x}) \rangle \tag{3}$$

where $\langle \mathbb{T}_j.\mathbf{v}, F(\mathbf{x}) \rangle$ is the acute angle between the weight vector of jth node and the objective vector. Then the node cursor $\mathbb{P}$ is mapped to the child node $\mathbb{T}_{j^*}$. While the solution $\mathbf{x}$ is marked as a dominated solution, we directly transmitted it to the child node and need not compare with the solution corresponded to this node.

Finally, when the node cursor $\mathbb{P}$ maps a leaf node, there are two case for the updating of the solutions. If there is no solution corresponds to this leaf node,

Algorithm 2. Update the solutions in the tree by a given solution

---

Input :
  - The tree $\mathbb{T}$;
  - The solution **x**.

Output: The updated tree $\mathbb{T}$.
1 $\mathbb{P} \to \mathbb{T}_0$; /*mapping the node point to the root of the tree*/
2 $flag \leftarrow 1$.
3 **while** 1 **do**
4   **if** $\mathbb{P}$ *is a leaf node* **then**
5   **if** $\mathbb{P}.\mathbf{x}$ *is empty* **then**
6              $\mathbb{P}.\mathbf{x} \leftarrow \mathbf{x}$;   ❶
7   **else**
8   **if** $F(\mathbf{x})^T \mathbb{P}.\mathbf{v} < F(\mathbb{P}.\mathbf{x})^T \mathbb{P}.\mathbf{v}$ **then**
9                  $\mathbb{P}.\mathbf{x} \leftarrow \mathbf{x}$;   ❷
10   **end**
11   **end**
12   break;
13   **else**
14   **if** $flag == 1$ **then**
15   **if** $\mathbb{P}.\mathbf{x}$ *is empty* **then**
16                 $\mathbb{P}.\mathbf{x} \leftarrow \mathbf{x}$; break;   ❸
17   **else**
18   **if** $\mathbf{x} \prec \mathbb{P}.\mathbf{x}$ **then**
19                     $\mathbb{P}.\mathbf{x} \rightleftharpoons \mathbf{x}$; /*Swapping solutions*/   ❹
20                     $flag \leftarrow 0$;
21   **else if** $\mathbb{P}.\mathbf{x} \prec \mathbf{x}$ **then**
22                     $flag \leftarrow 0$;   ❺
23   **else**
24   **if** $\langle \mathbb{P}.\mathbf{v}, F(\mathbf{x}) \rangle < \langle \mathbb{P}.\mathbf{v}, F(\mathbb{P}.\mathbf{x}) \rangle$ **then**
25                         $\mathbb{P}.\mathbf{x} \rightleftharpoons \mathbf{x}$;   ❻
26   **end**
27   **end**
28   **end**
29   **end**
30         $j^* = arg \min\limits_{j \in \text{N}.Children} \langle \mathbb{T}_j.\mathbf{v}, F(\mathbf{x}) \rangle$;   ❼
31         $\mathbb{P} \to \mathbb{T}_{j^*}$ /*mapping the node point to the next closest node*/
32   **end**
33 **end**

---

we directly assign the solution **x** into this leaf node (cf. ❶); Otherwise, we select a better solution from **x** and $\mathbb{P}.\mathbf{x}$ by the value of the scalar aggregating objective (cf. ❷). In this paper, the scalar aggregating objective is defined as the weight sum of the objective vectors. The weight vector is the one assigned into this leaf node. Obviously, other aggregation approaches, such as Tchebycheff approach and penalty-based boundary intersection (PBI) approach [22], also can be used to aggregate the objectives.

Figure 1 presents a simple example to illustrate the updating procedure. A set of solutions $x_1, \ldots, x_8$ whose objective vectors shown in Fig. 1(a) are assigned into the nodes of the tree one by one. The detail operations of each solution are presented in Table 1. Figure 1(b) shows the final correspondence between the solutions and the nodes of the tree.

Table 1. The updating procedure of the solutions $x_1, \ldots, x_8$ of an example shown in Fig. 1

Solutions	Updating procedure	Solutions	Updating procedure
x_1	❸	x_2	❻ x_1 ❼ v_4 ❸
x_3	❹ x_2 ❼ v_9 ❼ v_7 ❼ v_8 ❶	x_4	❼ v_4 ❼ v_2 ❸
x_5	❼ v_4 ❼ v_2 ❹ x_4 ❼ v_3 ❶	x_6	❼ v_9 ❸
x_7	❼ v_9 ❺ ❼ v_{11} ❼ v_{10} ❶	x_8	❼ v_4 ❼ v_2 ❻ x_5 ❼ v_3 ❷

2.4   Mating Selection

Mating selection is implemented to select some promising solutions for recombination. We consider the solution with smaller value of level has a better fitness. When the number of solutions in the tree is smaller than N, all solutions is composed of the mating pool, where N is the mating pool size. Otherwise, the mating pool is the solutions with smaller value of level. Specifically, let P_i is the solutions in the ith level of the tree, and $|P_i|$ is the count of solutions in set P_i. For set P_i, if the count of solutions in sets from P_1 to P_i is smaller than N, i.e., $\sum_{k=1}^{i} | P_k | < N$, the solutions from the set P_i are chosen for the mating pool. Otherwise, we randomly chose $N - \sum_{l=1}^{i-1} | P_i |$ solutions from P_i and add to the mating pool.

The simulated binary crossover (SBX) and polynomial mutation (PM) [5] are used in all the algorithms for generating offspring in this paper. Two parent solutions Q are randomly selected from the mating pool for generating one new solution.

2.5   Computational Complexity Analysis

Given an MaOP with M objectives and a binary tree with size $\mathbb{N}$, the time complexity of updating one candidate solution of the proposed algorithm is as follows: The time complexity of computing the dominance relationship of two solutions is $\mathcal{O}(M)$ (lines 19 and 22 in Algorithm 2). In the worst case, we need compare the candidate solutions with the solutions on the path from root to a leaf node. Since the constructed is a comparatively balanced tree, the total time complexity of the comparison solutions is $\mathcal{O}(Mlog(\mathbb{N}))$. Furthermore, we need assign the solution to the child node by computing the inner product of objective vector and weight vector (line 31 in Algorithm 2). It's time complexity also is $\mathcal{O}(Mlog(\mathbb{N}))$. In summary, the computational complexity of the proposed algorithm is $\mathcal{O}(Mlog(\mathbb{N}))$. In this paper, $\mathbb{N}$ is set to be CN, and $C > 1$ is a constant. In other word, the computational complexity of the proposed algorithm is $\mathcal{O}(Mlog(N))$. Compared the state-of-the-art algorithms, e.g. NSGA-II [6] requiring $\mathcal{O}(MN)$ and MOEA/D [22] requiring $\mathcal{O}(MT)$ for updating one candidate solution, the proposed algorithm has low computational complexity.

3   Experimental Settings

This section will conduct the experiments to investigate the performance of the proposed algorithm. We compared the proposed algorithm with six state-of-the-art MaOEAs, i.e., HypE [2], AGE-II [20], NSGA-III [7], MOEA/D [22], IBEA [23] and SRA2 [15] on two well-known benchmark problem sets: DTLZ and WFG test suites [12]. The problems DTLZ1-DTLZ4 and WFG1-WFG9 with 5 objectives are used for empirical studies. The parameter settings of these problems as described in [15].

3.1   Performance Metrics

The Inverted Generational Distance (IGD) [3] and Hypervolume indicator (HV) [9] are used to evaluate the performance of the compared algorithms in this paper. In the following, we give a brief introduction of these two metrics.

IGD: Let Q^* be a set of points which are uniformly distributed along the PF in the objective space, and Q be an estimate of Q^* obtained by an algorithm. The distance between Q^* and Q is defined as:

$$IGD(Q|Q^*) = \frac{\sum\limits_{v \in Q^*} d(v, Q)}{|Q^*|}, \tag{4}$$

where $d(v, Q)$ is the minimum Euclidean distance from the point v to Q. Since the PF is known apriori for problem sets DTLZ1-DTLZ4 and WFG1-WFG9, we sample 500000 points on the PF as described in [21] to form Q^*. Obviously, the IGD metric can measure the convergence and diversity of an solution set simultaneously. The smaller value of IGD is, the better the algorithm performs.

HV: Let $\mathbf{z}^r = (z_1^r, \ldots, z_M^r)$ be a reference point in the objective space which is dominated by any Pareto optimal objective vectors. Let Q be the obtained approximation to the PF in the objective space. Then, $H(Q|\mathbf{z}^r)$ is the value of Q (with regard to $\mathbf{z}^r$) is the volume of the region which is dominated by Q and dominates $\mathbf{z}^r$. That is,

$$H(Q|\mathbf{z}^r) = Vol\left(\bigcup_{\mathbf{x} \in Q} [f_1(\mathbf{x}), z_1^r] \times \ldots \times [f_M(\mathbf{x}), z_M^r]\right),$$

where $Vol(.)$ indicates the Lebesgue measure. The larger the HV is, the better the approximation is. In our experiments, the objective vectors are first normalized using the $1.1 \times \mathbf{z}^{nadir}$, where $\mathbf{z}^{nadir} = (z_1^{nadir}, \ldots, z_M^{nadir})$ and z_i^{nadir} is the scale of ith objective over the PF, $i = 1, \ldots, M$. After that, the hypervolume is computed using $\mathbf{z}^r = (1.0, \ldots, 1.0)^T$ as the reference point.

3.2 Parameter Settings

All the algorithms ran 20 times independently for each test instance. The parameters of the algorithms were given as follows:

- The simulated binary crossover (SBX) and polynomial mutation (PM) are used in all the algorithms for generating offspring. The control parameters in these two operators are the same in all algorithms. The crossover rate is set at 1 and the mutation rate is 0.1. The distribution index of crossover and mutation operators are $\eta_c = 15$ and $\eta_m = 15$, respectively.
- All algorithms stop when the number of the function evaluation reaches the maximum number 90,000 of function evaluation for all test instances.
- The population size N of MOEA/D and SRA2 is set to be 210. For the other compared algorithms, the population size is set to be 212 as used in NSGA-III [7].
- The weight vectors used in MOEA/D, NSGA-III, SRA2 are generated by a systematic approach proposed in [16]. The number of weight vectors is set to be 210.
- The neighborhood size is set to 20 and the maximum replacement number is set to 2 for MOEA/D and SRA2 [15] and the ϵ in AGE-II is set to 0.1 [20].
- The weight vectors of the proposed algorithm are also generated the systematic approach proposed in [16] and it's number $\mathbb{N}$ is set to be 1366.
- The size of the mating pool in the proposed algorithm is the same with the population size used in NSGA-III for all test instances.

3.3 Experimental Results and Analysis

The results of the compared algorithms obtained in [15] are directly applied in this paper. Table 2 lists the mean IGD values of the final solutions obtained by the compared algorithms in the 20 independent runs for all test instances. The values of IGD for each test instance are sorted in an ascending. The number in the brackets of these tables are their ranks. The total ranks and the final ranks for the problems are listed in the last two row in the tables, separately. Table 3 lists the mean HV values of the final solutions obtained by the compared algorithms in the 20 independent runs for all the test instances. The HV values for each test instance are sorted in a descending. The number in the brackets of these tables are their ranks. The total ranks and the final ranks are listed in the last two row in the table, separately.

From the above results, we can obtained the following observations for the proposed algorithm.

Table 2. Performance comparison of the proposed algorithm with six state-of-the-art algorithms in term of the average IGD values on DTLZ and WFG problems. The numbers in the brackets are their ranks. The total ranks and the final ranks of the algorithms for the problems are listed in the last two row.

Instance	Our	HypE	AGE-II	NSGA-III	MOEA/D	IBEA	SRA2
DTLZ1	0.0322(1)	0.188(6)	0.0954(2)	0.111(4)	0.109(3)	0.487(7)	0.113(5)
DTLZ2	0.107(1)	0.277(6)	0.161(2)	0.184(5)	0.183(4)	0.293(7)	0.182(3)
DTLZ3	0.119(1)	6.43(7)	0.315(4)	2.00(6)	0.227(2)	0.611(5)	0.255(3)
DTLZ4	0.108(1)	0.279(6)	0.164(2)	0.184(4)	0.183(3)	0.340(7)	0.184(4)
WFG1	0.174(1)	0.703(6)	0.698(5)	0.724(7)	0.576(4)	0.487(2)	0.569(3)
WFG2	0.127(3)	0.366(6)	0.250(4)	0.115(2)	0.555(7)	0.0995(1)	0.292(5)
WFG3	0.132(5)	0.152(6)	0.0889(3)	0.0921(4)	0.0810(2)	0.810(7)	0.0777(1)
WFG4	0.132(1)	0.194(5)	0.189(4)	0.177(3)	0.328(6)	0.523(7)	0.176(2)
WFG5	0.133(1)	0.190(4)	0.193(5)	0.173(2)	0.299(7)	0.226(6)	0.174(3)
WFG6	0.135(1)	0.197(5)	0.191(4)	0.179(2)	0.354(7)	0.283(6)	0.179(2)
WFG7	0.132(1)	0.197(5)	0.191(4)	0.177(3)	0.369(7)	0.250(6)	0.175(2)
WFG8	0.156(1)	0.219(5)	0.199(3)	0.203(4)	0.277(7)	0.267(6)	0.197(2)
WFG9	0.139(1)	0.184(5)	0.179(4)	0.170(3)	0.291(7)	0.211(6)	0.169(2)
Total	19	72	46	49	66	73	37
Final Rank	1	6	3	4	5	7	2

- From Table 2, in terms of IGD values, we can see that the proposed algorithm outperformed the other algorithms and obtained the best results for most of test instances. The reason of the performance of the proposed algorithm is better than that of the other algorithms maybe it can conserve more non-dominant solutions to achieve a good approximation of the PF. The number of the nondominant solutions used to compute the IGD values generally is greater than the population size of other algorithms.
- From Table 3, we can see that the proposed algorithm also achieved a promising results in term of HV values. Moreover, it still obtained the best results for DTLZ suite test instances.

The proposed algorithm cannot obtain a promising result for the problem with incomplete PF, e.g., WFG2 and WFG3. It is because the Pareto relationship works as the primary evaluation mechanism and the distance between the weight vectors and the objective vector of the solutions as secondary evolution mechanism for updating the solutions in the interior node. For MaOPs, the solutions are generally nondominated with each other. This make the distance plays a decisive role in comparing the solutions in the interior node. It make the proposed algorithm can not find a well-converged set of solutions. Some adaptive weight design methods [10] can be used to get around this problem.

Table 3. Performance comparison of the proposed algorithm with six state-of-the-art algorithms in term of the average HV values on DTLZ and WFG problems. The numbers in the brackets are their ranks. The total ranks and the final ranks of the algorithms are listed in the last two row.

Instance	Our	HypE	AGE-II	NSGA-III	MOEA/D	IBEA	SRA2
DTLZ1	0.999(1)	0.955(5)	0.723(6)	0.978(3)	0.979(2)	0.684(7)	0.974(4)
DTLZ2	0.841(1)	0.766(6)	0.703(7)	0.806(3)	0.810(2)	0.791(5)	0.805(4)
DTLZ3	0.809(1)	0.0036(7)	0.668(4)	0.0715(6)	0.741(3)	0.441(5)	0.765(2)
DTLZ4	0.842(1)	0.766(5)	0.748(7)	0.811(2)	0.811(2)	0.762(6)	0.808(4)
WFG1	0.753(1)	0.469(5)	0.346(6)	0.268(7)	0.568(3)	0.604(2)	0.500(4)
WFG2	0.943(4)	0.981(1)	0.925(5)	0.954(3)	0.922(6)	0.879(7)	0.965(2)
WFG3	0.578(6)	0.681(1)	0.601(5)	0.624(4)	0.638(3)	0.238(7)	0.643(2)
WFG4	0.756(2)	0.778(1)	0.635(6)	0.716(3)	0.669(5)	0.533(7)	0.702(4)
WFG5	0.734(3)	0.752(1)	0.633(7)	0.700(4)	0.661(6)	0.745(2)	0.682(5)
WFG6	0.746(2)	0.749(1)	0.620(7)	0.684(4)	0.625(6)	0.723(3)	0.665(5)
WFG7	0.780(3)	0.798(1)	0.659(7)	0.746(4)	0.660(6)	0.788(2)	0.730(5)
WFG8	0.677(2)	0.689(1)	0.568(7)	0.626(4)	0.606(6)	0.633(3)	0.608(5)
WFG9	0.665(2)	0.674(1)	0.621(6)	0.650(4)	0.597(7)	0.638(5)	0.659(3)
Total	29	36	80	51	57	61	49
Final Rank	1	2	7	4	5	6	3

4   Conclusion

In this paper, we proposed a hierarchical decomposition-based EMO algorithm for solving MaOPs. It constructed a relatively balance binary tree on a set of uniform weight vectors. Each node was associated a weight vector. For each candidate solution, we only compared it with the solutions on a path from the root to a leaf of the tree to assign the candidate solution into a node. The complexity of the proposed algorithm was $\mathcal{O}(Mlog(\mathbb{N}))$ for dealing with a new candidate solution and had a low computational complexity. Since the number of the survive individuals in the tree was incremental, it can provide more solutions for approximating the PF. We compared the proposed algorithm with six state-of-the-art EMO algorithms on thirteen benchmark problems. The experimental results showed the effectiveness of the proposed approach.

References

1. Asafuddoula, M., Ray, T., Sarker, R.: A decomposition based evolutionary algorithm for many objective optimization. IEEE Trans. Evol. Comput. **19**(3), 445–460 (2015)
2. Bader, J., Zitzler, E.: HypE: an algorithm for fast hypervolume-based many-objective optimization. Evol. Comput. **19**(1), 45–76 (2011)

3. Bosman, P.A., Thierens, D.: The balance between proximity and diversity in multiobjective evolutionary algorithms. IEEE Trans. Evol. Comput. **7**(2), 174–188 (2003)
4. Cheung, Y.M., Gu, F., Liu, H.L.: Objective extraction for many-objective optimization problems: algorithm and test problems. IEEE Trans. Evol. Comput. **20**(5), 755–772 (2016)
5. Deb, K.: Multiobjective Optimization Using Evolutionary Algorithms. Wiley, New York (2001)
6. Deb, K., Pratap, A., Agarwal, S., Meyarivan, T.: A fast and elitist multiobjective genetic algorithm: NSGA-II. IEEE Trans. Evol. Comput. **6**(2), 182–197 (2002)
7. Deb, K., Jain, H.: An evolutionary many-objective optimization algorithm using reference-point-based nondominated sorting approach, part I: solving problems with box constraints. IEEE Trans. Evol. Comput. **18**(4), 577–601 (2014)
8. Eckart, Z., Marco, L., Lothar, T.: SPEA2: improving the strength pareto evolutionary algorithm for multiobjective optimization. In: Proceedings of Evolutionary Methods for Design Optimization and Control with Applications to Industrial Problems, pp. 95–100 (2001)
9. Emmerich, M., Beume, N., Naujoks, B.: An EMO algorithm using the hypervolume measure as selection criterion. In: Coello Coello, C.A., Hernández Aguirre, A., Zitzler, E. (eds.) EMO 2005. LNCS, vol. 3410, pp. 62–76. Springer, Heidelberg (2005). doi:10.1007/978-3-540-31880-4_5
10. Gu, F., Cheung, Y.M.: Self-organizing map-based weight design for decomposition-based many-objective evolutionary algorithm. IEEE Trans. Evolutionary Computation (2017). doi:10.1109/TEVC20172695579
11. Hadka, D., Reed, P.: Diagnostic assessment of search controls and failure modes in many-objective evolutionary optimization. Evol. Comput. **20**(3), 423–452 (2012)
12. Huband, S., Hingston, P., Barone, L., While, L.: A review of multiobjective test problems and a scalable test problem toolkit. IEEE Trans. Evol. Comput. **10**(5), 477–506 (2006)
13. Ishibuchi, H., Masuda, H., Nojima, Y.: Pareto fronts of many-objective degenerate test problems. IEEE Trans. Evol. Comput. (2015) doi:10.1109/TEVC20152505784
14. Li, B., Li, J., Tang, K., Yao, X.: Many-objective evolutionary algorithms: a survey. ACM Comput. Surv. **48**(1), 13:1–13:35 (2015)
15. Li, B., Tang, K., Li, J., Yao, X.: Stochastic ranking algorithm for many-objective optimization based on multiple indicators. IEEE Trans. Evol. Comput. **20**(6), 924–938 (2016)
16. Li, K., Deb, K., Zhang, Q., Kwong, S.: An evolutionary many-objective optimization algorithm based on dominance and decomposition. IEEE Trans. Evol. Comput. **19**(5), 694–716 (2015)
17. Nicola, B., Naujoks, B., Emmerich, M.: SMS-EMOA: multiobjective selection based on dominated hypervolume. Eur. J. Oper. Res. **181**(3), 1653–1669 (2007)
18. Schutze, O., Lara, A., Coello Coello, C.A.: On the influence of the number of objectives on the hardness of a multiobjective optimization problem. IEEE Trans. Evol. Comput. **15**(4), 444–455 (2011)
19. Trivedi, A., Srinivasan, D., Sanyal, K., Ghosh, A.: A survey of multiobjective evolutionary algorithms based on decomposition. IEEE Trans. Evol. Comput. (2016). doi:10.1109/TEVC.2016.2608507
20. Wagner, M., Neumann, F.: A fast approximation-guided evolutionary multiobjective algorithm. In: Proceedings of 2013 Conference on Genetic and Evolutionary Computation, pp. 687–694 (2013)

21. Wang, H., Jiao, L., Yao, X.: Two-Arch2: an improved two-archive algorithm for many-objective optimization. IEEE Trans. Evol. Comput. **19**(4), 524–541 (2015)
22. Zhang, Q., Li, H.: MOEA/D: a multiobjective evolutionary algorithm based on decomposition. IEEE Trans. Evol. Comput. **11**(6), 712–731 (2007)
23. Zitzler, E., Künzli, S.: Indicator-based selection in multiobjective search. In: Yao, X., et al. (eds.) PPSN 2004. LNCS, vol. 3242, pp. 832–842. Springer, Heidelberg (2004). doi:10.1007/978-3-540-30217-9_84

Adjusting Parallel Coordinates for Investigating Multi-objective Search

Liangli Zhen[1,2]([✉]), Miqing Li[2], Ran Cheng[2], Dezhong Peng[1], and Xin Yao[2,3]

[1] Machine Intelligence Laboratory, College of Computer Science,
Sichuan University, Chengdu 610065, China
llzhen@outlook.com, pengdz@scu.edu.cn
[2] CERCIA, School of Computer Science,
University of Birmingham, Birmingham B15 2TT, UK
limitsing@gmail.com, ranchengcn@gmail.com, x.yao@cs.bham.ac.uk
[3] Department of Computer Science and Engineering,
Southern University of Science and Technology, Shenzhen 518055, China

Abstract. Visualizing a high-dimensional solution set over the evolution process is a viable way to investigate the search behavior of evolutionary multi-objective optimization. The parallel coordinates plot which scales well to the data dimensionality is frequently used to observe solution sets in multi-objective optimization. However, the solution sets in parallel coordinates are typically presented by the natural order of the optimized objectives, with rare information of the relation between these objectives and also the Pareto dominance relation between solutions. In this paper, we attempt to adjust parallel coordinates to incorporate this information. Systematic experiments have shown the effectiveness of the proposed method.

1 Introduction

Multi-objective optimization problems (MOPs), which involve several (conflicting) objectives to be optimized, widely exist in real-world applications [14]. Since the multiple objectives in an MOP can be in conflict with each other, there often exist a set of trade-off solutions, known as the Pareto optimal solutions. In order to solve such MOPs, a variety of multi-objective evolutionary algorithms (MOEAs) have been proposed, where the aim is to obtain (or approximate) the Pareto optimal solutions during one single run [3]. To investigate the search behavior of different MOEAs, the classic visualization technique, i.e., scatter plot, is used for the visualization of the population throughout the evolution process [11]. Despite that the scatter plot allows us to observe important information such as the shape and distribution of the candidate solutions and the conflict between objectives, its applicability is only limited to MOPs with two or three objectives.

With the aim of visualizing high-dimensional candidate solutions in evolutionary multi-objective search, another widely adopted visualization method is known the parallel coordinates [7], which places the objective axes parallel to

© Springer International Publishing AG 2017
Y. Shi et al. (Eds.): SEAL 2017, LNCS 10593, pp. 224–235, 2017.
https://doi.org/10.1007/978-3-319-68759-9_19

each other rather than orthogonally such that an arbitrary number of dimensions can be displayed inside one 2D plane. Specifically, to show a solution set of an m-objective optimization problem, parallel coordinates map them into a coordinate system with m parallel axes, typically vertical and equally spaced. One candidate solution is represented as a polyline with m vertices on these parallel axes, and the position on the ith axis corresponds to the value of the solution on the ith objective. Recently, the parallel coordinates plot has been dominantly used in high-dimensional data visualization [13], e.g., the multi-objective optimization with more than three objectives, in spite of the emergence of various visualization techniques [5,6,15,16].

Despite its popularity, the parallel coordinates plot is not straightforward as the scatter plot to show the information contained in solution sets [13]. In a parallel coordinates plot, each vertical axis has at most two neighboring axes, and different order of objective axes provide different information about the conflict between objectives. The parallel coordinates plot only shows $(m-1)$ relationships of a total of C_m^2 relationships existing in m objectives. How to show the conflict between objectives clear becomes critical and challenging to the parallel coordinates plot. Take Fig. 1 as an example, which shows the parallel coordinates plots of two different order of the same solution set. In Fig. 1(a) where the order of objectives is f_1, f_2, f_3, and f_4, the conflict between any two adjacent objectives is mild. Conversely, in Fig. 1(b) where the order of objectives is f_1, f_3, f_2, f_4, the conflict between f_1 and f_3 and the conflict between f_2 and f_4 are intense, and imply that f_1 is negatively linear with f_3, and f_2 is negatively linear with f_4. Moreover, during the evolution process, the solutions are not mutually non-dominated, and the dominance relation between solutions are not considered in parallel coordinates plot makes the gradual improvement of the solution set invisible. In this paper, we aim to address these two problems in the parallel coordinates plot by adjusting parallel coordinates. The proposed parallel coordinates adjustment (APC) is capable of clearly presenting the relation between objectives and the dominance relation between candidate solutions.

The rest of this paper is organized as follows. Section 2 provides the background, including a general definition of MOPs, concepts of Pareto dominance and Pareto optimal set, and some related work. Section 3 is devoted to the

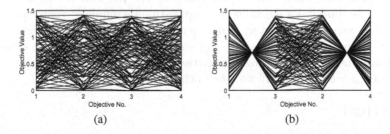

(a)   (b)

Fig. 1. Two different order of objective axes of a solution set in parallel coordinates.

description of the proposed method. Section 4 provides some results of the investigation of MOEAs. Section 5 concludes the paper.

2   Background

A multi-objective optimization problem (MOP) can be generally formulated as a minimization problem and defined as follows:

$$
\min \ F(\mathbf{x}) = (f_1(\mathbf{x}), f_2(\mathbf{x}), \ldots, f_M(\mathbf{x}))^T
$$
$$
\text{s.t. } \mathbf{x} \in \Omega,
$$
(1)

where $\mathbf{x} \in \mathbb{R}^n$ consists of n decision variables representing the values which are to be chosen in the optimization, $\Omega \subseteq \mathbb{R}^n$ is the decision space, and $F : \Omega \to \mathbb{R}^M$ consists of M (conflicting) objective functions $f_i : \mathbb{R}^n \to \mathbb{R}, (i = 1, \ldots, M)$.

For any two feasible solutions $\mathbf{a}$ and $\mathbf{b}$ of the MOP, it says that $\mathbf{a}$ is better than $\mathbf{b}$ if the following conditions hold:

$$
\forall i \ f_i(\mathbf{a}) \leq f_i(\mathbf{b}) \ \text{ and } \ \exists j \ f_j(\mathbf{a}) < f_j(\mathbf{b}),
$$
(2)

where $i, j \in \{1, 2, \ldots, M\}$. In other words, $\mathbf{a}$ is not worse than $\mathbf{b}$ on all objectives and $\mathbf{a}$ is better than $\mathbf{b}$ on at least one objective. We can also say that $\mathbf{a}$ dominates $\mathbf{b}$, and denote it as $\mathbf{a} \prec \mathbf{b}$. A solution that is not dominated by any other solutions is denoted as Pareto optimal. The set of the Pareto optimal solutions in the decision space is denoted as the Pareto set, and the corresponding outcome in objective space is denoted as the Pareto front. From the formulation in (1), we can see that the conflicts between objectives prevent us from having a single optimal solution but rather a Pareto set for an MOP.

MOEAs optimize MOPs by producing a solution set at each generation and evolving the candidate set gradually. The parallel coordinates plot is frequently used to view these high-dimensional solutions, but it suffers from the visual clutter problem [9]. To address this problem in parallel coordinates, Ankerst *et al.* proposed to reorder the axes such that similar dimensions are positioned close to each other [1]. They modeled the reordering of axes as a traveling salesman problem (TSP) and applied a heuristics to solve it. In [2], Artero *et al.* presented a method, called similarity-based attribute arrangement (SBAA), to select two dimensions with the largest similarity as the initial axes, and then to search for the dimensions which will be positioned to the left and the right of them. The SBAA method has a much lower computational complexity comparing with the previous methods. However, it may leads to some intense conflict between objectives being invisible. Actually, the most desirable order of the objectives should make the most conflicting information visible that every objective at most can only be placed adjacently with two other objectives.

3   Method

3.1   Reordering of Objectives

In this section, we present an algorithm to arrange the order of objectives such that the most significant conflict (harmony) between objectives can be visualized.

Since the conflict between objectives is local rather than global on the population from different generations, we need to re-evaluate the conflict between objectives during the evolution process. In this paper, we assess the conflict/harmony between two objectives according to the Spearman's rank correlation between the objectives of all candidate solutions. The Spearman's rank correlation coefficient is a nonparametric technique for evaluating the degree of rank correlation between two variables. It equals the Pearson correlation between the rank values of the two variables. Technically, the variables A and B are converted to rank variables r_A and r_B, respectively, according to the ranks of their observations. The Spearman's rank correlation coefficient is defined as

$$\rho(A, B) = \frac{cov(r_A, r_B)}{\sigma_{r_A} \sigma_{r_B}}, \tag{3}$$

where σ_{r_A} and σ_{r_B} are the standard deviation of r_A and r_B, respectively, and $cov(r_A, r_B)$ is the covariance of r_A and r_B. Intuitively, the Spearman's correlation between two variables will be high when observations have a similar rank between the two variables and low when observations have a dissimilar rank between the two variables. As it operates on the ranks of the data, the Spearman's correlation coefficient is appropriate for both continuous and discrete variables and is insensitive to the operations of translation/scaling on the data.

In the evolution process, the most conflicting/harmonious information between objectives is desirable for the users. For a solution set, we calculate the Spearman's rank correlation between objectives, and then we use the absolute values of the correlation to represent the harmony/conflict between two objectives. To arrange the order of these objectives in a parallel coordinates plot, we use a greedy strategy and propose an algorithm listed in Algorithm 1.

From the algorithm, we see that it consists of three stages: calculation of the Spearman's rank correlation, correlation sorting, and the arrangement of the order of objectives according to the sorted result. The third stage (Step 4 to Step 22) is the essential part of the proposed method. It handles a pair of two objectives at each iteration. It differs from the SBAA method, which iteratively adds one objective in one iteration. In our method, the two objectives may be both added in the system at one iteration as shown at Step 7. It may also add one objective at a time, as Step 11 and Step 14, if only one of the objectives at one side of a group and another objective is not joined in any group, as the conditions at Step 10 and Step 13. If both of the objectives are at the side of two different groups, the algorithm will merge these two groups by placing these two objectives adjacent. However, if both of these two objectives are at the side of the same group or one of the objectives has already connected to two other objectives, the algorithm will do nothing and go to the next step. Overall, after rearranging the order of objectives with Algorithm 1, the objective would be adjacent to the two objectives which have clearest (conflicting/harmonous) relation with except that these objectives have stronger relation with other objectives.

Algorithm 1. The proposed procedure of arranging the order of objectives in parallel coordinates

---

Require: The objective vectors of the solution sets $y_i = f_i(x_1, x_2, \ldots, x_N) \in \mathbb{R}^N, i \in \{1, \ldots, M\}$.

Ensure: The rearranged order of objectives.

1: $t \leftarrow 1$, $p(i) \leftarrow 0, i \in \{1, \ldots, M\}$; // t denotes the index of the current iteration, and $p(i)$ denotes the number of the connected adjacent objectives for the i-th objective.

2: Calculate the Spearman's rank correlation $R_{ij} \leftarrow \rho(y_i, y_j)$ via (3), **for all** $i > j \in \{1, \ldots, M\}$;

3: $list \leftarrow$ the sorting result on the absolute value of the correlation in descending order;

4: **while** exist one objective is not arranged **do**

5:     Denote two objectives whose correlation corresponding to the $list(t)$ as a and b;

6:     **if** $p(a) = 0$ and $p(b) = 0$ **then**

7:         Create a new group which includes a and b;

8:         $p(a) \leftarrow p(a) + 1$;

9:         $p(b) \leftarrow p(b) + 1$;

10:     **else if** $p(a) = 1$ and $p(b) = 0$ **then**

11:         Insert objective b to the same group with a;

12:         $p(b) \leftarrow p(b) + 1$;

13:     **else if** $p(a) = 0$ and $p(b) = 1$ **then**

14:         Insert objective a to the same group with b;

15:         $p(a) \leftarrow p(a) + 1$;

16:     **else if** $p(a) = 1$ and $p(b) = 1$ and a is not in the same group with b **then**

17:         Merge these two groups;

18:         $p(a) \leftarrow p(a) + 1$;

19:         $p(b) \leftarrow p(b) + 1$;

20:     **end if**

21:     $t \leftarrow t + 1$;

22: **end while**

23: **return** the order of the objectives in the group.

3.2 Involving Dominance Relation

Since the optimal solution of an MOP is a set of Pareto optimal vectors, the Pareto dominance relation between candidate solutions naturally becomes a criterion to distinguish different solutions. In the evolution process, the candidate solutions can be sorted into different levels according to the non-dominance relation by using the non-dominated sorting approaches, such as the efficient non-dominated sorting method in [17]. We represent the candidate solutions with different colors according to their non-dominated levels such that the dominance relation can be easily observed. Figure 2 shows an example of six solutions in a 3D objective space with parallel coordinates. From Fig. 2(a), it can be hard to observe the solutions which belong to the first non-dominated front, but we can easily do from Fig. 2(b) where the solutions with blue color lie in the first non-dominated front and the solutions with red color are located at the second non-dominated front.

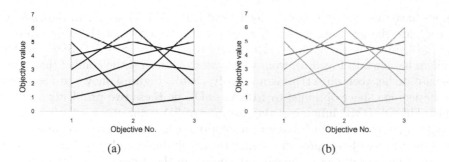

Fig. 2. Six solutions in 3D objective space with parallel coordinates plot. (a) presents the results without special colors about the dominance relation; (b) is the results with special colors according to the non-dominated levels of the solutions. (Color figure online)

With this simple color annotating method, we can obtain more information of the population, such as the number of individuals in different non-dominated front, how these candidates evolve, and the solutions at the boundaries. They are helpful for investigating the behavior of the MOEAs.

4   Results

In order to demonstrate the main properties of the proposed method and illustrate how to use it to show solution sets and to investigate the search process of multi-objective optimization, a series of experiments are conducted on the test problems of DTLZ5(I,M) [4], multi-line distance minimization problem (ML-DMP) [13], and multi-point minimization problem (MP-DMP) [8,10]. Specifically, the experiments to be conducted consist of two parts. In the first part, we demonstrate the result of the proposed method on rearranging the order of objectives for the solution sets of the DTLZ5(I,M) and ML-DMP via a many-objective optimizer, i.e., the strength Pareto evolutionary algorithm (SPEA2) [18] with the shift-based density estimation (SDE) [12] strategy (SPEA2+SDE)[1]. In the second part, we apply the proposed method to investigate the behavior of the SPEA2+SDE on the MP-DMP. The experimental setting is as follows: for the SPEA2+SDE, the maximum number of evaluation is used as the termination condition, which is set to 50000, 50000 and 100000 for the DTLZ5(I, M), MP-DMP, and ML-DMP, respectively, and the corresponding population sizes are 100, 100, and 200.

4.1   Visualization of Solution Sets

To analyze the conflict/harmony between objectives of a solution set, we conduct the experiment on the output of the SPEA2+SDE on DTLZ5(3, 5) problem, 5-objective ML-DMP, and 10-objective ML-DMP. From the definition of DTLZ5(I,

---

[1] SPEA2+SDE has shown its good performance on this problem [11].

M), we have that the first three objectives of DTLZ5(3, 5) are linear dependent. To evaluate the proposed method, we exchange the order of the objectives in DTLZ5(3, 5) to f_1, f_4, f_3, f_5, f_2. The solution set of the SPEA2+SDE on this problem is shown in Fig. 3(a), from which we can see that the conflict/harmony information between objectives is not easily visible. Figure 4 shows two solution sets in decision space obtained by SPEA2+SDE on these two problems, respectively. The DL-DMP minimizes the distance of 2D points to a set of multiple straight lines, each of which passes through one edge of the given regular polygon. One feature of this problem is that these solutions are located in a regular polygon and their objective images are similar in the sense of Euclidean geometry. This allows us to observe the distribution of the solutions in the objective space via viewing them in the 2D decision space. We will use this feature of ML-DMP to analyze the results of the reordering of the objectives in parallel coordinates.

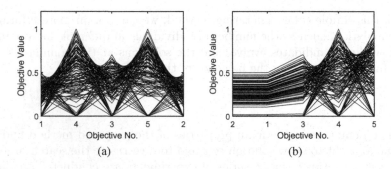

Fig. 3. The solutions of the SPEA2+SDE for DTLZ5(3,5) with different order of objectives. The results before and after the rearranging of the order of objectives are shown at left and right, respectively.

Results on the DTLZ5(3, 5) Problem. From the definition of the DTLZ5(I, M) problem, we have that the first three objectives of DTLZ5(3, 5), i.e., f_1, f_2, and f_3, are linear dependent. The result after rearranging the order of objectives with the proposed method is shown in Fig. 3(b). We can see that the first three objectives are arranged in the adjacent positions, and it is consistent with our goal that placing the most conflicting/harmonious objectives in adjacent positions. Comparing with the result in Fig. 3(a), the result given by the proposed method provides important information between objectives that the first three objectives are harmonious, and the objectives f_3 and f_4 are conflicting, as well as f_4 and f_5.

Results on the 5-Objective ML-DMP. In Fig. 5(a) where the order of objectives is f_1, f_2, f_3, f_4, f_5, the conflict between any two adjacent objectives is rather mild. On the other hand, in Fig. 5(b) where the order of objectives is f_3, f_1, f_4, f_2, f_5, the conflicts between any two adjacent objectives are intense. Inspecting the result in Fig. 4(a), we find that the adjacent objectives automatically be rearranged by the proposed method are the most conflicting objectives, i.e., most of the points which are closer to L1 would be far away from L3 and L4, and most of the points which are closer to L2 would be far away from L4 and L5. This is caused by the fact that f_1 and f_3 are not completely conflicted. Similar situations hold for f_1 and f_4, f_4 and f_2, and f_2 and f_5. From Figs. 4(a) and 5(b), we obtain that the proposed method detects the most desirable information between objectives. This can bring some insights to the solution sets and the investigated MOEAs, which can be helpful to algorithm designers and decision makers.

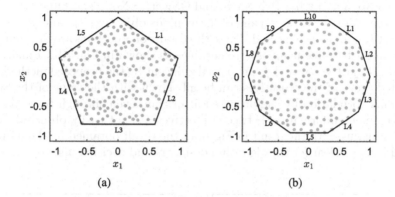

Fig. 4. The solutions of the SPEA2+SDE in the decision space for 5-objective ML-DMP and 10-objective ML-DMP at left and right, respectively.

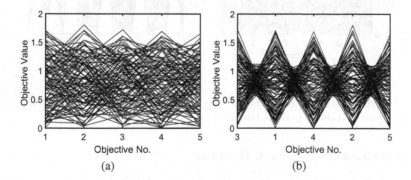

Fig. 5. The solution set of SPEA2+SDE on the 5-objective ML-DMP with different order of objective axes in parallel coordinates.

Results on the 10-Objective ML-DMP. In Fig. 6(a) where the order of objectives is f_1, f_2, f_3, f_4, f_5, f_6, f_7, f_8, f_9, f_{10}, the conflict between any two adjacent objectives is mild. In some area, the adjacent objectives are even harmonious, but they are not harmonious in the whole optimal region. In contrast, in Fig. 6(b) where the order of objectives is f_1, f_6, f_5, f_{10}, f_9, f_4, f_3, f_8, f_2, f_7, some pair of adjacent objectives are completely conflicting. From Fig. 4(b), we find that f_1 is negatively linear with f_6, i.e., any point which moves more closely to L1 would have a longer distance to L6 because these two lines are parallel and placed at two sides of optimal solutions. The objectives f_5 and f_{10}, f_9 and f_4, f_3 and f_8, f_2 and f_7 have similar relation. These five pairs of objectives are completely conflicting, respectively. It leads to the result in Fig. 6(b) that the lines of the solutions are intersected at one point between axes of Objective No. 1 and Objective No. 6, Objective No. 5 and Objective No. 10, Objective No. 9 and Objective No. 4, Objective No. 3 and Objective No. 8, and Objective No. 2 and Objective No. 7, respectively. Moreover, three pairs of harmonious objectives, f_6 and f_5, f_{10} and f_9, f_4 and f_3, are then connected. These three pairs of objectives are the minimization distances to three pairs of adjacent lines as shown in Fig. 4(b). Finally, two conflicting objectives f_8 and f_2 are placed adjacent by the proposed method. The connected order of the objectives can be all shown with the value of the Spearman's rank correlation by the proposed algorithm, even through these conflicting/harmonious information between objectives are not easily observed by the user. Comparing with the result in Fig. 6(a), the result obtained by the proposed method is much clear for the algorithm designers and decision makers.

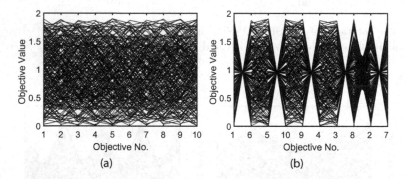

Fig. 6. The solution set of SPEA2+SDE on the 10-objective ML-DMP with different order of objective axes in parallel coordinates.

4.2 Investigation of Search Behavior

In this subsection, we demonstrate how to investigate the search behaviors of MOEAs using the proposed adjusted parallel coordinates method. To exemplify, we apply the SPEA2+SDE to solve a six-objective MP-DMP whose goal is to minimize the distance to the six vertexes of a polygon. The results are shown in Fig. 7, from which we have the following observations: (1) for the initial population, the individuals are fairly uniformly distributed in the whole objective space and they are sorted to many non-dominated fronts; (2) for the population in the 5th generation, the number of non-dominated fronts are fewer than

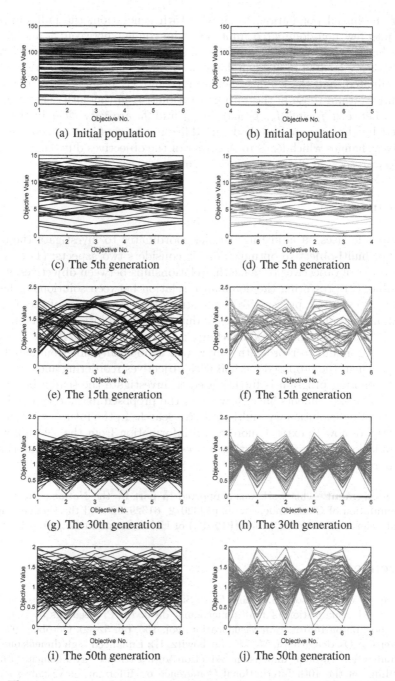

Fig. 7. The populations of the SPEA2+SDE method on the 6-objective MP-DMP during the evolution process. The subplots at the left column are the results by using the original parallel coordinates, and the subplots at the right side are the results obtained by the proposed method.

that of the initial population; (3) in the 15th generation, the individuals are sorted into few non-dominated fronts and the conflict between f_3 and f_6, and the conflict between f_1 and f_4 are fairly intense; (4) in the 30th generation, the individuals are located in one non-dominated front, i.e., all of they are mutually non-dominated, and the conflicts between f_1 and f_4, f_2 and f_5, f_3 and f_6 are more intense than those in the 15th generation; (5) in the 50th generation, the conflicts between f_1 and f_4, f_2 and f_5, f_3 and f_6 are very clear in the result obtained by the proposed method. In addition, the conflict/harmony between objectives changes which leads to the order of the objectives different during the evolution process (as shown in the right column of Fig. 7).

5   Conclusion

This paper focuses on adjusting parallel coordinates to investigate the search process of multi-objective optimization. It considers two aspects: (1) rearranging the order of objectives to make the relationships between objectives as clear as possible; (2) presenting the dominance relation between solutions to help us to know the evolution process. To demonstrate the effectiveness of the proposed method, a series of experiments have conducted on the solution sets or the population of the MOEAs on several benchmarks. It firstly illustrated how to use the proposed algorithm to reorder the objectives of mutually non-dominated solution sets. Then, the proposed method with objectives reordering and dominance relation denoting program is further used to investigate the search behavior of MOEAs. The experiments have shown that the proposed method can be helpful in investigating evolutionary multi-objective search. In the future, we would like to investigate how to extract more useful information from the solution sets or the population during the evolution process and then present this information in the parallel coordinates.

Acknowledgment. This work was supported in part by the National Natural Science Foundation of China under grants 61432012, 61329302, and the Engineering and Physical Sciences Research Council (EPSRC) of UK under grant EP/J017515/1.

References

1. Ankerst, M., Berchtold, S., Keim, D.A.: Similarity clustering of dimensions for an enhanced visualization of multidimensional data. In: Proceedings of 1998 IEEE Symposium on Information Visualization, vol. 153, pp. 52–60, October 1998
2. Artero, A.O., de Oliveira, M.C.F., Levkowitz, H.: Enhanced high dimensional data visualization through dimension reduction and attribute arrangement. In: Proceedings of the 10th International Conference on Information Visualisation, pp. 707–712, July 2006
3. Coello, C.C.: Evolutionary multi-objective optimization: a historical view of the field. IEEE Comput. Intell. Mag. 1(1), 28–36 (2006)

4. Deb, K., Saxena, D.: Searching for pareto-optimal solutions through dimensionality reduction for certain large-dimensional multi-objective optimization problems. In: Proceedings of 2006 IEEE Congress on Evolutionary Computation, pp. 3352–3360, July 2006
5. de Freitas, A.R., Fleming, P.J., Guimares, F.G.: Aggregation trees for visualization and dimension reduction in many-objective optimization. Inf. Sci. **298**, 288–314 (2015)
6. He, Z., Yen, G.G.: Visualization and performance metric in many-objective optimization. IEEE Trans. Evol. Comput. **20**(3), 386–402 (2016)
7. Inselberg, A., Dimsdale, B.: Parallel coordinates: a tool for visualizing multi-dimensional geometry. In: Proceedings of the 1st IEEE Conference on Visualization, pp. 361–378, October 1990
8. Ishibuchi, H., Yamane, M., Akedo, N., Nojima, Y.: Many-objective and many-variable test problems for visual examination of multiobjective search. In: Proceedings of 2013 IEEE Congress on Evolutionary Computation, pp. 1491–1498. IEEE, July 2013
9. Johansson, J., Forsell, C.: Evaluation of parallel coordinates: overview, categorization and guidelines for future research. IEEE Trans. Vis. Comput. Graph. **22**(1), 579–588 (2016)
10. Köppen, M., Yoshida, K.: Substitute distance assignments in NSGA-II for handling many-objective optimization problems. In: Obayashi, S., Deb, K., Poloni, C., Hiroyasu, T., Murata, T. (eds.) EMO 2007. LNCS, vol. 4403, pp. 727–741. Springer, Heidelberg (2007). doi:10.1007/978-3-540-70928-2_55
11. Li, M., Grosan, C., Yang, S., Liu, X., Yao, X.: Multi-line distance minimization: a visualized many-objective test problem suite. IEEE Trans. Evol. Comput. (2017)
12. Li, M., Yang, S., Liu, X.: Shift-based density estimation for pareto-based algorithms in many-objective optimization. IEEE Trans. Evol. Comput. **18**(3), 348–365 (2014)
13. Li, M., Zhen, L., Yao, X.: How to read many-objective solution sets in parallel coordinates. CoRR abs/1705.00368 (2017)
14. Miettinen, K.: Nonlinear Multiobjective Optimization, vol. 12. Springer Science & Business Media, Heidelberg (2012)
15. Tuar, T., Filipi, B.: Visualization of pareto front approximations in evolutionary multiobjective optimization: a critical review and the prosection method. IEEE Trans. Evol. Comput. **19**(2), 225–245 (2015)
16. Walker, D.J., Everson, R., Fieldsend, J.E.: Visualizing mutually nondominating solution sets in many-objective optimization. IEEE Trans. Evol. Comput. **17**(2), 165–184 (2013)
17. Zhang, X., Tian, Y., Cheng, R., Jin, Y.: An efficient approach to nondominated sorting for evolutionary multiobjective optimization. IEEE Trans. Evol. Comput. **19**(2), 201–213 (2015)
18. Zitzler, E., Laumanns, M., Thiele, L.: SPEA2: improving the strength Pareto evolutionary algorithm for multiobjective optimization. In: Evolutionary Methods for Design, Optimisation and Control, pp. 95–100. International Center for Numerical Methods in Engineering (2002)

An Elite Archive-Based MOEA/D Algorithm

Qingling Zhu$^{(\boxtimes)}$, Qiuzhen Lin, and Jianyong Chen

Shenzhen University, Shenzhen 518060, China
zhuqingling@email.szu.edu.cn,
{qiuzhlin, jychen}@szu.edu.cn

Abstract. MOEA/D is a novel multiobjective evolutionary algorithm based on decomposition approach, which has attracted much attention in recent years. However, when tackling the problems with irregular (e.g., disconnected or degenerated) Pareto fronts (PFs), MOEA/D is found to be ineffective and inefficient, as uniformly distributed weight vectors used in decomposition approach cannot guarantee the even distribution of the optimal solutions on PFs. In this paper, an elite archive-based MOEA/D algorithm (ArchMOEA/D) is proposed to tackle the above problem. An external archive is used to store non-dominated solutions that help to spread the population diversity. Moreover, this external archive is evolved and used to compensate the search area that decomposition-based approaches cannot reach. The external archive and the main population cooperate with each other using Pareto- and decomposition-based techniques during the evolutionary process. Some experiments in solving benchmark problems with various properties have been used to verify the efficiency and effectiveness of ArchMOEA/D. Experimental results demonstrate the superior performance of ArchMOEA/D over other kinds of MOEA/D variants.

Keywords: Evolutionary algorithm · Irregular problems · Co-evolution strategy

1 Introduction

A multiobjective optimization problem (MOP) can be mathematically formulated, as follows:

$$\text{minimize } F(x) = (f_1(x), \ldots, f_m(x))^T \tag{1}$$

where $x = (x_1, x_2, \ldots, x_n) \in \Omega$ is a decision vector with n variables, the mapping function $F : \Omega \to R^m$ defines m objective functions, Ω and R^m are respectively the decision space and the objective space. As the natural conflicts may exist among the objectives, no single solution is able to give the optimal results for all the objectives and generally there exist a set of equally-optimal solutions. Such set in decision space is termed Pareto-optimal set (PS), and their mapping on objective space is termed as Pareto-optimal front (PF). Over the last two decades, evolutionary algorithms (EAs) have been widely investigated as a major approach for solving MOPs, namely MOEAs, due to their population-based search ability and the possibility of obtaining a set of Pareto optimal solutions in a single run [1].

© Springer International Publishing AG 2017
Y. Shi et al. (Eds.): SEAL 2017, LNCS 10593, pp. 236–247, 2017.
https://doi.org/10.1007/978-3-319-68759-9_20

Generally, most of MOEAs can be classified into three kinds, *i.e.*, Pareto-based MOEAs, indicator-based MOEAs and decomposition-based MOEAs. The representatives of these three types of MOEAs include NSGA-II [2], IBEA [3], and MOEA/D [4], respectively. Especially, the development of MOEA/D has attracted a lot of attention in recent years. It transfers an MOP into a number of single objective optimization sub-problems using decomposition approach and then optimizes them in a collaborative manner. The study of MOEA/D is a hot topic in the research field of evolutionary computation and many enhanced strategies were designed for MOEA/D. For example, an ensemble approach of different neighborhood sizes was presented for MOEA/D, namely ENS-MOEA/D [5], which is able to decrease the impact of neighborhood size on MOEA/D. A novel bandit-based adaptive operator selection was reported for MOEA/D (MOEA/D-FRRMAB) [6], to adaptively choose the suitable recombination operator using their recent performance. A stable matching model [7] and an improved inter-relationship model [8] were also built for MOEA/D, which help to match each individual with one unique sub-problem.

In MOEA/D, a weight vector used in decomposition approach generally defines a sub-problem to be solved. That is to say, the distribution of weight vectors can greatly affect the spread of solutions on the true PF. The most commonly-used strategy in many MOEA/D algorithms is to produce a set of uniformly distributed weight vectors. However, this strategy may not work well on some MOPs with irregular PFs. If a PF can be well approximated by the optimal solutions of single objective sub-problems defined by a set of uniformly distributed weight vectors, we call this PF is a regular PF. Otherwise, it is called an irregular PF [9]. The examples with regular PFs are DTLZ1-DTLZ4 [10], while some examples with irregular PFs include ZDT3 [11] and DTLZ7 [10] (disconnection), DTLZ5-DTLZ6 [10] (degeneration), SCH [12] (sharp peak and low tail), and WFG1-WFG9 [13] (different scales in two objectives). For the above mentioned irregular problems, decomposition-based MOEAs meet some difficulty, as analyzed in Sect. 2.

To address the lack of uniformity when tackling the problems with irregular PFs using MOEA/D, an adaptive weight adjustment method was proposed in [14] and a random weight approach was reported in [9]. These methods can provide a better performance in solving the problems with irregular PFs; however, as demonstrated in their experiments, their performance in tackling the problem with regular PFs is greatly affected. This is because it is difficult to distinguish whether a search area is real sparse or pseudo sparse, *e.g.*, discontinuous regions [14]. Other strategies, e.g., [9, 15], use the external archive as the supplement for the main population, which is aimed at searching the sparse region that MOEA/D is difficult to reach. Following this research direction, an elite archive-based MOEA/D algorithm is designed in this paper, named ArchMOEA/D, which is based on a cooperative manner and is able to provide a superior performance. The elite archive is also evolved to compensate the search of sparse area that MOEA/D cannot reach. The elite archive and the main population are cooperatively evolved to accelerate the evolutionary process. The elite archive is updated using the Pareto-ranking approach, while the main population is renewed using the decomposition approach. The experimental results demonstrate that the proposed algorithm has superior performance over two state-of-the-art MOEAs (*i.e.*, NSGA-II and MOEA/D-DE) and two recently proposed MOEA/D variants (*i.e.*, MOEA/D-GR and ED/DPP).

The remainder of this paper is organized as follows. In Sect. 2, we give a brief analysis of the problems that decomposition-based MOEAs encounter when tackling MOPs with irregular PFs. The proposed algorithm is introduced in Sect. 3 and some experimental results are reported in Sect. 4. At last, the final section concludes this paper.

2 Analysis

In the early study of MOPs, the PF shapes in most of test problems are relatively simple [9]. For example, the PFs of ZDT1 and ZDT4 are a one-dimensional connected and convex curve, and that of ZDT2 is concave. All these problems have the same scales in two objectives. MOEA/D using uniformly distributed weight vectors can well handle the above simple MOPs. However, when tackling MOPs with irregular PFs, the uniformly distributed weight vectors in MOEA/D cannot guarantee the even spread of the optimal solutions on the PFs [14].

ZDT3 is a bi-objective test problem characterized with disconnected PFs and different scales in two objectives. To visualize the problems of decomposition-based MOEAs in solving such kind of MOPs, Fig. 1 gives the final results of MOEA/D-DE on ZDT3 using a population with 50 individuals. The dash lines are the weight vectors used in MOEA/D-DE and the circles are the individuals. From Fig. 1, it is observed that MOEA/D-DE shows two challenges in solving ZDT3. The first one is that some redundant weight vectors is not intersected with the true PF of ZDT3, such as the vectors $\lambda^4 - \lambda^6$, $\lambda^{11} - \lambda^{15}$, $\lambda^{22} - \lambda^{24}$, $\lambda^{35} - \lambda^{36}$. This will lead to the case that one

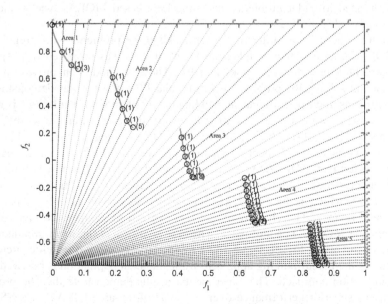

Fig. 1. An illustration of MOEA/D-DE on ZDT3 problem

individual is assigned to solve several different sub-problems. This problem happens not only in solving MOPs with disconnected PFs, but even more seriously, in MOPs with degenerated PFs, as there are more redundant sub-problems for degenerated problems. The second challenge is that the uniformly distributed weight vectors cannot guarantee the even spread of the optimal solutions on the PFs [14]. Regarding the MOPs with different objective scales, the Pareto-optimal solutions are not uniformity allocated in PFs. For example, Area1 and Area2 plotted in Fig. 1 are too sparse, while Area 4 and Area 5 are too crowded. For the MOPs characterized with a sharp peak and low tail, the second challenge also exists. In Fig. 2, the final results of MOEA/D-DE in solving Schaffer [12] problem are also plotted as an example. In this case, the extreme sides of PF are sparse, while the central region of PF is crowded.

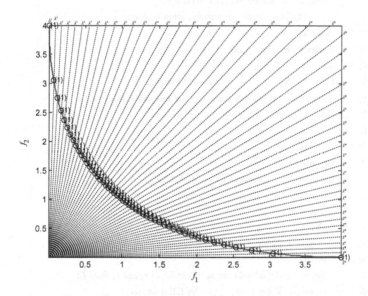

Fig. 2. An illustration of MOEA/D-DE on Schaffer problem

3   The Proposed Algorithm

To address the problems discussed in Sect. 2, an elite archive is used to preserve the non-dominated solutions found during the evolutionary process. The pseudo-code of the proposed algorithm ArchMOEA/D is given in Algorithm 1.

At first, the main population P, the weight vectors W, the ideal point z^* and the neighbor B_i for each individual $i \in \{1, \ldots, N\}$, are initialized, and then the elite archive A is update by the main population P using Algorithm 2. Here, the popular archive update approach in [1, 2, 16] is adopted, which is selected based on both of Pareto dominance and crowding distance. In Algorithm 2, the function **CheckDominance**(x,y) returns the Pareto dominance relationship between solutions x and y. It will return 1 when x dominates y. Otherwise, It will return -1. Another function **CrowdingDistanceAssignment** (A) will calculate the crowding distance value [2] for each solution in A.

Algorithm 1: ArchMOEAD: Archive-based MOEA/D

1:    Initialize $P = \{x^1, ..., x^N\}$, $W = \{w^1, ..., w^N\}$, $z^*, A=\{\}$, $neval = 0$;
2:    **for** $i = 1$ to N
3:        $B_i = \{i_1, ..., i_T\}$ // $w^{i_1}, ..., w^{i_T}$ are the T closest weight vectors to w^i;
4:    **end for**
5:    $A = $**ArchiveUpdate**$(P, A)$;
6:    **while** $neval < maxneval$
7:        **for** i=1 to $|A|$
8:            Generate a random integer j in $[1, |A|]$;
9:            $\{C_1, C_2\}$=SBX(A_i, A_j);   //simulated binary crossover
10:            Generate a random integer k in $[1, 2]$;
11:            S_i=PM(C_k);   //polynominal mutation operator
12:        **end for**
13:        A=**ArchiveUpdate**(S, A);
14:        $neval = neval + |A|$;
15:        **for** i=0 to N //use A to update P
16:            Find the most suitable solution s for sub-problem i in A;
17:            **if** $g^{te}(s \mid w^i, z^*) \le g^{te}(x^i \mid w^i, z^*)$
18:                x^i=s;
19:            **end if**
20:        **end for**
21:        **for** i=1 to N //evolve P use MOEA/D
22:            **if** $rand < \delta$
23:                $E = B_i$;
24:            **else**
25:                $E = \{1, ..., N\}$;
26:            **end if**
27:            Set r_1=i and randomly select two indexes r_2 and r_3 from E;
28:            Generate $\bar{y}$ from $x^{r_1}, x^{r_2}, x^{r_3}$ by DE operator;
29:            y =PM$(\bar{y})$;   //polynomial mutation operator
30:            evaluate y and set $neval = neval + 1$;
31:            update z^* by y;
32:            find the most suitable sub-problem j for y;
33:            **if** $g^{te}(y' \mid w^j, z^*) \le g^{te}(x^j \mid w^j, z^*)$
34:                $x^j = y$;
35:            **end if**
36:        **end for**
37:        $A = $**ArchiveUpdate**$(P, A)$;   //Use P to Update A
38:    **end while**
39:    **return** A;

After the initialization, ArchMOEA/D turns into the loop of evolutionary process until the number of function evaluation *neval* reaches the predefined maximum counts *maxneval*. During the evolutionary phase, the archive A is evolved by simulated binary crossover (SBX) and polynomial mutation (PM) operator to generate an offspring population S (lines 7–12). After that, the offspring population S is employed to update A as described in Algorithm 2. At the same time, the elite archive A is used to update the main population P based on decomposition-based technique (lines 15–19). Then, P is further evolved by DE operator and updated using decomposition-based approach [17] (lines 21–36). At last, the archive A is also renewed by P (line 37) using Algorithm 2. The above evolutionary phase will repeat until the predefined maximum counts *maxneval* are achieved. At the end of algorithm, the non-dominated solutions in A or P are reported as the final result.

Algorithm 2: A = **ArchiveUpdate**(S, A)

1:    **for** i=1 to $|S|$
2:        $flag$ =0;
3:        **for** j=1 to $|A|$
4:            $flag$ = **CheckDominance**(S_i, A_j);
5:            **if** $flag$ == −1   //S_i is dominated by or equal to A_j
6:                Break;
7:            **else if** $flag$ == 1 // S_i dominates A_j
8:                Delete A_j //delete the solution dominated by S_i;
9:            **end if**
10:      **end for**
11:      **if** $flag$!= −1   // if have not a individual in A dominate S_i
12:          Add S_i to A;
13:          **if** $|A| > N$
14:              **CrowdingDistanceAssignment**(A);
15:              Delete the most crowded one;
16:          **end if**
17:      **end if**
18: **end for**
19: Return A;

---

4   Experimental Studies

In this section, the performance of ArchMOEA/D is compared to two state-of-the-art MOEAs (*i.e.*, NSGA-II [2] and MOEA/D-DE [4]) and two recently proposed MOEA/D variants (*i.e.*, MOEA/D-GR [17] and ED/DPP [15]), in solving a number of MOPs characterized with different features.

4.1   Benchmark Problems and Performance Metrics

In our experiments, a set of 18 test MOPs with various properties, including ZDT3 [11], Schaffer [12], WFG [13] and DTLZ series problems [10], are used to evaluate the performance of all the compared algorithms. It is noted that the numbers of decision variables are set to 30 for ZDT3, and to 10 for WFG1-WFG9, DTLZ1-DTLZ7 problems. Especially, 10 decision variables in all the WFG problems include 8 position parameters and 2 distance parameters. These test problems are characterized with different features. For example, ZDT3, WFG2, and DTLZ7 are disconnected problems; Schaffer [12] has a sharp peak and low tail; DTLZ5 and DTLZ6 have the degenerated PFs; WFG1-WFG9 own different scale values in two objectives.

One widely used metric, inverted generational distance (IGD) [18], is adopted in this paper to evaluate the performance of an MOEA. As the IGD metric can examine both of convergence and diversity, it was used in most of MOEAs for performance comparison [2, 4]. It calculates the average Euclidean distance from each individual of P^* (a subset of the true PF) to the set P (non-dominated solutions found by a certain algorithm). The IGD metric is defined as follows

$$IGD(P, P^*) = \frac{\sum_{i=1}^{|P^*|} d(P_i^*, P)}{|P^*|} \qquad (2)$$

where $|P^*|$ indicates the size of P^* and $d(P_i^*, P)$ returns the minimum Euclidean distance in objective space between P_i^* and the individuals in P. In general, a lower value of $IGD(P, P^*)$ is preferred as it indicates that P obtains a more even coverage and is closer to true PF.

4.2   The Parameter Settings

In this paper, four competitive MOEAs are selected for performance comparison, such as NSGA-II [2] using a Pareto-based method, MOEA/D [4] and MOEA/D-GR [17] using a decomposition-based method, and ED/DPP [15] using both Pareto-based and decomposition-based methods. All the algorithms are implemented by Java programming language under the framework of jMetal [19]. The parameters in our experimental studies are set, as suggested in their references [2, 4, 15, 17].

The population size N and maximum number of function evaluations are respectively set to 100 and 25000 for 2-objective problems and set to 300 and 50000 for 3-objective problems. The crossover probability for SBX is set to 0.9 and the mutation probability for PM is set to $1/n$ (n is the number of decision variables), as suggested in [2]. The distribution indexes for SBX and PM are all set to 20. The crossover probability CR and scale factor F for DE operator are respectively set to 0.5 and 0.5, as recommended in [8]. In MOEA/D-DE and MOEA/D-GR, the neighborhood size T is set to 20 [4, 17]. All the simulations are run 30 times, in which the median and interquartile range (IQR) values are collected for comparison.

4.3   Comparisons with Other MOEAs

The comparison results obtained by all the compared algorithms are given in Table 1, regarding the IGD metric. When compared to the decomposition-based algorithms (MOEA/D-DE and MOEA/D-GR), ArchMOEA/D shows the superiority as it wins on all the test instances in Table 1. According to the Wilcoxon's rank sum test, ArchMOEA/D obtains the better IGD values with statistical significance for most of test MOPs. Regarding the comparison with the Pareto-based algorithm (NSGA-II), ArchMOEA/D gets the better results on 16 out of 18 test problems and obtains the statistically similar results only on WFG2 and DTLZ7 based on the Wilcoxon's rank sum test. At last, regarding the comparison with ED/DPP that also incorporates both Pareto-based and decomposition-based techniques, ArchMOEA/D performs better on 16 out of 18 test problems, worse on WFG2 and similarly on WFG1. In summary, ArchMOEA/D shows the superior performance when compared to these four MOEAs.

Table 1. Performance comparison results of IGD values

	NSGA-II	MOEA/D-DE	MOEA/D-GR	ED/DPP	ArchiveMOEA/D
	Median $_{IQR}$	Median $_{IQR}$	Median $_{IQR}$	Median $_{IQR}$	Median $_{IQR}$
ZDT3	5.34e$-$3 $_{2.9e}$ $_{-4}{}^-$	1.06e$-$2 $_{1.2e}$ $_{-4}{}^-$	1.06e$-$2 $_{8.3e}$ $_{-5}{}^-$	1.10e$-$2 $_{4.4e}$ $_{-4}{}^-$	4.45e$-$3 $_{8.1e-5}$
SCH	2.00e$-$2 $_{8.9e}$ $_{-4}{}^-$	4.81e$-$2 $_{2.2e}$ $_{-4}{}^-$	4.77e$-$2 $_{7.9e-5}{}^-$	5.49e+0 $_{1.9e}$ $_{+1}{}^-$	1.70e$-$2 $_{1.6e-4}$
WFG1	1.57e+0 $_{1.7e}$ $_{-1}{}^-$	2.00e$-$2 $_{2.9e}$ $_{-3}{}^-$	2.12e$-$2 $_{4.3e}$ $_{-1}{}^-$	1.96e$-$2 $_{5.0e}$ $_{-4}{}^{\approx}$	1.59e$-$2 $_{1.4e-2}$
WFG2	1.52e$-$1 $_{1.6e}$ $_{-1}{}^{\approx}$	2.45e$-$1 $_{1.6e}$ $_{-1}{}^-$	2.45e$-$1 $_{1.3e}$ $_{-3}{}^-$	1.70e$-$1 $_{1.6e}$ $_{-1}{}^+$	2.32e$-$1 $_{1.6e-1}$
WFG3	1.50e$-$2 $_{1.6e}$ $_{-3}{}^-$	1.26e$-$2 $_{8.3e}$ $_{-5}{}^-$	1.26e$-$2 $_{1.5e}$ $_{-4}{}^-$	1.26e$-$2 $_{1.6e}$ $_{-4}{}^-$	1.17e$-$2 $_{1.8e-4}$
WFG4	1.54e$-$2 $_{1.1e}$ $_{-3}{}^-$	1.57e$-$2 $_{2.1e}$ $_{-4}{}^-$	1.57e$-$2 $_{1.8e}$ $_{-4}{}^-$	1.57e$-$2 $_{3.4e}$ $_{-4}{}^-$	1.20e$-$2 $_{1.5e-4}$
WFG5	6.84e$-$2 $_{5.5e}$ $_{-4}{}^-$	6.75e$-$2 $_{5.8e}$ $_{-5}{}^-$	6.75e$-$2 $_{5.0e}$ $_{-5}{}^-$	6.75e$-$2 $_{4.4e}$ $_{-5}{}^-$	6.70e$-$2 $_{1.6e-4}$
WFG6	1.56e$-$2 $_{1.4e}$ $_{-3}{}^-$	1.67e$-$2 $_{3.2e}$ $_{-3}{}^-$	1.70e$-$2 $_{2.4e}$ $_{-3}{}^-$	1.71e$-$2 $_{2.3e}$ $_{-3}{}^-$	1.25e$-$2 $_{2.3e-3}$
WFG7	2.50e$-$2 $_{5.5e}$ $_{-3}{}^-$	1.92e$-$2 $_{1.3e}$ $_{-3}{}^-$	1.92e$-$2 $_{1.1e}$ $_{-3}{}^-$	1.97e$-$2 $_{8.2e}$ $_{-4}{}^-$	1.50e$-$2 $_{8.2e-3}$
WFG8	3.44e$-$2 $_{6.3e}$ $_{-3}{}^-$	2.48e$-$2 $_{3.6e}$ $_{-3}{}^-$	2.67e$-$2 $_{4.4e}$ $_{-3}{}^-$	2.73e$-$2 $_{4.5e}$ $_{-3}{}^-$	2.32e$-$2 $_{5.0e-3}$
WFG9	1.54e$-$2 $_{1.1e}$ $_{-3}{}^-$	1.51e$-$2 $_{2.4e}$ $_{-4}{}^-$	1.50e$-$2 $_{2.3e}$ $_{-4}{}^-$	1.50e$-$2 $_{1.1e}$ $_{-4}{}^-$	1.25e$-$2 $_{3.1e-4}$
DTLZ1	4.96e$-$1 $_{7.0e}$ $_{-1}{}^-$	4.40e$-$1 $_{6.8e}$ $_{-1}{}^-$	1.84e$-$2 $_{1.0e}$ $_{-2}{}^-$	2.10e$-$1 $_{1.3e}$ $_{-1}{}^-$	1.10e$-$2 $_{9.4e-5}$

(continued)

Table 1. (*continued*)

	NSGA-II	MOEA/D-DE	MOEA/D-GR	ED/DPP	ArchiveMOEA/D
	Median $_{\text{IQR}}$	Median $_{\text{IQR}}$	Median $_{\text{IQR}}$	Median $_{\text{IQR}}$	Median $_{\text{IQR}}$
DTLZ2	3.94e$-$2 $_{1.7e-3^-}$	3.85e$-$2 $_{3.9e-4^-}$	3.85e$-$2 $_{3.0e-4^-}$	3.81e$-$2 $_{3.7e-4^-}$	2.87e$-$2 $_{5.1e-4}$
DTLZ3	1.26e+0 $_{1.4e+0^-}$	1.21e+0 $_{1.6e+0^-}$	3.90e$-$2 $_{2.2e-3^-}$	4.00e+1 $_{1.2e+1^-}$	3.74e$-$2 $_{2.6e-3}$
DTLZ4	3.80e$-$2 $_{9.4e-4^-}$	3.77e$-$2 $_{9.1e-4^-}$	3.79e$-$2 $_{5.8e-4^-}$	3.68e$-$2 $_{7.8e-4^-}$	3.00e$-$2 $_{5.9e-3}$
DTLZ5	1.75e$-$3 $_{1.0e-4^-}$	4.80e$-$3 $_{3.7e-5^-}$	4.83e$-$3 $_{1.0e-4^-}$	3.06e$-$2 $_{1.0e-3^-}$	1.37e$-$3 $_{4.7e-5}$
DTLZ6	4.73e$-$1 $_{3.1e-2^-}$	4.52e$-$3 $_{1.6e-5^-}$	4.55e$-$3 $_{5.8e-5^-}$	2.85e$-$2 $_{5.3e-4^-}$	1.30e$-$3 $_{8.6e-5}$
DTLZ7	4.07e$-$2 $_{2.3e-3\approx}$	1.13e$-$1 $_{1.2e-3^-}$	1.13e$-$1 $_{2.4e-1^-}$	1.17e$-$1 $_{1.1e-3^-}$	4.00e$-$2 $_{1.7e-3}$
+/$-$/$\approx$	0/16/2	0/18/0	0/18/0	1/16/1	-/-/-

"+" indicates that the corresponding algorithm significantly outperforms ArchMOEA/D at a 0.05 level by the Wilcoxon's rank sum test, where "$-$" indicates the opposite, i.e., ArchMOEA/D shows significant improvements over the corresponding algorithm. If no significant difference is detected, it will be marked by the symbol "$\approx$".

To be specific, regarding the disconnected problems, i.e., ZDT3, WFG2, and DTLZ7, their final results obtained by all the algorithms are respectively plotted in Figs. 3, 4 and 5. It is noted that ZDT3 and WFG2 have disconnected PFs and different scales in two objectives. As observed from Figs. 3 and 4, MOEA/D-DE and MOEA/D-GR fail to find the uniformly distributed solution sets along the true PF. Especially for WFG2, NSGA-II, MOEA/D-DE, and MOEA/D-GR are unable to cover the entire true PF. DTLZ7 is a 3-objective disconnected problem, as illustrated in Fig. 5. It can be found that MOEA/D-DE and MOEA/D-GR only find some boundary solutions for DTLZ7. ArchMOEA/D and NSGA-II are successful to find the better results and they perform similarly on DTLZ7, as shown in Table 1. From these three figures, it validates that ArchMOEA/D can compensate the search of sparse area that the decomposition-based algorithms are difficult to explore due to the existence of many redundancy sub-problems in MOPs with disconnected PFs (as analyzed in Sect. 2).

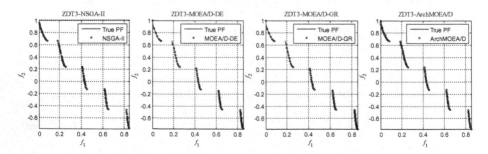

Fig. 3. Final solutions obtained by different MOEAs on ZDT3

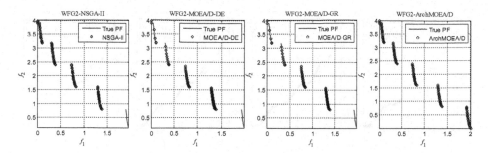

Fig. 4. Final solutions obtained by different algorithms on WFG2

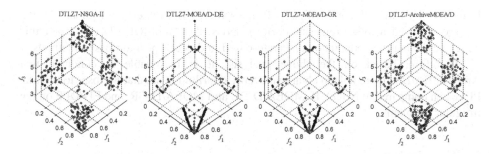

Fig. 5. Final solutions obtained by different MOEAs on DTLZ7

For SCH, it is a representative MOP with a sharp and low tail. Figure 6 plots the final solutions of all the algorithms in a single run when solving SCH. SCH has a convex Pareto optimal curve in the range f_1, f_2 belonging to [0, 4]. As illustrated in Fig. 4, MOEA/D-DE and MOEA/D-GR is difficult to maintain the even distribution of the solutions, especially around the edges of the true PF, as their solutions are concentrated in the range of [0, 3]. However, the proposed algorithm ArchMOEA/D performs much better. All the final solutions of ArchMOEA/D are uniformly distributed along the entire true PF. This is mainly due to the fact that the elite archive is further evolved in ArchMOEA/D to compensate the search of sparse area that decomposition-based algorithms are difficult to explore.

WFG1 owns different scales in two objectives. The final results of WFG1 are respectively plotted in Fig. 7. Regarding the WFG1 test problem, the final solutions

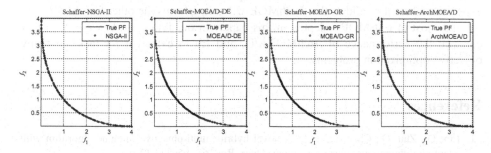

Fig. 6. Final solutions obtained by different MOEAs on Schaffer

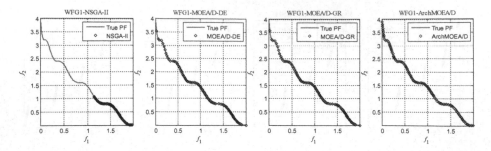

Fig. 7. Final solutions obtained by different MOEAs on WFG1

found by MOEA/D-DE and MOEA/D-GR are sparse in one dimension with large scale, but are crowded in other dimension with small scale. ArchMOEA/D can repair this deficiency using the cooperation of Pareto-based and decomposition-based methods.

Therefore, based on the above analysis, it is reasonable to conclude that ArchMOEA/D is more able to obtain an evenly distribution set that is closer to the true PF, when compared to NSGA-II, MOEA/D-DE and MOEA/D-GR, and ED/DPP on the irregular problems.

5   Conclusion

This paper analyzes some deficiency of decomposition-based MOEAs, and then proposes an elite archive-based MOEA/D algorithm to solve the MOPs with various features, such as disconnected PFs, degenerated PFs, and different scales in different objectives. An elite archive is used to maintain the non-dominated solutions founded during the evolutionary process. Moreover, this elite archive is further evolved using SBX and PM, which is expected to compensate the search of sparse area that the decomposition-based algorithms are unable to reach. For example, most of decomposition-based MOEAs are not good at solving the SCH problem with sharp peak and long tail, the ZDT3, WFG, DTLZ7 problems with disconnected PFs, and the DTLZ5, DTLZ6 problems with degenerated PFs. Four competitive MOEAs, *i.e.*, a baseline Pareto-based algorithm (NSGA-II), two decomposition-based algorithms (MOEA/D-DE and MOEA/D-GR), and a novel ED/DPP algorithm that is also based on both Pareto-based and decomposition-based approaches, are used for performance comparison, in solving 18 test MOPs. Our experimental results validate that ArchMOEA/D outperforms the other four MOEAs in solving most of test MOPs adopted in this paper. In our future work, we will further enhance the performance of ArchMOEA/D, and try to extend it for tackling many objective optimization problems.

References

1. Lin, Q., Zhu, Q., Chen, J., et al.: A novel hybrid multi-objective immune algorithm with adaptive differential evolution. Comput. Oper. Res. **62**, 95–111 (2015)

2. Deb, K.: A fast and elitist multiobjective genetic algorithm: NSGA-II. IEEE Trans. Evol. Comput. **6**(2), 182–197 (2002)
3. Zitzler, E., Künzli, S.: Indicator-based selection in multiobjective search. In: Yao, X., et al. (eds.) PPSN 2004. LNCS, vol. 3242, pp. 832–842. Springer, Heidelberg (2004). doi:10. 1007/978-3-540-30217-9_84
4. Li, H., Zhang, Q.: Multiobjective optimization problems with complicated Pareto sets, MOEA/D and NSGA-II. IEEE Trans. Evol. Comput. **12**(2), 284–302 (2009)
5. Zhao, S., Suganthan, P., Zhang, Q.: Decomposition based multiobjective evolutionary algorithm with an ensemble of neighborhood sizes. IEEE Trans. Evol. Comput. **16**(3), 422–446 (2012)
6. Li, K., Fialho, A., Kwong, S., Zhang, Q.: Adaptive operator selection with bandits for multiobjective evolutionary algorithm based decomposition. IEEE Trans. Evol. Comput. **19**, 114–130 (2014)
7. Li, K., Kwong, S., Li, M., Wang, R.: Stable matching-based selection in evolutionary multiobjective optimization. IEEE Trans. Evol. Comput. **18**(6), 909–923 (2014)
8. Li, K., Kwong, S., Zhang, Q., Deb, K.: Inter-relationship based selection for decomposition multiobjective optimization. IEEE Trans. Cybern. **45**(10), 2076–2088 (2015)
9. Li, H., Ding, M., Deng, J., Zhang, Q.: On the use of random weights in MOEA/D. In: Proceedings of the 2015 IEEE Congress on Evolutionary Computation (CEC), Sendai, Japan, pp. 978–985 (2015)
10. Deb, K., Thiele, L., Laumanns, M., Zitzler, E.: Scalable test problems for evolutionary multiobjective optimization. In: Abraham, A., Jain, L., Goldberg, R. (eds.) Evolutionary Multiobjective Optimization. Advanced Information and Knowledge Processing, pp. 105–145. Springer, London (2005). doi:10.1007/1-84628-137-7_6
11. Zitzler, E., Deb, K., Thiele, L.: Comparison of multiobjective evolutionary algorithms: empirical results. Evol. Comput. **8**(2), 173–195 (2000)
12. Schaffer, J.: Multiple objective optimization with vector evaluated genetic algorithms. In: Proceedings of the First International Conference on Genetic Algorithms, pp. 93–100 (1985)
13. Huband, S., Hingston, P., Barone, L., While, L.: A review of multiobjective test problems and a scalable test problem toolkit. IEEE Trans. Evol. Comput. **10**(5), 477–506 (2006)
14. Qi, T., et al.: MOEA/D with adaptive weight adjustment. Evol. Comput. **22**(2), 231–264 (2014)
15. Li, K., Kwong, S., Deb, K.: A dual-population paradigm for evolutionary multiobjective optimization. Inf. Sci. **309**, 50–72 (2015)
16. Lin, Q., et al.: A hybrid evolutionary immune algorithm for multiobjective optimization problems. IEEE Trans. Evol. Comput. **20**(5), 711–729 (2016)
17. Wang, Z., Zhang, Q., Zhou, A., Gong, M., Jiao, L.: Adaptive replacement strategies for MOEA/D. IEEE Trans. Cybern. **46**(2), 474–486 (2016)
18. Bosman, P., Thierens, D.: The balance between proximity and diversity in multiobjective evolutionary algorithms. IEEE Trans. Evol. Comput. **7**(2), 174–188 (2003)
19. Durillo, J., Nebro, A., Alba, E.: The jMetal framework for multi-objective optimization: design and architecture. In: Proceedings of the 2010 IEEE Congress on Evolutionary Computation (CEC), Barcelona, Spain, pp. 1–8 (2010)

A Constraint Partitioning Method Based on Minimax Strategy for Constrained Multiobjective Optimization Problems

Xueqiang Li[1], Shen Fu[2(✉)], and Han Huang[2]

[1] Dongguan University of Technology, Dongguan 523000, Guangdong, China
[2] South China University of Technology,
Guangzhou 510006, Guangdong, China
306059483@qq.com

Abstract. Constrained multiobjective optimization problem (CMOP) is an important research topic in the field of evolutionary computation. In terms of constraint handling, most of the existing evolutionary algorithms consider more about the proportion of infeasible solutions in population, but less concern about the distribution of infeasible solutions. Therefore, we propose a constraint partitioning method based on minimax strategy (CPM/MS) to solve CMOP. Firstly, we analyze the impact of the distribution of infeasible solutions on selecting solutions and give a preconditioning method for infeasible solutions. Secondly, we divide the preconditioned solutions into different regions by minimax strategy. Finally, we update individuals based on feasibility criteria method in each region. The effectiveness of CPM/MS algorithm is extensively evaluated on a suite of 10 bound-constrained numerical optimization problems, where the results show that CPM/MS algorithm is able to obtain considerably better fronts for some of the problems compared with some the state-of-the-art multiobjective evolutionary algorithms.

Keywords: CMOP · Evolutionary computation · Minimax strategy · Constraint handling

1 Introduction

There are a lot of CMOPs in real production and application. The CMOP considered in this paper is defined as follows [1]:

$$
\begin{aligned}
\text{Minimize} \quad & f(x) = (f_1(x), f_2(x), \ldots, f_m(x))^{\mathrm{T}} \\
\text{Subject to} \quad & g_j(x) \leq 0 \; j = 1, 2, \cdots, p \\
& h_k(x) = 0 \; k = 1, 2, \cdots, q \\
& x = (x_1, x_2, \cdots, x_n) \in S \subseteq R^n
\end{aligned}
\tag{1}
$$

where $f : R^n \to R^m$ is the target vector of m dimensions, $g_j(x)$ is the jth inequality constraint, h_k is the kth equality constraint, feasible domain $S = \{x | g_j(x) \geq 0,$ $h_k(x) = 0, j = 1, \cdots, p$ and $k = 1, \cdots q\}$, $x \in R^n$, $x_i \in [l_i, u_i]$, l_i, u_i are the lower bound and upper bound of x_i, $i = 1, \cdots, n$.

© Springer International Publishing AG 2017
Y. Shi et al. (Eds.): SEAL 2017, LNCS 10593, pp. 248–259, 2017.
https://doi.org/10.1007/978-3-319-68759-9_21

The CMOP requires finding a set of feasible solutions uniformly distributed over Pareto Front (PF). The related content mainly involves two aspects: constraint handling and representative solutions searching. The first involves a tradeoff between feasible and infeasible solutions, the second is necessary to find a set of representative solutions uniformly spaced on the PF. At present, combining evolutionary algorithm to solve CMOPs has become a research hotspot, and many related research have been put forward by scholars.

Constraint handling in evolutionary algorithm mainly has the following methods: penalty function method, feasibility criteria method, random sorting method, ε constraint handling method, multiobjective optimization method and hybrid method [2–4]. Penalty function method is relatively easy to implement, and lots of adaptive penalty function evolution algorithms are proposed so far [5–7]. However, this method relies too heavily on penalty parameters. Multiobjective optimization method considers constraint as an objective [8–12], which greatly increases computing resources, but it shows prominent convergence performance for CMOPs. Consequently, multiobjective optimization method is suitable for solving problems with small feasible domain. Feasibility criteria method, random sorting method and ε constraint handling method are criteria-based constraint handling methods. In which feasibility criteria always set feasible solution superior to infeasible solution, and solution with a low degree of constraint violation is superior to solution with a high degree of constraint violation [1, 14, 15]; random sorting method chooses objective function value or the degree of constraint violation based on a probability for function comparison [16, 17]; ε constraint handling method sets an acceptance degree ε, when the degree of constraint violation does not exceed ε, selection is performed according to the objective function, otherwise selection is performed according to the degree of constraint violation [18–20].

Multiobjective evolutionary algorithms mainly fall into three categories: the algorithm based on weighted sum, the algorithm based on Pareto dominates principle, and the algorithm based on criteria. The weighted sum algorithm developed by Ishibuchi and Murata [21], who adopt a weighted sum method to design a fitness function. The second include NSGA-II [22], PESA-II [23], SPEA [24] and so on. The representative of the third are MOEA/D [25] and its derivative algorithms MOEA/DM2 M [26], EAG-MOEA/D [27], MOEA/D-SAS [28] and FV-MOEA [29], these algorithms, that based on minimax strategy, can get better results in solving multiobjective optimization problems.

For CMOPs, constraint handling and multiobjective optimization are interrelated and cannot be treated separately. In constraint handling, Different proportion and distribution of infeasible solutions requires different measurement of the solutions, which affect population updating, and thus affect the performance of new generated individuals. Meanwhile, different optimization strategies of evolutionary algorithm will affect the feasibility of new solutions and superiority of objective function values. Therefore, effective constraint handling and proper multiobjective optimization strategies are critical for solving CMOPs.

Considering that allocation proportions of infeasible solutions are usually different in solution space, we partition solutions and then handle constraints within each partition. This way of dealing with constraints can effectively avoid the loss of valid solutions in many regions. Thus, a constraint partitioning method based on minimax strategy is proposed. Firstly, all solutions are assigned to each sub region by minimax strategy, and then the partitioned solutions are selected by a feasibility criterion independently in each sub region. The partitioning of constraint handling and solutions updating are more accurate than that overall processing. It firstly reduces the impact of the distribution of infeasible solutions on population updating. The main contributions of this work as follows.

(1) We will analyze the impact of distribution of infeasible solutions on selecting solutions based on minimax strategy.
(2) We will design a constraint preconditioning method based on minimax strategy.
(3) Partition-based constraints handling will be proposed for individuals of population.

This paper is organized as follows. Section 2 summarizes the minimax strategy and the constraint handling method based on criteria. Section 3 analyzes the impact of the distribution of infeasible solutions on selecting solutions, proposes a constraint preconditioning method and gives the basic framework of the proposed algorithm. Section 4 tests the proposed algorithm on CMOPs and compares the results with other algorithms. Section 5 makes a conclusion.

2   Related Works

2.1   The Fitness Function Based on Minimax Strategy

The fitness function based on minimax strategy is defined as follow [30].

$$F(x) = \max_{1 \leq j \leq m} \left\{ w_j F_j(x) \right\} \tag{2}$$

where $w_j > 0$ is weight should be designed properly, $F_j = \frac{f_j - f_{minj}}{f_{maxj} - f_{minj}}, j = 1, 2, \cdots, m$ is monotonic transformation function of $f_j(x)$, f_{minj} and f_{maxj} are minimum and maximum value of the subobjective f_j in current population.

The weights of this paper are predefined based on generalized sphere require $w_1^2 + w_2^2 + \cdots + w_m^2 = 1$, which are different from the commonly used plane-based weights require $w_1 + w_2 + \cdots + w_m = 1$. Compared with plane-based weights, the sphere-based weights can select more evenly spaced objective solutions when PF is convex. The N m-dimensional weights can be uniformly designed according to formula (3) on generalized spherical coordinates [30].

$$
\begin{cases}
w_1(x) = \frac{1}{\cos \theta_1} \\
w_2(x) = \frac{1}{\sin \theta_1 \cos \theta_2} \\
\cdots \cdots \cdots \\
w_{m-1}(x) = \frac{1}{\sin \theta_1 \sin \theta_2 \cdots \sin \theta_{m-2} \cos \theta_{m-1}} \\
w_m(x) = \frac{1}{\sin \theta_1 \sin \theta_2 \cdots \sin \theta_{m-2} \sin \theta_{m-1}}
\end{cases}
\tag{3}
$$

where $(\theta_1, \theta_2, \cdots, \theta_{m-1})$ denotes the generalized unit spherical coordinates in objective space. The inverse $(\frac{1}{w_1}, \frac{1}{w_2}, \cdots, \frac{1}{w_m})$ of any weight vector corresponds to a point on generalized spherical surface. For example, when $m = 3$, the generalized spherical points are shown in Fig. 1.

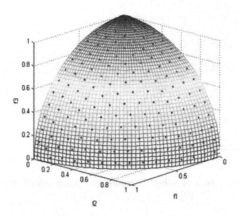

Fig. 1. The points corresponding to the weights in three-dimensional spherical surface

2.2   Calculation of the Degree of Constraint Violation

In order to evaluate the constraint violation reasonably and simplify the calculation for more than one constraint in CMOPs, it is necessary to unify different constraints. According to constraint condition in formula (1), for any of individual $x^i (i = 1, 2, \cdots, N)$, the degree of constraint violation usually defined as follow [4].

$$v^i = \sum_{j=1}^{p} \left(\frac{\max\{0, g_j(x^i)\}}{g_j^*} \right) + \sum_{k=1}^{q} \left| \frac{h_k(x^i)}{h_k^*} - \delta \right| \tag{4}$$

where $g_j^* = \max_{1 \leq i \leq N} \{g_j(x^i)\}$, $(j = 1, \cdots, p)$, $h_k^* = \max_{1 \leq i \leq N} \{h_k(x^i)\}$, $(k = 1, \cdots, q)$.

If x^i is a feasible solution, then $g_j(x^i) \leq 0$, $h_j(x^i) = 0$ for $\forall j$, it can be found that $v^i = 0$ by formula (4). If x^i is an infeasible solution, there $\exists j$ that makes $g_j(x^i) > 0$ or $|h_j(x^i)| > \delta$, and then $v^i > 0$ in this case. In order to reduce the differences between each constraint, the above formula is used for constraints unitization. In addition, the parameter δ is not discussed here because there is no equality constraint in the testing problems.

3   Population Updating and Constraint Handling Techniques

3.1   The Impact of Distribution of Infeasible Solutions on Selecting Solutions Based on Minimax Strategy

In CMOPs, the distribution of infeasible solutions often has a great impact on selecting solutions. It will be illustrated by means of Fig. 2. In Fig. 2, the white dots are

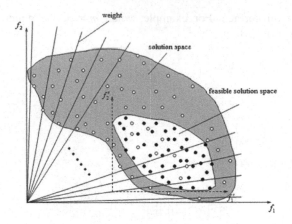

Fig. 2. Distribution of solution points and point-selection of weights

infeasible solutions, black dots are feasible solutions. The white region is the feasible solution space, and infeasible solutions also may be distributed in the white region or gray region.

In the process of selecting solutions according to the minimax strategy, if we do not handle infeasible solutions, taking f_1 and f_2 as coordinate axes, then a large number of infeasible solutions will be selected, and many valid feasible solutions will be lost. If solutions are selected with f_1' and f_2' as coordinate axes, the selected solutions will contain more feasible solutions, and obviously this approach is more reasonable. Therefore, the selection of axes in selecting solutions is critical. However, the coordinate axes are usually determined by the minimum value of each subobjective of solutions in current population, thus, the solutions with smaller subobjective function values but violate the constraints, must be preconditioned in CMOPs.

3.2 Constraint Preconditioning

As explained above, the function values of the infeasible solutions will affect the selection of coordinate axes, and result in a large number of feasible solutions losses. Meanwhile, by considering the superiority of objective function values of infeasible solutions, we only reserve the infeasible solutions near feasible solutions, and the other infeasible solutions that far away from the feasible solutions will be removed before population updating. The preconditioning approach is given as follow.

For any individual $x^i (i = 1, 2, \cdots, N)$, its jth subobjective function value is $f_j^i = f_j(x^i)$. Define the degree of x^i affects the coordinate offset as follow.

$$d(x^i) = \max_{j=1:m} \left\{ \frac{f_{minj}^* - f_j^i}{f_{maxj}^* - f_{minj}^*} \right\} \tag{5}$$

where $f^*_{\text{min}j}$ and $f^*_{\text{max}j}$ represent the minimum and maximum values of subobjective f_j of feasible individuals in current population, respectively, and the denominator $f^*_{\text{max}j} - f^*_{\text{min}j}$ is used to eliminate the impact of the range of jth subobjective.

For any individual $x^i (i = 1, 2, \cdots, N)$, if $f^i_j < f^*_{\text{min}j}$, then the corresponding $d^i > 0$, otherwise $d^i \leq 0$. The bigger d^i is, the greater impact of x^i on the axes selecting. If $d^i \leq 0$, then there is no effect of x^i on the axes. Therefore, in preconditioning of individuals in population, a certain number of bad infeasible individuals can be deleted according to descending order of d^i.

3.3   Constraint Handling and Population Updating

As mentioned in Subsect. 2.1, N weight vectors $\{w^1, w^2, \cdots, w^N\}$ are designed evenly spaced in an objective space. For any weight w^i, there must be a region of PF, where points on the region have better fitness values than other weights by formula (2). For this reason, all of the points on this region should be allocated to the weight w^i, but the points may not be assigned to w^i by traditional minimax strategy of weights select point. Thus, we use the updated minimax strategy that point select weights to partition individuals. To illustrate this further, detailed process is described by three steps.

Step 1: Transform each predesigned weight $w^i = (w^i_1, w^i_2, \cdots, w^i_m)^{\text{T}}$, $i = 1, 2, \cdots, N$ into point on the generalized sphere. The transformed point is set as $\tilde{f}^i$, $\tilde{f}^i = (\tilde{f}^i_1, \tilde{f}^i_2, \cdots, \tilde{f}^i_m)^{\text{T}} = (\frac{1}{w^i_1}, \frac{1}{w^i_2}, \cdots, \frac{1}{w^i_m})^{\text{T}}$ by formula (3).

Step 2: Turn each function value $f^i = (f^i_1, f^i_2, \cdots, f^i_m)^{\text{T}}$, $i = 1, 2, \cdots, N$ of individual in population into $F^i = (F^i_1, F^i_2, \cdots, F^i_m)^{\text{T}}$ by formula (2), and let $\tilde{w}^i = (\tilde{w}^i_1, \tilde{w}^i_2, \cdots, \tilde{w}^i_m)^{\text{T}} = (\frac{1}{F^i_1}, \frac{1}{F^i_2}, \cdots, \frac{1}{F^i_m})^{\text{T}}$ be the corresponding weigh of f^i.

Step 3: For each weight $\tilde{w}^i$ (corresponding to f^i), find an optimal point $\tilde{f}^k$ on the generalized sphere (corresponding to a pre-assigned weight w^k) by minimize the fitness value $F(x) = \max\limits_{1 \leq j \leq m} \{\tilde{w}^i_j \tilde{f}_j(x)\}$ according to formula (2). Then assign f^i (corresponding to $\tilde{w}^i$) to weight w^k (corresponding to $\tilde{f}^k$).

When every individual is partitioned to the corresponding weight, a feasibility criteria method is used for individual selecting in each region. Feasibility criteria are defined as follows [1].

(1) Any feasible solution is preferred to any infeasible solution.
(2) Among two feasible solutions, the one having better objective function value is preferred.
(3) Among two infeasible solutions, the one having smaller constraint violation is preferred.

In literature [1], population updating is selecting N optimal individuals from the whole population by above feasibility criteria. The update is not precise enough for that the number and the fitness values of feasible solutions do not consider in different regions of PF. In this case the selected individuals may be concentrated in a certain region of PF. It is obviously unreasonable. Based on the above consideration, we divide solutions into N regions, and then use feasibility criteria in each region to select the best solution. It avoids the selected solutions are concentrated in a small region of PF. Therefore, partition selection method is more scientific than not.

3.4   The Pseudo Code of CPM/MS Algorithm

The pseudo code of CPM/MS algorithm is shown in Fig. 3.

The proposed algorithm: CPM/MS

NP: Size of population.

$MaxFes$: Maximum number of function evaluations.

Fes: Number of function evaluations so far, set initial $Fes = 0$.

Output: A set of feasible non-dominated solutions.

1: Define fitness function by formula (2).

2: Define the degree of violation by formula (4).

3: Initialize population with N individuals.

4: While $Fes < MaxFes$

5:        For $i = 1$ to N

6:            Generate y^i through DE operator.

7:            Perform polynomial mutation on y^i.

8:            Calculate the fitness value of y^i.

9:            $Fes = Fes+1$

10:      End for

11:      Constraint preconditioning by subsection 3.2.

12:      Constraint handling and population evolving by subsection 3.3.

13: End while

Fig. 3. The pseudo code of CPM/MS algorithm

CPM/MS algorithm works as shown in Fig. 1. In input some parameters are set, a fitness function by minimax strategy and degree of constraint violation are defined. In output a set of feasible non-dominated solutions will be obtained by CPM/MS algorithm. In step 1 N individuals are initialized. From step 5 to step10, for each individual, a new individual y^i is generated by DE algorithm [30] and polynomial mutation [25], then the fitness value of y^i is calculated and Fes is updated. In step 11, constraint preconditioning is executed on both parent population and new generated individuals. In step 12, partitions processing of constraints and feasibility criteria are performed for population updating.

4   Experimental Results and Analysis

The benchmark test functions collected in 2009 IEEE congress on evolutionary computation (CEC2009) [31] were employed to demonstrate the capability of CPM/MS algorithm. These test functions are multimodal, many of which are discontinuous or segmented continuous multiobjective optimization problems. The maximal number of function evaluations is set to be 300,000 and each algorithm runs independently 30 times for each test function. The PF obtained by CPM/MS algorithm is shown in Fig. 4.

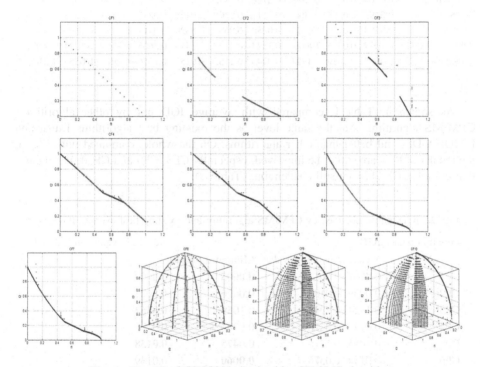

Fig. 4. The PF of CEC2009 obtained by CPM/MS algorithm

From the above, many PF of the test functions are sectional continuous or isolated points. A lot of optimal solutions of test functions and especially all optimal solutions of CF1 are obtained by CPM/MS algorithm. Also there are many optimal solutions are not gained within the limited number of function evolutions, particularly CF3 is difficult to be solved, which is a multiobjective optimization with deceptive imbalance.

IGD is introduced to measure the quality and uniformity of the feasible solution got by CPM/MS algorithm [32], meanwhile some of the state-of-the-art multiobjective evolutionary algorithms are compared [33]. The maximal number of the solutions in the approximate set, that produced by each algorithm for computing the IGD is 100 for two objective problems; 150 for three objective problems and 800 for five objective problems [31]. The mean, minimum and maximum values of IGD obtained by the other algorithms and CPM/MS algorithm are shown in Table 1.

Table 1. The average IGD metric obtained by 30 runs for the test function

Algorithms	CF1	CF2	CF3	CF4	CF5	CF6	CF7	CF8	CF9	CF10
MOEA DGM	0.0108	0.0080	0.5134	0.0707	0.5446	0.2071	0.5356	0.4056	0.1519	0.3139
LiuLi	0.0009	0.0042	0.1829	0.0142	0.1097	0.0139	0.1045	0.0607	0.0505	0.1974
DMOEA-DD	0.0113	0.0021	0.0563	0.0070	0.0158	0.0150	0.0191	0.0475	0.1434	0.1621
NSGAIILS	0.0069	0.0118	0.2399	0.0158	0.1842	0.0201	0.2335	0.1109	0.1056	0.3592
MTS	0.0192	0.0268	0.1045	0.0111	0.0208	0.0162	0.0247	1.0854	0.0851	0.1376
GDE3	0.0294	0.0160	0.1275	0.0080	0.0680	0.0620	0.0417	0.1387	0.1145	0.4923
DECMOSASQP	0.1077	0.0946	100000	0.1527	0.4128	0.1478	0.2605	0.1763	0.1271	0.5071
CPM/MS	0.0007	0.0039	0.1924	0.0143	0.1055	0.0155	0.1056	0.0613	0.0554	0.1968

As shown in Table 1, compared with average IGD got by other algorithms, CPM/MS algorithm is at the same level as the existing best algorithms LiuLi and DMOEA-DD, and better than other algorithms. On the whole, combined with Fig. 4, the results of IGD are still to be improved, especially CF3, CF9 and CF10. It indicates that complex CMOPs are still challenging (Table 2).

Table 2. IGD metric obtained by CPM/MS algorithm and existing best average IGD metric

Function name	IGD			Best IGD values in Table 1
	Mean	Maximum value	Minimum value	
CF1	0.0007	0.0011	**0.0005**	0.0009
CF2	0.0039	0.0103	0.0026	**0.0021**
CF3	0.1924	0.2948	0.1059	**0.0563**
CF4	0.0143	0.0216	0.0086	0.0070
CF5	0.1055	0.1716	0.0475	**0.0158**
CF6	0.0155	0.0376	**0.0060**	0.0139
CF7	0.1056	0.1857	0.0584	**0.0191**
CF8	0.0613	0.1018	**0.0443**	0.0475
CF9	0.0554	0.1014	**0.0460**	**0.0505**
CF10	0.1968	0.3967	**0.0955**	0.1376

From the above table we can see that the minimum value of IGD got by CPM/MS algorithm some are better than the best IGD values from Table 1, and the mean value of IGD got by CPM/MS algorithm is also competitive compared to other algorithms. It shows the effectiveness of CPM/MS algorithm in solving CMOPs.

In the above experiments, we use a constraint partitioning method based on minimax strategy for CMOPs and obtain good results compared with other algorithms, although some optimal solutions can be solved, but they cannot cover the whole PF as shown in Fig. 4, and this happens in other algorithms as well. We believe that the main reasons are: Firstly, the weights are designed uniform based on continuous functions, but the PF of the test functions are sectional continuous or isolated points, it means PF is not uniform. Therefore, evenly spaced weights will inevitably lead to many areas of PF without solutions, or too little, thus the method of selecting solutions will be improved in future. Secondly, since CMOPs are more and more complex, the search ability of the algorithm need to be stronger, thus the distribution information of solutions should be combined to guide the search of algorithm in later studies.

5 Conclusions

In this paper, a constraint partitioning method based on minimax strategy is proposed to compute CMOPs. By analyzing the impact of the distribution of infeasible solutions on selecting solutions, a method for population preconditioning is designed. The preconditioned population is then partitioned by minimax strategy, and the feasibility criteria are applied for selecting individuals in each region independently. This approach effectively avoids the valid solutions loss, which caused by infeasible solution allocation imbalance during population updating. Finally, the proposed CPM/MS algorithm is extensively tested on a suite of 10 bound-constrained numerical optimization problems of CEC2009. The results show that CPM/MS algorithm can solve complex CMOPs effectively.

References

1. Deb, K.: An efficient constraint handling method for genetic algorithms. Comput. Methods Appl. Mech. Eng. **186**(2–4), 311–338 (2000)
2. Cai, X., Hu, Z., Fan, Z.: A novel memetic algorithm based on invasive weed optimization and di_erential evolution for constrained optimization. Soft. Comput. **17**(10), 1893–1910 (2013)
3. Hu, Z., Cai, X., Fan, Z.: An improved memetic algorithm using ring neighborhood topology for constrained optimization. Soft. Comput. **18**(10), 2023–2041 (2013)
4. Li, Z.Y., Huang, T., Chen, S.M., Li, R.F.: Overview of constrained optimization evolutionary algorithms. J. Softw. (2017)
5. Farmani, R., Wright, J.A.: Self-adaptive fitness formulation for constrained optimization. IEEE Trans. Evol. Comput. **7**(5), 445–455 (2003)
6. Xiao, J.H., Xu, J., Shao, Z., Jiang, C.F., Pan, L.: A genetic algorithm for solving multi-constrained function optimization problems based on KS function. In: Proceedings of the 2007 IEEE Congress on Evolutionary Computation, Singapore, pp. 4497–4501. IEEE Press (2007)
7. Tessema, B., Yen, G.G.: A adaptive penalty formulation for constrained evolutionary optimization. IEEE Trans. Syst. Man Cybern. (A) **39**(3), 565–578 (2009)
8. Surry, P.D., Radcliffe, N.J.: The COMOGA method: Constrained optimization by multiobjective genetic algorithm. Control Cybern. **26**(3), 391–412 (1997)

9. Wang, Y., Cai, Z.X., Guo, G., Zhou, Y.R.: A dynamic hybrid framework for constrained evolutionary optimization. IEEE Trans. Syst. Man Cybern. (B) **42**(1), 203–217 (2012)

10. Cai, Z.X., Wang, Y.: Combining multiobjective optimization with differential evolution to solve constrained optimization problems. IEEE Trans. Evol. Comput. **16**(1), 117–134 (2012)

11. Gong, W.Y., Cai, Z.H.: A multiobjective differential evolution algorithm for constrained optimization. In: Proceedings of the 2008 IEEE Congress on Evolutionary Computation, Hong Kong, pp. 181–188. IEEE Press (2008)

12. Gao, W.F., Yen, G., Liu, S.Y.: A dual-population differential evolution with coevolution for constrained optimization. IEEE Trans. Cybern. **45**(5), 1108–1121 (2014)

13. Zielinski, R., Laur, R.: Constrained single-objective optimization using differential evolution. In: Proceedings of the 2006 IEEE International Conference on Evolutionary Computation, Vancouver, pp. 223–230. IEEE Press (2006)

14. Sarker, R.A., Elsayed, S.M., Ray, T.: Differential evolution with dynamic parameters selection for optimization problems. IEEE Trans. Evol. Comput. **18**(5), 689–707 (2014)

15. Wang, Y., Wang, B.C., Li, H.X., Yen, G.G.: Incorporating objective function information into the feasibility rule for constrained evolutionary optimization. IEEE Trans. Cybern. **46** (12), 2938–2952 (2015)

16. Runarsson, T.P., Yao, X.: Stochastic ranking for constrained evolutionary optimization. IEEE Trans. Evol. Comput. **4**(3), 284–294 (2000)

17. Zhang, M., Luo, W.J., Wang, X.: Differential evolution with dynamic stochastic selection for constrained optimization. Inf. Sci. **178**(15), 3043–3074 (2008)

18. Takahama, T., Sakai, S.: Constrained optimization by the ε constrained differential evolution with gradient-based mutation and feasible elites. In: Proceedings of the 2006 IEEE International Conference on Evolutionary Computation, Vancouver, pp. 372–378. IEEE Press (2006)

19. Bu, C., Luo, W., Zhu, T.: Differential evolution with a species-based repair strategy for constrained optimization. In: Proceedings of the 2014 IEEE Congress on Evolutionary Computation, Beijing, pp. 967–974. IEEE Press (2014)

20. Takahama, T., Sakai, S.: Efficient constrained optimization by the ε constrained rank-based differential evolution. In: Proceedings of the 2012 IEEE Congress on Evolutionary Computation, Brisbane, pp. 1–8. IEEE Press (2012)

21. Ishibuchi, H., Murata, T.: A Multiobjective genetic local search algorithm and its application to flowshop scheduling. IEEE Trans. Syst. Man Cybern. Part C Appl. Rev. **28**(3), 392–403 (1998)

22. Deb, K., Pratap, A., Agarwal, S., Meyarivan, T.: A fast and elitist multiobjective genetic algorithm: NSGA-II. IEEE Trans. Evol. Comput. **6**(2), 182–197 (2002)

23. Corne, D.W., Jerram, N.R., Knowles, J.D., Oates, M.J.: PESA-II: region-based selection in evolutionary multiobjective optimization. In: Proceedings of the 3rd Annual Conference on Genetic and Evolutionary Computation, pp. 283–290. Morgan Kaufmann Publishers Inc. (2001)

24. Zitzler, E., Thiele, L.: Multiobjective evolutionary algorithms: a comparative case study and the strength pareto approach. IEEE Trans. Evol. Comput. **3**(4), 257–271 (1999)

25. Ishibuchi, H., Murata, T.: A multiobjective genetic local search algorithm and its application to flowshop scheduling. IEEE Trans. Syst. Man Cybern. Part C Appl. Rev. **28**(3), 392–403 (1998)

26. Zhang, Q., Li, H.: MOEA/D: a multiobjective evolutionary algorithm based on decomposition. IEEE Trans. Evol. Comput. **11**(6), 712–731 (2007)

27. Liu, H.L., Gu, F., Zhang, Q.: Decomposition of a multiobjective optimization problem into a number of simple multiobjective subproblems. IEEE Trans. Evol. Comput. **18**(3), 450–455 (2014)

28. Cai, X., Li, Y., Fan, Z., Zhang, Q.: An external archive guided multiobjective evolutionary algorithm based on decomposition for combinatorial optimization. IEEE Trans. Evol. Comput. **19**(4), 508–523 (2015)
29. Cai, X., Yang, Z., Fan, Z., Zhang, Q.: Decomposition-based-sorting and angle-based-selection for evolutionary multiobjective and many-objective optimization. IEEE Trans. Cybern. **PP**(99), 1–14 (2016)
30. Jiang, S., Zhang, J., Ong, Y.S., Zhang, A.N., Tan, P.S.: A simple and fast hypervolume indicator-based multiobjective evolutionary algorithm. IEEE Trans. Cybern. **45**(10), 2202–2213 (2015)
31. Liu, H., Li, X., Chen, Y.: Multiobjective evolutionary algorithm based on dynamical crossover and mutation. In: Proceedings of International Conference on Computational Intelligence and Security, Suzhou, pp. 150–155. IEEE (2008)
32. Zhang, Q., Zhou, A.M., Suganthan, P.N., et al.: Multiobjective optimization test instances for the CEC 2009 special session and competition. School of Computer Science and Electrical Engineering, University of Essex, Essex (2009)
33. Zitzler, E., Thiele, L., Laumanns, M., et al.: Performance assessment of multiobjective optimizers: an analys is and review. IEEE Trans. Evol. Comput. **7**(2), 117–132 (2003)
34. Zhang, Q., Suganthan, P.N.: Final report on CEC'09 MOEA competition. School of Computer Science and Electrical Engineering, University of Essex, Essex (2009)

A Fast Objective Reduction Algorithm Based on Dominance Structure for Many Objective Optimization

Fangqing Gu[1], Hai-Lin Liu[1], and Yiu-ming Cheung[2,3(✉)]

[1] Guangdong University of Technology, Guangdong, China
{fqgu,lhliu}@gdut.edu.cn
[2] Department of Computer Science, Hong Kong Baptist University (HKBU),
Hong Kong SAR, China
ymc@comp.hkbu.edu.hk
[3] HKBU Institute of Research and Continuing Education, Shenzhen, China

Abstract. The performance of the most existing classical evolutionary multiobjective optimization (EMO) algorithms, especially for Pareto-based EMO algorithms, generally deteriorates over the number of objectives in solving many-objective optimization problems (MaOPs), in which the number of objectives is greater than three. Objective reduction methods that transform an MaOP into the one with few objectives, are a promising way for solving MaOPs. The dominance-based objective reduction methods, e.g. k-EMOSS and δ-MOSS, omitting an objective while preserving the dominant structure of the individuals as much as possible, can achieve good performance. However, these algorithms have higher computational complexity. Therefore, this paper presents a novel measure for measuring the capacity of preserving the dominance structure of an objective set, i.e., the redundancy of an objective to an objective set. Subsequently, we propose a fast algorithm to find a minimum set of objectives preserving the dominance structure as much as possible. We compare the proposed algorithm with its counterparts on eleven test instances. Numerical studies show the effectiveness of the proposed algorithm.

Keywords: Many-objective optimization · Evolutionary algorithm · Objective reduction

---

This work was supported by the National Natural Science Foundation of China under Grants 61672444, 61673121 and 61703108, in part by the Natural Science Foundation of Guangdong Province under Grant 2017A030310467, and in part by the Projects of Science and Technology of Guangzhou under Grant 201508010008, the SZSTI Grant: JCYJ20160531194006833, the Faculty Research Grant of Hong Kong Baptist University (HKBU) under Project: FRG2/16-17/051, and the MPCF Project of Knowledge Transfer Office in HKBU: MPCF-004-2017/18.

Y. Shi et al. (Eds.): SEAL 2017, LNCS 10593, pp. 260–271, 2017.
https://doi.org/10.1007/978-3-319-68759-9_22

1   Introduction

Without loss of generality, a multiobjective optimization problem (MOP) can be formulated as follows:

$$\min \ F(\mathbf{x}) = (f_1(\mathbf{x}), f_2(\mathbf{x}), \dots, f_m(\mathbf{x}))^T$$
$$s.t. \ \mathbf{x} \in \Omega, \tag{1}$$

where $\Omega \subset \mathbb{R}^n$ is the decision space and n is the dimension of the decision variable $\mathbf{x} = (x_1, x_2, \dots, x_n)^T$. $F : \Omega \to \mathbb{R}^m$ consists of m real-value objective functions, and T is the transpose of a matrix. When $m \geq 4$, the problem (1) is regarded as a many-objective optimization problem (MaOP). The optimality of a multi/many-objective optimization problem is defined by the concept of dominance [7]. That is, a solution $\mathbf{x}$ is said to *weakly dominate* a solution $\mathbf{y}$ with respect to objective set $\mathcal{F}' \subseteq \mathcal{F} : \{f_1, f_2, \dots, f_m\}$ (denoted as $\mathcal{F}'(\mathbf{x}) \preceq \mathcal{F}'(\mathbf{y})$) if for any $f_i \in \mathcal{F}'$, we have $f_i(\mathbf{x}) \leq f_i(\mathbf{y})$.

In the literature, a number of evolutionary multiobjective optimization (EMO) algorithms, such as Pareto-based methods NSGA-II [9] and SPEA2 [11], indicator-based methods HypE [1], SMS-EMOA [22] and decomposition-based methods MOEA/D [30], M2M [18] have been proposed for solving MOPs. However, the performance of most well-known EMO algorithms will seriously deteriorate over the number of objectives in solving MaOPs [26]. Recently, several algorithms have been developed to deal with MaOPs, which can be roughly divided into two categories: algorithm adaptation methods and problem transformation methods.

The algorithm adaptation methods modify the classical EMO algorithms for MaOPs. The classical EMO algorithm can be further divided into three categories according to the selection mechanism: Pareto-based methods, indicator-based methods and decomposition-based methods. Some effective measures have been proposed by analyzing the existing difficulties of the methods in dealing with MaOPs. Specifically, the Pareto-based methods may fail to converge to the Pareto front (PF) because the algorithms lose the selection pressure towards the PF [14]. A straightforward idea is to modify the Pareto dominance relation to enhance the selection pressure of the Pareto-based algorithms [32], e.g. ϵ-MOEA [8], k-optimality [12], and so on. The indicator-based EMO algorithms use a performance indicator to guide the search process [1, 22]. The hypervolume indicator has been widely used to guide the search process because it is the only metric known to be strictly monotonic to the Pareto dominance [1]. Unfortunately, it suffers from the high computational cost for solving MaOPs. In the literature, some improved strategies have been proposed in [24]. The last decomposition-based EMO algorithm aims at decomposing an MOP into a number of sub-problems and then optimizes simultaneously. MOEA/D [30], as one of the most well-known decomposition-based EMO algorithm, achieves a good performance when tacking unconstrained and constrained MaOPs. Recently, some excellent decomposition-based algorithms have been presented in [10, 17] for MaOPs. However, the weight vectors have a great impact on the performance of the algorithms and how to set the weight vectors is a burdensome task for solving MaOPs [15].

Furthermore, in some real applications [21], some objectives of the problems would be correlated or redundant. Accordingly, problem transformation methods are another technique for solving such MaOPs, which is objective reduction oriented through identifying the redundant objectives. As summarized in [25,27], a number of objective reduction methods have been presented in the past few years and these algorithms can be divided into two categories according to the measures of the redundancy of an objective.

The first one is the correlation-based objective reduction methods which use the correlation or mutual information of the objective values of the nondominated solutions to measure the conflict of objectives [28,29]. For example, Jaimes et al. [16,19] developed an objective reduction scheme based on unsupervised feature selection. A distance matrix based on the correlation matrix is defined to measure the conflict between the objectives. Saxena et al. [2,25] employed the Principal Component Analysis on the correlation matrix to identify the redundant objectives. Actually, we have also presented an online objective reduction algorithm based on the correlation matrix [5,6]. It formulates the reduced objectives as a nonnegative linear combination of the original objectives to maximize the conflict of reduced objectives. A new objective reduction strategy by employing the mutual information to measure the relationship between pairs of objectives is proposed in [13,23]. These algorithms do not take the underlying dominance structure into account. In general, as discussed in [6], the measure based on correlation matrix of the objectives is not totally equivalent to the conflict between objectives, especially for the problems with multiple essential objectives.

The other one is the dominance-based objective reduction methods which measure the conflict of objectives by employing the capacity of preserving the dominance structure of the individuals in a population. Generally, it can give a more accuracy measure to the redundancy of objectives. For example, Brockhoff and Zitzler [3,4] presented a criterion taking the maximum dominance error of the individuals to measure the degree of conflict of the objectives. Singh et al. [27] proposed a Pareto corner search evolutionary algorithm for MaOPs. It uses the number of nondominated solutions to measure the degree of conflict of the objectives. These algorithms have a high computational cost because of computing the dominant matrix.

The motivation of this paper is twofold. First, the existing measures have some shortcomings to measure the degree of conflict between the objectives. Therefore, we present a more accurate and effective measure for measuring the degree of conflict of objectives. Then, we propose a faster method to compute the proposed measure. Since the dominance relationship of the individuals on the reduced objective set needs to compute, some researchers have tried to reduce the computational complexity of the dominance relationship of individuals [20] thus far. Currently, Zhou et al. [31] proposed a new and efficient implementation of non-dominated sorting based on the dominance degree matrix. In this paper, we draw on the dominance degree matrix and design a simple but fast method to compute the dominance relationship of individuals on the reduced objectives, and then we present a fast dominance-based objective reduction algorithm. The proposed algorithm has a lower computational complexity, i.e. $\mathcal{O}(m^2 N^2)$, through the theoretical analysis. Experimental results show the effectiveness of the proposed algorithm.

The remainder of the paper is organized as follows: Section 2 proposes a measure for measuring the redundancy of objectives, and then presents a fast objective reduction method. Section 3 compares the proposed objective reduction method with k-EMOSS and δ-MOSS on DTLZ5 with the different numbers of objectives and essential objectives. Finally, we draw a conclusion in Sect. 4.

2   Measuring the Redundancy of an Objective to a Given Objective Set

Objective reduction refers to finding a minimum objective subset such that the dominance structure is preserved for a given solution set $\mathcal{X} \subset \Omega$. In other words, it can also refer to eliminating the objectives which do not affect the dominance structure of the original objectives set $\mathcal{F}$. In practice, one is often interested in a further objective reduction at a cost of slight changes in the dominance structure. To illustrate how the weak dominance structure is modified when one objective is removed from a objective set, we present a measure σ which is the changes in the dominance structure as adding/removing an objective to measure the redundancy of an objective to an objective set.

2.1 σ-Redundancy

The degree of the redundancy of objective $f_i \in \mathcal{F} \setminus \mathcal{F}'$ to objective set $\mathcal{F}'$ for a given solution set $\mathcal{X}$ with size N is defined as the capacity of preserving the dominance structure of the objective set $\mathcal{F}'$. That is

$$\sigma_{f_i 2 \mathcal{F}'} = \frac{|\preceq_{\mathcal{F}'}|}{\mathbb{N}} - \frac{|\preceq_{\mathcal{F}}|}{\mathbb{N}} \tag{2}$$

where $\preceq_{\mathcal{F}'} : \{(\mathbf{x}, \mathbf{y}) | \mathbf{x}, \mathbf{y} \in \mathcal{X} \wedge \mathcal{F}'(\mathbf{x}) \preceq \mathcal{F}'(\mathbf{y})\}$, $| \preceq_{\mathcal{F}'} |$ is the size of set $\preceq_{\mathcal{F}'}$, $\mathbb{N} = 0.5N(N-1)$ is the number of the pairs of solutions in $\mathcal{X}$. Obviously, we have $\sigma_{f_i 2 \mathcal{F}'} \in [0, 1]$. The smaller value of $\sigma_{f_i 2 \mathcal{F}'}$ is, the more degree of redundancy of objective f_i to objective set $\mathcal{F}'$ is.

Definition 1. For a given $\sigma \geq 0$, we call $f_i \notin \mathcal{F}'$ σ-redundancy with $\mathcal{F}' \subset \mathcal{F}$ iff $\frac{|\preceq_{\mathcal{F}'}|}{\mathbb{N}} - \frac{|\preceq_{\mathcal{F}}|}{\mathbb{N}} \leq \sigma$. Analogously, $\mathcal{F}'$ is σ-nonredundancy if there does not exist $f_i \in \mathcal{F} \setminus \mathcal{F}'$ is σ-redundancy to objective set $\mathcal{F}'$.

Let us consider an MOP used in [3] as depicted in Fig. 1 by a parallel coordinates plot. There are four objectives f_1, f_2, f_3 and f_4, and four solutions a, b, c and d, which are pairwisely incomparable with respect to the objective set $\mathcal{F} = \{f_1, f_2, f_3, f_4\}$. This means that $\frac{|\preceq_{\mathcal{F}}|}{\mathbb{N}} = 0$. Then, for each objective f_i, $i = 1, \ldots, 4$, its redundancy degree to each objective set is calculated by Eq. (2) and listed in Table 1, where the first row is the objective f_i, the first term is the objective set $\mathcal{F}'$, and the second term is the value of $\sigma_{f_i 2 \mathcal{F}'}$ in each cell.

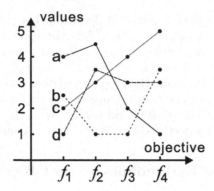

Fig. 1. Parallel coordinates plots for the given example with four solutions and four objectives.

Table 1. The values of $\sigma_{f_i 2 \mathcal{F}'}$ for a given example

f_1	f_2	f_3	f_4
$f_2 f_3 f_4$: 1/6	$f_1 f_3 f_4$: 1/6	$f_1 f_2 f_4$: 0	$f_1 f_2 f_3$: 1/6
$f_2 f_3$: 1/2	$f_1 f_3$: 1/3	$f_1 f_2$: 1/2	$f_1 f_2$: 1/2
$f_2 f_4$: 1/6	$f_1 f_4$: 1/3	$f_1 f_4$: 1/3	$f_1 f_3$: 1/3
$f_3 f_4$: 2/3	$f_3 f_4$: 2/3	$f_2 f_4$: 1/6	$f_2 f_3$: 1/2
f_2: 1	f_1: 1	f_1: 1	f_1: 1
f_3: 1	f_3: 1	f_2: 1	f_2: 1
f_4: 1	f_4: 1	f_4: 1	f_3: 1

$\sigma_{f_3 2 \{f_1 f_2 f_4\}} = 0$ means that all solutions a, b, c and d are also incomparable with respect to the objective set $\{f_1, f_2, f_4\}$. That is, f_3 is a redundant objective to the objective set $\{f_1, f_2, f_4\}$.

Based on the definition of $\sigma_{f_i 2 \mathcal{F}'}$, and the analysis of the given example, the proposed measures for measuring the redundancy of an objective have the following two properties:

(a) As $\sigma_{f_i 2 \mathcal{F}'} = 0$, the objective is redundant to objective set $\mathcal{F}'$. That is, the weak dominance structure of $\mathcal{X}$ with respect to objective set $\mathcal{F}'$ is the same as that to $\mathcal{F}$.

(b) The value of $\sigma_{f_i 2 \mathcal{F}'}$ monotonically increases with the objective set $\mathcal{F}'$ decreases, i.e., removing objective from objective set $\mathcal{F}'$, which is shown by Theorem 1.

Theorem 1. Let two objective set $\mathcal{F}_1, \mathcal{F}_2 \subseteq \mathcal{F}$, if $\mathcal{F}_1 \subseteq \mathcal{F}_2$. For any objective $f_i \notin \mathcal{F}_2$, we have $\sigma_{f_i 2 \mathcal{F}_1} \geq \sigma_{f_i 2 \mathcal{F}_2}$.

We first prove that $\preceq_{\mathcal{F}_2} \subseteq \preceq_{\mathcal{F}_1}$. For any $(\mathbf{x}, \mathbf{y}) \in \preceq_{\mathcal{F}_2}$ we have that $f_k(\mathbf{x}) \leq f_k(\mathbf{y})$ for any $f_k \in \mathcal{F}_2$. Since $\mathcal{F}_1 \subseteq \mathcal{F}_2$, it means that $f_k(\mathbf{x}) \leq f_k(\mathbf{y})$ for any $f_k \in \mathcal{F}_1$. That is $(\mathbf{x}, \mathbf{y}) \in \preceq_{\mathcal{F}_1}$. Thus, we have that $\preceq_{\mathcal{F}_2} \subseteq \preceq_{\mathcal{F}_1}$.

Algorithm 1. A greedy algorithm for σNR

Input :
- The objective values $F(\mathbf{x})$ for $\mathbf{x} \in \mathcal{X}$;
- The minimum value of the redundancy degree σ_r;

Output: The selected objective set $\mathcal{F}_s$.

1 $\diamond$ $\mathcal{F}_s := \emptyset$; $\mathcal{F}_c := \{f_1, f_2, \ldots, f_m\}$; $m' := m$;

2 **for** *each* $f_j \in \mathcal{F}_c$ **do**

3   Calculate the comparison matrix $\mathcal{A}^{f_i}$ by Eq. (3);

4 **end**

5 $\diamond$ $\mathcal{A} := \sum\limits_{f_i \in \mathcal{F}_c} \mathcal{A}^{f_i}$;

6 $\diamond$ $\sigma_0 := \dfrac{\sum\limits_{i=1}^{N} \sum\limits_{j=1}^{N} \mathbf{I}(\mathcal{A}(i,j)=m)}{N}$;

7 **while** $|\mathcal{F}_c| > 0$ **do**

8   **for** *each* $f_j \in \mathcal{F}_c$ **do**

9          $\mathcal{A}' := \mathcal{A} - \mathcal{A}^{f_j}$;

10          $\sigma_j := \dfrac{\sum\limits_{i=1}^{N} \sum\limits_{j=1}^{N} \mathbf{I}\big(\mathcal{A}(i,j)=m'-1\big)}{N} - \sigma_0$;

11   **if** $\sigma_j > \sigma_r$ **then**

12              $\mathcal{F}_s := \mathcal{F}_s \bigcup f_j$;

13              $\mathcal{F}_c := \mathcal{F}_c \setminus f_j$.

14   **end**

15   **end**

16   **if** $|\mathcal{F}_c| > 0$ **then**

17          $j^* := arg \min\limits_{f_j \in \mathcal{F}_c} \sigma_j$;

18          $\mathcal{F}_c := \mathcal{F}_c \setminus f_{j^*}$;

19          $\mathcal{A} := \mathcal{A} - \mathcal{A}^{f_{j^*}}$; $m' := m' - 1$.

20   **end**

21 **end**

Since $\preceq_{\mathcal{F}_2} \subseteq \preceq_{\mathcal{F}_1}$, this means that $|\preceq_{\mathcal{F}_2}| \leq |\preceq_{\mathcal{F}_1}|$. Then, we have:

$$\sigma_{f_i 2 \mathcal{F}_2} = \frac{|\preceq_{\mathcal{F}_2}|}{N} - \frac{|\preceq_{\mathcal{F}}|}{N}$$

$$\leq \frac{|\preceq_{\mathcal{F}_1}|}{N} - \frac{|\preceq_{\mathcal{F}}|}{N}$$

$$= \sigma_{f_i 2 \mathcal{F}_1}.$$

2.2 The Proposed Objective Reduction

Regarding objective reduction with the measure of the redundancy of objective as defined in the previous section, given $\sigma \geq 0$, one aims to find a minimum objective set $\mathcal{F}'$ which is σ-nonredundancy (σNR for short hereinafter). In this paper, we present a fast greedy algorithm for σNR.

The pseudocode of the proposed σNR is described in Algorithm 1. Firstly, we initialize the selected objective set $\mathcal{F}_s$ as an empty set and the candidate objective set $\mathcal{F}_c$ as all objectives. Then, we compute the comparison matrix $\mathcal{A}^{f_i}$ of each objective $f_i \in \mathcal{F}_c$. The comparison matrix $\mathcal{A}^f$ of a vector f is defined as:

$$\mathcal{A}^f(i, j) = \begin{cases} 1, \text{ if } f(i) \le f(j), i \ne j \\ 0, \text{ otherwise.} \end{cases} \tag{3}$$

We employ the example depicted in Fig. 1 to illustrate the above process. For the objectives $f_1 = (4, 2.5, 2, 1)$, $f_3 = (2, 1, 4, 3)$, we have:

$$\mathcal{A}^{f_1} = \begin{bmatrix} 0 & 0 & 0 & 0 \\ 1 & 0 & 0 & 0 \\ 1 & 1 & 0 & 0 \\ 1 & 1 & 1 & 0 \end{bmatrix} \text{ and } \mathcal{A}^{f_3} = \begin{bmatrix} 0 & 0 & 1 & 1 \\ 1 & 0 & 1 & 1 \\ 0 & 0 & 0 & 0 \\ 0 & 0 & 1 & 0 \end{bmatrix}.$$

Afterwards, we compute the dominance degree matrix $\mathcal{A}^{\mathcal{F}'}$ with respect to an objective set $\mathcal{F}'$ which is the sum of the comparison matrix of the objectives set, i.e., $\mathcal{A}^{\mathcal{F}'} = \sum_{f_i \in \mathcal{F}'} \mathcal{A}^{f_i}$. For each element $\mathcal{A}^{\mathcal{F}'}(i, j)$ of $\mathcal{A}^{\mathcal{F}'}$, if and only if $\mathcal{A}^{\mathcal{F}'}(i, j) = |\mathcal{F}'|$, the solution i weakly dominates solution j with respect to $\mathcal{F}'$. Based on the example shown in Fig. 1, we can obtain the dominance degree matrix of $\{f_1, f_3\}$:

$$\mathcal{A}^{\{f_1, f_3\}} = \begin{bmatrix} 0 & 0 & 1 & 1 \\ 2 & 0 & 1 & 1 \\ 1 & 1 & 0 & 0 \\ 1 & 1 & 2 & 0 \end{bmatrix}.$$

From $\mathcal{A}^{\{f_1, f_3\}}$, we can see that a dominates b and d dominates c with respect to the objective set $\{f_1, f_3\}$. Thus, it is easy to calculate the number of the pairs of the weakly dominated solutions. We firstly computate σ_0 of all candidate objectives (cf. line 6 of Algorithm 1). The function

$$\mathbf{I}(\mathcal{A}(i, j) = m) = \begin{cases} 1, \text{ if } \mathcal{A}(i, j) = m \\ 0, \text{ otherwise} \end{cases}$$

is an indicator function.

The main loop of the Algorithm 1 includes two parts: Add the objectives with $\sigma_j > \sigma_r$ from the candidate objectives to the selected objective set and remove the most redundancy objective from the candidate objectives. In the algorithm, $\mathcal{A}$ is the dominance degree matrixes of objectives $\mathcal{F}_s \bigcup \mathcal{F}_c$. We compute the degree σ_j of the redundancy of each objective $f_j \in \mathcal{F}_c$ to the objective set $\mathcal{F}_s \bigcup \mathcal{F}_c \setminus f_j$ (cf. line 10). If the value of σ_j is greater than a given threshold σ_r, then we add it into the selected objective set and remove it from the candidate objective set. By Theorem 1, if $\sigma_j > \sigma_r$ with respect to the current objective set $\mathcal{F}_s \bigcup \mathcal{F}_c$, σ_j must be greater than σ_r for the final selected objective set $\mathcal{F}_s$. Afterwards, if the candidate objective set is not empty, we remove the objective with the minimum value of σ_j and subtract the corresponding comparison matrix from the dominance degree matrix.

2.3 Computational Complexity Analysis

Algorithm 1 computes an objective subset $\mathcal{F}_s$ in a greedy way. Given a solution set $\mathcal{X}$ with the size N for an MaOP with m objectives, the time complexity of computing the comparison matrixes of objectives in the initial candidate objective set is $\mathcal{O}(mN log N)$. In the while loop, it requires $\mathcal{O}(N^2)$ integer comparisons to calculate σ_j for each objective $f_j \in \mathcal{F}_s$. In the worst case, the algorithm needs to perform the while loop $\mathcal{O}(m)$ times. Thus, the total computational complexity of the proposed algorithm is $\mathcal{O}(m^2 N^2)$. Compared the algorithms, e.g. k-EMOSS requiring $\mathcal{O}(m^3 N^2)$ and δ-MOSS requiring $\mathcal{O}(\min\{m^3 N^2, m^2 N^4\})$ [4], the proposed algorithm has low computational complexity.

3 Simulation Results

3.1 Experimental Settings

In order to investigate the performance of the proposed objective reduction algorithm, we compared the proposed algorithm with k-EMOSS and δ-MOSS on DTLZ5(I, m) [27]. DTLZ5(I, m) is a redundant problem, where I denotes the number of essential objectives and m is the number of original objectives of the problem. Eleven test instances whose m and I are listed in Table 2 are used in this paper. The other parameters of these test instances are set at the same values as those used in [6]. The essential objective set of this problem is $\{f_l, f_{m-I+1}, \ldots, f_m\}$, where $l \in \{1, \ldots, m - I + 1\}$. That is, the first $m - I + 1$ objectives are mutually nonconflicting.

The success of the algorithms to identify the essential objectives depends on the quality of the solutions set. In our experiments, 30 different solution set $\mathcal{X}$ with size 300 are obtained by NSGA-II for each test instance. In NSGA-II, the maximum number of function evaluations is set at 100000 for all test instances. The simulated binary crossover (SBX) and polynomial mutation are used for generating offspring. The crossover rate is set at 1 and the mutation rate is $1/n$, where n is the dimension of the variables. The distribution index of crossover and mutation operators are $\eta_c = 20$ and $\eta_m = 20$, respectively. Moreover, in order to investigate the performance of the proposed algorithm in the best circumstances, a solution set with the size 1000 is randomly sampled from the true PF of the problem for each test instance to symbolize a noise-free signal.

The parameters of the compared objective reduction methods are set as follows: In the proposed algorithm, the minimum value of the redundancy degree is set at $\sigma_r = 0.1$ for the solutions obtained by NSGA-II and $\sigma_r = 0$ for the solutions sampled on the true PF. In k-EMOSS, the number of reduced objectives is set as the number of essential objectives and the error δ in δ-MOSS is set at 0 for all test instances.

3.2   Experimental Results and Analysis

Table 2 lists the results obtained by the compared algorithms. The result of k-EMOSS and δ-MOSS is obtained using the source code at:http://www.tik.ee.ethz.ch/sop/download/supplementary/objectiveReduction/, where $\mathcal{F}_T$ denotes the number of successful case in 30 runs. Time is the average of run time for each test instance and μ is the average of the number of reduced objectives.

Table 2. The result obtained by the compared algorithms. $\mathcal{F}_T$ denotes the number of successful case in 30 runs. Time is the average of run time for each test instance. μ is the average of the number of reduced objectives

		The proposed algorithm			k-EMOSS		δ-MOSS		
m	I	$\mathcal{F}_T$	Time	μ	$\mathcal{F}_T$	Time	$\mathcal{F}_T$	Time	μ
5	2	30	0.00618	2.000	30	0.02217	0	0.05584	4.833
5	3	30	0.00540	3.000	30	0.02516	0	0.05910	4.967
10	2	18	0.01753	2.400	30	0.06191	0	0.20640	9.433
10	3	30	0.01803	3.000	30	0.07769	0	0.20772	9.933
10	5	25	0.01506	5.000	30	0.10347	0	0.20655	9.300
10	7	0	0.01464	5.033	30	0.11872	0	0.20867	9.833
20	2	9	0.05870	2.700	30	0.20972	0	0.76033	12.633
20	3	29	0.06109	3.000	30	0.26247	0	0.75984	12.800
20	5	7	0.05538	5.000	30	0.34875	0	0.69269	10.733
20	7	0	0.05507	5.000	30	0.41607	0	0.71880	11.167
50	2	5	0.33017	2.833	30	1.19422	0	4.00120	14.500

From this table, we can see that the average running time of the proposed algorithm is much smaller than that of the compared algorithms. It demonstrates that the proposed algorithm has a lower computational complexity. k-EMOSS can successfully identify the essential objectives for all test instances. However, the value of k is unknown for the real-world problems. In the proposed algorithm, one need not provide the number of the reduced objectives. Compared with its counterpart, i.e., δ-MOSS, the number of times that $\mathcal{F}_T$ is accurately identified in 30 runs is greater than that of δ-MOSS for almost all test instances. Moreover, the average of the number of reduced objectives obtained by the proposed algorithm is close to the number of essential objectives. This demonstrates the effectiveness of the proposed algorithm. Please note that, corresponding the solution set without noise, i.e., the solution set sampled from the true PF, all algorithms could accurately identify the essential objectives for all test instances.

4   Conclusion

In this paper, we have presented a more accurate and effective measure for measuring the degree of conflict between the objectives. Subsequently, we have proposed a fast objective reduction algorithm based on preserving the dominance structure for many-objective optimization. The proposed algorithm has a lower computational complexity and its computational complexity is $\mathcal{O}(m^2 N^2)$ through the theory analysis. We compared the proposed algorithm with k-EMOSS and δ-MOSS on eleven test instances. The experimental results have shown the effectiveness of the proposed approach. In future work, we will test the proposed algorithm on more problems and some real-world problems. Also, we will focus on investigating the behavior of different measures for measuring the conflict of the objectives, e.g. δ error proposed in [4] and η error proposed in [27].

References

1. Bader, J., Zitzler, E.: HypE: an algorithm for fast hypervolume-based many-objective optimization. Evol. Comput. **19**(1), 45–76 (2011)
2. Bandyopadhyay, S., Mukherjee, A.: An algorithm for many-objective optimization with reduced objective computations: a study in differential evolution. IEEE Trans. Evol. Comput. **19**(3), 400–413 (2015)
3. Brockhoff, D., Zitzler, E.: Are all objectives necessary? On dimensionality reduction in evolutionary multiobjective optimization. In: Runarsson, T.P., Beyer, H.-G., Burke, E., Merelo-Guervós, J.J., Whitley, L.D., Yao, X. (eds.) PPSN 2006. LNCS, vol. 4193, pp. 533–542. Springer, Heidelberg (2006). doi:10.1007/11844297_54
4. Brockhoff, D., Zitzler, E.: Objective reduction in evolutionary multiobjective optimization: theory and applications. Evol. Comput. **17**(2), 135–166 (2009)
5. Cheung, Y.M., Gu, F.: Online objective reduction for many-objective optimization problems. In: Proceedings of IEEE Congress on Evolutionary Computation, pp. 1165–1171 (2014)
6. Cheung, Y.M., Gu, F., Liu, H.L.: Objective extraction for many-objective optimization problems: algorithm and test problems. IEEE Trans. Evol. Comput. **20**(5), 755–772 (2016)
7. Deb, K.: Multiobjective Optimization using Evolutionary Algorithms. Wiley, New York (2001)
8. Deb, K., Mohan, M., Mishra, S.: Evaluating the ε-domination based multi-objective evolutionary algorithm for a quick computation of pareto-optimal solutions. Evol. Comput. **13**(4), 501–525 (2005)
9. Deb, K., Pratap, A., Agarwal, S., Meyarivan, T.: A fast and elitist multiobjective genetic algorithm: NSGA-II. IEEE Trans. Evol. Comput. **6**(2), 182–197 (2002)
10. Deb, K., Jain, H.: An evolutionary many-objective optimization algorithm using reference-point-based nondominated sorting approach, part I: solving problems with box constraints. IEEE Trans. Evol. Comput. **18**(4), 577–601 (2014)
11. Eckart, Z., Marco, L., Lothar, T.: SPEA2: improving the strength pareto evolutionary algorithm for multiobjective optimization. In: Proceedings of Evolutionary Methods for Design Optimization and Control with Applications to Industrial Problems, pp. 95–100 (2001)
12. Farina, M., Amato, P.: A fuzzy definition of "optimality" for many-criteria optimization problems. IEEE Trans. Syst. Man Cybern. Part A Syst. Hum. **34**(3), 315–326 (2004)

13. Guo, X., Wang, X., Wang, M., Wang, Y.: A new objective reduction algorithm for many-objective problems: employing mutual information and clustering algorithm. In: Proceedings of 2012 Eighth International Conference on Computational Intelligence and Security, pp. 11–16 (2012)
14. Ishibuchi, H., Akedo, N., Nojima, Y.: Behavior of multi-objective evolutionary algorithms on many-objective knapsack problems. IEEE Trans. Evol. Comput. **19**(2), 264–283 (2014)
15. Ishibuchi, H., Masuda, H., Nojima, Y.: Pareto fronts of many-objective degenerate test problems. IEEE Trans. Evol. Comput. **20**(5), 807–813 (2016)
16. Jaimes, A.L., Coello, C.A.C., Urías Barrientos, J.E.: Online objective reduction to deal with many-objective problems. In: Ehrgott, M., Fonseca, C.M., Gandibleux, X., Hao, J.-K., Sevaux, M. (eds.) EMO 2009. LNCS, vol. 5467, pp. 423–437. Springer, Heidelberg (2009). doi:10.1007/978-3-642-01020-0_34
17. Li, K., Deb, K., Zhang, Q., Kwong, S.: An evolutionary many-objective optimization algorithm based on dominance and decomposition. IEEE Trans. Evol. Comput. **19**(5), 694–716 (2015)
18. Liu, H.L., Gu, F., Zhang, Q.: Decomposition of a multiobjective optimization problem into a number of simple multiobjective subproblems. IEEE Trans. Evol. Comput. **18**(3), 450–455 (2014)
19. López Jaimes, A., Coello Coello, C.A., Chakraborty, D.: Objective reduction using a feature selection technique. In: Proceedings of 10th Annual Conference on Genetic and Evolutionary Computation, pp. 673–680 (2008)
20. McClymont, K., Keedwell, E.: Deductive sort and climbing sort: new methods for non-dominated sorting. Evol. Comput. **20**(1), 1–26 (2012)
21. Narukawa, K., Rodemann, T.: Examining the performance of evolutionary many-objective optimization algorithms on a real-world application. In: Proceedings of 2012 Sixth International Conference on Genetic and Evolutionary Computing, pp. 316–319 (2012)
22. Nicola, B., Naujoks, B., Emmerich, M.: SMS-EMOA: multiobjective selection based on dominated hypervolume. Eur. J. Oper. Res. **181**(3), 1653–1669 (2007)
23. Freitas, A.R., Fleming, P.J., Guimaraes, F.: A non-parametric harmony-based objective reduction method for many-objective optimization. In: Proceedings of 2013 IEEE International Conference on Systems, Man, and Cybernetics, pp. 651–656 (2013)
24. Russo, L.M.S., Francisco, A.P.: Quick hypervolume. IEEE Trans. Evol. Comput. **18**(4), 481–502 (2014)
25. Saxena, D.K., Duro, J.A., Tiwari, A., Deb, K., Zhang, Q.: Objective reduction in many-objective optimization: linear and nonlinear algorithms. IEEE Trans. Evol. Comput. **17**(1), 77–99 (2013)
26. Schutze, O., Lara, A., Coello Coello, C.A.: On the influence of the number of objectives on the hardness of a multiobjective optimization problem. IEEE Trans. Evol. Comput. **15**(4), 444–455 (2011)
27. Singh, H.K., Isaacs, A., Ray, T.: A pareto corner search evolutionary algorithm and dimensionality reduction in many-objective optimization problems. IEEE Trans. Evol. Comput. **15**(4), 539–556 (2011)
28. Wang, H., Yao, X.: Objective reduction based on nonlinear correlation information entropy. Soft. Comput. **20**(6), 2393–2407 (2016)
29. Yuan, Y., Ong, Y.S., Gupta, A., Xu, H.: Objective reduction in many-objective optimization: evolutionary multiobjective approaches and comprehensive analysis. IEEE Trans. Evol. Comput. (2017). doi:10.1109/TEVC.2017.2672668

30. Zhang, Q., Li, H.: MOEA/D: a multiobjective evolutionary algorithm based on decomposition. IEEE Trans. Evol. Comput. **11**(6), 712–731 (2007)
31. Zhou, Y., Chen, Z., Zhang, J.: Ranking vectors by means of the dominance degree matrix. IEEE Trans. Evol. Comput. **21**(1), 34–51 (2017)
32. Zhu, C., Xu, L., Goodman, E.D.: Generalization of Pareto-optimality for many-objective evolutionary optimization. IEEE Trans. Evol. Comput. **20**(2), 299–315 (2016)

A Memetic Algorithm Based on Decomposition and Extended Search for Multi-Objective Capacitated Arc Routing Problem

Ronghua Shang[✉], Yijing Yuan, Bingqi Du, and Licheng Jiao

Key Laboratory of Intelligent Perception and Image Understanding of Ministry of Education, International Research Center for Intelligent Perception and Computation, Joint International Research Laboratory of Intelligent Perception and Computation, Xidian University, Xi'an 710071, Shanxi, China
rhshang@mail.xidian.edu.cn

Abstract. The capacitated arc routing problem is a classical NP-hard problem to solve in the field of combinatorial optimization. In recent years, due to its extensive use in our daily life, its importance has gradually emerged. Multi-objective capacitated arc routing problem (MO-CARP) is more close to real life, so it arouses widespread concern. The Multi-objective evolution algorithm based on decomposition provides a suitable frame for solving MO-CARP. In this paper, a memetic algorithm based on decomposition and extended search (ED-MAENS) is proposed to deal with MO-CARP. Firstly, decompose the MO-CARP into many single-objective sub-problems using weight vectors. Then assign represent solution for each single-objective problem. To make sure that each single-objective problems can get a reasonable represent solution, the rank conception is proposed. After that, MAENS algorithm is adopted to solve each single-objective problem using the information of its neighborhood. Finally, we proposed an extended search operator to enlarge the searching space to improve the solution quality. The new proposed algorithm is evaluated on medium and large scale instance set and experimental results demonstrate the proposed method can obtain the better non-dominated solution than compared algorithms especially on large-scale instance.

Keywords: Extended search · Problem decomposition · Priority rank · MO-CARP

1 Introduction

The capacitated arc routing problem (CARP) [1] is a classic problem in vehicle routing planning, which has a wide range of applications in real life. Golden and Assad listed a number of practical applications related to capacitated arc routing problems in literature [2]. For example, there are transport path planning, street garbage collection, inspection and replacement of oil passages, inspection of energy lines, etc. [3, 4]. To be more abstract, CARP can be defined as: Given a non-directional network, each side of the network has a non-negative travel costs, while there are still some tasks need to be served. The purpose of solving CARP is to look for the route that make sure each task

© Springer International Publishing AG 2017
Y. Shi et al. (Eds.): SEAL 2017, LNCS 10593, pp. 272–283, 2017.
https://doi.org/10.1007/978-3-319-68759-9_23

is served and with the minimum cost under the constraints of vehicle capacity. This kind of CARP, which only takes the total cost as the optimization goal, is called single-objective capacitated arc routing optimization problem. However, in the real world, single-objective CARP often cannot meet people's needs, and people sometimes also consider some other goals, such as the cost of services and manpower, the cost of vehicle repairs, the number of vehicles to be used, the cost of overtime penalties, the minimization of the longest sub-route distance or the cost of the whole cycle, and so on. Considering these objectives, it becomes a multi-objective capacitated-arc optimization problem (MO-CARP) [5–9]. In this regard, many domestic and foreign scholars have given a lot of attention and research to the MO-CARP.

Lacomme et al. [10] proposed a modified route segmentation process combined with the memetic algorithm proposed by himself to deal with a number of MO-CARP and minimize the completion time with a limited number of vehicles. They tested the algorithm on *gdb* test set and get the average difference of 6%, but also referred to that the lower bound results of this simple approach are not ideal. Lacomme et al. considered a two-objective CARP problem in [11], whose first objective function is to minimize the total time or total distance cost in the transport process, and the second goal is to minimize the maximum distance spent or the maximum time spent in sub-route. The second objective function means that it is better to balance the transit time to allow the driver to complete the task earlier. In this paper, a multi-objective genetic algorithm (MOGA) is proposed. This genetic algorithm is based on the method proposed in [5] for the undirected capacitated arc routing problem, and it also added some local search strategy. For example, by limiting the search to a small clustering range to ensure that the local search does not disrupt the overall mechanism of MOGA. The experimental results show that although this algorithm is designed for multi-objective problems, and the best version of MOGA can produce some better lower bounds than solutions obtained by single-objective algorithm on some instances.

In 2011, a memetic algorithm based on decomposition [12] was proposed by Mei et al. to solve the problem of two-objective CARP in [11]. In the decomposition framework, the multi-objective problem is decomposed into many single-objective problems using weight vectors. In this way, a lot of sub-problems will have the different emphasis on the two objective functions. In the optimization of the sub-problem, a sub-population is maintained for each sub-problem, and each sub-problem has a representative solution. Then the sub-problems are solved by the MAENS algorithm [13]. The experimental results show that D-MAENS is better than MOGA algorithm Lacomme proposed. However, in the process of assigning representative solutions to each sub-problem, D-MAENS just considered the second objective function, so that the representation of each sub-problem is unreasonable and cannot effectively use the computational resources and neighborhood information to make a more efficient search. In addition, due to the multi-objective problem is decomposed into multiple sub-problems, in the search process with the MAENS algorithm, the global search process with crossover operator will limit the search field in a small scale. The global solution is easy to miss the global optimal solution of the problem. In 2014, Shang Ronghua et al. proposed a more effective improved memetic algorithm (ID-MAENS) based on the D-MAENS algorithm [14]. ID-MAENS updates the solution of offspring timely and an elite strategy is added to prevent the loss of the optimal solution. The experimental results show that ID-MAENS achieve better results than D-MAENS. But it still has the same defects as D-MAENS: the allocation of represent solution for each sub-problem is unreasonable and the small search field in global search process lead to the loss of excellent solution.

In order to solve the problem, this paper proposes a memetic algorithm based on decomposition and extended search to solve the MO-CARP. The algorithm uses a multi-objective optimization framework based on MOEA/D [12]. Firstly, we use a series of weight vectors to decompose multi-objective problems into many single-objective problems. Then, candidate solution in the non-dominated solution is sorted first according to the solution's priority rank, and the representative solution is assigned to each sub-problem according to the priority of the solution, so that each sub-problem can be allocated to the reasonable representative solution. As a result of the reasonable assignment of represent solution for each sub-question, the search resource is balanced, and the search efficiency is improved. Then, we use the MAENS to solve each sub-problem. We also add an extended search operator to the global search, and expand the search space to improve the search ability as much as possible. After that, the progeny of the sub-problem and the parent individual are merged, and then adopt the strategy of fast non-dominated sorting and crowding distance to sort the merged solutions. Finally, a certain number of preferred solutions are selected to participate in the evolution of the next generation.

2   Related Work

In this section, we will briefly introduce the mathematical model of MO-CARP and the framework of new proposed algorithm is also presented.

2.1   Mathematical Model of MO-CARP

CARP can be described as follows: given an weighted connected graph $G = (V, E)$, where V is the set of vertex, E represents the set of edges, and the set $V = \{v_0, v_1, ..., v_n\}$ composed of all vertex, in which there is a special vertex v_0 called depot. To describe the model briefly, we uniformly name the edges without direction as "edge" and the directional edges are called "arc". Each edge e in the graph has three non-negative attributions including service cost $sc(e)$, demand $d(e)$ and traverse cost $dc(e)$ caused by traversing from one vertex to another. Here CARP can be easily depicted as follows: there are n vehicles with capacity Q starting from depot, serving all the arc task and edge task in the graph, and finally return to the depot. The objective is to find the optimal path with a minimum total cost including serving cost and traversing cost. At the same time, three constraints must be satisfied.

1. Each vehicle must start from depot and end with the depot.
2. Each arc task and edge task must be served only once.
3. The total cost including serving cost and traversing cost can't exceed the vehicle's capacity Q.

In order to describe the mathematical model of multi-objective CARP more concisely, we first assume that there are T routes in a feasible solution. We use a decision variable M_e^t to denote whether the edge e in the t-th route ($t \in T$) is served. Secondly, we use a decision variable N_e^t to represent the number of times that through e in the t-th route. With the above definition, the mathematical model of the multi-objective CARP problem can be described as follows [12]:

$$\min f_1(t, e) = \left(\sum_{t \in T} \sum_{e \in E_R} s(e) \cdot M_e^t + \sum_{t \in T} \sum_{e \in E} c(e) \cdot N_e^t \right) \tag{1}$$

$$\min f_2(t, e) = \left(\sum_{e \in E_R} s(e) \cdot M_e^t + \sum_{e \in E} c(e) \cdot N_e^t \right), \forall t \in T \tag{2}$$

$$s.t. \quad \sum_{t \in T} M_e^t = 1, \forall e \in E_R \tag{3}$$

$$\sum_{e \in E_R} s(e) \cdot M_e^t + \sum_{e \in E} c(e) \cdot N_e^t \leq Q, \forall t \in T \tag{4}$$

where the formula (1) represents the sum of all the cost of the service and the travel cost spent in a solution, (2) represents the sum of all the cost in one route, and the formula (3) ensures each task is served. Formula (4) ensures that the cost in each route does not exceed the capacity limit Q.

2.2 The Frame of ED-MAENS

ED-MAENS adopts the framework of MOEA/D, which is similar to D-MAENS. The idea of MOEA/D is to decompose a multi-objective problem into a number of sub-problems by a certain method, and then optimize these sub-problems at the same time. This optimization process can only considers the information of its neighborhood sub-problems, so it can reduce the computational complexity to perform more efficient searches [15], and find the non-dominated solution of the original multi-objective problem in the optimization of different sub-problems.

In ED-MAENS, we assume that our multi-objective optimization function G $(x) = (G_1(x), G_2(x))$, the original multi-objective problem is divided into many single-objective problem optimization by a series of two-dimensional weight vectors $\alpha_i = (\alpha_{i1}, \alpha_{i2})$. α_{i1} is the weight coefficient of the first optimization function $G_1(x)$ in the multi-objective optimization problem, and α_{i2} is the weight coefficient of the second optimization function $G_2(x)$ in the multi-objective optimization problem. Then, the function of the decomposed single-objective optimization problem can be expressed as follows:

$$g_i(x) = \alpha_{i1} G_1(x) + \alpha_{i2} G_2(x) \tag{5}$$

The Pseudo code of ED-MAENS is as follows (Table 1):

Table 1. The Pseudo code of ED-MAENS

Algorithm 1: The main flow of ED-MAENS

Input: Instance, weight vectors α_i, i=1, 2, ..., n, initial population P
Output: Non-dominated solution set P^*
Begin
1. Decompose the original MO-CARP into many single-objective sub-problems;
2. Initialize population P={$P_1, P_2, P_3, ..., P_n$};
3. Assign the population for each sub-problem according to the Euclidean Distance between weight vectors;
4. **While** (ite<ite$_{max}$)
5.   Assign one represent solution selected from P for each sub-question;
6.   Apply the extended search operator and obtain the new population P_{new};
7.   If the solution in P_{new} is better than solution in P^*, let this solution in P^*;
8.   **for** (i=1: n) **do**
9.   Select two individuals from the population of i-th sub-problem to do a crossover operation and produce the new individual;
10.   Do the local search for the new individual to obtain the new solution S_i;
11.   If S_i is better than solution in P^*, let S_i in P^*;
12.   **end for**
13.   Merge P and S_i and sort the merged population according to crowding distance and NSGA-II;
14.   Select n individuals to form the population of next generation.
15. **end while**
end

2.3   The Mechanism of Assigning Represent Solution

In step 3 of Algorithm 1, we need to allocate a solution for each sub-problem from the evolutionary population. From the point of view of each sub-problem optimization, because it is a single-objective problem, we should regard the optimal solution on the sub-problem as its representative solution, which will be more conducive to the optimization of this problem. But such a distribution mechanism will have some defects. First of all, this allocation mechanism may lead to the situation that one individual may be allocated to more than one sub-problems, and some individuals may not be allocated to any one of the sub-problems resulting in inefficiency of search. Then, in the process of problem optimization, this mechanism will lead to the loss of population diversity in the evolution process, which is not conducive to the further optimization of the problem. In order to solve this problem, we consider the global information of the population, and propose a mechanism based on the priority rank. The individual is assigned to each sub-problem according to the priority, and the representative solution of sub-problem and the individual in evolutionary population have a one-to-one relationship.

According to the observation of ED-MAENS decomposition framework, we find that the weight coefficient vector plays an important role in the process of problem decomposition. It not only decomposes multi-objective problem into many single-objective problem, but also determines the search emphasis of sub-problem. Here we will use a series of uniform vectors as weight vectors and defined as follows:

$$\alpha_i = (\alpha_{i1}, \alpha_{i2}) = \left(1 - \frac{n-i}{n-1}, \frac{n-i}{n-1}\right) \qquad (6)$$

where n is the number of decomposed sub-problems, we can see from the formula (6), $\alpha_{i1} + \alpha_{i2} = 1$. In addition, considering the decomposed single-objective function in Eq. (5), we also find that as the number i increases, the searching emphasis on the first objective function increases. Instead, the emphasis on the second objective function is reduced. Therefore, for the sub-problem with a larger i, we should allocate the solution which has a smaller value of first objective or a larger value of second objective. But here we cannot consider the first or second objective function only as D-MAENS algorithm when we assign a representative solution to a sub-problem. In the process of sub-problem representation of solution, we must take into account the priority of the two objective functions, and give the corresponding priority order according to the two objective functions of each solution. So as to better balance the search direction, to make a reasonable allocation of search resources. To this end, we propose the following mechanism based on priority rank to allocate represent solution for each sub-problem, and pseudo-code is shown in Table 2.

2.4 Extended Search Operator

In step 9 of Algorithm 1, a global search is carried out for each sub-problem after assigning a represent solution. Because if the two weight vectors are closer, then the solution of sub-problems represented by the two weight vectors should be very close, and the exchange of information between the closed sub-problem contributes to the evolutionary of the sub-problem. Therefore, the sub-problem's population consists of the solution of its neighboring sub-problems. Thus, the parent individual for global search is selected from the sub-problem population. Assuming that the size of each sub-problem is 9, and the distribution of the sub-problem population is shown in Fig. 1.

The size of the sub-problem population is 9, and the sub-problem population is centered on the representative solution of the sub-problem, and get 4 represent solutions of the four closed sub-problems from counter-clockwise and clockwise. For example, the population of weight vector α_{30} corresponding to the representative solutions of sub-problem α_{26}, α_{27}, α_{28}, α_{29}, α_{30}, α_{31}, α_{32}, α_{33}, α_{34}. If one of the directions is less than four sub-problems, then get more in another direction until the size of population up to 9 (including the representative of the sub-problem itself). That is, the population of weight vector α_1 corresponding to the representative solution of sub-problem α_1, α_2, α_3, α_4, α_5, α_6, α_7, α_8, α_9. The communication of the search information is realized between the neighboring sub-problems. Due to the similarity of the search directions, the sub-problem can be promoted of collaborative evolution for more efficient search.

However, it can be seen from Fig. 1 that the weight vector α_1 places all the search focus on the first objective function value, that is $G_1(x)$, and the value of the first objective function corresponding to the solution should be ideal. The weight of α_{60} put all the focus on the second objective function, so the solution it searched should has a

Table 2. The assign mechanism of represent solution for sub-problem

---

Algorithm 2: The assign mechanism of represent solution for sub-problem

Input: Weight vectors α_i, i=1, 2, ..., n, population P
Output: The population P={P_1, P_2, ..., P_i, ..., P_n}, P_i is the represent solution i-th sub-problem
Begin
1. **for** i=1: n-1 **do**
2.   **for** j=i+1: n **do**
3.   **if** $(G_1(P_j)>G_1(P_i)$ or $G_1(P_j)=G_1(P_i)$ and $G_2(P_j)>G_2(P_i))$
4.   Swap the position of P_i and P_j;
5.   **end if**
6.   **end for**
7. **end for**
8. Record the first priority of the solution which is the order number in sorted solution sequence R_{1i}
        (i=1, 2, ..., n);
9. **for** i=1: n-1 **do**
10.   **for** j=i+1: n **do**
11.   **if** $(G_2(P_j)>G_2(P_i)$ or $G_2(P_j)=G_2(P_i)$ and $G_1(P_j)>G_1(P_i))$
12.   Swap the position of P_i and P_j;
13.   **end if**
14.   **end for**
15. **end for**
16. Record the first priority of the solution which is the order number in sorted solution sequence R_{2i}
        (i=1, 2, ..., n);
17. Compute the final priority R_i=R_{1i}+R_{2i};
18. **for** i=1: n-1 **do**
19.   **for** j= i+1: n **do**
20.   **if** $(R_j<R_i)$
21.   Swap the position of P_i and P_j;
22.   **end if**
23.   **end for**
24. **end for**
End
Output the sorted solution sequence P= {P_1, P_2, ..., P_i, ..., P_n}, where P_i is the representative solution of i-th sub-problem.

---

better value of second objective function. However, according to the above-mentioned global search process, the parent individual is selected from the adjacent sub-problems. Thus the two sub-problems corresponding to the two vectors of α_1 and α_{60} will not be possible to make an exchange of information. Therefore, in the global search process of sub-problem, it will result in the loss of the optimal solution. In order to solve this problem, this algorithm designs a search operator based on the extended neighborhood. The pseudo-code is shown in Table 3:

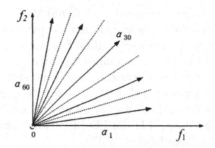

Fig. 1. Distribution of sub-problem population

Table 3. The search operator based on extended neighborhood

Algorithm 3: Extended search operator

Input: Population $P=\{P_1, P_2, ..., P_i, ..., P_n\}$, P_i is the representative solution i-th sub-problem
Output: Non-dominated solution set P^*
Begin
1. Let array $A=\{A_1, A_2, A_3, A_4\}=\{0, n/16, n/8, n/4\}$;
2. **for** $i=1$: 4
3. Select the representative solution of i-th sub-problem, that is P_i, as the first parent individual;
4. Select the representative solution of $(n-A_i)$-th sub-problem, as the second parent individual;
5. Do a global search for the two parent individual selected above to obtain the new offspring P_0 ;
6. **if** $(P_0$ is better than solutions in P^*)
7.   Let P_0 in P^*.
8. **end if**
9. **end for**
end

---

3   Experiment

In order to test the performance of ED-MAENS for solving MO-CARP, this algorithm is compared with D-MAENS [12], ID-MAENS [14], which two algorithms have now obtained excellent solution performance. This algorithm and the two contrast algorithms are compared with the results in the commonly used data sets *egl* [16] and EGL-G [17]. Because the algorithm has the characteristics of random algorithm, so the three algorithms in each case carry on 10 independent run, the average performance indicators will be compared.

Here we select the following three indicators to evaluate the multi-objective algorithm: the distance I_D from the non-dominated set of solutions to the reference set [18], the purity indicated by P [19], the super-volume HV [20]. If R_D is smaller, then the tested algorithm is better; if purity is higher, the convergence performance of tested algorithm is better; if HV is higher, the degree of fit between tested solution set and the optimal set of problems is higher.

In the performance comparison process of ED-MAENS and two other contrast algorithms, the average of the three indexes in ten independent runs is compared. If a certain algorithm of an indicator is superior to other contrast algorithms, then indicate bold. If an algorithm is superior to other contrast algorithms on two or more metrics, it is considered that the algorithm is superior. If there is no such algorithm, then all the algorithms are marked as superior, and the results will be presented in the "winner" column. In addition, for the sake of display more concise, the following "D" for D-MAENS, "ID" for ID-MAENS, "ED" for ED-MAENS, if the three algorithms win at the same time, "winner" column labeled "All".

egl is a mid-size test set containing 24 test cases. As can be seen from the results in Table 4, the overall performance of ED-MAENS in 23 test cases is superior to ID-MAENS algorithm and D-MAENS algorithm. The ED-MAENS did not achieve optimal performance on only one instance (S2-C), and ID-MAENS achieved the best results. From the single indicator, ED-MAENS achieved 23 optimal results on the index "Distance to the reference set". ID-MAENS achieved the optimal value only on

Table 4. The performance comparison of three algorithms on *egl*

Name	D-MAENS			ID-MAENS			ED-MAENS			Winner
	I_D	P	HV	I_D	P	HV	I_D	P	HV	
e1-A	5	0.62	16343	6	0.66	**25331**	**4**	**0.86**	25133	ED
e1-B	15	0.23	219	10	0.59	330	**6**	**0.82**	**361**	ED
e1-C	39	0.15	813	56	0.1	679	**23**	**0.85**	**920**	ED
e2-A	42	0.24	**128257**	39	0.31	120320	**21**	**0.72**	117385	ED
e2-B	53	0.13	18693	40	0.27	**19860**	**26**	**0.74**	18210	ED
e2-C	49	0.33	2666	46	0.44	2652	**28**	**0.53**	**3346**	ED
e3-A	78	0.15	123916	82	0.16	**137863**	**57**	**0.72**	122684	ED
e3-B	58	0.26	13678	64	0.15	14105	**33**	**0.58**	**15185**	ED
e3-C	94	0	4885	54	0.02	**7466**	**22**	**0.9**	3697	ED
e4-A	80	0.16	70361	79	0.18	**76241**	**37**	**0.73**	75695	ED
e4-B	34	0.11	15956	26	0.2	16035	**17**	**0.7**	**18125**	ED
e4-C	175	0	366	191	0	1036	**37**	**0.9**	**2856**	ED
s1-A	81	0.27	**333258**	82	0.2	312809	**42**	**0.75**	273153	ED
s1-B	63	0.19	67839	76	0.18	**76745**	**31**	**0.69**	71849	ED
s1-C	163	0.09	39440	115	0.39	42322	**90**	**0.58**	**44845**	ED
s2-A	139	0.16	150723	150	0.39	**163394**	**117**	**0.6**	145525	ED
s2-B	82	0.1	**58935**	71	0.21	53169	**43**	**0.73**	51861	ED
s2-C	342	0	7200	**115**	0.34	**9471**	143	**0.63**	9253	ID
s3-A	126	0.06	**170559**	135	0.31	158423	**97**	**0.63**	154206	ED
s3-B	104	0.09	42391	105	0.26	43466	**86**	**0.69**	**47424**	ED
s3-C	302	0.1	11356	231	0.2	**17370**	**155**	**0.77**	16564	ED
s4-A	77	0.03	10447	49	0.39	10512	**35**	**0.59**	**10977**	ED
s4-B	177	0	414	112	0.05	**1102**	**48**	**0.9**	361	ED
s4-C	333	0.2	0	483	0.3	0	**297**	**0.4**	**37**	ED

one test case (S2-C). It shows that ED-MAENS can obtain the solutions more close to the reference set than compared algorithms. On the index "purity", ED-MAENS obtain the best performance on the 24 examples, indicating that the convergence performance of ED-MAENS is better than other compared algorithms. On the index "HV", ED-MAENS achieved best performance on 10 instances (e1-B, e1-C, etc.), D-MAENS achieved the best results in the four test cases (e2-A, s1-A, etc.), and ID-MAENS in 10 test cases (e1-A, e2-B, etc.) obtain the best performance. All these indicate that the HV of ED-MANES and ID-MAENS is better than D-MAENS, and the two algorithms is closer to the optimal set of non-dominated solutions. On the whole, in egl, compared to D-MAENS and ID-MANES, ED-MAENS's performance is better and more competitive.

Here's the performance analysis of the three algorithms on a large test set EGL-G, as shown in Table 5.

EGL-G is a large-size test set containing 10 test cases. As can be seen from the results in Table 5, the overall performance of ED-MAENS in 10 test cases is superior to ID-MAENS algorithm and D-MAENS algorithm. From a single indicator, ED-MAENS achieved 10 optimal results on the index I_D. It shows that ED-MAENS can obtain the solutions closer to the optimal reference set than compared algorithms. On the index "purity", ED-MAENS obtains the best performance on 10 examples, indicating that the convergence performance of ED-MAENS is better than other compared algorithms. On the index "HV", ED-MAENS achieved best performance on 4 instances (G1-E, G2-A, G2-C, G2-E), D-MAENS achieved the best results on the four test cases (G1-A, G1-B, G2-B, G2-D), and ID-MAENS in 2 test cases (G1-C, G1-D) obtains the best performance. All these indicate that the HV of ED-MANES and D-MAENS is better than ID-MAENS, and these two algorithms are closer to the optimal set of non-dominated solutions. On the whole, in EGL-G, compared with D-MAENS and ID-MANES, ED-MAENS's performance is better and more competitive.

Table 5. The performance comparison of three algorithms on EGL-G

Name	D-MAENS			ID-MAENS			ED-MAENS			Best
	I_D	P	HV	I_D	P	HV	I_D	P	HV	
G1-A	38992	0	**816625846**	14986	0.13	788686488	**6105**	**0.89**	749451656	ED
G1-B	17637	0.04	**649485682**	14691	0.03	474793838	**7051**	**0.96**	504214047	ED
G1-C	25721	0.07	99268990	25409	0	**135366358**	**6230**	**1**	115349341	ED
G1-D	21391	0.3	11913003	16722	0.3	**15116013**	**12426**	**0.4**	14984211	ED
G1-E	28641	0.1	14187981	25509	0	14821722	**10810**	**0.9**	**21472371**	ED
G2-A	66286	0	415851290	53259	0.27	327561425	**10978**	**0.87**	**416597259**	ED
G2-B	40044	0	**261953981**	33569	0.2	185471545	**12109**	**0.9**	219024289	ED
G2-C	217578	0	40568721	213140	0	67368474	**16084**	**1**	**265419695**	ED
G2-D	25362	0	**36809661**	27547	0	29914501	**6553**	**1**	31404277	ED
G2-E	26519	0	7379590	18908	0	1806694	**6337**	**1**	**9954202**	ED

We can see from the comparison about three indicators that ED-MAENS has a obvious advantage than compared algorithms on I_D and purity, indicating ED-MAENS is closer to the optimal solution set and with a better convergence performance. This is because ED-MAENS allocates the reasonable represent solution for each sub-problem according to the priority, and thus balance the distribution of compute resource improving the search efficiency. Besides, the extended searching operator also enlarges the search space and improves the searching ability. In index HV, ED-MAENS did not show a absolutely advantage, but it is not worse than other algorithms. In a word, ED-MANES has a better performance than compared algorithms in three indicators and is more competitive.

4   Conclusion and Outlook

In this paper, a memetic algorithm based on decomposition and extended search (ED-MAENS) is proposed to solve MO-CARP problem. The algorithm decomposes the multi-objective problem into multiple single objective problems by weighted vectors. Then for each single objective sub-problem, allocate a reasonable represent solution. In this process, to ensure that each sub-problem can be assigned to a suitable representative solution, the concept of solution priority rank is introduced. In addition, an extended search operator is added to the algorithm to extend the solution space to improve the quality of the solution. Experiment shows ED-MAENS is competitive than other two compared algorithms. Next, we will consider more limited factor, like such as the middle of the transfer station in MO-CARP, as well as periodic CARP problem, with the time window of ARP, etc.

Acknowledgments. This work was partially supported by the National Basic Research Program (973 Program) of China under Grant 2013CB329402, the National Natural Science Foundation of China, under Grants 61371201, 61203303 and 61272279.

References

1. Golden, B.L., Wong, R.T.: Capacitated arc routing problems. Networks **11**(3), 305–315 (1981)
2. Assad, A.A., Golden, B.L.: Arc routing methods and applications. In: Handbooks in Operations Research and Management Science, pp. 375–483 (1995). (Chapter 5)
3. Shang, R., Ma, H., Wang, J., Jiao, L., Stolkin, R.: Immune clonal selection algorithm for capacitated arc routing problem. Soft. Comput. **20**(6), 1–28 (2016)
4. Handa, H., Lin, D., Chapman, L., Yao, X.: Robust solution of salting route optimization using evolutionary algorithms. In: IEEE Congress on Evolutionary Computatio, pp. 3098–3105 (2006)
5. Lacomme, P., Prins, C., Sevaux, M.: Multiobjective capacitated arc routing problem. In: Fonseca, C.M., Fleming, P.J., Zitzler, E., Thiele, L., Deb, K. (eds.) EMO 2003. LNCS, vol. 2632, pp. 550–564. Springer, Heidelberg (2003). doi:10.1007/3-540-36970-8_39
6. Eydi, A., Javazi, L.: Model and Solution Approach for multi objective-multi commodity capacitated arc routing problem with fuzzy demand. J. Ind. Syst. Eng. **5**(4), 208–229 (2012)

7. Shang, R., Wang, Y., Wang, J., Jiao, L., Wang, S., Qi, L.: A multi-population cooperative coevolutionary algorithm for multi-objective capacitated arc routing problem. Inform. Sci. **277**(2), 609–642 (2014)
8. Lyckander, I.: A hybrid metaheuristic for a multi-objective mixed capaciatated general routing problem. NTNU (2014)
9. Mandal, S.K., Pacciarelli, D., Løkketangen, A., Hasle, G.: A memetic NSGA-II for the bi-objective mixed capacitated general routing problem. J. Heur. **21**(3), 359–390 (2015)
10. Lacomme, P., Prins, C., Ramdane-Cherif, W.: Competitive memetic algorithms for arc routing problems. Ann. Oper. Res. **131**(1–4), 159–185 (2004)
11. Lacomme, P., Prins, C., Sevaux, M.: A genetic algorithm for a bi-objective capacitated arc routing problem. Comput. Oper. Res. **33**(12), 3473–3493 (2006)
12. Mei, Y., Tang, K., Yao, X.: Decomposition-based memetic algorithm for multiobjective capacitated arc routing problem. IEEE Trans. Evol. Comput. **15**(2), 151–165 (2011)
13. Mei, Y., Tang, K., Yao, X.: A global repair operator for capacitated arc routing problem. IEEE Trans. Syst. Man Cybern. B Cybern. **39**(3), 723–734 (2009)
14. Shang, R., Wang, J., Jiao, L., Wang, Y.: An improved decomposition-based memetic algorithm for multi-objective capacitated arc routing problem. Appl. Soft Comput. **19**(1), 343–361 (2014)
15. Zhang, Q., Li, H.: MOEA/D: a multiobjective evolutionary algorithm based on decomposition. IEEE Trans. Evol. Comput. **11**(6), 712–731 (2007)
16. Eglese, R.W.: Routing winter gritting vehicles. Discrete Appl. Math. **48**(3), 231–244 (1994)
17. Shang, R., Dai, K., Jiao, L., Stolkin, R.: Improved memetic algorithm based on route distance grouping for multiobjective large scale capacitated arc routine problems. IEEE Trans. Cybern. **46**(4), 1000–1013 (2016)
18. Czyzżak, P., Jaszkiewicz, A.: Pareto simulated annealing—a metaheuristic technique for multiple objective combinatorial optimization. In: Proceeding of Multi-Criteria Making, pp. 297–307 (1998)
19. Bandyopadhyay, S., Pal, S.K., Aruna, B.: Multiobjective GAs, quantitative indices, and pattern classification. IEEE Trans. Syst. Man Cybern. B Cybern. **34**(5), 2088–2099 (2004)
20. Zitzler, E., Laumanns, M., Thiele, L.: SPEA2: improving the strength Pareto evolutionary algorithm. In: Proceeding of Evolutionary Methods Design, Optimisation and Control With Applications to Industrial Problems (EUROGEN), Athens, Greece, pp. 95–100 (2001)

Improvement of Reference Points for Decomposition Based Multi-objective Evolutionary Algorithms

Hemant Kumar Singh[1]([✉]) and Xin Yao[2]

[1] School of Engineering and Information Technology,
The University of New South Wales, Canberra, ACT 2600, Australia
h.singh@adfa.edu.au
[2] Shenzhen Key Lab of Computational Intelligence,
Department of Computer Science and Engineering,
Southern University of Science and Technology, Shenzhen 518055, China
xiny@sustc.edu.cn

Abstract. A multi-objective optimization problem (MOP) involves simultaneous minimization or maximization of more than one conflicting objectives. Such problems are commonly encountered in a number of domains, such as engineering, finance, operations research, etc. In the recent years, algorithms based on decomposition have shown commendable success in solving MOPs. In particular they have been helpful in overcoming the limitation of Pareto-dominance based ranking when the number of objectives is large. Decomposition based evolutionary algorithms divide an MOP into a number of simpler sub-problems and solve them simultaneously in a cooperative manner. In order to define the sub-problems, a *reference point* is needed to construct reference vectors in the objective space to guide the corresponding sub-populations. However, the effect of the choice of this reference point has been scarcely studied in literature. Most of the existing works simply construct the reference point using the minimum objective values in the current nondominated population. Some of the recent studies have gone beyond and suggested the use of *optimistic*, *pessimistic* or dynamic reference point specification. In this study, we first qualitatively examine the implications of using different strategies to construct the reference points. Thereafter, we suggest an alternative method which relies on *identifying* promising reference points rather than *specifying* them. In the proposed approach, each objective is individually minimized in order to estimate a point close to the true *ideal* point to identify such reference points. Some initial results and analysis are presented to demonstrate the potential benefits and limitations of the approach. Overall, the approach demonstrates promising results but needs further development for achieving more significant improvements in solving MOPs.

Keywords: Multi-objective optimization · Reference vector · Reference point

© Springer International Publishing AG 2017
Y. Shi et al. (Eds.): SEAL 2017, LNCS 10593, pp. 284–296, 2017.
https://doi.org/10.1007/978-3-319-68759-9_24

1   Introduction and Related Work

It is common to encounter situations in real-world design problems where multiple conflicting criteria need to be optimized simultaneously, often subject to a given set of constraints. Such problems are referred to as multi-objective optimization problems (MOP), and are relevant to several domains including engineering, logistics, finance, management, etc. [5]. The solution to an MOP comprises a set of designs representing the best trade-off, referred to as the Pareto optimal front (PF) in the objective space and the Pareto optimal set (PS) in the variable (design) space. Population based metaheuristic approaches such as multi-objective evolutionary algorithms (MOEAs) have been commonly chosen to solve MOPs due to their ability to search for global optimum and deal with non-linear, black-box optimization problems. Through evolution, MOEAs attempt to obtain a set of designs which are good in two attributes: *convergence*, i.e., closeness to the true PF, and *diversity*, i.e., a relatively uniform coverage of the entire PF. Pareto-ranking is a technique employed in some of the most popular MOEAs, such as the Non-dominated sorting genetic algorithm II (NSGA-II) [4] and Strength Pareto evolutionary algorithm 2 (SPEA2) [21], which have shown great success in solving 2–3 objective problems. However, their performance is reported to scale poorly when number of objectives increases [9]. The key limitation arises from the use of non-dominance as the primary ranking measure. A number of other challenges also come into play, such as difficulty in visualization the PF, and the computational complexity and reliability of the performance metrics themselves. Due to these challenges, MOPs with ≥ 4 objectives are now more specifically referred to as *many*-objective optimization problems (MaOP).

Some of the approaches that have been used to address the above challenges include modified/secondary ranking [12,17], indicator based selection [2] and objective reduction [15,16]. While these approaches had reasonable success in targeted aspects of MaOP, the concept of *decomposition* has attracted significant research attention in the last few years for generic many-objective optimization. Decomposition based approaches solve an MOP/MaOP as a set of several sub-problems guided by a set of reference vectors. Multi-objective optimization based on decomposition (MOEA/D) [20] is among the most popular of such algorithmic frameworks, although some of the earlier studies [8] have also reported the use of this general principle. Since its inception, a number of related developments and advancements have been proposed [18]. These include studies on the scalarizing functions, generation and adaptation of reference vectors, selection operators, constraint handling etc. [18].

However, one of the important aspects that has received less attention is the specification of reference point used for defining the reference vectors [10,19], and consequently the sub-problems. The de-facto approach in this regard has been to simply use the point with minimum[1] objective values of the current population ($\mathbf{z}^{min}$). However, some recent studies have demonstrated that this

---

[1] Without loss of generality, all objectives are considered to be minimized in this study.

may not always be the best approach [10,19]. Both the studies focused on specifying different levels of offsets (ε) from the $\mathbf{z}^{min}$ to construct the reference points during optimization. That is to say, the reference point $\mathbf{z}^R$ is constructed as $\mathbf{z}_i^R = \mathbf{z}_i^{min} - \varepsilon$ for $i = 1, 2, \ldots M$, where M is the number of objectives. Effectively, most of the conventional studies can be thought of as having used $\varepsilon = 0$ or a very small value, for example [3,13] used $\varepsilon = 10^{-7}$ and 10^{-6} respectively (in the normalized space). The reason for doing so is often to circumvent the special cases where the objective vectors in the population are very close or coinciding [7] with each other, rather than any specific considerations about convergence/diversity itself. In [10,19], experiments were conducted using a range of values of ε (up to $\varepsilon = 10$) to study the effect of reference point specification on convergence and diversity. Both static and dynamic values using a pre-specified schedule were investigated, showing noticeable benefits for some problems.

In this study, we explore the idea of using reference points other than $\mathbf{z}^{min}$ further. However, instead of *specifying* the values of ε, we propose that a better initial estimate of the true ideal point ($\mathbf{z}^I$) itself could be used as the reference point, and such estimates could be obtained through fast local searches on individual objectives. By doing so, an external specification of ε (and the subjectivity associated with its chosen values or ranges), can be circumvented. In a way, this can be also thought of as ε being completely self-adaptive instead of being fixed to a particular value or annealing schedule used in [10,19]. We illustrate the principle qualitatively in Sect. 2 by observing different strategies for setting the reference point. Thereafter, in Sect. 3 we integrate the proposed idea in the framework of the existing Decomposition Based Evolutionary Algorithm (DBEA) [1,14] and present some a proof-of-concept results. Concluding remarks and future directions are outlined in Sect. 4.

2   Overview of the Proposed Idea

2.1   Preliminaries

A generic MOP can be formally defined as shown in Eq. 1.

$$\text{Minimize: } f_i(\mathbf{x}), i = 1, 2, \ldots \ldots M$$
$$\text{Subject to}$$
$$c_j(\mathbf{x}) \geq 0, j = 1, 2, \ldots \ldots p$$
$$h_j(\mathbf{x}) = 0, j = 1, 2, \ldots \ldots \ldots q \tag{1}$$
$$\mathbf{x}^{(L)} \leq \mathbf{x} \leq \mathbf{x}^{(U)}$$

Here, $f_1(\mathbf{x}), f_2(\mathbf{x}), f_3(\mathbf{x}), \ldots \ldots f_M(\mathbf{x})$ are the M objective functions. The number of inequality and equality constraints are denoted by p and q respectively. The upper and lower bounds of the variables are denoted as $\mathbf{x}^{(U)}$ and $\mathbf{x}^{(L)}$ respectively. For every solution, the sum of constraint violations is denoted by CV, where $CV = 0$ indicates a feasible solution. The theoretical solution to the problem is a Pareto Front (PF) consisting of feasible solutions which are not dominated by any other feasible solutions in the objective space. Two key points with regard to the PF are the *ideal point* ($\mathbf{z}^I$) and the *nadir point* ($\mathbf{z}^N$). The former is an unattainable vector constructed using minimum (best) value corresponding to each objective from the PF, while the latter is constructed using the maximum (worst) values.

2.2   The Implications of Reference Point Specification

Within the existing algorithms based on decomposition, sub-problems are typically (but not necessarily) defined using systematic sampling on a normalized hyperplane as shown in Fig. 1a. For each sub-problem, usually one (or a combination) of the scalarization functions such as PBI, Tchebychev, Weighted Sum [20] etc. is used for environmental selection. A simple example is shown in Fig. 1b, where two distances d_1 and d_2 are calculated for a solution and a reference vector to quantify how competitive it is for this particular sub-problem. To compare between solutions, PBI [20] uses a measure $d_1 + \theta d_2$ (where θ can be adjusted), while the DBEA [1] uses a precedence of d_2 over d_1 among nondominated solutions. The intent is to minimize both in order to obtain a Pareto-optimal point along each reference vector. Both of these distances are calculated in a normalized objective space (between 0 and 1) using the reference point $\mathbf{z}^R$ and the nadir point of the current non-dominated population $\mathbf{z}^N$. The true solution of this sub-problem (i.e., $d_2 = 0$ and d_1 is minimum) will give a Pareto optimal solution to the original problem.

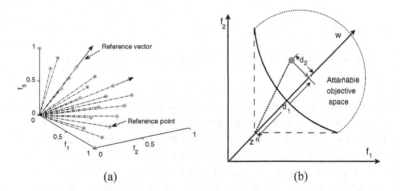

(a)   (b)

Fig. 1. (a) Uniformly distributed reference vectors; and (b) distance measures

However, it is notable that the optimum solution(s) to the above subproblem(s) is in-fact *not always* a Pareto-optimal solution to the *original problem* – this will heavily depend on the choice of $\mathbf{z}^R$. Consider, for example the three cases shown in Fig. 2, where $\mathbf{z}^R$ is taken very close to $\mathbf{z}^{min}$, i.e., $\varepsilon \approx 0$. This is termed as *pessimistic* specification in [19]. Shown in each of the plots are

10 solutions, which could be considered a pool of solutions (either parent or parent+child) at any given generation. For Case 1, all solutions are far from the PF and $\mathbf{z}^{min}$ does not dominate any of the points on the PF. Therefore, if the reference point $\mathbf{z}^R$ is set as $\mathbf{z}^{min}$, then the true solution of each of the sub-problems will be $\mathbf{z}^{min}$ itself, which is not a Pareto solution for the original problem (Fig. 2a). For the case 2 shown in Fig. 2b, $\mathbf{z}^{min}$ dominates some points on the PF. The optimization of each sub-problem in this case will result in a solution on the PF, but they will tend to be more concentrated rather then well spread out on the front. For case 3 (Fig. 2c), $\mathbf{z}^{min}$ almost coincides with the true ideal point $\mathbf{z}^I$, and therefore each of the sub-problems are uniformly distributed as originally intended and the solution of each will result in an overall good distribution of points on the PF. For completeness, it is to be noted that these intermediate problems are not actually *solved* to completion, but the *selection* is made based on them. Thus the extent of impact of the above specifications is that the selection is based on a problem which may not (if solved to optimality) give a solution to the original problem instead of one that does.

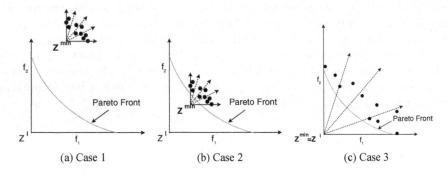

(a) Case 1   (b) Case 2   (c) Case 3

Fig. 2. The reference point $\mathbf{z}^R$ set to $\mathbf{z}^{min} - \varepsilon$, where $\varepsilon \cong 0$

A key inference from these different scenarios is that the construction of the sub-problems (which implicitly involves $\mathbf{z}^R$) can immensely affect the search. For example, for the populations that are in states shown in Cases 1 and 2, the sub-problems *change* very frequently, because the $\mathbf{z}^{min}$ has not yet reached the true ideal point and hence moves around significantly. In strategies where extreme objective values are not explicitly preserved, this may in-fact lead to even more undesirable cases where $\mathbf{z}^{min}$ does not *monotonically* move closer to the $\mathbf{z}^I$ over the generations. Frequent change of sub-problems is not helpful for the search as it does not give sufficient opportunity to evolve solutions suited to a particular problem long enough. This was observed in the context of *adaptive* distribution of reference vectors in [6], but from the above discussions the same can be inferred even when the distribution of reference vectors is kept fixed. On the other hand, if population for a given problem resembles distribution as shown in Case 3, the expected results are likely to be better compared to that in Case 1, because (a) more appropriate sub-problems are being targeted and (b) the sub-problems are not changing frequently. Also to be noted is that the irrespective of the distribution of solutions in Case 3, the presence of solutions with (close to) the true lowest objective values will be sufficient to allow construction of a reference point $\mathbf{z}^R$ close to $\mathbf{z}^I$.

Now, let us consider a large ε for the same populations, referred to as *optimistic* specification in [19]. The resulting scenarios are shown in Fig. 3. In can be observed that depending on the location of the population, some of the sub-problems which did not yield a solution on PF earlier now do have some solutions on it (Cases 1, Fig. 3a); but the phenomenon may be reversed for some in other situations (Case 3, Fig. 3c).

In some problems, it is likely that the population starts off far from the PF in the initial generations (such as Case 1), and moves close to the PF in the later generations (Cases 2 and 3). So in the beginning, a using a high value of ε may be beneficial as it creates the possibility of $\mathbf{z}^R$ dominating $\mathbf{z}^{min}$. On the other hand, in the later generations, it may be likely that $\mathbf{z}^{min}$ is close to $\mathbf{z}^I$, and hence $\varepsilon \cong 0$ works well, as suggested in [19]. However, it is also plausible for some other problems that the population does not show the above behavior and/or the ε is not in the range to create the desired sub-problems. For example, if the initial population itself looks somewhat like Case 3 (Fig. 2c) then using a large ε may not be beneficial even in the initial generations. Similarly, if the population is too far from PF then the initial value of ε maybe too small to convert sub-problems in Fig. 2a to those in Fig. 3a. Therefore, specifying an arbitrary value of ε may not always work as desired, and there remains a scope of further improvement in this aspect.

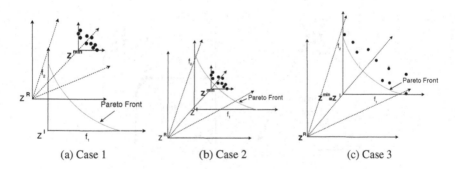

(a) Case 1   (b) Case 2   (c) Case 3

Fig. 3. The reference point $\mathbf{z}^R$ set to $\mathbf{z}^{min} - \varepsilon$, where ε is a large value.

2.3   Proposed Approach

Considering the above observations, it is apparent that setting $\mathbf{z}^R = \mathbf{z}^I$ is likely to be the most advantageous strategy to construct the sub-problems. This is mainly because *irrespective* of which region the population lies in, the optimum solutions to *all* sub-problems constructed in this way will have a corresponding solution on the PF. In fact, an experimental validation of this can be observed from results presented in [19], where using $\mathbf{z}^R = \mathbf{z}^I$ obtains close to best performance for the three instances of WFG4.[2]

The obvious obstacle in setting $\mathbf{z}^R = \mathbf{z}^I$ is that the ideal point is not known in advance. This brings us to an interesting proposition: Is it worth searching *actively* for the *true* ideal point to set the reference point(s) for the search instead of relying on the multi-objective search itself to find it? While the definitive answer to this question may depend on several factors that require an in-depth study, we explore one possibility here. The ideal point can be searched for by minimizing each objective individually through a single-objective search. While it is not expected that all such searches will give the global optimum, they might still be able to provide quick *estimates* of individual optimum each function to construct the $\mathbf{z}^{Ies}$ (i.e., estimated $\mathbf{z}^I$), which is likely to be much closer to the true ideal point than the initial random population. The starting point of each of the single-objective searches could be set as the one with best value in a given objective. This is schematically shown in Fig. 4, and two possible approaches could be taken. The first one is a one-time optimization of each objective to construct the $\mathbf{z}^{Ies}$ and use it throughout the search. However, the performance in this case may heavily depend on the efficiency of this single optimization run. For some cases, the population members may start far enough that optimization once does not achieve a solution close to $\mathbf{z}^I$. Therefore, a more reliable approach could be to perform such local searches each time the range of the evolving population surpasses the current $\mathbf{z}^{Ies}$. An illustration is shown in Fig. 4b, where $\mathbf{z}^{Ies1}$ is found initially and used as a reference point. During a later stage in the search, once the solutions with lower f_1 or f_2 values are found, the individual

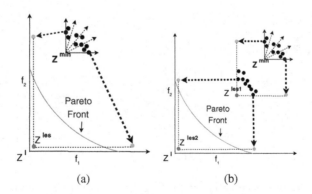

(a)   (b)

Fig. 4. Illustration of the proposed idea: (a) One time estimation of $\mathbf{z}^{Ies}$ (b) Iterative estimation of $\mathbf{z}^{Ies}$

---

[2] The performance using $\mathbf{z}^R = \mathbf{z}^I$ is reported to be *marginally* inferior to $\varepsilon = 1$ for L-WFG and $\varepsilon = 5$ for K-WFG in [19]. There is a possibility that this minor variation could have resulted due to finite population size, stochastic nature of the search, as well as the nature of the HV metric itself (i.e. a higher HV doesn't necessarily always imply better distribution).

single-objective searches are invoked again from the lowest extreme values in the child population to find the next estimate $\mathbf{z}^{Ies2}$ which is close to $\mathbf{z}^I$.

Two prominent features of the above approach may be noted:

1. Effectively, the approach can be thought of as using $\varepsilon = \mathbf{z}^{min}$ (before local search)$-\mathbf{z}^{Ies}$, which gets automatically set and updated/adapted based on the estimate of $\mathbf{z}^{Ies}$. A difference, however, is that the two extreme solutions are also obtained (during search for $\mathbf{z}^{Ies}$) which change the $\mathbf{z}^{min}$ after local search.
2. If a local search algorithm is used with appropriate termination criteria (such as improvement of objective values is below threshold), the search effort in finding $\mathbf{z}^{Ies}$ could be reasonably controlled. For example, if the initial population looks like that in Fig. 2c, then the single-objective searches will not yield a (significantly) better solution that current population, and the algorithm can be set for quick termination. On the other hand, for Fig. 2a, the search effort might be slightly larger, but given the scope of improvement in $\mathbf{z}^{Ies}$, it is also more beneficial. Thus, the search effort can be adjusted based on how much benefit it brings in estimating the ideal point.

3   Case Studies Using DBEA

The above mentioned strategies could be embedded in any of the existing decomposition based frameworks. For the proof-of-concept studies presented in this paper, we use the generational version of decomposition based evolutionary algorithm (DBEA) presented in [1,14] as the base framework. DBEA uses normal boundary intersection for generating the reference vectors and a precedence of d_2 over d_1 among the non-dominated solutions for environmental selection (Fig. 1). The description of individual components of DBEA are omitted for the sake of brevity, and interested readers are referred to [1,14] for more details. The key aspect of DBEA relevant to this study is that like most other algorithms, DBEA uses minimum value of current population to construct the reference point (i.e., $\varepsilon \approx 0$).

We embed the iterative reference point update discussed above (Fig. 4b) in DBEA. Thus, $\mathbf{z}^{Ies}$ is constructed initially based on a local search in each of the objectives from the starting points that are best in each respective objective (i.e. M local searches for $M-$objective problem). Thereafter, whenever any member in the new child population achieves a lower value in any of the objectives, the local search is invoked again on each objective to obtain the new reference point. The best solutions obtained through these local searches are also added to the population. For ease of reference, we label the the proposed approach using extreme points for reference point update as DBEA_E.

The sequential quadratic programming (SQP) implemented in the fmincon package of Matlab is used for the current study for each local search, with termination criteria set as the change in function value $FTol = 10^{-3}$ or maximum of $20n$ evaluations, whichever occurs sooner. The other parameters used for the study are listed in Table 1.

Table 1. Parameter settings used for the study

Parameter	Value
Population size (N)	100
Number of generations (T)	200
Max. function evaluations (FE_{max})	$N \times G \times M$ (M = No. of objectives)
Crossover and Mutation probabilities (p_c, p_m)	0.9, $1/n$ (n = No. of variables)
Crossover (SBX) and Mutation (Polynomial) index	30,20
Number of variables n	32
Number of independent runs (N_r)	11

For the numerical experiments, we choose three types of WFG4 instances, similar to that used in the previous study [19]. The three instances represent problems with different type of behaviors. The first instance, referred to simply as WFG4 uses $k = 16, l = 16$, where the total number of variables is $n = k + l$. This difficulty of achieving convergence and diversity is roughly comparable for this setting. The second instance uses $k = 28, l = 4$ and features more difficulty in achieving diversity than convergence, and is referred to as K-WFG4. On the contrary, the third instance uses $k = 4, l = 28$ and features more difficulty in convergence than diversity, referred to as L-WFG4. For each instance, two and three objective problems are solved using DBEA and DBEA$_E$, and the performance is compared using the hypervolume metric. For hypervolume calculation, $1.1 \times \mathbf{z}^N$ is used as the reference point.

The statistics of hypervolume across multiple runs are shown in Table 2. It is seen that DBEA$_E$ obtains better mean/median hypervolume than DBEA for WFG4 and K-WFG4, whereas it is inferior for the case of L-WFG4. The behavior is consistent for both two and three objective problems. To get better insight into individual performance, the Pareto front approximations obtained by each of the algorithms is plotted in Fig. 5. The figure shows a collation of the final populations of 11 out of 25 runs in order to observe the general trend (plotting all 25 reduces clarity due to large number of overlapping solutions).

Table 2. Comparison of hypervolume obtained using conventional v/s proposed approach. The statistics are across 25 runs.

Prob.	Obj.	DBEA				DBEA$_E$			
		Mean	Median	Best	Worst	Mean	Median	Best	Worst
WFG4	2	3.1156	3.1174	3.1629	3.012	**3.131**	**3.1391**	3.2212	3.0051
K-WFG4	2	2.9999	3.0113	3.091	2.8894	**3.0273**	**3.035**	3.1271	2.9216
L-WFG4	2	**3.2613**	**3.2626**	3.2818	3.2264	3.2083	3.2081	3.2501	3.1409
WFG4	3	29.4881	29.5561	30.4956	28.4647	**30.094**	**30.1141**	30.8729	29.2925
K-WFG4	3	29.6219	29.5506	30.4562	28.6438	**31.0446**	**31.1483**	32.2919	29.5651
L-WFG4	3	**32.3564**	**32.3353**	32.8373	31.8131	32.2201	32.2613	33.1525	31.138

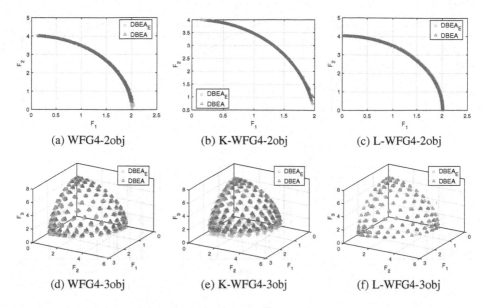

(a) WFG4-2obj   (b) K-WFG4-2obj   (c) L-WFG4-2obj

(d) WFG4-3obj   (e) K-WFG4-3obj   (f) L-WFG4-3obj

Fig. 5. The distribution of final populations obtained using DBEA and DBEA$_E$ (Note: only 11 out of 25 runs are plotted for better visibility).

From Fig. 5, a visible improvement in spread can be clearly seen for WFG4 and K-WFG4 problems using the proposed approach. Since K-WFG4 problem poses more difficulty in achieving diversity, an early improvement in reference point creates a significant advantage in extending the range of the population. The behavior can be referred back to Fig. 2, where a pessimistic specification of reference point (as done in DBEA) could result in the sub-problems having solutions closer together, in contrast with when the reference point is close(r) to the ideal point. For L-WFG4 on the other hand, the diversity is easy to achieve, therefore, the local searches that are conducted as part of the reference point update do not provide any significant benefits over what the population would have already obtained through pessimistic specification. However, because these reference point updates consume function evaluations (for local search) from the total computation budget, DBEA$_E$ ends up running for fewer generations than DBEA, resulting in slightly inferior convergence. For WFG4 instance, the difficulties are somewhat comparable, and the proposed scheme achieved a favorable balance.

The above inferences are also validated by observing the magnitude of improvements obtained for the three instances as shown in Fig. 6. The plots show the location of the reference point before and after each of the reference point updates were invoked for a typical (randomly chosen) run, for the 2-objective problems. For WFG4 and K-WFG4, it can be seen that the improvements in reference points are relatively large compared to that seen in the case of L-WFG4. Also shown in Fig. 6(d–e) are the corresponding function evaluations that were spent in performing the reference point update. For L-WFG4, it can be seen

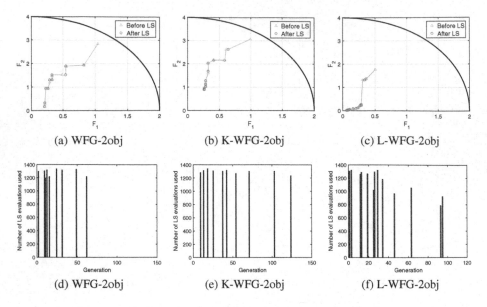

Fig. 6. (a–c) Reference points before and after local search (LS). PF is shown in black; (d–e) The corresponding function valuations used for each reference point update

that the updates were invoked more frequently, but improvements were minor. At times the search was also terminated earlier than the set maximum, however, collectively a significant number of evaluations were spent trying to improve the reference point, which affected the evaluations left for other operations.

Overall, based on the initial experiments, the proposed approach shows some promise, particularly in improving diversity early in the search. It can be considered as an alternative to the reference point specification strategies proposed in the earlier works, but the relative performance needs further in-depth studies.

4   Concluding Remarks and Future Work

In this study, we proposed a new approach for improving the reference points used for decomposition based multi-objective evolutionary algorithms. The main contribution of this study is to qualitatively analyze the impact of various types of reference point specifications, and to instigate the idea of actively searching for the true ideal point instead of specifying it using user defined offsets from z^{min}. This could possibly be a better approach, for example, when the objectives are of different order and a single value of ε at any given point may not be suitable for all objectives (which would mean a separate value will need to be specified for each objective). The limitation on the other hand, is that the proposed approach, unlike specification, consumes some of the computational budget. Therefore it becomes necessary that the maximum possible gain in reference point updates be achieved using fewest possible evaluations by using strong single-objective optimizers. Overall it seems unlikely that either of the above strategies, including dynamic specification, will be ubiquitously better than the others. The primary reason for this is not only the parameters involved in each of these strategies, but also that the PFs of many problems do not adhere to the regularity assumptions under the traditional decomposition based approaches. They may be highly nonlinear, discontinuous or "inverted", due to which they cannot be fully mapped by the fixed set of uniformly distributed reference vectors (Fig. 1). This issue is discussed in more detail in [11], but is not considered in the scope of this study. However, an interesting future direction could be to investigate the proposed strategy with or *for* reference vector adaptation to deal with more generic cases. Another interesting direction will be to investigate the scalability of the proposed approach for large number of objectives.

Acknowledgements. The first author would like to acknowledge the *Australian Bicentennial Fellowship* from the Menzies Centre, Kings College London, which supported his research visit to the University of Birmingham for this work, where the second author holds a concurrent position. The work was also partially supported by Science and Technology Innovation Committee Foundation of Shenzhen (Grant No. ZDSYS201703031748284) and NSFC (Grant No. 61329302).

References

1. Asafuddoula, M., Ray, T., Sarker, R.: A decomposition-based evolutionary algorithm for many-objective optimization. IEEE Trans. Evol. Comput. **19**(3), 445–460 (2015)
2. Bader, J., Zitzler, E.: HypE: an algorithm for fast hypervolume-based many-objective optimization. Evol. Comput. **19**, 45–76 (2011)
3. Bhattacharjee, K.S., Singh, H.K., Ray, T.: A novel decomposition-based evolutionary algorithm for engineering design optimization. J. Mech. Des. **139**(4), 041403 (2017)
4. Deb, K., Pratap, A., Agarwal, S., Meyarivan, T.: A fast and elitist multiobjective genetic algorithm: NSGA-II. IEEE Trans. Evol. Comput. **6**(2), 182–197 (2002)
5. Deb, K.: Multi-Objective Optimization Using Evolutionary Algorithms. Wiley, Hoboken (2005)
6. Giagkiozis, I., Purshouse, R.C., Fleming, P.J.: Towards understanding the cost of adaptation in decomposition-based optimization algorithms. In: IEEE International Conference on Systems, Man, and Cybernetics (SMC), pp. 615–620 (2013)
7. Goulart, F., Campelo, F.: Preference-guided evolutionary algorithms for many-objective optimization. Inf. Sci. **329**, 236–255 (2016)
8. Hughes, E.J.: Multiple single objective Pareto sampling. IEEE Congr. Evol. Comput. **4**, 2678–2684 (2003)
9. Ishibuchi, H., Tsukamoto, N., Nojima, Y.: Evolutionary many-objective optimization: a short review. In: IEEE World Congress Computational Intelligence, pp. 2419–2426 (2008)
10. Ishibuchi, H., Doi, K., Nojima, Y.: Reference point specification in MOEA/D for multi-objective and many-objective problems. In: IEEE International Conference on Systems, Man, and Cybernetics, pp. 4015–4020 (2016)

11. Ishibuchi, H., Setoguchi, Y., Masuda, H., Nojima, Y.: Performance of decomposition-based many-objective algorithms strongly depends on pareto front shapes. IEEE Trans. Evol. Comput. **21**(2), 169–190 (2017)
12. Köppen, M., Yoshida, K.: Substitute distance assignments in NSGA-II for handling many-objective optimization problems. In: Obayashi, S., Deb, K., Poloni, C., Hiroyasu, T., Murata, T. (eds.) EMO 2007. LNCS, vol. 4403, pp. 727–741. Springer, Heidelberg (2007). doi:10.1007/978-3-540-70928-2_55
13. Qi, Y., Ma, X., Liu, F., Jiao, L., Sun, J., Wu, J.: MOEA/D with adaptive weight adjustment. Evol. Comput. **22**(2), 231–264 (2014)
14. Ray, T., Asafuddoula, M., Singh, H.K., Alam, K.: An approach to identify six sigma robust solutions of multi/many-objective engineering design optimization problems. J. Mech. Des. **137**(5), 051404 (2015)
15. Saxena, D.K., Duro, J.A., Tiwari, A., Deb, K., Zhang, Q.: Objective reduction in many-objective optimization: linear and nonlinear algorithms. IEEE Trans. Evol. Comput. **17**(1), 77–99 (2013)
16. Singh, H.K., Isaacs, A., Ray, T.: A Pareto corner search evolutionary algorithm and dimensionality reduction in many-objective optimization problems. IEEE Trans. Evol. Comput. **15**(4), 539–556 (2011)
17. Singh, H.K., Isaacs, A., Ray, T., Smith, W.: An improved secondary ranking for many objective optimization problems. In: Genetic and Evolutionary Computation Conference, pp. 1837–1838 (2009)
18. Trivedi, A., Srinivasan, D., Sanyal, K., Ghosh, A.: A survey of multiobjective evolutionary algorithms based on decomposition. IEEE Trans. Evol. Comput. **21**(3), 440–462 (2017)
19. Wang, R., Xiong, J., Ishibuchi, H., Wu, G., Zhang, T.: On the effect of reference point in MOEA/D for multi-objective optimization. Appl. Soft Comput. **58**, 25–34 (2017)
20. Zhang, Q., Li, H.: MOEA/D: a multiobjective evolutionary algorithm based on decomposition. IEEE Trans. Evol. Comput. **11**(6), 712–731 (2007)
21. Zitzler, E., Laumanns, M., Thiele, L.: SPEA2: improving the strength Pareto evolutionary algorithm for multi-objective optimisation. In: Evolutionary Methods for Design, pp. 95–100. Optimisation and Control with Application to Industrial Problems (2002)

Multi-Objective Evolutionary Optimization for Autonomous Intersection Management

Kazi Shah Nawaz Ripon[✉], Jostein Solaas, and Håkon Dissen

Department of Computer Science, Norwegian University of Science and Technology,
Trondheim, Norway
ksripon@ntnu.no, josteinsolaas@gmail.com, hakon.dissen@gmail.com

Abstract. This paper investigates the real-time application of multi-objective evolutionary algorithm (MOEA) for managing traffic at an intersection with its focus on autonomous vehicles. Most of the existing works on intersection management emphasize using MOEAs to optimize parameters for traffic-light based intersections, or they target human drivers. However, the advent of autonomous vehicles has changed the field of intersection management. To maximize the use of autonomous vehicles, the intersections should be autonomous also. This paper proposes an autonomous intersection management (AIM) system that controls the speed for each vehicle approaching at an intersection by using MOEA. The proposed system first looks at splitting the continuous problem of intersection management into smaller independent scenarios. Then it utilizes the MOEA to find solutions for each scenario by optimizing multiple objectives with different goals in terms of overall performance. In order to give the MOEA low level control of traffic at intersections, the autonomous vehicles are modelled as travelling along a predefined path, with a speed determined by the MOEA.

Keywords: Multi-objective evolutionary optimization · Autonomous intersection management · Discrete time steps · Autonomous vehicle

1 Introduction

The automobile has become a dominant mode of traveling nowadays. However, the increasing number of households along with the increasing number of cars that a household owns hastens the increasing rate of traffic delay, mostly at an traffic intersection [2]. Traffic jams and collisions at intersections lead to endless frustration, hinder mobility, contribute to air pollution, loss of time, waste fuel, and impede economic growth. In 2008, citizens of the USA spent an average of 46 h a year per capita in congested traffic, up from 16 h in 1982 [4]. In the EU, the total cost of traffic congestion was estimated at 1% of the total GDP in 2010 [5]. Americans burn approximately 5.6 billion gallons of fuel each year at intersections [4]. Considering these, the main motivation behind intersection management is to reduce the amount of time vehicles spent at traffic intersections

© Springer International Publishing AG 2017
Y. Shi et al. (Eds.): SEAL 2017, LNCS 10593, pp. 297–308, 2017.
https://doi.org/10.1007/978-3-319-68759-9_25

as a way to ease traffic congestion. In addition, intersection management reduces the total emissions of vehicles idling by or traversing an intersection.

The advent of autonomous vehicles has introduced capabilities far beyond the capabilities of human drivers. A few of the very important features of these new vehicles are the capabilities of cars to sense their locations accurately in the world, their precision and to use sophisticated measures to plan their travel paths [4,6]. Once autonomous vehicles are available, autonomous interactions amongst multiple vehicles will be possible. To take complete advantage of the increased sensitivity and precision of autonomous vehicles, the intersections should be autonomous also. Thereupon, current methods of vehicle coordination, which are all designed to work with human drivers or to optimize parameters for traditional intersection controllers, will be outdated soon. Therefore, the bottleneck for roadway efficiency will no longer be the drivers, rather it will be the mechanism by which those drivers' actions are coordinated. Consequently, current methods for controlling traffic, specifically at intersections, will not be able to take advantages of autonomous vehicles [6]. This paper suggests an alternative mechanism for coordinating the movement of autonomous vehicles through intersections as opposed to current intersection control technology – traffic lights and stop signs. Here we propose an *autonomous intersection management* (AIM) by using NSGA-II [3], an efficient multi-objective evolutionary algorithm (MOEA), to manage real time traffic at an intersection.

There exist a few recent methods of AIM [4,9,10] where cars can travel along predefined trajectories. However, these approaches are built on ideas and results from research on human drivers, and therefore have to be understood in that context. Wu et al. [8] showed that vehicles passing an intersection could be modelled as an ordering problem, and proposed a searching algorithm to find the optimal order for vehicles approaching an intersection. The computational expense for this method is too high and it is not suitable in real-world scenarios. Based on [8], Yan et al. proposed a genetic searching approach to reduce the complexity [10]. Still these approaches use only single objective function, namely overall evacuation time. There is no consideration of other important objectives. In this work, different objectives, with different goals in terms of overall performance, have been optimized at the same time. The proposed system involves dividing the continuous problem of intersection management into smaller independent time steps. Then it explores the application of MOEA to find solutions for each scenario. Ultimately, this work implements an AIM which regulates the behaviour of autonomous vehicles at an intersection by controlling the speed of each vehicle.

Our aim is to examine how splitting the continuous problem of intersection management into smaller scenarios affects the performance of the AIM based on the number of cars at intersections. To study this effect, we have introduced two time step parameters: (i) t_{main} that determines for how long each solution is deployed, and (ii) t_{sim} that specifies how much extra time, beyond t_{main}, each solution is evaluated for. This paper also studies the scaling capability of the proposed AIM to reveal its plausibility for real time use. In addition, the experimental results report the effects of the conflicting objectives to the overall performance of the AIM as well as finds the circumstances in which they conflict.

In order to fulfill these goals, it is necessary to implement an intersection manager (IM) that will use an MOEA to measure vehicle speeds in accordance with the given objectives. No simulator has been found that meets all requirements of this work. Thus, we have implemented a modified version of the AIM4 simulator [1]. To ensure a fair evaluation of the IM, it is tested with different values for t_{main} and t_{sim}. The IM is also tested for specific scenarios, and for continuous operation with different amounts of traffic. To compare the *effectiveness* of the IM in different settings, four performance metrics are used: (i) throughput, (ii) mean evacuation time (MET), (iii) total loss of kinetic energy, and (iv) the amount of collisions.

This work does not target a complete replication of the real world scenarios. Therefore, the simulator used to evaluate solutions will also be used to simulate the real world. Vehicle collision and control after traversing through the intersection is beyond the scope of this work. So are the interactions between multiple intersections. The rest of this paper is organized as follows. Section 2 explains the proposed system as well as the implementation details for the experiments. Section 3 provides the experimental results and discusses the findings. Section 4 concludes the paper with suggestions for future research.

2   Proposed System

As mentioned earlier, the goal of this work is to control the behaviour of autonomous vehicles at an autonomous intersection by controlling the speed of each vehicle. The speed is simultaneously optimized by four objectives: (i) maximize throughput at an intersection (tiny throughput), (ii) maximize the distance traveled, (iii) minimize the total stoppage time (starvation), and (iv) minimize the total kinetic energy lost. We implemented a system with a central IM that communicates with each vehicle. The system has three main parts (Fig. 1): (i) the intersection manager (IM), (ii) the evolutionary processor (EP), and (iii) the simulator. In Fig. 1, grey rounded squares signify entities, and yellow slanted rectangles are the information shared among them.

The IM reads the current *state* of the physical intersection and passes that to the EP, so that it can develop a *speed vector* **v**. The IM communicates with the vehicles using vehicle to infrastructure (V2I) protocol [7]. In V2I, all vehicles communicate with a central server that makes decisions with regard to intersection management or simply relays messages safely among the cars. In the context of the EP, each **v** is an individual – a solution to the problem that it is trying to solve. Note that **v** is not a multi-dimensional vector specifying the speed of a single vehicle, rather it is an n-dimensional vector describing the target speed of n vehicles. Using the MOEA, the EP evaluates the individuals by emulating them in multiple instances of the simulator. Once the stopping condition of the MOEA is met, a decision maker (DM) selects one of the available Pareto-optimal

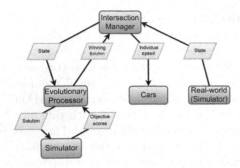
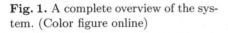
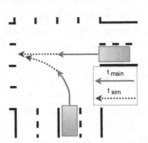

Fig. 1. A complete overview of the system. (Color figure online)

Fig. 2. A visual representation of t_{sim}, t_{main}, and $t_{evaluate}$. (Color figure online)

solutions, before a speed vector is returned to the IM. The IM then sets the target speed of each vehicle at an intersection in accordance with the solution. This determines how fast vehicles should travel for the next time step.

For managing the intersection, the IM is concerned with t_{main} and t_{sim}. Once the EP has decided on a solution, that solution is used for the next t_{main} seconds before the EP is ordered to come up with a new solution. However, if the EP only validates the solution for t (current time) $+ t_{main}$, there is no guarantee that the intersection will not end up in an *unsolvable state* (a state where a collision is unavoidable for the next t_{main}). In order to ensure that the IM never approves such an unsolvable state, the EP is designed to evaluate the solutions for an extra amount of time (t_{sim}). Therefore, the total amount of time that the EP evaluates each solution ($t_{evaluate}$) is $t_{main} + t_{sim}$. Figure 2 shows these time steps visually. As shown in this figure, $t_{evaluate}$ is the time taken by the cars to travel along both the solid blue line (t_{main}) and the dotted red line (t_{sim}).

Since autonomous vehicles have such fine control over their own movements, newer AIM research [4,9,10] use an intersection organizing system where cars have to travel along predefined trajectories. These trajectories traverse the intersection from one source lane to the destination lane. Our proposed IM is based on some of the ideas introduced in AIM4 [1], most importantly the cars can simulate their own behaviour based on parameters individual to each car. The vehicles are modelled as single entities travelling along predefined paths, where the only variable parameter is a target speed that the vehicle should accelerate/decelerate to. More details about the system is available in our earlier work [6]. It is important to mention that in order to deploy the proposed system in real world autonomous vehicles and in autonomous intersections surrounding them, some supporting infrastructure are necessary.

The genotype is an array of the speed of each vehicle (s_i) at the intersection. It is equivalent to the speed vector $\mathbf{v}$, and can be represented as:

$$\mathbf{v} = [s_1, s_2, \ldots, s_n]; \quad s_i \in [0, speedlimit] \tag{1}$$

Here n is the number of vehicles approaching at an intersection. The genotype is ordered so that new vehicles are appended to the right side; vehicle $i+1$ spawned right after vehicle i. A population P of size k is represented as:

$$P = [\mathbf{v}_1, \mathbf{v}_2, \ldots, \mathbf{v}_k] \tag{2}$$

The MOEA tries to optimize the speed of each vehicle based on four objectives as mentioned in Sect. 2. Worthy to mention, while these objectives are important in terms of performance, they are not the final performance metrics by which the system is evaluated. The goal of the IM itself is to optimize its performance in terms of the performance metrics. In this work, we used four performance metrics as mentioned in Sect. 1. Some of these are similar to the optimization objectives, but are calculated over longer periods of time.

There is no direct relation between performance metrics and optimization objectives. Hence, several distinct objectives are optimizied simultaneously, each contributing to improve the behaviour of the IM at single independent time step. It is another issue which motivated us to apply MOEA instead of regular EAs as in the existing works. MOEA can avoid convergence toward a solution adapted for just one of these partial objectives as well as can find a diverse Pareto-set for decision making, which are not possible by applying regular EAs.

During crossover, the tails of the parent genomes are switched from a random index. This results in two new individuals based on both parents. For mutation, each s_i in the new individual ($\mathbf{v}$) has a certain probability of mutating. If a mutation occurs, a new speed is picked based on a random draw. For this, a random number between -1 and speed limit $+1$ is generated and used as the new speed. However, if the number is below 0, the new speed is set at 0. If the number is above the speed limit, it is set to the speed limit. This is to enable the random selection easier access to full speed or complete stopping. Otherwise, with a continuous random draw, these values would be impossible to get.

In order to find the appropriate values for the parameters, the system was tested multiple times (each for 25000 evaluations) with the spawn rate set at 0.5 and with different values for crossover/mutation probability, population size and the objective weighting (α). The values mentioned below were selected as they were found not to cause any collisions, and produced acceptable values for MET and total kinetic energy lost. For our experiments, these values were: population size $= 100$, crossover probability $= 0.9$, mutation probability $= 0.1$, speed limit $= 25\,\mathrm{m\,s}^{-1}$, vehicle mass $= 1000\,\mathrm{kg}$, $\frac{evaluations}{second}$ (the amount of evaluations available per second of t_{main}) $= 50,000$, and $\alpha = 0.25$ (same weight for all objectives).

To automate the system, we have applied a simple decision maker (DM) that picks up a preferable solution from the Pareto-set returned by the MOEA. For this, the Pareto-set is first sorted based on the number of collisions. If the number of collisions is equal, a secondary sorting is applied. For this, each remaining objective score is multiplied by their corresponding weighting factor (α) and summed up. In a run where there is no collision, this function priorities the objectives based on the weights provided to the IM.

3   Results and Discussion

Because the state of an intersection can be incredibly complex, there is no simple way to calculate the minimum value for t_{sim} to keep the system safe. In our earlier work [6], we explored different values for these time step parameters to find the best performance with regard to performance metrics, mainly focusing on minimizing collisions at an intersection. The results suggested that a value of 1.5 s for t_{sim} in combination with $t_{main} = 1.5$ s should give the IM a good balance between security and efficiency. Finding these values is important, because they guide other experiments. The following sub-sections present the experiments conducted in this work along with the results and discussion for each experiment.

3.1   Experiment–1: Different Traffic Scenarios

Table 1 shows the performance for the proposed system at different traffic scenarios. To help describe the rest of this work, this table has been cited from [6]. This involves spawning cars probabilistically with a *spawn rates*—a simulator parameter that represents the probability that the spawn zone will spawn a vehicle in one second in the real world simulator. It is a number between 0 and 1. This experiment compares the performance of the IM for different spawn rates (in an increment of 0.1). The real world simulator ran in a continuous mode. Each spawn rate was tested five times, each for 300s, and did not terminate before the time ran out.

Table 1. IM performance metrics for different traffic levels

Spawn rate	Runs	MET (s)	Collisions	Collisions (%)	Throughput	Total kinetic energy lost (J)
0.1	5	13.37	0.00	0.00	236.20	4539.93
0.2	5	13.37	0.00	0.00	417.60	16923.33
0.3	5	13.44	0.00	0.00	578.60	54323.80
0.4	5	13.46	0.00	0.00	712.60	126729.28
0.5	5	13.64	0.00	0.00	820.40	343614.86
0.6	5	13.89	0.40	20.00	926.80	768865.80
0.7	5	14.17	0.80	20.00	1025.80	1641376.12
0.8	5	17.59	68.80	100.00	1042.60	4810951.97
0.9	5	25.08	189.20	100.00	943.00	9604215.88
1.0	5	28.08	204.00	100.00	943.60	11658489.02

It is expected that the IM would perform worse as the amount of cars increased. This should result in a higher MET and loss of kinetic energy as the spawn rate increases. Table 1 also justifies that MET, throughput, and total kinetic energy lost—all increase as the spawn rate increases. The vehicles start to collide when the spawn rate is above 0.6, as shown by collisions and collisions (%) – the percentage of the runs that collide.

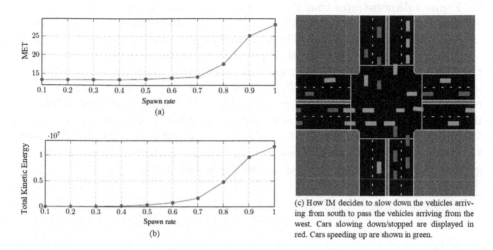

(c) How IM decides to slow down the vehicles arriving from south to pass the vehicles arriving from the west. Cars slowing down/stopped are displayed in red. Cars speeding up are shown in green.

Fig. 3. Effects of smaller time steps based on the number of cars in intersection. (Color figure online)

Figure 3 supports this claim. Two graphs (Fig. 3a and b) illustrate the nonlinear relationships between spawn rates and MET as well as total kinetic energy lost, where both MET and total kinetic energy lost increase sharply after spawn rate 0.6. For them, as long as the spawn rates are low enough, vehicles can route through intersection without much delay. The IM is also able to slow vehicles significantly allowing the passage for new cars. Manual observation also supports this result (Fig. 3c). From this figure, it is apparent that the IM slows the whole group of cars arriving from the south (represented as red) in order to speed up another group of cars (represented as green) arriving from the west.

3.2 Experiment–2: Scalability

The next experiment investigates how solving individual states of the intersection scales with the amount of traffic, considering collision avoidance. It is expected that the more vehicles will arrive at the intersection, the more evaluations the EP should, on average, need to find a solution without collision. Since the search space of the EP increases by an extra dimension when one more vehicle is introduced, the required number of evaluations will increase faster than linearly. The parameters for this experiment are similar to earlier experiment. The IM was run for 300 s for each of the spawn rates used in earlier experiment. We recorded the number of cars at an intersection and the number of evaluations needed before a solution without collisions was found. If the EP was unable to find any solution without collision, nothing was recorded. In other words, only states that could be solved within the given amount of evaluations were considered. Because the evaluations of individuals were done simultaneously, the granularity of the results were constrained to within one generation (100 evaluations).

Figure 4 demonstrates that the EP uses more evaluations to find a solution without collisions as the amount of vehicles at an intersection increases. There are two main reasons for this. The non-constraint violating part of the search space is considered as the full set of paths that can be travelled by all cars in the next $t_{evaluate}$ without causing a collision. Therefore, introducing another car anywhere at the intersection will decrease the number of valid paths for the existing vehicles or they will stay same. Thus, the number of valid solutions in the search space decreases or stays equal. In addition, introducing one more vehicle adds another dimension to the search space which drastically increases the search space as a whole. These effects together make each state harder to solve for the EP when the number of vehicles is increasing.

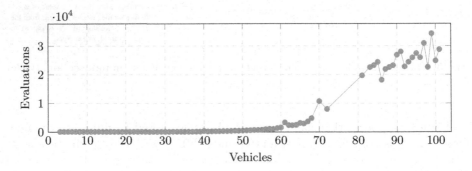

Fig. 4. Number of evaluations needed to avoid collisions based on the number of vehicles at an intersection.

Analysis of the same data, but, with regard to spawn rate (Fig. 5), presents a very similar scenario. Higher spawn rates indicate more cars, which in turn increase the average complexity of each state. This is in line with the earlier observation of higher spawn rates leading to more collisions. Higher amount of evaluations also negatively impacts on the amount of evaluations required for the MOEA to optimize other objectives. As a result, IM will more often fail to evacuate vehicles as fast as requires, further increasing the amount of vehicles at the intersection. This is also supported by our earlier finding—increase in the required evaluations strongly correlates with the performance metrics considering spawn rate (as shown in Fig. 3a and b).

3.3   Experiment–3: Conflicting Objectives

Our last experiment describes how the optimization objectives conflict in both complex and non-complex scenarios. It also investigates the circumstances under

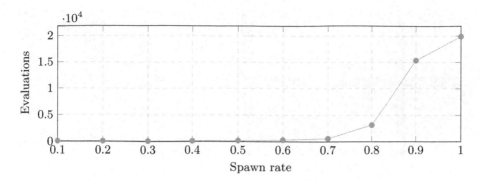

Fig. 5. Number of evaluations needed to avoid collisions based on spawn rates.

which the objectives conflict. As shown in [6], maximizing the distance traveled in each time step has a large effect on the overall performance of the IM, and the IM performs considerably worse when this objective is ignored. However, no significant changes are observed for tiny throughput and starvation. The extended experiments reported in this work are important to realize why and how the system fails/works.

These experiments analyze the behaviour of the system under different scenarios. The scenarios reflect the intersection with few cars as well as with many cars. The results show how the chosen objectives conflict in the varying situations encountered by the IM running continuously. Three different scenarios were used for this experiment. All scenarios were created by running the earlier experiment setup with the exception of spawn rate. The first scenario was generated with a spawn rate of 0.4 having few cars at the intersection. Thus, avoiding collisions was easy. The second scenario was generated with a spawn rate of 0.8 and with relatively more vehicles at the intersection. As a result, the EP would struggle avoiding collisions. The third scenario was generated with a spawn rate of 0.9 and had a lot of cars arriving at the intersection. Therefore, avoiding collisions would be the toughest. The generated scenarios were made by running the system before any car arrived at the intersection with a given spawn rate. The spawn rate only mattered when generating the scenarios. This is because, no vehicle would spawn while running this experiment, since the EP evaluated a small time segment. Ultimately, the spawn rate would not affect the actual evaluation of each scenario. Sample solutions obtained for each of the three scenarios are shown in Fig. 6.

The results for a simple scenario are presented in Table 2 and Fig. 6a. Given that the optimal solution for distance travelled and tiny throughput is −1.0 for each and for starvation and total kinetic energy lost is 0.0; it is clear that all objectives are either optimal or near-optimal. As the EP does not struggle avoiding collisions by stopping/slowing several vehicles, the result depends only on the speed vector evolved by the MOEA, where each value has the speed limit.

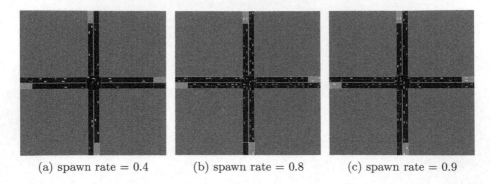

(a) spawn rate = 0.4   (b) spawn rate = 0.8   (c) spawn rate = 0.9

Fig. 6. Solutions found by optimizing the objectives using simple and complex scenarios

Table 2. Pareto-set found by the EP on a simple scenario with spawn rate = 0.4

Distance travelled	Total kinetic energy lost	Starvation	Tiny throughput
−0.9998	9.0464×10^{-5}	0.000	−1.000

This problem is similar to the well known *one-max* problem, and is a lot simpler than the more complex scenarios used later in this experiment.

Table 3. Pareto-set found by the EP on a complex scenario with spawn rate = 0.8

Distance travelled	Total kinetic energy lost	Starvation	Tiny throughput
−0.8935	0.0478	0.0000	−0.7500
−0.8962	0.0488	0.0000	−0.7500
−0.8948	0.0483	0.0000	−0.7500
−0.8916	0.0464	0.0000	−0.7500
−0.8895	0.0442	0.0120	−0.7500

Table 3 shows the Pareto-set produced by the EP on the complex scenario with a spawn rate of 0.8. Though these values seem relatively worse compared to the first scenario, they are close to the optimal values and are satisfactory, considering that the EP can still avoid collisions Fig. 6b. An interesting point to note in the Pareto-set is the last individual. Both starvation and distance travelled are worse than its peers, but total kinetic energy lost is better. This is because the EP decides to starve one car in order to prevent another from slowing down. Distance travelled is lower because the starved car had the opportunity to travel further than the favoured car if it were not starved.

The Pareto-set found for the most complex scenario with a spawn rate of 0.9 is presented in Table 4. As there are a lot of vehicles at the intersection, the objectives are expected to conflict. However, as shown in Fig. 6c, the proposed

Table 4. Pareto-set found by the EP on a complex scenario with spawn rate $= 0.9$

Distance travelled	Total kinetic energy lost	Starvation	Tiny throughput
−0.7942	0.1816	0.0000	−0.6471
−0.7855	0.1799	0.0000	−0.6471
−0.7702	0.1714	0.0148	−0.6471
−0.7775	0.1762	0.0148	−0.6471
−0.7850	0.1713	0.0281	−0.6471
−0.7695	0.1609	0.0428	−0.6471
−0.7790	0.1804	0.0000	−0.7059
−0.7849	0.1826	0.0000	−0.7059
−0.7859	0.1904	0.0000	−0.7059
−0.7770	0.1772	0.0134	−0.7059
−0.7755	0.1771	0.0151	−0.7059
−0.7644	0.1663	0.0281	−0.7059
−0.7656	0.1690	0.0281	−0.7059
−0.7714	0.1758	0.0281	−0.7059

AIM system can successfully manage the traffic at an intersection. Since avoiding collisions is difficult for this scenario and the search space is larger than other scenarios; the EP finds a larger Pareto-set. There are two reasons behind producing several non-dominated solutions than in earlier two scenarios (Tables 2 and 3). Either the EP has to compromise on one objective to improve another. Due to conflicts among the objectives, the EP has to prefer one objective over another based on relative importance. Or, because of the complexity in this scenario, the EP struggles finding a single dominating solution while avoiding collision within the given number of evaluations.

4   Conclusion

In order to take advantages of the capability of autonomous vehicles, it is time to take initiative for AIM. In this paper we proposed an AIM which is divided into two logical parts. One part controls the vehicles at an intersection by modulating their speed, and the other part analyzes a state of the intersection as well as finds a speed for each vehicle in the given state by using MOEA. This paper analyzes and reports the performance of the MOEA that manages the traffic at an intersection, given full control of the speeds of incoming vehicles. The experimental results show that the proposed system can efficiently and safely route vehicles through the intersection in different traffic scenarios. In fact, the results show that collisions could only be observed in scenarios with high amount of traffic. Considering the scaling capability of the system, the results demonstrate that the EP uses more evaluations to find a solution without collisions as the number of vehicles at the intersection increases. With regard to the objectives of the MOEA, it is evident that they do not conflict much when there are few vehicles at an intersection. This is because, the collision constraint can not be violated if no vehicle is on a colliding path, and the objectives themselves do not conflict. The objectives may conflict when the number of vehicles at an intersection is high or the state is complex. Accordingly, the EP finds a more diverse Pareto-set for a complex intersection state. In future, we would like to implement some external mechanisms to systematically reduce the number of vehicles at intersection in order to avoid any probable complex state.

References

1. IM: The aim4 simulator v1.0.3 (2016). http://www.cs.utexas.edu/aim/. Accessed 20 Jan 2016
2. Berisha, B.: Alleviating traffic congestion in Prishtina. Thesis, Rochester Institute of Technology (2016)
3. Deb, K., Pratap, A., Agarwal, S., Meyarivan, T.: A fast and elitist multiobjective genetic algorithm: NSGA-II. IEEE Trans. Evol. Comput. 6(2), 182–197 (2002)
4. Dresner, K., Stone, P.: A multiagent approach to autonomous intersection management. J. Artif. Intell. Res. 31, 591–656 (2008)
5. Gemeinschaften, K.E.: White paper-European transport policy for 2010: time to decide. Office for Official Publications of the European Communities (2001)
6. Ripon, K.S.N., Dissen, H., Solaas, J.: Real time traffic intersection management using multi-objective evolutionary algorithm. In: Martín-Vide, C., Mizuki, T., Vega-Rodríguez, M.A. (eds.) TPNC 2016. LNCS, vol. 10071, pp. 110–121. Springer, Cham (2016). doi:10.1007/978-3-319-49001-4_9
7. Vegni, A.M., Little, T.D.: Hybrid vehicular communications based on v2v–v2i protocol switching. Int. J. Veh. Inf. Commun. Syst. 2(3–4), 213–231 (2011)
8. Wu, J., Abbas-Turki, A., El Moudni, A.: Discrete methods for urban intersection traffic controlling. In: IEEE 69th Vehicular Technology Conference (VTC 2009), pp. 1–5. IEEE (2009)
9. Wuthishuwong, C., Traechtler, A., Bruns, T.: Safe trajectory planning for autonomous intersection management by using vehicle to infrastructure communication. EURASIP J. Wirel. Commun. Netw. 2015(1), 1–12 (2015)
10. Yan, F., Dridi, M., El Moudni, A.: An autonomous vehicle sequencing problem at intersections: a genetic algorithm approach. Int. J. Appl. Math. Comput. Sci. 23(1), 183–200 (2013)

Study of an Adaptive Control of Aggregate Functions in MOEA/D

Shinya Watanabe[1(✉)] and Takanori Sato[2]

[1] Department of Computer Science and Systems Engineering,
Muroran Institute of Technology, 27-1, Mizumoto-cho, Muroran 050-8585, Japan
sin@csse.muroran-it.ac.jp
[2] IBM Global Services Japan Solution and Services Company (ISOL), 2-2,
Nishi6chome, Kita5jo, Chuo-ku, Sapporo-shi, Hokkaido 060-0005, Japan
digimon07vr@gmail.com
http://is.csse.muroran-it.ac.jp/

Abstract. This paper proposed a new adaptive control mechanism of aggregation functions (scalarizing functions) in MOEA/D, "ADaptive control of Aggregation function dePending on a search condiTion (ADAPT)". Although MOEA/D has been well known as one of the most powerful EMO algorithms, it hasn't been resolved which aggregation function should be choose. It is strongly depended on characteristics of the problem which aggregation function of MOEA/D is best suited and very difficult to predict which one is best suited in advance. Our proposed ADAPT changes adaptively an aggregation function of MOEA/D according to the search condition. ADAPT uses multiple aggregation functions and multiple archives corresponding to each aggregation function. The important points of ADAPT is that the number of function calls is same as that of original MOEA/D.

In numerical examples, the characteristics and effectiveness of ADAPT were verified by comparing the performance of ADAPT with that of original MOEA/D (using a fixed aggregation function). The results of experiments indicated that ADAPT could obtain the solutions as same quality as that of original MOEA/D with the best suited aggregation function.

Keywords: Dynamic control of aggregate functions · MOEA/D · ADAPT

1 Introduction

There has been a great deal of progress in the study of evolutionary multi-criterion optimization (EMO) over the last two decade [4]. One of important reasons is performance improvements of EMO algorithms. MOEA/D (multiobjective evolutionary algorithm based on decomposition) [7] has been known as one of the most efficient EMO algorithms. MOEA/D decomposes multi-objective

© Springer International Publishing AG 2017
Y. Shi et al. (Eds.): SEAL 2017, LNCS 10593, pp. 309–320, 2017.
https://doi.org/10.1007/978-3-319-68759-9_26

problem into a number of single-objective problems by using aggregation function, such as Tchebycheff, weighted sum, PBI (penalty-based boundary intersection) and etc.

Although it has been known that the selection of aggregation functions (scalarizing functions) has a strong influence on a performance of MOEA/D [3,6], it hasn't established the way how to choice the best suited aggregation function in MOEA/D. The features of aggregation functions has been revealed partly, but it is very difficult to predict precisely the affinity between the aggregation function and the target problem.

Therefore, we presented a new mechanism to control adaptively the choice of aggregation functions in MOEA/D according to the condition of search. In this paper, this proposed mechanism is called "ADaptive control of Aggregation function dePending on a search condiTion -ADAPT-". In ADAPT, some different types of aggregation functions are prepared in advance and the same number of archive populations corresponding to each aggregation function's setting are used for reserving best individuals for each aggregation function's setting. The setting of aggregation function is replaced in a certain fixed period by calculating the HV (hyper volume) of each archive population. Two important points of our mechanism are that the number of function calls is same as that of original MOEA/D and its implementation is not complicated.

To investigate the effectiveness of ADAPT, we applied it to some well-known typical test suits and compared the results of ADAPT with those of original MOEA/D (using a fixed aggregation function).

2   MOEA/D-DU and Aggregation Function

In our mechanism, we choose a modified MOEA/D, MOEA/D-DU [6] as MOEA/D algorithm. In the selection of MOEA/D-DU, new created individuals are compared with not only a part of individuals but also the whole individuals in every sub-problem. The main reason of why to choose MOEA/D-DU (not MOEA/D) is that this feature in selection is very suitable for ADAPT.

The brief flow of MOEA/D-DU and the details of these aggregation functions were described as below.

2.1   The Flow of MOEA/D-DU

The procedure of MOEA/D-DU was briefly described as below.

step 1: Initialization
> **step 1.1:** Initializing external population (EP) as vacuity ($EP = \emptyset$).
> **step 1.2:** Calculate the Euclidean distances of every combination between uniformed weight vectors ($\boldsymbol{\lambda}^1, \ldots, \boldsymbol{\lambda}^N$) and defines T neighbor vectors $\boldsymbol{B}(i) = \{i_1, \ldots, i_T\}$ for each weight vectors.
> **step 1.3:** Create initial individuals $\boldsymbol{x}^1, \ldots, \boldsymbol{x}^N$ and evaluate these ($FV^i = F(\boldsymbol{x}^i)$).

step 1.4: Set reference point $z = (z_1, \ldots, z_m)^T (z_i = \min\{f_i\})$.

step 2: Genetic operations

The following operations are performed for every sub-problem ($\lambda^i, i = 1, \ldots, N$).

step 2.1: Select two individuals (x^k, x^l) as parents and create new children y using crossover operation.

step 2.2: Create y' by perturbing y.

step 2.3: If $z_j < f_j(y')$, then $z_j = f_j(y')(j = 1, \ldots, m)$.

step 2.4: Compare y' to every individual. When an individual dominated by y', then replaced the dominated one with y'. In the case y' dominates some individuals, only the dominated individual closest to y' would be replaced.

step 2.5: Delete the individuals dominated by $F(y')$ in EP. If there is no individual dominated, only add $F(y')$ to EP.

step 3: Terminal criterion

If terminal condition is satisfied, then end. Otherwise, go to step 2.

2.2   Aggregation Function

We explained four typical aggregation functions; weighted sum, Tchebycheff, PBI and IPBI. These four functions were used as aggregation function of MOEA/D in numerical examples of this paper.

Weighted Sum

Weighted sum is one of most widely-used aggregation function and calculates the sum of the values of evaluation functions. This function is very effective for convex problems but is impossible to get Pareto solutions of non-convex problems except extreme points.

$$g^{ws}(x) = \sum_{i=1}^{m} \lambda_i^j f_i(x) \tag{1}$$

Tchebycheff

Tchebycheff optimizes the differences between a current point and a reference point. The main feature of this is possible to obtain whole Pareto solutions in non-convex problems. However the approximation ability is not so strong.

$$g^{te}(x|\lambda, z^*) = \max_{1 \leq i \leq m} \{\lambda_i | f_i(x) - z_i^* |\} \tag{2}$$

PBI

Penalty-based Boundary Intersection (PBI) is to minimize the distance according to the search vector line starting from reference point. The main feature of PBI is to consider not only vertical direction of the search vector line

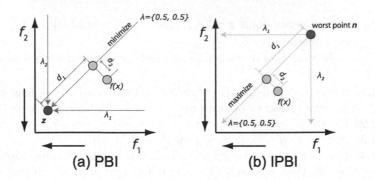

Fig. 1. Concept figures of PBI and IPBI

but also horizontal direction. The evaluation related to horizontal direction is controlled by penalty parameter θ. Larger value of θ means to strengthen a directivity of search, while lower value of θ is to get closer to weighted sum. The concept of PBI is illustrated in Fig. 1(a).

$$\text{minimize } g^{pbi}(\boldsymbol{x} \mid \lambda, z^*) = d_1 + \theta d_2 \tag{3}$$
$$\text{subject to} \qquad x \in \Omega \tag{4}$$

In above equation, d_1 and d_2 mean the distance between current point $\boldsymbol{x}$ and reference point z^* in vertical direction and horizontal direction, respectively.

$$d_1 = \frac{\|(z^* - F(\boldsymbol{x}))^T\|}{\lambda} \tag{5}$$
$$d_2 = \|F(\boldsymbol{x}) - (z^* - d_1\lambda)\| \tag{6}$$

IPBI

Inverted Penalty-Based Boundary Intersection (IPBI) has been proposed by Sato [5]. IPBI is an extension of the conventional PBI function and has completely an opposite feature of PBI. It is more clearly understandable when to contrast the concept figure of IPBI (Fig. 1(b)) with that of PBI (Fig. 1(a)). While PBI tries to minimize the distance from reference point, IPBI tries to maximize the distance from nadir point.

$$\text{maximize} g^{ipbi}(\boldsymbol{x}|\lambda, z^*) = d_1 - \theta d_2 \tag{7}$$
$$d_1 = \frac{\|(\boldsymbol{n} - F(\boldsymbol{x}))^T\lambda\|}{\lambda} \tag{8}$$
$$d_2 = \|(\boldsymbol{n} - F(\boldsymbol{x})) - d_1\lambda\| \tag{9}$$

In the above equation, $\boldsymbol{n}$ means nadir point having the worst objective values in solutions.

3 Dynamic Control Approach of Aggregation Function in MOEA/D

In this section, we explained a details of the proposed approach, "A Dynamic control of Aggregation function dePending on a search condiTion -ADAPT-". ADAPT realizes an adaptive control of aggregation function's setting in MOEA/D.

3.1 The Outline of ADAPT

ADAPT prepares some different settings of aggregation function in advance and chooses one from these depending on a search condition. In this paper, ADAPT used twelve different settings of aggregation functions. These are Tchebycheff, Weighted Sum, five types of PBI($\theta = 1, 2, 3, 4, 5$) and five types of IPBI($\theta = 1, 2, 3, 4, 5$).

Through previous our works of MOEA/D, we confirmed a change of an aggregation function in the process of search would result in worsening of search efficiency. One reason of this is to share same individuals despite these aggregation functions having different directional characteristics.

Therefore, ADAPT tries to overcome this problem by preparing several archive populations corresponding to each aggregation function's setting. In ADAPT, the selected aggregation function must be always one when parents are selected for creating new children, but every archive population would be updated no matter which set of aggregation function is chosen. Therefore, the information of every archive population could be kept up to date. Figure 2 indicates that ADAPT keeps several populations corresponding to each aggregation function's setting in each subproblem. In Fig. 2, the number of evaluation values for each sub problem $\lambda_i = \{\omega_i, 1 - \omega_i\}$ is twelve in total; Tchebycheff, Weighted Sum, 5 types of PBI($\theta = 1, 2, 3, 4, 5$) and 5 types of IPBI($\theta = 1, 2, 3, 4, 5$). And

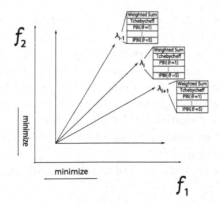

Fig. 2. Concept figure of each sub problem having several solutions in ADAPT.

ADAPT would choose which aggregation function to be used according to the value of HV (hyper volume) in certain intervals.

The details of ADAPT were described below.

3.2   The Flow of ADAPT

The flow of ADAPT was described in the same way of that of MOEA/D-DU (in Sect. 2.1).

step 1: Initialization
  step 1.1-1.2: Perform the same initialization procedure of MOEA/D-DU in Sect. 2.1.
  step 1.3: Create initial solutions $x^1, \ldots, x^N$ and evaluate these by using $FV^i = F(x^i)$. Copy these initial solutions to each archives respond to each aggregation function.
  step 1.4: Set reference point $z = (z_1, \ldots, z_m)^T (z_i = \min\{f_i\})$ in the same way of MOEA/D-DU in Sect. 2.1.
step 2: Selection of aggregation function
  In a certain interval (or initial generation), select the aggregation function from the prepared set of aggregation functions according to the following steps.
  step 2.1: Calculate Hyper Volume (HV) values of archive populations corresponding to each aggregation function's setting separately.
  step 2.2: Select the aggregation function's setting having the highest HV value as the best suited one.
  Figure 3 shows the image of this selection in ADAPT. The selected function has a important role when to select parent solutions in crossover operator.
step 3: Renewing solutions
  The following operations are performed for every sub-problems ($\lambda^i, i = 1, \ldots, N$).
  step 3.1-3.3: Perform the same genetic operations of MOEA/D-DU in Sect. 2.1.
  step 3.4: Compare the new created child y' to each archive population and update the solutions in each archive if y' could dominate these. Figure 4 presents that a new child is created by the selected aggregation's solutions (archive). In Fig. 5, the created solution is shared to other aggregation's solutions (archives).
  step 3.5: Perform the same updating of EP of MOEA/D-DU in Sect. 2.1.
step 4: Terminal criterion
  Perform the same judgement of terminal condition as that of MOEA/D-DU.

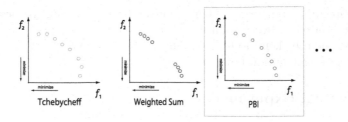

Fig. 3. Selection of aggregation function in ADAPT.

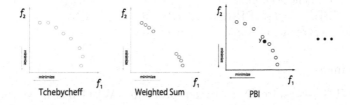

Fig. 4. Concept figure of creating a new child in ADAPT.

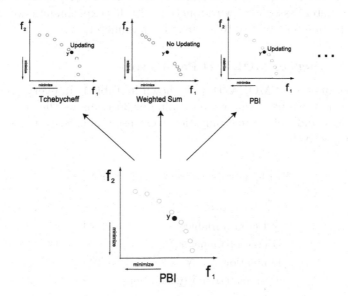

Fig. 5. Sharing information of a new child to other aggregation's solutions (archives) in ADAPT.

By changing the aggregation function according to the HV value of archive population corresponding to each aggregation function's setting, ADAPT could select adaptively a best suited aggregation function on a search situation of MOEA/D.

In ADAPT, each sub problem has several solutions corresponding to each aggregation function's setting. These several solutions could be seen as archive of each aggregation function's setting. Since the information of new created children are shared in every solutions (every archive), every solutions in each sub problem could be kept up to date. This is a key to prevent the bad influence by switching of aggregation function.

4   Numerical Experiments

We investigated the effectiveness of ADAPT through numerical examples. In this experiments, ADAPT was compared with twelve kinds of MOEA/D that used Weighted Sum, Tchebycheff, PBI($\theta = 1$), PBI($\theta = 2$), PBI($\theta = 3$), PBI($\theta = 4$), PBI($\theta = 5$), IPBI($\theta = 1$), IPBI($\theta = 2$), IPBI($\theta = 3$), IPBI($\theta = 4$) and IPBI($\theta = 5$) as an fixed aggregation function, respectively.

4.1   Instances

We used WFG test suite [2] as target problems. WEG has been widely used as typical test problems and could change not only the number of objectives and variables but also the difficulty and characteristics of problems by tuning internal parameters associated with functions. In this experiments, we set $k = 10$ as position parameter and $l = 10$ as distance parameter.

4.2   The Settings of MOEA/D Parametres

The used parameters of MOEA/D were shown in Table 1. In every approach, In this experiments, we used the average value of 30 trials as the results of each approach. SBX and polynomial mutation were used as crossover and mutation methods, respectively.

Table 1. Used parameters of MOEA/D

# Objectives	2
# Design variables	20
Division parameter H	99
Population size N	100
Terminal criteria (generations)	1000

4.3   Measure Methods

We used Inverted Generational Distance (IGD) [1] and Hypervolume (HV) [8] as measure methods. The details of these were described as below.

Inverted Generational Distance. IGD is a measure index for representing the distance between solutions and Pareto solutions (Pareto front). IGD could be defined as Eq. (10) and lower value of IGD means that solutions is closer to Pareto front.

$$IGD(S,R) = \frac{1}{R} \sum_{r \in R} \min_{s \in S} \sqrt{\sum_{i=1}^{k} [\max(0, r_i - s_i)]^2} \qquad (10)$$

Hypervolume. Hypervolume (HV) indicator is to calculate the size of the objective space covered by solutions. Therefore HV can be used as a comprehensive measure index considering "accuracy","width", and "uniformity". In this experiments, the reference point of HV was set as (3, 5). The equation of HV is defined by Eq. 11.

$$\text{Hypervolume} = \text{volume}(\cup_{i=1}^{nPF} v_i) \qquad (11)$$

4.4 The Results of Numerical Examples

The results of comparison experiments between original MOEA/D and the proposed ADAPT were shown in Tables 2 and 3. Table 2 presented the results of IGD and Table 3 was those of HV. We used the average value of 30 trials as the results of Tables 2 and 3. In these experiments, we sat the interval of calculating HV in ADAPT as one. That is, ADAPT performed step2 of Sect. 3.2 at every generation in these experiments.

In these results, twelve kinds of MOEA/D with the fixed aggregation function were used as original MOEA/D. These aggregation functions are weighted sum, Tchebycheff, 5 different types of PBI and 5 different types of IPBI. Also, the bold fonts in these results mean the best result of these original MOEA/D in each problem and underline fonts mean the result of ADAPT is better than that of best of these original MOEA/D.

Table 2. Results of IGD

	WFG1	WFG2	WFG3	WFG4	WFG5	WFG6	WFG7	WFG8	WFG9
Weighted sum	**1.291**	0.272	0.676	0.167	0.249	0.278	0.261	0.346	0.145
Tchebycheff	1.538	0.223	0.693	0.230	0.285	0.291	0.266	0.333	0.216
PBI($\theta = 1$)	1.699	0.317	0.408	**0.059**	**0.079**	**0.095**	**0.110**	0.423	**0.118**
PBI($\theta = 2$)	1.574	0.327	0.206	0.104	0.080	0.102	0.132	0.273	0.129
PBI($\theta = 3$)	1.619	0.271	**0.199**	0.125	0.085	0.108	0.189	0.228	0.152
PBI($\theta = 4$)	1.606	0.234	0.213	0.147	0.092	0.100	0.188	**0.204**	0.170
PBI($\theta = 5$)	1.608	**0.217**	0.211	0.147	0.102	0.098	0.220	0.206	0.170
IPBI($\theta = 1$)	2.040	0.433	0.717	0.292	0.355	0.336	0.349	0.393	0.300
IPBI($\theta = 2$)	2.132	0.529	0.753	0.335	0.388	0.379	0.406	0.414	0.368
IPBI($\theta = 3$)	2.167	0.612	0.788	0.357	0.387	0.393	0.418	0.430	0.377
IPBI($\theta = 4$)	2.190	0.647	0.803	0.363	0.395	0.405	0.465	0.443	0.411
IPBI($\theta = 5$)	2.201	0.689	0.801	0.367	0.405	0.402	0.476	0.467	0.429
ADAPT	1.607	__0.200__	__0.185__	__0.059__	__0.070__	__0.081__	__0.086__	__0.167__	__0.094__

Table 3. Results of HV

	WFG1	WFG2	WFG3	WFG4	WFG5	WFG6	WFG7	WFG8	WFG9
Weighted sum	**4.984**	8.722	8.132	5.484	5.967	6.107	5.889	4.977	6.687
Tchebycheff	3.947	8.879	8.140	5.197	5.803	6.059	5.391	4.985	6.260
PBI($\theta = 1$)	3.675	8.510	9.273	7.830	7.761	7.572	6.580	4.334	7.411
PBI($\theta = 2$)	4.121	8.564	10.192	**8.017**	**7.998**	7.716	**7.119**	5.167	**7.467**
PBI($\theta = 3$)	3.887	8.779	**10.259**	7.885	7.981	7.699	7.032	5.496	7.384
PBI($\theta = 4$)	3.881	8.933	10.204	7.791	7.934	7.750	7.043	5.790	7.273
PBI($\theta = 5$)	3.855	**9.027**	10.235	7.789	7.881	**7.762**	7.005	**5.819**	7.301
IPBI($\theta = 1$)	2.041	8.019	7.787	4.892	5.496	5.856	5.408	4.616	5.777
IPBI($\theta = 2$)	1.603	7.465	7.575	4.672	5.296	5.609	4.708	4.513	5.204
IPBI($\theta = 3$)	1.447	7.109	7.433	4.560	5.298	5.438	4.628	4.413	5.228
IPBI($\theta = 4$)	1.352	6.924	7.339	4.542	5.242	5.421	4.471	4.360	5.044
IPBI($\theta = 5$)	1.306	6.743	7.350	4.525	5.155	5.383	4.438	4.248	4.902
ADAPT	3.846	**9.160**	**10.376**	**8.174**	**8.041**	**7.861**	**7.224**	**6.093**	**7.649**

From the results of Tables 2 and 3, ADAPT could get the best or second best results in most of problems. These results indicated that ADAPT could get almost same quality result of original MOEA/D with the best suited aggregation function in most of problems. In the case of original MOEA/D, it needs many preliminary surveys for finding the best aggregation function and setting. Therefore, ADAPT could be said to have high value as an adaptive MOEA/D algorithm.

Also, when to focus on twelve original MOEA/D using the fixed aggregation function, the best suited aggregation function was different in problems and the differences of θ value associated with PBI and IPBI would have some effect on the result of search from the results of Tables 2 and 3. However, it was very difficult to catch definitive trends from these results and the best suited aggregation function and the value of θ are very difficult to predict in advance.

Figure 6 showed the transitions of the selected aggregation function of ADAPT in WFG2, 4 and 9. In these figures, two cases of 30 trials having the best and worst IGD values were illustrated as black and gray lines.

In Fig. 6, PBI was most used while IPBI was least used. In WFG4, the both of best and worst cases used the same aggregation function (PBI) after 200 generations. Therefore, we could estimate the best suited aggregation function in WFG4 is PBI with $\theta = 1$. Also, when to compare Fig. 6 with Table 2, the best suited aggregation of original MOEA/D was most frequently selected in ADAPT. This fact indicated that ADAPT could work as we had expected. Since ADAPT could get better results than those of original MOEA/D with the best suited aggregation function in some problems and the selected functions of ADAPT was changed according to the search process in Fig. 6, ADAPT would have high potential to exceed the search performance of original MOEA/D. The reason of this is that ADAPT could change adaptively the aggregation function according

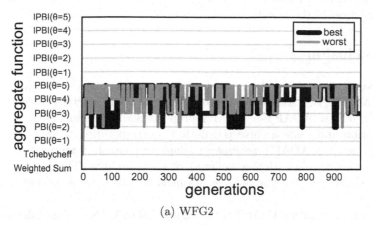

(a) WFG2

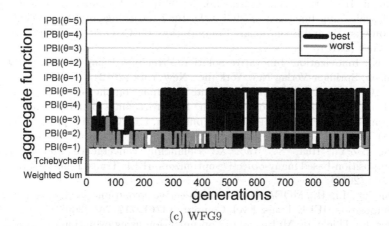

(b) WFG4

(c) WFG9

Fig. 6. Transitions about the selected aggregate function

the search condition, while original MOEA/D cannot change the selected aggregation function in the whole of search process.

5   Conclusion

In this paper, we presented a new adaptive control approach of aggregate functions in MOEA/D, "ADaptive control of Aggregation function dePending on a search condiTion -ADAPT-". ADAPT prepares some different kinds of aggregation function and some archive populations corresponding to each aggregation function's setting. ADAPT realizes an adaptive control of aggregation function by calculating the HV (hyper volume) of each archive. The most important point of ADAPT is that the number of function calls is same as that of original MOEA/D.

Through comparing ADAPT with original MOEA/Ds having different aggregation function, ADAPT could get the same or better than results of original MOEA/D with the best suited aggregation function in most of problems. Therefore, we could say ADAPT is very practical and promising as an adaptive MOEA/D approach.

References

1. Bosman, P.A.N., Thierens, D.: The balance between proximity and diversity in multiobjective evolutionary algorithms. IEEE Trans. Evol. Comput. **7**(2), 174–188 (2003)
2. Huband, S., Barone, L., While, L., Hingston, P.: A scalable multi-objective test problem toolkit. In: Coello Coello, C.A., Hernández Aguirre, A., Zitzler, E. (eds.) EMO 2005. LNCS, vol. 3410, pp. 280–295. Springer, Heidelberg (2005). doi:10.1007/978-3-540-31880-4_20
3. Ishibuchi, H., Sakane, Y., Tsukamoto, N., Nojima, Y.: Simultaneous use of different scalarizing functions in MOEA/D. In: Proceedings of 12th Annual Conference on Genetic and Evolutionary Computation, GECCO 2010, pp. 519–526. ACM, New York (2010)
4. Deb, K.: Innovization: Innovative Solution Principles Using Multiobjective Optimization. Springer-Verlag New York Inc., New York (2012)
5. Sato, H.: Inverted PBI in MOEA/D and its impact on the search performance on multi and many-objective optimization. In: Proceedings of 2014 Annual Conference on Genetic and Evolutionary Computation, GECCO 2014, pp. 645–652. ACM (2014)
6. Yuan, B.Z.Y., Hua, X., Yao, X.: Balancing convergence and diversity in decomposition-based many-objective optimizers. IEEE Trans. Evol. Comput. **20**(2), 180–198 (2016)
7. Zhang, Q., Li, H.: MOEA/D: a multiobjective evolutionary algorithm based on decomposition. IEEE Trans. Evol. Comput. **11**(6), 712–731 (2007)
8. Zitzler, E., Thiele, L.: Multiobjective optimization using evolutionary algorithms - a comparative case study. In: Eiben, A.E., Bäck, T., Schoenauer, M., Schwefel, H.-P. (eds.) PPSN 1998. LNCS, vol. 1498, pp. 292–301. Springer, Heidelberg (1998). doi:10.1007/BFb0056872

Use of Inverted Triangular Weight Vectors in Decomposition-Based Many-Objective Algorithms

Ken Doi[1], Ryo Imada[1], Yusuke Nojima[1(✉)], and Hisao Ishibuchi[1,2]

[1] Department of Computer Science and Intelligent Systems,
Graduate School of Engineering, Osaka Prefecture University,
Sakai, Osaka 599-8531, Japan
{ken.doi, ryo.imada}@ci.cs.osakafu-u.ac.jp,
{nojima, hisaoi}@cs.osakafu-u.ac.jp
[2] Department of Computer Science and Engineering,
Southern University of Science and Technology (SUSTech),
Nanshan, Shenzhen, Guangdong, China

Abstract. A number of decomposition-based algorithms have been proposed for many-objective problems using a set of uniformly distributed weight vectors in the literature. In those algorithms, a many-objective problem is decomposed into single-objective problems. Each single-objective problem is optimized in a cooperative manner with other single-objective problems. Their performance strongly depends on the Pareto front shape of a test problem. This is because weight vectors are generated using a triangular simplex lattice structure. It is easy for decomposition-based algorithms to obtain uniformly distributed solutions on triangular Pareto fronts. However, it is not easy for them to handle non-triangular Pareto fronts such as inverted-triangular and disconnected Pareto fronts. In our former study, we examined the performance of MOEA/D when the triangular simplex lattice structure was replaced with the inverted triangular structure for generating weight vectors. The use of those weight vectors deteriorated the performance of MOEA/D for almost all test problems including those with inverted triangular Pareto fronts. In this paper, we examine the use of the inverted triangular simplex lattice structure in two variants of MOEA/D (MOEA/D-DE and MOEA/D-STM) and other four decomposition-based algorithms (NSGA-III, θ-DEA, MOEA/DD, and Global WASF-GA). Their performance is reported for many-objective problems with triangular and inverted triangular Pareto fronts.

Keywords: Evolutionary many-objective optimization · Decomposition-based many-objective algorithms · Inverted triangular Pareto fronts

1 Introduction

Evolutionary multiobjective optimization (EMO) has been actively studied in the last two decades [1]. Various EMO algorithms have been developed to obtain a set of non-dominated solutions over the entire Pareto front for multiobjective optimization

© Springer International Publishing AG 2017
Y. Shi et al. (Eds.): SEAL 2017, LNCS 10593, pp. 321–333, 2017.
https://doi.org/10.1007/978-3-319-68759-9_27

problems. There are mainly three approaches existed for EMO algorithm design: Pareto dominance-based [2, 3], indicator-based [4, 5], and decomposition-based [6–13]. Recently, the application of EMO algorithms to many-objective optimization problems with four or more objectives has been a hot topic in the EMO community. Good performance has frequently been reported from a number of decomposition-based EMO algorithms for many-objective problems.

Decomposition-based algorithms need a set of weight vectors, which are also referred to as reference points. In those algorithms, a multiobjective problem is decomposed into a number of single-objective problems using a set of uniformly distributed weight vectors. In Fig. 1(a), a two-objective problem is decomposed into six single-objective problems using six weight vectors (w_1, w_2, w_3, w_4, w_5, w_6). A solution for each single-objective problem is usually obtained on the reference line (one of l_1, l_2, l_3, l_4, l_5, and l_6) which is generated by extending the corresponding weight vector from the ideal point z^*.

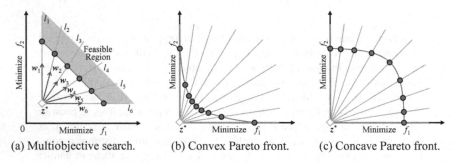

(a) Multiobjective search.   (b) Convex Pareto front.   (c) Concave Pareto front.

Fig. 1. Illustration of multiobjective search and examples of Pareto fronts where a set of uniformly distributed weight vectors is not the best choice.

Figure 1(b) and (c) show typical examples of Pareto fronts where a set of well-distributed solutions cannot be obtained from the uniformly distributed weight vectors. An appropriate set of weight vectors strongly depends on the curvature property of the Pareto front (convex, concave, and so on) [14]. Of course, this issue also exists in multiobjective problems with three or more objectives whereas we illustrate it for two-objective problems in Fig. 1.

In multiobjective problems with three or more objectives, an appropriate distribution of weight vectors strongly depends on not only the curvature properties but also the geometric shape properties of Pareto fronts (e.g., triangular, inverted triangular, etc.) [10, 14, 15]. Examples of multiobjective problems with inverted triangular Pareto fronts are inverted DTLZ1 [10], Minus-DTLZ and Minus-WFG [14]. In Fig. 2, we show the Pareto front of the standard three-objective DTLZ1 [16], the inverted triangular Pareto front of the Minus-DTLZ1 and a set of weight vectors used in decomposition-based algorithms. Intuitively, we can see that the set of weight vectors in Fig. 2(c) is problematic for the Minus-DTLZ1 with the inverted triangular Pareto front in Fig. 2(b) whereas it is suitable for the DTLZ1 with the triangular Pareto front in

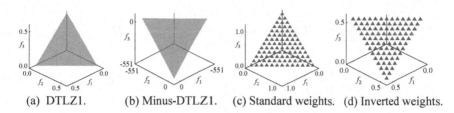

(a) DTLZ1.   (b) Minus-DTLZ1.   (c) Standard weights.   (d) Inverted weights.

Fig. 2. Pareto fronts of the three-objective DTLZ1 and Minus-DTLZ1 problems, a set of standard triangular weight vectors and a set of inverted triangular weight vectors.

Fig. 2(a). In fact, it was clearly demonstrated in [14] that decomposition-based algorithms could obtain good results for DTLZ1-4 and WFG1-9 while they showed poor performance for most of Minus-DTLZ1-4 and Minus-WFG1-9. This is because the standard weight vector distribution in Fig. 2(c) is not suitable for those test problems with inverted triangular Pareto fronts [14].

In our former study [15], we examined the performance of MOEA/D with the standard weight vectors in Fig. 2 (c) and the inverted triangular weight vectors in Fig. 2 (d) on the test problems with triangular Pareto fronts in Fig. 2(a) and inverted triangular Pareto fronts in Fig. 2(b). Whereas MOEA/D with inverted weight vectors looks suitable for test problems with inverted triangular Pareto front, good results cannot be obtained from MOEA/D with inverted triangular weight vectors. This is because the search for the ideal point is difficult for the inverted weight vectors (since only a single weight vector in the inverted triangular weight vectors is used for the search for the best value of each objective whereas multiple weight vectors are used in the case of the triangular weight vectors: for details, see [15]).

In this paper, we examine the effect of the inverted weight vectors on the search ability of various decomposition-based algorithms (i.e., MOEA/D-DE [7], MOEA/D-STM [8], NSGA-III [9], θ-DEA [11], MOEA/DD [12], and Global WASF-GA [13]).

This paper is organized as follows. We first explain the standard triangular weight vectors (which are commonly used in decomposition-based algorithms) and the inverted triangular weight vectors (which are generated from the standard triangular weight vectors) in Sect. 2. In Sect. 3, we briefly explain the characteristics of each decomposition-based algorithm examined in this paper. In Sect. 4, we report experimental results by the examined decomposition-based algorithms on DTLZ1-4, WFG1-4, Minus-DTLZ1-4 and Minus-WFG1-4 test problems with 3, 5, 8 and 10 objectives. Finally, we summarize this paper in Sect. 5.

2   Weight Vector Specification

In decomposition-based evolutionary many-objective algorithms, a set of weight vectors is generated in a triangular simplex lattice based on the following equations:

$$\sum_{i=1}^{M} w_i = 1 \text{ and } 0 \le w_i \le 1 \quad \text{for } i = 1, 2, \ldots, M, \tag{1}$$

$$w_i \in \left\{ 0, \frac{1}{H}, \frac{2}{H}, \ldots, \frac{H}{H} \right\} \quad \text{for } i = 1, 2, \ldots, M, \tag{2}$$

where M is the number of objectives, w_i is the ith weight value, and H is a positive integer. The number of weight vectors generated from (1) and (2) is $_{H+M-1}C_{M-1}$. Figure 2(c) shows 91 weight vectors generated from (1) and (2) for three-objective problems when H is specified as $H = 12$. These weight vectors are referred to as the "standard weights" in this paper.

The inverted triangular weight vectors $v = (v_1, v_2, \ldots, v_M)$ are generated from the standard weights $w = (w_1, w_2, \ldots, w_M)$ using the following transformation:

$$r_i = 1 - w_i \text{ for } i = 1, 2, \ldots, M, \tag{3}$$

$$v_i = r_i \left/ \sum_{j=1}^{M} r_j = r_i / (M - 1) \quad \text{for } i = 1, 2, \ldots, M. \tag{4} \right.$$

In Fig. 2(d), 91 weight vectors are generated by (3) and (4) from the standard weights in Fig. 2(c). Weight vectors generated by (3) and (4) are referred to as the "inverted weights" in this paper. Decomposition-based algorithms search for a solution of each single-objective problem along the corresponding weight vector as shown in Fig. 1. Thus, one may think that the inverted weights are more suitable than the standard weights for inverted triangular Pareto fronts.

3   Decomposition-Based Evolutionary Algorithms

In this section, we explain various decomposition-based evolutionary many-objective algorithms used in this paper.

MOEA/D-DE [7] and MOEA/D-STM [8]: These algorithms have been proposed using the framework of MOEA/D [6]. These algorithms can maintain the population diversity by selecting parent solutions from the whole population with a small probability (i.e., not only from the neighborhood). Both of them use DE operator [17] to further maintain the population diversity. MOEA/D-STM has a stable matching model (STM). Each solution can be assigned to only a single weight vector by STM. Thus, MOEA/D-STM can promote the diversity.

NSGA-III [9] and θ-DEA [11]: These algorithms have been proposed for many-objective problems. They have similar structures and may be classified as hybrid algorithms of decomposition-based and dominance-based approaches. In these algorithms, the population is divided into several non-domination levels using the Pareto dominance relation for the first criterion. By using the second criterion, each solution is assigned to a weight vector (i.e., a reference point).

MOEA/DD [12]: MOEA/DD may be also classified as hybrid algorithms of decomposition-based and dominance-based approaches. NSGA-III and θ-DEA generate N offspring from N parent solutions and then a non-dominated sorting is applied to 2 N individuals in each iteration. However, MOEA/DD generates n offspring ($n = 2$ in the available code on the Internet by the author of MOEA/DD from [18]) from the neighborhood parent solutions and then a non-dominated sorting is applied to $(N + n)$ individuals (i.e., the sorting is applied to $(N + 2)$ individuals in the source code [18]). In other words, the generated solutions depend strongly on the distribution of the neighborhood parent solutions.

Global WASF-GA [13]: In Global WASF-GA, the achievement scalarizing function (ASF) which is based on the Tchebycheff function is used as a scalarizing function. In this algorithm, there are two definitions of ASF: using the ideal point or the nadir point. One half of the population is evaluated by using the ideal point and the other half is evaluated by using the nadir point. In this way, Global WASF-GA can search for multiple search directions at the same time.

4   Computational Experiments

In this section, we compare two types of weight vector distributions in decomposition-based evolutionary algorithms for DTLZ1-4, WFG1-4, Minus-DTLZ1-4 and Minus-WFG1-4 with 3, 5, 8 and 10 objectives. The parameter settings in NSGA-III, θ-DEA, MOEA/DD, MOEA/D variants are the same as in Ishibuchi et al. [14]: the polynomial mutation with the distribution index 20 (the mutation probability is 1/ n where n is the string length) and the simulated binary crossover (SBX) with the distribution index 20 (30 in NSGA-III, θ-DEA and MOEA/DD) and the crossover probability 1.0. The neighborhood selection probability is 0.9, and the PBI function and the Tchebycheff function are used in MOEA/D variants. $CR = 1.0$ and $F = 0.5$ are used for the DE operator. We use available codes on the Internet: θ-DEA and NSGA-III from [19] by the authors of the θ-DEA paper [11], MOEA/DD from [18] by the authors of the MOEA/DD paper [12], and the other algorithms from jMetal [20].

We use the hypervolume as a performance measure because the hypervolume is one of the best performance measures especially for high-dimensional objective problems. However, it is important to specify the reference point for calculating the hypervolume [21]. The objective vector is normalized using the ideal point z^I and the nadir point z^N of the exact (i.e., true) Pareto front. Thus, the range of the Pareto front in the normalized objective space is from 0.0 to 1.0. We specify the reference point for hypervolume calculation as (1.1, 1.1, ..., 1.1) on the DTLZ1-4 and the WFG1-4 problems. This specification is not the best choice for the high-dimensional objective problems with the inverted Pareto front as in [21]. Therefore, we specify the reference point for hypervolume calculation as (1.1, 1.1, ..., 1.1) on the three- and five-objective problems and as (2.0, 2.0, ..., 2.0) on the eight- and ten-objective problems.

The average hypervolume values over 51 runs on the DTLZ1-4 and the WFG1-4 problems using MOEA/D variants and other algorithms are summarized in Tables 1 and 2. Figures 3 and 4 show the obtained solutions by a single run with the median hypervolume value on the three-objective DTLZ1 problem.

In almost all problems, the better results are obtained from the standard weights in Tables 1 and 2. This is because the weight vector distribution is suitable for those problems with the triangular Pareto fronts. We can also see that almost all algorithms using the standard weights can obtain solutions over the entire Pareto front while these algorithms using the inverted weight vectors cannot obtain solutions distributed over the entire Pareto front as in Figs. 3 and 4.

The average hypervolume values over 51 runs on the Minus-DTLZ1-4 and the Minus-WFG1-4 problems using MOEA/D variants and other algorithms are summarized in Tables 3 and 4. Figures 5 and 6 show the obtained solutions by a single run with the median hypervolume value on the three-objective Minus-DTLZ1 problem. As we mentioned in Sect. 1, one may expect better results by using the inverted weight vectors. However, MOEA/D variants cannot obtain better results in Table 3 and Fig. 5. This is because the ideal point could not be obtained by MOEA/D variants with the

Table 1. Average hypervolume values over 51 runs on DTLZ and WFG using MOEA/D variants. The better results between the two weight vector specification methods (SW: Standard weight vector specification, IW: Inverted weight vector specification) are highlighted by red bold font ("$\times 10^{??}$" is omitted).

Problem	M	MOEA/D-DE-PBI SW	IW	MOEA/D-DE-Tch SW	IW	MOEA/D-STM-PBI SW	IW	MOEA/D-STM-Tch SW	IW
DTLZ1	3	**1.060**	0.939	**1.063**	0.960	**1.026**	0.901	**1.065**	0.960
	5	**1.567**	1.239	**1.136**	1.066	**1.567**	1.243	**1.203**	1.068
	8	**2.132**	1.648	**2.054**	1.206	**2.132**	1.646	**2.008**	1.215
	10	**2.592**	2.013	**2.516**	1.475	**2.592**	2.022	**2.515**	1.534
DTLZ2	3	**0.671**	0.554	**0.701**	0.614	**0.680**	0.556	**0.701**	0.614
	5	**1.022**	0.545	**1.131**	0.843	**1.042**	0.547	**1.133**	0.839
	8	**1.289**	0.468	**1.173**	0.631	**1.368**	0.471	**1.182**	0.612
	10	**2.090**	0.482	**1.444**	0.708	**2.137**	0.495	**1.430**	0.729
DTLZ3	3	**0.534**	0.433	**0.693**	0.590	**0.449**	0.422	**0.687**	0.591
	5	**0.868**	0.514	0.421	**0.796**	**0.812**	0.484	0.396	**0.800**
	8	**1.222**	0.424	**1.118**	0.548	**1.078**	0.389	**1.076**	0.505
	10	**2.118**	0.459	**1.403**	0.533	**2.175**	0.468	**1.373**	0.492
DTLZ4	3	**0.690**	0.550	**0.690**	0.622	**0.698**	0.568	**0.688**	0.626
	5	**1.231**	0.608	**1.105**	0.990	**1.233**	0.628	**1.117**	0.982
	8	**1.919**	0.637	1.321	**1.587**	**1.928**	0.645	1.318	**1.570**
	10	**2.481**	0.671	1.557	**2.032**	**2.484**	0.656	1.539	**2.000**
WFG1	3	**0.375**	0.309	**0.359**	0.321	**0.388**	0.308	**0.373**	0.325
	5	**0.472**	0.404	**0.475**	0.383	**0.514**	0.405	**0.834**	0.396
	8	**1.144**	0.493	**1.560**	1.014	**1.467**	0.519	**1.880**	1.344
	10	**2.297**	0.919	**2.452**	1.854	**2.287**	1.146	**2.423**	2.365
WFG2	3	**1.081**	0.887	**1.128**	1.081	**1.091**	0.897	**1.137**	1.091
	5	**1.505**	1.367	**1.523**	1.436	**1.511**	1.377	**1.537**	1.431
	8	**1.997**	1.957	**2.127**	2.002	**2.002**	1.965	**2.132**	1.991
	10	**2.457**	2.444	**2.592**	2.479	**2.462**	2.456	**2.592**	2.480
WFG3	3	**0.739**	0.529	**0.743**	0.649	**0.743**	0.530	**0.752**	0.652
	5	**0.820**	0.458	**0.855**	0.529	**0.831**	0.458	**0.862**	0.525
	8	**0.888**	0.438	**1.221**	0.456	**0.937**	0.438	**1.227**	0.462
	10	**0.863**	0.473	**1.675**	0.532	**0.916**	0.474	**1.696**	0.536
WFG4	3	**0.568**	0.373	**0.578**	0.498	**0.582**	0.382	**0.598**	0.517
	5	**0.929**	0.347	**0.750**	0.705	**0.981**	0.357	**0.817**	0.729
	8	**1.012**	0.340	**1.185**	0.961	**1.126**	0.350	**1.286**	0.983
	10	**1.333**	0.409	**1.831**	1.403	**1.473**	0.454	**1.717**	1.421

Table 2. Average hypervolume values over 51 runs on DTLZ and WFG using non-MOEA/D variants. The better results between the two weight vector specification methods (SW: Standard weight vector specification, IW: Inverted weight vector specification) are highlighted by red bold font ("$\times 10^{??}$" is omitted).

Problem	M	NSGA-III SW	NSGA-III IW	θ-DEA SW	θ-DEA IW	MOEA/DD SW	MOEA/DD IW	Global WASF-GA SW	Global WASF-GA IW
DTLZ1	3	**1.116**	0.933	**1.116**	0.910	**1.119**	0.975	1.093	**0.981**
	5	**1.577**	1.138	**1.578**	1.193	**1.578**	1.258	**1.561**	1.308
	8	**2.138**	1.596	**2.138**	1.567	**2.138**	1.664	**2.113**	1.698
	10	**2.593**	2.129	**2.593**	2.007	**2.593**	2.048	**2.586**	2.077
DTLZ2	3	**0.743**	0.551	**0.744**	0.560	**0.744**	0.585	**0.716**	0.706
	5	**1.303**	0.857	**1.307**	0.608	**1.308**	0.605	**1.262**	1.073
	8	**1.969**	0.502	**1.978**	0.504	**1.979**	0.553	**1.856**	0.848
	10	**2.509**	0.559	**2.514**	0.539	**2.515**	0.566	**2.439**	0.989
DTLZ3	3	**0.735**	0.530	**0.738**	0.514	**0.740**	0.583	**0.702**	0.650
	5	**1.300**	0.879	**1.304**	0.579	**1.307**	0.607	**1.246**	0.779
	8	**1.954**	0.793	**1.967**	0.456	**1.971**	0.543	**1.805**	0.785
	10	**2.507**	0.930	**2.513**	0.495	**2.515**	0.564	**2.416**	0.928
DTLZ4	3	**0.683**	0.611	**0.671**	0.567	**0.745**	0.586	**0.660**	0.632
	5	**1.308**	1.038	**1.309**	0.611	**1.309**	0.612	**1.264**	0.964
	8	**1.980**	0.881	**1.981**	0.742	**1.981**	0.561	**1.951**	0.989
	10	**2.515**	1.061	**2.515**	0.913	**2.515**	0.570	**2.505**	1.232
WFG1	3	**0.652**	0.512	**0.694**	0.536	**0.705**	0.519	**0.916**	0.570
	5	**0.851**	0.647	**1.148**	0.706	**1.233**	1.114	**1.526**	1.034
	8	**1.350**	0.855	**1.878**	1.328	**1.915**	1.753	**2.045**	1.615
	10	**2.215**	1.415	**2.386**	2.064	**2.359**	2.226	**2.470**	2.121
WFG2	3	**1.225**	1.059	**1.229**	1.074	**1.224**	1.087	**1.222**	1.157
	5	**1.598**	1.459	**1.597**	1.437	**1.556**	1.436	**1.603**	1.560
	8	**2.136**	1.969	**2.126**	1.959	**2.045**	2.000	**2.139**	2.085
	10	**2.589**	2.472	**2.577**	2.468	**2.492**	2.471	**2.591**	2.540
WFG3	3	**0.820**	0.230	**0.816**	0.489	**0.772**	0.600	0.838	**0.796**
	5	**1.009**	0.453	**1.027**	0.435	**0.954**	0.652	0.900	**0.939**
	8	**1.237**	0.636	**1.105**	0.542	**1.154**	0.788	**1.373**	1.180
	10	**1.574**	1.038	**1.555**	0.655	**1.382**	1.083	**1.689**	1.442
WFG4	3	**0.729**	0.509	**0.729**	0.563	**0.720**	0.496	**0.726**	0.596
	5	**1.285**	0.581	**1.287**	0.571	**1.261**	0.524	**1.226**	0.934
	8	**1.963**	0.476	**1.965**	0.481	**1.836**	0.551	**1.930**	1.319
	10	**2.503**	0.536	**2.503**	0.540	**2.237**	0.623	**2.499**	1.679

inverted weights as shown in Fig. 5. Even when we use DE and STM in MOEA/D for diversity maintenance, it is difficult for the MOEA/D variants to efficiently find the ideal point.

Global WASF-GA do not obtain the better results from the inverted weight vectors. NSGA-III, θ-DEA and MOEA/DD use the Pareto dominance relation for the first criterion. The weight vector is only used for the solution assignment for the second criterion, which maintains the population diversity. On the other hand, Global WASF-GA performs the search using a scalarizing function with weight vectors. This search mechanism is the same as MOEA/D. The search for the ideal point is difficult for the inverted weight vectors in the same way as MOEA/D as we mentioned in Sect. 1.

Although MOEA/DD has the same hybrid structure with dominance-based and decomposition-based approaches as NSGA-III and θ-DEA, MOEA/DD with the

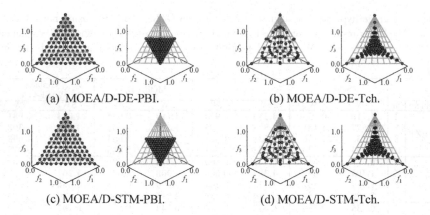

Fig. 3. Obtained solution sets in the normalized objective space by a single run on the three-objective DTLZ1 using MOEA/D variants with standard weight vectors (Left) and inverted weight vectors (Right).

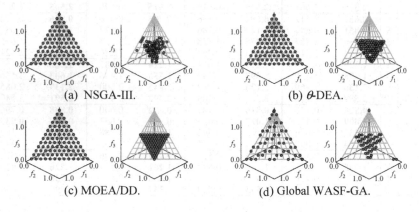

Fig. 4. Obtained solution sets in the normalized objective space by a single run on the three-objective DTLZ1 using non-MOEA/D variants with standard weight vectors (Left) and inverted weight vectors (Right).

inverted weights comparatively could not obtain the better results. One of the major differences between MOEA/DD and the other algorithms (i.e., NSGA-III and θ-DEA) is the presence of the neighborhood selection mechanism. Thanks to this mechanism, MOEA/DD can generate the similar offspring to the parent solutions. Whereas this mechanism seems to have a positive effect on uniformity, it may also have a negative effect on the search for the entire Pareto front. NSGA-III and θ-DEA do not have the neighborhood mechanism. The parent solutions to generate offspring are selected from the whole population so that they can search the whole objective space.

NSGA-III and θ-DEA can especially obtain the better results from the inverted weight vectors on the problems with the inverted triangular Pareto front whereas other algorithms cannot obtain the better results from the inverted weights on the

Table 3. Average hypervolume values over 51 runs on the Minus-DTLZ and Minus-WFG using MOEA/D variants. The better results between the two weight vector specification methods (SW: Standard weight vector specification, IW: Inverted weight vector specification) are highlighted by red bold font ("$\times 10^{??}$" is omitted).

Problem	M	MOEA/D-DE-PBI		MOEA/D-DE-Tch		MOEA/D-STM-PBI		MOEA/D-STM-Tch	
		SW	IW	SW	IW	SW	IW	SW	IW
Minus-DTLZ1	3	**2.293**	1.878	**2.297**	1.798	**2.398**	1.894	**2.356**	1.858
	5	**1.680**	1.078	**0.934**	0.426	**1.753**	1.121	**0.939**	0.458
	8	**0.652**	0.345	**1.477**	0.354	**0.656**	0.350	**1.469**	0.354
	10	**0.654**	0.332	**2.119**	0.363	**0.655**	0.339	**2.059**	0.363
Minus-DTLZ2	3	**6.883**	6.867	**6.821**	5.477	**6.893**	6.862	**6.821**	5.497
	5	1.596	**2.055**	**1.559**	1.073	1.602	**2.012**	**1.559**	1.042
	8	2.246	**3.649**	**3.956**	1.475	2.232	**3.676**	**3.961**	1.436
	10	3.130	**6.091**	**6.770**	1.814	3.143	**5.958**	**6.755**	1.775
Minus-DTLZ3	3	**5.984**	5.327	**5.767**	4.670	**5.998**	5.491	**5.928**	4.669
	5	**1.403**	0.951	**1.182**	0.673	**1.396**	1.065	**1.219**	0.702
	8	**1.858**	1.691	**2.559**	1.078	**1.878**	1.793	**2.630**	1.081
	10	**2.704**	2.441	**4.485**	1.333	2.833	**3.045**	**4.760**	1.291
Minus-DTLZ4	3	6.735	**6.828**	**6.777**	5.581	**6.908**	6.839	**6.805**	5.590
	5	1.405	**1.844**	**1.326**	1.228	1.457	**1.849**	**1.355**	1.247
	8	1.988	**2.051**	**3.614**	1.941	1.875	**2.051**	**3.634**	1.830
	10	2.599	**3.059**	**6.062**	3.069	2.541	**3.056**	**6.113**	2.802
Minus-WFG1	3	**1.119**	0.992	**1.275**	0.879	**1.111**	0.991	**1.275**	0.887
	5	**1.556**	0.772	**2.622**	1.091	**1.553**	0.789	**2.647**	1.102
	8	**0.562**	0.468	**1.201**	0.410	**0.556**	0.460	**1.207**	0.403
	10	**0.560**	0.519	**1.561**	0.421	**0.560**	0.511	**1.572**	0.397
Minus-WFG2	3	**2.709**	1.995	**3.473**	3.383	**2.870**	2.031	**3.562**	3.421
	5	**0.054**	0.016	**0.065**	0.029	**0.058**	0.016	**0.072**	0.031
	8	**0.766**	0.382	**1.611**	0.482	**0.786**	0.382	**1.620**	0.483
	10	**0.838**	0.383	**2.125**	0.462	**0.843**	0.382	**2.139**	0.463
Minus-WFG3	3	**2.300**	1.154	**1.965**	1.231	**2.379**	1.226	**2.020**	1.248
	5	**0.429**	0.061	**0.537**	0.125	**0.471**	0.065	**0.564**	0.129
	8	**0.593**	0.253	**1.418**	0.350	**0.598**	0.254	**1.445**	0.352
	10	**0.640**	0.256	**2.057**	0.359	**0.642**	0.255	**2.076**	0.358
Minus-WFG4	3	**6.796**	5.745	**6.598**	5.232	**6.806**	5.794	**6.618**	5.231
	5	**1.328**	0.602	**0.845**	0.492	**1.346**	0.620	**0.853**	0.474
	8	**1.689**	1.166	**3.470**	1.123	**1.697**	1.178	**3.488**	1.124
	10	**2.200**	1.573	**5.497**	1.438	**2.204**	1.578	**5.533**	1.434

Minus-DTLZ and the Minus-WFG. These algorithms have the hybrid structure with dominance-based and decomposition-based approaches. They do not have the neighborhood selection mechanism and the solutions are generated from the whole population. Thus, they have no difficulty of search for the best value of each objective by only one weight vector. In these algorithms, solutions with the last dominance rank in the population are assigned to the weight vectors for the second criterion and then the solutions are selected as the next population based on this criterion. One of the big differences between NSGA-III and θ-DEA is how to choose the assigned solutions.

In NSGA-III, the solutions already selected as the next population are assigned to the closest weight vector. Let ρ be the number of these solutions assigned to a weight vector. The solutions with the last dominance rank are assigned to the closest weight vector. Let ρ' be the number of these assigned solutions with the last dominance rank.

Table 4. Average hypervolume values over 51 runs on the Minus-DTLZ and Minus-WFG using non-MOEA/D variants. The better results between the two weight vector specification methods (SW: Standard weight vector specification, IW: Inverted weight vector specification) are highlighted by red bold font ("$\times 10^{??}$" is omitted).

Problem	M	NSGA-III SW	NSGA-III IW	θ-DEA SW	θ-DEA IW	MOEA/DD SW	MOEA/DD IW	Global WASF-GA SW	Global WASF-GA IW
Minus-DTLZ1	3	2.728	**2.748**	2.507	**2.955**	2.486	**2.934**	**2.697**	2.308
	5	1.250	**1.471**	0.893	**1.594**	0.989	**1.962**	0.925	**1.073**
	8	0.744	**2.048**	0.646	**2.057**	0.668	**0.793**	**1.077**	0.571
	10	0.782	**3.043**	0.396	**3.077**	0.733	**0.866**	**1.303**	0.655
Minus-DTLZ2	3	**6.907**	4.942	**6.925**	6.250	**6.892**	6.618	**6.828**	6.255
	5	1.400	**1.588**	1.322	**1.636**	0.845	**1.574**	0.836	**1.306**
	8	2.800	**3.479**	1.996	**3.517**	2.068	**2.368**	**3.455**	2.038
	10	4.623	**5.622**	3.307	**6.131**	2.748	**4.044**	**5.849**	3.377
Minus-DTLZ3	3	**6.926**	5.371	**6.953**	6.521	**6.898**	6.816	**6.826**	6.282
	5	1.295	**1.557**	1.382	**1.668**	0.801	**1.736**	0.830	**1.352**
	8	2.650	**3.400**	2.084	**3.603**	2.045	**2.567**	**3.461**	2.100
	10	4.341	**5.828**	3.349	**6.556**	2.730	**4.434**	**5.808**	3.518
Minus-DTLZ4	3	**6.937**	6.633	**6.954**	6.912	6.892	**6.992**	**6.827**	6.219
	5	1.216	**1.467**	1.153	**1.695**	0.723	**2.179**	0.827	**1.694**
	8	3.540	**4.220**	2.348	**4.434**	1.709	**3.832**	**3.368**	2.937
	10	**6.484**	3.598	4.205	**8.126**	2.429	**6.846**	**5.747**	5.567
Minus-WFG1	3	**1.119**	0.706	**0.925**	0.475	**0.813**	0.327	**1.196**	0.282
	5	**2.178**	2.080	**1.526**	1.430	**0.935**	0.464	**1.040**	0.345
	8	0.541	**0.772**	0.539	**0.575**	**0.339**	0.269	**0.523**	0.222
	10	0.549	**0.961**	0.512	**0.700**	**0.361**	0.293	**0.575**	0.224
Minus-WFG2	3	**3.837**	3.249	**3.838**	3.145	**3.810**	3.196	**3.768**	3.282
	5	**0.106**	0.094	0.080	**0.095**	**0.061**	0.037	**0.075**	0.055
	8	1.034	**1.484**	0.779	**1.414**	**0.891**	0.654	**1.352**	0.559
	10	1.053	**1.996**	0.621	**1.861**	**0.946**	0.738	**1.635**	0.611
Minus-WFG3	3	**2.652**	2.160	2.497	**2.922**	**2.330**	1.920	**2.643**	2.570
	5	**1.297**	1.075	0.906	**1.238**	**0.410**	0.110	0.444	**0.906**
	8	**0.832**	0.298	0.404	**0.857**	**0.631**	0.422	**1.235**	0.576
	10	0.824	**0.869**	0.384	**0.927**	**0.685**	0.456	**1.538**	0.631
Minus-WFG4	3	**6.623**	5.990	**6.881**	6.609	**6.632**	5.614	**6.678**	6.616
	5	1.286	**1.516**	**1.442**	1.380	**1.106**	0.363	0.502	**1.337**
	8	**3.039**	2.654	2.389	**3.354**	**1.510**	1.057	**3.028**	2.294
	10	**4.901**	3.095	2.585	**5.381**	**1.858**	1.225	**4.726**	3.180

If ρ is zero (a solution is yet selected as the next population) and ρ' is not zero, the closest solution to the weight vector is selected as the next population. If ρ is not zero (i.e., one or more solutions are already assigned to the weight vector) and ρ' is not zero, a solution is selected at random. If ρ' is zero (i.e., no solution with the last dominance rank is assigned to the weight vector), the weight vector is ignored for selecting solutions as the next population. In other words, if the weight vector has no solution with the last dominance rank, no solution is obtained for the corresponding weight vector. As in Fig. 7 (a), no solutions are assigned to the red weight vectors (because of the infeasible objective space) and the blue weight vectors can have some solutions. Thus, the solutions can be obtained for the blue weight vectors whereas a lot of solutions are randomly distributed over the Pareto front because ρ of the blue weight vectors is usually not zero and the red weight vectors are ignored for selecting the

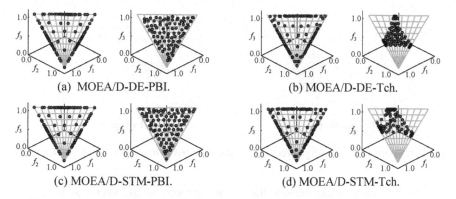

(a) MOEA/D-DE-PBI.   (b) MOEA/D-DE-Tch.

(c) MOEA/D-STM-PBI.   (d) MOEA/D-STM-Tch.

Fig. 5. Obtained solution sets in the normalized objective space by a single run on the three-objective Minus-DTLZ1 using MOEA/D variants with standard weight vectors (Left) and inverted weight vectors (Right).

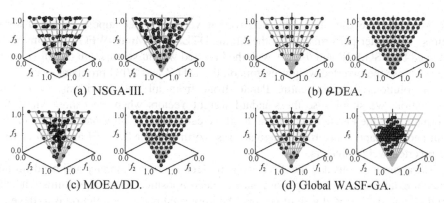

(a) NSGA-III.   (b) θ-DEA.

(c) MOEA/DD.   (d) Global WASF-GA.

Fig. 6. Obtained solution sets in the normalized objective space by a single run on the three-objective Minus-DTLZ1 using non-MOEA/D variants with standard weight vectors (Left) and inverted weight vectors (Right).

solutions as the next population. On the other hand, all the weight vectors are distributed on the Pareto front as in Fig. 7 (b) so that no weight vector is ignored in selection of the solutions. Thus, if the solution distribution is close to the Pareto front, the obtained solutions are well-distributed over the Pareto front.

In θ-DEA, the solutions with the last dominance rank are assigned to the closest weight vector. The assigned solutions are sorted using θ-dominance based on the distance between the corresponding weight vector and the solution. The weight vectors without any solution are ignored in θ-dominance sorting of θ-DEA in the same way as NSGA-III. Moreover, in θ-dominance, the closest solutions to each weight vector are selected to the next population. Thus, if the solutions are distributed near the Pareto front, the obtained solutions are usually distributed on the blue weight vectors in Fig. 7 (a). As a result, the solution distribution gets sparse as shown in Fig. 6(b). However, if

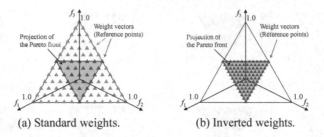

(a) Standard weights.   (b) Inverted weights.

Fig. 7. Relation between weight vectors and the inverted Pareto front. (Color figure online)

we use the inverted weight vectors, there is no ignored weight vector as in Fig. 7(b). Thus, we can obtain the well-distributed solutions as in Fig. 6(b).

5   Concluding Remarks

We examined the use of the inverted weight vectors in decomposition-based algorithms. The better performance on the Minus-DTLZ and Minus-WFG problems were obtained by NSGA-III and θ-DEA with the inverted weight vectors. On the other hand, when we use the inverted weight vectors on the DTLZ and WFG problems, we cannot obtain solutions over the entire Pareto front from all the algorithms. From this observation, we should use the standard weight vectors when we cannot know the information of the Pareto front. However, if we can know the information of the Pareto front and its shape is inverted triangular, it is worth to use NSGA-III and θ-DEA with the inverted weight vectors.

These observations and the discussions in Sect. 4 are preliminary and need further detailed examinations of the performance of decomposition-based algorithms with the standard and the inverted weight vectors. An important research direction is to develop an efficient and effective adaptation mechanism of weight vectors depending on the characteristics of each decomposition-based algorithm.

References

1. Deb, K.: Multi-Objective Optimization Using Evolutionary Algorithms. Wiley, Chichester (2001)
2. Deb, K., Pratap, A., Agarwal, S., Meyarivan, T.: A fast and elitist multiobjective genetic algorithm: NSGA-II. IEEE Trans. Evol. Comput. **6**, 182–197 (2002)
3. Zitzler, E., Laumanns, M., Thiele, L.: SPEA2: improving the strength Pareto evolutionary algorithm. TIK-Report 103, Computer Engineering and Networks Laboratory (TIK), Department of Electrical Engineering, ETH, Zurich (2001)
4. Beume, N., Naujoks, B., Emmerich, M.: SMS-EMOA: multiobjective selection based on dominated hypervolume. Eur. J. Oper. Res. **181**, 1653–1669 (2007)
5. Bader, J., Zitzler, E.: HypE: an algorithm for fast hypervolume-based many-objective optimization. Evol. Comput. **19**, 45–76 (2011)

6. Zhang, Q., Li, H.: MOEA/D: a multiobjective evolutionary algorithm based on decomposition. IEEE Trans. Evol. Comput. **11**, 712–731 (2007)
7. Li, H., Zhang, Q.: Multiobjective optimization problems with complicated Pareto sets, MOEA/D and NSGA-II. IEEE Trans. Evol. Comput. **13**, 284–302 (2009)
8. Li, K., Zhang, Q., Kwong, S., Li, M., Wang, R.: Stable matching-based selection in evolutionary multiobjective optimization. IEEE Trans. Evol. Comput. **18**, 909–923 (2014)
9. Deb, K., Jain, H.: An evolutionary many-objective optimization algorithm using reference-point-based non-dominated sorting approach, part I: solving problems with box constraints. IEEE Trans. Evol. Comput. **18**, 577–601 (2014)
10. Jain, H., Deb, K.: An evolutionary many-objective optimization algorithm using reference-point based non-dominated sorting approach, part II: handling constraints and extending to an adaptive approach. IEEE Trans. Evol. Comput. **18**, 602–622 (2014)
11. Yuan, Y., Xu, H., Wang, B., Yao, X.: A new dominance relation based evolutionary algorithm for many-objective optimization. IEEE Trans. Evol. Comput. **20**, 16–37 (2016)
12. Li, K., Deb, K., Zhang, Q., Kwong, S.: An evolutionary many-objective optimization algorithm based on dominance and decomposition. IEEE Trans. Evol. Comput. **19**, 694–716 (2015)
13. Saborido, R., Ruiz, A.B., Luque, M.: Global WASF-GA: an evolutionary algorithm in multiobjective optimization to approximate the whole Pareto optimal front. Evol. Comput. **25**, 309–349 (2017)
14. Ishibuchi, H., Setoguchi, Y., Masuda, H., Nojima, Y.: Performance of decomposition-based many-objective algorithms strongly depends on Pareto front shapes. IEEE Trans. Evol. Comput. **21**, 169–190 (2017)
15. Ishibuchi, H., Imada, R., Doi, K., Nojima, Y.: Use of inverted triangular weight vectors in decomposition-based multiobjective algorithms. In: Proceedings of 2017 IEEE International Conference on Systems, Man, and Cybernetics (in press)
16. Deb, K., Thiele, L., Laumanns, M., Zitzler, E.: Scalable multi-objective optimization test problems. In: Proceedings of 2013 Congress on Evolutionary Computation, pp. 825–830 (2002)
17. Price, K., Storn, R.M., Lampinen, J.A.: Differential Evolution: A Practical Approach to Global Optimization. Springer Natural Computing Series, Heidelberg (2005)
18. MOEA/DD Code. http://www.cs.bham.ac.uk/~likw/publications.html. Accessed 15 July 2016
19. Yuan's Many-Objective EA Codes. https://github.com/yyxhdy/ManyEAs. Accessed 15 July 2016
20. jMetal Website. http://jmetal.sourceforge.net/. Accessed 19 May 2017
21. Ishibuchi, H., Imada, R., Setoguchi, Y., Nojima, Y.: Reference point specification in hypervolume calculation for fair comparison and efficient search. In: Proceedings of 2017 Genetic and Evolutionary Computation Conference, pp. 585–592 (2017)

Surrogate Model Assisted Multi-objective Differential Evolution Algorithm for Performance Optimization at Software Architecture Level*

Du Xin[1], Ni Youcong[1(✉)], Wu Xiaobin[1], Ye Peng[2], and Xin Yao[3]

[1] Faculty of Software, Fujian Normal University, Fuzhou 350117, China
youcongni@foxmail.com
[2] College of Mathematics and Computer,
Wuhan Textile University, Wuhan 430200, China
[3] Department of Computer Science and Engineering,
Southern University of Science and Technology, Shenzhen 518055, China

Abstract. This paper proposes a surrogate model assisted differential evolutionary algorithm for performance optimization at the software architecture (SA) level, which is named SMDE4PO. In SMDE4PO, different strategies of crossover and mutation are adopted to enhance the algorithm's search capability and speed up its convergence. Random forests are used as surrogate models to reduce the time of performance evaluation (i.e., fitness evaluation). Our comparative experiments on four different sizes of cases between SMDE4PO and NSGA-II are conducted. From the results, we can conclude that (1) SMDE4PO is significantly better than NSGA-II according to the three quality indicators of Contribution, Generation Distance and Hyper Volume; (2) By using random forests as surrogates, the run time of SMDE4PO is reduced by up to 48% in comparison with NSGA-II in our experiments.

Keywords: Software architecture · Performance optimization · Differential evolution · Surrogate model

1 Introduction

The software architecture (SA) of a program or computing system is the structure or structures of the system, which comprise software elements, the externally visible properties of those elements, and the relationships among them [1]. Based on architecture-based performance analysis and evaluation, performance problems (e.g., high resource utilization rate, long response time and low throughput) are found and their negative effects can be mitigated at the early stages of the software lifecycle. With that in mind, architecture-based software performance optimization [2] has been a highlight topic among academia and industry in the field of software engineering and performance engineering. Especially, how to obtain the optimal SA in the huge space of performance improvement has become a hot research subject in academia and industry [3].

© Springer International Publishing AG 2017
Y. Shi et al. (Eds.): SEAL 2017, LNCS 10593, pp. 334–346, 2017.
https://doi.org/10.1007/978-3-319-68759-9_28

In recent years, rule-based and metaheuristic-based approaches to automatic per-formance optimization have been proposed [3]. The rule-based approaches [4] describe performance improvement knowledge in terms of machine processable rules at SA level. Due to the limitation of definition and usage of rules, the rule-based approaches can only search limited performance improvement space to exclude the optimal improvement solution. Although meta-heuristic methods can search the larger space and can obtain better performance improvement solution, most of them have not fully considered the following two problems: (1) the values of variable SA elements not only have different types, such as numeric and category, but also need to be limited in a certain range. This results in a high discontinuity of performance improvement space; (2) in the evolutionary process, it is a high-cost and time-consuming to obtain the values of performance indices (such as system response time, utilization) by architecture-based performance evaluation.

To solve the two problems mentioned above, this paper proposes SMDE4PO that takes Random Forests (RFs) as a surrogate model to reduce the run time of perfor-mance optimization, as well as improve the quality of optimized solution.

2   Related Work

2.1   Performance Evaluation at the SA Level

A few architecture-based performance evaluation methods adopting well-known per-formance models and analysis tools have been proposed in the past several years. These methods can be used during optimizing performance. Several well-known performance models adopted by these methods are Queuing Network (QN), Layered Queuing Network (LQN), Stochastic Petri Net (SPN) and so on [2]. It is noteworthy that performance evaluation is a time-consuming step with considerably high computational effort in the process of performance optimization. For simplicity, only the response time is discussed in this paper.

2.2   Metaheuristics-Based Performance Optimization Method at the SA Level

For different SA modeling languages, various metaheuristics-based performance optimization methods by designing different metaheuristics algorithms are proposed.

(1) **Methods for Palladio Component Model (PCM).** Martens [5] used hill climbing algorithm and particle swarm optimization algorithm to optimize the system response time respectively. Koziolek [6] used the NSGA-II algorithm to optimize the system response time and hardware cost. Martens used the NSGA-II algorithm to optimize the performance, availability/reliability and hardware cost of the system in [7].

(2) **Methods for East-AADL modeling language**. Li [8] used the NSGA-II algo-rithm to optimize data-flow latency, processor usage and cost of the system. Etemaadi [9] applied the NSGA-II algorithm to optimize system performance,

security and hardware cost. Walker [10] used the NSGA-II algorithm to optimize system performance, reliability, and hardware cost.

(3) **Methods for AADL modeling language**. Mccdcniya [11] and Rahmoun [12] used NSGA-II algorithm to optimize the system performance and reliability.

2.3   Surrogate Model for Evolutionary Algorithms

The surrogate model is constructed to estimate the value of objective function to reduce the call-frequency of the objective function. In [13], PRS, Kriging, RBFN, SVM and RF are pointed to be often used as the surrogate models for evolutionary algorithms. There are three control strategies for training a surrogate model in the evolutionary algorithms [13]. They are No Evolution Control (NEC), Fixed Evolution Control (FEC) and Adaptive Evolution Control (AEC). While FEC is widely used because of its good performance. SMDE4PO adopts the FEC to improve the accuracy of surrogate model.

3   Architecture-Based Performance Optimization

For the two objectives of response time and hardware cost, a formal description for architecture-based performance optimization is given as follows.

Definition 1 (Objective functions). The functions $rest(SA)$ and $cost(SA)$ can respectively obtain the value of the system response time and hardware cost by evaluating the performance and cost in terms of SA.

Definition 2 (Solution). Suppose that the number of variable elements in SA is D and each element can be taken as a certain variable integer or real within a certain range. Then the solution X of performance optimization problem at SA level can be formulated as a vector $(x_1, x_2, x_3, \cdots, x_D)$ whose dimension is D. The upper and lower bounds of the value of the jth dimension variable are represented by x_j^L and x_j^U in formula (1).

$$x_j^L \leq x_j \leq x_j^U, \, j = 1, 2, \cdots, D \tag{1}$$

The processing rate (PR) of each server can be regarded as a variable element. Its value often takes a real in a specified range. If the values of some variable elements which have category type (e.g. component deployment, component selection) are mapping into integer set starting from 1, then they can take an integer within a certain range.

Definition 3 (SA's Generation). The function $genSA(X)$ returns the resulting SA by modifying the SA_0 based on the values of variable elements defined by X.

Definition 4 (The architecture-based performance optimization). The architecture-based performance optimization can be abstracted as the two-objective optimization problem defined by formula (2). In formula (2), the objective functions of $f_1(X)$ and $f_2(X)$ respectively obtain the system response time and cost for improvement in terms of the result SA generated by X. Formulas (3) and (4) represent Pareto optimal solution set *Opt* for the problem defined by formula (2). In formulas (3) and (4), the notations $\prec$ and Ω represent dominance relation and the solution space, respectively.

$$f_1(X) = rest(genSA(X))$$
$$f_2(X) = cost(genSA(X))$$
$$\text{Minimize } F(X) = (f_1(X), f_2(X)) \tag{2}$$

$$X' \prec X \triangleq \left(f_1(X') \leq f_1(X) \bigwedge f_2(X') < f_2(X) \right) \vee \left(f_1(X') < f_1(X) \bigwedge f_2(X') \leq f_2(X) \right) \tag{3}$$

$$Opt = \left\{ X \,\middle|\, \nexists X' \in \Omega \bigwedge (X' \prec X) \right\} \tag{4}$$

4   Surrogate Model Assisted Multi-objective Differential Evolution Algorithm for Performance Optimization at the SA Level

To solve the problem defined in formula (2), a surrogate model assisted performance differential evolutionary optimization algorithm named SMDE4PO is proposed based on DEMO algorithm [14] in this paper.

4.1   Initial Population

The encoding of the ith individual $x_i(0) = \{x_{1,i}(0), x_{2,i}(0), \cdots, x_{D,i}(0)\}$ in the initial population can be randomly generated based on the formulas (5) and (6). In formulas (5) and (6), $x_{j,i}(0)$ is the encoding in the jth dimension of the ith individual, where $rand(0, 1)$ generates a uniformly distributed random variable in the range of 0 to 1, *ceil* is a ceiling function. The initial value of the jth dimension of real-coded and integer-coded can be randomly generated by formulas (5) and (6), respectively.

$$x_{j,i}(0) = x_j^L + rand(0, 1) \cdot \left(x_j^U - x_j^L \right) \tag{5}$$

$$x_{j,i}(0) = ceil\left(x_j^L + rand(0, 1) \cdot \left(x_j^U - x_j^L \right) \right) \tag{6}$$

4.2   Objective Function

The objective function takes the individual x as input and outputs the two objective values (response time and cost) of its corresponding candidate solution. Figure 1 shows the process of calculating the objective values. The calculation of hardware cost is divided into two steps. First, calculate the $genSA(x)$ to obtain the resulting software architecture SA^*; Second, calculate the $cost(SA^*)$ and output the value of hardware cost. Due to the high computational cost and long time-consuming of the system response time, the SMDE4PO algorithm takes the RFs as a surrogate model to predict the system response time. Specifically, the process of solving the system response time includes the solving phase, the prediction phase, and the transitions phase, which is shown in three dashed box of Fig. 1.

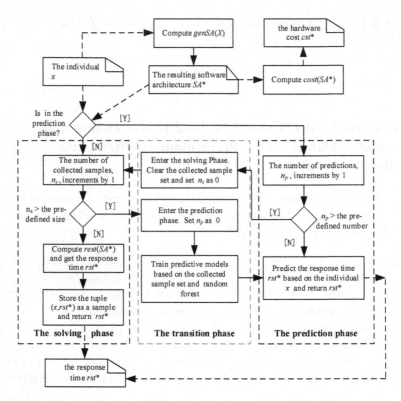

Fig. 1. The process of calculating the objective values in SMDE4PO algorithm

4.3 Mutation Operator

The mutation operator includes two steps. Firstly, a corresponding mutant vector v_i is produced by employing a mutation strategy selected randomly from a predefined differential strategy pool on the individual x_i. Secondly, each dimension j of $v_i(v_{j,i})$ is checked whether it is over-bounded based on Definition 2. The formulas (7) and (8) define the way to repair its value when $v_{j,i}$ disobeys Definition 2. The former is for the real-coded $v_{j,i}$ and the latter is for integer-coded $v_{j,i}$.

In SMDE4PO algorithm, four kinds of strategies are selected from the differential strategy pool defined in [15] to prevent the population from getting into local optimal solution and speed up the convergence rate. They are DE/best/2, DE/best/1, DE/rand/2 and DE/current-to-rand/1. In addition, F is the scaling factor [15], which guides the amplitude of the influence of the difference vector.

$$v_{j,i}(g) = \begin{cases} \frac{x_j^L + x_{j,i}(g)}{2}, & \text{if } v_{j,i}(g) < x_j^L \\ \frac{x_j^U + x_{j,i}(g)}{2}, & \text{if } v_{j,i}(g) > x_j^U \end{cases} \tag{7}$$

$$v_{j,i}(g) = \begin{cases} ceil\left(\frac{x_j^L + x_{j,i}(g)}{2}\right), & \text{if } v_{j,i}(g) < x_j^L \\ ceil\left(\frac{x_j^U + x_{j,i}(g)}{2}\right), & \text{if } v_{j,i}(g) > x_j^U \end{cases} \tag{8}$$

4.4 Cross Operator

In SMDE4PO, a crossover strategy is selected from a predefined crossover strategy pool composed of binomial distribution and exponential distribution crossover strategies. It is used to generate trail vector u_i based on each pair of target vector x_i and its corresponding mutation vector v_i.

The binomial crossover operator is shown as formula (9) where j_{rand} is a random integer in [1, NP] (NP is the population size) and CR is crossover probability. The exponential crossover is more complicated. Firstly, the initial crossover position k of $u_{j,i}(g)$ is generated randomly on [1, D] and the length l of consecutive crossover bits are generated, which is shown in Fig. 2. Secondly, the crossover range $[low, high]$ is determined by formulas (10) and (11). Finally, each bit in the crossover range of $u_i(g)$ is set to $v_{j,i}(g)$ and other bits are set to $x_{j,i}(g)$.

```
l = 0
Do
    l = l + 1
While (rand(0,1) < CR and l < D)
```

Fig. 2. The pseudocode for generating the length of crossover bits

$$u_{j,i}(g) = \begin{cases} v_{j,i}(g) & \text{if } \left(rand_j(0,1) \leq CR \text{ or } j = j_{rand}\right) \\ x_{j,i}(g) & \text{else} \end{cases} \tag{9}$$

$$low = \begin{cases} k & \text{if } (k+l) \leq D \\ (k+l) \mod D & \text{otherwise} \end{cases} \tag{10}$$

$$high = \begin{cases} (k+l) & \text{if } (k+l) \leq D \\ D & \text{otherwise} \end{cases} \tag{11}$$

4.5   Selection Operator

The greedy strategy shown in formula (12) is used to select the individuals in the next generation population. In formula (12), $\tilde{P}(g)$ represents the temporary population in g^{th} generation, which will be set to empty before the evolution of gth population. Here, $\prec$ denotes the domination relation, which is defined in formula (3).

$$\tilde{P}(g) = \begin{cases} \tilde{P}(g) \cup x_i(g), & if \; x_i(g) \prec u_i(g) \\ \tilde{P}(g) \cup u_i(g), & else \end{cases} \tag{12}$$

4.6   The Algorithm

The SMDE4PO algorithm is shown in Table 1. The truncation method on the temporary population $\tilde{P}(g)$ in row 12 is the same as that in [14]. They all use non-dominated rank and the crowding distance to sort individuals, and then select NP individuals (NP is the population size).

Table 1. The SMDE4PO algorithm

1	Evolutionary generation $t \leftarrow 0$
2	Generate random population $P(t)$, the population size is NP
3	Evaluate the objective values of each individual $x_i(t)$ in $P(t)$
4	While stopping criterion not met do
5	Empty the temporary population $\tilde{P}(t)$
6	$for(i := 1 \; to \; NP)$ do
7	Generate mutant vector $v_i(t)$ by mutation operator
8	Generate trail vector $u_i(t)$ by executing crossover operation on $v_i(t)$ and its corresponding target vector $x_i(t)$
9	Generate temporary population $\tilde{P}(t)$ by selecting individuals from $x_i(t)$ and $u_i(t)$
10	End for
11	If $|\tilde{P}(t)| > NP$ do
12	Generate new population whose size is NP by truncating $\tilde{P}(t)$
13	End if
14	$P(t + 1) \leftarrow \tilde{P}(t)$, and do the permutation of the individuals in $P(t + 1)$ randomly, $t \leftarrow t + 1$
15	End while
16	Solve the actual system response time of individual $x_i(t)$ in $P(t)$ and replace the corresponding target value with the actual response time
17	Output $P(t)$

5   Case Studies

5.1   Research Questions and Assessment Methods

Research Question 1 (RQ1): Which surrogate model is more suitable for SMDE4PO among the five popular predictive models, including PRS, Kriging, RBFN, SVM and

RF? In [13, 16], various surrogate models for evolutionary algorithms are summarized, and PRS, Kriging, RBFN, SVM and RF are regarded as five most popular surrogate models. So, these five models are considered as our candidates to be used in SMDE4PO.

We defines the Time of execution for Training and Prediction (TTP) and the Ranking Preservation (RP) as two indicators to answer RQ1. Here, TTP is the total execution time for training surrogate model and predicting the system response time. The value of TTP may vary with the size of samples of training and the number of inputs needed to be predicted. The smaller the TTP value is, the better the surrogate model is. While the RP [13] refers to the ability of surrogate model to maintain the same rank of the solutions with respect to the original function. The greater the RP value is, the better the surrogate model is.

Research Question 2 (RQ2): How effective is SMDE4PO compared to NSGA-II in terms of the response time and the hardware cost? NSGA-II not only is popular algorithm in performance optimization at SA level but also can obtain good solutions in the different cases. Therefore, we can verify the effectiveness and usefulness of SMDE4PO algorithm by answer the RQ2.

To provide the quantitative assessment for RQ2, we employ three quality indicators [17] for solution set, namely Contribution (I_C), Hypervolume (I_{HV}), and Generational Distance (I_{GD}). The larger the values of I_C and I_{HV} are, the better the quality of solution is. To let I_{GD} has the same range of values and changes of direction for good or bad as I_{HV} and I_C, the value of I_{GD} quality indicator in is reversed. Thus, the larger the value of I_{GD} is, the better the solution quality is.

Research Question 3 (RQ3): Does SMDE4PO significantly reduce the running time, compared with the NSGA-II algorithm, while maintaining a higher solution quality? The efficiency and effectiveness of the surrogate model are further studied by this research question.

5.2 Four Cases

The Business Reporting System (BRS) [7], Multimedia File Access System(MS) [18], Process Control System(PCS) [18] and Simple Design Policy Example(STE) [19] are selected to answer the above three questions RQ1, RQ2 and RQ3.

5.3 Statistical Methods Used

The nonparametric Wilcoxon rank-sum test is used to analyze and compare our experimental data. We set the confidence limit α at 0.05. The Wilcoxon rank-sum test can give statistically significant differences in the compared data. To further observe the degree of difference (effect size), $\hat{A}_{12}$ of Vargha-Delaney [20] is used as the intuitive measurement of the effect size. The value range of $\hat{A}_{12}$ is [0, 1]. The larger the value is, the greater the difference of compared algorithms is.

5.4 Experimental Setup

(1) The parameter setting for training surrogate model

To avoid the unfairness caused by improper parameter setting, each surrogate model is trained based on the parameters in Table 2. After training, there are five obtained surrogate models whose mean square error (MSE) is smallest for PRS, Kriging, RBFN, SVM and RF.

Table 2. The value or range of parameters used to train surrogate model

PRS	Degree	2
Kriging	Correlation function	{Gaussian, Cubic Exponential, Linear, Spherical, Spline}
RBFN	The number of neurons in the hidden layer	{3:100}
SVM	C	$\{2^{-5} : 2^{15}\}$
	γ	{0.1:2}
	ϵ	$\{2^{-10} : 2^5\}$
RF	Tree numbers	{1:1000}
	Features	{1:dimension size}

(2) The parameter setting of algorithms

The common parameters in NSGA-II and SMDE4PO algorithms are set as follows. The population size, crossover rate, mutation rate and generation are 30, 0.8, 0.6 and 200. The scaling factor F, the size of training samples and the times of prediction in each phase for SMDE4PO are [0.5, 1], 400 and 400 respectively. To realize the fair comparison, the number of individual evaluation of each algorithm is 6,000 in each run. For each case, the NSGA-II and SMDE4PO algorithms run independently 30 times.

5.5 Experimental Results

Experimental environment: Inter (R) Core (TM) 2 2.66 GHz processor, 2G memory and Win8.1 operating system.

(1) Answers to RQ1

The values of two quality indicators RP and TTP obtained by PRS, Kriging, RBFN, SVM and RF with the optimal train parameters are shown in Table 3. Table 3 shows that the values of two quality indicators RP and TTP acquired by RF are better than other values acquired by other four models.

To compare conveniently, not only the best values of two quality indicators RP and TTP in the row of RF but also the second best values of two quality indicators RP and TTP in each case are marked bold in Table 3. The experimental results show that RF is more suitable for surrogate model of performance evolutionary optimization algorithm at SA level than PRS, Kriging, RBFN and SVM models.

Table 3. The values of TTP and RP applied to PRS, Kriging, RBFN, SVM and RF models in BRS, MS, PCS, and STE cases

	BRS		MS		PCS		STE	
	RP	TTP	RP	TTP	RP	TTP	RP	TTP
PRS	**0.689**	393	**0.842**	262	0.808	382	0.514	**21**
Kriging	0.523	360	0.525	640	0.494	710	0.307	659
RBFN	0.492	306	0.527	**94**	0.532	**101**	0.558	93
SVM	0.679	**108**	0.831	110	**0.817**	122	**0.609**	101
RF	**0.751**	70	**0.844**	**66**	**0.818**	97	**0.614**	9

(2) Answers to RQ2

Table 4 shows the p-values obtained in Wilcoxon experiments by applying NSGA-II and SMDE4PO algorithms to BRS, MS, PCS and STE cases. From Table 4, we observe that the quality indicators of I_C, I_{GD} and I_{HV} gotten by SMDE4PO are significantly better than those of NSGA-II. This conclusion is consistent with the results of the statistical boxplot in Fig. 3. Table 5 presents the corresponding effect size for I_C, I_{GD} and I_{HV} indicators. The experimental results show that SMDE4PO is more effective than NSGA-II in terms of the response time and the hardware cost.

Table 4. The p-value obtained in Wilcoxon experiments applying NSGA-II and SMDE4PO algorithms to BRS, MS, PCS and STE cases

Case	I_C	I_{GD}	I_{HV}
BRS	7.0266e−07	7.0541e−07	7.0541e−07
MS	6.7193e−08	1.4309e−07	4.5031e−07
PCS	2.1802e−06	3.3918e−06	6.1516e−06
STE	6.7956e−08	5.8959e−05	0.7557

(3) Answers to RQ3

Table 6 and Fig. 4 show the average time-consuming of the NSGA-II and SMDE4PO algorithms in the BRS, MS, PCS and STE cases for 30 runs. Table 6 shows that the decreasing ratios of SMDE4PO on time-consuming compared with NSGA-II vary from 43% of the PCS case to 48% of the BRS case. The experimental results show that the surrogate model can reduce the running time because the number of performance evaluation is declined.

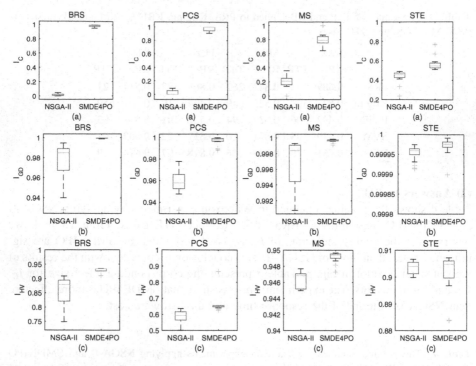

Fig. 3. Boxplots using the quality indicators I_C, I_{GD} and I_{HV} applied to NSGA-II and SMDE4PO algorithms in BRS (a), PCS (b), MS (c) and STE (d) cases.

Table 5. The effect size obtained in Wilcoxon experiments applying NSGA-II and SMDE4PO algorithms to BRS, MS, PCS and STE cases

Case	I_C	I_{GD}	I_{HV}
BRS	1.0	1.0	1.0
MS	1.0	0.9875	0.9850
PCS	1.0	1.0	0.9867
STE	1.0	0.8725	0.5300

Table 6. The comparison of the average time-consuming between NSGA-II and SMDE4PO algorithms by 30 runs in BRS, PCS, MS, and STE cases

	BRS	MS	PCS	STE
Average time-consuming of NSGA-II	4452	3693	5356	1860
Average time-consuming of SMDE4PO	2320	2007	3052	1020
The decreasing ratio of SMDE4PO on time-consuming compared with NSGA-II	48%	46%	43%	45%

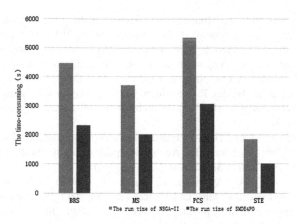

Fig. 4. The time-consuming comparison between NSGA-II and SMDE4PO in BRS, PCS, MS and STE cases

6   Conclusions and Future Work

In this paper, we propose a novel algorithm called SMDE4PO. SMDE4PO uses a variety of crossover and mutation strategies to enhance the search capability and improve the convergence rate. In addition, SMDE4PO adopts random forests as the surrogate model to estimate the response time. From the comparative experiments between SMDE4PO and NSGA-II, it can be concluded that SMDE4PO can obtain better solutions and reduce the running time. In the future, we will extend SMDE4PO to optimize performance, hardware cost, availability, and reliability simultaneously.

References

1. Taylor, R.N., Medvidovic, N., Dashofy, E.M.: Software Architecture: Foundations, Theory, and Practice. Wiley, Hoboken (2009)
2. Aleti, A., Buhnova, B., Grunske, L., Koziolek, A., Meedeniya, I.: Software architecture optimization methods: a systematic literature review. IEEE Trans. Softw. Eng. **39**(5), 658–683 (2013)
3. Koziolek, A.: Automated Improvement of Software Architecture Models for Performance and Other Quality Attributes. KIT Scientific Publishing, Karlsruhe (2014)
4. Du, X., Yao, X., Ni, Y., Minku, L.L., Ye, P., Xiao, R.: An evolutionary algorithm for performance optimization at software architecture level. In: 2015 IEEE Congress on Evolutionary Computation (CEC), pp. 2129–2136. IEEE, Sendai (2015)
5. Martens, A., Koziolek, H.: Automatic, model-based software performance improvement for component-based software designs. Electron. Notes Theoret. Comput. Sci. **253**(1), 77–93 (2009)
6. Koziolek, A., Koziolek, H., Reussner, R.: PerOpteryx: automated application of tactics in multi-objective software architecture optimization. In: Proceedings of Joint ACM SIGSOFT Conference–QoSA and ACM SIGSOFT Symposium–ISARCS, pp. 33–42. ACM, Boulder (2011)

7. Koziolek, A., Ardagna, D., Mirandola, R.: Hybrid multi-attribute QoS optimization in component based software systems. J. Syst. Softw. **86**(10), 2542–2558 (2013)

8. Li, R., Etemaadi, R., Emmerich, M.T., Chaudron, M.R.: An evolutionary multiobjective optimization approach to component-based software architecture design. In: 2011 IEEE Congress on Evolutionary Computation (CEC), pp. 432–439. IEEE, New Orleans (2011)

9. Etemaadi, R., Lind, K., Heldal, R., Chaudron, M.R.: Quality-driven optimization of system architecture: industrial case study on an automotive sub-system. J. Syst. Softw. **86**(10), 2559–2573 (2013)

10. Walker, M., Reiser, M.-O., Tucci-Piergiovanni, S., Papadopoulos, Y., Lönn, H., Mraidha, C., Parker, D., Chen, D., Servat, D.: Automatic optimisation of system architectures using EAST-ADL. J. Syst. Softw. **86**(10), 2467–2487 (2013)

11. Meedeniya, I., Aleti, A., Avazpour, I., Amin, A.: Robust archeopterix: architecture optimization of embedded systems under uncertainty. In: 2012 2nd International Workshop on, Software Engineering for Embedded Systems, pp. 23–29. IEEE, Zurich (2012)

12. Rahmoun, S., Borde, E., Pautet, L.: Automatic selection and composition of model transformations alternatives using evolutionary algorithms. In: Proceedings of 2015 European Conference on Software Architecture Workshops. p. 25. ACM, Dubrovnik (2015)

13. Díaz-Manríquez, A., Toscano-Pulido, G., Gómez-Flores, W.: On the selection of surrogate models in evolutionary optimization algorithms. In: 2011 IEEE Congress on Evolutionary Computation (CEC), pp. 2155–2162. IEEE, New Orleans (2011)

14. Robič, T., Filipič, B.: DEMO: differential evolution for multiobjective optimization. In: Coello Coello, C.A., Hernández Aguirre, A., Zitzler, E. (eds.) EMO 2005. LNCS, vol. 3410, pp. 520–533. Springer, Heidelberg (2005). doi:10.1007/978-3-540-31880-4_36

15. Mendes, R., Mohais, A.S.: DynDE: a differential evolution for dynamic optimization problems. In: 2005 IEEE Congress on Evolutionary Computation. pp. 2808–2815. IEEE, Edinburgh (2005)

16. Díaz-Manríquez, A., Toscano, G., Barron-Zambrano, J.H., Tello-Leal, E.: A review of surrogate assisted multi-objective evolutionary algorithms. Comput. Intell. Neurosci. **2016**, 1–14 (2016)

17. Zitzler, E., Thiele, L.: Multiobjective evolutionary algorithms: a comparative case study and the strength Pareto approach. IEEE Trans. Evol. Comput. **3**(4), 257–271 (1999)

18. Brosig, F., Meier, P., Becker, S., Koziolek, A., Koziolek, H., Kounev, S.: Quantitative evaluation of model-driven performance analysis and simulation of component-based architectures. IEEE Trans. Softw. Eng. **41**(2), 157–175 (2015)

19. https://svnserver.informatik.kit.edu/i43/svn/code/Palladio/Examples/ SimpleHeuristicsExample. Accessed 6 Aug 2017

20. Grissom, R.J., Kim, J.J.: Effect Sizes for Research: A Broad Practical Approach. Lawrence Erlbaum Associates, Mahwah (2005)

Normalized Ranking Based Particle Swarm Optimizer for Many Objective Optimization

Shi Cheng[1(✉)], Xiujuan Lei[1], Junfeng Chen[2], Jiqiang Feng[3], and Yuhui Shi[4]

[1] School of Computer Science, Shaanxi Normal University, Xi'an, China
cheng@snnu.edu.cn
[2] College of IOT Engineering, Hohai University, Changzhou, China
[3] Institute of Intelligent Computing Science, Shenzhen University, Shenzhen, China
[4] Shenzhen Key Lab of Computational Intelligence,
Department of Computer Science and Engineering,
Southern University of Science and Technology, Shenzhen, China
shiyh@sustc.edu.cn

Abstract. Nearly all solutions are Pareto non-dominated for multi-objective problems with more than three conflicting objectives. Thus, the comparison of solutions is a critical issue in many objective optimization. A simple but effective normalized ranking metric based method is proposed to compare solutions in this paper. All solutions are ranked by the sum of normalized fitness value of each objective. A solution with a small value is considered to be a good solution for minimum optimization problems. To enhance the population diversity of all solutions, the solutions with small values and the solutions with better fitness values on each objective are kept in an archive and updated per iteration. This ranking metric is further utilized in a particle swarm optimization algorithm to solve multiobjective and many objective problems. Four benchmark problems are utilized to test the proposed algorithm. Experimental results demonstrate that the proposed algorithm is a promising approach for solving the multiobjective and many objective optimization problems.

Keywords: Diversity maintaining · Multiple/many objective optimization · Particle swarm optimizer · Normalized ranking

1 Introduction

Many objective optimization refer to algorithms which solve problems with more than three conflicting objectives [2,10,17]. Unlike the multiobjective optimization, the Pareto optimality is not effective because nearly all solutions are Pareto non-dominated for problems with more than three objectives. The solution comparison, or the selection guidance of solutions is an essential issue in many objective optimization. Many algorithms and strategies have been proposed to handle the many objective optimization problems [1,20], such as two archive algorithm [17], objective reduction [19], and two stage strategy [11], etc.

© Springer International Publishing AG 2017
Y. Shi et al. (Eds.): SEAL 2017, LNCS 10593, pp. 347–357, 2017.
https://doi.org/10.1007/978-3-319-68759-9_29

The Pareto non-dominated solutions are stored in an external archive to guide the search. Compared to other solutions, these solutions are good samples from the objective space. In this paper, the normalized ranking metric based method is used to select more representative solutions by utilizing a new metric to guide the search.

Particle swarm optimization (PSO) is a swarm intelligence algorithm [9,13]. New strategies in PSO algorithm are proposed to solve different kinds of algorithms [5,16]. Normalized ranking metric based particle swarm optimizer (RPSO), which replaces the Pareto optimality, is proposed to solve many objective optimization problems in this paper. To give a simple illustration of the proposed metric, the RPSO algorithm is tested on four multiobjective optimization problems and three many objective optimization problems. Experiments are conducted for the comparison of the RPSO with Pareto optimality relation based multiobjective particle swarm optimizer (MOPSO) [6].

The remaining of this paper is organized as follows: In Sect. 2, the normalized ranking metric will be introduced and the diversity maintaining will be discussed. A particle swarm optimizer (PSO) based on normalized ranking metric for many objective optimization will be proposed in Sect. 3. Experiments of the proposed particle swarm optimizer on benchmark functions will be conducted in Sect. 4. Finally, conclusions and future research directions will be given in Sect. 5.

2   Normalized Ranking Metric

Pareto optimality relation is an effective way to compare solutions with less than three objectives in multiobjective optimization. However, almost all solutions are Pareto non-dominated in many objective optimization. The comparison of solutions, or the choice of more representative solutions to guide the search, is an essential issue in many objective optimization. Ranking strategy could be a good way to choose more representative solutions from nondominated solutions [7,12].

2.1   Solution Comparison

The minimum problem is used as an example to illustrate the normalized ranking metric. Thus, the smaller the value, the better the solution. Figure 1 gives an illustration on the normalized ranking of solutions for a problem with seven objectives. The solution x_1 performs best on objectives f_1, f_3, and f_6, the solution x_2 performs the best on objectives f_2 and f_4, and solution x_3 performs best on objectives f_5 and f_7. All these three solutions are not able to be compared based on the concept of Pareto optimality, because all these solutions are Pareto non-dominated.

A ranking metric based on the sum of normalized value on each objective is proposed to compare Pareto non-dominated solutions. The calculation of normalized value a_{ik} is given in Eq. (1):

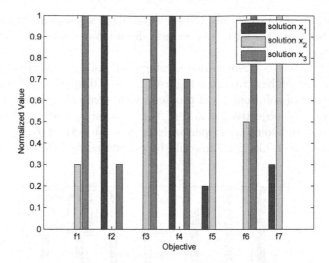

Fig. 1. An illustration on the normalized ranking of solutions for a problem with seven objectives

$$a_{ik} = \begin{cases} \frac{f_k(x_i)-f_{k,\min}}{f_{k,\max}-f_{k,\min}} & f_{k,\max} \neq f_{k,\min} \\ \text{tiny value} & f_{k,\max} = f_{k,\min} \end{cases} \tag{1}$$

where $f_k(x_i)$ is the fitness value of solution x_i on the kth objective. The $f_{k,\max}$ and $f_{k,\min}$ are the maximum value and the minimum value of all current solutions obtained on the kth objective, respectively. All solutions are ranked by the sum of calculated value on each objective. The aim of many objective optimization is to optimize all objectives at the same time. All objectives are considered equally in Fig. 1. For objectives with user preferences, a weight strategy may be needed on the normalization. After the calculation of normalized value on each objective, the goodness of each solution could be ranked by its sum value on all objectives. For three solutions in Fig. 1, the ranking value could be calculated as follows:

$$
\begin{aligned}
\text{solution } x_1 \quad & 0.0 + 1.0 + 0.0 + 1.0 + 0.2 + 0.0 + 0.3 = 2.5 \\
\text{solution } x_2 \quad & 0.3 + 0.0 + 0.7 + 0.0 + 1.0 + 0.5 + 1.0 = 3.5 \\
\text{solution } x_3 \quad & 1.0 + 0.3 + 1.0 + 0.7 + 0.1 + 1.0 + 0.0 = 4.0
\end{aligned}
$$

Thus, there is a ranking among the three solutions: $x_1 \prec x_2 \prec x_3$.

2.2 Maintaining Diversity

The population diversity is an important issue in many objective optimization [14,18] and particle swarm optimization algorithms [3,4]. Compared to the single objective optimization, it has different meaning in multiobjective and many objective optimization. Not only the solutions have a good distribution in decision space, but also the objective values should have a good distribution in objective space.

Without a diversity maintaining strategy, all solutions will be guided to a solution with the highest ranking. Figure 2 gives a simple illustration on maintaining diversity of solutions for a problem with seven objectives. The solution x_1 performs best on objectives f_5 and f_6, the solution x_2 performs best on objectives f_4 and f_7, and solution x_3 performs best on objectives f_1, f_2, and f_3. For three solutions, the ranking value could be calculated as follows:

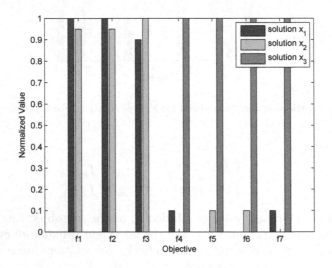

Fig. 2. An illustration on the maintaining diversity of solutions for a problem with seven objectives

$$
\begin{aligned}
\text{solution } x_1 \quad & 1.0 + 1.0 + 0.9 + 0.1 + 0.0 + 0.0 + 0.1 = 3.1 \\
\text{solution } x_2 \quad & 0.95 + 0.95 + 1.0 + 0.0 + 0.1 + 0.1 + 0.0 = 3.1 \\
\text{solution } x_3 \quad & 0.0 + 0.0 + 0.0 + 1.0 + 1.0 + 1.0 + 1.0 = 4.0
\end{aligned}
$$

The ranking is $x_1 \doteq x_2 \prec x_3$. However, the solution x_1 and x_2 have the similar results on all objectives. To obtain a good diversity or distribution on objective space, the solution x_3 may need be kept and the solution x_1 or x_2 may need be abandoned in the archive.

3   Ranking Based Particle Swarm Optimizer

3.1   Classical Particle Swarm Optimizer

Particle swarm optimization emulates the swarm behavior and the individuals represent points in the n-dimensional search space. A particle represents a potential solution. Each particle is associated with two vectors, $i.e.$, the velocity vector and the position vector. For the purpose of generality and clarity, i is used to index the particles or solutions (from 1 to m), j is used to index the dimensions (from 1 to n), m represents the number of particles and n the number of dimensions. The position of a particle i is represented as $\boldsymbol{x}_i$, $\boldsymbol{x}_i = [x_{i1}, x_{i2}, \ldots, x_{ij}, \ldots, x_{in}]^T$. The velocity of a particle i is represented as $\boldsymbol{v}_i = [v_{i1}, v_{i2}, \ldots, v_{ij}, \ldots, v_{in}]^T$, $i = 1, \cdots, m$, and j is the jth dimension, $j = 1, \cdots, n$.

The velocity and position update equations in canonical PSO algorithm are as follow [9,13]:

$$\boldsymbol{v}_i \leftarrow w\boldsymbol{v}_i + c_1\text{rand}()(\boldsymbol{p}_i - \boldsymbol{x}_i) + c_2\text{rand}()(\boldsymbol{p}_n - \boldsymbol{x}_i) \tag{2}$$

$$\boldsymbol{x}_i \leftarrow \boldsymbol{x}_i + \boldsymbol{v}_i \tag{3}$$

where w denotes the inertia weight, c_1 and c_2 are two positive acceleration constants, rand() is a random function to generate uniformly distributed random numbers in the range $[0, 1)$ and are different for each dimension and each particle, $\boldsymbol{x}_i$ represents the ith particle's position, $\boldsymbol{v}_i$ represents the ith particle's velocity, $\boldsymbol{p}_i$ is termed as personal best, which refers to the best position found by the ith particle, and $\boldsymbol{p}_n$ is termed as local best, which refers to the position found by the members in the ith particle's neighborhood that has the best fitness evaluation value so far.

The basic procedure of PSO is shown as Algorithm 1. A particle updates its velocity according to Eq. (2), and updates its position according to Eq. (3). The $c_1\text{rand}()(\boldsymbol{p}_i - \boldsymbol{x}_i)$ part can be seen as a cognitive behavior, while $c_2\text{rand}()(\boldsymbol{p}_n - \boldsymbol{x}_i)$ part can be seen as a social behavior.

Algorithm 1. The basic procedure of particle swarm optimizer

---

1 **Initialization**: Initialize velocity and position randomly for each particle in every dimension;

2 **while** $have\ not\ found\ "good\ enough"\ solution\ or\ not\ reached\ the\ pre\text{-}determined$ $maximum\ number\ of\ iterations$ **do**

3   Calculate each particle's fitness value;

4   Compare fitness value between current position and the best position in history (personal best, termed as $\boldsymbol{p}_i$);

5   **for** $each\ particle$ **do**

6   **if** $the\ fitness\ value\ of\ the\ current\ position\ is\ better\ than\ \boldsymbol{p}_i$ **then**

7   update $\boldsymbol{p}_i$ to be the current position;

8   Select the particle which has the best fitness value among current particle's neighborhood, this particle is called the neighborhood best (termed as $\boldsymbol{p}_n$); Update each particle's velocity and position, respectively;

3.2   Normalized Ranking Based Particle Swarm Optimizer

An essential issue in utilizing particle swarm optimizer to solve multiobjective or many objective problems is the setting of the personal best p_i and the neighborhood best p_n.

Personal Best. The personal best is selected from the existed personal best and the new position. The Pareto optimality relation is utilized to determine p_i the in the traditional multiobjective optimization. The number of better objective values is utilized to select personal best, instead of Pareto optimality relation. For problems with more than one objective, a solution x_i has m improved objectives and n worsen objectives simultaneously after iteration. The update of personal best p_i is given in Eq. (4). The new position will be the new personal best when the value m is bigger than n. In addition, to enhance the population diversity, the new position will be the new personal best with probability 50% when m equals to n.

$$\text{Personal best } p_i = \begin{cases} \text{New position } x_i, & m > n \\ \text{Existed } p_i, & m < n \\ \text{New position } x_i \text{ or Existed } p_i, & m = n \end{cases} \quad (4)$$

Neighborhood Best. In the traditional multiobjective optimization, many Pareto non-dominated solutions are used as neighborhood best and stored in an external archive. In the normalized ranking metric based particle swarm optimizer (RPSO), the neighborhood best solutions are selected from the collection of current solutions and the existed neighborhood best. The archive of neighborhood best is updated after each iteration.

The update of neighborhood best p_n is given in Eq. (5). The archive of neighborhood best is formed by three parts: the solutions with better sum value of all objectives, the solutions with better value on each objective, and the random solutions. There are some overlapped solutions between the first two parts, thus, the random solutions could be used to fill the archive and to enhance the population diversity. In the normalized ranking metric based particle swarm optimizer, the percentage for solutions with best sum value is 40% and the percentage of solutions with better value on each objective is 60%.

$$\text{Neighborhood best } p_n = \text{the solutions}$$
$$\begin{cases} \text{with better sum value on all objectives} & 40\% \\ \text{with better value on each objective} & 60\% \\ \text{randomly selected} & \text{overlap of the first two groups} \end{cases} \quad (5)$$

4   Experimental Study

The Pareto optimality relation based particle swarm optimizer (MOPSO) and the normalized ranking metric based particle swarm optimizer (RPSO) have the same settings on the experimental study.

4.1   Multiobjective Optimization

Benchmark Functions. Four problems, the ZDT1, ZDT2, ZDT4, and ZDT6 benchmark functions, are utilized to test the proposed algorithm.

Parameter Settings. The parameter settings are as follows:

- weight $w = 0.72984$, $c_1 = c_2 = 1.496172$;
- population size: 250;
- number of dimension: 10;
- iteration number: 2000;
- archive size: 100.

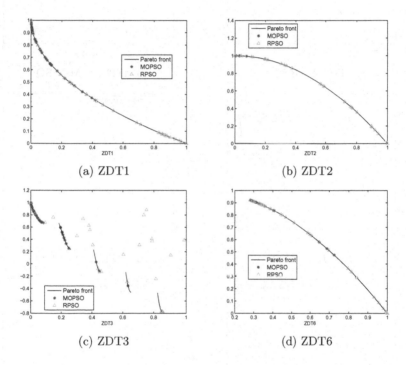

(a) ZDT1   (b) ZDT2

(c) ZDT3   (d) ZDT6

Fig. 3. The result of Pareto metric based MOPSO and normalized ranking metric based RPSO.

Experimental Results. Figure 3 gives the result of Pareto optimality relation based MOPSO and normalized ranking metric based RPSO. The solutions are from the archive of a randomly selected single run. For ZDT1, ZDT2, and ZDT6 functions, the RPSO could find many optimal solutions at the same time, and all solutions have a good distribution. Because the population diversity is considered during the form of archive. For ZDT4 function, the real Pareto front is separated into five parts. The MOPSO algorithm finds more Pareto non-dominated solutions than RPSO algorithm. However, RPSO could find solutions at each part, which means it has a good distribution. Several Pareto dominated solutions are kept in the final results of RPSO algorithm, which is due to the concept of Pareto optimality is not used in RPSO.

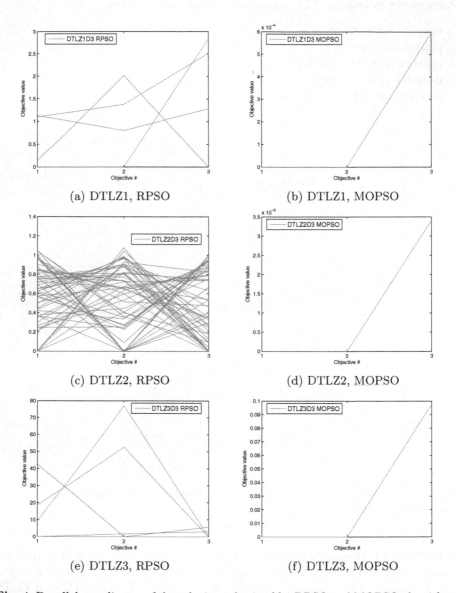

(a) DTLZ1, RPSO   (b) DTLZ1, MOPSO

(c) DTLZ2, RPSO   (d) DTLZ2, MOPSO

(e) DTLZ3, RPSO   (f) DTLZ3, MOPSO

Fig. 4. Parallel coordinates of the solutions obtained by RPSO and MOPSO algorithms on DTLZ1–DTLZ3 functions with three objectives.

4.2 Many Objective Optimization

Benchmark Functions. Three problems, the DTLZ1, DTLZ2, and DTLZ3 function [8], are utilized to test the proposed algorithm. The parameter $M = 3$ and $M = 5$ are tested respectively, which indicates that the functions have 3 or 5 objectives. The number of problem dimensions $n = M + k - 1$, k is 5, therefore, the test functions have 7 or 9 decision variables, respectively.

Parameter Settings. The parameter settings are as follows:

- weight $w = 0.72984$, $c_1 = c_2 = 1.496172$;
- population size: 200 for 3 objectives, 400 for 5 objectives;
- number of dimension: 7 for 3 objectives, 9 for 5 objectives;
- iteration number: 2000 for 3 objectives, 4000 for 5 objectives;
- archive size: 200 for 3 objectives, 400 for 5 objectives.

Experimental Results. The parallel coordinates of the solutions obtained by RPSO and MOPSO algorithms on DTLZ1–DTLZ3 functions with three objectives are shown in Fig. 4. The RPSO could obtain multiple solutions at the end of

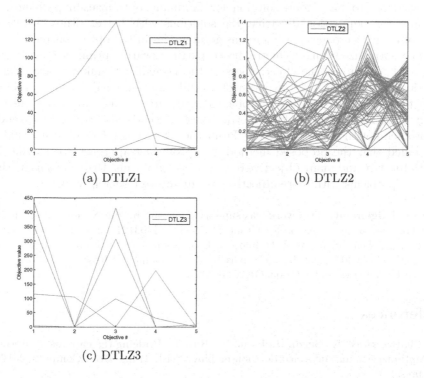

(a) DTLZ1   (b) DTLZ2

(c) DTLZ3

Fig. 5. Parallel coordinates of the solutions obtained by RPSO algorithms on DTLZ1–DTLZ3 functions with five objectives.

search, but the MOPSO is easily converged to a single solution after iterations. The performance of RPSO on DTLZ1 and DTLZ3 should be improved. The experimental results on the number of obtained solutions and the distribution of solutions should be enhanced.

The parallel coordinates of the solutions obtained by RPSO algorithms on DTLZ1–DTLZ3 functions with five objectives are shown in Fig. 5. This is only a preliminary study for the RPSO on solving many objective optimization problems. More methods, such as cooperative co-evolutionary strategy [15], could be combined to obtain better performance.

From the experimental results, it could be demonstrated that the proposed algorithm is a promising approach for solving the multiobjective and many objective optimization problems.

5   Conclusions

Solution comparison is a hard task in many objective optimization. The simple but effective normalized ranking metric based solution comparison method was proposed in this paper to replace Pareto optimality relation in many objective optimization. The solutions were compared by the normalized ranking of the sum of normalized fitness value of each objective. A solution with a small value is considered to be a good solution for minimum optimization problems. To enhance the population diversity, the solutions with better fitness values on each objective were also considered as good guides in the optimization.

The normalized ranking metric based particle swarm optimizer (RPSO) was proposed to validate the effectiveness of the normalized ranking metric based solutions comparison. The experimental study is conducted on four problems with two objectives and three problems with three or five objectives, respectively. The normalized ranking metric based methods also could be extended to problems with more objectives. From the experimental results, it could be concluded that the proposed method is a promising approach for solving the multiobjective and many objective optimization problems. Utilizing this method to solve problems with more objectives is our future research work.

Acknowledgement. This work was supported in part by the National Natural Science Foundation of China under Grant 61672334, 61403121, and 61273367; in part by the Shenzhen Science and Technology Innovation Committee under grant number ZDSYS201703031748284; and in part by the Fundamental Research Funds for the Central Universities under Grant GK201703062.

References

1. Bhattacharjee, K., Singh, H., Ryan, M., Ray, T.: Bridging the gap: many-objective optimization and informed decision-making. IEEE Trans. Evol. Comput. (2017, in press)
2. Cheng, R., Jin, Y., Olhofer, M., Sendhoff, B.: Test problems for large-scale multi-objective and many-objective optimization. IEEE Trans. Cybern. (2017, in press)

3. Cheng, S., Shi, Y., Qin, Q.: Experimental study on boundary constraints handling in particle swarm optimization: from population diversity perspective. Int. J. Swarm Intell. Res. **2**(3), 43–69 (2011)
4. Cheng, S., Shi, Y., Qin, Q.: Population diversity based study on search information propagation in particle swarm optimization. In: Proceedings of 2012 IEEE Congress on Evolutionary Computation (CEC 2012), pp. 1272–1279. IEEE, Brisbane (2012)
5. Cheng, S., Zhang, Q., Qin, Q.: Big data analytics with swarm intelligence. Ind. Manag. Data Syst. **116**(4), 646–666 (2016)
6. Coello, C.A.C., Pulido, G.T., Lechuga, M.S.: Handling multiple objectives with particle swarm optimization. IEEE Trans. Evol. Comput. **8**(3), 256–279 (2004)
7. Corne, D., Knowles, J.: Techniques for highly multiobjective optimisation: some nondominated points are better than others. In: Proceedings of the 2007 Genetic and Evolutionary Computation Conference (GECCO 2002), London, pp. 773–780 (2007)
8. Deb, K., Thiele, L., Laumanns, M., Zitzler, E.: Scalable multi-objective optimization test problems. In: Proceedings of 2002 IEEE Congress on Evolutionary Computation (CEC 2002), pp. 825–830 (2002)
9. Eberhart, R., Shi, Y.: Computational Intelligence: Concepts to Implementations. Morgan Kaufmann Publishers, San Francisco (2007)
10. Farina, M., Amato, P.: On the optimal solution definition for many-criteria optimization problems. In: Proceedings of the 2002 Annual Meeting of the North American Fuzzy Information Processing Society (NAFIPS-FLINT 2002), pp. 233–238 (2002)
11. Hu, W., Yen, G.G., Luo, G.: Many-objective particle swarm optimization using two-stage strategy and parallel cell coordinate system. IEEE Trans. Cybern. **47**(6), 1446–1459 (2017)
12. Jaimes, A.L., Quintero, L.V.S., Coello, C.A.C.: Ranking methods in many-objective evolutionary algorithms. In: Chiong, R. (ed.) Nature-Inspired Algorithms for Optimisation. Studies in Computational Intelligence, vol. 193, pp. 413–434. Springer, Heidelberg (2009). doi:10.1007/978-3-642-00267-0_15
13. Kennedy, J., Eberhart, R., Shi, Y.: Swarm Intelligence. Morgan Kaufmann Publishers, San Francisco (2001)
14. Li, M., Yang, S., Liu, X.: Diversity comparison of Pareto front approximations in many-objective optimization. IEEE Trans. Cybern. **44**(12), 2568–2584 (2014)
15. Peng, X., Liu, K., Jin, Y.: A dynamic optimization approach to the design of cooperative co-evolutionary algorithms. Knowl.-Based Syst. **109**, 174–186 (2016)
16. Qin, Q., Cheng, S., Zhang, Q., Li, L., Shi, Y.: Particle swarm optimization with interswarm interactive learning strategy. IEEE Trans. Cybern. **46**(10), 2238–2251 (2016)
17. Wang, H., Jiao, L., Yao, X.: Two_Arch2: an improved two-archive algorithm for many-objective optimization. IEEE Trans. Evol. Comput. **19**(4), 524–541 (2015)
18. Wang, H., Jin, Y., Yao, X.: Diversity assessment in many-objective optimization. IEEE Trans. Cybern. **47**(6), 1510–1522 (2017)
19. Yuan, Y., Ong, Y.S., Gupta, A., Xu, H.: Objective reduction in many-objective optimization: evolutionary multiobjective approaches and comprehensive analysis. IEEE Trans. Evol. Comput. (2017, in press)
20. Zou, X., Chen, Y., Liu, M., Kang, L.: A new evolutionary algorithm for solving many-objective optimization problems. IEEE Trans. Syst. Man Cybern. Part B (Cybern.) **38**(5), 1402–1412 (2008)

Evolutionary Machine Learning

A Study on Pre-training Deep Neural Networks Using Particle Swarm Optimisation

Angus Kenny and Xiaodong Li[(✉)]

School of Science, RMIT University, Melbourne, Australia
{angus.kenny,xiaodong.li}@rmit.edu.au

Abstract. Deep learning is a "hot-topic" in machine learning at the moment. Currently deep learning networks are constrained in their size and complexity due to the algorithms used to optimise being computationally expensive. This paper examines the potential of optimising deep neural networks using particle swarm optimisation (PSO) as a substitute for the most common methods of contrastive divergence (CD) or stochastic gradient descent. It investigates the problems caused by using PSO in such high-dimensional problem spaces and the issues around applying *divide-and-conquer* techniques to neural networks. A novel network architecture is proposed to overcome the limitations caused by the low dimensional capabilities of PSO, dubbed *semi-disjoint expanded networks* (SdENs). A comparative analysis is performed between the proposed model and more popular techniques. Our experiment results suggest that the proposed techniques could perform similar functions to the more traditional pre-training technique of CD, however it is identified that the deeper networks required suffer from the *vanishing gradient* problem. This paper serves to highlight the issues prevalent in this new and fertile ground of research.

1 Introduction

Ever since Hinton developed his contrastive divergence algorithm [8], the field of artificial intelligence, and neural networks specifically, has been abuzz with the words "deep learning". Deep neural networks are useful in solving a variety of machine learning problems; in particular computer vision and similar related problems [7]. In such problems low level point and edge detectors can be combined in deeper layers to detect higher-level features [9].

Traditional methods of training deep neural network architectures, such as by gradient descent, are time consuming, require the transfer function to be differentiable and rely on tuned parameters such as a learning rate [22]. From the field of evolutionary computation, there is some research to be found on the use of genetic algorithms (GA) to learn deep neural networks [6,16,18,20], however there is little research in the literature on applying particle swarm optimisation (PSO) techniques to these sorts of problems, despite PSO being a good candidate because of its generality, fast convergence, simplicity of implementation and the fact that it does not place restrictions on the transfer function. While there

© Springer International Publishing AG 2017
Y. Shi et al. (Eds.): SEAL 2017, LNCS 10593, pp. 361–372, 2017.
https://doi.org/10.1007/978-3-319-68759-9_30

has been significant research on optimising feed-forward neural networks with PSO [15, 19, 24], there is very little research into using these same techniques to optimise deep learning neural networks.

Image processing problems often contain tens of thousands of variables, requiring the use of deep nets with thousands of hidden nodes and connection weights, a large scale optimisation problem that is challenging for PSO. This research investigates if it is possible to apply *divide-and-conquer* techniques in order to reduce the network pre-training problem to a size that is manageable by PSO; and if applying these techniques improves the accuracy of operation or training efficiency when learning a deep neural network. This is a preliminary study of using PSO as a substitute for standard deep neural network training algorithms and so serves to identify a number of the issues and challenges that arise when applying these techniques to such problems.

2   Related Works

This section gives a brief introduction into deep learning networks, methods of training them and particle swarm optimisation. These are the three main aspects drawn upon in developing the model proposed in this paper.

2.1   Deep Stacked Autoencoder Networks

Autoencoder networks are a subset of feed-forward artificial neural networks which have two visible layers and one hidden layer and are able to learn without supervision [25]. They achieve this by processing an input using a weight matrix, $\mathbf{W}$, and then reconstructing the input in the output layer by processing the information in the hidden layer by the weight matrix $\mathbf{W}^\top$. The squared error between the actual and the reconstructed input is used to evaluate solutions.

The basis of an autoencoder is the Restricted Boltzmann Machine (RBM). An RBM is a simple two layer network, with one visible layer and one hidden layer [10]. Like RBMs, autoencoders can also be "stacked" in order to create deep networks; this is done by "freezing" the weights of the already trained layers and using their outputs as the input for the next layer (Fig. 1).

2.2   Training Deep Networks

Deep networks are trained in a greedy, layer-wise fashion. The connection weights for each layer are pre-trained using an unsupervised training method before being "frozen" and used to pre-train the weights for subsequent layers. Once all layers have been pre-trained, the layers are stacked on top of each other and "fine-tuned" using backpropagation [2]. The reason for this pre-training is to give the backpropagation algorithm a "head start" by giving it some initial values to start with, rather than purely random connection weights. This greatly reduces the amount of time taken by the backpropagation algorithm and also diminishes the risk that it will become stuck in a local optimum [3].

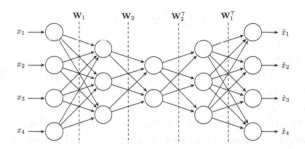

Fig. 1. Autoencoder network - x_i is the input data and $\hat{x}_i$ is the reconstructed input. By processing the data with the transpose matrix $\mathbf{W}_i^\top$ in the reverse order to which it was processed by $\mathbf{W}_i$, the original input data can be reconstructed in a network with multiple layers.

An autoencoder is trained with the aim of being able to encode its input in the hidden layer, such that the original input can be reconstructed from that encoding [1]. This is done by using the same connection weights that encoded the information to decode it, except that the input and output have been swapped for each weight. Once decoded, the reconstruction error is calculated using the mean square error as the cost function:

$$C = \frac{1}{2n} \sum_i^n (x_i - \hat{x}_i)^2, \tag{1}$$

$$\frac{\partial C}{\partial \hat{x}_i} = \hat{x}_i - x_i. \tag{2}$$

where n is the number of training examples, x_i is the original input and $\hat{x}_i$ is the reconstructed output. The derivative of this cost function (Eq. 2) can be used to perform gradient descent with backpropagation to determine the connection weights that best allow the network to give a faithful reconstruction of the input [21].

2.3 Particle Swarm Optimisation

Particle swarm optimisation (PSO) is a metaheuristic search technique that uses a population of particles to perform an iterative, stochastic search of a solution space in order to find an optimal solution to a given problem [14]. It achieves this by updating the position of each particle in parallel according to a linear combination of the current velocity of each particle, the personal best position of each particle and the position of the best informant for each particle [5]. This information is used to update the position of each particle iteratively, in accordance with the following equations [13]:

$$\mathbf{v}_{i+1} \leftarrow \chi(\omega \mathbf{v}_i + \varphi_1 \odot (\mathbf{p}_i - \mathbf{x}_i) + \varphi_2 \odot (\mathbf{p}_g - \mathbf{x}_i)), \tag{3}$$

$$\mathbf{x}_{i+1} \leftarrow \mathbf{x}_i + \mathbf{v}_{i+1}. \tag{4}$$

where $\odot$ is the element-wise, or Hadamard, product operator, $\mathbf{x}_i$ is the position of the current particle, $\mathbf{p}_i$ is the personal best position of the current particle, $\mathbf{p}_g$ is the position of the best informant to the current particle, $\mathbf{v}$ is the velocity of the current particle, $\varphi_1 = c_1 \cdot \mathbf{R}_1$ and $\varphi_2 = c_2 \cdot \mathbf{R}_2$ where c_1 and c_2 are acceleration coefficients, $\mathbf{R}_1$ and $\mathbf{R}_2$ are vectors of random values sampled from a uniform distribution in the range $[0, 1]$, χ is the constriction coefficient and ω is the inertia weight. A more complete derivation and description of these terms can be found in [4,5].

3   Semi-disjoint Expanded Networks

This section presents the model developed in order to answer the research questions posed in the introduction. It first introduces the topology of the network and then describes its method of training.

3.1   Separating the Network

It is well-known that metaheuristics such as PSO are not suitable for high dimensional optimisation problems such as image processing. The most obvious technique to reduce problem size is to use *divide-and-conquer*. The hypothesis is that if the network can be divided up into a number of smaller networks while still retaining its functionality, PSO could be used to train these smaller networks and optimise this smaller number of connection weights.

Every input unit in a neural network has some degree of influence on every output unit; therefore separating a network into N completely disjoint sets of units would effectively split the image processing problem into N different image processing problems that are completely unrelated (Fig. 2 *centre*).

By adding an "intermediate" layer to the network, grouping the neurons and offsetting the connections between groups such that each group connects to two other groups (hence, *semi*-disjoint). Each of the units in the input layer has an effect on each unit in the output layer (Fig. 2, *right*).

In order to maintain the fully-connectedness of SdENs, an intermediate layer must be added for every group. The example in Fig. 2, *right* shows a network with 8 input units, divided into 2 groups of 4 units; meaning that only one extra layer was needed. If this example had been of a 12 input network divided into 3 groups of 4 units, then two extra layers would need to be added in order to keep it fully connected from input to output. This means that the complexity of the network increases linearly with the number groups.

3.2   Training Semi-disjoint Expanded Networks

Each separate group of units in a SdEN can be trained as an individual autoencoder by propagating the portion of the input data corresponding to that group

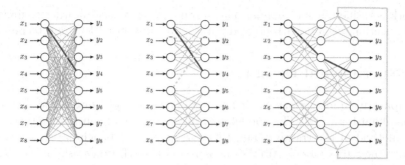

Fig. 2. Fully connected network *(left)*; fully disjoint network *(centre)*. The red and blue lines represent two possible paths between layers; while there remains a path from input unit x_1 to output unit y_4; there is no longer a connected path from input unit x_5 to output unit y_2 indicating the influence of x_5 on y_2 has been removed; semi-disjoint expanded network (SdEN) *(right)*, by adding an intermediate layer and offsetting the connections by half the size of the group, there is now a connected path from any input unit to any output unit. (Color figure online)

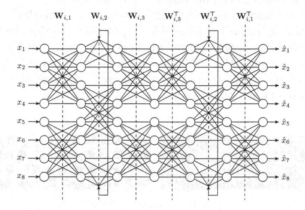

Fig. 3. Deep stacked semi-disjoint expanded network - each layer is trained greedily and stacked one after another. The transpose of the layer weight matrices are used to decode the information into a reconstruction.

forward to the hidden layer using the connection weight matrix and then using the transpose of that matrix to reconstruct the input. Because the layers of neurons have been separated into groups, they can be trained using PSO techniques instead of the typical method of contrastive divergence.

Once each group is trained such that it is able to reconstruct its input faithfully, the weights in the trained layer are frozen and the output of those groups are used as the input for the groups of the next layer; the connections having been offset. Once complete, the network should be able to reconstruct any input by propagating it forwards through the layers, using the trained weights, and then using the transpose of the weights in reverse order (Fig. 3). After the network is trained in this manner, back-propagation is used in order to fine tune the connection weights with labeled data using supervised learning techniques.

4   Experimental Design

A comparative analysis was carried out against the model developed by Hinton and Salakhutdinov [11]. This model uses the technique of contrastive divergence as its method of pre-training, and therefore is a good benchmark by which to compare the SdEN model. Alterations were made to Hinton's original *MATLAB* code to make the architectures as similar as possible across the models and also to accommodate downsampled and reduced datasets. Due to the large differences in the architectures and function between Hinton's model and the SdEN model, the only common point of comparison is the final reconstruction error after training so this was selected as the metric to compare the models. All experiments were carried out ten times recording the mean and standard deviation across the population. The results from the Hinton model was then compared against the SdEN model with various combinations of parameters.

The two main parameters used for this comparison were PSO type (*g-best*, *l-best*) and number of groups per layer. The population size (for the SdEN model) and number of training epochs (for all models) were set at 10. The input images were four classes from the MNIST handwritten digit dataset [17] which had been downsampled from 28×28 to 12×12 pixels, so each layer of the models was constructed with 144 neurons (Fig. 4, *left*).

Fig. 4. MNIST handwritten digit dataset *(left)* - the dataset has been reduced to four classes and downsampled from 28×28 pixels to 12×12. Random samples of noisy test data *(right)* - input data which has been corrupted by flipping a pre-defined number of random bits (uncorrupted dataset is in top row).

The ungrouped layers each consist of 144 neurons, requiring 20,736 (144×144) connection weights per layer, however separating the layers into groups drastically reduces the number of connection weights. For the tests, the layers of the network were separated into 8 or 12 groups so each PSO population need only optimise 324 (18×18) or 144 (12×12) weights per group per layer. These group sizes were chosen because 324 variables was found to be close to the upper bound that allowed the chosen PSO algorithms to work effectively.

As well as the comparison against Hinton's model, an investigation of the effect that different parameters have on the SdEN model was also conducted. For this, a smaller dataset was constructed and used to run tests on the model.

The need for this is because the model reduces the dimensionality of the search space by increasing the depth of the network, so in order to avoid the vanishing gradient problem caused by too-deep networks, the dimensionality of the original search space must be as low as possible. This dataset consists of 4 distinct images in the training set with dimensions 4×4, only requiring 256 connection weights per unseparated layer. The testing set consisted of 100 versions of each image with varying degrees of corruption caused by flipping a set number of random bits (Fig. 4, *(left)*). The noise is to determine if the network has learnt how to recognise the classes even when the image has been changed; the idea being that if it is able to do this, it has learned some meaningful feature about the class, rather than just the exact pixels. In this second set of experiments, the effect of the number of epochs, the number of groups, the number of layers, the population size and the PSO type were all tested and compared.

5   Results

5.1   Testing on Scaled-down MNIST Dataset

Table 1 gives the data obtained from experiments that compare the reconstruction error between the Hinton model [11] which uses contrastive divergence as its training method and variants of the SdEN model employing *g-best* and *l-best* PSO. Table 1 presents some strange results; it appears that regardless of the parameters used, the reconstruction error of the SdEN model will always be around 12.5% across both the training set and the testing set, and further experimentation confirmed this pattern. This apparent anomaly can be explained by looking at the cost function used to evaluate the reconstruction error, Eq. 1. This Equation works by taking vectors of classifications (e.g. $[0.23\ 0.81\ 0.05\ 0.12]$) and expected values (e.g. $[0\ 1\ 0\ 0]$), finds the average square difference between all of the elements and halves it to give the reconstruction error (the half being a scalar factor included to simplify the derivative of the cost function). When the classification vector is $[0.5\ 0.5\ 0.5\ 0.5]$ the reconstruction error is 0.125, or 12.5%.

Because the classification result is the average reconstruction error over the entire dataset and the value that an element in the classification vector can

Table 1. Comparative analysis between the Hinton's model and SdEN. Results shown are the mean and standard deviation of the classification error on the test set across a population of 10 experimental trials.

	Reconstruction error (%)					
	Hinton model		SdEN_*g-best*		SdEN_*l-best*	
	2 layers	3 layers	8 groups	12 groups	8 groups	12 groups
Mean	2.04	1.23	12.37	12.47	12.24	12.94
Std dev	0.38	0.17	1.73	2.04	1.88	1.73

take is between 0 and 1; it makes sense that the elements in the classification vector would all take the value 0.5 if the network was purely "guessing" at random. Further investigation confirmed this hypothesis; a sample of images from the training set were taken at random and reconstructions generated using the trained network (Fig. 5). This figure shows that there is very little difference between reconstructions of different classes and it appears that the network has actually learned an *average* across the whole training set. This phenomenon is illustrated more clearly in the third and fourth rows of Fig. 5. Here the network has been trained only on instances of the one class (all 0's), the third row of Fig. 5 shows a random sample of the training set and the fourth row displays the reconstruction of the training image above, from this it can be seen clearly that the network is reconstructing an average across the whole training set. The reason for this is something called the *vanishing gradient problem* [23] or *exponential gradient decay* [12] and it occurs when trying to fine-tune a very deep architecture using standard backpropagation. The deeper the architecture, the harder it is to propagate the error back through the layers, until the gradient is so weak that it no longer has any effect on the weights of the network and disrupts the training process. It appears that using such a deep network makes SdENs prone to this effect, so further work will be needed to overcome this issue if the model is going to be effective on real-world problems.

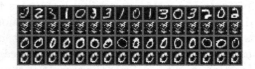

Fig. 5. Training images (top row) and their reconstructions (second row). There is very little discernable difference between the reconstructions of the different classes, implying that the network has learned an average across the whole training set. This effect is illustrated more clearly by the third and fourth rows.

5.2   PSO as Contrastive Divergence Substitute

The vanishing gradient problem occurs when fine-tuning the network after pre-training. While there were issues with learning features from multiple classes of images on a large scale, PSO is still a potential candidate replacement for CD and can be used to transfer the training data to the network. To prove this, a toy experiment was used that trained the network on one single training image. As the function of an autoencoder is to learn to reconstruct its input faithfully; if the model could be shown to be able to reconstruct an image that it had been trained on, this would be evidence that some form of learning had occurred.

Figure 6 shows the reconstructions obtained after training a network on a single image with varying layers and epochs. It can be seen that as the number of epochs increases, so does the reconstruction fidelity, implying that the system

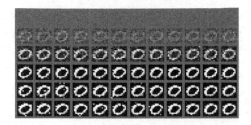

Fig. 6. Reconstructions of a network trained on a single image. From left to right shows the reconstructions from networks with increasing numbers of layers from 1 to 12 and top to bottom shows reconstructions with increasing numbers of epochs from the set $\{1, 5, 10, 25, 50, 100\}$.

is learning with each epoch that passes. It can also be seen that as the number of layers increases, there is not much change in the quality of the reconstruction for the same amount of epochs. The bottom right image in the figure represents a 12 layer network being trained over 100 epochs. The fact that the reconstruction error is very low even after 12 layers indicates that training with PSO is not significantly affected by the vanishing gradient problem. This result implies that the issue lies with the backpropagation fine-tuning step.

5.3   Testing on Small-Scale Custom Dataset

In order to demonstrate a proof of concept and show that the model developed does actually work, albeit in a limited capacity; a further set of experiments were devised using a smaller, more basic dataset as described in Fig. 4 *(right)*. These experiments are designed to illustrate the effects of the various parameters in the model on its performance. The first experiment shows the effect that varying the PSO population size has on the model; the number of groups or hidden layers has been set at 2 and the number of training epochs has been set at 50. Once again, the mean has been taken across a population of 10 experimental trials. As illustrated in Fig. 7a, variations in the population size do not make much difference to the results on the training set ($n = 0$). As the test data becomes more noisy however, the difference in performance is amplified with the general trend of the results plot becoming steeper. The second experiment conducted is designed to investigate the effect that variations on the number of training epochs has on the performance of the model. Here, the population size was set at 10 and the number of groups/layers remained at 2. The results shown are the mean over 10 experimental trials. As with the previous experiment, it appears that the effect of varying the number of pre-training epochs is amplified as the number of random bits are flipped. This can be seen clearly in Fig. 7b with the trend of the plot for $n = 3$ being much steeper than the plot for $n = 0$. One difference between the two experiments though, is that there does seem to be a difference even on the training set ($n = 0$) between pre-training with 1 epoch, and pre-training with 100. This makes sense as varying the number of pre-training epochs has an effect on the amount of time (or, more accurately, connection weight updates) to learn the training data; whereas varying the population size only has an effect on the efficiency with which the solution space is searched.

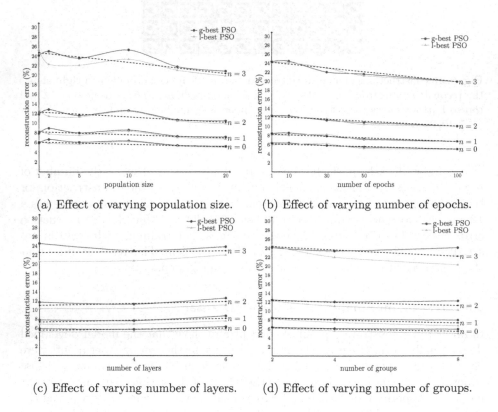

(a) Effect of varying population size.

(b) Effect of varying number of epochs.

(c) Effect of varying number of layers.

(d) Effect of varying number of groups.

Fig. 7. Experimental results on small-scale custom dataset. n is the number of random bits flipped in each image of the set being tested.

The number of intermediate hidden layers is directly proportional to the number of groups that each layer is split into ; it is this property that the third experiment conducted is designed to investigate. The experiment uses a population size of 10, 50 pre-training epochs and 2 groups; the number of layers tested is 2, 4 and 6. Figure 7c shows that as the number of layers are increased, so does the reconstruction error; supporting the fact that the model is able to train deeper architectures, up until the vanishing gradient problem arises.

One final experiment that was undertaken was one designed to test the effect of varying the number of groups that a layer is divided into has on the model. As number of layers is directly related to number of groups per layer, the number of layers could not be fixed for this experiment, however the population size was fixed at 10 and each experiment was run over 50 pre-training epochs. The results are presented below and each value is the mean of a population of 10 runs.

Figure 7d shows some results which look quite surprising on the surface. Interestingly, the reconstruction error seems reduce as the number of groups increases, despite the fact that a network that is split into 8 groups requires there to be 8 hidden layers in order to maintain fully connectedness and therefore should be susceptible to the vanishing gradient problem. However, in this toy example there are only 16 neurons per layer, so splitting the layer into 8 groups results in groups of only 2 neurons with 4 connecting weights per group, making it an extremely easy optimisation problem for the system to solve. It appears that the network is able to learn the features of the training set very well.

6   Conclusions and Future Work

Our research findings show that it is not as straightforward a matter as "plugging" PSO into an established deep neural network training algorithm. The "curse of dimensionality" associated with image processing problems is too great an issue for PSO to surmount on its own, implying a method of decomposition is needed to overcome this problem. Although the model performed adequately on the toy problem, the overall performance was not satisfactory enough to indicate the model developed is a suitable replacement for traditional training methods of deep neural networks; it did however, serve to highlight some of the main issues and problems associated with training in this manner. Because the method of decomposition requires the network to become very deep, the gradient information is lost at the deeper levels. Future work could investigate different decomposition techniques that do not require such a deepening of the network, or alternatively, a new technique for fine-tuning the network after pre-training could be found that is not susceptible to the vanishing gradient problem.

References

1. Bengio, Y.: Learning deep architectures for AI. Found. Trends Mach. Learn. **2**(1), 1–127 (2009)
2. Bengio, Y.: Practical recommendations for gradient-based training of deep architectures. In: Montavon, G., Orr, G.B., Müller, K.-R. (eds.) Neural Networks: Tricks of the Trade. LNCS, vol. 7700, 2nd edn, pp. 437–478. Springer, Heidelberg (2012). doi:10.1007/978-3-642-35289-8_26
3. Bengio, Y.: Evolving culture versus local minima. Grow. Adapt. Mach. - Stud. Comput. Intell. **557**, 109–138 (2014)
4. Blum, C., Li, X.: Swarm intelligence in optimization. In: Blum, C., Merkle, D. (eds.) Swarm Intelligence - Introduction and Applications. NCS, pp. 43–86. Springer, Heidelberg (2008). doi:10.1007/978-3-540-74089-6_2
5. Clerc, M.: Particle Swarm Optimization. ISTE Ltd. (2006)
6. David, O.E., Greental, I.: Genetic algorithms for evolving deep neural networks. In: GECCO 2014 - Proceedings of the 2014 Conference on Genetic and Evolutionary Computation, pp. 1451–1452. Association for Computing Machinery Special Interest Group on Genetic and Evolutionary Computation (2014)

7. Deng, L., Yu, D.: Deep learning: methods and applications. Found. Trends Sig. Process. **7**(3–4), 197–387 (2014)
8. Hinton, G.E.: Training products of experts by minimizing contrastive divergence. Neural Comput. **14**(8), 1771–1800 (2002)
9. Hinton, G.E.: To recognize shapes, first learn to generate images. Prog. Brain Res. **165**, 535–547 (2007)
10. Hinton, G.E.: A practical guide to training restricted boltzmann machines. Momentum **1**, 926 (2010)
11. Hinton, G.E., Salakhutdinov, R.: Reducing the dimensionality of data with neural networks. Science **313**, 504–507 (2006)
12. Hochreiter, S., Bengio, Y., Frasconi, P., Schmidhuber, J.: Gradient flow in recurrent nets: the difficulty of learning long-term dependencies. In: A Field Guide to Dynamical Recurrent Neural Networks (2001)
13. Kennedy, J.: Swarm intelligence. In: Zomaya, A.Y. (ed.) Handbook of Nature-Inspired and Innovative Computing. Springer, Boston (2006). doi:10.1007/0-387-27705-6_6
14. Kennedy, J., Eberhart, R.: Particle swarm optimization. In: Proceedings of IEEE International Conference on Neural Networks, vol. 4, pp. 1942–1948 (1995)
15. Kuok, K.K., Harun, S., Shamsuddin, S.M.: Particle swarm optimization feed forward neural network for hourly rainfall-runoff modeling in Bedup Basin, Malaysia. Int. J. Civil Environ. Eng. **9**(10), 9–18 (2010)
16. Lamos-Sweeney, J.: Deep learning using genetic algorithms. Master's thesis, Rochester Institute of Technology (2012)
17. LeCun, Y., Bottou, L., Bengio, Y., Haffner, P.: Gradient-based learning applied to document recognition. Proc. IEEE **86**(11), 2278–2324 (1998)
18. Levy, E., David, O.E., Netanyahu, N.S.: Genetic algorithms and deep learning for automatic painter classification. In: GECCO 2014 - Proceedings of 2014 Conference on Genetic and Evolutionary Computation, pp. 1143–1150. Association for Computing Machinery Special Interest Group on Genetic and Evolutionary Computation (2014)
19. Mendes, R., Cortez, P., Rocha, M., Neves, J.: Particle swarms for feedforward neural network training. In: Proceedings of 2002 International Joint Conference on Neural Networks (2002)
20. Morse, G., Stanley, K.O.: Simple evolutionary optimization can rival stochastic gradient descent in neural networks. In: Proceedings of Genetic and Evolutionary Computation Conference 2016, GECCO 2016, pp. 477–484. ACM, New York (2016)
21. Nielsen, M.A.: Neural Networks and Deep Learning. Determination Press (2014)
22. Porto, V.W., Fogel, D.B.: Alternative neural network training methods. IEEE Expert **10**(3), 16–22 (1995)
23. Squartini, S., Cecchi, S., Rossini, S., Piazza, F.: Comparing different recurrent neural architectures on a specific task from vanishing gradient effect perspective. In: Proceedings of 2006 IEEE International Conference on Networking, Sensing and Control, pp. 380–385 (2006)
24. Tsou, D., MacNish, C.: Adaptive particle swarm optimisation for high-dimensional, highly convex search spaces. In: 2003 Congress on Evolutionary Computation, vol. 2, pp. 783–789 (2003)
25. Vincent, P., Larochelle, H., Lajoie, I., Bengio, Y., Manzagol, P.: Stacked denoising autoencoders: learning useful representations in a deep network with a local denoising criterion. J. Mach. Learn. Res. **11**, 3371–3408 (2010)

Simple Linkage Identification Using Genetic Clustering

Kei Ohnishi[1(✉)] and Chang Wook Ahn[2]

[1] Kyushu Institute of Technology, 680-4 Kawazu, Iizuka, Fukuoka 820-8502, Japan
ohnishi@cse.kyutech.ac.jp
[2] Gwangju Institute of Science and Techology (GIST), 123 Cheomdangwagi-ro,
Buk-gu, Gwangju 61005, Korea
cwan@gist.ac.kr

Abstract. The paper proposes a simple linkage identification method for binary optimization problems. The method is basically equivalent to the genetic clustering method, called GC, inspired by the speciation due to segregation distortion genes that was previously proposed by us. A genetic algorithm using the method, called GAuGC, is also proposed. The GAuGC is applied to decomposable, nearly decomposable, and indecomposable problems. The results show that the GAuGC better solves problems with weak decomposability than the linkage tree genetic algorithm for comparison and also show that it cannot handle the deception well.

Keywords: Genetic algorithm · Genetic clustering · Linkage identification · Data clustering · Decomposability

1   Introduction

To efficiently solve a decomposable binary optimization problem that consists of sub-problems by a genetic algorithm (GA), the GA first needs to identify a linkage that represents a set of variables forming a sub-problem and then utilize the identified linkage to produce solution candidates. If GA disrupts linkages during search frequently, it cannot achieve efficient search [18]. One such GA for achieving efficient search is model-building GA. The model-building GA builds a model representing linkages using some machine learning technique and produces solution candidates using the built model. The model-building GA using a probabilistic model is called the probabilistic model-building GA [16] or the estimation distribution algorithm [11].

Recently, several efficient model-building GAs have been developed for solving hard decomposable binary problems [13,15,17,19]. For instance, hBOA [15], DSMGA [19], LTGA [17] have been shown to have high scalability against hierarchical decomposable problems. However, it is generally time-consuming to identify linkages in a complicated hard problem. So, GA is required to be able to solve problems with less computational time. The model-building GAs have also

© Springer International Publishing AG 2017
Y. Shi et al. (Eds.): SEAL 2017, LNCS 10593, pp. 373–384, 2017.
https://doi.org/10.1007/978-3-319-68759-9_31

been applied to nearly decomposable hard problems [3,9,19] and indecomposable problems [12]. However, it has been shown that the GAs cannot solve those problems as efficiently in terms of function evaluations as the decomposable problems. So, GA is required to be able to efficiently solve not only decomposable problems but ones with weak decomposability.

In this paper, toward realizing GA that can not only identify linkages in a decomposable problem with less computational time but also solve problems with weak decomposability efficiently, we first propose a simple linkage identification method and then propose GA using it. Then, we apply the proposed GA to decomposable, nearly decomposable, and indecomposable problems. The proposed linkage identification method is basically equivalent to the genetic clustering method, called GC, that we previously proposed in [14]. We, therefore, call the proposed GA the genetic algorithm using the genetic clustering method, GAuGC.

The remainder of the paper is organized as follows. We describe the GC and the GAuGC in Sects. 2 and 3, respectively. We show simulation results in Sect. 4. Section 5 mentions the conclusions and future work.

2   Linkage Identification Using Genetic Clustering

In this section we propose a new simple linkage identification method for binary optimization problems. The method is basically equivalent to the genetic clustering method (GC) that we proposed previously in [14].

2.1   Genetic Clustering Method (GC)

The GC was previously proposed by us [14] and is an unsupervised clustering method. It is based on one of mechanisms for yielding a reproductively isolated group of individuals in biological world, that is, the speciation. The mechanism is the effect of genes causing *segregation distortion*.

The segregation distortion is a phenomenon that when a genome includes different alleles coming from a male and a female on a particular locus, one of the alleles is selectively inherited into offsprings, which means that the so-called Mendel's law breaks. The segregation distortion occurs in meiosis. One of the mechanisms for causing the segregation distortion is that some genes make only gametes where particular alleles survive and kill the others. For example, in a case where gametes with an allele coming from a male survive, gametes with another allele coming from a female at the same locus are killed by genes coming from the male, where the allele coming from the female and the genes coming from the male have been combined by recombination in meiosis. These genes coming from the male, which do not allow another allele coming from the female to survive, increase the rate of the gametes including the particular allele. We call such genes *segregation distortion genes* hereinafter.

The basic mechanism by which the segregation distortion contributes to the speciation is roughly as follows. Suppose that there exists a segregation distortion gene coming from a male that kills a gamete including an allele coming from a female at a certain locus. At the same time, we can also theoretically suppose that there exists a segregation distortion gene coming from a female that kills a gamete including an allele coming from a male at another locus. If there exist segregation distortion genes coming from both of a male and a female as mentioned above, no gamete is produced.

As the basic principle of the reproductive isolation (speciation) mentioned above, the GC classifies data by producing the segregation distortion genes and then utilizing them. However, a procedure to produce the segregation distortion genes in the GC is not based on biological knowledge at all. In addition, for simplicity, a haploid chromosome is assumed here and it is considered whether a gamete is produced from a pair of haploid male and female chromosomes.

The algorithm flow of the GC for binary data is not described in the paper due to the page limitation. The algorithm flow is described in our previous work [14]. In addition, the algorithm flow of the GAuGC will be shown in Sect. 3 and it includes most parts of the algorithm flow of the GC.

2.2 Linkage Identification

The GC explained in Sect. 2.1 is used for linkage identification. The GC includes the GA procedures such as crossover and mutation, but the linkage identification method proposed herein focuses only on the procedure of generating the segregation distortion genes in the GC. In addition, the linkage identification method is combined with GA, as mentioned in Sect. 3, so chromosomes mentioned in the explanation below stand for ones selected by a selection operator of the GA.

The GC identifies a locus at which a particular allele more relatively frequently appears and then limits the application of crossover and mutation to the chromosomes that have the particular allele at the locus. The allele that relatively frequently appeared at the locus becomes the segregation distortion gene. The GC repeats this identification and limitation. We expect that the locus at which the segregation distortion gene appeared forms some linkage. The generated segregation distortion gene narrows the possible space for producing new chromosomes by crossover and a new segregation distortion gene is generated based on chromosomes produced in the narrowed space. We also expect that the locus at which the new segregation gene appeared forms some linkage.

The GC provides the appearance order of the segregation distortion gene at each locus. For example, suppose that an chromosome is a 5-bit string. Then, the order in which the segregation distortion genes appeared at the loci is represented in a vector form using sequential numbers as $(2, 1, 1, 3, 3)$. The vector form, $(2, 1, 1, 3, 3)$, indicates that the segregation distortion gene firstly appeared at the second and the third loci simultaneously and secondly appeared at the first locus and thirdly appeared at the fourth and fifth loci simultaneously. Each locus has two alleles, 0 or 1, but earlier order among the two alleles becomes the order for that locus.

The linkage identification method utilizes the appearance order of the segregation distortion genes at the loci for identifying the linkage. The method regards the loci having close orders as a particular linkage. This simple linkage identification cannot specify a clear border between two linkages. However, as we will mention in Sect. 3, genes at all loci on a chromosome are arranged in the appearance order for one point crossover not to seriously disrupt sub-strings of genes on identified linkages and to effectively mix the sub-strings, where the loci having the same appearance order are arranged in the order of locus number.

As described above, the linkage identification method simply relies on the appearance number of times of alleles. However, by the clustering function of the GC, we can expect that counting the appearance number of times of alleles is limited to chromosomes in a promising search space, which means that the clustering function facilitates local search.

3   Genetic Algorithm Using Genetic Clustering (GAuGC)

In the explanation below, we use the terms of individuals, positions, and values, which are equal to chromosomes, loci, and alleles in the linkage identification method and the GC, respectively.

The GAuGC is obtained by introducing GA procedures into the linkage identification method, so is similar to the GC. However, there are several differences between the two. First, unlike the GC, the GAuGC evaluates individuals using a fitness function. Second, one feature of the GC is to increase individuals by applying genetic operators to them while clustering the target individuals, but the GAuGC does not increase individuals. That is, the population size in the GAuGC is fixed. Third, the GAuGC uses tournament selection and one point crossover, but does not use mutation. Forth, unlike the GC, the GAuGC initializes the population whenever a certain condition is met. The condition is that a complete appearance order of segregation distortion genes at all positions has been determined.

Moreover, fifth, when producing new two individuals by the one point crossover, the values of the two individuals are first arranged in the appearance order of the segregation distortion genes at all ℓ positions. Then, the one point crossover is applied to the arranged ones. To realize such crossover, two arrays to record the appearance order of the segregation distortion genes at the ℓ positions, which are v_p and v_c with the length of ℓ, are prepared. The determination of the complete appearance order is repeatedly done. The latest complete appearance order is recorded in v_p and the current appearance order that is being determined is recorded in v_c. At the beginning, a vector of position numbers, $(1, 2, \ldots, \ell)$, is stored only in v_p, but nothing is stored in v_c.

The algorithm flow of the GAuGC is as follows.

1. The algorithm randomly generates the initial population of size P.
2. Every individual is evaluated by a given fitness function. Then, if the stop condition is met, the algorithm stops running. Otherwise, if the segregation distortion genes have been generated at all ℓ positions, the population is randomly re-generated. Furthermore, v_c that records the complete appearance order of those segregation distortion genes is copied onto v_p for recording the

latest complete appearance order of them. Then, the segregation distortion genes generated so far are all discarded and v_c is set to be empty. Regardless of whether the segregation distortion genes have been generated at all ℓ positions, the algorithm then selects $P/2$ pairs of individuals by the tournament selection operator of size K.

3. For each pair of selected individuals, the steps (a) and (b) are executed.

   (a) The algorithm judges if only one of the two selected individuals has the segregation distortion gene at some position. If so, they are reproductively isolated. Then, there is noting to do for the pair in the step (a). Otherwise, the selected individuals are not reproductively isolated, that is, are of the same species. Then, the algorithm updates the cumulative number of times that the same value, 0 or 1, appeared at each position on the selected two individuals of the same species. This record is conducted for all possible values, 0 and 1. After updating the record, if the cumulative number of times on each value (0 or 1) at each position exceeds a

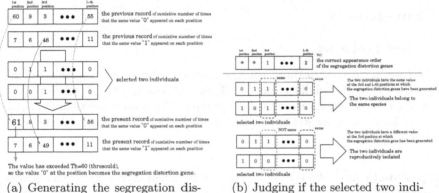

(a) Generating the segregation distortion gene.

(b) Judging if the selected two individuals are reproductively isolated.

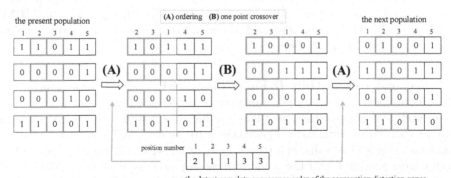

(c) Applying the one point crossover operator.

Fig. 1. Example of the procedures of the GAuGC.

threshold value, T_h, given in advance, the value at the position becomes the segregation distortion gene (see the example in Fig. 1(a)).

   If the segregation distortion gene newly appears at a position in the step, the appearance order of that new segregation distortion gene at the position is recorded in $\boldsymbol{v}_c$, and then, the cumulative number of times for every position is reset to be zero.

(b) If the two selected individuals are reproductively isolated, then the algorithm just returns the two selected individuals to the population. Otherwise, the algorithm conducts the one point crossover between the selected two individuals of the same species to produce new two individuals (see the example in Fig. 1(b)). The one point crossover operator is applied to the individuals that are arranged according to the linkage information, that is, $\boldsymbol{v}_p$ representing the latest complete appearance order of the segregation distortion genes. Then, the algorithm returns the newly produced two individuals to the population (see the example in Fig. 1(c)).

4. Go back to the step 2.

4 Simulations

4.1 Test Problems

All test problems used in the simulations were maximization problems and shuffled versions. In the shuffled version all variables of the problem are randomly positioned on the string of a solution candidate. The shuffled versions of problems are very hard for conventional fixed-operation-based evolutionary algorithms to optimize.

Trap Function (TRAP) [6]. This test problem is the uniformly-scaled 4-bit deceptive trap function. The problem consists of multiple 4-bit deceptive problems. The 4-bit deceptive problem gives 1 when the solution candidate has four 1s, gives 0 when it has three 1s, gives 0.25 when it has two 1s, gives 0.5 it has one 1, gives 0.75 when it has no 1, as fitness. We call this problem **TRAP** hereinafter. TRAP is a non-hierarchical decomposable problem. As the problem size of ℓ, we use 24, 32, 40 here.

Hierarchical If-And-Only-If Function (HIFF) [15,17]. The structure of the Hierarchical If-And-Only-If function is represented as a balanced binary tree. Each leaf node of the tree takes a value 0 or 1 and a set of leaf nodes is equal to a solution candidate. The fitness value of each leaf node is 1 no matter what its value is. The value of a parent node in the tree is 0 when all its children nodes have a value 0 and the value of a parent node is 1 when all its children nodes have a value 1. In all other cases, a parent node is not assigned any value. The internal and parent nodes have the fitness $2^{height(X)}$, where X is a node and $height(X)$ is a distance from its leaf nodes, if and only if all their children nodes have either 0 or 1. Otherwise, they have the fitness 0. The entire fitness value of a solution candidate is the sum of the fitnesses of all nodes in the tree and each level of the tree contributes to the entire fitness at the same magnitude.

We call this problem **HIFF** hereinafter. HIFF is a hierarchical decomposable problem. As the problem size of ℓ, we use 32, 64, 128 here.

Hierarchical Trap Function (HTRAP) [15,17]. The structure of the Hierarchical Trap function is represented as a balanced k-*ary* tree with $k \geqq 3$. Each leaf node of the tree takes a value 0 or 1 and a set of leaf nodes is equal to a solution candidate. The bit length of a solution candidate is k to the a-th power, where a is a positive integer. The value of a parent node in the tree is 0 when all its children nodes have a value 0 and the value of a parent node is 1 when all its children nodes have a value 1. In all other cases, a parent node is not assigned any value. In the tree, k nodes in every level of the tree is regarded as the k-bit deceptive problem and the fitness value of a parent node of the k nodes is given by $f(u(X)) \times k^{height(X)}$, where X is a parent node of focus and $f(u(X))$ is the fitness of the k-bit deceptive problem represented by Eq. (1).

$$f(u) = \begin{cases} f_{high} & u = k, \\ f_{low} - u \times \frac{f_{low}}{k-1} & otherwise. \end{cases} \tag{1}$$

At the root node $f_{high} = 1$ and $f_{low} = 0.9$, while for all other internal nodes $f_{high} = f_{low} = 1$. The global optimal solution is thus the string of all ones. However, this problem biases the search to the solution of all zeroes on each but the top level. In addition, the top level is fully deceptive with the all zeroes solution as deceptive attractor.

We call this problem **HTRAP** hereinafter. HTRAP is a hierarchical decomposable problem. As the problem size of ℓ, we use 9, 27, 81 here.

Hierarchically Dependent Function (HDEP) [7]. The test problem was devised by us. The test problem includes hierarchical dependency among variables in terms of fitness values, and is hard to determine values of variables at higher hierarchies correctly due to a sort of deception included in the problem, and leads to incorrect determination of values of variables at lower hierarchies if the determination at higher hierarchies is incorrect. How to generate the instance of this test problem and the details of the problem instance used in the preset paper is described in our previous work [7].

To generate the instance of the test problem here, a connected graph using the algorithm described in [4] is first generated. The topology of the generated graph follows a power law [1] with respect to the distribution of degree. Then, a 2-bit problem that includes a sort of deception is assigned to every edge between two nodes in the graph. The total number of the 2-bit problems assigned on the generated graph is equal to the number of the edges of the graph. The fitness of a solution candidate is obtained by dividing the sum of the fitnesses of all the 2-bit problems by the number of the edges.

We call this problem **HDEP** hereinafter. HDEP is a hierarchical nearly decomposable problem in which two sub-problems shares just one variable. As the problem size of ℓ, we use 20, 30, 40 here.

N-K Landscape Function (K = 4) (NKL-K4) [10]. This problem is a problem with dependencies between variables. N represents the size of problem and is equivalent to ℓ that is used as the notation of the problem size in this paper. Each variable of the problem takes 0 or 1 and the fitness of each variable depends on its K neighboring variables. In this paper we use $K = 4$. We call this problem **NKL-K4** hereinafter. NKL-K4 is a non-hierarchical indecomposable problem in which two sub-problems shares four variable. As the problem size of ℓ, we use 20, 30, 40 here.

In NKL-K4, the fitness of g in the sequential five bits, $(g_{r1}, g_{r2}, g, g_{\ell1}, g_{\ell2})$, is determined by referring to Table 1, in which all possible combinations of values of $(g_{r1}, g_{r2}, g, g_{\ell1}, g_{\ell2})$ and their corresponding fitness values are presented. In addition, the most-right bit (the most-left bit) is connected to the most-left bit (the most-right bit). The fitness of a solution candidate is obtained by dividing the sum of fitness of all variables by $N(= \ell)$.

Table 1. The fitness of g in the sequential five bits, $(g_{r1}, g_{r2}, g, g_{\ell1}, g_{\ell2})$, in NKL-K4.

5-bit	Fitness	5-bit	Fitness	5-bit	Fitness	5-bit	Fitness
00000	0.036486	01000	0.258027	10000	0.315626	11000	0.101828
00001	0.833081	01001	0.467604	10001	0.575035	11001	0.533017
00010	0.267900	01010	0.243886	10010	0.704985	11010	0.118997
00011	0.011235	01011	0.040266	10011	0.283613	11011	0.546785
00100	0.882766	01100	0.178573	10100	0.66152	11100	0.516638
00101	0.213545	01101	0.803215	10101	0.175868	11101	0.707389
00110	0.778439	01110	0.903812	10110	0.979191	11110	0.038014
00111	0.537816	01111	0.262323	10111	0.886160	11111	0.452097

Multidimensional Knapsack Problem (MKP) [5,12]. The multidimensional knapsack problem is a non-hierarchical indecomposable problem. We call this problem **MKP** hereinafter. Unlike a conventional knapsack problem, MKP introduces multiple knapsacks (resources) with their own capacities, in which an item is stuffed simultaneously. The problem instances can be downloaded from [2] and we use the 20th and 30th problem instances that have a tightness ratio α of 0.50 and 0.75, respectively, described in "mknapcb1.txt". The smaller the value of α, the harder the problem. The problem size of ℓ is 100.

4.2 Algorithms for Comparison and Algorithm Configurations

We used the extended compact genetic algorithm (ECGA) [8] and the linkage tree genetic algorithm (LTGA) [3] as algorithms for comparison. We made the program of the ECGA by ourselves, but downloaded the program of the LTGA from the Web page of the first author of [3].

The population size P of the GAuGC was 5000, 10000, or 20000. The value of the parameter T_h of the GAuGC was $P/5$. The stop conditions for the GAuGC with P = 500, P = 10000, P = 20000 were 800, 400, 200 generations, respectively. For any case, the maximum number of function evaluations is four hundred millions, but since the GAuGC does not produce new individuals when parent individuals are productively isolated, the total number of function evaluations in a simulation run usually in between three hundred millions and four hundred millions.

The population size P of the ECGA was 5000 and that of the LTGA was 200, 300, or 400. The stop condition of the ECGA and the LTGA was four hundred millions function evaluations. However, both algorithms judge if the population is converged, and if judging so, they stop running even if the stop condition is not met.

4.3   Results and Discussion

The simulation results are shown in Table 2. Each algorithm ran 30 times for each problem. However, we did not obtain the results of the ECGA for HIFF with $\ell = 128$ and MKP with $\ell = 100$ because the ECGA takes very long time for larger size of problems. The results of the LTGA for HIFF and HTRAP were read from the result graphs presented in [17].

We can observe from Table 2 that the GAuGC obtained better solutions against NKL-K4 and MKP compared to the ECGA and the LTGA. We assume the reason for that is related to the proposed linkage identification method. The basis of the proposed linkage identification method is local search that examines which variable value converges relatively earlier than others first, then fixes the variable value mandatorily, and facilitates the convergence of other variables under the fixation. This local search strategy is thought to be one of promising approaches to solving hard problems with weak decomposability, NKL-K4 and MKP in the paper, because it is difficult to determine appropriate values for all or most variables simultaneously in such problems.

Meanwhile, we can also observe from Table 2 that the GAuGC did not obtain better solutions against problems with strong decomposability compared especially to the LTGA. For such problems, accurate linkage identification is though to contribute to finding better solutions. However, the proposed linkage identification method does not directly examine if there is a linkage between variables but examine which variable value converges relatively earlier and consider variables with close convergence order to be a linkage, and therefore, cannot conduct accurate linkage identification.

In addition, we can observe from Table 2 that the GAuGC had much worse search performance against TRAP, HTRAP, and HDEP that include the factor of deception compared to the LTGA. The reason for that would be also related to the proposed linkage identification. It is generally hard to obtain optimum solutions for all sub-problems that form an entire problem including the factor

Table 2. Simulation results. N_r represents the number of success runs out of 30 runs. N_e represents the average number of function evaluations for N_r success runs. F_a represents the average of the best fitness values ever-obtained at the end.

Population size			GAuGC			ECGA	LTGA		
			5000	10000	20000	5000	200	300	400
TRAP	$\ell = 24$	N_r	29	30	30	30	30	25	0
		N_e	1.1×10^6	6.1×10^5	9.5×10^5	2.1×10^4	8.4×10^3	1.2×10^4	-
		F_a	5.9910	6	6	6	6	5.9583	5.5583
	$\ell = 32$	N_r	2	1	0	29	30	16	0
		N_e	2.0×10^6	8.4×10^5	-	3.7×10^4	1.5×10^4	1.8×10^4	-
		F_a	7.7666	7.7583	7.75	7.9833	8	7.8833	7.1750
	$\ell = 40$	N_r	0	0	0	17	26	0	0
		N_e	-	-	-	5.7×10^4	1.9×10^4	-	-
		F_a	9.75	9.75	9.75	9.8583	9.9583	8.7083	8.7583
HIFF	$\ell = 32$	N_r	30	30	30	30	30	-	-
		N_e	8.4×10^4	1.5×10^5	2.7×10^5	5.4×10^4	2.0×10^3	-	-
		F_a	192	192	192	192	192	-	-
	$\ell = 64$	N_r	30	30	30	1	30	-	-
		N_e	4.4×10^5	5.1×10^5	9.0×10^5	1.3×10^5	9.0×10^3	-	-
		F_a	448	448	448	338.4	448	-	-
	$\ell = 128$	N_r	0	6	9	-	30	-	-
		N_e	-	2.6×10^6	2.5×10^6	-	2.5×10^4	-	-
		F_a	7.5×10^2	8.6×10^2	8.9×10^2	-	1024	-	-
HTRAP	$\ell = 9$	N_r	30	30	30	30	-		
		N_e	5.8×10^2	5.3×10^2	4.8×10^2	4.0×10^2	-	-	-
		F_a	6	6	6	6	-	-	-
	$\ell = 27$	N_r	12	11	16	27	30		
		N_e	1.6×10^6	1.5×10^6	1.8×10^6	3.7×10^4	1.0×10^4	-	-
		F_a	26.4	26.4	26.5	26.9	27	-	-
	$\ell = 81$	N_r	0	0	0	0	30		
		N_e	-	-	-	-	6.0×10^4	-	-
		F_a	105.3	105.3	105.3	105.3	108	-	-
HDEP	$\ell = 20$	N_r	22	21	24	17	30	30	29
		F_a	1.7×10^6	1.2×10^6	1.5×10^6	2.8×10^4	3.8×10^3	3.8×10^3	3.3×10^3
		F_a	9.88	9.87	9.91	9.79	10	10	9.98
	$\ell = 30$	N_r	0	1	0	0	30	30	12
		N_e	-	2.9×10^6	-	-	7.4×10^3	1.0×10^4	7.6×10^3
		F_a	9.44	9.45	9.44	9.69	10	10	9.82
	$\ell = 40$	N_r	0	0	0	0	30	3	1
		N_e	-	-	-	-	1.1×10^4	6.3×10^3	4.2×10^3
		F_a	9.16	9.11	9.07	9.15	10	9.64	9.71
NKL-K4	$\ell = 20$	N_r	30	30	30	30	30	30	28
		N_e	4.2×10^4	3.9×10^4	4.3×10^4	5.7×10^4	2.3×10^3	2.2×10^3	2.7×10^3
		F_a	0.6591	0.6591	0.6591	0.6591	0.6591	0.6591	0.6578
	$\ell = 30$	N_r	30	29	28	4	18	19	3
		N_e	6.3×10^5	6.9×10^5	7.4×10^5	1.6×10^5	1.3×10^4	1.6×10^4	8.1×10^3
		F_a	0.6591	0.6587	0.6582	0.6422	0.6539	0.6543	0.6433
	$\ell = 40$	N_r	16	13	12	0	1	0	0
		N_e	1.6×10^6	1.4×10^6	1.9×10^6	-	1.6×10^4	-	-
		F_a	0.6545	0.6536	0.6532	0.6354	0.6447	0.6343	0.6325
MKP ($\ell = 100$)	$\alpha = 0.50$	F_a	44351	44468	44495	-	40185	40279	40371
	$\alpha = 0.75$	F_a	59751	59868	59900	-	56886	57078	57099

of deception unless the algorithm identifies linkages accurately and then utilizes the identified linkage information for producing solution candidates. Since the GAuGC determines values of variables that form the identified linkage based simply on the appearance frequency of the values of the variables while conducting rough linkage identification, it would be hard for the GAuGC to obtain optimum solutions for all sub-problems including the factor of deception, especially when the number of sub-problems is large.

Lastly, the LTGA stops running if the variance of the fitness values of the population becomes zero, besides reaching four hundred millions function evaluations. We observed during the simulations that the larger the population size became, the more frequently such stop before obtaining global optimum occurred. At this moment, we cannot guess the reason for that, and will investigate it in future work.

5 Concluding Remarks

We have proposed the simple linkage identification method based on the genetic clustering method and the genetic algorithm using the proposed linkage identification method, called the GAuGC. We have also applied the GAuGC to decomposable, nearly decomposable, and indecomposable problems. The results have shown that the GAuGC better solves problems with weak decomposability than the linkage tree genetic algorithm for comparison and have also shown that it cannot handle the deception well.

In the future work, we will investigate the search performance of the GAuGC against problems with weak decomposability in more details. Meanwhile, we will improve the search performance of the GAuGC against problems with the factor of deception by making the procedure of the linkage identification and that of determining values for variables that form the identified linkage independent. More concretely, we will consider a method for initializing a population by which initial individuals are produced using past better individuals and the latest linkage information. Since the initialization of a population is done many times in one run of the GAuGC, the method would contribute to better search performance.

References

1. Barabasi, A.L., Albert, R.: Emergence of scaling in random networks. Science **286**, 509–512 (1999)
2. Beasley, J.E.: Or-library, multidimensional knapsack problem (1990). http://people.brunel.ac.uk/~mastjjb/jeb/orlib/mknapinfo.html
3. Bosman, P.A.N., Thierens, D.: More concise and robust linkage learning by filtering and combining linkage hierarchies. In: 2013 Genetic and Evolutionary Computation Conference (GECCO 2013), pp. 359–366 (2013)
4. Bu, T., Towsley, D.: On distinguishing between internet power law topology generators. In: Proceedings of IEEE INFOCOM 2002, pp. 638–647 (2003)

5. Chu, P.C., Beasley, J.E.: A genetic algorithm for the multidimensional knapsack problem. Heuristics **4**, 63–86 (1998)
6. Deb, K., Goldberg, D.E.: Analyzing deception in trap functions. Found. Genet. Algorithms **2**, 93–108 (1993)
7. Hamano, K., Ohnishi, K., Köppen, M.: Evolution of developmental timing for solving hierarchically dependent deceptive problems. In: Dick, G., et al. (eds.) SEAL 2014. LNCS, vol. 8886, pp. 58–69. Springer, Cham (2014). doi:10.1007/978-3-319-13563-2_6
8. Harik, G.: Learning via probabilistic modeling in the ECGA. IlliGAL Report No. 99010, Illinois Genetic Algorithms Lab., Univ. of Illinois, Urbana, IL (1999)
9. Hsu, S.H., Yu, T.L.: Optimization by pairwise linkage detection, incremental linkage set, and restricted/back mixing: DSMGA-II. In: 2015 Genetic and Evolutionary Computation Conference (GECCO 2015), pp. 519–526 (2015)
10. Kauffman, S.A., Weinberger, E.D.: The NK model of rugged fitness landscapes and its application to maturation of the immune response. Theoret. Biol. **141**(2), 211–245 (1989)
11. Larranaga, P., Lozano, J.A.: Estimation of Distribution Algorithms: A New Tool for Evolutionary Computation. Kluwer Academic Publishers, Dordrecht (2001)
12. Martins, J.P., Fonseca, C.M., Delbem, A.C.: On the performance of linkage-tree genetic algorithms for the multidimensional knapsack problem. Neurocomputing **146**(C), 17–29 (2014)
13. Munetomo, M.: Linkage identification with epistasis measure considering monotonicity condition. In: 4th Asia-Pacific Conference on Simulated Evolution and Learning, pp. 550–554 (2002)
14. Ohnishi, K., Koeppen, M., Ahn, C.W., Yoshida, K.: Genetic clustering based on segregation distortion caused by selfish genes. In: Proceedings of 2012 IEEE International Conference on Systems, Man, and Cybernetics (IEEE SMC 2012) (2012)
15. Pelikan, M., Goldberg, D.E.: Hierarchical problem solving and the Bayesian optimization algorithm. In: Proceedings of Genetic and Evolutionary Computation Conference (GECCO 2000), pp. 267–274 (2000)
16. Pelikan, M., Goldberg, D.E., Lobo, F.: A survey of optimization by building and using probabilistic models. IlliGAL Report No. 99018, Illinois Genetic Algorithms Lab., Univ. of Illinois, Urbana, IL (1999)
17. Thierens, D., Bosman, P.: Hierarchical problem solving with the linkage tree genetic algorithm. In: Proceedings of Genetic and Evolutionary Computation Conference (GECCO 2013), pp. 877–884 (2013)
18. Thierens, D., Goldberg, D.E.: Mixing in genetic algorithms. In: Proceedings of 5th International Conference on Genetic Algorithms (ICGA-1993). pp. 38–45 (1993)
19. Yu, T.L., Goldberg, D.E., Sastry, K., Lima, C.F., Pelikan, M.: Dependency structure matrix, genetic algorithms, and effective recombination. Evol. Comput. **17**(4), 595–626 (2009)

Learning of Sparse Fuzzy Cognitive Maps Using Evolutionary Algorithm with Lasso Initialization

Kai Wu and Jing Liu[✉]

Key Laboratory of Intelligent Perception and Image Understanding of Ministry of Education, Xidian University, Xi'an 710071, China
kaiwu@stu.xidian.edu.cn, neouma@163.com

Abstract. Fuzzy cognitive maps (FCMs), characterized by a great deal of abstraction, flexibility, adaptability, and fuzzy reasoning, are widely used tools for modeling dynamic systems and decision support systems. Research on the problem of finding sparse FCMs from observed data is outstanding. Evolutionary algorithms (EAs) play a key role in learning FCMs from time series without expert knowledge. In this paper, we first involve sparsity penalty in the objective function optimized by EAs. To improve the performance of EAs, we develop an effective initialization operator based on the Lasso, a convex optimization approach. Comparative experiments on synthetic data with varying sizes and densities compared with other state-of-the-art methods demonstrate the effectiveness of the proposed approach. Moreover, the proposed initialization operator is able to promote to performance of EAs in learning sparse FCMs from time series.

Keywords: Fuzzy cognitive maps · Evolutionary algorithm · Lasso

1 Introduction

Fuzzy cognitive maps (FCMs), introduced by Kosko [1], inheriting main aspects of fuzzy logic and neural networks, are a kind of graph models that visualize expert knowledge as weighted directed graphs. The nodes in the graph are utilized to stand for real world concepts (variables, attributes etc.) and weighted edges represent the relations between nodes. The causal relationships among concepts can be determined by experts' knowledge or by learning approaches when historical data are available. Benefiting from their advantages in terms of abstraction, flexibility, adaptability, and fuzzy reasoning, FCMs have been applied in a variety of applications, i.e., time series analysis [2, 3], control [4], political and social sciences [5], decision making [8], and gene regulatory networks [9, 10].

There are many learning algorithms which have been used to develop FCMs [11]. Indeed, because of the subjective beliefs of expert(s), there are some deficiencies in the underlying theoretical framework that develop FCMs always based on human knowledge [12, 13]. These pitfalls imply that there is a genuine need to come up with learning schemes using which FCMs can be designed on the basis of observed data.

© Springer International Publishing AG 2017
Y. Shi et al. (Eds.): SEAL 2017, LNCS 10593, pp. 385–396, 2017.
https://doi.org/10.1007/978-3-319-68759-9_32

Over the years, automatic learning approaches, such as evolutionary approaches, have been proposed to handle the FCM learning problem.

There are many preeminent automatic learning algorithms, such as real-coded genetic algorithm (RCGA) [16], ant colony optimization (ACO) [17], and competent memetic algorithm (CMA) [21], and so forth. However, the weight matrix generated by automated learning approaches are much denser than the real weight matrix [22]. Stach *et al.* [22] proposed the sparse real-coded genetic algorithm (SRCGA) to learn sparse FCMs, but the predefined density parameter in SRCGA is not known in real-world applications. Being different from single-objective approaches, Chi and Liu [23] proposed the multi-objective evolutionary algorithm (MOEA-FCM) incorporating both measurement error and link density to learn sparse FCMs. In terms of single-objective EAs, none of them considers incorporating the sparsity of FCM into objective function of EAs. Thus, similar to previous work (LASSO$_{FCM}$) [6], in this paper, we optimize the objective of LASSO$_{FCM}$, which transforms the sparsity of FCM and measurement error into one by multiplying each objective function by a weighting factor and then summingup all contributions. Prior knowledge can effectively promote the performance of EAs. Therefore, different from initializing the population randomly, we propose a novel initialization operator based on the Lasso [6] for EAs to learn sparse FCMs. The performances of the proposed framework have been validated on synthetic data with various sizes and densities. Extensive experimental studies compared with other state-of-the-art approaches prove that the proposed method is effective.

The remainder of this paper is organized as follows. Section 2 gives an introduction on FCMs. Section 3 describes our learning framework for FCMs and the proposed initialization operator in detail. Section 4 presents experimental data, and compares Lasso initialization against random initialization. Section 5 concludes the work in this paper.

2   Fuzzy Cognitive Maps

An FCM is assigned fuzzy graph, structured as N concepts, and a vector C can represent these concepts,

$$C = [C_1, C_2, C_3, \ldots, C_N] \tag{1}$$

Each concept takes value in the range [0, 1]. The value of a concept reflects the degree to which the concept is active in the system at a particular time moment. The casual relationships between concepts are defined as an $N \times N$ weight matrix W

$$W = \begin{bmatrix} w_{11} & w_{12} & \cdots & w_{1N} \\ w_{21} & w_{22} & \cdots & w_{2N} \\ \vdots & \vdots & \ddots & \vdots \\ w_{N1} & w_{N1} & \cdots & w_{NN} \end{bmatrix} \tag{2}$$

where w_{ij} is in the range of $[-1, 1]$, and represents the relationship between concepts i and j, $i, j = 1, \ldots, N$. Each edge has a weight which indicates how much one concept affects another. There are three possible types of causal relationships, which express the type of influence from one concept to the others.

The value of concept i at the $(t + 1)$th iteration is influenced by the weight matrix and the state values of connected concept nodes at the tth iteration. The state vector in a particular iteration t, denoted as $A(t)$, contains the activation level of each concept (node) in that particular iteration. Formally, the activation level at the iteration $t + 1$ for each concept C_i is determined by the following equation,

$$A_i(t+1) = \psi \left(\sum_{j=1}^{N} w_{ji} A_j(t) \right) \tag{3}$$

where $A_i(t)$ is the activation degree of node i at the tth iteration, N is the number of nodes, w_{ij} is the edge weight between nodes i and j, and ψ is a transfer function that bounds the activation degree to the range of [0, 1]. To let the system evolve, the state vector A is passed repeatedly through the FCM weight matrix W. Equation (3) can be rewritten as $A = \psi(\Phi \times W)$. For data with S response sequences with T time point search, Φ is defined as,

$$\Phi = \begin{bmatrix} A_1^1(1) & A_2^1(1) & \cdots & A_N^1(1) \\ \vdots & \vdots & \ddots & \vdots \\ A_1^1(T-1) & A_2^1(T-1) & \cdots & A_N^1(T-1) \\ \vdots & \vdots & \ddots & \vdots \\ A_1^S(1) & A_2^S(1) & \cdots & A_N^S(1) \\ \vdots & \vdots & \ddots & \vdots \\ A_1^S(T-1) & A_2^S(T-1) & \cdots & A_N^S(T-1) \end{bmatrix} \tag{4}$$

where $A_i^k(t)$ is the state value of the ith concept at certain iteration t in the kth observed sequence.

Various transfer functions can be used, such as bivalent function, trivalent function, sigmoid function, and wavelet function [15]. According to the comparison study in [7], the sigmoid transformation function outperforms the others in general. Thus, the following sigmoid transformation function is employed,

$$\psi(x) = \frac{1}{1 + e^{-lx}} \tag{5}$$

where l is a parameter used to characterize the steepness of the function around zero. Usually a small l is suitable for highly nonlinear system. In this paper, l is set to 5.

3   The Proposed Method

3.1   Problem Formulation

$A = \psi(\Phi \times W)$ can be rewritten as $Y = \Phi \times W$ [6], where Y contains $\psi^{-1}(A)$ and ψ^{-1} is an inverse function for ψ. Due to decomposition strategy, this leads to N independent equations (sub-problems):

$$Y_i = \Phi \times W_i \tag{6}$$

$Y = [Y_1, Y_2, \ldots, Y_N]$, $W = [W_1, W_2, \ldots, W_N]$, where A_i contains $A_i(t)$ at different t, W_i is the weight vector from all nodes to the ith node. The vector Y_i and the matrix Φ can be obtained from historical data and the vector W_i to be learnt is sparse. For each sub-problem, considering the sparse constraint and measurement error as two factors, this problem can be formulated as

---

Algorithm 1 Framework of RCGA

Input:
maximum generation: *maxgen*;
population size: *pop*;
mating pool size: *pool*;
tournament size: *tour*;
crossoverprobability: *pc*;
mutation probability: *pm*;
lambda: λ;
the data: Y and A;
Output: weight matrix W.

Step 1) Node $i \leftarrow 1$;
Step 2) Optimize (7) using RCGA;

    Step 2.1)   Population initialization: $P^0 = \left\{ P_1^0, P_2^0, \cdots, P_{pop}^0 \right\}^T$;

    Step 2.2)   Obtain the best individual initialization: $P_{best}^0 = P_i^0$;

    Step 2.3)   Generation $t \leftarrow 0$;

    Step 2.4)   Select parental chromosomes for mating:
        $P_{Selection}^t = Selection\left(P^t, pool, tour \right)$;

    Step 2.5)   Perform genetic operators:
        $P_{GO}^t = GeneticOperation\left(P_{Selection}^t, pc, pm \right)$;

    Step 2.6)   Update population:
        $P^{t+1} = UpdatePopulation\left(P_{GO}^t, P^t \right)$;

    Step 2.7)   Update the best individual P_{best}^{t+1};

    Step 2.8)   If $t <$ *maxgen* and the fitness of $P_{best}^{t+1} >= 0.01$, then $t \leftarrow t+1$ and go to
        Step 2.4);
Step 3) $W_i \leftarrow P_{best}^{t+1}$;
Step 4) If ($i > N$), stop and output W; otherwise, $i \leftarrow i+1$ and go to **Step 2)**.

$$\min_{W_i}\left(\|\Phi W_i - Y_i\|_2^2 + \lambda\|W_i\|_1\right) \tag{7}$$

The first objective means minimizing the differences between the observed data and the historical data for concept i. The second objective is L_1-norm of W_i which represents the sparsity of local connections from the pool of all concepts to concept i.

3.2 Optimization Algorithm

To solve Eq. (7), we employ RCGA [16]. The whole framework of RCGA is shown in Algorithm 1. In Step (1), we set $i = 1$. In Step (2), RCGA is employed to dealing with Eq. (7). In Step (2.1) and Step (2.2), RCGA completes the population initialization task and selects the individual with the minimum fitness. In Step (2.4), RCGA first uses the deterministic tournament selection method to select parental individuals for mating in genetic algorithm. Then in Step (2.5), RCGA performs crossover and mutation operation on the chosen parental individuals $P_{Selection}^t$. The genetic operator can be the combination of BLX-α crossover [18] and non-uniform mutation operation [19], termed RCGA-U-B. We also use the another combination of simulated binary crossover (SBX) operator and polynomial mutation [20] for RCGA, termed RCGA-P-S. Step (2.6) is to refresh the current population by taking the best pop individuals from $P_{GO}^t \cup P^t$. In Step (2.7), we update the best individual and λ. In Step (3), when the stopping criterion satisfies, RCGA stops and outputs W_i. In step (4), when $i > N$, RCGA stops and outputs W.

3.3 Lasso Initialization

In this paper, we design a new operator to initialize population. For each sub-problem, consider LASSO$_{FCM}$ [6], which solves Eq. (7). Clearly, different choices for λ in the above equation will yield different optimal solutions and it is not easy to know the optimal λ, which will result in the best estimation of the ground-truth signal. However, we still get a set of solutions by using Lasso with different values of λ. For example, in order to generate pop individuals, we need to set pop different value of $\lambda_i \in [0, 1]$, $i = 1, 2, 3,..., pop$, and then solve Eq. (7) using LASSO$_{FCM}$ to generate pop solutions. The procedure for initialization operator is summarized in Algorithm 2. Note that we consider the condition that FCM cannot be fully reconstructed. Thus, EAs is used to optimize the results of LASSO$_{FCM}$ with different λ.

4 Experiments

This section consists of three parts. Section 4.1 introduces several measures to evaluate the performance of the proposed method and parameters setting for RCGA. Section 4.2 presents data that analyzes the effect of λ on the performance of RCGA. Section 4.3 compares the performance of RCGA with Lasso initialization against RCGA with random initialization. Section 4.4 compares the performance of the proposed method against other state-of-the-art methods.

Algorithm 2 Initialization Operator
Input:Φ (the sensing matrix), Y_i (the measurement vector), $\lambda_i \in [0,1], i = 1,2,3,\ldots, N_n$.
Output: the initial population P^0.
Step 1: $i \leftarrow 1$;
Step 2: $P_i^0 \leftarrow \text{LASSO}_{\text{FCM}}$ (Φ, Y_i, λ_i), solve this problem using LASSO$_{\text{FCM}}$ with λ_i and P_i^0 represents ith individual in the initial population;
Step 3: $i \leftarrow i+1$;
Step 4:If ($i > N_n$), stop; otherwise, go to Step 2.

4.1 Performance Measures and Parameter Settings

To evaluate the performance of the proposed initialization operator, the following measures are used. The first measure is *Data_Error*, which is used to evaluate the difference between available response sequences and generated response sequences,

$$Data\_Error = \frac{1}{NS(T-1)}(Y - Y^*)^2 \tag{8}$$

where Y^* is the state value of all concepts with S simulated sequence generated by candidate FCM, and Y is the state value of all concepts with S observed sequence, and each response sequence has T time points.

Model_Error is used to compare the weight matrix of learnt FCMs and target FCMs directly,

$$Model\_Error = \frac{1}{N^2}|W - W^*| \tag{9}$$

where W is weight matrix in input FCM, and W^* is weight matrix in candidate FCM. Note that $|\cdot|$ stands for l_1 norm.

In order to predict the existence of a link between two concepts, the learned weight needs to be transformed to binary one. In the following experiments, if the absolute value of a weight is less than 0.05, then there is no link; otherwise there is a link. Based on this, the measure *SS_Mean* is calculated,

$$SS\_Mean = \frac{2 \times Specificity \times Sensitivity}{Specificity + Sensitivity} \tag{10}$$

where

$$Specificity = \frac{TP}{TP + FN} \tag{11}$$

$$Sensitivity = \frac{TN}{TN + FP} \tag{12}$$

where TP is the number of true positives, FN is the number of false negatives, TN is the number of true negatives, and FP is the number of false positives (see Table 1). The value of SS_Mean is in the range of [0, 1], and the larger the value is, the better the performance is.

Table 1. The definition of TP, FP, FN, and TN.

Candidate FCM	Input FCM	
	0	1
0	TP	FP
1	FN	TN

To generate synthetic data with various scales and properties, first, the percent of nonzero weights is set, which is the target density. Then, each nonzero weight is generated randomly from $[-1, 1]$, and the abstract value of each nonzero weight needs to be larger than 0.05. Second, the initial state value of each concept node is randomly generated from [0, 1]. Then, the response sequences are generated using Eq. (3). These are the target response sequences and also the available data for the learning algorithms. More than one response sequence can be generated for an FCM.

For RCGA, we have chosen a reasonable set of values. The parameters of RCGA are showed in Table 2.

Table 2. The parameter settings of RCGA.

Parameter	Meaning	Value
$maxgen$	The maximum generation	10000
pop	Population size	100
$pool$	Size of the mating pool	50
$tour$	Tournament size	2
pc	Crossover rate (RCGA-U-B)	0.5
pm	Mutation rate (RCGA-U-B)	0.2
pc	Crossover rate (RCGA-P-S)	0.9
pm	Mutation rate (RCGA-P-S)	0.1
ηc	Distribution index for crossover	20
ηm	Distribution index for mutation	20

4.2 Effect of λ on Lasso Initialization

We conduct the following experiments to show the effect of λ on the proposed initialization operator. The generation method of mentioned FCM and data are described in Sect. 4.1. The experiments are conducted on FCMs with 10 nodes and 20 nodes and density = 20% and 40%. N_M is set to 2, where N_M is the total data length M divided by FCM size N. λ is increased from 0.00001 to 0.1 in steps of 0.005. For each setup, 10 independent runs are conducted with different input FCMs. We exhibit the corresponding *Data_Error*, *Model_Error*, and *SS_Mean* of RCGA with the Lasso initialization operator, as shown in Fig. 1.

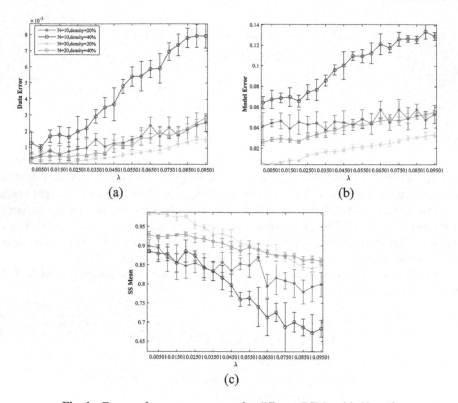

(a)   (b)

(c)

Fig. 1. Four performance measures for different FCMs with $N_M = 2$.

As seen, the value of λ has an important effect on the performance of Lasso initialization, even for small value of N_M, most links and weights can be identified. The greater value of λ contributes to lower value of *SS_Mean*, and higher values of *Data_Error* and *Model_Error*. With increasing N_M, this trend can be more clear. So wouldn't the best choice of lambda be zero? As is well known, to obtain a sparse W_i, we must increase λ properly. When $\lambda = 0$, this means that W_i is not the sparsest. In practice, there are many elements of W_i greater than zero but smaller than 0.05. In practice, when $|w_{ij}| < 0.05$, we set it to zero.

4.3   Comparison of Lasso Initialization Against Random Initialization

We conduct the following experiments to show the advantage of the proposed initialization operator. The number of nodes (N) is set to 10, 20, and 40, respectively, and the density is set to 20% and 40% for each scale. In this experiment, three types of response sequences are tested, namely 1 response sequence with 20 time points ($S = 1$, $T = 20$), 5 response sequences with 4 time point search ($S = 5$, $T = 4$), and 40 response sequences with 10 time points each ($S = 40$, $T = 10$). The performance of RCGAs with Lasso initialization is compared with those of RCGAs with random initialization in terms of *Data_Error* and *Model_Error* which are reported in Tables 3 and 4, respectively. Random Initialization stands for the initial population obtained by initializing population randomly, and Lasso Initialization stands for the initial population obtained by initializing population using LASSO$_{FCM}$. Without loss of generality, we set $\lambda = 0.005$.

Table 3. The experimental results in terms of *Data_Error*.

#Nodes	Density	S-T	Random initialization		Lasso initialization	
			RCGA-P-S	RCGA-U-B	RCGA-P-S	RCGA-U-B
10	20%	1-20	**0.002 ± 0.000**	0.001 ± 0.000	**0.002 ± 0.000**	0.006 ± 0.005
		5-4	0.013 ± 0.003	0.002 ± 0.000	**0.000 ± 0.000**	**0.000 ± 0.000**
		40-10	0.264 ± 0.080	0.084 ± 0.025	**0.009 ± 0.000**	**0.013 ± 0.001**
	40%	1-20	**0.016 ± 0.012**	0.002 ± 0.000	0.132 ± 0.000	**0.001 ± 0.000**
		5-4	**0.000 ± 0.002**	0.007 ± 0.000	**0.000 ± 0.000**	**0.001 ± 0.000**
		40-10	0.238 ± 0.048	0.141 ± 0.025	**0.061 ± 0.000**	**0.064 ± 0.003**
20	20%	1-20	**0.014 ± 0.002**	0.003 ± 0.000	0.021 ± 0.000	**0.002 ± 0.000**
		5-4	0.022 ± 0.001	0.007 ± 0.000	**0.004 ± 0.000**	**0.001 ± 0.000**
		4-10	0.467 ± 0.069	0.307 ± 0.021	**0.038 ± 0.000**	**0.059 ± 0.005**
	40%	1-20	**0.015 ± 0.000**	0.005 ± 0.000	0.074 ± 0.000	**0.003 ± 0.000**
		5-4	0.086 ± 0.003	0.016 ± 0.003	**0.015 ± 0.000**	**0.002 ± 0.000**
		40-10	1.943 ± 0.271	0.395 ± 0.033	**0.047 ± 0.000**	**0.078 ± 0.005**

From the results showed in Table 3, Lasso initialization outperforms random initialization except for 7 cases where $S = 1$ and $T = 20$. When $S = 1$ and $T = 20$, the *Data_Error* of RCGA-P-S with Lasso initialization performs worse than RCGA-P-S with random initialization except for one case. As seen, in terms of *Model_Error*, Lasso initialization outperforms random initialization in all cases.

4.4 Comparison of the Proposed Method Against Other Methods

In this section, we use the dataset described in Sect. 4.3. The performance of our method is compared with those of ACO$_{RD}$ [17], RCGA [16], D&C RCGA [14], and dMAGA [10] in terms of *SS_Mean*, which are reported in Table 5. P-S stands for RCGA-P-S and U-B represents RCGA-U-B. In terms of *SS_Mean*, P-S outperforms or matches U-B in 8 of 12 cases. Among the 4 cases with *S-T* = 1-20, dMAGA is the best in one cases. Among the 4 cases with *S-T* = 40-10, ACO$_{RD}$ is the best in all cases. P-S outperforms RCGA and D&C RCGA in all cases.

Table 4. The experimental results in terms of *Model_Error*.

#Nodes	Density	S-T	Random initialization		Lasso initialization	
			RCGA-P-S	RCGA-U-B	RCGA-P-S	RCGA-U-B
10	20%	1-20	0.106 ± 0.010	0.134 ± 0.012	**0.074 ± 0.000**	**0.086 ± 0.005**
		5-4	0.066 ± 0.005	0.062 ± 0.023	**0.018 ± 0.000**	**0.018 ± 0.000**
		40-10	0.100 ± 0.008	0.093 ± 0.016	**0.011 ± 0.000**	**0.024 ± 0.002**
	40%	1-20	0.218 ± 0.014	0.157 ± 0.010	**0.195 ± 0.010**	**0.110 ± 0.006**
		5-4	0.146 ± 0.015	0.108 ± 0.010	**0.028 ± 0.000**	**0.051 ± 0.003**
		40-10	0.159 ± 0.018	0.121 ± 0.011	**0.057 ± 0.000**	**0.075 ± 0.003**
20	20%	1-20	0.128 ± 0.009	0.120 ± 0.006	**0.097 ± 0.002**	**0.088 ± 0.003**
		5-4	0.102 ± 0.003	0.127 ± 0.011	**0.055 ± 0.000**	**0.036 ± 0.001**
		40-10	0.114 ± 0.009	0.119 ± 0.006	**0.023 ± 0.000**	**0.038 ± 0.002**
	40%	1-20	0.172 ± 0.006	0.217 ± 0.010	**0.147 ± 0.002**	**0.215 ± 0.009**
		5-4	0.180 ± 0.006	0.201 ± 0.012	**0.068 ± 0.000**	**0.095 ± 0.001**
		40-10	0.175 ± 0.002	0.151 ± 0.004	**0.035 ± 0.000**	**0.052 ± 0.002**

Table 5. The experimental results in terms of *SS_Mean*.

#Nodes	Density	S-T	P-S	U-B	dMAGA	D&C RCGA	ACO$_{RD}$	RCGA
10	20%	1-20	0.51	**0.61**	0.54	0.16	0.24	0.19
		5-4	**0.93**	0.86	0.81	0.16	0.86	0.17
		40-10	0.94	0.83	0.88	0.11	**0.95**	0.13
	40%	1-20	0.44	0.43	**0.46**	0.18	0.24	0.20
		5-4	**0.93**	0.92	0.53	0.10	0.87	0.23
		40-10	**0.86**	0.83	0.47	0.23	**1.00**	0.12
20	20%	1-20	**0.52**	0.50	0.46	0.08	0.24	0.16
		5-4	**0.83**	**0.83**	0.53	0.14	0.25	0.15
		40-10	**0.88**	**0.88**	0.33	0.14	**0.97**	0.15
	40%	1-20	0.47	**0.49**	0.48	0.08	0.16	0.15
		5-4	**0.80**	0.73	0.43	0.09	0.18	0.14
		40-10	**0.91**	0.86	0.50	0.10	**0.93**	0.16

5   Conclusions

In this paper, we have proposed a problem-specific initialization operator, based on the Lasso, to initialize the population of RCGA. Extensive experiments on FCMs with various sizes and densities have demonstrated the effectiveness of Lasso initialization compared with random initialization. As seen, Lasso initialization provides two additional heuristics for EAs: one with greater chance to increase speed of convergence toward the optimal solution, and another with higher probability to avoid local optimal solution. The experimental results also demonstrate that the proposed method with sparsity and Lasso initialization outperforms other methods.

Here, we analyze the computational complexity of Lasso initialization operator. As introduced in Subsect. 3.3, the proposed initialization operator needs O (pop • $(n^3 + n^2m)$) basic operations, where n stands for the number of nodes and m represents the sample size. However, random initialization operator just needs O (n) basic operations. Although Lasso initialization has higher computational complexity than random initialization, Lasso initialization can obtain better performance than random initialization.

Acknowledgements. This work is partially supported by the Outstanding Young Scholar Program of National Natural Science Foundation of China (NSFC) under Grant 61522311, the Overseas, Hong Kong & Macao Scholars Collaborated Research Program of NSFC under Grant 61528205, and the Key Program of Fundamental Research Project of Natural Science of Shaanxi Province, China under Grant 2017JZ017.

References

1. Kosko, B.: Fuzzy cognitive maps. Int. J. Man Mach. Stud. **24**(1), 65–75 (1986)
2. Song, H., Miao, C., Roel, W., Shen, Z., Catthoor, F.: Implementation of fuzzy cognitive maps based on fuzzy neural network and application in prediction of time series. IEEE Trans. Fuzzy Syst. **18**(2), 233–250 (2010)
3. Stach, W., Kurgan, L.A., Pedrycz, W.: Numerical and linguistic prediction of time series with the use of fuzzy cognitive maps. IEEE Trans. Fuzzy Syst. **16**(1), 61–72 (2008)
4. Stylios, C.D., Groumpos, P.P.: Modeling complex systems using fuzzy cognitive maps. IEEE Trans. Syst. Man Cybern. Part A: Syst. Hum. **34**(1), 155–162 (2004)
5. Andreou, A.S., Mateou, N.H., Zombanakis, G.A.: Soft computing or crisis management and political decision making: the use of genetically evolved fuzzy cognitive maps. Soft. Comput. **9**(3), 194–210 (2005)
6. Wu, K., Liu, J.: Robust learning of large-scale fuzzy cognitive maps via the lasso from noisy time series. Knowl.-Based Syst. **113**, 23–38 (2016)
7. Tsadiras, K.: Comparing the inference capabilities of binary, trivalent and sigmoid fuzzy cognitive maps. Inf. Sci. **178**, 3880–3894 (2008)
8. Salmeron, J.L., Papageorgiou, E.I.: A fuzzy grey cognitive maps-based decision support system for radiotherapy treatment planning. Knowl.-Based Syst. **30**, 151–160 (2012)
9. Chen, Y., Mazlack, L.J., Minai, A.A., Lu, L.J.: Inferring causal networks using fuzzy cognitive maps and evolutionary algorithms with application to gene regulatory network reconstruction. Appl. Soft Comput. **37**, 667–679 (2015)
10. Liu, J., Chi, Y., Zhu, C.: A dynamic multi-agent genetic algorithm for gene regulatory network reconstruction based on fuzzy cognitive maps. IEEE Trans. Fuzzy Syst. **24**(2), 419–431 (2016)
11. Papageorgiou, E.I.: Learning algorithms for fuzzy cognitive maps - a review study. IEEE Trans. Syst. Man Cybern. Part C **42**(2), 150–163 (2012)
12. Papageorgiou, E.I., Stylios, C.D., Groumpos, P.P.: Fuzzy cognitive map learning based on nonlinear Hebbian rule. In: Proceedings of Australian Conference on Artificial Intelligence, pp. 256–268 (2003)
13. Stach, W., Kurgan, L.A., Pedrycz, W.: Data-driven nonlinear Hebbian learning method for fuzzy cognitive maps. In: Proceedings of 2008 IEEE International Conference on Fuzzy Systems, pp. 1975–1981 (2008)

14. Stach, W., Kurgan, L., Pedrycz, W.: A divide and conquer method for learning large fuzzy cognitive maps. Fuzzy Sets Syst. 161(19), 2515–2532 (2010)
15. Wu, K., Liu, J., Chi, Y.: Wavelet fuzzy cognitive maps. Neurocomputing 232, 94–103 (2017)
16. Stach, W., Kurgan, L., Pedrycz, W., Reformat, M.: Genetic learning of fuzzy cognitive maps. Fuzzy Sets Syst. 153(3), 371–401 (2005)
17. Chen, Y., Mazlack, L.J., Lu, L.J.: Learning fuzzy cognitive maps from data by ant colony optimization. In: Proceedings of Genetic and Evolutionary Computation Conference, pp. 9–16 (2012)
18. Neubauer, A.: A theoretical analysis of the non-uniform mutation operator for the modified genetic algorithm. In: Proceedings of IEEE Congress on Evolutionary Computation, pp. 93–96 (1997)
19. Eshellman, L.J.: Real-coded genetic algorithms and interval-schemata. Found. Genet. Algorithms 2, 187–202 (1993)
20. Deb, K., Agrawal, R.B.: Simulated binary crossover for continuous search space. Complex Syst. 9(3), 1–15 (1994)
21. Acampora, G., Pedrycz, W., Vitiello, A.: A competent memetic algorithm for learning fuzzy cognitive maps. IEEE Trans. Fuzzy Syst. 23(6), 2397–2411 (2015)
22. Stach, W., Pedrycz, W., Kurgan, L.A.: Learning of fuzzy cognitive maps using density estimate. IEEE Trans. Syst. Man Cybern. Part B 42(3), 900–912 (2012)
23. Chi, Y., Liu, J.: Learning of fuzzy cognitive maps with varying densities using a multi-objective evolutionary algorithm. IEEE Trans. Fuzzy Syst. 24(1), 71–81 (2016)

A Bayesian Restarting Approach to Algorithm Selection

Yaodong He[⊠], Shiu Yin Yuen, and Yang Lou

Department of Electronic Engineering,
City University of Hong Kong, Hong Kong, China
{yaodonghe2-c, felix.lou}@my.cityu.edu.hk,
kelviny.ee@cityu.edu.hk

Abstract. A Bayesian algorithm selection framework for black box optimization problems is proposed. A set of benchmark problems is used for training. The performance of a set of algorithms on the problems is recorded. In the beginning, an algorithm is randomly selected to run on the given unknown problem. A Bayesian approach is used to measure the similarity between problems. The most similar problem to the given problem is selected. Then the best algorithm for solving it is suggested for the second run. The process repeats until n algorithms have been run. The best solution out of n runs is recorded. We have experimentally evaluated the property and performance of the framework. Conclusions are (1) it can identify the most similar problem efficiently; (2) it benefits from a restart mechanism. It performs better when more knowledge is learned. Thus it is a good algorithm selection framework.

Keywords: Evolutionary algorithm · Algorithm selection · Optimization problems · Bayesian approach · Monte Carlo method

1 Introduction

Typically, optimization problems lacking algebraic expressions are called black box optimization problems. The derivative information for these problems is not available. Evolutionary algorithms (EAs) are inspired by biological evolution. Since EAs treat an optimization problem as a black box, an optimization problem can be solved even though the algebraic expression and the gradient are unknown. On the other hand, most EAs are simple and easy to implement. Thus EAs are effective methods to solve optimization problems.

Nowadays, many powerful EAs have been invented. These EAs include genetic algorithm (GA) [1], evolutionary strategy (ES) [2], artificial bee colony algorithm (ABC) [3], differential evolution (DE) [4], particle swarm optimization (PSO) [5], etc. Moreover, new EAs are being invented each year. Although most of them are efficient, these algorithms are mainly improved from some old EAs. Famous algorithms such as composite DE [6] and self-adaptive DE [7] are evolved from DE. PSO2011 [8, 9] and Comprehensive learning particle swarm optimizer (CLPSO) [10] are evolved from PSO. Covariance matrix adaptation evolutionary strategy (CMA-ES) [11] is evolved from ES, etc. The explosion of EAs provides us with more choices, but it cannot solve

© Springer International Publishing AG 2017
Y. Shi et al. (Eds.): SEAL 2017, LNCS 10593, pp. 397–408, 2017.
https://doi.org/10.1007/978-3-319-68759-9_33

the issue that an EA may not perform well for certain problems. The no free lunch (NFL) theorems [12] inform us that no algorithm can perform well on all problems. On the other hand, some algorithms are designed to win competitions such as CEC [13] and BBOB [14]. Thus an algorithm may perform badly on solving real-world problems even though it performs very well on the benchmark suites. Therefore we need different algorithms for different types of problems. However, it is extremely difficult for a practitioner from other fields to choose a suitable algorithm. Also, it is unwise to try algorithms one by one since running an algorithm on the problem is frequently computationally intensive.

2 Related Works

Algorithm portfolio is one of the approaches proposed to deal with the issue mentioned above. A portfolio of algorithms is a collection of different algorithms which aims to fully utilize the advantages of these algorithms. It has been shown that combining multiple algorithms into a portfolio may perform better than a single algorithm [15]. So far, many effective ideas have been proposed. Tang et al. [16] and Yuen and Zhang [17] propose meta-algorithms that can compose a portfolio automatically for a given problem class.

Another reasonable approach called algorithm selection is to map problem space and algorithm space, and suggests suitable algorithms for different problems [18]. However, the work is not easy due to the complexity of mapping the two spaces.

One tries to construct such a map by measuring problem characteristics and algorithm performance, using machine learning models. The framework of algorithm selection was proposed by Rice [19]. There are three spaces: problem space, algorithm space, and performance space. A problem space consists of a set of problems. An algorithm space consists of a set of algorithms for solving the problems. A performance space is a set of values to measure algorithm performance such as the quality of the found solutions, how much resource is needed to find a good solution, or the robustness of the algorithm, etc. In this paper, the quality of the found solutions is used.

Given a problem, a set of features can be extracted. Although different methods may use different features, many researches focus on landscape characterization. Explorative landscape analysis (ELA) methods can be used to extract features such as the number of optima, the size of the basins of attraction, the magnitude of change in fitness within a neighborhood [20]. Bischl et al. [21] propose an algorithm selection approach which incorporates a cost sensitive learning method. A set of features is computed by ELA. The features are mapped to the best algorithm by the learning method. Muñoz et al. [22] propose a robust information content-based method for continuous landscape. The method is tested on the BBOB 2010 benchmark functions. It classifies the functions into five groups. The classification accuracy is greater than 90%.

Although ELA seems good, it has a shortcoming: ELA methods consume the function evaluation budget. The methods can be expensive if sufficient and accurate information is required [19]. To overcome it, recently Kerschke et al. [23] propose a low-budget ELA method. In this paper, we try to overcome the problem by a different method.

Recently, we proposed a sequential learnable evolutionary algorithm (SLEA) [24] for solving black box continuous single objective optimization problems. The framework of SLEA is shown in Fig. 1. Let $A = \{A_1, \ldots, A_q\}$ be a set of q algorithms. Let $P = \{P_1, \ldots, P_r\}$ be a set of r problems. Assume a given optimization problem $\wp$ is unknown. In the beginning, algorithm A_{r1} ($r1$ stands for the first run) is selected from A to run on $\wp$. After T evaluations, feature(s) and the fitness values are obtained in the feature extraction process. As these features are specific to the algorithm, we coin the term algorithm-problem features to describe them. The idea is most similar to landmarking in machine learning [25], except that in landmarking, a set of simple algorithms are used to extract features. In the problem identification process, feature(s) is used to measure the similarity between problems. SLEA will map $\wp$ to the most similar problem. According to the mapping result, SLEA will suggest a suitable EA as the second algorithm A_{r2} to run on $\wp$. The process repeats until n algorithms have been run, where n is a user defined number.

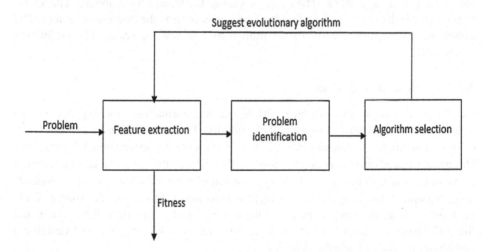

Fig. 1. General framework of SLEA and SLEA-b

SLEA is an algorithm with n restarts. Algorithm selection is done in each restart using all existing knowledge about the problem. When one tries to solve an optimization problem, it is reasonable to run an EA several times and choose the best result. In a single run, an algorithm may fall into a local optimum that will take exponential time to escape and thus return a bad result. Running an algorithm with restarts may avoid these shortcomings. Apart from SLEA, some existing approaches [26, 27] also use restarts to improve performance and robustness.

The rest of this paper is organized as follows. In Sect. 3, we propose a novel approach called Bayesian sequential learnable evolutionary algorithm (SLEA-b). Section 4 reports experimental results. Section 5 recaps our findings and brings the paper to a conclusion.

3   Bayesian Sequential Learnable Evolutionary Algorithm

In this section, we describe the SLEA-b. It inherits the advantages of SLEA and uses a Bayesian approach to measure the similarity between problems. It is able to identify similar problems more efficiently. The general framework of SLEA-b is the same as SLEA. It includes three main steps: feature extraction, problem identification, and algorithm selection. Compared with SLEA, the main improvement of SLEA-b lies in problem identification. A Bayesian approach is reported to measure the similarity between two problems.

3.1   Feature Extraction

In the feature extraction process, a suggested EA is run on $\wp$. SLEA-b will suggest $n-1$ algorithms which might be the same or different. The algorithm for the first run is randomly selected from the algorithm set. We record the convergence curve of an algorithm solving a problem. The curve is used as the feature for mapping. The x-axis of the curve is the number of evaluations, the y-axis records the best fitness values. The fitness values are normalized to span from 0 to 1 to achieve scale and translational invariance.

3.2   Problem Identification

In SLEA, the mean squared error (MSE) of the normalized convergence curves between problems is used to measure the similarity. The normalized convergence curve of $A_j \in A$ solving $\wp$ is denoted as $C(\wp, A_j)$. Two curves are more similar if they have less mean squared error. $\wp$ is mapped to $P_i \in P$ which has the most similar convergence curve to $C(\wp, A_j)$. In this method, the comparison of the most similar problem depends on comparing convergence curves, which may be noisy. Moreover, the choice of the next algorithm to run purely depends on the result of the last run. In SLEA-b, we would like the choice to depend on all previous runs. In the following, we will describe a Bayesian approach to achieve this.

The normalized convergence curve $C(\wp, A_j)$ of applying algorithm A_j to unknown problem $\wp$ is compared with the median normalized convergence curve $C(P_i, A_j)$, where P_i is a known problem in the knowledge database. (The method to select the median normalized convergence curve will be detailed in the next section.) Since $C(\wp, A_j)$ is obtained in a single run, it is noisy. Let the mean squared error between the two curves be e. During off-line training, we can let $\wp = P_i$. One can plot the probability of the error being e. We can use a Monte Carlo method to calculate the approximate conditional probability $Pr(e|\wp = P_i)$ for each problem i off-line.

The procedure is as follows: Algorithm A_j is run on problem P_i. The normalized convergence curve is obtained and compared with the median normalized convergence curve $C(P_i, A_j)$ in the knowledge base. We define the convergence curve which has the median fitness result out of the convergence curve in the knowledge base as the median convergence curve. Let e be the error. We can use a histogram to store the error. After many Monte Carlo trials, one can normalize the histogram to obtain $Pr(e \mid \wp = P_i)$. For this method to work, it is necessary to determine the bin size, and the number of trials should be large to approximate $Pr(e \mid \wp = P_i)$ and $Pr(e)$ well.

This process is repeated m times. Then the histogram is normalized such that the sum of the bins is 1. This gives an approximate $Pr(e \mid \wp = P_i)$. Let r be the number of problems in the knowledge base. The process is repeated for each of the r problems in the knowledge base. This gives r probability curves as a function of e, $Pr(e \mid \wp = P_1).,\ldots, Pr(e \mid \wp = P_r)$. By computing the average of these functions, we can obtain an approximate $Pr(e)$. If we assume $Pr(\wp = P_1) = Pr(\wp = P_2)\ldots = Pr(\wp = P_r) = \frac{1}{r}$, we can estimate $Pr(\wp = P_i \mid e)$ using the Bayes' rule since $Pr(\wp = P_i \mid e) = \frac{Pr(e \mid \wp=P_i)Pr(\wp=P_i)}{Pr(e)}$.

When A_j is run on unknown problem $\wp$, a normalized convergence curve is obtained. It is compared with the median normalized convergence curve of each of the r problems in the knowledge base. This gives r errors $e_1,\ldots, e_r$. The r conditional probabilities $Pr(\wp = P_1 \mid e_1),\ldots, Pr(\wp = P_r \mid e_r)$ are computed using the r probability curves. Problem $P^* = \underset{P_i}{argmax} \{Pr(\wp = P_1 \mid e_1),\ldots, Pr(\wp = P_i \mid e_i),\ldots, Pr(\wp = P_r \mid e_r)\}$ which has the largest conditional probability is selected to be the most similar problem to $\wp$.

The following gives an illustrative example. Let P be the CEC 2013 benchmark suite with 28 problems, and $\wp$ be most similar to $P_3 \in P$ in this example. Suppose ABC [3] is the selected algorithm for the first run. ABC is run on $\wp$ to generate a convergence curve. The normalized convergence curve $C(\wp, \text{ABC})$ is compared with 28 median normalized convergence curves respectively. Then the mean squared errors between them are computed. We can obtain 28 errors $e_1,\ldots, e_{28}$. If $Pr(\wp = P_3 \mid e_3)$ is the highest conditional probability, P_3 is selected to be the most similar problem to $\wp$.

Moreover, suppose $k < n$ runs have been made. The problem P^* which has the largest conditional probability averaged over k runs is selected as the most similar problem. Thus the Bayesian approach can integrate all knowledge learned in the previous k inferences to make the next decision.

3.3 Algorithm Selection

After the most similar problem P^* is selected, SLEA-b will suggest the best algorithm for P^*. To select the best algorithm, a knowledge table that records the best EA(s) on each problem is necessary. The number of rows and columns is the size of P and A respectively. Table 1 is an example that is trained by the CEC 2013 benchmark suite. We will describe the method to generate the table in the next section. The ith row records the rank of algorithms on problem P_i. After the most similar problem is selected, the best algorithm will be suggested by searching the ith row.

4 Experimental Results

We use the CEC 2013 benchmark suite as the training data which includes 28 minimization problems. In this section, we use f_i to represent P_i. There are three different

Table 1. Rank table of the nine algorithms on the CEC 2013 benchmark suite

	ABC	CLPSO	CMA-ES	CoDE	JADE	jDE	PSO 2011	RGA	SaDE
f_1	4	9	4	4	4	4	4	8	4
f_2	7	9	1	5	2	4	3	8	6
f_3	7	9	1	4	2	3	6	8	5
f_4	8	7	1	2	6	3	4	9	5
f_5	5	9	6	2.5	2.5	2.5	7	8	2.5
f_6	6	9	1	3	2	5	4	8	7
f_7	8	6	7	3	2	1	5	9	4
f_8	7	8	5	1	3	4	2	6	9
f_9	6	7	8	1	5	4	3	9	2
f_{10}	5	9	1	2	3	4	6	8	7
f_{11}	3	9	7	5	1.5	1.5	8	4	6
f_{12}	8	7	4	2	1	5	6	9	3
f_{13}	8	7	5	2	1	3	6	9	4
f_{14}	3	8	7	5	2	1	9	6	4
f_{15}	2	9	4	3	1	7	6	5	8
f_{16}	2	8	3	1	5	7	6	4	9
f_{17}	3	9	7	4	1.5	1.5	8	6	5
f_{18}	7	8	2	1	3	5	6	9	4
f_{19}	1	9	6	5	3	4	8	2	7
f_{20}	8	6	9	7	1	3	4	5	2
f_{21}	1	9	8	6	2	4	7	3	5
f_{22}	1	9	7	5	2	3	8	6	4
f_{23}	4	9	3	2	1	6	5	8	7
f_{24}	8	7	4	5	2	1	6	9	3
f_{25}	8	7	5	2	4	1	6	9	3
f_{26}	2	3	9	7	5	1	6	8	4
f_{27}	1	8	6	5	4	3	7	9	2
f_{28}	1	8	6	3.5	3.5	3.5	7	9	3.5

classes of continuous single objective problems. $f_1 - f_5$ are unimodal functions. $f_6 - f_{20}$ are basic multimodal functions. $f_{21} - f_{28}$ are composition functions. The dimension for each function is set to $D = 30$. The search range is set to $[-100, 100]^D$. The fitness evaluations (FES) is set to $10000 \times D$. To compose our knowledge database, we initially select 9 algorithms including ABC [3], CLPSO [10], CMA-ES [11], Composite Differential Evolution (CoDE) [6], JaDE [28], jDE [29], Real-coded Genetic Algorithm (RGA) [30, 31], Self-adaptive Differential Evolution (SaDE) [7], and standard Particle Swarm Optimization 2011 (PSO2011) [8, 9]. The population sizes of ABC, CLPSO, CMA-ES, CoDE, JaDE, jDE, RGA, SaDE and PSO2011 are 15, 40, 13, 30, 100, 100, 20, 50 and 21 which follow their recommended parameter settings in the above references. For each algorithm, each f_i has been run for 401 independent times. We choose a median normalized convergence curve which stands for a median convergence performance of A_j on f_i from the 401 curves. It records the median fitness result out of these 401 curves for each generation. The rest of the curves are compared with the median curve to estimate $Pr(e|\wp = f_i)$ and $Pr(e)$. The bin size of the histograms is set to 0.1.

Table 1 records the rank of the algorithms on the problems. In Table 1, there may be two or more algorithms performing the same on a problem. In that case, the ranks are shared amongst these algorithms. For example, the averaged ranks of ABC, CMA-ES, CoDE, JADE, jDE, PSO2011, SaDE on f_1 are $(1 + 7)/2$. The winner-take-all strategy is applied in SLEA-b. When the most similar problem is selected, only the best algorithm(s) for it will be suggested for the next run. When two or more algorithms are the best for a problem, SLEA-b picks one of them randomly. Because of the winner-take-all strategy, we care more about the best algorithm(s) than the ranking. The best algorithm(s) for each problem is marked with gray shading in Table 1. Note that neither CLPSO nor RGA is the best for any problem, so we remove them from the algorithm set. Thus the final algorithm set consists of 7 algorithms rather than 9 algorithms. We use a similar method as [32] in selecting algorithms, namely, the algorithms selected should be the best for at least one training problem. However, the main difference is that the performance data of CLPSO and RGA are still kept in the knowledge base, and it makes no difference whether we remove them from the algorithm set or not. This flexibility allows the scenario that later, CLPSO or RGA may be used once a benchmark problem is found for which it does best.

In the first experiment, SLEA-b is compared with SLEA. SLEA uses the mean squared error between two normalized convergence curves to measure the similarity. The 28 problems from the CEC 2013 suite are tested by SLEA and SLEA-b. The purpose is to investigate the performance of the two approaches on a small set of problems which has been seen before. The two approaches are set with 20 restarts, running 30 independent times. The percentage of identifying the same problem as the most similar problem is recorded in Tables 2 and 3 respectively. On most of the problems, SLEA-b performs better than SLEA. The average percentage that SLEA successfully identifies the most similar problems approximates to 48.0%. The average percentage of SLEA-b is higher which approximates to 63.7%. If the problems are selected by random, the percentage should approximate to $\frac{1}{28} = 3.57\%$. The high

Table 2. Accuracy of SLEA with 20 restarts on the CEC 2013 suite. The 2nd column to the 8th column record the percentage of finding the best algorithm for each problem.

$f_1 - f_7$	65.3%	33.8%	68.2%	8.00%	17.3%	68.8%	18.5%
$f_8 - f_{14}$	20.0%	33.7%	24.3%	81.7%	57.2%	45.8%	72.3%
$f_{15} - f_{21}$	43.2%	39.8%	87.3%	90.3%	47.2%	86.5%	54.8%
$f_{22} - f_{28}$	84.3%	62.7%	24.2%	56.7%	8.3%	32.5%	11.5%
Average	48.0%						

Table 3. Accuracy of SLEA-b with 20 restarts on the CEC 2013 suite. The 2nd column to the 8th column record the percentage of finding the best algorithm for each problem.

$f_1 - f_7$	96.0%	30.8%	91.2%	0.5%	11.3%	84.7%	10.2%
$f_8 - f_{14}$	46.0%	86.8%	41.2%	98.5%	79.8%	54.8%	88.8%
$f_{15} - f_{21}$	44.2%	72.7%	99.2%	98.2%	84.8%	92.8%	79.2%
$f_{22} - f_{28}$	88.5%	71.0%	80.0%	76.8%	9.67%	21.7%	45.2%
Average	63.7%						

percentage shows that: (1) both SLEA and SLEA-b can measure the similarity between problems efficiently; (2) the ability to measure the similarity is improved by the Bayesian approach.

Recall that the winner-take-all strategy is applied in SLEA-b, i.e., the suggested EA is the best for the selected problem. Thus finding the most similar problem is equivalent to finding the best algorithm for SLEA-b. If the average percentage of identifying the most similar problems is 63.7%, the average percentage of suggesting the best algorithm should not be lower than 63.7%. Thus we can conclude that SLEA-b is a good approach to suggest the best algorithm for problems that have been seen before.

We design SLEA-b which integrates all knowledge it has learned in the previous k runs. In the next experiment, we would investigate the effectiveness of the idea. We run SLEA-b with 5, 10 and 15 restarts on the CEC 2013 suite for 10 independent times. The average percentages of identifying the most similar problem by SLEA-b with 5, 10 and 15 restarts are 56.2%, 57.7%, and 62.0%. Tables 4, 5 and 6 record the detailed percentages. Figure 2 is the plot of average percentage versus number of runs. In the figure, the average percentage increases when the number of runs increases. It shows that SLEA-b performs better when more knowledge is learned. Thus we have experimentally shown that integrating all knowledge is an effective method. Also, we can conclude that SLEA-B performs better when more resource is allocated to it.

Table 4. Accuracy of SLEA-b with 5 restarts on the CEC 2013 suite. The 2nd column to the 8th column record the percentage of finding the best algorithm for each problem.

$f_1 - f_7$	88.0%	30.0%	84.0%	0.00%	12.0%	88.0%	0.00%
$f_8 - f_{14}$	40.0%	64.0%	38.0%	96.0%	70.0%	66.0%	98.0%
$f_{15} - f_{21}$	44.0%	70.0%	100%	98.0%	76.0%	70.0%	68.0%
$f_{22} - f_{28}$	94.0%	30.0%	56.0%	36.0%	2.00%	40.0%	16.0%
Average	56.2%						

Table 5. Accuracy of SLEA-b with 10 restarts on the CEC 2013 suite. The 2nd column to the 8th column record the percentage of finding the best algorithm for each problem.

$f_1 - f_7$	92.0%	20.0%	80.0%	2.00%	2.00%	81.0%	24.0%
$f_8 - f_{14}$	27.0%	72.0%	42.0%	95.0%	57.0%	68.0%	86.0%
$f_{15} - f_{21}$	60.0%	79.0%	98.0%	95.0%	88.0%	86.0%	93.0%
$f_{22} - f_{28}$	94.0%	28.0%	49.0%	53.0%	15.0%	16.0%	13.0%
Average	57.7%						

Table 6. Accuracy of SLEA-b with 15 restarts on the CEC 2013 suite. The 2nd column to the 8th column record the percentage of finding the best algorithm for each problem.

$f_1 - f_7$	94.0%	40.0%	86.7%	1.33%	0.00%	86.7%	26.0%
$f_8 - f_{14}$	46.7%	92.0%	38.7%	96.7%	73.3%	59.3%	96.0%
$f_{15} - f_{21}$	31.3%	80.7%	98.0%	100%	76.7%	85.3%	57.3%
$f_{22} - f_{28}$	91.3%	47.3%	62.7%	60.7%	0.00%	22.7%	84.0%
Average	62.0%						

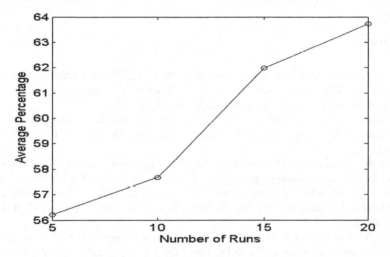

Fig. 2. Average percentage vs number of runs

5 Conclusion

Evolutionary algorithms (EAs) are efficient methods to solve optimization problems. Although many EAs have been invented, the no free lunch (NFL) theorems suggest that no one EA can perform well on all problems. To solve this, we propose a novel approach named Bayesian sequential learnable evolutionary algorithm (SLEA-b). The basic idea is to run the algorithms sequentially, and choose the best solution out of the multiple runs. SLEA-b allows different EAs for each run. Algorithm-problem feature, which are features specific to an algorithm, is extracted in each run. The EA to be run is based on the both the offline and online knowledge that SLEA-b has learned. Offline learning is achieved by a Monte Carlo approach. Online learning is achieved by applying Bayesian reasoning.

In the first experiment, SLEA-b is compared with sequential learnable evolutionary algorithm (SLEA). The two algorithms are tested on the CEC 2013 suite. We compare the percentage of finding the most similar problems. SLEA-b performs very well. We also test SLEA-b with different numbers of restarts on the CEC 2013 suite. The performance of SLEA-b is better when the number of restarts is greater. This suggests that SLEA-b is able to use the knowledge that has been learned to make a better decision.

In this paper, general EAs are included in SLEA-b. We can also include stronger algorithms such as BIPOP-CMAES [33] and L-Shade [34] in our framework which may further improve performance of SLEA-b.

Acknowledgement. The work described in this paper was supported by a grant from the Research Grants Council of the Hong Kong Special Administrative Region, China [Project No. CityU 125313]. Yaodong He acknowledges the Institutional Postgraduate Studentship from City University of Hong Kong. Yang Lou acknowledges the Institutional Postgraduate Studentship and the Institutional Research Tuition Grant from City University of Hong Kong.

References

1. Mitchell, M.: An Introduction to Genetic Algorithms. MIT Press, Cambridge (1998)
2. Auger, A.: Convergence results for the $(1, \lambda)$-SA-ES using the theory of ϕ-irreducible Markov chains. Theoret. Comput. Sci. **334**(1–3), 35–69 (2005)
3. Karaboga, D.: An idea based on honey bee swarm for numerical optimization. Technical report-tr06, Engineering Faculty, Computer Engineering Department, Erciyes University (2005)
4. Storn, R., Kenneth, P.: Differential evolution–a simple and efficient heuristic for global optimization over continuous spaces. J. Glob. Optim. **11**(4), 341–359 (1997)
5. Kennedy, J.: Particle swarm optimization. In: Sammut, C., Webb, G.I. (eds.) Encyclopedia of Machine Learning, pp. 760–766. Springer, New York (2011). doi:10.1007/978-0-387-30164-8_630
6. Wang, Y., Cai, Z., Zhang, Q.: Differential evolution with composite trial vector generation strategies and control parameters. IEEE Trans. Evol. Comput. **15**(1), 55–66 (2011)
7. Qin, A.K., Huang, V.L., Suganthan, P.N.: Differential evolution algorithm with strategy adaptation for global numerical optimization. IEEE Trans. Evol. Comput. **13**(2), 398–417 (2009)
8. Particle Swarm Central: http://www.particleswarm.info. Accessed 04 Nov 2016
9. Zambrano-Bigiarini, M., Clerc, M., Rojas, R.: Standard particle swarm optimization 2011 at CEC-2013: a baseline for future PSO improvements. In: Proceedings of IEEE Congress on Evolutionary Computation, pp. 2337–2344 (2013)
10. Liang, J.J., Qin, A.K., Suganthan, P.N., Baskar, S.: Comprehensive learning particle swarm optimizer for global optimization of multimodal functions. IEEE Trans. Evol. Comput. **10**(3), 281–295 (2006)

11. Hansen, N.: The CMA evolution strategy: a comparing review. In: Lozano, J.A., Larrañaga, P., Inza, I., Bengoetxea, E. (eds.) Towards a New Evolutionary Computation. SFSC, vol. 192, pp. 75–102. Springer, Heidelberg (2006). doi:10.1007/3-540-32494-1_4

12. Wolpert, D.H., Macready, W.G.: No free lunch theorems for optimization. IEEE Trans. Evol. Comput. **1**(1), 67–82 (1997)

13. CEC Benchmarks. http://www.ntu.edu.sg/home/epnsugan/index_files/cec-benchmarking. htm. Accessed 04 Nov 2016

14. BBOB Benchmarks. http://coco.gforge.inria.fr/doku.php. Accessed 04 Nov 2016

15. Burke, E.K., Gendreau, M., Hyde, M., et al.: Hyper-heuristics: a survey of the state of the art. J. Oper. Res. Soc. **64**(12), 1695–1724 (2013)

16. Tang, K., Peng, F., Chen, G., Yao, X.: Population-based algorithm portfolios with automated constituent algorithms selection. Inf. Sci. **279**, 94–104 (2014)

17. Yuen, S.Y., Zhang, X.: On composing an algorithm portfolio. Memet. Comput. **7**, 203–214 (2015)

18. Kotthoff, L.: Algorithm selection for combinatorial search problems: a survey. AI Mag. **35**, 48–60 (2014)

19. Rice, J.R.: The algorithm selection problem. Adv. Comput. **15**, 65–118 (1976)

20. Muñoz, M.A., Sun, Y., Kirley, M., Halgamuge, S.K.: Algorithm selection for black-box continuous optimization problems: a survey on methods and challenges. Inf. Sci. **317**, 224–245 (2015)

21. Bischl, B., Mersmann, O., Trautmann, H., Preuss, M.: Algorithm selection based on ELA and cost-sensitive learning. In: Proceedings of International Conference on Genetic and Evolutionary Computation, pp. 313–320 (2012)

22. Muñoz, M.A., Kirley, M., Halgamuge, S.K.: Explorative landscape analysis of continuous space optimization problems using information content. IEEE Trans. Evol. Comput. **19**, 74–87 (2015)

23. Kerschke, P., Preuss, M., Wessing, S., Trautmann, H.: Low-budget exploratory landscape analysis on multiple peaks models. In: Proceedings of 2016 on Genetic and Evolutionary Computation Conference, pp. 229–236. ACM (2016)

24. Yuen, S.Y., Zhang, X., Lou, Y.: Sequential learnable evolutionary algorithm: a research program. In: 2015 IEEE International Conference on Systems, Man, and Cybernetics, Kowloon, pp. 2841–2848 (2015)

25. Pfahringer, B., Hilan B., Giraud-Carrier, C.: Tell me who can learn you and I can tell you who you are: landmarking various learning algorithms. In: Proceedings of 17th International Conference on Machine Learning, pp. 743–750 (2000)

26. Auger, A., Hansen, N.: A restart CMA evolution strategy with increasing population size. In: 2005 IEEE Congress on Evolutionary Computation, pp. 1769–1776 (2005)

27. Sun, J., Garibaldi, J.M., Krasnogor, N., Zhang, Q.: An intelligent multi-restart memetic algorithm for box constrained global optimisation. Evol. Comput. **21**(1), 107–147 (2013)

28. Zhang, J., Sanderson, A.C.: JADE: adaptive differential evolution with optional external archive. IEEE Trans. Evol. Comput. **13**(5), 945–958 (2009)

29. Brest, J., Greiner, S., Bošković, B., Mernik, M., Žumer, V.: Self-adapting control parameters in differential evolution: a comparative study on numerical benchmark problems. IEEE Trans. Evol. Comput. **10**(6), 646–657 (2006)

30. Eshelman, L.J., Schaffer, J.D.: Real-coded genetic algorithms and interval-schemata. In: Proceedings of International Conference on Genetic Algorithms (ICGA), pp. 187–202 (1992)

31. Lihu, A., Holban, S., Popescu, O.A.: Real-valued genetic algorithms with disagreements. Memet. Comput. **4**(4), 317–325 (2012)

32. Muñoz, M.A., Kirley, M.: ICARUS: identification of complementary algorithms by uncovered sets. In: 2016 IEEE Congress on Evolutionary Computation (CEC), pp. 2427–2432 (2016)
33. Hansen, N.: Benchmarking a BI-population CMA-ES on the BBOB-2009 function testbed. In: Proceedings of 11th Annual Conference Companion on Genetic and Evolutionary Computation Conference: Late Breaking Papers, pp. 2389–2396. ACM (2009)
34. Tanabe, R., Fukunaga, A.S.: Improving the search performance of SHADE using linear population size reduction. In: Proceedings of IEEE Congress on Evolutionary Computation, pp. 1658–1665 (2014)

Evolutionary Learning Based Iterated Local Search for Google Machine Reassignment Problems

Ayad Turky[1(✉)], Nasser R. Sabar[2], Abdul Sattar[3], and Andy Song[1]

[1] School of Computer Science and I.T., RMIT University, Melbourne, Australia
{ayad.turky,andy.song}@rmit.edu.au
[2] Queensland University of Technology, Brisbane, Australia
nasser.sabar@qut.edu.au
[3] Griffith University, Nathan, Australia
a.sattar@griffith.edu.au

Abstract. Iterated Local Search (ILS) is a simple yet powerful optimisation method that iteratively invokes a local search procedure with renewed starting points by perturbation. Due to the complexity of search landscape, different ILS strategies may better suit different problem instances or different search stages. To address this issue, this work proposes a new ILS framework which selects the most suited components of ILS based on evolutionary meta-learning. It has three additional components other than ILS: meta-feature extraction, meta-learning and classification. The meta-feature and meta-learning steps are to generate a multi-class classifier by training on a set of existing problem instances. The generated classifier then selects the most suitable ILS setting when performing on new instances. The classifier is generated by Genetic Programming. The effectiveness of the proposed ILS framework is demonstrated on the Google Machine Reassignment Problem. Experimental results show that the proposed framework is highly competitive compared to 10 state-of-the-art methods reported in the literature.

Keywords: Iterated Local Search · Meta-learning · Google machine reassignment problem · Genetic programming

1 Introduction

The aim of this paper is to improve Iterated Local Search (ILS) using evolutionary learning for optimisation tasks especially clouding computing. As a large industry sector cloud computing is a recent emerging technology which has impact on many application domains such as industry computing, scientific research and business analytics [3]. It aims to provide a real time services access to a shared pool of computing resources including storage, processing and network bandwidth [3,5]. Service providers like Google and Amazon need to manage a large-scale data centres of which the computing resources are to be shared by end users with high quality of service.

© Springer International Publishing AG 2017
Y. Shi et al. (Eds.): SEAL 2017, LNCS 10593, pp. 409–421, 2017.
https://doi.org/10.1007/978-3-319-68759-9_34

More recently, a benchmark problem on cloud computing resource optimisation has been proposed by Google which is called Google machine reassignment problem (GMRP) [1]. GMRP aims to improve machine usage by reassigning a set of processes across a pool of servers while satisfying a set of constraints. A number of studies have been addressed this problem using various optimisation algorithms [4,8,9,13–16,18,19,21–25]. More details about all the participated teams in ROADEF/EURO challenge 2012 can be found in [2]. However, there is no absolute winner and there is still plenty of room for further improvement.

Following to this line of thought, this paper introduces a new ILS framework based on meta-learning for GMRP. ILS iteratively invokes a local search procedure with a perturbation operator to find the optimal solution with renewed starting points during search. As the search landscape of an optimisation problem is often highly complex, different problem instances or different search stages may have different best ILS settings. To address this issue, we propose to use evolutionary meta-learning to learning problem characteristics, then apply the suitable ILS based on the characteristic of the new problem instance. The new ILS framework consists of three major steps: meta-feature extraction, meta-learning and classification. The meta-feature and meta-learning steps are to generate a multi-label classifier by training on a set of existing problem instances to select ILS. Genetic programming (GP) is chosen as the classification method in our framework as GP has demonstrated its capability in classification and more importantly in constructing heuristics.

In GMRP, Google proposed 30 instances which are all used in this study for evaluating the performance of the proposed framework. These instances are very diverse in size and features. To further verify the benefit of the proposed meta-learning approach, state-of-the-art methods are used for comparison.

The rest of the paper is organized as such. Section 2 is the detailed problem description. Section 3 presents the proposed framework. Section 4 shows the experimental Settings. Section 5 are the results and discussions. Finally, we conclude this study in Sect. 6.

2   Problem Description

The French Operational Research and Decision Aid society (ROADEF) and the European Operational Research society (EURO) organise a challenge contest every two years since 1999. The challenge is called ROADEF/EURO. In 2012, Google proposed a machine reassignment problem (GMRP) for this challenge. GMRP is a recent combinatorial optimisation problem [1]. The main elements of this problem are a set of machines M and a set of processes P. The goal of this problem is to find the optimal way to assign process $p \in P$ to machines $m \in M$ in order to improve the usage of a given set of machines. One machine consists of a set of resources such as CPUs and RAM. One process can be moved from one machine to another to improve overall machine usage. The allocation of processes must not violate the following hard constraints:

- *Capacity constraints*: the sum of requirements of resource of all processes does not exceed the capacity of the allocated machine.
- *Conflict constraints*: processes of the same service must be allocated into different machines.
- *Transient usage constraints*: if a process is moved from one machine to another, it requires adequate amount of capacity on both machines.
- *Spread constraints*: the set of machines is partitioned into locations and processes of the same service should be allocated to machines in a number of distinct locations.
- *Dependency constraints*: the set of machines are partitioned into neighbourhoods. Then, if there is a service depends on another service, then the process of first one should be assigned to the neighbouring machine of second one or vice versa.

A feasible solution to GMRP is a process-machine assignment which satisfies all hard constraints and minimises the weighted cost function as much as possible which is calculated as follows:

$$f = \sum_{r \in R} weight_{loadCost}(r) \times loadCost(r)$$
$$+ \sum_{b \in B} weight_{balanceCost}(b) \times balanceCost(b)$$
$$+ weight_{processMoveCost} \times processMoveCost$$
$$+ weight_{serviceMoveCost} \times serviceMoveCost$$
$$+ weight_{machineMoveCost} \times machineMoveCost \qquad (1)$$

where R is a set of resources, *loadCost* represents the used capacity by resource r which exceeds the safety capacity, *balanceCost* represents the use of available machine, *processMoveCost* is the cost of moving a process from its current machine to a new one, *serviceMoveCost* represents the maximum number of moved processes over services and *machineMoveCost* represents the sum of all moves weighted by relevant machine cost. $weight_{loadCost}$, $weight_{balanceCost}$, $weight_{processMoveCost}$, $weight_{serviceMoveCost}$ and $weight_{machineMoveCost}$ define the importance of each individual cost.

For more details about the constraints, the costs and their weights can be found on the challenge documentation [1]. Note that the quality of a solution is evaluated by the given solution checker, which returns fitness measure to the best solution generated by our proposed algorithm. Another important aspect of this challenge is the time limit. All methods have to finish within the 5-min time frame to ensure the fairness of the comparison.

3   Evolutionary Learning Based Iterated Local Search (EL-ILS)

The selection of the most suitable search algorithm for a particular problem instances is not an easy task and often time consuming. Hence we introduce a new ILS framework based on evolutionary meta-learning, called $EL - ILS$. The proposed framework has two phases which are training and application phases. The general framework is shown in Fig. 1.

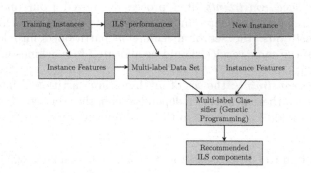

Fig. 1. Structure of the proposed EL-ILS framework

The given GMRP instances are divided into training and application (or test) sets. The following subsections discuss the main components of the proposed framework.

3.1   Instance Features

In this step, a set of GMRP instances is used to compute a numerical characteristics that describe a problem instance so-called *instance features*. These features are the basis for selecting suitable ILS. Nine types of features are extracted from the GMRP instances. They are shown in Table 1.

Table 1. Nine types of GMRP instance features

Feature	Description
M	Number of machines
R	Number of resources
P	Number of processes
S	Number of services
N	Number of neighbourhoods
SD	Number of dependencies
L	Number of locations
B	Number of balance costs
TR	Number of resources needing transient usage

3.2 ILS' Performances

ILS algorithm is a simple, yet effective, single solution based heuristic introduced by [10]. ILS has been successfully used to solve various optimisation problems and produced competitive results when compared to other algorithms [20]. An ILS search process starts from an initial solution and then iteratively explore its neighbour, searching for a better solution. ILS escapes from a local optima point by perturbing the current local optima instead of generating a new one. A traditional ILS iteratively applies the following three procedures: (1) local search procedure to explore the neighbour of a given solution, (2) perturbation procedure to provide a starting solution for the local search procedure and (3) acceptance criterion to either accept or reject the newly generated solution. Algorithm 1 shows the pseudocode of basic ILS [12]. More details of the ILS algorithm can be found in [11,12]. In order to improve the effectiveness of the proposed algorithm by accommodating various changes in the search landscape, we introduce four different neighbourhood structures in this framework. At each iteration of the algorithm a random neighbourhood structure is selected and the feasibility of the solution is maintained throughout the neighbourhood search process. The neighbourhood structures for the GMRP are:

Algorithm 1. Basic Iterated Local Search (ILS)

---

1 %scriptsize Set $MaxIter$; $Iter = 0$;
2 $S_0 \leftarrow GenerateInitialSolution()$;
3 $S_1 \leftarrow Localsearch(S_0)$;
4 **while** $Iter < MaxIter$ **do**
5    $S_2 \leftarrow$ Perturbation procedure (S_1);
6    $S_3 \leftarrow$ Local search procedure (S_2) ;
7    $S_1 \leftarrow$ Acceptance criterion procedure $(S_1, S_3, history)$;
8    $Iter = Iter + 1$;
9 **end**
10 Return the best solution;

- **Single swap.** Selects two processes from two different machines and interchanges them.
- **Double swap.** Selects four processes from two different machines and interchanges them.
- **Single move.** Selects a process from a machine and moves it to a different machine.
- **Double move.** Selects two processes from a machine and moves them to a different machine.

In addition, the perturbation operator also plays a big role on ILS performance. Its main role is to help the search in escaping from a local optima point by providing a new starting position to continue the search. The perturbation operators are:

- **Random perturbation**. Randomly move some processes from machines to another machines.
- **Guided perturbation**. It uses the problem knowledge to generate a starting solution. Using a guided perturbation may significantly improve the search performance through exploring and exploiting a new promising area in the search space. This guided perturbation is based on the idea of reassigning the processes with large sizes. The size of each process is equal to the summation of its requirements over all resources.

We run ILS algorithm with different components e.g. 4 different neighbourhood structure and 2 different perturbation operators, in total 8 variations, for 30 runs. A maximum of 5 min is set for each run as required in the Google challenge. As one algorithm or more may be recommended for each instance, the meta-learning problem can be addressed from a multi-label learning perspective. In contrast with single label, where only one class label can be assigned to an instance, in multi-label learning multiple target labels can be associated to each instance. In order to deal with the multi-label, a binary representation is used in this work where each label becomes a new binary classification problem [6].

3.3 Multi-label Data Set

A matrix is used to store the multi-label data for training and application. Its rows show the given instances. Each column stores the features as described in Table 1 for that instance and the label of class, meaning which ILS variation achieved the best on this instance. If multiple methods achieved the same best performance on the instance, then this instance will have multiple labels.

3.4 Training Classifiers Using Genetic Programming

Based on labeled dataset the training of classifiers then can proceed. As mentioned before, the classification method in the proposed EL-ILS method is Genetic Programming. Multi-label and multi-class classification is decomposed as multiple binary classification tasks.

The representation of GP in this classification is straightforward. The fitness of a GP classifier is simply the classification accuracy on the training cases. The terminals are numeric values of attributes from the training data and the functions are simply arithmetic operators. The division is protected so there will be no divide by zero errors. The classification boundary of those evolved binary GP classifiers is zero. So any negative output from a classifier indicates one class while an non-negative output means an ILS class.

The termination conditions of the training process is reaching the maximum number of generations or the perfect classification accuracy.

3.5 Features of New Unseen GMRP Instances

New instances in the test set also have the same features listed in Table 1, but with different feature values. The process of obtaining the feature value for a new instance is the same as described in Sect. 3.1. These feature values of an instance has no label and will be used as the input for the evolved Genetic Programming Classifiers that are evolved as in Sect. 3.4.

3.6 Recommending an ILS

When the GP classifiers apply on a new instance, one type of ILS will be selected by the classifier or classifiers (multi-label). This ILS then is applied on the corresponding instance to search for an optimised machine arrangement.

4 Experimental Settings

In this section, the GMRP instances used in our experiments are discussed. In total 30 different instances provided by Google for ROADEF/EURO 2012 challenge named as a, b and x. Theses instances have various characteristics in terms of number of machines, the number of processes and so on. We divided these instances into two sets, one for training and one for testing the EL-ILS methodology.

Tables 2 and 3 show the instances from these two sets with their feature values. The features are the same mentioned in Table 1. It can be seen from these two tables that the instances of training are quite different with the instances for test. In general the test set is more complex that the training set. In the case of dataset a, the number of resources R in Table 3 are much larger than

Table 2. The characteristics of instances for training

Instance	R	TR	M	P	S	L	N	B	SD
a1_1	2	0	4	100	79	4	1	1	0
a1_2	4	1	100	1000	980	4	2	0	40
a1_3	3	1	100	1000	216	25	5	0	342
a1_4	3	1	50	1000	142	50	50	1	297
a1_5	4	1	12	1000	981	4	2	1	32
b_1	12	4	100	5000	2512	10	5	0	4412
b_2	12	0	100	5000	2462	10	5	1	3617
b_3	6	2	100	20000	15025	10	5	0	16560
b_4	6	0	500	20000	1732	50	5	1	40485
b_5	6	2	100	40000	35082	10	5	0	14515
x_1	12	4	100	5000	2529	10	5	0	4164
x_2	12	0	100	5000	2484	10	5	1	3742
x_3	6	2	100	20000	14928	10	5	0	15201
x_4	6	0	500	20000	1190	50	5	1	38121
x_5	6	2	100	40000	34872	10	5	0	20560

Table 3. The characteristics of new instances

Instance	R	TR	M	P	S	L	N	B	SD
a2_1	3	0	100	1000	1000	1	1	0	0
a2_2	12	4	100	1000	170	25	5	0	0
a2_3	12	4	100	1000	129	25	5	0	577
a2_4	12	0	50	1000	180	25	5	1	397
a2_5	12	0	50	1000	153	25	5	0	506
b_6	6	0	200	40000	14680	50	5	1	42081
b_7	6	0	4000	40000	15050	50	5	1	43873
b_8	3	1	100	50000	45030	10	5	0	15145
b_9	3	0	1000	50000	4609	100	5	1	43437
b_10	3	0	5000	50000	4896	100	5	1	47260
x_6	6	0	200	40000	14504	50	5	1	39890
x_7	6	0	4000	40000	15273	50	5	1	43726
x_8	3	1	100	50000	44950	10	5	0	12150
x_9	3	0	1000	50000	4871	100	5	1	45457
x_10	3	0	5000	50000	4615	100	5	1	47768

that in Table 2, while the latter has much diver of N which is the number of neighbourhoods. In the case of datasets b and x, the number of machines M in training is much less than that in test. The number of processes P seems also quite different in these two sets.

The GP run-time parameters used in our experiments are the number of generations G $(G = 100)$, Population size P $(P = 30)$, Maximal depth M $(M = 8)$, Crossover rate CR $(CR = 0.85)$, Mutation rate MR $(MR = 0.05)$, Elitism E $(E = 0.10)$, Parent selection is *Binary tournament*, Fitness function is *Accuracy*, Terminal is Feature value and Function is $(/, *, +, \%)$. The choice of parameter settings for GMRP is empirical and based on default settings in some cases. The optimisation process is not seriously affected by these settings which are just set for the evolution of search algorithms. Certainly it is possible to search for the best combination of these settings. However that is not the focus of this study.

5   Results and Comparison

In order to verify the effectiveness of the proposed EL-ILS framework, we evaluate its performance by comparing with the state-of-the-art algorithms that we can find in the literature. In total ten other algorithms are involved in the comparison [4, 8, 14, 15, 17–19, 21, 22, 25].

Tables 4 and 5 shows the experimental results on the 3 groups of instances from the test set. The aforementioned ten existing algorithms are split into these two tables. The algorithms in Table 5 did not report their results on group x.

Table 4. Comparison between the proposed EL-ILS with the state of the art algorithms - Part I

Instance	EL-ILS	MNLS	VNS	CLNS	LNS	MILS
a2_1	**164**	225	199	196	1,869,113	167
a2_2	**720,671,513**	793,641,799	720,671,548	803,092,387	858,367,123	970,536,821
a2_3	**1,190,713,414**	1,251,407,669	**1,190,713,414**	1,302,235,463	1,349,029,713	1,452,810,819
a2_4	**1,680,587,592**	1,680,744,868	1,680,615,425	1,683,530,845	1,689,370,535	1,695,897,404
a2_5	309,714,531	337,363,179	**309,714,522**	331,901,091	385,272,187	412,613,505
b_6	**9,525,857,712**	9,525,885,495	9,525,900,218	9,525,867,169	9,525,862,018	9,525,913,044
b_7	**14,835,031,810**	14,842,926,007	14,835,031,813	14,838,521,000	14,868,550,671	15,244,960,848
b_8	**1,214,411,945**	1,214,591,033	1,214,416,705	1,214,524,845	1,219,238,781	1,214,930,327
b_9	15,885,541,409	**15,885,541,403**	15,885,548,612	15,885,734,072	15,887,269,801	15,885,617,841
b_10	**18,048,499,611**	18,055,765,224	18,048,499,616	18,049,556,324	18,092,883,448	18,093,202,104
x_6	**9,546,945,498**	9,546,966,175	-	-	9,546,945,537	9,546,992,887
x_7	**14,259,657,569**	14,259,657,575	-	-	14,330,862,773	14,701,830,252
x_8	83,713	**83,711**	-	-	98,054	309,080
x_9	16,125,675,271	**16,125,675,266**	-	-	16,128,419,926	16,125,753,242
x_10	**17,824,568,849**	17,824,568,855	-	-	17,861,616,489	17,867,789,754

Table 5. Comparison between the proposed EL-ILS with the state of the art algorithms - Part II

Instance	EL-ILS	SA	P-LAHC	ESA	MA	GE-SA
a2_1	**164**	222	166	167	**164**	181
a2_2	**720,671,513**	877,905,951	720,671,543	720,671,545	720,671,537	720,671,552
a2_3	**1,190,713,414**	1,380,612,398	1,192,054,462	1,194,261,501	1,193,311,432	1,193,311,446
a2_4	**1,680,587,592**	1,680,587,608	1,680,587,596	**1,680,587,592**	1,680,596,746	1,680,587,593
a2_5	309,714,531	310,243,809	310,287,633	310,243,641	312,124,226	310,243,857
b_6	**9,525,857,712**	9,525,861,951	9,525,859,949	9,525,859,941	9,525,857,758	9,525,857,758
b_7	**14,835,031,810**	14,836,763,304	14,835,122,152	14,835,122,181	14,836,237,140	14,835,031,806
b_8	**1,214,411,945**	1,214,563,084	1,214,416,691	1,214,416,703	1,214,411,947	1,214,416,698
b_9	15,885,541,409	15,886,083,835	15,885,545,683	15,885,545,712	15,885,546,811	15,885,548,592
b_10	**18,048,499,611**	18,049,089,128	**18,048,499,611**	180,512,416,401	18,051,241,638	18,048,499,610

Hence this table only shows test instances of a and b. In fact only $MNLS$, LNS, $MILS$ have results on group x available. The symbol "-" in Table 4 indicates that the method did not report its performance on the instance.

A value in Tables 4 and 5 is the cost of the best solution achieved by the corresponding algorithm on that instance within 5 min. For GMRP the lower the cost the better the solution. The best results achieved on one instance is highlighted in bold, meaning that algorithm outperformed other 10 algorithms. Multiple results on a row may be highlighted if the same best objective was achieved by serval methods. As can be seen in the two tables, our proposed EL-ILS was highlighted 11 times out of 15 cases. Among them EL-ILS achieved cost lower than other all other algorithms in 7 cases. On 4 instances, a2_1, a2_3, a2_4 and b_10, EL-ILS equalised the best known results. On instances a2_5, b_9, x_8 and x_9, EL-ILS did not reach the best known results. However EL-ILS is still the runner up on all these four instance. The differences between EL-ILS and the best are rather marginal, much smaller than the difference between EL-ILS and other 8 algorithms in the tables.

A further statistical analysis was carried out to see the significance of the difference between EL-ILS and the 10 algorithms from the literature. Friedman's test [7] was first applied, as the full results from other methods are not available for parametric tests. Then Holm and Hochberg tests were performed as post hoc methods to obtain the adjusted p-values for each comparison (if significant differences are detected). Note that this statistical test was only performed on a and b sets as majority of methods including VNS, CLNS, SA, P-LAHC, ESA, MA and GE-SA did not report their results on x set.

The rankings obtained by the Friedman's test are EL-ILS = 1.6, P-LAHC = 3.65, GE-SA = 3.95, MA = 4.3, ESA = 4.8, VNS = 5.25, SA = 7.4, MNLS = 7.7, CLNS = 7.8, LNS = 9.7 and MILS = 9.85. We can see that our proposed EL-ILS ranked first, with only 1.6 ranking index. Followed EL-ILS are P-LAHC, GE-SA, MA, ESA, VNS, SA, MNLS, CLNS, LNS and MILS. The p-values computed by the Friedman test is 0.000, which is way below the significance interval of 95% ($\alpha = 0.05$). This result shows that there is a significant difference among the observed results listed in Tables 4 and 5.

Post hoc methods, Holm and Hochberg tests, were also performed on the results using EL-ILS as the control method. Table 6 shows the adjusted p-values from the tests. We can see that Holm and Hochberg procedures reveal significant differences when using EL-ILS as a control algorithm, where proposed framework is better than all the algorithms in the comparison. Such difference is significant in majority cases including MILS, LNS, CLNS, SA and VNS. The p-values from these test show the difference between EL-ILS and P-LAHC, GE-SA and MA are not significant, while VNS and ESA are arguably board-line. Still EL-ILS found better solutions than these methods as shown in Tables 4 and 5. That matters in optimisation and the proposed EL-ILS is indeed a high competitive methodology.

Table 6. Adjusted p-values from the comparison between EL-ILS and existing methods by Friedman test

Instance	Algorithm	Unadjusted p	p_{Holm}	$p_{Hochberg}$
1	MILS	0	0	0
2	LNS	0	0	0
3	CLNS	0.000029	0.000233	0.000233
4	MNLS	0.000039	0.000274	0.000274
5	SA	0.000092	0.000553	0.000553
6	VNS	0.013862	0.069308	0.069308
7	ESA	0.030971	0.123886	0.123886
8	MA	0.068707	0.206122	0.166938
9	GE-SA	0.11311	0.226219	0.166938
10	P-LAHC	0.166938	0.226219	0.166938

6   Conclusion and Future Work

In this study we proposed a learning based search method to improve optimisation performance. The basic idea is to learn the correlations between problem instances and suitable search techniques. By examining the characteristics of the instances for training, a classifier can be established which can assess an new problem instance and determine which search technique is to be used for this particular instance. The learning method used in this initial work is Genetic Programming, which can assign a suitable Iterated Local Search for instances from Google Machine Reassignment Problem.

The experimental results clearly show the feasibility of this approach. Based on the comparison between the proposed EL-ILS framework with 10 existing methods reported in the literature on 15 GMRP instances, it can be seen that EL-ILS has the best performance. The Friedman test shows the significance in this leading performance although the significance was not that strong in other tests. Nevertheless such results can lead to a conclusion that learning based search approach is a highly competitive approach and can achieve better outcomes. The proposed evolutionary learning based iterated local search is a good demonstration of this approach. EL-ILS is a strong candidate for resource optimisation problem GMRP.

References

1. Roadef/euro challenge 2012: Machine reassignment. http://challenge.roadef.org/2012/en/
2. Afsar, H.M., Artigues, C., Bourreau, E., Kedad-Sidhoum, S.: Machine reassignment problem: the ROADEF/EURO challenge 2012. Ann. Oper. Res. **242**(1), 1–17 (2016)
3. Armbrust, M., Fox, A., Griffith, R., Joseph, A.D., Katz, R., Konwinski, A., Lee, G., Patterson, D., Rabkin, A., Stoica, I., et al.: A view of cloud computing. Commun. ACM **53**(4), 50–58 (2010)
4. Brandt, F., Speck, J., Völker, M.: Constraint-based large neighborhood search for machine reassignment. Ann. Oper. Res. **242**(1), 63–91 (2016)
5. Calheiros, R.N., Ranjan, R., Beloglazov, A., De Rose, C.A., Buyya, R.: Cloudsim: a toolkit for modeling and simulation of cloud computing environments and evaluation of resource provisioning algorithms. Softw.: Practice Experience **41**(1), 23–50 (2011)
6. de Carvalho, A.C.P.L.F., Freitas, A.A.: A tutorial on multi-label classification techniques. In: Abraham, A., Hassanien, AE., Snásel, V. (eds.) Foundations of Computational Intelligence, Studies in Computational Intelligence, vol. 5, pp. 177–195. Springer, Heidelberg (2009). doi:10.1007/978-3-642-01536-6_8
7. García, S., Fernández, A., Luengo, J., Herrera, F.: Advanced nonparametric tests for multiple comparisons in the design of experiments in computational intelligence and data mining: experimental analysis of power. Inf. Sci. **180**(10), 2044–2064 (2010)
8. Gavranović, H., Buljubašić, M., Demirović, E.: Variable neighborhood search for Google machine reassignment problem. Electron. Notes Discrete Math. **39**, 209–216 (2012)

9. Lopes, R., Morais, V.W.C., Noronha, T.F., Souza, V.A.A.: Heuristics and matheuristics for a real-life machine reassignment problem. Int. Trans. Oper. Res. **22**(1), 77–95 (2015)
10. Lourenço, H.R., Martin, O., Stützle, T.: A beginners introduction to iterated local search. In: Proceedings of MIC, pp. 1–6 (2001)
11. Lourenço, H.R., Martin, O.C., Stützle, T.: Iterated local search. In: Glover, F., Kochenberger, G.A. (eds.) Handbook of Metaheuristics. International Series in Operations Research and Management Science, vol. 57, pp. 320–353. Springer, Heidelberg (2003). doi:10.1007/0-306-48056-5_11
12. Lourenço, H.R., Martin, O.C., Stützle, T.: Iterated local search: framework and applications. In: Gendreau, M., Potvin, J.Y. (eds.) Handbook of Metaheuristics. International Series in Operations Research and Management Science, vol. 146, pp. 363–397. Springer, Heidelberg (2010). doi:10.1007/978-1-4419-1665-5_12
13. Malitsky, Y., Mehta, D., O'Sullivan, B., Simonis, H.: Tuning parameters of large neighborhood search for the machine reassignment problem. In: Gomes, C., Sellmann, M. (eds.) CPAIOR 2013. LNCS, vol. 7874, pp. 176–192. Springer, Heidelberg (2013). doi:10.1007/978-3-642-38171-3_12
14. Masson, R., Vidal, T., Michallet, J., Penna, P.H.V., Petrucci, V., Subramanian, A., Dubedout, H.: An iterated local search heuristic for multi-capacity bin packing and machine reassignment problems. Expert Syst. Appl. **40**(13), 5266–5275 (2013)
15. Mehta, D., O'Sullivan, B., Simonis, H.: Comparing solution methods for the machine reassignment problem. In: Milano, M. (ed.) CP 2012. LNCS, pp. 782–797. Springer, Heidelberg (2012). doi:10.1007/978-3-642-33558-7_56
16. Portal, G.M., Ritt, M., Borba, L.M., Buriol, L.S.: Simulated annealing for the machine reassignment problem. Ann. Oper. Res. **242**(1), 93–114 (2016)
17. Ritt, M.R.P.: An algorithmic study of the machine reassignment problem. Ph.D. thesis, Universidade Federal do Rio Grande do Sul (2012)
18. Sabar, N.R., Song, A.: Grammatical evolution enhancing simulated annealing for the load balancing problem in cloud computing. In: Proceedings of the 2016 on Genetic and Evolutionary Computation Conference, pp. 997–1003. ACM (2016)
19. Sabar, N.R., Song, A., Zhang, M.: A variable local search based memetic algorithm for the load balancing problem in cloud computing. In: Squillero, G., Burelli, P. (eds.) EvoApplications 2016. LNCS, vol. 9597, pp. 267–282. Springer, Cham (2016). doi:10.1007/978-3-319-31204-0_18
20. Turky, A., Moser, I., Aleti, A.: An iterated local search with guided perturbation for the heterogeneous fleet vehicle routing problem with time windows and three-dimensional loading constraints. In: Wagner, M., Li, X., Hendtlass, T. (eds.) ACALCI 2017. LNCS, vol. 10142, pp. 279–290. Springer, Cham (2017). doi:10.1007/978-3-319-51691-2_24
21. Turky, A., Sabar, N.R., Sattar, A., Song, A.: Parallel late acceptance Hill-Climbing algorithm for the Google machine reassignment problem. In: Kang, B.H., Bai, Q. (eds.) AI 2016. LNCS, vol. 9992, pp. 163–174. Springer, Cham (2016). doi:10.1007/978-3-319-50127-7_13
22. Turky, A., Sabar, N.R., Song, A.: An evolutionary simulating annealing algorithm for Google machine reassignment problem. In: Leu, G., Singh, H.K., Elsayed, S. (eds.) Intelligent and Evolutionary Systems. PALO, vol. 8, pp. 431–442. Springer, Cham (2017). doi:10.1007/978-3-319-49049-6_31
23. Turky, A., Sabar, N.R., Song, A.: Cooperative evolutionary heterogeneous simulated annealing algorithm for Google machine reassignment problem. In: Genetic Programming and Evolvable Machines, pp. 1–28 (2017). doi:10.1007/s10710-017-9305-0

24. Turky, A., Sabar, N.R., Song, A.: Neighbourhood analysis: a case study on Google machine reassignment problem. In: Wagner, M., Li, X., Hendtlass, T. (eds.) ACALCI 2017. LNCS, vol. 10142, pp. 228–237. Springer, Cham (2017). doi:10. 1007/978-3-319-51691-2_20

25. Wang, Z., Lü, Z., Ye, T.: Multi-neighborhood local search optimization for machine reassignment problem. Comput. Oper. Res. **68**, 16–29 (2016)

Geometric Semantic Genetic Programming with Perpendicular Crossover and Random Segment Mutation for Symbolic Regression

Qi Chen[✉], Mengjie Zhang, and Bing Xue

School of Engineering and Computer Science, Victoria University of Wellington,
PO Box 600, Wellington 6140, New Zealand
{Qi.Chen,Mengjie.Zhang,Bing.Xue}@ecs.vuw.ac.nz

Abstract. Geometric semantic operators have been a rising topic in genetic programming (GP). For the sake of a more effective evolutionary process, various geometric search operators have been developed to utilise the knowledge acquired from inspecting the behaviours of GP individuals. While the current exact geometric operators lead to overgrown offsprings in GP, existing approximate geometric operators never consider the theoretical framework of geometric semantic GP explicitly. This work proposes two new geometric search operators, i.e. perpendicular crossover and random segment mutation, to fulfil precise semantic requirements for symbolic regression under the theoretical framework of geometric semantic GP. The two operators approximate the target semantics gradually and effectively. The results show that the new geometric operators bring a notable benefit to both the learning performance and the generalisation ability of GP. In addition, they also have significant advantages over Random Desired Operator, which is a state-of-the-art geometric semantic operator.

Keywords: Genetic programming · Symbolic regression · Geometric semantic operators

1 Introduction

Semantic Genetic Programming (SGP) [8], which is a recently developed variant of Genetic Programming (GP) [5], makes use of semantic-aware search operators to produce offsprings that are highly correlated with their parents in behaviour. The definition of semantics in GP is different from domain to domain. In symbolic regression, the semantics of a GP program refers to a vector, the elements of which are the corresponding outputs of the program for the given samples [8]. The semantics of GP individuals form the semantic space. The fitness function (i.e. a kind of distance measure) spanning over the semantic space has a conic shape, thus search in such a unimodal space should be easy in principle [6]. However, it is not the case in practice, since the semantic space is not the space being searched in SGP. One particular category of SGP, Geometric Semantic GP

© Springer International Publishing AG 2017
Y. Shi et al. (Eds.): SEAL 2017, LNCS 10593, pp. 422–434, 2017.
https://doi.org/10.1007/978-3-319-68759-9_35

(GSGP) [7], opens a new direction to utilise the semantics of GP individuals. GSGP implements the exact geometric semantic operators, which generate offsprings that lie either on the segment of the parents in the semantic space or in the interval bound defined by one parent. In this way, GSGP makes the desired semantics as the main driving force of the evolutionary process.

Research on GSGP mainly focuses on two aspects: *the theoretical framework* which poses the geometric requirement to the offspring, and *the implementation algorithm of* the geometric operators. Previous work [9] has figured out that the implementation algorithm in GSGP [7], which is a linear combination of parents, typically leads to over-grown offsprings, while the theoretical framework of it is the principle of many successful applications [2,10]. The over-grown offsprings are expensive to execute in both memory and time, which makes GSGP difficult to use in practice. Recent research has proposed variants of geometric operators to overcome this limitation. Random Desired Operator (RDO) [11] is one of the state-of-the-art geometric operators. Although these approximate geometric operators can eliminate over-grown individuals to certain extent, they never follow the theoretical framework of GSGP to further improve the effectiveness of the semantic operators. This work aims to fulfil this gap to some extent.

The overall goal of this work is to develop new geometric semantic operators for crossover and mutation to fulfil new semantic requirements under the theoretical framework of GSGP. The new desired semantics for offspring individuals will be much more precise than that in GSGP, and more diverse than that in RDO (which only consider the target semantics). The newly desired semantics are expected to guide the evolutionary search in a more effective way. A comparison between the proposed geometric operators and RDO will be conducted to investigate the effect of the new operators. Specifically, three research objectives emerge in this work:

- whether the proposed geometric operators can improve the learning performance of RDO on the training data,
- whether the proposed geometric operators can generalise better than RDO on new/unseen test data, and
- whether the new geometric operators can evolve programs with a smaller program size, and accordingly being more understandable.

2   Related Work

2.1   Geometric Semantic Genetic Programming

The definition of the theoretical framework of GSGP is as follows [7]:

Definition 1. *Given two parent individuals P_1 and P_2, geometric semantic crossover generates offspring $O_j(j \in 1, 2)$ having semantics $S(O_j)$ on the segment between the semantics of their parents, i.e., $\|S(P_1), S(P_2)\| = \|S(P_1), S(O_j)\| + \|S(O_j), S(P_2)\|$.*

Definition 2. *Given a parent P, r-geometric semantic mutation produces off-spring O in a ball of radius r centered in P i.e., $\|S(P), S(O)\| \leq r$.*

Moraglio et al. [7] proposed an algorithm to implement the exact geometric operators. This implementation is a linear combination of the parent(s) and one/two randomly created programs. The proposal of the exact geometric semantic operators opens a new direction in SGP, since geometric semantic operators aim to search directly in the semantic space. However, the excessive growth in the size of the offspring produced by these operators is an obstacle to the application of GSGP, since it leads to an expensive computational cost and decreases the interpretability of the evolved models. In addition, the exact geometric crossover is criticised to contribute little to improving the generalisation ability of GP [4].

2.2 RDO and Semantic Backpropagation

Variants of GSGP have been proposed to overcome the limitation of GSGP. Pawlak et al. [11] proposed a semantic operator named Random Desired Operator (RDO), which generates offspring individuals with the target semantics as their desired semantics. The rationale behind RDO is that achieving a subtarget (part of the whole target) is much easier than the whole target. Based on a randomly selected node of a GP individual, the desired semantics of the GP individual is split into two parts, which are the semantics of the fixed suffix and the desired semantics of the selected node. Then RDO only needs to approximate the semantics of the selected node. To this end, a semantic backpropagation (SB) algorithm was proposed [11]. The SB algorithm obtains the desire semantics of the selected node by backpropagating through a chain of nodes from the root to the node. Then a new subtree with the desired semantics is obtained from a predefined semantic library, and replaces the original subtree. Although the SB algorithm provides a sensible way to obtain the subtarget semantics, RDO can potentially lead to a limitation of quickly losing the semantic diversity, which might be caused by the unique desired semantics for all the offspring. Furthermore, RDO has a greedy nature in chasing a lower training error, which might make GP suffer from overfitting and can not generalise well on the test data.

3   The Proposed Geometric Semantic Operators

This work proposes two new geometric operators named *perpendicular crossover* and *random segment mutation* to fulfil new semantic requirements for the offspring individuals. The new requirements are either more effective in approximating the target semantics or easier to achieve than the originally desired semantics in both GSGP and RDO. The semantics of the children individuals rely on their parent(s) in GSGP, while RDO only considers the target semantics. The new geometric operators utilise both types of semantics. For presentation convenience, GP with the two new geometric operators is named *NGSGP*.

3.1   Perpendicular Crossover

To have a more precisely semantic control and approximate the target semantics more effectively than the exact geometric semantic crossover operator, we propose a new semantic crossover operator called—*perpendicular crossover*. Given two parent individuals, perpendicular crossover (PC) generates offsprings having two geometric properties in semantic space. The first property is that the semantics of offsprings (i.e. represented as a point in semantic space) need to stand on the line defined by the semantics of their parents. The second one is that the line defined by the target semantics and the offspring point should be perpendicular to the given line of their parents. The first three columns in Fig. 1 illustrate the three possible positions of offspring O. Suppose the target semantic is T, and the semantics of the two parents are P_1 and P_2. As shown in the figure, the three points define a triangle. α refers to the angle between the relative semantics of P_2 and T to P_1, while β is its counterpart to P_2. The angle α and β are defined as follows:

$$\alpha = \arccos\left(\frac{(T - P_1) \cdot (P_2 - P_1)}{\|T - P_1\| \cdot \|P_2 - P_1\|}\right) \quad \beta = \arccos\left(\frac{(T - P_2) \cdot (P_1 - P_2)}{\|T - P_2\| \cdot \|P_1 - P_2\|}\right) \quad (1)$$

where $(T - P_1) \cdot (P_2 - P_1) = \sum_{i=1}^{n}(t_i - p_{1i}) \cdot (p_{2i} - p_{1i})$, $\|T - P\| = \sqrt{\sum_{i=1}^{n}(t_i - p_i)^2}$ and $\|P_2 - P_1\| = \sqrt{\sum_{i=1}^{n}(p_{1i} - p_{2i})^2}$. p_{1i}, p_{2i} and t_i are the values of P_1, P_2 and T in the ith dimension, respectively. The semantics of the offspring O is corresponding to the base of the perpendicular dropped from T to the relative semantics $P_2 - P_1$. In the first case (as shown in Fig. 1(a)), when α and β are both smaller than $90°$, the offspring O (represented by the green point in the figure) stands on the segment of $P_2 - P_1$. In the other two cases, where either α or β is larger than $90°$, the offspring stands along the segments on the P_1 or P_2 side. Now, a key step is to obtain point O on the line P_1P_2.

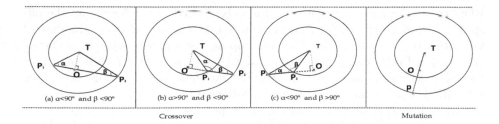

(a) α<90° and β <90°   (b) α>90° and β <90°   (c) α<90° and β >90°

Crossover   Mutation

Fig. 1. PC and RSM (Color figure online)

In the scenario of obtaining a point on the line defined by two given points, the parametric equation, which is the most versatile equation to define a line in an n dimensional space, is a good choice to express a line. Then once the distance from O to one of the given points is calculated, it is easy to obtain O. Specifically, suppose L is the line given by two points P and Q in an n dimensional space. A particular point in line L is given in Eq. (2).

$$O = P + k \cdot (Q - P) \tag{2}$$

where $Q - P$ gives the direction of L, the elements of which are defined as $\{q_1 - p_1, q_2 - p_2, \ldots, q_n - p_n\}$. $k = \|O - P\|/\|Q - P\|$ is a real number parameter, which stands for the relative distance between O and P. When $0 < k < 1$, O is a point on the segment between P and Q. Further, if $k < 0$, O is outside the segment on the P side, while if $k > 1$, O is outside on the Q side. The procedure of obtaining the semantics of O is showing in Algorithm 1.

Algorithm 1. Obtaining the Desired Semantics in Perpendicular Crossover

---

Input   : Target semantics T, and the semantics of the two parents P_1 and P_2
Output: The desired semantics of the offspring O
Obtain the $P_2 - P_1$, $\|P_2 - P_1\|$, $\|T - P_1\|$ and $\|T - P_2\|$;
Calculate the angle α and β according to Equation (1);
if $\alpha < 90$ *and* $\beta < 90$ then
  $\|O - P_1\| = \|T - P_1\| \cdot cos(\alpha)$;
  $O = P_1 + \|O - P_1\|/\|P_2 - P_1\| \cdot (P_2 - P_1)$;
else
  if $\alpha > 90$ then
    $\|P_1 - O\| = \|T - P_1\| \cdot cos(180 - \alpha)$;
    $O = P_1 - \|P_1 - O\|/\|P_2 - P_1\| \cdot (P_2 - P_1)$;
  else
    if $\beta > 90$ then
      $\|O - P_2\| = \|T - P_2\| \cdot cos(180 - \beta)$;
      $O = P_2 + \|O - P_2\|/\|P_2 - P_1\| \cdot (P_2 - P_1)$;

3.2   Random Segment Mutation

RDO treats the target semantics as the only desired semantics for all the off-spring. To utilise the target semantics in a better way and make the desired semantics to be more achievable, we propose the *random segment mutation* (RSM). RSM makes a small but important change to RDO, which is to utilises the target semantics in an implicit way. The rationale for this change is twofold. First RSM aims to maintain the semantic diversity of the population by assigning vary desired semantics to offspring. Rapid loss of semantic diversity has been considered as a major cause for the premature convergence of GP. Thus, maintaining a high semantic diversity is important for GP to escape from local optima. Secondly, RSM intends to approximate the target gradually. When tackling real-world data containing noise, the property of less greedy to the target semantics is expected to help GP to avoid the issue of overfitting.

In RSM, the desired semantics of the offspring individual stands on the segment of the parent and the target point in the semantic space. As shown in the last column in Fig. 1, given a parent P, RSM firstly needs to find the segment between the target semantics T and P. Then a random point is obtained along this segment, which is treated as the desired semantics of the offspring O. Then O is obtained according to $O = P + k \cdot (T - P)$, $k \in (0, 1)$.

3.3 Fulfilling the Semantic Requirements

Both PC and RSM rely on semantic backpropagation to fulfil the semantic requirements of the offspring individuals.

Figure 2 gives an example of semantic backpropagation. Given a randomly selected node in a GP individual, semantic backpropagation decomposes the individual into two parts: the prefix expressed by the subtree rooted at the selected node and the suffix corresponding to the rest of the individual. Accordingly, the desired semantics of the GP individual is achieved by the combination of the fixed semantics of the suffix and a new semantics of the prefix. This new semantics is the semantic difference between the target and the fixed suffix. Specifically, to calculate the desired semantics of the prefix, semantic backpropagation starts from the desired semantics of the whole individual (like D_1 shown in Fig. 2), then backpropagates through a chain of nodes from the root to the selected node, i.e., in order to obtain D_3, which is the desired semantics of the selected subtree, the semantics of its parent node, which is referred to D_2, is needed beforehand. The same requirement is propagated to the root node $D1$. For the given example, the backpropagation chain is from D_1 to D_2, then to D_3. In addition, the inverted function operator is applied, which is the invert of the original operators. For example, in Fig. 2, the output of the parent node ("+") of the selected node ("2") is equal to $S_2 + D_3$, then accordingly $D_3 = D_2 - S_2$, thus "−" is the inverted operator of "+", and vice versa.

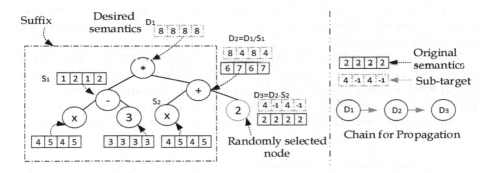

Fig. 2. One example for semantic backpropagation.

After obtaining the desired semantics, the prefix will be replaced by a new subtree from a predefined semantic library. Specifically, an exhaustive search will perform on the library to find a subtree with the desired semantics. If a subtree with the exact desired semantics does not exist, the search will return a subtree with the closest Euclidean distance to the desired semantics among the library. The diversity of the semantic library is important for the success of the exhaustive search, thus the semantic library is updated and filled with subtrees taken from individuals at every generation. These subtrees have unique semantics. When two subtrees have the same semantics, the small one is preferred.

Compared with GSGP and RDO, the proposed NGSGP algorithm has the following properties. First NGSGP utilises both the target semantics and the semantics of the parent(s) to have a precise control over the semantics of the offspring individuals. Meanwhile, in contrast with driven by a uniform target semantics, the precise control has been conducted in a way of fulfilling various semantic requirements, which are more achievable and maintain more diverse semantics of the GP population. Second instead of relying on a linear combination of parent(s) and randomly generated trees, NGSGP fulfils the semantic requirement by semantic backpropagation and selects appropriate subtrees from a semantic library. With these significant improvements, NGSGP is expected to not only achieve a good learning ability but also generalise well.

4   Experiment Design

To investigate the effectiveness of NGSGP, it is compared with RDO. In addition, to have a more precise investigation, the performance of GP with only one of the two operators, i.e. GP with only PC (denoted as PC) and GP with only RSM (denoted as RSM), are also examined. Standard GP is used as a baseline for comparison. All the GP methods are implemented under the GP framework provided by Distributed Evolutionary Algorithms in Python (DEAP) [3]. The five GP methods are tested on six commonly used synthetic datasets, which are taken from previous work on GSGP [6,11]. The target functions and sampling strategies are shown in Table 1. In addition, we are also interested in testing the proposed method on real-world datasets [1,12] shown in Table 2, which have not been widely used in GSGP.

Parameter settings for all the GP methods are summarised in Table 3. Most of these parameters are common settings in GP [5,7]. In the four GSGP methods (RDO, RSM, PC and NGSGP), the Euclidean metric is adopted to measure the distance between two points. For an easy comparison, at every generation, the root mean square error (RMSE) of the best-of-generation model on the training

Table 1. Synthetic datasets. (The training samples are drawn using regular intervals from the interval range, while the test samples are drawn randomly within the same interval. Each of them have 20 samples. The interval range is $[-1; 1]$ (except for Nguyen-7, which has a range of $[0; 2]$).)

Problem	Function	Problem	Function
Septic	$x^7 - 2x^6 + x^5 - x^4 + x^3 - 2x^2 + x$	Nonic	$\sum_{i=1} 9x^i$
Nguyen-7	$log(x+1) + log(x^2+1)$	R1	$(x+1)^3/(x^2 - x + 1)$
R2	$(x^5 - 3x^3 + 1)/(x^2 + 1)$	R3	$(x^6 + x^5)/(x^4 + x^3 + x^2 + x + 1)$

Table 2. Real-world problems

Name	# Features	#Total instances	#Training instances	#Test instances
LD50	626	234	163	71
DLBCL	7399	240	160	80

Table 3. Parameter settings for GP

Parameter	Value	Parameter	Value
Population size	256	Generations	100
Crossover rate	0.9	Mutation rate	0.1
Elitism	1	Maximum tree depth	17
Initialisation	Ramped half-and-half	Initialisation depth	2–6
Function set	$+, -, *,$ %protected, exp, log, sin, cos	Fitness function	Euclidean distance, RMSE

set and its corresponding test error are recorded. 100 independent runs has been conducted for each method on each dataset.

5 Results and Discussions

This section compares and discusses the experiment results obtained by the five GP methods. The comparison will be presented in terms of training performance, generalisation ability and the size of the evolved programs by the GP methods. The non-parametric statistical significance test—Wilcoxon test, which has a significance level of 0.05, is conducted to compare the training RMSEs and test RMSEs of the 100 best-of-run models.

5.1 Overall Results

The mean and standard deviation of RMSEs achieved by the best-of-run programs on the training sets and the corresponding results on the test sets are shown in Tables 4 and 5, respectively. The best (i.e. smallest) values among the five methods are marked in bold.

As shown on Table 4, the four GSGP methods all have much smaller training RMSEs than standard GP on most of the datasets. On seven of the eight training sets (except for LD50), NGSGP obtains smaller mean RMSEs than RDO. On LD50, NGSGP has a higher training error than RDO. The difference between NGSGP and RDO on the eight datasets are all significant. RSM and PC both have better training performance than RDO on five of the eight problems.

Table 5 shows clearly that the four GSGP methods can generalise better than standard GP on all the synthetic benchmarks. The advantages are all significant. However, it is not the case on the two real-world datasets. On LD50 and DLBCL,

Table 4. Training errors of the 100 best-of-run programs

Problem	GP	RDO	RSM	PC	NGSGP
	Mean ± Std	Mean ± Std	Mean ± Std	Mean ± Std	Mean ± Std
Septic	0.07 ± 0.04	0.01 ± 0.01	0.02 ± 0.01	0.01 ± 0.01	**2.1E−3 ± 1.7E−3**
Nonic	0.06 ± 0.03	0.01 ± 0.02	4E−3 ± 2.3E−3	0.01 ± 0.01	**2.9E−3 ± 1.8E−3**
Nguyen7	0.01 ± 0.01	2.1E−3 ± 3E−3	3.6E−4 ± 3.1E−4	9.5E−4 ± 1.2E−3	**3.3E−4 ± 3.3E−4**
R1	0.05 ± 0.03	0.01 ± 0.01	3.2E−3 ± 2.8E−3	3.6E−3 ± 3.2E−3	**2.6E−3 ± 2.3E−3**
R2	0.05 ± 0.03	3E−3 ± 3.1E−3	1.4E−3 ± 8.9E−4	1.5E−3 ± 1.3E−3	**1.3E−3 ± 8.8E−4**
R3	0.01 ± 3.9E−3	2.1E−3 ± 0.01	**8E−4 ± 6.1E−4**	1.9E−3 ± 4.2E−3	8.8E−4 ± 1.4E−3
LD50	1950.94 ± 67.66	**1692.2 ± 317.1**	1888.59 ± 108.26	1952.63 ± 51.68	1844.52 ± 88.5
DLBCL	0.65 ± 0.02	0.63 ± 0.07	0.65 ± 0.04	0.62 ± 0.03	**0.57 ± 0.08**

Table 5. Corresponding test errors of the 100 best-of-run programs

Problem	GP	RDO	RSM	PC	NGSGP
	Mean ± Std	Mean ± Std	Mean ± Std	Mean ± Std	Mean ± Std
Septic	0.07 ± 0.05	0.03 ± 0.01	0.05 ± 0.07	0.04 ± 0.07	**0.02 ± 0.03**
Nonic	0.06 ± 0.04	0.02 ± 0.02	0.06 ± 0.18	0.02 ± 0.02	**0.01 ± 0.02**
Nguyen7	0.01 ± 0.01	0.01 ± 0.02	**6.8E−4 ± 5.4E−4**	3.2E−3 ± 0.01	0.01 ± 0.03
R1	0.06 ± 0.04	0.01 ± 0.02	0.01 ± 0.02	0.01 ± 0.01	**3.2E−4 ± 7E−3**
R2	0.05 ± 0.03	0.02 ± 0.05	0.01 ± 0.02	0.03 ± 0.08	**0.01 ± 0.03**
R3	0.01 ± 0.01	0.02 ± 0.05	0.24 ± 1.43	4.8E−3 ± 0.01	**4.4E−3 ± 0.01**
LD50	2007.5 ± 67.1	4354.9 ± 9236.7	1996.8 ± 79.4	2020.7 ± 83.3	**1987.88 ± 87.5**
DLBCL	0.7 ± 0.04	0.71 ± 0.04	0.7 ± 0.04	0.69 ± 0.05	**0.62 ± 0.07**

while RDO generalises much worse than standard GP, GP equipped with the two new operators (solely or together) can generalise better than standard GP. Particularly on LD50, where all the GSGP methods can have much better training performance than standard GP, only RSM and NGSGP can generalise slightly better than standard GP. On DLBCL, while RDO still can not generalise better than standard GP, the other three methods can generalise significantly better than standard GP. On these two real-world datasets, PC, RSM and NGSGP all have significantly better generalisation performance than RDO. The ranking of the generalisation performance of the five GP methods on the synthetic datasets is consistent with that on the training set, which indicates the geometric semantic methods are resistant to overfitting on the comparatively simple problems. On the real-world datasets, which might contain noise, RDO is prone to overfitting and NGSGP has a much better generalisation ability than RDO.

5.2   Behavior Analysis—Training/Evolutionary Process

The evolutionary plots on the training sets, which are drawn using the median of training errors of the 100 best-of-generation individuals, are shown in Fig. 3. On five of the seven training sets, except for Septic and R3, NGSGP outperforms

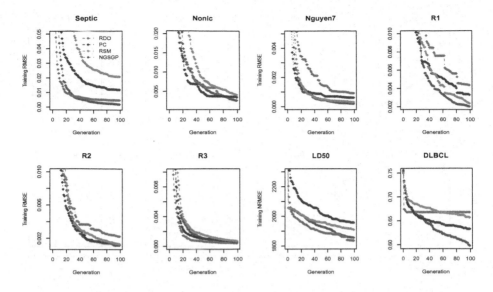

Fig. 3. Training/Evolutionary process on the training sets.

RDO in an early stage and this advantage becomes larger over generations. This might be due to the less greedy nature of NGSGP for achieving the target semantics. NGSGP is driven by vary target semantics, which are a kind of intermediate target under the theoretical requirement of GSGP. These intermediate targets are different from individual to individual, which can help maintain the semantic diversity of the population better than utilising only one target. Higher semantic diversity will lead to a better exploration ability of GP and has a positive effect on enhancing the effectiveness of the evolutionary search. Furthermore, these intermediate targets are generally closer to the parents than the target semantics. Searching from a semantic library, which consists of semantic uniquely subtrees from the population, the semantics of these intermediate targets are easier to match. Following these reliable and achievable intermediate targets, NGSGP is able to get even closer to the target semantics than RDO gradually and smoothly.

Comparing PC and RSM with RDO, it can be observed that both new geometric operators generally have a positive effect on enhancing the training performance of RDO to some extent. Combining the new geometric crossover, which is relatively stable, with the new geometric mutation operator, which brings randomness, can lead to even better learning performance.

5.3   Analysis of Generalisation Behaviour

The generalisation performance of the evolved models on unseen data is a key metric to measure the effectiveness of the proposed GP method. Figure 4 shows the evolutionary plots on the generalisation performance. The overall pattern on the test sets is similar to that on the training sets. Clearly, NGSGP is the winner

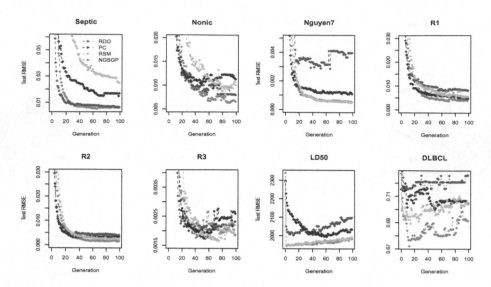

Fig. 4. Results on the test sets against the evolution.

on the generalisation performance among the four geometric semantic methods. On seven of the eight benchmarks (except for Septic), NGSGP generalises significantly better than RDO. On Septic, no significant difference can be found between the two methods. On Nonic, R1 and R2, where RDO generalises well, NGSGP can generalise even better than RDO. On the other four datasets, where RDO overfits the training data, NGSGP can either overfit less (i.e. on R3, LD50 and DLBCL) or resistant to overfitting (on Nguyen7). On these datasets, before the 40th generation on LD50 and the 20th generation on DLBCL, both method do not overfit, NGSGP still has much smaller generalisation error than RDO. On LD50, RDO achieves the best training performance but the worst generalisation performance, which indicates it overfits to the training set the severest among the four methods.

Compared PC and RSM with RDO, on five of the eight benchmarks, except for Septic, Nonic and R3, both PC and RSM have better generalisation performance than RDO. Clearly, the advantage of NGSGP over RDO on the generalisation performance is brought by both the perpendicular crossover and random segment mutation. Compared with RDO, which uses the target semantics in an explicit way, the two semantic operators in NGSGP intend to approximate the target gradually. When tackling the real-world data containing noise, the property of NGSGP, i.e. being less greedy, to the target semantics will surely lead it to less overfit the training set, thus generalise better.

5.4   Comparison on the Program Size

The average and minimum sizes of the best-of-run individuals are presented in Table 6. Not surprisingly, the modes evolved by GSGP methods have a much

Table 6. Program size of the evolved models

Problem	GP	RDO	NGSGP	Problem	GP	RDO	NGSGP
	Mean(Min)				Mean(Min)		
Septic	215.04 (111)	1180.32 (39)	702.16 (239)	Nonic	184.12 (59)	1050.28 (31)	1016.4 (471)
Nguyen7	115.8 (51)	2152.63 (15)	1111.0 (571)	R1	168.92 (67)	1715.9 (29)	1670.16 (325)
R2	144.32 (47)	1261.88 (39)	1008.16 (151)	R3	200.76 (63)	1141.43 (17)	1085.0 (485)
LD50	179.76 (39)	947.2 (23)	78.04 (7)	DLBCL	60.2 (3)	205.56 (3)	46.0 (5)

larger size than standard GP on most of the datasets, which is 5–15 times larger. However, it is interesting to see that, on the two real-world datasets, NGSGP has the smallest average program size, which is even smaller than standard GP. These smaller models generally have better interpretability, which is a desired property in many real-world problems. Comparing the program size of RDO and NGSGP, it is clear that on all the eight benchmarks, NGSGP has a smaller average program size but much higher minimum size than RDO. This indicates that the programs evolved by the different runs in NGSGP are more stable than RDO in size, and NGSGP is less likely to generate oversize programs.

6 Conclusions and Future Work

This work aimed to address the limitations of GSGP and RDO, which are either a loosely or a uniformly semantic control over the offspring individuals and can potentially lead to premature convergence and overfitting in GP. The goal has been achieved by developing two new geometric semantic operators named perpendicular crossover and random segment mutation to conduct a precise semantic control under the theoretical requirement of GSGP. The behavioural analysis of the evolved models releases that NGSGP, which employs the two operators, outperforms RDO at an early stage of learning process and this advantage increases along with generations. More importantly, NGSGP has a much better generalisation ability than RDO shown by obtaining lower testing errors and eliminating/releasing overfitting. In addition, NGSGP also evolves more compact models than RDO.

For future work, we are interested in speeding up the new operators, as the overall computational cost of the new geometric operators is much higher than the canonical form of GP operators. The major expense is in searching the semantic library and evaluating the large individuals. Thus, we would like to improve the algorithm on semantic library search and introduce bloat free mechanism to the new operators in the near future. In addition, this work only compares with one kind of geometric operators, a more comprehensive comparison between the new operators and other variants of geometric operators on improving the performance of GP will be performed in the future.

References

1. Archetti, F., Lanzeni, S., Messina, E., Vanneschi, L.: Genetic programming for computational pharmacokinetics in drug discovery and development. Genetic Program. Evol. Mach. **8**(4), 413–432 (2007)
2. Chen, Q., Xue, B., Mei, Y., Zhang, M.: Geometric semantic crossover with an angle-aware mating scheme in genetic programming for symbolic regression. In: McDermott, J., Castelli, M., Sekanina, L., Haasdijk, E., García-Sánchez, P. (eds.) EuroGP 2017. LNCS, vol. 10196, pp. 229–245. Springer, Cham (2017). doi:10.1007/978-3-319-55696-3_15
3. Fortin, F.A., Rainville, F.M.D., Gardner, M.A., Parizeau, M., Gagné, C.: DEAP: evolutionary algorithms made easy. J. Mach. Learn. Res. **13**, 2171–2175 (2012)
4. Gonçalves, I., Silva, S., Fonseca, C.M.: On the generalization ability of geometric semantic genetic programming. In: Machado, P., Heywood, M.I., McDermott, J., Castelli, M., García-Sánchez, P., Burelli, P., Risi, S., Sim, K. (eds.) EuroGP 2015. LNCS, vol. 9025, pp. 41–52. Springer, Cham (2015). doi:10.1007/978-3-319-16501-1_4
5. Koza, J.R.: Genetic Programming: on the Programming of Computers by Means of Natural Selection, vol. 1. MIT Press, Cambridge (1992)
6. Krawiec, K., O'Reilly, U.M.: Behavioral programming: a broader and more detailed take on semantic GP. In: Proceedings of the 16th Annual Conference on Genetic and Evolutionary Computation Conference (GECCO), pp. 935–942 (2014)
7. Moraglio, A., Krawiec, K., Johnson, C.G.: Geometric semantic genetic programming. In: Coello, C.A.C., Cutello, V., Deb, K., Forrest, S., Nicosia, G., Pavone, M. (eds.) PPSN 2012. LNCS, vol. 7491, pp. 21–31. Springer, Heidelberg (2012). doi:10.1007/978-3-642-32937-1_3
8. Nguyen, Q.U., Nguyen, X.H., O'Neill, M.: Semantic aware crossover for genetic programming: the case for real-valued function regression. In: Vanneschi, L., Gustafson, S., Moraglio, A., De Falco, I., Ebner, M. (eds.) EuroGP 2009. LNCS, vol. 5481, pp. 292–302. Springer, Heidelberg (2009). doi:10.1007/978-3-642-01181-8_25
9. Pawlak, T.P.: Geometric semantic genetic programming is overkill. In: Heywood, M.I., McDermott, J., Castelli, M., Costa, E., Sim, K. (eds.) EuroGP 2016. LNCS, vol. 9594, pp. 246–260. Springer, Cham (2016). doi:10.1007/978-3-319-30668-1_16
10. Pawlak, T.P., Krawiec, K.: Guarantees of progress for geometric semantic genetic programming. In: Semantic Methods in Genetic Programming, Ljubljana, Slovenia, vol. 13 (2014)
11. Pawlak, T.P., Wieloch, B., Krawiec, K.: Semantic backpropagation for designing search operators in genetic programming. IEEE Trans. Evol. Comput. **19**(3), 326–340 (2015)
12. Rosenwald, A., Wright, G., Chan, W.C., Connors, J.M., Campo, E., Fisher, R.I., Gascoyne, R.D., Muller-Hermelink, H.K., Smeland, E.B., Giltnane, J.M., et al.: The use of molecular profiling to predict survival after chemotherapy for diffuse large-B-cell lymphoma. N. Engl. J. Med. **346**(25), 1937–1947 (2002)

Constrained Dimensionally Aware Genetic Programming for Evolving Interpretable Dispatching Rules in Dynamic Job Shop Scheduling

Yi Mei[1(✉)], Su Nguyen[1,2], and Mengjie Zhang[1]

[1] Victoria University of Wellington, Wellington, New Zealand
{yi.mei,su.nguyen,mengjie.zhang}@ecs.vuw.ac.nz
[2] Advanced Analytics Lab, La Trobe University, Melbourne, Australia

Abstract. This paper investigates the interpretability of the Genetic Programming (GP)-evolved dispatching rules for dynamic job shop scheduling problems. We incorporate the physical dimension of the features used in the terminal set of GP, and assume that the rules that aggregate the features with the same physical dimension are more interpretable. Based on this assumption, we define a new interpretability measure called dimension gap, and develop a Constrained Dimensionally Aware GP (C-DAGP) that optimises the effectiveness and interpretability simultaneously. In C-DAGP, the fitness is defined as a penalty function with a newly proposed penalty coefficient adaptation scheme. The experimental results show that the proposed C-DAGP can achieve better tradeoff between effectiveness and interpretability compared against the baseline GP and an existing DAGP.

1 Introduction

Job Shop Scheduling (JSS) [18] has applications in a variety of real-world domains such as manufacturing [3], project scheduling [23] and cloud computing. It aims to schedule the jobs arriving at a job shop (e.g. factory) subject to some constraints (e.g. each job much follow a pre-specified routing, and each machine can process no more than one job at one time) and optimise some criteria such as flowtime and tardiness.

In the real world, the job arrival process is an ongoing process. Therefore, it is more realistic to consider the *Dynamic* JSS (DJSS), in which there are unpredicted job arrivals occurring in real time. More specifically, in DJSS, at any given time point, only the information of the jobs that have arrived before the current time is available, while the future jobs are still unknown. In this paper, we focus on solving DJSS, which is closer to reality than the *static* JSS counterpart.

For solving DJSS, traditional optimisation approaches such as mathematical programming and genetic algorithms are not directly applicable since they are trying to obtain a solution (schedule). When the environment changes, e.g. a new

© Springer International Publishing AG 2017
Y. Shi et al. (Eds.): SEAL 2017, LNCS 10593, pp. 435–447, 2017.
https://doi.org/10.1007/978-3-319-68759-9_36

job arrives, it is non-trivial to effectively adjust the current schedule to adapt to the new environment. *Dispatching Rules* (DRs), on the other hand, are promising heuristics for solving DJSS due to their low complexity, scalability and flexibility. Instead of optimising the schedule as a whole, a DR gradually builds the schedule step by step by taking the latest information into account. Specifically, a DR uses a *priority function* to decide for each idle machine which job in its waiting queue should be processed next. Common DRs include First-Come-First-Serve (FCFS), Earliest Due Date (EDD), Shortest Processing Time (SPT), etc. A lot of DRs have been designed manually (e.g. [10, 20, 22]) by considering job shop attributes such as operation processing time, due date, work remaining and slack. However, the existing manually designed DRs are normally not effective enough, and restricted to the particular job shop scenario they are designed for.

The effectiveness of DRs depends on various factors such as objective, due date tightness and job shop utilisation [22]. Therefore, it is hard to design effective DRs *manually* under a given job shop scenario. To address this issue, Genetic Programming (GP) is a promising approach to automatically design DRs as a hyper-heuristic. Evolving DRs with GP has achieved some success in scheduling [2, 15], and the GP-evolved DRs have shown to be much more effective than the manually designed rules.

Most existing related works focused on the effectiveness of DRs. However, they ignored another important property of the GP-evolved DRs, which is *interpretability*. As a result, the GP-evolved DRs are too complicated to be interpreted and understood. The practitioners may feel less confident of using the DRs due to the lack of understanding of the inner mechanism, despite of their effectivenesses shown on the training instances.

In this paper, we aim to consider both *effectiveness* and *interpretability* of the DRs during the GP process. We employ the Dimensionally Aware GP (DAGP), which considers the *physical dimensions* (time, count and weight) of the job shop attributes, and favours the combinations between the attributes with the same physical dimension. Specifically, we have the following research objectives:

- Develop a Constrained DAGP (C-DAGP) algorithm for DJSS based on the physical dimensions of the job shop attributes.
- Propose a new penalty coefficient adaptation scheme for C-DAGP.
- Compare between the penalty adaptation schemes for C-DAGP, and compare C-DAGP with an existing DAGP and the baseline GP.

The rest of the paper is organised as follows: Sect. 2 gives the background introduction. Then, the proposed C-DAGP is described in Sect. 3. Experimental studies are carried out in Sect. 4. Finally, Sect. 5 gives the conclusions and future work.

2 Background

2.1 Job Shop Scheduling

JSS is to process a set of jobs with a set of given machines subject to some constraints. Each job has an arrival time, a due date, and a sequence of operations.

Each operation has an eligible machine which is the only machine that can process it, as well as a processing time. An operation cannot be processed before the completion before its precedent operations. Each machine can process at most one operation at a time. The commonly considered JSS objectives include minimising the makespan ($C_{\max}$), total flowtime ($\sum C_j$), total weighted tardiness ($\sum w_j T_j$), number of tardy jobs, etc. [18].

2.2   Related Works

So far, there have been extensive studies [5,7,9,14,17] in evolving DRs for DJSS using GP, and successfully achieved much better DRs than the previously manmade rules. Comprehensive reviews can be found in [2,15].

Most existing works focused on the effectiveness (i.e. the test performance) of the GP-evolved DRs. Only a few recent works tried to improve the *interpretability* of the DRs. Nguyen et al. [14] investigated different representations and proposed a grammar-based representation to evolve more meaningful rules. Some studies tried to use *feature selection* to implicitly improve the interpretability of the evolved rules, assuming that using fewer terminals tends to generate more meaningful rules. Along this direction, Mei et al. [13] proposed to a feature selection algorithm that obtained more compact terminal set for GP. Riley et al. [21] proposed a similar feature selection approach.

To focus on more meaningful combinations of terminals, Hunt et al. [8] considered the physical dimensions of the job shop attributes (e.g. time, count and weight), and developed a strongly-typed GP that evolves DRs that only allows the "meaningful" combinations between the attributes with the same physical dimension. Following similar ideas, Durasević et al. [4] developed a DAGP that considers the compatibility between the physical dimensions of the terminals. They designed initialisation and evolutionary operators so that no semantically incorrect rule (e.g. adding time to weight) is generated.

However, it has been shown [4,8] that when restricting the combination between terminals of GP, the rules obtained by the strongly-typed GP and DAGP had worse test performance than the baseline GP. The main reason is that the restrictions on the combinations of terminals make a huge part of the search space infeasible, and the resultant search space consists of many isolated feasible regions. It may be hard to jump from one feasible region to another. Thus, the final rule largely depends on the initial rules, and the search gets stuck into poor local optima easily.

Keizer and Babovic [1,11] proposed a dimension-based brood selection scheme for DAGP, which addressed the overly restricted search space to some extent. The proposed algorithm allows dimensional inconsistent combinations, and uses a *culling function* to measure the total *dimensional inconsistency* (i.e. dimensional violations) of each individual. Then, each crossover/mutation operator generates $m(>1)$ offsprings, and the best one in terms of dimensional inconsistency is selected as the offspring produced by the operator.

However, the culling function is not flexible enough, and our preliminary studies showed that in DJSS, even $m = 2$ can lead to a dramatic deterioration in test performance. In this paper, we propose to improve the flexibility of DAGP by considering the dimensional consistency as a constraint.

3   Constrained Dimensionally Aware Genetic Programming

The framework of the proposed C-DAGP is given in Algorithm 1. There are two important features in the framework, highlighted in lines 3 and 4. The first feature is the *dimension gap* (line 3), which reflects the degree of dimension inconsistency based on the *physical dimensions* (or *units*) of each terminal introduced in DAGP [11]. The calculation of the dimension gap will be described in detail in Sect. 3.1. The second feature is the *constrained fitness function* defined by both the objective value and the dimension gap. The two terms are aggregated by a *penalty coefficient* α on the dimension gap. Since the objective value and dimension gap have significantly different scales, an open issue is to set a proper α value to achieve good balance between the objective value and dimension gap. We propose a new penalty coefficient adaptation scheme, which will be described in Sect. 3.2.

Algorithm 1. The framework of C-DAGP.

---

1 Initialise a population using Grow method;
2 **while** *Stopping criteria not met* **do**
3 | Calculate the objective value $\mathtt{obj}(x)$ and the **dimension gap** $\mathtt{dimGap}(x)$ for each individual x in the population;
4 | **Calculate the fitness of each individual using a penalty function** $\mathtt{fit}(x) = \mathtt{obj}(x) + \alpha \cdot \mathtt{dimGap}(x)$;
5 | Generate a new population by selection and evolutionary operators;
6 **end**
7 **return** The best individual in the population;

3.1   Calculation of Dimension Gap

First, we introduce the physical dimensions of the terminals used in GP for evolving DRs in DJSS. We define three physical dimensions as follows:

1. `TIME`: including terminals such as processing time, due date, slack, etc.
2. `COUNT`: including terminals such as number of operations remaining, number of jobs in the queue, etc.
3. `WEIGHT`: the weight of a job.

Each node in the GP-tree is associated with a 3D vector $\boldsymbol{\theta} = (T, C, W)$, representing its exponentials of the three dimensions. For example, a terminal `PT` (processing time) is associated with a vector $(1, 0, 0)$, since it belongs to the `TIME` dimension, that is, its dimension exponential is 1 in `TIME`, and 0 in all the other dimensions. The dimension exponential values of a non-terminal node depends on that of its children and the function that the node represents. Table 1 shows how the calculation is conducted for the functions used in the proposed C-DAGP. For multiplication (division), the exponentials of the two children are added (subtracted). For addition, subtraction, max and min operators, since we allow children with inconsistent exponentials, we set the exponentials of the result to be the average of that of the two children. If the two children have the same dimension exponentials, then the result will have the same dimension exponentials with the children as well.

Table 1. The calculation of the dimension vector values of a non-terminal node.

Function(s)	Children vector values	Result
$+$, $-$, max and min	$(T_1, C_1, W_1), (T_2, C_2, W_2)$	$\left(\frac{T_1+T_2}{2}, \frac{C_1+C_2}{2}, \frac{W_1+W_2}{2}\right)$
$\times$	$(T_1, C_1, W_1), (T_2, C_2, W_2)$	$(T_1 + T_2, C_1 + C_2, W_1 + W_2)$
$/$	$(T_1, C_1, W_1), (T_2, C_2, W_2)$	$(T_1 - T_2, C_1 - C_2, W_1 - W_2)$

Then, we calculate the dimension gaps for each node and the entire GP-tree. For multiplication and division, the dimension gap is always zero since these two operators have no restriction on the dimensions of the children. For the other operators, the dimension gap is the sum of the differences between the children in all the dimensions. The dimension gaps are calculated as follows:

$$\text{dimGap(node)} = \begin{cases} 0, & \text{if node} = \times \text{ or } / \\ \delta(\boldsymbol{\theta}(\mathbf{c_1}), \boldsymbol{\theta}(\mathbf{c_2})), & \text{otherwise.} \end{cases} \tag{1}$$

$$\text{dimGap(tree)} = \sum_{\text{node} \in \text{tree}} \text{dimGap(node)}, \tag{2}$$

where $\delta(\boldsymbol{\theta}_1, \boldsymbol{\theta}_2) = |T_1 - T_2| + |C_1 - C_2| + |W_1 - W_2|$.

Figure 1 gives an example of the dimension gap calculation. In this example, all the terminals have zero dimension gaps. Then, according to Eq. (1), the dimension gaps of the "$*$" and "$/$" non-terminal nodes are 0, and that of the root "$-$" is 2.

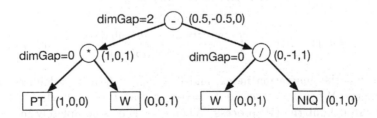

Fig. 1. An example of the dimension gap calculation.

3.2 Penalty Coefficient Adaptation

It is a non-trivial task to set a proper penalty coefficient to achieve a good balance between the test performance and interpretability (represented by dimension gap). Specifically, the penalty coefficient should be set according to the distribution of the current population. If the current population is located in regions with high dimension gap, then the coefficient should be high to push the search towards the more interpretable areas. On the other hand, if most individuals in the current population have zero dimension gap, then the coefficient should be low to encourage the search to jump out of the current region of zero dimension gap ("feasible" region in terms of dimension consistency) through the intermediate area with positive dimension gap ("infeasible" regions). Here, we extend a mechanism proposed for bloating control in GP [19]. In that work, to keep the average program size in the population staying at the same level during the GP process, a *parsimony pressure* method is used and the adjusted fitness of a solution x is defined as $\texttt{fit}(x) = \texttt{obj}(x) + \alpha \cdot \texttt{size}(\texttt{x})$, where the parsimony coefficient α at generation t is determined by

$$\alpha(t) = -\frac{\mathrm{cov}(\texttt{size}, \texttt{obj})}{\mathrm{var}(\texttt{size})} \tag{3}$$

where the covariance $\mathrm{cov}(\texttt{size}, \texttt{obj})$ and variance $\mathrm{var}(\texttt{size})$ are calculated empirically using the program sizes and objective values of the individuals in the current population [19].

In this paper, we borrow this idea and design the penalty coefficient adaptation so that the average dimension gap of the individuals in the population stays at the same level during the GP process. To this end, we simply replace $\texttt{size}$ with $\texttt{dimGap}$ in Eq. (3). Furthermore, to reduce the empirical estimation bias of the covariance and variance, we propose the following two strategies:

1. Instead of using all the individuals in the population, we use the top 10% individuals in terms of the objective value in the population for estimating the covariance and variance measures. This way, we expect to reduce the effect of the individuals with very poor objective values.
2. The penalty coefficient is updated by a *moving average* technique as follows:

$$\alpha(0) = -\frac{\mathrm{cov}(\texttt{dimGap}(pop_0), \texttt{obj}(pop_0))}{\mathrm{var}(\texttt{dimGap}(pop_0))}, \tag{4}$$

$$\alpha(t+1) = \alpha(t) - \eta \left(\frac{\mathrm{cov}(\texttt{dimGap}(pop_t), \texttt{obj}(pop_t))}{\mathrm{var}(\texttt{dimGap}(pop_t))} + \alpha(t) \right). \tag{5}$$

where t is the generation index, and $0 \leq \eta \leq 1$ is a user-defined step size parameter. When $\eta = 0$, $\alpha(t+1) = \alpha(t)$ for all $t \geq 0$, i.e. the coefficient is fixed throughout the GP process. When $\eta = 1$, α is completely memoryless, and $\alpha(t+1)$ is independent of $\alpha(t)$.

4   Experimental Studies

To evaluate the effectiveness of the proposed C-DAGP, we first conduct sensitivity analysis on the parameter η. Then, we compare C-DAGP with the baseline GP (denoted as BaselineGP) and the GP with culling function [11] (denoted as CullingGP). For CullingGP, each crossover/mutation operator generates 2 offsprings, and the one with least dimension gap is selected.

In the experiments, we consider 3 objectives: maximal tardiness (Tmax), mean tardiness (Tmean) and total weighted tardiness (TWT). For each objective, we consider utilisation levels of 0.85 and 0.95. This results in $3 \times 2 = 6$ different job shop scenarios. The configuration parameters of the simulation model are given in Table 2, which has been used in previous studies [6,12,16]. The parameter setting of the compared GP algorithms is given in Table 3.

Table 2. The DJSS simulation configuration.

Parameter	Value	Parameter	Value
#machines	10	#jobs	5000
#warmup jobs	1000	#operations/job	Random from 2 to 10
Job arrival	Poisson process	Utilisation level	{0.85, 0.95}
Due date	4× total processing time	Processing time	$U[1, 99]$

Table 3. The parameter setting of the compared GP algorithms.

Parameter	Value	Parameter	Value
Terminal set	See Table 4	Function set	$\{+, -, *, /, \min, \max\}$
Population size	1024	Maximal depth	8
Crossover rate	80%	Mutation rate	15%
Reproduction rate	5%	#generations	51

During the training process, an individual is evaluated using a randomly generated simulation. To improve generalisation, the random seed for generating the training simulation changes per generation. In addition, the fitness is normalised by the objective value of the reference rule. The reference rule is set to EDD, ATC and WATC for Tmax, Tmean and TWT, respectively. Finally, the best individual in the last generation is selected as the best individual of the GP run.

For testing, a test set of 50 simulation replications is randomly generated for each scenario. The test fitness of a rule x is defined as the normalised total objective value over the test replications, i.e. $\Gamma(x, \Pi, F) = \frac{\sum_{\pi \in \Pi} F(x, \pi)}{\sum_{\pi \in \Pi} F(\text{RefRule(Obj)}, \pi)}$, where $F \in \{\text{Tmax}, \text{Tmean}, \text{TWT}\}$.

Table 4. The terminals used in the GP algorithms.

Notation	Description	Dimension
WIQ	Work In Queue	TIME
MWT	Machine Waiting Time	TIME
PT	Processing Time	TIME
NPT	Next Processing Time	TIME
OWT	Operation Waiting Time	TIME
NWT	Next Machine Waiting Time	TIME
WKR	Work Remaining	TIME
WINQ	Work In Next Queue	TIME
rFDD	Relative FDD	TIME
rDD	Relative DD	TIME
TIS	Time In System	TIME
SL	Slack	TIME
NIQ	Number of operations In Queue	COUNT
NOR	Number of Operations Remaining	COUNT
NINQ	Number of operations In Next Queue	COUNT
W	Weight	WEIGHT

All the compared GP approaches were implemented in Java using the ECJ library. The experiments were run on desktops with Intel(R) Core(TM) i7 CPU @3.60 GHz. Both algorithms were run 30 times independently for each scenario.

4.1 Parameter Sensitivity Analysis

First, we conducted the sensitivity analysis to study the effect of the step size η on the performance of the algorithm. To this end, we compared the test performance and the dimension gap of the rules obtained by the C-DAGP with $\eta = 1$, 0.1 and 0.01, as shown in Tables 5 and 6. We conducted Wilcoxon's rank sum test

Table 5. The mean and standard deviation (in brackets) of the **test performance** obtained by the C-DAGP with $\eta = 1$, 0.1 and 0.01.

Scenario	Dimension gap		
	$\eta = 1$	$\eta = 0.1$	$\eta = 0.01$
$\langle T_{max}, 0.85, 4 \rangle$	0.49(0.02)	0.49(0.01)	0.49(0.01)
$\langle T_{mean}, 0.85, 4 \rangle$	0.51(0.06)	0.51(0.06)	0.51(0.05)
$\langle TWT, 0.85, 4 \rangle$	0.59(0.10)	0.57(0.08)	0.59(0.09)
$\langle T_{max}, 0.95, 4 \rangle$	0.72(0.02)	0.71(0.02)	0.70(0.02)
$\langle T_{mean}, 0.95, 4 \rangle$	0.69(0.02)	0.68(0.02)	0.69(0.03)
$\langle TWT, 0.95, 4 \rangle$	0.80(0.04)	0.81(0.04)	0.80(0.04)

Table 6. The mean and standard deviation (in brackets) of the **dimension gap** obtained by the C-DAGP with $\eta = 1$, 0.1 and 0.01.

Scenario	Dimension gap		
	$\eta = 1$	$\eta = 0.1$	$\eta = 0.01$
$\langle T_{max}, 0.85, 4 \rangle$	9.11(6.89)	5.35(6.07)	11.54(9.54)
$\langle T_{mean}, 0.85, 4 \rangle$	15.42(8.11)	12.69(7.36)	15.61(7.59)
$\langle TWT, 0.85, 4 \rangle$	13.12(6.31)	11.92(6.45)	14.31(7.88)
$\langle T_{max}, 0.95, 4 \rangle$	10.31(9.97)	9.10(7.91)	13.69(8.79)
$\langle T_{mean}, 0.95, 4 \rangle$	16.10(8.95)	15.29(7.83)	15.21(6.27)
$\langle TWT, 0.95, 4 \rangle$	16.77(8.03)	15.27(6.09)	16.95(6.63)

with significance level of 0.05, and found no statistical significance between the compared η values in terms of both test performance and dimension gap. Table 6 shows that $\eta = 0.1$ tends to achieve smaller (although not significant due to the high standard deviation) dimension gap than $\eta = 1$ and $\eta = 0.01$. Therefore, we choose $\eta = 0.01$ in the subsequent experiments.

4.2 Results and Discussions

The proposed C-DAGP is compared with BaselineGP and CullingGP [11]. BaselineGP does not consider dimension gap at all. CullingGP is a DAGP that reduces the dimension gap by repeatedly generating several (2 in the experiment) offsprings in each crossover and mutation, and selecting the one with the minimal dimension gap. It is not flexible in adjusting the balance between test performance and dimension gap.

Figures 2 and 3 show the convergences curves of the compared BaselineGP, CullingGP [11] and C-DAGP in terms of test performance and dimension gap. For each curve, the center is the mean value, and the ribbon is the standard error In Fig. 2, the curves for the last 5 generations are zoomed in and shown in the blocks inside.

From Fig. 2, one can see that in terms of performance of C-DAGP (blue) was generally better than CullingGP (green). It outperformed CullingGP in $\langle T_{mean}, 0.85, 4 \rangle$, $\langle TWT, 0.85, 4 \rangle$, $\langle T_{mean}, 0.95, 4 \rangle$ and $\langle TWT, 0.95, 4 \rangle$, and almost the same as CullingGP in other cases. C-DAGP was slightly worse than BaselineGP (red). It was outperformed by BaselinGP in $\langle T_{mean}, 0.95, 4 \rangle$ and $\langle TWT, 0.95, 4 \rangle$, performed better in $\langle T_{mean}, 0.85, 4 \rangle$, and achieved comparable performance as BaselineGP in other cases.

Figure 3 clearly shows that the dimension gap obtained by C-DAGP is between the dimension gaps of BaselineGP and CullingGP. BaselineGP ignores the dimension gap during the evolutionary process, and thus obtained very high dimension gaps. CullingGP, on the other hand, focused too much on the dimension gap. As a result, it achieved very low dimension gap (close to zero) at the cost of significantly worse test performance than BaselineGP (the green curves v.s. red curves in Fig. 2).

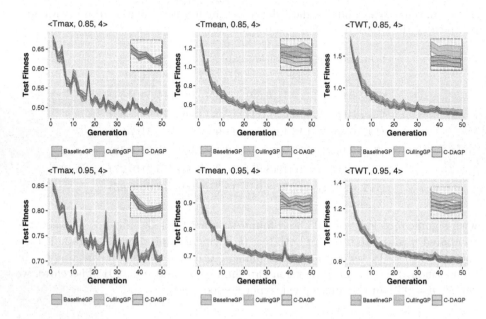

Fig. 2. The convergence curves (mean and standard error) of the **test performance** of BaselineGP, CullingGP and C-DAGP, with the last 5 generations zoomed in. (Color figure online)

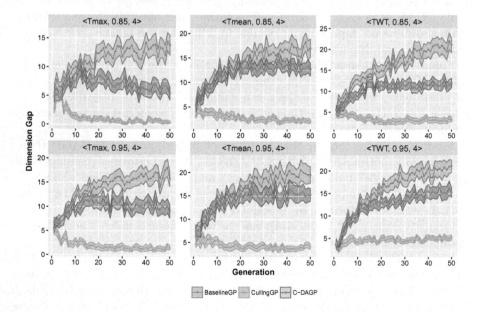

Fig. 3. The convergence curves (mean and standard error) of the **dimension gap** of BaselineGP, CullingGP and C-DAGP.

Overall, C-DAGP sat in the middle of BaselineGP and CullingGP. It achieved better test performance than CullingGP and smaller dimension gap than BaselineGP. Although the current results do not clearly show the advantage of C-DAGP, the new constrained optimisation framework enables a finer control on the balance between the test performance and dimension gap than CullingGP (it is reduced to BaselineGP when $m = 1$).

4.3   Further Analysis

As a further analysis, we investigated the structure of a rule obtained by C-DAGP for $\langle \text{TWT}, 0.85, 4 \rangle$, which obtained both promising test performance (0.47 versus the mean of 0.57 over 30 runs) and dimension gap ($\text{dimGap} = 2$). The structure of the rule is as follows.

$$\text{rule} = B_1/B_2,$$
$$B_1 = \max((\text{SL} + \text{PT}) * \max(\min(\text{SL}, \text{WINQ}), \text{PT})/\text{WKR}, \text{PT}),$$
$$B_2 = \text{W} * \text{WKR}/(\max((\text{SL} + \text{PT}), \text{WKR}) * \mathbf{\max(W, PT)})$$

One can see that the rule contains important features for the weighted tardiness (PT, W, SL, WINQ, WKR), and similar patterns to the WSPT rule (PT/W), which is a promising rule for minimising the weighted tardiness. The only dimension inconsistency occurred in $\max(\text{W}, \text{PT})$ in B_2.

5   Conclusions and Future Work

In this paper, we propose a Constrained Dimensionally Aware GP (C-DAGP) to optimise both test performance and interpretability of job shop scheduling rules. Based on the physical dimension of the job shop attributes, we define a *dimension gap* measure to reflect the degree of interpretability of the evolved rules. Then, we develop a new penalty coefficient adaptation scheme to achieve a good balance between the performance and dimension gap during the GP search process. The experimental results show that the proposed C-DAGP sits between the baseline GP and an existing DAGP (CullingGP [11]) in terms of test performance and dimension gap. Although C-DAGP did not show consistent outperformance in both test performance and dimension gap, the new constrained optimisation framework enables a finer control on the balance between test performance and dimension gap.

In the future, we will investigate more penalty adaptation schemes to further improve the performance of C-DAGP. In addition, we will consider multi-objective frameworks and treat dimension gap as an objective rather than a constraint.

References

1. Babovic, V., Keijzer, M.: Genetic programming as a model induction engine. J. Hydroinf. **2**(1), 35–60 (2000)

2. Branke, J., Nguyen, S., Pickardt, C., Zhang, M.: Automated design of production scheduling heuristics: a review. IEEE Trans. Evol. Comput. **20**(1), 110–124 (2016)
3. Ceberio, J., Irurozki, E., Mendiburu, A., Lozano, J.A.: A distance-based ranking model estimation of distribution algorithm for the flowshop scheduling problem. IEEE Trans. Evol. Comput. **18**(2), 286–300 (2014)
4. Durasević, M., Jakobović, D., Knežević, K.: Adaptive scheduling on unrelated machines with genetic programming. Appl. Soft Comput. **48**, 419–430 (2016)
5. Hildebrandt, T., Heger, J., Scholz-Reiter, B.: Towards improved dispatching rules for complex shop floor scenarios: a genetic programming approach. In: Proceedings of Genetic and Evolutionary Computation Conference, pp. 257–264. ACM (2010)
6. Hildebrandt, T., Branke, J.: On using surrogates with genetic programming. Evol. Comput. **23**(3), 343–367 (2015)
7. Hunt, R., Johnston, M., Zhang, M.: Evolving less-myopic scheduling rules for dynamic job shop scheduling with genetic programming. In: Proceedings of the 2014 Conference on Genetic and Evolutionary Computation, pp. 927–934. ACM (2014)
8. Hunt, R., Johnston, M., Zhang, M.: Evolving dispatching rules with greater understandability for dynamic job shop scheduling. Technical report ECSTR-15-6 Victoria University of Wellington, Wellington, NZ (2015)
9. Jakobović, D., Budin, L.: Dynamic scheduling with genetic programming. In: Collet, P., Tomassini, M., Ebner, M., Gustafson, S., Ekárt, A. (eds.) EuroGP 2006. LNCS, vol. 3905, pp. 73–84. Springer, Heidelberg (2006). doi:10.1007/11729976_7
10. Jayamohan, M., Rajendran, C.: New dispatching rules for shop scheduling: a step forward. Int. J. Prod. Res. **38**(3), 563–586 (2000)
11. Keijzer, M., Babovic, V.: Dimensionally aware genetic programming. In: Proceedings of the 1st Annual Conference on Genetic and Evolutionary Computation, vol. 2, pp. 1069–1076. Morgan Kaufmann Publishers Inc. (1999)
12. Mei, Y., Nguyen, S., Zhang, M.: Evolving time-invariant dispatching rules in job shop scheduling with genetic programming. In: McDermott, J., Castelli, M., Sekanina, L., Haasdijk, E., García-Sánchez, P. (eds.) EuroGP 2017. LNCS, vol. 10196, pp. 147–163. Springer, Cham (2017). doi:10.1007/978-3-319-55696-3_10
13. Mei, Y., Zhang, M., Nyugen, S.: Feature selection in evolving job shop dispatching rules with genetic programming. In: Proceedings of Genetic and Evolutionary Computation Conference, pp. 365–372. ACM (2016)
14. Nguyen, S., Zhang, M., Johnston, M., Tan, K.: A computational study of representations in genetic programming to evolve dispatching rules for the job shop scheduling problem. IEEE Trans. Evol. Comput. **17**(5), 621–639 (2013)
15. Nguyen, S., Mei, Y., Zhang, M.: Genetic programming for production scheduling: a survey with a unified framework. Complex Intell. Syst. **3**(1), 41–66 (2017)
16. Nguyen, S., Zhang, M., Johnston, M., Tan, K.C.: Dynamic multi-objective job shop scheduling: a genetic programming approach. In: Uyar, A., Ozcan, E., Urquhart, N. (eds.) Automated Scheduling and Planning. SCI, vol. 505, pp. 251–282. Springer, Heidelberg (2013). doi:10.1007/978-3-642-39304-4_10
17. Pickardt, C., Hildebrandt, T., Branke, J., Heger, J., Scholz-Reiter, B.: Evolutionary generation of dispatching rule sets for complex dynamic scheduling problems. Int. J. Prod. Econ. **145**(1), 67–77 (2013)
18. Pinedo, M.L.: Scheduling: Theory, Algorithms, and Systems. Springer, New York (2012). doi:10.1007/978-3-319-26580-3
19. Poli, R., McPhee, N.F.: Parsimony pressure made easy. In: Proceedings of the 10th Annual Conference on Genetic and Evolutionary Computation, pp. 1267–1274. ACM (2008)

20. Rajendran, C., Holthaus, O.: A comparative study of dispatching rules in dynamic flowshops and jobshops. Eur. J. Oper. Res. **116**(1), 156–170 (1999)
21. Riley, M., Mei, Y., Zhang, M.: Feature selection in evolving job shop dispatching rules with genetic programming. In: IEEE Congress on Evolutionary Computation, pp. 3362–3369. IEEE (2016)
22. Sels, V., Gheysen, N., Vanhoucke, M.: A comparison of priority rules for the job shop scheduling problem under different flow time-and tardiness-related objective functions. Int. J. Prod. Res. **50**(15), 4255–4270 (2012)
23. Xiong, J., Liu, J., Chen, Y., Abbass, H.A.: A knowledge-based evolutionary multi-objective approach for stochastic extended resource investment project scheduling problems. IEEE Trans. Evol. Comput. **18**(5), 742–763 (2014)

Visualisation and Optimisation of Learning Classifier Systems for Multiple Domain Learning

Yi Liu$^{(\boxtimes)}$, Bing Xue, and Will N. Browne

Victoria University of Wellington, Wellington, New Zealand 6014
liuyi4@myvuw.ac.nz

Abstract. Learning classifier system (LCSs) have the ability to solve many difficult benchmark problems, but they have to be applied individually to each separate problem. Moreover, the solutions produced, although accurate, are not compact such that important knowledge is obscured. Recently a multi-agent system has been introduced that enables multiple, different LCSs to address multiple different problems simultaneously, which reduces the need for human system set-up, recognises existing solutions and assigns a suitable LCS to a new problem. However, the LCSs do not collaborate to solve a problem in a compact or human observable manner. Hence the aim is to extract knowledge from problems by combining solutions from multiple LCSs in a compact manner that enables patterns in the data to be visualised. Results show the successful compaction of multiple solutions to a single, optimum solution, which shows important feature knowledge that would otherwise have been hidden.

Keywords: Learning classifier systems · Multiple domain learning

1 Introduction

Learning Classifier Systems (LCSs) are a family of evolutionary computation techniques that evolve a population of 'condition-action' heuristics that cooperate to address classification tasks. They have the ability to provide solutions in domains exhibiting epistasis (e.g. non-linear feature interaction) and heterogeneity (e.g. different combinations of features producing the same class). The transparent nature of the heuristic (rule) format enables humans to interrogate the knowledge discovered.

LCSs have been shown to be accomplished at solving many different and difficult problem domains [11], such as salient object detection, game policy design, patient care and so forth [16]. However, as with many artificial intelligence approaches, they require humans to carefully set the parameters for each pre-selected problem domain. Furthermore, the solutions produced, albeit accurate, often require post-processing to obtain the most compact (condensed) solution. This reduces the transparency of knowledge to human users, although the additional time for processing and memory storage for the non-condensed solution is minimal nowadays.

© Springer International Publishing AG 2017
Y. Shi et al. (Eds.): SEAL 2017, LNCS 10593, pp. 448–461, 2017.
https://doi.org/10.1007/978-3-319-68759-9_37

Recently, the advances in fast and large memory computation have enabled system comprising of multiple LCSs to be realised [13]. This has the advantage of allowing multiple LCS setups to coexist so that one suited to an individual problem can be selected autonomously and quickly. Moreover, problem types can be identified, best matches to past solutions determined and new problems assigned to appropriate LCS setups. However, the problem remains of storing the best solution to a problem in a compact and human understandable manner.

The research question addressed here is whether each solution to one problem from multiple different setup LCSs can be combined into a single solution, improving both the understanding (i.e. visualisation) and compactness (i.e. condensation). The objectives are to generate novel algorithms/methods to combine multiple LCS populations together into a single solution for the first time. Secondly, to design methods for human understanding of the knowledge from multiple LCS solutions in order to aid transparency of the knowledge discovered.

LCSs have been applied to many types of problem including Boolean, integer, real-valued and categorical encoded domains. This can be coupled with either supervised or reinforcement learning and instantaneous or delayed reward environmental interaction. As an initial investigation of the novel methods, Boolean domains are selected as the solutions are well understood, varied and straightforward to visually judge the worth of evolved solutions. Stimulus-response (i.e. instantaneous) learning is often used in knowledge discovery tasks so is appropriate here. As the multi-agent system can contain both supervised and reinforcement learning based LCSs, reinforcement learning was selected as arguably the more complex problems due to the absence of a known class. It is worth noting that although the system has been tested up to and including 70-bit problems, only 6-bit results are presented due to space restrictions (2^6 vs. 2^{70} long optimal solutions) and (6 feature wide graphs vs. 70 wide graphs).

2   Background

Learning Classifier Systems (LCSs) produce cooperative solutions of 'if condition then action' rules as specified by the Michigan approach adopted here [16]. Evolutionary search is used for global exploration for the best forms of solution for an environmental niche (an area of solution space that has common characteristics). While reinforcement learning is used to fine tune the parameter values, such as rule fitness, in order to guide this local search. When an environmental state is passed to an LCS it searches its population of rules to determine while rules match this input in order to form the match set $[M]$. Initially, $[M]$ may be empty, such that the *covering* method is called to generate a rule with generality to cover the input space.

Not all rules will match an input, hence the need for a cooperating population. Alternating between deterministic and guided stochastic selection an action (e.g. proposed class of data) will be selected from those advocated in $[M]$. All rules (termed classifiers when supporting parameters are included) advocating this action are placed in the action set $[A]$. Once the action is effected on the environment (e.g. the proposed class is checked for appropriateness) then the parameters of classifiers in [A] are updated through reinforcement learning (e.g. a recency-weighted filter or a Q-learning like policy update for multistep problems). Once the classifiers in a niche have been tested sufficiently to obtain their relative worth to the system an evolutionary search algorithm is used, often in this niche (e.g. only classifiers currently in [A] are evolved).

This project is based on two assumptions. Firstly, LCS can extract information from Boolean problems [9], which is plausible from previous results [12]. According to Iqbal [6–8,10], reinforcement based LCS [2], e.g. XCS [18], can solve many complex Boolean problems, but they often express the target solution in a rich way making knowledge hard to observe. Secondly, the solutions can be non-optimal if the parameters are poorly set-up, such that different partially correct information is discovered in different runs [5].

Recently, different LCSs have been combined into a multi-agent system, affectionately known as Original Intelligence System (OIS) as it approaches the task of learning multiple problems in a novel manner [13]. This is different to the GALE system [1] for individual problems as OIS seeks continuous learning using multiple agents for multiple problems, see Fig. 1.

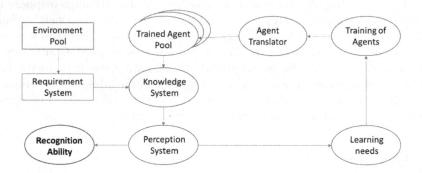

Fig. 1. Original Intelligence System [13]

OIS forms the base of the novel methods, which are related to compaction [3,4] and visualisation [15,17] of extracted knowledge, although unusually as a combination of multiple agents rather than one. These techniques are also not competitors as they can be used within OIS without loss of benefits.

3   Method

The novel contribution is split into three main parts. The first part uses different versions of standard LCSs (in this case different XCSs) to learn a benchmark problem several times. The second part selects reasonably high fitness rules from all the trained agents. The last part is using our novel search technique, termed *attribute-search* to discover the unique best classifier set among the whole good performance rules.

To collect the candidate classifiers, four strategies are employed in sequence. 1. Elite selection, 2. Experience assessment 3. Consistency assessment and 4. Correctness Partition. Therefore, the acronym for these four strategies is EECC, see Fig. 2.

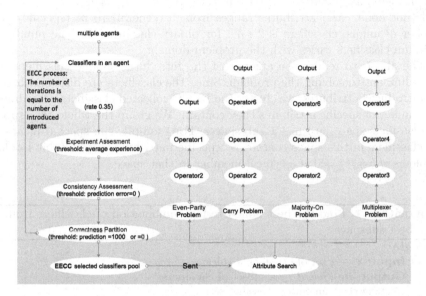

Fig. 2. EECC and Attribute search: firstly, multiple agents produce final classifiers which EECC sub-selects to send to attribute search. Currently, the best operation combination for a specific problem domain is set manually, e.g. for the even-parity problem, all the EECC selected classifiers will undergo operator2 and operator1 in turn.

Elite Selection. The elite selection algorithm firstly ranks all classifiers in an agent according to their value of numerosity (a parameter that stores the number of duplicates of a unique classifier) from high to low. The classifiers are selected according to their rank above a threshold based on population size and training number.

Experience Assessment. In XCS, the parameter experience indicates the number of training instances for every classifier. We only consider classifiers with an experience greater than the average to remove poorly tested rules.

Consistency Assessment. We delete any classifiers whose prediction error is higher than 0 as they are not considered accurate. This could be tuned for noisy domains.

Correctness Partition. In XCS, both completely correct and incorrect classifiers can reduce their prediction error to 0. We employ the best action map strategy to only use correct classifiers [14].

Attribute-Search: In Boolean problems, every bit can be considered as an attribute according to their location. Therefore, an m-bit Boolean problem can be considered as [Attribute0, Attribute1, ... Attribute$_m$]. The number of specified (not don't care) attributes ranges from 0 (general) to m (specific). The number of unique classifiers is $2 * 3^m$ for binary classification. The number of optimum classifiers varies with the problem domain.

The aim is to reduce the amount of the introduced unique classifiers that are redundant to solving the problem. Since the classifiers are distinguished by the introduced attributes, we cluster the EECC collected classifiers according to the number of specific attributes they contain. We group the whole corresponding classifiers space into m + 1 sub-spaces. For example, sub-space 0 means all the classifiers in this space contain no specified attribute, e.g. in 6-bit Boolean problems ######:0 is a typical member in that space.

Algorithm 1. Find the best none-overlap combination of classifiers from the best subspace

---

1 **begin**
2   **Input:** $S \leftarrow$ a set of classifier n rules;
3   **Output:** $BestSubset \leftarrow$ a subset of classifiers;
4      $BestSubset \leftarrow$ an empty classifier set;
5      $MaximumNumerosity \leftarrow 0$;
6   Rank the n rules in S in a descending order, according to their numerosity values;
7   **foreach** $s \in S$ **do**
8          $S_{temp} \leftarrow S$;
9          $Subset \leftarrow$ an empty rule set;
10   Add s to $Subset$; // **every rule has a chance to be a priority rule to be returned**
11   Remove s from S_{temp};
12   **foreach** $s' \in S_{temp}$ **do**
13   **if** s' *does not have overlap with any rule in Subset* **then**
14   Add s' to $Subset$;
15         $TotalNumerosity \leftarrow$ calculate the total Numerosity of rules in $Subset$;
16   **if** $TotalNumerosity > MaximumNumerosity$ **then**
17   Update $MaximumNumerosity \leftarrow TotalNumerosity$;
18   Update $BestSubset \leftarrow Subset$;
19   Return $BestSubset$;

Attribute-search is an umbrella name for a set of simple operations, which focus on search a reasonable classifiers combination among the EECC selected classifiers. This search technique includes 6 operations:

1. Error detection operation
2. Correct and incorrect group merge operation
3. Most reasonable sub-search space detection operation
4. Best none-overlap classifiers combination detection
5. Removal of over-general and over-specific rules
6. Subsumption operation.

Error Detection Operation. This operation focus on detecting the potential over-general classifiers in EECC selected classifiers. The basic idea of this operation is to compare each classifier (termed the target) with the classifiers in the higher sub-search space. The sum of the numerosity of any contrasting classifiers in the higher sub-search space that have an overlapping condition, but different action, with the target classifier is termed the conflict value. When the conflict value surpasses the target classifier's numerosity, we define the target classifier as an over-general classifier and delete this classifier.

Correct and Incorrect Group Merge Operation. A best action map is formed by flipping the action of any completely incorrect classifier (i.e. 0 prediction) then merge into the correct classifier set. Any classifiers having the same condition and action are combined into one classifier with summed numerosity.

Most Reasonable Sub-space Detection. The process of this strategy is to firstly cluster the EECC selected classifiers according to the number of attributes contained in the condition part. To solve an m-bit Boolean problem, we create m+1 sub-search spaces from minimum 0 to maximum m. For example, in 6-bit multiplexer problem, the attribute interval we obtained is [3, 5]. Then we calculate the total numerosity value for every remaining sub-space in the attribute interval, e.g. [5832, 17, 36] corresponding to sub-spaces [3, 4, 5]. We select the most important sub-spaces, e.g. sub-space 3, by a percentage threshold.

Best None-Overlap Classifiers Combination Detection. In string based condition, the overlap space between two classifiers can be calculated. Therefore, the overlapping classifiers can be detected. We search each rank from top to bottom and delete the classifiers that have overlap between the previous kept classifiers. Then we calculate the total numerosity value of each ranked combination of the remaining classifiers. The ranked combination with the highest numerosity is returned.

Removal of Over-General and Over-Specific Rules. The next step is to remove the over-general classifiers in the lower sub-search space, and the over-specific classifiers in the higher sub-search space. We can calculate the over-lap space between classifiers and detect a non-overlapping classifier in the best sub-space. Therefore, we detect whether a classifier-rule in the lower sub-search space can be expressed in the best sub-space.

Any classifier that has over-lap between a classifier in the best non-overlap classifier combination in the condition part and their action is different will be considered as an over-general classifier and it will be deleted. For example, in Table 3 the number 3 classifier (i.e. 000###:0) which belongs to the best sub-search space 3. We detect a classifier in the lower sub-search space, which is 00####:1 where its condition over-laps and its action is different so it will be removed.

Subsumption Operation. The subsumption operation in Attribute-search is the same as the subsumption in the XCS - if we can find a more general accurate classifier in a lower sub-space then we can directly delete a matching higher sub-space classifier.

4   Results and Discussion

In our experiment, standard XCSs are employed to generate the 360 agents for 6-bit problems, i.e. 30 runs (to statistically reduce variability) of three different XCSs were used for four problems. The three different versions of standard XCS only differed by the probability of generating don't care symbol, $P_\#$, see Fig. 3. Importantly, the training runs had a limited number of iterations in order to generate a variety of populations for the EECC system to merge, see Fig. 4.

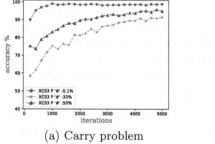
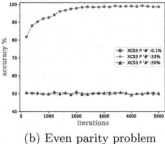

(a) Carry problem   (b) Even parity problem

Fig. 3. Example training plots showing deliberately compromised performance

Imperfect agents were introduced to test whether our strategy can select the optimal classifiers when there are poor classifiers in the whole classifier set. This is because in real problems there is no guarantee that every trained agent can completely solve the target problem.

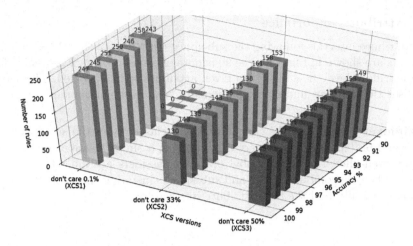

Fig. 4. The distribution of global agents' accuracy.

Table 1. XCS (accuracy)

Problems	XCS1	XCS2	XCS3	EECC and attribute-search
Even parity	[94.5%, 100%]	[43.8%, 54.5%]	[46.4%, 56.3%]	[100%, 100%]
Carry	[95.5%, 100%]	[76.3%, 98.7%]	[89.4%, 100%]	[100%, 100%]
Majority on	[95.9%, 100%]	[66.9%, 94.2%]	[74.3%, 96.2%]	[100%, 100%]
Multiplexer	[97.2%, 100%]	[72.7%, 100%]	[94.5%, 100%]	[100%, 100%]

Table 2. XCS (classifiers)

Problems	XCS1	XCS2	XCS3	EECC and attribute-search
Even parity	[845, 913]	[215, 288]	[322, 455]	64
Carry	[214, 262]	[135, 196]	[168, 223]	18
Majority on	[421, 480]	[209, 264]	[235, 332]	35
Multiplexer	[243, 258]	[130, 161]	[140, 154]	8

The performance results in terms of training accuracy and number of rules produced are shown in Tables 1 and 2 respectively. Note that as the purpose of LCSs is extraction of patterns through classification that a separate test set is not used as no claims on predictive ability to unseen data are being made. The tables show that non-optimal knowledge has been combined to generate optimal and compact rule sets, which can be interrogated, using the introduced methods.

4.1   Attribute Importance

The Attribute intervals following the sub-space clustering of the EECC collected classifiers are shown in Fig. 5 for the 90 agents of each problem. Essentially, for a given attribute level, how likely is a given attribute to be specified. This clearly visualises the different underlying patterns in each problem domain.

Multiplexer Problem. We cannot find any classifiers in the sub-space 0, 1, 2, 4, 5 and 6. Thus, the number of attributes in a single classifier is limited to [3]. It is well-known that the global optimal classifiers are indeed in the sub-space3. When we combine EECC and sub-space clustering together, the system can automatically find the best attribute interval for us.

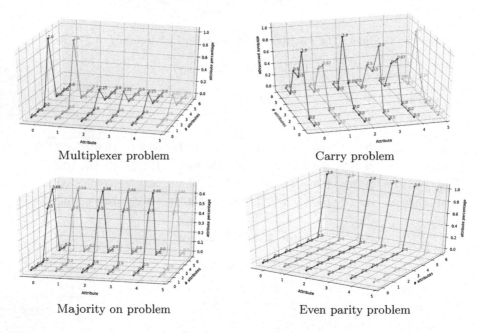

Multiplexer problem   Carry problem

Majority on problem   Even parity problem

Fig. 5. The attribute importance change according to different attribute space in attribute-search selected classifiers for certain problem

Carry Problem. The parameter settings for EECC used to analyze the Carry problem were the same as the setting in the multiplexer problem. Firstly, the methods reduced the number of introduced classifiers from 150 to 18. Secondly, according to the results in Table 6, the attribute interval of Carry problem is [2, 4]. Thus the attribute-space for the Carry problem is narrowed by the EECC. Thirdly, the attribute importance distribution for the most reasonable sub-search space, i.e. based on highest numerosity, was [1 0 0 1 0 0]. This shows the importance of the most significant bits in the Carry problem, which autonomously shows the nature of the problem.

Majority on Problem. A sample of the rule set produced, which is optimal, is shown in Table 5. Again the attribute interval, Fig. 5, shows the distribution of attribute importance, where no rules with attribute [0, 1, 2, 5, 6] are present. This demonstrates that both over-general and over-specific rules have been eliminated.

Even Parity Problem. When generating the result for the Even parity problem, the EECC needed three adjustments. Firstly, the Elite selection threshold was increased to 0.8 from the standard 0.35 as low numerosity classifiers were being produced by the agents. Moreover, if we set the threshold to 0.3, none of the classifiers were selected from EECC indicating a too strict threshold that needed relaxing. Secondly, in the Experience assessment part, we need to discount the experience threshold (or run the experiments for more iterations). Thirdly, in the Consistency assessment part, the prediction error was set raised to 1 as the lack of experience meant the parameter value had not converged.

The correct total of 64 classifiers was discovered where, as necessary, all are in sub-search space6, i.e. fully specified (table not shown due to length as fully enumerated 6-bit Boolean domain). Therefore the attribute interval for the Even parity problem is [6], see Fig. 5. This discovery supports that LCS can not generate any general classifiers suitable for this problem. EECC can detect the nature of the Even parity problem.

4.2   Specific Search

Since XCS generated classifiers can be grouped based on the number of attributes contained by the condition. Then we create the sub-search space for each XCS. In a m-bit Boolean problem, each of the $m + 1$ sub-space has the ability to express the whole problem domain. The extended OIS can detect which sub-space is more reasonable for solving the target problem. Also which sub-spaces are too over-general and which sub-spaces are too specific. Thus, it is practical for extended OIS to limit the search space. Thus, three strategies are introduced to complete the attribute-search. First one is the most reasonable attribute-space detection, we achieved this goal by finding the sub-space which has the highest totally numerosity value among all the sub-spaces detected in the attribute interval. Then we implement a strategy named as best non-overlap classifiers combination detection. Since in a string-based condition, we can calculate the overlap between classifiers, if no overlap classifiers combination can be detected, among all the non-overlap classifiers combination, we select the best one means the one has the highest total numerosity value. After this step, all the classifiers in the higher search space (greater number of attributes) we implement the decomposed operation, then any of the classifiers, which can be expressed in the best classifiers combination will be deleted. For any classifiers in the lower sub-search space (less number of attributes) we implement the conflict operation if a conflict occurs this classifier will be deleted (Table 4).

Table 3. Raw classifiers after EECC is applied in 6-bit multiplexer problem

ID	Condition	Action	Numerosity
0	01#1##	1	624
1	001###	1	593
2	10##1#	1	526
3	000###	0	486
4	11###0	0	452
...	...	...	...
21	110#00	0	7
22	01#010	0	6
23	#00101	0	6
24	#00001	0	5

Table 4. The final result for the Multiplexer problem

ID	Condition	Action	Numerosity
0	01#1##	1	624
1	001###	1	593
2	10##1#	1	526
3	000###	0	486
4	11###0	0	452
5	11###1	1	451
6	01#0##	0	394
7	10##0#	0	311

Time. Using XCS to train one 6-bit Boolean problem with maximum iterations as 3000 and maximum population 500 needs 1 to 2 min. By utilizing GRID computing, training 90 agents only take us 5 to 10 min. EECC and attribute-specific only spend 40 s to finish their tasks. Compared with the previous XCSs, we only introduce 4 to 8 addition minutes in the training step, but we can reduce more than 100 classifiers in our final result. In addition, our agent is much more compressed than the agents trained from previously XCSs. Therefore, when we reuse them to solve problems, they compute much more quickly than the previous agents speeding-up OIS.

5   Discussion

The Attribute-search for the Multiplexer problem is operation 3, operation 4 and operation 5. Firstly, we find the most reasonable sub-search space. Secondly, we find the best unique classifiers combination to obtain a unique classifiers combination in the best sub-search space. The reason is that the Multiplexer problem does not need any overlapping classifiers to solve the problem. Lastly, we run the decompose operation to delete all the classifiers in the higher sub-search space, which can be expressed totally in the most-reasonable sub-search space.

The Attribute-search for the Carry problem and the Majority on problem is operation 2, operation 1, and operation 6. Firstly, we merged the incorrect classifier set and correct classifier set from EECC selected classifiers. Then implement the error detect to delete the noise classifiers. Lastly, we run the subsumption operation to delete any classifiers in the higher sub-search space that can be subsumed by the classifiers that are in the lower sub-search space. The reason for the Carry problem and the Majority on problem use the same Attribute-search process is that they all need overlapping classifiers to address the target problem.

Table 5. Sample rules for the Majority on problem

Condition	Action	Numerosity
0	00###0	22
0	#0#00#	22
0	#000##	13
0	##0#00	8
1	#1#111	63
1	1#11#1	63
1	#11#11	59
1	#111#1	55

Table 6. The final result of the Carry problem, the attribute interval is [2, 4]

Condition	Action	Numerosity
1	1##1##	1312
0	0##0##	923
1	11##1#	215
1	#1#11#	185
0	0###00	156
0	0#0#0#	124
0	00##0#	75
0	###000	61
0	00###0	59
0	#0#0#0	58
0	000###	58
0	#000##	57
0	#0#00#	46
0	##000#	28
1	##1111	29
1	#111#1	23
1	1#1#11	21
1	111##1	13

The Attribute-search for the Even parity problem only uses the operation 1 and operation 2. We merge the correct and incorrect classifier sets and then detect the erroneous classifiers. A very interesting phenomenon is that almost all the EECC selected classifiers are in the incorrect classifier set. It appears that the system tends to solve the Even parity problem by combining over-general classifiers and incorrect specific classifiers.

6   Conclusion

The novel methods demonstrate that it is both practical and beneficial to combine the results of multiple LCSs as they have differing viewpoints into the same problem. This is related to ensembles of 'weak classifiers', albeit each LCS may be a collection of powerful classifiers in its own right. Results show the successful compaction of multiple solutions to a single, optimum solution, which highlights important feature knowledge that would otherwise have been hidden.

Future work will introduce more styles of LCS, e.g. supervised learners, and different types of problem, e.g. real-valued, into OIS in order to seamlessly improve its capabilities.

References

1. Bernadó, E., Llorà, X., Garrell, J.M.: XCS and GALE: a comparative study of two learning classifier systems on data mining. In: Lanzi, P.L., Stolzmann, W., Wilson, S.W. (eds.) IWLCS 2001. LNCS, vol. 2321, pp. 115–132. Springer, Heidelberg (2002). doi:10.1007/3-540-48104-4_8
2. Browne, W., Scott, D.: An abstraction algorithm for genetics-based reinforcement learning. In: Proceedings of the 7th annual conference on Genetic and evolutionary computation, pp. 1875–1882. ACM (2005)
3. Butz, M.V., Lanzi, P.L., Wilson, S.W.: Function approximation with XCS: Hyperellipsoidal conditions, recursive least squares, and compaction. Trans. Evol. Comput. **3**(12), 355–376 (2008)
4. Dixon, P.W., Corne, D.W., Oates, M.J.: A preliminary investigation of modified XCS as a generic data mining tool. In: Lanzi, P.L., Stolzmann, W., Wilson, S.W. (eds.) IWLCS 2001. LNCS, vol. 2321, pp. 133–150. Springer, Heidelberg (2002). doi:10.1007/3-540-48104-4_9
5. Ioannides, C., Browne, W.: Investigating scaling of an abstracted LCS utilising ternary and s-expression alphabets. In: Bacardit, J., Bernadó-Mansilla, E., Butz, M.V., Kovacs, T., Llorà, X., Takadama, K. (eds.) IWLCS 2006-2007. LNCS, vol. 4998, pp. 46–56. Springer, Heidelberg (2008). doi:10.1007/978-3-540-88138-4_3
6. Iqbal, M., Browne, W.N., Zhang, M.: Extracting and using building blocks of knowledge in learning classifier systems. In: Proceedings of the 14th Annual Conference on Genetic and Evolutionary Computation, pp. 863–870. ACM (2012)
7. Iqbal, M., Browne, W.N., Zhang, M.: Evolving optimum populations with XCS classifier systems. Soft. Comput. **17**(3), 503–518 (2013)
8. Iqbal, M., Browne, W.N., Zhang, M.: Extending learning classifier system with cyclic graphs for scalability on complex, large-scale boolean problems. In: Proceedings of the 15th Annual Conference on Genetic and Evolutionary Computation, pp. 1045–1052. ACM (2013)
9. Iqbal, M., Browne, W.N., Zhang, M.: Learning overlapping natured and niche imbalance boolean problems using XCS classifier systems. In: 2013 IEEE Congress on Evolutionary Computation (CEC), pp. 1818–1825. IEEE (2013)
10. Iqbal, M., Browne, W.N., Zhang, M.: Reusing building blocks of extracted knowledge to solve complex, large-scale boolean problems. IEEE Trans. Evol. Comput. **18**(4), 465–480 (2014)
11. Iqbal, M., Naqvi, S.S., Browne, W.N., Hollitt, C., Zhang, M.: Salient object detection using learning classifiersystems that compute action mappings. In: Proceedings of the 2014 Annual Conference on Genetic and Evolutionary Computation GECCO 2014, pp. 525–532 (2014)
12. Lanzi, P.L.: Mining interesting knowledge from data with the XCS classifier system. In: Proceedings of the 3rd Annual Conference on Genetic and Evolutionary Computation, pp. 958–965. Morgan Kaufmann Publishers Inc. (2001)
13. Liu, Y., Iqbal, M., Alvarez, I., Browne, W.N.: Integration of code-fragment based learning classifier systems for multiple domain perception and learning. In: 2016 IEEE Congress on Evolutionary Computation (CEC), pp. 2177–2184 (2016)
14. Orriols-Puig, A., Bernadó-Mansilla, E.: A further look at UCS classifier system. In: GECCO06, pp. 8–12 (2006)
15. Urbanowicz, R.J., Granizo-Mackenzie, A., Moore, J.H.: An analysis pipeline with statistical and visualization-guided knowledge discovery for Michigan-style learning classifier systems. Comput. Intell. Mag. **7**(4), 35–45 (2012)

16. Urbanowicz, R.J., Browne, W.N.: Introduction to Learning Classifier Systems. Springer, Heidelberg (2017)
17. Urbanowicz, R.J., Moore, J.H.: Exstracs 2.0: description and evaluation of a scalable learning classifier system. Evol. Intell. **8**(2–3), 89–116 (2015)
18. Wilson, S.W.: Classifier fitness based on accuracy. Evol. Comput. **3**(2), 149–175 (1995)

Adaptive Memetic Algorithm Based Evolutionary Multi-tasking Single-Objective Optimization

Qunjian Chen[1], Xiaoliang Ma[1], Yiwen Sun[2], and Zexuan Zhu[1(✉)]

[1] College of Computer Science and Software Engineering, Shenzhen University,
Shenzhen 518060, China
zhuzx@szu.edu.cn
[2] School of Medicine, Shenzhen University, Shenzhen 518060, China

Abstract. Evolutionary multitasking optimization has recently emerged as an effective framework to solve different optimization problems simultaneously. Different from the classic evolutionary algorithms, multi-task optimization (MTO) is designed to take advantage of implicit genetic transfer in a multi-tasking environment. It deals with multiple tasks simultaneously by leveraging similarities and differences across different tasks. However, MTO still suffers from a few issues. In this paper, a multifactorial memetic algorithm is introduced to solve the single-objective MTO problems. Particularly, the proposed algorithm introduces a local search method based on quasi-Newton, reinitializes a port of worse individuals, and suggests a self-adapt parent selection strategy. The effectiveness of the proposed algorithm is validated by comparing with the multifactorial evolutionary algorithm proposed in CEC'17 competition.

Keywords: Multi-tasking optimization · Memetic algorithm · Multifactorial evolutionary algorithm

1 Introduction

Evolutionary algorithms (EAs) are inspired by Darwinian's principle of "survival of the fittest" [1, 2]. EAs search optimal solutions based on reproduction and mutation to produce the offspring. In each evolution generation, fitter individuals are more likely to survive and be selected to generate offspring [1].

In classic EAs, different optimization problems are normally solved independently. However, like human possessing the most excellent capacity to manage and implement multiple tasks at the same time, a good solver of optimization problems is favorable to deal with multiple problems simultaneously. This desirable multitasking ability has motivated new computational methodologies to tackle multiple tasks simultaneously based on the correlation among different tasks, such that the tasks can be better solved together than solved separately.

Recently, the notion of evolutionary multitasking has been proposed in [3] with a paradigm namely multifactorial optimization (MFO). Each component task in the MFO possesses a unique function landscape and provides a particular factor influencing the evolutionary process. MFO takes full advantage of the implicit parallelism on the basis

© Springer International Publishing AG 2017
Y. Shi et al. (Eds.): SEAL 2017, LNCS 10593, pp. 462–472, 2017.
https://doi.org/10.1007/978-3-319-68759-9_38

of the population-based search. Accordingly, the solving of one optimization problem help to solve other optimization problems if these problems possess commonality and/or complementarity.

Each component task is considered as a single optimization solver and different single optimization solvers can learn from each other in the evolutionary process [5]. The corresponding pattern has been implemented in the multifactorial evolutionary algorithm (MFEA). In MFEA, one of the basic concepts is that all the individuals in the population are encoded in a unified search space [3]. The previous studies have shown the superiority of MFEA over traditional mode of solving each task [3, 4].

However, the MFEA still has some limitations. In this paper, a multifactorial memetic algorithm is introduced to solve some of these issues. Firstly, to improve the effectiveness of the learning in MFEA, a new local search strategy is proposed based on the knowledge learning among tasks. Secondly, to reduce the issue of premature convergence in MFEA, a re-initialization technique is introduced for a port of individuals whose ranks on the bottom. Finally, a self-adapt parent selection strategy is suggested aiming to fit different search stages. Compared with MFEA, the proposed algorithm can obtain better solutions for CEC'17 competition on evolutionary multi-task optimization [24].

The following sections are described below. In Sect. 2, we introduce the framework of the algorithm that contains definition of the properties and description of the procedure. In Sect. 3, we describe the benchmark problems that are used as a test suite. In Sect. 4, numerical experiments are carried out for showing the efficacy of the improved algorithm. Section 5 concludes the paper.

2 Adaptive Memetic Algorithm

2.1 Preliminary

In the multitasking environment, we suppose that K distinct optimization tasks are executed simultaneously, and all tasks are minimization problems. The j-th task is denoted as T_j, and each task has its unique search space X_j and objective function $F_j : X_j \rightarrow R$. Through such a setting, MFO is defined as an evolutionary multitasking paradigm that builds on the implicit parallelism of population-based search:

$$\{x_1, x_2, \ldots, x_{K-1} x_K\} = \arg \min\{F_1(x), F_2(x), \ldots, F_{K-1}(x), F_K(x)\}$$

where x_j is a feasible solution in X_j. Each component task F_j in the MFO possesses a particular factor influencing the evolutionary process. Therefore, the composite optimization problem can be referred to as a K-factorial problem.

In order to distinguish the population members in a multitasking environment effectively, it is important to formulate a general method to evaluate each individual. Each individual $p_i, i \in \{1, 2, \ldots, |P|\}$, in a population P has a set of properties. Every individual is encoded in a unified search space Y encompassing $X_1, X_2, \ldots, X_K$, and is decoded into a task-specific solution that can be written as $\{x_{i1}, x_{i2}, \ldots, x_{iK}\}$, where $x_{i1} \in X_1, x_{i2} \in X_2, \ldots, x_{iK} \in X_K$. Correspondingly, the description of five properties is given below.

- Factorial Cost: Define a formula $\psi_{ij} = \lambda \delta_{ij} + F_{ij}$. Which corresponds to task T_j and individual p_i. F_{ij} is the objective value, λ and δ_{ij} are the large penalizing multiplier and the total constraint violation.
- Factorial Rank: For a given task T_j, sorting the individuals in ascending order with respect to factorial cost. The rank r_{ij} of p_i is the index of p_i in j-th task T_j.
- Skill Factor: The τ_i of p_i is one of the tasks that need to be evaluated, i.e. $\tau_i = \min\limits_{1 \le j \le K} \{r_{ij}\}$.
- Scalar Fitness: The scalar fitness is $\varphi_{ij} = 1/r_{ij}$ for task T_j and individual p_i.
- Multifactorial Optimality: a solution is optimum in multitasking environment if it is the globally optimum in at least one task.

2.2   Basic Framework of Adaptive Memetic Algorithm (AMA)

In this subsection, we introduce three improved strategies for MFEA. Compared with solving each task respectively, MFEA has been proved to be more effective [3, 4]. In the multitasking optimization environment, all the tasks evolve a single population whose individuals are encoded in a unified search space. Using the unified individual encode is benefit for the transfer of genetic material [6]. Different tasks can learn from each other to improve their algorithmic performance [5].

The pseudocode of the adaptive memetic algorithm is presented in Algorithm 1, which base on multifactorial evolution. Lines 1–7 are the initialization stage. An initial population is first generated randomly in line 1. Each individual consist of a D_{max}-dimensional vector and each variable is a continuous value in the range [0, 1]. We need to evaluate every individual for all tasks in line 3, and then assign a skill factor for it according to factorial rank for each task in lines 4–5. Lines 8–16 are a typical evolution stages. The current population P_t is used to generate offspring by crossover and mutation in line 9, and the next parent population based on selection operator in line 16. The skill factor of offspring individual is inherited from its parents randomly in line 10. To reduce the computational resource, each of offspring is evaluated only for one task in line 11. The status for all tasks in the multitasking environment is recorded first in the line 17. The initial status of task is assigned 0. For task T_j, if the current best solution of T_j equals to its previous best solution (i.e. the best solution has not changed), the task status of T_j is recorded as 1, and otherwise it will be recorded as 0.

The above steps are similar to MFEA that has a few limitations. Firstly, the transferred knowledge can make the recipient achieve great success, but it is also possible to obtain no reward. It is important to choose an appropriate way to improve the effectiveness of learning [18–23]. Thus, line 18 of Algorithm 1 uses a new learning strategy among tasks described in Algorithm 2. Secondly, MFEA may be trapped into a local optimum making the search stagnation over a period of time. Thus, how to overcome the premature convergence is a key issue of MFEA. Line 19 applies a re-initialization technique, which is introduced in Algorithm 3, for a port of individuals whose ranks on the bottom. Finally, to fit different search stages, line 20 uses a self-adapt parent selection strategy introduced in Algorithm 4.

Algorithm 1. Pseudocode of the AMA

1. Randomly generate an initial population P_0 of n individuals.
2. **for every** p_j in P_0 **do**
3.   Evaluate p_j for all tasks
4.   Compute factorial rank r_{ij} for p_j, $j=1,2,...,k$
5.   Assign skill factor τ_i for p_j, $j=1,2,...,k$
6. **end for**
7. Set $t=0$
8. **While** stopping conditions are not satisfied **do**
9. C_t=Crossover + Mutate(P_t)
10.   **for every** c_j in C_t **do**
11.   Inherit skill factor τ_i of c_j from its parents
12.   Evaluate c_j for task τ_i only
13.   **end for**
14. $R_t=C_t + P_t$
15.   Compute scalar fitness φ_{ii} for all individuals
16.   Select N members from R_t to P_{t+1}
17.   Record tasks status
18.   Learning strategy among tasks on P_{t+1} – (see Algorithm 2)
19.   Broaden the search region – (see Algorithm 3)
20.   Self-adaptive selection strategy – (see Algorithm 4)
21.   Set $t=t+1$
22. **end while**

2.3 Learning Strategy Among Tasks

In Algorithm 2, an effective learning strategy among tasks is introduced. In the above three strategies, it provides best performance. After all the individuals are evaluated, we can get the current best individual for each task T_j in step 1. Suppose there are K optimization tasks, we can get at most K best individuals in step 1. Step 3 implements a quasi-Newton method to improve the current best individual of each task. Step 4 exchanges their skill factors of these best individual with ring topology. To reduce the computation resource, the proposed algorithm evaluates b_j for task τ_j only in step 5. Through such operations, we obtain at most K new individuals. This process can be regarded as a learning process among tasks.

Algorithm 2 can be explained further as follows. Each task can transfer a part of its genetic material to the other tasks [7–9]. It can be represented as the transfer of skill factor. If too much genetic material of one task is transferred, the evolution of individuals will be slow. For this reason, we only consider the best individual of each task. One situation is that the tasks in the multitasking environment have similar or even same optimum solution. If a task obtains a good solution, other tasks can benefit from it. Moreover, their genetic material will have a lasting influence on recipient [10, 11]. A quasi-Newton method [12] is introduced to efficiently use the exchanged of skill factor.

Algorithm 2. Learning strategy among tasks

Input: population information of tasks.
Output: the learned individual of each task.
1. Calculate the current best individual b_j of each task T_j, $j=1,...,K$
2. **for every** b_j, $j=1,...,K$
3.   Apply a quasi-Newton method
4.   Exchange the skill factors of these best individuals
5.   Evaluate b_j for task τ_j only, $j=1,...,K$
6. **end for**

2.4   Broaden the Search Region

In Algorithm 3, we describe a method to broaden the search region when the algorithm is trapped into local minima. The status for all tasks has been record in line 17 of Algorithm 1. After an iteration, if the best solution of task T_j has not changed (i.e. status equals to 1), we need to improve the diversity of population for task T_j. We first rank these individuals whose skill factor is j in line 6. As shown in the line 7, we make the good individuals remain the same, and randomly reinitialize those individuals whose ranks at the bottom. Therefore, in such settings, the individuals who have the same skill factor include a majority of the elite individuals and a few random individuals. On the one hand, space for local search is retained. On the other hand, the diversity of the population increases.

Algorithm 3. Broaden the search region

Consider the tasks status
1. **for every** task T_j **do**
2.   **if** the best solution of task T_j has not changed **then**
3.   **for every** p_j **do**
4.   Compute factorial rank r_{ij} for T_j
5.   **end for**
6.   Rank the individuals of skill factor$= j$
7.   Randomly update a part of individuals whose
          rank at the bottom but their skill factor stay the same
8.   **end if**
9. **end for**

2.5   Self-adaptive Selection Strategy

In Algorithm 4, we introduce a self-adaptive selection strategy based on the status of each task (in line 17 of Algorithm 1, a vector records the status for all tasks). In the beginning of the AMA, we adopt the elite selection operator. If the best solution of task T_j has not changed in an iteration, lines 3 of Algorithm 4 uses the roulette wheel selection to improve the diversity of generated offspring. Otherwise, line 5 applies the elite selection in next generation.

A MTO problem contains multiple optimization tasks. It is reasonable to provide multiple selection strategies in the multitasking optimization because the best selection strategy varies with optimization tasks. If a task in the problem is no improvement in an iteration, the effectiveness of the used selection operator has declined. Therefore, it is necessary to change the selection operator for getting more excellent individuals.

Algorithm 4. Self-adaptive selection strategy

Consider the tasks status
1. **for every** task T_j **do**
2.   **if** the best individual of task T_j has not changed **then**
3.   selection strategy = roulette wheel
4.   **else**
5.   selection strategy = elitist
6.   **end if**
7. **end for**

---

3 Individual Tasks in Test Suite

In this section, we describe seven typical optimization functions used in the numerical experiment as follows. All the optimization functions are the single-objective continuous functions. The MTO test suite [24] has been designed for single-objective continuous optimization tasks, it consists of nine MTO benchmark problems. Each benchmark problem contains two out of the sever single-objective continuous optimization functions. For more details of the benchmark problems, the reader is referred to [24].

(1) S*pere* :

$$F_1(x) = \sum_{i=1}^{D} x_i^2, \ x \in [-100, 100]^D$$

(2) *Rosenbrock* :

$$F_2(x) = \sum_{i=1}^{D-1} (100(x_i^2 - x_{i+1})^2 + (x_i - 1)^2), \ x \in [-50, 50]^D$$

(3) *Ackley* :

$$F_3(x) = -20\exp(-0.2\sqrt{\frac{1}{D}\sum_{i=1}^{D}x_i^2}) - \exp(\frac{1}{D}\sum_{i=1}^{D}\cos(2\pi x_i)) + 20 + e, \ x$$
$$\in [-50, 50]^D$$

(4) *Rastrgin* :

$$F_4(x) = \sum_{i=1}^{D}(x_i^2 - 10\cos(2\pi x_i) + 10), x \in [-50, 50]^D$$

(5) *Schwefel* :

$$F_5(x) = 418.9829 \times D - \sum_{i=1}^{D}x_i\sin(|x_i|^{\frac{1}{2}}), \ x \in [-500, 500]^D$$

(6) *Griewank* :

$$F_6(x) = 1 + \frac{1}{4000}\sum_{i=1}^{D}x_i^2 - \prod_{i=1}^{D}\cos(\frac{x_i}{\sqrt{i}}), \ x \in [-100, 100]^D$$

(7) *Weierstrass* :

$$F_7(x) = \sum_{i=1}^{D}(\sum_{k=0}^{k_{max}}[a^k\cos(2\pi b^k(x_i + 0.5))]) - D\sum_{k=0}^{k_{max}}[a^k\cos(2\pi b^k \bullet 0.5)],$$
$$a = 0.5, b = 3, k_{max} = 20, x \in [-0.5, 0.5]^D$$

4 Experimental Results

In this section, we provide the comparative results based on MFEA and AMA for nine benchmark problems. We adopt the same crossover operator, mutation operator, population size in the MFEA and the AMA. For these benchmark problems in test suite, every algorithm is required to be executed for 30 runs. In addition, for all 9 benchmark problems, the maximal number of function evaluations is set to 300,000.

Part of the experimental results are shown below. Figures 1, 2, 3 and 4 provide the convergence trends of MFEA and AMA, each of the figures represents a benchmark problem which consist of two tasks. In the Fig. 1, the convergence trends of task 1 and task 2 in AMA are similar. Through observation of the iteration process, it can be explained that task 2 can get the most useful knowledge from task 1 by learning. Generally, in Figs. 2, 3 and 4, AMA gets the better performance than MFEA.

We provide the statistical analysis for the experiment results. We test two algorithms in our study. As shown in Table 1, for all the benchmark problems, it present the mean and the best objective in 30 runs on MFEA and AMA. We can see that the AMA

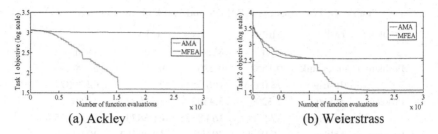

(a) Ackley   **(b) Weierstrass**

Fig. 1. Convergence trends for MFEA and AMA on Ackley and Weierstrass

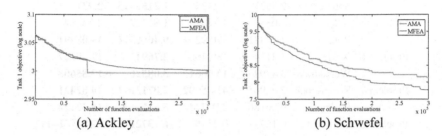

(a) Ackley   **(b) Schwefel**

Fig. 2. Convergence trends for MFEA and AMA on Ackley and Schwefel

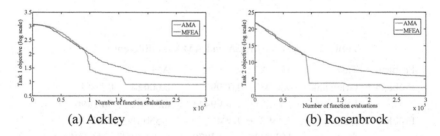

(a) Ackley   **(b) Rosenbrock**

Fig. 3. Convergence trends for MFEA and AMA on Ackley and Rosenbrock

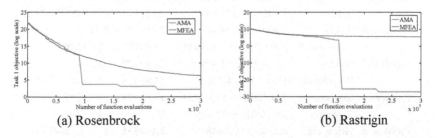

(a) Rosenbrock   **(b) Rastrigin**

Fig. 4. Convergence trends for MFEA and AMA on Rosenbrock and Rastrigin

Table 1. Performances of MFEA and AMA on different tasks

Problem	Task	MFEA		AMA	
		Best	Mean	Best	Mean
Problem 1	Griewank	0.1552	0.2203	**0**	**0.00024**
	Rastrigin	78.0593	166.3511	**0**	**6.59987**
Problem 2	Ackley	**2.5295**	**3.4302**	2.67647	3.55061
	Rastrigin	87.5465	**163.8335**	**61.68741**	181.67955
Problem 3	Ackley	20.0179	20.0826	**19.99782**	**20.03115**
	Schwefel	**1997.6938**	**2841.1228**	2016.24131	3336.01226
Problem 4	Rastrigin	266.0987	405.1913	**174.11712**	**351.99791**
	Sphere	2.5521	3.7426	**1.215E-13**	**2.937E-13**
Problem 5	Ackley	2.0382	2.8807	**1.02712**	**2.36924**
	Rosenbrock	219.8812	370.9291	**9.406E-11**	**19.08991**
Problem 6	Ackley	3.2114	18.8466	**2.76912**	**17.69127**
	Weierstrass	3.4792	15.6661	**3.08526**	**12.85608**
Problem 7	Rosenbrock	246.9659	414.5092	**2.0713E-10**	**14.82421**
	Rastrigin	93.6166	241.7448	**5.33E-14**	**15.32234**
Problem 8	Griewank	0.1624	0.2546	**6.1372E-12**	**2.19455E-11**
	Weierstrass	18.6733	24.5647	**16.47132**	**22.65889**
Problem 9	Rastrigin	260.9278	421.1149	**243.76351**	**417.23502**
	Schwefel	2166.1976	**2909.1464**	**2025.49772**	3063.33834

Table 2. T-test for MFEA and AMA on different tasks

Problem	Task	MFEA	AMA
Problem 1	Griewank	0.2203 ± 0.0399-	**0.00024 ± 0.0014**
	Rastrigin	166.3511 ± 44.9443-	**6.59987 ± 36.1490**
Problem 2	Ackley	**3.4302 ± 0.4949**	3.55061 ± 0.8611 ≈
	Rastrigin	**163.8335 ± 52.3870**	181.67955 ± 56.9666 ≈
Problem 3	Ackley	20.0826 ± 0.0516-	**20.03115 ± 0.0686**
	Schwefel	**2841.1228 ± 413.0272**	3336.01226 ± 617.4879-
Problem 4	Rastrigin	405.1913 ± 65.4625-	**351.99791 ± 71.2085**
	Sphere	3.7426 ± 0.7653-	**2.937E-13 ± 1.0486E-13**
Problem 5	Ackley	2.8807 ± 0.5074-	**2.36924 ± 0.3153**
	Rosenbrock	370.9291 ± 107.1941-	**19.08991 ± 21.8288**
Problem 6	Ackley	18.8466 ± 4.0909 ≈	**17.69127 ± 5.6641**
	Weierstrass	15.6661 ± 4.2013-	**12.85608 ± 4.2240**
Problem 7	Rosenbrock	414.5092 ± 115.7751-	**14.82421 ± 26.3293**
	Rastrigin	241.7448 ± 71.7191-	**15.32234 ± 32.2250**
Problem 8	Griewank	0.2546 ± 0.0448-	**2.19455E-11 ± 1.6164E-1**
	Weierstrass	24.5647 ± 4.2787 ≈	**22.65889 ± 4.1134**
Problem 9	Rastrigin	421.1149 ± 74.1779 ≈	**417.23502 ± 84.1061**
	Schwefel	**2909.1464 ± 375.5420**	3063.33834 ± 546.5655 ≈

can get better performance in a majority of benchmark problems. Specially, AMA has substantial improvements in problem 1, problem 5, and problem 7.

To examine the distinction of the running results, the Student's t test is adopted and the experimental results are shown in Table 2 (-/≈: the average performance of the corresponding method is significantly worse than or similar to the highlighted best average performance at level p = 0.05 in t-test). The proposed algorithm outperforms MFEA on most of the test problems.

5 Conclusions

This paper points out the adaptability problems for multitasking optimization. From this point of view, we have presented the AMA for improving the MFEA. The proposed algorithms provide some changes in both genetic and cultural [13]. Experimental results are presented for demonstrating the effectiveness of AMA. Evolutionary computing has been applied in many interesting ways [14–17], how to solve practical problems with multi-tasking method is a noticeable direction.

Acknowledgments. This work was supported by National Natural Science Foundation of China [61471246, 61603259, 61575125], Guangdong Special Support Program of Top-notch Young Professionals [2014TQ01X273, 2015TQ01R453], Guangdong Foundation of Outstanding Young Teachers in Higher Education Institutions [Yq2015141], China Postdoctoral Science Foundation [2016M592536], and Shenzhen Fundamental Research Program [JCYJ2015032 4141711587, JCYJ20170302154328155].

References

1. Back, T., Hammel, U., Schwefel, H.P.: Evolutionary computation: comments on the history and current state. IEEE Trans. Evol. Comput. **1**(1), 3–17 (1997)
2. Dawkins, R.: The selfish gene. Q. Rev. Biol. **110**(466), 781–804(24) (1989)
3. Gupta, A., Ong, Y.S., Feng, L.: Multifactorial evolution: toward evolutionary multitasking. IEEE Trans. Evol. Comput. **20**(3), 343–357 (2016)
4. Ong, Y.-S., Gupta, A.: Evolutionary multitasking: a computer science view of cognitive multitasking. Cogn. Comput. **8**(2), 125–142 (2016)
5. Caruana, R.: Multitask learning. Mach. Learn. **28**(1), 41–75 (1997)
6. Gupta, A., Ong, Y.S.: Genetic transfer or population diversification? Deciphering the secret ingredients of evolutionary multitask optimization. In: 2016 IEEE Symposium Series on Computational Intelligence, pp. 1–7 (2016)
7. Chen, X., Ong, Y.S., Lim, M.H., Tan, K.C.: A multi-facet survey on memetic computation. IEEE Trans. Evol. Comput. **15**(5), 591–607 (2011)
8. Cavalli-Sforza, L.L., Feldman, M.W.: Cultural versus biological inheritance: phenotypic transmission from parents to children. (A theory of the effect of parental phenotypes on children's phenotypes). Am. J. Hum. Genet. **25**(6), 618–637 (1973)
9. Feldman, M.W., Laland, K.N.: Gene-culture coevolutionary theory. Trends Ecol. Evol. **11** (11), 453 (1996)

10. Iqbal, M., Browne, W.N., Zhang, M.: Reusing building blocks of extracted knowledge to solve complex, large-scale boolean problems. IEEE Trans. Evol. Comput. **18**(4), 465–480 (2014)

11. Mills, R., Jansen, T., Watson, R.A.: Transforming evolutionary search into higher-level evolutionary search by capturing problem structure. IEEE Trans. Evol. Comput. **18**(5), 628–642 (2014)

12. Yi, A.Z., Jianhong, C.S., Xiuxia, D.Y., Pei, B.S.: Quasi-Newton iterative learning control and its application. In: 2008 IEEE International Conference on Automation and Logistics, pp. 656–660 (2008)

13. Cloninger, C.R., Rice, J., Reich, T.: Multifactorial inheritance with cultural transmission and assortative mating. II. A general model of combined polygenic and cultural inheritance. Am. J. Hum. Genet. **31**(2), 176–198 (1979)

14. Cai, Q., Ma, L., Gong, M.: A survey on network community detection based on evolutionary computation. Int. J. Bio-Inspired Comput. **8**(2), 84–98 (2014)

15. Bijani, V., Khosravi, A., Sarhadi, P.: A optimal acceleration autopilot design for non-minimum phase missiles using evolutionary algorithms. Int. J. Bio-Inspired Comput. **8**(4), 221–227 (2014)

16. Ma, X., Zhang, Q., Yang, J., Zhu, Z.: On Tchebycheff decomposition approaches for multi-objective evolutionary optimization. IEEE Trans. Evol. Comput. 1–1 (2017)

17. Ma, X., Liu, F., Qi, Y., Wang, X., Li, L., Jiao, L., Yin, M., Gong, M.: A multiobjective evolutionary algorithm based on decision variable analyses for multiobjective optimization problems with large-scale variables. IEEE Trans. Evol. Comput. **20**(2), 275–298 (2016)

18. Zhu, Z., Ong, Y.S., Dash, M.: Wrapper-filter feature selection algorithm using a memetic framework. IEEE Trans. Syst. Man Cybern. Part B Cybern. **37**(1), 70–76 (2007)

19. Zhu, Z., Zhou, J., Ji, Z., Shi, Y.H.: DNA sequence compression using adaptive particle swarm optimization-based memetic algorithm. IEEE Trans. Evol. Comput. **15**(5), 558–643 (2011)

20. Zhu, Z., Xiao, J., He, S., Ji, Z., Sun, Y.: A multi-objective memetic algorithm based on locality-sensitive hashing for one-to-many-to-one dynamic pickup-and-delivery problem. Inf. Sci. Int. J. **329**(C), 73–89 (2016)

21. Zhu, Z., Xiao, J., Li, J.Q., Wang, F., Zhang, Q.: Global path planning of wheeled robots using multi-objective memetic algorithms. Integr. Comput. Aided Eng. **22**(4), 387–404 (2015)

22. Zhu, Z., Wang, F., He, S., Sun, Y.: Global path planning of mobile robots using a memetic algorithm. Int. J. Syst. Sci. **46**(11), 1982–1993 (2015)

23. Zhu, Z., Jia, S., He, S., Sun, Y., Ji, Z., Shen, L.: Three-dimensional Gabor feature extraction for hyperspectral imagery classification using a memetic framework. Inf. Sci. **298**(C), 274–287 (2015)

24. Da, B., Ong, Y.S., Feng, L., Qin, A.K., Gupta, A., Zhu, Z., Ting, C.K., Tang, K., Yao, X.: Evolutionary multitasking for single-objective continuous optimization: benchmark problems, performance metric, and baseline results. arXiv preprint arXiv:1706.03470 (2017)

Effective Policy Gradient Search
for Reinforcement Learning Through NEAT
Based Feature Extraction

Yiming Peng[✉], Gang Chen, Mengjie Zhang, and Yi Mei

School of Engineering and Computer Science, Victoria University of Wellington,
Wellington, New Zealand
{yiming.peng,gang.chen,mengjie.zhang,yi.mei}@ecs.vuw.ac.nz

Abstract. To improve the effectiveness of commonly used Policy Gradient Search (PGS) algorithms for Reinforcement Learning (RL), many existing works considered the importance of extracting useful state features from raw environment inputs. However, these works only studied the feature extraction process, but the learned features have not been demonstrated to improve reinforcement learning performance. In this paper, we consider NeuroEvolution of Augmenting Topology (NEAT) for automated feature extraction, as it can evolve Neural Networks with suitable topologies that can help extract useful features. Following this idea, we develop a new algorithm called NEAT with Regular Actor Critic for Policy Gradient Search, which integrates a popular Actor-Critic PGS algorithm (i.e., Regular Actor-Critic) with NEAT based feature extraction. The algorithm manages to learn useful state features as well as good policies to tackle complex RL problems. The results on benchmark problems confirm that our proposed algorithm is significantly more effective than NEAT in terms of learning performance, and that the learned features by our proposed algorithm on one learning problem can maintain the effectiveness while it is used with RAC on another related learning problem.

Keywords: NeuroEvolution · NEAT · Policy Gradient Search · Actor-Critic · Reinforcement learning · Feature extraction

1 Introduction

In many real-world applications such as robotics control, game playing, and system optimization, Reinforcement Learning (RL) has attracted increasingly attentions from both academic researchers and industrial practitioners [20, 22]. In a typical RL setting, an intelligent agent is designed to consecutively interact with an unknown environment. In one interaction, the agent observes at any state and takes an action, then it enters another state meanwhile perceives an instant reward to assess the action. Through such continuous interactions, the agent aims to learn suitable behaviors (a.k.a., policies) that can maximize the expected total rewards (a.k.a., value function) [20].

© Springer International Publishing AG 2017
Y. Shi et al. (Eds.): SEAL 2017, LNCS 10593, pp. 473–485, 2017.
https://doi.org/10.1007/978-3-319-68759-9_39

The paper is focused on a widely-used Actor-Critic Policy Gradient Search (AC-PGS) framework, where the critic defines the value function learner whereas the actor defines the policy learner [5,21]. Both models share the same collection of state features represented as numerical vectors. Such features are extracted from the raw environmental inputs. However, most of existing AC-PGS algorithms mainly focus on improving the critic via various gradient-descent algorithms without significantly enhancing the feature extraction process. Traditionally, it is often assumed that good state features can be designed by experienced domain experts, which is usually time-consuming and error-prone [2,14,15,22].

In view of this, many researchers have considered to automate the feature extraction process [6,15]. This is normally achieved through two steps. First, a parametric function is chosen carefully as a feature base, including Radial Basis Function Network [15], Fourier Basis Function [11] and other types of bases [20]. Next, the feature function parameters are learned by optimizing carefully-designed score functions such as the Bellman Error [14,15], and Mean Squared Error [6]. However, the aim of these methods is to accurately approximate the value function based on given solutions to the RL problems. Therefore, they do not aim to solve the RL problems by finding effective policies. Motivated by this, we intend to develop a new algorithm that can seamlessly integrate automatic feature extraction with effective policy search.

For the purpose of extracting useful features, we particularly consider an Evolutionary Computation (EC) method, i.e., NeuroEvolution of Augmenting Topology (NEAT) because of two reasons. First, NEAT produces Neural Networks (NNs) which are widely applicable with proven effectiveness as feature extraction models [2,20]. Second, compared to other EC methods, NEAT has the capability of maintaining the structural simplicity of NNs. The structural simplicity of an NN can help to reduce the variances of its outputs [1]. In doing so, we expect to stabilize the learning of value function and policy [9].

For the purpose of learning effective policies, we use a popular algorithm called Regular Actor-Critic (RAC-PGS) [3]. We choose RAC-PGS due to its simplicity and proven effectiveness [3]. More importantly, it can be easily adapted to accommodate NEAT as a feature extractor during the entire learning process.

Goals: The overall goal of the paper is to develop an effective RAC-PGS algorithm through NEAT based feature extraction called NEAT with Regular Actor Critic for Policy Gradient Search (NEAT-RAC-PGS). Through developing this algorithm, we intend to achieve four specific objectives:

- To design a new method to automatically extract suitable state features through NNs evolved by NEAT.
- To utilize state features extracted by the evolved NNs in RAC-PGS for effective policy search.
- To evaluate the effectiveness of NEAT-RAC-GPS on two benchmark problems.
- To examine the usefulness of the feature learned by NEAT-RAC-PGS on one learning problem in improving the effectiveness of RAC on a related learning problem.

2   Related Work

In literature, the applicability of EC techniques to the RL domain has already been widely studied. NEAT and its variations (e.g., Hyper-NEAT) have reported outstanding performances on solving classic control problems and intelligent game-play problems [18,19]. Genetic Programming has been integrated as an RL agent to solve real-world robotic problems with notable success [10]. Many other evolutionary algorithms, such as Learning Classifier Systems, have also been successfully applied to addressing sophisticated RL problems [4,12]. Unlike NEAT-RAC-PGS, these methods only focus on improving learning performance, but their outputs cannot be used to solve other different but similar problems. NEAT-RAC-PGS can not only solve the problem effectively, but also produce useful feature extractors that can be applied to similar problems.

We are not the first to consider using NEAT for feature learning during RL. For example, FS-NEAT [23] and its variations [13] are limited to perform only feature selection rather than feature extraction, where no high level features are explicitly evolved. NEAT+Q [22] takes feature extraction into consideration, but different from NEAT-RAC-PGS, it is a value function based indirect search which does not explicitly learn a policy. In addition, as the extracted features of NEAT+Q are embedded in value functions, they cannot be reused for other learning algorithms. This paper will address these gaps by developing the NEAT-RAC-PGS algorithm.

3   A New NEAT Based Policy Gradient Search Algorithm

In this section, we propose the NEAT-RAC-PGS algorithm to tackle RL problems. Firstly, we present the overall design of NEAT-RAC-PGS. Next, we describe details of NEAT-RAC-PGS with support of algorithmic descriptions. Lastly, we discuss the new characteristics of NEAT-RAC-PGS with comparison to existing RL algorithms.

3.1   Overall Design

Figure 1 shows an overall design of our NEAT-RAC-PGS algorithm. As shown in the figure, NEAT-RAC-PGS evolves a population of RL learning agents, $P = \{A_1, \ldots, A_p\}$. Each agent A_i consists of three components: an NN $\phi(s) \in \mathbb{R}^z$, a parameter vector for value function ω_i, and a parameter vector for policy θ_i. Based on the extracted features $\phi(s)$, the value function in each agent is approximated as,

$$V^\pi(s) \approx \omega^{\pi T} \cdot \phi(s), \tag{1}$$

and is learned following the reducing direction of Temporal Difference (TD) error at every t time when the agent reaches a new state at $t + 1$, i.e.,

$$\delta_t^\pi = r_{t+1} + \gamma V^\pi(s_{t+1}) - V^\pi(s_t). \tag{2}$$

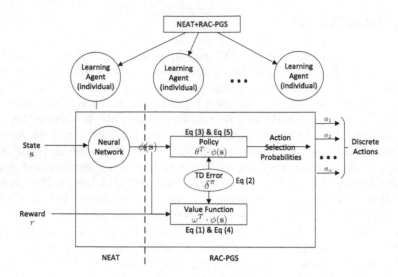

Fig. 1. The overall design of NEAT-RAC-PGS.

Additionally, the policy for action selection is formulated as,

$$\pi_{\boldsymbol{\theta}}(a|\boldsymbol{s}) = \frac{1}{\sigma\sqrt{2\pi}} e^{-\frac{(a-\mu)^2}{2\sigma^2}}, \tag{3}$$

where $\mu = \boldsymbol{\theta}^T \cdot \phi(\boldsymbol{s})$. $\sigma = 1.0$ is used to control the level to explore new actions. Note that, π at the RHS of (3) is the circumference ratio.

In association with (1), (2) and (3), the updating rule for value function parameters is,

$$\boldsymbol{\omega}_{t+1}^{\pi} \leftarrow \boldsymbol{\omega}_t^{\pi} + \alpha_t \delta_t^{\pi} \phi(\boldsymbol{s}_t), \tag{4}$$

and the rule for policy parameters is

$$\boldsymbol{\theta}_{t+1} \leftarrow \boldsymbol{\theta}_t + \beta_t \delta_t^{\pi} \Phi(\boldsymbol{s}, a), \tag{5}$$

respectively. Note, α_t and β_t are the learning rates, and $\Phi(\boldsymbol{s}, a) = \nabla_{\boldsymbol{\theta}} \ln \pi(\boldsymbol{s}, a) = \frac{a_t - \boldsymbol{\theta} \cdot \phi(\boldsymbol{s}_t)}{\sigma^2} \cdot \phi(\boldsymbol{s}_t)$ [21].

3.2   Policy Gradient Search Through NEAT Based Feature Extraction

NEAT-RAC-PGS is designed with four learning stages, namely *initialization, evolution, evaluation,* and *termination.*

Initialization. The initialization stage of NEAT-RAC-PGS is to initialize a population with p learning agents (i.e., individuals). For the NN in each agent, its inputs and outputs are defined as states $\boldsymbol{s}$ and extracted state features $\phi(\boldsymbol{s})$

respectively. Additionally, its input nodes are directly connected to its output nodes without any hidden nodes, and weights of each NN are randomly initialized. For the critic and actor model in each agent, the value function parameters and policy parameters are initialized to ω_0 and θ_0 respectively. Note, ω_0 and θ_0 are vectors with arbitrary values.

Evolution. NEAT-RAC-PGS evolves a new population of agents by performing two sequential tasks according to Sect. 3.1. The first task is to evolve p NNs ($\{\phi_1, \ldots, \phi_p\}$) based on the standard evolutionary operators of NEAT defined in [19]. The second task is to initialize ω_i and θ_i to 0 for every agent A_i in the new population. This ensures a fair evaluation across all agents.

Evaluation. The evaluation stage of the NEAT-RAC-PGS has two objectives, one is to compute the fitness value for a single individual, and the other is to find good policies. The fitness value of each individual is directly computed by averaging total rewards obtained by the learning agent over all episodes. Using an average value can help reduce the variance as rewards are collected in a stochastic environment. To search for the good policies, we use the RAC-PGS to learn the critic and actor models for an individual from its continuous interactions with the environment. This stage is presented in Algorithm 1.

Termination. The termination stage manages stop criteria for the learning process of NEAT-RAC-PGS. To stop the feature extraction process, we define two stop criteria: the first is to stop when the predefined maximum number of generations is reached, and the second is when the fitness values of all individuals do not improve over 10 generations. To cease the policy search process, we setup the maximumly allowed learning episodes for an RL agent to interact with an environment. Each episode is composed of multi interaction steps, and it terminates at the situations when either the predefined maximum number of steps is reached, or the target RL problem is solved (see Sect. 4.1). A full algorithmic description for NEAT-RAC-PGS is given in Algorithm 2.

3.3 Key Characteristics of NEAT-RAC-PGS

In this subsection, we discuss three key characteristics of NEAT-RAC-PGS in contrast to traditional PGS approaches and EC based RL methods, namely *multiple diverse learning agents, automated feature extraction*, and *reusable features extractors*. These three characteristics enable each of NEAT-RAC-PGS learning agent to produce useful and reusable state features meanwhile to find good policies that solve sophisticated RL problems.

Multiple Diverse Learning Agents. As explained in Sect. 3.1, NEAT-RAC-PGS is a population-based method composed of multiple diverse learning agents whereas traditional PGS methods are often constructed as a single learning

---

Algorithm 1. NEAT-RAC-PGS Evaluation

Require: P: a population of learning agents, p: population size, e_g: maximum training
    episodes per generation, T: maximum training steps per episode, α: value function
    learning rate, β: policy learning rate, $\tilde{R}$: total rewards
Ensure: P: a population of learning agents
 1: **function** EVALUATION(P, p, e_g, T, α, β)
 2:    **for** $k = 1, 2, ..., p$ **do**
 3:        $\tilde{R} \leftarrow 0$
 4:        **for** $j = 1, 2, ..., e_g$ **do**
 5:            $s_t \leftarrow s_0$
 6:            **for** $t = 0, 1, ..., T - 1$ **do**
 7:                $a_t \sim \pi_\theta(a|s_t)$ ▷ See (3)
 8:                Take action a_t, observe reward r_{t+1} and new state s_{t+1}
 9:                $\delta_t \leftarrow r_{t+1} + \gamma\omega_t^T \cdot \phi(s_{t+1}) - \omega_t^T \cdot \phi(s_t)$ ▷ See (2)
                      ▷ Note: $\phi = P[k].N$, $\omega_t = P[k].\omega$, $\theta_t = P[k].\theta$
10:                $\omega_{t+1} \leftarrow \omega_t + \alpha\delta_t \cdot \phi(s_t)$ ▷ See (4)
11:                $\theta_{t+1} \leftarrow \theta_t + \beta\delta_t \cdot \Phi(s_t, a_t)$ ▷ See (5)
12:                $\tilde{R} \leftarrow \tilde{R} + r_{t+1}$
13:                **if** TERMINAL-STATE(s_{t+1}) **then**
14:                    **break**
15:                **end if**
16:            **end for**
17:        **end for**
18:        $P[k].N.fitness \leftarrow \frac{\tilde{R}}{e_g}$
19:    **end for**
20:    **return** P
21: **end function**

---

agent. In dosing so, NEAT-RAC-PGS has better potential to find good policies,
even when several learning agents are stuck in local optima.

Automated Feature Extraction. Unlike those PGS methods [5] where feature extractors are predetermined and are fixed through the entire reinforcement learning process, NEAT-RAC-PGS incorporates NEAT as a new component to automatically learn suitable feature extractors along the policy search process as shown in Fig. 1. This helps the learning agent to find useful features which can further enhance its ability to find good policies.

Reusable Feature Extractors. Unlike many existing EC based RL methods where feature extraction and policy search are mingled together, NEAT-RAC-PGS treats them as two subsequent stages. To do so, the RAC algorithm is wrapped as a fitness evaluator for each individual. Following this design principle, we can explicitly represent the feature extractors as NNs. Thus, after learning these feature extractors on one problem, it becomes possible to reuse them for various RL algorithms on a related problem.

Algorithm 2. NEAT-RAC-PGS Algorithm

Require: an MDP $\langle \mathcal{S}, \mathcal{A}, \mathcal{P}, \mathcal{R}, \gamma \rangle$, p: population size, g: number of generations, e_g: maximum training episodes per generation, T: maximum training steps per episode, d: state dimension, z: feature dimension, α: value function learning rate, β: policy learning rate, ω_0: initial value function parameters, β_0: initial policy parameters
Ensure: P: the population of individuals, N^*: the optimal Neural Network ($\phi(s)$), ω^*: the best value function parameter, θ^*: the best policy parameter
1: *Initialization:*
2: $P \leftarrow$ INITIALIZATION(p, d, z, ω_0, β_0)   ▷ See Sect. 3.2
3: *Learning Process:*
4: **for** $i = 1, 2, ..., g$ **do**
5:     $P \leftarrow$ EVALUATION(P, p, e_g, T, α, β)   ▷ See Algorithm 1
6:     **if** $i < g$ **then**   ▷ Stop evolution at the final generation
7:         $P \leftarrow$ EVOLUTION(P)   ▷ See [19]
8:     **end if**
9: **end for**
10: $k^* \leftarrow \text{argmax}_k(P[k].N.fitness)$
11: $N^* \leftarrow P[k^*].N$
12: $\omega^* \leftarrow P[k^*].\omega$
13: $\theta^* \leftarrow P[k^*].\theta$
14: **return** P, N^*, ω^*, θ^*

---

4   Experiment Design

In this section, we present our experiment design. We first describe the two continuous benchmark problems, i.e., the Cart-Pole problem and the Mountain Car problem. We then describe detailed setups for the experiments. Lastly, we present two separate experiment designs to examine the usefulness of extracted features and to evaluate the effectiveness of learned policies respectively.

4.1   Benchmark Problems

We choose two continuous benchmark problems, i.e., the Mountain Car problem [20] and the Cart Pole problem [20] for experiments. Because they are widely exploited to examine effectiveness of new RL algorithms. In addition, neural networks have already been successfully used as feature extractors on these problems [20,22].

Mountain Car Problem [20]. The Mountain Car problem, as shown in Fig. 2(a), models a two-dimensional environment where the two dimensions of the state represent the position of the car x and the velocity of the car $\dot{x}$. The goal of the problem is to thrust a car from the bottom of the valley to a steep mountain at the right side. As the power of the car's engine is weaker than the gravity, the car needs the descending acceleration generated by sliding from the opposite slope at the left side. The top of the mountain is set as a goal region, and the car aims to use the minimum steps to reach the region. In the problem, the car

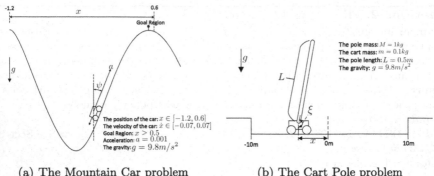

(a) The Mountain Car problem   (b) The Cart Pole problem

Fig. 2. The two benchmark problems drawn based on description in [20]

moves a step meanwhile receives a penalty "-1", a reward "$+100$" is given until the car reaches the goal region. The car updates its location and speed following the equation below,

$$\ddot{x} = \dot{a}\mathcal{F} - 0.0025 \cos(3x),$$

where $\dot{a} = 0.001$ denotes the sliding acceleration obtained by the car. $\mathcal{F}$ represents a force (i.e., continuous action $a \in [-1.0, 1.0]$) performed by the system.

Note that, the initial state for the Mountain Car problem is fixed as $s = [-5.0, 0.0]$, and the terminative condition of a learning episode is defined as either the maximum learning steps or the goal regions is reached.

Cart Pole Problem [20]. In the Cart Pole problem shown in Fig. 2(b), a learning agent learns to generate an action $\mathcal{F}$ (i.e., $a \in [-10, 10]$) in the form of a horizontal force that drives a cart to move along a fixed length track. Meanwhile, it aims to balance the hinged rigid pole on the cart to the up-right position. The state contains four dimensions, including x_t (the relative position of the center of the cart to the center of the track), $\dot{x}_t$ (the velocity of the cart), ξ_t (the relative angle of the pole to the up-right position), and $\dot{\xi}_t$ (the angular velocity of the pole). Accompanied with the cart's current movement, the environment provides an instant reward determined by

$$r_{t+1} = \begin{cases} 0.0, & \text{if } |\xi| > 0.628 \text{ or } |x| > 10.0 \\ 0.2\pi - \xi, & \text{otherwise} \end{cases}. \tag{6}$$

In addition, the dynamics of cart and pole can be defined as,

$$\ddot{\xi} = \frac{g \cdot sin(\xi) - cos(\xi)(F + M \cdot L \cdot \dot{\xi}^2 sin(\xi))}{\frac{4}{3}L - \frac{m \cdot cos(\xi^2)}{m + M}}$$
$$\ddot{x} = \frac{\mathcal{F} + M \cdot L \cdot \dot{\xi}^2 \cdot sin(\xi) - M \cdot L \cdot \ddot{\xi} \cdot cos(\xi)}{m + M}.$$

Moreover, a learning episode for the Cart Pole problem is alway starts from the initial state $s = [0.0, 0.0, 0.15, 0.0]$, and it terminates whenever a maximum number of learning steps have been conducted in the episode, or the terminating condition (i.e., $|\xi| > 0.628$ or $|x| > 10.0$) is satisfied.

4.2 Experiment Setup

To identify any significant performance difference, for each benchmark problem, we conduct 30 independent runs for our algorithms. Among all runs, the population size and the number of generations are set to 100 and 100 respectively. For the Mountain Car problem, we perform 1000 learning episodes with 200 steps in each episode and 25 independent testing episodes where each has 200 testing steps. For the Cart Pole problem, we perform 200 learning steps in each of the 5000 learning episodes. Also, we conduct 1000 testing steps in each of 25 independent testing episodes. All independent tests are performed by the best learning agent of each generation.

Some important meta parameter settings are summarized as follows. Firstly, for meta parameters of NEAT and NEAT component of NEAT-RAC-PGS, we adopt identical settings reported in [22] where the effectiveness of NEAT with these settings has been verified on several benchmark problems. Secondly, we choose the commonly used settings ($\alpha = 0.1$, $\beta = 0.01$, $\gamma = 0.99$) reported in [3, 16] for RAC-PGS algorithm and RAC-PGS component of NEAT-RAC-PGS. These meta parameter settings are used for experiments on both benchmark problems described in Sect. 4.1.

4.3 Experiment Design

In this paper, driven by the last two research objectives, we will conduct two different types of experiments. In the first type of experiment, as discussed in Sect. 4.2, we evaluate the performance of NEAT-RAC-PGS on each benchmark problem to understand the effectiveness of the algorithm. The performance is measured by the number of steps for balancing the pole, or the number of steps to drive the car to mountain top.

In the meantime, driven by the last objective, we intend to evaluate the usefulness of the state features on a relevant problem. We expect that the learned useful state features can be reused on a related problem and still can maintain or improve the learning performance. For this purpose, in our feature evaluation, we firstly maintain the feature extractor of the current best learning agent by NEAT-RAC-PGS (i.e., the NN evolved by NEAT) on Cart Pole. Next, we modify the Cart Pole problem described in Sect. 4.1 to obtain a relevant problem. To do so, we uniformly set an arbitrary value from $[-0.05, 0.05]$ for every dimension of initial states at the beginning of every learning episode. Lastly, we adopt the RAC-PGS learning algorithm with the maintained feature extractor on the modified Car Pole problem to observe the learning performance for understanding the usefulness of state features.

5   Results and Discussion

The experimental results are presented and analyzed in this section. We firstly analyze the learning effectiveness of NEAT-RAC-PGS contrary to NEAT on the two benchmark problems. Next, we discuss the usefulness of learned features by NEAT-RAC-PGS.

5.1   Learning Effectiveness Evaluation

To evaluate the learning effectiveness, we present the learning performances obtained by NEAT-RAC-PGS and NEAT on the Mountain Car problem in Fig. 3(a) and on the Cart Pole problem in Fig. 3(b) respectively.

As shown in Fig. 3(a), after a certain period of time, both NEAT-RAC-PGS and NEAT achieve reasonably good performance (around 120 steps), which is consistent with the results of NEAT reported in [22]. The two high peaks of NEAT-RAC-PGS do not imply that it performs sometimes worse than NEAT, as no significance can be found after the 53-th generation according to a statistical test. Meanwhile, owing to the capability of NEAT-RAC-NEAT to make more effective use of learned features, eventually it achieved better performance than NEAT.

Figure 3(b) evidently shows that NEAT-RAC-PGS outperforms NEAT with averaging 1000 steps after the 10-th generation. As a matter of fact, NEAT achieves the desirable performance (approximately 100 steps) according to the OpenAI GYM benchmark [7]. Without comparing it with NEAT-RAC-PGS, NEAT should be treated as an effective algorithm. However, our NEAT-RAC-PGS algorithm can achieve significantly higher performance than many recently developed algorithms that cannot compete on the same benchmark.

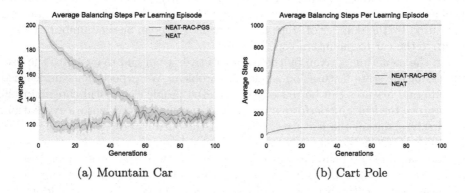

(a) Mountain Car   (b) Cart Pole

Fig. 3. The comparison of learning performance of NEAT-RAC-PGS and NEAT on two benchmark problems: (a) displays the averaging steps to reach the goal region on Mountain Car (the smaller the better), (b) displays the averaging steps to balance the pole to the upright position on Cart Pole (the larger the better).

5.2   Feature Usefulness Evaluation

To evaluate the usefulness of features, in Fig. 4, we compare the learning performances of RAC-PGS with two different feature extractors on the standard Cart Pole problem and on the modified Cart Pole problem respectively. The first feature extractor is a learned NN by the NEAC component of an NEAT-RAC-PGS learning agent on the standard Cart Pole with the highest fitness value. The second feature extractor is the widely-used discretization feature extractor where each dimension of environment state is discretized into 20 bins as described in [20].

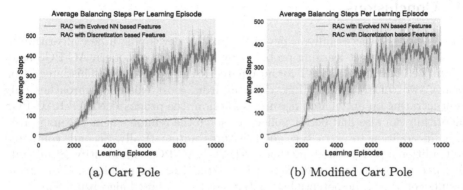

(a) Cart Pole   (b) Modified Cart Pole

Fig. 4. The comparison of learning performance of RAC-PGS with two different feature extractors (an evolved NN feature extractor and a predefined discretized feature extractor) on the two related problems (see Sect. 4.2): (a) displays learning performances obtained on the standard Cart Pole problem, (b) displays learning performances obtained on the modified Cart Pole problem.

Figure 4(a) reveals that, on the standard Cart Pole problem, RAC with evolved NN features performs significantly and consistently better than RAC with discretized features after the 2370-th generation. On the other hand, when the learning environment is changed to the modified Cart Pole problem, we are still able to find a similar observation in Fig. 4(b) that RAC with evolved NN features outperforms RAC with discretized features after the 2214-th generations. Statistical tests reject the null hypothesis after the time points. The RAC with discretized features achieves averaging 100 steps on both problems, which can be regarded effective as reported in [17]. These results suggest that the features learned by NEAT-RAC-PGS on one problem can not only be used to solve the original problem, but also be adopted to solve similar but different problems.

Nevertheless, on both problems, the RAC-PGS with evolved NN features appears to fluctuate. Actually, the step-based learning process of NNs has already been reported unstable in literature [8], because step-based learning always picks up the recent state transitions for estimating gradients, which may bring bias into gradient estimation resulting in the unstable updating. A possible solution to address the issue is experience replay, but this is not the focus of this paper.

The reason that evolved NN features are superior to discretized features is given below. Firstly, the real-word environment (e.g., Cart Pole) often exhibits high non-linearity, NN is well known as suitable non-linear models in comparison to other models. Secondly, the raw environment input is continuous, some intrinsic information, that is useful for finding good policies, may be lost during the discretization. On the other hand, NN is capable of smoothly producing continuous values as high level features. More importantly, NEAT can evolve both weights and structures for NNs, which further provides higher chances to find suitable state features.

6   Conclusions

This paper has successfully achieved the goal of developing a new algorithm to tackle reinforcement learning problems by integrating a modern AC-PGS algorithm, i.e., RAC, with NEAT for automated feature extraction. This integration brings two contributions. First, different from most existing approaches only concentrating on automated feature extraction, the proposed NEAT-RAC-PGS algorithm can also find better policies to solve the reinforcement learning problems in addition to extracting good features automatically. Second, compared to traditional policy search methods, NEAT-RAC-PGS can identify useful state features that can be further reused in related learning problems. Experiment results confirmed the potential advantages of the proposed algorithm. This work opens possibilities of exploiting other cutting-edge AC-PGS algorithms based on the same design principle of NEAT-RAC-PGS. More comprehensive experiments involving a wide range of benchmarks can also help truly understand the real efficacy of NEAT-RAC-PGS.

References

1. Balduzzi, D., Frean, M., Leary, L., Lewis, J.P.: The shattered gradients problem: if resnets are the answer, then what is the question? arXiv.org (2017)
2. Bengio, Y., Courville, A., Vincent, P.: Representation learning: a review and new perspectives. IEEE Trans. Pattern Anal. Mach. Intell. **35**(8), 1798–1828 (2013)
3. Bhatnagar, S., Sutton, R.S., Ghavamzadeh, M., Lee, M.: Natural actor-critic algorithms. Automatica **45**(11), 2471–2482 (2009)
4. Chen, G., Douch, C.I.J., Zhang, M.: Accuracy-based learning classifier systems for multistep reinforcement learning: a fuzzy logic approach to handling continuous inputs and learning continuous actions. IEEE Trans. Evol. Comput. **20**(6), 953–971 (2016)
5. Deisenroth, M.P., Neumann, G., Peters, J.: A survey on policy search for robotics. Found. Trends Robot. **2**(1–2), 1–142 (2013)
6. Castro, D., Mannor, S.: Adaptive bases for reinforcement learning. In: Balcázar, J.L., Bonchi, F., Gionis, A., Sebag, M. (eds.) ECML PKDD 2010. LNCS (LNAI), vol. 6321, pp. 312–327. Springer, Heidelberg (2010). doi:10.1007/978-3-642-15880-3_26

7. Grondman, I., Busoniu, L., Lopes, G.A.D., Babuška, R.: A survey of actor-critic reinforcement learning: standard and natural policy gradients. IEEE Trans. Syst. Man Cybern. Part C Appl. Rev. **42**(6), 1291–1307 (2012)

8. Gu, S., Lillicrap, T.P., Sutskever, I., Levine, S.: Continuous deep q-learning with model-based acceleration. In: ICML, pp. 2829–2838 (2016)

9. Hermundstad, A.M., Brown, K.S., Bassett, D.S., Carlson, J.M.: Learning, memory, and the role of neural network architecture. PLoS Comput. Biol. **7**(6), e1002063 (2011)

10. Kamio, S., Iba, H.: Adaptation technique for integrating genetic programming and reinforcement learning for real robots. IEEE Trans. Evol. Comput. **9**(3), 318–333 (2005)

11. Konidaris, G., Osentoski, S., Thomas, P.: Value function approximation in reinforcement learning using the fourier basis. In: 2011 AAAI, pp. 380–385 (2011)

12. Lanzi, P.L.: Learning classifier systems: then and now. Evol. Intell. **1**(1), 63–82 (2008)

13. Loscalzo, S., Wright, R., Yu, L.: Predictive feature selection for genetic policy search. AAMAS **2014**, 1–33 (2014)

14. Menache, I., Mannor, S., Shimkin, N.: Basis function adaptation in temporal difference reinforcement learning. Ann. Oper. Res. **134**(1), 215–238 (2005)

15. Parr, R., Painter-Wakefield, C., Li, L.: Analyzing feature generation for value-function approximation. In: ICML, pp. 737–744 (2007)

16. Peng, Y., Chen, G., Zhang, M., Pang, S.: A sandpile model for reliable actor-critic reinforcement learning. In: IJCNN, pp. 4014–4021. IEEE (2017)

17. Peng, Y., Chen, G., Zhang, M., Pang, S.: Generalized compatible function approximation for policy gradient search. In: Hirose, A., Ozawa, S., Doya, K., Ikeda, K., Lee, M., Liu, D. (eds.) ICONIP 2016. LNCS, vol. 9947, pp. 615–622. Springer, Cham (2016). doi:10.1007/978-3-319-46687-3_68

18. Schrum, J., Miikkulainen, R.: Discovering multimodal behavior in ms. pac-man through evolution of modular neural networks. IEEE Trans. Comput. Intell. AI Games **8**(1), 67–81 (2016)

19. Stanley, K.O., Miikkulainen, R.: Evolving neural network through augmenting topologies. Evol. Comput. **10**(2), 99–127 (2002)

20. Sutton, R.S., Barto, A.G.: Reinforcement learning: An introduction, vol. 1. MIT press, Cambridge (1998)

21. Sutton, R.S., Mcallester, D., Singh, S., Mansour, Y.: Policy gradient methods for reinforcement learning with function approximation. In: NIPS, pp. 1057–1063 (1999)

22. Whiteson, S., Stone, P.: Evolutionary function approximation for reinforcement learning. J. Mach. Learn. Res. **7**(5), 877–917 (2006)

23. Whiteson, S., Stone, P., Stanley, K.O., Miikkulainen, R., Kohl, N.: Automatic feature selection in neuroevolution. In: 2005 GECCO, pp. 1225–1232 (2005)

Generalized Hybrid Evolutionary Algorithm Framework with a Mutation Operator Requiring no Adaptation

Yong Wee Foo[1,2], Cindy Goh[2], Lipton Chan[2], Lin Li[3,4], and Yun Li[2,4(✉)]

[1] School of Engineering, Nanyang Polytechnic, Singapore 569830, Singapore
Foo_Yong_Wee@nyp.edu.sg
[2] School of Engineering, University of Glasgow, Glasgow G12 8LT, UK
Cindy.Goh@glasgow.ac.uk, Dr.Lipton.Chan@gmail.com,
Yun.Li@ieee.org
[3] School of Computer Science and Engineering,
South China University of Technology, Guangzhou 510006, Guangdong, China
LinLi@ieee.org
[4] School of Computer Science and Network Security,
Dongguan University of Technology, Songshanhu 523808, Guangdong, China

Abstract. This paper presents a generalized hybrid evolutionary optimization structure that not only combines both nondeterministic and deterministic algorithms on their individual merits and distinct advantages, but also offers behaviors of the three originating classes of evolutionary algorithms (EAs). In addition, a robust mutation operator is developed in place of the necessity of mutation adaptation, based on the mutation properties of binary-coded individuals in a genetic algorithm. The behaviour of this mutation operator is examined in full and its performance is compared with adaptive mutations. The results show that the new mutation operator outperforms adaptive mutation operators while reducing complications of extra adaptive parameters in an EA representation.

Keywords: Optimization algorithms · Evolutionary algorithms · Evolutionary computation · Derivative-free optimization · Heuristic search

1 Introduction

Conventional optimisation algorithms are often deterministic and are restricted to numerical optimisation with one objective and one optimum [1, 2]. Lifting much of the restriction with nondeterministic search, evolutionary algorithms (EAs) are able to deal with extra-numerical, multi-objective and multimodal problems [3]. However, an inevitable cost an EA pays for this is that it converges far more slowly around a local optimum. Therefore, combining the global aspect of EAs with the local strength of conventional algorithms has been an active research topic in evolutionary computation, resulting in hybrid algorithms with both merits and deficiencies [4, 5].

© Springer International Publishing AG 2017
Y. Shi et al. (Eds.): SEAL 2017, LNCS 10593, pp. 486–498, 2017.
https://doi.org/10.1007/978-3-319-68759-9_40

Historically, the development of EAs originated from three initial paradigms: the genetic algorithm (GA), the evolution strategy (ES), and the evolutionary programming (EP) [6]. These algorithms have much in common but also have differences. Merging these three EAs, this paper develops a generalized hybrid EA (GHEA) with customizable operations to commission EAs with differing behaviors for different applications. Without the need for adaptation, a simulated binary mutation (SBM) operator is proposed for the GHEA framework. This framework is to improve the flexibility of a maturing population via a number of different selection techniques, so as to enhance both local and global search.

The remainder of this paper is organized as follows. Section 2 analyzes the merits and deficiencies of hybrid EAs reported so far. Based on these analyses, Sect. 3 develops the details of the GHEA. The SBM operator is detailed in Sect. 4. Section 5 presents test results and discussions. Section 6 concludes the paper with recommendations for future work.

2 Merits and Deficiencies of Existing Hybrid EAs

A number of hybrid EA techniques were summarized in the *Handbook of Evolutionary Computation* [7]. Subsequently, many effective hybrid EA algorithms have been developed for specific applications. One example is a hybrid EA with fitness approximation for solving the two-stage capacitated facility location problem, which uses genetic operations with a restarting strategy and extreme machine learning to approximate the fitness of most of the individuals [8]. Another example incorporates a tabu search procedure into the framework of an evolutionary algorithm in solving a job shop scheduling problem [9]. For tackling continuous multiobjective optimization problems, a recombination operator is proposed to at the gene level to combine the advantages of simulated binary crossover with local search and differential evolution with global search [10]. However, these hybrid EAs rely on GA operators, and do not accommodate ES or EP for customizability or flexibility.

A hybridized EA framework should take the advantage of the global search capability of the EA and the search speed as well as accuracy of local search algorithms such as hill-climbing. Further, Baldwin effect and Lamarckian evolution also help achieve this goal [11–13]. With the Baldwin effect, individuals will learn locally but the learning does not affect their genetic code. With the Lamarckian principle of "use and disuse", however, each individual will pass much of the learning results in genetic code to offspring. Hence, a hybrid EA framework should readily support both of these options.

Alternative, conventional optimization algorithms can also be incorporated into a hybrid EA, so that whenever appropriate the EA can evaluate an individual for local optimization with resulting solutions stored back into the individual. Conventional algorithms are deterministic in nature and are dependent of their initial starting position. This strengthens exploitation of the exploration results brought about by the EA population. For example, gradient guided algorithms such as the Quasi-Newton methods and the conjugate gradient methods. Quasi-Newton methods store an estimate of the Hessian internally and iterate it using Newton's method whereas conjugate gradient methods use line optimisations in directions that are conjugate to previously tried directions. These methods are very fast at locating optima, but the derivative function is required.

3 Generalized Hybrid EA Framework

Based on the analyses of the merits and deficiencies of hybrid EAs in the literature, a generalized hybrid EA framework is proposed in this paper, as shown in Fig. 1. The framework also includes other basic elements that are part of applying an EA, such as objective, constraints and other housekeeping tasks. It is to allow customization of EAs with different behaviours, to improve flexibility for the formation of adult population via a number of different selection techniques, and to enhance EA performance through integration of both local and global optimization algorithms. The framework also implements a new non-adaptive mutation operator which does not require any evolving scaling parameters.

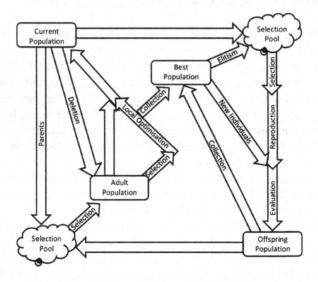

Fig. 1. Generalization of hybrid EAs

In the GHEA framework, once an offspring population is created, an adult population follows from it, which will eventually replace the current population. A number of different techniques exist to create this adult population. In (μ, λ) ES, for example, the best μ offspring individuals are used to create the adult population. In (μ + λ) ES, however, the parents and the offspring are aggregated and the best μ individuals are used. From GAs, the notion of generation gap was created to describe the formation of the adult population. The generation gap is the percentage of individuals in the current population to be deleted and replace by offspring to form the adult population [7]. The GHEA framework accommodates for all these variations in adult population creation.

A replacement selection pool of individuals is created from the offspring population and the current population can optionally be included. A number of individuals are then selected from this pool and the same number of individuals is selected for deletion from the current population. These replacement individuals and remainder individuals then form the adult population.

4   Simulated Binary Mutation for Improved Efficiency

4.1   Adaptive Mutations

A commonly used real-value mutation scheme in an EA involves a Gaussian distribution, as given by:

$$x_i[t+1] = x_i[t] + N_i(0, \eta_i[t]) \tag{1}$$

where $N(\mu, \sigma)$ is a normal distribution of mean μ and standard deviation σ. Another mutation operator which appears to be better than the Gaussian mutation, especially for multimodal problems, is the Cauchy mutation [14, 15], as given by:

$$x_i[t+1] = x_i[t] + \eta_i[t]\delta_i[t] \tag{2}$$

where δ_i is a sample from the Cauchy density function:

$$f(x) = \frac{1}{\pi(x^2+1)} \tag{3}$$

These two mutation operators can be made to adapt their shapes according to the landscape of the objective function, in a way similar to the Estimation of Distribution Algorithm (EDA). Such adaptive mutation operators have generally been found to outperform their static counterparts.

For the adaptive versions, each real-value parameter of the objective function is replaced by a 2-tuple of real values, $x_i \rightarrow (x_i, \eta_i)$. The new parameter, η_i, is the scaling parameter for the adaptive mutation and is itself mutated using the following update:

$$\eta_i[t+1] = \eta_i[t]\exp(N(0, \tau') + N_i(0, \tau)) \tag{4}$$

where the recommended values of τ and τ' are $(4n)^{-1/4}$ and $(2n)^{-1/2}$, respectively [16].

4.2   Simulated Binary Mutation

To reduce overhead of the scaling parameters especially for real-time applications of an EA, a new static mutation operator is developed in this section. Binary coding has been used in GAs, where the accuracy of the resulting solutions has been limited by the chromosome length. The mutated bit in an individual chromosome can be the LSB, MSB, or any other bit. Thus the mutation has equal probability of making large changes as of making small changes.

In binary coding, when a real value, $x \in [a, b]$, is represented by a string of l bits, $s \in \{0, 1\}^l$, the real value is given by:

$$x = a + r \sum_{i=1}^{l} 2^{i-1} s_i \qquad (5)$$

$$r = \frac{b - a}{2^l - 1} \qquad (6)$$

If the ith bit in s is flipped, i.e., $s_i[t+1] = 1 - s_i[t]$, then:

$$x[t+1] = x[t] \pm |\Delta_i| \qquad (7)$$

$$|\Delta_i| = 2^{\wedge}(i - 1) r \qquad (8)$$

In a real value representation, however, there may not be any bounds on the value and thus no resolution is set. Therefore, the smallest or largest resolution for a real value parameter is dependent on the order of magnitude of the value itself without the original value losing significance

$$r[t] = 2^{-m} |x[t]| \qquad (9)$$

m is the bits of significance. The perturbation amount due to the mutation can then be defined for real value parameters as:

$$|\Delta[t]| = 2^i |x[t]| \qquad (10)$$

where $i \in [-m, m]$. This can be converted to base-10 so that:

$$|\Delta[t]| = 10^j |x[t]| \qquad (11)$$

and $j \in [-k, k]$ where $k = m \frac{\ln 2}{\ln 10}$. Now k is the number of significant digits in base-10. The perturbation amount is now proportional to the value of the parameter and this will result in a perturbation of zero always when the value is zero. Thus, the zero case has to be treated specially and the mutation of the real value is defined as:

$$|\Delta[t]| = \begin{cases} 10^{kU(-1,1)} |x[t]| & \text{if } x[t] \neq 0 \\ 10^{kU(-1,1)} |x_{small}| & \text{if } x[t] = 0 \end{cases} \qquad (12)$$

$$p[t] = U(-1, 1) \qquad (13)$$

$$x[t+1] = \begin{cases} x[t] + |\Delta[t]| & \text{if } p[t] \geq 0 \\ x[t] - |\Delta[t]| & \text{if } p[t] < 0 \end{cases} \qquad (14)$$

where $U(a,b)$ is a sample from a uniform distribution in the interval [a,b] and x_{small} is the smallest number greater than zero that can be represented.

The probability of mutation for each individual is set as, where n is the number of real-value parameters in the individual. Thus, in probability there will on average be one real value parameter mutated in each individual. The probability distribution function of the new value of the mutated parameter is thus:

$$\Pr(x[t+1]) \begin{cases} 4k(x[t+1]-x[t]\ln 10)^{-1} & \text{if } x[t](1+10^{-k}) \le x[t+1] \le x[t](1+10^k) \\ 4k(x[t]-x[t+1]\ln 10)^{-1} & \text{if } x[t](1+10^{-k}) \le x[t+1] \le x[t](1+10^k) \\ 0 & \text{otherwise} \end{cases}$$

$$(15)$$

This p.d.f. is illustrated in Fig. 2. The range of this mutation is determined by the constant k which as mentioned previously is the number of significant digits that this mutation will perturb to. In most cases, after considering the floating-point implementation and accumulated round-off errors, the constant k can be determined.

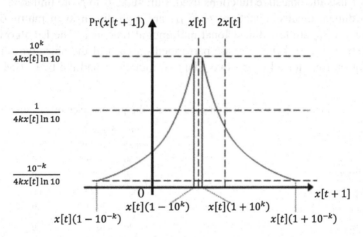

Fig. 2. Probability distribution of the mutated real value where there is on average one real parameter mutated in each individual

If, however, true arbitrary preci sion is desired, then a variant of this mutation can be used instead where (12) is replaced by the following

$$|\Delta[t]| = \begin{cases} 10^{N(0,k)}|x[t]| & \text{if } x[t] \ne 0 \\ 10^{N(0,k)}|x_{small}| & \text{if } x[t] = 0 \end{cases}$$

$$(16)$$

where the uniform distribution is replaced by the Gaussian distribution. The mutation operator defined by (12) will be referred to as the simulated binary mutation – uniform or SBM-U(k) for short, and the mutation operator defined by (16) will be referred to as SBM-G(k).

Now that the SBM operators have been defined, their performance is compared with those of the adaptive Gaussian and the adaptive Cauchy mutations in the next section.

5 Tests and Result Discussions

In order to evaluate their performance of SBM operators on different functions, it is further compared with those of the adaptive Gaussian and the adaptive Cauchy mutations. The adaptive mutations require a coding representation that stores both the real value parameters and their corresponding scaling parameters. The SBMs, however, does not require any evolving scaling parameters and the coding requires nothing other than the real value parameters themselves. For the SBMs, k was set to 5, and for the adaptive mutations the scaling parameters were bounded to the interval $[10^{-5}, 10^5]$ with the initial scaling set to 3.

Table 1 lists the objective functions used. Functions f_1 to f_7 are unimodal functions with high dimensionality. Functions f_8 to f_{11} are high dimensional multimodal functions and f_{12} to f_{16} are low dimensional multimodal functions. The EP algorithm with the population size, μ, being 100 are performed on each of the objective functions in Table 1 for 50 runs for all of the two adaptive mutations and the two SBMs.

Table 1. Benchmark objective function used to test the performance of mutation operators

Test function	n	Range	f_{min}
$f_1(x) = \sum_{i=1}^{n} x_i^2$	30	$[-100, 100]^n$	0
$f_2(x) = \sum_{i=1}^{n} |x_i| + \prod_{i=1}^{n} |x_i|$	30	$[-10, 10]^n$	0
$f_3(x) = \sum_{i=1}^{n} \left(\sum_{j=1}^{i} x_j \right)^2$	30	$[-100, 100]^n$	0
$f_4(x) = max_i\{|x_i|, 1 \leq i \leq n\}$	30	$[-100, 100]^n$	0
$f_5(x) = \sum_{i=1}^{n-1} \left(100(x_{i+1} - x^2)^2 + (x_i - 1)^2 \right)$	30	$[-30, 30]^n$	0
$f_6(x) = \sum_{i=1}^{n} (\lfloor x_i + 0.5 \rfloor)^2$	30	$[-100, 100]^n$	0
$f_7(x) = \sum_{i=1}^{n} i x_i^4 + U[0, 1)$	30	$[-1.28, 1.28]^n$	0
$f_8(x) = -\sum_{i=1}^{n} x_i sin\sqrt{|x_i|}$	30	$[-500, 500]^n$	-1.2569.5
$f_9(x) = 10n + \sum_{i=1}^{n} \left(x_i^2 - 10cos(2\pi x_i) \right)$	30	$[-5.12, 5.12]^n$	0
$f_{10}(x) = 20 + e - 20exp\left(-\sqrt{\frac{1}{25n}\sum_{i=1}^{n} x_i^2} \right) - exp\left(\frac{1}{n}\sum_{i=1}^{n} cos(2\pi x_i) \right)$	30	$[-32, 32]^n$	0
$f_{11}(x) = 1 + \frac{1}{4000}\sum_{i=1}^{n} x_i^2 - \prod_{i=1}^{n} cos\frac{x_i}{\sqrt{i}}$	30	$[-600, 600]^n$	0
$f_{12}(x) = \left(\frac{1}{500} + \sum_{j=1}^{25} \left(j + \sum_{i=1}^{2} (x_i - a_{ij})^6 \right)^{-1} \right)^{-1}$	2	$[-65.536, 65.536]^n$	~ 1
$f_{13}(x) = \sum_{i=1}^{11} \left(a_i - \frac{x_i(b_i^2 + b_i x_2)}{b_i^2 + b_i x_3 + x_4} \right)^2$	4	$[-5, 5]^n$	3.075×10^{-4}
$f_{14}(x) = 4x^2 - 2.1x_1^4 + \frac{1}{3}x_1^6 + x_1 x_2 - 4x_2^2 + 4x_2^4$	2	$[-5, 5]^n$	-1.0316285
$f_{15}(x) = \left(x^2 - \frac{5.1}{4\pi^2}x_1^2 + \frac{5}{\pi}x_1 - 6 \right)^2 + 10\left(1 - \frac{1}{8\pi}\right)cosx_1 + 10$	2	$[-5, 10] \times [0, 15]$	0.398
$f_{16}(x) = \left(1 + (x_1 + x_2 + 1)^2(19 - 14x_1 + 3x_1^2 - 14x_2 + 6x_1 x_2 + 3x_2^2)\right)$ $\times \left(30 + (2x_1 - 3x_2)^2(18 - 32x_1 + 12x_1^2 + 48x_2 - 36x_1 x_2 + 27x_2^2)\right)^2$	2	$[-2, 2]^n$	3

In the unimodal tests, $f_1 - f_7$, there was very little difference in the performance of SBM-U and SBM-G. Both of them outperformed the adaptive Gaussian and the adaptive Cauchy mutations for most of these benchmark problems. However, the SBMs' convergence has been seen worse in benchmark functions f_3 and f_5. The averaged best results are plotted against the generation number in Fig. 3 and the average final results are tabulated in Table 2. Thus, to be fair, the SBMs results are also compared with the published results of [15] in Table 2. Again, the SBMs performed better in all but functions f_3 and f_5. On average and for almost all the unimodal benchmark problems, SBMs converges linearly with increasing generations.

The results of the tests on the four high-dimensional multimodal benchmark functions, $f_8 - f_{11}$, show that both of the SBMs performed significantly better than the

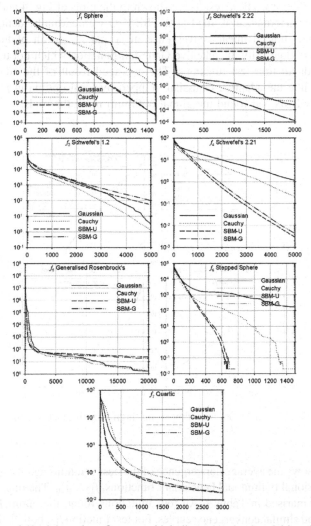

Fig. 3. Average of 50 trials on best fitness on high dimensional unimodal benchmark problems

Table 2. Comparison of best results averaged over 50 trials for unimodal benchmark functions

Functions	Gen	Gaussian	Cauchy	SBM-U	SBM-G	Yao et al. [17]	
						Gaussian	Cauchy
f_1	1500	8.79×10^{-2}	4.55×10^{-3}	5.56×10^{-6}	6.22×10^{-6}	2.2×10^{-4}	5.7×10^{-3}
f_2	2000	6.51×10^{-4}	2.55×10^{-3}	1.61×10^{-6}	1.63×10^{-6}	2.6×10^{-3}	8.1×10^{-3}
f_3	5000	3.05	1.26	53.5	101.6	5.0×10^{-2}	1.6×10^{-2}
f_4	5000	1.14	0.205	2.95×10^{-3}	4.20×10^{-3}	2.0	0.3
f_5	20000	1.59	1.72	22.8	16.3	6.17	5.06
f_6	1400	169.4	0.02	0	0	577.8	0
f_7	3000	0.147	2.64×10^{-2}	1.77×10^{-2}	1.86×10^{-2}	1.8×10^{-2}	7.6×10^{-3}

two adaptive mutations. These results are shown in the plots of Fig. 4 and are tabulated in Table 3. The performance of SBM-U and SBM-G were virtually identical in this set of functions and showed linear convergence in f_9 and f_{10}. In all of these the worst performer was undoubtedly the adaptive Gaussian mutation which got trapped in poor local optima for all four test functions. The averaged result of the adaptive Cauchy mutation was, like the adaptive Gaussian, trapped by local optima in f_9. For this test function, both SBMs had found the global optimum in all the trials.

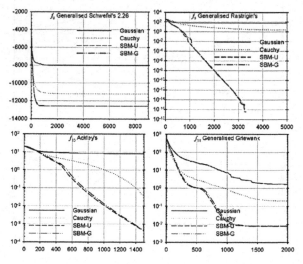

Fig. 4. Average of 50 trials on best fitness on high dimensional multimodal benchmark problems

Figure 5 shows the average convergence of the best solutions against generations for the low dimensional multimodal benchmark functions, $f_{12} - f_{16}$. The final averaged best results are summarised in Table 4. All four mutations found the optimal solutions for $f_{14} - f_{16}$ and had similar convergence curves. For test function f_{12}, both SBMs performed

Table 3. Comparison of best results averaged over 50 trials for high dimensional multimodal benchmark functions

Functions	Gen	Gaussian	Cauchy	SBM-U	SBM-G	Yao et al. [17]	
						Gaussian	Cauchy
f_8	9000	-8001.1	−11218.5	−12569.5	−12569.5	−7917.1	−12554.5
f_9	5000	66.9	2.41	0	0	89.0	4.6×10^{-2}
f_{10}	1500	8.17	3.94×10^{-2}	4.33×10^{-2}	4.45×10^{-4}	9.2	1.8×10^{-2}
f_{11}	2000	1.64	0.199	8.03×10^{-3}	7.97×10^{-3}	8.6×10^{-2}	1.6×10^{-2}

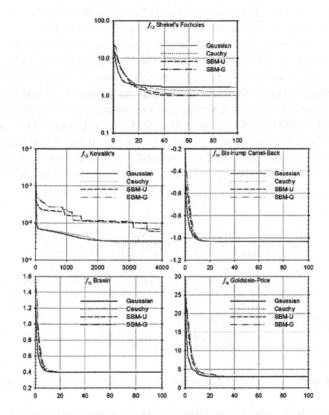

Fig. 5. Average of 50 trials on best fitness on low dimensional multimodal benchmark problems

better than the two adaptive mutations and found the global optimum. However, the performances of the SBMs were worse than both adaptive mutations for test function f_{13}.

Overall the SBMs performed better than the adaptive mutations while having a linear convergence rate in many of the test functions. This is achieved without the added complexity of having scaling parameters for each objective parameter in every individual. [15] also introduced the improved fast evolutionary programming (IFEP) algorithm in which each parent individual produces two individuals by adaptive Gaussian and by adaptive Cauchy mutations and the better of the two is kept as the

Table 4. Comparison of the best results averaged over 50 trials for the low dimensional multimodal benchmark functions

Functions	Gen	Gaussian	Cauchy	SBM-U	SBM-G	Yao et al. [17] Gaussian	Cauchy
f_{12}	100	1.68	1.27	0.998	0.998	1.66	1.22
f_{13}	4000	3.28×10^{-4}	3.07×10^{-4}	5.84×10^{-4}	6.84×10^{-4}	4.7×10^{-4}	5.0×10^{-4}
f_{14}	100	−1.03	−1.03	−1.03	−1.03	−1.03	−1.03
f_{15}	100	0.398	0.398	0.398	0.398	0.398	0.398
f_{16}	100	3	3	3	3	3	3.02

offspring. To allow for fair comparison the IFEP algorithm used half the population size and results were published for the IFEP for test functions f_1, f_2, f_{10}, and f_{11} [15].

The results of both of the SBMs were also better than those of the IFEP algorithm. The similarity of the results of SBM-U and SBM-G suggests that the order k has only a small effect on the convergence. There are however three of the test functions that the SBMs performed worse than the adaptive mutations, namely f_3, f_5 and f_{13}. By looking into the landscapes of these test functions and the mechanism of the SBMs, the type of problems that the SBMs perform less well in and why it is so can be found. Contour plots of two dimensional versions of f_3 and f_5 are shown in Fig. 6 The minimum of f_3 is elliptical with its major and minor axis rotated from, and thus unaligned with, the parameter axes. The Rosenbrock function, f_5, is sometimes known as the banana function due to its minimum being located within a curved valley.

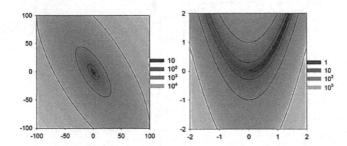

Fig. 6. Contour plots of f_3 and f_5 with $n = 2$, left and right respectively

As mentioned previously, the SBM is derived from binary mutation and hence inherited its mutation rate method. That is, only one of the objective parameters in each individual will undergo mutation, hence the SBM suffers from the same problem as performing line optimisations along axes directions only. In problems like f_3, where the ellipse's principal axis is at an angle to the parameter axis, the algorithm has to zigzag, constantly crossing the ellipse's principal axis, to reach the minimum. In such problems, it is necessary to simultaneously adjust many parameters to be able to converge efficiently and traverse the direction closer to the minimum. The adaptive mutations performed better here because all of the objective parameters undergo mutation and thus individuals can travel diagonally.

Likewise, for f_5, individuals mutated by the SBM must zigzag around the bent valley to reach the optimum which is very inefficient. These types of functions are probably best tackled with the adaptive mutations with correlated mutations, i.e., rotation angles. For the SBM to be more efficient in these types of functions, it may be necessary to abandon the one mutation-per-individual mutation rate and adopt an alternative approach to selecting which parameters to undergo mutation.

6 Conclusions

By factoring out the common denominators of the three originating branches of evolutionary algorithms (EA) and identifying their particularities, a generalised HEA structure has been created, which behaves like any of the three original EA paradigms. The customisability and flexibility of the library makes it a more comprehensive tool in the application and research of EAs.

The mutation of chromosomes in a binary-coded GA is very good in its ability to produce mutations of different magnitudes. The simulated binary mutation has been created to simulate this binary-coded mutation for real-value parameters. SBM is seen to perform very well comparing with adaptive mutations for real-value parameters showing good convergence on many benchmark functions, although it is identified that certain landscapes can cause SBM a difficulty. In these landscapes, the SBM would have to zigzag slowly along a valley. This behaviour is due to the typical one mutation per chromosome inherited from binary-coded mutation of GAs, but increasing the mutation rate would allow individuals to traverse at a higher speed.

References

1. Conn, A.R., Scheinberg, K., Vicente, L.N.: Introduction to Derivative-Free Optimization. SIAM, Philadelphia (2009)
2. Powell, M.J.D.: Direct search algorithms for optimisation calculations. Acta Numer. **7**, 287–336 (1998). doi:10.1017/S0962492900002841
3. Fogel, D.B.: Evolutionary computation: towards a new philosophy of machine intelligence. IEEE Press, New York (1995). doi:10.1002/0471749214
4. Grosan, C., Abraham, A.: Hybrid Evolutionary Algorithms: Methodologies, Architectures, and Reviews. In: Abraham, A., Grosan, C., Ishibuchi, H. (eds.) Hybrid Evolutionary Algorithms. Studies in Computational Intelligence, vol. 75, pp. 1–17. Springer, Heidelberg (2007). doi:10.1007/978-3-540-73297-6_1
5. Lin, Q., Chen, J., Zhan, Z.H.: A hybrid evolutionary immune algorithm for multiobjective optimization problems. IEEE Trans. Evol. Comput. **20**(5), 711–729 (2016). doi:10.1109/TEVC.2015.2512930
6. Chen, G., Low, C.P., Yang, Z.H.: Preserving and exploiting genetic diversity in evolutionary programming algorithms. IEEE Trans. Evol. Comput. **13**, 661–673 (2009). doi:10.1109/TEVC.2008.2011742
7. Bäck, T., Fogel, D.B., Michalewicz, Z. (eds.): Handbook of Evolutionary Computation. Institute of Physics Publishing Ltd/Oxford University Press, Bristol/Oxford (1997)

8. Guo, P., Cheng, W., Wang, Y.: Hybrid evolutionary algorithm with extreme machine learning fitness function evaluation for two-stage capacitated facility location problem. Expert Syst. Appl. **71**, 57–68 (2016). doi:10.1016/j.eswa.2016.11.025

9. Cheng, T.C.E., Peng, B., Lü, Z.: A hybrid evolutionary algorithm to solve the job shop scheduling problem. Ann. Oper. Res. **242**(2), 223–237 (2016). doi:10.1007/s10479-013-1332-5

10. Zhu, Q., Lin, Q., Du, Z.: A novel adaptive hybrid crossover operator for multiobjective evolutionary algorithm. Inf. Sci. **345**, 177–198 (2016). doi:10.1016/j.ins.2016.01.046

11. Anderson, R.W.: The Baldwin effect. In: Bäck, T., Fogel, D.B., Michalewicz, Z. (eds.): Handbook of Evolutionary Computation, pp. C3.4:1–C3.4:7. Institute of Physics Publishing Ltd/Oxford University Press (1997)

12. Li, L., Zhang, C.Z., Li, Z.N., Li, Y.: Particle filter with Lamarckian inheritance for nonlinear filtering. In: 2016 IEEE Congress on Evolutionary Computation, pp. 2852–2857. IEEE, Vancouver (2016). doi:10.1109/CEC.2016.7744149

13. Li, L., Li, Y.: Particle filter track-before-detect algorithm with Lamarckian inheritance for improved dim target tracking. In: 2017 IEEE Congress on Evolutionary Computation, pp. 1158–1164. IEEE, San Sebastián (2017). doi:10.1109/CEC.2017.7969437

14. Yao, X., Liu, Y.: Fast evolution strategies. Control Cybern. **26**(3), 467–496 (1997). doi:10.1007/BFb0014808

15. Yao, X., Liu, Y., Lin, G.: Evolutionary programming made faster. IEEE Trans. Evol. Comput. **3**(2), 82–102 (1999). doi:10.1109/4235.771163

16. Bäck, T.: Evolutionary Algorithms in Theory and Practice: Evolution Strategies, Evolutionary Programming, Genetic Algorithms. Oxford University Press, Oxford (1996)

A Multitree Genetic Programming Representation for Automatically Evolving Texture Image Descriptors

Harith Al-Sahaf[⊠], Bing Xue, and Mengjie Zhang

School of Engineering and Computer Science, Victoria University of Wellington,
P.O. Box 600, Wellington 6140, New Zealand
{harith.al-sahaf,bing.xue,mengjie.zhang}@ecs.vuw.ac.nz

Abstract. Image descriptors are very important components in computer vision and pattern recognition that play critical roles in a wide range of applications. The main task of an image descriptor is to automatically detect micro-patterns in an image and generate a feature vector. A domain expert is often needed to undertake the process of developing an image descriptor. However, such an expert, in many cases, is difficult to find or expensive to employ. In this paper, a multitree genetic programming representation is adopted to automatically evolve image descriptors. Unlike existing hand-crafted image descriptors, the proposed method does not rely on predetermined features, instead, it automatically identifies a set of features using a few instances of each class. The performance of the proposed method is assessed using seven benchmark texture classification datasets and compared to seven state-of-the-art methods. The results show that the new method has significantly outperformed its counterpart methods in most cases.

Keywords: Multitree · Image classification · Feature extraction

1 Introduction

Discriminating between texture images is highly dependent on the detected micro-patterns, i.e., keypoints, such as lines, spots and homogeneous regions presented in those images. Designing a method to automatically identify or detect such micro-patterns is often require human intervention to carry out this task. The detection can be performed either manually, where a domain expert highlights the coordinates of those keypoints, or automatically by using keypoint detectors such as corner detection [21] and local binary patterns (LBP) [18]. Over the past 50 years, image descriptors have emerged to automatically detect a set of predetermined micro-patterns in order to extract the feature vector for an image [11]. The majority of those image descriptors have two limitations. Firstly, they are designed to detect a specific set of micro-patterns such as corners; secondly, they are hand-crafted where domain expert intervention is needed to design and develop those descriptors.

© Springer International Publishing AG 2017
Y. Shi et al. (Eds.): SEAL 2017, LNCS 10593, pp. 499–511, 2017.
https://doi.org/10.1007/978-3-319-68759-9_41

Genetic Programming (GP) is an evolutionary computation technique that mimics the principles of natural selection and survival of the fittest, where a population of computer programs are evolved over generations to find a solution for a user-defined problem [10].

Conventionally, a GP individual is represented by tree structure, where the leaf nodes are populated from the *terminal* set and the internal nodes are populated from the *function* set. The tree-based representation is one of the most commonly used individual representations in GP [20], but it is not the only one. Over the past 30 years, different individual representations have been investigated such as linear GP, multitree GP, and cartesian GP [20].

Automatically evolving interest point detectors by utilising GP has been proposed in [7], and further studied by Olague and Trujillo [19].

Fu *et al.* [8] proposed a GP method to construct invariant features for edge detection. In order to improve the extracted features from raw pixel values, the distributions of the observations from GP programs are used. Their results show that the constructed features by GP with distribution estimation have improved the detection performance compared to the combination of linear support vector machine and a Bayesian model.

Cordelia *et al.* [6] proposed a multitree based GP method for generating prototypes in classification problems, where a dynamic representation is used to allow each individual to have different number of trees. This dynamic representation allows the method to cope with situation where one or more classes comprise subclasses. Using three well-known datasets and compared to another GP based method, their method has achieved significantly better performance as shown in [6].

Broic and Estevez [3] utilised multitree GP and information theory to perform clustering. In their method, an information theory based fitness function is developed to measure the goodness of an evolved program. Moreover, probabilistic based interpretation of the trees' output is used in order to avoid the requirement for a *conflict resolution* phase. The results of their experiments show the superiority of this method compared to k-means clustering using 10 clustering benchmark datasets.

Utilising multitree GP to automatically discover some patterns for self-assembling swarm robots is proposed in [14]. Promising results have been achieved by this method, which reflect its effectiveness.

Recently, Al-Sahaf *et al.* [1] utilised GP to automatically evolve LBP-like rotation-invariant image descriptors using a set of arithmetic operators, first-order statistics and a special *code* node. Strongly-typed GP (STGP) [16] is required in order to specify the structure of an evolved program by this method. Their results reveal the ability of the automatically evolved descriptors to outperform their counterpart hand-crafted descriptors.

The proposed method in [1] represents the baseline for the newly introduced method in this paper, where the representation of an evolved program is the main difference between the two methods.

The overall goal of this study is to utilise multitree GP to the task of automatically evolving rotation-invariant image descriptors. The proposed method uses simple arithmetic operators and first-order statistics, and only two instances per class to build a GP program that scans an image using a sliding window to generate the feature vector. Specifically, this study aims at providing answers for the following questions.

- How a descriptor can be represented using a multitree GP representation?
- What fitness function can be used when there are only a few instances per class in the training set?
- Is the proposed method able to evolve image descriptors that can outperform the hand-crafted descriptors?

2   Background

The baseline method *rotation-invariant GP descriptor* (GP-criptor^{ri}) [1] is discussed in this section.

GP-criptor^{ri} is a GP based method that aims at automatically evolving rotation-invariant image descriptors using only two instances per class. GP-criptor^{ri} uses a tree based representation, where each individual is represented by a single tree. The function set comprises the four arithmetic operators $+$, $-$, $\times$ and $/$, and a special *code* node type. Apart from *code*, these functions takes two arguments and they have their corresponding arithmetic meaning. A *code* node takes a predefined number of children and returns a binary code by substituting the value returned by each of its children by 0 if it is negative, and 1 otherwise. The terminal set in GP-criptor^{ri} consists of four node types $min(\cdot)$, $max(\cdot)$, $mean(\cdot)$, and $stdev(\cdot)$ each of which operates on a vector of values and returns the minimum, maximum, mean and standard deviation, respectively. The order-invariant property of these four operators allowed GP-criptor^{ri} to evolve rotation-invariant image descriptors [1].

The distances of between-class and within-class are used in the fitness function of GP-criptor^{ri} in order to allow the method to cope with having a small number of training instances. The fitness function of GP-criptor^{ri} is defined as:

$$fitness' = 1 - \left(1 \Big/ \left(1 + e^{-5\left(D'_b - D'_w\right)} \right) \right) \tag{1}$$

where D'_b and D'_w are, respectively, the average distance of between-class and the average distance of within-class. These two distances are defined as:

$$D'_b = \frac{1}{z(z-n)} \sum_{u \in R} \sum_{v \in R \backslash u} \chi^2(u, v), \quad \{u \in u, v \in v\} \tag{2}$$

$$D'_w = \frac{1}{z(n-1)} \sum_{u \in R} \sum_{u,v \in u} \chi^2(u, v), \quad \{u \neq v\} \tag{3}$$

where z is the total number of instances in the training set, n is the number of instances per class, and $\mathbf{R} = \{(v_i, \ell_i)\}$ is the training set. v_i denotes the feature vector of the ith instance and the corresponding class label is denoted by ℓ_i, where $\boldsymbol{v}_i \in \mathbb{R}_{\geq 0}$, $\ell_i \in \{1, 2, \ldots, c\}$, c is the number of classes, and $i \in \{1, 2, \ldots, z\}$. The distance between two feature vectors is measured by the widely used *Chi-square* (χ^2) measure [5], which is defined as:

$$\chi^2 (\boldsymbol{u}, \boldsymbol{v}) = \frac{1}{2} \sum_{i=1}^{E} \frac{(\boldsymbol{u}_i - \boldsymbol{v}_i)^2}{(\boldsymbol{u}_i + \boldsymbol{v}_i)} \tag{4}$$

where E is the number of elements, $\boldsymbol{u}$ and $\boldsymbol{v}$ are two feature vectors of the same length, i.e., consist of equal umber of elements, and $\boldsymbol{u}_i$ and $\boldsymbol{v}_i$ are, respectively, the ith element in $\boldsymbol{u}$ and $\boldsymbol{v}$.

3 The Proposed Method

The proposed *multitree GP rotation-invariant image descriptor* ($\text{MGPD}_{t,w}^{\text{ri}}$) method is explained in this section.

3.1 Overall Algorithm

Similar to other machine learning methods, the overall algorithm can be divided into five parts as depicted in Fig. 1. In the first part (dataset preprocessing), the system divides the dataset equally into two subsets each of which comprises 50% of the total instances in each class. The system *randomly* selects two instances of each class from the first subset to form the training set ($\mathbf{S_{tr}}$); whereas the second subset will be used for evaluating the performance of the system, i.e., the test set ($\mathbf{S_{ts}}$). In the second part (image descriptor evolution), the system feeds the training set ($\mathbf{S_{tr}}$) into GP to evolve an image descriptor. The evolved descriptor is then used to transform the training and test sets, i.e., generates the feature vector for each image in the two sets, which is the third part of the overall algorithm (dataset transformation). The transformed training and test sets are, respectively, denoted as $\mathbf{R}$ and $\mathbf{S}$. The fourth part (building a classifier) concerns with building a classifier by feeding the transformed training set ($\mathbf{R}$) into a classification algorithm. The fifth and final part of the overall algorithm (evaluation) uses the transformed test set ($\mathbf{S}$) and the built classifier in order to assess the goodness of the evolved descriptor to generate feature vectors that are sufficient to be classified by the built classifier. More details regarding these five parts are provided in the following subsections.

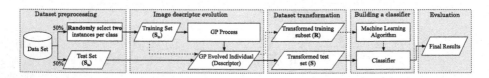

Fig. 1. The overall algorithm of the proposed method.

3.2   Program Representation

Here, a tree-based GP representation [20] is used, where a tree is a set of connected nodes. Unlike conventional GP representation where each individual is represented by a single tree, each individual in multitree GP (MGP) [6] is represented by a *set* of trees as depicted in Fig. 2. Each individual in $\text{MGPD}^{\text{ri}}_{t,w}$ comprises a set of predefined number of trees (t), where the leaf nodes are drawn from the *terminal* set and the internal nodes are drawn from the *function* set. Similar to GP-criptor[ri] [1], the terminal set comprises four first-order statistic node types $min(\cdot)$, $max(\cdot)$, $mean(\cdot)$, and $stdev(\cdot)$. The aim of each of these node types is to perform feature extraction as they aggregate a set of pixels and return a single value. The function set consists of the arithmetic operators that are often used in GP such as $+$, $-$, $\times$, and protected $/$ (returns 0 if the denominator is zero). One of the main differences between $\text{MGPD}^{\text{ri}}_{t,w}$ and the baseline GP-criptor[ri] method is that the *code* node type has been omitted, which represents the root node of an individual evolved by GP-criptor[ri]. Having the *code* node type requires the use of STGP in order to define restrictions on the inputs and outputs of the different node types. Moreover, special care is required to ensure the closure property when applying the mutation and crossover operators. The *code* node converts the output of its children to a binary code by using the 0 value as a threshold. As this node is not used in $\text{MGPD}^{\text{ri}}_{t,w}$, the system applies the same rule, i.e., uses the 0 value as a threshold, on the output of the root node of each tree of the individual in order to generate a binary code from the outputs of those trees. More details on this operation are provided in Sect. 3.4.

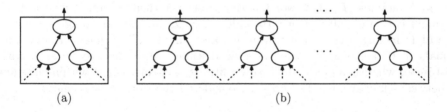

(a)   (b)

Fig. 2. GP individual representations (a) single tree; and (b) multitree.

3.3   Fitness Function

The fitness of an individual often reflects its ability to tackle the user-defined problem. Hence, the design of the fitness function is highly dependent on some factors such as the problem at hand (e.g. classification or regression) and the restrictions (e.g. number of training examples). For classification tasks, the accuracy measure, or its variations, is often used as a fitness function. However, relying on the accuracy is inappropriate in some situations such as when there are only a few training instances [1], or the dataset is highly imbalanced [2], i.e., the instances of one class are outnumbered by the instances in the other classes. Similar to GP-criptor[ri], the fitness function in $\text{MGPD}^{\text{ri}}_{t,w}$ is designed to consider the distance between instances from different classes as well as the distance between instances of the same class, which is defined as

$$fitness = \alpha \times D_{\mathrm{w}} + (1 - \alpha) \times (1 - D_{\mathrm{b}}) \tag{5}$$

where α is a scale factor $\in [0, 1]$, and D_{w} and D_{b} are, respectively, the within-class and between-class distance components.

Unlike GP-criptor^{ri}, MGPD$_{t,w}^{\mathrm{ri}}$ does not measure the average distance between each instance and *all* instances from the same and other classes; instead, the D_{w} component measures the average distance between each instance and only the *farthest* (most dissimilar) instance from the same class and calculated using Eq. (6); whilst D_{b} measures the average distance between each instance and only the *closest* (most similar) instance from all other classes and is calculated using Eq. (7). This design was motivated by the concepts of margins in support vector machines.

$$D_{\mathrm{w}} = \frac{1}{z} \sum_{\mathbf{u} \in \mathbf{R}} \sum_{u \in \mathbf{u}} \max_{v} \chi^2 (\boldsymbol{u}, \boldsymbol{v}), \quad \{\boldsymbol{v} \in \mathbf{u}, \boldsymbol{u} \neq \boldsymbol{v}\} \tag{6}$$

$$D_{\mathrm{b}} = \frac{1}{z(c-1)} \sum_{\mathbf{u} \in \mathbf{R}} \sum_{v \in \mathbf{R} \backslash \mathbf{u}} \min_{u,v} \chi^2 (\boldsymbol{u}, \boldsymbol{v}), \quad \{\boldsymbol{u} \in \mathbf{u}, \boldsymbol{v} \in \mathbf{v}\} \tag{7}$$

Here a bold letter, e.g., $\mathbf{u}$ and $\mathbf{v}$, is used to indicate the set of all instances belonging to one class.

In MGPD$_{t,w}^{\mathrm{ri}}$, the aim is to minimise the fitness value, i.e., the smaller the fitness value the better the individual. Hence, the system will try to minimise D_{w} and maximise D_{b}. It is worth noting that χ^2 returns a value between 0 and 1 (inclusive), and subsequently the values for D_{w} and D_{b} are ranging between 0 and 1. Ideally, the system will evolve an individual that has a fitness value equals to 0 (i.e. 0 within-class average distance and 1 between-class average distance); whereas an individual with a fitness value of 1 (i.e. 1 within-class and 0 between-class average distances) is considered the worst case scenario.

3.4   Feature Vector Extraction

Each individual in MGPD$_{t,w}^{\mathrm{ri}}$ is an image descriptor that operates directly on the raw pixel values of an image and generates a feature vector. The individual scans the image being evaluated in a pixel-by-pixel manner from left to right and from top to bottom using a window of size w (i.e. $w \times w$ pixels). At each pixel (window position), the system calculates the terminals required by invoking the *min*, *max*, *mean* and *stdev* functions on the pixel values of the current window. The calculated terminals are then fed into the trees of the individual and recursively each tree will be evaluated from the leaf nodes to the root node. The value obtained from each root node will be substituted by 0 if it is negative and 1 otherwise. This will form a binary code that comprises t bits, where t is the number of trees. The binary code is then converted to decimal and the corresponding bin of the histogram is incremented as presented in Fig. 3.

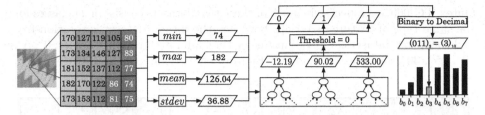

Fig. 3. An example demonstrates the steps to extract the feature vector from an image.

4 Experiment Design

To assess the performance of $\mathrm{MGPD}_{t,w}^{ri}$, experiments are conducted using seven datasets for texture image classification. This section provides details regarding the benchmark datasets, methods for comparison, and parameter settings.

4.1 Benchmark Datasets

The proposed method is designed to handle grey-scale images, where the intensity of each pixel is ranging between 0 (black) and 255 (white). Hence, seven widely-used datasets for texture classification are selected in this study.

The first dataset in this study (BrNoRo) is formed from the widely used *Brodatz Texture*[1] [4] dataset. Originally, the Brodatz Texture dataset comprises 112 classes each of which consists of a single image of size 640×640 pixels. The single instance of 20 randomly selected classes is divided into 84 non-overlapping tiles each of which with size 64×64 pixels. The second dataset (BrWiRo) is formed by rotating the instances of BrNoRo around the centre at successive $30°$ angles, i.e., $\{0°, 30°, \dots, 330°\}$. Figure 4 presents samples from BrNoRo.

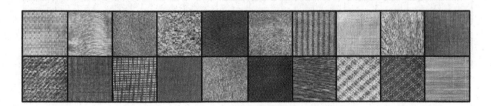

Fig. 4. Samples from the BrNoRo dataset.

The *Outex Texture Classification*[2] [17] test suites consist of 16 texture classification benchmark datasets that vary in illumination, rotation, spatial scale and colour. The third (OutexTC00) and fourth (OutexTC10) datasets in this study are formed using the instances of Outex_TC_00000 and its rotated version

---

[1] Available at: http://multibandtexture.recherche.usherbrooke.ca.

[2] Available at: http://www.outex.oulu.fi/index.php?page=classification.

Outex_TC_00010, respectively. Each of these two datasets consist of 24 classes for the same type of texture materials; however, the former dataset is rotation-free and the latter dataset comprises instances that fall into 9 rotation angles: $0°$, $5°$, $10°$, $15°$, $30°$, $45°$, $60°$, $75°$ and $90°$. Figure 5 shows examples from OutexTC00.

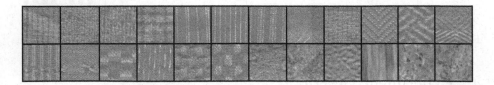

Fig. 5. Samples from the OutexTC00 dataset.

The fifth dataset in this study (KySinHw) is formed using the instances of *Kylberg Sintorn Rotation*[3] [13], which consists of 25 classes each of which comprises instances that were rotated at successive $40°$ angles, i.e., $\{0°, 40°, \ldots, 320°\}$. Figure 6 shows examples from this dataset.

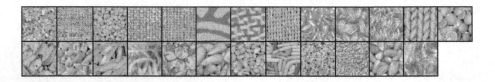

Fig. 6. Samples from the KySinHw dataset.

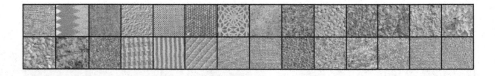

Fig. 7. Samples from the KyNoRo dataset.

The *Kylberg Texture*[4] [12] dataset comprises two groups: with rotation, and without rotation. The two groups consist of the same number of classes (28) and for the same type of materials as depicted in Fig. 7. The main difference between the content of these two groups is that the instances of each class in the former (without rotation) are all captured under the same rotation angle; whilst the instances of each class in the latter group (with rotation) are rotated in

---

[3] Available at: http://www.cb.uu.se/~gustaf/KylbergSintornRotation/.
[4] Available at: http://www.cb.uu.se/~gustaf/texture/.

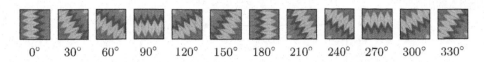

0°   30°   60°   90°   120°   150°   180°   210°   240°   270°   300°   330°

Fig. 8. A sample from the KyWiRo dataset presented in 12 rotation angles.

12° at successive 30° angles, i.e., $\{0°, 30°, \ldots, 330°\}$. Figure 8 shows an example taken from the with rotation group rotated in 12 angles. The sixth (KyNoRo) and seventh (KyWiRo) datasets in this study are, respectively, formed using the instances of the without and with rotation groups.

4.2 Methods for Comparison

The $\text{MGPD}_{t,w}^{\text{ri}}$ method aims at evolving dense image descriptors, therefore, six the-state-of-the-art dense hand-crafted image descriptors are used in this study in addition to the baseline method (GP-criptor^{ri}). The methods are uniform local binary pattern ($\text{LBP}_{p,r}^{\text{u2}}$) [18], uniform and rotation-invariant LBP ($\text{LBP}_{p,r}^{\text{u2ri}}$) [18], completed LBP ($\text{CLBP}_{p,r}$) [9], local binary count ($\text{LBC}_{p,r}$) and completed LBC ($\text{CLBC}_{p,r}$) [22], and dominant rotation LBP ($\text{DRLBP}_{p,r}$) [15].

4.3 Parameter Settings

Both $\text{MGPD}_{t,w}^{\text{ri}}$ and GP-criptor^{ri} are evolutionary-based methods. The evolutionary parameters for both methods were kept identical as summarised in Table 1. Moreover, these methods comprise other non-evolutionary parameters. The window size (w) and number of trees (t), which is also the number of children of *code* in GP-criptor^{ri}, are experimentally set to 5×5 pixels and 9, respectively. The value of α in the fitness function of $\text{MGPD}_{t,w}^{\text{ri}}$ ranges between 0 and 1, which specifies the importance of the within-class and between-class distance components. Hence, 11 different values with a step of size 0.1 are used as shown in Fig. 9. As depicted in Fig. 9, the value of $\alpha \in [0.0, 0.6]$ gives good performance; therefore, the scale factor has been set to 0.1 in this study.

Table 1. The GP parameters

Parameter	Value	Parameter	Value
Generations	50	Minimum tree depth	2
Population size	300	Maximum tree depth	10
Crossover rate	80%	Mutation rate	20%
Selection type	Tournament	Tournament size	7
Elitism	Keep the best 10 individuals	Initial population	Ramped half-and-half

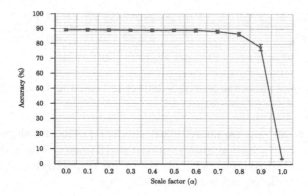

Fig. 9. The sensitivity of the scale factor (α) on KyNoRo.

Parameters of the benchmark methods have been investigated in [1], and therefore, they have been set at those values were observed to give the best performance. For $\text{LBP}_{p,r}^{\text{u2ri}}$, $\text{CLBP}_{p,r}$, $\text{LBC}_{p,r}$ and $\text{CLBC}_{p,r}$ methods, the radius (r) and number of neighbouring pixels (p) parameters have been, respectively, set to 3 and 24, i.e., $\text{LBP}_{24,3}^{\text{u2ri}}$, $\text{CLBP}_{24,3}$, $\text{LBC}_{24,3}$ and $\text{CLBC}_{24,3}$; whereas $\text{LBP}_{p,r}^{\text{u2}}$ and $\text{DRLBP}_{p,r}$ are set to $p = 8$ and $r = 1$, i.e., $\text{LBP}_{8,1}^{\text{u2}}$ and $\text{DRLBP}_{8,1}$.

4.4 Experiments

The main role of an image descriptor is to generate the feature vector for an image. The classification accuracy is widely adopted to measure the goodness of a descriptor [18]. Hence, the k-Nearest Neighbours classifier with $k = 1$ (1-NN) is used in this study. Apart from GP-criptor^{ri} and $\text{MGPD}_{t,w}^{\text{ri}}$, all other methods are deterministic that require only a single run. The run for each of the stochastic methods, i.e., GP-criptor^{ri} and $\text{MGPD}_{t,w}^{\text{ri}}$, is repeated independently 30 times using different seed values and the average performance is reported. The training set ($\mathbf{S_{tr}}$) is formed by randomly selecting two instances from each class (Sect. 3.1); therefore, the same process is further repeated 10 times and the mean and standard deviation are reported. In total, there are 4620 runs (= [(30 (runs)$\times$2 (methods))+(1 (run)$\times$6 (methods))]$\times$10 (repeats)$\times$7 (datasets)).

5 Results and Discussions

The results of the eight methods on the seven datasets are presented in Fig. 10. Each block in this figure groups the results of a single dataset. To test the significance of the obtained results, Mann-Whitney-Wilcoxon Test is used with 0.05 significance level. The symbols "+", "−" and "=" are used in Fig. 10 to indicate that the proposed method is significantly better, significantly worse, and not significant, respectively, compared to the corresponding method.

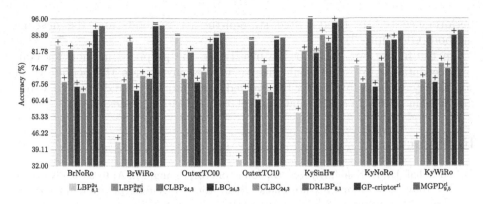

Fig. 10. The average accuracy (%) of eight image descriptors on seven texture datasets.

On the first dataset (BrNoRo), the proposed method has significantly outperformed all the other image descriptors, and achieved on average 93.00% accuracy. The minimum difference between $MGPD_{9,5}^{ri}$ and the other methods ranges between 2.08% (GP-criptor^{ri}) and 29.38% (CLBP$_{24,3}$).

The results on the second dataset (BrWiRo) show that $MGPD_{9,5}^{ri}$ has achieved the best performance (92.94%). Apart from GP-criptor^{ri}, $MGPD_{9,5}^{ri}$ has significantly outperformed the other methods.

The results on the third dataset (OutexTC00) show that $MGPD_{9,5}^{ri}$ has achieved on average 89.75% accuracy, which is significantly better than the performance of the competitor methods, apart from LBP$_{8,1}^{u2}$ and GP-criptor^{ri}.

The results on the fourth dataset (OutexTC10) show similar pattern compared to that of the rotation-free dataset (OutexTC00) with on average performance of 87.82%, where $MGPD_{9,5}^{ri}$ has significantly outperformed five methods and show comparable, yet better, result to CLBP$_{24,3}$ and GP-criptor^{ri}.

The proposed method has achieved the second best performance (95.88%) on the fifth dataset (KySinHw), which is significantly outperformed the other methods apart from CLBP$_{24,3}$ (97.31%).

The results on the sixth (KyNoRo) and seventh (KyWiRo) datasets show that $MGPD_{9,5}^{ri}$ has significantly outperformed the competitor methods apart from CLBP$_{24,3}$. The proposed method has achieved on average 90.53% on KyNoRo and 90.91% on KyWiRo.

6 Conclusions

This paper has successfully utilised multitree GP to automatically evolve rotation-invariant image descriptors. Relying on the between-class and within-class distances, the proposed method uses only two instances per class to evolve a descriptor. The results of the experiments on seven texture datasets show that the proposed method has significantly outperformed, or achieved comparable performance to, six hand-crafted state-of-the-art methods and the baseline method (GP-criptor[ri]).

In the future, we would like to investigate the proposed method for non-texture datasets. We also would like to further investigate the possibility of completely or partially transfer the evolved descriptors on one dataset to a similar domain (texture) or different, but related, domain (non-texture).

References

1. Al-Sahaf, H., Al-Sahaf, A., Xue, B., Johnston, M., Zhang, M.: Automatically evolving rotation-invariant texture image descriptors by genetic programming. IEEE Trans. Evol. Comput. **21**(1), 83–101 (2016)
2. Bhowan, U., Johnston, M., Zhang, M., Yao, X.: Reusing genetic programming for ensemble selection in classification of unbalanced data. IEEE Trans. Evol. Comput. **18**(6), 893–908 (2014)
3. Boric, N., Estevez, P.A.: Genetic programming-based clustering using an information theoretic fitness measure. In: Proceedings of 2007 IEEE Congress on Evolutionary Computation, pp. 31–38. IEEE (2007)
4. Brodatz, P.: Textures: A Photographic Album for Artists and Designers. Dover Publications, Mineola (1999)
5. Cha, S.-H.: Comprehensive survey on distance/similarity measures between probability density functions. Int. J. Math. Models Methods Appl. Sci. **1**(4), 300–307 (2007)
6. Cordella, L.P., de Stefano, C., Fontanella, F., Marcelli, A.: Genetic programming for generating prototypes in classification problems. In: Proceedings of 2005 IEEE Congress on Evolutionary Computation, pp. 1149–1155. IEEE (2005)
7. Ebner, M., Zell, A.: Evolving a task specific image operator. In: Poli, R., Voigt, H.-M., Cagnoni, S., Corne, D., Smith, G.D., Fogarty, T.C. (eds.) EvoWorkshops 1999. LNCS, vol. 1596, pp. 74–89. Springer, Heidelberg (1999). doi:10.1007/10704703_6
8. Fu, W., Johnston, M., Zhang, M.: Distribution-based invariant feature construction using genetic programming for edge detection. Soft Comput. **19**(8), 2371–2389 (2015)
9. Guo, Z., Zhang, L., Zhang, D.: A completed modeling of local binary pattern operator for texture classification. IEEE Trans. Image Process. **19**(6), 1657–1663 (2010)
10. Koza, J.R.: Genetic Programming: On the Programming of Computers by Means of Natural Selection. MIT Press, Cambridge (1992)
11. Krig, S.: Computer Vision Metrics: Survey, Taxonomy, and Analysis, 1st edn. Apress, New York (2014)
12. Kylberg, G.: The Kylberg texture dataset v. 1.0. External report (Blue series) 35, Centre for Image Analysis, Swedish University of Agricultural Sciences and Uppsala University, Uppsala, Sweden (2011)
13. Kylberg, G.: Automatic virus identification using TEM: image segmentation and texture analysis. Ph.D. thesis, Division of Visual Information and Interaction, Uppsala University, Uppsala, Sweden (2014)
14. Lee, J.-H., Ahn, C.W., An, J.: An approach to self-assembling swarm robots using multitree genetic programming. Sci. World J. **2013**, 1–10 (2013)
15. Mehta, R., Egiazarian, K.: Dominant rotated local binary patterns (DRLBP) for texture classification. Pattern Recogn. Lett. **71**(1), 16–22 (2016)

16. Montana, D.J.: Strongly typed genetic programming. Evol. Comput. **3**(2), 199–230 (1995)
17. Ojala, T., Mäenpää, T., Pietikäinen, M., Viertola, J., Kyllonen, J., Huovinen, S.: Outex - new framework for empirical evaluation of texture analysis algorithms. In: Proceedings of 16th International Conference on Pattern Recognition, vol. 1, pp. 701–706. IEEE (2002)
18. Ojala, T., Pietikäinen, M., Mäenpää, T.: Gray scale and rotation invariant texture classification with local binary patterns. In: Vernon, D. (ed.) ECCV 2000. LNCS, vol. 1842, pp. 404–420. Springer, Heidelberg (2000). doi:10.1007/3-540-45054-8_27
19. Olague, G., Trujillo, L.: A genetic programming approach to the design of interest point operators. In: Melin, P., Kacprzyk, J., Pedrycz, W. (eds.) Bio-inspired Hybrid Intelligent Systems for Image Analysis and Pattern Recognition. SCI, vol. 256, pp. 49–65. Springer, Heidelberg (2009). doi:10.1007/978-3-642-04516-5_3
20. Poli, R., Langdon, W.B., McPhee, N.F.: A Field Guide to Genetic Programming (2008). Published via http://lulu.com. (With contributions by J.R. Koza)
21. Willis, A., Sui, Y.: An algebraic model for fast corner detection. In: Proceedings of 12th IEEE International Conference on Computer Vision, pp. 2296–2302. IEEE (2009)
22. Zhao, Y., Huang, D.-S., Jia, W.: Completed local binary count for rotation invariant texture classification. IEEE Trans. Image Process. **21**(10), 4492–4497 (2012)

Theoretical Developments

Running-Time Analysis of Particle Swarm Optimization with a Single Particle Based on Average Gain

Wu Hongyue[1], Huang Han[1], Yang Shuling[1(✉)], and Zhang Yushan[2]

[1] School of Software Engineering, South China University of Technology,
Guangzhou 510006, China
694712017@qq.com
[2] School of Mathematics and Statistics, Guangdong University of Finance
and Economics, Guangzhou 510320, China

Abstract. Running-time analysis of the particle swarm optimization (PSO) is a hard study in the field of swarm intelligence, especially for the PSO whose solution and velocity are encoded continuously. In this study, running-time analysis on particle swarm optimization with a single particle (PSO-SP) is analyzed. Elite selection strategy and stochastic disturbance are combined into PSO-SP in order to improve optimization capacity and adjust the direction of the velocity of the single particle. Running-time analysis on PSO-SP based on the average gain model is applied in two different situations including uniform distribution and standard normal distribution. The theoretical results show running-time of the PSO-SP with stochastic disturbance of both distributions is exponential. Besides, in the same accuracy and the same fitness difference value, running-time of the PSO-SP with stochastic disturbance of uniform distribution is better than that of standard normal distribution.

Keywords: Swarm intelligence · Particle swarm optimization · Running-time analysis · Average gain model

1 Introduction

Particle Swarm Optimization (PSO) proposed by Kennedy and Eberhart in 1995 is an algorithm inspired by social insects and animals [3]. In 1998, Shi improved the algorithm framework [5]. In this paper, the PSO we analyze is under this framework. Those insects and animals are considered as flying particles searching optimal solutions in a multi-dimensional search space. There are three important factors, individual information, global information and inertia, which influence flight paths of particles in PSO algorithm. While using PSO to solve optimization problems, individual information generally adopt individual optimal solutions; global information record optimal solutions of the whole; inertia is expressed as velocity.

Running-time analysis is a difficult challenge in the research field of evolutionary computation [4]. Although PSO is applied widely in engineering design and engineering optimization, the study of time complexity obviously lags behind. There are some literatures to analyze time complexity for bio-inspired optimization algorithms.

© Springer International Publishing AG 2017
Y. Shi et al. (Eds.): SEAL 2017, LNCS 10593, pp. 515–527, 2017.
https://doi.org/10.1007/978-3-319-68759-9_42

For example, Oliveto [9] presented a simple and easy method which can analyze computational time complexity of $(1 + 1)$ EA and obtain an exponential lower bound of time according to drift analysis proposed by He et al. [6–8]. Rowe and Sudholt presented the relationship between the offspring population size and running-time in the $(1, \lambda)$ EA [17]. Qian et al. [12, 13] presented an analysis in evolutionary multi-objective optimization. They found that recombination helped find approximate solutions faster [12] and provided theoretical support for selection hyper-heuristics in multi-objective optimization [13]. Evolutionary optimization in noisy environments were analyzed by Qian et al. [14, 15]. Runtime complexity analysis for ant colony optimization (ACO) is proposed by Gutjahr [10]. Doerr analyzed running-time analysis of 1-ANT ACO algorithm [11]. Sudholt et al. presented runtime analysis of binary PSO and gave time complexity [12]. Witt [18] proved expected polynomial time on Sphere for a PSO algorithm using a self-adapting scheme. Lehre and Witt [19] compared the expected first hitting time between a basic PSO and the Noisy PSO.

This study proposes a special algorithm named PSO with a single particle (PSO-SP) and analyzes running-time complexity with average gain model when the algorithm solves Sphere function. In Sect. 2, PSO with a single particle will be introduced. In Sect. 3, sphere function and average gain model will be illustrated. Running-time analyses for PSO-SP in two situations are compared. The last section concludes the study.

2   PSO with a Single Particle (PSO-SP) Algorithm

A traditional PSO algorithm stores information of optimal solution gbest, and every individual keeps information of individual optimal solution pbest. Each particle guided by those information approaches a best solution in a search space.

It is complicated to analyze running-time complexity for PSO with multiple particles. Thus, this study focuses on a single particle. PSO with a single particle (PSO-SP) algorithm applies elite selection strategy to strengthen its own performance. It makes gbest and pbest equal to a current solution, so direction of velocity of particles will not change. Therefore, stochastic disturbance will be employed in PSO-SP. The algorithm pseudo-code will be given as following.

Algorithm 1 PSO-SP

1: Initialize $x_0, v_0, t = 0$

2: while (termination conditions are not met)

3:   $v_{t+1} = \omega v_t, x'_{t+1} = x_t + v_{t+1}$

4:   if $f(x'_{t+1}) > f(x_t)$ then $x'_{t+1} = x_t$

5:   $x_{t+1} = x'_{t+1} + u$

6:   if $f(x_{t+1}) > f(x'_{t+1})$ then $x_{t+1} = x'_{t+1}$

7:   $v_{t+1} = x_{t+1} - x_t$

8:   $t = t + 1$

9: output the solution

---

x_t is equal to gbest and pbest because of elite selection strategy. Updating v_{t+1} is related to v_t of a previous generation and a parameter ω which can control the proportion of the velocity of this generation in the velocity of the next generation. u provided a stochastic disturbance to a particle is an independent and identically distributed n-dimensional vector in order to change direction of velocity of the particle. Termination conditions are set according to different problems.

3 Running-Time Analysis for PSO-SP

3.1 Problem Description and Average Gain Model

Definition 1 (Minimization problem). Let $S \subseteq R^n$ be a subspace on n-dimensional real number field R^n. $f : S \to R$ is expressed as n-dimensional real number function. (S, f) means to find a n-dimensional vector $x_{min} \in S$ to obtain $\forall x \in S, f(x_{min}) \le f(x)$.

Sphere Function Expression is as following:

$$f(x) = \sqrt{\sum_{i=1}^{n} x_i^2}$$

while $x = (x_1, x_2, \ldots, x_n) \in R^n$, $f(x)$ is equal to Euclidean distance of x to origin.

$f(x)$ is regarded as a target function of PSO-SP. In each iteration, the algorithm calculates x_{t+1} based on the current solution x_t.

Definition 2 (Fitness difference). Let $d : S \to R$ satisfies $d(x) = f(x) - f(x^*)$, $\forall x \in S$. x^* represents an optimum solution, d represents fitness difference function [2].

It is obvious that $d(x^*)$ equals to 0. For example, S is n-dimensional real space R^n in sphere function. $f(x^*)$ equals to 0, thus, $d(x)$ equals to $f(x)$.

Definition 3 (Average running time). For $0 \le a < b$, if a fitness difference of an initial solution $d(x_0) = b$, then $T|_a^b = min\{t | d(x_t) \le a\}$ means running time of the algorithm through the interval $[a, b]$. $E\left(T|_a^b\right)$ represents average running time when PSO-SP runs from fitness difference b to fitness difference a. Assume $d(x_0) = \sqrt{n}$, then the mean time of PSO-SP is $E\left(T|_\varepsilon^{\sqrt{n}}\right)$. Under satisfaction of accuracy $\varepsilon > 0$, average running-time is expressed as $E\left(T|_\varepsilon^{\sqrt{n}}\right)$ [2].

Lemma 1. Let $V := min\{E(d(x_t) - d(x_{t+1})) | t \in N\} > 0$, running-time of fitness difference of PSO-SP is $T|_0^{d(x_0)}$ through $[0, d(x_0)]$ and expectation $E\left(T|_0^{d(x_0)}\right)$ satisfies [2]

$$E\left(T|_0^{d(x_0)}\right) \le \frac{d(x_0)}{V}$$

While x_t is a stochastic variable of the tth generation in a variable space S, x_0 equals to an initial individual. See Appendix A for proof.

Definition 4 (Average Gain Model). $G(r,t) = E(d(x_t - x_{t+1}|x_t = r)$ is average gain about fitness difference in t moment for PSO-SP. u has no connection with iteration time t because every dimension of u in PSO-SP is independent and subjects to uniform distribution or standard normal distribution. Thus, $G(r,t)$ is not related with iteration time t, called $G(r)$ [2].

$G(r)$ represents expectation fitness difference between x_t and x_{t+1}. Evolutional individuals of PSO-SP can approach to mean velocity of global best solution. Definition 4 and Lemma 1 provide a method of average calculation time of PSO-SP. Theorems 1 and 2 and Corollary 1 can illustrate it. Compared to average drift [16], average gain model is suitable to be used to analyze running-time of algorithm whose solution is continuously.

Theorem 1. Set $d(x_0) = L$, if $G(r)$ is integrable, average calculation time reached accuracy ε satisfies $E(T|_\varepsilon^L) \leq \int_\varepsilon^L 1/G(r)dr$. See Appendix B for proof [2].

Theorem 2. Set $d(x_0) = L$, if $G(r)$ is integrable, average calculation time reached accuracy ε satisfies $E(T|_\varepsilon^L) \geq \int_\varepsilon^L 1/G(r)dr$. See Appendix C for proof [2].

Proof. Theorems 1 and 2 can obtain $E(T|_\varepsilon^L) = \int_\varepsilon^L 1/G(r)dr$.

Distribution density functions are expressed as [2]

$$f_1(x) = \frac{1}{\sqrt{2\pi}}e^{-\frac{x^2}{2}}$$

$$f_2(x) = \begin{cases} \frac{1}{2}, x \in (-1,1), \\ 0, x \notin (-1,1). \end{cases}$$

u satisfies $(-1, 1)$ of uniform distribution for PSO-SP which is called PSO-SP-I. In addition, u satisfies standard normal distribution for PSO-SP which is named PSO-SP-II. Initial solutions of PSO-SP-I and PSO-SP-II set $x_0 = \left(\frac{1}{2\sqrt{n}}, \frac{1}{2\sqrt{n}}, \cdots, \frac{1}{2\sqrt{n}}\right)$ and $d(x_0) = 0.5$. Thus, average calculation time of PSO-SP-I is $E\left(T|_\varepsilon^{0.5}\right)$.

3.2   Running-Time Analysis for PSO-SP-I of Uniform Distribution

Lemma 2. $E[d(x'_{t+1}) - d(x_{t+1})|d(x'_{t+1}) = r]$ satisfies [2]:

$E[d(x'_{t+1}) - d(x_{t+1})|d(x'_{t+1}) = r] = 2^{-n} \cdot r^{n+1} \cdot \sqrt{\pi}^n/(\Gamma(\frac{n}{2}+1) \cdot (n+1))$. See Appendix D for proof.

Lemma 3. In PSO-SP-I, $G(r)$ satisfies:

$$\begin{aligned} G(r) &= E[d(x_t) - d(x_{t+1})|d(x_t) = r] \\ &= E[d(x'_{t+1}) - d(x_{t+1})|d(x'_{t+1}) = r'] + r - r' \\ &\geq E[d(x'_{t+1}) - d(x_{t+1})|d(x'_{t+1}) = r] \end{aligned}$$

See Appendix F for proof.

Average gain $G(r)$ of PSO-SP-I is obtained from Lemmas 2 and 3.

Lemma 4. If $r \leq 0.5$, average gain of PSO-SP-I satisfies [2]:

$$G(r) \geq 2^{-n} \cdot r^{n+1} \cdot \sqrt{\pi}^n / \left(\Gamma \left(\frac{n}{2} + 1 \right) \cdot (n+1) \right)$$

It can be proved by Lemmas 2 and 3.

According to Lemma 4, average gain G(r) of PSO-SP-I is integrable in real number field. Therefore, Theorem 3 can be concluded from Corollary 1.

Theorem 3. In PSO-SP-I, the initial solution satisfies $d(x_0) = 0.5$, the accuracy of average calculation time reached $d(x_t) \leq \varepsilon$ satisfies [2]:

$$E\left(T|_\varepsilon^{0.5} \right) \leq \Gamma \left(\frac{n}{2} + 1 \right) \cdot (n+1)/n \cdot 2^n / \sqrt{\pi}^n \cdot \left(\frac{1}{\varepsilon^n} - \frac{1}{0.5^n} \right)$$

See Appendix G for proof.

Thus, running-time complexity of PSO-SP-I is $\Theta \left(\Gamma \left(\frac{n}{2} + 1 \right) \cdot \left(\frac{2}{\varepsilon \sqrt{\pi}} \right)^n \right)$.

3.3   Running-Time Analysis for PSO-SP-II of Standard Normal Distribution

Lemma 5. A mathematical expectation $E\left[d(x'_{t+1}) - d(x_{t+1}) | d(x'_{t+1}) = r \right]$ in PSO-SP-II satisfies [2]:

$$\frac{e^{-\frac{r^2}{2}} \cdot r^{n+1}}{\Gamma \left(\frac{n}{2} + 1 \right) \cdot (\sqrt{2})^n \cdot (n+1)} \leq E\left[d(x'_{t+1}) - d(x_{t+1}) | d(x'_{t+1}) = r \right]$$

$$\leq \frac{r^{n+1}}{\Gamma \left(\frac{n}{2} + 1 \right) \cdot (\sqrt{2})^n \cdot (n+1)}$$

See Appendix H for proof.

Lemma 6. G(r) in PSO-SP-II satisfies

$$\begin{aligned} G(r) &= E[d(x_t) - d(x_{t+1}) | d(x_t) = r] \\ &= E\left[d(x'_{t+1}) - d(x_{t+1}) | d(x'_{t+1}) = r' \right] + r - r' \\ &\geq E\left[d(x'_{t+1}) - d(x_{t+1}) | d(x'_{t+1}) = r \right] \end{aligned}$$

The proof process is similar with Lemma 3.

Lemma 7. if $r \leq 0.5$, Average gain $G(r)$ of PSO-SP-II satisfies [2]

$$G(r) \geq \frac{e^{-\frac{r^2}{2}} \cdot r^{n+1}}{\Gamma(\frac{n}{2}+1) \cdot (\sqrt{2})^n \cdot (n+1)}$$

The proof can be obtained according to Lemmas 5 and 6.

Theorem 4. Initial solution x_0 satisfies $d(x_0) = 0.5$, the accuracy of average calculation time reached $d(x_t) \leq \varepsilon$ in PSO-SP-II satisfies [2]

$$E\left(T|_{\varepsilon}^{0.5}\right) < \Gamma\left(\frac{n}{2}+1\right) \cdot (n+1)/n \cdot \left(\sqrt{2}\right)^n \cdot \frac{1}{n \cdot \varepsilon^n}$$

See Appendix I for proof.

Thus, running-time complexity of PSO-SP-II is $\Theta\left(\Gamma(\frac{n}{2}+1) \cdot \left(\frac{\sqrt{2}}{\varepsilon}\right)^n\right)$.

3.4 Comparative Analysis of Running-Time Complexity

Given the same accuracy ε and initial fitness difference $d(x_0) = 0.5$, running-time complexity of two algorithms can be obtained according to Theorem 4 and Theorem 5. t_1 represents average calculation time of PSO-SP-I, t_2 represents average calculation time of PSO-SP-II, they satisfy:

$$\lim_{n \to +\infty} \frac{t_2}{t_1} = \lim_{n \to +\infty} \frac{\Gamma(\frac{n}{2}+1) \cdot \left(\frac{\sqrt{2}}{\varepsilon}\right)^n}{\Gamma(\frac{n}{2}+1) \cdot \left(\frac{2}{\varepsilon\sqrt{\pi}}\right)^n} = \left(\sqrt{\frac{\pi}{2}}\right)^n = +\infty, \quad \lim_{n \to +\infty} \frac{t_1}{t_2} = 0.$$

Running-time complexity of PSO-SP-I is lower than PSO-SP-II's. That means stochastic disturbance with uniform distribution is better than that with standard normal distribution when the algorithm solves sphere function.

In order to verify the validity of the theoretical analysis, an experiment that compares the running-time on PSO-SP-I and PSO-SP-II for sphere function. The dimension of the problem n = 5 and n = 10. The parameter of velocity w is 0.8. The result is shown in Fig. 1. The left one is n = 5, and the right one is n = 10. The result show that the running-time of PSO-SP-I is smaller than that of PSO-SP-II.

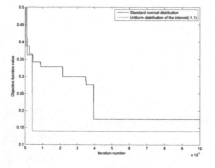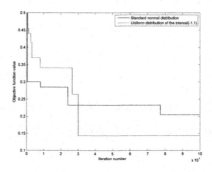

Fig. 1. Comparison of the running-time on PSO-SP-I and PSO-SP-II

4 Conclusion

In the field of swarm intelligence, running-time analysis of PSO is a difficult challenge. In this study, we conduct running-time analysis of PSO-SP based on average gain model. We estimate average gain of PSO-SP with stochastic disturbance in two situations. Then, the mean of average calculation time is estimated. Last, running-time analyses for PSO-SP with stochastic disturbance in two situations are compared. Solving sphere function, running-time of PSO-SP with stochastic disturbance of standard normal distribution is better than that of uniform distribution.

In the future, the research will focus on running-time analysis of general PSO. The effect of the own best and the global best should be studied.

Acknowledgement. This work is supported by National Natural Science Foundation of China (61370102), Guangdong Natural Science Funds for Distinguished Young Scholar (2014A030 306050), the Ministry of Education - China Mobile Research Funds (MCM20160206) and Guangdong High-level personnel of special support program (2014TQ01X664).

Appendix A Proof of Lemma 1

$T|_0^{d(x_0)}$ is simply equal to T, the probability of calculation time t is $P(T = t)$ and the difference of fitness difference is $D_t = d(x_t) - d(x_{t+1})$, $d(x_0)$ satisfies

$$d(x_0) \geq E\left(\sum_{t=0}^{T-1} D_t\right) = \sum_{t=0}^{+\infty} P(T = t) \cdot E\left(\sum_{i=0}^{T-1} D_i | T = t\right)$$

$$= \sum_{t=0}^{+\infty} P(T = t) \cdot \sum_{i=0}^{T-1} E(D_i | T = t)$$

$$= \sum_{t=0}^{+\infty} \sum_{i=0}^{t} P(T = t) \cdot E(D_i | T = t)$$

$$= \sum_{i=0}^{+\infty} \sum_{t=i}^{+\infty} P(T = t) \cdot E(D_i | T = t)$$

$$\geq \sum_{i=0}^{+\infty} \sum_{t=i}^{+\infty} P(T \geq i) \cdot P(T = t | T \geq i) \cdot E(D_i | T = t)$$

$$= \sum_{i=0}^{+\infty} P(T \geq i) \cdot \sum_{t=i}^{+\infty} P(T = t | T \geq i) \cdot E(D_i | T = t \wedge T \geq i)$$

$$= \sum_{i=0}^{+\infty} P(T \geq i) \cdot E(D_i | T = t) \geq V \cdot \sum_{i=0}^{+\infty} P(T \geq i)$$

$$= V \cdot \sum_{i=0}^{+\infty} \sum_{j=i}^{+\infty} P(T = j) = V \cdot \sum_{i=0}^{+\infty} i \cdot P(T = t) \geq V \cdot E(T)$$

Thus, when $V \neq 0$, $E(T) \leq \frac{d(x_0)}{V}$.

Appendix B Proof of Theorem 1

Given l $(\varepsilon < l < L)$, consider a subinterval $Z' = \{x | l < d(x) \leq l + \Delta l\}$, difine a fitness difference function $d'(x) = d(x) - l$. Begin right point of the subinterval $d(x_0 = l + \Delta l)$, reach left subinterval through $T|_l^{l+\Delta l}$. Average calculation time $E\left(T|_l^{l+\Delta l}\right)$ satisfies when $V' := min\{E(d'(x_t) - d'(x_{t+1}) | t \in N\}$

$$E\left(T|_l^{l+\Delta l}\right) \leq \frac{d'(x_0)}{V} = \frac{\Delta l}{min\{E(d'(x_t) - d'(x_{t+1}) | 0 \leq d'(x_t) \leq \Delta l\}}$$

$$= \frac{\Delta l}{min\{E(d(x_t) - d(x_{t+1}) | l \leq d(x_t) \leq l + \Delta l\}}$$

$$= \frac{\Delta l}{min\{G(r) | l \leq r \leq l + \Delta l\}}$$

$G(r)$ is an increasing function, $min\{G(r) | l \leq r \leq l + \Delta l\} = G(l)$, thus $E\left(T|_l^{l+\Delta l}\right)$
$\leq \frac{\Delta l}{G(l)}$.

According to Riemann integral, average calculation time of PSO-SP is

$$E(T|_\varepsilon^L) = \lim_{n \to +\infty} \sum_{i=1}^n E\left(T|_{y_i-1}^{y_i}\right) \leq \lim_{\gamma \to 0} \sum_{i=1}^n 1/G(y_{i-1})^{\Delta y_i} = \int_\varepsilon^L 1/G(r)^{dr}$$

The interval is separated n: $\varepsilon = y_0 < y_1 < \ldots < y_{n-1} < y_n = L$.

Appendix C Proof of Theorem 2

According to Riemann integral, The interval is separated to n subinterval: $\varepsilon = y_0 < y_1 < \ldots < y_{n-1} < y_n = L$, $E(T|_\varepsilon^L) = \lim_{n \to +\infty} \sum_{i=1}^n E\left(T|_{y_i-1}^{y_i}\right)$ can be given while $i = 1, 2, \ldots, n$,

$$E\left(T|_{y_i-1}^{y_i}\right) = \int_0^{+\infty} t \cdot g_T(t) dt = \int_0^{+\infty} g_{D_t}(r) \cdot \frac{\Delta y_i}{r} dr$$

$g_T(t)$ means a probability density function through $[y_{i-1}, y_i]$, $g_{D_t}(r)$ represents a probability density function of current steps and satisfies $t = \frac{\Delta y_i}{r}$.

Cauchy inequality: $\int_0^{+\infty} g_{D_t}(r) \cdot \frac{1}{r} dr \cdot \int_0^{+\infty} g_{D_t}(r) \cdot r dr \geq \left(\int_0^{+\infty} g_{D_t}(r) dr\right)^2 = 1$, and then $\int_0^{+\infty} g_{D_t}(r) \cdot \frac{\Delta y_i}{r} dr \geq \frac{\Delta y_i}{\int_0^{+\infty} g_{D_t}(r) \cdot r dr} = \frac{\Delta y_i}{G(x_i)}$.

Thus it can prove:

$$E(T|_\varepsilon^L) = \lim_{n \to +\infty} \sum_{i=1}^n E\left(T|_{y_i-1}^{y_i}\right) \geq \lim_{n \to +\infty} \sum_{i=1}^n \frac{\Delta y_i}{G(x_i)} = \int_\varepsilon^L 1/G(r) dr$$

Appendix D Proof of Lemma 2

$$E[d(x'_{t+1}) - d(x_{t+1})|d(x'_{t+1}) = r] = \int_{\delta_1} f_{x_{t+1}}(x|d(x'_{t+1}) = r)(r - d(x))dx$$

while $\delta_1 = \{x|d(x) < r\}$, if $d(x'_{t+1}) = r$, probability density function of x_{t+1} is $f_{x_{t+1}}(x|d(x'_{t+1}) = r)$.

Let $\delta_2 = \{x||(x - x'_{t+1})_i| \leq 1, i = 1, 2, \ldots, n\}$, a random process of uniform distribution in $(-1, 1)$, if $|x_i| > 1 (i = 1, 2, \ldots, n)$, $f_u(x) = 0$ ($f_u(x)$ means probability density function of u). Thus, in the space of $R^n - \delta_2 = \{x||(x - x'_{t+1})_i| > 1, i = 1, 2, \ldots, n\}, f_{x_{t+1}}(x|d(x'_{t+1}) = r) = 0$, it satisfies

$$E[d(x'_{t+1}) - d(x_{t+1})|d(x'_{t+1}) = r] = \int_{\delta} f_{x_{t+1}}(x|d(x'_{t+1}) = r)(r - d(x))dx$$

Here, $\delta = \delta_1 \cap \delta_2$. Because $|x| \neq 0$ and $r \leq 0.5$, there is $|d(x)| < |x|$, that means $\delta_1 \cap \delta_2 = \delta_1$, $\delta = \delta_1$.

$\delta_1 = \{x|d(x) < r\}$ is a high-dimensional sphere, its integration satisfies

$$\int_{\delta} f_{x_{t+1}}(x|d(x'_{t+1}) = r)(r - d(x))dx = \left(\frac{1}{2^n}\right) \int_{\delta} (r - d(x))dx$$

According to Appendix E, when $r \leq 0.5$, there is

$$E[d(x'_{t+1}) - d(x_{t+1})|d(x'_{t+1}) = r] = 2^{-n} \cdot r^{n+1} \cdot \sqrt{\pi}^n / \left(\Gamma\left(\frac{n}{2} + 1\right) \cdot (n + 1)\right)$$

Appendix E Calculate $\int_{\delta}(r - d(x))dx$

According to definition B function $B(m+1, n+1) = 2\int_0^{\pi/2}(cosx)^{2m+1}(sinx)^{2n+1}dx$, thus $\int_0^{\pi/2}(sinx)^k dx = \frac{1}{2} \cdot B\left(\frac{1}{2}, \frac{k+1}{2}\right), k \in N$.

Because $B(m, n) = \Gamma(m) \cdot \Gamma(n)/\Gamma(m+n)$, $\Gamma(1/2) = \sqrt{\pi}$, there is

$$\int_0^{\pi} (sinx)^k dx = 2\int_0^{\pi/2}(sinx)^k dx = B\left(\frac{1}{2}, \frac{k+1}{2}\right) = \sqrt{\pi} \cdot \frac{\Gamma\left(\frac{k}{2} + \frac{1}{2}\right)}{\Gamma\left(\frac{k}{2} + 1\right)}$$

l replaces r in order to calculate easily $\int_{\delta}(r - d(x))dx$,

$$\int_{r=0}^{l}\int_{\beta_n=0}^{\pi}\int_{\beta_{n-1}=0}^{\pi}\cdots\int_{\beta_3=0}^{\pi}\int_{\alpha=0}^{2\pi}(l-r)dr(rsin\beta_n\ldots sin\beta_3 d\alpha)\ldots(rd\beta_n)$$

$$=\int_{r=0}^{l}\int_{\beta_n=0}^{\pi}\int_{\beta_{n-1}=0}^{\pi}\cdots\int_{\beta_3=0}^{\pi}\int_{\alpha=0}^{2\pi}(l-r)dr(rsin\beta_n\ldots sin\beta_3 d\alpha)(rsin\beta_n\ldots sin\beta_4 d\beta_3)\ldots(rd\beta_n)$$

$$=l\int_{r=0}^{l}\int_{\beta_n=0}^{\pi}\int_{\beta_{n-1}=0}^{\pi}\cdots\int_{\beta_3=0}^{\pi}\int_{\alpha=0}^{2\pi}dr(rsin\beta_n\ldots sin\beta_3 d\alpha)(rsin\beta_n\ldots sin\beta_4 d\beta_3)\ldots(rd\beta_n)$$

$$-\int_{r=0}^{l}\int_{\beta_n=0}^{\pi}\int_{\beta_{n-1}=0}^{\pi}\cdots\int_{\beta_3=0}^{\pi}\int_{\alpha=0}^{2\pi}dr(rsin\beta_n\ldots sin\beta_3 d\alpha)(rsin\beta_n\ldots sin\beta_4 d\beta_3)\ldots(rd\beta_n)$$

$$=l\int_{r=0}^{l}dr\cdot r^{n-1}\cdot 2\pi\cdot\prod_{i=0}^{n-2}\int_{\beta=0}^{\pi}(sin\beta)^i d\beta-\int_{r=0}^{l}rdr\cdot r^{n-1}\cdot 2\pi$$

$$\cdot\prod_{i=1}^{n-2}\int_{\beta=0}^{\pi}(sin\beta)^i d\beta$$

$$=l\int_{r=0}^{l}dr\cdot r^{n-1}\cdot 2\pi\cdot\prod_{i=1}^{n-2}B\left(\frac{1}{2},\frac{i+1}{2}\right)-\int_{r=0}^{l}rdr\cdot r^{n-1}\cdot 2\pi\cdot\prod_{i=1}^{n-2}B\left(\frac{1}{2},\frac{i+1}{2}\right)$$

$$=l\int_{r=0}^{l}dr\cdot r^{n-1}\cdot 2\sqrt{\pi}^n/\Gamma(n/2)-\int_{r=0}^{l}rdr\cdot r^{n-1}\cdot 2\sqrt{\pi}^n/\Gamma(n/2)$$

$$=l\cdot\sqrt{\pi}^n\cdot l^n/\Gamma(n/2+1)-1/(n+1)\cdot l^{n+1}\cdot 2\sqrt{\pi}^n/\Gamma(n/2)$$

$$=l^{n+1}\cdot\sqrt{\pi}^n/\Gamma(n/2)\cdot 2/n-1/(n+1)\cdot l^{n+1}\cdot 2\sqrt{\pi}^n/\Gamma(n/2)$$

$$=l^{n+1}\cdot\sqrt{\pi}^n/(\Gamma(n/2+1)\cdot(n+1))$$

Appendix F Proof of Lemma 3

$$E[d(x'_{t+1})-d(x_{t+1})|d(x'_{t+1})=r]-E[d(x'_{t+1})-d(x_{t+1})|d(x'_{t+1})=r']$$

$$-(r-r')=\frac{r^{n+1}-r'^{n+1}}{2^n\cdot\Gamma\left(\frac{n}{2}+1\right)\cdot(n+1)}-(r-r')$$

$$=\frac{(r-r')\cdot\sum_{i=1}^{n}r^{n-i}\cdot r'^{i-1}}{2^n\cdot\Gamma\left(\frac{n}{2}+1\right)\cdot(n+1)}-(r-r')$$

$$=\left(\frac{\sum_{i=1}^{n}r^{n-i}\cdot r'^{i-1}}{2^n\cdot\Gamma\left(\frac{n}{2}+1\right)\cdot(n+1)}-1\right)\cdot(r-r')$$

Obviously:

$$\frac{\sum_{i=1}^{n}r^{n-i}\cdot r'^{i-1}}{2^n\cdot\Gamma\left(\frac{n}{2}+1\right)\cdot(n+1)}-1<0$$

Therefore:

$$E\left[d\left(x'_{t+1}\right) - d(x_{t+1}) \mid d\left(x'_{t+1}\right) = r\right] - E\left[d\left(x'_{t+1}\right) - d(x_{t+1}) \mid d\left(x'_{t+1}\right) = r'\right]$$

$$- (r - r') = \left(\frac{\sum_{i=1}^{n} r^{n-i} \cdot r'^{i-1}}{2^n \cdot \Gamma\left(\frac{n}{2} + 1\right) \cdot (n+1)} - 1\right) \cdot (r - r') \leq 0$$

$$E\left[d\left(x'_{t+1}\right) - d(x_{t+1}) \mid d\left(x'_{t+1}\right) = r'\right] + r - r' \geq E\left[d\left(x'_{t+1}\right) - d(x_{t+1}) \mid d\left(x'_{t+1}\right) = r\right]$$

Appendix G Proof of Theorem 3

$$
\begin{aligned}
E\left(T\big|_{\varepsilon}^{0.5}\right) &\leq \int_{\varepsilon}^{0.5} \frac{1}{G_1(r)}\, dr = \int_{\varepsilon}^{0.5} \Gamma\left(\frac{n}{2}+1\right) \cdot (n+1) \cdot r^{-(n+1)} \cdot \frac{\sqrt{\pi}^{-n}}{2^{-n}}\, dr \\
&= \Gamma\left(\frac{n}{2}+1\right) \cdot (n+1) \cdot \int_{\varepsilon}^{0.5} r^{-(n+1)} \cdot \sqrt{\pi}^{-n} \cdot 2^n dr \\
&= \Gamma\left(\frac{n}{2}+1\right) \cdot (n+1) \cdot \sqrt{\pi}^{-n} \cdot 2^n \cdot \int_{\varepsilon}^{0.5} r^{-(n+1)} dr \\
&= \Gamma\left(\frac{n}{2}+1\right) \cdot \frac{(n+1)}{n} \cdot \sqrt{\pi}^{-n} \cdot 2^n \cdot \left(-\frac{1}{n} \cdot r^{-n}\big|_{r=\varepsilon}^{0.5}\right) \\
&= \Gamma\left(\frac{n}{2}+1\right) \cdot \frac{(n+1)}{n} \cdot \sqrt{\pi}^{-n} \cdot 2^n \cdot \left(\varepsilon^{-n} - 0.5^{-n}\right) \\
&= \Gamma\left(\frac{n}{2}+1\right) \cdot (n+1)/n \cdot 2^n / \sqrt{\pi}^{n} \cdot \left(\frac{1}{\varepsilon^n} - \frac{1}{0.5^n}\right)
\end{aligned}
$$

Appendix H Proof of Lemma 5

$$E\left[d\left(x'_{t+1}\right) - d(x_{t+1}) \mid d\left(x'_{t+1}\right) = r\right] = \int_{\delta} f_{x_{t+1}}\left(x \mid d\left(x'_{t+1}\right) = r\right)(r - d(x))dx \quad \text{(H1)}$$

While $\delta = \{x \mid d(x) < r\}$, if $d\left(x'_{t+1}\right) = r, f_{x_{t+1}}\left(x \mid d\left(x'_{t+1}\right) = r\right)$ represents probability density function of x_{t+1}.

While $d(x_{t+1}) < d\left(x'_{t+1}\right) = r$, x_{t+1} belongs to δ, $x_{t+1} = x'_{t+1} + u$, thus $f_{x_{t+1}}\left(x \mid d\left(x'_{t+1}\right) = r\right)$ equals to $f_u(x)$. While $u = x_{t+1} - x'_{t+1}$, $f_u(x)$ is probability density function of u.

$$f_u(x) = \prod_{i=1}^{n} f_2(x_i) = \frac{1}{\left(\sqrt{2\pi}\right)^n} \cdot e^{-\frac{d(x)^2}{2}}$$

$f_u(x)$ decreases when u decreases, $0 \le d(u) \le 2d(x'_{t+1}) = 2r$, thus

$$\frac{1}{\left(\sqrt{2\pi}\right)^n} \cdot e^{-\frac{d(x)^2}{2}} \le f_u(x) \le \frac{1}{\left(\sqrt{2\pi}\right)^n}$$

$$\frac{1}{\left(\sqrt{2\pi}\right)^n} \cdot e^{-\frac{d(x)^2}{2}} \le f_{x_{t+1}}\left(x|d(x'_{t+1}) = r\right) \le \frac{1}{\left(\sqrt{2\pi}\right)^n}$$

Into H1, there is

$$\frac{1}{\left(\sqrt{2\pi}\right)^n} \cdot e^{-\frac{d(x)^2}{2}} \cdot \int_{\delta} f_{x_{t+1}}\left(x|d(x'_{t+1}) = r\right) dx \le E\left[d(x'_{t+1}) - d(x_{t+1})|d(x'_{t+1}) = r\right]$$

$$\le \frac{1}{\left(\sqrt{2\pi}\right)^n} \cdot \int_{\delta} f_{x_{t+1}}\left(x|d(x'_{t+1}) = r\right) dx$$

Combine Appendix E, it can obtain

$$\frac{e^{-\frac{2}{2}} \cdot r^{n+1}}{\Gamma\left(\frac{n}{2} + 1\right) \cdot \left(\sqrt{2}\right)^n \cdot (n+1)} \le E\left[d(x'_{t+1}) - d(x_{t+1})|d(x'_{t+1}) = r\right]$$

$$\le \frac{r^{n+1}}{\Gamma\left(\frac{n}{2} + 1\right) \cdot \left(\sqrt{2}\right)^n \cdot (n+1)}$$

Appendix I Proof of Theorem 4

$$E\left(T|_{\varepsilon}^{0.5}\right) \le \int_{\varepsilon}^{0.5} \frac{1}{G_l(r)} dr \le \Gamma\left(\frac{n}{2} + 1\right) \cdot (n+1) \cdot \left(\sqrt{2}\right)^n \int_{\varepsilon}^{0.5} r^{-(n+1)} \cdot e^{2r^2} dr$$

$$< \Gamma\left(\frac{n}{2} + 1\right) \cdot (n+1) \cdot \left(\sqrt{2}\right)^n \cdot e^2 \cdot \int_{\varepsilon}^{0.5} r^{-(n+1)} dr$$

$$= \Gamma\left(\frac{n}{2} + 1\right) \cdot (n+1) \cdot \left(\sqrt{2}\right)^n \cdot e^2 \cdot \left(\frac{-1}{n \cdot (0.5)^n} + \frac{1}{n \cdot \varepsilon^n}\right)$$

$$< \Gamma\left(\frac{n}{2} + 1\right) \cdot (n+1)/n \cdot \left(\sqrt{2}\right)^n \cdot \frac{1}{n \cdot \varepsilon^n}$$

References

1. Jägersküpper, J.: How the $(1 + 1)$ ES using isotropic mutations minimizes positive definite quadratic forms. Theor. Comput. Sci. **361**(1), 38–56 (2006)
2. Huang, H., Xu, W.D., Zhang, Y.S., Lin, Z.Y., Hao, Z.F.: Runtime analysis for continuous $(1 + 1)$ evolutionary algorithm based on average gain model. Sci. China **44**, 811–824 (2014)
3. Kennedy, J., Eberhart, R.: Particle swarm optimization. In: 1995 IEEE International Conference on Neural Networks, pp. 1942–1948 (1995)
4. Yao, X., Xu, Y.: Recent advances in evolutionary computation. J. Comput. Sci. Technol. **21**, 1–18 (2006)
5. Shi, Y., Eberhart, R.: A modified particle swarm optimizer. In: 1998 IEEE International Conference on Evolutionary Computation Proceedings. IEEE World Congress on Computational Intelligence, pp. 69–73. IEEE (1998)
6. He, J., Yao, X.: Drift analysis and average time complexity of evolutionary algorithms. Artif. Intell. **127**(1), 57–85 (2002)
7. He, J., Yao, X.: From an individual to a population: an analysis of the first hitting time of population-based evolutionary algorithms. IEEE Trans. Evol. Comput. **6**(5), 495–511 (2008)
8. Oliveto, Pietro S., Witt, C.: Simplified drift analysis for proving lower bounds in evolutionary computation. In: Rudolph, G., Jansen, T., Beume, N., Lucas, S., Poloni, C. (eds.) PPSN 2008. LNCS, vol. 5199, pp. 82–91. Springer, Heidelberg (2008). doi:10.1007/978-3-540-87700-4_9
9. Gutjahr, W.J.: First steps to the runtime complexity analysis of ant colony optimization. Comput. Oper. Res. **35**(9), 2711–2727 (2008)
10. Doerr, B., Neumann, F., Sudholt, D., Witt, C.: On the runtime analysis of the 1-ANT ACO algorithm. In: Conference on Genetic and Evolutionary Computation. vol. 65, pp. 33–40. ACM (2007)
11. Sudholt, D., Witt, C.: Runtime analysis of binary PSO. In: Conference on Genetic and Evolutionary Computation, pp. 135–142. ACM (2008)
12. Qian, C., Yu, Y., Zhou, Z.H.: An analysis on recombination in multi-objective evolutionary optimization. Artif. Intell. **204**(204), 99–119 (2013)
13. Qian, C., Tang, K., Zhou, Z.-H.: Selection hyper-heuristics can provably be helpful in evolutionary multi-objective optimization. In: Handl, J., Hart, E., Lewis, P.R., López-Ibáñez, M., Ochoa, G., Paechter, B. (eds.) PPSN 2016. LNCS, vol. 9921, pp. 835–846. Springer, Cham (2016). doi:10.1007/978-3-319-45823-6_78
14. Qian, C., Yu, Y., Zhou, Z.H.: Analyzing evolutionary optimization in noisy environments. Evol. Comput. 1 (2013)
15. Qian, C., Yu, Y., Jin, Y., Zhou, Z.H.: On the effectiveness of sampling for evolutionary optimization in noisy environments. In: Parallel Problem Solving from Nature – PPSN XIII. Springer, Heidelberg, pp. 33–55 (2014)
16. He, J., Yao, X.: Average drift analysis and population scalability. IEEE Trans. Evol. Comput. **21**(3), 426–439 (2017)
17. Rowe, J.E., Sudholt, D.: The choice of the offspring population size in the $(1, \lambda)$ EA. Theor. Comput. Sci. **545**(545), 20–38 (2014)
18. Witt, C.: Why standard particle swarm optimisers elude a theoretical runtime analysis. In: ACM SIGEVO International Workshop on Foundations of Genetic Algorithms, FOGA 2009, Proceedings, Orlando, Florida, USA, January 9–11, 2009, pp. 13–20. DBLP (2009)
19. Lehre, P.K., Witt, C.: Finite first hitting time versus stochastic convergence in particle swarm optimisation. **53**, 1–20 (2011)

Evolutionary Computation Theory for Remote Sensing Image Clustering: A Survey

Yuting Wan, Yanfei Zhong, Ailong Ma$^{(\boxtimes)}$, and Liangpei Zhang

State Key Laboratory of Information Engineering in Surveying, Mapping,
and Remote Sensing, Wuhan University, Wuhan 430000, China
Csu_wyt@163.com, {zhongyanfei,maailong007}@whu.edu.cn

Abstract. This paper presents a survey of evolutionary computation theory for remote sensing image clustering. With the ongoing development of Earth observation techniques, remote sensing data has entered the era of big data, so it is difficult for researchers to get more prior knowledge. In recent years, many experts and scholars have a strong interest in remote sensing clustering due to it does not require training samples. However, remote sensing image clustering has always been a challenging task because of the inherent complexity of remote sensing images, the huge amount of data and so on. Normally, the clustering problem of remote sensing images is transformed into the optimization problem of fuzzy clustering objective function, the goal of which lies in the identification of correct cluster centers in the eigenspace. But traditional clustering approaches belong to hill climbing methods, which are greatly affected by initial values and easily get stuck in local optima. Evolutionary computation techniques are inspired by biological evolution, which can provide possible solutions to find the better clustering centers. So, researchers have carried out a series of related studies. Here, we provide an overview, including: (1) evolutionary single-objective; (2) evolutionary multi-objective; (3) memetic algorithm.

Keywords: Remote sensing clustering · Evolutionary computation · Evolutionary algorithms

1 Introduction

Clustering, that is unsupervised classification, has been a hot and difficult topic in the field of machine learning and data mining. For remote sensing domain, clustering can solve the remote sensing image classification problem without training samples. The main task of remote sensing clustering is dividing the different ground features in images without any prior information based on some similarity/dissimilarity metric, making the image pixels that belong to the same object category be as similar as possible, while the pixels of different objects are different [1]. In recent years, remote sensing image clustering is attracting more and more attention of researchers.

In other words, the target of remote sensing image clustering can be implemented by finding a set of cluster centers, then the distance metrics are used to assign all the pixels to the corresponding cluster centers. So, the task of clustering a remote sensing image can be transformed into an optimization problem. However, traditional

© Springer International Publishing AG 2017
Y. Shi et al. (Eds.): SEAL 2017, LNCS 10593, pp. 528–539, 2017.
https://doi.org/10.1007/978-3-319-68759-9_43

clustering approaches such as K-means, ISODATA and FCM, as shown in Fig. 1, often make prior assumptions about the cluster structure and adopt a corresponding suitable objective function that is optimized through classical techniques, which are greatly affected by the initial values and easily get stuck in local optima. In [2], it presented a survey of EAs for clustering, indicated EAs have powerful global search capability, and can jump out of the local optimal. So, it demonstrates the effectiveness for finding the cluster center set, and can be transferred to remote sensing image clustering. Of course, EAs based remote sensing image clustering methods also have many outspread applications,such as feature selection for hyper-spectral images classification [3], SAR Image segmentation [4] and retrieval [5], change detection [6] and so on.

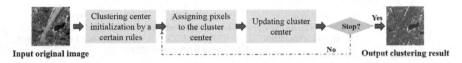

Fig. 1. Frame diagram of remote sensing image clustering

Table 1 gives a summary of the problems in remote sensing image clustering and corresponding solutions through evolutionary computation approaches. In (2), the DB index is the clustering function, which the minimal DB value can indicate the optimal number of categories. In (3), it considers more clustering objective functions, which can represent more image data structure information. In (4), it adds local searcher, which can increase the probability of searching for the superior solutions.

Table 1. The problems in remote sensing image clustering and corresponding solutions

Problems	Corresponding solutions
(1) Lack of global optimization capability in traditional clustering methods	Using evolutionary algorithms (EAs)
(2) Number of clusters requires manual input	Automatic clustering [8, 11]
(3) Clustering algorithms lack robustness to remote sensing image data or lack consideration for multi-objective functions	Adding the objective functions of spatial information [16]; simultaneously optimizing multiple objective functions (such as Jm, XB and DB, represent a specific structure on the image) by NSGA-II, etc. [23, 37]
(4) The process of clustering optimization lacks local search capability	Introducing memetic algorithms (MAs) [36]

In the next three sections, the second section will respectively elaborate the research progress of three aspects: evolutionary single-objective clustering, evolutionary multi-objective clustering and memetic algorithm based clustering for remote sensing image. The third section will give an experimental comparison of different evolutionary computation based clustering methods. The forth section is a conclusion and outlook.

2 Evolutionary Computation Approaches in Remote Sensing Image Clustering

Firstly, here give a time-ordered research development, as shown in Fig. 2 following.

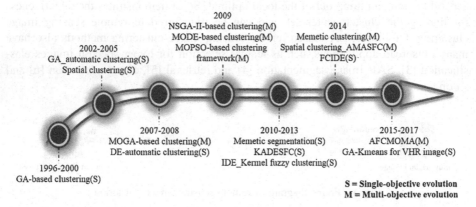

Fig. 2. The research development for EAs-based remote sensing image clustering.

Then, in EAs-based clustering of remote sensing images, the clustering centers are encoded as gene loci for each individual [2], as shown in Fig. 3(c). The ultimate goal of the EAs-based clustering algorithms is to produce an optimal individual through continuous evolution, and take the points in the individual as the clustering centers.

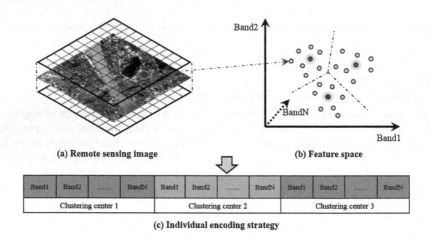

Fig. 3. Encoding strategy for the EAs-based remote sensing image clustering approaches.

In addition, the main idea of the improved clustering algorithms is transforming the remote sensing image clustering process into the optimization process for clustering functions. Evolutionary computation is a stochastic search method based on population, the search process in the solution and the objective space is shown in Fig. 4 (a); the frame of EAs-based remote sensing image clustering is shown in Fig. 4(b).

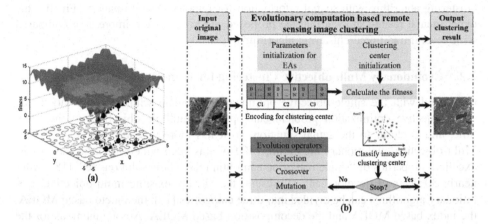

Fig. 4. (a) The search process of individuals in solution space and objective space, (b) frame diagram of EAs-based remote sensing image clustering

Next, the following three parts will be introduced separately.

2.1 Evolutionary Single-Objective Clustering for Remote Sensing Imagery

In the early stage, the complexity of remote sensing data structure was not very high, and because single-objective evolution was simple and effective, so it was first used in remote sensing image clustering. Currently speaking, it has already existed more researches on single-objective optimization based remote sensing image clustering.

As early as in 1996, Murthy and Chowdhury firstly applied genetic algorithm to remote sensing image clustering, attempted to optimize related clustering function in K-means, and tested this approach on both synthetic and real-life data sets [7]. In the next years, on this basis, researchers have carried out many related studies. In [8, 9], Das et al. and Zhang et al. applied the differential evolution algorithm to remote sensing image clustering, where the former used DB index as the clustering objective function while XB index was used in [9]. In [10], Zhong and Zhang proposed clonal selection algorithm based clustering approaches, where the Jm was used as the clustering objective function. In [11–13], Bandyopadhyay and Pakhira et al. applied the genetic algorithm in remote sensing image clustering. The above methods achieved better clustering performance than traditional clustering methods. Among them, in [8, 11, 14], in order to solve the lack of automaticity and intelligence of the clustering process, respectively proposed a novel DE, GA and an improved binary artificial bee colony algorithm based clustering method for automatic evolution of clusters.

And then, considering the abundant spatial information of remote sensing image, researchers considered adding the spatial information to the clustering process to improve the clustering accuracy. In [15], Ma et al. proposed an adaptive differential evolution fuzzy clustering algorithm with spatial information and kernel metric for remote sensing imagery. In [16], Zhong et al. proposed an adaptive memetic fuzzy clustering algorithm with spatial information for remote sensing imagery. Finally, the experimental results showed that the proposed algorithms were impressive compared with several traditional clustering algorithms.

2.2   Evolutionary Multi-objective Clustering for Remote Sensing Imagery

Compared with the single objective optimization problem with only one target, the multi-objective optimization problem can optimize multiple objectives at the same time, and is closer to the actual situation, so it has more practical significance [17]. Multi-objective evolutionary algorithm, MOEA, has been widely used because of its excellent properties of "single operation can obtain the whole solutions set" [18]. After nearly 30 years of development, at present, the already existing multi-objective evolutionary algorithms can be divided into three categories [19]: the Pareto based MOEA, the index based MOEA and the decomposition based MOEA. Among them, as for the traditional Pareto dominated method, the mapping from the decision space to the objective space and the Pareto front is shown in Fig. 5:

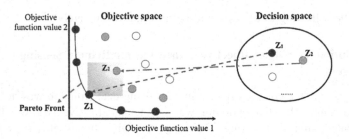

Fig. 5. Pareto dominating and Pareto front.

Similarly, in the field of remote sensing image clustering, when we consider the complex structure of remote sensing data, there may be no single objective function that can perform well on every remote sensing image. Thus, it is natural to simultaneously optimize multiple objective functions to make them complement each other, and achieve a balance between them. Compared with the single-objective clustering methods, multi-objective clustering methods can acquire better results because the multi-objective optimization technique can take more information into consideration.

In [20], Bandyopadhyay et al. firstly used the multi-objective evolution framework—NSGA-II [21] in the remote sensing image clustering, the clustering objective functions Jm and XB were optimized simultaneously. And it achieved better performance than single-objective optimization and traditional remote sensing image clustering methods. After that, more scholars devoted more effort to multi-objective evolutionary clustering for remote sensing image. In [22], Mukhopadhyay and Maulik proposed a clustering method, which combined multi-objective fuzzy clustering scheme (NSGA-II based multi-objective fuzzy clustering) and support vector machine (SVM) classifier in unsupervised classification of satellite images with many homogeneous regions. In [23], Kaushik et al. added the differential evolution algorithm to the multi-objective optimization framework to perform the task of automatic fuzzy clustering. In [24], Paoli et al. designed a new method for clustering the hyper-spectral images within a multi-objective PSO framework, which can simultaneously implement band selection, determination of the cluster number and clustering by simultaneously optimized three clustering objective functions. In [25], Li et al. proposed a quantum-inspired multi-objective evolutionary clustering algorithm for SAR image segmentation. A similar task was implemented in a multi-objective PSO framework in [26]. In addition, in order to improve the stability of decision strategy for clustering numbers in the algorithm mentioned above, Zhong et al. designed a two-layer clustering system comprising an optimization layer and a classification layer [27]. In the optimization layer, the Xie-Beni (XB) index was optimized to acquire the optimal cluster number. In the classification layer, NSGA-II was utilized to minimize the Jm value and the XB index.

Generally speaking, multi-objective clustering methods are preferred over single-objective clustering methods. However, when the remote sensing data structure becomes more complex, which means that it needs more objective functions, the decision and objective space will also be more complex. But at present, for solving high-dimensional optimization problems, the existing methods still fail to obtain satisfactory results, and there are still few related studies. Besides, as for the multi-objective solution set, it is needed a strategy to select the most appropriate solution from the solution set. These years, researcher have presented some decision-making strategy, such as the "technique for order of preference by similarity to ideal solution" (TOPSIS) [26], ratio cut [28] and the angle-based method proposed in [29], which are used to locate these solutions. But in a way, it is still an open issue because these decision-making techniques do not consistently function well in multi-objective clustering methods for remote sensing images. So, when we face the more and more massive and complex remote sensing image data, it still needs a great deal of efforts to improve the multi-objective evolutionary clustering for remote sensing image.

2.3   Memetic Algorithm Based Clustering for Remote Sensing Imagery

Nowadays, researchers generally believe that the performance of an optimization algorithm is determined by two capabilities: exploration and exploitation [30]. The exploration capability ensures the algorithms have global search ability, which can provide a reliable estimate of the global optimal solution; exploitation capability ensures the ability of local search, which can search the neighborhoods of the current optimal solution, the optimal solution with higher quality can be obtained. As early as in 1989, Moscato firstly proposed the concept of memetic algorithm [31]. In [32], it indicated that MAs were a combination of population based hybrid genetic algorithms and a learning that can perform partial improvement, which were proposed to solve the problem by taking advantage of both global and local search. The search process of solutions in objective space is shown in Fig. 6. The effectiveness of the advanced MAs has been demonstrated in many areas, such as feature selection [33], vehicle routing [34] and multi-dimensional knapsack problem [35] and so on.

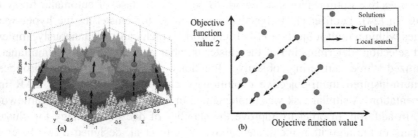

Fig. 6. (a) The search process of MAs in single, (b) multi-objective optimization problems.

In remote sensing image clustering, the performance relies on the optimizer chosen to select the clustering centers. A large number of related researches indicated, the MAs-based clustering methods can achieve better performances than the clustering methods based on individual EAs, due to the fact that MAs can capture a more balanced optimization between global search and local search. In [36], a new image segmentation method based on memetic algorithm was proposed. In this method, the objects were regarded as the processing unit instead of the pixels, local search operations were performed by redistributing the object's tags. Experimental results showed that the proposed method can achieve better performance in preserving details for segmentation results. In [16, 37], a local searcher was designed to combine with DE in single-objective clustering and multi-objective clustering, in which Gaussian mutation was performed on each dimension of the individual, and a new individual was then generated, as shown in Fig. 7. Then, comparing newly generated individuals with old individuals, individuals with higher fitness values were able to survive, the experimental consequences showed that the clustering performance got improved.

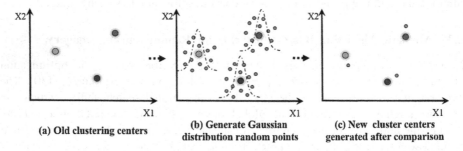

(a) Old clustering centers   (b) Generate Gaussian distribution random points   (c) New cluster centers generated after comparison

Fig. 7. Gaussian local search process

Currently speaking, there are less researches on the MAs based remote sensing image clustering, due to it is indeed a challenging work. In [38], it indicated that it should be careful and adaptive to select local searcher. In a way, an inappropriate choice of local searcher may destroy the diversity of the population and converge to a bad solution. From the existing achievement, although the MAs can introduce the local searchers to improve the performance of the EAs-based remote sensing image clustering, it is hard to automatically achieve an excellent balance between global search and local search. However, in [39], it emphasized that it was a matter of time before we see more demonstrative and ground-breaking applications in this rich research area.

3 Experimental Comparison

In order to empirically compare the above-mentioned clustering methods, we used a 30-m resolution multi-spectral Landsat TM image of Wuhan City, China, with a size of 400 × 400 pixels, and six bands. The selected region of the image was expected to contain five classes, which are listed in Table 2. The original Wuhan TM image and the ground-truth image are shown in Fig. 8(a) and (b).

Table 2. Groundtruth and the corresponding numbers of training samples.

Class	River	Vegetation	Lake	Bare soil	Building
Number	2577	4098	1559	3037	1666

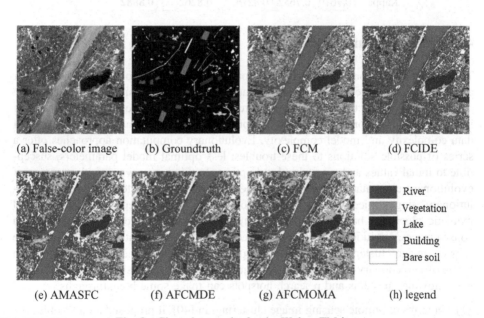

(a) False-color image   (b) Groundtruth   (c) FCM   (d) FCIDE

(e) AMASFC   (f) AFCMDE   (g) AFCMOMA   (h) legend

River
Vegetation
Lake
Building
Bare soil

Fig. 8. Clustering results for the Wuhan TM image

The compared clustering methods were FCM, the automatic fuzzy clustering using an improved differential evolution algorithm (FCIDE) [8], the adaptive memetic fuzzy clustering algorithm with spatial information (AMASFC) [16], the automatic fuzzy clustering method based on adaptive multi-objective differential evolution (AFCMDE)

[27], and the adaptive multi-objective memetic fuzzy clustering algorithm (AFC-MOMA) [37]. A comparison between the different clustering methods with the Wuhan TM image is shown in Fig. 8(c)–(g) and Table 3, where it can be seen that the evolutionary computation based clustering methods can acquire a better clustering accuracy than FCM (81.66%). For FCM, many Building pixels are misclassified as Vegetation pixels. In addition, the multi-objective clustering methods, AFCMDE (86.38%) and AFCMOMA (91.29%), perform better than the single-objective clustering method, FCIDE (81.75%), due to the fact that they can take more information (characterized by the multiple objectives) into consideration. In Fig. 8(g), AFCMOMA obtains better visual results, particularly for the Vegetation class. Finally, the memetic algorithm based clustering methods, AMASFC (86.55%) and AFCMOMA (91.29%), obtain higher OA and Kappa values than the corresponding single-objective clustering method (i.e. FCIDE (81.75%)) and multi-objective clustering method (i.e. AFCMDE (86.38%)).

Table 3. Comparison between different clustering methods for the Wuhan TM image.

	FCM	FCIDE	AMASFC	AFCMDE	AFCMOMA
OA (%)	81.66	81.75	86.55	86.38	**91.29**
Kappa	0.7619	0.7652	0.8276	0.8262	**0.8882**

4 Conclusion and Outlook

These years, the booming earth observation techniques, multi-platform, multi-sensor and multi-angle observation means promote the remote sensing images hold the character of high spectral-spatial-temporal resolution. At the same time, remote sensing image clustering as one of the important processing contents, facing the problems of data complexity and model complexity. Evolutionary computation approaches offer a series of possible solutions to these troubles: less optimal model parameters, susceptible to initial values and trapped in local optima. In this paper, we provide a survey of evolutionary computation theory in remote sensing image clustering, including evolutionary single-objective clustering, evolutionary multi-objective clustering and memetic algorithm based clustering for remote sensing image. From the research consequences, evolutionary computation technique has shown its potential in remote sensing image clustering, and has made preliminary achievement. In the future, in terms of evolutionary computation technique based remote sensing image clustering, the following problems and research hotspots can make some breakthroughs.

(1) In terms of remote sensing image clustering, in [40], it proposed a multi-objective optimization framework for ill-posed inverse problems in image processing. An ill-posed problem can be defined as follows: a problem is well-posed if its solution exists and is unique and stable; a problem is ill-posed if at least one of the three conditions does not hold [41]. So, it can also use the multi-objective optimization framework in remote sensing image clustering, such as intra-class distance and

interclass distance can be used as the objective function of clustering problem, both of which can achieve the purpose of automatic clustering.

(2) As for the efficiency of evolutionary computation based optimization, it can consider software acceleration and hardware acceleration. Firstly, in software acceleration, we can introduce more ideas of machine learning and mathematic planning into the process of evolutionary computation based remote sensing image clustering, which can improve clustering efficiency. Such as, we can introduce the estimation of distribution algorithms (EDA) in the process of producing offspring, and update the offspring by establishing a probabilistic model and sampling [42, 43]; In the selection process, we can use classification based approaches, training the classifier through positive and negative samples, the number of evaluations can be reduced for improving the efficiency of the algorithm [44, 45]. Secondly, as for hardware acceleration, as the evolutionary algorithms have good parallelism, which can be accelerated through the GPU. In addition, FPGA methods can also be achieved on the efficiency of time to meet the needs of the actual production [46].

References

1. Jain, A.K.: Data clustering: 50 years beyond k-means. In: Daelemans, W., Goethals, B., Morik, K. (eds.) ECML PKDD 2008. LNCS, vol. 5211, pp. 3–4. Springer, Heidelberg (2008). doi:10.1007/978-3-540-87479-9_3
2. Hruschka, E.R., Campello, R.J.G.B., Freitas, A.A.: A survey of evolutionary algorithms for clustering. IEEE Trans. Syst. Man Cybern. Part C **39**(2), 133–155 (2009)
3. Zhang, M., Ma, J., Gong, M., Li, H., Liu, J.: Memetic algorithm based feature selection for hyperspectral images classification. In: 2017 IEEE Congress on Evolutionary Computation (CEC), pp. 495–502. IEEE (2017)
4. Yu, H., Jiao, L., Liu, F.: CRIM-FCHO: SAR image two-stage segmentation with multifeature ensemble. IEEE Trans. Geosci. Remote Sens. **54**(4), 2400–2423 (2016)
5. Jiao, L., Tang, X., Hou, B., Wang, S.: SAR images retrieval based on semantic classification and region-based similarity measure for earth observation. IEEE J. Sel. Top. Appl. Earth Obs. Remote Sens. **8**(8), 3876–3891 (2015)
6. Ghosh, A., Mishra, N.S., Ghosh, S.: Fuzzy clustering algorithms for unsupervised change detection in remote sensing images. Inf. Sci. **181**(4), 699–715 (2011)
7. Murthy, C.A., Chowdhury, N.: In search of optimal clusters using genetic algorithms. Pattern Recogn. Lett. **17**(8), 825–832 (1996)
8. Das, S., Abraham, A., Konar, A.: Automatic clustering using an improved differential evolution algorithm. IEEE Trans. Syst. Man Cybern. Part A Syst. Hum. **38**(1), 218–237 (2008)
9. Zhang, S., Zhong, Y., Zhang, L.: An automatic fuzzy clustering algorithm based on self-adaptive differential evolution for remote sensing image. Acta Geodaetica Cartogr. Sin. **42**(2), 239–246 (2013)
10. Zhong, Y., Zhang, L.: A new fuzzy clustering algorithm based on clonal selection for land cover classification. Math. Probl. Eng. **2011**(2), 253–266 (2011)
11. Bandyopadhyay, S.: Satellite image classification using genetically guided fuzzy clustering with spatial information. Int. J. Remote Sens. **26**(3), 579–593 (2005)

12. Bandyopadhyay, S.: Genetic algorithms for clustering and fuzzy clustering. Wiley Interdisc. Rev. Data Min. Knowl. Discov. **1**(6), 524–531 (2011)
13. Pakhira, M.K., Bandyopadhyay, S., Maulik, U.: A study of some fuzzy cluster validity indices, genetic clustering and application to pixel classification. Fuzzy Sets Syst. **155**(2), 191–214 (2005)
14. Ozturk, C., Hancer, E., Karaboga, D.: Dynamic clustering with improved binary artificial bee colony algorithm. Appl. Soft Comput. **28**(C), 69–80 (2015)
15. Ma, A., Zhong, Y., Zhang, L.: Adaptive differential evolution fuzzy clustering algorithm with spatial information and kernel metric for remote sensing imagery. In: Yin, H., Tang, K., Gao, Y., Klawonn, F., Lee, M., Weise, T., Li, B., Yao, X. (eds.) IDEAL 2013. LNCS, vol. 8206, pp. 278–285. Springer, Heidelberg (2013). doi:10.1007/978-3-642-41278-3_34
16. Zhong, Y., Ma, A., Zhang, L.: An adaptive memetic fuzzy clustering algorithm with spatial information for remote sensing imagery. IEEE J. Sel. Top. Appl. Earth Observ. Remote Sens. **7**(4), 1235–1248 (2014)
17. Marler, R.T., Arora, J.S.: Survey of multi-objective optimization methods for engineering. Struct. Multidiscip. Optim. **26**(6), 369–395 (2004)
18. Deb, K.: Scope of stationary multi-objective evolutionary optimization: a case study on a hydro-thermal power dispatch problem. J. Glob. Optim. **41**(4), 479–515 (2008)
19. Wagner, T., Beume, N., Naujoks, B.: Pareto-, aggregation-, and indicator-based methods in many-objective optimization. In: Obayashi, S., Deb, K., Poloni, C., Hiroyasu, T., Murata, T. (eds.) EMO 2007. LNCS, vol. 4403, pp. 742–756. Springer, Heidelberg (2007). doi:10.1007/978-3-540-70928-2_56
20. Bandyopadhyay, S., Maulik, U., Mukhopadhyay, A.: Multiobjective genetic clustering for pixel classification in remote sensing imagery. IEEE Trans. Geosci. Remote Sens. **45**(5), 1506–1511 (2007)
21. Deb, K., Pratap, A., Agarwal, S., et al.: A fast and elitist multiobjective genetic algorithm: NSGA-II. IEEE Trans. Evol. Comp. **6**(2), 182–197 (2002)
22. Mukhopadhyay, A., Maulik, U.: Unsupervised pixel classification in satellite imagery using multiobjective fuzzy clustering combined with SVM classifier. IEEE Trans. Geosci. Remote Sens. **47**(4), 1132–1138 (2009)
23. Kaushik, S., Debarati, K., Sayan, G., Swagatam, D., Ajith, A., Han, S.Y.: Multi-objective differential evolution for automatic clustering with application to micro-array data analysis. Sensors **9**(5), 3981–4004 (2009)
24. Paoli, A., Melgani, F., Pasolli, E.: Clustering of hyperspectral images based on multiobjective particle swarm optimization. IEEE Trans. Geosci. Remote Sens. **47**(12), 4175–4188 (2009)
25. Li, Y., Feng, S., Zhang, X., Jiao, L.: SAR image segmentation based on quantum-inspired multiobjective evolutionary clustering algorithm. Inf. Process. Lett. **114**(6), 287–293 (2014)
26. Naeini, A.A., Homayouni, S., Saadatseresht, M.: Improving the dynamic clustering of hyperspectral data based on the integration of swarm optimization and decision analysis. IEEE J. Sel. Top. Appl. Earth Observ. Remote Sens. **7**(6), 2161–2173 (2014)
27. Zhong, Y., Zhang, S., Zhang, L.: Automatic fuzzy clustering based on adaptive multi-objective differential evolution for remote sensing imagery. IEEE J. Sel. Top. Appl. Earth Observ. Remote Sens. **6**(5), 2290–2301 (2013)
28. Luo, J., Jiao, L., Lozano, J.A.: A sparse spectral clustering framework via multiobjective evolutionary algorithm. IEEE Trans. Evol. Comput. **20**(3), 418–433 (2016)
29. Li, L., Yao, X., Stolkin, R., Gong, M., He, S.: An evolutionary multiobjective approach to sparse reconstruction. IEEE Trans. Evol. Comput. **18**(6), 827–845 (2014)
30. Črepinšek, M., Liu, S.H., Mernik, M.: Exploration and exploitation in evolutionary algorithms: a survey. ACM Comput. Surv. **45**(3), 1–33 (2013)

31. Moscato, P.: On evolution, search, optimization, genetic algorithms and martial arts: towards memetic algorithms. Caltech concurrent computation program. C3P Report 826 (1989)
32. Chen, X., Ong, Y.S., Lim, M.H., Tan, K.C.: A multi-facet survey on memetic computation. IEEE Trans. Evol. Comput. 15(5), 591–607 (2011)
33. Zhu, Z., Jia, S., Ji, Z.: Towards a memetic feature selection paradigm. IEEE Comput. Intell. Mag. 5(2), 41–53 (2010)
34. Chen, X., Feng, L., Soon Ong, Y.: A self-adaptive memeplexes robust search scheme for solving stochastic demands vehicle routing problem. Int. J. Syst. Sci. 43(7), 1347–1366 (2012)
35. Özcan, E., Başaran, C.: A case study of memetic algorithms for constraint optimization. Soft. Comput. 13(8), 871 (2009)
36. Jiao, L., Gong, M., Wang, S., Hou, B.: Natural and remote sensing image segmentation using memetic computing. IEEE Comput. Intell. Mag. 5(2), 78–91 (2010)
37. Ma, A., Zhong, Y., Zhang, L.: Adaptive multiobjective memetic fuzzy clustering algorithm for remote sensing imagery. IEEE Trans. Geosci. Remote Sens. 53(8), 4202–4217 (2015)
38. Ong, Y.S., Lim, M.H., Zhu, N., Wong, K.W.: Classification of adaptive memetic algorithms: a comparative study. IEEE Trans. Syst. Man Cybern. Part B Cybern. Publ. IEEE Syst. Man Cybern. Soc. 36(1), 141–152 (2006)
39. Ong, Y.S., Lim, M.H., Chen, X.: Research frontier: memetic computation-past, present and future. IEEE Comput. Intell. Mag. 5(2), 24–31 (2010)
40. Gong, M., Li, H., Jiang, X.: A multi-objective optimization framework for ill-posed inverse problems in image processing ★. CAAI Trans. Intell. Technol. 1(3), 225–240 (2016)
41. Kabanikhin, S.I.: Definitions and examples of inverse and ill-posed problems. J. Inverse Ill-posed Probl. 16(4), 317–357 (2008)
42. Hauschild, M., Pelikan, M.: An introduction and survey of estimation of distribution algorithms. Swarm Evol. Comput. 1(3), 111–128 (2011)
43. Zhou, A., Zhang, Q., Jin, Y.: Approximating the set of pareto-optimal solutions in both the decision and objective spaces by an estimation of distribution algorithm. IEEE Trans. Evol. Comput. 13(5), 1167–1189 (2009)
44. Zhang, J., Zhou, A., Zhang, G.: A multiobjective evolutionary algorithm based on decomposition and preselection. In: Gong, M., Pan, L., Song, T., Tang, K., Zhang, X. (eds.) BIC-TA 2015. CCIS, vol. 562, pp. 631–642. Springer, Heidelberg (2015). doi:10.1007/978-3-662-49014-3_56
45. Lin, X., Zhang, Q., Kwong, S.: A decomposition based multiobjective evolutionary algorithm with classification. In: 2016 IEEE Congress on Evolutionary Computation (CEC), Canada, pp. 3292–3299. IEEE (2016). doi:10.1109/CEC.2016.7744206
46. Mussi, L., Daolio, F., Cagnoni, S.: Evaluation of parallel particle swarm optimization algorithms within the CUDA TM architecture. Inf. Sci. 181(20), 4642–4657 (2011)

Feature Selection and Dimensionality Reduction

New Representations in Genetic Programming for Feature Construction in k-Means Clustering

Andrew Lensen[✉], Bing Xue, and Mengjie Zhang

School of Engineering and Computer Science, Victoria University of Wellington,
PO Box 600, Wellington 6140, New Zealand
{Andrew.Lensen,Bing.Xue,Mengjie.Zhang}@ecs.vuw.ac.nz

Abstract. k-means is one of the fundamental and most well-known algorithms in data mining. It has been widely used in clustering tasks, but suffers from a number of limitations on large or complex datasets. Genetic Programming (GP) has been used to improve performance of data mining algorithms by performing feature construction—the process of combining multiple attributes (features) of a dataset together to produce more powerful constructed features. In this paper, we propose novel representations for using GP to perform feature construction to improve the clustering performance of the k-means algorithm. Our experiments show significant performance improvement compared to k-means across a variety of difficult datasets. Several GP programs are also analysed to provide insight into how feature construction is able to improve clustering performance.

Keywords: Cluster analysis · Feature construction · Genetic programming · k-means · Evolutionary computation

1 Introduction

Clustering is a common data mining task which groups similar data items (instances) of a dataset into homogeneous groups (clusters) [1,2]. k-means [1,3] is one of the most widely used clustering algorithms due to its simple design and low computational cost. However, it suffers from several limitations: clustering solution (partition) quality is heavily dependent on the initial cluster centroids, and cluster quality quickly decreases as the number of clusters (K) increases. k-means also cannot produce non-hyper-spherical clusters [1], as it uses a distance measure to assign instances to clusters based on the cluster centres. Hyper-spherical clusters have instances which lie in a region enclosed by a hyper-sphere around the cluster mean; in a 2D space, this would be a circle. Data may naturally contain clusters of various shapes (e.g. elliptical, spiral, ring, etc. [4]).

Feature construction (FC) is a common technique used to improve the performance of learning algorithms in data mining [5]. FC algorithms produce powerful high-level CFs (CFs) by combining features from the original feature set.

© Springer International Publishing AG 2017
Y. Shi et al. (Eds.): SEAL 2017, LNCS 10593, pp. 543–555, 2017.
https://doi.org/10.1007/978-3-319-68759-9_44

By only using a few CFs instead of the full feature set, data mining algorithms can train more efficiently (due to a smaller search space) and more effectively, while generally producing more concise and understandable solutions [6].

Genetic Programming (GP) [7] is an Evolutionary Computation (EC) [8] technique, which has been shown to be effective at performing FC, especially on classification problems [9,10]. GP, like other EC algorithms, produces solutions to a problem by performing a population-based heuristic search, using Darwinian inspired principles to encourage co-operation between solutions. Tree-based GP has been extensively used for FC as its representation can easily combine features in different ways [10]. One of the most successful approaches in classification tasks has been to use a *wrapper* approach, where GP is used to construct features which are then fed into an existing classifier. This allows the performance of an existing, well-founded classifier to be improved by using a smaller number of more powerful features.

Unlike in classification tasks, there has been very little work conducted using GP for FC for clustering [11]. Most existing work does not examine the clustering performance on a large number of clusters, and no work has been proposed using a wrapper approach where GP produces CFs that are fed to an existing clustering algorithm. The performance of k-means could be improved by using such an approach, where a GP individual produces several CFs which are then fed into k-means to perform clustering. In this way, the performance of k-means can be improved beyond what is possible with the original features alone. Traditional GP program designs output only a single value from a single individual, meaning only a single CF is created. While a single CF may be adequate on easy datasets with a small K, when there are many clusters it would be very difficult to accurately partition the dataset using a single value. Hence, new GP representations would need to be developed to produce multiple CFs. The evolved system can also be taught to produce good clusters according to any measure of cluster quality, as GP individuals will learn to produce CFs to maximise the fitness of the wrapped k-means algorithm. In contrast, standard k-means simply minimises intra-cluster variance without considering any other indicators of cluster quality. As clustering will be performed on a constructed feature space, using a clustering algorithm more advanced than k-means may not be necessary, as GP should learn to produce features tailored to the clustering algorithm used.

This paper aims to explore the potential of using GP for FC with a wrapper approach to improve the clustering performance of k-means. We will:

- Propose new GP representations for producing multiple CFs from a single GP individual,
- Investigate suitable fitness functions for improving cluster quality,
- Evaluate our proposed representations and fitness functions across a variety of datasets, and
- Analyse evolved GP trees to understand the usefulness of the CFs they produce.

A variety of clustering algorithms have been proposed which are effective on different datasets and problems [12]. These can be generally grouped into a number of categories such as hierarchical [12], density [13], partitional [3], or graph-based algorithms [14]. This paper focuses on applying GP to FC with k-means, a centroid-based, partitional clustering algorithm.

When GP is used for FC, terminal nodes generally draw from the feature set, and function nodes are operators which operate on real values, such as the arithmetic functions. The small amount of work using GP for clustering uses a variety of approaches [11], several of which perform FC within the GP tree [15,16]. However, no existing work uses a wrapper approach where an existing clustering algorithm is used for clustering.

2   Proposed Method

In this section, we propose two new representations for performing FC using GP for clustering. We also introduce two fitness functions which can be used to train GP with k-means to improve clustering performance.

2.1   Multi-tree Representation

To allow multiple CFs to be produced by one GP individual, we propose an extension to the standard single-tree GP representation, so that an individual contains multiple trees, producing multiple CFs. The number of trees (t) is dependent on the dataset used—generally, a higher K requires a higher t.

The function set used contains a number of standard arithmetic operators $(+, -, \times, \div, | + |, | - |)$, as well as the max and min operators. Each of these operators take two children and produce a single output. The $\div$ operator is protected division; if the second child (the divisor) is 0, the operator returns 1. The final operator in the function set is if, which takes three children and returns the value of $child_2$ if $child_1$ is positive; otherwise it returns the value of $child_3$. The if operator is used to allow conditional behaviour in the GP program. The terminal nodes consist of the features of the dataset (f_1 through to f_m for m features) as well as a random double in the range $[0, 1]$.

When a multi-tree approach is used, the crossover and mutation operators in the evolutionary process must be adapted. In this work, we use a common approach whereby crossover is performed by selecting two random individuals, selecting a random tree from each of the individuals, and then selecting a random sub-tree from each tree to use for crossover. Mutation is performed by choosing a random tree from a random individual to be mutated.

While the multi-tree approach is reasonably straightforward to design, it has a number of limitations; most notably, t must be set in advance. The crossover operator used may also be problematic; as any two random trees can be chosen for crossover, trees being crossed over may not correspond to similar CFs, and so the CFs produced are unlikely to be fully distinct from each other. Redundancy across a constructed feature set may affect the efficiency and interpretability of a given solution.

2.2   Vector Representation

To address these issues, we also propose a single-tree approach which utilises a vector representation to produce multiple CFs from a single tree. The vector representation has no t parameter and so no parameter tuning is required. We use a similar function set as in the previous approach, but adapt each function to take two vectors as input and produce a vector as output. Each function operates on the input vectors in a pairwise manner, and the output vector has length equal to that of the smaller vector. We also introduce a *concat* function which takes two vectors as input and outputs a vector which is the result of appending the second vector to the end of the first. This *concat* function allows vectors of variable length to be generated, allowing GP to automatically generate a dynamic number of CFs. By using several *concat* functions in a single tree, the constructed feature vector will grow as the tree is evaluated from bottom to top. The terminal set remains the same as in the previous approach, however each terminal node now outputs a **vector** containing the terminal value.

2.3   Fitness Function

When K is fixed, the most common fitness function is the $\sum$ Intra fitness [12]:

$$\sum \text{Intra} = \sum_{i=1}^{K} \sum_{I_a \in C_i} d(I_a, Z_i) \tag{1}$$

where C_i represents the ith cluster, $I_a \in C_i$ represents an instance in the ith cluster and Z_i represents the mean of the ith cluster. This fitness function is what is minimised by k-means—when K is known, we should encourage all clusters to be as compact as possible, by minimising $\sum Intra$. One limitation of this measure is that clusters are encouraged towards hyper-sphericality; clusters will be unlikely to form non-spherical shapes that can occur on certain datasets.

One way of avoiding this problem is to use a fitness function based on connectedness. Connectedness measures the extent to which instances are in the same cluster as their immediate neighbours; close instances are similar and should fall in the same cluster. We propose a new fitness function, based on that proposed by Handl and Knowles [17], that computes the mean connectedness of all clusters in a partition:

$$\text{Connectedness} = \frac{1}{K} \sum_{i=1}^{K} \frac{1}{|C_i|} \sum_{I_a, I_b \in C_i} d_{inverse}(I_a, I_b) \tag{2}$$

$$d_{inverse}(I_a, I_b) = min\left[\frac{1}{d(I_a, I_b)}, 10\right] \tag{3}$$

The above fitness function, which should be maximised, encourages clusters to contain instances which are close together. Equations (2) and (3) contain a number of extensions to the one proposed by Handl and Knowles [17]:

1. Closer neighbours are weighted more strongly, by directly using the distance between neighbours in the fitness calculation. The inverse distance is capped to a maximum of 10 (i.e. when dist ≤ 0.1) to prevent very similar/identical instances overly affecting fitness. The value of 10 was chosen empirically.
2. The mean connectedness is calculated across the set of clusters, instead of summing over all instance pairs. This discourages solutions with one very large cluster (with very good connectedness) and several very small clusters.
3. The mean connectedness within a cluster is used (instead of summing), to prevent very close instances from being over-represented in the fitness.

It is hoped that by using connectedness, GP will produce features that allow for non-hyper-spherical clustering—although k-means itself will create hyper-spherical clusters in terms of the CFs, the CFs created by GP need not be linear transformations of the original features. The ability of our wrapper approach to train k-means based on different fitness measures allows k-means to be adapted to perform well on datasets that it would otherwise struggle on, especially when it is used with only a few CFs.

3   Experiment Design

Each combination of the two representations and two fitness functions were evaluated on a range of datasets using a variety of metrics. k-means was evaluated as a baseline, using all features. Each method is non-deterministic, and so is run 30 times using different seeds, and the mean result for each metric is computed.

Table 1 shows the evolutionary parameters used for all the GP methods across all the datasets. For the multi-tree approach, t is set to 7—this was found empirically to be the required number of trees in order to give good performance across all datasets. k-means is also run for 100 iterations, or until convergence is reached (i.e. when cluster centres do not move across iterations). The initial cluster centres for k-means are randomly selected from the dataset. The seed of k-means is determined using a hashing function applied to a GP tree so that each tree produces consistent partitions.

Table 1. GP parameter settings

Parameter	Value	Parameter	Value
Generations	100	Crossover Rate	80%
Population Size	1024	Mutation Rate	20%
Minimum Depth	2	Elitism	top-10
Maximum Depth	8	Selection Type	Tournament
Initial Population	Half-and-half	Tournament Size	7

3.1   Datasets

A range of synthetic and real-world datasets were used to comprehensively evaluate the proposed methods, as shown in Table 2 Datasets were scaled so that each feature had values in $[0, 1]$, to prevent bias towards features with large ranges.

The synthetic datasets are chosen from a widely-used study by Handl and Knowles [17]. These datasets contain 10, 50, or 100 features and 10, 20, or 40 clusters. The synthetic datasets are used to test the performance of the proposed methods when K is high; k-means (and other methods) perform poorly on high K values.

The real-world classification datasets were chosen from the UCI machine learning repository [18], which has been commonly used in clustering studies. We use these real-world datasets to evaluate how well our proposed methods can re-create the known classifications (as is common in the literature); the class labels are **not** used during training, and are only used to evaluate how well the partitions produced match the known classes. As clustering a classification dataset is harder than clustering a specifically designed clustering dataset, we generally use real-world datasets with small K, but also include the Movement Libras dataset (with $K = 15$) to give an indication of performance on hard classification problems.

Table 2. Datasets used in the experiments.

Real-World UCI datasets from [18].				Synthetic datasets from [17].			
Name	No. of Features	No. of Instances	No. of Classes	Name	No. of Features	No. of Instances	No. of Classes
Iris	4	150	3	10d10c	10	2730	10
Wine	13	178	3	10d20c	10	1014	20
Movement Libras	90	360	15	10d40c	10	1938	40
				50d10c	50	2699	10
Breast Cancer	9	683	2	50d20c	50	1255	20
				50d40c	50	2335	40
Image Segmentation	18	683	7	100d10c	100	2893	10
				100d20c	100	1339	20
Dermatology	34	359	6	100d40c	100	2212	40

3.2   Evaluation Metrics

Clustering performance is measured using the two *internal* metrics defined previously, which directly measure the quality of a cluster partition. Connectedness (see Eq. (2)) evaluates how well neighbouring instances are allocated to the same cluster, and $\sum$ Intra Distance (see Eq. (1)) indicates how compact the clusters are.

In addition, we use two *external* metrics to measure how well the cluster partitions produced correspond to the dataset's class labels. These are class purity, which measures the homogeneity of each cluster with respect to the class labels, and the F-measure, which measures how well pairs of instances agree in terms of the clusters they are allocated to and their class labels. These measures are defined as follows:

1. Class purity: computed according to the following steps:
   (a) For each cluster, find the majority class label of that cluster's instances.
   (b) Count the number of correctly classified instances in the cluster, where an instance is correctly classified if it belongs to the majority class.
   (c) Calculate class purity as the fraction of correctly classified instances across the dataset.
2. F-measure: We adapt the F-measure used in classification. We consider each pair of instances in turn (as it is not possible to directly decide if a given instance is in the "right" cluster) and select from the following cases:
   (a) Same class label, assigned the same cluster: true positive (TP).
   (b) Same class label, assigned **different** clusters: false negative (FN).
   (c) **Different** class labels, assigned **different** clusters: true negative (TN).
   (d) **Different** class labels, assigned the same cluster: false positive (FP).

The F-measure is calculated using the total number of TPs, FPs, and FNs:

$$\text{F-measure} = 2 \times \frac{\text{precision} \times \text{recall}}{\text{precision} + \text{recall}} \tag{4}$$

$$\text{precision} = \frac{TPs}{TPs + FPs} \quad (5) \qquad \text{recall} = \frac{TPs}{TPs + FNs} \quad (6)$$

4   Results and Analysis

Tables 3 and 4 show the performance of the four GP methods and k-means (using all features (AF)) across the six real-world and nine synthetic datasets respectively. MTConn and MTIntra are the multi-tree approaches using the connectedness and $\sum$ Intra fitness function respectively, with $t = 7$. VectorConn and VectorIntra are the two vector approaches, each using one of the fitness functions proposed. Each metric is labelled with an "↑" or "↓" if it should be maximised or minimised respectively. The four metrics are: Conn (connectedness), $\sum$ Intra ($\sum$ intra distance), Purity (class purity), and FM (the F-measure). For the GP methods, each result is labelled with a "+" or a "−" if it is significantly better or worse than the k-means baseline according to a Student's t-test performed with a 95% confidence interval. A lack of a "+" or "−" indicates no significant difference.

Table 3. Performance on Real-World datasets.

Method	Conn ↑	Intra ↓	Purity ↑	FM ↑	Conn ↑	Intra ↓	Purity ↑	FM ↑
		Iris				Wine		
MTConn7	223.4$^+$	29.59$^+$	0.8989$^+$	0.8308$^+$	90.13$^+$	88.99$^-$	0.9723$^+$	0.9444$^+$
MTIntra	26.49$^-$	29.28$^+$	0.8867$^+$	0.8111$^+$	7.621$^+$	88.7$^+$	0.9663$^+$	0.933$^+$
VectorConn	223.1$^+$	29.59$^+$	0.9502$^+$	0.9086$^+$	90.12$^+$	89.01$^-$	0.9697$^+$	0.9392$^+$
VectorIntra	26.49$^-$	29.28$^+$	0.8867$^+$	0.8111$^+$	7.618$^+$	88.7$^+$	0.9661$^+$	0.9325$^+$
k-means AF	26.77	31.39	0.8116	0.7544	7.561	88.74	0.9491	0.8998
		Movement Libras				Breast Cancer		
MTConn7	19.28$^+$	424.9$^-$	0.4424$^-$	0.3417	895.8$^+$	369.7$^-$	0.9101$^-$	0.8445$^-$
MTIntra	5.473$^+$	400.2$^+$	0.472	0.3527	15.63$^+$	331.6$^+$	0.9675$^+$	0.9423$^+$
VectorConn	19.1$^+$	414.3	0.4583	0.3434	898.1$^+$	376.7$^-$	0.8972$^-$	0.824$^-$
VectorIntra	5.486$^+$	399.0$^+$	0.4749$^+$	0.3542$^+$	15.64$^+$	331.6$^+$	0.9669$^+$	0.9413$^+$
k-means AF	5.134	414.5	0.4619	0.3439	15.52	332.0	0.9609	0.9313
		Image Segmentation				Dermatology		
MTConn7	798.4$^+$	877.1$^+$	0.6832$^+$	0.5886$^+$	42.28$^+$	377.1$^+$	0.946$^+$	0.9324$^+$
MTIntra	25.39$^+$	869.5$^+$	0.6654$^+$	0.5717$^+$	3.176$^+$	376.2$^+$	0.8655$^+$	0.7915
VectorConn	797.1$^+$	873.8$^+$	0.6859$^+$	0.5894$^+$	41.7$^+$	382.8	0.9063$^+$	0.8764$^+$
VectorIntra	25.38$^+$	872.2$^+$	0.6655$^+$	0.5726$^+$	3.063	380.9$^+$	0.8538	0.7839
k-means AF	24.78	908.6	0.6383	0.5582	3.022	386.5	0.8349	0.7569

4.1 Results on Real-World Datasets

The GP methods generally perform well compared to k-means across the real-world datasets. All four of the GP methods are significantly better in terms of the F-measure on the Iris, Wine, and Image Segmentation datasets. At least one of the GP methods is significantly better than k-means on all remaining real-world datasets; GP is only significantly worse than k-means when using connectedness on the Breast Cancer dataset, where the $\sum$ Intra fitness measure gives much better performance. The connectedness fitness measure, however, gives very good results on the Dermatology dataset, improving performance over k-means significantly. The fact that different fitness functions perform better on different datasets shows the usefulness of our proposed methods to train using a range of criteria, unlike the original k-means algorithm. Both the multi-tree and the vector approaches appear to perform similarly on the real-world datasets, with an exception on the Iris dataset, where the vector approach is superior when connectedness is used in terms of the external metrics.

4.2 Results on Synthetic Datasets

The GP methods continue to perform well compared to k-means on the synthetic datasets. All four methods have a significantly higher F-measure value than k-means on the datasets with 20 or 40 clusters. These datasets are the most difficult as they require separating the dataset into the greatest number

Table 4. Performance on Synthetic Datasets.

Method	Conn ↑	Intra ↓	Purity ↑	FM ↑	Conn ↑	Intra ↓	Purity ↑	FM ↑
	10d10c				10d20c			
MTConn	823.3+	719.1-	0.9019-	0.7836-	177.0+	213.2+	0.9948+	0.9919+
MTIntra	17.67-	710.1+	0.9294	0.878	16.5+	213.0+	0.9948+	0.9919+
VectorConn	827.3+	713.9	0.9153-	0.8025-	177.0+	213.5+	0.9941+	0.9887+
VectorIntra	18.05+	706.3+	0.9404+	0.8926+	16.48+	213.5+	0.9938+	0.9906+
k-means AF	17.88	712.4	0.9291	0.8571	15.29	254.8	0.8732	0.7969
	10d40c				50d10c			
MTConn	173.2+	406.5+	0.9747+	0.9311+	589.4+	1480.0-	0.7325-	0.5167+
MTIntra	16.34+	405.0+	0.977+	0.9456+	17.14-	1220.0+	0.7392	0.4785-
VectorConn	173.6+	403.3+	0.9789+	0.9409+	587.3+	1437.0-	0.7278-	0.5005
VectorIntra	16.32+	404.1+	0.9771+	0.9494+	17.22-	1216.0+	0.7397	0.4795-
k-means AF	15.75	436.8	0.9182	0.8628	17.49	1317.0	0.744	0.4939
	50d20c				50d40c			
MTConn	163.3+	583.2-	0.7138+	0.4996+	163.3+	894.7-	0.685	0.4397+
MTIntra	17.43	493.8+	0.7456+	0.4776+	18.95-	833.8+	0.6952+	0.4269+
VectorConn	162.5+	555.7	0.7212+	0.4832+	165.4+	850.4+	0.7082+	0.4106+
VectorIntra	17.52	487.2+	0.7412+	0.4351+	19.3+	797.1+	0.7165+	0.3759+
k-means AF	17.33	546.5	0.6868	0.3823	19.16	865.2	0.6791	0.2618
	100d10c				100d20c			
MTConn	521.8+	2123.0-	0.7598	0.5311	126.0+	885.4-	0.7084	0.4657+
MTIntra	15.81+	1776.0+	0.7835+	0.5825+	13.66+	764.9+	0.7481+	0.4598+
VectorConn	519.5+	2077.0-	0.7595	0.5446	125.5+	850.5	0.7122	0.4451+
VectorIntra	15.89+	1771.0+	0.7839+	0.5854+	13.74+	749.6+	0.7466+	0.4331+
k-means AF	15.14	1968.0	0.748	0.5255	13.31	844.2	0.7033	0.38
	100d40c							
MTConn	114.8+	1234.0-	0.6963	0.4629+				
MTIntra	14.18-	1118.0+	0.7181+	0.462+				
VectorConn	116.0+	1159.0	0.7142+	0.4418+				
VectorIntra	14.45	1061.0+	0.7344+	0.4028+				
k-means AF	14.55	1184.0	0.6904	0.2675				

of distinct groups. k-means performs very poorly when there is a large number of clusters (e.g. $K = 40$); GP is able to effectively perform FC to significantly improve the performance of k-means on the hardest datasets, while only using a small subset of the feature set. Some GP methods perform significantly worse on the simple 10d10c and 50d10c datasets, but at least one GP method is still significantly better than k-means in these cases.

The connectedness and $\sum$ Intra fitness measures are again superior on different datasets. The method using connectedness are significantly better than k-means on the 50d10c dataset, whereas those using $\sum$ Intra fitness are significantly worse. The inverse is true on the 10d10c dataset, however. In general, the multi-tree approach seems slightly better than the vector approach, especially on the datasets with highest dimensionality such as 100d20c and 100d40c. Future testing is required to evaluate which method is superior, and more work could be done to improve each method by further exploring alternative representations or fitness functions.

5   Evolved Program Analysis

It is often useful when using GP to evaluate and analyse some of the high-performing individuals produced during the evolutionary process. Doing so allows us to understand what properties of a given tree allow it to perform well, which leads to a better understanding of the problem as well allowing the GP method to be improved further. In addition, analysing evolved programs increases the confidence in our proposed method by demonstrating how it is able to achieve the good results we claim. In this section, we analyse a number of GP trees with high F-measure across a range of datasets.

An example of the multi-tree approach can be seen in Fig. 1. The seven trees produced by an individual with a very high F-measure value of 0.9947 is shown, along with the constructed feature set generated which consists of seven features, one from each tree. Of these trees, three are simply performing feature selection of a single feature, two add a constant value to a single feature, and the remaining two are performing more advanced FC. In total, seven of the original 10 features are used. Although the dimensionality has not been greatly reduced, performance is still much higher than that of the original k-means algorithm (which achieves an F-measure value of 0.7969). This further highlights the ability of GP to improve performance by selecting the most important features, and creating more powerful high-level features.

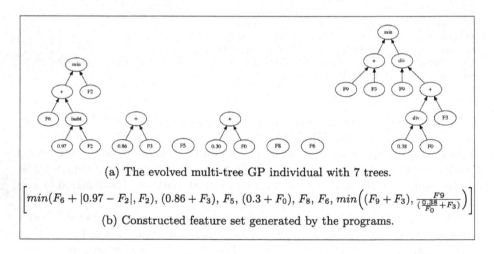

(a) The evolved multi-tree GP individual with 7 trees.

$$\left[min(F_6 + |0.97 - F_2|, F_2), (0.86 + F_3), F_5, (0.3 + F_0), F_8, F_6, min\left((F_9 + F_3), \frac{F_9}{(\frac{0.38}{F_0} + F_3)}\right)\right]$$

(b) Constructed feature set generated by the programs.

Fig. 1. An evolved *multi-tree* individual on the 10d20c dataset (FM: 0.9947).

Figure 2 shows a GP individual using the vector approach with high performance on the hardest synthetic dataset (100d40c). The individual is a reasonably concise tree, with a maximum width of eight nodes and a depth of seven. The tree itself is shown in Fig. 2a, and the output of the tree as shown in Fig. 2b. The tree selects feature values as terminal nodes, and outputs a constructed feature vector of length 12, containing 11 "constructed" features and one constant value. Of these CFs, one is an arithmetic combination of two selected features and two constants, two are operations applied to a selected feature and a constant value, and the remaining nine are unchanged selected features. k-means achieved an F-measure value of 0.2618 on average; this GP individual produced nearly double the F-measure value while only using 12 features compared to the 100 original features that k-means used. This large increase in performance shows the power of GP in improving performance by creating more powerful high-level features while also reducing dimensionality.

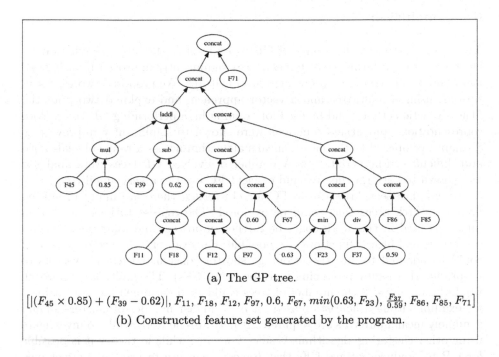

(a) The GP tree.

$$[|(F_{45} \times 0.85) + (F_{39} - 0.62)|, F_{11}, F_{18}, F_{12}, F_{97}, 0.6, F_{67}, min(0.63, F_{23}), \tfrac{F_{37}}{0.59}, F_{86}, F_{85}, F_{71}]$$

(b) Constructed feature set generated by the program.

Fig. 2. An evolved *vector* individual on the 100d40c dataset (FM: 0.499).

A useful property of the vector approach is its ability to dynamically produce a variable number of CFs. For example, on the Iris dataset which has only three classes, it is unnecessary to have seven CFs (as occurs for $t = 7$ in the multi-tree approach) and having so many features may reduce the interpretability of the solution. Figure 3 shows a high performing, very simple GP individual produced on the Iris dataset. This tree is very easy to analyse: it simply selects two of the four features in the dataset (F_3 and F_2). By not selecting the other misleading or redundant features, this GP tree significantly improves the ability of k-means to produce a good cluster partition.

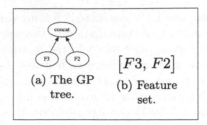

(a) The GP tree. (b) Feature set. $[F3, F2]$

Fig. 3. An evolved *vector* individual on the Iris dataset (FM: 0.9233).

6 Conclusion

This work showcased the ability of GP to be used for feature construction for clustering; the performance of k-means was significantly improved by using GP to automatically construct a few high-level features. We proposed two representations, using a multi-tree and a vector approach, and explored two potential fitness functions that could be used for training high performing GP trees. Both representations and fitness functions were shown to significantly improve performance compared to the base k-means algorithm across a range of real-world and difficult synthetic datasets. A number of evolved GP trees were analysed and shown to perform effective and efficient FC even in a very small tree.

As GP has seen little use in FC for clustering, there are many promising future research areas that could be explored. The representations and fitness functions used in this work could be further improved, and many other representations and fitness functions are possible. For example, the vector approach could be adapted to directly encourage shorter constructed feature vectors to be produced (thereby producing more powerful CFs). The multi-tree approach would be improved if the number of trees could be determined automatically—for example, using a heuristic based on K (a higher number of clusters should genuinely mean more CFs are required). It may also be worthwhile to investigate using other clustering algorithms besides k-means; while in theory it is possible for GP to produce optimal CFs that k-means can use to produce perfect partitions, other algorithms may be more powerful and perform well with a wider range of CFs. The methods we proposed were all designed to work when K was pre-defined, as k-means requires K to be known. This is somewhat inflexible, and extending these methods to automatically determine K would be beneficial.

References

1. Jain, A.K.: Data clustering: 50 years beyond k-means. Pattern Recogn. Lett. **31**(8), 651–666 (2010)
2. García, A.J., Gómez-Flores, W.: Automatic clustering using nature-inspired metaheuristics: a survey. Appl. Soft Comput. **41**, 192–213 (2016)
3. Hartigan, J.A., Wong, M.A.: Algorithm AS 136: a k-means clustering algorithm. J. R. Stat. Soc. Ser. C (Appl. Stat.) **28**(1), 100–108 (1979)

4. Tseng, L.Y., Yang, S.B.: A genetic clustering algorithm for data with non-spherical-shape clusters. Pattern Recogn. **33**(7), 1251–1259 (2000)
5. Liu, H., Motoda, H.: Feature Extraction, Construction and Selection: A Data Mining Perspective. Springer Science & Business Media, Heidelberg (1998)
6. Espejo, P.G., Ventura, S., Herrera, F.: A survey on the application of genetic programming to classification. IEEE Trans. Syst. Man Cybern. Part C **40**(2), 121–144 (2010)
7. Koza, J.R.: Genetic programming: on the programming of computers by means of natural selection, vol. 1. MIT press, Cambridge (1992)
8. Eiben, A.E., Smith, J.E.: Introduction to Evolutionary Computing. Natural Computing Series. Springer, Heidelberg (2015)
9. Neshatian, K., Zhang, M., Andreae, P.: A filter approach to multiple feature construction for symbolic learning classifiers using genetic programming. IEEE Trans. Evol. Comput. **16**(5), 645–661 (2012)
10. Tran, B., Xue, B., Zhang, M.: Genetic programming for feature construction and selection in classification on high-dimensional data. Memet. Comput. **8**(1), 3–15 (2016)
11. Nanda, S.J., Panda, G.: A survey on nature inspired metaheuristic algorithms for partitional clustering. Swarm Evol. Comput. **16**, 1–18 (2014)
12. Aggarwal, C.C., Reddy, C.K. (eds.): Data Clustering: Algorithms and Applications. CRC Press, Boca Raton (2014)
13. Ester, M., Kriegel, H., Sander, J., Xu, X.: A density-based algorithm for discovering clusters in large spatial databases with noise. In: Proceedings of the Second International Conference on Knowledge Discovery and Data Mining (KDD-96), Portland, pp. 226–231 (1996)
14. Hartuv, E., Shamir, R.: A clustering algorithm based on graph connectivity. Inf. Process. Lett. **76**(4–6), 175–181 (2000)
15. Boric, N., Estévez, P.A.: Genetic programming-based clustering using an information theoretic fitness measure. In: Proceedings of the IEEE Congress on Evolutionary Computation (CEC), pp. 31–38 (2007)
16. Ahn, C.W., Oh, S., Oh, M.: A genetic programming approach to data clustering. In: Kim, T., Adeli, H., Grosky, W.I., Pissinou, N., Shih, T.K., Rothwell, E.J., Kang, B.-H., Shin, S.-J. (eds.) MulGraB 2011. CCIS, vol. 263, pp. 123–132. Springer, Heidelberg (2011). doi:10.1007/978-3-642-27186-1_15
17. Handl, J., Knowles, J.D.: An evolutionary approach to multiobjective clustering. IEEE Trans. Evol. Comput. **11**(1), 56–76 (2007)
18. Lichman, M.: UCI machine learning repository (2013)

Transductive Transfer Learning in Genetic Programming for Document Classification

Wenlong Fu, Bing Xue$^{(\boxtimes)}$, Mengjie Zhang, and Xiaoying Gao

School of Engineering and Computer Science, Victoria University of Wellington,
PO Box 600, Wellington, New Zealand
wenlong.fu@msor.vuw.ac.nz,
{bing.xue,mengjie.zhang,xiaoying.gao}@ecs.vuw.ac.nz

Abstract. Document classification tasks generally have sparse and high dimensional features. It is important to effectively extract features. In document classification tasks, there are some similarities existing in different categories or different datasets. It is possible that one document classification task does not have labelled training data. In order to obtain effective classifiers on this specific task, this paper proposes a Genetic Programming (GP) system using transductive transfer learning. The proposed GP system automatically extracts features from different source domains, and these GP extracted features are combined to form new classifiers being directly applied to a target domain. From experimental results, the proposed transductive transfer learning GP system can evolve features from source domains to effectively apply to target domains which are similar to the source domains.

Keywords: Genetic programming · Document classification · Transfer learning · Text classification

1 Introduction

Document classification, as a task of natural language processing, has been addressed by many artificial intelligence algorithms [1,11,14,19]. Since many different words are used in documents, document classification tasks generally have high dimensional and sparse features. In a document classification task, pre-processing, feature construction, feature selection, and model building are normally included. How to select and extract features is very important in document classification [1]. One popular approach is to use the frequency of words to construct a high dimensional and sparse set of basic features [14]. However, there is no sufficient work of how to effectively and automatically extract the frequencies of words to combine as high-level features [6,22].

Genetic programming (GP) has been successfully employed to select features for different tasks, such as edge detection [7], symbolic regression problems [4,5] and a question-answer ranking task [2]. In a web document ranking task [2], GP can effectively select a smaller set of features based on the domain knowledge

© Springer International Publishing AG 2017
Y. Shi et al. (Eds.): SEAL 2017, LNCS 10593, pp. 556–568, 2017.
https://doi.org/10.1007/978-3-319-68759-9_45

than other feature selection methods. Also, GP has been used to evolve programs of combining existing features for document classification [6,22]. It shows
that GP has potential to automatically extract features in text classification to
construct effective classifiers.

In document classification tasks, we might have pre-defined labels for some
datasets, but no labels for other datasets. If these datasets have similar targets and the categories in these datasets are relatively similar to each other,
the features extracted from the datasets with pre-defined labels might be helpful for those datasets without labels. Transfer learning has been investigated in
this field [18,20]. Transfer learning techniques [18,20] have been used to train
models from one source domain, then transfer learnt knowledge to other similar
domains [17]. When a transductive transfer learning technique is used to build
classifiers, pre-defined category labels are considered in source domains, but category labels are not considered in target domains. It is promising to employ GP
to automatically extract features from source domains (including predefined category labels) to apply to a target domain (without considering category labels).

1.1 Goals

The overall goal of this paper is to initially investigate transductive transfer
learning in GP for automatically extracting features for document classification.
GP is used to automatically extract features from source domains when category
labels exist in these source domains, then the extracted features are directly
applied to a target domain without training. Features extracted by GP from
these source domains are combined to classify documents from target domains.
Here, we will investigate the performance on single or multiple features extracted
by GP from different source domains and being used to a target domain. Specifically, we would like to investigate the following research objectives.

- Whether extracted features from source domains can be directly applied to
  target domains.
- Whether combining a set of features extracted by GP from source domains
  can compete with the features directly extracted by GP on a target domain.
- Whether increasing of the number of features extracted by GP from source
  domains and used for a target domain can improve test accuracy performance
  on the target domain.

1.2 Organisation

In the remainder of this paper, Sect. 2 briefly describes the background of document classification, transfer learning and GP for text classification. Section 3
introduces the proposed GP system to automatically extract features for document classification and directly apply extracted features to target domains. After
Sect. 4 presents the design of the experiments, Sect. 5 provides the experimental
results with discussions. Section 6 draws conclusions and addresses future work
directions.

2   Background

2.1   Document Classification and Transfer Learning

The task of document classification is to classify a document to a predefined category based on the texts in the document. Statistical algorithms and artificial intelligence techniques have been used to automatically classify documents from provided datasets [1,14,19]. In document classification tasks, the frequency of words or the letter combination is considered as an important attribute to construct basic features. In general, the number of letter combinations are huge, and the frequency of each combination is not high. In the stage of pre-processing, some texts will be filtered, such as "and". In the process of feature extraction, it is popular to use n-gram techniques [1,3]. If we only consider the word specific combination, the bag-of-words model can be considered as a special case in the n-gram model. The number of occurrences of each word is a general and basic feature in a bag-of-words model. Considering the frequency of each word is not high and the set of words is large in a document classification task, we need effective feature selection techniques to select small sets of features from a high dimensional and sparse set of basic features. Traditional feature selection methods, such as information gain [21], are generally employed [1]. After a small set of features is selected, learning algorithms, such as Support Vector Machine (SVM) [13], are used to build classifiers.

In some document classification tasks, some topics (categories) are similar and usually include similar words. When the same input feature space is applied to these tasks and the distributions of the input features are different, the domain adaptation technique has been developed for similar topics [17]. When models (or features) are obtained from datasets which are considered as source domains, the models (or features) can be transferred to target domains including similar categories [18,20]. When training data is expensive or difficult to collect, we need an effective technique to obtain models (or features) with more easily obtained data from different domains. This technique is transfer learning.

In transfer learning, there are many types of methods for transferring knowledge from source domains to target domains [18,20]. Categorising transfer learning techniques mainly focuses on the difference between the source domain and the target domain. In a transfer learning task, when the input features in the source and target domains are different, the task is considered as heterogeneous transfer learning; otherwise it is homogeneous transfer learning. When a task considers the predefined labels in the source and target domains, it is considered as inductive transfer learning. Inductive transfer learning includes semi-supervised (only using a few labels) and supervised transfer learning. When the labels in the target domains are not provided, it is considered as transductive transfer learning. Unsupervised transfer learning is also used for transductive transfer learning. Since no labels are used in target domains, transductive transfer learning is very challenging [9,18,20].

In document classification tasks, there are n source domains SD, and each source domain SD_i $(i = 1, \ldots, n)$ has basic features X_{SD_i} and a marginal probability distribution $P_{X_{SD_i}}$; and a target domain TD has a feature space X_{TD} and a marginal probability distribution $P_{X_{TD}}$. A subset feature space X_{sel,SD_i} from the source domain is selected by a feature selection algorithm; A model M_i is trained by using X_{sel,SD_i} to discriminate a document as category c. A category for a document is obtained by Eq. (1). Meanwhile, we can consider the model M_i as a high-level feature.

$$c = M_i(X_{sel,SD_i}) \tag{1}$$

Here, we only consider homogeneous transfer learning. In general, the source domain SD_i and the target domain TD have different marginal probability distributions. For the selected feature space X_{sel,SD_i}, SD_i has a marginal probability distribution $P_{X_{sel,SD_i}}$ and TD has a marginal probability distribution $P_{X_{sel,TD}}$. For a document from the source domain, its category c is obtained by Eq. (2). For a document from the target domain, its category c is obtained by Eq. (3) [17,20]. Here, TM (Transferred Model) is the model used in the target domain, which is generally driven from M. After $P_{X_{sel,TD_i}}$ is used to drive TM from M, Eq. (3) is adaptive to apply to the target domain.

$$c = M(X_{sel}, P_{X_{sel,SD_i}}) \tag{2}$$

$$c = TM(X_{sel}, P_{X_{sel,SD_i}}, P_{X_{sel,TD}}) \tag{3}$$

2.2   Related Work to GP for Text Classification

Based on the output and structure of GP programs, the categories of using GP for text classification are rule-based and value-based [6,10].

In a rule-based model (classifier), rules are easily understood by humans. So programs evolved by a rule-based GP system are normally readable. In [10,11], GP systems imitate the rule design from humans. In the GP systems, letters are used as terminals, and string operators and logical operators as functions. N-gram terms are generated by using an expand function and string connection function. Different from humans, the GP systems do not need an exhaustive search of all n-gram terms. GP will automatically find meaningful n-gram terms. However, since the evolved programs mainly focus on whether combinations of letters exist or not in a document, the frequencies of n-gram terms are not addressed, it is possible that complex and similar documents with different categories might not be handled well. Additionally, prior knowledge on rule-based text classification algorithms is required for setting up the GP system.

Similar to other value-based classification problem, a value-based GP system evolves programs to classify documents based on its output. In [6,22], predefined categories and existing features are provided to evolve binary GP programs. In the value-based GP systems, a small set of features are selected as terminals by feature selection algorithms. Common arithmetic operators, such as add, minus, times and division, are used to construct formulae. A threshold is used to discriminate whether a document belongs to a category or not based on the output of an evolved GP program. Different from a rule-based GP system, a value-based GP system considers the frequencies of words and n-gram terms. Therefore, a value-based GP system can generally achieve better performance than a rule-based GP system [6,15,22].

3   The Method

This section introduces the proposed GP system for document classification used for transductive transfer learning. Here, we use a strongly typed and tree-based GP system. Firstly, we introduce the sets of terminals and functions, then describe the fitness function. Also, how to use composite features evolved by GP for another similar domain is introduced.

3.1   Functions and Terminals

Since GP has the ability to select features [7], traditional feature selection process is not used to select basic features in the proposed GP system. The numbers of the occurrences of words from a predefined vocabulary in a document are directly considered as terminals. If a word does not exist in a document, its occurrence will be 0. The proposed GP system randomly selects terminals to construct a GP tree. Therefore, the proposed GP system will automatically select features based on the predefined vocabulary. When the vocabulary are built from all training documents, the basic features from the vocabulary are the same to the features from the bag-of-words model. One advantage of using a vocabulary is that we can filter useless features, such as comma and full stop. Also, random constants are used in the GP system.

To construct a value-based GP tree, the function set contains four common arithmetic operators $\{+, -, \times, \div\}$. For example, we have two topics (categories) "food" and "motor". In order to classify a document from "food" or "motor", we have a GP program $\#[meal] - \#[wheel]$. Here, $\#[meal]$ and $\#[wheel]$ are the number of the occurrences of the word "meal" and the word "wheel" existing in the document. If the output of $\#[meal] - \#[wheel]$ is larger than threshold $th = 0$, the document is classified as label "food"; otherwise "motor".

In a binary document classification problem, there are positive label (class) "1" and negative label "0". A binary GP program from source domain SD_i in Eq. (4) classifies a document as "1" (the output of GP being larger than threshold th) or "0" (the output of GP not being larger than threshold th). Here c_i is the predicated label for the GP program evolved from source domain SD_i.

$$c_i = GP_{SD_i}(X_{SD_i}) > th?1 : 0 \qquad (4)$$

Note that the training data in this paper is considered as balanced data, and only binary classification problems are addressed. The accuracy of correctly classified documents is used as the GP fitness function. Equation (5) defines the fitness function f, where N_T is the total number of correctly classified documents and N is the total number of documents.

$$f = \frac{N_T}{N} \qquad (5)$$

3.2   Transductive Transfer Learning

GP evolves programs GP_{SD_i} from each source domain SD_i. However, the target domain TD is not totally the same to the source domain SD_i. The knowledge from a program evolved from SD_i might be partially helpful for predicating labels in the target domain. For the helpful part, it is considered as shared knowledge between source domain SD_i and the target domain TD. It is expected that GP evolved programs from source domain SD_i to transfer the shared knowledge to the target domain TD. To utilise the shared knowledge from GP evolved programs, we combine GP evolved programs from multiple source domains. Equation (6) describes a GP program $GP_{SD_{i,j}}$ to predicate a document in target domain TD as label $c_{i,j}$ ("0" or "1"). Here, j indicates one of GP programs evolved from source domain SD_i and $j = 1, \ldots, p$. Equation (7) describes that we randomly select p GP programs as extracted features from each source domain SD_i to combine as a final classifier for the target domain TD. The number of source domains is n.

$$c_{i,j} = GP_{SD_{i,j}}(X_{TD}) > th?1 : 0 \tag{6}$$

$$c = \sum\nolimits_{i=1,\ldots,n, j=1,\ldots,p} c_{i,j} > 0.5 * n * p?1 : 0 \tag{7}$$

To indicate the number of extracted features from each source domain, we use GP for the standard GP system (without transfer learning), GP_{vp} to indicate p GP programs as features from each source domain to vote for a document from the target domain as "1" or "0".

4   The Design of the Experiment

4.1   Dataset

The 20 newsgroup dataset [16] has been widely used by researchers [1,14,17]. The dataset includes 20 categories, and some are very closely related to each other, such as "rec.autos" and "rec.motorcycles". In "rec" group, there are four subcategories, namely "rec.autos", "rec.motorcycles", "rec.sport.baseball" and "rec.sport.hockey". Two groups "rec" and "talk" in the dataset are selected in this paper. Here, we consider one binary task of classifying "rec" and "talk" ("rec" vs talk"). "rec" is considered as label "1", and "talk" as label "0". Table 1 provides the details of the binary classification tasks. For instance, in "rec vs talk", when "rec.autos" and "talk.politics.guns" is a source domain, the others as the relevant target domains. $data_1$ is used to indicate the binary dataset which only includes "rec.autos" and "talk.politics.guns". The 20 newsgroup dataset has three different types of files. Here, "20news-bydate" is used. In "20news-bydate", its training dataset and test dataset are independent. Also, a vocabulary is provided in the 20 newsgroup dataset. The vocabulary includes 61188 words from the 20 newsgroup dataset.

Here, we take three datasets as source domains, and the other one as the target domain. Therefore, for each dataset, when it is the target domain, the other

Table 1. Four datasets used for source domain SD or target domain TD

	1	0
$data_1$	rec.autos	talk.politics.guns
$data_2$	rec.motorcycles	talk.politics.mideast
$data_3$	rec.sport.baseball	talk.politics.misc
$data_4$	rec.sport.hockey	talk.religion.misc

three are source domains. GP_{vp} automatically extracts features (programs) from the source domains and directly applies them to the test dataset on the target domain. It is assumed that some features are helpful to classify documents in the source domains and target domain. It is expected that GP will extract these helpful features from the source domains then these features can be effectively applied to the target domain.

4.2   GP Settings

We select the numbers of GP programs from each source as followings: 1, 3, 5. Namely, we have GP_{v1}, GP_{v3} and GP_{v5} to classify documents from the target domain.

Based on the common GP parameter settings in [8], the probability for mutation is 0.15, the probability for crossover is 0.80, the probability for elitism (reproduction) is 0.05, the population size is 200, and the maximum generations is 200. Since GP will automatically select features from a sparse and large set, the maximum depth (of a program) is 10, There are 30 independent runs for each experiment.

5   Results and Discussions

This section describes the test performance on each dataset with discussions. The results based on each dataset set as the target data and the others as the source datasets are provided. Further discussions are also presented.

5.1   Test Performance

Table 2 presents the test accuracies from GP, GP_{v1}, GP_{v3} and GP_{v5}. The fist row indicates the target domain. When one dataset is selected as the target domain, the other three datasets are the source domains. For instance, in the column "$data_1$", the source domains are $data_2$, $data_2$ and $data_3$, and the target domain is $data_1$. Here, we use two-pair sampled t-tests to compare the results from GP_{vp} to GP. The significance level 0.05 is used, and ↑ indicates that the test results from GP_{vp} are all significantly better than the results from GP. As we can see, only GP_{v1} on the target domain $data_2$ has non-significant results with GP; the others from GP_{vp} are significantly better than GP. From the four datasets, it seems that the proposed GP system effectively extracts features from different source domains and effectively combines the extracted features as classifiers for similar target domains.

Table 2. Test accuracies on the target domain from GP, GP_{v1}, GP_{v3}, and GP_{v5}

	$data_1$	$data_2$	$data_3$	$data_4$
GP	0.7197 ± 0.0527	0.7516 ± 0.0447	0.7043 ± 0.0406	0.7389 ± 0.0444
GP_{v1}	0.7987 ± 0.0628 ↑	0.7339 ± 0.0954	0.7770 ± 0.0600 ↑	0.8014 ± 0.0806 ↑
GP_{v3}	0.8529 ± 0.0306 ↑	0.7812 ± 0.0503 ↑	0.8230 ± 0.0518 ↑	0.8552 ± 0.0478 ↑
GP_{v5}	0.8643 ± 0.0224 ↑	0.7880 ± 0.0337 ↑	0.8403 ± 0.0314 ↑	0.8675 ± 0.0315 ↑

There are also several interesting observations. Firstly, the test accuracies on $data_1$, $data_3$ and $data_4$ are improved more than 7%, comparing GP_{v1} with the standard GP method GP. Comparing the results from GP_{v3} and GP_{v5} with GP, the test accuracy improvement is more than 11% on datasets $data_1$, $data_3$ and $data_4$. Secondly, the test accuracy improvement on $data_2$ for GP_{vp} is not as large as the three datasets. It is possible that the three datasets $data_1$, $data_3$ and $data_4$ are close to each other. It is easier to find shared features for correctly classifying documents from the three datasets than $data_2$. Lastly, when the number of extracted programs is increasing, the test accuracy becomes higher; also, the standard deviations of the test accuracies become smaller. It seems that more features from the source domains can improve test performances on the accuracy and stability. More comparisons on the different numbers of features are given in the next subsection.

Figure 1 presents the details of the test accuracies of GP, GP_{v1}, GP_{v3} and GP_{v5} by box-plots.

First of all, when only one program evolved by GP from each source domain is combined together for a target domain, the test accuracy is not stable. Since these datasets do not have the same distribution on the input features, for a GP program evolved from a source domain, there might be limited shared knowledge between the source domain and a target domain.

Secondly, Fig. 1(2) shows one result with the test accuracy less than 0.5. It reveals that negative transfer occurs for the relevant combination. It is possible that the shared knowledge between a source domain and a target domain is not easily found. This paper only employs the voting strategy to classify documents. In order to avoid negative transfer when only single GP program is used for each source domain, the difference between the source domain and the target domain will be considered. Based on the difference, there are two potential ways to address the negative transfer issue. One way is to always to select evolved programs whose shared knowledge is easily found. The second way is to further handle with the evolved programs whose shared knowledge is not easily found so that the shared knowledge is easily used. Both ways are our future work directions.

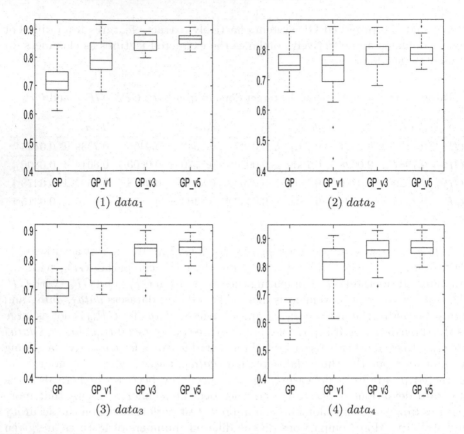

Fig. 1. Test Accuracies on the dataset from $data_1$ to $data_4$. In each figure, from the first to the fourth is the results from GP, GP_{v1}, GP_{v3}, and GP_{v5} respectively.

Thirdly, it also shows that the test accuracies are better when more the evolved GP programs are combined together for classifying documents from target domain. Since the evolved programs are different, there may also be difference of the shared knowledge from these programs. When more GP programs are used, the combination of the shared knowledge of these GP programs covers more for the dataset on the target domain. When the number of GP evolved programs reaches to a proper value, the coverage ratio of the knowledge on the target domain becomes stable. The experiments on the four datasets show that the test accuracy increment from GP_{v3} to GP_{v5} is obviously less than the increment from P_{v1} to GP_{v3}.

Fourthly, GP_{v3} and GP_{v5} do not have negative transfer based on the test accuracy on the four datasets. It seems that using multiple GP programs from each source domain can avoid negative transfer.

Finally, the best combinations can archive very high test performances. The results from the best combinations are higher than 0.9 on $data_1$, $data_3$ and $data_4$, and being close to 0.9 on $data_2$. It looks like that GP have potential to automatically extract very good features. However, how to make GP to always generate very good features needs further investigation.

5.2 Comparisons Among GP_{v1}, GP_{v3} and GP_{v5}

Table 3 gives the multiple comparisons among GP_{v1}, GP_{v3} and GP_{v5} on the four test datasets. The multiple comparisons based on t-tests use Holm's method [12] for p-value adjustment, and the overall significance level is 0.05. "↑" means that the relevant row item is significantly better than the relevant column item. From the comparison results, GP_{v3} and GP_{v5} have significantly test accuracy results than GP_{v1}. However, there are no significant differences between GP_{v3} and GP_{v5}. From the multiple comparisons among GP_{v1}, GP_{v3} and GP_{v5} on the four test datasets, it also shows that multiple features (programs) evolved by GP from different source domains can improve test performance on the target domain than only using single GP features from source domains. When the number of GP features from each sourced domain used to a target domain reaches to a proper value, there is no significant improvement.

Table 3. Multiple Comparison Among GP_{v1}, GP_{v3} and GP_{v5} on Four Datasets $data_1$, $data_2$, $data_3$, and $data_4$

	GP_{v1}	GP_{v3}	GP_{v5}
$data_1$			
GP_{v3}	↑		
GP_{v5}	↑	−	
$data_2$			
GP_{v3}	↑		
GP_{v5}	↑	−	
$data_3$			
GP_{v3}	↑		
GP_{v5}	↑	−	
$data_4$			
GP_{v3}	↑		
GP_{v5}	↑	−	

5.3 Discussions

When a single feature from each source domain is applied to a target domain, negative transfer might occur. One evolved program which has negative transfer includes sub-tree $\#[car] - \#[gun]$. From its training data $data_1$, it is helpful to classify a document from "rec.auto" or "talk.politics.gun". However, "gun" may be not a general word for other data in group "talk". Since we do not consider how to evaluate the difference between source domains and target domains, we do not know when negative transfer occurs. In [9], to obtain the same distribution for both domains, latent space construction aims to find the same distribution latent space between the feature spaces of the source and target domains. If the outputs of a GP feature is in a latent space, the distribution of the outputs of the GP feature may be helpful to check whether negative transfer occurs. In order to check whether a GP feature can be directly applied to a target domain, one potential way is to consider whether the outputs of the GP feature has a similar distribution to the raw source domain. This is our future work.

Also, the GP features are directly evolved from source domains without any information from a target domain. To make GP generate features which share knowledge between a source domain and a target domain, it is worth also considering the information from the target domain during an evolving stage. Evolved GP programs which are helpful for target domains include sub-trees, such as $\frac{\#[irregular]}{\#[technique]}$ and $\#[face] \times \#[improving]$. These words are general for groups "rec" and "talk". These general words are extracted by GP, and they are used as shared knowledge between source domains and target domains. Besides of the distributions of GP programs, it is worth to investigate how to integrate other information between the source and target domains into the GP fitness function.

6   Conclusions

This paper was to initially investigate transductive transfer learning in GP for automatically extract features for document classification based on four datasets. The GP evolved features from source domains were directly applied to a target domains. From the experimental results, when only a single GP evolved feature from each source domain is directly applied to the target domain, negative transfer might occur. However, from the overall results, the combinations of the GP evolved features from source domains have significantly better results on the target domain than the GP evolved single features directly from the target domain. Using multiple GP evolved features from each source domain can avoid negative transfer, also improves the test accuracy on the target domains, comparing the use of a single GP feature from the source domains to the target domain. More GP evolved features from each source domain to the target domain might not always significantly improve test accuracy.

In our future work, we will investigate how to avoid negative transfer. Also, the distribution difference between a source domain and a target domain will be considered into a GP fitness function so that evolved GP features can be adaptively applied to the target domain. Note that this paper only conducts investigation on the datasets being similar to each other. When source domains and a target domain are obviously different, how to effectively transfer the GP evolved features from the source domains to the target domain is future work.

References

1. Agarwal, B., Mittal, N.: Text classification using machine learning methods-a survey. In: Babu, B.V., Nagar, A., Deep, K., Pant, M., Bansal, J.C., Ray, K., Gupta, U. (eds.) Proceedings of the Second International Conference on Soft Computing for Problem Solving (SocProS 2012), December 28-30, 2012. AISC, vol. 236, pp. 701–709. Springer, New Delhi (2014). doi:10.1007/978-81-322-1602-5_75
2. Bhowan, U., McCloskey, D.J.: Genetic programming for feature selection and question-answer ranking in IBM watson. In: Machado, P., Heywood, M.I., McDermott, J., Castelli, M., García-Sánchez, P., Burelli, P., Risi, S., Sim, K. (eds.) EuroGP 2015. LNCS, vol. 9025, pp. 153–166. Springer, Cham (2015). doi:10.1007/978-3-319-16501-1_13
3. Cavnar, W.B., Trenkle, J.M.: N-gram-based text categorization. In: Proceedings of 3rd Annual Symposium on Document Analysis and Information Retrieval, SDAIR-1994, pp. 161–175 (1994)
4. Chen, Q., Xue, B., Niu, B., Zhang, M.: Improving generalisation of genetic programming for high-dimensional symbolic regression with feature selection. In: 2016 IEEE Congress on Evolutionary Computation (CEC), pp. 3793–3800 (2016)
5. Chen, Q., Zhang, M., Xue, B.: Feature selection to improve generalisation of genetic programming for high-dimensional symbolic regression. IEEE Trans. Evol. Comput. **PP**(99), 1 (2017)
6. Escalante, H.J., García-Limón, M.A., Morales-Reyes, A., Graff, M., Montes-y-Gómez, M., Morales, E.F., Martínez-Carranza, J.: Term-weighting learning via genetic programming for text classification. Knowl.-Based Syst. **83**, 176–189 (2015)
7. Fu, W., Johnston, M., Zhang, M.: Low-level feature extraction for edge detection using genetic programming. IEEE Trans. Cybern. **44**(8), 1459–1472 (2014)
8. Fu, W., Johnston, M., Zhang, M.: Distribution-based invariant feature construction using genetic programming for edge detection. Soft Comput. **19**(8), 2371–2389 (2015)
9. Gong, B., Grauman, K., Sha, F.: Learning kernels for unsupervised domain adaptation with applications to visual object recognition. Int. J. Comput. Vis. **109**(1), 3–27 (2014)
10. Hirsch, L., Saeedi, M., Hirsch, R.: Evolving rules for document classification. In: Keijzer, M., Tettamanzi, A., Collet, P., van Hemert, J., Tomassini, M. (eds.) EuroGP 2005. LNCS, vol. 3447, pp. 85–95. Springer, Heidelberg (2005). doi:10.1007/978-3-540-31989-4_8
11. Hirsch, L., Saeedi, M., Hirsch, R.: Evolving text classification rules with genetic programming. Appl. Artif. Intell. **19**(7), 659–676 (2005)
12. Holm, S.: A simple sequentially rejective multiple test procedure. Scand. J. Stat. **6**(2), 65–70 (1979)
13. Joachims, T.: Text categorization with support vector machines: learning with many relevant features. In: Nédellec, C., Rouveirol, C. (eds.) ECML 1998. LNCS, vol. 1398, pp. 137–142. Springer, Heidelberg (1998). doi:10.1007/BFb0026683
14. Khan, A., Baharudin, B., Lee, L.H., Khan, K., Tronoh, U.T.P.: A review of machine learning algorithms for text-documents classification. J. Adv. Inf. Technol. (2010)
15. Khodadi, I., Abadeh, M.S.: Genetic programming-based feature learning for question answering. Inf. Process. Manage. **52**(2), 340–357 (2016)
16. Lang, K.: Newsweeder: learning to filter netnews. In: Proceedings of the 12th International Machine Learning Conference (ML95) (1995)

17. Pan, S.J., Tsang, I.W., Kwok, J.T., Yang, Q.: Domain adaptation via transfer component analysis. IEEE Trans. Neural Netw. **22**(2), 199–210 (2011)
18. Pan, S.J., Yang, Q.: A survey on transfer learning. IEEE Trans. Knowl. Data Eng. **22**(10), 1345–1359 (2010)
19. Sebastiani, F.: Machine learning in automated text categorization. ACM Comput. Surv. **34**(1), 1–47 (2002)
20. Weiss, K., Khoshgoftaar, T.M., Wang, D.: A survey of transfer learning. J. Big Data **3**(1), 9 (2016)
21. Yang, Y., Pedersen, J.O.: A comparative study on feature selection in text categorization. In: Proceedings of the Fourteenth International Conference on Machine Learning, pp. 412–420 (1997)
22. Zhang, B., Fan, W., Chen, Y., Fox, E.A., Gonçalves, M.A., Cristo, M., Calado, P.: A genetic programming approach for combining structural and citation-based evidence for text classification in web digital libraries. In: Herrera-Viedma, E., Pasi, G., Crestani, F. (eds.) Soft Computing in Web Information Retrieval. Studies in Fuzziness and Soft Computing, vol. 197, pp. 65–83. Springer, Heidelberg (2006). doi:10.1007/3-540-31590-X_4

Automatic Feature Construction for Network Intrusion Detection

Binh Tran[1], Stjepan Picek[2], and Bing Xue[1(✉)]

[1] School of Engineering and Computer Science, Victoria University of Wellington,
600, Wellington 6140, New Zealand
{binh.tran,bing.xue}@ecs.vuw.ac.nz
[2] Cyber Security Research Group, Delft University of Technology,
Mekelweg 2, Delft, The Netherlands
stjepan@computer.org

Abstract. The notion of cyberspace became impossible to separate from the notions of cyber threat and cyberattack. Since cyberattacks are getting easier to run, they are also becoming more serious threats from the economic damage perspective. Consequently, we are evident of a continuous adversarial relationship between the attackers trying to mount as powerful as possible attacks and defenders trying to stop the attackers in their goals. To defend against such attacks, defenders have at their disposal a plethora of techniques but they are often falling behind the attackers due to the fact that they need to protect the whole system while the attacker needs to find only a single weakness to exploit. In this paper, we consider one type of a cyberattack – network intrusion – and investigate how to use feature construction via genetic programming in order to improve the intrusion detection accuracy. The obtained results show that feature construction offers improvements in a number of tested scenarios and therefore should be considered as an important step in defense efforts. Such improvements are especially apparent in scenario with the highly unbalanced data, which also represents the most interesting case from the defensive perspective.

1 Introduction

From its inception, the word cyberspace is used to represent an umbrella of phenomena occurring in computer networks. Besides the advantages stemming from the better connectivity and reachability, cyberspace also has its drawbacks and dangers, where cyberattacks represent one that cannot be neglected. Here, by cyberattacks we consider all deliberate exploitations of computer systems, since such attacks seem to be becoming easier to conduct while their severity grows. The proliferation of such threats on computers, mobile phones, etc. made us all beware that the connectivity we often take for a granted comes with a high price. As an example of that tendency, we mention a fact that NATO suffered from 500 cyber attacks every month in 2016, which represents an increase of 60% from 2015 [1]. One could postulate that the increase and severity of attacks is

© Springer International Publishing AG 2017
Y. Shi et al. (Eds.): SEAL 2017, LNCS 10593, pp. 569–580, 2017.
https://doi.org/10.1007/978-3-319-68759-9_46

evident only for large organizations, but that is not necessarily true. It is enough to consider the 2017 Wannacry ransomware case, where in only one day, more than 230 000 computers in more than 150 countries were infected [2]. Finally, the threats are not limited to only one type of hosts - the Wannacry example spreads over computers running Microsoft Windows operating system, while even more recent threat "Cloak and Dagger" was identified for the Android operating system [3]. We note there are also different types of attacks with respect to the attacker's goals. As an example, the attacker can conduct only a simple network scanning in order to detect some possible system weaknesses to be used later. Alternatively, he can launch massive Distributed Denial-of-Service (DDos) attacks with a goal of making network resources unavailable to its intended users by temporarily or indefinitely disrupting services of a host connected to the Internet.

To fight against such varying threats, there are numerous options one can consider. In the rest of this paper, we limit our attention to one type of threat – network intrusion attacks and consequently defenses against such attacks. A network intrusion attack is an activity, where a malicious user tries to make some sort of unauthorized activity on a computer network. Often, the first defense against it are network intrusion detection techniques. Intrusion detection techniques are usually divided into signature based and anomaly detection based approaches [4]. In the signature based approaches one relies on recognizing the signatures of attacks (for example, hash values that are characteristic for certain attack types). Such detection techniques are easily avoided by modifying the attack or using previously unknown attack (i.e., zero-day attack). Anomaly detection systems rely on recognizing what is normal traffic and categorizing all that does not fit the description of normal into anomaly.

When discussing anomaly detection systems, a great deal of research has been invested in utilizing machine learning and evolutionary computation techniques [5,6]. As far as we are aware, up to now there is no research considering how to use evolutionary algorithms to construct higher level features that can result in better classification accuracy for the network intrusion detection. We aim to fill this gap by providing the first results in several relevant scenarios and proposing further research directions.

Genetic programming (GP) is an evolutionary computation technique that can automatically evolve solutions based on the idea of the survival of the fittest. With a flexible representation such as trees and any kind of operators or functions to represent the model, GP is an excellent choice for feature construction. Features constructed by GP have been shown to obtain better discriminating power than the original features [7–9]. In this study, we investigate GP performance in constructing high-level features for the network intrusion detection. The constructed features are expected to improve the classification performance of common learning algorithms when compared with the original feature sets.

The area of network intrusion detection has several specificities which makes it a challenging scenario to consider. The first problem stems from the lack of good datasets since they are in most cases artificially constructed and difficult to correlate with the realistic scenarios. The second difficulty comes from the fact the classification accuracy is relatively high when compared to other problems and consequently possible improvements obtainable with feature construction are much smaller. Still, due to the importance of the highly-accurate intrusion detection systems and possible damages when anomalies are not detected, even small improvements in accuracy can be of extreme importance. Finally, being able to automatically construct features is beneficial since feature construction is most often done by human experts, which is far from being error prone and is a time consuming process.

The rest of this paper is organized in the following way. In Sect. 2 we discuss the attacker capabilities as well as the defender's goals. We also give details about the dataset we investigate. Section 3 gives a short overview of related work. In Sect. 4 we provide details about GP that is used for feature construction, an brief description of the two classification algorithms used in this paper. Section 5 gives experimental results for several intrusion detection scenarios and a comparison between the constructed features and the original ones. We also provide a discussion on results and remarks on possible future research directions. Finally, in Sect. 6 we give a brief conclusion and future work.

2   Background

2.1   Stages of a Cyberattack

When discussing cyber threats, it is important to realize that often they do not represent atomic actions leading to a success but are rather a succession of steps one needs to do in order to successfully attack a system. Although there are various understandings and attack stage granularities (usually ranging from five to ten stages), some common ones are defined in [10]. An attack usually starts with the reconnaissance phase, where the attacker's goal is to obtain knowledge about the system and find possible weaknesses. Next, incursion follows where the attacker actually penetrates the system. Within the system, the attacker moves laterally in order to discover and exploit the system. Finally, in the exfiltration phase the attacker tries to steal the sensitive data and leave the system undiscovered. We depict five stages of a cyberattack with an emphasis on attacker's goals in Fig. 1.

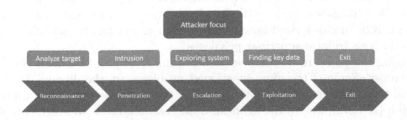

Fig. 1. Five stages of a cyberattack.

We aim to defend against a powerful attacker that has an unbounded number of IP addresses on his disposal, which enables him to run anything from a simple network scanning attacks up to massive DDoS attacks. We do not limit the attacker to be present in any specific stage of a cyber attack. In order to be able to recognize such wide set of threats, we train anomaly detectors for all available attack types as well as for the normal traffic. We assume that the attacker can mount already known attacks as well as the zero-day attacks. Finally, we assume that the attacker cannot interfere with the running of GP or classifiers.

Due to the fact that our system is not fast enough to work in an online setting (where as the new data instances are acquired, GP is able to update the set of constructed features) we consider here only the offline setting, where a number of training instances is acquired and on the basis of them, GP constructs features. Since we are not time-constrained, it is reasonable to assume that we can run additional classifiers on the obtained data in order to classify it into normal or anomaly data. Therefore, we work here only in the binary setting where we have both normal and anomaly data (regardless whether there are different types of anomalies or only one).

Anomaly detection is often considered in the one-class classification setting, where we assume not to have anomaly data at the time of the model training. Still, adding additional classifiers (i.e., building ensemble classifiers) as combinations among one-class, binary, and multi-class classifiers is an option that improves the accuracy of the intrusion detection system. Although it could be claimed that first running feature selection would enable GP to be faster and to work with only the most informative features, we use all available features and expect from GP to recognize the most important ones.

2.2 Datasets

All our experiments are based on the NSL-KDD dataset [11]. This dataset is on the other hand based on one older dataset called the KDD Cup dataset [12]. Here, we first briefly describe the KDD Cup dataset and then we discuss the differences between it and the NSL-KDD dataset.

The KDD Cup dataset is comprised from nine weeks of raw TCP dump data for a local-area network (LAN) simulating a typical U.S. Air Force LAN that was exposed to multiple attacks. Each instance is a sequence of TCP packets starting and ending at some well-defined times. Each record can be labeled into either normal or anomaly data, where anomaly data can be divided into four classes: DoS (denial-of-service attacks), Probe (surveillance and other probing attacks), R2L (unauthorized access from a remote machine), and U2R (unauthorized access to local superuser privileges).

During the years, researchers noticed a number of problems with the KDD Cup dataset. Some of the often mentioned problems are the dissimilarity from the real traffic and issues encountered due to the synthetic data generation and insertion [13]. Still, due to the artificial data creation, one advantage is that we can be sure the data to be correctly classified. Consider a "realistic" dataset where the only proof of an attack is to have some classifier reporting it. In the case that classifier misclassified, we would propagate errors to the next level of experiments – feature construction. Finally, the KDD Cup dataset offers a wide variety of attacks, which is not something one necessarily encounters in "realistic" scenarios. The improvements of NSL-KDD over the KDD Cup dataset are:

- the dataset does not include redundant records in the train set,
- there are no duplicate records in the proposed test sets,
- the number of selected records from each difficulty level group is inversely proportional to the percentage of records in the original KDD Cup dataset,
- the number of records in the train and test sets are smaller.

3   Related Work

Anomaly based detection is a well-researched topic in the last decade or more with many papers examining various defense types and algorithms to be used.

When using GP for anomaly detection, there is a line of works exploring binary and one-class classification. One-class GP is a technique introduced by Curry and Heywood [14] where they artificially create the second class (outliers) on the basis of the normal data that is available. Cao et al. [15] experiment with one-class classification by using kernel density function, where the density function is approximated by using GP symbolic regression. To and Elati [16] developed a one-class GP where they use only one class in the training. In their approach, GP tries to find a curve that fits all patterns in the training set and if an instance belonging to the testing set is close to the trained patterns, it is defined as belonging to the normal class. Song et al. use GP to detect anomalies in the KDD Cup dataset where the authors use hierarchical dynamic subset selection in order to train around 500 000 instances [17].

When considering feature selection, Wang et al. [18] experiment with several methods to find the most informative features for each of the four anomaly classes in the KDD Cup dataset. Zargari and Voorhis [19] conduct feature selection for the NSL-KDD dataset and suggest the most informative features for all anomaly classes.

When considering automatic feature construction for network intrusion detection, the works are sparse and do not consider genetic programming (or any kind of evolutionary algorithms). As an example of automatic feature construction technique, we mention the work by Lee and Stolfo [20], where the authors use several data mining algorithms to build a framework to construct features and models for intrusion detection.

4   Methodology

4.1   Classification Algorithms

We use two simple classifier techniques in order to investigate the performance of the constructed features. We decided to use these classifiers since they are fast and able to reach high accuracies. Note that using more powerful classifiers could improve the results but with a price of a longer classification process.

Naive Bayes (NB). NB classifier is a method based on the Bayesian rule that works under the simplified assumption that the predictor attributes (measurements) are conditionally independent among the features given the target class. Detailed information about the Naive Bayes algorithm can be found in [21].

C4.5. C4.5 is a divide-and-conquer algorithm that split features at tree nodes using the information gain ratio criterion [22]. The node splits in further branches if more information is gained (as measured by the gain ratio) by the split than by keeping all the instances at the node. The trees are first grown to full length and pruned afterwards in order to avoid data overfitting.

With the C4.5 algorithm, we investigate the influence of the confidence factor parameter c that is used for pruning, where smaller values relate to more pruning. We tested that parameter in the range $[0.05, 0.5]$ with a step of 0.05, where we conducted a separate tuning phase for each scenario. Due to the lack of space, we do not show the full tuning results but only the best obtained solutions. For normalVSanomaly we use $c = 0.3$, for normalVSdos $c = 0.35$, for normalVSprobe $c = 0.5$, for normalVSr2l $c = 0.5$, and for normalVSu2r $c = 0.2$.

4.2 Genetic Programming

We use a standard GP algorithm to construct one high-level feature using the single-tree representation as in [8,23]. GP works by maintaining a population of individuals, each of which represents a constructed feature.

To evaluate the goodness of a constructed feature, the evaluation procedure follows an embedded approach, where each individual is evaluated based on its classification performance on the training set. In other words, each individual or the corresponding constructed feature can also be considered as a classifier, which classifies an instance x by executing the following rule:

$$IF \;\; constructed \; F <= 0 \;\; THEN \;\; x \in class_0; \quad ELSE \;\; x \in class_1. \quad (1)$$

Since the network attack detection datasets are usually unbalanced, we use the balanced accuracy [24] as shown in Eq. (2) for fitness evaluation. It is an average of true positive rate (TPR) and true negative rate (TNR), where TPR (or TNR) is the proportion of correctly identified instances of positive (or negative) class.

$$fitness = \frac{1}{2} \left(TPR + TNR \right), \quad (2)$$

In order to avoid underfitting as well as overfitting, we use a dynamic stopping criterion. During the evolutionary process, if the validation accuracy does not improve after 50 generations, GP stops and returns the model with the best validation accuracy; otherwise, GP continues to run until a maximum number of generations is reached. After the evolutionary process, the GP individual having the best validation accuracy is returned as the best solution. Algorithm 1 shows the pseudo code of the GP-based feature construction method which returns a new constructed feature.

Algorithm 1. GP-based feature construction method

  Input : Training_data
  Output: The best constructed feature
1 **begin**
2 | Training data is equally split into *train_set* and *valid_set*;
3 | Initialize a population of GP individuals/trees;
4 | *not_improved* ← 0;
5 | **while** *Maximum iterations is not reached or the best solution is not found or not_improved < 50* **do**
6 | | **for** *i* = 1 to *Population Size* **do**
7 | | | *transf_train* ← Calculate constructed feature of individual *i* on *train_set* (*transf_train* has only one feature, i.e. the constructed feature) ;
8 | | | *fitness* ← classification accuracy of *transf_train* using Rule 1 and Eq. 2;
9 | | **end**
10 | | *best_gen_ind* ← individual that have the highest *fitness*;
11 | | *transf_valid* ← Calculate constructed feature of the *best_gen_ind* on *valid_set* (*transf_valid* has only one new feature) ;
12 | | *valid_acc* ← classification accuracy of *transf_valid* using Rule 1 ;
13 | | **if** *(valid_acc is improved)* **then**
14 | | | Update *valid_acc* ;
15 | | | *not_improved* ← 0;
16 | | **else**
17 | | | *not_improved* + +;
18 | | **end**
19 | | Select parent individuals using tournament for breeding;
20 | | Create offspring individuals by applying crossover or mutation on the selected parents;
21 | | Place new individuals into the population of the next generation;
22 | **end**
23 | *best_ind* ← individual that have the highest *valid_acc*;
24 | Return the *best_ind*;
25 **end**

Table 1. Datasets

Dataset	#Features	#Instances	Class-distribution
normalVSanomaly	40	47 736	48.52%–51.48%
normalVSdos	39	39 852	58.12%–41.88%
normalVSprobe	38	27 870	83.10%–16.90%
normalVSr2l	40	26 123	88.66%–11.34%
normalVSu2r	40	23 371	99.10%–0.90%

4.3 Dataset Details

To test the performance of our method, five binary class datasets are generated from the NSL-KDD dataset. To obtain the instances, we take 10% of all measurements (which are already labeled) and we create datasets by combining instances belonging to the Normal class with instances belonging to each of the four anomaly classes.

Finally, we combine Normal instances with all anomaly instances (belonging to all 4 classes) and simply assigning them to the anomaly class (i.e., the binary setting). After generating these datasets, we remove those features that have only a single value since it does not provide any usefuly information. The number of remaining features of each dataset is shown in Table 1. As it can be seen from the class distribution, three out of the five datasets are extremely unbalanced (normalVSu2r dataset has less than 1% of instances belonging to one class), which makes these problems more challenging for machine learning algorithms. Each dataset is stratified and equally split into three data subsets for training, validation, and testing. These subsets are standardized based on the training set before feeding it into GP for feature construction.

5   Experiments

5.1   Experiment Configuration and Parameter Settings

To test the performance of GP in constructing better discriminating features, we compare the performance of common classification algorithms including Naive Bayes and Decision Tree using the resulting feature sets and the original feature set. As GP is a stochastic algorithm, 30 independent runs with different random seeds are applied on each training set. The resulting feature sets are tested on the test set. To eliminate the statistical variations, all comparisons are done on the 30 test results using the Wilcoxon significance test.

Table 2 describes the parameter settings for GP. The function set comprises of 7 functions, 5 of which are arithmetic operators (addition, subtraction, multiplication, square root, and protected division). Function max returns the maximum values from the two inputs and if returns the second argument if the first argument is positive and returns the third argument otherwise. The terminal set comprises of all the original features. ECJ package [25] was used to implement the system. We used the standard crossover operator provided by the package, which swaps two randomly picked subtrees of two parents, and the standard mutation, which replaces a randomly picked subtree of the parent by a new subtree.

Table 2. GP parameters and experiment settings

Function set	$+, -, \times, /, \sqrt{}, max, if$
Initial population	Ramped half-and half
Maximum tree depth	10
Initial maximum tree depth	3
Generations	500
Population size	1 024
Crossover rate	0.4
Mutation rate	0.6
Elitism size	10
Selection method	Tournament method
Tournament size	7

5.2 Results and Analysis

Table 3 shows the test accuracy of NB and DT using the resulting constructed feature sets compared with the "Full" (i.e., using the original feature set) feature set. For each classification algorithm, the best (B), the average, and the standard deviation (A ± Std) over the 30 independent runs are reported. In this column, we also display the Wilcoxon significance test results of the corresponding feature set over Full feature set with significance level of 0.05. "+" or "–" means that the result is significantly better or worse than the Full set and "=" means that their results are similar. In other words, the more "+", the better the resulting feature sets. The time (in minutes) used to train the constructed features is shown under the dataset name. Column "#F" shows the average size of each feature set.

We can observe that the running time is correlated with the sample size of the dataset. Note that although the time to train the constructed features ranges from 38 to 92 min for each dataset, it is only run once and can be offline. After the constructed features are learned, the execution time of the tree to produce the new features is negligible.

Table 3. Test results using NB and DT

Dataset	Features	#F	B-NB	A ± Std-NB	B-DT	A ± Std-DT
normalVSanomaly	Full	40.00	84.40	84.40 ± 0.00	98.44	98.44 ± 0.00
92.21 (m)	FullCF	41.00	87.31	84.71 ± 0.84 =	98.53	98.37 ± 0.09 –
normalVSdos	Full	39.00	91.90	91.90 ± 0.00	99.83	99.83 ± 0.00
77.61 (m)	FullCF	40.00	95.62	92.50 ± 0.90 +	99.84	99.75 ± 0.06 –
normalVSprobe	Full	38.00	93.10	93.10 ± 0.00	99.17	99.17 ± 0.00
51.97 (m)	FullCF	39.00	95.27	93.62 ± 0.64 +	99.40	99.16 ± 0.09 =
normalVSr2l	Full	40.00	85.25	85.25 ± 0.00	96.10	96.10 ± 0.00
50.84 (m)	FullCF	41.00	89.83	87.00 ± 2.09 +	96.95	96.27 ± 0.37 +
normalVSu2r	Full	40.00	91.03	91.03 ± 0.00	89.27	89.27 + 0.00
38.98 (m)	FullCF	41.00	92.36	91.06 ± 0.60 =	95.67	92.06 ± 1.79 +

As can be seen from Table 3 that feature sets with added one constructed feature (FullCF) are able to outperform the original sets in all considered cases. There, when using the Naive Bayes classifier, the difference is relatively large, while when using Decision Tree classifier, the difference in the accuracy is less pronounced. The FullCF helps NB achieve significantly better results in three out of five cases. The remaining two datasets, namely normalVSanomaly and normalVSu2r, obtain a similar accuracy. We also notice that the best accuracy that NB achieves using FullCF is always higher than using Full set. Using FullCF and considering averaged values, DT performance is better on 2 datasets, similar on 1 and worse on the remaining 2. We emphasize that bigger differences can be seen in the last three datasets, where the imbalance between the classes is more significant. Note the last scenario – normalVSu2r where the accuracy improvement is more than 6% and the class distribution is 99.10%–0.90%.

To better assess the influence of the added constructed feature, next we present the testing results for scenarios, where we use only one feature (or GP tree) – "CF" set as a binary classifier. As can be seen from Table 4, using one constructed feature results on average in performance degradation for DT on the first three datasets when compared with the original or FullCF feature set. Still, considering the fact that we use only one feature, the results are promising for scenarios, where extremely fast classification is needed. On the other hand, in scenarios with highly unbalanced data as in the last two datasets, this binary classifier with only one constructed feature still achieves higher accuracy than DT using Full or FullCF feature set.

Table 4. Testing results, GP using CF, accuracy. 1 – normalVSanomaly, 2 – normalVSdos, 3 – normalVSprobe, 4 – normalVSr2l, 5 – normalVSu2r

Statistics	1	2	3	4	5
Best	97.13	99.64	99.08	97.28	96.82
Average	96.26	99.35	98.29	96.36	95.03
StdDev	0.75	0.21	0.34	0.48	0.92

Finally, in Table 5 we display the testing results for the FullCF scenario. Note that the results are averaged over 30 runs and we use the C4.5 parameters obtained after a tuning phase for each scenario. The tuning phase is done on a single (for each scenario) training set where we select those uniformly at random. Notice that the first three scenarios give similar accuracies as those where the tuning phase was done on Full feature set (see Table 3) but in the last two scenarios the improvement is even more significant (considering Best values) with the tuning done on FullCF feature set.

Table 5. Testing results, DT using FullCF, accuracy. 1 – normalVSanomaly, 2 – normalVSdos, 3 – normalVSprobe, 4 – normalVSr2l, 5 – normalVSu2r

Statistics	1	2	3	4	5
Best	98.32	99.78	99.96	98.62	99.76
Avg	94.95	98.98	99.14	96.66	99.05
StdDev	3.61	2.85	0.19	3.91	0.48

Since our work represents only a start of investigations on GP feature construction for intrusion detection, there are many possible research directions one could follow. We briefly discuss only three of those. An obvious continuation of this work would be to consider more complex classifiers like Support Vector

Machines. Naturally, this would come with an added cost in the evolutionary process. The second interesting option would be to investigate how to reduce the false positive rate. This could be done by incorporating appropriate term in the fitness function for GP. Finally, here we discuss binary setting but we believe it would be of extreme importance to consider one-class classification and GP feature construction. In such a scenario, one would build new features that better represent normal class and hopefully help to further discriminate between normal and anomaly data.

6   Conclusions

In this paper, we consider the task of automated construction of higher-level features via GP for the network intrusion detection problem. Although this work should be considered only as a preliminary investigation in that direction, our results show that constructed features are able to increase the accuracy especially in scenarios where we observe highly unbalanced data. Since such unbalanced data represents a usual scenario for network intrusion detection (where we have either many normal instances and only sparse anomalies as in the reconnaissance phase or where most of the instances belong to the anomaly class like in DDoS attack) the proposed can be considered highly beneficial. In the future, we will consider other scenarios and datasets to further examine the performance of the proposed algorithm. We also intend to develop new approaches to further investigate the potential of feature construction on solving complex network intrusion problems.

References

1. Browne, R.: Nato: we ward off 500 cyberattacks each month, January 2017. http://edition.cnn.com/2017/01/19/politics/nato-500-cyberattacks-monthly/
2. Symantec: Ransom.wannacry, March 2017. https://www.symantec.com/security_response/writeup.jsp?docid=2017-051310-3522-99
3. Fratantonio, Y., Qian, C., Chung, S., Lee, W.: Cloak and Dagger: from two permissions to complete control of the UI feedback loop. In: Proceedings of the IEEE Symposium on Security and Privacy, Oakland, San Jose, CA, May 2017
4. García-Teodoro, P., Díaz-Verdejo, J., Maciá-Fernández, G., Vázquez, E.: Anomaly-based network intrusion detection: techniques. Syst. Chall. Comput. Secur. **28**(1–2), 18–28 (2009)
5. Wu, S.X., Banzhaf, W.: Review: the use of computational intelligence in intrusion detection systems: a review. Appl. Soft Comput. **10**(1), 1–35 (2010)
6. Tsai, C.F., Hsu, Y.F., Lin, C.Y., Lin, W.Y.: Intrusion detection by machine learning: a review. Expert Syst. Appl. **36**(10), 11994–12000 (2009)
7. Al-Sahaf, H., Al-Sahaf, A., Xue, B., Johnston, M., Zhang, M.: Automatically evolving rotation-invariant texture image descriptors by genetic programming. IEEE Trans. Evol. Comput. **21**(1), 83–101 (2017)
8. Tran, B., Xue, B., Zhang, M.: Genetic programming for feature construction and selection in classification on high-dimensional data. Memet. Comput. **8**(1), 3–15 (2015)

9. Tran, B., Zhang, M., Xue, B.: Multiple feature construction in classification on high-dimensional data using GP. In: IEEE Symposium Series on Computational Intelligence (SSCI), pp. 210–218, December 2017
10. Symantec: preparing for a cyber attack, January 2017. http://www.symantec.com/content/en/us/enterprise/other_resources/b-preparing-for-a-cyber-attack-interactive-SYM285k_050913.pdf
11. Habibi, A., et al.: UNB ISCX NSL-KDD dataset. http://nsl.cs.unb.ca/NSL-KDD/
12. Tavallaee, M., Bagheri, E., Lu, W., Ghorbani, A.A.: A detailed analysis of the KDD CUP 99 data set. In: Proceedings of the Second IEEE International Conference on Computational Intelligence for Security and Defense Applications, CISDA 2009, Piscataway, NJ, USA, pp. 53–58. IEEE Press (2009)
13. Shiravi, A., Shiravi, H., Tavallaee, M., Ghorbani, A.A.: Toward developing a systematic approach to generate benchmark datasets for intrusion detection. Comput. Secur. **31**(3), 357–374 (2012)
14. Curry, R., Heywood, M.I.: One-class genetic programming. In: Vanneschi, L., Gustafson, S., Moraglio, A., De Falco, I., Ebner, M. (eds.) EuroGP 2009. LNCS, vol. 5481, pp. 1–12. Springer, Heidelberg (2009). doi:10.1007/978-3-642-01181-8_1
15. Cao, V.L., Nicolau, M., McDermott, J.: One-class classification for anomaly detection with kernel density estimation and genetic programming. In: Heywood, M.I., McDermott, J., Castelli, M., Costa, E., Sim, K. (eds.) EuroGP 2016. LNCS, vol. 9594, pp. 3–18. Springer, Cham (2016). doi:10.1007/978-3-319-30668-1_1
16. To, C., Elati, M.: A Parallel genetic programming for single class classification. In: Proceedings of the 15th Annual Conference Companion on Genetic and Evolutionary Computation, GECCO 2013 Companion, pp. 1579–1586. ACM, New York (2013)
17. Song, D., Heywood, M.I., Zincir-Heywood, A.N.: Training genetic programming on half a million patterns: an example from anomaly detection. IEEE Trans. Evol. Comput. **9**(3), 225–239 (2005)
18. Wang, W., Gombault, S., Guyet, T.: Towards fast detecting intrusions: using key attributes of network traffic. In: Proceedings of the 2008 The Third International Conference on Internet Monitoring and Protection, ICIMP 2008, pp. 86–91. IEEE Computer Society, Washington, DC (2008)
19. Zargari, S., Voorhis, D.: Feature selection in the corrected KDD-dataset. In: 2012 Third International Conference on Emerging Intelligent Data and Web Technologies, pp. 174–180, September 2012
20. Lee, W., Stolfo, S.J.: A framework for constructing features and models for intrusion detection systems. ACM Trans. Inf. Syst. Secur. **3**(4), 227–261 (2000)
21. Friedman, N., Geiger, D., Goldszmidt, M.: Bayesian network classifiers. Mach. Learn. **29**(2), 131–163 (1997)
22. Quinlan, J.R.: C4.5: Programs for Machine Learning. Morgan Kaufmann Publishers Inc., San Francisco (1993)
23. Tran, B., Xue, B., Zhang, M.: Using feature clustering for GP-based feature construction on high-dimensional data. In: McDermott, J., Castelli, M., Sekanina, L., Haasdijk, E., García-Sánchez, P. (eds.) EuroGP 2017. LNCS, vol. 10196, pp. 210–226. Springer, Cham (2017). doi:10.1007/978-3-319-55696-3_14
24. Bhowan, U., Johnston, M., Zhang, M., Yao, X.: Reusing genetic programming for ensemble selection in classification of unbalanced data. IEEE Trans. Evol. Comput. **18**(6), 893–908 (2014)
25. Evolutionary Computation Laboratory: ECJ: a Java-based evolutionary computation research system. https://cs.gmu.edu/eclab/projects/ecj/

A Feature Subset Evaluation Method Based on Multi-objective Optimization

Mengmeng Li, Zhigang Shang$^{(\boxtimes)}$, and Caitong Yue

School of Electrical Engineering, Zhengzhou University, Science Avenue 100,
Zhengzhou 450001, China
limengmeng1014@163.com, zhigang_shang@zzu.edu.cn

Abstract. To remove the irrelevant and redundant features from the high-dimensional data while ensuring classification accuracy, a supervised feature subset evaluation method based on multi-objective optimization has been proposed in this paper. Four aspects, sparsity of feature space, classification accuracy, information loss degree and feature subset stability, were took into account in the proposed method and the Multi-objective functions were constructed. Then the popular NSGA-II algorithm was used for optimization of the four objectives in the feature selection process. Finally the feature subset was selected based on the obtained feature weight vector according the four evaluation criteria. The proposed method was tested on 4 standard data sets using two kinds of classifier. The experiment results show that the proposed method can guarantee the higher classification accuracy even though only few numbers of features selected than the other methods. On the other hand, the information loss degrees of the proposed method are the lowest which demonstrates that the selected feature subsets of the proposed method can represent the original data sets best.

Keywords: Feature subset selection · Multi-objective optimization · Supervised learning · Redundancy · Regularization

1 Introduction

In supervised learning, there are always many irrelevant and redundant features in data sets, which not only result in an increase in computational complexity, but also affect the performance of classifiers. This is known as curse of dimensionality [1] in the field of pattern recognition. Feature selection is one of the key technologies to solve the problem [2]. In recent years, more and more experts and scholars have focused on feature selection and completed a great deal of related research. Many classical methods have been proposed to solve the problem. According to the different search strategies, feature selection methods can be divided into three categories: full search, random search and heuristic search. According to the different generation strategies of successors, feature selection methods can be divided into forward selection, backward selection, compound

© Springer International Publishing AG 2017
Y. Shi et al. (Eds.): SEAL 2017, LNCS 10593, pp. 581–590, 2017.
https://doi.org/10.1007/978-3-319-68759-9_47

selection, weighting selection and random selection. According to the evaluation measure, it can be divided into three broad categories: filter, wrapper and embedded method [3]. Filter methods are independent with specific classification algorithm, so they always have high generalization ability among different classification algorithms and computational efficiency, but the selected feature subsets may not be optimal, especially when the noise features are highly correlated with classifier. Wrapper methods can usually achieve high accuracy on the test set, but they rely on specific learning machine and the computational burden is quite large. In addition the overfitting problem of wrapper methods is terrible. Embedded methods are more efficient and faster than wrapper methods, but their disadvantages are that it is difficult to construct proper function optimization models and the computational complexity is greater.

Since feature selection in supervised learning often involves more than one objective, such as classification accuracy, number of features, and so on, more and more researches on feature selection using multi-objective optimization algorithms have been carried out recently. Hamdani et al. [4] used multi-objective optimization to minimize two objectives in feature selection, namely the number of features and the classification error, but they did not take some other objectives into account, such as the redundancy among the features. Vebkatadri and Rao [5] applied multi-objective optimization to search for nearly optimal subsets when taking different evaluation criteria into account, however they did not considerate the number of the features. Saroj [6] constructed three objective functions to optimize feature subset using multi-objective genetic algorithm, including maximizing information gain, non-redundancy and unused features. However they didn't focus on the stability of feature selection and the dimensionality of the used data sets were generally low.

In this paper, a supervised feature selection method based on multi-objective optimization was proposed to solve feature selection problem. Popular multi-objective evolutionary algorithms, called Non-dominated sorting genetic algorithm-II (NSGA-II) [7] was used. Four related criteria in the process of feature selection were considered fully and comprehensively and four objective functions were constructed to be optimized in the feature subset selection. The proposed method was applied to 4 different standard data sets and the feature effects were verified through different way.

The rest of this paper is organized as follows. Section 2 introduces NSGA-II, four feature selection criteria and the proposed method. Experiments set up and results analyses are presented in Sect. 3. Finally, the discussion and future work of the paper are given in Sect. 4.

2   Feature Subset Evaluation Method Based on NSGA-II

2.1   Feature Subset Evaluation Criteria and Objective Functions

There are always many feature subset evaluation criteria involved in the process of feature selection and they often conflict with each other. As we all know, multi-objective optimization can solve this problem. So suitable objective functions were constructed and multi-objective optimization algorithm was used to balance the conflicts among them in this paper. Four criteria of feature subset evaluation were taken into account to construct objective functions, which were described as follows. X represents the feature set and w stands for the weighted vector of the features. y represents the labels of the samples in the data set.

(1) Sparsity of Feature Space (Minimizing the Features Numbers):

$$f_1(X) = \|w\|_1. \tag{1}$$

$\|w\|_1$ represents the L_1 norm of w. L_0 regularization can achieve sparseness and is the ideal way to realize feature selection, but it is difficult to solve because it is a non-deterministic polynomial hard problem. L_1 regularization, also called Lasso regularization, is the optimal convex approximation of L_0 regularization. L_1 has been widely used because it is easier to be solved than L_0 [8].

(2) Classification Accuracy in Supervised Learning (Maximizing the Classification Accuracy):

$$f_2(X) = |\mathrm{corr}(X * w, y)|. \tag{2}$$

The correlation coefficient can directly reflect the correlation degree among variables. If two variables are completely linearly correlative, the absolute value of the correlation coefficient is 1; if they are entirely irrelevant, the value is 0. In the definition of the formula, the greater the correlation degree is, the better the $X * w$ feature space is to predict y. Therefore, f_2 is used to measure classification accuracy.

(3) Information Loss of Feature Selection (Maximizing the Sample Distribution Variance of the Compressed Single Variable Space):

$$f_3(X) = \mathrm{std}(X * w). \tag{3}$$

In essence, the information loss is the sample distribution variance of the compressed single variable space after the projection from the original sample space, which reflects the reconstruction error caused by this dimension reduction. To a certain extent, this criterion can reflect the information loss degree [9]. When the variance is the largest, it shows that the error caused by dimension reduction at this time is the least which also means that the information loss is the least; otherwise, the error is greater.

Two dimensional space is took as an example to illustrate this criterion. As shown in Fig. 1, when X is projected to the direction w_1, the sample distribution variance is greater than to w_2. So the information loss in w_1 is less than w_2.

(4) Stability of Feature Selection (Minimizing the Features L_2 Norm of the Weighted Vector to Maximize the Stability of Feature Selection):

$$f_4(X) = \|w\|_2. \tag{4}$$

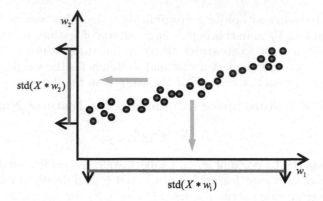

Fig. 1. An information loss example of a two dimensional space.

$\|w\|_2$ represents the L_2 norm of w. Its powerful function is to improve the important overfitting problem [10] in machine learning. L_2 regularization can improve the stability and generalization ability of the model.

Finally, the multi-objective feature subset criteria optimization functions can be concluded as

$$
\begin{cases}
\min & f_1 \\
\max & f_2 \\
\max & f_3 \\
\min & f_4
\end{cases}
. \tag{5}
$$

2.2   Multi-objective Optimization Based on NSGA-II

In order to consider the above multiple objectives comprehensively, multi-objective optimization algorithm is needed. NSGA-II is one of the most popular multi-objective evolutionary algorithms, which reduces the complexity of the non-dominated sorting genetic algorithm. It has the advantages of fast running speed and good convergence of the solution set. The sorting and selection process of NSGA-II is divided into two parts. Firstly, the population is divided into a series of Pareto ranks. The individuals in each rank are non-dominated with each other. Secondly, in each rank, all individuals are sorted by crowding distance, which is the sum of the distances between the individual with all adjacent individuals in each dimension. The procedure of NSGA-II is shown in Fig. 2. The sets of non-dominated solutions F are sorted by non-dominated order and F_1 is the best subset.

2.3   Feature Selection Based on Four Objectives

Iterative optimization were carried out according to the above objective functions using NSGA-II and Pareto set was obtained. We consider the compromise among

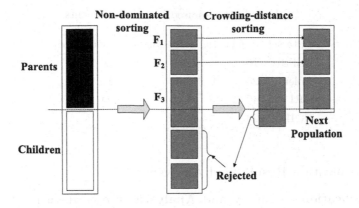

Fig. 2. The procedure of NSGA-II.

the four objectives and choose the knee point of the Pareto front as the final feature weight vector. Each value of the vector represents importance degree of corresponding feature, so feature subset selection can be completed according to the marshalling sequence of the ranked weight vector. The features in the front rank with higher weight are selected into the feature subset, however the features with lower weight are rejected.

3 Experiments and Results

In this section, numerical experiments on several data sets are provided to verify the validity of the proposed method. Firstly, data sets and experimental settings are presented. Then the experimental results and analysis are shown.

3.1 Data and Experimental Platform

In order to investigate the performances of the proposed method on different data sets, related numerical experiments were carried out. So as to make a full comparison of the experimental results, we made a diversity of the sample size and the number of features as far as possible. 4 different standard data sets were selected in the experiment. The detailed information of the data sets are shown in Table 1.

In addition, all of the experiments in this paper are carried out with MAT-LAB software programming. The experimental conditions are: Intel(R) Xeon(R) CPU E52667 v3 3.20 GHz/64.0 GB/ Windows 7 Professional/MATLAB R2014a. And the parameter setting for NSGA-II is: population size = 800, crossover probability = 0.9, mutation probability = 0.1 and maximal number of generations = 100.

Table 1. Data sets used in our experiments

Data set	# Classes	# Instances	# Attributes
USPS	10	7291	526
Isolet	26	7797	617
ORL	40	400	1024
COIL	20	1440	1024

3.2   Classification Results and Analysis

(1) Classification Accuracy and Analysis: To test whether our proposed feature selection method has good performance on various types of classifiers, two widely used classical classifiers, namely Naive Bayes (NB) and Support Vector Machine (SVM) were used in this paper. It should be noted that the LIBSVM package [11] which supports multiclass classification is used when it refers to SVM in the following texts.

We compared the performances of our method with several other feature selection methods on different data sets, including Fisher score [12] based method (FFS), Gini index [13] based method (GFS), Information Gain [14] based method (IGFS), Kruskal-Wallis test [15] based method (KWFS), ReliefF algorithm (ReliefF) [16] and T-test based method (TFS) [17]. Figure 3 shows the results of 4 data sets using different methods by different classifiers. Cross validation is used and seventy percent of the samples in each data set are randomly selected as the training set and the others as the test set. Twenty times random sampling are implemented in the experiments.

The results show that the feature subsets selected by the proposed method can obtain high classification accuracy than other methods when onlf few features are selected compared with other methods. For almost all of the data sets, Fig. 3 shows that the classification accuracy of the sub sets selected by the proposed method are highest when there are more than 50 features selected. In particular, on some data sets such as USPS (Fig. 3a) and Isolet (Fig. 3b), the proposed method can achieve highest classification accuracy compared with other methods when the features number is only 20. That is to say, compared with other methods, the features selected by the proposed method contribute more greatly to classification results, thus ensuring the classification accuracy high when the feature subsets selected by different methods contain the same number of features.

(2) Classification Stability and Analysis: Another point needs to be emphasized is that according to the comparison of the classification accuracy results on different classifiers, the classification stability of different feature subsets obtained by different methods can also be analyzed. The classification accuracy scatter line plot of different data sets on two classifiers were shown in the two-dimensional plane. Thus the classification consistency on different classifiers

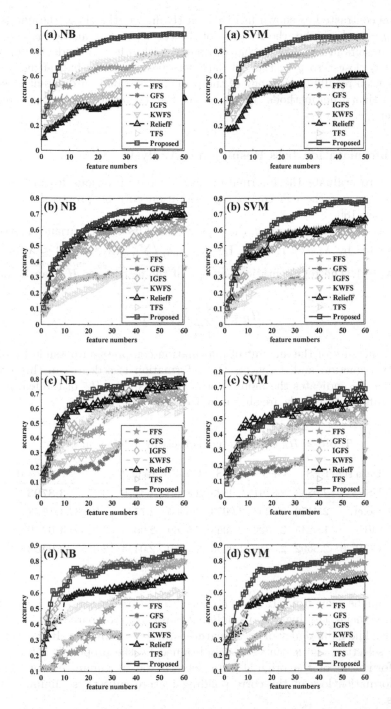

Fig. 3. Comparison of classification accuracies of feature subsets by different feature selection methods on different sets. (a) USPS. (b) Isolet. (c) ORL. (d) COIL20.

could be contrasted as shown in Fig. 4. In the figure, the closer the line is close to the $y = x$, the higher the stability of the corresponding method is.

The results in Fig. 4 show that compared with other methods, the proposed method is closest to $y = x$ in all data sets besides ORL, indicating that the classification results consistency of the proposed method on different classifiers is higher than other methods. That is to say, the stability of the proposed method is higher.

3.3   Informatation Loss Results and Analysis

In order to evaluate the information loss degree of various feature selection methods, we use the concept of representation entropy proposed by Devijve and Kittler [18].

Given a feature set of size d, the eigenvalues of its $d \times d$ covariance matrix can be presented by $\lambda_j, j = 1, \cdots, d$. Let $\tilde{\lambda}_j = \lambda_j / \sum_{j=1}^{d} \lambda_j$, then $0 \leq \tilde{\lambda}_j \leq 1$ and $\sum_{j=1}^{d} \lambda_j = 1$. The representation entropy of the feature set H_R can be defined as

$$H_R = -\sum_{j=1}^{d} \tilde{\lambda}_j \log \tilde{\lambda}_j. \tag{6}$$

H_R is a measure of the amount of information compression possible by dimensionality reduction and it reflects the information loss degree in this process. A smaller H_R indicates the more information loss. The H_R of the feature subsets by different methods are shown in Table 2.

Table 2. H_R of the feature subsets by different methods

Data set	FFS	GFS	IGFS	KWFS	ReliefF	TFS	Proposed
USPS	2.9853	2.8791	2.3826	2.8850	3.3176	3.1539	**3.8793**
Isolet	2.4152	2.8905	2.0053	2.8905	2.7741	1.9193	**4.1528**
ORL	1.9245	2.7822	2.2063	2.8569	2.9043	3.0299	**4.0779**
COIL20	2.3692	2.7250	1.9930	2.7250	2.0453	2.6637	**2.9408**

As can be seen from Table 2, H_R of the feature subsets by the proposed method remains the highest on different data sets compared with the other methods. The redundancy of these feature subsets is minimum. It shows that in feature selection, the feature subsets obtained by the proposed method retain the information of the original data sets to the maximum extent. That is, the information loss of the corresponding feature subsets is minimum in the process.

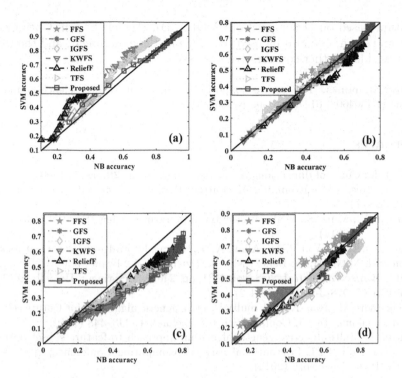

Fig. 4. Distribution of two classifiers accuracies by different feature selection methods on different sets. (a) USPS. (b) Isolet. (c) ORL. (d) COIL20.

4   Discussion and Future Work

In this paper we had applied the popular multi-objective optimization, NSGA-II to feature selection in supervised learning. Four objective functions involved in feature selection, the features numbers, classification accuracy, information loss and stability were contracted. Through the feature weight vector obtained by iterative optimization, important features could be selected finally. The results on 4 data sets using two classifiers verify the effectiveness of the proposed method.

In this paper, we only choose one Pareto solution as the feature weight vector. In fact, we have more other choices. According to our different needs of feature number, predictive power, non-redundancy and stability of the subsets, a range of diverse Pareto optimal solutions can be chosen.

On the other hand, in multi-objective optimization, the initial population is generated randomly in this paper, and in fact we can add constraints according to the prior knowledge, so that it can not only reduce the number of iterations, save operation time, but also can ensure the reliability of the obtained Pareto front and avoid falling into local optimum.

In addition, as mentioned above, the popular NSGA-II algorithm was used as the multi-objective optimization algorithm in this paper to select features. In fact, the other optimization algorithms, such as Multi-objective Evolutionary

Algorithm Based on Decomposition (MOEA/D), Particle Swarm Optimization (PSO) and so on, can also be used to carry out the experiment, and the results can be used for further comparative analysis.

Acknowledgments. The work is supported by National Nature Science Foundation of China (U1304602, 61473266 and 61305080).

References

1. Chen, L.: Curse of dimensionality. J. Ind. Eng. Chem. **29**, 48–53 (2009)
2. Theodoridis, S., Koutroumbas, K.: Pattern Recognition, 4th edn. Academic Press, Orlando (2008)
3. Kumar, V., Minz, S.: Feature selection: a literature review. Smart Comput. Rev. **4**, 211–222 (2014)
4. Hamdani, T.M., Won, J.-M., Alimi, A.M., Karray, F.: Multi-objective feature selection with NSGA II. In: Beliczynski, B., Dzielinski, A., Iwanowski, M., Ribeiro, B. (eds.) ICANNGA 2007. LNCS, vol. 4431, pp. 240–247. Springer, Heidelberg (2007). doi:10.1007/978-3-540-71618-1_27
5. Venkatadri, M., Rao, K.S.: A multiobjective genetic algorithm for feature selection in data mining. Int. J. Comput. Sci. Inf. Technol. **1**, 443–448 (2010)
6. Saroj, J.: Multi-objective genetic algorithm approach to feature subset optimization. In: 2014 IEEE International Advance Computing Conference, pp. 544–548. IEEE Press, New York (2014)
7. Deb, K., Pratap, A., Agarwal, S., et al.: A fast and elitist multiobjective genetic algorithm: NSGA-II. IEEE Trans. Evol. Comput. **6**, 182–197 (2002)
8. Indyk, P., Ruzic, M.: Near-optimal sparse recovery in the L_1 norm. In: 2008 Conference on Communication, pp. 199–207. IEEE Press, New York (2008)
9. Mitra, P., Murthy, C.A., Pal, S.K.: Unsupervised feature selection using feature similarity. IEEE Trans. Pattern Anal. Mach. Intell. **24**, 301–312 (2002)
10. Hawkins, D.M.: The problem of overfitting. J. Chem. Inf. Comput. Sci. **44**, 1 (2004)
11. Chang, C.C., Lin, C.J.: LIBSVM: a library for support vector machines. ACM Trans. Intell. Syst. Technol. **2**, 27 (2011)
12. Duda, R.O., Hart, P.E., Stork, D.G.: Pattern Classification, 2nd edn. Wiley, New York (2000)
13. Singh, S.R., Murthy, H.A., Gonsalves, T.A., et al.: Feature selection for text classification based on Gini coefficient of inequality. J. Mach. Learn. Res. Proc. Track **10**(10), 76–85 (2010)
14. Yang, Y., Pedersen, J.O.: A comparative study on feature selection in text categorization. In: Fourteenth International Conference on Machine Learning, pp. 182–197. Morgan Kaufmann, San Francisco (1998)
15. Wei, L.J.: Asymptotic conservativeness and efficiency of Kruskal-Wallis test for K dependent samples. J. Am. Stat. Assoc. **76**, 1006–1009 (1981)
16. Kononenko, I.: Estimating attributes: analysis and extensions of RELIEF. In: Bergadano, F., De Raedt, L. (eds.) ECML 1994. LNCS, vol. 784, pp. 171–182. Springer, Heidelberg (1994). doi:10.1007/3-540-57868-4_57
17. Tusher, V.G., Tibshirani, R., Chu, G.: Significance analysis of microarrays applied to the ionizing radiation response. Proc. Nat. Acad. Sci. **98**, 5116–5121 (2001)
18. Devijver, P.A., Kittler, J.: Pattern Recognition: A Statistical Approach. Prentice-Hall International, London (1982)

A Hybrid GA-GP Method for Feature Reduction in Classification

Hoai Bach Nguyen[(✉)], Bing Xue, and Peter Andreae

School of Engineering and Computer Science, Victoria University of Wellington,
PO Box 600, Wellington 6140, New Zealand
{Hoai.Bach.Nguyen,Bing.Xue,Peter.Andreae}@ecs.vuw.ac.nz

Abstract. Feature reduction is an important pre-processing step in classification and other artificial intelligent applications. Its aim is to improve the quality of feature sets. There are two main types of feature reduction: feature construction and feature selection. Most current feature reduction algorithms focus on just one of the two types because they require different representations. This paper proposes a new representation which supports a feature reduction algorithm that combines feature selection and feature construction. The algorithm uses new genetic operators to update the new representation. The proposed algorithm is compared with two conventional feature selection algorithms, a genetic algorithms-based feature selection algorithm, and a genetic programming-based algorithm which evolves feature sets containing both original and high-level features. The experimental results on 10 different datasets show that the new representation can help to produce a smaller number of features and improve the classification accuracy over using all features on most datasets. In comparison with other feature selection or construction algorithms, the proposed algorithm achieves similar or better classification performance on all datasets.

1 Introduction

One of the most important tasks of machine learning is classification [1] which assigns a class label to an instance. The classification is based on the instance's properties, known as features. The quality of the feature set significantly affects the classification performance. However, in many real-world problems, there are many irrelevant and redundant features that not only reduce the classification accuracy, but also increase the complexity of the learned classifier and the training time.

Feature reduction is typically a pre-processing step, which aims to create an informative feature set from the original one to improve the classification performance. In feature reduction, there are two main approaches including feature selection and feature construction. While feature selection aims at selecting a good feature subset from the original features, feature construction builds one or more high-level features with better discrimination ability. Since feature selection does not produce any new feature, it maintains the meanings of the original

© Springer International Publishing AG 2017
Y. Shi et al. (Eds.): SEAL 2017, LNCS 10593, pp. 591–604, 2017.
https://doi.org/10.1007/978-3-319-68759-9_48

features in each problem. On the other hand, feature construction aims to combine original features to achieve better classification performance.

Although feature reduction is a useful step, it is not an easy task. Given N original features, the task of feature selection is to find an optimal subset among 2^N possible feature subsets. So the search space of feature selection increases exponentially with respect to the number of features. Besides the large search space, the complex interactions between features make feature selection a challenging task. For example, two relevant features may provide the same information about the class label, which means it is redundant to select both features. Meanwhile, selecting two weakly relevant features may significantly improve the classification performance if they are complementary features [2]. In order to achieve feature construction, the first step is to select a good feature subset, based on which the new high-level features are built. Therefore the search space of feature construction is even larger than feature selection since it also needs to consider how to combine features. In summary, feature reduction has two main difficulties: large search spaces and complex feature interactions which are usually addressed by two key factors: the search technique and the evaluation criteria, respectively.

According to the evaluation criteria, feature reduction can be divided into two main categories: wrappers and filters [3]. Wrapper approaches usually evaluate feature subsets by a classification algorithm. On the other hand, filters do not involve any classification algorithm during the evaluation process. In filters, the goodness of a feature set is measured by characteristics of datasets. Filters are usually more efficient and result in more general feature sets. However, wrappers usually achieve higher classification accuracies. Therefore, in this work feature reduction is achieved by wrapper approaches.

Evolutionary computation (EC) has been widely applied to feature reduction because of its potential global search ability. EC-based feature construction is usually achieved by genetic programming (GP) [4] since GP can automatically evolve mathematic formulas without any assumptions about the structure of the formulas. In addition, the tree-like representation of GP is quite flexible, which makes it easy to express complex solutions with different kinds of operators and functions. For EC-based feature selection, genetic algorithms (GAs) and particle swarm optimization (PSO) are the most popular approaches [2]. Among EC algorithms, GAs were the earliest search mechanism applied to feature selection because of its natural representation of a binary string.

Most existing feature reduction works focus on either feature selection or feature construction. However, Tran et al. [5] showed that the combination of new high-level features and the original features appearing in the high-level features achieves a better classification performance than using only selected features or only constructed features. This suggests that it is promising to do feature construction and feature selection together so that we can take the advantages of both methods. This was partially done by Tran et al. [5] but only constructed features were evolved during the evolutionary process while the selected features were chosen at the end, which meant that the interactions between constructed and selected features were ignored. In this work, a new representation, which can be seen as a combination of bit vector and tree representations, is proposed to simultaneously perform feature selection and feature construction while taking into account the interactions between the two kinds of features.

Goal: The overall goal of this paper is to develop a new scheme for feature reduction to evolve small new feature sets with better classification performance than using all features. The new representation scheme and genetic operators are designed so that feature selection and feature construction can be performed simultaneously. The proposed feature reduction algorithm is then compared with a GA-based feature selection algorithm, a GP-based feature construction algorithm, and two conventional feature selection algorithms on 10 datasets with different numbers of features, classes and instances. Specifically, we will investigate:

- whether the new algorithm can reduce the number of features while increasing the classification performance over using all features,
- whether the new algorithm can evolve smaller feature sets with better classification accuracy than the GA-based feature selection algorithm,
- whether the new scheme helps to build a small feature set containing both high-level and original features that achieves better performance than the high-level feature and/or selected features evolved by GP,
- whether the new algorithm can outperform two traditional (non-EC) feature selection algorithms.

2 Background

2.1 Genetic Algorithms (GAs) and Genetic Programming (GP)

GAs [6] are one of the first EC algorithms, which are inspired by the natural selection from the Darwinian theory of evolution. In GAs, an optimization problem is solved by a population of candidate solutions. Each candidate solution is represented by a fixed-length bit string which is also known as a chromosome. The algorithm starts with a number of random chromosomes. During the evolutionary process, each candidate solution is evaluated by a fitness function. The *selection* scheme ensures that the chromosomes with better fitness values have higher chance to be selected or survival in the next generation. Some genetic operators such as *crossover* and *mutation* are applied to the selected chromosomes to produce new chromosomes for the next generation. It is expected that exchanging information between two good parents can result in better children. In addition, the fittest chromosomes is possibly preserved by the *elitism* mechanism. The new generation is then evaluated and enhanced in the following iteration. The algorithm terminates when a maximum number of iterations is reached, and/or a satisfactory fitness value has been achieved. It can be seen that GAs use a vector representation, which is a natural representation for feature selection. Specifically, in the binary vector representation, "1" shows the corresponding feature is selected and "0" means not selected.

Similar to GAs, GP [7] is a population-based optimization algorithm in which the candidate solutions are evolved by a number of genetic operators such as *selection, crossover, mutation* and *elitism*. The difference between GAs and GP is mainly on their representations. In GP, each candidate solution is usually represented by a tree, where the decision variables/features are the leaf nodes and each internal node is a function selected from a predefined function set. So each candidate solution, presented by a tree representation, can be seen as a high-level function, which maps from a number of original features to a high-level feature. GP is a domain-independent method since it does not require any domain knowledge such as any assumption about the model. Therefore, GP is usually used to achieve feature construction.

2.2 Related Work on Feature Reduction

The easiest way to achieve feature selection was to consider all possible feature subsets, which guaranteed to produce an optimal feature subset. However, this method was very computationally intensive and impossible when there was a large number of features. In order to reduce the computation cost, two sequential searches including forward (SFS) and backward (SBS) selection approaches were proposed [8]. Starting from an empty or full set of features, in each iteration SFS or SBS added or removed one feature from the current feature subset. The algorithms terminated when a pre-defined number of features was reached. However, the decision on a feature could not be changed once the feature was added or removed. The issue was addressed in two floating sequential forward (SFFS) and backward (SBFS) selection methods [8], which performed an additional step to remove or select features after each of the forward or backward step.

EC has been widely applied to feature selection. GAs [9,10] and PSO [11,12] are the two most popular techniques because of their natural representations for feature selection. Some works focused on improving the feature subset qualities by estimating good starting points for the population, such as [13,14]. The experimental results suggested that a good initialization strategy not only improved the classification performance but also shortened the training time. Representations were also modified to further enhance the feature subset qualities. For example, Vieira et al. [15] included a classifier's parameters into an individual's position in PSO to simultaneously optimize both feature subsets and the parameters. Statistical feature clustering information was also utilized to shorten the representation as in [16,17], which allowed to select the most important features in different runs consistently. Besides effectiveness, improving efficiency is also an important aspect in feature selection. Nguyen et al. [18] used a small number of training instances to estimate promising search regions before further exploring the regions using the whole training set. In addition, a local search mechanism was proposed to use information from the previous iterations to improve the current feature subsets. The proposed algorithm not only significantly reduced the computation time but also evolved better feature subsets than using the whole training set.

In terms of feature construction, GP was used to build a single high-level feature by using a single tree-representation for a given problem [19]. However, a single constructed feature usually did not contain enough information to well describe the problem. Therefore, GP was extended to construct multiple high-level features. A straight-forward way was to used a multi-tree representation [5], in which each individual consisted of more than one tree and each tree corresponded to one constructed feature. The experimental results showed that using the constructed and selected features resulted in better accuracies than using either of them. However, the selected features were chosen from features used as leaf nodes in the best constructed features in the last iteration, which were not explicitly evaluated during the evolutionary process. This means that their interactions might be ignored. For example, the selected features and constructed features might be redundant since the selected feature was already included in the constructed features. Furthermore, some original features, which were complementary with the constructed features, might not be selected since they were not used for constructing features. This work will address the above issues by proposing a new representation to achieve both feature selection and feature construction.

3   Proposed Approach

3.1   Hybrid GA-GP: A New Representation

This section describes a new representation scheme for feature reduction to conduct feature selection and feature construction simultaneously. The vector representation used in GAs is most appropriate for feature selection and the tree representation used in GP is most appropriate for feature construction. In order to achieve the two tasks at the same time, the new representation is designed as a combination of the vector and the tree representations. The reason for selecting GAs and GP over other EC algorithms such as PSO and differential evolution (DE) is that the similar evolutionary mechanisms of the two selected algorithms make it easier to combine them into a single algorithm.

In the new representation scheme, each individual includes two parts. The first component of the new representation (FS) is a bit string, as in GAs. Each bit corresponds to one original feature, so the length of the string is equal to the number of original features. A bit's value of "1" means the corresponding feature is selected, otherwise the feature is discarded. The second component of the new representation (FC) is a tree, as in GP, and represents a constructed feature. Therefore, each candidate solution is a feature set containing a subset of original features and a newly constructed feature. The essential difference between this representation and the work conducted by Tran et al. [5] is that the selected and constructed features are evaluated together as a single feature set. Therefore, the new representation is able to consider the interactions between selected features and the constructed feature. An example of the new representation with four original features, $\{f_0, f_1, f_2, f_3\}$, is given in Fig. 1. As can be seen in the figure, the FS part is a binary vector with a length of 4. The bit values indicate that

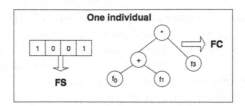

Fig. 1. An example of the new representation with a dataset including 4 features

two original features, f_0 and f_3, are selected. The FC part contains a single tree, which uses 3 original features f_0, f_1 and f_3 to construct a high-level feature, $(f_0 + f_1) * f_3$. Therefore, the individual defines a new feature set, which is $\{f_0, f_3, ((f_0 + f_1) * f_3)\}$.

3.2   Genetic Operators

The aim of the algorithm that uses this representation is to co-evolve the bit vector (FS) and the tree representation (FC) together so that the selected original features and the constructed feature in the final feature set are complementary in achieving better classification performance.

The *selection* operator of the algorithm works the same way as *selection* in traditional GAs and GP. In this work, a tournament selection is applied. Specifically, each time from the population, a number of individuals are picked, from which the fittest one is selected. This process is repeated to select a fixed number of individuals which work as parents for *crossover*, the next operator.

Since each individual has both a bit string (FS) and a tree (FC), the two operators *crossover* and *mutation* must be modified to cope with the new representation. In *crossover*, firstly two parents are randomly selected. After that, the *crossver* is performed on both FS and FC components, simultaneously. Specifically, a single crossover point on the two bit strings is selected and two crossover nodes in two trees are randomly selected. All bits beyond the crossover point are swapped and the two subtrees rooted at the two crossover nodes are exchanged to form two new trees. The results of the *crossover* operator is two new offspring and each of them contains a new bit string and a new tree. In Fig. 2, the vertical green dash-line shows the crossover point between the two bit strings and the 4th bits of the two strings are exchanged. The crossover node and its corresponding subtree are marked in green.

As in *crossover*, *mutation* is also changed so that both components in the new representation are mutated. Given a parent randomly selected from the population, its bit string is mutated by firstly selecting some bits randomly and then flipping the selected bits (change 1 to 0 and 0 to 1). Similarly, the tree from the FC part is mutated by replacing a random subtree by a small newly generated tree. Therefore, the *mutation* operator replaces a selected parent by an offspring, which also has both a bit string and a tree. An example of *mutation*

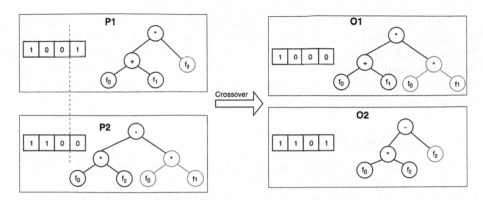

Fig. 2. An example of crossover for the new representation (Color figure online)

is shown in Fig. 3, where the bits and subtree selected for *mutation* are filled in green. Specifically, the subtree $\{f_2\}$ is replaced by another small tree, $\{f_0 * f_1\}$.

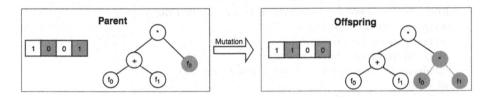

Fig. 3. An example of mutation for the new representation (Color figure online)

3.3   Fitness Function

In feature reduction, there are two main objectives: to minimize the classification error and to minimize the number of features. The algorithm combines the two objectives into a single fitness function, as shown in the following equation:

$$fitness = \alpha * ErrorRate + (1 - \alpha) * \frac{\#manipulatedFeatures}{\#originalFeatures} \qquad (1)$$

where *ErrorRate* is the classification error of the new feature set, *#manipulatedFeatures* and *#originalFeatures* represent the number of features in the new feature set and the total number of original features, respectively. α is used to control the contribution of the two objectives. The task of a feature reduction algorithm is to minimize the fitness value calculated by Eq. (1). The classification error is calculated based on the new feature set including selected original features from the bit string (FS) and constructed features from the tree (FC), which means that the interaction between the two parts of the new representation is considered.

Note that in a GA-based feature selection algorithm, the new feature set is actually a subset of features selected from the original feature set. So the features inside the new feature set are **not** new features. On the other hand, in the proposed feature reduction algorithm with the new representation, the new feature set contains a new constructed feature, along with a subset of the original features.

3.4   Overall Algorithm

Algorithm 1 shows the pseudo-code of the proposed algorithm, which combines GAs and GP together to perform feature selection and feature construction simultaneously. The proposed algorithm is called HGAGP. In the initialization, each bit in a bit string is randomly assigned to 0 or 1. Trees in FC components are initialized using the ramped half-and-half strategy.

Algorithm 1. Hybrid GA-GP for feature reduction (HGAGP)

1: Initialize the population;
2: Evaluate each individual according to Eq. (1);
3: **while** Maximum number of iterations is not reached **do**
4:    Perform selection operator;
5:    Perform crossover operator;
6:    Perform mutation operator;
7:    Evaluate the new population according to Eq. (1);
8: **end while**
9: Return the best individual including the selected and constructed features with its corresponding training and testing accuracies.

---

4   Experiment Design

To examine the performance of the proposed algorithm HGAGP, two traditional feature selection methods, which are floating sequential forward and backward selection (SFFS and SBFS) [8] and two feature reduction algorithms based on GAs and GP are used as benchmark techniques. Note that for the GP based algorithm, GP is used to construct a single feature. The feature set evolved by HGAGP is compared with a single constructed feature (GP), and the combination of the constructed feature with the selected original features used as leaf nodes in the constructed feature (GPWS).

The algorithms are compared on 10 different datasets selected from the UCI machine learning repository [20]. The datasets have different numbers of features, classes and instances (Table 1). For each dataset, the instances are divided into training and test sets with the proportions of 70% and 30%, respectively. The division ensures that the class distribution are roughly maintained in the two instance subsets. On each dataset, each algorithm is ran 50 independent times.

Table 1. Datasets

Dataset	No. of features	No. of classes	No. of instances
Wine	13	3	178
Vehicle	18	4	946
WBCD	30	2	569
Ionosphere	34	2	351
Sonar	60	2	208
Movementlibras	90	15	360
Hillvalley	101	2	606
Musk1	166	2	476
Arrhythmia	279	16	452
Isolet5	617	5	7797

All feature reduction algorithms in this work are wrapper approaches, in which each candidate solution is evaluated by the K-nearest neighbor (KNN) classification algorithm. K is set to 5 so that KNN can avoid the noisy instances while maintaining its efficiency. During the training process, 10-fold cross validation is applied to measure the classification error of a feature set to be used in the fitness function. The α value in Eq. (1) is set to 0.9 so that the search focuses more on improving the classification performance.

For all algorithms, the population size is set to three times the total number of original features since the search space size increases exponentially with respect to the number of features. However, the population size is limited to 100. The maximum initial depth of a tree is set to 7 and the maximum tree depth is 17 to avoid the bloating problem in GP. The crossover and mutation rates for GAs, GP and HGAGP are 0.8 and 0.2, respectively, which follows the parameter settings by Tran et al. [5] to ensure a fair comparison. In this work, followed the implementation by the DEAP package [21], *elitism* is not implemented. However the best solution evolved during the evolutionary process is recorded, which is returned at the end of each algorithm. All algorithms stop after 50 generations. Different algorithms are compared by a statistical significance test, Wilcoxon signed rank test with the significance level being set to 0.05.

5   Results and Discussions

5.1   Results on the Training Set

The average training accuracies of the feature sets evolved by the four algorithms over 50 independent runs are shown in Table 2. In the table, "Full" means that all the original features are used for classification. The significance test results are shown in the brackets, where "+"/"−" means that the corresponding algorithm is significantly better/ worse than the proposed algorithm, HGAGP; "="

Table 2. Training accuracies

Datset	Full	GAs	GP	GPWS	HGAGP
Wine	96.74 (−)	98.01 (−)	97.34 (−)	97.41 (−)	99.10
Vehicle	84.26 (−)	83.99 (−)	77.19 (−)	79.52 (−)	85.72
WBCD	97.22 (−)	97.73 (−)	98.13 (=)	97.68 (−)	97.96
Ionosphere	92.24 (−)	95.64 (−)	95.77 (−)	94.68 (−)	96.70
Sonar	91.66 (−)	97.13 (=)	88.73 (−)	89.93 (−)	97.08
Movementlibras	89.64 (−)	89.92 (=)	64.31 (−)	75.15 (−)	90.22
Hillvalley	78.15 (−)	80.77 (−)	99.57 (=)	95.80 (−)	99.49
Musk1	92.77 (−)	95.64 (=)	85.56 (−)	87.40 (−)	95.86
Arrhythmia	69.84 (−)	77.18 (−)	71.82 (−)	73.19 (−)	78.55
Isolet5	91.19 (−)	94.41 (=)	57.53 (−)	78.36 (−)	94.58

means not significantly different. As can be seen in the table, HGAGP achieves better training accuracies than using all features on all datasets. Especially on Hillvalley, the accuracy of HGAGP is 20% higher than using all features. Similarly, HGAGP is significantly better than GPWS on all datasets. In comparison with GAs and GP, HGAGP significantly outperforms them on a majority of the datasets. For example, on Isolet5, HGAGP's training accuracy is 94.58% which is almost twice higher than the one obtained by GP.

5.2   Results on the Test Set

Feature sets evolved by the four algorithms were evaluated on unseen instances from the test set. The average testing accuracies are shown in Table 3. As can

Table 3. Testing accuracies

Datset	Full	GAs	GP	GPWS	HGAGP
Wine	98.14 (+)	93.48 (−)	91.33 (−)	94.14 (−)	96.62
Vehicle	66.14 (−)	72.99 (−)	62.07 (−)	65.95 (−)	74.09
WBCD	98.83 (+)	95.99 (=)	96.10 (=)	96.37 (=)	95.82
Ionosphere	78.09 (−)	84.55 (=)	84.49 (=)	83.75 (=)	84.74
Sonar	77.77 (−)	79.65 (=)	64.76 (−)	69.84 (−)	80.66
Movementlibras	75.00 (=)	74.96 (=)	27.00 (−)	47.22 (−)	74.77
Hillvalley	58.24 (−)	61.76 (−)	99.13 (=)	90.72 (−)	98.92
Musk1	76.92 (−)	86.65 (=)	64.40 (−)	70.61 (−)	85.93
Arrhythmia	53.67 (−)	59.41 (−)	58.86 (−)	60.44 (−)	62.52
Isolet5	75.42 (−)	84.79 (−)	28.18 (−)	60.74 (−)	85.14

be seen from the table, on 7 out of the 10 datasets, HGAGP improves the testing accuracies over using all features. Especially on the Hillvalley dataset, in comparison with using all features, HGAGP is almost two times more accurate. Compared with GP and GPWS, on most datasets HGAGP performs significantly better. For example, on Isolet5, the largest dataset, HGAGP's accuracy is almost 60% and 25% higher than GP and GPWS, respectively. HGAGP is significantly better than GAs on 5 datasets and achieves similar performance on the other datasets. The most significant difference between the two algorithms is on Hillvalley, where HGAGP's accuracy is almost 40% better than that of GAs. Therefore, on all datasets the proposed algorithm is never significantly worse than GAs, GP or GPWS.

It can be seen that GAs, GP and GPWS do not perform consistently well on all datasets. On some datasets, feature selection with GAs is more suitable. On the other datasets, constructing features with GP is a better method. However, HGAGP shows that it can adapt with different datasets to consistently produce good features on all datasets since it does both feature selection and feature construction at the same time. Although GPWS also combines a constructed feature with original features, it does not consider the interaction between the two kinds of features, which results in its worse performance than HGAGP.

5.3   Size of New Feature Sets

The size of new feature sets evolved by the algorithms is shown in Table 4. Since the target is to select a small number of features, the smaller feature set the better the algorithm. GP necessarily produces the smallest feature set because it only constructs a single feature. It can be seen that on all datasets, HGAGP evolves feature sets containing less than 30% of the total number of original features. On the small datasets, HGAGP usually selects a similar or smaller number of features than other algorithms (except for GP). When the

Table 4. Number of features in the new feature set

Datset	Full	GAs	GP	GPWS	HGAGP
Wine	13.0 (−)	4.2 (=)	1.0 (+)	8.8 (−)	4.3
Vehicle	18.0 (−)	7.3 (=)	1.0 (+)	7.5 (=)	7.5
WBCD	30.0 (−)	6.1 (=)	1.0 (+)	10.8 (−)	5.7
Ionosphere	34.0 (−)	7.4 (=)	1.0 (+)	10.5 (−)	6.9
Sonar	60.0 (−)	19.7 (+)	1.0 (+)	20.4 (=)	21.7
Movementlibras	90.0 (−)	30.8 (=)	1.0 (+)	15.1 (+)	31.7
Hillvalley	100.0 (−)	30.4 (−)	1.0 (+)	14.5 (−)	5.1
Musk1	166.0 (−)	56.5 (=)	1.0 (+)	24.2 (+)	58.2
Arrhythmia	278.0 (−)	85.5 (+)	1.0 (+)	33.1 (+)	94.9
Isolet5	617.0 (−)	234.6 (=)	1.0 (+)	28.0 (+)	240.0

number of original features is increased, HGAGP tends to select more features to preserve its high classification performance. So the experimental results show that HGAGP can adapt with different numbers of features to maintain its high classification accuracies. Due to space limitations the computation cost is not included. In general, HGAGP is a little bit more expensive than GAs and GP since it needs to transform the original dataset using both bit strings and trees.

5.4   Further Comparison with Traditional Methods

A comparison between HGAGP and two sequential searches, SFFS and SBFS, is shown in Table 5. The number of features evolved by HGAGP is used as stopping criteria for the two sequential searches. In the table, on each dataset (each column) the best testing accuracy is marked in bold. As can be seen from the table, HGAGP achieves the best performance on 7 out of the 10 datasets. The largest difference between the three methods is on Hillvalley, where HGAGP is almost twice accurate than SFFS and SBFS. The experimental results show that the new representation helps HGAGP to better explore the search space than the two sequential algorithms.

Table 5. Results of SFFS and SBFS

Method	Wine	Vehicle	WBCD	Ionosphere	Sonar
SFFS	**98.15**	69.69	92.98	81.91	74.60
SBFS	**98.15**	68.90	92.98	84.70	**80.95**
HGAGP	96.62	**74.09**	**95.92**	**84.74**	80.66
Method	Movementlibras	Hillvalley	Musk1	Arrhythmia	Isolet5
SFFS	73.15	64.56	82.52	**64.71**	83.55
SBFS	73.15	59.34	82.52	55.88	76.92
HGAGP	**74.77**	**98.92**	**85.93**	62.52	**85.14**

6   Conclusions and Future Work

The goal of the research was to develop a new representation for feature reduction using EC, which not only performs feature construction and selection simultaneously but also considers the interaction between the two kinds of features. The goal has been achieved by combining a bit string and a tree together to form a new representation. The genetic operators were also redesigned to suit the new representation. The experimental results on 10 different datasets show that the proposed algorithm, HGAGP, can evolve smaller feature sets with better classification accuracy than using all features. Since HGAGP performs feature selection and construction at the same time, it can consistently achieve good performance on all datasets. In addition, considering the interactions between original and constructed features helps HGAGP to outperform using GAs for feature selection only, and using GP for feature construction and/or feature selection.

In the future, we will investigate on how to construct multiple features along with selecting features to further improve the classification performance. In addition, it will be interesting to exchange the information between two parts in the new representation. For example, the selected features in feature selection can be used to enhance the constructed features in feature construction and vice versa.

References

1. Lones, M.A., Smith, S.L., Alty, J.E., Lacy, S.E., Possin, K.L., Jamieson, D.S., Tyrrell, A.M.: Evolving classifiers to recognize the movement characteristics of Parkinson's disease patients. IEEE Trans. Evol. Comput. **18**(4), 559–576 (2014)
2. Xue, B., Zhang, M., Browne, W.N., Yao, X.: A survey on evolutionary computation approaches to feature selection. IEEE Trans. Evol. Comput. **20**(4), 606–626 (2016)
3. Nguyen, H.B., Xue, B., Andreae, P.: Mutual information for feature selection: estimation or counting? Evol. Intel. **9**(3), 95–110 (2016)
4. Neshatian, K., Zhang, M., Andreae, P.: A filter approach to multiple feature construction for symbolic learning classifiers using genetic programming. IEEE Trans. Evol. Comput. **16**(5), 645–661 (2012)
5. Tran, B., Xue, B., Zhang, M.: Genetic programming for feature construction and selection in classification on high-dimensional data. Memet. Comput. **8**(1), 3–15 (2015)
6. Goldberg, D.E., Holland, J.H.: Genetic algorithms and machine learning. Mach. Learn. **3**(2), 95–99 (1988)
7. Koza, J.R.: Genetic Programming II: Automatic Discovery of Reusable Subprograms. MIT Press, Cambridge (1994)
8. Niu, G.: Feature selection optimization. Data-Driven Technology for Engineering Systems Health Management, pp. 139–171. Springer, Singapore (2017). doi:10. 1007/978-981-10-2032-2_6
9. De Paula, L.C., Soares, A.S., de Lima, T.W., Coelho, C.J.: Feature selection using genetic algorithm: an analysis of the bias-property for one-point crossover. In: GECCO 2016 Companion, pp. 1461–1462 (2016)
10. Stefano, C.D., Fontanella, F., Marrocco, C., di Freca, A.S.: A GA-based feature selection approach with an application to handwritten character recognition. Pattern Recogn. Lett. **35**, 130–141 (2014). Frontiers in Handwriting Processing
11. Li, N.J., Wang, W.J., Hsu, C.C.J.: Hybrid particle swarm optimization incorporating fuzzy reasoning and weighted particle. Neurocomputing **167**, 488–501 (2015)
12. Mistry, K., Zhang, L., Neoh, S.C., Lim, C.P., Fielding, B.: A micro-GA embedded PSO feature selection approach to intelligent facial emotion recognition. IEEE Trans. Cybern. **47**(6), 1496–1509 (2017)
13. Bharti, K.K., Singh, P.K.: Opposition chaotic fitness mutation based adaptive inertia weight BPSO for feature selection in text clustering. Appl. Soft Comput. **43**, 20–34 (2016)
14. Xue, B., Zhang, M., Browne, W.N.: Particle swarm optimisation for feature selection in classification: novel initialisation and updating mechanisms. Appl. Soft Comput. **18**, 261–276 (2014)

15. Vieira, S.M., Mendonça, L.F., Farinha, G.J., Sousa, J.M.: Modified binary PSO for feature selection using SVM applied to mortality prediction of septic patients. Appl. Soft Comput. **13**(8), 3494–3504 (2013)
16. Nguyen, H.B., Xue, B., Liu, I., Andreae, P., Zhang, M.: Gaussian transformation based representation in particle swarm optimisation for feature selection. In: Mora, A.M., Squillero, G. (eds.) EvoApplications 2015. LNCS, vol. 9028, pp. 541–553. Springer, Cham (2015). doi:10.1007/978-3-319-16549-3_44
17. Nguyen, H.B., Xue, B., Liu, I., Zhang, M.: PSO and statistical clustering for feature selection: a new representation. In: Dick, G., et al. (eds.) SEAL 2014. LNCS, vol. 8886, pp. 569–581. Springer, Cham (2014). doi:10.1007/978-3-319-13563-2_48
18. Nguyen, H.B., Xue, B., Andreae, P.: Surrogate-model based particle swarm optimisation with local search for feature selection in classification. In: Squillero, G., Sim, K. (eds.) EvoApplications 2017. LNCS, vol. 10199, pp. 487–505. Springer, Cham (2017). doi:10.1007/978-3-319-55849-3_32
19. Guo, H., Nandi, A.K.: Breast cancer diagnosis using genetic programming generated feature. Pattern Recogn. **39**(5), 980–987 (2006)
20. Lichman, M.: UCI machine learning repository (2013)
21. Fortin, F.A., De Rainville, F.M., Gardner, M.A., Parizeau, M., Gagné, C.: DEAP: evolutionary algorithms made easy. J. Mach. Learn. Res. **13**, 2171–2175 (2012)

Kernel Construction and Feature Subset Selection in Support Vector Machines

Shinichi Yamada$^{(\boxtimes)}$ and Kourosh Neshatian

Department of Computer Science and Software Engineering,
University of Canterbury, Christchurch, New Zealand
shinichi.yamada@pg.canterbury.ac.nz, kourosh.neshatian@canterbury.ac.nz

Abstract. Kernel functions have an important role in the performance of Support Vector Machines (SVMs), since they form the geometry of the feature space. Manual designing of kernel functions is an expensive task and requires domain-specific knowledge. In this article, we propose a new method to automatically construct kernel functions and select optimal subsets of features. We achieve this by combining primitive kernels and subsets of features using Genetic Programming (GP). Our experiments show that the proposed method drastically improves the prediction accuracy of SVMs.

Keywords: Support Vector Machines · Multiple Kernel Learning · Kernel Construction · Feature Selection · Genetic Programming

1   Introduction

Support vector machines (SVMs) are state-of-the-art tools in machine learning delivering high performance in diverse areas such as computer vision and text mining. The successful applications of SVMs often depend on the choice of kernels. In problems where a domain expert is accessible, kernel functions can be hand-crafted, but in most cases generic kernels (with some adjustable parameters) are used.

Multiple Kernel Learning (MKL), a variant of SVM, was introduced so that multiple kernels with different parameters (and possibly different types) can be used at the same time. Lanckriet et al. [14] showed that the optimal combination of kernels and the optimal solutions of SVMs can be learned simultaneously. It implies that the MKL reduces one's burden to prepare the best kernel. However, the study of MKL has mainly focused on the linear combination of kernels. A common practice in MKL is to prepare a set of kernels which consists of kernels corresponding to each individual feature and a kernel corresponding to all the features. Therefore, the vast space of nonlinear combinations of kernels which correspond to arbitrary subsets of features still remains unknown. In this article, we consider a heuristic method to explore that huge space.

Genetic programming (GP) addresses the problem of program induction; it can be used to produce the right program or expression without explicitly specifying a template or pattern for the program. Koza [13] showed that a wide variety of problems in many different fields can be expressed as problems of creating

© Springer International Publishing AG 2017
Y. Shi et al. (Eds.): SEAL 2017, LNCS 10593, pp. 605–616, 2017.
https://doi.org/10.1007/978-3-319-68759-9_49

computer programs which can then be solved by domain-independent operations. Genetic programming searches for the better programs using the Darwinian principle of survival of the fittest and the genetic operation of crossover.
GP also "actively encourages a diverse set of clearly inconsistent and contradic-
tory approaches in attempting to solve a problem" (Koza [13]). The diversity is
a key element to arrive at better solutions in GP.

In this article, we use two types of GP systems:

1. a GP system to find the optimal subset of features; and
2. a GP system that takes the output of the first one and then finds an optimal
   combination of kernels.

Our results show that the combination of these two GP systems leads to a
significant improvement in the performance of SVMs.

This article is organized as follows. In Sect. 2, we start with a brief review
of relevant concepts and previous works related to this article. In Sect. 3, we
describe the proposed system of constructing optimal kernels. In Sect. 4, we
show the experimental results, and conclude the article in Sect. 5.

2 Background and Related Works

In this section, we outline the theory and formulation of SVMs, kernels and MKL
and review the previous works related to this paper.

2.1 Support Vector Machines

For a given set of data

$$(\mathbf{x}_1, y_1), (\mathbf{x}_2, y_2), \ldots, (\mathbf{x}_n, y_n),$$

where $\mathbf{x}_i = \{x_{i1}, \ldots, x_{id}\} \in \mathbb{R}^d$, and $y_i \in \{-1, 1\}$ for $i = 1, \ldots, n$, the standard
SVMs are formulated as

$$\min_{\mathbf{w}, b} \left(\frac{1}{2} \|\mathbf{w}\|^2 + C \sum_{i=1}^{n} \ell \left(\langle \mathbf{w}, \Phi(\mathbf{x}_i) \rangle + b, y_i \right) \right), \tag{1}$$

where $\Phi(\mathbf{x}_i)$ are nonlinear feature maps which map the input data $\mathbf{x} \in X \subset \mathbb{R}^d$
into a Hilbert space H; $\ell(\cdot)$ is a loss function which penalizes the devia-
tion between the output label y_i and the prediction based on the hyperplane
$\langle \mathbf{w}, \Phi(\mathbf{x}_i) \rangle + b$ in H; and the constant C is a regularization hyper-parameter.

A common choice of the loss function is the hinge loss function, in which case
the optimization problem is formulated as

$$\min_{\mathbf{w}, b, \boldsymbol{\xi}} \left(\frac{1}{2} \|\mathbf{w}\|^2 + C \sum_{i=1}^{n} \xi_i \right)$$
$$\text{s.t.}\ \ y_i(\langle \mathbf{w}, \Phi(\mathbf{x}_i) \rangle + b) \geq 1 - \xi_i, \tag{2}$$
$$\xi_i \geq 0, \quad i = 1, \ldots, n.$$

A standard method to solve the optimization problem (2) is to transform it to the dual form:

$$\max_{\boldsymbol{\alpha}} \left(\sum_{i=1}^{n} \alpha_i - \frac{1}{2} \left(\boldsymbol{\alpha} \circ \mathbf{y} \right)^T K \left(\boldsymbol{\alpha} \circ \mathbf{y} \right) \right)$$

$$\text{s.t.} \sum_{i=1}^{n} \alpha_i y_i = 0, \tag{3}$$

$$0 \le \alpha_i \le C, \quad i = 1, \dots, n,$$

where $\boldsymbol{\alpha} \circ \mathbf{y}$ is an Hadamard (element-wise) product between a vector $\boldsymbol{\alpha}$ and a vector $\mathbf{y}$. K is a *kernel matrix* whose elements are inner products of $\Phi(\mathbf{x})$:

$$K_{ij} = \langle \Phi(\mathbf{x_i}), \Phi(\mathbf{x_j}) \rangle, \quad i, j = 1, \dots, n.$$

2.2 Kernels

Definition 1. *Kernel (Steinwart and Christmann [22]).*
A function $k : X \times X \to \mathbb{R}$ is a kernel on a set X if there exists a Hilbert space H and a map $\Phi : X \to H$ such that

$$k(\mathbf{x}, \mathbf{y}) = \langle \Phi(\mathbf{y}), \Phi(\mathbf{x}) \rangle,$$

for all $\mathbf{x}, \mathbf{y} \in X$.

Definition 2. *Positive Definite Symmetric (PDS) functions (Cortes et al. [5]).*
A function $k : X \times X \to \mathbb{R}$ is PDS on a set X if it is symmetric:

$$k(\mathbf{x}, \mathbf{y}) = k(\mathbf{y}, \mathbf{x}),$$

for all $\mathbf{x}, \mathbf{y} \in X$, and

$$\sum_{i=1}^{n} \sum_{j=1}^{n} a_i a_j k(\mathbf{x}_i, \mathbf{x}_j) \ge 0$$

for all $n \ge 0$, $\{\mathbf{x}_1, \dots, \mathbf{x}_n\} \in X$ and $\{a_1, \dots, a_n\} \in \mathbb{R}$.

The basic criterion which characterizes kernels is called Mercer's condition.

Theorem 1. *Mercer's condition (Steinwart and Christmann [22]).*
A function $k : X \times X \to \mathbb{R}$ is a kernel if and only if it is PDS.

New kernels can be defined as functions of other kernels. For instance, given any two kernels k_1 and k_2 on a set X, ak_1 ($a \ge 0$) and $k_1 + k_2$ are also kernels on X. It has also been shown that $\exp(k(\mathbf{x}, \mathbf{y}))$ is a kernel if $k(\mathbf{x}, \mathbf{y})$ is a kernel (Cortes et al. [5]).

Theorem 2. *Products of kernels (Steinwart and Christmann [22]).*
Let k_1 be a kernel on X_1 and k_2 be a kernel on X_2. Then $k_1 k_2$ is a kernel on $X_1 \times X_2$.

The product of two PDS matrices is not necessary PDS (Meenakshi and Rajian [16]). However, from Theorem 2, the Hadamard product of two kernel matrices is also a kernel matrix in the corresponding tensor product space.

In our experiments, we use three types of kernels:

$$\text{Polynomial: } k(\mathbf{x}_i, \mathbf{x}_j) = (a\langle \mathbf{x}_i, \mathbf{x}_j \rangle + b)^c \qquad a, c > 0, b \geq 0 \tag{4}$$

$$\text{Gaussian: } k(\mathbf{x}_i, \mathbf{x}_j) = \exp\left(-\frac{\|\mathbf{x}_i - \mathbf{x}_j\|^2}{\sigma^2}\right) \tag{5}$$

$$\text{Exponential: } k(\mathbf{x}_i, \mathbf{x}_j) = \exp\left(\frac{\langle \mathbf{x}_i, \mathbf{x}_j \rangle}{\sigma^2}\right). \tag{6}$$

2.3 Multiple Kernel Learning

The ℓ_p-norm of a vector $\mathbf{x}$ is, for $p \geq 1$, defined as

$$\|\mathbf{x}\|_p = (|\mathbf{x}_1|^p + \cdots + |\mathbf{x}_n|^p)^{\frac{1}{p}}.$$

Using this notation, multiple kernel learning (MKL) is formulated as

$$\min_{\mathbf{w}, \boldsymbol{\xi}} \frac{1}{2} \left(\sum_{j=1}^{m} \|\mathbf{w}_j\|_2^p \right)^{\frac{2}{p}} + C \sum_{i=1}^{n} \xi_i$$

$$\text{s.t. } y_i \sum_{j=1}^{m} \langle \mathbf{w}_j, \Phi(\mathbf{x}_i) \rangle \geq 1 - \xi_i \tag{7}$$

$$\xi_i \geq 0, \quad i = 1, \dots, n,$$

where m is the number of kernels in MKL. Originally MKL was formulated for $p = 1$ (Bach et al. [1]). With $p = 1$, MKL returns sparse solutions in which a large proportion of $\mathbf{w}_1, \dots, \mathbf{w}_m$ are zero. For larger values of p, MKL returns less sparse solutions. Therefore, by adjusting the value of p, we can control the sparsity of solutions.

The optimization problem (7) can be equivalently formulated as

$$\min_{\hat{\mathbf{w}}, \boldsymbol{\xi}, \boldsymbol{\theta}} \sum_{j=1}^{m} \frac{\|\hat{\mathbf{w}}_j\|^2}{\theta_j} + C \sum_{i=1}^{n} \xi_i$$

$$\text{s.t. } y_i \sum_{j=1}^{m} \langle \hat{\mathbf{w}}_j, \Phi_j(\mathbf{x}_i) \rangle \geq 1 - \xi_i, \qquad i = 1, \dots, n \tag{8}$$

$$\xi_i \geq 0, \quad i = 1, \dots, n$$

$$\|\boldsymbol{\theta}\|_{\bar{p}} \leq 1, \bar{p} = p(2 - p)^2, \boldsymbol{\theta} \geq 0$$

(Micchelli and Pontil [17]). This formulation allows us to derive the dual form of (8) for a fixed $\boldsymbol{\theta}$:

$$\min_{\boldsymbol{\theta}:\boldsymbol{\theta}\geq 0} \max_{\boldsymbol{\alpha}} \sum_{i=1}^{n} \alpha_i - \frac{1}{2}(\boldsymbol{\alpha}\circ\mathbf{y})^T K_{\boldsymbol{\theta}}(\boldsymbol{\alpha}\circ\mathbf{y})$$

$$\text{s.t.} \sum_{i=1}^{n} \alpha_i y_i = 0 \tag{9}$$

$$0 \leq \alpha_i \leq C, \quad i = 1,\ldots,n$$

where $K_{\boldsymbol{\theta}} = \sum_{j=1}^{m} \theta_j K_j$. It is the same form as (3). For fixed $(\hat{\mathbf{w}}, \boldsymbol{\xi})$, $\boldsymbol{\theta}$ can be solved analytically. Therefore, the solutions of the optimization problem (8) can be obtained iteratively by fixing each of $(\hat{\mathbf{w}}, \boldsymbol{\xi})$ or $\boldsymbol{\theta}$. The coefficient vector $\boldsymbol{\theta}$ of the kernels provides useful information. Kernels with larger coefficients have more influence (importance) on the optimization problems.

The optimization problem (7) can also be solved directly in the primal form (Orabona et al. [18,20]). Using the stochastic gradient descent methods, the primal approach can solve the optimization problem more efficiently. It also has the strong advantage that the framework of the primal optimization problem is not affected by minor changes. For instance, the changes of loss functions do not require changing the whole computational process (Orabona and Luo [19]). In the primal form of optimization problems we use the weights vectors $\mathbf{w}_j, j = 1,\ldots,m$ instead of $\boldsymbol{\theta}$ to determine the relative importance of kernels.

2.4 Related Works

Genetic programming has been used to automatically discover a new form of kernel functions using the biological-inspired operations such as reproduction, crossover and mutations. The evolved kernels are expressed as tree structures in which internal nodes correspond to functional operations such as + and × and leaf nodes correspond to input vectors (Howley and Madden [9]; Dioşan et al. [6]; Koch et al. [11]) or kernels (Sullivan and Luke [23]; Dioşan et al. [7]), so that the obtained expressions satisfy Mercer's condition in Theorem 1.

Koch et al. [11] search for the optimal hyper-parameters using their software which implements genetic methods such as SPOT (Bartz-Beielstein et al. [2]) and TDM (Konen et al. [12]), and construct kernels using operators $(+, \times, \exp(\cdot))$ and input vectors. They conclude the experiments with the remark; "Our method rediscovered multiple standard kernels, but no significant improvements over standard kernels were obtained." Sullivan and Luke [23] use standard kernels (Polynomial, Gaussian, Sigmoid) instead of input vectors to construct composite kernels. In the tree representation of GP, the leaf nodes are input vectors, the internal nodes—which are one level above the leaf nodes—are the kernel functions, and the internal nodes—which are two or more levels above the leaf nodes—are functions $(+, \times, \exp(\cdot))$. Dioşan et al. [7] adopt the simpler configuration in which leaf nodes are standard kernels and random constants, and internal nodes are functions $(+, \times, \exp(\cdot))$.

Evolutionary algorithms have been successful at finding optimal subsets of features (Xue et al. [25]). GP has been used for feature selection in a variety ways. Suárez et al. [24] use two GP runs to first identify promising subsets of features and then use them in a classification problem. Gray et al. [8] use GP to evolve a classifier. The features that are actively used in the resulting classifier identify good predictors, and therefore, implicitly lead to feature selection. Bhowan and McCloskey [3] use a similar mechanism in order to evolve ranking functions and achieve comparable performance with fewer numbers of features.

3   Proposed System

In this section, we describe the proposed system of constructing optimal kernels. The system consists of two GP systems:

1. a GP system for selection of optimal subsets of features; and
2. a GP system for optimal combinations of kernels using the selected subsets.

3.1   Feature Selection (FS) Subsystem

In this subsystem, we use GP to evolve individuals (expressions) that are functions over sets and evaluate to sets of features. The primitive functions are set operators and the fitness function is based on the accuracy of an SVM classifier using the selected subset of features. Since the search space of the candidate subsets of features is exponentially larger than the number of features in the problem, we use an MKL system to make the probability distribution of selecting individual features non-uniform. The components of this subsystem are as follows.

(i) **Primitive Functions:** There are two binary functions where each takes two sets A and B and implement the following mappings:

- returns the union of the two sets: $A \cup B$; and
- returns the difference of the two sets: $A - B$.

(ii) **Terminals:** All the terminals are sets since the GP individual computes a function over sets. There are d sets of size one, each containing a single feature. We also used the MKL method with kernels corresponding to each single feature and determine the relative importance of features (i.e. the size of the coefficients of the kernels). This implicitly defines a permutation function p such that $\theta_{p(1)} \geq \theta_{p(2)} \cdots \geq \theta_{p(d)}$. Then, we construct $d - 1$ subsets: $\{x_{.p(1)}, x_{.p(2)}\}$, $\{x_{.p(1)}, x_{.p(2)}, x_{.p(3)}\}$, $\ldots \{x_{.p(1)}, x_{.p(2)}, \ldots, x_{.p(d)}\}$, where $x_{.j}$ is the j-th feature. In total, we provide $2d - 1$ subsets as the terminal nodes. We run the MKL method again with $2d - 1$ kernels corresponding to the terminal nodes. This time we use the obtained coefficients as the probability of the selection of the terminal nodes during evolution. The motivation is to incorporate the importance of single features in the evolution process.

(iii) **Fitness Function:** This function maps an individual to its fitness which is in the range $[0, 1]$ with 1 representing the highest fitness. An individual evaluates to a (candidate) subset of features. A Gaussian kernel (5) is constructed using this selected subset of features. Then an SVM model is constructed using this kernel function. The model is trained on the training data by solving the optimization problem (2). The prediction accuracy of the model on the validation set is returned as the fitness of the individual.

After the last generation of the feature selection subsystem, we have a set (or population) of subsets of features with their corresponding fitness measures. The top n subsets are used in the kernel construction subsystem.

3.2 Kernel Construction (KC) Subsystem

In this subsystem, we use GP to evolve individuals that are composite kernel functions and evaluate to kernel matrices. The components of this subsystems are as follows.

(i) **Primitive Functions:** There are two binary functions, each taking two kernel matrices K_1 and K_2, that implement the following mappings:

- the function returns the sum of the kernels: $K_1 + K_2$; and
- the function returns the Hadamard product of the kernels: $K_1 \circ K_2$.

(ii) **Variable Terminals:** All the terminals are basic kernel functions of one of the three types of kernels (4), (5) and (6).

Each basic kernel has a set of hyper-parameters that must be specified. A large number of basic kernel functions with various hyper-parameter settings are constructed and used in an MKL model to determine their relative importance (based on the magnitude of the corresponding coefficients). The m top basic kernels are chosen. Then, we construct $n \times m$ kernels combining the n subsets of features produced by the feature selection subsystem.

We use the MKL method again with $n \times m$ kernels corresponding to the terminal nodes to obtain coefficients that will be used as the probabilities of selecting the variable terminals during evolution. One reason for attempting to make the distribution non-uniform is that kernels with a larger number of parameters generate a larger number of basic kernels, and would therefore be more likely to be selected if the terminal nodes were chosen uniformly.

(iii) **Constant Terminals:** Random constants, i.e. uniformly generated random numbers in $(0, 1)$ (Koza [13]).

(iv) **Fitness Function:** As before, this function maps an individual to its fitness which is in the range $[0, 1]$. An individual is a kernel function. An SVM model is constructed using this kernel function. The model is trained on the training data by solving the optimization problem (2). The prediction accuracy of the model on the validation set is returned as the fitness of the individual.

After the last generation the best individual (i.e. a kernel function) is returned.

4 Experiments

We conduct a number of experiments in order to examine the prediction accuracy of the proposed system compared to some other alternatives. We compare the prediction accuracy of the following six methods:

1. **SVM:** standard SVM with Gaussian kernels;
2. **MKL 1:** MKL with a combination of the polynomial and Gaussian kernels with all the features. The parameters of the polynomial and Gaussian kernels are set as follows:
   - Polynomial kernel: $(a\langle \mathbf{x}_i, \mathbf{x}_j \rangle + b)^c$: $a = 1$; $b \in \{0, 1\}$; $c \in \{1, 2, \ldots, 4\}$;
   - Gaussian kernel: $\exp\left(-\frac{\|\mathbf{x}_i - \mathbf{x}_j\|^2}{\sigma^2}\right)$: $\sigma^2 \in \{2^{-10}, 2^{-8}, \ldots, 2^{10}\}$.
3. **MKL 2:** MKL with a combination of Polynomial kernels and Gaussian kernels which correspond to each single feature and all the features. If a dataset has m features, the MKL has a combination of $m + 1$ (subsets of features) $\times$ 19 kernels (8 Polynomial kernels and 11 Gaussian kernels as described above).
4. **FS:** SVMs with the optimal subset of features obtained by applying the FS subsystem.
5. **KC:** SVMs with the optimal constructed kernels obtained by applying the KC subsystem (using all the features). For kernel construction, we use the three types of primitive kernels (4), (5) and (6). The parameters of those kernels are specified as follows:
   - Polynomial kernel: $(a\langle \mathbf{x}_i, \mathbf{x}_j \rangle + b)^c$: $a \in \{2^{-2}, 2^{-1}, \ldots, 2^2\}$; $b \in \{0, 1\}$; $c \in \{1, 2, \ldots, 10\}$;
   - Gaussian kernel: $\exp\left(-\frac{\|\mathbf{x}_i - \mathbf{x}_j\|^2}{\sigma^2}\right)$: $\sigma^2 \in \{2^{-10}, 2^{-9}, \ldots, 2^{10}\}$;
   - Exponential kernel: $\exp\left(\frac{\langle \mathbf{x}_i, \mathbf{x}_j \rangle}{\sigma^2}\right)$: $\sigma^2 \in \{2^{-2}, 2^{-1}, \ldots, 2^2\}$.
6. **FS-KC:** SVMs with the optimal constructed kernels with the optimal subset of features obtained by applying both the FS and KC subsystems. For the variable terminals of the KC subsystem, we set $n = 30$ and $m = 30$.

For SVMs, the initial range for the regularization hyper-parameter C is $\{2^{-9}, 2^{-6}, \ldots, 2^9\}$ and for the width of the kernel σ^2 is $\{2^{-9}, 2^{-6}, \ldots, 2^9\}$. We conduct a two-stage sampling process to specify the optimal values of C and σ^2: We use the Bézier curve to estimate the surface of the prediction accuracy from the sample points, and then we compute the area under the curve (AUC) to identify the most relevant regions in which a second finer search is carried out (Yamada et al. [26]).

In our experiments, we use LIBSVM (Chang and Lin [4]) as the SVM solver, ℓ_p-norm MKL (Kloft et al. [10]) as the MKL solver for binary classification and UFO-MKL (Orabona et al. [19]) as the MKL solver for multi-class classification. For GP, we use GPLAB (Silva and Almeida [21]). Table 1 gives a summary of the settings in GPLAB.

We use benchmark datasets from the UCI Machine Learning Repository [15]. Training, validation, and test datasets are constructed as specified in Table 2. Validation datasets are used to compute the prediction accuracy in the training phase, and test datasets are used for the final evaluation. Our strategy is to use small sizes of training data, so that any difference among the methods is easily identifiable, and larger sizes of validation data and test data to obtain reliable results for the comparison. Experiments are repeated 100 times for each dataset.

Table 1. Summary of settings in GPLAB

Parameter	Value
Population size	200 (FS) / 50 (KC)
Generation number	30
Initialization	Ramped half-and-half
Maximum level of node depth	6
Maximum level for initialization	3
Selection for reproduction	Roulette
Expected number of children	Absolute
Elitism	Halfelitism
Survival	Fixedpopsize
Reproduction rate	0.1
Crossover/mutation rate	0.7/0.3

Table 2. Information of datasets

Dataset	Instances	Features	(Training/ validation/test)	Categories for binary classification
Banknote authentication	1372	5	(50/450/872)	
Svmguide1	7089	4	(50/1000/3000)	
Occupancy detection	20560	7	(50/1000/3000)	
MAGIC gamma telescope	19020	11	(100/1000/3000)	
Page blocks classification	5473	10	(50/1000/3000)	1 vs >1
Car evaluation	1728	6	(100/600/1128)	{unacc} vs {acc, good, v-good}
Statlog (shuttle)	58000	9	(50/1000/3000)	1 vs >1
Wine quality	4898	12	(100/1000/3000)	≤5 vs >5
Default of credit card clients	30000	24	(100/1000/3000)	
Optical recognition of handwritten digits	5620	62	(100/1000/3000)	Odd vs even
Pen-based recognition of handwritten digits	10992	16	(100/1000/3000)	Odd vs even

In Table 3, the binary classification is carried out for the first 10 datasets and the multi-class classification is conducted for the last two datasets. In the last three columns of Table 3, the second row in each cell shows the average difference between the prediction accuracy of (the standard) SVM and SVM using the method in the corresponding column.

The numbers in the parenthesis are the p-values of the paired t-test for the null hypothesis that the prediction accuracy of the corresponding methods are equal. The table shows that the prediction accuracy of FS-KC is significantly better than SVM and in most cases also outperforms KC.

Table 3. Prediction accuracy for binary and multi-class classification

Dataset	SVM	MKL 1	MKL 2	FS	KC	FS-KC
Banknote	98.48 ± 1.02	98.3 ± 1.04	98.06 ± 1.3	98.43 ± 1.31	**99.16 ± 0.74**	99.04 ± 1.04
				−0.04 ± 1.1	0.69 ± 0.77	0.56 ± 1.22
				(p = 0.709)	(p < 0.001)	(p < 0.001)
Svmguide1	94.76 ± 1.22	92.88 ± 4.07	94.5 ± 2.89	94.15 ± 2.2	95.39 ± 1.14	**96.14 ± 0.64**
				−0.6 ± 2.1	0.63 ± 1.03	1.38 ± 1.17
				(p = 0.005)	(p < 0.001)	(p < 0.001)
Occupancy	98.05 ± 1.14	98.08 ± 1	98.67 ± 0.55	97.96 ± 0.97	98.58 ± 0.63	**98.84 ± 0.45**
				−0.09 ± 1.12	0.53 ± 0.8	0.79 ± 1.1
				(p = 0.446)	(p < 0.001)	(p < 0.001)
MAGIC	81.1 ± 1.3	80.56 ± 1.58	80.26 ± 2.04	80.88 ± 2.06	**81.74 ± 1.33**	81.58 ± 1.49
				−0.22 ± 1.59	0.64 ± 1.06	0.48 ± 1.3
				(p = 0.174)	(p < 0.001)	(p < 0.001)
Page blocks	93.16 ± 0.95	92.38 ± 1.19	89.39 ± 9.78	92.24 ± 1.49	93.33 ± 1.04	**93.83 ± 1.21**
				−0.92 ± 1.38	0.17 ± 0.84	0.66 ± 1.16
				(p < 0.001)	(p = 0.046)	(p < 0.001)
Car	93.4 ± 1.33	93.03 ± 1.59	93.05 ± 1.69	93.61 ± 1.3	94.03 ± 1.22	**94.66 ± 1.3**
				0.21 ± 0.58	0.64 ± 0.7	1.26 ± 1.33
				(p < 0.001)	(p < 0.001)	(p < 0.001)
Statlog	97.21 ± 1.54	97.44 ± 1.43	92.74 ± 7.61	96.15 ± 3.08	98.14 ± 1.22	**99.03 ± 0.99**
				−1.06 ± 2.65	0.93 ± 0.91	1.81 ± 1.28
				(p < 0.001)	(p < 0.001)	(p < 0.001)
Wine	79.35 ± 0.85	79.49 ± 0.93	79.2 ± 0.97	79.25 ± 0.96	**80.32 ± 0.89**	80.28 ± 0.9
				−0.1 ± 0.66	0.97 ± 0.74	0.94 ± 0.87
				(p = 0.132)	(p < 0.001)	(p < 0.001)
Credit	79.65 ± 1.47	80.12 ± 1.58	79.64 ± 2.87	79.06 ± 1.71	79.74 ± 1.59	**80.69 ± 1.58**
				−0.59 ± 1.22	0.08 ± 0.85	1.04 ± 1.03
				(p < 0.001)	(p = 0.334)	(p < 0.001)
Pen digit	95.15 ± 1.26	94.94 ± 1.25	93.59 ± 1.59	95.37 ± 1.03	96.02 ± 1.08	**96.18 ± 0.87**
				0.22 ± 0.5	0.87 ± 0.62	1.02 ± 0.85
				(p < 0.001)	(p < 0.001)	(p < 0.001)
Opt digit	92.04 ± 1.09	92.21 ± 1.12	84.22 ± 3.69	90.5 ± 2.03	92.92 ± 1.05	**93.34 ± 0.98**
				−1.54 ± 1.51	0.88 ± 0.7	1.3 ± 0.78
				(p < 0.001)	(p < 0.001)	(p < 0.001)
Pen digit	90.63 ± 1.79	90.29 ± 1.6	89.07 ± 1.99	90.4 ± 1.95	91.8 ± 1.62	**91.86 ± 1.87**
				−0.23 ± 0.74	1.17 ± 0.85	1.24 ± 1.03
				(p = 0.003)	(p < 0.001)	(p < 0.001)

5   Conclusion and Future Work

We presented a heuristic method to explore a large space of nonlinear combinations of kernels with arbitrary subsets of features. Genetic programming provided a way to tackle this difficult task. Experiments show that the proposed method, with two types of GP operations for constructing kernels and selecting subsets of features, achieves a drastic improvement in comparison to the standard SVM with fine-tuned parameters.

In our experiments, we used the top $n = 30$ subsets of features and the top $m = 30$ nonlinear kernels. Scaling up the values of m and n is a valuable direction for future research.

References

1. Bach, F.R., Lanckriet, G.R.G., Jordan, M.I.: Multiple kernel learning, conic duality, and the SMO algorithm. In: Proceedings of 21st International Conference on Machine Learning, ICML 2004, p. 6. ACM, New York (2004)
2. Bartz-Beielstein, T., Lasarczyk, C., Preuss, M.: The sequential parameter optimization toolbox. In: Bartz-Beielstein, T., Chiarandini, M., Paquete, L., Preuss, M. (eds.) Experimental Methods for the Analysis of Optimization Algorithms, pp. 337–360. Springer, New York (2010). doi:10.1007/978-3-642-02538-9_14
3. Bhowan, U., McCloskey, D.J.: Genetic programming for feature selection and question-answer ranking in IBM Watson. In: Machado, P., Heywood, M.I., McDermott, J., Castelli, M., García-Sánchez, P., Burelli, P., Risi, S., Sim, K. (eds.) EuroGP 2015. LNCS, vol. 9025, pp. 153–166. Springer, Cham (2015). doi:10.1007/978-3-319-16501-1_13
4. Chang, C.-C., Lin, C.-J.: LIBSVM: a library for support vector machines. ACM Trans. Intell. Syst. Technol. **2**(3), 27:1–27:27 (2011)
5. Cortes, C., Haffner, P., Mohri, M., Bennett, K., Cesa-bianchi, N.: Rational kernels. J. Mach. Learn. Res. **5**, 1035–1062 (2004)
6. Diosan, L., Rogozan, A., Pecuchet, J.P.: Evolving kernel functions for SVMs by genetic programming. In: Sixth International Conference on Machine Learning and Applications (ICMLA 2007), pp. 19–24, December 2007
7. Dioşan, L., Rogozan, A., Pecuchet, J.-P.: Improving classification performance of support vector machine by genetically optimising kernel shape and hyper-parameters. Appl. Intell. **36**(2), 280–294 (2012)
8. Gray, H.F., Maxwell, R.J., Martnez-Prez, I., Ars, C., Cerdn, S.: Genetic programming for classication and feature selection: analysis of 1h nuclear magnetic resonance spectra from human brain tumour biopsies. NMR Biomed. **11**(4–5), 217–224 (1998)
9. Howley, T., Madden, M.G.: The genetic kernel support vector machine: description and evaluation. Artif. Intell. Rev. **24**(3), 379–395 (2005)
10. Kloft, M., Brefeld, U., Sonnenburg, S., Zien, A.: Lp-norm multiple kernel learning. J. Mach. Learn. Res. **12**, 953–997 (2011)
11. Koch, P., Bischl, B., Flasch, O., Bartz-Beielstein, T., Weihs, C., Konen, W.: Tuning and evolution of support vector kernels. Evol. Intel. **5**(3), 153–170 (2012)
12. Konen, W., Koch, P., Flasch, O., Bartz-Beielstein, T., Friese, M., Naujoks, B.: Tuned data mining: a benchmark study on different tuners. In: Proceedings of 13th Annual Conference on Genetic and Evolutionary Computation, GECCO 2011, pp. 1995–2002. ACM, New York (2011)

13. Koza, J.R.: Genetic Programming: On the Programming of Computers by Means of Natural Selection. MIT Press, Cambridge (1992)
14. Lanckriet, G.R., Cristianini, N., Bartlett, P., Ghaoui, L.E., Jordan, M.I.: Learning the kernel matrix with semidefinite programming. J. Mach. Learn. Res. **5**, 27–72 (2004)
15. Lichman, M.: UCI machine learning repository (2013)
16. Meenakshi, A.R., Rajian, C.: On a product of positive semidefinite matrices. Linear Algebra Appl. **295**(1), 3–6 (1999)
17. Micchelli, C.A., Pontil, M.: Learning the kernel function via regularization. J. Mach. Learn. Res. **6**, 1099–1125 (2005)
18. Orabona, F., Fornoni, M., Caputo, B., Cesa-Bianchi, N.: OM-2: an online multiclass multi-kernel learning algorithm Luo Jie. In: IEEE Conference on Computer Vision and Pattern Recognition, CVPR Workshops 2010, San Francisco, CA, USA, 13–18 June 2010, pp. 43–50. IEEE Computer Society (2010)
19. Orabona, F., Luo, J.: Ultra-fast optimization algorithm for sparse multi kernel learning. In: Proceedings of 28th International Conference on Machine Learning, no. Idiap-RR-11-2011, June 2011
20. Orabona, F., Luo, J., Caputo, B.: Online-batch strongly convex multi kernel learning. In: The 23rd IEEE Conference on Computer Vision and Pattern Recognition, CVPR 2010, San Francisco, CA, USA, 13–18 June 2010, pp. 787–794. IEEE Computer Society (2010)
21. Silva, S., Almeida, J.: GPLAB-a genetic programming toolbox for MATLAB. In: Proceedings of Nordic MATLAB Conference (NMC-2003), pp. 273–278 (2005)
22. Steinwart, I., Christmann, A.: Support Vector Machines, 1st edn. Springer Publishing Company Incorporated, New York (2008)
23. Sullivan, K.M., Luke, S.: Evolving kernels for support vector machine classification. In: Thierens, D., Beyer, H.-G., Bongard, J., Branke, J., Clark, J.A., Cliff, D., Congdon, C.B., Deb, K., Doerr, B., Kovacs, T., Kumar, S., Miller, J.F., Moore, J., Neumann, F., Pelikan, M., Poli, R., Sastry, K., Stanley, K.O., Stutzle, T., Watson, R.A., Wegener, I. (eds.) GECCO 2007: Proceedings of 9th Annual Conference on Genetic and Evolutionary Computation, vol. 2, pp. 1702–1707. ACM Press, London, 7–11 July 2007
24. Surez, R.R., Valencia-Ramrez, J.M., Graff, M.: Genetic programming as a feature selection algorithm. In: 2014 IEEE International Autumn Meeting on Power, Electronics and Computing (ROPEC), pp. 1–5, November 2014
25. Xue, B., Zhang, M., Browne, W.N., Yao, X.: A survey on evolutionary computation approaches to feature selection. IEEE Trans. Evol. Comput. **1**(99), 1 (2015)
26. Yamada, S., Neshatian, K., Sainudiin, R.: Optimal hyper-parameter search in support vector machines using Bézier surfaces. In: Pfahringer, B., Renz, J. (eds.) AI 2015. LNCS, vol. 9457, pp. 623–629. Springer, Cham (2015). doi:10.1007/978-3-319-26350-2_55

KW-Race and Fast KW-Race: Racing-Based Frameworks for Tuning Parameters of Evolutionary Algorithms on Black-Box Optimization Problems

Mang Wang, Xin Tong, and Bin Li[✉]

School of Information Science and Technology,
University of Science and Technology of China, Hefei, China
{mangwang,txt}@mail.ustc.edu.cn, binli@ustc.edu.cn

Abstract. Setting proper parameters is vital for using Evolutionary Algorithms (EAs) to optimize problems, while parameter tuning is a time-consuming task. Previous approaches focus on tuning parameter configurations that are suitable for multiple problems or problem instances. However, according to the No Free Lunch (NFL) theorem, there is no generic parameter configuration that is fit for all problems. Moreover, practitioners are usually concerned with their particular optimization problem at hand and desire to obtain an acceptable result with less computational cost. Therefore, in this paper, the KW-Race framework is first proposed for solving the parameter tuning task of EAs on certain black-box optimization problem. Then a measure of convergence speed is embedded in the preceding framework to form the Fast KW-Race (F-KW-Race) framework for further reducing the computational cost of the tuning procedure. Experimental studies illustrate remarkable results and further demonstrate the validity and efficiency of the proposed frameworks.

Keywords: Racing method · Kruskal-Wallis H test · Parameter tuning · Evolutionary Algorithms · Black-box optimization

1 Introduction

Performance of Evolutionary Algorithms (EAs) is strongly correlated with different parameter settings. Two sets of parameters, i.e., qualitative parameters and quantitative parameters, can be tuned simultaneously. Specifically, the former are often symbolic, e.g., the selection operator which can be chosen among a set of values {roulette wheel, tournament, elitism}. In contrast, the quantitative parameters are mostly numerical values, e.g., the mutation rate that locates in the interval $[0, 1]$. The main difference between these two parameters is that the quantitative parameters can form a searchable space that is analogous to the fitness landscape of optimization problems, which was named by Eiben and Smit [5] as the utility landscape. In this landscape, locations are the parameter

© Springer International Publishing AG 2017
Y. Shi et al. (Eds.): SEAL 2017, LNCS 10593, pp. 617–628, 2017.
https://doi.org/10.1007/978-3-319-68759-9_50

vectors and measures are their utility values. It is notable that the utility values are stochastic as they reflect the performance of an EA which is a stochastic searching algorithm.

Parameter tuning is usually a difficult task. The main difficulties can be summarized as follows: (1) it is a time-consuming process that generally requires multiple runs of the combination of parameters with different random seeds; (2) there is no generic parameter configuration that can fit for all optimization problems, which means the best parameter configuration depends on particular problem at hand. This is also demonstrated by the famous No Free Lunch (NFL) theorem [21]; (3) parameters are interrelated so that the behavior of different parameter configurations during optimization is complex, which is hard to be analyzed using traditional approaches such as statistical modeling.

Traditional approaches for parameter tuning include the simple brute-force tuning, hand-made tuning, tuning by analogy, experimental design based tuning, search based tuning, model-based tuning and hybrid tuning [18]. Concretely, the brute-force approach determines the best parameter configuration by evaluating the performance of a full factorial set of parameter configurations on a problem instance, which requires sufficiently high computation cost. Hand-made tuning is a common approach in the early stage of parameter tuning, which iteratively modifies one parameter to achieve improvements in performance. Tuning by analogy approach follows the typical guidelines recommended by other researchers. The mainstream parameter tuning approaches include the experimental design based tuning, the search based tuning and the model-based tuning. Particularly, the first approach is based on the experimental design to set parameter values, which includes the F-Race method [2] and the Sequential Parameter Optimization (SPO) method [1]; the second approach searches the utility landscape of parameter vectors, which contains the meta-GA [7], REVAC [19] and ParamILS [11]; the third approach generates better-performing parameter configurations by updating the parameters of pre-set models, which includes the EGO-based methods [12] such as SMAC [10]. Lastly, hybrid tuning combines the existing approaches to form more flexible methods.

The existing tuning methods have several limitations when being used in practice. REVAC and SPO can only tune the numerical parameters efficiently. F-Race, ParamILS and SMAC can tune both symbolic and numerical parameters, while they are all designed for multiple problems or instances. Given the above, in this paper, we present a parameter tuning approach that is not only for tuning both symbolic and numerical parameters of EAs, but also valid for certain black-box optimization problem. The idea of the proposed approach is derived from the F-Race method [2] while focusing on the actual requirements of algorithm practitioners. Compared with previous studies, the main contributions of this paper are as follows:

1. The KW-Race framework is proposed based on the Kruskal-Wallis H test [13], which is statistically sound for tuning parameters of EAs on a particular black-box problem;

2. A measure of convergence speed is embedded in the KW-Race framework to form the Fast KW-Race (F-KW-Race) framework, which can further reduce the computational cost of the tuning process;
3. Remarkable results of experimental studies demonstrate the validity and efficiency of the proposed frameworks.

The rest of this paper is organized as follows. Section 2 introduces the related work. Section 3 is devoted to the details of the proposed frameworks. Section 4 conducts experimental studies. Finally, Sect. 5 draws the conclusions.

2   Related Work

In the past several decades, approaches of parameter tuning have demonstrated their success in many applications. In this section, the F-Race method is described in detail as the idea of this article is derived from it.

2.1   F-Race Method

F-Race was first implemented in configuring parameters of metaheuristics by Birattari et al. [2] and further improved to form the Iterated F-Race (I/F-Race) [15]. It is inspired by the racing methods that initially used to solve the model selection problem for lazy learners in machine learning [17]. The motivation of racing methods is for better allocating the resources among candidate algorithms, so that they want to reduce the computational resources of poor candidates as early as possible. Specifically, F-Race eliminates poor parameter configurations based on statistical results coming from the Friedman test [6]. It eliminates the calibrations that show a statistical worse performance from the candidate set iteratively until there is only one parameter configuration left or the predefined budget is reached.

F-Race implements a block design to meet the requirements of Friedman test. In Friedman test [6], data is accumulated as a matrix with n rows and k columns. Each row is a block and each column is called a treatment. Within each block, the initial data is ranked first and tied values are assigned to average of their original ranks. Then the test statistic can be formulated as follows:

$$Q = \frac{(k-1)\sum\limits_{j=1}^{k}\left(R_j - \frac{n(k+1)}{2}\right)^2}{\sum\limits_{i=1}^{n}\sum\limits_{j=1}^{k}R_{ij}^2 - \frac{nk(k+1)^2}{4}} \tag{1}$$

where R_{ij} is the rank within the block i and $R_j = \sum\limits_{i=1}^{n} R_{ij}$ is the sum of the ranks over the treatment j. Under the null hypothesis that the effects of all treatments are equal, Q is approximately χ^2 distributed with $(k-1)$ degrees of freedom when n or k is large (i.e., $n > 15$ or $k > 4$). Then the p-value can be calculated from the upper α quantile of the preceding distribution. If the p-value of Friedman Test is less than the preset significance level, the null hypothesis can be rejected, which means that at least one treatment is better than at least one other. A post-hoc procedure can be used for multiple comparisons between pairs of treatments to obtain the stochastic dominance. Usually, the Conover [3] procedure is adopted as the post-hoc procedure following the Friedman Test, which is formulated as:

$$|R_i - R_j| > t_{1-\alpha} \sqrt{\frac{2n\left(1 - \frac{Q}{n(k-1)}\right)\left(\sum_{i=1}^{n}\sum_{j=1}^{k} R_{ij}^2 - \frac{nk(k+1)^2}{4}\right)}{(n-1)(k-1)}} \qquad (2)$$

where $t_{1-\alpha}$ is the upper α quantile of the Student's t-distribution with $(n-1)$ $(k-1)$ degrees of freedom. Then the obtained p-values are adjusted by the Holm procedure [9] to revise the family-wise error rate (FWER), which represents the probability of making one or more false conclusions among all hypotheses of multiple pair-wise tests.

In F-Race, at step i, the best candidate parameter configuration (i.e., the minimum R_j for a minimization problem) is first selected as the control treatment, then other parameter configurations are compared with this control treatment one by one. All candidates that are statistically worse than the control treatment will be discarded and not appear in the next step $(i + 1)$. The whole process terminates when there is only one parameter configuration left or the predefined budget is reached.

F-Race eliminates the poor candidates through a non-parameter statistical test procedure, where the normality of the tested data is not required. Moreover, through the block design, the variations among treatments in each block can be controlled. The traditional F-Race is designed for selecting parameter configurations on multiple problem instances, because each problem instance can be viewed as a natural block. However, according to the No Free Lunch (NFL) theorem [21], there is no generic parameter configuration that can fit for all problems. In practice, people usually concentrate on choosing proper parameter configurations for their particular optimization problem at hand, then the block design would be problematic. The reason is that randomness is the intrinsic characteristic of EAs, thus different random seeds or initialization can achieve diverse performance even using the same EA to optimize the same problem. Although we can set a same random seed for each run of all candidate parameter configurations, this will break the stochastic nature of EAs that leads to one-sided results. In addition, the computational cost of F-Race is still relatively high, especially for the situation in which multiple parameter configurations are not distinguishable based on the their performance.

3   Methods

Practitioners usually desire an algorithm that would solve their current problem well and fast. In this section, the KW-Race framework is first proposed to conquer the preceding issues of F-Race. Then a measure of convergence speed is introduced and embedded in the KW-Race framework to form the Fast KW-Race (F-KW-Race) framework to further reduce the computational cost of the tuning process.

3.1   The KW-Race Framework

As the name suggests, KW-Race is a racing method that implements the Kruskal-Wallis H test [13] (denoted as K-W test hereafter) to eliminate poor parameter configurations. K-W test is a non-parametric one-way ANOVA test based on ranks, which extends the Mann-Whitney U test (or Wilcoxon rank-sum test) [16] to more than two groups. The main difference between the K-W test and the Friedman test is that the former does not need the block design, which effectively ensure the stochastic nature of EAs. Concretely, the null hypothesis H_0 of K-W test is that all the distributions of k groups are equal, where k is the number of candidate parameter configurations. Then it ranks total N measures from all groups together and calculates the test statistic as follows:

$$H = \frac{12}{N(N+1)} \sum_{i=1}^{k} \frac{R_i^2}{n_i} - 3(N+1) \tag{3}$$

where n_i is the number of measures in group i and R_i is the sum of ranks of the ith group. Besides, all the tied ranks should be corrected. When $k > 3$, the p-value can be approximated by the χ^2 distribution with $(k-1)$ degrees of freedom. If the p-value of K-W test is less than the preset significance level, the post-hoc procedure that is the Conover-Iman test [3] can be employed for multiple comparisons between pairs of groups, which is formulated as:

$$S^2 = \frac{1}{N-1} \left[\sum_{l=1}^{N} r_l^2 - N \frac{(N+1)^2}{4} \right]$$

$$\left| \frac{R_j}{n_j} - \frac{R_i}{n_i} \right| > t_{1-\alpha} \sqrt{S^2 \frac{N-1-H}{N-k}} \sqrt{\frac{1}{n_i} + \frac{1}{n_j}} \tag{4}$$

where r_l is the global rank of the measure and t represents the Student's t-distribution with $(N-k)$ degrees of freedom. Then the p-value is calculated from the upper α quantile of the preceding t-distribution and adjusted by the Holm procedure [9] to revise the FWER.

The KW-Race framework performs the parameter tuning process as follows: at step i, each parameter configuration forms a group of K-W test. If the indicator H in (3) is statistically significant, the best preformed configuration is viewed as the control group and compared with other groups iteratively using (4). Then all configurations that are statistically worse than the control group will be eliminated and not participate in racing at step $(i+1)$. The whole process will continue until reaching certain termination criterion.

3.2   The Fast KW-Race Framework

In the field of theoretical analysis of EAs, drift analysis [8] is a typical approach to analyze computational time complexity of EAs. It analyzes the general conditions for an EA to solve a problem within polynomial time. In drift analysis, the first hitting time on an optimal solution is first defined and then the relationship between the expected first hitting time and the problem size is investigated. Inspired by the first hitting time, a measure that is the first hitting function evaluations (FEs) is used to indicate the convergence speed of EAs. Specifically, the first hitting FEs is defined as the number of FEs required for first hitting the global (or approximately global) best fitness value.

The first hitting FEs is expected to measure the convergence speed of EAs during optimization. Recall the KW-Race framework, as the racing proceeds, there is usually a stage that all remaining candidates are statistically with no differences. If the process continues, the number of eliminated configurations would usually be few, whereas the subsequent processes waste a lot of computational cost. Therefore, the F-KW-Race framework is proposed to terminate the racing process quickly while keeping the accuracy of the final results. Concrete descriptions of the F-KW-Race framework are illustrated in Algorithm 1.

4   Experimental Studies and Results

In this section, experimental studies are conducted to demonstrate the validity and efficiency of the proposed frameworks. Firstly, thirteen numerical black-box test problems are introduced. Then the parameters of Differential Evolution (DE) are described. Finally, the results of the proposed frameworks are compared with those of F-Race and the brute-force approach.

4.1   Problem Set

Thirteen typical numerical problems are chosen from the CEC 2013 benchmark function set [14]. All the functions are minimization problems and their search region are all bounded in $[-100, 100]^D$. The global optimum of these functions are randomly shifted in $[-80, 80]^D$ and the fitness value of the global optimum is respectively shifted to positive, zero and negative values. The test problems are all viewed as the black-box optimization problems and their dimensions are set to $D = 30$. Table 1 shows the test functions in this study in detail. It is notable that the first five functions are unimodal and the rest functions are multimodal.

4.2   Descriptions of the Parameter Configurations

Two kinds of categorical parameters and two numerical parameters of DE are configured as the candidate set. Concretely, for categorical parameters, the mutation operator can be selected from the set {rand/1, best/1, target-to-best/1, best/2, rand/2, rand/2/dir}; the crossover operator can use the binomial or

---

Algorithm 1. The Fast KW-Race (F-KW-Race) Framework

Require: C (candidate set of parameter configurations), r (amount of steps required to start racing), α (the significance level), b (the predefined budget to terminate the racing process)

1: step $s \leftarrow 1$
2: **while** termination criterion is not fulfilled **do**
3:   **for all** $c_j \in C$ **do**
4:     append the measure of c_j in run i to the ith index of group G_j
5:   **end for**
6:   **if** $s > r$ **then**
7:     **for all** k candidate groups at step s **do**
8:       ranking the measures from all groups
9:       $R_j \leftarrow$ sum of ranks of group j
10:    **end for**
11:    perform the K-W test according to (3)
12:    **if** null hypothesis of K-W test is rejected **then**
13:      $c_{cont} \leftarrow \operatorname{argmin} R_j$
14:      **for all** $c_j \in C \setminus c_{cont}$ **do**
15:        perform pair-wise test following (4), then the p-value is adjusted by the Holm procedure
16:        **if** adjusted p-value $< \alpha$ **then**
17:          $C \leftarrow C \setminus c_j$
18:        **end if**
19:      **end for**
20:    **else if** the H_0 of K-W test is accepted for two consecutive times **then**
21:      change the measure of performance to the combined measure (i.e., multiplying the measure of performance by the first hitting FEs) from now on
22:    **end if**
23: **end if**
24: $s \leftarrow s + 1$
25: **end while**
26: **return** the remaining set C

---

exponential methods. As to the numerical parameters, both the scale factor F and the crossover rate CR are sampled from the range $[0, 1]$ with five equal intervals, i.e., F and CR can be chosen from $\{0.1, 0.3, 0.5, 0.7, 0.9\}$. Therefore, the total number of parameter configurations is $6 \times 2 \times 5 \times 5 = 300$. The detailed descriptions of all these parameters can be found in [4].

4.3   Brute-Force Approach as the Golden Standard

The results of brute-force approach, which exhaustively runs all candidate parameter configurations on each test problem for the tuning task, are viewed as the golden standard as suggested by Naudts and Kallel [20]. Concretely, all candidate parameter configurations are executed for 50 independent runs on each test problem with the preset budget of FEs equals $10^4 \times D$. In addition, according to

Table 1. Thirteen test functions used in this study

Function	Definition	Transformation	f_i^*
Sphere Function	$f_1(x) = \sum\limits_{i=1}^{D} z_i^2 + f_1^*$	$z = x - o$	-600
High Conditioned Elliptic Function	$f_2(x) = \sum\limits_{i=1}^{D} (10^6)^{\frac{i-1}{D-1}} z_i^2 + f_2^*$	$z = T_{osz}(x - o)$	-500
Bent Cigar Function	$f_3(x) = z_1^2 + 10^6 \sum\limits_{i=2}^{D} z_i^2 + f_3^*$	$z = T_{asy}^{0.5}(x - o)$	-400
Discus Function	$f_4(x) = 10^6 z_1^2 + \sum\limits_{i=2}^{D} z_i^2 + f_4^*$	$z = T_{osz}(x - o)$	-300
Different Powers Function	$f_5(x) = \sqrt{\sum\limits_{i=1}^{D} |z_i|^{2+4\frac{i-1}{D-1}}} + f_5^*$	$z = x - o$	-200
Rosenbrock's Function	$f_6(x) = \sum\limits_{i=1}^{D-1} (100(z_i^2 - z_{i+1})^2 + (z_i - 1)^2) + f_6^*$	$z = \frac{2.048(x-o)}{100} + 1$	-100
Schaffers F7 Function	$f_7(x) =$ $\left(\frac{1}{D-1} \sum\limits_{i=1}^{D-1} (\sqrt{z_i} + \sqrt{z_i} \sin^2(50z_i^{0.2})) \right)^2 + f_7^*$	$z_i = \sqrt{y_i^2 + y_{i+1}^2}$ $y = \Lambda^{10} T_{asy}^{0.5}(x - o)$	0
Ackley's Function	$f_8(x) = -20 \exp\left(-0.2\sqrt{\frac{1}{D}\sum\limits_{i=1}^{D} z_i^2}\right) -$ $\exp\left(\frac{1}{D}\sum\limits_{i=1}^{D} \cos(2\pi z_i)\right) + 20 + e + f_8^*$	$z = \Lambda^{10} T_{asy}^{0.5}(x - o)$	100
Weierstrass Function	$f_9(x) =$ $\sum\limits_{i=1}^{D} \left(\sum\limits_{k=0}^{k_{max}} [a^k \cos(2\pi b^k (z_i + 0.5))]\right) -$ $D\sum\limits_{k=0}^{k_{max}} [a^k \cos(2\pi b^k \cdot 0.5))] + f_9^*$	$a = 0.5, b = 3, k_{max} = 20,$ $z = \Lambda^{10} T_{asy}^{0.5}\left(\frac{0.5(x-o)}{100}\right)$	200
Griewank's Function	$f_{10}(x) = \sum\limits_{i=1}^{D} \frac{z_i^2}{4000} - \prod\limits_{i=1}^{D} \cos(\frac{z_i}{\sqrt{i}}) + 1 + f_{10}^*$	$z = \Lambda^{100}\left(\frac{600(x-o)}{100}\right)$	300
Rastrigin's Function	$f_{11}(x) = \sum\limits_{i=1}^{D} (z_i^2 - 10\cos(2\pi z_i) + 10) + f_{11}^*$	$z =$ $\Lambda^{10}T_{asy}^{0.2}\left(T_{osz}\left(\frac{5.12(x-o)}{100}\right)\right)$	400
Schwefel's Function	$f_{12}(z) = 418.9829 \times D - \sum\limits_{i=1}^{D} g(z_i) + f_{12}^*$	$z = \Lambda^{10}\left(\frac{1000(x-o)}{100}\right) +$ 420.9687462275036	500
Katsuura Function	$f_{13}(x) =$ $\frac{10}{D^2} \prod\limits_{i=1}^{D} \left(1 + i\sum\limits_{j=1}^{32} \frac{|2^j z_i - round(2^j z_j)|}{2^j}\right)^{\frac{10}{D^{1.2}}}$ $-\frac{10}{D^2} + f_{13}^*$	$z = \Lambda^{100}\left(\frac{5(x-o)}{100}\right)$	600

o represents the random shift adding to the global optimum;
the definitions of Λ^α, T_{asy}^β, T_{osz} and $g(z_i)$ of f_{12} can be found to [14].

the IEEE Standard for Floating-Point Arithmetic (IEEE 754), the precision of the double-precision floating-point number has $15-17$ significant decimal digits. In this study, we set the precision to $1e-8$ and revise the performance as follows: if $f - f^* < 1e-8$, then $f = f^*$, where f^* denotes the global optimum.

Statistical analysis for the final performance is conducted through the K-W test which is similar to the procedure illustrated in (3) and (4). Specifically, the performance measures of each parameter constitute each group required by the K-W test. If the preceding test is rejected based on the preset significance level (0.05 in this study), the Conover-Iman post-hoc test is further used for pair-wise comparison. Holm procedure is also employed to adjust the obtained p-value. Finally, the best parameter configuration or a set of equally best configurations can be selected based on the results of statistical test.

4.4   Comparisons Between KW-Race and F-Race

As described in Sect. 2.1, F-Race may break the stochastic nature of EAs due to the blocking design, which could lead to incomplete results. Instead, the proposed KW-Race framework fully protects the randomness of EAs, thus is expected to have better results than F-Race when comparing with the golden standard.

Table 2 shows the results of the brute-force approach, F-Race and KW-Race on each test function, where the blocking design of F-Race is achieved by using the same random seed for each run of all parameter configurations. It first shows the number of remaining parameter configurations of both F-Race and KW-Race is usually less than that of the brute-force approach. Then for the computational cost, both F-Race and KW-Race can dramatically save the computational cost compared with the brute-force approach, and F-Race seems slightly better than KW-Race. While for the accuracy, i.e., the proportion of correctly selected parameter configurations referring to the golden standard, F-Race selects parameter configurations that are not contained in the set of golden standard on functions f_3, f_4, f_8, f_{12} and f_{13}. Particularly, on f_8, f_{12} and f_{13}, the accuracy of F-Race is only about 40%. On the contrary, KW-Race achieves 100% accuracy on all test functions, which demonstrates the proposed KW-Race framework is more accurate than the F-Race for tuning parameters on a particular black-box optimization problem.

Table 2. Tuning results of the brute-force, F-Race and KW-Race method

		f_1	f_2	f_3	f_4	f_5	f_6	f_7	f_8	f_9	f_{10}	f_{11}	f_{12}	f_{13}
Brute-force	Remaining	131	98	87	121	92	10	51	5	1	74	38	8	6
F-Race	Remaining	47	45	44	48	22	1	12	10	1	29	3	5	3
	Cost saving (%)	87.9	88.2	87.9	87.8	92.1	96.8	93.9	91.8	96.4	89.6	96.0	95.5	96.3
	Accuracy (%)	100	100	**98**	**98**	100	100	100	**40**	100	100	100	**40**	**33**
KW-Race	Remaining	131	93	85	118	87	2	46	2	1	67	37	3	1
	Cost saving (%)	72.4	79.2	80.9	74.4	80.6	96.4	88.2	97.2	96.5	82.2	90.2	96.8	97.5
	Accuracy (%)	100	100	**100**	**100**	100	100	100	**100**	100	100	100	**100**	100

4.5   Comparisons Between F-KW-Race and KW-Race

Compared with KW-Race, the F-KW-Race framework involves the first hitting FEs in the racing process and is expected to further reduce the computational cost. Table 3 illustrates the detailed results of F-KW-Race, where the computational cost of F-KW-Race is reduced by 95% in majority compared with the brute-force approach. Especially, on functions f_3, f_4, f_5, f_6, f_8, f_9, f_{12} and f_{13}, the computational cost are all saved more than 97%. Besides, recall the contents of Table 2, F-Race is already capable of saving remarkable computational cost compared with the brute-force approach and even better than KW-Race, while the F-KW-Race can further reduce the computational cost over F-Race, particularly on the functions that F-Race made mistakes (shown in bold face).

It is noteworthy that the accuracy of F-KW-Race is not decreased at all, which also remains 100% for all test functions except for f_9. After carefully examining the selected parameter configurations on f_9, {target-to-best/1, binomial, F = 0.5, CR = 0.1} is selected as the best one by the brute-force approach, while {$rand/1, binomial, F = 0.1, CR = 0.1$} is chosen as the best configuration via the F-KW-Race. Furthermore, the performance and the first hitting FEs of these two configurations are checked. As to the performance, the brute-force approach finds the global optimum for 44 times and F-KW-Race for 15 times, thus the brute-force approach undoubtedly selects the former parameter configuration. However, for the average first hitting FEs, the latter configuration only uses about half FEs compared with the former ($128840/230656 \approx 55.9\%$). From the perspective of algorithm practitioners, the configuration selected by F-KW-Race can find the global optimum and also converges faster, which is exactly the required solution for tuning parameters. Therefore, this is actually not a mistake made by F-KW-Race and is marked by asterisk in Table 3.

Table 3. Results of the F-KW-Race framework

	f_1	f_2	f_3	f_4	f_5	f_6	f_7	f_8	f_9	f_{10}	f_{11}	f_{12}	f_{13}
Remain	2	1	3	1	1	1	46	1	1	3	1	1	1
Cost saving over **brute-force** (%)	96.4	96.8	97.1	97.4	97.7	97.3	92.0	97.9	97.3	92.6	96.4	97.9	97.8
Cost saving over **F-Race** (%)		72.3	74.2	**79.3**	**79.1**	70.1	15.0	26.8	**74.5**	26.4	29.2	10.9	**52.2**	**38.8**
Accuracy (%)	100	100	**100**	**100**	100	100	100	**100**	100*	100	100	**100**	100

In order to give an intuitive demonstration, the racing process of KW-Race and F-KW-Race on functions f_4, f_5, f_8 and f_{12} are shown in Fig. 1a–d, respectively. From these figures, the difference between F-KW-Race and KW-Race can be summarized as follows: on one hand, on simple test functions such as f_4 and f_5 in Fig. 1a and b, F-KW-Race terminates the racing process much earlier than the KW-Race and also leaves less number of parameter configurations; on the other hand, on complicated problems such as f_8 and f_9 in Fig. 1c and d, F-KW-Race can terminated the racing process earlier as well, while the number of remaining parameter configurations is almost as same as that of KW-Race.

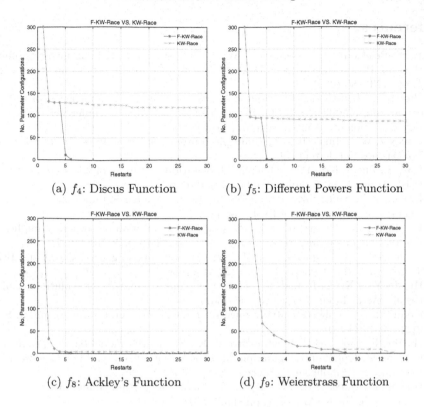

(a) f_4: Discus Function

(b) f_5: Different Powers Function

(c) f_8: Ackley's Function

(d) f_9: Weierstrass Function

Fig. 1. Visualization of the racing process of KW-Race and F-KW-Race.

5   Conclusions

In this article, the KW-Race framework is proposed to solve the parameter tuning task on a particular black-box optimization problem. Then the first hitting FEs is embedded in KW-Race to form the F-KW-Race framework. In practice, the KW-Race framework is expected to be used in the situation that the performance is the main focus, and the F-KW-Race framework is expected to select parameter configurations that can achieve acceptable performance while using less FEs.

Concerning with the future research, methods for automatically generating new and effective parameters for both symbolic and numerical parameters are remained to be explored. In this context, model-based tuning approaches may provide some inspirations.

Acknowledgments. This work was supported in part by National Natural Science Foundation of China under Grant 61473271.

628   M. Wang et al.

References

1. Bartz-Beielstein, T., Lasarczyk, C.W., Preuß, M.: Sequential parameter optimization. In: Proceedings of 2005 IEEE Congress on Evolutionary Computation, vol. 1, pp. 773–780 (2005)
2. Birattari, M., Stützle, T., Paquete, L., Varrentrapp, K.: A racing algorithm for configuring metaheuristics. In: Proceedings of 4th Annual Conference on Genetic and Evolutionary Computation, pp. 11–18 (2002)
3. Conover, W.J., Iman, R.L.: On multiple-comparisons procedures. Technical report, Los Alamos Sci. Lab (1979)
4. Das, S., Suganthan, P.N.: Differential evolution: a survey of the state-of-the-art. IEEE Trans. Evol. Comput. 15(1), 4–31 (2011)
5. Eiben, A.E., Smit, S.K.: Parameter tuning for configuring and analyzing evolutionary algorithms. Swarm Evol. Comput. 1(1), 19–31 (2011)
6. Friedman, M.: The use of ranks to avoid the assumption of normality implicit in the analysis of variance. J. Am. Stat. Assoc. 32(200), 675–701 (1937)
7. Grefenstette, J.J.: Optimization of control parameters for genetic algorithms. IEEE Trans. Syst. Man Cybern. 16(1), 122–128 (1986)
8. He, J., Yao, X.: Drift analysis and average time complexity of evolutionary algorithms. Artif. Intell. 127(1), 57–85 (2001)
9. Holm, S.: A simple sequentially rejective multiple test procedure. Scand. J. Stat. 6(2), 65–70 (1979)
10. Hutter, F., Hoos, H.H., Leyton-Brown, K.: Sequential model-based optimization for general algorithm configuration. In: Proceedings of International Conference on Learning and Intelligent Optimization, pp. 507–523 (2011)
11. Hutter, F., Hoos, H.H., Stützle, T.: Automatic algorithm configuration based on local search. In: AAAI, vol. 7, pp. 1152–1157 (2007)
12. Jones, D.R., Schonlau, M., Welch, W.J.: Efficient global optimization of expensive black-box functions. J. Glob. Optim. 13(4), 455–492 (1998)
13. Kruskal, W.H., Wallis, W.A.: Use of ranks in one-criterion variance analysis. J. Am. Stat. Assoc. 47(260), 583–621 (1952)
14. Liang, J., Qu, B., Suganthan, P., Hernández-Díaz, A.G.: Problem definitions and evaluation criteria for the CEC 2013 special session on real-parameter optimization. Technical report, Zhengzhou University and Nanyang Technological University (2013)
15. López-Ibáñez, M., Dubois-Lacoste, J., Cáceres, L.P., Birattari, M., Stützle, T.: The irace package: iterated racing for automatic algorithm configuration. Oper. Res. Perspect. 3, 43–58 (2016)
16. Mann, H.B., Whitney, D.R.: On a test of whether one of two random variables is stochastically larger than the other. Ann. Math. Stat. 18(1), 50–60 (1947)
17. Maron, O., Moore, A.W.: The racing algorithm: model selection for lazy learners. In: Aha, D.W. (ed.) Lazy Learning, pp. 193–225. Springer, Dordrecht (1997). doi:10.1007/978-94-017-2053-3_8
18. Montero, E., Riff, M.C., Neveu, B.: A beginner's guide to tuning methods. Appl. Soft Comput. 17, 39–51 (2014)
19. Nannen, V., Eiben, A.E.: Relevance estimation and value calibration of evolutionary algorithm parameters. In: IJCAI, vol. 7, pp. 975–980 (2007)
20. Naudts, B., Kallel, L.: A comparison of predictive measures of problem difficulty in evolutionary algorithms. IEEE Trans. Evol. Comput. 4(1), 1–15 (2000)
21. Wolpert, D.H., Macready, W.G.: No free lunch theorems for optimization. IEEE Trans. Evol. Comput. 1(1), 67–82 (1997)

Dynamic and Uncertain Environments

A Probabilistic Learning Algorithm
for the Shortest Path Problem

Yiya Diao[1], Changhe Li[1($\boxtimes$)], Yebin Ma[1], Junchen Wang[1], and Xingang Zhou[2]

[1] School of Automation and Hubei Key Laboratory of Advanced Control
and Intelligent Automation for Complex Systems,
China University of Geosciences, Wuhan, China
dwzxdjt@126.com, changhe.lw@gmail.com, benzalus@163.com,
jenswang@outlook.com
[2] Communication Security Group of Eastern Theater Command, Nanjing, China
pcm603@163.com

Abstract. Ant colony optimization (ACO) has been shown effectiveness
for solving combinatorial optimization problems. Inspired by the basic
principles of ACO, this paper proposes a novel evolutionary algorithm,
called probabilistic learning (PL). In the algorithm, a probability matrix
is created based on weighted information of the population and a novel
random search operator is proposed to adapt the PL to dynamic environments. The algorithm is tested on the shortest path problem (SPP) in
both static and dynamic environments. Experimental results on a set of
carefully designed 3D-problems show that the PL algorithm is effective
for solve SPPs and outperforms several popular ACO variants.

Keywords: Probabilistic learning · Ant colony optimization · Dynamic
shortest path problems

1 Introduction

The shortest path problem (SPP) is a classical combinatorial optimization problem. In this paper, the problem is defined as follows. Given a graph of a set of
nodes linked by directed edges, where each node is connected with eight neighbour nodes, the aim is to find the shortest path from a starting point to a
destination point. It is a simple problem and has been widely applied in many
applications, e.g., robot routing problem, the shortest path in games, the shortest
traffic route, etc.

The Dijkstra algorithm is widely used to find the shortest path in a completely known environment. However, when the environment is partially known,
unknown or changing, the Dijkstra algorithm seems unsuitable to solve this problem. To overcome these limitations, many heuristic approaches have been used
to address this problem, such as ant colony optimization (ACO).

Inspired by ACO, this paper proposes a novel probabilistic algorithm, namely
probabilistic learning (PL), for the SPP. A probabilistic matrix is created and

Y. Shi et al. (Eds.): SEAL 2017, LNCS 10593, pp. 631–643, 2017.
https://doi.org/10.1007/978-3-319-68759-9_51

updated according to weighted values of historical solutions. Each element in the matrix denotes the probability of an edge to be chosen. Different from ACO, PL neither follows the basic operations of ACO nor uses any geographical heuristic. An efficient random search operator is proposed to maintain the population diversity. The proposed algorithm is competitive in comparison with several ACO algorithms on the SPP.

The rest of this paper is organized as follows. Section 2 gives a brief review of related work. Section 3 describes the proposed algorithm in detail. Section 4 presents experimental results and discussions. Finally, conclusions and future work are discussed in Sect. 5.

2   Related Work

There are many research branches for combinatorial optimization problems. However, in this section, we mainly focus on the methods related to ACO. ACO simulates the foraging behavior of real ants for finding the shortest path from a food source to their nest by exploiting pheromone information. While walking, ants deposit pheromone chemicals, and follow, in probability, pheromone previously deposited by other ants.

Ant system (AS) [8] was the first ACO model proposed by Dorigo, and it has gained huge success. In order to simulate the foraging behavior, each ant chooses its next node by:

$$
p_{ij}^k(t) = \begin{cases} \frac{[\tau_{ij}(t)]^\alpha [\eta_{ij}]^\beta}{\sum_{l \in U} [\tau_{ij}(t)]^\alpha [\eta_{ij}]^\beta} & j \in U \\ 0 & j \notin U, \end{cases} \tag{1}
$$

where $p_{ij}^k(t)$ means the possibility of ant k moves from node i to node j. If ant k has visited node j, $p_{ij}^k(t)$ will be 0; otherwise, the ant will probabilistically choose a candidate node. τ_{ij} means the pheromone intensity of edge (i,j). η_{ij} means the visibility of edge (i,j), which equals to the reciprocal of the length of this edge. α is the weight of pheromone and β is the weight of the visibility. After all ants reach the food point, the pheromone matrix is updated by:

$$
\tau_{ij}(t+1) = \rho * \tau_{ij}(t) + \sum_{k=1}^{m} \Delta \tau_{ij}^k(t), \tag{2}
$$

where m is the number of ants, and ρ means the persistence of pheromone. After this update, all ants go back to the start point and repeat the above procedures until the algorithm stops.

AS has a strong ability in searching good solutions. However, it has shortcomings: the slow convergence speed and the stagnation issue. Inspired by the selection principle of genetic algorithms, an elitist AS (EAS) [2] was developed. Compared to AS, EAS takes an ant which performs best as an "elitist", and it leaves more pheromone than other ants. As a result, ants are more likely to choose the elitist path.

The ant colony system (ACS) [7] was proposed based on Ant-Q (AS with Q-learning) [6]. ACS provides two ways to update global pheromone: the local online update and the global offline update. The local online update is used after every ant moves a step, which means the pheromone of the map changes synchronously. On the other hand, the global offline update is used when all ants reach the food point, then the best ant is chosen to update the global pheromone. ACS is quick and it can obtain good solutions, but it is not stable.

A rank-based AS (RAS) [1] was proposed by sorting ants based on route lengths. Like EAS, ants with high rank leave more pheromone than the others as follows. RAS is more likely to find a better solution than EAS, but its convergence speed is slower than EAS. A min-max AS (MMAS) [12] was proposed. The amount of the pheromone of each edge is constrained within a range. Also, like EAS, only the ant with best performance can leave pheromone on its route. The rules of the node selection and pheromone update are the same as in EAS, except that it keeps the pheromone level in a dynamic range. A best-worst AS (BWAS) [3] was proposed where it rewards the best ant and punishes the worst one. In each generation, BWAS increases the pheromone level on the best ant's route and decreases the pheromone level of the worst route.

Recently, many other improvements for ACO have been proposed, such as ant colony system with a cooperative learning approach [7], a hybrid method combining ACO with beam search (Beam-ACO) [9], parallel ant colony optimization (PQACO) [15], a hybrid PS-ACO algorithm with the hybridization of the PSO [11], a novel two-stage hybrid swarm intelligence optimization algorithm [4], cooperative genetic ant systems [5], ACO with new fast opposite gradient search [10], advanced harmony search with ACO [16], and so on.

3   The Proposed Method

This section will introduce the PL algorithm in detail. Before the introduction of PL, we first describe the problem to be solved in this paper in a game scenario.

3.1   The Map for the SPP

Figure 1-a shows a game map, which is discretized into a grid shown in Fig. 1-b where each cross point in the grid is represented by a two dimensional integer coordinate (i, j). The color of the point stands for its height from the highest (red color) to the lowest (purple color). The yellow point at the left bottom corner is the home point, and the red point at the right top corner is the food point. The dotted path obtained is the shortest path from the home point to the food point. Figure 1-c shows a blue path, which constructed by an ant. Figure 1-d shows 3D ants moving on the map in the game, where an ant can only be placed on a cross point. Note that, an ant is only allowed to visit its 8-neighborhood points of the point where it is.

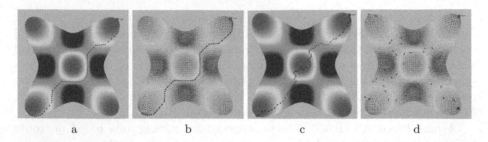

Fig. 1. An example of a 3D problem, where the dotted path is the shortest path from the home point to the food source labelled by the yellow point at the left bottom corner and the red point at the right top corner, respectively. (Color figure online)

3.2 Probabilistic Learning

In this paper, a population consists of a set of solutions constructed by ants from the home point to the food point. This paper introduces a probability matrix (PM) to learn promising edges found by ants. The idea of the PM was initially proposed in [13] and recently updated in [14] for solving the travelling sales problem. Each item in the PM denotes the probability of each edge to be chosen during the construction of a path. In this paper, we build the PM using a different strategy used in [14] to adapt it to the SPP.

In the SPP, each ant can only visit its 8-neighborhood points and the ant is allowed to revisit a point. A randomly constructed path may contain many loops. We need to design a method to avoid these loops to obtain an effective path.

The Probabilistic Matrix. An element in the PM indicates the frequency of an edge visited by ants. Initially, ants randomly construct their paths since there is no information in the PM. Each ant keeps its historical best path so far and update it once the ant finds a better path. Correspondingly, the PM will be also updated.

The PM in fact reflects the learning process as the evolutionary process goes on: (1) The number of good edges in a particular solution increases; (2) The frequency of appearance of a particular good edge increases in the population.

To implement the above idea, we assume that the shorter the path, the better the solution. So we use the length of a solution to evaluate its fitness. The fitness of a solution is obtained by:

$$F_i = \frac{L^{max} - L^i + 1}{L^{max} - L^{min} + 1} \tag{3}$$

where F_i is the fitness of the ith solution, L^{max} and L^{min} are the maximum and the minimum length of all the solutions, respectively. We assign each ant i a weight W_i based on its historical best solution as follow:

$$W_i = \frac{1}{1 + e^{-F_i}}, \tag{4}$$

Algorithm 1. Probabilistic Learning Algorithm

1: Initialize a population $X=[x_1,x_2,...,x_{PS}]$ with PS ants;
2: Initialize an archive population A;
3: Initialize a probability matrix PM with element values of zero;
4: **while** (termination criteria not satisfied) **do**
5:     **for** (each ant x_i) **do**
6:         **if** $rand() \leq \rho$ **then**
7:             Construct a new solution x_i' by Algorithm 2;
8:         **else**
9:             Construct a new solution x_i' by PM;
10:         **end if**
11:         **if** x_i gets better **then**
12:             Update x_i's personal best solution;
13:             Update DM_i by Algorithm 3;
14:         **end if**
15:     **end for**
16:     Update PM based on the archive population A;
17: **end while**

The higher value of the fitness, the higher value of the weight. Finally, we compute each element p_{ij} of the matrix as follows:

$$p_{ij} = \sum_{k=1}^{PS} W_k * o_{ij} / \sum_{k=1}^{PS} W_k, o_{ij} = \begin{cases} 1, edge(i,j) \in best\_path^k \\ 0, else \end{cases} \tag{5}$$

where p_{ij} means the possibility of each ant moves from node i to node j, PS is the population size and $best\_route^k$ is the historical best path of ant k.

3.3 Probabilistic Learning Algorithm

The framework of the PL algorithm is presented in Algorithm 1. An archive population is utilized to store the historical best solution of each ant. For each generation, a solution is constructed from the home point to the food point either by the PM or by Algorithm 2 (introduced later) depending on a probability ρ. After all ants obtain a valid path, the PM will be updated according to each ant's historical best solution.

Random Search Operator. Although an ant is able to construct a solution based on the PM, it cannot produce new edges. So we need to find an effective random search operator to maintain the population diversity. The aim is also to adapt PL to dynamic environments by using the diversity maintaining schemes as follows.

In this paper, we design two rules for an ant to efficiently construct a random path from the start point to the end point: (1) Each ant always head to the end point, which helps it avoid loops on its path. To achieve this, we suppose that each ant know the position of the end point; (2) The ant walks toward a fix direction for several steps unless it comes across a visited node, where a step means an ant moves to one of its 8-neighborhood points. A random direction is chosen from a set of neighbourhood nodes if $\overrightarrow{N_cN_e} \cdot \overrightarrow{N_cN_d} \geq 0$, where N_c, N_e,

Algorithm 2. Random search operator

1: Create an archive Cur to store the current position of the ant, which is initially the start point.
2: Create an archive Way to store the path constructed by this algorithm.
3: Add Cur to Way.
4: **while** Cur is not the end point **do**
5:     Randomly select an integer Len between 1 and the maximum number of the height and the width of the map.
6:     Randomly select a feasible direction Dir which heads to the end point.
7:     **for** $i = 1$ to Len **do**
8:         **if** next point is not feasible or C is the end point **then**
9:             exit from the loop
10:        **end if**
11:        Update Cur by Dir.
12:        Add Cur to Way.
13:    **end for**
14: **end while**

Algorithm 3. Update Local Distance Matrix

1: Create an archive W based on the path constructed by Algorithm 2.
2: Create an archive D to remember the distance and initialize it to zero.
3: Create an archive C to remember the current position of the ant and initialize it to the end point.
4: **while** W is not empty **do**
5:     get the last point P from W.
6:     remove P from W.
7:     add the distance between C and P to D
8:     **if** $D \leq DM[P])$ **then**   ▷ DM[P] is the distance between P and the end point
9:         $DM[P] \leftarrow D$
10:        $PreM[P] \leftarrow C$ ▷ P is the next node of node C
11:    **else**
12:        $D \leftarrow DM[P]$
13:    **end if**
14:    $C \leftarrow P$
15: **end while**

and N_d are positions of the current, ending, and next nodes, respective. An ant sometime might not be able to move forward since all its neighborhood points have been visited. In this case, we allow the ant to reconstruct its path.

Using these rules, this paper introduces a new random search operator to construct an effective path. Algorithm 2 presents the procedures for constructing a new solution. It works as follows. Each ant re-starts from the start point. It randomly select a feasible direction which heads to the end point and selects a random step between 1 and the maximum number between the height and the width of a map. It will change its direction if the next point has been visited. The process is repeated until it reaches the end point.

Local Distance Matrix. Although we can construct an effective path by Algorithm 2, the path may not always get improved since it is randomly created. To fully use the information we get during the random searching process, this paper introduces a matrix for each ant to remember the current shortest distance from each point in the map to the end point, and we will update the matrix DM whenever a shorter path is found.

Adaptation of Parameter ρ. In the beginning of the search, all ants randomly construct solutions, and learning too much from the PM may not benefit the search. As the run goes on, the population will improve as the number of good edges increases, and it will be helpful to increase the probability of learning from the PM. In this paper, we adaptively adjust ρ by the equation below:

$$\rho = \frac{S}{T} * \theta \tag{6}$$

where S is the total number of the points of the best paths found so far by all ants and T is the total number of points which appear in all the historical best paths found by all ants. θ is used to set the lowest possibility of random search.

4   Experimental Studies

Performance comparison between the proposed algorithm and several ACO variants is conducted on a set of 3D problems in this section.

4.1   Test Problems

To test the performance of an algorithm in a game scenario, we have carefully designed a set of 3D maps to simulate real-world environments. Figure 2 shows 15 test problems. We divide these test problems into two groups: asymmetrical and symmetrical. The difficulty of a problem mainly depends on the number of curve segments and the degree of the curvature of curve segments on the shortest path. The asymmetrical problems P00 and P01 have only one global optimum. P01 is more difficult than P00 due to the steep terrain. The symmetrical problems (P03-P14) have more than one global optimum because of its symmetrical characteristics, and are more difficult than the problem in the fist group. These maps are defined in Table 1, where H and W are the height and width of a map, respectively.

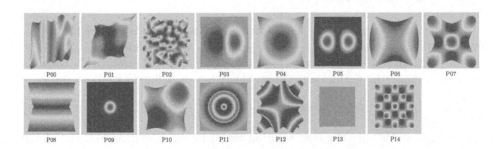

Fig. 2. The 3D maps for all the problems

Table 1. Test problems, where H and W are the height and width, respectively.

Problem	Description	Range
P00	$\frac{1}{10}(W+H)\left(3+3.5xy^3-4.7cos\left(3x-(2+x)t\right)sin\left(2.5\pi x\right)\right)$	$-0.9\leq x\leq 1.2,\ -1.2\leq y\leq 1.2$
P01	$\frac{1}{2}(W+H)\left(\left(4-2.1x^2+\frac{1}{3}x^4\right)x^x+xy+\left(-4+4y^2\right)y^2\right)$	$-1.9\leq x\leq 1.9,\ -1.1\leq y\leq 1.1$
P02	$rand()*(W+H)$	$-1\leq rand()\leq 1$
P03	$2*(W+H)\,x*\exp\left(x^2-y^2\right)$	$-2\leq x\leq 2,\ -2\leq y\leq 2$
P04	$\frac{1}{4}(W+H)\sqrt{x^2+y^2}$	$-5\leq x\leq 5,\ -5\leq y\leq 5$
P05	$2(W+H)\,|x|\exp\left(-x^2-\frac{4}{3}y^2\right)$	$-2\leq x\leq 2,\ -2\leq y\leq 2$
P06	$\frac{1}{4}(W+H)\left(x^2-y^2\right)$	$-2\leq x\leq 2,\ -2\leq y\leq 2$
P07	$(W+H)\cos x\cos y$	$-4\leq x\leq 4,\ -4\leq y\leq 4$
P08	$(W+H)\sqrt{|y-0.01x^2|+0.01*|x+10|}$	$-2\leq x\leq 2,\ -2\leq y\leq 2$
P09	$(W+H)\exp(x^x-y^y)$	$-4\leq x\leq 4,\ -4\leq y\leq 4$
P10	$\frac{1}{2}(W+H)\sin x\sin y$	$-3\leq x\leq 3,\ -3\leq y\leq 3$
P11	$(W+H)*\left(0.5+\dfrac{\left(0.5-sin\left(\sqrt{0.0001+x^2+y^2}\right)\right)^2}{\left(1+0.001(x^2+y^2)*(x^2+y^2)\right)^2}\right)$	$-6\leq x\leq 6,\ -6\leq y\leq 6$
P12	$\frac{1}{2}(W+H)\sin(xy)$	$-3\leq x\leq 3,\ -3\leq y\leq 3$
P13	0	-
P14	$\frac{3}{4}(W+H)\cos x\cos y$	$-8\leq x\leq 8,\ -8\leq y\leq 8$

4.2 Parameter Settings

We set the parameters of ACO variants based on the suggestions of their authors for TSPs. Parameter settings of involved algorithms are as follows. (1) AS: $\alpha = 1.0$, $\beta = 5.0$, $\rho = 0.5$, $Q = 100$, $\tau_{ij}(0) = \frac{2}{W+H}$; (2) ACS: $\alpha = 1.0$, $\beta = 2.0$, $\rho = 0.1$, $Q = 0.9$, $\tau_{ij}(0) = \frac{2}{(W+H)*L^{hunger}}$, L^{hunger} is the length of path constructed by hunger strategy, where we construct a path always by choosing the shortest edges; (3) MMAS: $\alpha = 1.0$, $\beta = 2.0$, $\rho = 0.02$, $length = 20$ (the length of the candidate list), $\lambda = 0.05$, $\tau_{max}^0 = \frac{1}{\rho*L^{hunger}}$, $\tau_{min}^0 = \frac{\tau_{max}^0}{4.0*(W+H)}$ where τ_{max0} and τ_{min0} is the initially min pheromone and the max pheromone respectively. For each iteration, $\tau_{max}^t = \frac{1}{\rho*L_{best}}$, where L_{best} is the length of global best solution, $\tau_{min}^t = \frac{\tau_{max}^t*(1-\exp(\frac{\log(0.05)}{n}))*2}{\exp(\frac{\log(0.05)}{n})*(length+1)}$, where n is the number of points in the global best solution.

All algorithms terminate when the number of iterations is greater than I_{max} or the population meets $L_{worst}-L_{best}\leq$1e-5 L_{best}, Len_{best} and Len_{worst} are the current best and worst solutions, respectively. The relative error (RE), which is used to evaluate the performance of an algorithm, is defined as follows.

$$RE = (Dis(x_{best}) - Dis(x^*))/Dis(x^*) \tag{7}$$

where x_{best} and x^* are the best solution found by an algorithm and the global optimum, respectively. All results are averaged over 30 independent runs in this paper. To test the statistical significance between the results of algorithms, the Wilcoxon rank sum test is performed at the significance level $\alpha = 0.05$ in this paper.

4.3 Experimental Results

Minimum Probability. In the PM, the possibility of an edge to be chosen is zero if it does not appear in any solution. To improve its global search ability, we set a lowest possibility of each edge to be selected.

In this test, we set $W = H = 50$, $I_{max} = 1000$, and $PS = 500$. If the possibility of an edge to be chosen is zero, then we use a minimum possibility $\lambda * W_{max}$, where W_{max} is the weight of the best so far solution and λ is a parameter to be tested. Figure 3 presents the effect of varying λ on all the problems.

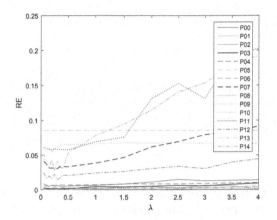

Fig. 3. The effect of varying λ.

The experiment shows that as the value of λ increases, the relative error also increases. The ants in PL will be more likely to perform random search as λ increase since all neighbour nodes have similar possibilities. For example, when the λ is small, e.g., between 0 and 4, its performance stays at almost the same level. In this paper, we set $\lambda = 0.2$ to make sure PL can achieve a good result in a relatively short time on most problems.

Performance Comparison. In this subsection, to compare the global search capability with AS, ACS, and MMAS, we only use the probability matrix for PL. In this test, we set $W = H = 50$, $PS = 500$, and $I_{max} = 1000$. Table 2 shows the performance comparison of all the algorithms, where Worst, Best, and Mean are the worst, the best, and the mean of RE over all runs. The Wilcoxons rank sum test is performed among algorithms on the best mean results on each problem, Y and N denote that the mean results of the best algorithm are significantly better than and statistically equivalent to other algorithms, respectively.

The Results show that PL outperforms ACS, AS, and MMAS on most problems. MMAS performs best on P07, P12, and P14 and ACS on P10 and P11. Although PL performs best on most problems, it could be improved in comparison with MMAS on hard problems P07, P12, and P14.

Table 2. Performance comparison of all the algorithms on SPP.

Algorithm	Problem	Mean	STD	T	Problem	Mean	STD	T	Problem	Mean	STD	T
ACS	P00	6.28e−2	1.41e−2	Y	P01	1.27e−1	1.77e−2	Y	P02	9.59e−2	1.04e−2	Y
AS		4.03e−1	2.78e−2	Y		6.06e−1	3.25e−2	Y		3.82e−2	1.75e−2	Y
MMAS		1.12e−2	4.70e−3	Y		5.02e−3	5.62e−3	Y		1.95e−2	7.51e−3	Y
PL		**6.36e−3**	3.54e−3	N		**5.24e−4**	1.21e−3	N		**1.59e−3**	3.18e−3	N
ACS	P03	4.60e−2	1.20e−2	Y	P04	3.40e−2	9.86e−3	Y	P05	1.19e−1	1.61e−2	Y
AS		2.43e−1	4.92e−2	Y		2.26e−1	2.52e−2	Y		3.38e−1	8.24e−2	Y
MMAS		6.10e−3	2.98e−3	Y		7.27e−3	8.14e−4	Y		8.69e−2	2.10e−3	Y
PL		**1.09e−3**	6.84e−4	N		**5.37e−3**	1.51e−3	N		**8.56e−2**	0.00e−0	N
ACS	P06	9.21e−2	3.00e−2	Y	P07	2.82e−2	6.39e−3	Y	P08	4.53e−2	1.60e−2	Y
AS		3.63e−1	3.27e−2	Y		2.10e−1	5.40e−2	Y		2.75e−1	3.20e−2	Y
MMAS		2.22e−2	5.83e−3	Y		**1.12e−2**	6.88e−3	Y		8.98e−3	6.18e−3	Y
PL		**2.54e−3**	1.40e−3	N		3.03e−2	6.99e−3	N		**1.93e−3**	1.43e−3	N
ACS	P09	3.96e−2	1.44e−2	Y	P10	**4.92e−2**	1.44e−2	Y	P11	**2.89e−2**	8.96e−3	Y
AS		2.82e−1	3.08e−2	Y		2.98e−1	1.95e−2	Y		2.82e−1	6.41e−2	Y
MMAS		2.02e−3	1.02e−3	Y		5.50e−2	1.19e−2	Y		6.49e−2	3.92e−3	Y
PL		**4.32e−5**	1.24e−4	N		5.91e−2	9.65e−3	N		5.98e−2	3.88e−3	N
ACS	P12	1.59e−2	5.42e−3	N	P13	9.55e−2	1.20e−2	Y	P14	7.08e−3	7.51e−3	Y
AS		2.76e−1	1.15e−1	Y		3.86e−1	1.65e−2	Y		1.37e−1	7.00e−2	Y
MMAS		**4.95e−3**	2.95e−3	Y		1.52e−2	6.33e−3	Y		**5.71e−4**	1.72e−3	Y
PL		1.24e−2	7.34e−3	N		**0.00e−0**	0.00e−0	N		4.41e−2	2.10e−2	N

The Possibility to Learn from PM. The PM helps PL quickly find a solution, which often is a local optimum. The random search operator has a strong global search capability but it takes a long time to converge. In this subsection, we test the sensitivity of parameter θ. Figure 4 presents the effect on varying θ on the performance of PL regarding the RE and the average number of iterations which PL takes. In this test, we set $W = H = 500$, $PS = 50$, and $I_{max} = 20000$. The results show that the PL takes less number of iterations to converge as θ increases, but it more likely get stuck at local optima, and vice versa for decreasing θ. From the results, the random search operator does help PL to improve the RE at the price of increasing the number of iterations. From the results, we suggest to take $\theta = 0.2$.

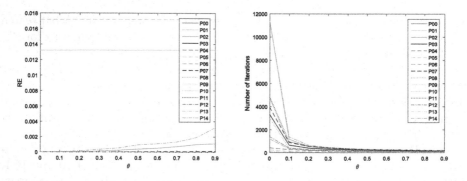

Fig. 4. The effect of varying parameter θ.

Experiment on Dynamic SPP. In this subsection, we carry out experiments on dynamic SPP, where the food point changes to a random location on the map every a certain number of iterations I_g. Given the knowledge that a large value of θ helps PL achieve a fast convergence speed, we set $\theta = 0.9$. The random search operator is enabled. In this test, we set $W = H = 500$ and $PS = 50$. The change interval I_g varies from 5 to 100.

Table 3 shows the results of PL on all problems with different change frequencies. From the results, we can have a common observation: the RE gets better as the change interval increases. It is reasonable since a greater change interval means a longer time for PL to search. PL achieves a good performance even in frequently changing environments. Take $I_g = 5$ for example, where the food point changes every five iterations, PL is able to achieve a small RE on most problems, e.g., $RE < 1\mathrm{e}{-2}$. Thanks to the random search operator, the PL is able to maintain the population diversity during the runtime. On the other hand, the

Table 3. Results of PL on dynamic SPP with different change frequencies.

I_g	Problem	Mean	STD	Problem	Mean	STD	Problem	Mean	STD
5	P00	4.87e−2	1.57e−2	P01	2.96e−2	1.02e−2	P02	7.02e−1	4.21e−2
10		1.04e−2	2.82e−3		1.24e−2	3.95e−3		2.53e−1	1.50e−2
20		2.49e−3	1.14e−3		7.80e−4	2.46e−4		1.37e−1	1.42e−2
50		2.90e−4	6.88e−5		1.20e−3	5.59e−4		9.65e−3	1.63e−3
100		1.41e−4	2.71e−5		1.13e−4	2.47e−5		5.40e−3	1.26e−3
5	P03	3.96e−3	1.45e−3	P04	1.18e−4	2.83e−5	P05	1.52e−2	4.94e−3
10		1.51e−3	4.00e−4		1.02e−4	2.80e−5		8.58e−3	3.76e−3
20		1.49e−4	1.78e−5		9.43e−5	6.16e−8		3.32e−4	8.65e−5
50		1.18e−4	1.56e−5		1.06e−4	6.70e−7		8.62e−3	6.55e−8
100		1.10e−4	4.58e−6		8.62e−5	6.55e−8		9.63e−5	2.81e−7
5	P06	3.64e−3	6.45e−3	P07	1.31e−1	1.85e−2	P08	2.24e−3	1.41e−3
10		3.70e−4	6.70e−4		3.97e−2	5.17e−3		1.01e−4	1.48e−5
20		1.08e−4	3.39e−5		4.01e−3	7.14e−4		1.11e−4	1.37e−5
50		9.03e−5	2.27e−7		3.77e−3	1.52e−3		8.87e−5	5.33e−6
100		1.05e−4	6.41e−6		9.00e−4	3.52e−4		8.03e−5	2.52e−9
5	P09	6.21e−4	1.74e−4	P10	7.65e−4	6.33e−4	P11	2.82e−2	4.30e−3
10		4.13e−4	1.28e−4		1.07e−4	1.86e−5		6.65e−3	7.87e−4
20		1.75e−4	4.17e−5		9.69e−5	6.62e−6		1.79e−3	4.45e−4
50		1.26e−4	2.31e−5		9.21e−5	2.51e−6		2.23e−4	4.33e−5
100		1.13e−4	7.78e−6		9.32e−5	2.30e−6		1.94e−4	3.91e−5
5	P12	1.14e−2	2.66e−3	P13	1.11e−4	1.56e−15	P14	6.64e−1	3.93e−2
10		3.98e−3	1.33e−3		9.55e−5	1.21e−15		2.58e−3	2.26e−2
20		3.78e−4	8.73e−5		9.99e−5	1.17e−15		1.32e−1	1.49e−2
50		3.40e−4	1.19e−4		1.01e−4	1.11e−15		3.34e−2	4.18e−3
100		8.96e−5	1.16e−5		1.02e−4	1.09e−15		8.83e−3	3.44e−3

PM helps PL quickly find a reasonable solution. These two components make PL easily adapt to dynamic environments without using extra dynamism handling techniques.

Compared with ACOs, PL has only two parameters (λ and θ) to set and it outperforms the ACOs on most problems. To handle dynamic problems, ACO should reconstruct the pheromone matrix or use some strategies to update its matrix. While PL calculates its matrix based on the ants' best solutions, which will change as the problem changes. Therefore, PL is more suitable to solve dynamic SPP than ACOs.

5   Conclusions

This paper proposes a probabilistic learning algorithm with a random search operator for solving the dynamic SPP. A set of 3D problems are also designed. PL shows competitive performance in comparison with several peer algorithm on static SPP and it also shows good performance on dynamic SPP. In the future, we will compare PL with other algorithm equipped with dynamism handling techniques.

Acknowledgement. This work was supported in part by the National Natural Science Foundation of China under Grant 61673355.

References

1. Bullnheimer, B., Hartl, R.F., Strauss, C.: A new rank based version of the ant system. A computational study (1997)
2. Bullnheimer, B., Hartl, R.F., Strauss, C.: An improved ant system algorithm for thevehicle routing problem. Ann. Oper. Res. **89**, 319–328 (1999)
3. Cordon, O., de Viana, I.F., Herrera, F., Moreno, L.: A new ACO model integrating evolutionary computation concepts: the best-worst ant system (2000)
4. Deng, W., Chen, R., He, B., Liu, Y., Yin, L., Guo, J.: A novel two-stage hybrid swarm intelligence optimization algorithm and application. Soft. Comput. **16**(10), 1707–1722 (2012)
5. Dong, G., Guo, W.W., Tickle, K.: Solving the traveling salesman problem using cooperative genetic ant systems. Expert Syst. Appl. **39**(5), 5006–5011 (2012)
6. Dorigo, M., Gambardella, L.M.: A study of some properties of Ant-Q. In: Voigt, H.-M., Ebeling, W., Rechenberg, I., Schwefel, H.-P. (eds.) PPSN 1996. LNCS, vol. 1141, pp. 656–665. Springer, Heidelberg (1996). doi:10.1007/3-540-61723-X_1029
7. Dorigo, M., Gambardella, L.M.: Ant colony system: a cooperative learning approach to the traveling salesman problem. IEEE Trans. Evol. Comput. **1**(1), 53–66 (1997)
8. Dorigo, M., Maniezzo, V., Colorni, A.: Ant system: optimization by a colony of cooperating agents. IEEE Trans. Syst. Man Cybern. Part B (Cybern.) **26**(1), 29–41 (1996)
9. López-Ibáñez, M., Blum, C.: Beam-ACO for the travelling salesman problem with time windows. Comput. Oper. Res. **37**(9), 1570–1583 (2010)

10. Saenphon, T., Phimoltares, S., Lursinsap, C.: Combining new fast opposite gradient search with ant colony optimization for solving travelling salesman problem. Eng. Appl. Artif. Intell. **35**, 324–334 (2014)
11. Shuang, B., Chen, J., Li, Z.: Study on hybrid PS-ACO algorithm. Appl. Intell. **34**(1), 64–73 (2011)
12. Stützle, T., Hoos, H.H.: Max-min ant system. Future Gener. Comput. Syst. **16**(8), 889–914 (2000)
13. Xia, Y., Li, C., Zeng, S.: Three new heuristic strategies for solving travelling salesman problem. In: Tan, Y., Shi, Y., Coello, C.A.C. (eds.) ICSI 2014. LNCS, vol. 8794, pp. 181–188. Springer, Cham (2014). doi:10.1007/978-3-319-11857-4_21
14. Yong Xia, C.L.: Memory-based statistical learning for the travelling salesman problem. In: 2016 IEEE Congress on Evolutionary Computation (CEC). IEEE (2016, accepted)
15. You, X.M., Liu, S., Wang, Y.M.: Quantum dynamic mechanism-based parallel ant colony optimization algorithm. Int. J. Comput. Intell. Syst. **3**(Sup01), 101–113 (2010)
16. Yun, H.Y., Jeong, S.J., Kim, K.S.: Advanced harmony search with ant colony optimization for solving the traveling salesman problem. J. Appl. Math. **2013**, 1–8 (2013)

A First-Order Difference Model-Based Evolutionary Dynamic Multiobjective Optimization

Leilei Cao[1], Lihong Xu[1(✉)], Erik D. Goodman[2], and Hui Li[3]

[1] Department of Control Science and Engineering, Tongji University,
Shanghai 201804, China
mcaoleilei@sina.com, xulhk@163.com
[2] BEACON Center, Michigan State University, East Lansing, MI 48824, USA
goodman@egr.msu.edu
[3] School of Mathematics and Statistics, Xi'an Jiaotong University,
Xi'an 710049, China
lihui10@mail.xjtu.edu.cn

Abstract. This paper presents a novel algorithm to solve dynamic multiobjective optimization problems. In dynamic multiobjective optimization problems, multiple objective functions and/or constraints may change over time, which requires a multiobjective optimization algorithm to track the moving Pareto-optimal solutions and/or Pareto-optimal front. A first-order difference model is designed to predict the new locations of a certain number of Pareto-optimal solutions based on the previous locations when an environmental change is detected. In addition, a part of old Pareto-optimal solutions are retained to the new population. The prediction model is incorporated into a multiobjective evolutionary algorithm based on decomposition to solve the dynamic multiobjective optimization problems. In such a way, the changed POS or POF can be tracked more quickly. The proposed algorithm is tested on a number of typical benchmark problems with different dynamic characteristics and difficulties. Experimental results show that the proposed algorithm performs competitively when addressing dynamic multiobjective optimization problems in comparisons with the other state-of-the-art algorithms.

Keywords: Prediction model · Dynamic multiobjective optimization · Evolutionary algorithm · Decomposition

1 Introduction

In real-world multiobjective optimization problems, particularly in optimal control problems or problems requiring an on-line optimization [1], many of them are dynamic in nature, whose objective functions, constraints, or decision variables may change over time [2, 3]. This kind of problem is usually known as a dynamic multiobjective optimization problem (DMOP), or considered as multiobjective optimization in dynamic environments [4]. DMOP challenges evolutionary algorithms (EAs) since any environmental change may affect the objective functions or constraints, which resulting in

© Springer International Publishing AG 2017
Y. Shi et al. (Eds.): SEAL 2017, LNCS 10593, pp. 644–655, 2017.
https://doi.org/10.1007/978-3-319-68759-9_52

that the Pareto-optimal solutions (POS) or Pareto-optimal front (POF) may change over time [2]. Therefore, the optimization goal for evolutionary algorithms (EAs) is to track the moving POS and/or POF and obtain a sequence of approximations over time [2, 4].

There are many different dynamic characteristics or uncertainties in optimization in nature. In this paper, we focus on the following class of DMOPs [5]:

$$minimize\ F(x,t) = (f_1(x,t), f_2(x,t), \cdots, f_m(x,t))^T$$
$$subject\ to\ x \in \prod_{i=1}^{n} [a_i, b_i] \tag{1}$$

where m is the number of objectives, $t = 0, 1, 2 \cdots$ represents discrete time instants. $\prod_{i=1}^{n} [a_i, b_i] \subset R^n$ defines the feasible region of the decision space, and $x = (x_1, x_2, \cdots, x_n)^T$ is the decision variable vector. $F(x,t)$ is the objective function vector that evaluates solution x at time t.

DMOP defined in (1) can be treated as a sequence of (stationary) multiobjective optimization problems [4], where the problem is considered stationary for some time period and an optimization algorithm be allowed to find optimal or near-optimal solutions within the time span in which the problem remains stationary [1].

This problem has been rapidly attracting the interest of the research community in recent years [2]. Many existing typical multiobjective optimization evolutionary algorithms (i.e., NSGA-II [1, 6], MOEA/D [7, 8], RE-MEDA [4]) have been modified to solve DMOPs. Adapting search behavior quickly to the environmental changes is a key issue in dealing with dynamic problems. In order to adapt the evolutionary algorithm to the new environment rapidly, diversity increasing [1], memory [8] and prediction [4, 7, 9, 10] are most used approaches in recent literature. Although a number of approaches have been proposed, the development of this research area is a relatively young field and more studies are greatly needed [2].

In this paper, we propose a simple first-order difference model incorporated into a multiobjective evolutionary algorithm based on decomposition (MOEA/D) to solve DMOPs. MOEA/D decomposes a multiobjective optimization problem into a number of single objective optimization subproblems through aggregation function and optimizes them simultaneously [11]. It has been paid widely attention since it was proposed. We use a simple yet effective model to predict the location of the new Pareto-optimal solutions based on the previous locations. The predicted locations of a number of solutions are mixed with some old solutions to form a new population once a change is detected. In such a way, the changed POS or POF can be found more quickly by the modified MOEA/D.

The remainder of this paper is organized as follows. Section 2 presents a brief overview on evolutionary dynamic multiobjective optimization algorithms in recent literature. Section 3 presents our proposed approach. A comparative study and related discussions based on a set of benchmark functions are given in Sect. 4. Finally, a conclusion is given in Sect. 5.

2 Related Work

A dynamic multiobjective optimization evolutionary algorithm (DMOEA) should be composed of three major components, including change detection, change reaction, and multiobjective optimization [4]. The main steps of a typical DMOEA are described as follows.

Step 0. Set time step g = 0, and time window: T = 1. Initialize a population: P^g;
Step 1. If a change is detected:
       1.1. Update the population: reuse memory, tune parameters, or predict solutions;
       1.2. T = T + 1;
Step 2. Optimize the T-th MOP by using an MOEA for one generation;
Step 3. If the stop criterion is met, stop; else set g = g + 1 and go to Step 1.

To detect the environmental change in Step1, some solutions are reevaluated in the beginning of each generation, which is used by many algorithms [2, 7, 10]. It is easy to implement but it is based on the assumption that there is no noise in function evaluations [4].

In Step 1.1, the algorithm performs reaction on the population. There are three major approaches to update the population: memory maintenance, parameter tuning and model-based prediction.

Memory Maintenance: Memory based approach in DMOEA uses an addition set to store Pareto-optimal solutions from the previous environment in order to reuse them when necessary [6]. This approach is effective when periodic changes occurred. [6] utilizes an explicit memory to store a number of non-dominated solutions to reuse in later stages to reinitialize part of the population when an environment change occurs. Similarly, [8, 12] use the memory scheme to store the old Pareto-optimal solutions. [13] hybrids explicit memory and local search memory scheme to store the old Pareto-optimal solutions.

Parameter Tuning: This approach increases or maintains diversity of population through tuning parameters of DMOEA. All population or part of it can be reinitialized randomly whenever a change is detected, which is used by DNSGA-II-A [1]. Another widely used method is randomly reinitializing a fixed of changed percent of population in each generation regardless of the detected change [6]. Hyper mutation operator is a typical method to increase the diversity of population, in which the mutation probability can be increased rapidly once a change is detected [14].

Model-Based Prediction: In real-world DMOPs, many of them change as some regular rules, but not randomly. Thereafter, prediction based algorithms were proposed to solve DMOPs. They try to estimate the next locations of POS from the past sequence locations of POS when a change is detected [6]. A linear model with a Gaussian noise is most adopted to predict the new locations of POS [2, 5, 10]. An autoregressive model is used as a forecasting method by [4, 9, 15]. In addition, [7, 16] adopts a Kalman filter model to predict the new locations of POS, which was incorporated into MOEA/D to solve DMOP.

3   Prediction Model-Based MOEA/D Algorithm

In order to predict the locations of the POS, we have to make some assumptions: (1) a DMOP remains stationary within a fixed time span; (2) the POS or POF of consecutive MOPs changes as a regular rule. Based on two assumptions, we propose a first-order linear model to predict the new location of the centroid of the POS.

In DMOEA, a tradeoff between diversity and convergence is an important task. Diversity is maintained inherently in a static multi-objective optimization algorithm. Thus, we concentrate on fast convergence to the new POF when a change is detected in the environment by predicting the new locations of the POS [5]. We assume that the recorded solutions in the previous time windows when a change is detected, i.e. $P_T, \cdots, P_1$, can provide information for predicting the new locations of the POS at time window T + 1. The locations of POS can be considered as a function of the locations $P_T, \cdots, P_1$:

$$P_{T+1} = F(P_T, \cdots, P_1, t) \tag{2}$$

where P_{T+1} denotes the new location of the POS for time window T + 1. In practice, function $F(\cdot)$ is not known and must be estimated using a certain technique [5].

We assume that each POS $(P_T, \cdots, P_1)$ is composed of N solutions, then $x_{i,t}(i = 1, 2 \cdots, N, t = 1, 2, \cdots, T)$ represents the i-th solution in the t-th POS $P_t, t = 1, 2, \cdots, T$. Accordingly, $x_{i,T}, x_{i,T-1}, \cdots, x_{i,1}$ are a series of solutions that describe the movement of the i-th solution in the POS over time, a prediction model can estimate its next location in the following time window $x_{i,T+1}$ by the former series solutions [5]. Theoretically, each solution should be estimated by a separate prediction model, therefore there will be N prediction models to describe the movement of N solutions in the POS exactly. However, it is too complex to use so many different prediction models. Actually in the real-world dynamic problems, the N solutions have similar moving characteristics, and the aim of prediction model is only to provide the initial solutions for the evolutionary algorithm, therefore a generic prediction model is enough for these N solutions. The generic model to predict the location of the initial i-th individual for the time window T + 1 can be formulated as follows [5]:

$$x_{i,T+1} = F\left(x_{i,T}, x_{i,T-1}, \cdots, x_{T-K+1}, t\right) \tag{3}$$

where K represents the number of the previous time windows that $x_{i,T+1}$ is dependent on in the prediction model.

3.1   A First-Order Difference Model

Any time series model can be used for modeling F in (3). The major problem in making a prediction is that it is very difficult to identify the relationship between the stored solutions in $P_T, \cdots, P_1$ to build a time series [5]. However, in MOEA/D, this problem can be ignored, since all solutions are arranged by weight vectors [17, 18]. Although each solution's location at time window T + 1 can be predicted through its historical locations, how can we guarantee the accuracy of these historical locations? In addition, each solution that obtained during the given evaluations may deviate its trajectory over time windows in different ways. To simplify the prediction model and enhance the predicting accuracy, the centroid of solutions is used to describe the movement of solutions over time [4]. We assume that each solution has the same movement as the centroid, including the moving direction and the moving step size. However this condition may be too strict, since the solutions may have similar movements to the centroid but not completely the same in most situations in nature [2]. We still can predict the new location of the centroid to represent the other solutions, since the prediction model is only used to provide the initial individuals to the evolutionary algorithm.

Let C_T be the centroid of the POS and P_T be the obtained approximation POS set at time window T, then C_T can be computed by:

$$C_T = \frac{1}{|P_T|} \sum_{x \in P_T} x \tag{4}$$

where $|P_T|$ is the cardinality of P_T, x is a solution in P_T.

Then the movement vector of C_T at the end of time window T is $\overrightarrow{C_T - C_{T-1}}$, which is considered as the inertia of C_T's movement. Consequently, the location of the centroid in the solution space for the next time window T + 1 is predicted as follows:

$$C_{T+1} = C_T + \overrightarrow{C_T - C_{T-1}} \tag{5}$$

This model can be treated as a first-order difference model that is also called linear model by many researchers in their algorithms [5, 10]. In most algorithms, a Gaussian noise is added to the linear model, which is used to compensate possible errors in the prediction [10] and intends to increase the probability of the reinitialized population to cover the POS in the new environment [2]. However, the noise is not needed when predicting since a prediction model is only to provide the initial individuals to the evolutionary algorithm as mentioned before. We don't need exactly accurate locations of the POS in the new environment, but the moving directions and a rough moving step-size are enough to provide valuable information to the evolutionary algorithm. The successful prediction locations are close to the next POS, which assists the algorithm in discovering the new POS quickly. Instead, a noise may perturb the original prediction locations and lead to wrong directions. Therefore, a Gaussian noise is not adopted by the first-order difference model.

3.2 Response to Change

Once an environmental change is detected, the population in the evolutionary algorithm must be updated to respond to the change. Instead of completely predicting all solutions, a part of old solutions are retained to the new population. In real-world DMOPs, the POS of consecutive MOPs are similar to each other in most cases [4]. Therefore, these solutions found just before the change can also be retained to the initial population in the new environment. The old solutions may perform better than the reinitialized population as done in most current DMOEAs.

The new population is composed of two kinds of solutions: the old solutions and the prediction solutions. In MOEA/D, all solutions found just before the change have been arranged by the uniformly distributed weight vectors automatically. Since each subproblem is optimized by using information only from its neighboring subproblems [17], the old solutions and the prediction solutions must be separately distributed, which intends to place the prediction solutions into the population uniformly. As mentioned before, the predicting solutions are assumed to have the same or similar movement with the centroid, therefore each predicting solution can refer to formula (5) to obtain a predicted location in the next time window. The algorithm of updating population works as follows:

1): **Input** P_T, N and the historic centroid points C_{T-1}, calculate C_T;
2): *for* i=1:N *do*
3):   *if* mod $(i,3)$==0 *do*
4): $x_i^{T+1} = x_i^T + \overrightarrow{C_T - C_{T-1}}$;
5):   Boundary check x_i^{T+1};
6):   *else* $x_i^{T+1} = x_i^T$;
7):   *end if*
8): *end for*
9): **Output** P_{T+1}.

3.3   Summary of the Proposed Algorithm

A first-order difference model is incorporated into MOEA/D (simplify as MOEA/D-FD) in this paper. There are many variants of MOEA/D in recent literature; MOEA/D with a differential evolution (DE) operator and a polynomial mutation operator is adopted in this paper [17]. The main steps of the proposed algorithm are described as follows. (The detail steps in MOEA/D-DE can refer to [17]).

Step 0. Initialize and evaluate an initial population P^0, then initialize the ideal point z;
Step 1. Detect the environmental change;
        Step 1.1. If the environment changes, go to Step 1.2, else go to Step 2.
        Step 1.2. Predict next location of the centroid, and update the current population;
        Step 1.3. Reevaluate the new population, and update the ideal point z;
Step 2. Update the population using DE and the polynomial mutation operator;
Step 3. If the stopping criterion is met, stop; else go to Step 1.

In Step 1, to detect the environmental change, 10% randomly selected population members are re-evaluated for change detection, which is widely used by many algorithms [2, 4, 7]. Note that the first-order difference model needs former two locations of the centroid to predict the next location, therefore Step 1.2 works beginning from the third time window. In the second time window, Step 1.2 is omitted, and all solutions of the POS are retained to be a new population.

4 Experimental Study

4.1 Benchmark Problems and Performance Metrics

The proposed algorithm is tested on six benchmark problems, including FDA1–FDA3 [19] and JY1–JY3 [20]. The FDA test suite is commonly used to evaluate the performance of DMOEAs. JY test suite is a recently proposed benchmark framework, which is able to tune a number of challenging characteristics, including mixed Pareto-optimal front, nonmonotonic and time-varying variable linkages, mixed types of changes [20]. The time instance t involved in these problems is defined as $t = (1/n_t) * \lfloor \tau/\tau_t \rfloor$ [19] (where n_t, τ_t, and τ represent the severity of change, the frequency of change, and the iteration counter, respectively). The definition of these problems can be found in [19, 20], respectively. Note that, FDA2 has been modified, and the modified version of FDA2 can be found in [1], but the time instance in this modified FDA2 is still defined as mentioned before. The dimensions of FDA1 and FDA2 are set to be 11 and 13, respectively. In FDA3, the dimension is set to be $|X_I| = 2$ and $|X_{II}| = 8$. The domains of decision variables in FDA test suites are set as [19]. The dimensions of JY test suites are set to be 10, and the domains are set as [20].

There are a number of metrics to be used for performance assessment of DMOEAs, i.e., Inverted Generational Distance (IGD), Schott's Spacing Metric, Maximum Spread and Hypervolume Difference. In this paper, a modified version of the IGD (MIGD) metric is used to assess the algorithms, which is suggested in [4, 7].

Let Q^{t*} be a set of uniformly distributed points in the true POF^t, and Q^t be an approximation of POF^t. The IGD metric is defined as:

$$IGD(Q^{t*}, Q^t) = \frac{\sum_{v \in Q^{t*}} d(v, Q^t)}{|Q^{t*}|} \tag{6}$$

where $d(v, Q^t) = \min_{u \in Q^t} \|F(v) - F(u)\|$ is the distance between v and Q^t, and $|Q^{t*}|$ is the cardinality of Q^{t*}. The IGD metric can measure both diversity and convergence. To have a low IGD value, Q^t should be very close to the true POF^t and cannot miss any part of the whole POF^t. In the experiments, 500 points are uniformly sampled from the true POF^t of biobjective problems for computing the IGD metrics.

The MIGD metric is defined as the average of the IGD values in some time windows over a single run:

$$MIGD = \frac{1}{|T|} \sum_{t \in T} IGD(Q^{t*}, Q^t) \tag{7}$$

where T is a set of discrete time instances in a run and $|T|$ is the cardinality of T.

4.2 Compared Algorithms and Parameter Settings

Three popular DMOEAs are used for comparison in our empirical studies, including MOEA/D [17], DNSGA-II-A [1] and DDS [10]. To adapt the dynamic change of problems, the original MOEA/D is modified. A part of population members are randomly reinitialized when the environmental changes, which is similar to the idea of DNSGA-II-A. DDS combined a linear prediction model as well as a directed local search with NSGA-II. These three compared algorithms also use DE and the polynomial mutation operator to generate new individuals. The problem and algorithms parameter settings are as follows.

(1) The problem parameters: To study the impact of change frequency and change severity, different parameters are adopted. The severity of changes is $n_t = 10, 5$. The frequency of changes is $\tau_t = 5, 10, 20$. Thereafter, each problem will have 6 different cases of changes, and the total number of changeable cases is 36.

(2) Common parameters in all algorithms: the population size is set as 100. $CR = 0.5$, $F = 0.5$ in the DE operator. $\eta = 20$, $p_m = 1/n$ in the polynomial mutation operator (n is the dimension of variables).

(3) Other parameters in MOEA/D-FD and MOEA/D: $T = 20$, $\delta = 0.8$, $n_r = |P|$ ($|P|$ is the cardinality of P). The meaning of P can refer to [17]. Note that the value of n_r in this paper is different from [17], which is a key parameter in solving DMOPs. Besides, the Techebycheff method is used to be as a decomposition approach in MOEA/D-FD and MOEA/D.

(4) In MOEA/D and DNSGA-II-A, 20% of population members are randomly reinitialized within the domain when the environment changes. The other parameters of DSS can refer to [10].

(5) Algorithm cost: The number of total generations in each run is fixed to be $40 * \tau_t$, which ensures that 40 changes will happen in each experiment. Each algorithm run 30 times for each test instance independently.

4.3 Comparative Study

Results on FDA: Table 1 shows the obtained average MIGD values and standard deviations over 30 runs by four algorithms on the FDA test instances, where the best values are highlighted in bold. The nonparametric statistical test results called Wilcoxon's rank sum test are in the brackets followed by the standard deviations in Table 1. The statistical test is conducted at the 5% significance level, and the results are marked as "+," "−," or "∼" when MOEA/D-FD is statistically significantly better than, worse than, or statistically equivalent to the corresponding algorithm, respectively. It is obvious that MOEA/D-FD performed best on the majority of the FDA instances, implying that it has the best tracking ability of changing POS and/or POF in most cases. MOEA/D performed better than MOEA/D-FD on FDA3 with three cases. The POS and POF of FDA3 changed over time, in which environmental changes shifted the POS and affected the density of points on the POF. The reinitialized approach for MOEA/D was better than prediction when the change frequency was relatively slow ($\tau_t = 20$) or the change severity was relatively smooth ($n_t = 10, \tau_t = 10$) on this problem, which implied that the diversity of population was more needed on these cases. However, when the change frequency was fast, the prediction approach could enhance the searching efficiency, in which the moving direction and the moving step-size may be predicted correctly. The prediction approach worked well, viewing

Table 1. Mean values and standard deviations of MIGD metric obtained by four algorithms on FDA1–FDA3

Problem	(n_t, τ_t)	MOEA/D-FD	MOEA/D	DNSGA-II-A	DSS
FDA1	(5,5)	**0.0261 ± 0.0016**	0.1080 ± 0.0044(+)	0.2472 ± 0.0002(+)	0.0942 ± 0.0093(+)
	(5,10)	**0.0106 ± 0.0005**	0.0211 ± 0.0022(+)	0.0966 ± 0.0027(+)	0.0484 ± 0.0010(+)
	(5,20)	**0.0063 ± 0.0001**	0.0077 ± 0.0002(+)	0.0286 ± 0.0014(+)	0.0195 ± 0.0022(+)
	(10,5)	**0.0187 ± 0.0055**	0.0374 ± 0.0017(+)	0.1458 ± 0.0016(+)	0.0817 ± 0.0027(+)
	(10,10)	**0.0080 ± 0.0005**	0.0134 ± 0.0006(+)	0.0551 ± 0.0001(+)	0.0283 ± 0.0013(+)
	(10,20)	**0.0055 ± 0.0001**	0.0072 ± 0.0001(+)	0.0214 ± 0.0024(+)	0.0127 ± 0.0011(+)
FDA2	(5,5)	**0.0204 ± 0.0013**	0.0283 ± 0.0022(+)	0.0525 ± 0.0021(+)	0.1880 ± 0.0087(+)
	(5,10)	**0.0083 ± 0.0001**	0.0114 ± 0.0003(+)	0.0244 ± 0.0002(+)	0.0434 ± 0.0027(+)
	(5,20)	**0.0058 ± 0.0001**	0.0070 ± 0.0002(+)	0.0125 ± 0.0003(+)	0.0148 ± 0.0004(+)
	(10,5)	**0.0114 ± 0.0009**	0.0137 ± 0.0001(+)	0.0317 ± 0.0008(+)	0.0716 ± 0.0072(+)
	(10,10)	**0.0072 ± 0.0001**	0.0083 ± 0.0001(+)	0.0168 ± 0.0005(+)	0.0203 ± 0.0001(+)
	(10,20)	**0.0053 ± 0.0001**	0.0059 ± 0.0001(+)	0.0103 ± 0.0001(+)	0.0123 ± 0.0009(+)
FDA3	(5,5)	**0.0973 ± 0.0102**	0.1035 ± 0.0128(+)	0.1588 ± 0.0117(+)	0.1202 ± 0.0090(+)
	(5,10)	**0.0559 ± 0.0011**	0.0716 ± 0.0084(+)	0.1083 ± 0.0045(+)	0.0928 ± 0.0002(+)
	(5,20)	0.0514 ± 0.0019	**0.0486 ± 0.0022(−)**	0.0867 ± 0.0023(+)	0.0788 ± 0.0060(+)
	(10,5)	**0.0741 ± 0.0072**	0.0816 ± 0.0097(+)	0.1374 ± 0.0052(+)	0.1064 ± 0.0082(+)
	(10,10)	0.0535 ± 0.0013	**0.0428 ± 0.0016(−)**	0.1009 ± 0.0036(+)	0.0776 ± 0.0033(+)
	(10,20)	0.0495 ± 0.0002	**0.0366 ± 0.0055(−)**	0.0779 ± 0.0010(+)	0.0695 ± 0.0047(+)

from the results of MOEA/D-FD and DSS. DSS performed better than DNSGA-II-A on FDA1 and FDA3, but worse on FDA2. When the change severity was fixed, the performance of all algorithms were better with slower change frequency (more evaluations were allowed). When the change frequency was fixed, all algorithms performed better if the change severity was smoother.

Figure 1(a)–(c) show the tracking of the IGD values with the environmental change obtained by four algorithms for FDA1-FDA3 with $n_t = 10, \tau_t = 10$, which is obtained from the average value over 30 runs. Observing from Fig. 1(a) and (b), the tracking ability of MOEA/D-FD was most stable, especially after the first two time windows (the prediction model works beginning from the third time window). The reinitialized MOEA/D also had better tracking ability than DNSGA-II-A and DSS. These two algorithms that based on NSGA-II could not steadily track the moving POS and/or POF, especially on FDA1. FDA3 challenged all algorithms, in which the IGD curves of four algorithms fluctuated a lot in Fig. 1(c). It is difficult to track the moving POS and POF on stable manners for these algorithms.

Results on JY: Table 2 shows the obtained average MIGD values and the standard deviations over 30 runs by four algorithms on the JY test instances, where the best values are highlighted in bold. The nonparametric statistical test results are also in the brackets. Unlike FDA, the JY test instances have nonlinear linkages between decision variables, and JY test suites introduce some new dynamic features that are not included in FDA. Obviously, DNSGA-II-A and DSS were challenged a lot on the JY test suites, comparing with their performance on FDA test suites. However, MOEA/D-FD and the reinitialized MOEA/D were not affected a lot by these new dynamic features and

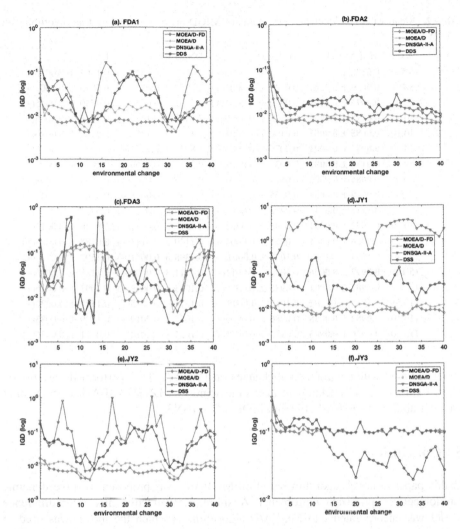

Fig. 1. Tracking the IGD values with the environmental change obtained by four algorithms for all test problems with $n_t = 10, \tau_t = 10$.

nonlinear linkages between decision variables. Similarly, MOEA/D-FD performed best on most test instances, while it was only slightly worse than the reinitialized MOEA/D on JY3 with $n_t = 5, \tau_t = 5$ and $n_t = 10, \tau_t = 5$. The fast change frequency $(\tau_t = 5)$ and the serve change severity $(n_t = 5)$ leaded to hard tracking the changing POS and/or POF for all algorithms on the JY test instances.

Figure 1(d)–(f) show the tracking of the IGD values with the environmental change obtained by four algorithms for JY1–JY3 with $n_t = 10, \tau_t = 10$, which is obtained from the average value over 30 runs. MOEA/D-FD and the reinitialized MOEA/D performed well and stably on JY1–JY3, in which their tracking abilities were not affected by the environmental changes too much. However, DNSGA-II-A and DDS

Table 2. Mean values and standard deviations of MIGD metric obtained by four algorithms on JY1–JY3

Problem	(n_t, τ_t)	MOEA/D-FD	MOEA/D	DNSGA-II-A	DSS
JY1	(5,5)	**0.0178 ± 0.0007**	0.0346 ± 0.0003(+)	2.4965 ± 0.1513(+)	0.1507 ± 0.0050(+)
	(5,10)	**0.0099 ± 0.0001**	0.0127 ± 0.0001(+)	2.3222 ± 0.0551(+)	0.0975 ± 0.0002(+)
	(5,20)	**0.0076 ± 0.0001**	0.0080 ± 0.0001(+)	2.1691 ± 0.0641(+)	0.0740 ± 0.0035(+)
	(10,5)	**0.0118 ± 0.0002**	0.0225 ± 0.0009(+)	2.3450 ± 0.1215(+)	0.1228 ± 0.0015(+)
	(10,10)	**0.0085 ± 0.0001**	0.0109 ± 0.0001(+)	2.1358 ± 0.1850(+)	0.0940 ± 0.0026(+)
	(10,20)	**0.0072 ± 0.0001**	0.0079 ± 0.0001(+)	1.8928 ± 0.1526(+)	0.0734 ± 0.0066(+)
JY2	(5,5)	**0.0154 ± 0.0002**	0.0032 ± 0.0001(+)	0.3917 ± 0.0169(+)	0.1075 ± 0.0028(+)
	(5,10)	**0.0086 ± 0.0003**	0.0117 ± 0.0004(+)	0.1773 ± 0.0201(+)	0.0693 ± 0.0009(+)
	(5,20)	**0.0060 ± 0.0001**	0.0065 ± 0.0001(+)	0.1589 ± 0.0058(+)	0.0383 ± 0.0040(+)
	(10,5)	**0.0115 ± 0.0011**	0.0208 ± 0.0007(+)	0.2199 ± 0.0053(+)	0.0852 ± 0.0014(+)
	(10,10)	**0.0072 ± 0.0001**	0.0098 ± 0.0001(+)	0.1297 ± 0.0052(+)	0.0548 ± 0.0012(+)
	(10,20)	**0.0056 ± 0.0001**	0.0062 ± 0.0001(+)	0.1149 ± 0.0118(+)	0.0283 ± 0.0001(+)
JY3	(5,5)	0.1054 ± 0.0010	**0.1027 ± 0.0001(−)**	0.1398 ± 0.0051(+)	0.1592 ± 0.0161(+)
	(5,10)	**0.0997 ± 0.0006**	0.1008 ± 0.0011(+)	0.1111 ± 0.0009(+)	0.1188 ± 0.0076(+)
	(5,20)	**0.0985 ± 0.0001**	0.0986 ± 0.0001(+)	0.1033 ± 0.0012(+)	0.1097 ± 0.0026(+)
	(10,5)	0.1037 ± 0.0015	**0.1021 ± 0.0009(−)**	0.1371 ± 0.0035(+)	0.1522 ± 0.0230(+)
	(10,10)	**0.0982 ± 0.0008**	0.0986 ± 0.0003(+)	0.1077 ± 0.0019(+)	0.1359 ± 0.0083(+)
	(10,20)	**0.0936 ± 0.0043**	0.0977 ± 0.0001(+)	0.1034 ± 0.0010(+)	0.0811 ± 0.0036(+)

fluctuated a lot with environmental changes on JY1–JY2. DSS performed unstably on JY3 in spite of good tracking on later time windows. DNSGA-II-A had the similar tracking ability to MOEA/D-FD and MOEA/D on JY3.

5 Conclusion

In this paper, a novel algorithm based on MOEA/D was proposed to solve dynamic multiobjective optimization problems. A simple yet effective first-order difference model was incorporated into MOEA/D algorithm, in which the model was used to predict the new location of the centroid of the POS based on its historical locations. The performance of the proposed algorithm was validated using six benchmark problems. The results show that MOEA/D-FD is competitive with other state-of-the-art dynamic algorithms in terms of tracking the POS and/or POF. The proposed prediction strategy for solving dynamic multiobjective optimization problems illustrates that a proper prediction approach is indeed effective to enhance the tracking ability of MOEAs in dynamic environments.

Acknowledgement. This work was supported in part by the National Natural Science Foundation of China under Grant 61573258, in part by the National High-Technology Research and Development Program (863 Program) of China under Grant 2013AA103006-2, and in part by U. S. National Science Foundation's BEACON Center for the Study of Evolution in Action, funded under Cooperative Agreement No. DBI-0939454.

References

1. Deb, K., Rao, N.U.B., Karthik, S.: Dynamic multi-objective optimization and decision-making using modified NSGA-II: a case study on hydro-thermal power scheduling. In: Obayashi, S., Deb, K., Poloni, C., Hiroyasu, T., Murata, T. (eds.) EMO 2007. LNCS, vol. 4403, pp. 803–817. Springer, Heidelberg (2007). doi:10.1007/978-3-540-70928-2_60
2. Jiang, S., Yang, S.: A steady-state and generational evolutionary algorithm for dynamic multiobjective optimization. IEEE Trans. Evol. Comput. **21**, 65–82 (2017)
3. Azzouz, R., Bechikh, S., Ben Said, L.: Multi-objective optimization with dynamic constraints and objectives : new challenges for evolutionary algorithms (2015)
4. Zhou, A., Jin, Y., Zhang, Q.: A population prediction strategy for evolutionary dynamic multiobjective optimization. IEEE Trans. Cybern. **44**, 40–53 (2014)
5. Zhou, A., Jin, Y., Zhang, Q., Sendhoff, B., Tsang, E.: Prediction-based population re-initialization for evolutionary dynamic multi-objective optimization. In: Obayashi, S., Deb, K., Poloni, C., Hiroyasu, T., Murata, T. (eds.) EMO 2007. LNCS, vol. 4403, pp. 832–846. Springer, Heidelberg (2007). doi:10.1007/978-3-540-70928-2_62
6. Shaaban, S., Haluk, T.R.: A memory based NSGA2 algorithm for DMOP. In: LNCS, pp. 296–310 (2016)
7. Muruganantham, A., Tan, K.C., Vadakkepat, P.: Evolutionary dynamic multiobjective optimization via Kalman filter prediction. IEEE Trans. Cybern. **46**, 2862–2873 (2016)
8. Chen, X., Zhang, D., Zeng, X.: A stable matching-based selection and memory enhanced MOEA/D for evolutionary dynamic multiobjective optimization. In: Proceedings of the International Conference on Tools with Artificial Intelligence, ICTAI 2016, pp. 478–485 (2016)
9. David, H.I.W.: Dynamic multi-objective optimization evolutionary algorithms: a forward-looking approach. In: GECCO 2006, pp. 456–459 (2006)
10. Wu, Y., Jin, Y., Liu, X.: A directed search strategy for evolutionary dynamic multiobjective optimization. Soft. Comput. **19**, 3221–3235 (2015)
11. Zhang, Q., Li, H.: MOEA/D: a multiobjective evolutionary algorithm based on decomposition. IEEE Trans. Evol. Comput. **11**, 712–731 (2007)
12. Liu, M., Zeng, W.-H.: Memory enhanced dynamic multi-objective evolutionary algorithm based on decomposition. J. Softw. **24**, 1571–1588 (2014)
13. Wang, Y., Li, B.: Investigation of memory-based multi-objective optimization evolutionary algorithm in dynamic environment. In: CEC 2009, pp. 630–637 (2009)
14. Nguyen, T.T., Yang, S., Branke, J.: Evolutionary dynamic optimization. a survey of the state of the art. Swarm Evol. Comput. **6**, 1–24 (2012)
15. Hatzakis, I., Wallace, D.: Topology of anticipatory populations for evolutionary dynamic multi-objective optimization. In: 11th AIAA/ISSMO Multidisciplinary Analysis and Optimization Conference, pp. 1–10 (2006)
16. Muruganantham, A., Zhao, Y., Gee, S.B., Qiu, X., Tan, K.C.: Dynamic multiobjective optimization using evolutionary algorithm with Kalman filter. Procedia Comput. Sci. **24**, 66–75 (2013)
17. Li, H., Zhang, Q.: Multiobjective optimization problems with complicated Pareto sets, MOEA/D and NSGA-II. IEEE Trans. Evol. Comput. **13**, 284–302 (2009)
18. Li, H., Zhang, Q., Deng, J.: Biased multiobjective optimization and decomposition algorithm. IEEE Trans. Cybern. **47**, 52–66 (2017)
19. Farina, M., Deb, K., Amato, P.: Dynamic multiobjective optimization problem: test cases, approximation, and applications. IEEE Trans. Evol. Comput. **8**, 425–442 (2004)
20. Jiang, S., Yang, S.: Evolutionary dynamic multiobjective optimization: benchmarks and algorithm comparisons. IEEE Trans. Cybern. **47**, 198–211 (2017)

A Construction Graph-Based Evolutionary Algorithm for Traveling Salesman Problem

Gang Li[1], Zhi feng Hao[1,2], Hang Wei[1,3], and Han Huang[4(✉)]

[1] School of Computer and Engineering, South China University of Technology,
Guangzhou, China
[2] School of Mathematics and Big Data, Foshan University, Foshan, China
[3] School of Medical Information Engineering,
Guangzhou University of Chinese Medicine, Guangzhou, China
[4] School of Software Engineering, South China University of Technology,
Guangzhou 510006, China
hhan@scut.edu.cn

Abstract. In a traveling salesman problem (TSP), the contribution of
a variable to fitness depends on the state of other variables. This characteristic can be referred to as entire linkage, utilizing which evolutionary algorithms can significantly enhance performance, especially in cases
of large scale problems. In this paper, a construction graph-based evolutionary algorithm (CGEA) to learn variable interactions in TSP is
presented. The proposed method employs real adjacency matrix-coding
based on construction graph to make population individuals as carriers of variable interaction degrees through evolution. Iteratively, variable interactions are discovered by a parameterless search scheme, called
matrix recombination-difference. In order to explore features of CGEA,
an entire linkage index (ELI) is proposed to measure the entire linkage
level of TSP. The experimental results show CGEA is promising for TSP,
especially with a high entire linkage level.

1 Introduction

The traveling salesman problem (TSP) is one of the most widely studied combinatorial optimization problems for its wide logistical applications, such as household waste collection, product distribution and postal deliveries, among others
[1]. In TSP, the contribution of a variable to fitness depends on the state of
other variables, referring to it in this way as entire linkage. This means that
it is impossible to tune one variable to find the optimal value independently
of the others. Studies have shown that interactions between decision variables
typically make an optimization problem difficult for an evolutionary algorithm
(EA) to solve [2]. As the dimensionality of a TSP instance increases, solving the
problem can be very challenging. Evolutionary algorithms are suitable for solving complex optimization problems because they belong to a class of heuristic
derivative-free optimization methods, which demand little for problem properties [3]. However, most evolutionary algorithms are predominately used to find

© Springer International Publishing AG 2017
Y. Shi et al. (Eds.): SEAL 2017, LNCS 10593, pp. 656–667, 2017.
https://doi.org/10.1007/978-3-319-68759-9_53

solutions in a continuous space. As many optimization problems are defined in the discrete space, research on extending these EAs to solve discrete COPs has become an attractive subject in recent years. The TSP is a classics COP for researchers to verify effectiveness of their EAs on COPs.

According to data structure, there are four existing data representational approaches in utilizing EAs for TSP, namely binary, integer, real and character encodings. Binary encoding is incorporated into genetic algorithm by means of binary vector [4] or binary matrix [5], so that the existing crossover operators can be harnessed. However the validity cannot be guaranteed. And, in case of binary vector, enough bytes must be supplied for every dimension, a stipulation which is a difficulty for large scale problems. The second type integer encoding is the conventional method through permutation of integers [6] because solutions to TSP can be naturally described using symbolic labels. However, the search and solution spaces are both discrete, leading to great constraints in searching behavior. Moreover, some powerful arithmetical operators must be redefined in discrete search space. The third type real encoding includes real vector and real matrix. At present there exist numerous excellent continuous optimization tools in EAs, such as particle swarm optimization (PSO) and differential evolution (DE) algorithm. Therefore, real vector is frequently employed as data representation in EAs for COPs. The key to success is the decoding scheme, which deals with the one-to-many relationship between phenotype and genotype, such as random key [7], relative position indexing [6] and smallest position value [6]. However, the existing decoding schemes cannot reflect the structure or variable information of the permutation COP. Real matrix coding was proposed by Wang et al. for TSP by PSO in [8] literature, which defines the position and velocity as a fuzzy matrix; and, the experimental results have shown success in small scale instances. The fourth type is character encoding in the form of an edge-set, which was proposed by Chen et al. for TSP by CLPSO [9], LIPS [10] and DE [11], and the corresponding operators are redefined to adapt to discrete data representation. The results are quite good in experiments, but in set-based EAs, the crisp edge-set is still imposed as discrete data presentation, so the convergence behaviors of the original EAs are given a big discount. Its also worth mentioning that ant colony optimization (ACO) algorithms utilize integer vector as population representation, but all the knowledge is stored in a pheromone matrix during evolution [12]. In ACO, a set of agents construct their walks- the so-called feasible solutions- step by step with certain transition probabilities, which vary with the rail levels stored in an array named pheromone matrix [12].

Although various data representation approaches have been proposed for EAs to solve TSP, they cannot thoughtfully utilize variable interactions and the entire linkage characteristic of TSP. Hence, their performance is generally unsatisfactory in cases of large scale problems. This paper presents a continuous optimization tool, named construction graph-based evolutionary algorithm (CGEA), to solve TSP. The algorithm employs real adjacency matrix-coding based on construction graph to make population individuals as carriers of variable interaction degrees through evolution. Iteratively, variable relations are discovered by a parameterless search scheme, called matrix recombination-difference. Hence, this search scheme can effectively realize knowledge of variable interactions in TSP evolve and accumulate in an evolutionary process. Terminally, the optimal, or nearly optimal variable interaction matrix of the TSP instance can be found. In addition, an entire linkage index (ELI) is proposed to characterize the synthetic interaction degree among variables in TSP, a measure which can help to explore how the proposed CGEA exploit interactions among variables in TSP.

2 Preliminary

In this section, we first give the mathematical formulations of TSP. Subsequently a brief introduction of the construction graph is presented.

2.1 TSP Prototype

The travelling salesman problem (TSP) can be defined on a completely undirected weighted graph $G = (V, E, D)$ if it is symmetric. On the other hand, TSP can be defined on a completely directed graph if it is asymmetric. The goal of TSP is to seek a Hamiltonian circuit with the least costs [1]. Vertex set $V = \{1, 2, \ldots, n\}$, arc set $E = \{<i, j> | i, j \in V\}$ and cost set $D = \{d_{ij} | d_{ij} \geq 0, i, j \in V\}$ correspond to cities, paths between city i and city j and Euclidean distances of paths, respectively. Let $s = \{s = (v_1, v_2, \cdots, v_n) | (v_1, v_2, \cdots, v_n)$ is a permutaion of V$\}$ be the solution space of TSP. The cost of circuit is total length of arcs at solution s, so the value of objective function is the length of s.

$$f(s) = \sum_{i=2}^{n} d_{v_{i-1}v_i} + d_{v_n v_1}. \tag{1}$$

2.2 Construction Graph

The concept of "construction graph" was first presented by Professor Gutjahr, and it's described in the following [13].

Definition 1. *Let an instance of a combinatorial optimization problem be given. By a construction graph for this instance, we understand a directed graph $G(V, E)$ together with a function Φ with the following properties:*

1. *In G, a unique node is marked as the so-called* start *node.*
2. *Let S be the set of (directed) paths s in G satisfying the following conditions:*
   (a) s starts at the start node of G,
   (b) s contains each node of G at most once,
   (C) the last node on s has no successor node in G that is not already contained in s (i.e. s cannot be prolonged without violating b.).

Then Φ maps a subset $\overline{S}$ of the set S onto the set of feasible solutions of the given problem instance [13]. Based on Definition 1, a feasible solution to the given TSP instance can be represented as a "walk" on the construction graph (G, Φ). It has been proven successful in ACO for COPs [13] and has effectively applied in web service composition [14].

Thus the concept of construction graph provides us with ideas about encoding for TSP. There are two parts in the encoding work: first, seeking suitable data structure for a population to store information of variable interactions, denoted as weight set X in the directed weighted graph $G(V, E, X)$ of the given problem instance; secondly, designing an appropriate function Φ to map the information of the corresponding construction graph to the feasible solution set of the given instance.

3 A Construction Graph-Based Evolutionary Algorithm for TSP

In this section, we present a construction graph-based evolutionary algorithm for TSP: a real adjacency matrix-coding is designed and a search scheme without parameters called matrix recombination-difference is proposed to learn variable interactions. The main process of CGEA for TSP are simplified in Fig. 1.

Fig. 1. Main stages of CGEA for TSP.

3.1 Real Adjacency Matrix-Coding Based on Construction Graph for TSP

According to the entire linkage among vertices in TSP, we define (G, Φ) as the construction graph of the given TSP instance: where V and E denote vertex set and arc set, respectively; weight set X stores the interaction degrees between vertices; and, function Φ maps the construction graph onto the set of feasible solutions of the TSP instance. Combined with swarm intelligence, individuals in the population are represented as weight set X in the construction graph of TSP in the form of a swarm of real adjacency matrices.

$$X_{i,t} = (x_{i,t})_{n \times n}, i = 1, 2, \ldots, NP, t = 1, 2, \ldots, t_{max}. \tag{2}$$

where n is the number of vertices, NP is population size, t_{max} is maximum generation, and represents the correlation weight between vertex v_j and vertex v_k in the construction graph, that is the decision weight of arc $<$j, k$>$. Hence search space can be defined as $\Omega = (R)^{n \times n}$. To map the construction graph onto the set of feasible solutions of the TSP instance, decoding scheme namely function Φ, is designed based on nearest neighbor heuristic for TSP. Algorithm 1 illustrates the procedure of real adjacency matrix-coding based on construction graph for TSP.

Algorithm 1. Real Adjacency Matrix-coding Based on Construction Graph for TSP

Input: $W \in (R^+)^{n \times n}$: individual in population, where n is the number of vertices; SR: sampling rate; q_0: a parameter $(0 \le q_0 \le 1)$ in pseudo-random-proportional rule.
Output: the fitness of individual X.
Procedure:

1: Calculate the standard deviation of $x_{ij} (j = 1, 2, \ldots, n)$;
2: **for** $k \leftarrow 1$ to $(SR \times n)$ **do**;
3: Choose starting vertex v_s by applying the pseudo-random-proportional rule given by Eqs. 3 and 4;
4: Repeat the following procedures until all the n vertices are added to the path: find a vertex not yet on the path which has the maximum weight with the vertex last added and connect these two vertices;
5: When n vertices have been all added to the path, add an arc connecting the starting vertex and the last vertex;
6: $k = k + 1$;
7: **end**;
8: **return** the fitness of individual $fit(X)$ and its correspondent solution x by Eqs. 5 and 6, respectively.

To choose the starting vertex v_{start}, pseudo-random-proportional rule is employed as follows.

$$start = \begin{cases} \text{argmax}_{j \in J} std(j), \text{if } q \le q_0, \\ \text{RAND, otherwise.} \end{cases} \qquad (3)$$

where J is the set of vertices mutually exclusive, chosen as starting vertices; $std(j)$ denotes the standard deviation of association weights between the vertex $j(j = 1, 2, \ldots, n)$ and other vertices; q is a random number, uniformly distributed in $[0,1]$; q_0 is a parameter $(0 \le q_0 \le 1)$; and, $RAND$ is a random variable, selected according to the probability distribution given in Eq. 4.

$$p(j) = \begin{cases} std(j)/\sum_{t \in J} std(t), \text{ if } t \in J, \\ 0, \text{ otherwise.} \end{cases} \qquad (4)$$

Applied nearest neighbor heuristic, $n_0 (n_0 = SR \times n)$ circuits are constructed, where SR is the sampling rate. Here the circuit of minimal length is defined as the solution of the corresponding individual matrix X to TSP, a solution which denotes as a permutation in Eq. 5. Fitness of individual matrix X is defined as the corresponding total length of s in Eq. 6.

$$s = \arg \min_{l=1,2\ldots,n_0} f(s_l). \tag{5}$$

$$fit(X) = f(s). \tag{6}$$

Algorithm 2. Procedure of CGEA for TSP

Input: NP: population size; $maxFEs$: max fitness evaluation times; SR: sampling rate; q_0: a parameter $0 \leq q_0 \leq 1$ of pseudo-random-proportional rule.
Output: best solution s^* and its objective value.
Procedure:

1: Initialize population using Eq. 7, $t = 0$, $fe = 0$ and $gBest_0 = X_{10}$
2: **for** $i \leftarrow 1$ to NP **do**
3:   $pBest_{i0} = X_{i0}$
4:   **if** $fit(pBest_{k0} < fit(gBest_0))$ **then**
5:     $gBest_0 = pBest_{k0}$
6:   **end**
7: **end**
8: $fe = fe + NP; t = t + 1$
9: **while** $fe < maxFEs$ **do**
10:   $fe = fe + NP$
11:   **for** $i \leftarrow 1$ to NP **do**
12:     Matrix recombination.
13:     Matrix difference.
14:     **if** $fit(X_{i,t}) < fit(pBest_{i,t-1})$ **then**
15:       $pBest_{i,t} = X_{i,t}$
16:     **end**
17:     **if** $fit(pBest_{it}) < fit(gBest_{t-1})$ **then**
18:       $gBest_t = pBest_{it}$
19:     **end**
20:   The solution is brought to a local minimum using a tour improvement 3-opt if $gBest_t$ is changed.
21:   **end**
22: return the fitness of individual $gBest_t$ and its correspondent solution s^*.

3.2 Population Initializing

Considering hints from distance matrix [15], one individual is initialized as reciprocal of distance matrix of the instance. To balance exploitation and exploration, other individuals are initialized randomly using Eq. 7.

$$x_{i,0}(j,k) = \begin{cases} 1/d_{jk}, & \text{if } i = 1; \\ lb + \lfloor rand \times (ub - lb) \rfloor, & \text{if } i = 2,3,\ldots NP. \end{cases} \quad j,k = 1,2,\ldots n. \tag{7}$$

3.3 Matrix Recombination

Inspired by swarm intelligence, matrix recombination executes after population initialization and encoding as Eq. 8, wherein $i = 1, 2, \ldots NP$, $t = 1, 2, \ldots t_{max}$.

$$x'_{i,t}(j,k) = \begin{cases} x_{i,t}(j,k) + \dfrac{n}{fit(gBest_t)}, & \text{if } arc <j,k> \in S_{gBest_t}; \\ x_{i,t}(j,k) + \dfrac{n}{fit(pBest_{i,t})}, & \text{if } arc <j,k> \in S_{pBest_{i,t}}; \\ x_{i,t}(j,k), & \text{otherwise.} \end{cases} \qquad (8)$$

wherein $gBest_t$ and $pBest_{i,t}$ are the denotations of best-so-far solution obtained by whole swarm and best solution yielded by the kth individual, S_{gBest_t} and $S_{pBest_{i,t}}$ are symbols for the circuits of $gBest_t$ and $pBest_i$, respectively. Through iterations, the arcs occur frequently in S_{gBest_t} or S_{pBest_i} will have relative priority to be chosen. When implementing matrix recombination, information of the local search results from the best-so-far global solution or the best-so-far solutions yielded by population individuals can be fed back to the present population individuals and be joined in the following evolution. This process improves convergence towards the global optimum interaction matrix.

3.4 Matrix Difference

To ensure diversity and interchange information of each individual, matrix difference operator is utilized after matrix recombination as follows.

$$X_{i,t+1} = X'_{r1,t} + (X'_{r2,t} - X'_{r3,t}), \; i = 1, 2, \ldots, NP, t = 1, 2, \ldots, t_{max}. \qquad (9)$$

wherein if $x_{i,t+1}(j,k) < 0$, $x_{i,t+1}(j,k) = randomized(0, min(x'_{r1,t}(j,k), x'_{r2,t}(j,k)))$. The existing deterministic individual $X'_{i,t}$ is mutated as $X_{i,t+1}$ by sampling three random individual matrices $X'_{r1,t}$, $X'_{r2,t}$ and $X'_{r3,t}$ from the population except current $X'_{i,t}$. Arithmetical operators also work here in the form of real matrices.

3.5 Procedure of CGEA for TSP

In evolutionary computing, arithmetical operators of CGEA are carried out sequentially in form of real matrices. If $gBest$ is improved in the current iteration, a local search procedure like 3-opt [9] can be applied. Algorithm 2 captures the framework of CGEA (Algorithm 2).

4 Entire Linkage Index

In this section, entire linkage index (ELI) is proposed to characterize the synthetic interaction degree among variables in TSP, to help explore as to how the proposed CGEA exploits interactions among variables in TSP. ELI is defined as follows.

$$ELI = \frac{1}{n}\sum_{i=1}^{n}(\frac{1}{n-1}\sum_{j=1}^{n}(d_{ij} - \overline{d_i})^2/\overline{d_i}). \tag{10}$$

where n is the number of vertices, d_{ij} is the Euclidean distance between vertex i and vertex j, and $\overline{d_i}$ is the average Euclidean distance between vertex i and other vertices. ELI utilizes average variation coefficient of distances between any two vertices in TSP to analyze the overall scatter degree among vertices.

5   Computational Experiments

A series of experiments were implemented using TSP instances from TSPLIB [16]. Parameters are set as follows: maxFEs is set as $(500 \times vertex\_number)$ [9–11]; $q_0 = 0.9$ [12]; $NP = 5$ and $SR = 20\%$ according to experiments.

5.1   Comparisons with EAs Using Different Data Representation Approaches

To illustrate the performance influenced by data representation, a series of comparison experiments were carried out with six EAs using different data representation approaches, including CGEA, SPV-RDE [6], ACS [12], MMAS [17], and S-CLPSO [9]. Results of S-CLPSO and E-DDE are taken from the literature [9,10], others are coding in Matlab according the original algorithms. To be fair, 3-opt local search operators were imposed on the $gBest$ in each iteration in all EAs. From the numerical outcomes of TSP instances shown in Table 1, the proposed CGEA obviously outperformed SPV-RDE; compared with ACS and MMAS, CGEA was superior in large problems and also has shown advantage in small scale problems; CGEA and S-CLPSO tied in most instances.

5.2   Analysis on Convergence Characteristics of CGEA

Convergence characteristics of CGEA are analyzed by comparison with S-CLPSO[1], whose outcomes of TSP values are similar in most cases. The convergent speed and change of fitness landscape are graphically illustrated in Fig. 2. CGEA tends to have achieved global optimums faster than S-CLPSO. Moreover, the vitality of CGEA is able to remain higher than that of S-CLPSO. To demonstrate convergent characteristics of CGEA in detail, average FEs utilization of 19 instances are displayed in Table 2. Being contrasted by max fitness evaluation times $(maxFEs)$, much fewer evaluation times were needed, a result which accounted for 4.38% to 35.17% of $maxFEs$. In this way, computing complexity as $O(n^2)$ in the decoding scheme of CGEA would be compensated to a large extent. For Fl1577 instance as example, a desired optimum could be found within 4.38% of $maxFEs$ by CGEA.

---

[1] Notes: Results of S-CLPSO were provided by Chen.

Table 1. Comparing EAs using different data representation on TSP instances (over 50 runs).

Instance	Best known	Error				
		CGEA	S-CLPSO	ACS	MMAS	SPV-RDE
eil51	426	0.26%	0.29%	1.63%	1.54%	22.17%
berlin52	7542	0.00%	0.03%	0.54%	3.20%	16.99%
st70	675	0.07%	0.21%	3.18%	3.86%	20.67%
eil76	538	3.11%	0.27%	2.05%	2.62%	34.77%
kroA100	21282	0.02%	0.31%	3.45%	6.30%	31.69%
eil101	629	0.60%	1.51%	7.23%	6.64%	25.84%
lin105	14379	0.00%	0.38%	1.87%	5.77%	40.03%
pr107	44303	0.66%	0.86%	2.42%	1.85%	22.16%
pr144	58537	0.42%	0.40%	1.20%	1.01%	16.66%
kroA150	26524	2.12%	1.54%	8.21%	9.62%	27.96%
d198	15780	0.16%	1.48%	7.56%	4.86%	26.22%
pr299	48191	0.51%	2.01%	14.59%	13.35%	41.25%
lin318	42029	1.59%	1.98%	20.61%	14.65%	35.40%
d493	35002	2.05%	3.10%	15.05%	11.54%	30.76%
d657	48912	2.65%	3.71%	22.37%	17.16%	109.31%
u724	41910	2.55%	2.53%	42.46%	36.60%	106.92%
d1291	50801	3.33%	1.88%	26.79%	25.54%	242.97%
fl1400	20127	6.17%	4.02%	51.38%	45.32%	379.17%
fl1577	22249	2.74%	2.57%	24.70%	21.98%	416.75%

Table 2. FEs utilization of CGEA.

Instance	MaxFEs	Average FEs	FEs utilization	Instance	MaxFEs	Average FEs	FEs utilization
eil51	25500	1307.4	5.13%	d198	99000	24612.53	24.86%
berlin52	26000	1599.93	6.15%	pr299	149500	31276.67	20.92%
st70	35000	1572.6	4.49%	lin318	159000	24991.93	15.72%
eil76	38000	5259.33	13.84%	d493	246500	61275.97	24.86%
kroA100	50000	10891.65	21.78%	d657	328500	52222.87	15.90%
eil101	50500	17758.5	35.17%	u724	362000	65007.08	17.96%
lin105	52500	5684.87	10.83%	d1291	645500	185387.6	28.72%
pr107	53500	5564	10.40%	fl1400	700000	145969.13	20.85%
pr144	72000	5961.6	8.28%	fl1577	788500	34513.7	4.38%
kroA150	75000	12962.15	17.28%				

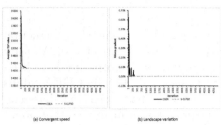
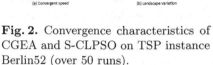

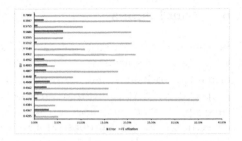

Fig. 2. Convergence characteristics of CGEA and S-CLPSO on TSP instance Berlin52 (over 50 runs).

Fig. 3. Distributions of performance by CGEA with ELI.

5.3 Analysis on How the Proposed CGEA Exploit Interactions Among Variables in TSP

The ELI values of 19 TSP instances are listed in Table 3 accompanied by FE utilization and error of CGEA. To visually illustrate the association between ELI and performance of CGEA, distributions of FE utilization and error in experiments are graphed by order of ELI values in clustered bar chart shown in Fig. 3. When ELI values are beyond 0.5, values of error tend to be quite low, such as berlin52, lin105, and kroA100 instances. By contrast, while the ELI values are below 0.5, values of error tend to be higher in most cases. Likewise, values of FE utilization with high ELI value ($\geq$0.5) tended to be lower than those with low ELI value ($<$0.5). It can be inferred that TSP instances of high ELI value are more appropriately solved by CGEA in most cases, especially for TSP instances of large scale. Taking fl1577 as an example, error values of CGEA and S-CLPSO are similar, but their FE utilization values are 4.38% and 99.92%, respectively.

Table 3. Comparison of ELI and Performance by CGEA.

Instance	ELI	FEs utilization	Error	Instance	ELI	FEs utilization	Error
eil51	0.4295	5.13%	0.26%	kroA150	0.4952	17.28%	2.12%
berlin52	0.5355	6.15%	0.00%	d198	0.7808	24.86%	0.16%
st70	0.4384	4.49%	0.07%	pr299	0.5312	20.92%	0.51%
eil76	0.4367	13.84%	3.11%	lin318	0.4526	15.72%	1.59%
kroA100	0.4962	21.78%	0.02%	d493	0.5937	24.86%	2.05%
eil101	0.4478	35.17%	0.60%	d657	0.4562	15.90%	2.65%
lin105	0.5249	10.83%	0.00%	u724	0.4807	17.96%	2.55%
pr107	0.5753	10.40%	0.66%	d1291	0.4608	28.72%	3.33%
pr144	0.4648	8.28%	0.42%	fl1400	0.5686	20.85%	6.17%
fl1577	0.4933	4.38%	2.74%				

6   Conclusions

In this paper, a variable interaction learning algorithm, named construction graph-based evolutionary algorithm (CGEA) for TSP, is introduced. A study of related work show that no efficient data representation approaches have been proposed for EAs to utilized variable interactions for TSP. The CGEA fulfills this gap on two counts: first, a real adjacency matrix-coding mechanism based on construction graph is proposed for routing optimization problems, so that population individuals in evolution become the carriers of correlation degrees among variables and search the optimal real correlation matrix through evolution; secondly, variable relations are discovered by a search scheme without parameters called matrix recombination-difference, so that information of the local search results from the best-so-far global solution or the best-so-far solutions yielded by population individuals can be fed back to the present population individuals and join in the following evolution. Besides, an entire linkage index (ELI) is proposed to explore how the proposed CGEA exploit interactions among variables in TSP. In experimental study, comparing with mainstreaming EAs using different data representation, superior behavior of CGEA is clearly demonstrated, especially with high entire linkage level.

The experiments also showed the drawback of CGEA: to evaluate an individual as real matrix each time costs $O(n_0 n^2)$. Although convergence of CGEA is quite good, some methods to decrease the computation cost are needed to be explore. Divide-and-conquer strategy can be utilized in fitness evaluation; on the other hand. Alternatively, statistics [2] and machine learning [18] can be introduced to guide the searching direction or range.

Acknowledgement. First of all, the writers are very thankful to Pro. Chen who provided computation results of some TSP instances by S-CLPSO.

This work is supported by National Natural Science Foundation of China (61370102), Guangdong Natural Science Funds for Distinguished Young Scholar (2014A030306050), the Ministry of Education - China Mobile Research Funds (MCM20160206) and Guangdong High-level personnel of special support program (2014TQ01X664).

References

1. Matai, R., Mittal, M.L., Singh, S.: Traveling Salesman Problem: An Overview of Applications, Formulations, and Solution Approaches. Intech Open Access Publisher, Rijeka (2010)
2. Sun, Y., Kirley, M., Halgamuge, S.: Quantifying variable interactions in continuous optimization problems. IEEE Trans. Evol. Comput. **99**, 1 (2016)
3. Eiben, A.E., Smith, J.: From evolutionary computation to the evolution of things. Nature **521**(7553), 476–482 (2015)
4. Huang, H., Yang, X., Hao, Z., Wu, C., Liang, Y., Zhao, X.: Hybrid chromosome genetic algorithm for generalized traveling salesman problems. In: Wang, L., Chen, K., Ong, Y.S. (eds.) ICNC 2005. LNCS, vol. 3612, pp. 137–140. Springer, Heidelberg (2005). doi:10.1007/11539902_16

5. Homaifar, A., Guan, S., Liepins, G.: A new approach to the traveling salesman problem by genetic algorithm. In: 5th International Conference on Genetic Algorithms, 1CGA 1993. University of Illinois at Urbana-Champaign, Champaign, IL, pp. 460–466 (1993)
6. Onwubolu, G.C., Davendra, D.: Differential Evolution: a Handbook for Global Permutation-Based Combinatorial Optimization. Spinger Publishing Company, Incorporated, Heidelberg (2009)
7. Samanlioglu, F., Kurz, M.B., Ferrell, W.G., et al.: A hybrid random-key genetic algorithm for a symmetric travelling salesman problem. Int. J. Oper. Res. **2**(1), 47–63 (2006)
8. Pang, W., Wang, K., Zhou, C., et al.: Fuzzy discrete particle swarm optimization for solving traveling salesman problem. In: 2004 The Fourth International Conference on Computer and Information Technology, CIT 2004, pp. 796–800. IEEE (2004)
9. Chen, W., Zhang, J., Chung, H.H., et al.: A novel set-based particle swarm optimization method for discrete optimization problems. IEEE Trans. Evol. Comput. **14**(2), 278–300 (2010)
10. Ma, Y., Gong, Y., Chen, W., et al.: A set-based locally informed discrete particle swarm optimization. In: Proceedings of the 15th Annual Conference Companion on Genetic and Evolutionary Computation, pp. 71–72. ACM (2013)
11. Liu, Y., Chen, W.N., Zhan, Z.H., et al.: A set-based discrete differential evolution algorithm. In: 2013 IEEE International Conference on Systems, Man, and Cybernetics (SMC), pp. 1347–1352. IEEE (2013)
12. Dorigo, M., Sttzle, T.: Ant Colony Optimization. MIT Press, Cambridge (2004)
13. Gutjahr, W.J.: A generalized convergence result for the graph-based ant system metaheuristic. Probab. Eng. Inf. Sci. **17**(04), 545–569 (2003)
14. Yan, L., Mei, Y., Ma, H., et al.: Evolutionary web service composition: a graph-based memetic algorithm. In: 2016 IEEE Congress on Evolutionary Computation (CEC), pp. 201–208. IEEE (2016)
15. Peng, G., Wang, H., Dong, J., et al.: Knowledge-based resource allocation for collaborative simulation development in a multi-tenant cloud computing environment. IEEE Trans. Serv. Comput. **99**, 1 (1939)
16. TSPLIB. http://www.iwr.uni-heidelberg.de
17. Sttzle, T., Hoos, H.H.: MAX-MIN ant system. Future Gener. Comput. Syst. **16**(8), 889–914 (2000)
18. Yu, Y., Qian, H., Hu, Y.Q.: Derivative-free optimization via classification. In: Proceedings of Thirtieth AAAI Conference on Artificial Intelligence. Phoenix (2016)

Real-world Applications

Bi-objective Water Cycle Algorithm for Solving Remanufacturing Rescheduling Problem

Kaizhou Gao[1,2], Peiyong Duan[3(✉)], Rong Su[2], and Junqing Li[1]

[1] School of Computer, Liaocheng University, Liaocheng, China
[2] School of Electrical and Electronic Engineering,
Nanyang Technological University, Singapore, Singapore
[3] School of Information Science and Engineering,
Shandong Normal University, Jinan, China
duanpeiyong@sdnu.edu.cn

Abstract. This paper researches on the remanufacturing rescheduling problems (RRP) for new job insertion. The objective is to minimize the total flow time and the instability at the same time. A bi-objective function is developed for RRP and water cycle algorithm (WCA) is employed and improved to solve the problem. A discretization strategy is proposed to make the WCA applicable for handling the RRP. An ensemble of local search operators is developed to improve the performance of the discrete WCA (DWCA) algorithm. Six real-life remanufacturing cases with different scales are solved by DWCA. The results and comparisons indicate the superiority of the proposed DWCA scheme over the famous bi-objective algorithm, NSGAII.

Keywords: Remanufacturing · Scheduling · Water cycle algorithm · Instability

1 Introduction

Flexible job shop scheduling problem (FJSP) is an extension of classical job shop scheduling problem (JSP) and includes two sub-problem, machine assignment and operation sequence [1, 2]. Machine assignment is to select a processing machine from a candidate set for each operation while operation sequence is to schedule all operations on all machines to obtain feasible and satisfactory schedules. FJSP is complicated and has been proven to be an NP-hard problem [3, 4].

FJSP exists in many industry fields with many practical and uncertainty related issues. Wang et al. [5, 6] studied FJSP with fuzzy processing time using artificial be colony (ABC) algorithm and estimation of distribution algorithm (EDA). Also for the FJSP with fuzzy processing time, Gao et al. [7] proposed a discrete harmony search

This work was supported by National Nature Science Foundation under Grant 61603169, 61374187. This work was conducted within the Delta-NTU Corporate Lab for Cyber-Physical Systems with funding support from Delta Electronics Inc and the National Research Foundation (NRF) Singapore under the Corp Lab@University Scheme.

Y. Shi et al. (Eds.): SEAL 2017, LNCS 10593, pp. 671–683, 2017.
https://doi.org/10.1007/978-3-319-68759-9_54

algorithm and compared against several existing algorithms for minimizing the maximum completion time objective. Xiong et al. [8] researched into robust scheduling multi-objective FJSP with random machine breakdowns. Ahmadi et al. [9] researched on the multi-objective FJSP with random machine breakdown by using NSGA-II and NRGA. The stability and makespan are optimized after machine breakdown. Gao et al. [10] researched on the FJSP with fuzzy processing time using ABC algorithm. Zheng and Wang [11] and Gao and Pan [12] studied the FJSP with dual resource constrained and multi-resource constrained by using fruit fly optimization algorithm and migrating birds optimizer, respectively. Karimi et al. [13] modelled the FJSP with transportation times and employed imperialist competitive algorithm with simulated annealing based local search operator to solve makespan objective.

In this study, the remanufacturing rescheduling problems (RRP) is considered as FJSP with new job insertion. Junior and Filho [14] reviewed the literatures on production planning and control in remanufacturing. There are few literatures on reprocessing scheduling in remanufacturing. New job insertion is one of seven major complicating characteristics in remanufacturing [15, 16]. In the real-life shop floor, rescheduling is necessary after new jobs insertion. The RRP is modelled from pump remanufacturing. The stability is an important metrics to evaluate the quality of rescheduling solutions [9]. Hence, how to guarantee the stability in the RRP after new jobs insertion is a significant topic.

In this study, a simple and novel metaheuristic, named water cycle algorithm (WCA) is implemented to solve the RRP. The WCA, inspired by the nature water cycle process, has been proposed as a metaheuristic optimization method [17]. The efficiency and validity of the WCA has been examined for unconstrained, constrained engineering design problems, and truss structures [17–19]. Recently, different applications and improved versions of WCA have been implemented in the literature, finding optimal operation of reservoir systems [20], urban traffic light scheduling problem [21].

To solve the RRP, a discrete versions of WCA (DWCA) algorithm is developed. Based on the feature of the RRP, two objective-oriented local search operators and ensemble of them are proposed to improve the performance of the proposed DWCA. To test the performance of the proposed DWCA algorithm, six real-life cases with different scales from pump remanufacturing are solved. A bi-objective for total flow time and instability is optimized.

The remainder of this paper is organized as follows. Section 2 describes the mathematical model of RRP. The standard WCAalgorithm is introduced in Sect. 3. In Sect. 4, the proposed DWCA algorithm is described in detail. Section 5 represents the experimental setup, comparisons and discussions of the obtained optimization results. Finally, Sect. 6 gives the conclusions of this study and potential future works.

2   Problem Model

2.1   FJSP

In a flexible job shop, each job consists of a sequence of operations. An operation can be executed on only one machine out of a set of candidate machines. Each operation of a job must be processed only on one machine at a time, while each machine can process only one operation at a time.

The following notations and assumptions are used for the formulation of FJSP.

Let $J = \{J_i\}$, $1 \leq i \leq n$, index i, be a set of n jobs to be scheduled. q_i denotes the total number of operations of job i. Let $M = \{M_k\}$, $1 \leq k \leq m$, index k, be a set of m machines. Each job J_i consists of a predetermined sequence of operations. Let $O_{i,h}$ be operation h of J_i. Each operation $O_{i,h}$ can be processed without interruption on one of the set of candidate machines $M(O_{i,h})$. Let $P_{i,h,k}$ be the processing time of $O_{i,h}$ on machine M_k. Decision variables

$$x_{i,h,k} = \begin{cases} 1, \text{ if machine } k \text{ is selected for the operation } O_{i,h} \\ 0, \text{ otherwise} \end{cases} \tag{1}$$

$c_{i,h}$ denotes the completion time of the operation $O_{i,h}$ and c_i denotes the completion time of the job J_i. The objective considered in this paper is total flow time: The total flow time, denoted by T_M, is the total completion time of all jobs.

$$Min \; C_{Total} = \sum_{1 \leq i \leq n} c_i \tag{2}$$

where c_i is the completion time of job J_i.

2.2 Rescheduling and Stability Metrics for New Job Insertion

To explain RRP problem with a new job insertion more clearly, an example is shown in Fig. 1. Figure 1(a) shows the result with no rescheduling after inserting Job4 directly. Existing scheduling scheme is retained and the Job4 is scheduled when the last operation on each machine is completed. Figure 1(b) shows rescheduling solution. Both new Job4 and all non-started operations of existing jobs are rescheduled when Job4 is inserted at time 3.

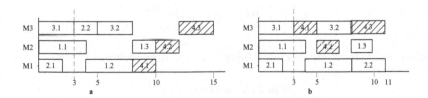

Fig. 1. An example of new job insertion

The stability metrics is to evaluate how many operations of existing jobs will be remained on the original assigned machine in rescheduling phase. More operations remaining the original machine means higher stability of rescheduling. For example, in Fig. 1(a), the operations of existing jobs are remained, the operations of new job, Job4, are scheduled after finishing the existing operations. The stability of the schedule is very high. If other scheduling objectives are considered, the stability of rescheduling solution may be decreased. For example, in Fig. 1(b), the Makespan is 11 which is less than that (15) in Fig. 1(a). The operation $O_{2,2}$ is moved from M_3 to M_1 and the stability is decreased. To describe the stability metrics more clearly, a model about instability of rescheduling solutions are proposed as follows:

$$F = 100 \times \frac{\sum_{i=1}^{n} \sum_{h=1}^{q_i} x_{i,h}}{\sum_{i=1}^{n} h(i)} \% \tag{3}$$

$$x_{i,h} = \begin{cases} 0, M_k \text{ is remained for } O_{i,h} \\ 1, M_k \text{ is changed for } O_{i,h} \end{cases} \tag{4}$$

where q_i is the operation number of job i and M_k is the process machine of operation $O_{i,h}$. The objective is to minimize the instability of rescheduling solution. The job number n here is the number of existing jobs before new job insertion. It is clear that smaller instability value means better stability of rescheduling solution.

2.3   Bi-objective Function

A multi-objective optimization problem can be stated as follows:

$$\text{Min } F(X) = (f_1(x), f_2(x), \cdots, f_m(x))^T \tag{5}$$

$$\text{Subject to } X \in \Omega \tag{6}$$

where the decision vector $x = (x_1, x_2, \cdots, x_n)$ belongs to the decision space Ω. The objective function vector $F : \Omega \to \Lambda$ consists of multiple objectives. In this study, functions f_1 is set as the total flow time mentioned in Sect. 2.1 while the instability of rescheduling solution is set as the fifth function f_2.

$$f_1 : C_{Total} = \sum_{1 \le i \le n} c_i \tag{7}$$

$$f_2 : F = 100 \times \frac{\sum_{i=1}^{n} \sum_{h=1}^{h(i)} x_{i,h}}{\sum_{i=1}^{n} h(i)} \% \tag{8}$$

Bi-objective function about instability f_2 and f_1 is defined as follows:

$$\text{Min } F(X) = (f_1(x), f_2(x))^T \tag{9}$$

Here, a widely used strategy, Pareto domination, is employed to compare and rank solutions for bi-objective function. For two solutions $x = (x_1, x_2, \cdots, x_n)$ and $x' = (x'_1, x'_2, \cdots, x'_n)$, x domimates x' (denotes as $x \prec x'$) if and only if $\forall p \in \{1, 2\}$, $f_p(x) \le f_p(x')$ and $\exists q \in \{1, 2\}, f_q(x) < f_q(x')$. Solution x is an optimal in the Pareto set if there is not any solution x' which dominates x. The Pareto optimal set is the collection of all Pareto optimal solutions and the corresponding image in the objective space is the Pareto front. In this paper, an archive set (AS) is used to record the non-dominated solutions during the iterations. During the search process in the following introduced algorithms, if a new solution dominates one or more solutions in AS, the new solution will replace the dominated solutions.

3   Water Cycle Algorithm

The idea of water cycle algorithm (WCA) [17] is inspired by the nature and observation of water cycle process, how rivers and streams flow downhill towards the sea in nature. Similar to other metaheuristic algorithms, the WCA begins with an initial population so called the population of streams. First, we assume that we have rain or precipitation. After that, the best individual (i.e., best stream) is chosen as a sea. Then, a number of good streams after sea (Nsr) are chosen as rivers. Indeed, Nsr is the summation of rivers and a sea. The original idea and the design details can be found in the literate [17]. The steps of WCA is shown as follows:

Step 1:   Initializing population (including streams, rivers, and sea) and parameters.
Step 2:   Calculate the cost of all solutions in population
Step 3:   Streams flow to rivers
Step 4:   Rivers flow to the sea which is the best solution in current iteration number.
Step 5:   Evaporation and raining to avoid getting trapped in local optimal.
Step 6:   If the stop criterion is satisfied, output the sea; otherwise, go to Step3.

Depending on their magnitude of flow (i.e., cost/fitness function), rivers and sea absorb water from streams. Indeed, streams flow to rivers and rivers flow to the sea. Also, some streams directly flow to the sea. Therefore, the new positions for streams and rivers have been proposed as follows [17].

$$\vec{X}_{Stream}^i(t+1) = \vec{X}_{Stream}^i(t) + rand \times C \times (\vec{X}_{Sea}^i(t) - \vec{X}_{Stream}^i(t)), \tag{10}$$

$$\vec{X}_{Stream}^i(t+1) = \vec{X}_{Stream}^i(t) + rand \times C \times (\vec{X}_{River}^i(t) - \vec{X}_{Stream}^i(t)), \ i = 1,2,3,\ldots, N_{Stream} \tag{11}$$

$$\vec{X}_{River}^i(t+1) = \vec{X}_{River}^i(t) + rand \times C \times (\vec{X}_{Sea}^i(t) - \vec{X}_{River}^i(t)), \ i = 1,2,3,\ldots,(N_{sr} - 1) \tag{12}$$

where rand is a uniformly distributed random number between 0 and 1 (1 < C < 2). If the solution given by a stream is better than its connecting river, the positions of river and stream are exchanged. Such exchange can similarly happen for rivers and sea, and sea and streams. For exploration phase, if norm distances among rivers, streams, and sea are smaller than a predefined value (dmax), new streams are generated flowing into the rivers and sea (i.e., evaporation condition) [19]. The schematic view of the WCA is demonstrated in Fig. 2, where circles, stars, and the diamond correspond to the streams,

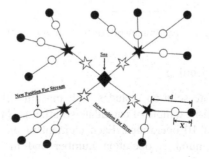

Fig. 2.   Schematic view of the WCA

rivers, and sea, respectively. Moreover, detailed comparisons concerning similarities and differences between the PSO, WCA, and other optimizers have been given in the literature [22].

4 Proposed Discrete WCA Algorithm

4.1 Framework of Discrete WCA

For RRP, the presented solution in Fig. 3 is a river or the sea or a stream in discrete WCA (DWCA). An ensemble of two local search operators is combined with the DWCA to improve the local search performance. Indeed, the raining process of the DWCA is replaced with the ensemble for solving the RRP. The framework of DWCA with the ensemble are shown in Fig. 3. The design details of DWCA are described in Sects. 4.2, 4.3 and 4.4.

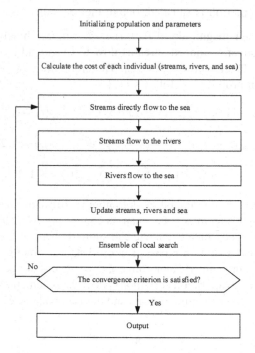

Fig. 3. The framework of the proposed DWCA

4.2 Encoding and Decoding

In DWCA, one candidate solution includes both machine assignment and operation sequence for the RRP. An example of candidate solution is shown in Fig. 4. There are 4 jobs, 3 machines and 10 operations. Each element in the solution includes three values, which are job number, operation number and the number of processing

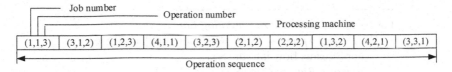

Fig. 4. An example for decoding

machine. The first element (1, 1, 3) means that the first operation of job 1 is processed on machine 3. The total number of elements is the total number of operations. In this encoding strategy, both operation sequence and machine assignment are considered at the same time. If the four jobs are new jobs inserted in to existing schedule at time 30 and the start time of three machines for rescheduling are 32, 34, and 33, respectively, the new jobs and the non-started operations of existing jobs will be rescheduled and the rescheduling solution can be decoded to a Gantt chart shown in Fig. 5.

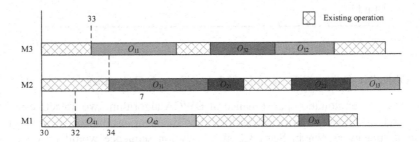

Fig. 5. An example for rescheduling solution decoding

4.3   Discretization Strategy

In the standard WCA, the generated solutions (i.e., streams) have been compared with the sea (i.e., the best temporal solution) and/or corresponding rivers (e.g., second or third best temporal solutions). Therefore, there is no comparison between the updated solutions (i.e., streams/rivers) with their current positions. This comparison has been taken into account in the current discrete version of WCA considered as an improvement in the solution quality for the RRP. Indeed, using this strategy, more exploitations (local search) have been performed around the best solution. After assigning each stream to rivers and sea based on their intensity of flow, for each iteration, the DWCA generates a random binary matrix of zero and one with size of (Npop − 1) × D.

The randomly generated matrix of zero and one is used for decision criterion of whether accepting the components of sea (i.e., best solution) or not. One means "Replace" and zero means "Do not replace". Therefore, for the new solutions, values corresponding to the one from sea/rivers are replaced with the corresponding components in the new solutions (e.g., new streams/rivers). Also, the pseudo-code of the DWCA in detail is shown as follows.

For $t \leq Max\_Iteration$ % *Updating Equations*
   For $i = 1$ to *Npop* % *Npop* stands for population size
      For Streams flow into the Sea
      Vector = Random binary (N_{Stream}, D) {0,1}
         New Stream (Vector == 1) = Sea (Vector == 1)
      End For
      For Streams flow into the Rivers
      Vector = Random binary (N_{Stream}, D) {0,1}
         New Stream (Vector == 1) = River (Vector == 1)
      End For
      For Rivers flow into the Sea
      Vector = Random binary (N_{sr}, D) {0,1}
         New River (Vector == 1) = Sea (Vector == 1)
      End For
   End For
End For

4.4   Objective-Oriented Ensemble of Local Search Operators

To improve the exploitation performance of DWCA algorithm, two objective-oriented local search operators are proposed for total flow time and instability. According to the encoding strategy shown in Sect. 4.1, the operation sequence would be updated or improved in each iteration. To balance the machine assignment and operation sequence, the local search operators focus on machine assignment part. Considering the computing complexity, the local search operators will be stopped once the objective is improved. The two local search operators are presented as follows.

LS1: Local search operator for total flow time

For a solution X, count the completion time of all jobs and C_{Total}, $h = q_i$
For $1 \leq i \leq n$
   If $O_{i,h}$ has more than one candidate machines
      Move $O_{i,h}$ to a different machine M' and obtain a new solution X'
   If C'_{Total} is less than C_{Total}
      X' replaces X and update C_{Total}
   Else
      $i = i + 1$
      If $i > n$
      $i = 1, h = h - 1$
      Endif
   Endif
   Endif
Endfor

LS2: Local search operator for instability

> For a solution X, select one operation $O_{i,h}$ on machine M randomly
> If $O_{i,h}$ has more than one candidate machines
> Find the processing machine M' before rescheduling
> If M' is different to M
> Move $O_{i,h}$ to M'
> Endif
> Else
> Execute above operators for other operations on M.
> Endfor

To match the bi-objective function in Sect. 2.3, an ensemble is developed by integrating the local search operator for instability (LS2) and other local search operators (LS1). The detail procedures of the ensemble is shown as follows.

Ensemble:

Select one solution X from population
Execute the LS2 to obtain a new solution X'
Execute one local search operator among LS1, get a new solution X''
Check the domination relationship among X, X', and X''
If $X' \prec X, X'' \prec X$
    Randomly select X' or X'' to replaces X and put another one into AS if it is not dominated by others in AS
Else
    If $(X' \prec X, X \prec X'')$ or $(X \prec X', X'' \prec X)$
    Select the one dominated X' or X'' to replaces X
    Else
    If X, X', and X'' cannot dominated with each other
        Randomly select X' or X'' to replaces X and put other two into AS if they are not dominated in AS
    Endif
    Endif
Endif

5 Experiments and Comparisons

5.1 Experimental Setup

Six cases from the real-life orders are solved. The scales are from 10 jobs, 6 machines and 81 operations to 20 jobs, 15 machines and 355 operations. There are 13 new jobs inserted into existing schedule of six instances with different inserting time, job number and operation number. The DWCA algorithm is compared to NSGAII [23]. Two algorithms are coded in C++ and run on an Intel 3.40 GHz PC with 8 GB memory. The population size and maximum iteration number are set to 50 and 1000 for the sake of having fair comparisons. All experiments are carried out with 30 replications. For each algorithm, the non-dominated solutions in 30 repeats are used to generate a new non-dominated solution set which is used for the following comparisons.

A widely used performance indicator, inverted generational distance (IGD) [24] is used to evaluate the quality of non-dominated solutions. For each algorithm, there is a set of non-dominated solutions in 30 runs. The actual Pareto front (PF) is unknown for RRP. Here, the approximation of the PF is obtained by comparing non-dominated solutions by two algorithms. Let P^* be the set of uniformly distributed points in PF while P is the set of non-dominated solutions by compared algorithms. The IGD is defined as follows:

$$IGD(P^*, P) = \frac{\sum_{v \in P^*} d(v, P)}{|P|} \tag{13}$$

where, $d(v, P)$ is the minimum Euclidean distance in the objective v and the points in P. To have a low IGD value, P must be very close to the PF.

The PF is obtained by comparing all non-dominated solutions of two algorithms. One algorithm has better performance if this algorithm can found larger number of solutions in PF. Hence, the proportion of the solutions in PF found by the ith algorithm is evaluated by the following equation.

$$P(i) = \frac{n(i)_{Non-domi}}{N(All)_{Non-domi}} \times 100 \tag{14}$$

where, the $N(All)_{Non-domi}$ is the number of solutions in PF, $n(i)_{Non-domi}$ is the number of solutions in PF which are found by i^{th} algorithm. It is obvious that the larger $P(i)$ means the better performance.

5.2   Comparisons and Discussions

To show the differences of the non-dominated solutions by NSGAII and DWCA, the non-dominated results are shown in Fig. 6. It can be seen from Fig. 6 that the DWCA obtains better solutions than NSGAII. With the increasing of case-scale, the superiority of DWCA is more obvious.

The IGD and proportion metrics values of NSGAII and DWCA are shown in Table 1. It can be reported from Table 1 that the IGD values of NSGAII are non-zero for all cases while the corresponding values of DWCA are zero for all cases. It means that all non-dominated solutions by DWCA are in Pareto front (PF). The number of non-dominated solutions by DWCA is the same to that in PF for each case. For the proportion metrics, the values of NSGAII are zero for call cases while the values of DWCA are 100 for all cases. It means that all results by DWCA are those in PF and the NSGAII cannot find the results in PF.

Based on the above comparisons and discussions, it is clear that the proposed DWCA with ensemble of local search operators has better performance than the NSGAII for solving RRP.

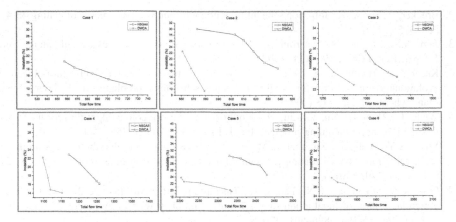

Fig. 6. Pareto results of total flow time vs instability

Table 1. IGD values for total flow time vs instability

Case	PF No	NSGAII			Djaya		
		No	IGD	P(i) %	No	IGD	P(i) %
1	3	5	1.96	0.0	3	0.00	100
2	3	7	1.28	0.0	3	0.00	100
3	3	4	1.39	0.0	3	0.00	100
4	4	4	1.27	0.0	4	0.00	100
5	5	6	1.50	0.0	5	0.00	100
6	4	4	3.03	0.0	4	0.00	100

6   Conclusions

This study researched on remanufacturing rescheduling problem (RRP) by using discrete water cycle algorithm (DWCA). A bi-objective function related to total flow time and instability were optimized. A discretization strategy was proposed to make DWCA applicable for RRP. An ensemble of objective-oriented local search operators was proposed to improve the performance of the DWCA. The DWCA was verified by comparing against NSGAII. It can be concluded that the DWCA is effective and efficiency for solving the RRP.

As the future studies, the following directions will be considered. 1. Solve the remanufacturing rescheduling problem with more different objectives. 2. Develop more problem feature based local search operators and ensembles to improve the convergence of the DWCA. 3. Develop more heuristics for RRP.

References

1. Garey, M.R., Johnson, D.S., Sethi, R.: The complexity of flow hop and job shop scheduling. Math. Oper. Res. **1**(2), 117–129 (1976)

2. Brucker, P., Schlie, R.: Job-shop scheduling with multi-purpose machines. Computing **45**(4), 369–375 (1990)
3. Jain, A.S., Meeran, S.: Deterministic job-shop scheduling: past, present and future. Eur. J. Oper. Res. **113**(2), 390–434 (1998)
4. Kacem, I., Hammadi, S., Borne, P.: Approach by localization and multi-objective evolutionary optimization for flexible job shop scheduling problems. IEEE Trans. Syst. Man Cybern. **32**(1), 1–13 (2002)
5. Wang, L., Zhou, G., Xu, Y., Liu, M.: A hybrid artificial bee colony algorithm for the fuzzy flexible job-shop scheduling problem. Int. J. Prod. Res. **51**(12), 3593–3608 (2013)
6. Wang, S.Y., Wang, L., Xu, Y., Liu, M.: An effective estimation of distribution algorithm for the flexible job shop scheduling problem with fuzzy processing time. Int. J. Prod. Res. **51** (12), 3778–3793 (2013)
7. Gao, K.Z., Suganthan, P.N., Pan, Q.K., Tasgetiren, M.F.: An effective discrete harmony search algorithm for flexible job shop scheduling problem with fuzzy processing time. Int. J. Prod. Res. **53**(19), 5896–5911 (2015)
8. Xiong, J., Xing, L.N., Chen, Y.W.: Robust scheduling for multi-objective flexible job shop problems with random machine breakdown. Int. J. Prod. Econ. **141**(1), 112–126 (2013)
9. Ahmadi, E., Zandieh, M., Farrokh, M., Emami, S.M.: A multi objective optimization approach for flexible job shop scheduling problem under random machine breakdown by evolutionary algorithms. Comput. Oper. Res. **73**, 56–66 (2016)
10. Gao, K.Z., Suganthan, P.N., Pan, Q.K., et al.: An improved discrete artificial bee colony algorithm for flexible job shop scheduling problem with fuzzy processing time. Expert Syst. Appl. **65**, 52–67 (2016)
11. Zheng, X.L., Wang, L.: A knowledge-guided fruit fly optimization algorithm for dual resource constrained flexible job shop scheduling problem. Int. J. Prod. Res. **54**(18), 5554–5566 (2016)
12. Gao, L., Pan, Q.K.: A shuffled multi-swarm micro-migrating birds optimizer for a multi-resource-constrained flexible job shop scheduling problem. Inf. Sci. **372**, 655–676 (2016)
13. Karimi, S., Ardalan, Z., Naderi, B., Mohammadi, M.: Scheduling flexible job-shops with transportation times: mathematical models and a hybrid imperialist competitive algorithm. Appl. Math. Model. **41**, 667–682 (2017)
14. Junior, M.L., Filho, M.G.: Production planning and control for remanufacturing: literature review and analysis. Prod. Plan. Control Manag. Oper. **23**(6), 419–435 (2012)
15. Krupp, J.A.: Structuring bills of material for automotive remanufacturing. Prod. Inventory Manag. J. **34**, 46–52 (1993)
16. Ferguson, M.: The value of quality grading in remanufacturing. Prod. Oper. Manag. **18**(3), 300–314 (2009)
17. Eskandar, H., Sadollah, A., Bahreininejad, A., Hamdi, M.: Water cycle algorithm – a novel metaheuristic optimization method for solving constrained engineering optimization problems. Comput. Struct. **110–111**, 151–161 (2012)
18. Sadollah, A., Eskandar, H., Bahreininehad, A., Kim, J.H.: Water cycle, mine blast and improved mine blast algorithms for discrete sizing optimization of truss structures. Comput. Struct. **149**, 1–16 (2015)
19. Sadollah, A., Eskandar, H., Bahreininehad, A., Kim, J.H.: Water cycle algorithm with evaporation rate for solving constrained and unconstrained optimization problems. Appl. Soft Comput. **30**, 58–71 (2015)
20. Haddad, O.B., Moravej, M., Locaiciga, H.A.: Application of the water cycle algorithm to the optimal operation of reservoir systems. J. Irrig. Drain. Eng. **141**(5), 04014064 (2014)

21. Gao, K.Z., Zhang, Y.C., Sadollah, A., Lentzakis, A.: Jaya, harmony search and water cycle algorithms for solving large-scale real-life urban traffic light scheduling problem. Swarm Evol. Comput. https://doi.org/10.1016/j.swevo.2017.05.002
22. Sadollah, A., Eskandar, H., Bahreininehad, A., Kim, J.H.: Water cycle algorithm for solving multi-objective optimization problems. Soft. Comput. 19(9), 2587–2603 (2015)
23. Deb, K., Pratap, A., Agarwal, S., Meyarivan, T.: A fast and elitist multiobjective genetic algorithm: NSGAII. IEEE Trans. Evol. Comput. 6(2), 182–197 (2002)
24. Zhang, Q.F., Li, H.: MOEA/D: a multiobjective evolutionary algorithm based on decomposition. IEEE Trans. Evol. Comput. 11(6), 712–713 (2007)

A New Method for Constructing Ensemble Classifier in Privacy-Preserving Distributed Environment

Yan Shao[1](✉), Zhanjun Li[1], and Ming Li[2]

[1] School of Computer Science and Technology,
University of Science and Technology of China, Hefei 230027, China
{shaoy,lily79}@mail.ustc.edu.cn
[2] Academy of National Defense Information, Wuhan 430010, China
liming_yu2008@163.com

Abstract. How to build a classifier on datasets that are distributed across different sites under privacy constrains has attracted much attention during the past few years. In this paper, a new method for constructing classifier ensemble for privacy-preserving distributed data mining is proposed. Different from existing methods, the proposed method can obtain, without any auxiliary assumption and releasing the original data of stakeholders, the optimal weights for classifier combination. Experiments show that the ensemble based on our approach achieved high performance.

1 Introduction

A major feature of the big data era is that data stored at different locations, from different sources and stakeholders could be combined and analyzed for a common purpose. However, combining data from different sites or different stakeholders may cause privacy issues, especially for sensitive data, such as medical data, insurance data, etc. Hence, although stakeholders may all benefit from analysis on the combined data, they are usually hesitant to share their data. For this reason, Privacy Preserving Distributed Data Mining (PPDDM) [1–4], which aims to mine potential knowledge while without explicitly sharing data among stakeholders, has attracted more and more attentions lately.

Based on the partitioning mechanism, PPDDM can be grouped into vertically partitioned and horizontally partitioned PPDDM [5]. In vertically partitioned datasets, different sites contain the same set of records with different sets of attributes. In horizontally partitioned datasets, different sites have different sets of records with the same set of attributes. Many machine learning algorithms have been proposed for horizontally partitioned PPDDM, such as Decision Tree [6–8], Association Rule [9], Neural Network [10], Naïve Bayes [11], SVM [12] etc. The key goal of these methods is to implement computation of useful aggregate statistics over the entire dataset while preserving the privacy of the individual datasets within the different participants. However, these algorithms depend much on secure multiparty computation [13, 14] which is a field in cryptography and originates with Yao's Millionaires' problem [15].

© Springer International Publishing AG 2017
Y. Shi et al. (Eds.): SEAL 2017, LNCS 10593, pp. 684–693, 2017.
https://doi.org/10.1007/978-3-319-68759-9_55

Thus lots of encryption and decryption operation and data transmission are required in these methods which also lead to a significant cost in model implementation [13]. Especially when there are a great number of participants and the size of each stakeholder's dataset is huge, this problem will become even more serious.

Different from the above-mentioned methods that aim to train a single learner on horizontally distributed datasets, the concept of ensemble learning naturally fits the need of horizontally partitioned PPDDM [16]. To be specific, each participant can train a base learner on their own data, and then share their base learners rather than data, such that each participant could build an ensemble that can potentially outperform their single base learner, while the entire process does not need sharing the data that greatly reduces the risk of privacy leakage.

In the literature, there have been some attempts to apply ensemble learning to PPDDM [17–19]. For instance, to analyze the diabetes electronic medical records of the United States, Li et al. [18] proposed a method to filtrate and then integrate base learners that are trained by each participant state. When combining the base learners using a method similar to weighted averaging, the weight of a selected base learner is determined solely based on the size of dataset on which the learner is trained. Since no other information is shared when determine the weights for base learners, the whole process is secure, while the weights might be sub-optimal and thereby affect the performance of the ensemble which is an important factor to considerate for PPDDM. Xie et al. [19] assumed that there exists a public accessible dataset, on which the optimal weights of base learners can be identified. However, such a public accessible dataset may not exist in real environment.

In this work, we propose a new distributed ensemble method, namely Secure Optimal Weighting (SOW), for horizontally partitioned PPDDM. Basically, SOW takes both privacy and performance of the ensemble into account when learning the weights for combining base learners. To be specific, when a participant receives other participants' base classifiers, it first calculates the predictive values of each base classifier on part of its own samples, and then send the information about the predicted values and related class labels to a server which is designed to seek the optimal weights of base classifiers. According to the result of optimization on the server, each participant can integrate an ensemble with high performance. Although a third-party server is required in our method, each participant does not need to contact with the server frequently and only a few information has to be transmitted in the entire process. Most of all, there is no need for a publicly accessible dataset and besides the base classifiers, no other information can be guessed by the server or any participant. Therefore it is more practical than the method proposed in paper [19]. Same as paper [19], in this paper we only discuss the binary classification problem, and assume that the data of each site is identically distributed.

The rest of this paper is organized as follows. In Sect. 2, the problem is described in detail. Section 3 introduces our new method SOW. Experimental results are shown in Sect. 4. Finally, Sect. 5 concludes our work with some future research directions.

2 Problem Description and Analyses

Let $\{p_1, p_2, \ldots, p_n\}$ denote $n \geq 2$ different sites or participants in a distributed system, and $D_i = \{(x_{i,1}, y_{i,1}), (x_{i,2}, y_{i,2}), \ldots, (x_{i,m_i}, y_{i,m_i})\}$ denote the dataset of p_i where feature vector $x_{i,j} \in R^d$ and $y_{i,j} \in \{+1, -1\}$. Without loss of generality, all datasets are assumed to be independent and identically distributed. Let $h_i(\cdot)$ be the base classifier trained based on D_i. We focus on problem of ensemble classifier: the goal is to find a set of weights $W = \{w_1, w_2, \ldots, w_n\}$ with leaking information about each participant's dataset as little as possible, and at the same time, the ensemble $H(x) = \sum_{i=1}^{n} w_i \cdot h_i(x)$ can be integrated with high performance. In addition, the computational complexity and the network traffic generated throughout the entire process should also be considered.

For the problem above, in paper [18], once the base classifiers are built, all the participants share the classifiers and the size of each dataset D_i with one another. For each participant p_i, when received the other $n-1$ base classifiers, it first computes the testing error rate of others' base classifiers on its own dataset D_i, i.e.

$$\in_{p_i}^{p_j} = \frac{1}{m_i} \left[\sum_{k=1}^{m_i} I\left(sign\{h_j(x_{i,k})\} \neq y_{i,k}\right) \right], (j = 1, \ldots, i-1, i+1, \ldots, n), \quad (1)$$

where $I(.)$ is the indicator function. Then it calculates the difference between $\in_{p_i}^{p_j}$ and its training error rate

$$\in_{p_i} = \frac{1}{m_i} \left[\sum_{k=1}^{m_i} I\left(sign\{h_i(x_{i,k})\} \neq y_{i,k}\right) \right]. \quad (2)$$

If $(\in_{p_i}^{p_j} - \in_{p_i})$ is less than a certain threshold τ, then $h_j(\cdot)$ is selected to construct the ensemble. Otherwise, it is discarded. Finally, based on the selected base classifiers and related sample sizes, the weight assigned to h_j when integrate model for p_i are obtained by

$$w_{i,j} = \begin{cases} \frac{\lambda_j^2}{\lambda_{max}^2} \cdot \left\lceil \frac{\lambda_{max}^2}{\lambda_{min}} \right\rceil & \text{if } j = i \\ 1 & \text{if } j \neq i \end{cases}, \quad (3)$$

where $\lambda_j = m_j / \sum_{s \in S^{(i)}} m_s, j \in S^{(i)}$ and $S^{(i)}$ is the set of base classifiers selected by p_i. Since this method determines the weights solely by the size of each participant's dataset, it is referred to as Size Dependent Weights (SDW) hereafter. In paper [19], in order to weight the base classifiers, a public accessible dataset D_0 is assumed whose size is large enough. That is to say, when the base classifiers are shared, the weights can be obtained by minimizing $L(\sum_{i=1}^{n} w_i \cdot h_i(x), D_0)$ where L is a loss function which denotes the loss of ensemble $\sum_{i=1}^{n} w_i \cdot h_i(x)$ on D_0. This approach is simple and the weights obtained are also good. However, the weights depends much on the assumed D_0 that this method will not work once D_0 does not exist.

3   The SOW Method

The idea of SOW is using a little information, which is obtained from part of each participant's dataset and no privacy can be guessed from, to optimize the weights of base classifiers. In order protect the participants' respective data, the information used for optimization and base classifiers should be separated, thus a special server is designed in our method to seek the optimal weights. To facilitate the narrative, some notations used in SOW are given in Table 1 as below.

Table 1. Notations used in SOW

Notation	Description
n	The number of participants
p_i	The i-th participant
D_i	The dataset of i-th participant
m_i	The sample size of D_i
h_i	The base classifier trained by i-th participant
os_i	The subset extracted from D_i
$SC(os_i)$	The sequence of labels of os_i
om_i	The size of os_i
OS	The set of os_i
OM	The size of OS
$h_j(os_i)$	The sequence of $h_j(x_k)$ where $x_k \in os_i$
or_i	The information used for optimization generated by p_i
w_i	The weight of h_i
$H(x)$	The ensemble classifier

Same as general ensemble methods for PPDDM, in SOW, participants first train their base classifiers and share them with each other. However, when p_i received $n-1$ base classifiers from other participants, it extracts part of samples from its dataset which are labeled as os_i in this paper and take the follow forms:

$$os_i = \left\{ \left(x_{os_i,1}, y_{os_i,1} \right), \left(x_{os_i,2}, y_{os_i,2} \right), \ldots, \left(x_{os_i,om_i}, y_{os_i,om_i} \right) \right\}. \tag{4}$$

Then, it computes $\cup_j h_j(os_i)$ and sends the information or_i used for optimization to the designed server to seek the optimal weights. Here, or_i is defined as follow:

$$or_i = \left\{ \cup_j h_j(os_i), SC(os_i) \right\} \cdot random\{+1, -1\}$$
$$= \left\{ \begin{array}{c} \left(h_1\left(x_{os_i,1}\right), h_2\left(x_{os_i,1}\right), \ldots, h_n\left(x_{os_i,1}\right), y_{os_i,1} \right) \cdot r_1 \\ \ldots, \ldots, \ldots \\ \left(h_1\left(x_{os_i,om_i}\right), h_2\left(x_{os_i,om_i}\right), \ldots, h_n\left(x_{os_i,om_i}\right), y_{os_i,om_i} \right) \cdot r_{om_i} \end{array} \right\}, \tag{5}$$

where $random\{+1, -1\}$ is a function which returns +1 or −1 randomly and $r_k = random\{+1, -1\}$, $k = 1,2,\ldots,om_i$.

For the server, when it receives or_i from the n participants, it can find the optimal weights by minimizing the loss function:

$$
\begin{aligned}
L(W) &= \tfrac{1}{2}\sum_{i=1}^{OM}\left(\left(\sum_{j=1}^{n} w_j h_j(x_i)\cdot r_i\right) - y_i \cdot r_i\right)^2 \\
&= \tfrac{1}{2}\sum_{i=1}^{OM}\left(\left(\sum_{j=1}^{n} w_j h_j(x_i)\right) - y_i\right)^2 \\
&\quad \text{s.t } 0 \le w_j \le 1 \\
&\quad\quad \sum_{j=1}^{n} w_j = 1 \\
&\text{where } (x_i, y_i) \in OS, \text{ and } OS = \cup_i(os_i)
\end{aligned}
\tag{6}
$$

At last, the server sends the acquired weights to the n participants, and each participant get the ensemble $H(x) = \sum_{i=1}^{n} w_i \cdot h_i(x)$. The specific steps and flowchart are as follows (Fig. 1).

Algorithm 1 : secure optimal weights algorithm

Input : $\{D_1, D_2, \ldots, D_n\}$
Output: the final classifier $H(x)$
1   for each participant p_i parallel do:
2   train classifier h_i based on D_i
3   share h_i with each other
4   extract os_i from D_i & compute or_i
5   send or_i to the server for weights optimization
6   end
7   When the server found and shared the result weights, for each participant parallel do:
8   build ensemble classifier $H(x)=sign(\sum_i w_i * h_i(x))$
9   End

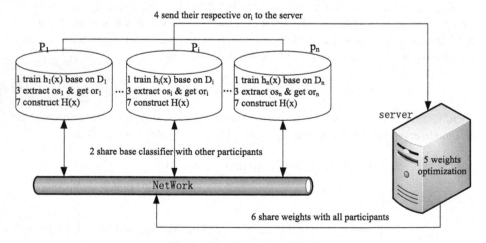

Fig. 1. The flowchart of SOW

In our method, the information about part of samples in each dataset is released to the server, but it is difficult for the server to get any useful information from it because the predicted values and labels of samples in os_i are randomized. At the same time, suppose that nothing can be guessed from the base classifiers and the mining result, each participant also cannot get anything of value about others' datasets. Thus, SOW is highly secure. Different from SDW, the weights of the base classifiers are obtained by optimization on part of samples extracted from the total dataset. That means the integrated weights are optimal for the extracted samples. Thus, in theory, the weights of SOW are more appropriate than that of SDW as long as the distribution of extracted dataset is identically to that of the total dataset. Throughout the entire process, apart from the traffic generated by sharing base classifiers between each participant and the result weights, only $(n+1)^*OM$ bits are required in all to transmitted from n participants to the server.

4 Experiment

The security of SOW and the performance of the ensemble built based on it have been explained theoretically above. In this section, empirical studies have been conducted to compare the proposed SOW with SDW in paper [18]. The experiment results show that our proposed method is superior to SDW in classification when the number of participants and the size of each dataset are both identical.

4.1 Experiment Design

Generally, the number of participants and the size of each dataset are two important influencing factors for the integrated classifier. In order to test the performance of the ensemble constructed by SOW, two groups of experiments on three UCI datasets are designed:

Experiment (1) Divide each UCI dataset into N parts more or less equally and select n parts as the participants' datasets randomly. Change the number of participants to check the ensemble performance of SOW against SDW.

Experiment (2) Fix the number of participants n. Then extract samples from each UCI dataset incrementally and divide them into the n participants to see the ensemble performance of SOW against SDW.

In every experiment, each algorithm is repeated 100 times and the mean is taken as result. For each participant, ID3 is selected to train the base classifier. In SDW, the ensemble performance of each participant may be different and we take the mean of n participants' results as the classification accuracy of one experiment.

4.2 Description of the Experimental Datasets

Three UCI datasets are selected in our experiments: "car-evaluation (car)", "adult" and "contraceptive-method-choice (cmc)". Basic information about the datasets is described in Table 2.

Table 2. Basic info about the three datasets from UCI

Data-set	Number of attribute	Total size
Adult	14	48842
Contraceptive-method-choice	9	1473
Car evaluation	6	1728

For dataset "car", the samples whose class value is "unacc" are labeled as "+1", and others as "−1".For "cmc", the samples whose class value is "1" are labeled as "+1", and others as "−1". In order to make the UCI dataset "adult" apply to ID3, discretize the continuous attribute values of samples first, and then delete the conflicting and repetitive samples. The samples with default attributes also should be removed. At last, for "car" and "cmc", we split the dataset into training samples and test samples at the ratio of 4:1. For "adult", there is no need to split because the dataset itself contains training and test samples.

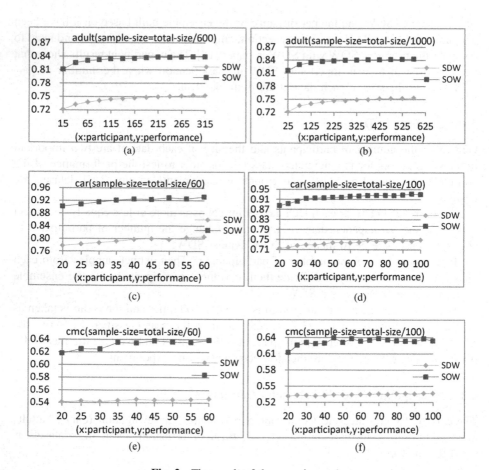

Fig. 2. The result of the experiment 1.

4.3   Experiments Results

To demonstrate the ensemble performance of SOW against SDW clearly, in our experiments, the total training samples extracted from the UCI datasets are divided into variable numbers of subsets equally according to their respective sample sizes. Specially, for "adult", it is divided into 600 or 1000 shares, which are distributed to corresponding sites, while "car" and "cmc" are divided into 60 or 100 shares. For experiment (1), the x-axis in the figure denotes the actual number of participants. While for experiment (2), the x-axis denotes the percentage of UCI dataset used as total training data. The result figures are as follows.

Figure 2 shows that when the size of each participant's dataset is fixed, the ensemble performance based on SOW is stably superior to that based on SDW no matter what the number of participants is.

Figure 3 presents that when the number of participants is fixed, the ensemble performance based on SOW has a distinct advantage against on SDW no matter how the sample size of each participant changes.

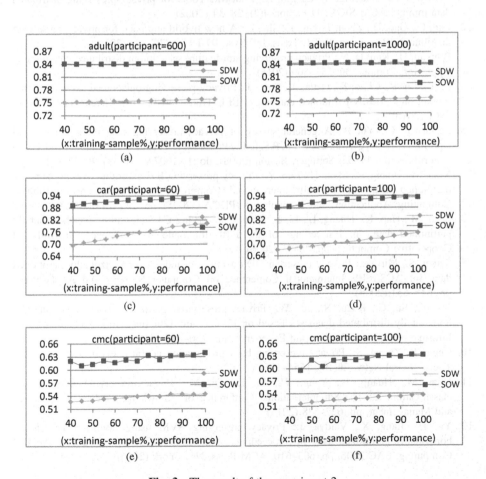

Fig. 3. The result of the experiment 2.

5   Conclusions

Based on the idea of ensemble learning, we present a secure and practicable approach for PPDDM in this paper. The basic idea is to take advantages of a little information about part of each participant's dataset to optimize the weights of base classifiers. In our method, a set of weights which is more optimal than that acquired by method SDW can be found privately without any auxiliary assumption. The network traffic generated in the whole process is also acceptable. However, we have not considered the privacy issues that may be caused by sharing the base classifiers between participants [20]. In follow-up study, we will make a deep research on this privacy problem, and improve our approach.

References

1. Clifton, C., Kantarcioglou, M., Lin, X., Zhu, M.: Tools for privacy-preserving distributed data mining. ACM SIGKDD Explor. **4**(2), 28–34 (2002)
2. Sun, C., Gao, H., Zhou, J., Hu, Y., She, L.: A new hybrid approach for privacy preserving distributed data mining. IEICE Trans. Inf. Syst. **97-D**(4), 876–883 (2014)
3. Bhuyan, H., Kamila, N.: Privacy preserving sub-feature selection in distributed data mining. Appl. Soft Comput. **36**, 552–569 (2015)
4. Li, L., Lu, R., Choo, K., Datta, A., Shao, J.: Privacy-preserving-outsourced association rule mining on vertically partitioned databases. IEEE Trans. Inf. Forensics Secur. **11**(8), 1847–1861 (2016)
5. Aggarwal, C., Yu, P.: A general survey of privacy-preserving data ming models and algorithms. In: Aggarwal, C.C., Yu, P.S. (eds.) Privacy-Preserving Data Mining: Models and Algorithms, pp. 11–52. Springer, Boston (2008). doi:10.1007/978-0-387-70992-5_2
6. Xiao, M., Huang, L., Shen, H., Luo, Y.: Privacy preserving ID3 algorithm over horizontally partitioned data. In: The 6th International Conference on Parallel and Distributed Computing, Applications and Technologies (PDCAT 2005), pp. 239–243 (2005)
7. Xiao, M., Han, K., Huang, L., Li, J.: Privacy preserving C4.5 algorithm over horizontally partitioned data. In: Proceedings of the Fifth International Conference on Grid and Cooperative Computing, pp. 78–85 (2006)
8. Samet, S., Miri, A.: Privacy preserving ID3 using Gini index over horizontally partitioned data. In: ACS/IEEE International Conference on Computer Systems and Applications, pp. 645–651 (2008)
9. Jin, Y., Su, C., Ruan, N., Jia, W.: Privacy-preserving mining of association rules for horizontally distributed databases based on FP-tree. In: 12th International Conference on Information Security Practice and Experience, pp. 300–314 (2016)
10. Chen, T., Zhong, S.: Privacy preserving back propagation neural network learning. IEEE Trans. Neural Netw. **20**(10), 1554–1564 (2009)
11. Huai, M., Huang, L., Yang, W., Li, L., Qi, M.: Privacy-preserving naive Bayes classification. In: The 8th International Conference on Knowledge Science, Engineering and Management, pp. 627–638 (2015)
12. Yu, H., Jiang, X., Vaidya, J.: Privacy preserving SVM using nonlinear kernels on horizontally partitioned data. In: Proceedings of the 2006 ACM Symposium on Applied Computing, SAC 2006, pp. 603–610. ACM Press, New York (2006)

13. Kantarcioglou, M.: A survey of privacy-preserving methods across horizontally partitioned data. In: Aggarwal, C.C., Yu, P.S. (eds.) Privacy-Preserving Data Mining: Models and Algorithms, pp. 311–335. Springer, Boston (2008). doi:10.1007/978-0-387-70992-5_13
14. Lindell, Y., Pinkas, B.: Secure multiparty computation for privacy-preserving data mining. In: IACR Cryptology ePrint Archive (2008)
15. Yao, A.: How to generate and exchange secrets. In: Proceedings of the 27th IEEE Symposium on Foundations of Computer Science, pp. 162–167 (1986)
16. Zhou, Z.: Ensemble Methods Foundations and Algorithms, pp. 15–17. CRC, Boca Raton (2012)
17. Gambs, S., Kégl, B., Aïmeur, E.: Privacy-preserving boosting. Data Mining Knowl. Discov. 14(1), 131–170 (2007)
18. Li, Y., Bai, C., Reddy, C.: A distributed ensemble approach for mining healthcare data under privacy constraints. Inf. Sci. 330, 245–259 (2016)
19. Xie, L., Plis, S., Sarwate, A.: Data-weighted ensemble learning for privacy-preserving distributed learning. In: IEEE International Conference on Acoustics, Speech and Signal Processing, pp. 2309–2313 (2016)
20. Kantarcioglou, M., Jin, J., Clifton, C.: When do data mining results violate privacy? In: Proceedings of the 2004 ACM SIGKDD International Conference on Knowledge Discovery and Data Mining, pp. 599–604 (2004)

Greedy Based Pareto Local Search for Bi-objective Robust Airport Gate Assignment Problem

Wenxue Sun[1], Xinye Cai[1(✉)], Chao Xia[1], Muhammad Sulaman[1], Mustafa Mısır[1], and Zhun Fan[2]

[1] College of Computer Science and Technology,
Nanjing University of Aeronautics and Astronautics, Nanjing, China
sunwenxue2013@163.com, {xinye,mmisir}@nuaa.edu.cn,
heaveneleven@126.com, sulman0909@gmail.com
[2] School of Engineering, Shantou University, Guangdong, China
zfan@stu.edu.cn

Abstract. The present paper proposes a Greedy based Pareto Local Search (GB-PLS) algorithm for the bi-objective robust airport gate assignment problem (bRAGAP). The bRAGAP requires to minimize the total passenger walking distance and the total robust cost of gate assignment. The robust cost is measured through our proposed evaluation function considering the impact of delay cost on the allocation of idle time. GB-PLS uses the Random and Greedy Move (RGM) as a neighborhood search operator to improve the convergence and diversity of the solutions. Two populations are maintained in GB-PLS: the external population (EP) stores the nondominated solutions and the starting population (SP) maintains all the starting solutions for Pareto local search (PLS). The PLS is applied to search the neighborhood of each solution in the SP and the generated solutions are used to update the EP. A number of extensive experiments has been conducted to validate the performance of GB-PLS over Pareto Simulated Annealing (PSA).

Keywords: Bi-objective optimization · Robust airport gate assignment · Pareto Local Search · Neighborhood search

1 Introduction

Aircrafts have turned into a major means of transportation with the changing customer needs, varying traveling prices and increasing number of airports. The aircraft stand positions (Gates) have a significant effect on the efficient utilization of aircrafts. The assignment of gates to the aircrafts should be carefully handled for both the optimal use of airports and the passengers' satisfaction. This assignment task has been studied as the airport gate assignment problem (AGAP) [1]. The AGAP aims at delivering gate schedules by taking various factors into account, including the flights' arrival and departure times, the aircraft types, the attribute of flight (domestic or international), the number of

© Springer International Publishing AG 2017
Y. Shi et al. (Eds.): SEAL 2017, LNCS 10593, pp. 694–705, 2017.
https://doi.org/10.1007/978-3-319-68759-9_56

passengers, as well as the gate preferences [2]. This paper further focuses on the deterministic factors where the arrival and departure times of each flight are fixed with no existing flight cancellations and delays.

The gate assignments should be determined such that the un-gated flights and passenger walking distance are minimized while the robustness is maximized. The terminal gates are usually equipped with the passenger bridges and the apron needs buses to transfer the passengers. In order to shorten the walking distance of passengers, assigning the terminal gates to the flights should be preferred over aprons [1]. For improving the passengers' satisfaction, the walking distance should be minimized [3]. Regarding robustness, the gate schedules should be insensitive to the minor changes on the aforementioned factors [2].

Maintaining the balance between the airports' operational efficiency and the passengers' satisfaction is a complex multi-objective combinatorial optimization problem. A number of studies [1,3–9] on this problem have been performed in the literature. Some of these studies tackled this multi-objective problem as a single-objective optimization problem by the weighted-sum approach. For generating multiple solutions, they have been executed many times to produce different solutions [10]. Pareto Simulated Annealing (PSA) [1] is the first algorithm that directly solves the AGAP as a multi-objective optimization problem. Despite its success on solving the AGAP and avoiding from the local optima, the exchange of information between the solutions is inadequate. Since this information can be used to speed up the convergence speed while improving the diversity of the solutions.

Pareto Local Search (PLS), as an extension of the single objective local search [11,12], is commonly used to explore the neighborhood of each non-dominated solution for approximating the Pareto front (PF). Neighborhood search determines the performance of PLS. Xu and Bailey [13] designed three types of neighborhood search moves: Insert, Exchange_1 and Exchange_2. However, these moves struggle to find good-quality solutions especially when the number of flights to assign in a short time period is high [6]. To overcome the shortcomings of these moves, the Interval Exchange move [6], which is based on partially swapping two sequences of flights, was proposed. An Apron Exchange move was additionally introduced to exchange a flight that assigned to the apron with a flight that has been assigned to a terminal gate. However, the Interval Exchange move is computationally expensive or may be ineffective when the feasibility constraint (Sect. 2) is considered.

The robust gate assignment has been particularly studied in the literature [14–18]. In [14,15], the robustness is measured by the idle period between two successive utilisations of one gate. A model for robust gate assignment was proposed by minimizing the variance of the idle times. However, the proposed model lacks practicality, since it is unable to handle the problems with more than 80 aircrafts and 20 gates in a reasonable amount of time [17]. Robustness was incorporated into scheduling by a stochastic programming model with stochastic arrival and departure time in [16]. The weakness of this model is that only one constraint of assigning each aircraft to one and only one gate is considered.

In [17], a cost function, which is very effective in evaluating the robustness of gate scheduling, was introduced for penalizing very small idle-times with very high cost and mildly penalize the large idle times.

For evaluating the robustness of the gate assignment, a practical evaluation function is needed. The existing evaluation functions are impractical as mentioned above. For better practicality, we design a novel evaluation function considering the impact of delay cost on the idle time allocation based on the cost function provided by [17]. The proposed evaluation function can take into account the airports' operational efficiency and the passengers' satisfaction to meet the actual requirements of the airport. We introduce a Greedy based Pareto Local Search (GB-PLS) to solve the bi-objective robust airport gate assignment problem (bRAGAP) more efficiently than the existing studies. The Random and Greedy Move (RGM) is designed in a way that it can guide the PLS for generating the high quality solutions as well as avoiding it to be stuck in the local optima. An empirical comparison provided against the PSA reveals the capabilities of GB-PLS in terms of solution quality.

This paper is organized as follows. Section 2 introduces the bRAGAP with a model. The proposed approach, i.e. GB-PLS, is explained in Sect. 3. The computational results are provided in Sect. 4. Section 5 concludes the paper with a summary and the future research plan.

2 The Bi-objective Robust Airport Gate Assignment Problem

This section provides a mathematical model for the bi-objective robust airport gate assignment problem (bRAGAP). All the notations are given in Table 1. Similar to [3], two dummy gates are introduced in our model. Gate 0 represents the entrance or exit of the airport. Gate $m + 1$ represents the apron assigned to the flights when terminal gates are all occupied. The binary variable $x_{i,k} = 1$ denotes that the flight i is assigned to gate k, where $1 \leq k \leq m + 1$, and $x_{i,k} = 0$ otherwise. According to [19], the delay cost of the flights is consisted of explicit cost and hidden cost. The explicit cost is composed of operating costs of delayed flights, passenger economic loss and profit loss of delayed flights [19]. The operating cost varies with the aircraft type. The delayed operating cost for all types of aircrafts is shown in Table 2. The flights can be divided into three types by collecting the maximum take-off weight of the aircraft. In [19], it was pointed out that the average delay cost per passenger for domestic and international flights are 50 and 100 per hour, respectively. So the passengers' economic loss can be calculated by gaining the average maximum passengers for specific type of aircraft. For calculating the profit per hour earned by each type of aircraft, a method was additionally introduced as in Eq. 1.

$$L_i = \gamma_i \times PLR \times APrice \times ANPM/AFLY \tag{1}$$

In Eq. 1, PLR represents the ratio of the number of passengers carried by the aircraft to the number of seats available for the aircraft which reflects the

Table 1. Notations in bRAGAP

Parameter	Description
n	Total number of flights
m	Total number of gates
a_i	Arrival time of flight i
d_i	Departure time of flight $i(a_i < d_i)$
$w_{k,l}$	Walking distance of passengers from gate k to gate l
$p_{i,j}$	Number of passengers transferring from flight i to flight j
$S_{i,k}$	The latest idle time of gate k before the arrival of flight i
$c(S_{i,k})$	The robust cost of idle time $S_{i,k}$
Co_i	Weight coefficient for the robust cost of flight i
γ_i	Maximum passengers of flight i
PLR	Passenger load factor
$APrice$	Average price for ticket
$ANPM$	Average net profit margin
$AFLY$	Average flying time
L_i	The unit time profit loss for flight i
$DisapRate$	The disappointment rate of passengers
$MAXApron$	The maximum number of allowed flights park at the apron
η	The minimum allowed safety interval in minutes

Table 2. Delay operating cost of different type of aircrafts

Aircraft type	Sign	Max takeoff weight/t	Wake type	Delay operating cost (RMB/hr)
Large aircraft	H	>136	Heavy wake	4167
Medium aircraft	M	7–136	Medium wake	2916
Small aircraft	L	<7	Light wake	208

degree of aircraft utilization. $ANPM$ is a measure of profitability. $AFLY$ means the average flight time from source to destination.

The concept of passenger disappointment spillover cost to express the hidden cost caused by the flight delay, was investigated in [20]. The flight delay causes the delay of passengers' arrival to the destination as originally planned, resulting the bad influence of the company. The spillover cost can be computed by $\gamma_i \times APrice \times DisapRate$. The $DisapRate$ refers to a measure coefficient of the loss of the airline's interest due to the passengers' disappointment because of flight delay. The coefficient is between 0 and 1, reflecting the relationship between flight delay time and passenger disappointment spillover cost. The $DisapRate$ can be calculated by the formula as follows [20]:

$$DisapRate = \sqrt[3]{(t/60)^2}/29 \tag{2}$$

where t represents the delay time in minutes. Hence, we can get the passenger disappointment spillover cost per hour by setting the delay time equals to 60. The delay cost of each flight can be calculated by using above formula. We choose the smallest cost as base cost and weight coefficient can be obtained by comparing the ratio with the minimum cost.

The objective function of the bRAGAP is given as follows:

$$
\begin{aligned}
min\ z_1 = &\sum_{i=1}^{n}\sum_{j=1}^{n}\sum_{k=1}^{m+1}\sum_{l=1}^{m+1} p_{i,j}w_{k,l}x_{i,k}x_{j,l} \\
&+ \sum_{i=1}^{n}\sum_{k=1}^{m+1} p_{0,i}w_{0,k}x_{i,k} + \sum_{i=1}^{n}\sum_{k=1}^{m+1} p_{i,0}w_{k,0}x_{i,k}
\end{aligned} \tag{3}
$$

$$min\ z_2 = \sum_{k=1}^{m}\sum_{i=2}^{n} Co_i c(S_{i,k})x_{i,k} \tag{4}$$

Equation 3 represents the total passenger walking distance. Equation 4 indicates the total robust cost of gate assignment. The robust cost $c(S_{i,k})$ can be calculated as follows [17]:

$$
c(S_{i,k}) = \begin{cases} 1000(\arctan(0.21(5 - S_{i,k})) + \dfrac{\pi}{2}), & S_{i,k} \geq \eta \\ \infty, & otherwise \end{cases} \tag{5}
$$

The first type of constraints can be applied as follows:

$$\sum_{k=1}^{m+1} x_{i,k} = 1, \quad 1 \leq i \leq n \tag{6}$$

$$x_{i,k}x_{j,k}(d_j - a_i)(d_i - a_j) \leq 0, \quad 1 \leq i,j \leq n,\ k \neq m+1 \tag{7}$$

$$x_{i,k} \in \{0,1\}, \quad 1 \leq i,j \leq n,\ 1 \leq k \leq m+1 \tag{8}$$

Equation 6 ensures that each flight must be assigned to one and only one gate. It will be assigned to the apron when no terminal gate is available. Equation 7 ensures that the flights assigned to the same terminal gate are not overlapped. Equation 8 specifies that each flight is either assigned to a gate or not.

The second type of constraints can be applied as follows:

$$x_{i,k} \leq f_{i,k}, \quad 1 \leq i \leq n,\ 1 \leq k \leq m \tag{9}$$

where $f_{i,k}$ is a binary variable indicating whether a terminal gate k can be assigned to the flight i or not. A terminal gate can only be allocated to the flight if the airline of the flight is in the list of permitted airlines to the corresponding gate. Furthermore, the flight attribute must be match with the terminal gate attribute (domestic or international). Moreover, the terminal gate type must be supported to the type of the aircraft. We applied an additional constraint to bound the number of flights to the apron which can be implemented as in Eq. 10.

$$\sum_{i=1}^{n} x_{i,k+1} \leq MAXApron \tag{10}$$

$MAXApron$ can be set by the airport manager and can be revised if required.

3   Greedy Based Pareto Local Search

At each generation, our Greedy based Pareto Local Search (GB-PLS) (Algorithm 1) maintains two populations: the starting population (SP) and the external population (EP). The SP consists of the starting solutions for PLS whereas all the non-dominated solutions are stored in the EP. The symbol $\downarrow$ represents the input whereas $\updownarrow$ represents the input and output.

Algorithm 1. Greedy based Pareto Local Search (GB-PLS)

Input: a stopping criterion;
N: the number of the solutions;
Υ: neighborhood search range;
P: the probability of choosing greedy gate.
Output: EP.
/* Initialize SP and EP   */
1 $Initialization(SP \updownarrow, EP \updownarrow)$
   /* Pareto Local search   */
2 $ParetoLocalSearch(SP \downarrow, EP \updownarrow)$
3 If stopping criteria is satisfied, stop and output the EP. Otherwise go to Step 2.

The Algorithm 2 describes the population initialization procedure. In order to initialize each solution $x \in EP$, the flights are sorted with respect to the arrival time. A gate is randomly selected for each flight from its available gates. If all terminal gates are busy, flights are assigned to the apron. The SP is initialized by all non-dominated solutions from EP.

Algorithm 2. *Initialization*

Input : SP, EP.
Output: SP, EP.
1 For each $i = 1, \ldots, N$, solution x^i is generated randomly.
2 Initialize $EP = \{x^1, \ldots, x^N\}$.
3 SP is set by the nondominated solutions in EP;

In Algorithm 3, to generate the neighborhood $NS(x)$, a neighborhood search method is applied to the each solution x in SP. The EP is updated by each newly generated solution. The SP is composed of all the newly added solutions in EP. If the size of SP is zero, the SP is set by copying all solutions from EP.

Algorithm 3. *ParetoLocalSearch*

   Input : SP, EP
   Output: EP.
1 Set $TP = EP$.
2 **for** *each $x \in SP$* **do**
       /* $NS(x)$:The neighborhood of x   */
3       $NS(x) = NeighborhoodSearch(x \downarrow)$;
4   **for** *each $x' \in NS(x)$* **do**
5 | $UpdateEP(x' \downarrow, EP \updownarrow)$
6   **end**
7 **end**
8 $SP = EP \backslash TP$.
9 **if** $|SP| == 0$ **then**
10 | $SP = EP$;
11 **end**

The Algorithm 4 describes the RGM neighborhood search approach. Initially, all the flights in solution x are grouped by the gates (line 1). Then, the flights are randomly selected in the range of Υ to form a search flight set Φ (line 2). Next, for each flight in Φ, the available gates are sorted randomly or greedily depending on the random number r (line 5–8). If $r \leq P$, the gates are sorted by the greedy method. Otherwise, the gates are randomly sorted. The greedy method operates based on the number of flights that the gate can be allocated to. The gates with a comparatively less number of flights are preferred so that the risk of conflicts between the flights can be degraded. Hence, the greedy method initially assigns the gate with the minimum number of flights. According to the gates order, the algorithm checks all of the available gates for the corresponding flight (line 9–21). A gate is chosen after ensuring that the arrival and departure time of a selected flight do not overlap with the existing flights.

Algorithm 5 shows how the EP is updated. A newly generated solution x' will be added to the EP if it is not dominated by any solution in EP. Meanwhile, all the solutions dominated by x' are removed from EP.

4   Computational Experiments

This section provides the experimental settings, computational results and performance analysis. To evaluate the performance of our proposed algorithm, i.e. Greedy based Pareto Local Search (GB-PLS), a real-world case from the Baiyun Airport (CAN), China is targeted. The Baiyun Airport is one of three major international hub airports in China as well as one of the most busiest airports in

---

Algorithm 4. *NeighborhoodSearch*

    Input : x.
    Output: $NS(x)$.

1 Group the flights in solution x by gates.
2 Randomly select flights in the range of Υ to form search flight set Φ.
      /* f_i: the *ith* flight in search flight set Φ */
3 **for** *each $f_i \in \Phi$* **do**
        /* $Gate(f_i)$:All the gates can be assigned to f_i */
4   Generate a random number $r \in [0, 1]$.
5   **if** $r \leq P$ **then**
6 | $Gate(f_i)$ are sorted by greedy;
7   **else**
8 | $Gate(f_i)$ are sorted randomly;
9   **for** *each $g \in Gate(f_i)$* **do**
10   Let *isFound* = *true*;
          /* $Fly(g)$:All flights park at gate g */
11   **for** *each $f' \in Fly(g)$* **do**
12   **if** *f_i overlaps with f'* **then**
13   set *isFound* = *false*;
14   break;
15   **end**
16   **end**
17   **if** *isFound* **then**
18   g is assigned to f_i ;
19   break;
20   **end**
21   **end**
22 **end**

Algorithm 5. *UpdateEP*

    Input : x',EP.
    Output: EP.

1 **for** *each $x^i \in EP$* **do**
2   **if** $x^i \prec x'$ **then**
3 | return;
4   **end**
5   **if** $x' \prec x^i$ **then**
6 | remove x^i from EP;
7   **end**
8 **end**
9 add x' into EP;

---

the world with 68 fixed terminal gates. In this paper, the three days real-world instances are used. These test instances are named as Data-1, Data-2 and Data-3 consisting of 402, 427 and 400 flights, respectively.

GB-PLS was compared against Pareto Simulated Annealing (PSA) [1]. PSA was applied to optimize the objectives of the walking distance and total gate assignment preferences after performing a greedy method to minimize the number of flights assigned to the apron. However, the objective of the bRAGAP relates to assigning flights to the apron by limiting the maximum allowed number of flights. For a fair comparison, the same procedure is used to initialize the population and $MAXApron$ is set to 45 for both algorithms. In GB-PLS, we set $\eta = 10$, $N = 100$, $\Upsilon = 10$ and $P = 0.8$. The same settings are used for the neighborhood search move for PSA, referred as Mixed, which is a combination of the Interval Exchange, Insert and Apron Exchange moves. A flight number and a terminal gate number are randomly chosen. If a flight is assigned to an apron, the Apron Exchange move will be performed, otherwise the Insert move is applied. If the latter fails, the Interval Exchange move will be executed. As given in [1], the initial annealing temperature $T_0 = 2 * (the\ number\ of\ flights)$, cooling schedule $T_q = 0.998 \times T_0$, the acceptance probability a and b are set to 1. Both algorithms, implemented in Java, are run 20 times on each test instance for 300 s. The experiments are performed on a PC equipped with Intel 3.4 GHz CPU and 16 GB of RAM.

Figure 1a–c show the convergence graphs of PSA and GB-PLS on three instances. The convergence speed of GB-PLS is faster than PSA. Figure 2a–c illustrate the distribution of final solutions obtained by the both algorithms in the objective space. It can be clearly seen that GB-PLS outperforms PSA in terms of both convergence and diversity. In GB-PLS, the newly added non-dominated solutions in EP are used as the starting solutions for PLS to generate the good quality solutions. This procedure helps reduce the computational overhead and improve the convergence speed of the solutions. On the other hand in PSA, to keep the solutions from local optima, some worse solutions may be preserved which are used as the starting solutions for the next iteration. This may cause the reproduction of bad quality solutions resulting the slow convergence speed.

Figure 3a and b illustrate the performance of RGM with the Interval Exchange and Mixed moves. We compare these three moves based on PSA framework with the same parameter setting as mentioned above. Figure 3a indicates that the convergence speed of PSA with RGM is faster than that obtained by the compared ones. Figure 3b displays the final obtained solutions of PSA. It can be noticed that the RGM outperforms the other two moves in terms of both convergence and diversity. Considering the feasibility constraints (Sect. 2), the Interval Exchange Move becomes computationally expensive while finding two compatible intervals. The Insert and Apron Exchange moves become inefficient when a large number of flights is required to be assigned in a short interval of time. For handling this issue, the greedy method is accommodated in RGM while the random method is employed to avoid getting stuck at local optima.

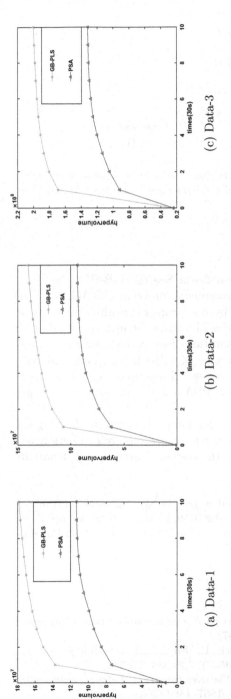

Fig. 1. Convergence graphs of GB-PLS and PSA in terms of hypervolume value on three instances.

(a) Data-1   (b) Data-2   (c) Data-3

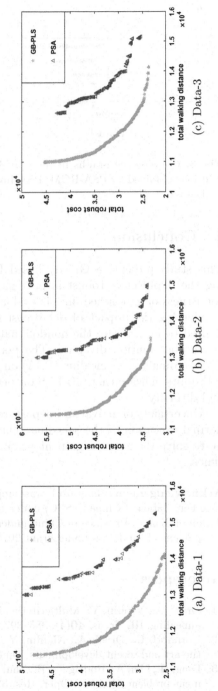

Fig. 2. Plots of the nondominated solutions of GB-PLS and PSA on three instances

(a) Data-1   (b) Data-2   (c) Data-3

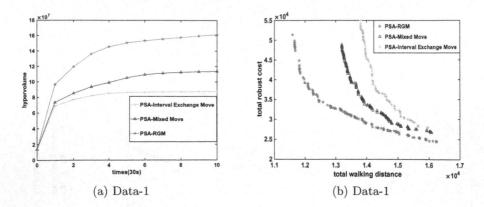

(a) Data-1   (b) Data-1

Fig. 3. Convergence graphs in terms of hypervolume value and final nondominated solutions obtained by PSA-RGM, PSA-Interval Exchange Move and PSA-Mixed Move on Data-1.

5   Conclusion

This study presents a Greedy based Pareto Local Search (GB-PLS) for solving the bi-objective robust airport gate assignment problem (bRAGAP). The robustness of gate scheduling is evaluated by our proposed evaluation function considering the impact of delay cost on the allocation of idle time. GB-PLS is used to incorporate the nondominated solutions for accelerating the convergence and solution diversity. The performance of GB-PLS is compared with Pareto Simulated Annealing (PSA) on the real-world instances. The experimental results indicate that GB-PLS outperforms PSA in terms of both convergence and diversity.

Uncertainty of arrival and departure time is an important factor affecting the normal execution of the schedule. Therefore, the future research direction will be to solve the gate assignment problem with stochastic arrival and departure times.

Acknowledgement. This work was supported in part by the National Natural Science Foundation of China (NSFC) under grant 61300159, by the Natural Science Foundation of Jiangsu Province of China under grant BK20130808 and by China Postdoctoral Science Foundation under grant 2015M571751.

References

1. Drexl, A., Nikulin, Y.: Multicriteria airport gate assignment and pareto simulated annealing. IIE Trans. **40**(4), 385–397 (2007)
2. Dorndorf, U., Drexl, A., Nikulin, Y., Pesch, E.: Flight gate scheduling: state-of-the-art and recent developments. Omega **35**(3), 326–334 (2007)
3. Ding, H., Lim, A., Rodrigues, B., Zhu, Y.: The over-constrained airport gate assignment problem. Comput. Oper. Res. **32**(7), 1867–1880 (2005)

4. Yan, S., Huo, C.M.: Optimization of multiple objective gate assignments. Transp. Res. Part A Policy Pract. **35**(5), 413–432 (2001)
5. Ding, H., Lim, A., Rodrigues, B., Zhu, Y.: Aircraft and gate scheduling optimization at airports. In: Proceedings of the 37th Annual Hawaii International Conference on System Sciences, pp. 74–81. IEEE (2004)
6. Ding, H., Lim, A., Zhu, Y.: New heuristics for over-constrained flight to gate assignments. J. Oper. Res. Soc. **55**(7), 760–768 (2004)
7. Nikulin, Y., Drexl, A.: Theoretical aspects of multicriteria flight gate scheduling: deterministic and fuzzy models. J. Sched. **13**(3), 261–280 (2010)
8. Gupet, J., Acuna-Agost, R., Briant, O., Gayon, J.P.: Exact and heuristic approaches to the airport stand allocation problem. Eur. J. Oper. Res. **246**(2), 597–608 (2015)
9. Dorndorf, U., Jaehn, F., Pesch, E.: Flight gate assignment and recovery strategies with stochastic arrival and departure times. OR Spectrum **39**(1), 65–93 (2017)
10. Deb, K., Agrawal, S., Pratab, A., Meyarivan, T.: A fast elitist non-dominated sorting genetic algorithm for multi-objective optimization: NSGA-II. KanGAL report 200001, Indian Institute of Technology, Kanpur, India (2000)
11. Lust, T.: Speed-up techniques for solving large-scale bTSP with the two-phase pareto local search. In: Genetic and Evolutionary Computation Conference (GECCO), Atlanta, USA, pp. 761–762. ACM Press (2008)
12. Lust, T., Teghem, J.: Two-phase pareto local search for the biobjective traveling salesman problem. J. Heuristics **16**(3), 475–510 (2010)
13. Xu, J., Bailey, G.: The Airport Gate Assignment Problem: Mathematical Model and a Tabu Search Algorithm (2001)
14. Bolat, A.: Assigning arriving flights at an airport to the available gates. J. Oper. Res. Soc. **50**(1), 23–34 (1999)
15. Bolat, A.: Procedures for providing robust gate assignments for arriving aircrafts. Eur. J. Oper. Res. **120**(1), 63–80 (2000)
16. Lim, A., Wang, F.: Robust airport gate assignment. In: IEEE International Conference on TOOLS with Artificial Intelligence, pp. 74–81 (2005)
17. Diepen, G., Akker, J.M.V.D., Hoogeveen, J.A., Smeltink, J.W.: Finding a robust assignment of flights to gates at amsterdam airport schiphol. J. Sched. **15**(6), 703–715 (2012)
18. Castaing, J., Mukherjee, I., Cohn, A., Hurwitz, L., Nguyen, A., Ller, J.J.: Reducing airport gate blockage in passenger aviation. Comput. Oper. Res. **65**(C), 189–199 (2014)
19. Xu, X., Xiong, L.: Cost analysis of flight delays and simulation in ground-holding model. J. Nanjing Univ. Aeronaut. Astronaut. **38**(1), 115–120 (2006)
20. Zhao, X.L., Zhu, J.F., Mei, G.: Study on modelling and algorithm of irregular flight delay operation. Syst. Eng.-Theory Pract. **4**, 018 (2008)

Multi-neighbourhood Great Deluge for Google Machine Reassignment Problem

Ayad Turky[1]([⊠]), Nasser R. Sabar[2], Abdul Sattar[3], and Andy Song[1]

[1] School of Computer Science and I.T., RMIT University, Melbourne, Australia
{ayad.turky,andy.song}@rmit.edu.au
[2] Queensland University of Technology, Brisbane, Australia
nasser.sabar@qut.edu.au
[3] Griffith University, Brisbane, Australia
a.sattar@griffith.edu.au

Abstract. Google Machine Reassignment Problem (GMRP) is a recent real world problem proposed at ROADEF/EURO challenge 2012. The aim of this problem is to maximise the usage of the available machines by reassigning processes among those machines while a numerous constraints must be not violated. In this work, we propose a great deluge algorithm with multi-neighbourhood operators (MNGD) for GMRP. Great deluge (GD) algorithm is a single solution based heuristic that accept non-improving solutions in order to escape from the local optimal point. The proposed algorithm uses multi-neighbourhood operators of various characteristics to effectively navigate the search space. The proposed algorithm is evaluated on a total of 30 instances. Computational results disclose that our proposed MNGD algorithm performed better than GD with single neighbourhood operator. Furthermore, MNGD algorithm obtains best results compared with other algorithms from the literature on some instances.

Keywords: Google machine reassignment problem · Great deluge · Multi-neighbourhood

1 Introduction

One of the fast growing technology is a cloud computing which aims to provide network access to computing resources including storage, processing and network bandwidth [2,4]. Service providers like Google and Amazon need to manage a large-scale data centers of which the computing resources are to be shared by end users with high quality of service. Recently, with the steady growth of cloud services and Internet, the importance of solving such resource management problems becomes one the most important targets in the optimisation community [4]. In this work, we investigate a recent combinatorial optimisation problem proposed at ROADEF/EURO challenge 2012 called google machine reassignment problem (GMRP) [1]. The main aim of this problem is to enhance the usage of the resources by reassigning a set of processes across a pool of server

© Springer International Publishing AG 2017
Y. Shi et al. (Eds.): SEAL 2017, LNCS 10593, pp. 706–715, 2017.
https://doi.org/10.1007/978-3-319-68759-9_57

machines subject to a set of constraints which must be satisfied. Several algorithms have been proposed to solve GMRP. These include simulated annealing [11,12,16,17], variable neighbourhood search [7], steepest descent [18], constraint programming-based large neighbourhood search [10], large neighbourhood search [3], multi-start iterated local search [9], memetic algorithm [13], late acceptance hill-climbing [15] and restricted iterated local search [8].

In this work, we propose a great deluge algorithm with multi-neighbourhood operators (MNGD) for GMRP. Great deluge (GD) algorithm is a single solution based heuristic proposed by Dueck [6], which has been successfully used in various optimisation problems [5,6,13,14]. GD always accepts improved solutions while worse solutions may also be accepted if it is a better than the threshold. To improve the search performance of GD, we utilise a multi-neighbourhood operators instead of single operator with the aim of gaining significant improvements in solution quality.

The performance of the proposed MNGD algorithm is assessed using 30 instances of GMRP which are very diverse in size and features. To verify the effectiveness of our proposed MNGD algorithm, we compare its performance over four variants of GD. Experimental results show that the proposed MNGD achieved outperforms all the variants of GD (implemented herein). Further comparison with other algorithms in the literature shows that the proposed MNGD is capable of obtaining good results on some instances.

The rest of this article is organised as follows. The formulation of google machine reassignment problem is described in Sect. 2. Section 3 presents the proposed algorithm MNGD. The experiment setup is discussed in Sect. 4. The results are presented and discussed in Sect. 5, followed by the conclusion and some remarks in Sect. 6.

2 Problem Description

The French Operational Research and Decision Aid society (ROADEF) and the European Operational Research society (EURO) organise a challenge contest every two years since 1999. The challenge is called ROADEF/EURO. In 2012, Google proposed a machine reassignment problem (GMRP) for this challenge. GMRP is a recent combinatorial optimisation problem [1]. The main elements of this problem are a set of machines M and a set of processes P. The goal of this problem is to find the optimal way to assign process $p \in P$ to machines $m \in M$ in order to improve the usage of a given set of machines. One machine consists of a set of resources such as CPUs and RAM. One process can be moved from one machine to another to improve overall machine usage. The allocation of processes must not violate the following hard constraints:

- *Capacity constraints*: the sum of requirements of resource of all processes does not exceed the capacity of the allocated machine.
- *Conflict constraints*: processes of the same service must be allocated into different machines.

- *Transient usage constraints*: if a process is moved from one machine to another, it requires adequate amount of capacity on both machines.
- *Spread constraints*: the set of machines is partitioned into locations and processes of the same service should be allocated to machines in a number of distinct locations.
- *Dependency constraints*: the set of machines are partitioned into neighbour-hoods. Then, if there is a service depends on another service, then the process of first one should be assigned to the neighbouring machine of second one or vice versa.

A feasible solution to GMRP is a process-machine assignment which satisfies all hard constraints and minimises the weighted cost function as much as possible which is calculated as follows:

$$f = \sum_{r \in R} weight_{loadCost}(r) \times loadCost(r)$$
$$+ \sum_{b \in B} weight_{balanceCost}(b) \times balanceCost(b)$$
$$+ weight_{processMoveCost} \times processMoveCost$$
$$+ weight_{serviceMoveCost} \times serviceMoveCost$$
$$+ weight_{machineMoveCost} \times machineMoveCost \qquad (1)$$

where R is a set of resources, $loadCost$ represents the used capacity by resource r which exceeds the safety capacity, $balanceCost$ represents the use of available machine, $processMoveCost$ is the cost of moving a process from its current machine to a new one, $serviceMoveCost$ represents the maximum number of moved processes over services and $machineMoveCost$ represents the sum of all moves weighted by relevant machine cost. $weight_{loadCost}$, $weight_{balanceCost}$, $weight_{processMoveCost}$, $weight_{serviceMoveCost}$ and $weight_{machineMoveCost}$ define the importance of each individual cost.

For more details about the constraints, the costs and their weights can be found on the challenge documentation [1]. Note that the quality of a solution is evaluated by the given solution checker, which returns fitness measure to the best solution generated by our proposed algorithm. Another important aspect of this challenge is the time limit. All methods have to finish within the 5-minute timeframe to ensure the fairness of the comparison.

3   Multi-neighbourhood Great Deluge - MNGD

GD is a single solution based heuristic was introduced by [6]. It uses an initial solution as a starting basis and then generated a neighbourhood solution. GD always accepts improved solutions while worse solutions may also be accepted if it is better than the threshold. In this work, four different neighbourhood operators are used generate a neighbourhood solution. At each iteration, one neighbour-hood operator is randomly selected. Given an initial solution, S_0, generates a neighbourhood solution, S_1, using the selected neighbourhood operator. Replace S_1 with the S_0 if the quality of S_1 is better than S_0 or lower than the *level*. Initially, the value of *level* is set equal to the fitness value of the initial solution. At each iteration, the value of *level* is decreased by ε as follows:

$$level = level - \varepsilon \tag{2}$$

and

$$\varepsilon = (f(S_1) - f(best_{sol}))/NI \tag{3}$$

where NI is the number of iterations which is fixed to 1000 (the 1000 was determined based on a preliminary test). The search process will stop when the *level* value is lower than the best solution found so far.

The overview of the proposed MNGD algorithm is shown in Fig. 1.

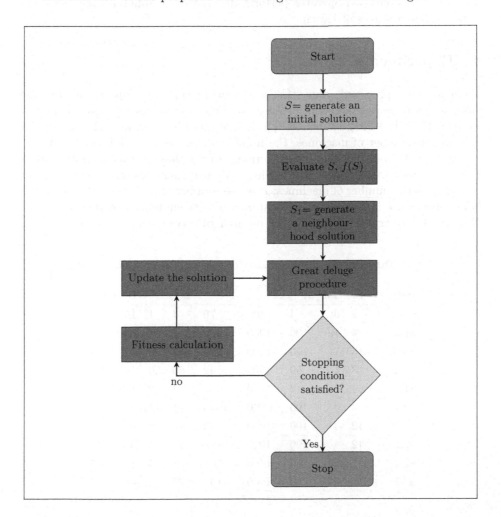

Fig. 1. Flowchart of Great Deluge (GD) algorithm

Google provides an initial solution for every problem instance and evaluated using Eq. 1 [1]. The neighbourhood operates used in the work are:

- **Single swap.** Selects two processes from two different machines and interchanges them.
- **Double swap.** Selects four processes from two different machines and interchanges them.
- **Single move.** Selects a process from a machine and moves it to a different machine.
- **Double move.** Selects two processes from a machine and moves them to a different machine.

The reason of using different neighbourhood operator at each iteration is because neighbourhood operates perform differently for different instances and under different stages of search.

4 Experiments

To test the proposed algorithm's performance, we applied it to the Google machine reassignment problem instances that were proposed for the ROADEF/EURO 2012 challenge. These instances have various characteristics in terms of number of machines, the number of processes, neighbourhood, and so on. Table 1 shows the main characteristics of the these instances. In the table, R is the number of resources; TR is the number of resources that need transient usage; M is the number of machines; P is the number of processes; S is the number of services; L is the number of locations; N is the number of neighbourhoods; B is number of triples and SD is the number of service dependencies.

Table 1. The characteristics of the problem instances

Instance	R	TR	M	P	S	L	N	B	SD
a1_1	2	0	4	100	79	4	1	1	0
a1_2	4	1	100	1000	980	4	2	0	40
a1_3	3	1	100	1000	216	25	5	0	342
a1_4	3	1	50	1000	142	50	50	1	297
a1_5	4	1	12	1000	981	4	2	1	32
a2_1	3	0	100	1000	1000	1	1	0	0
a2_2	12	4	100	1000	170	25	5	0	0
a2_3	12	4	100	1000	129	25	5	0	577
a2_4	12	0	50	1000	180	25	5	1	397
a2_5	12	0	50	1000	153	25	5	0	506

(*continued*)

Table 1. (*continued*)

Instance	R	TR	M	P	S	L	N	B	SD
b_1	12	4	100	5000	2512	10	5	0	4412
b_2	12	0	100	5000	2462	10	5	1	3617
b_3	6	2	100	20000	15025	10	5	0	16560
b_4	6	0	500	20000	1732	50	5	1	40485
b_5	6	2	100	40000	35082	10	5	0	14515
b_6	6	0	200	40000	14680	50	5	1	42081
b_7	6	0	4000	40000	15050	50	5	1	43873
b_8	3	1	100	50000	45030	10	5	0	15145
b_9	3	0	1000	50000	4609	100	5	1	43437
b_10	3	0	5000	50000	4896	100	5	1	47260
x_1	12	4	100	5000	2529	10	5	0	4164
x_2	12	0	100	5000	2484	10	5	1	3742
x_3	6	2	100	20000	14928	10	5	0	15201
x_4	6	0	500	20000	1190	50	5	1	38121
x_5	6	2	100	40000	34872	10	5	0	20560
x_6	6	0	200	40000	14504	50	5	1	39890
x_7	6	0	4000	40000	15273	50	5	1	43726
x_8	3	1	100	50000	44950	10	5	0	12150
x_9	3	0	1000	50000	4871	100	5	1	45457
x_10	3	0	5000	50000	4615	100	5	1	47768

5   Results and Discussions

This section is divided into two subsections. The first section compares the performance of the proposed MNGD algorithm and four variants of GD. The second section compares the results of our proposed MNGD algorithm with those of state-of-the-art algorithms.

5.1   Comparison Between the Variants of GD and MNGD

Table 2 presents the results of the variants of GD and MNGD algorithms. The results in term of cost of the best solution over 31 runs are reported. It can be seen in Table 2 that MNGD outperforms GD with single swap, GD with double swap, GD with single move and GD with double move over all instances. We believe this is due to the use of multi-neighbourhood operators in which to effectively explore the search space.

Table 2. The results of MNGD compared to the variants of GD on set a

Instance	GD with single swap	GD with double swap	GD with single move	GD with double move	MNGD
a1_1	44307107	44306804	44306501	44306501	**44306501**
a1_2	821045884	810089799	830249794	832618718	**777533310**
a1_3	583006826	583006918	583416892	583416992	**583005818**
a1_4	280990927	282367659	317088470	328814612	**251015180**
a1_5	727579618	727580017	727579110	727579210	**727578320**
a2_1	4545708	3265321	25530997	33577222	**167**
a2_2	1159386224	1191587413	1108165322	1120495815	**720671547**
a2_3	1571979990	1583717940	1517915037	1538035564	**1194261506**
a2_4	1818732313	1746131472	2100564985	2176917544	**1680587610**
a2_5	482371701	507282889	627974888	645847866	**309714528**

5.2   Comparison Between State-of-the-art Algorithms and MNGD

In this section, the comparisons between MNGD with the state-of-the-art algorithms. The algorithms in comparison are:

1. **MNLS**: Multi-neighborhood local search [19].
2. **VNS**: Variable neighbourhood search [7].
3. **CLNS**: CP-based large neighbourhood search [10].
4. **LNS**: Large neighbourhood search [3].
5. **MILS**: Multi-start iterated local search [9].
6. **SA**: Simulated annealing [11].
7. **EM-LAHC**: Late acceptance hill-climbing [15].
8. **ESA**: Evolutionary Simulated Annealing [16].
9. **GE-SA**: Simulated Annealing [12].
10. **RILS**: Restricted iterated local search [8].
11. **MA**: Memetic algorithm [13].

The computational results over 31 runs of the proposed MNGD algorithm for all instances from are summarised in Table 3. The results are compared in term of the cost of the best solution and the search has to be finished within 5 min. In the table, we indicate in boldfont the best results obtained by algorithms. There might be multiple results shown in bold for the same instance as all of them reached the same best value. For GMRPs the lower the cost the better the solution. A close scrutiny of Table 3 reveals that, the proposed MNGD is very competitive compared to the reference algorithms. MNGD achieved the lowest cost on 8 out of 30 instances. On instances a1_1, b_2, b_8, x_2, x_7 and x_10 the proposed MNGD achieved the best result equivalent to the reference algorithms.

Table 3. The results MNGD compared to the state of the art algorithms

instance	MNGD	MNLS	VNS	CLNS	LNS	MILS	SA	EM-LAHC	ESA	GE-SA	RILS	MA
a1.1	44,306,501	44,306,501	44,306,501	44,306,501	44,306,575	44,306,501	44,306,935	44,306,501	44,306,501	44,306,501	-	44,306,501
a1.2	777,533,310	777,535,597	777,536,907	778,654,204	788,074,333	780,499,081	777,533,311	777,533,309	777,533,310	777,533,310	-	777,533,308
a1.3	583,005,818	583,005,717	583,005,818	583,005,829	583,006,204	583,006,015	583,009,439	583,005,810	583,005,814	583,005,813	-	583,005,810
a1.4	251,015,180	248,324,245	251,524,763	251,189,168	278,114,660	258,024,574	260,693,258	251,015,185	251,015,178	250,866,958	-	250,866,958
a1.5	727,578,320	727,578,309	727,578,310	727,578,311	727,578,362	727,578,412	727,578,311	727,578,310	727,578,311	727,578,314	-	727,578,310
a2.1	167	225	199	196	1,869,113	167	222	166	167	181	-	164
a2.2	720,671,547	793,641,799	720,671,548	803,092,387	858,367,123	970,536,821	877,905,951	720,671,543	720,671,545	720,671,552	-	720,671,537
a2.3	1,194,261,506	1,251,407,669	1,190,713,414	1,302,235,463	1,349,029,713	1,452,810,319	1,380,612,398	1,192,054,462	1,194,261,501	1,193,311,446	-	1,193,311,432
a2.4	1,680,587,610	1,680,744,868	1,680,615,425	1,663,530,845	1,689,370,535	1,695,897,404	1,680,587,608	1,680,587,596	1,680,587,592	1,680,587,593	-	1,380,596,746
a2.5	309,714,528	337,363,179	309,714,522	337,901,091	385,272,187	412,613,505	310,243,809	310,287,633	310,243,641	310,243,857	-	312,124,226
b.1	3,302,947,421	3,354,204,707	3,307,124,603	3,357,329,571	3,421,883,971	3,516,215,373	3,455,971,935	3,305,899,993	3,305,899,957	3,307,124,640	3,511,150,815	3,302,947,648
b.2	1,010,949,451	1,021,230,060	1,015,517,386	1,022,043,596	1,031,415,191	1,027,393,159	1,015,763,028	1,010,949,451	1,015,489,174	1,015,517,397	1,017,134,891	1,011,789,473
b.3	156,978,421	157,127,101	156,978,411	157,273,705	163,547,097	158,027,548	215,060,097	156,978,421	156,978,415	156,978,402	161,557,602	158,102,214
b.4	4,677,819,387	4,677,895,984	4,677,961,007	4,677,817,475	4,677,869,484	4,677,940,374	4,677,985,338	4,677,819,387	4,677,819,354	4,677,819,137	4,677,999,380	4,677,819,137
b.5	923,299,281	923,427,881	923,610,156	923,335,604	940,312,257	923,857,499	923,299,310	923,299,306	923,299,290	923,311,250	923,732,659	923,311,250
b.6	9,525,859,941	9,525,885,495	9,525,900,218	9,525,867,169	9,525,862,018	9,525,913,044	9,525,861,951	9,525,859,949	9,525,859,941	9,525,857,758	9,525,937,918	9,525,867,758
b.7	14,835,031,801	14,842,926,007	14,835,031,813	14,838,521,000	14,868,550,671	15,244,960,848	14,836,763,304	14,835,122,152	14,835,122,181	14,835,031,806	14,835,597,627	14,836,237,140
b.8	1,214,411,947	1,214,591,033	1,214,416,705	1,214,524,845	1,219,238,781	1,214,930,327	1,214,563,084	1,214,416,691	1,214,416,703	1,214,416,698	1,214,900,909	1,214,411,947
b.9	15,885,541,357	15,885,541,403	15,885,548,612	15,885,734,072	15,887,269,801	15,885,617,841	15,886,083,835	15,885,545,683	15,885,545,712	15,885,548,592	15,885,632,605	15,885,546,811
b.10	18,048,499,596	18,055,765,224	18,048,499,616	18,049,556,324	18,092,883,448	18,093,202,104	18,049,089,128	18,048,499,611	180,512,416,401	18,048,499,610	18,052,239,907	18,051,241,638
x.1	3,044,418,078	3,060,461,509	-	-	3,119,249,147	3,209,874,890	-	-	-	-	3,341,920,446	-
x.2	1,008,340,365	1,010,050,981	-	-	1,018,164,308	1,018,646,825	-	-	-	-	1,008,340,365	-
x.3	493,984	493,917	-	-	4,784,450	1,965,401	-	-	-	-	1,359,493	-
x.4	4,721,591,023	4,721,727,496	-	-	4,721,702,912	4,721,786,173	-	-	-	-	4,721,833,040	-
x.5	615,241	518,250	-	-	391,923	615,277	-	-	-	-	385,150	-
x.6	9,546,956,965	9,546,966,175	-	-	9,546,945,537	9,546,992,887	-	-	-	-	9,547,002,140	-
x.7	14,253,835,332	14,259,657,575	-	-	14,330,862,773	14,701,836,252	-	-	-	-	14,253,835,332	-
x.8	98,024	83,711	-	-	98,054	309,083	-	-	-	-	96,936	-
x.9	16,125,675,266	16,125,675,266	-	-	16,128,419,926	16,125,755,242	-	-	-	-	16,125,780,091	-
x.10	17,819,116,915	17,824,568,855	-	-	17,861,616,489	17,867,789,754	-	-	-	-	17,819,116,915	-

6   Conclusion

This paper introduced a multi-neighbourhood operators great deluge algorithm (MNGD) for Google machine reassignment problem. The proposed solution algorithm used a four neighbourhood operators to effectively explore the search space. At each iteration, one operator is randomly selected to generate a neighbourhood solution. The proposed MNGD algorithm is compared with four variants of GD and with the state-of-the-art algorithms. MNGD produces high-quality solutions for Google machine reassignment benchmark instances that were used during the ROADEF/EURO 2012 challenge. We conclude that the MNGD is a good method for solving google machine reassignment problem.

References

1. Roadef/euro challenge 2012: Machine reassignment. http://challenge.roadef.org/2012/en/
2. Armbrust, M., Fox, A., Griffith, R., Joseph, A.D., Katz, R., Konwinski, A., Lee, G., Patterson, D., Rabkin, A., Stoica, I., et al.: A view of cloud computing. Commun. ACM **53**(4), 50–58 (2010)
3. Brandt, F., Speck, J., Völker, M.: Constraint-based large neighborhood search for machine reassignment. Ann. Oper. Res. **242**(1), 63–91 (2016)
4. Calheiros, R.N., Ranjan, R., Beloglazov, A., De Rose, C.A., Buyya, R.: CloudSim: a toolkit for modeling and simulation of cloud computing environments and evaluation of resource provisioning algorithms. Softw.: Pract. Exp. **41**(1), 23–50 (2011)
5. Paul, P.C., Beasley, J.E.: A genetic algorithm for the multidimensional knapsack problem. J. Heuristics **4**(1), 63–86 (1998)
6. Dueck, G.: New optimization heuristics: the great deluge algorithm and the record-to-record travel. J. Comput. Phys. **104**(1), 86–92 (1993)
7. Gavranović, H., Buljubašić, M., Demirović, E.: Variable neighborhood search for google machine reassignment problem. Electron. Notes Discrete Math. **39**, 209–216 (2012)
8. Lopes, R., Morais, V.W., Noronha, T.F., Souza, V.A.: Heuristics and matheuristics for a real-life machine reassignment problem. Int. Trans. Oper. Res. **22**(1), 77–95 (2015)
9. Masson, R., Vidal, T., Michallet, J., Penna, P.H.V., Petrucci, V., Subramanian, A., Dubedout, H.: An iterated local search heuristic for multi-capacity bin packing and machine reassignment problems. Expert Syst. Appl. **40**(13), 5266–5275 (2013)
10. Mehta, D., O'Sullivan, B., Simonis, H.: Comparing solution methods for the machine reassignment problem. In: Milano, M. (ed.) CP 2012. LNCS, vol. 7514, pp. 782–797. Springer, Heidelberg (2012). doi:10.1007/978-3-642-33558-7_56
11. Ritt, M.R.P.: An algorithmic study of the machine reassignment problem. Ph.D. thesis, Universidade Federal do Rio Grande do Sul (2012)
12. Sabar, N.R., Song, A.: Grammatical evolution enhancing simulated annealing for the load balancing problem in cloud computing. In: Proceedings of the 2016 on Genetic and Evolutionary Computation Conference, pp. 997–1003. ACM (2016)
13. Sabar, N.R., Song, A., Zhang, M.: A variable local search based memetic algorithm for the load balancing problem in cloud computing. In: Squillero, G., Burelli, P. (eds.) EvoApplications 2016. LNCS, vol. 9597, pp. 267–282. Springer, Cham (2016). doi:10.1007/978-3-319-31204-0_18

14. Turabieh, H., Abdullah, S., McCollum, B.: Electromagnetism-like mechanism with force decay rate great deluge for the course timetabling problem. In: Wen, P., Li, Y., Polkowski, L., Yao, Y., Tsumoto, S., Wang, G. (eds.) RSKT 2009. LNCS, vol. 5589, pp. 497–504. Springer, Heidelberg (2009). doi:10.1007/978-3-642-02962-2_63

15. Turky, A., Sabar, N.R., Sattar, A., Song, A.: Parallel late acceptance hill-climbing algorithm for the Google machine reassignment problem. In: Kang, B.H., Bai, Q. (eds.) AI 2016. LNCS (LNAI), vol. 9992, pp. 163–174. Springer, Cham (2016). doi:10.1007/978-3-319-50127-7_13

16. Turky, A., Sabar, N.R., Song, A.: An evolutionary simulating annealing algorithm for Google machine reassignment problem. In: Leu, G., Singh, H.K., Elsayed, S. (eds.) Intelligent and Evolutionary Systems. PALO, vol. 8, pp. 431–442. Springer, Cham (2017). doi:10.1007/978-3-319-49049-6_31

17. Turky, A., Sabar, N.R., Song, A.: Cooperative evolutionary heterogeneous simulated annealing algorithm for Google machine reassignment problem. Genetic Program. Evolvable Mach. 1–28 (2017). doi:10.1007/s10710-017-9305-0

18. Turky, A., Sabar, N.R., Song, A.: Neighbourhood analysis: a case study on Google machine reassignment problem. In: Wagner, M., Li, X., Hendtlass, T. (eds.) ACALCI 2017. LNCS, vol. 10142, pp. 228–237. Springer, Cham (2017). doi:10.1007/978-3-319-51691-2_20

19. Wang, Z., Lü, Z., Ye, T.: Multi-neighborhood local search optimization for machine reassignment problem. Comput. Oper. Res. **68**, 16–29 (2016)

Evolutionary Optimization of Airport Security Inspection Allocation

Zheng-Jie Fan and Yu-Jun Zheng[✉]

College of Computer Science and Technology, Zhejiang University of Technology,
Hangzhou 310023, China
yujun.zheng@computer.org
http://www.compintell.cn/en/

Abstract. Airport security inspection plays a vital role in protecting flights and passengers. However, assigning a large number of baggages to different inspection devices and personnel can be a difficult problem. In this paper, we present a security inspection assignment problem (SIAP) for maximizing the overall probability of detecting hazardous goods within a limited time period. We then propose a hybrid evolutionary algorithm, named DE-DNSPSO, which combines differential evolution (DE) with the diversity enhanced particle swarm optimization with neighborhood search (DNSPSO) to efficiently solve the problem. In DE-DNSPSO, DE operators are used to further improve the diversity enhancing mechanism of DNSPSO and thus better balance exploration and exploitation of the algorithm. Experimental results show that DE-DNSPSO performs better than DNSPSO and some other well-known algorithms on a set of test instances, and our approach contributes to the improvement of inspection capability of airports.

Keywords: Security inspection · Particle Swarm Optimization (PSO) · Differential Evolution (DE) · Hybrid evolutionary algorithm · Optimal assignment

1 Introduction

Airport security inspection is an important line of defense against hazardous goods, such as explosives, corrosives, radioactive materials, guns and knives, which can cause terrible damages to flights and passengers. Such hazardous goods may be carried intentionally by terrorists or unintentionally by normal passengers in their baggages. In general, an airport is equipped with a number of security inspection devices and personnel for detecting hazardous goods from baggages. However, hazardous goods can have different hazard levels and different probabilities of being contained in different baggages, and different inspection devices and personnel have different efficiencies in inspecting hazardous goods. Moreover, the time for checking through all the baggages is always very limited to avoid congestion and flight delay. Thus, it is a challenging problem to assign

© Springer International Publishing AG 2017
Y. Shi et al. (Eds.): SEAL 2017, LNCS 10593, pp. 716–726, 2017.
https://doi.org/10.1007/978-3-319-68759-9_58

baggages to inspection devices and personnel such that hazardous goods can be detected as much as possible while the inspection timespan does not exceed the predefined limit.

In the literature, there are a number of studies that have been devoted to different aspects of security inspection. Virta et al. [18] proposed a cost model to evaluate the tradeoffs between screening all baggage and screening baggage of only those passengers selected by the Computer-Assisted Passenger Prescreening System (CAPPS) [10], and their results indicated that the marginal increase in security per dollar spent is significantly lower when non-selectee checked bags are screened than when only selectee checked bags are screened. Babu et al. [3] studied a problem for grouping passengers based on their perceived threat probabilities and then assigning them with different screening, and their main conclusion was that passenger grouping can be beneficial even when the threat probability is assumed constant across all passengers. The study of McLay et al. [13] further revealed that that fewer security classes for passenger screening may be more effective. Cavusoglu et al. [5] analyzed how the addition of a profiler to a security setup that employs screening devices and physical inspections affects various performance indicators, and proposed a two-screening-device setup where classified attackers and classified normal passengers are sent separate devices for screening to ensure the benefit of profiling. The problem of passenger classification for aviation security has also been studied in [1,6,14,23,25].

The paper presents a security inspection allocation problem (SIAP), where each baggage needs to be assigned to exact one inspection device and can be assigned to at most one inspection personnel, which is a commonly used mode in most airports. That is, if a device detects hazardous goods in a baggage, the baggage and its owner are forbidden; otherwise, the baggage might be allowed on board or be sent to a personnel for further checking. The aim of the problem is to find an assignment solution that maximizes the overall probability of detecting hazardous goods within a given time limit. The problem can be regarded as a variation of the well-known resource allocation problem which has been proved to be *NP*-hard [4,11]. Therefore, traditional exact algorithms only apply to small-size instances. In recent decades a variety of evolutionary algorithms, including genetic algorithms (GA) [2], particle swarm optimization (PSO) [9], ant colony optimization (ACO) [7], etc., have been studied for and shown promising performance on a variety of resource allocation problems. For effectively solving this special problem, we propose a hybrid evolutionary algorithm, named DE-DNSPSO, which combines differential evolution (DE) [16] with the diversity enhanced particle swarm optimization with neighborhood search (DNSPSO) [19]. DE-DNSPSO, we use DE operators to further improve the diversity enhancing mechanism of DNSPSO and thus better balance the exploration (global search) and exploitation (local search) of the algorithm. The experiments on a set of SIAP instances show that the DE-DNSPSO performs better than the original DNSPSO and some other well-known algorithms. This work has practical significance in improving inspection capability for airport security.

In the rest of paper, Sect. 2 presents the SIAP model, Sect. 3 proposes the DE-DNSPSO algorithm, Sect. 4 describes the experiments, and Sect. 5 concludes.

2   The Formulation of SIAP

We consider that, in a given period T, an airport needs to check N pieces of baggages. The arrival time of each baggage j is denoted by t_j^0, and the length and the volume of baggage j are denoted by L_j and V_j, respectively ($j = 1, 2, \ldots, N$). Our aim is to try to find baggages that contain hazardous goods and prohibit them being carried on board. Suppose there are M types of hazardous goods, each with an importance weight w_i ($i = 1, 2, \ldots, M$) that represents its hazard level: The larger the w_i, the higher the hazard level is (e.g., explosives are typically more dangerous than small knives). The probability that baggage j contains hazardous goods i is denoted by α_{ij}, which can be estimated based on factors such as the sizes and weights of baggages and hazardous goods, the suspicion levels to the passengers owning the baggages, etc. For example, a handbag is unlikely to contain big knives, a baggage containing guns can be unusually heavy, and the baggages of passengers that are identified as dangerous (by classifiers such as [25]) are more likely to contain hazardous goods.

Assume that the airport has K security inspection devices, and each baggage should be assigned to exact one device. The devices may have different detection speeds and different detection effects on different hazardous goods. For instance, X-ray machines have high detection probabilities for flammable and explosive materials, while metal detectors have high detection probabilities for metal knives. We use S_k to denote the average detection speed of device k, and use β_{ik} to denote the probability of hazardous goods i being detected by device k, which is estimated by the characteristics of the security inspection devices ($i = 1, 2, \ldots, M; k = 1, 2, \ldots, K; 0 \leq \beta_{ik} \leq 1$).

In addition, some suspicious baggages can be further assigned to security inspection personnel (inspectors) for manually checking. Assume that the airport has Q inspectors, and each baggage can be assigned to at most one inspector. The probability of hazardous goods i being manually detected by inspector q is denoted by γ_{iq}, which can be estimated by the visual characteristics of hazardous goods and the abilities of the inspectors ($i = 1, 2, \ldots, M; q = 1, 2, \ldots, Q; 0 \leq \gamma_{iq} \leq 1$).

The problem has two classes of decision variables: x_j representing to which security inspection device the baggage j is assigned, and y_j representing to which inspector the baggage j is assigned ($1 \leq x_j \leq K, 0 \leq y_j \leq Q$, $y_j = 0$ denotes that baggage j will not be manually inspected, i.e., $\gamma_{i0} = 0$).

The time for device k to check baggage j, denoted by t_{jk}, is calculated as:

$$t_{jk} = \frac{L_j}{S_k} \tag{1}$$

And the time for an inspector to check baggage j, denoted by t'_j, is empirically estimated as:

$$t'_j = \lambda \cdot \sqrt{V_j} \tag{2}$$

where λ is a coefficient. The higher the λ, the lower the ability of the inspector, and our empirical data suggests that the value of λ is 5–10.

For each baggage j, let $Pre(j) = \{1 \leq j' \leq N | x_{j'} = x_j \land t_{j'}^0 < t_j^0\}$, i.e., the set of baggages that are assigned to the same device as baggage j and that arrive earlier than j. The baggages should be inspected in the same order of arrival, and thus the time that baggage j has been inspected by device x_j, denoted by t_j^1, is calculated as:

$$t_j^1 = \sum_{j' \in Pre(j)} t_{j' x_j} \tag{3}$$

Consequently, after being checked by the devices, the set $B_q = \{1 \leq j \leq N | y_j = q\}$ of the baggages assigned to inspector q should be sorted in increasing order of t_j^1. Let $pre(j)$ be the baggage previous to j in this set, the time that baggage j has been inspected by inspector y_j, denoted by t_j^2, is iteratively calculated as:

$$t_j^2 = \begin{cases} t_j^1 + t_j' & \text{if } j \text{ is the first one in } B_{y_j} \\ \max(t_j^1, t_{pre(j)}^2) + t_j' & \text{otherwise} \end{cases} \tag{4}$$

Given β_{ix_j} and γ_{iy_j}, the probability P_{ij} that hazardous goods i in baggage j will be detected is $\left(1 - (1 - \beta_{ix_j})(1 - \gamma_{iy_j})\right)$. The problem is to maximize the overall detection probability of all potential hazardous goods. Therefore, the problem can be formulated as follows:

$$\max f(X) = \sum_{i=1}^{M} w_i \sum_{j=1}^{N} \alpha_{ij}(1 - (1 - \beta_{ix_j})(1 - \gamma_{iy_j})) \tag{5}$$

s.t.   Eqs.(1) $-$ (4)

$$\max_{1 \leq j \leq N}(t_j^2) \leq T \tag{6}$$

$$1 \leq x_j \leq K; 0 \leq y_j \leq Q; \qquad j = 1, 2, ..., N \tag{7}$$

Equation (6) indicates that the time that the last baggage has been checked should not exceed the predefined period.

As we can see, each solution to the problem is a $2N$-dimensional integer vector $\{x_1, y_1, ..., x_j, y_j, ..., x_N, y_N\}$.

3   A Hybrid DE-NSPSO Algorithm for the SIAP

For efficiently solving the above SIAP, we propose DE-DNSPSO, a hybrid algorithm that combines DE with DNSPSO.

3.1   The Original DNSPSO

DNSPSO is an improved PSO algorithm proposed by Wang et al. [19], which employs a diversity enhancing mechanism and neighborhood search strategies to achieve a trade-off between exploration and exploitation abilities. The diversity is enhanced by making each dimension of each particle has a probability p_r

of being the new position (produced by the PSO movement operation) and a probability $(1 - p_r)$ of being unchanged. Here p_r is used to control the swarm diversity: The smaller the value of p_r, the higher the swarm diversity.

DNSPSO maintain particles with a ring neighborhood structure such that each particle has two neighbors, and a adopts two special neighborhood search strategies, local neighborhood search (LNS) and global neighborhood search (GNS), for enhancing exploitation and exploration, respectively. At each iteration, each particle X_i has a probability of p_n of being conducted neighborhood search. GNS is done by randomly selecting two other particles X_a and X_b from the entire swarm, $a, b \in [1, N] \wedge a \neq b \neq i$ (N denotes the population size), and then using the following movement equation to generate the new position for the particle (where r_1, r_2 and r_3 are three numbers randomly distributed in $[0, 1]$):

$$X_i = r_1 \cdot X_i + r_2 \cdot gbest + r_3 \cdot (X_a - X_b) \tag{8}$$

LNS is similar to GNS except that X_a and X_b are selected from the k-neighborhood radius of X_i, and the $gbest$ is replaced by $pbest_i$ in Eq. (8).

3.2   Combining DE for Diversity Enhancement

Our experiments show that, for the considered SIAP, the diversity of the original DNSPSO is still not enough. Although DNSPSO uses the parameter p_r to control the swarm diversity, it is difficult to determine the value of p_r. Some previous studies show that DE operators including mutation, crossover, and selection, if appropriately used, can effectively enhance the population diversity of many other metaheuristics [21,24]. At each iteration of the DE algorithm, the mutation operator generates a temporary mutant vector V_i for each solution X_i in the population as Eq. (9) (where X_{r_4}, X_{r_5} and X_{r_6} are three solutions randomly selected from the population), the crossover operator mixes the V_i and X_i to produce a trial vector U_i as Eq. (10), and the selection operator chooses the better one for the next generation as Eq. (11):

$$V_i = X_{r_4} + \delta \cdot (X_{r_5} - X_{r_6}) \tag{9}$$

$$U_i^j = \begin{cases} V_i^j & \text{if } rand(0,1) < C_r \text{ or } j = r_i, \\ X_i^j & \text{otherwise} \end{cases} \tag{10}$$

$$X_i = \begin{cases} U_i & \text{if } f(U_i) \geq f(X_i), \\ X_i & \text{otherwise} \end{cases} \tag{11}$$

3.3   Algorithm Framework

The basic framework of DE-DNSPSO is shown in Algorithm 1, where NFEs denotes the current number of function evaluations, and MAX_NFEs denotes the maximum number of function evaluations, i.e., the termination criterion of the algorithm. In our algorithm, DE operations in Lines 6–12 replace the original diversity enhancing mechanism in DNSPSO [19].

When evaluating the fitness value of a solution, we use the following penalty function to handle the constraint (6):

$$p(X) = \begin{cases} \left(\max_{1 \le j \le N}(t_j^2) \right) - T & \text{if } \max_{1 \le j \le N}(t_j^2) > T, \\ 0 & \text{otherwise} \end{cases} \tag{12}$$

And the objective function (5) is transformed as:

$$\max fit(X) = \left(\sum_{i=1}^{M} w_i \sum_{j=1}^{N} \alpha_{ij}(1 - (1 - \beta_{ix_j})(1 - \gamma_{iy_j})) \right) - C \cdot p(X) \tag{13}$$

where C is a large positive constant.

Algorithm 1. The DE-DNSPSO algorithm

1: Randomly initialize a population of solutions;
2: Determine *gbest* of the population and *pbest*$_i$ of each solution;
3: Let NFEs=0;
4: **while** NFEs $\le$ MAX_NFEs **do**
5:     **for all** X_i in the population **do**
6:         Generate a mutant vector V_i according to Eq.(9);
7:         Generate a trial vector U_i according to Eq.(10);
8:         Round each dimension of U_i to its nearest integer;
9:         Calculate the fitness value of U_i;
10:        NFEs++;
11:        Select a better one between U_i and X_i as the new X_i according to Eq.(11);
12:        Update *pbest*$_i$ and *gbest*;
13:    **end for**
14:    **for all** X_i in the population **do**
15:        **if** $rand(0,1) \le p_n$ **then**
16:            Use LNS to generate a trial particle L_i;
17:            Use GNS to generate a trial particle G_i;
18:            Round each dimension of L_i and G_i to the nearest integer;
19:            Calculate the fitness values of L_i and G_i;
20:            NFEs = NFEs + 2;
21:            Select the best one among X_i, L_i and G_i as the new X_i;
22:        **end if**
23:        Update *pbest*$_i$ and *gbest*;
24:    **end for**
25: **end while**
26: **return** *gbest*.

---

4   Computational Experiment

4.1   Experimental Settings and Comparative Methods

The experiments use eight SIAP instances as summarized in Table 1, where F denotes the value range of α_{ij} and $D = 2N$ denotes the dimension of the instance.

We have also implemented the following five popular evolutionary algorithms for comparison (most control parameters are fine-tuned on the test instances):

- The original DE algorithm [16]. The amplification coefficient $\delta = 0.5$, the crossover probability $C_r = 0.9$, and the population size is set to 50.
- The original DNSPSO algorithm [12,15,19]. The acceleration factor c_1 and c_2 are both set to 1.49618, the inertia weight w is set to 0.729844, the swarm diversity control parameter p_r is set to 0.9, the neighborhood search probability p_n is set to 0.6, and the population size is set to 50.
- A Birnbaum-importance based genetic local search (BIGLS) algorithm [20], which combines the original genetic algorithm with an embedded BI-based local search method to increase the solution quality. The elitist rate $\sigma = 0.04$, fitness scaling factor $S_f = 3$, crossover probability $P_{cro} = 0.8$, and mutation probability $P_{mut} = 0.05$, and the population size is set to 50.
- A hybrid fireworks and DE algorithm (FADE) [24], which improves the fireworks algorithm (FA) [17] by incorporating DE operators to increase the information sharing among individual solutions. The spark control parameters are set as $m = 25$, $\hat{m} = 5$, $S_{\max} = 20$, $S_{\min} = 2$, the scale factor $F = 0.5$, the crossover probability $C_r = 0.9$, and the population size is set to 50.
- The water wave optimization (WWO) algorithm [22], a new evolutionary algorithm inspired by the shallow water wave theory. WWO searches in a high-dimensional solution space through three operators named propagation, refraction, and breaking. The maximum wave height $h_{\max} = 12$, the wavelength reduction coefficient $\eta = 1.0026$, the breaking coefficient θ linearly decreases from 0.25 to 0.001, and the population size is also 50.

For our DE-DNSPSO algorithm, we set the mutation probability $\delta = 0.5$, the crossover probability $C_r = 0.9$, and the other parameters as consistent with the original DNSPSO. All the other algorithms use the same penalty function to handle the problem constraint as our DE-DNSPSO. Moreover, all the solution vectors generated during the execution of the algorithms are always rounded to integer vectors, as the SIAP is an integer programming problem.

For fairness, for all the algorithms we set the same termination condition as that the NFEs reach the MAX_NFEs specified in the last column in Table 1. All the algorithms are executed 50 times on each instance on the SIAP, and evaluation is based on the average performance over the 50 runs. The experimental environment is a computer of Intel Core i7-6700 8 processors and 8GB DDR3 memory, and the program is developed using the IntelliJ IDEA.

4.2   Experimental Results

Table 2 presents the maximum, minimum, mean, standard deviation of the objective values obtained by six algorithms as well as the computational time (in seconds) over 50 runs on each test instance. The symbol † before a mean value indicates that the result of DE-DNSPSO is statistically significantly different from that of the corresponding algorithms at 95% confidence level, according to the nonparametric Wilcoxon rank sum test [8].

Table 1. Summary of different experiment instances.

Instance	M	N	K	Q	T	F	D	MAX_NFEs
#1	5	24	3	4	120	[0.160, 0.234]	48	10000
#2	6	50	6	8	160	[0.132, 0.200]	100	20000
#3	9	130	13	9	200	[0.108, 0.117]	260	50000
#4	12	245	18	15	300	[0.079, 0.088]	490	100000
#5	23	450	42	30	400	[0.041, 0.045]	900	150000
#6	33	752	51	35	450	[0.029, 0.032]	1504	200000
#7	45	1024	64	40	500	[0.021, 0.023]	2048	250000
#8	57	1501	120	80	550	[0.017, 0.018]	3002	300000

As we can see from the results, the DE-DNSPSO can obtain the best mean detection probability among the six algorithms on every instance. In general, the DNSPSO performs well on small-size instances #1 and #2 but shows poor performance on the remaining instances, and the overall performance of the DE algorithms is the worst. The low performance of DE is mainly because of the lack of local search ability, as the other algorithms all have specific local search mechanisms.

Nevertheless, by elaborately combining DE with DNSPSO, our DE-DNSPSO achieves significant performance improvement over the two individual algorithms. For instance #1, there is no statistical difference between the results of DE-DNSPSO and DNSPSO, but DE-DNSPSO is significantly better than the other four algorithms. As the instance size increases, the performance advantage of DE-DNSPSO over others also increase. This also demonstrates that incorporating DE operators can effectively improve the exploration ability of the algorithm in high-dimensional search spaces where the solution diversity is important.

Among the other five algorithms, the DNSPSO performs best on small-size instances #1 and #2, the WWO performs best on moderate-size instances #3 and #4, and the FADE performs best on large-size instances #5–#8. The performance of FADE also shows the effectiveness of DE operators for exploring in high-dimensional search spaces. However, since the DNSPSO has higher convergence speed and better diversity than FADE, the hybrid DE-DNSPSO shows better performance than FADE.

In terms of computational time, the BIGLS is the fastest algorithm, and DE-DNSPSO often consumes a bit more time than other algorithms. However, there is no significant different between the time used by the comparative algorithms, since they use the same MAX_NFEs as the termination condition.

In summary, the experimental results show that DE-DNSPSO can balance the exploration and exploitation much better than the original DE and DNSPSO, and its performance is also better than some other state-of-the-arts including FADE and WWO.

Table 2. The experimental results of the six algorithms on the eight instances.

		DE_DNSPSO	DNSPSO	FADE	WWO	DE	BIGLS
#1	max	8.4148E−01	8.4335E−01	8.3000E−01	8.3914E−01	8.2343E−01	8.3991E−01
	min	8.2203E−01	8.2643E−01	8.0594E−01	8.2171E−01	8.0504E−01	8.1245E−01
	mean	8.3495E−01	8.3549E−01	†8.1784E−01	†8.2906E−01	†8.1302E−01	†8.2955E−01
	std	4.3868E−03	3.7667E−03	5.8138E−03	3.8677E−03	4.8508E−03	4.5439E−03
	time	0.4967	0.5525	0.4840	0.5304	0.5372	0.4361
#2	max	8.5368E−01	8.4011E−01	8.4016E−01	8.3687E−01	8.1137E−01	8.4103E−01
	min	8.0977E−01	8.1562E−01	8.0093E−01	7.9620E−01	7.9310E−01	7.9793E−01
	mean	8.3623E−01	†8.2863E−01	†8.2059E−01	†8.1677E−01	†8.0226E−01	†8.2046E−01
	std	1.2088E−02	6.6586E−03	9.2093E−03	9.1534E−03	4.7236E−03	6.9920E−03
	time	2.3713	2.4536	2.1999	2.2604	2.4616	2.0419
#3	max	8.8458E−01	8.5752E−01	8.6961E−01	8.5652E−01	8.3540E−01	8.5778E−01
	min	8.2794E−01	8.2020E−01	8.2342E−01	8.3177E−01	8.2379E−01	8.3017E−01
	mean	8.5271E−01	†8.4296E−01	8.4924E−01	†8.4518E−01	†8.2902E−01	†8.4633E−01
	std	1.7482E−02	7.7610E−03	1.0315E−02	5.9399E−03	2.7932E−03	6.8301E−03
	time	27.128	27.402	26.255	26.662	27.148	25.661
#4	max	8.6918E−01	8.4257E−01	8.3616E−01	8.4271E−01	8.2783E−01	8.2887E−01
	min	8.0755E−01	8.1133E−01	8.0387E−01	8.2544E−01	8.1259E−01	8.1497E−01
	mean	8.4668E−01	†8.2334E−01	†8.2444E−01	†8.3309E−01	†8.1692E−01	†8.2326E−01
	std	1.6514E−02	6.4289E−03	7.6277E−03	4.3754E−03	3.7436E−03	3.8303E−03
	time	144.99	144.85	140.76	140.38	143.68	141.12
#5	max	8.6969E−01	8.4648E−01	8.5025E−01	8.4032E−01	8.4494E−01	8.4747E−01
	min	8.3348E−01	8.3265E−01	8.2911E−01	8.3453E−01	8.1077E−01	8.3170E−01
	mean	8.5953E−1	†8.4005E−01	†8.3827E−01	†8.3732E−01	†8.2892E−01	†8.3823E−01
	std	6.4534E−03	3.8311E−03	5.9352E−03	1.6484E−03	1.2810E−02	3.1178E−03
	time	518.71	518.33	506.87	510.51	511.21	515.53
#6	max	8.6470E−01	8.4549E−01	8.4943E−01	8.4599E−01	8.2962E−01	8.4698E−01
	min	8.3646E−01	8.3253E−01	8.3190E−01	8.3516E−01	8.2404E−01	8.3510E−01
	mean	8.4894E−01	†8.3851E−01	†8.4005E−01	†8.3954E−01	†8.2671E−01	†8.4213E−01
	std	8.4878E−03	2.5333E−03	3.8850E−03	2.8098E−03	1.6035E−03	3.0178E−03
	time	695.72	674.41	625.92	640.68	671.64	683.12
#7	max	8.6331E−01	8.4799E−01	8.5008E−01	8.4828E−01	8.3627E−01	8.5086E−01
	min	8.3998E−01	8.3912E−01	8.3929E−01	8.4468E−01	8.3191E−01	8.4401E−01
	mean	8.5577E−01	†8.4257E−01	†8.4505E−01	†8.4651E−01	†8.3349E−01	†8.4687E−01
	std	6.3886E−03	2.1937E−03	2.6552E−03	1.0553E−03	1.0842E−03	1.7518E−03
	time	1480.3	1310.1	1301.0	1437.5	1419.1	1459.4
#8	max	8.6166E−01	8.5494E−01	8.5198E−01	8.5215E−01	8.4415E−01	8.5188E−01
	min	8.4836E−01	8.4673E−01	8.4740E−01	8.5105E−01	8.4227E−01	8.4770E−01
	mean	8.5551E−01	†8.5022E−01	†8.4995E−01	†8.5147E−01	†8.4313E−01	†8.5011E−01
	std	5.1176E−03	2.5451E−03	1.6247E−03	3.1966E−04	5.8018E−04	8.4481E−04
	time	3698.2	3634.6	3590.4	3398.3	3665.1	3446.7

5 Conclusion

This paper presents a SIAP for assigning baggages to inspection devices and personnel on order tries to maximize the overall probability of detecting various hazardous goods within a limited time period. We propose a hybrid algorithm which combines diversity enhanced particle swarm optimization with neighborhood search (DE-DNSPSO) algorithm with DE operators to solve the SIAP. The experimental results show that the DE-DNSPSO performs better on a set of test instances than DNSPSO and some other well-known algorithms.

In future research, we will introduce more realistic but complex characteristics, such as multi-device inspection and variable speed of devices, to our SIAP model. We will also study more accurate means for evaluating the inspection time and the detection probability.

Acknowledgements. This work is supported by National Natural Science Foundation under Grant No. 61473263 of China.

References

1. Adikariwattage, V., de Barros, A.G., Wirasinghe, S.C., Ruwanpura, J.: Airport classification criteria based on passenger characteristics and terminal size. J. Air Transp. Manag. **24**, 36–41 (2012)
2. Alcaraz, J., Maroto, C.: A robust genetic algorithm for resource allocation in project scheduling. Ann. Oper. Res. **102**(1–4), 83–109 (2001)
3. Babu, V.L., Batta, R., Lin, L.: Passenger grouping under constant threat probability in an airport security system. Oper. Res. **168**(2), 633–644 (2006)
4. Bretthauer, K.M., Shetty, B.: The nonlinear resource allocation problem. Oper. Res. **43**(4), 670–683 (1995)
5. Cavusoglu, H., Koh, B., Raghunathan, S.: An analysis of the impact of passenger profiling for transportation security. Oper. Res. **58**(5), 1287–1302 (2010)
6. Cavusoglu, H., Kwark, Y., Mai, B., Raghunathan, S.: Passenger profiling and screening for aviation security in the presence of strategic attackers. Decis. Anal. **10**(1), 63–81 (2013)
7. Chaharsooghi, S.K., Kermani, A.H.M.: An effective ant colony optimization algorithm (ACO) for multi-objective resource allocation problem (MORAP). Appl. Math. Comput. **200**(1), 167–177 (2008)
8. García, S., Molina, D., Lozano, M., Herrera, F.: A study on the use of nonparametric tests for analyzing the evolutionary algorithms behaviour: a case study on the CEC 2005 special session on real parameter optimization. J. Heuristics **15**(6), 617–644 (2009)
9. Gong, Y.J., Zhang, J., Chung, H.S.H., Chen, W.N., Zhan, Z.H., Li, Y., Shi, Y.H.: An efficient resource allocation scheme using particle swarm optimization. IEEE Trans. Evol. Comput. **16**(6), 801–816 (2012)
10. Hahn, R.W.: The economics of airline safety and security: an analysis of the white house commission's recommendations. The. Harv. JL & Pub. Pol'y. **20**, 791–828 (1997)
11. Ibaraki, T., Katoh, N.: Resource Allocation Problems: Algorithmic Approaches. MIT Press, Cambridge (1988)

12. Kennedy, J., Eberhart, R.: Particle swarm optimization. In: IEEE International Conference on Neural Networks, vol. 4, pp. 1942–1948 (1995)
13. Mclay, L.A., Jacobson, S.H., Kobza, J.E.: A multilevel passenger screening problem for aviation security. Naval Res. Logist. **53**(3), 183–197 (2010)
14. Mclay, L.A., Lee, A.J., Jacobson, S.H.: Risk-based policies for airport security checkpoint screening. Transp. Sci. **44**(3), 333–349 (2010)
15. Shi, Y., Eberhart, R.C.: A modified particle swarm optimizer. In: IEEE Congress Evolutionary Computation, pp. 69–73 (1998)
16. Storn, R., Price, K.: Differential evolution: a simple and efficient heuristic for global optimization over continuous spaces. J. Global Optim. **11**(4), 341–369 (1997)
17. Tan, Y., Zhu, Y.: Fireworks algorithm for optimization. In: Tan, Y., Shi, Y., Tan, K.C. (eds.) ICSI 2010. LNCS, vol. 6145, pp. 355–364. Springer, Heidelberg (2010). doi:10.1007/978-3-642-13495-1_44
18. Virta, J.L., Jacobson, S.H., Kobza, J.E.: Analyzing the cost of screening selectee and non-selectee baggage. Risk Anal. **23**(5), 897–908 (2003)
19. Wang, H., Sun, H., Li, C., Rahnamayan, S., Pan, J.S.: Diversity enhanced particle swarm optimization with neighborhood search. Inf. Sci. **223**(2), 119–135 (2013)
20. Yao, Q., Zhu, X., Kuo, W.: A Birnbaum-importance based genetic local search algorithm for component assignment problems. Ann. Oper. Res. **212**(1), 185–200 (2014)
21. Zhang, W.J., Xie, X.F.: DEPSO: hybrid particle swarm with differential evolution operator. In: Proceedings of the IEEE International Conference on Systems, Man and Cybernetics, vol. 4, pp. 3816–3821. IEEE (2003)
22. Zheng, Y.J.: Water wave optimization: a new nature-inspired metaheuristic. Comput. Oper. Res. **55**(1), 1–11 (2015)
23. Zheng, Y.J., Ling, H.F., Xue, J.Y., Chen, S.Y.: Population classification in fire evacuation: a multiobjective particle swarm optimization approach. IEEE Trans. Evol. Comput. **18**(1), 70–81 (2014)
24. Zheng, Y.J., Xu, X.L., Ling, H.F., Chen, S.Y.: A hybrid fireworks optimization method with differential evolution operators. Neurocomputing **148**, 75–82 (2015)
25. Zheng, Y.J., Sheng, W.G., Sun, X.M., Chen, S.Y.: Airline passenger profiling based on fuzzy deep machine learning. IEEE Trans. Neural Netw. Learn. Syst. (2016, in press). doi:10.1109/TNNLS.2016.2609437

Evolving Directional Changes Trading Strategies with a New Event-Based Indicator

Michael Kampouridis[✉], Adesola Adegboye, and Colin Johnson

School of Computing, University of Kent, Medway, UK
M.Kampouridis@kent.ac.uk

Abstract. The majority of forecasting methods use a physical time scale for studying price fluctuations of financial markets, making the flow of physical time discontinuous. An alternative to this is event-based summaries. Directional changes (DC), which is a new event-based summary method, allows for new regularities in data to be discovered and exploited, as part of trading strategies. Under this paradigm, the timeline is divided in directional change events (upwards or downwards), and overshoot events, which follow exactly after a directional change has been identified. Previous work has shown that the duration of overshoot events is on average twice the duration of a DC event. However, this was empirically observed on the specific currency pairs DC was tested with, and only under the specific time periods the tests took place. Thus, this observation is not easily generalised. In this paper, we build on this regularity, by creating a new event-based indicator. We do this by calculating the average duration time of overshoot events on each training set of each individual dataset we experiment with. This allows us to have tailored duration values for each dataset. Such knowledge is important, because it allows us to more accurately anticipate trend reversal. In order to take advantage of this new indicator, we use a genetic algorithm to combine different DC trading strategies, which use our proposed indicator as part of their decision-making process. We experiment on 5 different foreign exchange currency pairs, for a total of 50 datasets. Our results show that the proposed algorithm is able to outperform its predecessor, as well as other well-known financial benchmarks, such as a technical analysis.

Keywords: Directional changes · Algorithmic trading · Financial forecasting · Genetic algorithms

1 Introduction

The majority of traditional methods to observe price fluctuations in financial time series are based on physical time changes, e.g., daily data summaries. However, important price movements (and thus potential profit) might be lost due to the creation of such artificial price summaries. For example, if we are using daily

© Springer International Publishing AG 2017
Y. Shi et al. (Eds.): SEAL 2017, LNCS 10593, pp. 727–738, 2017.
https://doi.org/10.1007/978-3-319-68759-9_59

prices, we would not be able to observe the 6 May 2010 Flash Crash, which was a US trillion-dollar stock market crash that lasted for approximately 36 min.[1]

Directional Changes (DC) is based on the idea that an event-based system can capture significant points in price movements that the traditional physical time methods cannot. Instead of looking the market from an interval-based perspective, DC record the key events in the market (e.g., changes in the stock price by a pre-specified percentage) and summarise the data based on these events. Under this new paradigm, a threshold θ is defined, expressed by a percentage of the price. The market is then fragmented and summarised into upward and downward trends.

As a result of DC summaries, new market regularities have been observed. One such regularity, is the observation regarding the duration of events. Such knowledge is beneficial to traders, because it can allow them to anticipate trend reversal and thus increase their profitability margin. In this work, we exploit this regularity, by building a new event-based indicator, which predicts the expected duration of DC events. We provide more information about this in Sect. 3. We use this indicator as part of a genetic algorithm based trading strategy. This strategy combines multiple DC thresholds, and uses the genetic algorithm to optimise the parameters of the above multi-threshold strategy. Our goal is to show that the proposed indicator, under the DC paradigm, can lead to profitable strategies that outperform popular financial benchmarks. We test our proposed algorithm on 50 different datasets from 5 different foreign exchange (FX) currency pairs, and compare its results to a technical analysis based trading strategy, and also buy and hold.

The rest of this paper is organised as follows: Sect. 2 presents related work in the field of directional changes, and Sect. 3 gives an overview of the concept of directional changes, and also presents the proposed event-based indicator. Section 4 then discusses how we used the genetic algorithm to generate trading strategies. Section 5 presents our experiments, and Sect. 6 concludes the paper and discusses future work.

2   Related Work

The first works to use the concept of directional changes were proposed in [7, 16]. In these works, new empirical scaling laws in foreign exchange data series were discovered. These scaling laws aimed to establish mathematical relationships among price moves, duration and frequency. Then, directional changes and the scaling laws from the above works were used to develop new trading models in [6]. However, those models were not used for any financial forecasting purposes and were only used to derive statistics from potential trading. Furthermore, [1] demonstrated the effectiveness of directional changes in capturing periodic market activities. In addition, [8] presented an approach to forecasting the daily closing price of financial markets by combing directional changes and genetic

---

[1] http://blogs.wsj.com/marketbeat/2010/05/11/nasdaq-heres-our-timeline-of-the-flash-crash/ Last access: 13 May 2017.

programming. The work in [17] introduced new trading indicators for profiling markets under directional changes. Lastly, [2,3,13] were the first works that presented extensive experiments on algorithmic trading by utilising the DC paradigm. As we can observe, initial works had been focusing on theoretical aspects of directional changes—e.g. establishing mathematical relationships and developing new indicators. More recently, there have been attempts to generate trading strategies based on the DC concept. The current paper builds on these attempts, and particularly on [13], by presenting a new event-based indicator that predicts the expected duration of an event and comparing its trading performance to its predecessor's. We also compare the trading results to popular financial benchmarks. More information about the new indicator follow in the next section. First, Sect. 3.1 presents an overview of the DC methodology. Then, Sect. 3.2 presents the new indicator.

3   Directional Changes

3.1   Overview

The directional change (DC) approach is an alternative approach for summarising market price movements. A DC event is identified by a change in the price of a given financial instrument. This change is defined by a threshold value, which was in advance decided by the trader. Such an event can be either an upturn or a downturn event. After the confirmation of a DC event, an overshoot (OS) event follows. This OS event finishes once an opposite DC event takes place.

Figure 1 presents an example of how a physical-time price curve is dissected into DC and OS events. As we can observe, two different thresholds are used, and each threshold generates a different event series. Thus, each threshold produces a unique series of events. The idea behind the different thresholds is that each trader might consider different thresholds (price percentage changes) as significant. A smaller threshold creates a higher number of directional changes, while a higher thresholds produces fewer directional changes.

Looking at the events generated by a threshold of $\theta = 0.01\%$ (events connected via solid lines), we can observe that any price change less than this threshold is not considered a trend. On the other hand, when the price changes above that threshold, then the market is divided accordingly, to uptrends and downtrends. DC events are in red lines, and OS events are in green lines. So an downturn DC event starts at Point A and lasts until Point B, when the downturn OS events starts. The downturn OS lasts until Point C, when there is a reverse in the trend, and an uptrend starts, which lasts until Point D. From Point D to E we are in an upturn OS event, and so on.

It is important to note that the change of a trend can only be confirmed retrospectively, i.e. only after the price has changed by the pre-specified threshold θ. For example, under $\theta = 0.01\%$ we can only confirm that we are in a upward trend from Point D onwards. Point D is thus called a *confirmation point*. Before Point D, the directional change had not been confirmed (i.e. the market price had not changed by the pre-specified threshold value), thus a trader summarising the

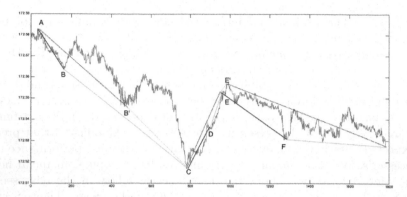

Fig. 1. Directional changes for tick data for the GBP/JPY currency pair. The solid lines denote a set of events defined by a threshold $\theta = 0.01\%$, while the dotted lines refer to events defined by a threshold $\theta = 0.018\%$. There red lines indicate the DC events, and the green lines indicate the OS events. (Color figure online)

data by the DC paradigm would continue believing we are in a downward trend, which started from Point A. So what becomes important here is to be able to anticipate the change of the trend as early as possible, i.e. before Points C and E have been reached. In addition, since different thresholds generate different event series, we hypothesise that the combined information from these series would lead to profitable trading strategies.

The advantage of this new way of summarising data is that it provides traders with new perspectives to price movements, and allows them to focus on those key points that an important event took place, blurring out other price details which could be considered irrelevant or even noise. Furthermore, DC have enabled researchers to discover new regularities in markets, which cannot be captured by the interval-based summaries [7]. Therefore, these new regularities give rise to new opportunities for traders, and also open a whole new area for research.

3.2 A New Event-Based Indicator

One of the most interesting regularities that was discovered in [7] was the observation that on average a DC takes t amount of physical time to complete, the OS event will last twice, i.e., $2t$. This observation *was only made under DC-based price summaries*, and not under phycical-time summaries.

The main advantage of the above observation is the fact that we can anticipate when trend is going to reverse, since we can expect when the OS event will end. However, this observation is only an approximation and it only applies to the specific currency pairs it was tested with, and only under the specific time periods it was tested. This thus makes it inflexible and rather static. We propose to have more tailored expected OS durations, by looking into each currency pair and time period separately. Therefore, we calculate the average time of each OS event for every period and dataset we experiment with. This makes this duration indicator more dynamic, as its duration estimates adapt to each dataset we experiment with. We create two variables, expressed as the average ratio of the OS event length over the DC event length. These two variables are r_u and r_d, where r_u is the average ratio of the upwards OS event, and r_d is the average ratio of the downwards OS event.

After obtaining these ratios, we are able to anticipate the end of a trend (approximately) and as a result make trading decisions once an OS event had reached the average ratio of r_u or r_d. Of course, in reality things are not that simple. The r_u and r_d ratios are just average approximations, so many times the OS event might last longer or shorter than anticipated. In an attempt to address this issue, we have created two user-specified parameters, namely b_1 and b_2, which define a range of time within the OS period, where trading is allowed. For instance, if a trader expects the OS event to last for 2 hours, then we can define an *action* range of $[b_1, b_2] = [0.90, 1.0]$, which effectively means we are going to trade at the last 10% of the 2 hours duration, i.e. in the last 12 min. By introducing b_1 and b_2, we are essentially attempting to anticipate the approximation errors that might have been created during the calculation of r_u and r_d. Equation 1 presents the formulas for these starting and ending for upward and downward OS periods:

$$
\begin{aligned}
t_0^U &= (t_1^{dc} - t_0^{dc}) \times r_u \times b_1 \\
t_1^U &= (t_1^{dc} - t_0^{dc}) \times r_u \times b_2 \\
t_0^D &= (t_1^{dc} - t_0^{dc}) \times r_d \times b_1 \\
t_1^D &= (t_1^{dc} - t_0^{dc}) \times r_d \times b_2
\end{aligned}
\tag{1}
$$

where t_0^U, t_1^U are the start and end times for upwards overshoot period, respectively, and t_0^D, t_1^D are the start and end times for downwards overshoot period, respectively. In addition, t_0^{dc} and t_1^{dc} are the start and the end times of the current DC event, after the confirmation of the event has taken place at time t_1^{dc}. Their difference $t_1^{dc} - t_0^{dc}$ returns the length of the current DC event. Also, r_u and r_d are the average ratios of the upwards and downwards OS period lengths, respectively, over the current DC period. Lastly, b_1 and b_2 are the two parameters defining the action range within the OS periods, as explained above.

Although b_1 and b_2 define a window for trading, a problem that exists with high-frequency data is that there can still be hundreds of points to trade, even if that trading window is very narrow. This could be problematic, because trading at multiple price levels will not return the highest profit. What is more effective is to sell (buy) at a price as expensive (cheap) as possible. To achieve this, we introduced another variable b_3, which prevents traders from doing expensive trades. To ensure this, we only allow the system to sell at the most expensive (peak) price P_{peak} and buy at the cheapest recorded price (trough) P_{trough}, or in prices in close range. This range is determined by the value of b_3. Therefore a trader would sell when the price is equal to $P_{peak} \times b_3$, or buy when the price is equal to $P_{trough} \times (1 - b_3)$. Essentially, b_3 is a value within the range of $[0, 1]$

and defines the range of prices close to P_{peak} and P_{tough} that the system will perform an action.

4   Generating GA-Based Directional Changes

4.1   Step 1: Creating a Multi-threshold DC Trading Strategy

As we discussed in Sect. 3, a DC event is identified by a change in the price by a given threshold value. The use of different DC thresholds provides a different view of the data: smaller thresholds allow the detection of more events and, as a result, actions can be taken promptly; larger thresholds detect fewer events, but provide the opportunity of taking actions when bigger price variations are observed. We will thus combine the use of different threshold values in an attempt to take advantage of the different characteristics of smaller and larger thresholds.

From the proposed duration indicator in the previous section, we know that under a specific threshold we should buy towards the end of a downtrend and sell towards the end of an uptrend (i.e. towards the end of the respective OS events). Since now we are dealing with multiple thresholds, each threshold summarises the data in a unique way. For example, at one point in time the trading strategy under one threshold could be recommending a buy action, while under a different threshold recommend a sell action.

In order to decide which recommendation to follow, we associate each DC threshold to an equal weight of $\frac{1}{N_\theta}$, where N_θ is the total number of thresholds used. Therefore, $W_1 = W_2 = W3 = ... = W_{N_\theta} = \frac{1}{N_\theta}$. As a result, at any point in time the trading strategy is able to make a buy/sell/hold recommendation based on the combined recommendations of all thresholds. As we already know, each threshold produces DC events; thus each threshold is able to make this buy/sell/hold recommendation. Since we have N_θ thresholds, this means that at any point in time we receive N_θ recommendations. In order to decide which recommendation to follow, we sum the weights of the thresholds: if the sum of the weights for all thresholds recommending a buy (sell) action is greater than the sum of the weights for all thresholds recommending a sell (buy) action, then the strategy's action will be to buy (sell). The hold action is a special case of both buy and sell and it happens when we are outside the price range recommended by b_3, or when there is not enough quantity to act.

In addition, the multi-threshold trading strategy is able to make recommendations on the trading quantity Q_{trade}. The decision for this quantity is a dynamic decision, taken by the number of DC thresholds that are advising to sell (buy) at a certain point in time: if many thresholds are advising to sell (buy), then the algorithm sells (buys) a higher quantity of the given currency pair. Equations 2a and 2b present the relevant formulas, for buy and sell, respectively:

$$Q_{trade} = (1 + \frac{N_\downarrow}{N_\theta}) \times Q \tag{2a}$$

$$Q_{trade} = (1 + \frac{N_\uparrow}{N_\theta}) \times Q \tag{2b}$$

where Q_{trade} is the quantity to trade, $N_\downarrow$ and $N_\uparrow$ are the number of thresholds recommending to buy and sell, respectively, N_θ is the total number of thresholds used in our experiments, and Q is a user-specified quantity, which is fixed through tuning and controls the trading quantity. As we can see, by taking into account the recommendations given by the DC thresholds, we are giving more or less weight to the Q quantity, resulting to a new quantity Q_{trade}. Lastly, it should be mentioned that our trading strategy allows short selling. However, in order to avoid excess short selling, which can lead to significant losses, we have introduced a stop loss mechanism that is called *short selling allowance*. This allowance is a percentage of our budget and allows short selling activities up to this pre-specified percentage. This percentage is decided during parameter tuning.

4.2 Step 2: Optimising Multi-threshold Strategies via a Genetic Algorithm

While the multi-threshold strategy presented above has the advantage of combining recommendations from different thresholds, a problem that exists is that we do not know how much weight we should give to each threshold and how to update them in time. Some thresholds might be more useful than others, hence we should give them more weight. Thus, we use a genetic algorithm (GA) to evolve *real values* for the weight of each DC threshold. In addition, we also evolve some other DC parameters that are crucial to the success of the trading strategy. All these are discussed next, where the GA representation, operators and fitness function are presented.

Representation. Each chromosome consists of $4 + N_\theta$ genes, where N_θ is the number of different threshold values of the multi-threshold strategy. The number 4 denotes that in addition to the thresholds, there are also 4 parameters to be optimised: Q (first gene), b_1 (second gene), b_2 (third gene), and b_3 (fourth gene). Q, b_1, b_2 and b_3 refer to the DC-related parameters presented in Sects. 3.2 and 4.1. A reminder that b_1 and b_2 are directly linked to the proposed duration indicator, as they control our expectations about trend reversal and the specific time period we should act. Each remaining gene in the chromosome (positions 5 to $[4 + N_\theta]$) represents the weight associated to a given threshold.

As a result, at any point in time a GA individual is able to make a buy/sell/hold recommendation based on the combined recommendations of all thresholds by using the majority vote mechanism we presented in the previous section. An example of an 8-gene GA chromosome is presented in Fig. 2.

Based on this example, the GA recommends buying/selling a quantity of Q equal to 10, and only acting in the period $[0.9, 1.0]$ of the estimated duration of the OS event (i.e., in the last 10% of the length of the OS event). In addition, the fourth gene recommends to only consider prices that are within a 20% range (the value of b_3 is 0.8, so $1.0 - 0.8 = 0.20$ or 20%) of the highest (lowest) recorded price P_{peak} (P_{trough}). In addition, to decide the trading action, we would check the recommendation of each individual threshold. For this example, let us assume

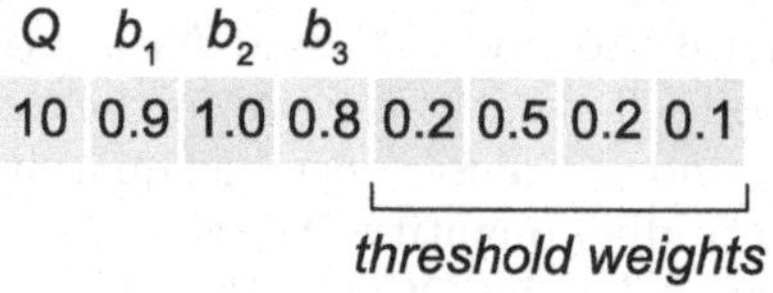

$$Q \quad b_1 \quad b_2 \quad b_3$$

10 0.9 1.0 0.8 0.2 0.5 0.2 0.1

threshold weights

Fig. 2. An example of a 8-gene GA chromosome. The first four genes are: Q, b_1, b_2 and b_3, respectively. The remaining four genes are the weights for the DC thresholds: W_1, W_2, W_3, and W_4.

that the first threshold recommends buy, the second threshold recommends sell, the third threshold recommends buy, and the fourth threshold recommends hold. We would then sum up the weights of the thresholds, according to each action. Therefore, the weight for buying W_B is equal to $W_1 + W_3 = 0.2 + 0.2 = 0.4$, and the weight for selling W_S is equal to $W_2 = 0.5$.[2] Since $W_S > W_B$, the GA's recommendation would be to sell.

Operators. We are using elitism, uniform crossover and uniform mutation.

In elitism, the best-performing individual (in terms of fitness) is copied to the next generation. In uniform crossover, two parents are selected via a tournament selection. In this type of crossover, the genes between the two parents are swapped with a fixed probability of 0.5. In addition, we ensure that the value of the third gene is always greater than the value of the second gene, i.e. b_2 always has to be greater than b_1. Lastly, for the uniform mutation operator a single parent is selected, again by tournament selection. With a probability of 0.5, each gene of the chromosome is mutated, and a different value is obtained. It should be clarified here that for the first gene (quantity Q), the mutated value can be any integer up to a pre-specified maximum quantity value; whereas for the remaining genes (i.e., b_1, b_2, b_3 and all weights W), the mutated values are real numbers randomly drawn between 0 and 1, where $b_2 > b_1$.

Fitness Function. Several different metrics have been used in the literature as fitness function in algorithmic trading. Some examples are: wealth, profit, return, Sharpe ratio, information ratio [4,5]. In this paper, we set our fitness equal to the total return minus the maximum drawdown, presented in Eq. 3:

$$ff = Return - \alpha \times MDD$$
$$MDD = \frac{P_{trough} - P_{peak}}{P_{peak}}, \tag{3}$$

where $Return$ is the return of the investment, MDD is the maximum drawdown, and α is a tuning parameter. Maximum drawdown is defined as the maximum cumulative loss since commencing trading with the system. It is used to penalise

---

[2] As explained earlier, the hold action is an exceptional case that is considered as an alternative to buy and sell actions.

volatile trading strategies in terms of return. Its value is given as the percentage of $\frac{P_{trough}-P_{peak}}{P_{peak}}$, where P_{trough} the trough value of the price, and P_{peak} is the peak value of the price. Lastly, the tuning parameter α is used to define how much risk-averse the strategy is. The more risk-averse in terms of wishing to avoid a catastrophic loss, the higher the value of α.

5   Experiments

We use 10-min interval high frequency data for the following currency pairs[3]: EUR/GBP, EUR/USD, EUR/JPY, GBP/CHF, and GBP/USD. The period is June 2013 to May 2014. Every month is split into its own dataset, with the first 70% of the data being the training set, and the remaining 30% being the testing set. We should also note that r_u and r_d (ratios for OS over DC duration) are only calculated for the training period during pre-processing; the resulted values are then used during the evolution of the GA individuals.

Our goal is to demonstrate that the proposed duration indicator, under the GA-optimised multi-threshold DC paradigm, can lead to profitable trading strategies that can also outperform popular financial benchmarks. We will be presenting experimental results for two variations of the DC strategy. The first will be using the static duration indicator [7], which assumes that the OS length is on average twice as long as the DC length. We denote this as $DC+GA_S$. The second DC algorithm will be using the new dynamic indicator, which uses tailored OS lengths for each dataset, denoted as $DC + GA_D$. We will also be presenting results from two common financial benchmarks: buy and hold (BH), and technical analysis. For the latter, there are numerous indicators that one can use. We use a genetic programming [14] algorithm, named EDDIE, to combine different indicators and formulate trading strategies [9–12]. This algorithm has shown in all of the above works its ability to generate profitable strategies.

5.1   Experimental Parameters

We used the I/F-Race package [15] for parameter tuning. I/F-Race automatically configures optimisation algorithms by finding the most appropriate settings, given a set of instances of an optimisation problem. It should be noted that BH is a simple process with no parameters that require tuning.

In order to avoid biased results, we used the first two months of our data (June and July 2013) for each currency pair for tuning purposes. Thus, I/F-Race was applied to the data of June and July 2013. The remaining ten months (August 2013–May 2014) were used only with the tuned parameters, after I/F-Race was complete. At the end of the tuning process, we picked the best parameters returned by I/F-Race. These parameters constitute the experimental parameters for our algorithms. These parameters are presented in Table 1. The buy and hold setup did not have any parameters, so it is not present in Table 1.

---

[3] All data was purchased by OlsenData: http://www.olsendata.com.

Table 1. Experimental parameters determined using I/F-Race.

Parameter	EDDIE	$DC + GA_S/DC + GA_D$
Population	500	1000
Generations	30	35
Tournament size	2	7
Crossover probability	0.90	0.90
Mutation probability	0.10	0.10
Number of thresholds	N/A	5
Short selling allowance	0.25	0.25
MDD weight	0.20	0.20

5.2   Results

Table 2 presents the mean return for EDDIE, $DC + GA_S$ and $DC + GA_D$ under the 10-min interval datasets, over 50 individual runs. We should also note that BH's average return was 0.01274%. The first observation we can make is that the DC paradigm outperforms technical analysis, as all best mean returns (boldface) come from either $DC + GA_S$ or $DC + GA_D$. EDDIE has a negative mean return of -0.00873%; it is also worth noting that for all five currency pairs EDDIE's mean return is negative. On the other hand, $DC + GA_S$ has a positive return for three currency pairs: EUR/GBP, EUR/USD, and GBP/CHF. However, overall, $DC + GA_S$'s mean return is negative: -0.00930%. This mainly because of the algorithm's very bad performance for the EUR/JPY currency pair. With respect to $DC + GA_D$, there's again 3 currency pairs with positive average returns (EUR/GBP, EUR/JPY, GBP/USD), and 2 pairs with negative average returns (EUR/USD, GBP/CHF). But these negative returns are minimal and thus, the mean return for all 5 currency pair is positive, at 0.01046. In addition, by looking into the standard deviation values, which are also presented in Table 2 inside the brackets, we can observe that $DC + GA_D$ has the lowest average standard deviation, making it the least volatile algorithm.

To further investigate the algorithms' performance, we applied Friedman's non-parametric statistical test to compare multiple algorithms. We present the results in Table 3. For each algorithm, the table shows the average rank according to the Friedman test (first column) over the 50 datasets, and the adjusted p-value of the statistical test, when that algorithm's average rank is compared to the average rank of the algorithm with the best rank (control algorithm) according to the Hommel post-hoc test (second column). The ranks presented in the table confirm that $DC + GA_D$ has the best overall performance, with a rank of 1.40. $DC + GA_S$ ranks second, and EDDIE ranks third. However, as we can observe from the p-value Friedman test (0.1250), the test was close to reject the null hypothesis at the 10% significance level; however, the p-value was slightly higher, which means that the differences in the ranks are not statistically significant. Nevertheless, the fact remains that $DC + GA_D$ was ranked first across the majority of the tests. More importantly, $DC + GA_D$ had a positive mean return

Table 2. Mean return results for EDDIE, $DC + GA_S$ and $DC + GA_D$. 10-min interval data. BH's average return (not included in the table) was 0.01274%. Results shown in % values. Best return value per currency pair is shown in bold. Standard deviation is presented inside the brackets.

	EDDIE	$DC + GA_S$	$DC + GA_D$
EUR/GBP	−0.00141 (0.007)	**0.00341** (0.008)	0.00063 (0.004)
EUR/JPY	−0.01644 (0.357)	−0.07723 (0.055)	**0.05387** (0.210)
EUR/USD	−0.00840 (0.018)	**0.02455** (0.276)	−0.00125 (0.009)
GBP/CHF	−0.01114 (0.015)	**0.00903** (0.027)	−0.00388 (0.014)
GBP/USD	−0.00628 (0.011)	−0.00580 (0.018)	**0.00293** (0.025)
Mean	−0.00873 (0.082)	−0.00930 (0.077)	**0.01046** (0.053)

Table 3. Statistical test results according to the non-parametric Friedman test with the Hommel's post-hoc test. 10-min interval data.

Friedman p-value	0.1250	
Algorithm	Average rank	Adjusted p_{Homm}
$DC + GA_D$ (c)	1.40	-
$DC + GA_S$	2.10	0.26838
EDDIE	2.50	0.16398

over the 50 datasets it was tested, while both of the other two algorithms had a negative mean return. This thus makes $DC + GA_D$ a much more attractive algorithm and also a promising algorithm for future experimentation. To sum up, our results demonstrate two things: (i) the DC paradigm can be a profitable one when tuned appropriately, and (ii) our proposed method of having tailored OS length estimates improves the mean return results of the trading algorithm.

6   Conclusion

To conclude, this paper presented a new tailored event-based indicator, which was used within the context of directional changes. DC is a new way of summarising physical-time data. After creating different summaries, based on different DC thresholds, we used a genetic algorithm to optimise their recommendations. Our experiments, over 50 datasets from 5 different FX currency pairs showed that our approach was able to yield positive returns in the majority of datasets tested, and outperformed both its predecessor, and also a technical analysis based trading algorithm. It also performed similarly to buy and hold.

We believe that this is a very positive result and that more research should go towards this direction. For example, it would be interesting to use a genetic programming algorithm for symbolic regression, to produce new equations describing the relationship of the length of DC and OS events. Also, we plan to test our algorithm with more datasets for generalisation purposes.

References

1. Aloud, M., Tsang, E., Olsen, R., Dupuis, A.: A directional-change events approach for studying financial time series. Economics Discussion Paper No. 2011-28 (2011). doi:10.2139/ssrn.1973471
2. Bakhach, A., Tsang, E., Ng, W.L., Chinthalapati, V.L.R.: Backlash agent: a trading strategy based on directional change. In: 2016 IEEE Symposium Series on Computational Intelligence (SSCI) (2016)
3. Bakhach, A., Tsang, E.P.K., Jalalian, H.: Forecasting directional changes in the FX markets. In: 2016 IEEE Symposium Series on Computational Intelligence (SSCI) (2016)
4. Brabazon, A., O'Neill, M.: Biologically Inspired Algorithms for Financial Modelling. Springer, Heidelberg (2006). doi:10.1007/3-540-31307-9
5. Bradley, R., Brabazon, A., O'Neill, M.: Dynamic high frequency trading: a neuro-evolutionary approach. In: Giacobini, M., et al. (eds.) EvoWorkshops 2009. LNCS, vol. 5484, pp. 233–242. Springer, Heidelberg (2009). doi:10.1007/978-3-642-01129-0_27
6. Dupuis, A., Olsen, R.: High frequency finance: using scaling laws to build trading models. In: James, J. (ed.) Handbook of Exchange Rates. Wiley, Hoboken (2012). (Chapter 20)
7. Glattfelder, J., Dupuis, A., Olsen, R.: Patterns in high-frequency FX data: discovery of 12 empirical scaling laws. Quant. Finan. **11**(4), 599–614 (2011)
8. Gypteau, J., Otero, F.E.B., Kampouridis, M.: Generating directional change based trading strategies with genetic programming. In: Mora, A.M., Squillero, G. (eds.) EvoApplications 2015. LNCS, vol. 9028, pp. 267–278. Springer, Cham (2015). doi:10.1007/978-3-319-16549-3_22
9. Kampouridis, M., Alsheddy, A., Tsang, E.: On the investigation of hyper-heuristics on a financial forecasting problem. Ann. Math. Artif. Intell. **68**(4), 225–246 (2013)
10. Kampouridis, M., Tsang, E.: EDDIE for investment opportunities forecasting: extending the search space of the GP. In: Proceedings of the IEEE World Congress on Computational Intelligence, Barcelona, Spain, pp. 2019–2026 (2010)
11. Kampouridis, M., Tsang, E.: Investment opportunities forecasting: extending the grammar of a GP-based tool. Int. J. Comput. Intell. Syst. **5**(3), 530–541 (2012)
12. Kampouridis, M., Otero, F.E.B.: Heuristic procedures for improving the predictability of a genetic programming financial forecasting algorithm. Soft. Comput. **21**, 1–16 (2015)
13. Kampouridis, M., Otero, F.E.B.: Evolving trading strategies using directional changes. Expert Syst. Appl. **73**, 145–160 (2017)
14. Koza, J.: Genetic Programming: On the Programming of Computers by Means of Natural Selection. MIT Press, Cambridge (1992)
15. Lopez-Ibanez, M., Dubois-Lacoste, J., Stutzle, T., Birattari, M.: The irace package, iterated race for automatic algorithm configuration. Technical report TR/IRIDIA/2011-004, IRIDIA, Université Libre de Bruxelles, Belgium (2011)
16. Olsen, R.B., Muller, U.A., Dacorogna, M.M., Pictet, O.V., Dave, R.R., Guillaume, D.M.: From the bird's eye to the microscope: a survey of new stylized facts of the intra-day foreign exchange markets. Finan. Stochast. **1**(2), 95–129 (1997)
17. Tsang, E., Tao, R., Serguieva, A., Ma, S.: Profiling high-frequency equity price movements in directional changes. Quant. Finan. **17**(2), 217–225 (2016)

Constrained Differential Evolution for Cost and Energy Efficiency Optimization in 5G Wireless Networks

Rawaa Dawoud AL-Dabbagh[✉] and Ahmed Jasim Jabur

University of Baghdad, Baghdad, Iraq
rawaa.dabbagh@ieee.org, ahmedcoomdr@gmail.com

Abstract. The majority of real-world problems involve not only finding the optimal solution, but also this solution must satisfy one or more constraints. Differential evolution (DE) algorithm with constraints handling has been proposed to solve one of the most fundamental problems in cellular network design. This proposed method has been applied to solve the radio network planning (RNP) in the forthcoming 5G Long Term Evolution (5G LTE) wireless cellular network, that satisfies both deployment cost and energy savings by reducing the number of deployed micro base stations (BSs) in an area of interest. Practically, this has been implemented using constrained strategy that must guarantee good coverage for the users as well. Three differential evolution variants have been adopted to solve the 5G RNP problem. Experimental results have shown that the constrained DE/best/1/bin has achieved best results over other variants in terms of deployment cost, coverage rate and quality of service (QoS).

Keywords: Evolutionary algorithms · Green network · Power consumption

1 Introduction

In the common practice, wireless cellular network administrators contribute enormous totals of capital on keeping up their systems in a request to guarantee aggressive execution and high client fulfillment. Radio network planning (RNP) is one fundamental challenge for administrators to send remote cell organizes in a cost and coverage effective way. Dealing with RNP begins generally with a set of input parameters including the area to be covered, the estimated traffic load, base station configurations (antenna patterns and transmit power capabilities), path loss models, and frequency reuse patterns. The output of RNP would be, generally, the system configuration, including the number and locations of base stations (BSs) over the region to be served [1, 2].

Recently, there is a significant increase in attention towards the development of cellular networks generations and their related issues. For example, the current 3G and 4G communication advancements were acquainted to satisfy the huge interest of improving the speed of data traffic [3]. In spite of the fact that the present interchanges innovation has advanced astonishingly in the current 4G/IMT, it is as yet confronting the expanding requests because of the improvement of smart devices; as such, different serious reviews towards 5G networks are being created [4, 5]. Much emphasis on research focuses on cellular networks has been placed latterly. This research has mainly

© Springer International Publishing AG 2017
Y. Shi et al. (Eds.): SEAL 2017, LNCS 10593, pp. 739–750, 2017.
https://doi.org/10.1007/978-3-319-68759-9_60

focused on the different approaches that can be utilized in the deployment of possible number of BSs, as this issue essentially affects the quality of service (QoS), deployment cost, and power consumption. For example, in [6], the authors proposed an enhancement to their earlier models to a more advanced one using Tabu search method and based on the signal-to-interference ratio (SIR) as evaluation measure for the UMTS (Universal Mobile Telecommunication System) BSs location problem. Artificial bee colony has been applied to minimize interference among BSs and optimize energy consumption in the WiMAX (Worldwide Interoperability for Microwave Access) network [7]. An attempt to solve the RNP problem in the context of 5G is presented in [2, 8]; where heuristic algorithms have been applied to optimize the locations of fixed BSs in a simulated geographical area. These algorithms have successfully achieved both objectives in providing good QoS and outage percentage, as well as reducing power consumption. Another study on the use of evolutionary algorithms (EAs) in the planning of wireless networks is presented in [9]. In this study a modified genetic algorithm (GA) is suggested to optimize the configuration of BSs locations which offers a good coverage based on minimizing the transmitted power.

In conclusion, one very hectic issue among all various problems of 5G networks is the deployment of BSs. As this problem has many related issues that might appear while finding an appropriate BSs configuration, for example, types of BSs, deployment cost, QoS, transmitted power and received power of every mobile station (MS). The complexity of this problem increases dramatically as the number and types of BSs increase. Also, in contrast with existing cellular networks, the real amendment that is demanded in the 5G development presents huge difficulties to the RNP, such as expanding interest to speed data rates and spurred bandwidths. In addition, the millimeter wave groups guarantee a gigantic measure of unlicensed range at 28 GHz and 38 GHz, and are probable frequency bands for 5G cellular systems [4].

The main contribution in this work is to apply and test multiple variants of constrained differential evolution (DE) algorithms to solve RNP problem in the 5G wireless networks. These strategies are performed in terms of reducing cost, power consumption, jointly with maintaining coverage ratio for every MS. This is an attempt to provide a good QoS for many users in several dense areas, called urban areas by using least number of BSs and least outage coverage ratio by locating BSs to their optimal or near optimal places using the new features available in the 5G networks.

This paper is organized as follows: in Sect. 2, the adopted system model in the context of 5G networks is introduced. The implementation of constrained DE algorithms for optimizing the cost and coverage of BSs is presented in Sect. 3. The results and analyses of the 5G RNP are presented and discussed in Sect. 4.

2   5G System Model

In this section, we adopted the 5G system model presented in [2, 10]. As this model is the most common one in many related studies. This model includes a given collection of candidate BSs β which is composed of $\beta macro$ macros and $\beta micro$ micros BSs. Macro and micro BSs may live together within the same geographical area and are deployed in the planning process. Macro BSs have transmission power higher than that of a micro BS and thus will cover bigger regions. In this study, we consider orthogonal frequency division multiple access (OFDMA) as an accessing scheme. Take note of that, the 5G networks accessing scheme is not realized yet, however, the utilization of OFDMA is helpful for evaluation assessment and for comparison with 4G systems. Assuming that there are K_{sub} subcarriers accessible for downlink transmission and a predefined number of users distributed uniformly in an area of interest. However, our framework model is adaptable and can take in any future unified access schemes for the next cellular generation. In addition, the model used to represent the users distributed in the geographical area is a snapshot model. Snapshot means the use of physical channel by a set of users at a given instant of time. Our aim is to find the minimum number of BSs that still guarantee minimum cost, coverage and capacity requirements based on their locations in the proposed area. The downlink signal to interference and noise ratio (SINR) over a given subcarrier k assigned to user u is,

$$SINR_u = \frac{P_{u,bs(u)}}{\sigma^2 + I_u},$$ (1)

where $P_{u,bs(u)}$ is the received power for user u on subcarrier k by its serving BS $bs(u)$, σ^2 is the thermal noise power, and I_U is the intercell interference from neighboring BSs. Equation 2 represents the power received by MS u from BS i.

$$P_{u,i}(dB) = 10\,log_{10}\left(\frac{P_{BS}}{K_{BS}}\right) - L_{u,i},$$ (2)

where P_{BS} is the amount of power in Watt served by BS i. K_{BS} is the maximum number of connected users to this BS. Both values are fixed and they depend on the type of BS in use. $L_{u,i}$ is the model of path loss between BS i and MS u and is formulated as

$$L_{u,i}(dB) = 92.4 + 20\,log_{10}\left(d_{u,i}\right) + 20\,log_{10}(f) + \varphi + h_{u,i},$$ (3)

where $d_{u,i}$ is the Euclidean distance between Cartesian coordinates of BS i (x_i, y_i) and MS u (w_u, z_u) as

$$d_{u,i} = \sqrt{(x_i - w_u)^2 + (y_i - z_u)^2}$$ (4)

The carrier frequency f in this work is set to 28 GHz. φ is the atmospheric attenuation which is almost ignored in 28 GHz. In this work, φ is set to 0.06 db/Km [11]. $h_{u,i}$ is the channel loss between BS i and MS u, such as shadowing and fading. Since the OFDMA is considered in this system, the subcarriers are assumed to be orthogonal per cell; as such, the interference I_u in Eq. 1 depends only on the intercell interference. This term represents the interference received power at MS u from neighboring BSs i as

$$I_u = \sum\nolimits_{i=1, i\neq bs(u)}^{N_B} c_i P_{u,i},$$ (5)

where c_i is a flag either 1 or 0 to indicate whether BS i is active or not. N_B is the number of neighboring BSs. Finally, as good quality signal to be received at MS u, the downlink SINR needs to satisfy the condition of the expression,

$$SINR_u \geq SINR_{thr} \tag{6}$$

3 Differential Evolution for Cost and Energy Savings

Differential evolution (DE) is a very competitive EAs approach. It has drawn the attention of many researches all over the globe due to its efficient performance over other EA variants [12]. For many years, it has proved to produce superior results when it applies to many fields such as engineering problems [13, 14]. For this reason, DE and its multiple variants has been considered as method of choice in this work. In this section, we will handle the problem formulation of the system in hand. Then, a proposed system using DE algorithm is suggested to tackle this problem.

3.1 Problem Formulation

Generally speaking, radio network planning (RNP) is considered very hard to solve because the complexity of this problem increases exponentially with the problem dimension. Formally speaking, it is considered as NP-hard problem. In the current system, RNP is associated with many constraints related to the 5G wireless network. These constraints increase the problem complexity as many solutions are considered infeasible solutions and the proposed system must have the ability to exclude these solutions during the searching process. Some recent researches have been done trying to handle RNP using heuristic approaches [2, 8]. These researches have tried to simplify the problem by performing RNP on fixed BSs locations. The task of the planner (heuristic approach) is to switch off/on BSs according to the traffic load, i.e. no deployment of new BSs has been considered. Its main idea is to reduce the number of BSs by one each time the system configuration is evaluated. Then, according to the evaluation results (outage ratio) the plan is considered feasible or infeasible.

Before we provide the problem's list of constrains, we must first determine the input and output parameters of the 5G RNP wireless network. As input parameters: a geographical area to be covered, varying traffic load (number of users distributed in the area of interest), and a pre-defined number of BSs (**macro cells**) located in a fixed locations. These BSs are considered exist from the 3G/4G prior deployment that must be taken into account because we are trying to simulate a real environment. The output of the system (system objective Φ) is to find the minimum number of BSs (**micro cells**) and their candidate locations that could be deployed in the area of interest and still satisfying the QoS requirements as

$$\Phi = min \sum_{i=1}^{N_{micro}} c_i \tag{7}$$

where c_i is a flag in which its value is either 0 if the BS is inactive and 1 otherwise. As follows, the list of constrains that must be considered when dealing with 5G RNP.

(1) Received Power of MS (P_{MS}): each cellular device should have a received power signal $P_{MS} \geq P_{thr}$; otherwise, this MS is considered not connected.
(2) Signal-to-interference-noise ratio of MS ($SINR_{MS}$): each cellular device should satisfy $SINR_{MS} \geq SINR_{thr}$. This constraint determines the QoS for a given MS.
(3) Outage percentage of the system configuration ($outp$): this parameter determines the percentage of users out of coverage; therefore, the outage target should be $\leq \rho$.
(4) Number of connected MSs per one BS (U_{bs}): each BS serves a pre-defined number of MS $U_{bs} \leq U_{BSMacro}$ or $U_{bs} \leq U_{BSMicro}$ depending on the type of BS.
(5) Each MS_i can be served by BS_j if and only if this BS_j is active.

Finally, a MS is considered served by a given BS if the power it receives from this BS is the maximum power among all neighboring BSs and within the P_{thr}.

3.2 Constrained DE as a Proposed Solution

The main idea of DE is it starts with an arbitrarily initial population of size Np of R^D space. The result of DE is the best individual achieved after $MAXG$ generations. Each parameter in the individual has certain range generated by the recommended least and most extreme parameters' limits: $\vec{X}_{min}$ and $\vec{X}_{max}$. Hence, we may initialize the components of each vector using the expression,

$$x_{i,j,0} = x_{j,min} + rand_{i,j}[0, 1] \cdot (x_{j,max} - x_{j,min}), \tag{8}$$

where $rand_{i,j}[0, 1]$ is a uniformly distributed random number generator. Then, DE enters a loop of evolutionary operations: mutation, crossover, and selection.

Problem Representation and Initialization. The problem representation or the individual representation should describe the plan that will be deployed on the area of interest. Based on our objective which is to minimize the number of deployed BSs and also to find the optimal BSs locations that will satisfy the coverage requirements, the individual representation is depicted in Fig. 1. From this figure, it can be seen that the main parts of the problem is to determine the appropriate locations (Cartesian coordinates) of the deployed BSs. Then, to minimize the cost by deactivating the flag parameter ($c_i = 0$) of the BSs that do not have significant effect on the outage target probability. This can be achieved by creating a counter for each BS that counts the number of connected users to this BS. If $count_{bsi} < count_{thr}$ then $c_i = 0$; otherwise, $c_i = 1$. For the initialization process, the same Eq. 8 can be used to initialize randomly the coordinates of the micro cells with respect to the pre-specified two-dimensional map. For initializing the flags values, a mapping technique has been adopted. Equation 8 is used to generate uniformly random numbers between 0 and 1. If the random number ≥ 0.5 then 1 is assigned to the flag; otherwise, it assigned to 0. This procedure is implemented for the micro cells only. Finally, the total number of genes (BSs) in one individual is $N_{BS} = N_{micro} + N_{Macro}$.

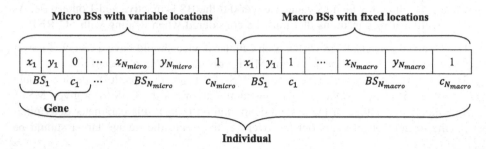

Fig. 1. DE individual representation for RNP problem

Modified Mutation and Crossover Operations. In this study, three DE variants (DE/rand/1/bin, DE/current-to-best/1/bin, and DE/best/1/bin) have been proposed to handle the 5G RNP, as in Eqs. 9, 10 and 11, respectively.

$$v_{i,g} = x_{r_1,g} + F \cdot \left(x_{r_2,g} - x_{r_3,g} \right), \tag{9}$$

where r_1, r_2 and r_3 are mutually different indices, randomly chosen from the range $[1, NP]$, and they are different from the base index i. The scale factor F is often set to 0.5. The new individual $v_{i,g}$ is called the donor vector.

$$v_{i,g} = x_{best,g} + F \cdot \left(x_{r_1,g} - x_{r_2,g} \right), \tag{10}$$

$$v_{i,g} = x_{i,g} + F \cdot \left(x_{best,g} - x_{r_1,g} \right) + F \cdot \left(x_{r_2,g} - x_{r_3,g} \right), \tag{11}$$

where $x_{best,g}$ is the best individual in the current generation. The general framework of these DE variants has been modified based on the problem requirements. The standard procedure of the mutation is to modify the individual gene by gene if these genes represent one parameter only. In the 5G RNP problem and as already depicted in Fig. 1, each gene represents three parameters. Each parameter has its own limits: the first parameter represents the x-axis, the second parameter represents the y-axis, and the third parameter is the flag c. From Fig. 1, it can be observed that c value for the micro cell can be changed either to 0 or 1 during the run depending on the configuration constraints; whereas, the c value of the macro cell is always 1 because these cells are considered active from the previous deployment of the 3G/4G network. This applies to the macro cell coordinates too. The macro cells information will not undergo mutation operation. As a result, the mutation is implemented on the parameters indexed from 1 to $3 \times N_{micro}$.

   After mutation operation, a binomial crossover (bin) operation forms the final trial vector $u_{i,g}$ using the formula

$$u_{i,j,g} = \begin{cases} v_{i,j,g}, & \text{if } rand_{i,j}(0,1) \leq CR \quad \text{or} \quad j = j_{rand} \\ x_{i,j,g} & \text{otherwise} \end{cases}, \tag{12}$$

where $rand_{i,j}(0,1)$ is a uniformly distributed random number. CR is the crossover rate and it is usually set to 0.8. $j_{rand} \in [1, 2, \ldots, D]$ is a randomly chosen index, which ensures that $u_{i,G}$ gets at least one component from $v_{i,G}$. In 5G RNP system, the gene's index is considered and not the parameter's index as in the mutation operation. This process should carefully be implemented if we want to extract the 3-parameters gene from the target individual or the donor individual according to Eq. 12 to produce the trial individual. The same what has already been implemented in the mutation process the macro cells will not undergo the crossover operation. As a result, the crossover operation will be implemented on the genes indexed from 1 to N_{micro}.

Evaluation and Constrained Selection. Each individual is evaluated using Eq. 7. This equation represents the main objective of this work. Its main idea is that the minimum number of BSs is deployed, the least cost of deployment it takes. However, this objective is subject to many constraints as listed in the problem formulation sub-section. After the evaluation process the selection operation is performed as

$$X_{i,g+1} = \begin{cases} U_{i,g} & \text{if } f(U_{i,g}) \leq f(X_{i,g}) \\ X_{i,g} & \text{if } f(X_{i,g}) < f(U_{i,g}) \end{cases}, \tag{13}$$

where $f(X)$ is the objective function to be minimized. This equation will determine which individual is going to survive based on the objective function and its associated constraints. The main reason of using constraints is to classify the solutions to feasible and infeasible. The solution that satisfies all constraints is called feasible, and the solution that violates any constraints is called infeasible regardless of its fitness value. In simple terms, Lampinen in [15] has suggested a direct constraints handling method or feasibility rules with DE. This method is considered very popular among other methods of constraints handling because of its simple and effective implementation. In this work, this method has been applied to the 5G RNP problem, more specifically; it has been added to the selection part.

Before we start to describe the constrained selection operation, we must define the main constraint of this problem. Achieving good coverage is another critical issue in the RNP process. This must be considered besides minimizing the deployment cost. Equation 14 expresses how to calculate the outage rate of a candidate plan.

$$outp\% = \frac{no.\ of\ unconnected\ users\ (P_{MS} \leq P_{thr})}{total\ no.\ of\ users\ in\ AoI} \times 100 \leq \rho \tag{14}$$

The cost function in Eq. 7 jointly with these outage value in Eq. 14 constitutes the proposed constrained handling system. The proposed mechanism consists of three selection criteria (see Eq. 15 which is a modified version of Eq. 13), as follows.

$$
X_{g+1} = \begin{cases} U_g & \begin{cases} \Phi(U_g) \leq \Phi(X_g) & if \quad outp(U_g), outp(X_g) \leq \rho \\ \Phi(U_g) & if \quad outp(U_g) \leq \rho \\ outp(U_g) \leq outp(X_g) & otherwise \end{cases} \\ X_g & \begin{cases} \Phi(X_g) < \Phi(U_g) & if \quad outp(U_g), outp(X_g) \leq \rho \\ \Phi(X_g) & if \quad outp(X_g) \leq \rho \\ outp(X_g) < outp(U_g) & otherwise \end{cases} \end{cases} \tag{15}
$$

From Eq. 15, it can be seen that when two feasible solutions (i.e. their outage rate are within the threshold) are compared, the individual with the best cost function is selected. When infeasible solution is compared with feasible solution, the feasible solution is selected regardless of its cost function value. If the two individuals are both infeasible, the individual with the lowest outage is selected.

Algorithm 1 depicts the main steps of applying constrained DE to the 5G RNP problem. In this algorithm, the DE/rand/1/bin has been selected to depict the main steps of the complete RNP process.

4 Experimental Results and Discussion

Results are generated for an area of 2.5 km × 2.5 km with different scenarios. Firstly, we assume that there are 4 macro BSs already exist from the current 4G/IMT Advanced standards, and micro BSs are uniformly distributed in the area upon implementing DE algorithm. Our aim is to minimize and optimize the number and locations of the initially deployed micro BSs to give a service to many users taking into consideration outage probability constraints, as well as SINR as a quality of service. Variants of constrained DE have been applied to allocate the micro BSs efficiently in the simulated area. The simulation parameters of the 5G RNP problem are shown in Table 1. Other parameters related to the problem are considered variable depending on the adopted scenario, i.e. number of users distributed in the area of interest. Table 2 lists the decision variables related to DE such as population size, control variables (F,CR) and individual length D ($N_{micro} + N_{macro}$) which reflects the plan to be deployed or the initially deployed micro BSs. The testing analysis was conducted on a PC with Intel Core 2 Duo 2.10 GHz and 2 GB of memory running Microsoft Windows 8. The simulation results are performed by using MATLAB (R2013a).

Starting with network scenario 1 which is an area of interest constitutes 35 randomly initially located micro BSs and 250 uniformly distributed users. Results show that the number of micro BSs is minimized by applying constrained DE algorithm reaching 18 micro BSs from 35 initially deployed as shown in Table 3, with DE/current-best/1 outperforms other DE variants. In scenario 2, the number of users has been increased to 350 uniformly distributed with the same initialized number of micro cells. As can be seen from Table 3, additional micro BSs are deployed to satisfy the capacity requirement. This has made the number of BSs increases to 19 micro cells with DE/best/1 outperforms other variants. In scenario 4, the problem has become more challenging as the number of users is increased to 400 MSs. From Table 3, we can observe that it is the same DE strategy which is DE/best/1/bin that gains the best performance so far. It has reduced the number of deployed micro BSs from 35 to 20 with good coverage percentage. In the last scenario, where the number of uniformly distributed users reaches 500 the DE/current-to-best/1 could manage to produce the best results in both number of deployed BSs and coverage percentage. Though, DE/best/1 also has comparable results.

Figure 2 shows the results of the 4 scenarios through visualizing the Cartesian coordinates of the deployed macro and micro cells. The coverage range of each cell has been depicted using circle. The radius of this circle represents the estimated distance in meter of the power received by each MS within this range.

Algorithm 1 Constrained DE/rand/1/bin algorithm for 5G RNP problem

---

1: **Input:** Set DE initial parameters, individual length D or number of BSs N_B, population size NP, crossover rate CR, mutation rate F, upper and lower boundaries for each problem parameter, no. of generations $MAXG$, and no. of macro cells N_{macro}.

2: Generate a uniformly distributed random population of size $NP(X_g)$ using (8) by selecting the corresponding upper and lower boundary for each parameter.

3: Set the generation counter $g = 1$

4: **While ($g \leq MAXG$) do**

5: Determine using (9) the mutant vectors V_g

   for $i = 1, \dots, (N_B - N_{macro}) \times 3$ do

   $v_g^i = x_g^{r_1} + F \cdot (x_g^{r_2} - x_g^{r_3})$

6: Determine using (12) the donor vector U_g

   for $i = 1, \dots, (N_B - N_{macro})$ do

    for $j = 1, \dots, 3$ do

      if $rand_i(0,1) \leq CR$ or $j = j_{rand}$ then $u_g^{i,j} = v_g^{i,j}$

                else $u_g^{i,j} = x_g^{i,j}$

7: Evaluate $\Phi(X_g)$, $outp(X_g)$, $\Phi(U_g)$ and $outp(U_g)$ using (7) and (14)

8: Determine the next X_{g+1} using (15)

   for $i = 1, \dots, N_B$ do

   if $(outp(U_g^i) \leq \rho)$ and $(outp(X_g^i) \leq \rho)$ then

    if $\Phi(U_g^i) \leq \Phi(X_g^i)$ then $X_{g+1} = U_g^i$

           else $X_{g+1} = X_g$

   if $(outp(U_g^i) \leq \rho)$ and $(outp(X_g^i) > \rho)$ then $X_{g+1} = U_g^i$

    else if $(outp(U_g^i) > \rho)$ and $(outp(X_g^i) \leq \rho)$ then $X_{g+1} = X_g^i$

      if $(outp(U_g^i) > \rho)$ and $(outp(X_g^i) > \rho)$ then

        if $outp(U_g^i) \leq outp(X_g^i)$ then $X_{g+1} = U_g^i$

              else $X_{g+1} = X_g^i$

9: $g = g + 1$

end while

Output: Elite individual from $MAXG$ generations

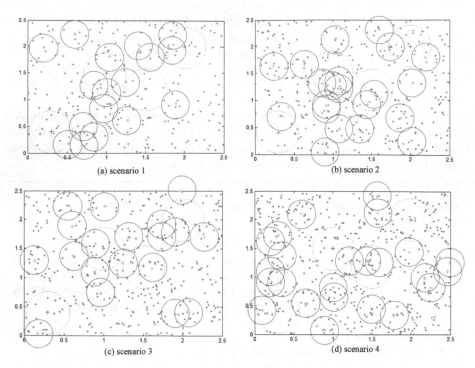

Fig. 2. The four scenarios that has been used for the experimental results of DE/best/1/bin. (a) scenario 1 with 250 MSs (b) scenario 2 with 350 MSs (c) scenario 3 with 400 MSs (d) scenario 4 with 500 MSs. The (·) represents users, (*) deployed micro cells, and (+) fixed macro cells. The circle with the solid line represents the coverage range of the micro cell. The circle with the intermitted line represents the coverage range of the macro cell.

Table 1. 5G RNP system parameters

Parameter	Value	Parameter	Value
N_{macro}	4	N_{micro}	35
$P_{BSmacro}$	40 W	$P_{BSmicro}$	10 W
$K_{BSmacro}$	27	$K_{BSmicro}$	15
σ^2	5.97×10^{-15} W	$SINR_{thr}$	-9 dB
P_{thr}	-80 dBm	ρ	0.15

Table 2. Constrained DE parameters

Parameter	Value
Pop_{size}	50
F	0.9
CR	0.5
$MAXG$	50
D	35 micros + 4 macros

For example, the radius length is 225 m for micro cell and 320 m for macro cell. However, from the same figure we can observe that our proposed DE needs to be improved in order to provide better coverage for all MSs in the AoI. This can also be implemented by adding more constraints to the formulation of the RNP in hand. Finally, the SINR on average is 1.74 dB in scenario 4 which is quite high, as a good QoS.

Table 3. Average results of three constrained DE strategies for the 5G RNP over 5 runs.

DE strategy	MSs in AoI	Avg. SINR (dB)	Avg. received power (dB)	Active micro BSs	Avg. outage
DE/rand/1	250	1.9	−77.87	20	0.132
	350	2.29	−66.21	24	0.128
	400	1.73	−70.80	24	0.120
	500	2.59	−77.98	29	0.126
DE/current-to-best/1	**250**	**1.49**	**−74.10**	**18**	**0.130**
	350	1.18	−73.80	19	0.130
	400	1.37	−74.21	21	0.126
	500	**1.79**	**−74.73**	**25**	**0.11**
DE/best/1	250	1.10	−74.32	20	0.132
	350	**1.09**	**−74.40**	**19**	**0.128**
	400	**1.74**	**−74.37**	**20**	**0.127**
	500	1.73	−74.37	25	0.118

5 Conclusion

In this paper, we addressed the problem of RNP in the 5G LTE wireless network with respect to deployment cost, energy consumption and coverage rate as the main constraints in the whole process. This problem has been considered as NP-hard that demands non-classical algorithms such as meta-heuristic algorithms. A framework of DE was proposed by modifying the conventional DE from the aspects of representation/initialization, mutation/crossover, evaluation/constrained (*feasible rules*) selection according to the problem at hand. Three DE variants were realized according to such framework. Experimental results have shown that the greedy DE/best/1/bin outperforms other variants in terms of deployment cost (i.e. minimizing the number of BSs), average outage percentage and respects the desired QoS when applied to different scenarios. As future work suggestions, we may consider using different constrained strategies, e.g. infeasible driven strategies EAs and stochastic ranking. It may also be interesting to consider some of the constraints as objectives and study if they offer any better results. Finally, when the problem became more complex existing adaptive DE can be considered upon the scalability of the classical DE. Then a comparison can be established to measure the performance of each method.

References

1. Yaacoub, E., Imran, A., Dawy, Z.: A genetic simulation-based dimensioning approach for planning hetrogenous LTE cellular networks. In: IEEE Mediterranean Electrotechnical Conference (2014)

2. El-Beaino, W., El-Hajj, A.M., Dawy, Z.: On radio network planning for next generation 5G networks: a case study. In: International Conference on Communications, Signal Processing, and Their Applications (ICCSPA) 2015, pp. 1–6. IEEE (2015)
3. Mitra, R.N., Agrawal, D.P.: 5G mobile technology: a survey. ICT Express 1, 132–137 (2015)
4. Akyildiz, I.F., Nie, S., Lin, S.-C., Chandrasekaran, M.: 5G roadmap: 10 key enabling technologies. Comput. Netw. 106(2016), 17–48 (2016)
5. Panwara, N., Sharmaa, S., Singh, A.K.: A survey on 5G: the next generation of mobile communication. Phys. Commun. 18(2016), 64–84 (2016)
6. Amaldi, E., Capone, A., Malucelli, F.: Improved models and algorithms for UMTS radio planning. In: Vehicular Technology Conference, VTC 2001, Atlantic City, NJ, USA, pp. 920–924. IEEE (2001)
7. Berrocal-Plaza, V., Vega-Rodríguez, M.A., Gómez-Pulido, J.A., Sánchez-Pérez, J.M.: Artificial bee colony algorithm applied to WiMAX network planning problem. In: 11th International Conference on Intelligent Systems Design and Applications (ISDA), Cordoba, Spain, pp. 504–509. IEEE (2011)
8. El-Beaino, W., El-Hajj, A.M., Dawy, Z.: A proactive approach for LTE radio network planning with green considerations. In: 19th International Conference on Telecommunications (ICT), Jounieh, Lebanon, pp. 1–6. IEEE (2012)
9. Sachan, R., Choi, T.J., Ahn, C.W.: A genetic algorithm with location intelligence method for energy optimization in 5G wireless networks. Discrete Dyn. Nat. Soc. 2016(2016), 1–9 (2016)
10. Haenggi, M., Andrews, J.G., Baccelli, F.: Stochastic geometry and random graphs for the analysis and design of wireless networks. IEEE J. Sel. Areas Commun. 27(7), 1029–1046 (2009)
11. MacCartney, G.R., Zhang, J., Nie, S.: Path loss models for 5G millimeter wave propagation channels in urban microcells. In: IEEE Global Communications Conference (GLOBECOM), Atlanta, GA, USA. IEEE (2014)
12. Price, K., Storn, R.: Differential evolution: a simple evolution strategy for fast optimization. Dr. Dobb's J. Softw. Tools 22(4), 18–24 (1997)
13. Develi, I., Yazlik, E.N.: Optimum antenna configuration in MIMO systems: a differential evolution based approach. Wirel. Commun. Mob. Comput. 12(6), 473–480 (2012)
14. Niu, M., Xu, Z.: Efficiency ranking-based evolutionary algorithm for power system planning and operation. IEEE Trans. Power Syst. 29(3), 1437–1438 (2014)
15. Lampinen, J.: Solving problems subject to multiple nonlinear constraints by the differential evolution (2001)

Evolutionary Computation to Determine Product Builds in Open Pit Mining

Adam Ghandar[✉]

University of Adelaide, Adelaide, Australia
adam.ghandar@adelaide.edu.au

Abstract. This paper describes an approach to optimising processing and stockpiling decisions in an open pit mine in order to minimise the deviation from production targets. The solution involves determining decisions on the destination of ore as it is mined: whether to use ore in a product directly as it is extracted from the ground, or to stockpile and use later. Experimental results are provided for a variable threshold based selection heuristic and an approach that applies evolutionary computation to find better solutions.

Keywords: Computational intelligence · Evolutionary computation · Mining · Supply chain

1   Introduction

Mining is the work of extracting materials from the earth to obtain profit. It has been a human activity since pre-history. The process of mining includes stages of prospecting and exploration to identify possible sites, the development of mines and resource exploitation and finally reclaiming or restoring natural state of the land once mining ceases. In modern times the complexity of mining operations has increased significantly.

Although companies in the mining industry are among the most profitable in the world, precipitous falls in commodity prices have altered the fiscal environment. Oil for example is in 2017 trading at less than half the price it was 2 years prior, iron fell from a peak of over $153 in April 2013 to $41 in December 2015, copper and other commodities have recorded similar drawdowns. At the same time there is a strong sense of the need for technology and to modernise operations in order to be competitive [8]. Price volatility and at times the boom bust nature of the industry create strong pressures for production to be flexible and adaptive to demand, maintain business growth, increase efficiency and reduce costs. Innovative approaches to planning and scheduling with computational intelligence are a cost effective way for achieving dramatic business outcomes and of leveraging advances being rolled out in sensors, real time operations systems and remote operations.

There are three main types of material that is commonly mined: metallic ores, non-metallic minerals, and fossil fuels. There are two main mining methodologies

© Springer International Publishing AG 2017
Y. Shi et al. (Eds.): SEAL 2017, LNCS 10593, pp. 751–762, 2017.
https://doi.org/10.1007/978-3-319-68759-9_61

for ores and minerals: surface and underground mining. Surface mining can be used when the valuable material is close to the surface. The discussions in this paper are with a context of open pit mines for metallic ores.

Optimisation and simulation have been applied in scheduling and planning mine operations since the 1960s, see [6] for a survey encompassing classical and modern methods. Classical approaches to mine planning specify the blocks included in pits (i.e. the material that will be mined); and more recent techniques built on these approach to set a sequence for extracting blocks; an additional level of detail is in the usage of equipment. Further approaches still consider data uncertainty such as of the quality of material in the geological model on extraction.

Some context on consideration of heuristics and mathematical or large scale optimisation is provided in [3], along with some useful heuristic techniques. A major obstacle in solving the problem is the large solution space, thus heuristic and hybrid approaches are quite common. Another issue that has been reported is difficulty in optimising to obtain a schedule such that it can be realistically applied in practice. See [10] for a hybrid algorithm that incorporates several heuristic techniques to solve the haulage aspects. An application of an evolutionary algorithm for longer term mine planning and scheduling is in [7], an application of evolutionary computation is described in [5]. A further application that combines integer programming with a heuristic model is described in [9], this solution includes a detailed model of haulage and digging.

In this paper evolutionary learning is applied to the "destination problem": given a fixed mining sequence where should material go. This innovation in the problem formulation enables the mine optimisation problem to be divided to components. In addition, the formulation is useful in tactical scheduling where the aim is to implement a strategic plan including a fixed mining sequence, or to determine detailed operations within time buckets. The solution uses evaluation of a simulation and simulated evolution to build a realistic problem model in minimal development time, see also [4] for application of similar techniques on a financial problem.

Section 2 introduces the destination problem as it exists in the application domain. Section 3 describes modelling aspects and the solution formulation. Section 4 contains experimental analysis to validate the learning approaches and compare the evolutionary computation search based method and the lighter weight threshold heuristic. Finally Sect. 5 concludes the paper.

2   Problem Description

Figure 1 shows the main locations of an open pit mine: excavation pits; re-handle stockpiles; the processing plant which carries out an initial stage of ore refinement in the mine; and the product stockyard where product builds are ready for further transportation to eventually reach customers (after possible additional blending and processing with product from other mines).

The objective is to make product builds using material coming the pit and re-handle stockpiles to meet produce grade targets. The re-handle stockyard creates scope for flexibility in the dig sequence as equipment is slow, subject to material availability, and geological constraints.

Some of the subproblems in a pit to port scheduling problem can include: pit design; the sequence to process blocks to be ready for excavation by drilling and blasting; the sequence to extract blocks from the ground; material to stack in re-handle stockpiles; material to send directly to the processing from the pit; material to reclaim from stockpiles to feed the processing plant; and the handling of material through intermediate stockpiling and processing via rail, port and ships on to further processing by customers.

The "destination problem" takes place after extraction before material is processed at the mine processing plant and its optimal resolution is significant in attaining production targets over time and in maintaining the overall performance of the pit to port supply chain.

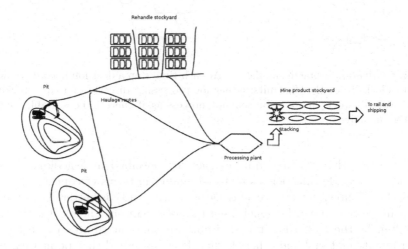

Fig. 1. Mine locations: pits, re-handle stockyard, processing equipment, and mine stockyard.

3 Methodology

This section describes the approach that is developed including a simulation of the problem, a decision rule heuristic solution and the solution approach based on an evolutionary algorithm.

3.1 Simulation

A simulation of the destination problem was developed to test and evaluate different solution approaches. The implementation is based on time steps of equal duration. Figure 2 gives an overview, blocks are pushed on to product stockyard builds from the pit via the extraction of material by dig units. The re-handle stockyard contains a number of stockpiles that are a buffer between the material coming out of the pit and the processing plant and builds. One build is stacked at a time in the mine stockyard.

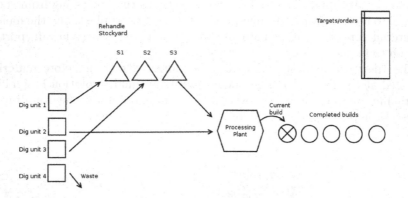

Fig. 2. Destination problem simulation. At each time step a decision is made on where to send blocks from the dig units: either for processing directly or to be stockpiled. Blocks already stockpiled can be sent for processing if there is no suitable material from the dig units.

The blocks that the dig units extract are specified in a geological model and include a grade that defines material quality in terms of concentration of a chemical attributes. In this case a higher percentage of Fe is better. The approach that is implemented can be generalised to more than one chemical attribute, it may often be the case that it is desirable for some attributes to be lower in higher quality material and others higher. It is also noted that point targets are used - a solution that exceeds the target is not considered better than one that is exactly on target as this would be a sign of "wasting" high grade material in practice. The test data includes equally sized blocks of size $25 \times 25 \times 5\,\mathrm{m}$, and the rates of equipment (including digging and processing) are set in terms of a number of blocks per unit of time. A cut-off grade is used to distinguish between valuable ore and waste, waste is discarded and cannot be used to contribute to builds or stockpiled.

The re-handle stockyard model includes a number of stockpiles that follow a first in first out protocol and are required to maintain a "build and destroy" logic which means that they must be stacked up to a certain size before reclaim can take place. The simulation allows for a variable number of stockpiles each with a lower and upper threshold to limit the grade that can be stacked.

The processing plant transformation is modelled in the data by including for each block a pre and post processing quality. The output of the plant is stacked onto the product stockyard builds. A new build is started as soon as a previous one has been completed (defined by a parameter n blocks per build). Targets are set in terms of a vector of target chemical attribute concentration for the tonnage weighted average grade of material in each builds.

3.2   Selection Cone Heuristic

The selection cone heuristic is designed to manage block selection by placing upper and lower thresholds on the acceptable block grade to include in a build. The idea is to accept a wide range of material quality early in the build and progressively tighten the acceptance criteria to restrict to blocks that can bring the average of the build onto target as the build progresses. This allows the use of a wider range of material quality and allows the potential to use all types of material quality in constructing builds (rather than say only using material that is near the target this approach would potentially allow high and low grade material to be used in a way that they "cancel" each other out and bring the build average to the target quality).

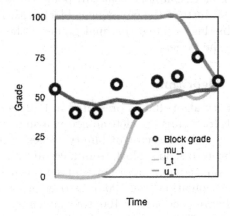

Fig. 3. Threshold heuristic decision rule parameters and build quality guiding block grade selection during a build. The figure shows the sequence of block selections to make up a build that has a target for the average quality on completion is 55% Fe.

The lower and upper thresholds for accepting blocks by grade is set with the formula:

$$l_t := \max[0, n \times T - n_b \times \mu_t - (n - n_b - 1) \times H],$$

$$u_t := \min[100, n \times T - n_b \times \mu_t - (n - n_b - 1) \times L],$$

where n is the number of blocks targeted to be contained in the build on completion, T is the target for attributes, μ_t is the build average at t, n_b is the number of blocks already in the build, L is a parameter that represents lower bound on quality possible, and H is the highest possible bound. μ_t is determined at a time step t:

$$\mu_t = ((n_b - 1) \times \mu_{t-1} + G)/n_t,$$

where G is the grade of a block being added to the build. Note the approach can work with a vector of several quality attributes.

Figure 3 gives an example of the adapting threshold heuristic in action for setting destinations of a sequence of 11 blocks received from the pit with Fe concentration (percent) as follows: 55, 40, 58, 40, 60, 63, 75, 60, 40, 62. The build target is 55% Fe. Any blocks with a concentration of Fe that falls outside the upper and lower thresholds is rejected from the build. For instance the block number 2, with grade 40% Fe, has calculation as follows:

- $\mu_t := (1 \times 55 + 40)/2 = 47.5$
- $l_t := \max[0, 10 \times 55 - 2 \times 47.5 - (10 - 2 - 1) \times 70] = \max[0, -35] = 0$
- $u_t := \min[100, 10 \times 55 - 2 \times 47.5 - (10 - 2 - 1) \times 40] = \min[100, 175] = 100$

As the grade of the 2nd block is within the range 0 to 100% Fe it is included in the build. The 10-th block also has grade 40% Fe and by this time the build is almost complete and has an aggregate quality of 53.875. The lower threshold is at this time 59%. Although this concentration was usable previously when the build only contained 2 blocks, 40% Fe is at this point below the lower threshold so the block is rejected. Instead the subsequent block with Fe = 62% is used to make up the build. In this example the final grade of the build was 55.3%, a 0.3% deviation above the target.

3.3 Evolutionary Algorithm

A canonical evolutionary algorithm as presented in [1, 2] is applied to minimise the deviation of builds from target as determined in a simulation, see also Fig. 4. Solutions are represented by a vector of binary values each element of which corresponds to a decision to send a block from a certain dig unit in a particular time step to the processing equipment or not. Elitism was used in addition to the following parameters: population size: 100, crossover probability: 0.5, mutation probability: 0.2, number of generations: 100, tournament size: 3. A standard two point crossover was used that randomly selects two points within the length of the parent vectors and then swaps the values of the elements between these points to produce two new offspring. Mutation was to flip bits randomly in the parent individual with probability 1 over the number of bits (corresponds to 1 over the total number of time periods times the number of dig units).

Evaluation was by using the simulation and assigning individuals fitness to be the SSE of target adherence for each build completed in the scenario:

$$\sum (T_i - A_i)^2,$$

where T_i is the target for the $i - th$ build, and A_i is the actual result obtained. Penalties can be applied to influence characteristics of the solutions obtained in the simulation, for example the number of blocks assigned to stockpiles, any blocks whose ideal stockpile was not available or caused overflow due to build logic. In the approach implemented in this paper a penalty is used to bias the search solutions that complete more builds in the same amount of time to create an incentive to maximise production.

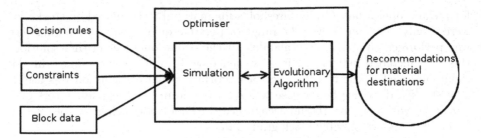

Fig. 4. Evaluation function and input data for the evolutionary algorithm.

4 Results

This section includes empirical results for a sample test using real mine data, and an extended scaled test with extended data. Figure 5 shows the sample test data consisting of a sub-structure extracted from an actual geological model of an iron ore mine in Western Australia. The data specifies 38 blocks ranging in Fe concentration 47% to 60%. A digging sequence for excavation was determined for the structure using a topological sorting algorithm with precedence specified by the physical constraints that the 9 blocks immediately above any block b must be dug out before b is able to be mined. The objective is to produce product builds with target grade 55%.

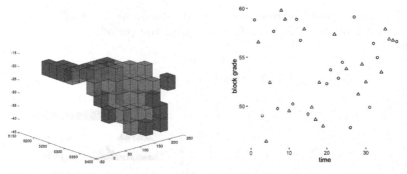

(a) Sample problem, highest grade blocks are blue. Source: MISG 2016.

(b) Destinations set by EA and block quality. Blocks sent to stockpile are triangles.

Fig. 5. Block model and the grade of material in the EAs optimised extraction sequence. (Color figure online)

In the tests based on the real dataset the stockyard was set to contain 7 rehandle stockpiles each with capacity three blocks, the build and destroy stockpile logic meant the stockpiles have to be stacked with 3 blocks before being available for reclaim operations. Grade thresholds for material to be placed on stockpiles were evenly distributed over the range of possible quality values. Another test was performed to study the scalability of the evolutionary algorithm solution, this test included 500 blocks in a sequence with grades set to values in the range observed in the real data set (a uniform random distribution was used). The stockyard in this larger case was set to contain 28 stockpiles: 4 sets of 7 stockpiles with capacity 10 and acceptance thresholds for each group of 7 set to cover the range of possible block grade values.

Figure 6 shows product builds and re-handle stockpile activity in tests with destinations set by the EA. 4 complete builds of 7 blocks were produced with Fe%: 54.42, 54.57, 54.06 and 54.78 (target was 55%). To compare, Fig. 7 shows the selection cone result: also 4 builds but with Fe% 53.91, 51.79, 55.57 and 54.07. The re-handle stockpiles, panels (b) in the figures, were fairly similar:

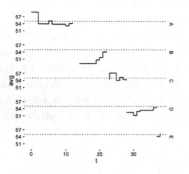
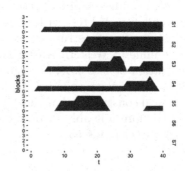

(a) Average grade as blocks are added to product builds A - E. Target: 55.

(b) Re-handle stockpile activity during test period.

Fig. 6. Evolutionary algorithm

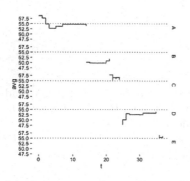
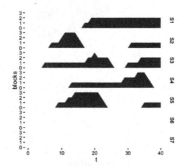

(a) Average grade as blocks are added to product builds A - E. Target: 55.

(b) Re-handle stockpile activity during test period.

Fig. 7. Selection Cone Heuristic

the business rules applied in the simulation give preference to directly feeding processing with material from the pit by considering direct feed before reclaim (direct feed is more economical, requires less material handling). It is also notable that the schedule the EA developed was "global" in the sense that it showed forward planning in stockpiling decisions over time. For example to keep build B on target in the EA schedule, some lower grade was diverted from the pit to stockpile $S2$ during build B and higher grade material from $S5$ that had been stockpiled in advance is used to keep the build on the target.

Table 1 summarises the results in the sample data case and extended case with randomly generated block grades. It is clear that the EA is performed well in comparison with the simpler adapting threshold approach with builds on average nearer to target and the production of an additional 4 builds in the same amount of time. Figure 8 describes the population fitness during the evolutionary algorithm runs for the large and small test cases. In the longer test 1000 generations were run, in the smaller case 100.

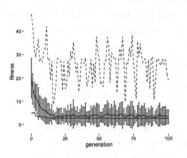

(a) Population summary for sample data case.

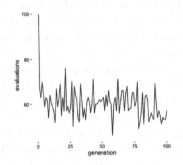

(b) Number of evaluations for sample data case.

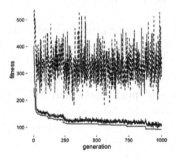

(c) Population summary for extended test case.

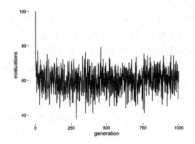

(d) Number of evaluations for extended test case.

Fig. 8. Summary of the population fitness during running the evolutionary algorithm. The average fitness with confidence interval is marked, along with the best/minimum and maximum fitness individual in the population.

Table 1. Summary statistics of the performance of the EA and the selection cone.

	n builds	Sum target diff.	Average target diff. per build
EA			
Sample data	4	2.17	0.30 (0.54)
Extended case	63	55.9	1.16 (1.18)
Selection cone			
Sample data	4	5.8	1.19 (1.45)
Extended case	59	81.48	1.38 (1.51)

5   Conclusion

This paper contributes two approaches for solving the "destination problem". It also defined this problem as a series of decisions for processing and stockpiling material as it is mined in order to minimise the deviation between actual production and target grades. The dataset and the implementation of the simulation and solution approaches are accessible online, see: https://github.com/adamnant/destination.

The selection cone approach is a based on the assumption that when a build is empty or contains only a few blocks it is desirable to be less restrictive on the quality of material that is added because it is more likely to be possible to correct the grade with blocks added later. The heuristic will result in worse solutions if it is not possible to source the particular grade required to bring the build back to target when needed. This approach is contrasted with solutions that were generated using an evolutionary algorithm. This approach determines the builds by having the evolutionary algorithm learn a sequence of decisions on material destination for a scenario by evaluating potential decision sequences in a simulation.

The two methods were evaluated in a particular example derived from a real world block model and in an extended test case that is produced with randomly generated data (a uniform random distribution is used to set the quality of a long sequence of blocks). In the real data case, the selection cone heuristic allocates slightly more blocks to production and performed well in 3 out of 4 product builds, in the second of the builds however the selection heuristic was significantly far from the target (Fig. 7). The EA approach performed better in adherence to targets of the product builds although this was at a cost of allocating more blocks to stockpiles. In the extended test the EA performed better overall including in completing more builds in the period and also the sum of the absolute quality deviations from the build target was 55.9 compared with 81.48 for the selection cone.

In the small example tested runtime is insignificant, in larger problems the time required for simulation increases and becoming an issue that potentially makes an approach wholly based on an EA impractical. Figure 8 shows population statistics, the EA (certainly the generational algorithm applied) takes a longer time to evaluate large simulations, this could be optimised significantly but would still be longer than a rule based heuristic. As the selection cone heuristic is able to perform fairly well much of the time, an approach to implementation in an application where runtime is an important criteria could be for the EA to be applied for constructing parts of the schedule that need correction or refinement (similar to the data case described in the results), or possibly the part of a schedule closest to the present before it is implemented.

Further work in the direction of this paper could include the development of methods to optimise separate sub-problems in the mining supply chain in jointly. Such as the stockyard design and for instance thresholds for the stockpiles, the digging sequence, and the haulage and material movement, the mine to port processing, and the rail and shipping transportation. A co-evolutionary algorithm could be used to optimise the stockyard parameters and digging sequence in conjunction with setting the material destinations. Another interesting aspect is in considering the uncertainty associated with the geological model in developing the production schedule.

Acknowledgement. This work was supported by the Australian Research council through grant DP130104395. Some of the methods used in this paper are based on work done by delegates at the 2016 Mathematics in Industry Study Group workshop, in particular the contributions to developing the simulation and the selection cone heuristic method are gratefully acknowledged.

References

1. Bäck, T., Fogel, D.B., Michalewicz, Z. (eds.): Evolutionary Computation 1: Basic Algorithms and Operators. Institute of Physics Publishing, Bristol (2000)
2. Fortin, F., De Rainville, F.-M., Gardner, M., Parizeau, M., Gagné, C.: DEAP: evolutionary algorithms made easy. J. Mach. Learn. Res. **13**, 2171–2175 (2012)
3. Gershon, M.: Heuristic approaches for mine planning and production scheduling. Geotech. Geol. Eng. **5**(1), 1–13 (1987)
4. Ghandar, A., Michalewicz, Z., Tô, T.-D., Zurbruegg, R.: The performance of an adaptive portfolio management system. In: IEEE Congress on Evolutionary Computation, CEC 2008 (IEEE World Congress on Computational Intelligence), pp. 2208–2216. IEEE (2008)
5. Myburgh, C., Deb, K.: Evolutionary algorithms in large-scale open pit mine scheduling. In: Proceedings of the 12th Annual Conference on Genetic and Evolutionary Computation, GECCO 2010, pp. 1155–1162. ACM, New York (2010)
6. Newman, A.M., Rubio, E., Caro, R., Weintraub, A., Eurek, K.: A review of operations research in mine planning. Interfaces **40**(3), 222–245 (2010)
7. Riff, M.-C., Alfaro, T., Bonnaire, X., Grandón, C.: EA-MP: an evolutionary algorithm for a mine planning problem. In: IEEE Congress on Evolutionary Computation, CEC 2008 (IEEE World Congress on Computational Intelligence), pp. 4011–4014. IEEE (2008)
8. Sganzerla, C., Seixas, C., Conti, A.: Disruptive innovation in digital mining. Procedia Eng. **138**, 64–71 (2016)

9. Souza, M.J.F., Coelho, I.M., Ribas, S., Santos, H.G., Merschmann, L.H.C.: A hybrid heuristic algorithm for the open-pit-mining operational planning problem. Eur. J. Oper. Res. **207**(2), 1041–1051 (2010)
10. Tolwtnski, B., Underwood, R.: A scheduling algorithm for open pit mines. IMA J. Manag. Math. **7**(3), 247–270 (1996)

An Evolutionary Vulnerability Detection Method for HFSWR Ship Tracking Algorithm

Pengju Zhang, Kun Wang$^{(\boxtimes)}$, Ling Zhang, Zexiao Xie, and Liqin Zhou

College of Engineering, Ocean University of China, Qingdao, China
kafchang@outlook.com, kunwang@ouc.edu.cn

Abstract. A high-frequency surface-wave radar (HFSWR) ship tracking algorithm's performance is significantly affected by the dynamics of ships, in which track fragmentation can be frequently observed. However, it is still unclear about in which scenarios the dynamics of ships sabotages the tracking performance. In this paper, an evolutionary-based vulnerability detection method is proposed to automatically collect scenarios of different ship motion dynamics that can cause quantitative failures in a HFSWR ship tracking algorithm. Firstly, a grammar-based scenario model which can describe multiple types of temporal relationships and generate autonomous motion of any number of ships with comparatively low-dimension data is proposed. Secondly, an encoding scheme of scenario is proposed and corresponding grammar-guided genetic programming (GGGP) algorithm is designed to evolve scenarios that can sabotages the tracking performance. Results show the effectiveness of this method in evolving and collecting scenarios that can cause more serious track fragmentation in the tracking results, with insights into the vulnerability of ship tracking algorithm provided.

Keywords: Vulnerability detection · HFSWR ship tracking · Multi-target model · Scenario grammar · GGGP

1 Introduction

These last decades see a great interest toward low-power high-frequency surface-wave radars (HFSWR) for ocean remote sensing. By virtue of their over-the-horizon coverage capability and continuous-time mode of operation, HFSWRs are also effective long-range early warning tools in maritime situational awareness applications providing an additional source of information for ship target detection and subsequent tracking [1]. The objective of a HFSWR-based ship tracking algorithm [1–9] is to associate consecutive detected state points of ship targets into corresponding tracks.

It has been shown that the dynamics of ships, as well as the background clutter and noise environment, plays a significant role in determining tracking performance. For instance, the phenomenon of track fragmentation (TF) is evident even in ship tracking algorithms with good overall performance [10,11]. Also, tracking performance may suffer seriously due to the interference when

© Springer International Publishing AG 2017
Y. Shi et al. (Eds.): SEAL 2017, LNCS 10593, pp. 763–773, 2017.
https://doi.org/10.1007/978-3-319-68759-9_62

ships are in close proximity or the residual effects of disappearing ships [8]. However, it is still unclear about how the dynamics of ships affect the tracking performance and in which degree the effect is, especially about which types of "scenarios"[1] can cause failures in a ship tracking algorithm.

Existing works rely on two types of scenarios to test the performance of a HFSWR ship tracking algorithm—the measured ships' dynamic trajectory data from sea trials [1,6], and the simulated data generated from specific motion model, such as Markov model and straight line model [8], with the initial states manually assigned. One possible problem of these works is that they fail to incorporate diversified scenarios that can reflect the autonomous movement of ships in the radar's surveillance area. Moreover, they lack a mechanism that can facilitate the detection and collection of vulnerabilities of a ship tracking algorithm (i.e. scenarios that can cause failures in this algorithm).

As detecting vulnerabilities of HFSWR ship tracking algorithms is necessary for both the algorithm designers and users, in this paper, we regard this vulnerability detection problem as finding multiple scenarios that can cause failures in a HFSWR ship tracking algorithm. Especially, we focus on the effect of ship motion dynamics on ship tracking performance by automatically collecting different scenarios of ship dynamics that can cause failures in a ship tracking algorithm.

However, finding interesting scenarios of ship dynamics is not a trivial task because of the complexity of scenarios and vast scenario space. For one thing, the number of ship targets in the scenario is uncertain, ranging from 1 to hundreds and thousands. For another, every ship target can move autonomously to a great extent.

To solve this scenario search problem and fill in the gap in existing ship tracking work on vulnerability detection, we propose an evolutionary-based vulnerability detection method for HFSWR ship tracking algorithm. The main contributions of this paper are twofold:

Firstly, a grammar-based scenario model is proposed to describe and generate autonomous motion of any number of ships, with multiple types of temporal relationships represented. Compared with motion states arranged chronologically in the measured radar data or simulated data, scenarios generated by this model enjoy concise form and comparatively low dimension thus facilitates more efficient search. The grammar representation of the proposed scenario model also facilitates easy encoding of a scenario into a genome for evolution to work on.

Secondly, an encoding scheme of scenario is proposed and corresponding grammar-guided genetic programming (GGGP) algorithm is designed to evolve scenarios that can cause quantitative failures of a HFSWR ship tracking algorithm and achieve vulnerability detection.

The rest of the paper is organised as follows. Sections 2 and 3 addresses the above-mentioned first and second contributions of this paper, respectively. The

---

[1] A scenario is a description of a variety of possible futures. It can be represented as a simple sampling in the parameter space, or a complex story (i.e. a sequence of events) that describes the future.

details of the experiment design and result analysis are presented in Sect. 4. Finally, some concluding remarks are made and future work is discussed in Sect. 5.

2 Scenario Modelling and Generation

This section addresses the first contribution of this paper by proposing a grammar-based scenario model. Building blocks of this scenario model are firstly provided, followed by a grammar presentation that describes local and global rules about how these building blocks can be combined to form a whole concise and comparatively low-dimension scenario of multiple ships moving autonomously.

2.1 Building Blocks of the Scenario Model

Building blocks of the scenario model are defined as the uncertain factors of ship dynamics that may affect the performance of the HFSWR ship tracking algorithm, which falls into four categories: parameters (denoting entities), initial states, events and relationships.

Parameters are introduced to denote different ship targets.

Initial States denote initial motion states of a ship target, including initial velocity, azimuth (i.e. angle between the ship and the normal direction of radar), positions in longitude and latitude.

Events are defined as the changes of states of the ship targets, or the appearance of new ships.

Relationships are divided into affiliation of a parameter (i.e. a ship target) to an initial state or an event, and temporal relationships between events.
For example, $i_0(1)$ denotes the affiliation of parameter 1 (i.e. ship target 1) to its initial states i_0, which means the initial states of ship 1 is i_0. $d_\Delta(2)$ denotes the affiliation of parameter 2 (i.e. ship target 2) to event d_Δ, which means ship 2 changes its moving direction by d_Δ.
Three types of temporal relationships can be represented in this model:

- $t_\Delta(1)$ denotes that, in the scenario of ship 1, current time advances by t_Δ from the last time reference point.
- $t_d(1)$ represents a time delay relation, which means time delays for t_d from the initial time of ship 1 (represented by the parameter in the brackets).
- $[\ldots + \ldots]$ represents a time synchronisation relation, which follows a time reference point. For example, $t_0\,[\,i_0(2)\,A(2) + i_0(3)\,A(3)]$ denotes synchrony between the initial states of ship 2 and 3 at time point t_0, which means the two ships appear at the same time, with $A(2)$ and $A(3)$ implying possible further events.

2.2 Representing Scenario Model into CFG

We introduce a parameterised version of the traditional context-free grammar (CFG) [12] to represent the above scenario model. As these parameters can be used to identify initial states and events of different ship targets, and to represent various types of temporal relationships, this grammar is suitable for generating complex maritime situation of variable number of ship targets with variable length of events and multiple types of temporal relationships.

The parameterised-CFG-based scenario grammar is defined as a quadruple $G = (N(X), \Sigma(X), P, S)$, in which X is the newly introduced parameter set, with $()$ denoting affiliation relationship of a parameter to corresponding terminals or non-terminals.

$N(X)$ is the non-terminal set. Only one non-terminal—A attached by a parameter—is defined, which allows more events to happen in this scenario.

$\Sigma(X)$ is the terminal set, including $t_0, t_\Delta, t_d, [,], +, i_0, v_\Delta, d_\Delta, \varepsilon$ attached by a parameter or not. $t_0, t_\Delta, t_d, [,], +$ are defined to describe temporal relationship (see Sect. 2.1 for explanations). i_0, v_Δ, d_Δ denotes the initial states, change of velocity event, change of moving direction event, respectively. ε is a placeholder.

S is the starting symbol.

The production rules P of this grammar are as follows:

$$S \to t_0\, i_0(x)\, A(x) \tag{1}$$

$$A(x) \to t_\Delta(x)\, v_\Delta(x)\, A(x) \tag{2}$$

$$A(x) \to t_\Delta(x)\, d_\Delta(x)\, A(x) \tag{3}$$

$$A(x1) \to A(x1) + t_d(x1)\,[\,i_0(x2)\,A(x2) + i_0(x3)\,A(x3) + i_0(x4)\,A(x4) \\ + i_0(x5)\,A(x5) + i_0(x6)\,A(x6)\,] \tag{4}$$

$$A(x1) \to A(x1) + t_d(x1)\,[\,i_0(x2)\,A(x2) + i_0(x3)\,A(x3)\,] \tag{5}$$

$$A(x1) \to A(x1) + t_d(x1)\, i_0(x2)\, A(x2) \tag{6}$$

$$A(x) \to \varepsilon \tag{7}$$

The function of each rule is described as follows: Rule (1) provides the initial time reference—t_0—for this scenario and ship x shows up at $t = t_0$. Rule (2) allows ship x to change its velocity after time elapses for t_Δ. Rule (3) allows ship x to change its moving direction after time elapses for t_Δ. Rule (4) introduces five more ships, with their initial time referred from that of $x1$ and their initial states provided. Similarly, Rule (5) and (6) introduces two and one more ship, respectively. Rule (7) terminates any further derivation of scenario from ship x.

2.3   Generating Scenarios by Grammar Derivation and Instantiation

Scenarios of ship dynamics can be generated in four steps:

First, the defined CFG-based scenario grammar is derived to obtain the derivation tree and derived tree. A traditional CFG derivation process is applied, with only one extra work—instantiating the parameters. The parameter instantiation can be implemented as follows: the first parameter—x in rule (1) which denotes the first ship in this scenario—is assigned to 1; in each of the rules, parameters that denote newly introduced/appearing ships ($x1$, $x2$ etc.) are assigned to the next bigger integer; and during the grammar derivation process, every time we replace a non-terminal by calling another production rule, the parameter of this non-terminal passes down to this rule. Figure 1 illustrates this derivation process.

Second, the derived tree is traversed and the string of parameterised terminals is obtained to form the "scenario skeleton". The scenario skeleton obtained from Fig. 1 is "$t_0\, i_0(1)\, t_\Delta(1)\, d_\Delta(1)\, \varepsilon\, t_d(1)\, [\, i_0(2)\, t_\Delta(2)\, v_\Delta(2)\, \varepsilon\, t_d(2)\, [\, i_0(3)\, t_\Delta(3)\, d_\Delta(3)\, \varepsilon\,]\,]$".

The scenario skeleton can be explained as: ship 1 appeared at $t=t_0$ in initial state $i_0(1)$, changed its direction by $d_\Delta(1)$ degree after $t_\Delta(1)$ time period, and kept moving without any change of direction or speed. After $t_d(1)$ since ship 1 firstly appeared, ship 2 showed up in initial state $i_0(2)$, changed its velocity by $v_\Delta(2)$ km/h, and kept moving. After $t_d(2)$ since ship 2 firstly appeared, ship 3 started to play in initial state $i_0(3)$, changed its direction by $d_\Delta(3)$ degree, and kept moving.

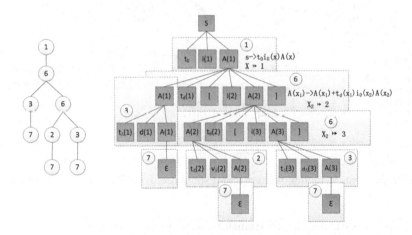

Fig. 1. An example of derivation and derived tree of scenario grammar.

Third, the scenario of each ship is obtained by inferring the initial time of each ship and separating the terminals parameterised by different ships from this skeleton in its original occurrence order.

Finally, the values of the terminals in each ship scenario are assigned.

3   Scenario Evolution Using GGGP

The above-proposed CFG-based scenario model facilities the design of evolutionary algorithm to evolve scenarios that can cause quantitative failure of a HFSWR ship tracking algorithm. As the scenario grammar is represented in a parameterised version of CFG, a corresponding revised grammar-guided genetic programming (GGGP) algorithm is designed in this section.

3.1   Encoding and Decoding Scheme

The derivation tree in Sect. 2.3 is defined as the genome of scenario. The phenotype is defined as the input of the HFSWR ship tracking algorithm—the consecutive motion states of ship targets that depict their motion dynamics, including their positions, directions, radial velocities and radial distances to the radar. The genotype-phenotype mapping can be achieved through a simulation process that transforms the scenario of each ship into temporally sampled motion states.

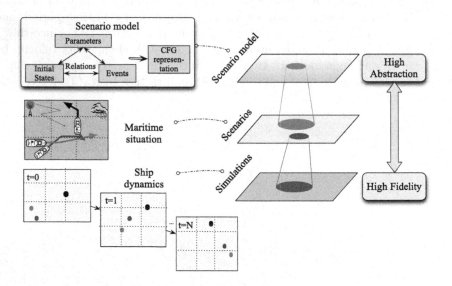

Fig. 2. Scenario model, scenarios and simulations in HFSWR ship tracking.

Figure 2 illustrates the relationship between our proposed scenario model, scenarios (i.e. the genotype) and simulations (i.e. the phenotype). It is worth noticing that compared with motion states arranged chronologically in simulations, scenarios generated by the scenario model enjoy concise form and comparatively low dimension thus facilitates more efficient search.

3.2   Genetic Operators

A binary tournament selection is applied to select scenarios for crossover or mutation.

The traditional subtree crossover of GGGP is applied, with an extra work of reassigning the values of parameters to maintain the parameter consistency after crossover. Figure 3 illustrate this process. It is worth mentioning that after crossover, the values assigned to each of the terminals remain unchanged.

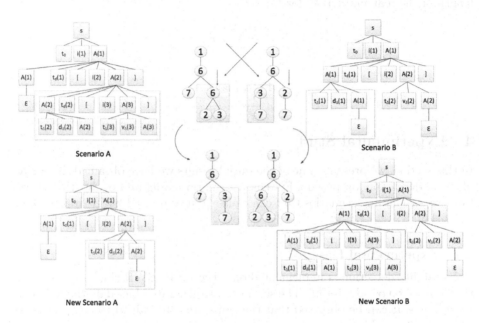

Fig. 3. Example of subtree crossover process.

Three types of mutation operators are applied, including the traditional subtree reallocation, node replacement, and value change of the terminal.

3.3   Fitness Evaluation

Scenarios are evaluated in the following steps:

The scenarios are firstly transformed into simulated ship dynamics through the genotype-phenotype mapping process explained in Sect. 3.1. The simulation data serves as the input of the HFSWR ship tracking algorithm. The algorithm outputs the tracking results and ship tracking performance metrics, such as number of track fragmentation (N_{TF}), can be calculated. It is worth mentioning that existing ship tracking performance metrics need to be transformed considering that the objective of our evolution is to detect vulnerability, that is to find scenarios that can cause failures in the HFSWR ship tracking algorithm.

Two fitness functions are defined in Eqs. F1 and F2, in which n denotes the number of ships in the scenario, l_{TF} denotes the output length of track fragment of a ship, l_T is the length of the real ship track, and n_{TF} is the output number of track fragments of a ship.

Both equations measure the degree of track fragmentation of ship targets in a scenario. They are defined based on the fact that if the ship tracking algorithm works perfectly, the output number of track fragments for each ship will be 1 (for Eq. F1) and the maximum length of track fragments will be the same to the length of the real ship track (for Eq. F2).

$$f = \frac{1}{n} \sum_{i=1}^{n} n_{TF} \tag{F1}$$

$$f = \frac{1}{n} \sum_{i=1}^{n} \frac{\max l_{TFi}}{l_{Ti}} \tag{F2}$$

4   Experimental Study

In this section, we present some of the initial results we have obtained. In particular, we derive our proposed CFG-based scenario model and evolve the derivation trees to finding scenarios that can cause failures in a HFSWR ship tracking algorithm.

4.1   Experimental Design

Vulnerability detection is implemented on a typical HFSWR ship tracking algorithm based on $\alpha - \beta$ filter [9]. The scenarios are generated based on the following value rages. It can be observed that the ships are constrained to comparatively small manoeuvrability.

- **Initial velocity**: 0–9.1 km/h
- **Initial positions**: longitude 120° E–21.5° E, latitude 37.5° N–38.5° N
- **Velocity change**: −1.55 km/h–2.25 km/h
- **Direction change**: −10°–10°
- **Ship number limit**: 50
- **Simulation time range**: 4 h
- **Simulation sampling time**: 1/60 h

Fitness functions in terms of track fragmentation defined in Eqs. F1 and F2 are applied, respectively, to guide the scenario evolution.

After testing the performance of the scenario evolutionary process under different parameter settings, the following are selected.

- **Population size**: 20
- **Generation limit**: 400
- **Crossover rate**: 0.7
- **Mutation rate**: 0.3, in which the node replacement and value change of the terminal are both implemented.

4.2   Results and Analysis

The performance of the designed GGGP is firstly tested to verify our proposed evolutionary-based vulnerability detection method in its ability to automatically find scenarios that can cause failures in a HFSWR ship tracking algorithm.

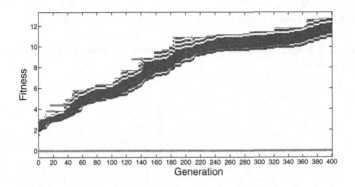

Fig. 4. Transition of track fragmentation fitness 1.

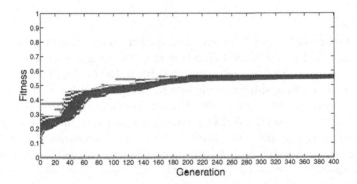

Fig. 5. Transition of track fragmentation fitness 2.

The transition of each fitness functions defined in Eqs. F1 and F2 during the evolutionary process is illustrated in Figs. 4 and 5. The box plot of each generation shows the distributions of the fitness values of the population. It can be observed that the evolutionary process succeeded in evolving failure scenarios, i.e., collecting scenarios with more serious track fragmentation, reflected in the increasing trend in the plots in the two figures.

Furthermore, typical scenarios before and after evolution are compared to discuss the effects of the scenario evolution process in this section.

Figure 6 presents the comparison of track fragmentation fitness 1, in which the lines denote the trajectories of ships and the circles mark the fragmentation

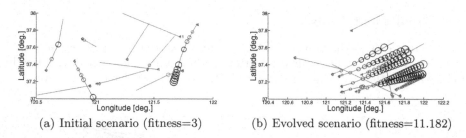

(a) Initial scenario (fitness=3)   (b) Evolved scenario (fitness=11.182)

Fig. 6. Scenarios before and after evolution guided by track fragmentation fitness 1. (Color figure online)

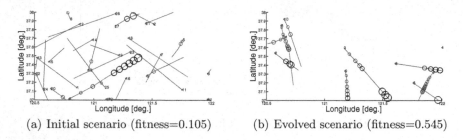

(a) Initial scenario (fitness=0.105)   (b) Evolved scenario (fitness=0.545)

Fig. 7. Scenarios before and after evolution guided by track fragmentation fitness 2.

points of tracks, with the bigger size and darker colour denoting later time. It can be observed that the tested HFSWR ship tracking algorithm suffers from significant average track fragmentation by ships in the evolved scenario. Possible reasons include multiple ships moving in a parallel way within certain adjacency.

Figure 7 presents the comparison of track fragmentation fitness 2. It can be observed that the tested HFSWR ship tracking algorithm suffers from significant average track fragmentation by ships in the evolved scenario. Possible reasons include trajectory crossing and disappearing from the surveillance areas.

It is noticeable that compared with the randomly generated scenarios, the evolved ones show significant degree of track fragmentation. Also, scenarios evolved with different fitness functions of track fragmentation metrics present diversified characteristics, which may imply multiple types of vulnerability of the tested HFSWR ship tracking algorithm.

5   Conclusion and Future Work

An evolutionary-based vulnerability detection method for HFSWR ship tracking algorithm is proposed in this paper. Results show the effectiveness of this method in evolving and collecting scenarios with more serious track fragmentation of the tested ship tracking algorithm. Also, scenarios evolved with different fitness functions of track fragmentation metrics present diversified characteristics, which may imply multiple types of vulnerability of the studied HFSWR ship tracking algorithm. Future work involves introducing more trajectory shape (e.g. arcs, not restricted to combinations of straight lines in this paper) to the scenario model and mining the collected failure scenarios to find vulnerability characteristics of the ship tracking algorithm.

Acknowledgement. This work is financially supported by the National Natural Science Foundation of China (Project number: 61601428) and the National Science Foundation of China (Project number: 41506114).

References

1. Vivone, G., Braca, P., Horstmann, J.: Knowledge-based multitarget ship tracking for HF surface wave radar systems. IEEE Trans. Geosci. Remote Sens. **53**(7), 3931–3949 (2015)
2. Mahler, R.P.S.: Multitarget bayes filtering via first-order multitarget moments. IEEE Trans. Aerosp. Electron. Syst. **39**(4), 1152–1178 (2004)
3. Kreucher, C., Kastella, K., Hero, A.O.: Multitarget tracking using the joint multitarget probability density. IEEE Trans. Aerosp. Electron. Syst. **41**(4), 1396–1414 (2005)
4. Pulford, G.W.: Taxonomy of multiple target tracking methods. IEE Proc.-Radar, Sonar Navig. **152**(5), 291–304 (2005)
5. Morelande, M.R., Kreucher, C.M., Kastella, K.: A Bayesian approach to multiple target detection and tracking. IEEE Trans. Signal Process. **55**(5), 1589–1604 (2007)
6. Dzvonkovskaya, A., Gurgel, K.W., Rohling, H., Schlick, T.: Low power high frequency surface wave radar application for ship detection and tracking. In: International Conference on Radar, pp. 627–632 (2008)
7. Ponsford, A.M., Wang, J.: A review of high frequency surface wave radar for detection and tracking. Turk. J. Electr. Eng. Comput. Sci. **18**, 409–428 (2010)
8. Yi, W., Morelande, M.R., Kong, L., Yang, J.: An efficient multi-frame track-before-detect algorithm for multi-target tracking. IEEE J. Sel. Topics Signal Process. **7**(3), 421–434 (2013)
9. Sun, W., Ji, Y., Zhang, X., Yu, C., Dai, Y.: Ship target tracking based on adaptive alpha-beta filter in HFSWR. Adv. Mar. Sci. **33**(3), 394–402 (2015)
10. Braca, P., Grasso, R., Vespe, M., Maresca, S., Horstmann, J.: Application of the JPDA-UKF to HFSW radars for maritime situational awareness. In: International Conference on Information Fusion, pp. 2585–2592 (2012)
11. Maresca, S., Braca, P., Horstmann, J., Grasso, R.: Maritime surveillance using multiple high-frequency surface-wave radars. IEEE Trans. Geosci. Remote Sens. **52**(8), 5056–5071 (2014)
12. Chomsky, N.: Three models for the description of language. IRE Trans. Inf. Theory **2**(3), 113–124 (2002)

Genetic Programming for Lifetime Maximization in Wireless Sensor Networks with a Mobile Sink

Ying Li[1], Zhixing Huang[1], Jinghui Zhong[1(✉)], and Liang Feng[2]

[1] School of Computer Science and Engineering,
South China University of Technology, Guangzhou, China
jinghuizhong@scut.edu.cn
[2] College of Computer Science, Chongqing University, Chongqing, China

Abstract. Maximizing the lifetime of Wireless Sensor Network (WSN) with a mobile sink is a challenging and important problem that has attracted increasing research attentions. In the literature, heuristic based approaches have been proposed to solve the problem, such as the Greedy Maximum Residual Energy (GMRE) based method. However, existing heuristic based approaches highly rely on expert knowledge, which makes them inconvenient for practical applications. Taking this cue, in this paper, we propose an automatic method to construct heuristic for sink routing based on Genetic Programming (GP) approach. Empirical study shows that the proposed method can generate promising heuristics that achieve superior performance against existing methods with respect to the global lifetime of WSN.

1 Introduction

Wireless Sensor Network (WSN) is a network formed by sensor nodes (SNs) that communicate via wireless signals [1,2]. Compared with wired network, WSN has the advantage of less cost, higher robustness, plummy traceability and portability [3]. Owning to these advantages, WSN has been used in a range of real-world applications, such as earthquake monitoring [4], communication supervising [5], climate changing [6], smart home [7] and smart city design [8], etc.

In a WSN, the SNs are usually battery-powered and it is often difficult or even impossible to recharge the SNs. Thus, maximizing the lifetime of WSN is an important issue in many WSN applications [9–11]. In the literature, one of the effective and popular techniques to prolong the lifetime of WSN is using a mobile sink to collect information from the network. In particular, by moving the sink to proper locations (i.e., sink sites) of the network, the energy consumption of the network can be reduced and its lifetime can be prolonged [12,13]. However, how to schedule the moving paths of the sink, i.e., the Mobile Sink Scheduling Problem (MSSP), become a challenging and hop research topic recently.

Over the past decades, a number of efforts have been proposed in the literature to solve the MSSP. Existing works mainly adopted centralized approaches

---

The first author and the second author contributed equally to this work.

© Springer International Publishing AG 2017
Y. Shi et al. (Eds.): SEAL 2017, LNCS 10593, pp. 774–785, 2017.
https://doi.org/10.1007/978-3-319-68759-9_63

which require knowing the global information of the WSN such as network topology, communication costs, etc. For example, Wang et al. [14] proposed a linear programming optimization model to optimize the moving path of the sink. Similar work that uses LP methods to solve the MSSP can be found in [15,16]. Zhong and Zhang [17] proposed an Ant Colony Optimization approach to solve the MSSP. The centralized methods are capable of finding the globally optimal or near global optimal solutions, but they require large memory and long computational time. To overcome these limitations, decentralized approach have also been proposed recently. The key idea is to design heuristic rules to schedule the movements of the sink step-by-step. For example, Basagni et al. [18] proposed a Greedy maximum Residual Energy (GMRE) which moves the sink in rounds. At the end of each round, the sink makes a constant movement towards the node that has the most residual energy. Typically, the heuristic rules are designed in a fairly ad-hoc manner, and relies on expert intuition. However, these intuition often mislead the sink routing since the WSN is a complex system and the relationship between the heuristic rule and the final network lifetime are unintuitive. How to automatically design effective heuristic rule is still challenging.

To address the above issue, in this paper, a GP based approach is proposed to solve the MSSP. Our key idea is using GP to automatically learn a heuristic function that can dynamically schedule the movements of the sink node. GP is an evolutionary algorithm (EA) that solves user-defined tasks by the evolution of computer programs. It has been shown to be highly efficient in many applications, including symbolic regression [19,20], Job Shop Scheduling Problem (JSP) [21] and workflow scheduling [22], etc. However, to the best of our knowledge, there is little work in the literature that uses GP for the sink mobility optimization. Thus, this paper makes an attempt to apply the GP to solve this kind of problem.

In our proposed method, the "sense-think-act" paradigm is adopted to schedule the sink. In particular, the sink node detects the environment features first, and a high-level heuristic (HH) is then utilized to determine the moving strategy based on the input features. Finally, the sink will either remain stationary or move to the next location according to the strategy. The above steps are repeated until the WSN become "dead". To build effective heuristic, four environment features are defined and the Self-Learning Gene Expression Programming (SL-GEP) [23] is utilized to construct a HH. These environment features are combined by the common numerical functions. The proposed method is tested on WSNs with different scales and deployment strategies. The empirical results demonstrated that our method can achieve superior performance over several other approaches, in terms of maximizing the network lifetime.

2   Problem Definition

In this paper, we consider that there are two kinds of nodes in WSN: sink node and sensor node (SN). The SNs are static, battery-powered and deployed over the monitoring region to sense the physical world, while the sink node is mobile and used to collect data from the SNs. The sink node has unlimited power and move over the candidate locations (i.e. sink sites). According to [24], we evenly divide the monitoring region into discrete grids and use the intersection points of the grids as sink sites. Figure 1 shows a typical example of the WSN with 19 SNs and 35 sink sites.

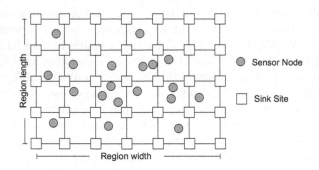

Fig. 1. A WSN with a single sink.

The maximum communication radius of the sink node is R. That is, a SN can communicate with the sink node in one hop if its distance to the sink node is less than or equal to R. If a SN is out of the communication radius of the sink node, its data can send to the sink node via a multi-hop manner. To minimize the energy consumption, a minimum spanning tree (MST) is constructed for message routing, whose root is the sink and nodes are SNs. Every sink site is associated with a corresponding MST.

As in [25], the energy consumption of transmitting one package data is given by:

$$C_{ij} = a * d_{ij}^2 + b. \tag{1}$$

where a and b are constants coefficient of communication energy consumption, C_{ij} is the energy consumption of transmitting one package data from the ith sensor to the sink node which is in the jth sink site. Since the real distance of package transmitting of ith sensor is the Euclidean distance between the ith sensor and its parent node in particular MST, d_{ij} represents the actual transmitting distance of the ith SN when sink node is in the jth sink site, i.e.,

$$d_{ij}^2 = (i_x - k_x)^2 + (i_y - k_y^2) \tag{2}$$

where x, y are the coordinate value and k is the parent node of the ith SN in the corresponding MST whose root is jth sink site.

When a WSN starts working, the sink node is initialized to a particular sink site. We assume that each SN has an initial energy of e_0 joule. Then, the sink node will stay at the sink site for certain time interval and move to a new sink site. Every time the sink moves to a new sink site, all SNs need to send a package to the sink node to construct a new MST. Since the model implements the multi-hop manner to transmit the packages, the energy consumption F for the ith SN in setting up the MST is the product of the number of SNs in the ith SN's sub-tree in MST and the energy consumption of the ith SN to transmit one package, i.e.,

$$F_{ij} = C_{ij} * N_{ij}. \tag{3}$$

where F_{ij} is the energy consumption for setting up the new MST for the ith SN when the sink node moves to the j sink site and N_{ij} is the number of SNs in the subtree of node i in MST when the sink node moves to the jth sink site.

The sink will stay at the site at least t_{min}. The sink judge whether it need to move to other sink site every t_{min}, to balance the energy consumption among the nodes. The broadcasting procedure will be omitted if the sink is remained in the original location. The maximum distance that sink can travel from one site to another is denoted as d.

According to [18], a WSN is deemed as dead when there is at least one SN running out of energy. Thus, the lifetime of a WSN can be expressed by

$$T = t_{min} * n, \tag{4}$$

where n is the number of the rounds (each round is a time interval of t_{min}) the WSN can work before it dies. The MSSP requires scheduling the moving paths of the sink properly so as to maximize the network lifetime.

3   Proposed Method

3.1   General Framework

In this paper, we adopt the "Sense-think-act" paradigm to schedule the sink mobility. Based on this paradigm, the sink will sense the environment features at the end of each round. Then, a high-level heuristic (HH) is utilized to determine the next sink site. Finally, the sink will move to the next sink site and stay there for a time interval of t_{min}. The HH is formed by various environment features (or terminals) and numerical functions such as sin and +. Based on the above scheduling mechanism, the problem of maximizing the lifetime of a WSN can be converted to a combinatorial optimization problem: *Given the terminal and function set, find the best HH $\Gamma*$ to determine the next location of the sink so that the network lifetime can be maximized, i.e.,*

$$\Gamma^* = \arg \min_{\Gamma} T(\Gamma), \tag{5}$$

where $T(\Gamma)$ is the network lifetime of the WSN that uses Γ as the HH to schedule the sink.

To search for the best Γ^*, the GP approach is used in the proposed method because GP is quite suitable for finding tree structure heuristic rules and formula

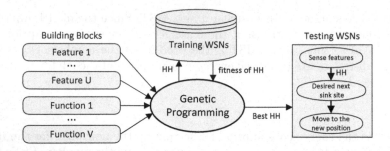

Fig. 2. The general structure of the proposed GP-based framework

[19,22]. Figure 2 illustrates the general structure of the proposed framework. The terminals and functions are defined in advance based on domain knowledge. They are used to build blocks to construct the HH. WSNs with different scales and deploying strategies are generated to evaluate the fitness (or quality) of a HH. That is, the fitness value of a HH is the average network lifetime of the training WSNs where the sink node is scheduled by the HH. Guided by this fitness function, the GP attempts to find a near global optimal HH via an iterative search process. At the end of the GP, the best HH is decoded for practical use.

3.2   Terminal Definition

To facilitate GP constructing promising HH, four low-level heuristics (or terminals) are defined as follows:

– *Minimum nodes energy (λ)* this terminal represents the minimum energy of the nodes covered by the candidate sink site.

$$\lambda = \min \{node\ i's\ energy | \text{SNs covered by the current sink site}\} \qquad (6)$$

– *Local global network lifetime (κ)* this terminal represents the network lifetime if sink remain in the candidate sink site till the network dies. The value of κ is computed by:

$$\kappa = \min \left\{ \frac{node\ i's\ energy}{C_{xi}} | \text{SNs covered by the current sink site} \right\} \qquad (7)$$

– *Average node energy (μ)* - the average node energy is calculated by:

$$\mu = \frac{\sum_{i=0}^{maxNode} e_i}{maxNode} \qquad (8)$$

where $maxNode$ is the number of nodes covered by the candidate sink site and e_i is the ith node's current energy.

– *Average energy consumption of nodes* (ν) -the average energy consumption is calculated by:

$$\nu = \frac{\sum_{i=0}^{maxNode} C_{ix}}{maxNode} \tag{9}$$

where C_{ix} is the energy consumption of transmitting one package from node i to site x.

3.3 Framework Implementation

In this paper, a recent published GP variant named SL-GEP [23] is adopted to search for the optimal HH. In SL-GEP, each chromosome represents a candidate heuristic, which is a fixed-length string that comprises of two parts. The first part is the main program which gives the final output, and the second part contains sub functions to be used in the main program. Both the main program and the sub-function parts can be translated into a mathematical formula by using the Breadth-First-traversal scheme. A typical example of the chromosome of SL-GEP can be expressed as:

$$[ADF_1, *, ADF_2, ADF_2, \kappa, \lambda, \sin, \kappa, \mu, \nu, +, *, b, a, b, -, a, b] \tag{10}$$

Figure 3 illustrates the decoded expression trees of the chromosome.

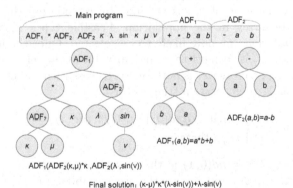

Fig. 3. The illustration of chromosome and tree structure demonstration

Based on the above chromosome representation, the SL-GEP evolves the chromosomes in the following procedures.

The first step is to generate a random initial population. Each chromosome in the population is represented by a vector of symbols:

$$X_i = [x_{i,1}, x_{i,2}, \ldots, x_{i,n}] \tag{11}$$

where n is the chromosome length. The value of $x_{i,j}$ is set as a feasible value (e.g., function, terminal, or ADF) randomly.

The second step is mutation which generates a mutant vector for each parent chromosome. In particular, the "DE/current-to-best/1" mutation is adopted to generate the mutant vectors:

$$Y_i = X_i + F \cdot (X_{best} - X_i) + \beta \cdot (X_{r1} - X_{r2}). \tag{12}$$

where X_{best} is the best-so-far chromosome, X_{r1} and X_{r2} are two random individuals selected from the population. X_i, X_{r1}, X_{r2}, and X_{best} are discrete vectors, the numerical operators such as $\cdot$ and $+$ are redefined in SL-GEP to evolve tree-structure solutions. Based on the newly defined operators, each element of Y_i is assigned by mutating the corresponding element in X_i. The mutation probability φ is calculated by the following two sub-steps: sub-step 1: randomly set the values of F and β, i.e., $F = rand(0,1), \beta = rand(0,1)$, where $rand(a,b)$ returns a random value uniformly distributed within $[a,b]$; sub-step 2: For each $x_{i,j}$, a mutation probability is calculated by

$$\varphi = 1 - (1 - F \cdot \psi(x_{best,j}, x_{i,j})) * (1 - \beta \cdot \psi(x_{r1,j}, x_{r2,j})) \tag{13}$$

where $\psi(a,b)$ is defined as

$$\psi(a,b) = \begin{cases} 1, \text{if } a \neq b \\ 0, \text{otherwise} \end{cases} \tag{14}$$

If $y_{i,j} \in$ sub-function, it will be set to a random value, as done in the initialization step. Otherwise, the type of $y_{i,j}$ is set first by considering the frequencies of feasible types appearing in the population. Feasible types that appear more often in the population are more likely to be selected. Once the feasible type of $y_{i,j}$ is determined, $y_{i,j}$ is then set to a random value of the selected feasible type.

In the third step, a crossover is performed to cross each target vector X_i with its mutant vector Y_i to generate a trial vector U_i. i.e.,

$$u_{i,j} = \begin{cases} y_{i,j}, \text{if } rand(0,1) < CR \quad \text{or} \quad j = k \\ x_{i,j}, \text{otherwise} \end{cases} \tag{15}$$

where CR with $CR = rand(0,1)$ is the crossover rate, k is a random integer between 1 and n, $u_{i,j}, y_{i,j}$ and $x_{i,j}$ are the jth variables of U_i, Y_i and X_i, respectively.

Finally, the selection operation selects the fitter solution between each pair of the target and trial vector to form a new population for the next generation, i.e.,

$$X_i = \begin{cases} U_i, \text{if } f(U_i) > f(X_i) \\ X_i, \text{otherwise} \end{cases} \tag{16}$$

where $f(X)$ is the fitness evaluation function which returns the network lifetime.

The second to fourth operations are repeated until the terminated conditions are met.

4   Experiment Studies

4.1   Training and Testing Data

In the simulation studies, we generate WSNs with different features for training and testing. For all WSNs, the SNs are deployed in a rectangle region which is evenly divided into discrete grids. The size of the discrete grids is 6 m and the intersect points of the discrete grids are regarded as candidate sink sites. The initial settings of all WSNs are set to be: $e_0 = 50000$ J, $t_{min} = 500$ s, $R = 25$ m, and $d = 10$ m. The SNs are distributed uniformly or with a gaussian distribution. Figure 4 illustrates two examples of the WSNs.

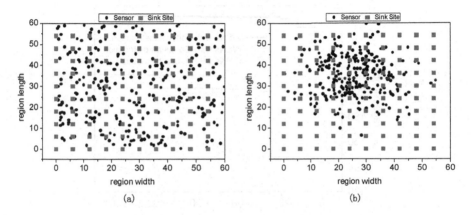

Fig. 4. Typical examples of the training WSNs. (a) a WSN with SNs in uniform distribution. (b) a WSN with SNs in Gaussian distribution.

During the training process, we learn heuristics from three different datasets respectively. The first dataset contains 100 WSNs with uniform distribution of SNs. The second dataset contains 100 WSNs with Gaussian distribution of SNs are used for training. The third dataset contains 100 WSNs with hybrid distribution (i.e., 50 WSNs with uniform distribution and 50 WSNs with Gaussian distribution). Our goal is to investigate which dataset is better for learning general heuristic rule. After the training process, the heuristics learned are test on testing datasets. We generate 60 WSNs with different scales and deploying strategies for testing. Among them, 30 testing WSNs contain SNs with uniform distribution and the remaining 30 WSNs contains SNs with Gaussian distribution. It should be noted that the number of SNs and the size of the regions are different for different testing WSNs.

To investigate the effectiveness of the proposed method, seven heuristics rules are used for comparison. The GMRE is a well-known heuristic proposed in [18]. The RM is a heuristic which selects the next sink site randomly. The four terminals, i.e., κ, λ, μ, and υ are also regarded as heuristic rules for comparison. In addition, we manually design a heuristic by multiplying the four terminals as the last heuristic. As in [18], the network lifetime is considered as the most important metric for performance evaluation.

4.2 Results and Analysis

For each training strategy, the SL-GEP is performed for 100 runs on the training data accordingly. Figure 5 illustrates the evolution of the best network lifetime (in round). It can be observed that for both three cases, the best network lifetime become longer as the evolution goes on, which means that the heuristic rule found by the proposed method become better and better.

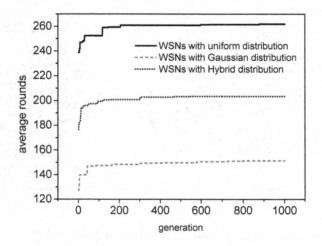

Fig. 5. Fitness value in training

Denote the best heuristics rule learned from the three datasets as Γ_U, Γ_G, and Γ_H respectively. Three typical examples of Γ_U, Γ_G, and Γ_H are expressed in (17), (18), and (19) respectively.

$$
\begin{aligned}
\Gamma_U =&((((((((\kappa - \lambda)/(\kappa - \lambda)) + ((\kappa - \lambda) * ((\kappa/\mu) * (\kappa * \mu)))) \\
&/(((\mu/\mu) * (\mu * \mu)) * \mu)) * ((((\kappa - \lambda)/(\kappa - \lambda)) + (\kappa - \lambda) \\
&* ((\kappa/\mu) * (\kappa * \mu)))) * (((\mu/\mu) * (\mu * \mu)) * \mu)))/(((\lambda/\nu)/ \\
&(\kappa + \nu)) * ((\lambda/\nu) * (\kappa + \nu)))) * ((((((\kappa - \lambda)/(\kappa - \lambda)) + ((\kappa \\
&- \lambda) * ((\kappa/\mu) * (\kappa * \mu))))/(((\mu/\mu) * (\mu * \mu)) * \mu)) * ((((\kappa - \lambda) \\
&/(\kappa - \lambda)) + ((\kappa - \lambda) * ((\kappa/\mu) * (\kappa * \mu)))) * (((\mu/\mu) \\
&* (\mu * \mu)) * \mu))) * (((\lambda/\nu)/(\kappa + \nu)) * ((\lambda/\nu) * (\kappa + \nu)))))
\end{aligned} \tag{17}
$$

$$
\begin{aligned}
\Gamma_G =&((((((((\kappa/\mu)*(\mu*\kappa))/(\nu*\lambda))*((\nu*\lambda)*((\kappa/\mu)*(\mu*\kappa))))\\
&-((\kappa*\kappa)+\lambda))/(((\mu*\lambda)/(\mu*\nu))*((\mu*\nu)*(\mu*\lambda))))*\\
&((((\mu*\lambda)/(\mu*\nu))*((\mu*\nu)*(\mu*\lambda)))*(((((\kappa/\mu)*(\mu*\kappa))/\\
&(\nu*\lambda))*((\nu*\lambda)*((\kappa/\mu)*(\mu*\kappa))))-((\kappa*\kappa)+\lambda))))
\end{aligned}
\tag{18}
$$

$$
\begin{aligned}
\Gamma_H =&(((\mu-((\mu-((\kappa+\mu)*\mu))+((\kappa+\mu)*\mu)))+(((\kappa-\\
&((\kappa+\lambda)*\lambda))+((\kappa+\lambda)*\lambda))/\lambda))*(((\kappa-((\kappa+\lambda)*\lambda))\\
&+((\kappa+\lambda)*\lambda))/\lambda))
\end{aligned}
\tag{19}
$$

Next, we test the performance of the best HH found by using the testing WSNs. Since the number of rounds is in proportion to network lifetime, we use the average rounds to represent the network lifetime. We apply the three heuristics learned from the three datasets to the 60 testing cases (30 WSNs with uniform distribution and 30 WSNs with Gaussian distribution).

Table 1. Comparison results

Function	Case	
	Uniform case	Gaussian case
κ	199.7	87.8
λ	193.3	70.6
μ	193.3	78.8
ν	197.9	74.7
GMRE	193.4	80.7
RM	190.3	71.5
Human designed	193.3	80.7
Γ_U	**211.2**	**99.7**
Γ_G	**207.3**	**106.6**
Γ_H	**210.7**	**103.8**

Table 1 lists the final comparison results. It can be observed that the heuristics generated by SL-GEP can improve the network lifetime by about 8% in uniform distribution and 30% in Gaussian distribution. In addition, the heuristics learned by the SL-GEP can outperform other heuristics designed by human. An interesting discovery is that Γ_U performs better than Γ_G on uniform case, while Γ_G performs better than Γ_U on Gaussian case. These results indicate that the heuristic learned from one dataset performs better in testing WSNs that are of the same types.

5   Conclusion

In this paper, we have proposed a GP based approach to maximize the lifetime of WSNs with a mobile sink. In particular, the self-learning gene expression programming is utilized to construct high-level heuristic which can dynamically schedule the moving path of the sink node. To evaluate the proposed approach, empirical study on WSNs with different scales and deployment strategies are conducted. The superior performance obtained against several other approaches confirmed the efficacy of our proposed method. As for future work, an interesting research direction to extend the proposed framework to optimize multiple objectives, such as the path length of the sink and the readability (or complexity) of the solution.

Acknowledgment. This work is partially supported under the National Natural Science Foundation of China (Grant Nos. 61602181, 61603064), Fundamental Research Funds for the Central Universities (Grant No. 2017ZD053), Frontier Interdisciplinary Research Fund for the Central Universities (Grant No. 106112017CDJQJ188828).

References

1. Bouyahi, M., Ezzedine, T.: Design of smart Bridge based on WSN for efficient measuring of temperature, strain and humidity. In: 2016 4th International Conference on Control Engineering Information Technology (CEIT), pp. 1–5 (2016)
2. Boubrima, A., Bechkit, W., Rivano, H.: Optimal WSN deployment models for air pollution monitoring. IEEE Trans. Wirel. Commun. **16**(5), 2723–2735 (2017)
3. Ren, G.L., Khairi, N.A.B.F., Ismail, W.: Design and implementation of environmental monitoring using RFID and WSN platform. In:2016 IEEE Asia-Pacific Conference on Applied Electromagnetics (APACE), pp. 328–333 (2016)
4. Lu, M., Zhao, X., Huang, Y.: Fast localization for emergency monitoring and rescue in disaster scenarios based on WSN. In: 2016 14th International Conference on Control, Automation, Robotics and Vision (ICARCV), pp. 1–6. (2016). doi:10. 1109/ICARCV.2016.7838790
5. Agemura, S., Katayama, K., Ohsaki, H.: On the effect of wireless communication range heterogeneity on WSN performance. In: International Conference on Information Networking (ICOIN), pp. 35–40 (2017)
6. Arunachalam, B., Arjun, D., Prahlada, R.B., Pasupuleti, H., Dwarakanath, V.: Sensing service framework for climate alert system using WSN-cloud infrastructure. In: 2015 9th International Conference on Sensing Technology (ICST), pp. 671–676 (2015)
7. Alaiad, A., Zhou, L.: Patients' adoption of WSN-based smart home healthcare systems: an integrated model of facilitators and barriers. IEEE Trans. Prof. Commun. **60**(1), 4–23 (2017)
8. Alvi, A.N., Bouk, S.H., Ahmed, S.H., Yaqub, M.A., Sarkar, M., Song, H.: BEST-MAC: bitmap-assisted efficient and scalable TDMA-based WSN MAC protocol for smart cities. IEEE Access **4**, 312–322 (2016)
9. Ye, Y., Luo, H., Cheng, J., Lu, S., Zhang, L.: A two-tier data dissemination model for large-scale wireless sensor networks. In: Proceedings of the 8th Annual International Conference on Mobile Computing and Networking, pp. 148–159. ACM (2002)
10. Lin, C.-J., Chou, P.-L., Chou, C.-F.: HCDD: hierarchical cluster-based data dissemination in wireless sensor networks with mobile sink. In: Proceedings of the 2006 International Conference on Wireless Communications and Mobile Computing, pp. 1189–1194. ACM (2006)

11. Jea, D., Somasundara, A., Srivastava, M.: Multiple controlled mobile elements (data mules) for data collection in sensor networks. In: Prasanna, V.K., Iyengar, S.S., Spirakis, P.G., Welsh, M. (eds.) DCOSS 2005. LNCS, vol. 3560, pp. 244–257. Springer, Heidelberg (2005). doi:10.1007/11502593_20

12. Kushal, B.Y., Chitra, M.: Cluster based routing protocol to prolong network lifetime through mobile sink in WSN. In: 2016 IEEE International Conference on Recent Trends in Electronics, Information Communication Technology (RTEICT), pp. 1287–1291 (2016)

13. Ren, J., Zhang, Y., Zhang, K., Liu, A., Chen, J., Shen, X.S.: Lifetime and energy hole evolution analysis in data-gathering wireless sensor networks. IEEE Trans. Ind. Inform. **12**(2), 788–800 (2016)

14. Wang, Z.M., Basagni, S., Melachrinoudis, E., Petrioli, C.: Exploiting sink mobility for maximizing sensor networks lifetime. In: Proceedings of the 38th Annual Hawaii International Conference on System Sciences, HICSS 2005, p. 287a. IEEE (2005)

15. Yun, Y., Xia, Y.: Maximizing the lifetime of wireless sensor networks with mobile sink in delay-tolerant applications. IEEE Trans. Mob. Comput. **9**(9), 1308–1318 (2010)

16. Shi, Y., Hou, Y.T.: Theoretical results on base station movement problem for sensor network. In: The 27th Conference on Computer Communications INFOCOM 2008, pp. 1–5. IEEE (2008)

17. Zhong, J., Zhang, J.: Ant colony optimization algorithm for lifetime maximization in wireless sensor network with mobile sink. In: Proceedings of the 14th Annual Conference on Genetic and Evolutionary Computation, pp. 1199–1204. ACM (2012)

18. Basagni, S., Carosi, A., Melachrinoudis, E., Petrioli, C., Wang, Z.M.: Controlled sink mobility for prolonging wireless sensor networks lifetime. Wirel. Netw. **14**(6), 831–858 (2008)

19. Zhong, J., Cai, W., Lees, M., Luo, L.: Automatic model construction for the behavior of human crowds. Appl. Soft Comput. **56**, 368–378 (2017)

20. Zhong, J., Feng, L., Ong, Y.-S.: Gene expression programming: a survey. IEEE Comput. Intell. Mag. **12**(3), 54–72 (2017)

21. Tay, J.C., Ho, N.B.: Evolving dispatching rules using genetic programming for solving multi-objective flexible job-shop problems. Comput. Ind. Eng. **54**(3), 453–473 (2008)

22. Xiao, Q., Zhong, J., Chen, W.N., Zhan, Z.H., Zhang, J.: Indicator-based multi-objective genetic programming for workflow scheduling problem. In: 2017 Genetic and Evolutionary Computation Conference Companion (GECCO), pp. 217–218 (2017)

23. Zhong, J., Ong, Y.S., Cai, W.: Self-learning gene expression programming. IEEE Trans. Evol. Comput. **20**(1), 65–80 (2016)

24. Bhatti, R., Kaur, G.: Virtual grid based energy efficient mobile sink routing algorithm for WSN. In: 2017 11th International Conference on Intelligent Systems and Control (ISCO), pp. 30–33 (2017)

25. Heinzelman, W.R., Chandrakasan, A., Balakrishnan, H.: Energy-efficient communication protocol for wireless microsensor networks. In: Proceedings of the 33rd Annual Hawaii International Conference on System Sciences, pp. 1–10 (2000)

Unsupervised Change Detection for Remote Sensing Images Based on Principal Component Analysis and Differential Evolution

Mi Song, Yanfei Zhong, Ailong Ma$^{(\boxtimes)}$, and Liangpei Zhang

State Key Laboratory of Information Engineering in Surveying,
Mapping and Remote Sensing, Wuhan University, Wuhan 430000, China
whusongmi@hotmail.com,
{zhongyanfei,maailong007}@whu.edu.cn

Abstract. This paper proposed a novel method for unsupervised change detection of remote sensing images using principal component analysis and differential evolution (PDECD). PDECD consists of two main steps. Firstly, an eigenvector space is generated by principal component analysis (PCA) of image blocks. Difference image is projected onto the eigenvector space to extract image local features, which is essentially composed of local smoothing feature and edge fidelity features. Then PDECD regards change detection as an optimal clustering problem and utilizes the differential evolution algorithm (DE) to search for the optimal change detection results without any priori knowledge. Compared with the existing methods, PDECD is not only robust to image noise, but also sensitive to small changed details. In addition, PDECD can avoid tracking to the local optima in change detection process and improve the detection performance due to the powerful global optimization capability of DE. Considering the image data belonging to two clusters cannot separated by sharp boundaries, so the *Jm* index of standard fuzzy clustering method is used as the objective function of DE. In order to improve the robustness and automatic detection capability of PDECD, control parameters of DE have been adjusted adaptively. Experiments conducted on real SAR and optical remote sensing images demonstrate the effectiveness of the proposed method.

Keywords: Change detection · Detail preserving · Differential evolution · Principal component analysis · Noise-robust · Remote sensing imagery

1 Introduction

Change detection is a process aims at identifying differences in the state of land cover by analyzing a pair of images acquired on the same geographical area at different times [1]. It has been widely used in urban expansion monitoring, disaster loss assessment, burned area identification, and environment protection [2]. Many change detection techniques for remote sensing images of coarse spatial resolution have been developed. No need of priori assumption and estimation of data distribution, clustering-based methods regard change detection problem as unsupervised classification or segmentation process. Considering the image data belonging to two clusters cannot separated

© Springer International Publishing AG 2017
Y. Shi et al. (Eds.): SEAL 2017, LNCS 10593, pp. 786–796, 2017.
https://doi.org/10.1007/978-3-319-68759-9_64

by sharp boundaries, so one of the most popular clustering-based methods is fuzzy c-means (FCM) algorithm [3], which can retain more information than hard clustering in some cases. However, the standard FCM algorithm is very sensitive to noise and initial value, thus it may sometimes get stuck at a suboptimal clusters. Celik proposed a computationally simple yet effective automatic change detection method [4], in which PCA is employed to extract image local features and the feature vector space is clustered into two clusters using k-means algorithm. However, k-means is a hard clustering method and it will affect detection accuracy.

In order to search for the optimal clusters and improve the detection performance, evolutionary algorithm has been introduced to solve change detection problem. In [5], a method based on genetic algorithms (GA) is proposed for change detection of satellite images. This method directly optimizes the binary change detection mask without any assumptions, thus it can be applied to different sensors. Anyway, long individual leads to low efficiency and spatial information is not taken into account in the objective function. The change detection approach proposed by Li et al., which is based on multiobjective evolutionary algorithm [6], achieved high accuracy in SAR image testing, but mean filtering as the spatial feature may lead to edge blur and detail loss. In summary, existing methods may get stuck into the local optima in change detection process, or the spatial information is improperly used, which will affect the detection accuracy.

To overcome the problems mentioned above, this paper proposed an unsupervised change detection method combined local PCA and differential evolution. PCA is employed to project the difference image onto eigenvector space and extract image local features [4], then adaptive DE is employed to automatically search for the optimal clusters in eigenvector space. Output is a binary map (0: unchanged, 1: changed). Actually the eigenvector space is composed of local smoothing feature and edge fidelity features, thus the proposed method is robust to image noise while sensitive to small change details.

This paper is organized as follows. Section 2 describes the methodology of proposed method. Section 3 describes the data sets and analyze experiment results. Section 4 concludes this paper.

2 Proposed Methodology

PDECD consists of three steps: (1) Generating difference images. (2) Constructing local PCA feature thought projecting the difference image onto eigenvector space. (3) Difference analysis base on adaptive DE, and produce the binary change map. The framework of proposed PDECD is shown in Fig. 1. Steps are described in detail as follows.

2.1 Generating Difference Image

The first step of the proposed algorithm is create the difference image. Assuming X_{T1} and X_{T2} are two images taken at difference times T_1 and T_2 but cover the same geographical area and coregistered with each other, X_{T1} and X_{T2} have the same size

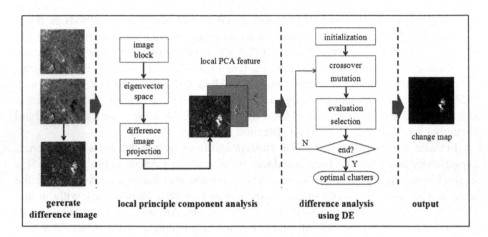

Fig. 1. Framework of proposed change detection method PDECD

$H \times W$. Let Xd be the difference image, and it can be defined according to the type of input image. For the optical images, Xd is defined using absolute-valued difference of intensity of two images.

$$Xd = |X_{T1} - X_{T2}| \tag{1}$$

As for SAR images, we use the log-ratio operator to create the difference image because it can reduce the multiplicative noise effectively. The operator is defined using (2). Where Xd_i correspond to the gray values of the ith pixel of image Xd

$$Xd = |\log X_{T1} - \log X_{T2}| \tag{2}$$

2.2 Local Principal Component Analysis

Challenges of change detection include details maintaining and noise removing, so the algorithm should be noise-insensitive meanwhile keeping change details (e.g., edge). So local PCA is applied to the difference image to create an eigenvector space.

Difference image is divided into $h \times h$ non-overlapping image blocks. The block centers on pixel $Xd(m,n), 1 \leq m \leq H, 1 \leq n \leq W$ is defined using (3), where $\lfloor \rfloor$ and $\lceil \rceil$ are mathematical ceiling operator which round a number up or down to the nearest integer, respectively.

$$B(m,n) = \{Xd(p,q) \mid m - \lceil h/2 \rceil + 1 \leq p \leq m + h - \lceil h/2 \rceil, n - \lceil h/2 \rceil + 1 \leq q \leq n + h - \lceil h/2 \rceil\} \tag{3}$$

Stretching each block into a column vector and the average vector ψ is defined using (4), where $M = \lfloor (H \times W)/(h \times h) \rfloor$ is the total number of blocks. The difference vector Δ_p is calculated using (5). Then the covariance matrix C can be calculated using (6), where $(\bullet)^T$ denotes transposition of the vector.

$$\psi = \frac{1}{M}\sum_{p=1}^{M} B_p \tag{4}$$

$$\Delta_p = B^p - \psi \tag{5}$$

$$C = \frac{1}{M}\sum_{p=1}^{M} \Delta_p \Delta_p^T \tag{6}$$

Through eigenvalue decomposition, the eigenvalues and eigenvectors are obtained. Sorting eigenvalues in descending order and select the corresponding eigenvector e_s to construct the eigenvector space. Then the difference image is projected onto eigenvector space using (7), where $X_{PCA}(m,n)$ is the corresponding point to image pixel $Xd(m,n)$ in PCA eigenvector space.

$$X_{PCA}(m,n) = e_s^T(B(m,n) - \psi) \tag{7}$$

Without losing generality, Bern data set is taken as an example, wen can find that local PCA feature X_{PCA} is essentially consisted of smooth feature and edge features in different direction, as shown in Fig. 2. Therefore, local PCA feature can be used for both denoising and edge enhancement.

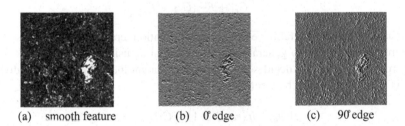

(a)   smooth feature   (b) $0°$ edge   (c) $90°$ edge

Fig. 2. Local PCA features of difference image

After extracting the local PCA feature X_{PCA} mentioned above, change detection process is to divide the feature space into two classes (changed and unchanged), so change detection problem can be transformed into a optimal clustering problem in the feature space.

2.3   Difference Image Analysis Using Differential Evolution

Differential evolution algorithm (DE) proposed by Storn and Price [7], is a floating point encoded evolutionary algorithm with powerful global optimization ability. DE has demonstrated good convergence properties and it is easy to understand [8]. Xu *et al.* proposed a hybrid computational model based on a modified probability collectives and DE algorithms for the purpose of improved solutions for real-valued optimization problems [9]. Coletta *et al.* employed differential evolution algorithm to optimise the combination of classifier and cluster ensembles [10]. Zhong *et al.* proposed a differential evolution-based clustering algorithm for remote sensing imagery and proved that DE can achieve high accuracy in image clustering [11]. Therefore, DE is employed to search for the optimal clusters in local PCA feature space X_{PCA}. Four main steps of PDECD are described as follows.

Initialization. The population of DE is consisted of NP individuals, $G = \{G_1, G_2, \ldots, G_{NP}\}$. Each individual is a vector, which represents two clusters. Individual is randomly generated in the solution space as follows:

$$G_{ij} = \min X_{PCA} + rand(0, 1) \cdot (\max X_{PCA} - \min X_{PCA}) \tag{8}$$

where $i = 1, 2, \ldots, NP, j = 1, 2, \ldots, D$, G_{ij} represents the jth dimension of ith individual in current population, D is the dimension of solution.min Xd and max Xd correspond to the minimum and maximum value in image Xd respectively, $rand(a, b)$ is a random value between a and b.

Mutation and Crossover. For each target individual G_i, randomly pick three exclusive parent individuals G_{r1}, G_{r2}, G_{r3} from current population and generate a mutant individual v_i using (9), where $F \in [0, 1]$ is the scaling factor and it can decide the degree of mutation and improve diversity of population. v_i has to be constrained after mutation.

$$v_i = G_{r1} + F \cdot (G_{r2} - G_{r3}) \tag{9}$$

In order to spread desirable genes among population, crossover operator is applied to the mutant individual to generate a trial individual q_{ij} using (10), where $CR \in [0, 1]$ is the crossover rate and it decides the influence of parent individual on trial individual. *randj* is a random integer between $[0, D]$.

$$q_{ij} = \begin{cases} v_{ij}, & if(rand(0,1) \leq CR \, or \, j = randj) \\ G_{ij} & if(rand(0,1) > CR) \end{cases} \tag{10}$$

It should be mentioned that a self-adaptive strategy (refers to [12]) is employed to adjusted the control parameters (F, CR) for the purpose of enhance the robustness and automatic detection capability PDECD.

Evaluation. Objective function value of each individual determines its likelihood of surviving into the next generation. Considering the feature data belonging to two clusters cannot separated by sharp boundaries, so the objective function is defined using Jm index of standard FCM.

$$f(G_i) = \sum_{k=1}^{N} \sum_{c=\{0,1\}} u_{ck}^m \|X_{PCA}(k) - G_i^c\| \tag{11}$$

where $N = H \times W$ is the size of image, G_i^0 and G_i^1 correspond to clusters of changed and unchanged class, respectively. u_{ck} is the fuzzy membership degree of the kth pixel to cluster G_i^c, u_{ck} and G_i^c can be obtained using (12) and (13). m denotes fuzzy component and usually set to 2. $\|\bullet\|$ represents the Euclidean distance. u_{ck} satisfies the constraints $\sum_{c=0}^{1} u_{ck} = 1$, $0 \le u_{ck} \le 1$. If $Xd_k = G_i(c)$, it indicates that the pixel belongs to class c, and u_{ck} should be set to 1.

$$u_{ck} = \frac{\|X_{PCA}(k) - G_i^c\|^{-1/(m-1)}}{\sum_{c=\{0,1\}} \|X_{PCA}(k) - G_i^c\|^{-1/(m-1)}} \tag{12}$$

$$G_i^c = \frac{\sum_{k=1}^{N} u_{ck}^m X_{PCA}(k)}{\sum_{k=1}^{N} u_{ck}^m} \tag{13}$$

After evaluating the quality of each individual, to keep the population size a constant, DE selects a set of solutions pass into next generation. Selection is executed between target individual and trial individual using (14), where G_i' is the ith individual in next generation, $f(\cdot)$ represents the objective function value.

$$G_i' = \begin{cases} q_i, & if(f(q_i) \le f(G_i)) \\ G_i & if(f(q_i) > f(G_i)) \end{cases} \tag{14}$$

If the number of iterations has reach the maximum threshold, then the evolution should be terminated and output the optimal clusters. Otherwise, repeat evolutionary steps.

Generating Change Detection Map. Image pixels and data points in local PCA feature space are one-to-one corresponding in position. Assigned label (0: unchanged, 1: changed) to each pixel according its fuzzy membership degree to the optimal clusters using (15), where $N = H \times W$ is the size of image.

$$M_k = \begin{cases} 0, & if(u_{0,k} \ge u_{1,k}) \\ 1 & if(u_{0,k} < u_{1,k}) \end{cases}, k = 1, 2, \ldots, N \tag{15}$$

3   Experiments and Analysis

In order to verify the effectiveness of the proposed PDECD, real SAR and optical data sets are selected for testing. All the images have been through radiometric correction, geometric correction and geometric registration. Meanwhile, the experimental results of

FCM (fuzzy c-means algorithm [3]), PCA-K (PCA is employed to extract the image local features and the feature vector space is clustered using k-means algorithm [4]), and GA (encoding the change mask and evolving it using genetic algorithm [5]) will also be presented to compare with PDECD.

Change maps have been compared with reference map in order to quantitatively analyze the experimental results. Commonly used Evaluation indexes are adopted to access the effect of image change detection, include false alarm (FA), miss alarm (MA), overall accuracy (OA) and Kappa coefficient. FA is the number of pixels which are misjudged to be changed and MA is the number of pixels which are misjudged to be unchanged.

3.1   Data Set Description

Optical Data Set. The first data set is consist of two optical images, which were obtained by Landsat 5 in 1986 and Landsat 7 in 2000, respectively. This data set covers Shahu area in Wuhan. Image size of 250 * 250 pixels with 30 m spatial resolution. Channel 3 is selected for testing. The change was caused by surrounding new buildings. The two images and corresponding available ground truth, which has 7116 changed pixels, are shown in Fig. 3.

    (a)   1986   (b)   2000   (c)   reference

Fig. 3. Shahu data set. (a) Image acquired in 1986. (b) Image acquired in 2000. (c) Reference map

SAR Data Set. Different from optical image, SAR image is affected by speckle noise. In order to verify the applicability of this method for SAR images, the second data set consists of two single band SAR images with size of 301 * 301 acquired by ERS-2in April 1999 and May 1999, respectively. Between the two dates, the River Aare inundated parts of Bern and Thun. So the valley between Bern and Thun is chosen as a test place to extract the flooded region. The two images and corresponding available ground truth, which has 1155 changed pixels, are shown in Fig. 4.

(a) Apr. 1999   (b) May. 1999   (c) reference

Fig. 4. Bern data set. (a) Image acquired in April 1999. (b) Image acquired in May 1999. (c) Reference map.

3.2 Parameters Setting

Parameters of PDECD are set according to Table 1 and the parameters of compared methods are adjusted to the best as follows:

FCM: fuzzy component is 2, the number of iterations is 1000.
GA: population consists of 20 individuals, crossover rate is 0.8, mutation rate is 0.01, and the maximum iterations is set to be 200,000.
PCA-K: neighborhood size of PCA is 3 × 3, the maximum iterations is set to be 1000.

Table 1. Parameters setting

Parameter	Meaning	Value
NP	Population size	20
$maxgen$	Maximum iterations	100
F_0	Initial scale factor	0.8
CR_0	Initial crossover rate	0.2
h	PCA feature dimension	3
m	Fuzzy component	2

3.3 Experiment Results

The results of the experiments on the Shahu data set are shown in Fig. 4 and listed in Table 2. In Shahu data set, noise interruption is small, water changes are significant, but changes caused by new buildings are relatively weak. We can find that FCM (see Fig. 5(a)), and GA (see Fig. 5(b)) are context-insensitive, so some new building changes are not detected. Because these methods do not take into account the local information. It is obvious that the change objects are more complete in change maps of PCA-K (see Fig. 5(c)), and proposed PDECD (see Fig. 5(d)), because both of them utilize local PCA feature, which contains edge feature. From Table 2, we can find that PDECD can achieve higher accuracy than PCA-K, because PCA-K is easy to fall into local optima in change detection process, while PDECD can obtain the global optimal change detection result due to the utilization of DE.

The results of the experiments on the Bern data set are shown in Fig. 5 and listed in Table 2. Bern data set is suffer from speckle noise and the change is strong but the object is relatively small. FCM (see Fig. 6(a)) is not only sensitive to noise, but also leave many change area undetected. GA (see Fig. 6(b)) detect the change object more completely, but it cannot resist image noise. PCA-K (see Fig. 6(c)), and PDECD (see Fig. 6(d)) generate satisfactory change maps with less white noise points, meanwhile preserving change details. From Table 2, the overall accuracy of PDECD is better than PCA-K, due to the powerful optimization capability of DE.

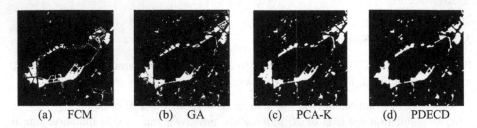

   (a)   FCM   (b)   GA   (c)   PCA-K   (d)   PDECD

Fig. 5. Change maps of Shahu data set. (a) FCM. (b) GA. (c) PCA-K. (d) PDECD

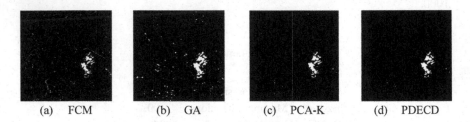

   (a)   FCM   (b)   GA   (c)   PCA-K   (d)   PDECD

Fig. 6. Change maps of Bern data set. (a) FCM. (b) GA. (c) PCA-K. (d) PDECD

Table 2. Quantitative evaluation.

Dataset	Index	FCM	GA	PCA-K	PDECD
Shahu	OA(%)	93.5040	94.2848	94.9216	**95.0480**
	MA	3238	2623	**2025**	2038
	FA	**822**	949	1149	1057
	Kappa	0.6222	0.6844	0.7341	**0.7389**
Bern	OA(%)	98.9724	98.9526	99.6645	**99.7020**
	MA	324	**58**	146	158
	FA	607	891	158	**112**
	Kappa	0.6358	0.6931	0.8674	**0.8792**
Noise	OA(%)	70.2233	93.1568	99.5442	**99.6391**
	MA	38	152	143	167
	FA	26940	6048	270	**160**
	Kappa	0.0533	0.2275	0.8282	**0.8562**

The optimal results for each indicator are bolded.

3.4 Noise Robustness Test

In order to verify the noise robustness PDECD, a comparative test is conducted. To make the result more obvious, we add Gaussian noise, which obeys to the Gaussian distribution N (0, 0.01), into Bern data set. The change detection maps generated by each method are shown in Fig. 7. It can be find that FCM (see Fig. 7(a)) and GA (see Fig. 7(b)) cannot resist image noise at all, and the detection maps contain a large number of white noise points. PDECD can effectively resist noise interference while maintaining a few missed detected points, which demonstrates that the local PCA feature has a significant denoising and detail preserving effect.

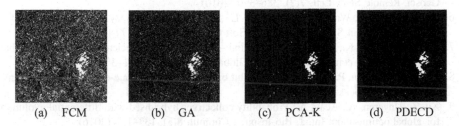

(a) FCM   (b) GA   (c) PCA-K   (d) PDECD

Fig. 7. Change maps of Bern-noise test. (a) FCM. (b) GA. (c) PCA-K. (d) PDECD

From the statistical results listed in Table 2, it can be seen that PDECD is obvious superior to the compared methods, because it has the lowest false alarm and highest overall accuracy. PDECD obtain the best results in all the data sets which proves the robustness and effective of proposed method.

4   Conclusion

This paper proposed an unsupervised change detection method PDECD, which combines local principal component analysis and differential evolution algorithm. PCA is employed to extract local features of difference image, which essentially contain both smooth feature and edge feature. Thus the proposed method is not only robust to image noise, but also sensitive to detail changes (e.g., weak edge). PDECD obtained the optimal clusters in the feature space using DE without any priori knowledge. In addition, due to the self-adaptive strategy, PDECD can produce satisfactory change detection result even without parameters tuning. Experiments conducted on real data sets show that the proposed methods consistently performs well on both SAR and optical images.

However, the proposed method have some weakness that the accuracy is not much improved. Therefore, we intend to continually explore the utilization of image information and further improve detection performance in the near future.

References

1. Singh, A.: Digital change detection techniques using remotely sensed data. Int. J. Remote Sens. **10**(6), 989–1003 (1989)
2. Bruzzone, L., Fernàndez Prieto, D.: Automatic analysis of the difference image for unsupervised change detection. IEEE Trans. Geosci. Remote Sens. **38**(3), 1171–1182 (2000)
3. Bezdek, J.C., Ehrlich, R., Full, W.: FCM: the fuzzy c-means clustering algorithm. Comput. Geosci. **10**(2–3), 191–203 (1984)
4. Celik, T.: Unsupervised change detection in satellite images using principal component analysis and k-means clustering. IEEE Geosci. Remote Sens. Lett. **6**(4), 772–776 (2009)
5. Celik, T.: Change detection in satellite images using a genetic algorithm approach. IEEE Geosci. Remote Sens. Lett. **7**(2), 386–390 (2010)
6. Li, H., Gong, M., Wang, Q., Liu, J., Su, L.: A multiobjective fuzzy clustering method for change detection in SAR images. Appl. Soft Comput. **46**, 767–777 (2016)
7. Storn, R., Price, K.: Differential evolution—A simple and efficient heuristic for global optimization over continuous spaces. J. Global Optim. **11**(4), 341–359 (1997)
8. Das, S., Suganthan, P.N.: Differential evolution: a survey of the state-of-the-art. IEEE Trans. Evol. Comput. **15**(1), 4–31 (2011)
9. Xu, Z., Unveren, A., Acan, A.: Probability collectives hybridised with differential evolution for global optimisation. Int. J. Bio-Inspired Comput. **8**(3), 133–153 (2016)
10. Coletta, L.F., Hruschka, E.R., Acharya, A., Ghosh, J.: A differential evolution algorithm to optimise the combination of classifier and cluster ensembles. Int. J. Bio-Inspired Comput. **7**(2), 111–124 (2015)
11. Zhong, Y., Zhang, S., Zhang, L.: Automatic fuzzy clustering based on adaptive multi-objective differential evolution for remote sensing imagery. IEEE J. Sel. Topics Appl. Earth Observ. Remote Sens. **6**(5), 2290–2301 (2013)
12. Zhong, Y., Zhang, L.: Remote sensing image subpixel mapping based on adaptive differential evolution. IEEE Trans. Syst. Man Cybern. Part B Cybern. **42**(5), 1306–1329 (2012)

Parallel Particle Swarm Optimization for Community Detection in Large-Scale Networks

Shanfeng Wang[1], Maoguo Gong[1(✉)], Yue Wu[2], and Xiaolei Qin[1]

[1] Key Laboratory of Intelligent Perception and Image Understanding of Ministry of Education, International Research Center for Intelligent Perception and Computation, Xidian University, Xi'an 710071, Shaanxi, China
omegawangsf@gmail.com, gong@ieee.org, omegaqinxl@gmail.com
[2] School of Computer Science and Technology,
Xidian University, Xi'an 710071, Shaanxi, China
ywu@xidian.edu.cn
http://web.xidian.edu.cn/mggong

Abstract. Community detection has great applications in many areas. Many algorithms have been proposed to solve this problem, while these algorithms could not detect communities in large-scale networks effectively and efficiently. In this paper, a parallel particle swarm optimization algorithm based on Apache Spark for community detection is put forward. In this algorithm, an effective representation and a specific updating strategy of discrete particle swarm optimization for parallel computing are designed. Modularity density is used as the objective function and GraphX is used to optimize modularity density parallel. To demonstrate the effectiveness of the proposed algorithm, various experiments on small real-world networks with ground-truth communities are carried out. At the same time, we test the performance of the proposed algorithm on large-scale networks. The experimental results indicate that the proposed method is effective and suitable for community detection in large-scale networks.

Keywords: Parallel particle swarm optimization algorithm · Apache Spark · Community detection · Large-scale networks

1 Introduction

Many complex systems such as the World Wide Web, neural networks and collaboration networks can be represented as complex networks. Community detection or complex network clustering aims to partition the network into several groups. These nodes in the same group are linked densely with each other and these among different groups are sparsely linked. So it is important to understand how a network is organized and the cooperation between these nodes.

There are many objective functions for community detection. The most wildly used quality function is modularity given by Grivan and Newman [1].

Y. Shi et al. (Eds.): SEAL 2017, LNCS 10593, pp. 797–809, 2017.
https://doi.org/10.1007/978-3-319-68759-9_65

Nevertheless, there is resolution limit of community optimization [2]. In other word, modularity optimization fails to identify modules smaller than a scale. Li et al. [3] proposed a new quality function called modularity density. The authors have introduced an adjustable parameter to explore the network community structure at different resolutions.

Many community detection algorithms have been proposed in recent years [4]. For modularity optimization is a NP-hard problem, evolutionary algorithms (EAs) have been widely and successfully used for community detection [5–8]. Apart from EA-based optimization techniques, swarm intelligence based methods have also been adopted [9,10]. These algorithms are with good performance but they could not deal with community detection problem in large-scale networks.

For large-scale optimization problems, Spark, an open-source platform is usually adopted. Apache Spark is a popular open-source platform for large-scale data processing that is well-suited for iterative machine learning tasks [11].

In this paper, we propose a parallel discrete particle swarm optimization algorithm for community detection in large-scale networks called PDPSO. An effective representation and a specific updating strategy of discrete particle swarm optimization for parallel computing are designed. Moreover, to further improve the ability of handling real-world large-scale networks, GraphX, a new Spark API for graphs and graph-parallel computation is applied. Experiments show that the proposed algorithm could detect community effectively and is efficient for community detection in large-scale networks.

2   Background

2.1   Particle Swarm Optimization

Particle swarm optimization (PSO) is a computational method that optimizes a problem iteratively to improve a candidate solution with regard to a given measure of quality. It was originally proposed for continuous single objective optimization problems [12]. In PSO, particles move in the search space to find the potential solutions. Each particle will adjust its position according to some simple formulas which are inspired by the movement of bird flock or fish school. The movement of the particles is directed by the best historical position of each particle and the entire population's best known position.

Let $V_i = \{v_i^1, v_i^2, ..., v_i^n\}$ and $X_i = \{x_i^1, x_i^2, ..., x_i^n\}$ respectively be the ith ($i = 1, 2, ..., p$) particle's velocity and position. Then in the standard PSO, particle's velocity and position are given:

$$\begin{cases} V_i = V_i + c_1 r_1 \cdot (Pbest_i - X_i) + c_2 r_2 \cdot (Gbest - X_i) \\ X_i = X_i + V_i \end{cases} \tag{1}$$

where $Pbest_i$ is the best solution of the ith particle and $Gbest_i$ is the best solution up-to-now over all these particles.

2.2   Modularity Density

In this section, we introduce the concept of modularity density [3] proposed by Li et al. Given a network $G = (V, E)$ with $|V| = n$ vertices and $|E| = e$ edges. The adjacency matrix A represents the structure relationship of the graph whose element $a_{ij} = 1$, if node i and node j are linked with each other, otherwise 0. Given two subsets V_1 and V_2, we define $L(V_1, V_2) = \sum_{i \in V_1, j \in V_2} A_{ij}$, $L(V_1, V_1) = \sum_{i \in V_1, j \in V_1} A_{ij}$, $L(V_1, \overline{V_1}) = \sum_{i \in V_1, j \in \overline{V_1}} A_{ij}$ where $\overline{V_1} = V - V_1$. The modularity density is then defined as:

$$D = \sum_{i=1}^{m} \frac{L(V_i, V_i) - L(V_i, \overline{V_i})}{|V_i|} \tag{2}$$

In this equation, each augend means ratio between the difference value of the internal and external degrees of subgraph G_i and the size of each subgraph. If the D value is large, it means that the internal relationships are tight and the external connections are sparse.

The authors also proved the equivalence of modularity density and kernel k means. A more general modularity density was proposed, and can be calculated as follows:

$$D_\lambda = \sum_{i=1}^{m} \frac{2\lambda L(V_i, V_i) - 2(1 - \lambda)L(V_i, \overline{V_i})}{|V_i|} \tag{3}$$

where λ is a parameter of resolution controlling. When $\lambda = 0$, D_λ means the ratio cut [13]; when $\lambda = 0.5$, D_λ is equivalent to the modularity density D; when $\lambda = 1$, D_λ means the ratio association. Currently, the optimization of ratio association always leads to many small communities and ratio cut can hardly separate the graph, which will discover many communities. Otherwise, by varying parameter λ, it is hopeful to analyze the network structure and discover more information of complex network.

3   The Proposed Method

In this section, we will describe the proposed PDPSO method for community detection. We aim to achieve a segmentation with maximizing modularity density, and the framework of PDPSO is given as Algorithm 1.

First, the raw data as distributed data format which is graph with property will be loaded. This corresponds to the parameter of graphinfo. This step makes the proposed algorithm suitable for Spark platform. Second, initialize the population of PSO. The $InitialPopulation$ procedure uses a heuristic method to initialize population. The $UpdateFitness$ procedure is the most important part of the proposed algorithm. We use a directed multi-graph with properties attached to each vertex and edge, because the specific data format of each node has its own information that can be used in fitness calculation. As the data format is a directed graph, we treat undirected graph as directed graph with each edge represents two directed edges. Last but not least, we use $UpdatePbestandGbest$ process to update the Pbest and Gbest of the population.

Algorithm 1. Framework of the proposed method

Input: Max generation: $maxgen$; Population size: $popSize$; Network structure $graphinfo$;

Output: The list of cluster ID for each nodes.

1: $graph \leftarrow$ LoadGraph(graphinfo)
2: $P \leftarrow$ InitialPopulation(popSize,graph)
3: **repeat**
4:    $P \leftarrow UpdateVelocity(P)$
5:    $P \leftarrow UpdatePosition(P)$
6:    $P \leftarrow UpdateFitness(P, graph)$
7:    $P \leftarrow UpdatePbestandGbest(P)$
8: **until** Termination criterion is satisfied or generation over
9: Cluster ID list $\leftarrow$ Best position of the population.

3.1   Representation and Initialization of Population

In this section, the representation of particle and the population are given. Each particle represents a solution of the community detection. The position is defined as $X_i = \{x_1, x_2, x_3, ..., x_n\}$, where n is the number of nodes, and x_i is the cluster ID. For $x_a = x_b$, node a and node b are in the same community. We define velocity as a set of binary number $V_i = \{v_1, v_2, v_3, ..., v_n\}$ where each v_a is 0 or 1. If $v_a = 1$, the corresponding location of a will be changed in the next iteration, otherwise, node a will stand its cluster ID.

In order to make the algorithm parallel, we redesign the data format of the whole population. The whole population is organized as a Resilient Distributed Data sets (RDD). Element of the RDD is defined as the information of node including position, velocity, best position in the history and the best position in the whole population. The definition makes it possible to calculate parallel. Figure 1 illustrates the representation of population.

From Fig. 1, we can see that each element in the RDD is the ID and information of each node. The number of the elements in RDD equals to the number of nodes in the network. The ID in each element means the unique index of each node. The information part includes the cluster ID in each particle. This structure makes it possible to represent the calculation parallel. In this structure, we combine all the particles together into the population.

At $UpdateVelocity$ process, each node's position is only related to the information of the velocity, $pBest$ and $Gbest$. All these information can be found from the same element. For a RDD, all these elements can calculate parallel.

The initialization procedure is described as follows. At the beginning, we generate the particle and initialize the position according to the ID of each node so that all these particles are the same as others. For each particle, we randomly choose one node and change its cluster to the majority clusters of its neighbours. This process is repeated several times. The label propagation-based initialization makes the convergence of algorithm faster. The population initialization is given in Algorithm 2.

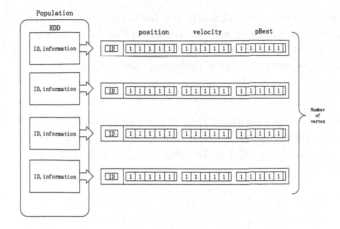

Fig. 1. Illustration of population representation.

3.2 Update Velocity and Position

After renewing the velocity, the position is updated according to the new velocity. Here we adopt the updating rules of DPSO [9].

$$V_i = sig(\omega V_i + c_1 r_1(pBest_i \oplus X_i) + c_2 r_2(gBest_i \oplus X_i)) \tag{4}$$

where ω is inertia weight, c_1 is cognitive weight, c_2 is social component, r_1 and r_2 are randomly chosen from $[0–1]$. Here we use $\oplus$ to represent xor operation; v_i is always binary, so that the sig method is described as below:

$$sig = \frac{1}{1 + e^{-x}} \tag{5}$$

Algorithm 2. Population initialization

Input: Max process: Network structure *graph*; *maxNum*; Population size: *popSize*; *graphinfo*;

Output: Population after initialization.

1: Generate Population P
2: Position initialization: $Position = \{x_1, x_2...x_n\}$,
   where $x_i = i$
3: Velocity initialization: $Velocity = \{v_1, v_2...v_n\}$,
   where $v_i = 0 \ or \ 1$
4: $graph \leftarrow$ LoadGraph(graphinfo)
5: **for all** chromosome **do**
6:    **repeat**
7:      *random select a vertex a from 1 to n*
8:      *change the position$_a$ to Nbest$_a$*
9:    **until** maxNum
10: **end for**

The inertia weight ω is randomly set between $[0, 1]$ and the cognitive and social component parameters are set to the typical value 1.494.

From the updating rules of velocity above, we can get a new velocity. Based on the velocity, we define the new updating rule of position:

$$x_i^{t+1} = x_i^t \otimes v_i^t \tag{6}$$

The operation $\otimes$ is important for the performance of the algorithm. It could represent the tendency of the amelioration of the community detection. Given a position $X_i^t = \{x_1^t, x_2^t, x_3^t...x_n^t\}$ and a velocity $V_i^t = \{v_1^t, v_2^t, v_3^t...v_n^t\}$, each element in X_i^t is defined:

$$\begin{cases} x_i^{t+1} = x_i^t & if \ v_i^t = 0 \\ x_i^{t+1} = Nbest_i & if \ v_i^t = 1 \end{cases} \tag{7}$$

where $Nbest_i$ means the cluster owned by the majority of the neighbor vertices of node i. Suppose node i has a neighbour set $N = \{n_1, n_2, ...n_m\}$ and $Nbest_i$ is defined as:

$$Nbest_i = arg \max_k \sum_{j \in N} \varphi(x_j^t, k) \tag{8}$$

where $\varphi(i, j) = 1$, if $i = j$, else 0. The $Nbest_i$ value can be easily computed during the $UpdateFitness$ process. Its significance is that it is highly possible for one to take part in the community formed by the majority of its neighbors.

3.3   Fitness Calculation and Updating

We propose a new way to calculate the objective function D_λ. From the definition, we can see the value is related to the inner relationships of communities

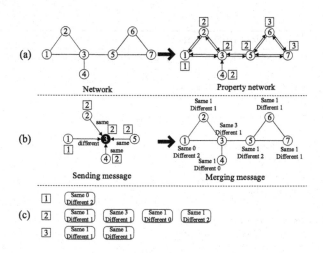

Fig. 2. The fitness calculation process

and the outer relationships between different ones. In this consideration, we use the way of aggregating message for fitness calculation. First, join the position with the property graph, and add the vertex property with position. Then each node will send a message to its neighbors, and if the node has same cluster label with its neighbors, his neighbors will receive a *same* message. Otherwise, the node gets a *different* message. After the sending message process, the merging message process is activated. Each node will count the number of the *same* and *different* it gets. The process is shown in Algorithm 3. Figure 2 also gives the whole procedure of the computing fitness.

Algorithm 3. Update Fitness

Input: Network structure *graph*; Population : P;
Output: Population with updated fitness and *Nbest*.
1: $newGraph \leftarrow JoinPwithgraph$
2: $Nbest, fitness \leftarrow AggregrateMessage(newGraph)$
3: *update Population*

During the sending message process along with the same or different information, the label of the node is also sent to the node's neighbors. After this step, it is easy to get the *Nbest* of the node.

4   Experiment Results

In this section, we will use two small real-world networks with known communities and seven large-scale real-world networks without real partitions to test the performance of the proposed algorithm.

These experiments on small-scale networks aim at proving the effectiveness of the proposed algorithm and these experiments on large-scale networks are used to prove the effectiveness and efficiency of the proposed algorithm for community detection in large scale networks.

In these experiments, two evaluation metrics are adopted. The first one is the modularity (Q) [1]. The definition is given as follows:

$$Q = \frac{1}{2m} \sum_{i,j} (A_{ij} - \frac{k_i k_j}{2m}) \delta(i, j) \tag{9}$$

where m is the dimension of the edges in the network, A_{ij} is the adjacent matrix of the whole network and k_i is the number of the degree of node i and $\delta(i, j)$ is binary. Node i and node j are in the same community, if $\delta(i, j) = 1$.

The second evaluation metric is normalized mutual information (NMI) [14]. NMI is used to estimate the similarity between the true clustering structure and the predicted ones. Assume that P_a and P_b be two partitions of a network. Let C be the confusion matrix whose element C_{ij} is the number of nodes which is in community i of partition P_a and also in community j of partition P_b. The normalized mutual information $NMI(A, B)$ is defined as:

$$NMI = \frac{-2\sum_{i=1}^{C_{P_a}} \sum_{j=1}^{C_{P_b}} C_{ij} log(\frac{C_{ij}N}{C_{i.}C_{.j}})}{\sum_{i=1}^{C_{P_a}} C_{i.} log(\frac{C_{i.}}{N}) + \sum_{j=1}^{C_{P_b}} C_{.j} log(\frac{C_{.j}}{N})} \tag{10}$$

where $C_{P_a}(C_{P_b})$ is the number of clusters in partition $P_a(P_b)$, $C_{i.}.(C_{.j})$ is the sum of elements of C in row i (column j) and N is the number of nodes in the network. While A is totally the same like B, then $NMI(P_a, P_b) = 1$; if A and B are completely different, $NMI(P_a, P_b) = 0$.

4.1   Experience on Small Real-World Networks

In this section, we give the performance of PDPSO on two small real-world networks, i.e. the Zachary's karate club network [15], and the dolphin social network [16] (Table 1). These two small real-world networks all have ground-truth communities, and the results will be compared with those of some other algorithms like Label Propagation Algorithm (LPA) [17], Genetic Algorithm (GA) [5], MOGA [7], and CND [18]. The experimental environment includes eight worker nodes and one driver node of Apache Spark plant form and each node has 64G memory, 2.6 GHz E5-2630 cpu with 10 cores. To run the proposed algorithm, it takes 50 cores totally and enough memory.

Table 1. Network properties of two small real-world networks including node number, edge number and real cluster number.

Network	♯ Node	♯ Egde	♯ Real cluster
Karate	34	78	2
Dolphin	62	159	2

We set λ from 0.1 to 0.7 in the objective function D_λ. We run the proposed algorithm 30 times for each small real-world network, and record the values of modularity, NMI and the cluster numbers of communities which is determined by the maximum D_λ. Table 2 gives the results of Q and NMI of the proposed algorithm on two networks with parameter λ from 0.1 to 0.7. When $\lambda = 0.1$ in the Zachary's karate club network, the proposed algorithm clusters the whole nodes in one community. The proposed algorithm can discover the real community structure when $\lambda = 0.2$. For dolphin data set, the proposed algorithm can find the true community when $\lambda = 0.1$ or $\lambda = 0.2$.

Table 3 shows the results of different algorithms on karate data set. We can find that the proposed algorithm can find the real community structure when D_λ is maximum, though the modularity of the proposed algorithm is the smallest one. The proposed algorithm is better than any other algorithms. Table 4 shows

Table 2. Results of Q and NMI of the proposed algorithm on two real-world networks for different values of λ.

Networks	λ	Q	NMI	Cluster number
Karate	0.1	0	0	1
	0.2	0.1328	0.2260	2
	0.3	0.3715	1	2
	0.4	0.4020	0.6995	3
	0.5	0.4020	0.6995	3
	0.6	0.3991	0.8255	3
	0.7	0.4020	0.7226	4
Dolphin	0.1	0.3787	1	2
	0.2	0.3787	1	2
	0.3	0.3735	0.8888	2
	0.4	0.4779	0.6803	3
	0.5	0.5096	0.5314	5
	0.6	0.5096	0.5314	5
	0.7	0.5096	0.5314	5

the results of different algorithms on dolphin data set. From Table 4, we can find that the proposed algorithm reaches the maximum of NMI. This is because our objective function is modularity density but not modularity. A large modularity does not mean a good community clustering.

Table 3. Results of different algorithms on karate data set.

Algorithm	Q_{max}	Q_{avg}	NMI_{avg}
PDPSO	0.3715	0.3715	1.0000
LPA	0.4151	0.3264	0.6623
GA	0.4198	0.4198	0.6681
MOGA	0.5085	0	0.9442
CNM	0.3800	0.3800	0.5730

4.2 Experience on Large-Scale Networks

In this section, we will apply the proposed algorithm on large-scale networks. These networks start with "ca" are from the e-print arXiv and cover scientific collaborations between authors papers. The numbers of nodes are range from 5,242 to 23,133. Table 5 shows properties about these large-scale networks.

The distributed system Spark has the feature of scalability, which enables the proposed algorithm to deal with large-scale networks. As Spark provides the

Table 4. Results of different algorithms on dolphin data set.

Algorithm	Q_{max}	Q_{avg}	NMI_{avg}
PDPSO	0.3787	0.3787	1.0000
LPA	0.5285	0.4964	0.6194
GA	0.5825	0.5280	0.5892
MOGA	0.5085	0.4098	0.9442
CNM	0.4950	0.4950	0.5730

Table 5. Network properties of large scale networks

Network	♯ Vertex	♯ Egde
ca-GrQc	5, 242	14, 496
ca-HepTh	9, 877	25, 998
ca-HepPh	12, 008	118, 521
ca-AstroPh	18, 772	198, 110
ca-CondMat	23, 133	93, 497
email-Enron	36, 692	183, 831
com-DBLP	317, 080	1, 049, 866
com-Amazon	334, 863	925, 872

algorithm LPA, we can compare the proposed algorithm fairly with it in dealing with these large-scale networks. In this part, we will compare the proposed algorithm with LPA with the modularity. The results are shown in Table 6. We use $\lambda = 0.3$ in D_λ for all these networks. From the results, we can see that the results of the proposed algorithm are completely better than those of LPA.

Figure 3 shows the execution time of the proposed algorithm on each network. It is found that the proposed algorithm could deal with the network with 334,863 nodes within 45 min. While the number of nodes increases from dozens to hundreds of thousands, the execution time only increases twice. This means that the execution time of the proposed algorithm is not directly proportional with the scale of the network. This phenomenon is very important in dealing with large-scale networks. The phenomenon is related to the data structure of our population. We consider the whole RDD as our population. Figure 1 gives the brief representation of population. Each arithmetic unit of RDD has all information about the data needed in the update process, which makes it easy to update particles parallel. This means this process takes few time in calculation. The distributed system needs to collect all results in each workers through internet transmission, which takes a lot of time. We also describe the calculation of the objective function D_λ, and we use aggregating message to compute the fitness values. The computation of objective function is based on the GraphX library and it takes a lot of time in the proposed algorithm. We need to calculate

Table 6. Results of the proposed algorithm on large-scale real-world networks.

Algorithm	Network	Modularity	Cluster number
PDPSO	ca-GrQc	0.7704	797
LPA	ca-GrQc	0.6723	1164
PDPSO	ca-HepTh	0.6465	1349
LPA	ca-HepTh	0.5988	1635
PDPSO	ca-HepPh	0.5105	1024
LPA	ca-HepPh	0.4474	911
PDPSO	ca-AstroPh	0.5212	1274
LPA	ca-AstroPh	0.2812	938
PDPSO	ca-CondMat	0.6005	2490
LPA	ca-CondMat	0.4764	2524
PDPSO	dblp	0.6967	23501
LPA	dblp	0.6170	34330
PDPSO	amazon	0.7828	22377
LPA	amazon	0.6207	30588

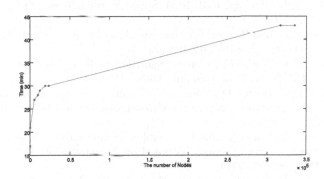

Fig. 3. Execution time of the proposed algorithm on each network.

the objective function for each particle, so that the execution time is directly related to the number of particles in the population and the iteration number.

5   Conclusions

In this work, we introduced a parallel particle swarm optimization algorithm based on Apache Spark for community detection. To design an effective PSO for community detection in large scale networks, we proposed a novel population representation and a novel method to compute objective functions. To show the performance of the proposed algorithm, the proposed algorithm was tested on small real-world networks and large-scale real-world networks. The proposed algorithm performed well on small real-world data sets with high value of NMI. It can also deal with the large-scale real-world networks with 330 thousand nodes fast.

Acknowledgements. This work was supported by the National Natural Science Foundation of China (Grant no. 61422209), the National Program for Support of Top-notch Young Professionals of China, and the National key research and development program of China (Grant no. 2017YFB0802200).

References

1. Girvan, M., Newman, M.E.: Community structure in social and biological networks. Proc. Nat. Acad. Sci. **99**(12), 7821–7826 (2002)
2. Fortunato, S., Barthelemy, M.: Resolution limit in community detection. Proc. Nat. Acad. Sci. **104**(1), 36–41 (2007)
3. Li, Z., Zhang, S., Wang, R.S., Zhang, X.S., Chen, L.: Quantitative function for community detection. Phys. Rev. E **77**(3), 036109 (2008)
4. Fortunato, S.: Community detection in graphs. Phys. Rep. **486**(3), 75–174 (2010)
5. Pizzuti, C.: GA-Net: a genetic algorithm for community detection in social networks. In: Rudolph, G., Jansen, T., Beume, N., Lucas, S., Poloni, C. (eds.) PPSN 2008. LNCS, vol. 5199, pp. 1081–1090. Springer, Heidelberg (2008). doi:10.1007/978-3-540-87700-4_107
6. Gong, M., Fu, B., Jiao, L., Du, H.: Memetic algorithm for community detection in networks. Phys. Rev. E **84**(5), 056101 (2011)
7. Pizzuti, C.: A multiobjective genetic algorithm to find communities in complex networks. IEEE Trans. Evol. Comput. **16**(3), 418–430 (2012)
8. Gong, M., Ma, L., Zhang, Q., Jiao, L.: Community detection in networks by using multiobjective evolutionary algorithm with decomposition. Phys. A **391**(15), 4050–4060 (2012)
9. Gong, M., Cai, Q., Chen, X., Ma, L.: Complex network clustering by multiobjective discrete particle swarm optimization based on decomposition. IEEE Trans. Evol. Comput. **18**(1), 82–97 (2014)
10. Cai, Q., Gong, M., Ma, L., Ruan, S., Yuan, F., Jiao, L.: Greedy discrete particle swarm optimization for large-scale social network clustering. Inf. Sci. **316**, 503–516 (2015)
11. Meng, X., Bradley, J., Yuvaz, B., Sparks, E., Venkataraman, S., Liu, D., Freeman, J., Tsai, D., Amde, M., Owen, S., et al.: Mllib: machine learning in apache spark. J. Mach. Learn. Res. **17**(34), 1–7 (2016)
12. Eberhart, R.C., Kennedy, J., et al.: A new optimizer using particle swarm theory. In: Proceedings of 6th International Symposium on Micro Machine Human Science, vol. 1, pp. 39–43 (1995)
13. Dhillon, I.S., Guan, Y., Kulis, B.: Kernel k-means: spectral clustering and normalized cuts. In: Proceedings of tenth ACM SIGKDD International Conference Knowledge Discovery and Data Mining, pp. 551–556. ACM (2004)
14. Wu, F., Huberman, B.A.: Finding communities in linear time: a physics approach. Eur. Phys. J. B **38**(2), 331–338 (2004)
15. Zachary, W.W.: An information flow model for conflict and fission in small groups. J. Anthropol. Res. **33**(4), 452–473 (1977)

16. Lusseau, D., Schneider, K., Boisseau, O.J., Haase, P., Slooten, E., Dawson, S.M.: The bottlenose dolphin community of Doubtful Sound features a large proportion of long-lasting associations. Behav. Ecol. Sociobiol. **54**(4), 396–405 (2003)
17. Bagrow, J.P., Bollt, E.M.: A local method for detecting communities. Phys. Rev. E **72**(2), 046108 (2005)
18. Clauset, A., Newman, M.E., Moore, C.: Finding community structure in very large networks. Phys. Rev. E **70**(6), 066111 (2004)

Multi-objective Memetic Algorithm Based on Three-Dimensional Request Prediction for Dynamic Pickup-and-Delivery Problem with Time Windows

Yanming Yang[1], Xiaoliang Ma[1], Yiwen Sun[2], and Zexuan Zhu[1(✉)]

[1] College of Computer Science and Software Engineering,
Shenzhen University, Shenzhen 518060, China
zhuzx@szu.edu.cn
[2] Department of Biomedical Engineering, School of Medicine,
Shenzhen University, Shenzhen 518060, China

Abstract. A multi-objective memetic algorithm based on three-dimensional request prediction is proposed in this paper to solve dynamic pickup-and-delivery route problems with time windows. Dynamic requests are predicted in three dimensions including two space coordinates and time based on the statistical distribution of historical data. The predictive routes are planned firstly and tuned subsequently when the real requests occur. Tri-objective route planning problem based on route length, served time and workload is optimized by the proposed multi-objective memetic algorithm based on prediction, which combines multi-objective genetic algorithm with a locality-sensitive hashing based local search. The proposed algorithm is compared with the other two popular algorithms on two test problems and the experimental results show the efficiency of the proposed algorithm.

Keywords: Memetic algorithm · Multi-objective optimization · Dynamic pickup-and-delivery problem · Time windows · Locality-sensitive hashing · Three-dimensional dynamic request prediction

1 Introduction

The pickup and delivery problem with time window (PDPTW) is an extension of the classical vehicle route problem (VRP) proposed by Savelsbergh and Sol [9]. PDPTW can be described as follows: A vehicle start from a depot to serve a number of customers with pickup and/or delivery demands within different time windows at different geographic locations. This vehicle finally returns to the same depot. The objective of such problem is to find a route of the vehicle for serving customers requests at a minimal cost (in terms of travel distance, served time, and so on) without violating the capacity and travel time constraints of vehicle. PDPTW has been proven by Lenstra and Kan [6] to be NP-hard so it is difficult to obtain the global optimal solution in restricted time.

© Springer International Publishing AG 2017
Y. Shi et al. (Eds.): SEAL 2017, LNCS 10593, pp. 810–820, 2017.
https://doi.org/10.1007/978-3-319-68759-9_66

Due to the NP-hard nature of PDPTW, many meta-heuristic algorithms have been proposed to solve PDPTW. Cherkesly et al. [1] proposed population-based meta-heuristic algorithm to solve the pickup and delivery problem with time windows and last-in-first-out (LIFO) loading. Kachitvichyanukul et al. [5] extended a previously published PSO algorithm [13,14,20] for solving the generalized multi-depot vehicle routing problem with multiple pickup and delivery requests (GVRP-MDPDR). Their preliminary results have shown that the proposed method is capable of providing good solutions on most of test problems. Wang et al. [12] proposed the multi-objective local search (MOLS) to solve multi-objective vehicle routing problems simultaneous with delivery and pickup and time windows.

Currently, very few methods were proposed to solve the dynamic PDPTW (DPDPTW), i.e., PDPTW with dynamic customer requests. In this study, we present a multi-objective memetic algorithm to solve DPDPTWs considering route length, served time, and workload of a single vehicle. In real-world applications, pickup-and-delivery problems usually are dynamic. It is difficult to optimize DPDPTW in minimal cost as dynamic demands appear in different locations and time intervals. Nevertheless, the dynamic requests, as the Allibaba *The Last Kilometer in Logistics* routing planning competition data[1] shown in Fig. 3(a), show regular patterns in some specific residential and commercial districts. So it is reasonable to predict the upcoming dynamic requests according to historical data. Based on accurate prediction, the proposed multi-objective memetic algorithm is able to plan a good predictive route that can be easily tuned to fit the real requests subsequently. The multi-objective memetic algorithm is a hybridization of multi-objective genetic algorithm and a locality-sensitive hashing (LSH) based local search [18]. Particularly, a population of individual candidate routes/solutions are evolved by a genetic algorithm and the individuals are refined by the LSH-based local search in each generation. The proposed method is tested on two benchmark datasets and the experimental results show the efficiency of the proposed method.

The rest of this paper is organized as follows. The formulation of the tri-objective DPDPTW is provided in Sect. 2. Section 3 provides the details of the proposed algorithm. The experimental results are presented in Sect. 4. Finally, the conclusion of this paper is given in Sect. 5.

2   Problem Formulation

Figure 1(a) shows one depot and seven customer nodes including four static demands and three dynamic demands. A vehicle starts from the depot, and then crosses the customer nodes, and finally returns to the same depot. The vehicle must carry delivery commodities on off-line demands before leaving the depot, and then serve delivery and/or pickup demands. Once new dynamic demands appear, the vehicle could respond the demands by re-planning the route or just ignore the requests. Let us introduce the following nomenclature.

---

[1] https://tianchi.aliyun.com/competition/introduction.htm?raceId=231581.

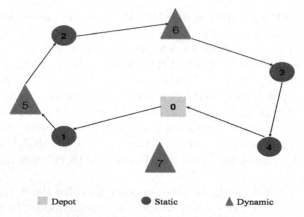

Depot   Static   Dynamic

(a) Single-vehicle working in DPDPTW

(b) Route encoding

Fig. 1. An illustration of single-vehicle DPDPTW

$E = \{e_i \mid i = 0, \ldots, n\}$	Environment of DPDPTW
$S = \{e_i \mid i = 0, \ldots, m \ and \ m \leq n\}$	e_0 is the depot and others are static nodes
$D = \{e_i \mid i = m + 1, \ldots, n\}$	Dynamic customers
$P \ where \ S \subseteq P \subseteq E$	A path consisting of a set of nodes
C	Vehicle capacity
$[a_i, b_i]$	a_i means the appear time of the request of customer i and b_i is the latest leave time
g_i	Delivery demand of customer i
p_i	Pickup demand of customer i
$d_{i,j}$	Distance between customers i and j
$t_{i,j}$	Travel time from customer i to j

In this case, the total route length $L(P)$ is defined as:

$$L(P) = \sum_{i=0}^{|P|-1} d_{i,i+1} \tag{1}$$

Let at_{i-1} be the arrival time of at the $i - 1$th. Thus, the arrival time of ith customer is

$$at_i = \begin{cases} at_{i-1} + t_{i-1,i}, & (at_i \geq a_i) \\ a_i, & otherwise \end{cases} \tag{2}$$

Total served time $T(P)$ is defined as:

$$T(P) = \sum_{e_i \in D \cap P} \begin{cases} 0, & (at_{e_i} \leq a_{e_i}) \\ at_{e_i} - a_{e_i}, & (a_{e_i} < at_{e_i} \wedge at_{e_i} \leq b_{e_i}) \\ b_{e_i} - a_{e_i} + \lambda \times (at_{e_i} - b_{e_i}), & (b_{e_i} < at_{e_i}) \end{cases} \qquad (3)$$

where the λ indicate the penalty factor and in this paper set $\lambda = 10$.
Total workload $W(P)$ is defined as:

$$W(P) = \sum_{i=0}^{|P|-1} (g_i + p_i) \qquad (4)$$

Real-time workload $\Omega(e_i)$ is defined as:

$$\Omega(e_i) = \sum_{i=0}^{i} (p_i - g_i) \qquad (5)$$

Thus, the DPDPTW with three optimization objectives in this paper can be summarized as $minF(P)$, where

$$\begin{cases} \min F(P) = (L(P), T(P), -W(P)) \\ subject\ to\ \forall e_i \in P : \Omega(e_i) \leq C \end{cases} \qquad (6)$$

minimization of the vector function $F(P)$ is supposed here.

3   The Proposed Algorithm

Memetic algorithms have shown promising performance in solving various complex optimization problems [15–17, 19]. A new multi-objective memetic algorithm based on dynamic request prediction and locality-sensitive hashing (LSH)-based local search, namely three-dimensional dynamic request prediction-LSH-MOMA (3DDP-LSH-MOMA), is proposed in this section. Figure 2 shows the algorithmic flowchart of the proposed algorithm. First of all, the request prediction analyzes the position of the potential dynamic nodes based on historical data and generates the virtual customer nodes to represent the dynamic request nodes. Second, a population of feasible routes is generated randomly considering the virtual customer nodes and the static nodes. The multi-objective memetic algorithm is used to find a set of non-dominated solutions of tri-objective DPDPTW. In the process of evolution, the real dynamic requests appear and are replaced by the closest predicted nodes. The candidate routes are adopted to involve the real dynamic nodes only. Each individual is refined by LSH based local improvement operator in each generation. Algorithm 1 provides the pseudo-code of the proposed algorithm. The key operators of the proposed algorithm are introduced subsequently.

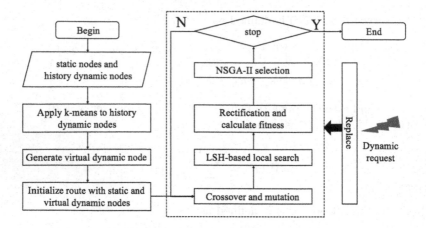

Fig. 2. The flowchart of the proposed algorithm.

Algorithm 1. The proposed algorithm: 3DDP-LSH-MOMA

1: Cluster the historical data of dynamic nodes into K clusters;
2: Randomly generate the predicted dynamic nodes in each clustering with 3-dimensional normal distribution;
3: Create LSH-based identified library by static node, dynamic nodes and predict nodes [18]
4: Randomly initialize a population of candidate routes P_i for optimizing the demand of static nodes only;
5: Evaluate the fitness of each individual by Eq.(6);
6: **while** the stop criterion is not reached **do**
7:    **if** newly dynamic requests arrive **then**
8:       Update LSH-based library by dynamic nodes;
9:       Replace the nearest predicted nodes by dynamic requests (Algorithm 2);
10:   **end if**
11:   Generate an offspring population P_i using crossover and adaptive mutation in Algorithm 3;
12:   Rectify the illegal nodes of P_i [18];
13:   Evaluate the fitness of each offspring individual;
14:   Use LSH-based local improvement operator [18] for each offspring;
15:   Select new population based on non-dominated sorting and crowding distance of NSGA-II [3];
16: **end while**

3.1   Prediction Operator

To quick respond to the dynamic request, predicting customer requests where and when they appear is helpful. We predict the new dynamic requests based on the Gaussian distribution of historical data as shown in Fig. 3. Figure 3(a) shows the historical data of dynamic requests, which are clustered by k-means clustering algorithm [4] in Fig. 3(b), where occurring time, latitude, and longitude are three features of the historical data. For each clustering, its mean and covariance matrix based on Gaussian distribution is calculated first and then used to predict the future dynamic requests as shown in Fig. 3(c).

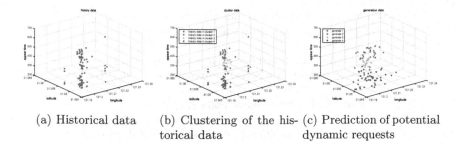

(a) Historical data   (b) Clustering of the his-   (c) Prediction of potential
                          torical data   dynamic requests

Fig. 3. An instance of dynamic requests prediction, its clustering result, and predicted result.

When dynamic nodes appear, the closest predicted nodes should be replaced. Due to different measures in the occurrence time and route length, a normalization method is used. In this study, the linear transformation function is adopted to normalize, i.e.,

$$x' = \frac{x - x_{min}}{x_{max} - x_{min}} \qquad (7)$$

After normalization, the distance between predicted node j and dynamic node is calculate as follow:

$$d_j = \min_{i \in virtul\ nodes\ of\ P} \sqrt{d_{i,j}'^2 + (a_i' - a_j')^2} \qquad (8)$$

where a_i' is the normalization time by Eq. (7) which represents the earliest appear time a_i of customer i, similarly, the $d_{i,j}'$ means the normalized distance of $d_{i,j}$ which represents the distance between customers i and j. Node i is the predicted one and node j is the real dynamic node. The closest predicted custom node is replaced by the real one and the corresponding routes are updated accordingly. The pseudo-code is shown in Algorithm 2.

3.2   Adaptive Mutation Operator

As shown in Fig. 1(b), the paper uses integer coding for route planing. In each generation, order-based crossover [11] and adaptive mutation are performed on each individual for creating an offspring population. Although the route with different number of customer nodes appear especially fix the dynamic nodes, we can simply select the route, with minimal numbers of customer nodes, as a reference length to crossover which guarantees both chromosomes have the same position. The details of adaptive mutation are described in Algorithm 3. To effectively jump out of local minima, the proposed algorithm applies four widely adopted mutation operators with the same used probability. The four used

---

Algorithm 2. Insert dynamic nodes

Input: Dynamic node j, all candidate routes Ps;
 1: **for** each route P **in** Ps **do**
 2:   **if** P has virtual nodes **then**
 3:     Get virtual nodes with minimal and maximal occurrence time in P;
 4:     Get minimal and maximal route length between dynamic node j and virtual nodes in route P;
 5:     Formate the route length and occurrence time by Eq.(7);
 6:     Get the closest distance d_j between virtual node i and dynamic node j by Eq.(8);
 7:     Replace virtual node i by dynamic node j;
 8:   **else**
 9:     Select a nearest node's position in route P to insert dynamic node j to P;
10:   **end if**
11: **end for**

---

mutation operators include randomly segment reversion, swapping two nodes, deleting a dynamic node, and adding a dynamic node.

After crossover and mutation, LSH-based revision are applied to repair the time window and capacity constraint violations. LSH-based local improve operator is subsequently used to enhance the quality of the offspring. NSGA-II [3] is used to select the next parent population from the union of current parent population and its offspring population.

Algorithm 3. Adaptive mutation operator

Input: All candidates route in offspring Ps;
Output: Offspring after mutation Ps;
 1: **for** P **in** Ps **do**
 2:   Generate a random number $r \in [0, 1]$;
 3:   **if** $0 \leq r < 0.25$ **then**
 4:     Insert dynamic node by algorithm 2
 5:   **else if** $0.25 \leq r < 0.5$ **then**
 6:     Randomly remove a dynamic node from P;
 7:   **else if** $0.5 \leq r < 0.75$ **then**
 8:     Randomly swap the orders of two nodes in P;
 9:   **else**
10:     Randomly select a segment in P and reverse it;
11:   **end if**
12: **end for**

---

4 Experiment Designed and Analysis

The performance of the proposed algorithm is tested on two benchmark problems of different scales using a real map of New York. Google map API is used to calculate the distances between different customer nodes. Following the suggestion in [18], we generate the static customer requests, dynamic customer requests, and ten times of historical data for request prediction by Gaussian distribution. Table 1 gives the settings of two benchmark problems.

Table 1. The benchmark problems in different scales

Benchmark	Number of static nodes	Number of dynamic nodes
DPDPTW1	30	50
DPDPTW2	50	50

LSH-MOMA [18] without prediction and MOGA without prediction are used as the compared algorithm. All of compared algorithms use the same setting including 200 for the population size, $\lambda = 10$ for penalty factor, 30 for the number of independent run, and the same number of function evaluations for all the compared algorithms. Tables 2 and 3 provide the comparison results.

Table 2. The results in terms of mean route length, workload, serviced time, convergence metric and spacing metric of the proposed algorithm, LSH-MOMA and MOGA in two DPDPTWs over 30 runs. ($-/\approx$: the average performance of the corresponding method is significantly worse than or similar to the highlighted best average performance at level $p = 0.05$ in Welch's t-test.)

		3DDP-LSH-MOMA	LSH-MOMA	MOGA
DPDPTW1	$\overline{L(P)}(\times 10^4)$	**9.03 ± 1.17**	10.51 ± 1.31-	11.92 ± 1.17-
	$\overline{W(P)}(\times 10^3)$	**3.54 ± 0.58**	3.47 ± 0.02≈	3.40 ± 0.08≈
	$\overline{T(P)}(\times 10^0)$	**5.68 ± 3.83**	24.79 ± 8.99-	17.56 ± 9.01-
	$\overline{M_C(P)}(\times 10^{-2})$	**5.83 ± 3.94**	10.18 ± 2.82-	11.20 ± 3.69-
	$\overline{M_S(P)}(\times 10^{-2})$	**3.98 ± 0.47**	4.08 ± 0.65-	5.68 ± 2.17-
DPDPTW2	$\overline{L(P)}(\times 10^4)$	**9.84 ± 0.83**	13.69 ± 1.71-	14.10 ± 1.45-
	$\overline{W(P)}(\times 10^3)$	**4.55 ± 0.67**	4.29 ± 0.00≈	4.23 ± 0.06≈
	$\overline{T(P)}(\times 10^0)$	**6.97 ± 3.90**	21.20 ± 9.86-	14.98 ± 6.13-
	$\overline{M_C(P)}(\times 10^{-2})$	**8.17 ± 5.51**	12.71 ± 3.97-	13.91 ± 3.32-
	$\overline{M_S(P)}(\times 10^{-2})$	**3.93 ± 0.49**	4.01 ± 0.42≈	5.60 ± 2.68-

The performances of the algorithms are evaluated based on the following six criteria:

1. Minimal route length (L).
2. Maximal workload (W).
3. Minimal served time (T).

Table 3. The results in terms of coverage-of-two-sets metric of the proposed algorithm, LSH-MOMA and MOGA in the two DPDPTWs over 30 runs. ($-/ \approx$: the average performance of the corresponding method is significantly worse than or similar to the highlighted best average performance at level p = 0.05 in Welch's t-test.)

| | 3DDP-LSH-MOMA vs LSH-MOMA | | 3DDP-LSH-MOMA vs MOGA | |
	$I(A, B)$	$I(B, A)$	$I(A, C)$	$I(C, A)$
DPDPTW1	**0.48 ± 0.35**	0.27 ± 0.23-	**0.53 ± 0.37**	0.23 ± 0.27-
DPDPTW2	**0.55 ± 0.32**	0.32 ± 0.23-	**0.66 ± 0.30**	0.24 ± 0.21-

4. Convergence metric (M_C) [2] of non-dominant solutions: M_C is a criterion measuring the distance between the obtained non-dominant solution set and the true Pareto-optimal front. Thus, smaller value of this metric means the obtain solutions with closer distance to the true pareto-optimal front.
5. Spacing metric (M_S) [7,8,10]: M_S estimates the variance of the distance from each member of non-dominant solutions to its closest neighbor.
6. Coverage-of-two-sets metric ($MC2S$) [21]: $MC2S$ compares the rate of non-dominant solutions in the union of two solution sets found by the compared algorithms. The higher this metric value is the better.

The results obtained by the three compared algorithms on the two problems are provided in Table 2. This table shows that the proposed algorithm obtains the best results in each objectives including minimal route length, workload, and service time. What is more, Table 2 also shows that the solutions obtained by the proposed algorithm have better convergence and diversity. Additionally, the proposed algorithm has better performance than other compared algorithms in terms of coverage-of-two-sets metric in Table 3. In a world, the results show that the proposed algorithm performs better than LSH-MOMA and MOGA in terms of all of the six criteria. Last but not least, the non-dominated solutions obtained by the three algorithms are plotted in Fig. 4 also show the efficiency of

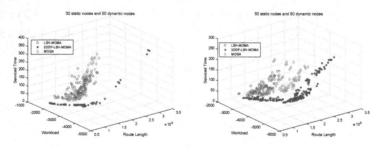

(a) Non-dominant solutions in   (b) Non-dominant solutions in
DPDPTW1   DPDPTW2

Fig. 4. Non-dominant solutions of the three algorithms

the proposed algorithm. Thus the request prediction and LSH-based local search working together can improve the quality of the solution set significantly.

5 Conclusion

This paper proposes a multi-objective memetic algorithm with dynamic request prediction and LSH-based techniques for solving dynamic pickup and delivery problem with time windows. The proposed request predict strategy is used to deal with the dynamic requests. The LSH-based rectification and local search are applied to fix the constraint violations and improve the algorithmic performance. Experimental results on two benchmark problems show the effectiveness of the proposed method.

Acknowledgments. This work was supported by National Natural Science Foundation of China [61471246, 61603259, 61575125], Guangdong Special Support Program of Top-notch Young Professionals [2014TQ01X273, 2015TQ01R453], Guangdong Foundation of Outstanding Young Teachers in Higher Education Institutions [Yq2015141], China Postdoctoral Science Foundation [2016M592536], and Shenzhen Fundamental Research Program [JCYJ20150324141711587, JCYJ20170302154328155].

References

1. Cherkesly, M., Desaulniers, G., Laporte, G.: A population-based metaheuristic for the pickup and delivery problem with time windows and LIFO loading. Comput. Oper. Res. **62**, 23–35 (2015)
2. Deb, K., Jain, S.: Running performance metrics for evolutionary multi-objective optimization. In: Proceedings of the Fourth Asia-Pacific Conference on Simulated Evolution and Learning (SEAL 2002), pp. 13–20 (2002)
3. Deb, K., Pratap, A., Agarwal, S., Meyarivan, T.: A fast and elitist multiobjective genetic algorithm: NSGA-II. IEEE Trans. Evol. Comput. **6**(2), 182–197 (2002)
4. Jain, A.K.: Data clustering: 50 years beyond K-means. Pattern Recogn. Lett. **31**(8), 651–666 (2010)
5. Kachitvichyanukul, V., Sombuntham, P., Kunnapapdeelert, S.: Two solution representations for solving multi-depot vehicle routing problem with multiple pickup and delivery requests via PSO. Comput. Ind. Eng. **89**, 125–136 (2015)
6. Lenstra, J.K., Kan, A.: Complexity of vehicle routing and scheduling problems. Networks **11**(2), 221–227 (1981)
7. Ma, X., Liu, F., Qi, Y., Wang, X., Li, L., Jiao, L., Yin, M., Gong, M.: A multiobjective evolutionary algorithm based on decision variable analyses for multiobjective optimization problems with large-scale variables. IEEE Trans. Evol. Comput. **20**(2), 275–298 (2016)
8. Ma, X., Zhang, Q., Tian, G., Yang, J., Zhu, Z.: On Tchebycheff decomposition approaches for multi-objective evolutionary optimization. IEEE Trans. Evol. Comput. (2017, in press). doi:10.1109/TEVC.2017.2704118
9. Savelsbergh, M.W., Sol, M.: The general pickup and delivery problem. Transp. Sci. **29**(1), 17–29 (1995)
10. Schott, J.R.: Fault tolerant design using single and multicriteria genetic algorithm optimization. Cell. Immunol. **37**(1), 1–13 (1995)

11. Tan, K.C., Lee, L.H., Zhu, Q.L., Ou, K.: Heuristic methods for vehicle routing problem with time windows. Artif. Intell. Eng. **15**(3), 281–295 (2001)
12. Wang, J., Zhou, Y., Wang, Y., Zhang, J., Chen, C.P., Zheng, Z.: Multiobjective vehicle routing problems with simultaneous delivery and pickup and time windows: formulation, instances, and algorithms. IEEE Trans. Cybern. **46**(3), 582–594 (2016)
13. Zhang, Y., Gong, D.W., Cheng, J.: Multi-objective particle swarm optimization approach for cost-based feature selection in classification. IEEE/ACM Trans. Comput. Biol. Bioinf. **22**(99), 64–75 (2015)
14. Zhang, Y., Gong, D., Hu, Y., Zhang, W.: Feature selection algorithm based on bare bones particle swarm optimization. Neurocomputing **148**, 150–157 (2015)
15. Zhu, Z., Jia, S., He, S., Sun, Y., Ji, Z., Shen, L.: Three-dimensional Gabor feature extraction for hyperspectral imagery classification using a memetic framework. Inf. Sci. **298**, 274–287 (2015)
16. Zhu, Z., Ong, Y.S., Dash, M.: Wrapper–filter feature selection algorithm using a memetic framework. IEEE Trans. Syst. Man Cybern. Part B Cybern. **37**(1), 70–76 (2007). (A Publication of the IEEE Systems Man and Cybernetics Society)
17. Zhu, Z., Wang, F., He, S., Sun, Y.: Global path planning of mobile robots using a memetic algorithm. Int. J. Syst. Sci. **46**(11), 1982–1993 (2015)
18. Zhu, Z., Xiao, J., He, S., Ji, Z., Sun, Y.: A multi-objective memetic algorithm based on locality-sensitive hashing for one-to-many-to-one dynamic pickup-and-delivery problem. Inf. Sci. **329**, 73–89 (2016)
19. Zhu, Z., Xiao, J., Li, J.Q., Wang, F., Zhang, Q.: Global path planning of wheeled robots using multi-objective memetic algorithms. Integr. Comput.-Aided Eng. **22**(4), 387–404 (2015)
20. Zhu, Z., Zhou, J., Ji, Z., Shi, Y.H.: DNA sequence compression using adaptive particle swarm optimization-based memetic algorithm. IEEE Trans. Evol. Comput. **15**(5), 643–658 (2011)
21. Zitzler, E., Thiele, L.: Multiobjective optimization using evolutionary algorithms a comparative case study. In: International Conference on Parallel Problem Solving from Nature, pp. 292–301 (1998)

Optimization of Spectrum-Energy Efficiency in Heterogeneous Communication Network

Fangqing Gu[2,3], Ziquan Liu[2], Yiu-ming Cheung[1,2($\boxtimes$)], and Hai-Lin Liu[3]

[1] Department of Computer Science, Hong Kong Baptist University,
Hong Kong SAR, China
ymc@comp.hkbu.edu.hk
[2] HKBU Institute of Research and Continuing Education, Shenzhen, China
[3] Guangdong University of Technology, Guangzhou, China

Abstract. Green communication has become a hot topic in the field of wireless communication. This paper aims to improve the Quality of Service (QoS) of the system and minimizes the energy consumption by the spectrum-energy cooperation between adjacent base stations. We formulate the proposed spectrum-energy cooperation model as a hybrid constrained many-objective optimization problem (MaOP). To improve the efficiency of optimization algorithm, an alternate optimization algorithm is presented to address the proposed complex MaOP. The evolutionary multiobjective algorithm is employed for spectrum cooperation optimization which is discrete optimization problem, meanwhile classical optimization method is employed for energy consumption optimization and energy cooperation optimization that are continuous optimization problems. Simulation results show the effectiveness of the algorithm.

Keywords: Green communication · Spectrum-energy cooperation · Evolutionary algorithm

1 Introduction

With the growing demand for social and economic connection, a number of wireless communication subscribers have been dramatically increased in the last decade. Correspondingly, the energy consumption of wireless communication also climbs at an unprecedented speed. The large amount of conventional energy consumption brings severe damage to global climate and constitutes a significant part of network operators' expenditures. According to [8], the total CO_2 emission of global mobile communication will amount to 235 megaton in 2020, which is

This work was supported by the National Natural Science Foundation of China under Grants 61672444, 61673121 and 61703108, in part by the Natural Science Foundation of Guangdong Province under Grant 2017A030310467, the Projects of Science and Technology of Guangzhou under Grant 201508010008, the SZSTI Grant: JCYJ20160531194006833, and the Faculty Research Grant of Hong Kong Baptist University (HKBU) under Project: FRG2/16-17/051.

© Springer International Publishing AG 2017
Y. Shi et al. (Eds.): SEAL 2017, LNCS 10593, pp. 821–832, 2017.
https://doi.org/10.1007/978-3-319-68759-9_67

approximately 3 times of the figure in 2007. Besides the growing number of subscribers, new technologies, such as internet of things and automatic drive, require higher data rate and lower block probability. To meet the challenge of mobile communication in the future, academia and network operators both try to push 5G's energy efficiency to a new level. For example, EARTH (Energy Aware Radio and Network Technologies) [11] is launched by European commission to reduce the energy consumption of mobile communication by 50%.

In the past few years, some efforts have been made to improve the energy efficiency. Energy cooperation technique, base stations (BSs) sleeping strategy, and utilization of renewable energy are three main methods for improving the energy efficiency. Energy cooperation between BSs is a promising technology to improve the energy efficiency. Some energy cooperation strategies in [2, 7, 9, 10, 14, 24] have been proposed to reduce green house gas emission. For instance, Smart Grid (SG) is an energy cooperation mechanism through power grid [9, 24]. When a cell, which is a land area supplied with radio service, has redundant renewable energy, sell the energy to the grid, while buying conventional energy from the grid when a cell has deficit in energy. Also, Xu Jie et al. [24] have proposed an improved energy transaction strategy in coordinated multi-point communication system with SG. Furthermore, BS sleeping strategy [15] switches off the idle or low-load BSs. For example, Ghazzai Hakim et al. [9] have presented an energy management technology in 5G, including BS sleeping and smart grid. Gong Jie et al. [10] have introduced a BS sleeping strategy in renewable powered BSs.

In addition, renewable energy harvesting is also one of the important method to improve the energy efficiency. As conventional energy brings more expenditures to cellular operators and more green house gas to our environment, renewable energy from solar panels or wind turbines has been becoming an alternative to power BSs [16]. A comprehensive report on current issues of BSs powered by solar energy is presented in [2]. However, as a result of undeveloped energy harvest and erratic natural condition, renewable energy supply is not as stable as conventional energy supply. Under the circumstances, a realistic method to use renewable energy is to power BSs with traditional power grid and renewable energy harvest both. Energy cooperation is proposed to coordinate energy supplies for such BSs: transfer surplus energy of low-load cells to energy-deficit high-load cells.

On the other hand, spectrum cooperation is becoming one of the mainstream technologies in communication research to improve the spectrum efficiency. Due to the physical characteristics of wireless communication, spectrum available for wireless communication is limited [21]. Without spectrum cooperation, one cell's available spectrum is static and will not change with its traffic load. Through spectrum cooperation, high-load cells can make use of the spectrum of low-load cells to satisfy their QoS demands. In the literature, e.g. see [2, 7, 9, 10, 14–17, 24], most researchers only focus on energy cooperation, while ignoring spectrum cooperation.

Thus far, some works have been done for the spectrum cooperation in different situations [6,18]. For example, Akshay et al. [19] have proposed a dynamic resource allocation algorithm for efficient spectrum utilization. A contract-based cooperative spectrum sharing mechanism is presented to exploit transmission opportunities for the Device-to-Device (D2D) links, and meanwhile achieving the maximum profit of the cellular links in [23]. In [20], a spectrum sharing model was presented for cognitive wireless network to maximize the sum of throughput. A spectrum allocation strategy is considered in heterogeneous cell to enhance total throughput of each cell in [3].

Most of the existing works have studied on energy efficiency optimization and spectrum efficiency optimization individually, but not both. In fact, only few studies have considered both energy efficiency and spectrum efficiency simultaneously. For example, Guo et al. [14] considered both spectrum and energy cooperation, but the model is formulated as a single objective optimization problem to minimize the total energy consumption as given the minimum Quality of Service (QoS), which limits the potential of improving QoS. An energy-spectrum optimization strategy has been proposed in [1] for massive multiple-input multiple-output (MIMO) network. The secondary user nodes harvest energy from the primary user transmissions, and then access and utilize the primary network spectrum for information transmission. Moreover, these models only consider two systems at the same time.

In this paper, we model spectrum-energy cooperation in heterogeneous wireless network as a many-objective optimization problem (MaOP). In general, a single BS cannot provide high QoS for indoor and edge users, heterogeneous network with picocells will be a competitive track of 5G communication. The energy efficient usually conflicts with the spectrum efficiency in a cell. Meanwhile, different cells conflict with the requirements of energy and spectrum. Therefore, modeling the energy-spectrum cooperation as an MaOP can further improve the QoS and reduce the energy consumption. To the best of our knowledge, our work is the first one that formulates the spectrum-energy cooperation as an MaOP to maximize QoS and minimize conventional energy consumption at the same time, considering multiple (i.e. more than 2 cells) wireless communication heterogeneous cells cooperations. The proposed model is hybrid constrained MaOP. The spectrum cooperation between the cells is a discrete optimization problem, and energy consumption and energy cooperation are continuous optimization problems. The evolutionary multiobjective optimization (EMO) algorithms [4,5,12,13] have promising performance on the discrete optimization problems, but the convergence speed is slower than that of classical optimization methods. In order to improve the efficiency of evolutionary algorithm, an alternate optimization algorithm is proposed accordingly to solve the proposed model. A decomposition-based EMO algorithm [22], i.e., MOEA/D-M2M, is employed for spectrum cooperation optimization, and a classical optimization method is employed for energy consumption optimization and energy cooperation optimization.

The main contributions of this paper are summarized as follows:

1. A spectrum-energy cooperation model is developed for heterogeneous network powered by both renewable energy and power grid. It is formulated as an MaOP to achieve high QoS and low energy consumption.
2. A high-efficiency wireless resources allocation algorithm is proposed to achieve fair and high QoS in each cell.
3. An alternate optimization algorithm is proposed to solve the proposed model.

The remainder of this paper is organized as follows: Section 2 gives the proposed spectrum-energy cooperation model in heterogeneous communication network. Section 3 analyzes the problem and proposes an alternate optimization algorithm for solving the proposed model. Section 4 shows the simulation results. Finally, we draw a conclusion in Sect. 5.

2 The Spectrum-Energy Cooperation Model

In this section, we propose the spectrum-energy cooperation model in heterogeneous communication network.

2.1 Problem Formulation

We consider the QoS and energy consumption of each cell as the optimization objectives. The QoS usually conflicts with the energy consumption in a cell. That is, a higher transmit power can improve the QoS, but brings more energy consumption. Moreover, different cells also conflict with the requirements of energy and spectrum. Therefore, the optimization problem of spectrum-energy cooperation is formulated as an MaOP in this paper. It is worth noting that we handle the problem in a time slot so that energy and power can be stated equally.

There are several energy-consumption units in a BS: power amplification, radio transmission, digital signal processing, cooling, and so on. The power amplification is related to traffic of the BS. There are B cells are considered in this paper. The energy consumption of each cell can be formulated as:

$$P_0 + \sum_{i=1}^{u_e^{(b)}} p_e^{(b)} + \sum_{i=1}^{u_c^{(b)}} p_c^{(b)} = P_u^{(b)} \tag{1}$$

for $b = 1, \ldots, B$, where P_0 is the non-transmit power, $p_c^{(b)}$ and $p_e^{(b)}$ are transmit power allocated to center users and edge users, respectively. $u_c^{(b)}$ and $u_e^{(b)}$ are number of center and edge users in the bth cell. There is a gap between $p_c^{(b)}$ and $p_e^{(b)}$ due to the transmit power difference between macro BS and pico BS. As 6 p BSs can serve edge users, there is a BS selection strategy for edge users. Here, we let edge users choose the nearest pico BS to serve them. The available energy of a cell $P^{(i)}$ comes from power grid P_G^i and renewable energy P_H^i. That is,

$$P^{(i)} = P_G^i + P_H^{(i)} - e_{ij} \tag{2}$$

where e_{ij} is the amount of energy the ith cell transfers to jth cell. Hence, there is an energy constraint:

$$P_u^{(b)} \le P^{(b)} \tag{3}$$

For spectrum cooperation, we set a spectrum sharing vector $\boldsymbol{\alpha} = (\alpha_1, \alpha_2, \ldots, \alpha_B)$ which means sharing rate of center spectrum of cells. The sum of shared subcarriers is computed as:

$$\sum_{i=1}^{B} \alpha_i N_{BS} \tag{4}$$

where N_{BS} denotes the total available subcarrier of each cell. Subcarriers and transmit power are wireless communication resources that should be allocated to center users and edge users in each cell. We denote subcarrier allocation and transmit power allocation as:

$$\begin{cases} \boldsymbol{n_e^{(b)}} = (n_{e,1}^{(b)}, n_{e,2}^{(b)}, \ldots, n_{e,u_e^{(b)}}^{(b)}) \\ \boldsymbol{n_c^{(b)}} = (n_{c,1}^{(b)}, n_{c,2}^{(b)}, \ldots, n_{c,u_c^{(b)}}^{(b)}) \\ \boldsymbol{p_e^{(b)}} = (p_{e,1}^{(b)}, p_{e,2}^{(b)}, \ldots, p_{e,u_e^{(b)}}^{(b)}) \\ \boldsymbol{p_c^{(b)}} = (p_{c,1}^{(b)}, p_{c,2}^{(b)}, \ldots, p_{c,u_c^{(b)}}^{(b)}) \end{cases} \tag{5}$$

where $n_{e,i}^{(b)}$ and $p_{e,i}^{(b)}$ means the allocated subcarriers of the ith edge user and the transmit power in the bth cell. QoS is measured by the maximum data transmission rate ($r_{c,i}^{(b)}$ for center user, $r_{e,i}^{(b)}$ for edge user). The following equations:

$$r_{c,i}^{(b)} = n_{c,i}^{(b)} \cdot \Delta f \cdot (1 + SINR_{c,i}^{(b)}) \tag{6}$$

$$SINR_{c,i}^{(b)} = \frac{\Gamma \cdot (d_{c,i}^{(b)})^{-l} \cdot p_{c,i}^{(b)}}{n_{c,i}^{(b)} \cdot \Delta f \cdot N_0 + \frac{n_{c,i}^{(b)}}{\Sigma_{b=1}^{B} \cdot N_{BS}} \Sigma_{d \neq b} \Gamma \cdot (d_{c,i}^{(d)})^{-l} \cdot \Sigma_{j=1}^{u_c^{(d)}} p_{c,j}^{(d)}} \tag{7}$$

are QoS and SINR for the ith center user in the bth cell, where Γ denotes the channel power gain, l is the path loss factor, $d_{c,i}^{(b)}$ denotes the distance between the ith center user and the bth macro BS, Δf is the bandwidth of a subcarrier, and N_0 denotes the power spectral density of additive Gaussian white noise. Suppose the inference is averaged on the spectrum, the inference is proportional to the spectrum of the user. For edge user, QoS has the same form. We assign an edge user to its nearest pico BS so that the inference for edge user comes from two adjacent pico BSs. To express the available energy in a simple way, we denote the power matrix M_p as:

$$M_p = \begin{pmatrix} P^{(1)} & e_{12} & e_{13} & \cdots & e_{1B} \\ -e_{12} & P^{(2)} & \cdots & \cdots & e_{2B} \\ -e_{13} & -e_{23} & P^{(3)} & \cdots & \vdots \\ \vdots & \vdots & \cdots & \ddots & \vdots \\ -e_{1B} & -e_{2B} & \cdots & \cdots & P_{(b)} \end{pmatrix} \tag{8}$$

where $P^{(b)} = P_G^{(b)} + P_H^{(b)}$. Then, the bth cell's available energy, i.e. Eq. (2), can be rewritten as:

$$\sum_{r=1}^{B} M_{p,rb}. \tag{9}$$

The objectives in the proposed optimization problem are to maximize the data transmission rate $F_R^{(b)}$ and minimize the total transmit energy consumption $F_E^{(b)}$ for the bth cell as shown in Eqs. (10) and (11):

$$F_R^{(b)} = \sum_{i=1}^{u_c^{(b)}} r_{c,i}^{(b)} + \sum_{i=1}^{u_e^{(b)}} r_{e,i}^{(b)} \tag{10}$$

$$F_E^{(b)} = \sum_{i=1}^{u_c^{(b)}} p_{c,i}^{(b)} + \sum_{j=1}^{u_e^{(b)}} p_{e,i}^{(b)}. \tag{11}$$

Then, the proposed model can be formulated as the following optimization problem:

$$MOP: \min_{\alpha, n_e^{(b)}, n_c^{(b)}, p_e^{(b)}, p_c^{(b)}, e_{ij}} \left(-F_R^{(1)}, -F_R^{(2)}, \cdots, -F_R^{(b)}, F_E^{(1)}, F_E^{(2)}, \cdots, F_E^{(b)} \right)$$

$$s.t. \sum_{i=1}^{u_e^{(b)}} n_{e,i}^{(b)} \leq (1 - \alpha_b) \cdot N_{BS} \tag{12}$$

$$\sum_{i=1}^{u_c^{(b)}} n_{c,i}^{(b)} \leq \sum_{b=1}^{B} \alpha_b \cdot N_{BS} \tag{13}$$

$$P_0 + \sum_{i=1}^{u_e^{(b)}} p_{e,i}^{(b)} + \sum_{i=1}^{u_c^{(b)}} p_{c,i}^{(b)} \leq \sum_{r=1}^{B} M_{p,rb} \tag{14}$$

$$r_{e,i}^{(b)} \geq r_{e0}^{(b)} \tag{15}$$

$$n_{c,i}^{(b)}, n_{e,i}^{(b)} \in \{0, 1, 2, \cdots\} \tag{16}$$

$$p_{c,i}^{(b)}, p_{e,i}^{(b)} \geq 0 \tag{17}$$

$$\mathbf{0 \leq \alpha \leq 0.92} \tag{18}$$

Constraints (12), (13) and (14) are the edge users' subcarrier constraint, center users' subcarrier constraint, and energy constraint, respectively. Constraint (15) ensure that data transmission rate should be greater than its lower boundary $r_{e0}^{(b)}$. In constraint (18), inequality means the element-wise inequality of a vector. The upper boundary 0.92 ensures that edge users have subcarriers to communicate. As this many-objective optimization problem is too complicated to be solved directly, we therefore divide the problem into three subproblems as described in the next section.

Algorithm 1. Transmission Power Optimization in Energy Consumption Optimization

---

Input:
- BS_{Arr}: Cell Parameters;
- Ind: The best individual in a population;

Output:

- $P_e^{(b)}$: Transmission power allocation for edge users, $e = 1, 2 \ldots u_e^{(b)}$, $b = 1, 2 \ldots B$;
- $P_c^{(b)}$: Transmission power allocation for center users, $c = 1, 2 \ldots u_c^{(b)}$, $b = 1, 2 \ldots B$;
- $r^{(b)}$: QoS of a cell, $b = 1, 2 \ldots B$;

1 %Optimize transmission power for edge user.
2 Get $P_{e0}^{(b)}$ and $r_{e,min}^{(b)}$ from BS_{Arr};
3 **for** $b \leftarrow 1$ **to** B **do**
4 | **while** *The stopping criterion is not satisfied* **do**
5 | | **for** $e \leftarrow 1$ **to** $u_e^{(b)}$ **do**
6 | | | $P_e^{(b)} = P_{e0}^{(b)}$;
7 | | | **while** $r_e^{(b)} > r_{e,min}^{(b)}$ **do**
8 | | | | Calculate gradient *grad*;
9 | | | | $d = -grad$;
10 | | | | Determine step size t via backtracking search;
11 | | | | $P_e^{(b)} = P_e^{(b)} + t \cdot d$;
12 | | | | Calculate $r_e^{(b)}$;
13 | | | **end**
14 | | **end**
15 | **end**
16 **end**
17 %Optimize transmission power for center user.
18 Get $P_{c0}^{(b)}$ and $r_{c,min}^{(b)}$ from BS_{Arr};
19 **while** *The stopping criterion is not satisfied* **do**
20 | **for** $b \leftarrow 1$ **to** B **do**
21 | | **for** $c \leftarrow 1$ **to** $u_0^{(b)}$ **do**
22 | | | **while** $r_c^{(b)} > r_{c,min}^{(b)}$ **do**
23 | | | | Calculate gradient *grad*;
24 | | | | $d = -grad$;
25 | | | | Determine step size t via backtracking search;
26 | | | | $P_c^{(b)} = P_c^{(b)} + t \cdot d$;
27 | | | | Calculate $r_c^{(b)}$;
28 | | | **end**
29 | | **end**
30 | **end**
31 **end**
32 **for** $b \leftarrow 1$ **to** B **do**
33 | Calculate lowest QoS of bth cell, denoted as $r^{(b)}$;
34 **end**
35 Output $P_c^{(b)}, P_e^{(b)}$ and $r^{(b)}$

3   Optimization Algorithm Based on MOEA

We solve MOP by dividing it into three subproblems: spectrum cooperation optimization (Subproblem 1), energy consumption optimization (Subproblem 2), energy cooperation optimization (Subproblem 3), and then alternately optimize these three subproblems.

3.1   Spectrum Cooperation Optimization

We firstly optimize the variables in spectrum cooperation, namely $\alpha, n_{c,i}^{(b)}$, and $n_{e,i}^{(b)}$. Transmit power for each user is arbitrarily determined at first so that energy consumption is determined and optimization objectives only include $F_R^{(b)}, b = 1, \cdots, B$. We denote this MaOP as Subproblem 1 and solve it via MOEA/D-M2M [22]. To allocate subcarriers in a reasonable way, $n_{c,i}^{(b)}$ and $n_{e,i}^{(b)}$ are not searched in evolutionary algorithm randomly but assigned using greedy strategy. Subcarriers are allocated iteratively and, in each iteration, one subcarrier is assigned to the user with minimum QoS. Subproblem 1 can be formulated as follows:

$$Subproblem1: \min_{\alpha, n_e^{(b)}, n_c^{(b)}} (F_R^{(1)}, F_R^{(2)}, \cdots, F_R^{(B)})$$

$$s.t. \text{ Constraints } (12), (13), (16), (18).$$

Through spectrum cooperation optimization, we can get spectrum sharing vector α, subcarriers allocation $n_{c,i}^{(b)}$ and $n_{e,i}^{(b)}$. Based on the result of this step, we can run energy consumption optimization.

3.2   Energy Consumption Optimization

We optimize the transmit power $p_e^{(b)}$ and $p_c^{(b)}$ by:

$$Subproblem2: \min_{p_e^{(b)}} p_e^{(b)}$$

$$s.t. \text{ Constraints } (14), (15), (17)$$

for $b = 1, \ldots, B$ and $i = 1, 2, \ldots, u_e^{(b)}$. For center users, we have the same optimization problem. As the gradient of $r_{e,i}^{(b)}$ with respect to $p_e^{(b)}$ is complicated to calculate, we therefore omit 1 in Eq.(6) and get the approximate gradient as:

$$\frac{\partial r_{c,i}^{(b)}}{\partial p_{c,i}^{(b)}} \approx \frac{n_{c,i}^{(b)} \cdot \Delta f}{In2 \cdot p_{c,i}^{(b)}}. \tag{19}$$

Edge user's gradient has the same form. We use backtracking strategy to determine an appropriate step size in the gradient descent method. Algorithm 1 is the pseudocode for energy consumption optimization.

Through 3.2 and 3.1, we obtain the spectrum sharing vector and wireless resources allocation variables. In the next section, we will optimize energy cooperation variables e_{ij}'s.

3.3   Energy Cooperation Optimization

After the previous optimization steps, only energy cooperation variables e_{ij}'s are undetermined. As $p_{c,i}^{(b)}$ and $p_{e,i}^{(b)}$ are obtained, we have energy consumption of each cell. Besides that, we generate renewable energy supply in some interval randomly. The energy cooperation can be optimized by the follow problem:

$$Subproblem3: \min_{P_G^{(b)}} \sum_{b=1}^{B} P_G^{(b)} \qquad (20)$$

$$s.t. \text{ Constraint (15)}$$

for $b = 1, 2, \cdots, B$. This problem is a typical linear programming (LP) one, thus we can use LP toolbox of Matlab to optimize it. To improve the accuracy of our algorithm, we iterate step 3.1 and step 3.2, input the outcomes of the iteration to LP programme, and get the final result.

4   Numerical Simulation

We evaluate the proposed algorithm using an example with 4 cells, in which the numbers of users are given in Table 1. The Inter-Site Distance of each cell is 1000 m. Number of available subcarriers is 600, which means each cell has a spectrum of 900 MHz. Initial transmit power is 30 W and 10 W for center user and edge user, respectively. Non-transmit power of heterogeneous cell is set at 500 W. Path loss l and attenuation Γ are 2 and $(3/32\pi)^2$. We run the first two steps 19 times and get the average QoS and transmit energy consumption for each iteration as illustrated in Fig. 1.

Table 1. Simulated cell users

	Edge users	Center users	Users
Cell1	5	8	13
Cell2	31	18	49
Cell3	25	27	52
Cell4	35	43	48

It can be observed that: (1) the first round of iteration makes the most significant energy reduction in all 20 iterations and the efficiency of energy consumption optimization is low at iteration 5–10; (2) QoS decreases dramatically after iteration 8 or 9. QoS in iteration 15–20 decreases to a relatively low level although the energy consumption drops significantly at the same time. This kind of energy reduction is ill reduction. Hence, we need to avoid ill reduction and make use of valuable energy reduction. Based on the experimental results, it can be seen that 5–8 is the best iteration number because 5–8 iterations can decrease

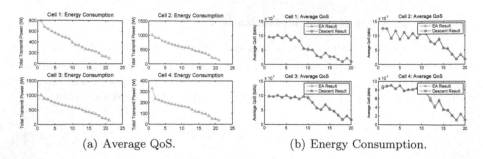

(a) Average QoS.   (b) Energy Consumption.

Fig. 1. Iteration result.

the energy consumption meanwhile maintaining QoS. Considering computation complexity, we will set the iteration number at 5 hereinafter.

Table 2 shows the result of energy cooperation (EC). Renewable energy is generated randomly from 700–800 W. It can be seen that, with EC, conventional energy consumption can be reduced to 68% compared to that without EC.

Table 2. Energy cooperation result

	Energy Consumption(W)	Renewable Energy(W)	Grid Power with EC(W)	Grid Power without EC(W)
cell1	607.22	763.23	79.33	0
cell2	770.07	709.75	83.99	63.71
cell3	922.56	727.85	84.66	194.71
cell4	987.04	754.69	83.37	232.35

Next, we investigated the impact of inter-site distance (ISD) on energy consumption and QoS and more importantly determined the best ISD setting. By changing ISD from 100–2000 m and maintaining other parameters fixed, we can get the following results. Energy consumption comprises of transmission energy and non-transmission energy, which is set at 500 W. Energy efficiency is measured by energy consumption per Mbps. Lower energy consumption per Mbps means higher energy efficiency. From the comparison, ISD400 m is approximately the best size of cell when traffic is heavy. Actually, ISD400 m achieves high average QoS and energy efficiency at the same time.

5   Conclusion

This paper has studied the spectrum-energy cooperation optimization in heterogeneous communication network to improve the communication quality and reduce the carbon emission through the spectrum-energy cooperation.

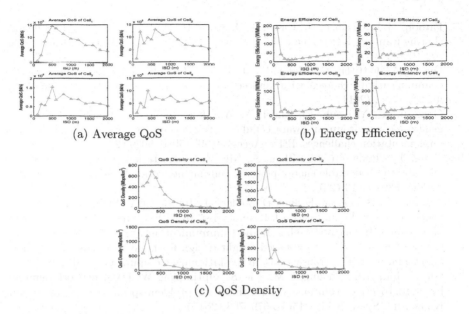

(a) Average QoS   (b) Energy Efficiency

(c) QoS Density

Fig. 2. ISD comparison

A spectrum-energy cooperation model based on the characteristics of heterogeneous cell has been proposed by formulating it as a hybrid constrained MaOP. Accordingly, an alternate optimization algorithm has been proposed for solving such complex problem. The simulation results have shown that the proposed energy-spectrum cooperation optimization algorithm can accomplish the expected target (Fig. 2).

References

1. Al-Hraishawi, H., Baduge, G.A.A.: Wireless energy harvesting in cognitive massive MIMO systems with underlay spectrum sharing. IEEE Wirel. Commun. Lett. **6**(1), 134–137 (2017)
2. Chamola, V., Sikdar, B.: Solar powered cellular base stations: current scenario, issues and proposed solutions. IEEE Commun. Mag. **54**(5), 108–114 (2015)
3. Chandrasekhar, V., Andrews, J.G.: Spectrum allocation in tiered cellular networks. IEEE Trans. Commun. **57**(10), 3059–3068 (2009)
4. Cheung, Y.M., Gu, F., Liu, H.L.: Objective extraction for many-objective optimization problems: algorithm and test problems. IEEE Trans. Evol. Comput. **20**(5), 755–772 (2016)
5. Deb, K.: Multiobjective Optimization using Evolutionary Algorithms. Wiley, New York (2001)
6. Deng, Y., Kim, K.J., Duong, T.Q., Elkashlan, M., Karagiannidis, G.K., Nallanathan, A.: Full-duplex spectrum sharing in cooperative single carrier systems. IEEE Trans. Cogn. Commun. Netw. **2**(1), 68–82 (2016)

7. Farooq, M.J., Ghazzai, H., Kadri, A., ElSawy, H., Alouini, M.S.: A hybrid energy sharing framework for green cellular networks. IEEE Trans. Commun. **65**(2), 918–934 (2017)
8. Fehske, A., Fettweis, G., Malmodin, J., Biczok, G.: The global footprint of mobile communications: the ecological and economic perspective. IEEE Commun. Mag. **49**(8), 55–62 (2011)
9. Ghazzai, H., Yaacoub, E., Kadri, A., Yanikomeroglu, H., Alouini, M.S.: Next-generation eenvironment-aware cellular networks: modern green techniques and implementation challenges. IEEE Access **4**(99), 5010–5029 (2016)
10. Gong, J., Thompson, J.S., Zhou, S., Niu, Z.: Base station sleeping and resource allocation in renewable energy powered cellular networks. IEEE Trans. Commun. **62**(11), 3801–3813 (2014)
11. Gruber, M., Blume, O., Ferling, D., Zeller, D., Imran, M.A., Strinati, E.C.: Earth-energy aware radio and network technologies. In: IEEE International Symposium on Personal, Indoor and Mobile Radio Communications, pp. 1–5 (2009)
12. Gu, F., Cheung, Y.M.: Som-based weight design for many-objective evolutionary algorithm. In: IEEE Transactions on Evolutionary Computation (2017)
13. Gu, F., Liu, H.L., Cheung, Y.M., Xie, S.: Optimizing WCDMA network planning by multiobjective evolutionary algorithm with problem-specific genetic operation. Knowl. Inf. Syst. (KAIS) **45**(3), 679–703 (2015)
14. Guo, Y., Xu, J., Duan, L., Zhang, R.: Joint energy and spectrum cooperation for cellular communication systems. IEEE Trans. Commun. **62**(10), 3678–3691 (2013)
15. Han, F., Zhao, S., Zhang, L., Wu, J.: Survey of strategies for switching off base stations in heterogeneous networks for greener 5G systems. IEEE Access **4**, 4959–4973 (2016)
16. Han, T., Ansari, N.: Powering mobile networks with green energy. IEEE Wirel. Commun. **21**(1), 90–96 (2014)
17. Hasan, Z., Boostanimehr, H., Bhargava, V.K.: Green cellular networks: a survey, some research issues and challenges. IEEE Commun. Surv. Tutor. **13**(4), 524–540 (2011)
18. Jia, Y., Zhang, Z., Tan, X., Liu, X.: Asymmetric active cooperation strategy in spectrum sharing game with imperfect information. Int. J. Commun. Syst. **28**(3), 414–425 (2015)
19. Kumar, A., Sengupta, A., Tandon, R., Clancy, T.C.: Dynamic resource allocation for cooperative spectrum sharing in LTE networks. IEEE Trans. Veh. Technol. **64**(11), 5232–5245 (2015)
20. Lee, S., Zhang, R.: Cognitive wireless powered network: spectrum sharing models and throughput maximization. IEEE Trans. Cogn. Commun. Netw. **1**(3), 335–346 (2015)
21. Liu, H.L., Gu, F., Cheung, Y.M., Xie, S., Zhang, J.: On solving WCDMA network planning using iterative power control scheme and evolutionary multiobjective algorithm. IEEE Comput. Intell. Mag. **9**(1), 44–52 (2014)
22. Liu, H.L., Gu, F., Zhang, Q.: Decomposition of a multiobjective optimization problem into a number of simple multiobjective subproblems. IEEE Trans. Evol. Comput. **18**(3), 450–455 (2014)
23. Ma, C., Li, Y., Yu, H., Gan, X., Wang, X., Ren, Y., Xu, J.J.: Cooperative spectrum sharing in D2D-enabled cellular networks. IEEE Trans. Commun. **64**(10), 4394–4408 (2016)
24. Xu, J., Zhang, R.: Cooperative energy trading in comp systems powered by smart grids. IEEE Trans. Veh. Technol. **65**(4), 2142–2153 (2016)

Large Scale WSN Deployment
Based on an Improved Cooperative Co-evolution
PSO with Global Differential Grouping

Yazhen Zhang and Wei Fang[✉]

School of IoT Engineering, Jiangnan University, Wuxi, China
fangwei@jiangnan.edu.cn

Abstract. With the development of wireless sensor networks (WSNs), the applications of WSNs are becoming more and more, especially in military monitoring, target tracking and traffic control. Coverage is one of the key metrics for WSNs performance. As a number of typical WSN applications such as forest fire or hostile environments monitoring are likely to expand their service coverage, they have to deploy a large number of sensor nodes in the interest area. However, with the number of sensor nodes increase the dimensions of the problem are also getting higher, traditional WSNs deployment algorithms can not achieve the desired results. In this paper, we propose an improved cooperative co-evolution global differential grouping particle swarm optimization (ICC-GDG-PSO) algorithm to solve the problem of large scale deployment. Global Differential Grouping (GDG) algorithm has good performance in large scale problem optimization, especially when the WSN contains thousands of sensors. We using the GDG decomposition strategy on a cooperative coevolution (CC) framework. But GDG algorithm won't update the grouping since the grouping information confirmed, we integrate the random grouping mechanism after the GDG algorithm to get more accurate grouping of variables. Experimental results show that our proposed ICC-GDG-PSO algorithm is superior to other algorithms in the large scale deployment problem.

Keywords: Large scale sensor networks · Dynamic deployment · Particle swarm optimization · Cooperative coevolution · Global differential grouping

1 Introduction

Wireless sensor networks (WSNs) consisting of a large number of sensor nodes deployed in the monitoring area, with computing power, sensing and communication capability. These sensor nodes communicate with each other to monitor physical or environmental conditions cooperatively [1]. WSN has been successfully applied in target tracking, monitoring and classification. Coverage is one of the key metrics for WSN performance. The dynamic deployment of sensor nodes is a major hotspot in research and will directly affect the performance of WSN.

© Springer International Publishing AG 2017
Y. Shi et al. (Eds.): SEAL 2017, LNCS 10593, pp. 833–842, 2017.
https://doi.org/10.1007/978-3-319-68759-9_68

In many cases the sensor nodes is randomly thrown in the monitoring area, the initial location of the sensor nodes can not be guaranteed to achieve effective coverage. To tackle this problem, various dynamic deployment algorithms have been studied by researchers. The virtual force (VF) algorithm [2] was introduced as one of main approaches for dynamic deployment offering outstanding performance for improving the coverage of WSN. However, their experiments based on the VF algorithm [2–4] consisting only of mobile sensor nodes, but WSNs in practice consist of mobile sensor nodes and stationary sensor nodes to reduce the cost and energy consumption [5]. In the experiment, the performance of the VF algorithm will be deteriorated because the force exerted by stationary sensor nodes will hinder the movements of mobile sensor nodes.

Swarm intelligence has also been used for solving WSNs deployment problems. In [6,7], particle swarm optimization (PSO) algorithms were proposed to find the optimal deployment of sensor nodes. However, with the increase in deployment area, the performance of the PSO algorithm will decrease because of the large quantity of sensor nodes. Since it suffers from the "curse of dimensionality", which implies that it's performance deteriorates rapidly as the dimensionality of the search space increases [8]. Specially, in [6] authors combined the virtual forces with co-evolutionary particle swarm optimization (CPSO) algorithm, CPSO is an improvement of the PSO algorithm where the dimensions are divided into subsets and each subset is given to a swarm. This is referred to fixed grouping strategy, each subset as a group, their experimental results are superior. CCPSO2 [9] (Cooperatively Co-evolution Particle Swarm) is a recent state-of-the-art CPSO variant that has been successfully used to solve large scale optimization problems. CCPSO2 adopt the random grouping, which equally distribute the decision variables to each group at random, this algorithm unable to placing interacting variables in the same group accurately. The Global Differential Grouping (GDG) [10] method is extended from the differential grouping method [11], which groups the variables based on the interaction between them. This is an automatic decomposition strategy and is capable of solving large scale optimization problem.

This work proposes an Improved Global Differential Grouping based Cooperatively Co-evolution PSO (ICC-GDG-PSO) algorithm to deal with large scale WSNs deployment problems. In our work, the WSNs consist thousands of sensor nodes, this is a high-dimensional optimization problem. We use cooperative coevolution (CC) framework to decompose a high-dimensional objective vector into smaller subcomponents that can be handled by conventional evolutionary algorithms (EAs). The improved GDG automatic decomposition strategy was used to get the ideal grouping of the sensor nodes location, and the PSO algorithm was introduced to optimize the subcomponents of the nodes location to improve the coverage of the network.

The rest of this paper is organized as follows. Section 2 gives the sensor detection model. Section 3 details the proposed approach. Experiments and results are discussed in Sect. 4, while Sect. 5 concludes the paper.

2 Sensor Detection Model

The performance of WSNs depends primarily on where the sensor nodes are placed in the region of interest. Because there is no a priori knowledge of terrain or obstacles in the area of interest, all sensor nodes are randomly scattered in the sensing area while initializing. The WSNs consist of static sensor nodes and N mobile sensor nodes $S = \{s_1, s_2, ..., s_i, ..., s_N\}, i = 1, ..., N$, all sensor nodes are assumed to have the same sensing radius R_s and communication radius R_c, to guarantee the connectivity of the whole network, the communication radius is twice of the sensing radius [12]. The sensing area is considered to be divided into $m \times n$ grids. The coverage of the whole area is proportional to the number of grid points that can be covered. Considering a sensor s_i deployed at point (x_i, y_i), for grid point $G(x, y)$, the Euclidean distance between s_i and G is:

$$d(s_i, G) = \sqrt{(x_i - x)^2 + (y_i - y)^2} \tag{1}$$

There are two detection models in WSNs: the binary detection model and the probabilistic detection model. Some uncertainty factors may contained in the sensor readings because of the noise or obstacles, for more realistic, the probabilistic model is used to describe the sensor detection. For the grid point $G(x, y)$, the possibility that it can be covered based on the probabilistic model by a sensor s_i as shown in Fig. 1 is described by [13]:

$$p_{(x,y,s_i)} = \begin{cases} 1 & , \text{ if } d(s_i, G) \leq R_s - r_e \\ e^{-\alpha\lambda^\beta} & , \text{ if } R_s - r_e < d(s_i, G) < R_s + r_e \\ 0 & , \text{ if } d(s_i, G) \geq R_s + r_e \end{cases} \tag{2}$$

r_e is the detection error range, α and β are parameters measuring the detection probability, their values depend on the characteristics of various types of physical sensors, λ is input parameter and given by:

$$\lambda = r_e - R_s + d(s_i, G) \tag{3}$$

The above model determines that it is necessary to calculate the overlap sensor detection areas. Considering a grid point (x, y) lying in the overlap region of a set of sensors S_{ov}. Its joint detection probability is presented as follows:

$$P_{x,y}(S_{ov}) = 1 - \prod_{s_i \in S_{ov}} (1 - p_{(x,y,s_i)}) \tag{4}$$

where $p_{(x,y,s_i)}$ is the detection probability of s_i at grid point (x, y). The grid point (x, y) can be effectively covered if

$$min\{P_{x,y}(S_{ov})\} \geq P_{th} \tag{5}$$

where P_{th} is the defined threshold. Finally, if the monitoring area is quantized as $m \times n$ points, the coverage rate can be described as:

$$R = \frac{\sum_{x=1}^{m} \sum_{y=1}^{n} P_{x,y}(S_{ov}) | \forall P_{x,y}(S_{ov}) \geq P_{th}}{m \times n} \tag{6}$$

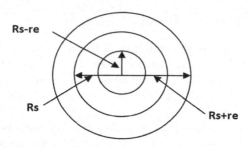

Fig. 1. Probabilistic detection model.

3   An Improved CC-GDG-PSO Based WSNs Deployment

3.1   Particle Swarm Optimization

Particle Swarm Optimization (PSO) algorithm is a swarm-intelligence-based evolutionary algorithm, inspired by the dynamic of a bird flock, which has the characteristic of quickly converging to a local minimum. Each particle represents a potential solution to the optimization problem. Let s denote the swarm size. For particle $i(1 \leqslant i \leqslant s)$, define y_i as its own local best position, and x_i denote its current position. The global best position found by any particle is presented as $\hat{y}$. At every iteration t, each particle updates its current velocity v_i toward y_i and $\hat{y}$ with the bounded random acceleration. y_i and $\hat{y}$ are updated as follows:

$$y_i\left(t+1\right) = \begin{cases} y_i\left(t\right), & \text{if } f\left(x_i\left(t+1\right)\right) \geq f\left(y_i\left(t\right)\right), \\ x_i\left(t+1\right), & \text{if } f\left(x_i\left(t+1\right)\right) < f\left(y_i\left(t\right)\right). \end{cases} \tag{7}$$

$$\hat{y}\left(t+1\right) = \underset{y_i}{\arg\min} f\left(y_i\left(t+1\right)\right), \quad 1 \leq i \leq s \tag{8}$$

Then velocity and position of particle are updated as follows:

$$\begin{aligned} v_{i,d}\left(t+1\right) = {} & \omega\left(t\right) v_{i,d}\left(t\right) + c_1 r_{1i}\left(t\right)\left(y_{i,d}\left(t\right) - x_{i,d}\left(t\right)\right) \\ & + c_2 r_{2i}\left(t\right)\left(\hat{y}\left(t\right) - x_{i,d}\left(t\right)\right) \end{aligned} \tag{9}$$

$$x_{i,d}\left(t+1\right) = x_{i,d}\left(t\right) + v_{i,d}\left(t+1\right) \tag{10}$$

The parameters c_1 and c_2 are the acceleration coefficients that control the particle direction, $r_{1i}(t)$ and $r_{2i}(t)$ are two separate random functions in the range $[0,1]$, $x_{i,d}(t)$ and $v_{i,d}(t)$ represent the position and velocity of ith particle in dth dimension at time t, $y_{i,d}(t)$ is the local best position of ith particle in dth dimension, and $\hat{y}(t)$ is the global best position. Variable $\omega(t)$ is the inertia weight used to balance local and global search, where $MaxNumber$ is the number of maximum iterations.

The vector $X_i = (x_{i1}^1, x_{i1}^2, x_{i2}^1, x_{i2}^2, ..., x_{iN}^1, x_{iN}^2)$ present the position coordinates of all mobile sensor nodes as shown in Table 1, where N is the total number of mobile sensor nodes, the fitness of the vector is presented by the effective coverage area.

Table 1. PSO particle representation.

Sensor nodes	s_1	s_2	s_3	s_4	s_5	s_6	...	s_N
Sensors location	$x_1^1 x_1^2$	$x_2^1 x_2^2$	$x_3^1 x_3^2$	$x_4^1 x_4^2$	$x_5^1 x_5^2$	$x_6^1 x_6^2$	...	$x_N^1 x_N^2$

3.2 Cooperative Coevolution with Improved Global Differential Grouping

Cooperative Coevolution (CC) is a general framework for applying EAs to large and complex problems using a divide-and-conquer strategy [14]. In CC, the objective vector is decomposed into smaller modules and each of them is assigned to a subpopulation. These subpopulation are evolved separately with the only cooperation happening during fitness evaluation. The framework of CC for optimization can be summarised as follows:

Problem decomposition: Decompose a high-dimensional objective vector into smaller subcomponents that can be handled by conventional EAs. **Subcomponent optimization**: Evolve each subcomponent separately using a certain EA. **Subcomponents coadaptation**: It is essential for coadaptation to capture the interdependencies between subcomponents during the optimization.

A critical step in the above framework is problem decomposition, here we use the improved Global Differential Grouping (GDG) to discover the underlying interaction structure of the decision variables. Algorithm 1 shows the complete algorithm design. Firstly, in the step of initialization, parameters are set up and particles are initialized randomly distributed in the interest area A, each particle represents a set of locations of sensor nodes. All locations of sensor nodes are encoded, since each location is two-dimensional, the dimension of each particle is twice of the number of sensor nodes. After a location is generated, then analyze the effective coverage area. Secondly, in the grouping stage, the GDG was introduced as the *grouping* function to discover the underlying interaction structure of the decision variables and the subcomponents are formed accordingly. During the optimization stage, the subcomponents that are formed in the grouping stage, we use PSO combined with the provided grouping information to optimize the fitness function f for a predetermined number of cycles. All particles are evaluated according to the fitness function. Using Eq. (1) to calculate the distance between each point and each sensor node, using Eqs. (4), (5) to determine whether one point is covered by the WSN, using Eq. (6) to calculate the fitness value of the particle. Finally, once the grouping is determined by GDG algorithm, the grouping information will no longer update. In order to further improve the grouping accuracy, we update the grouping information with random grouping mechanism [9] after the execution of GDG algorithm. Line 22 Variable best records the maximum coverage and the locations of all mobile sensor nodes can be found in $best_{val}$. Algorithm 1 describes the proposed ICC-GDG-PSO dynamic deployment algorithm for WSNs.

Algorithm 1. Pseudocode of ICC-GDG-PSO dynamic deployment algorithm for WSNs:

1: Initialize the parameters: number of static nodes n_s, number of mobile nodes n_m, detection radius R_s, size of the area A, maximum number of iterations $MaxNumber$ and so on.

2: Deploy all sensor nodes including the static and mobile sensors at random then analyze the effective coverage area

3: groups $= grouping(f,$ lbounds, ubounds, n)

4: pop=rand(popsize, n)

5: (best, $best_{val}$) $= \max f$

6: repeat:

7: for i=1 to Cycles do

8: for j=1 to size(groups) do

9: indicies=groups[j]

10: subpop=pop[:, indicies]

11: subpop=PSO((best, $best_{val}$), subpop, f)

12: pop[:, indicies] = subpop

13: (best, $best_{val}$) =max f

14: end for

15: end for

16: Create and initialize K swarms, each with s dimensions, where s is randomly chosen from a set S, ensure n $= K \times s$, the jth swarm is denoted as P_j, $j \in [1, ..., K]$

17: if the coverage has not improved then randomly choose s from S and let $K= n/s$

18: randomly permutate all n dimension indices, construct K swarm, each with s dimensions

19: for each swarm $j \in [1, ..., K]$ do

20: for each particle $i \in [1, ..., swarmSize]$ do

21: Calculate the coverage using the fitness function f

22: update (best, $best_{val}$) if the effective coverage area increase

23: end for

24: end for

25: until termination criterion is met

---

4 Experimental Results

In order to verify the validity of the proposed algorithm for large scale WSNs deployment, the experiment is conducted for VF, PSO, VFCPSO, CCPSO2, CC-DG-PSO and ICC-GDG-PSO algorithms. The experiment is implemented using Matlab R2014a, to eliminate the experimental error caused by randomness, the experiment was run for 30 independent runs and the average of results is calculated.

4.1 Parameter Settings

In our experiment, a WSN including $n_s = 300$ stationary nodes and $n_m = 1000$ mobile nodes. The sensor nodes are deployed in a square area $A = 500 \times$

$500 = 250000\text{m}^2$. The parameters of the probabilistic detection model are $R_s = 9\,\text{m}$, $R_c = 2\ R_s = 18\,\text{m}$, $r_e = 0.5\ R_s = 4.5\,\text{m}$, $\alpha = 0.5$, $\beta = 0.5$, $c_{th} = 0.9$. The acceleration constants of PSO are set as $c_1 = c_2 = 1$, $MaxNumber = 600$. The number of particles used in all PSO algorithms is set to 15. For CCPSO2, the S set is configured as $\{2, 5, 10, 50, 100, 250\}$.

4.2   Results and Analysis

Figure 2 (a) shows the initial deployment of WSN, we scattered the sensor nodes randomly, where the effective coverage area is 65.16%. During the algorithm optimization process, through redeploy the mobile nodes to increase the coverage and the location of stationary nodes won't be changed.

In an independent experiment, the final results carried out by VF, PSO, VFCPSO, CCPSO2, CC-DG-PSO and ICC-GDG-PSO are shown in Figs. 2(b) to 5(a) respectively. Accordingly, the effective coverage of these algorithms are 75.99%, 88.99%, 91.44%, 92.93%, 94.26%, 96.13%, and Fig. 5(b) is the average coverage curve in 30 independent runs, it shows the detailed comparison of convergence speed with the improvement of effective coverage. Obviously, the proposed ICC-GDG-PSO algorithm outperforms the other algorithms in terms

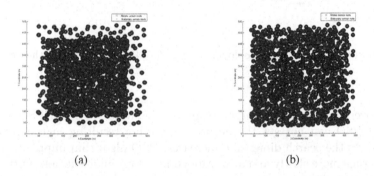

(a)   (b)

Fig. 2. Results of (a) initial random deployment and (b) after dynamic deployment by VF.

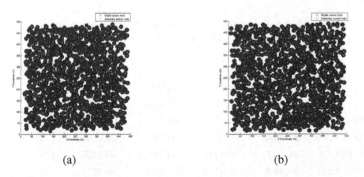

(a)   (b)

Fig. 3. Results of (a) dynamic deployment by PSO, and (b) VFCPSO.

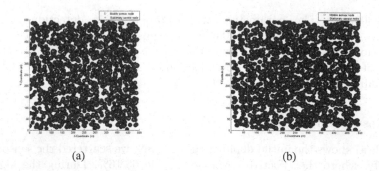

(a)   (b)

Fig. 4. Results of (a) dynamic deployment by CCPSO2, and (b) CC-DG-PSO.

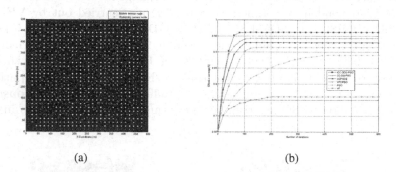

(a)   (b)

Fig. 5. Results of (a) dynamic deployment by ICC-GDG-PSO, and (b) the final average coverage curve.

of the coverage and the convergence speed. Meanwhile, CC-DG-PSO, CCPSO2 and VFCPSO can not get the accurate grouping resulting in the suboptimal solution. As the search dimension increases, PSO algorithm improves the effective coverage more slowly and also trapped in suboptimal solution. Furthermore, the force exerted by stationary sensor nodes will hinder the movements of mobile sensor nodes, so VF algorithm can not get the ideal solution too.

Table 2. Results of the Average, Best, Worst effective coverage and the standard deviation of all algorithms in 30 independent runs.

	Average	Std	Best	Worst	Average iterations
VF	75.02%	0.0892	75.99%	74.96%	251
PSO	88.55%	0.0754	90.01%	88.03%	402
VFCPSO	91.40%	0.0795	92.04%	91.11%	138
CCPSO2	92.89%	0.0523	93.10%	92.09%	113
CC-DG-PSO	94.12%	0.0433	94.58%	93.97%	108
ICC-GDG-PSO	96.88%	0.0336	97.85%	96.05%	75

Table 2 shows the average and standard deviation of effective coverage, the best and worst situations are also list in the table. Average iterations reflect the mean number of iterations that the algorithms get the maximum effective coverage. As seen from Table 2, the proposed ICC-GDG-PSO algorithm is more successful than the other algorithms for the large scale WSNs dynamic deployment.

5   Conclusion

In this paper, an improved cooperative co-evolution global differential grouping particle swarm optimization (ICC-GDG-PSO) algorithm is proposed to solve the dynamic deployment problem in large scale WSNs including mobile and static sensors. For large scale WSNs deployment, this is a high-dimensional optimization problem. Optimal solution corresponds to the ideal grouping of decision variables: each subcomponent should consist of tightly interacting variables while the interaction among subcomponents should be weak. We use CC framework to decompose the objective vector into smaller subcomponents that can be handled by conventional evolutionary algorithms. The improved GDG automatic decomposition strategy was used to get the ideal grouping of the sensor nodes location besides improving the coverage. Compared to the traditional algorithms, the experiment results illustrate the outstanding performance of the proposed algorithm for large scale WSNs dynamic deployment.

Acknowledgment. This work was partially supported by the National Natural Science foundation of China (Grant Nos. 61673194, 61105128), Key Research and Development Program of Jiangsu Province, China (Grant No. BE2017630), the Postdoctoral Science Foundation of China (Grant No. 2014M560390), Six Talent Peaks Project of Jiangsu Province (Grant No. DZXX-025).

References

1. Akyildiz, I.F., Su, W., Sankarasubramaniam, Y., Cayirci, E.: A survey on sensor networks. IEEE Commun. Mag. **40**(8), 102–114 (2002)
2. Zou, Y., Chakrabarty, K.: Sensor deployment and target localization based on virtual forces. In: Twenty-Second Annual Joint Conference of the IEEE Computer and Communications, INFOCOM 2003, vol. 2, pp. 1293–1303. IEEE Societies (2003)
3. Wong, T., Tsuchiya, T., Kikuno, T.: A self-organizing technique for sensor placement in wireless micro-sensor networks. In: 2004 18th International Conference on Advanced Information Networking and Applications, AINA 2004, vol. 1, pp. 78–83. IEEE (2004)
4. Li, S., Xu, C., Pan, W., Pan, Y.: Sensor deployment optimization for detecting maneuvering targets. In: 2005 8th International Conference on Information Fusion, vol. 2, p. 7. IEEE (2005)
5. Wang, X., Ma, J.J., Wang, S., Bi, D.W.: Prediction-based dynamic energy management in wireless sensor networks. Sensors **7**(3), 251–266 (2007)

6. Wang, X., Wang, S., Ma, J.J.: An improved co-evolutionary particle swarm optimization for wireless sensor networks with dynamic deployment. Sensors **7**(3), 354–370 (2007)
7. Ab Aziz, N.A.B., Mohemmed, A.W., Alias, M.Y.: A wireless sensor network coverage optimization algorithm based on particle swarm optimization and Voronoi diagram. In: 2009 International Conference on Networking, Sensing and Control, ICNSC 2009, pp. 602–607. IEEE (2009)
8. VandenBergh, F., Engelbrecht, A.P.: A cooperative approach to particle swarm optimization. IEEE Trans. Evol. Comput. **8**(3), 225–239 (2004)
9. Li, X., Yao, X.: Cooperatively co-evolution particle swarms for large scale optimization. IEEE Trans. Evol. Comput. **16**(2), 210–224 (2012)
10. Mei, Y., Omidvar, M.N., Li, X., Yao, X.: A competitive divide-and-conquer algorithm for unconstrained large-scale black-box optimization. ACM Trans. Math. Softw. (TOMS) **42**(2), 13 (2016)
11. Omidvar, M.N., Li, X., Mei, Y., Yao, X.: Cooperative co-evolution with differential grouping for large scale optimization. IEEE Trans. Evol. Comput. **18**(3), 378–393 (2014)
12. Wang, B.: Coverage problems in sensor networks: a survey. ACM Comput. Surv. (CSUR) **43**(4), 32 (2011)
13. Feng, J.: Wireless Networks: Research, Technology and Applications. Nova Science Publishers, Inc., New York (2009)
14. Yang, Z., Tang, K., Yao, X.: Large scale evolutionary optimization using cooperative coevolution. Inf. Sci. **178**(15), 2985–2999 (2008)

Adaptive Systems

Learning Fuzzy Cognitive Maps Using a Genetic Algorithm with Decision-Making Trial and Evaluation

Xumiao Zou and Jing Liu[✉]

Key Laboratory of Intelligent Perception and Image Understanding of Ministry of Education, Xidian University, Xi'an 710071, China
neouma@163.com

Abstract. Fuzzy cognitive maps (FCMs) are inference networks, which are the combination of fuzzy logic and neural networks. Various evolutionary-based learning algorithms have been proposed to learn FCMs. However, evolutionary algorithms have shortcomings, such as easy to become premature and the local search ability is weak where the search may trap into local optima. Decision-making trial and evaluation laboratory (DEMATEL) has been widely accepted as one of the best tools to analyze the causal and effect relationships between concepts. Therefore, we combine real-coded genetic algorithm (RCGA) with DEMATEL method, termed as RCGA$_{DEMATEL}$-FCM, to learn FCM models. In RCGA$_{DEMATEL}$-FCM, the DEMATEL method is used as a directed neighborhood search operator to steer the search to the right direction in the objective space, which can overcome the premature problem and make the search jump out of the local optimum. Experimental results on both synthetic and real life data demonstrate the efficiency of the proposed algorithm. The comparison with existing learning algorithms shows that RCGA$_{DEMATEL}$-FCM can learn FCMs with higher accuracy without expert knowledge.

Keywords: Fuzzy cognitive maps · Real-coded genetic algorithm · Decision-making trial and evaluation laboratory · Directed neighborhood search

1 Introduction

Fuzzy cognitive maps (FCMs), firstly proposed by Kosko [1], are a kind of powerful tools for analyzing and depicting human perception of an available system. An FCM is a directed weighted graph with feedback loops, which comprises a set of nodes and weighted edges. Nodes in the graph represent concepts used to describe the behavior of a given domain and weighted edges stand for the causal relationships between concept nodes. Due to their flexibility, adaptability, and fuzzy reasoning, FCMs have been applied in various scientific fields [2–4].

In the last few years, many FCM learning methods have been proposed [5]. The main task of the learning process is to learn the connection weighted matrix. Base on the different types of knowledge used, most learning algorithms for FCM learning can be divided into three types, i.e., Hebbian-based methods [6, 7], evolutionary-based methods [8–16], and hybrid methods that combining Hebbian-based and evolutionary-based

© Springer International Publishing AG 2017
Y. Shi et al. (Eds.): SEAL 2017, LNCS 10593, pp. 845–857, 2017.
https://doi.org/10.1007/978-3-319-68759-9_69

methods [17, 18]. Hebbian-based methods, such as nonlinear Hebbian learning algorithm (NHL) [6] and data-driven NHL (DD-NHL) [7], require expert knowledge to establish an initial map before FCM learning. However, expert knowledge is unknown or limited for some application domains. Therefore, evolutionary-based learning algorithms, such as genetic algorithm (GA) [8], differential evolution (DE) [10], ant colony optimization (ACO) [11], and big bang-big crunch (BB-BC) [13] for FCM learning, have gained the interest by researchers. Experimental results show that most of the evolutionary-based learning algorithms can learn FCM models with less simulation errors. However, evolutionary algorithms have shortcomings, such as easy to become premature and the local search ability is weak where the search may be trapped into local optima.

To solve these problems, we propose a new FCM learning method, applied decision making trial and evaluation laboratory (DEMATEL) into RCGA, termed as $RCGA_{DEMATEL}$-FCM, to learn FCM models. The DEMATEL [19] method is a modeling method to solve complex real-world problems with graph theory and matrices. Due to the practicality and effectiveness of the DEMATEL method, it has been successfully applied in many fields. In $RCGA_{DEMATEL}$-FCM, the DEMATEL method is used as a directed neighborhood search operator which can expend the local search space and guide the searching process to the right direction to make the search process jump out local optima by analyzing the causal and effect relationships between concepts in FCMs. In general, RCGA tends to converge when it approaches terminal time but does not achieve the optimal solution. At this point, we apply the DEMATEL method into RCGA to obtain the influence degree of each concept by analyzing the current optimal weighted matrix. According to the influence degree of each concept, we fine-tune the weight values of the causal links to directed expend the local search space with many suboptimal solutions. Experiments on both synthetic and real life data validate the performance of $RCGA_{DEMATEL}$-FCM. Compared with the existing learning algorithms, $RCGA_{DEMATEL}$-FCM can learn FCMs with higher accuracy without expert knowledge.

Alizadeh et al. in [20] proposed a learning method to construct FCMs using data mining and the DEMATEL method. However, DEMATEL in their method is used as a clustering tool to reduce the number of nodes in a map after the FCM learning process, whereas DEMATEL in $RCGA_{DEMATEL}$-FCM is employed as a directed neighborhood search operator in RCGA to guide the searching process to the right direction and make the search jump out local optima in the FCM learning process.

The rest of this paper is organized as follows. Section 2 describes the FCM learning problem. A detailed description of $RCGA_{DEMTEL}$-FCM is presented in Sect. 3. In Sect. 4, experiments on synthetic and real life models are reported. Finally, conclusions are given in Sect. 5.

2 FCM Learning Problem

FCMs are the signed directed graphs which consist of nodes and weighted edges. An FCM is structured as a number of nodes, which can be defined as a vector C,

$$C = [C_1, C_2, \ldots, C_N] \tag{1}$$

where $C_i \in [0, 1]$, $i = 1, 2, \ldots, N$ is the state value of node i and N is the total number of nodes. The casual relationships between nodes are denoted as an $N \times N$ weighted matrix W,

$$W = \begin{bmatrix} w_{11} & w_{12} & \cdots & w_{1N} \\ w_{21} & w_{22} & \cdots & w_{2N} \\ \vdots & \vdots & \ddots & \vdots \\ w_{N1} & w_{N2} & \cdots & w_{NN} \end{bmatrix} \tag{2}$$

where the value of the weight $w_{ij} \in [-1, 1]$, $i, j = 1, 2, \ldots, N$ represents the strength of the casual relationship between nodes i and j. The value of each node is influenced by its previous value and the weighted matrix. Therefore, the value of each concept can be calculated as follows,

$$C_i(t + 1) = f\left(\sum_{j=1}^{n} w_{ji} C_j(t)\right) \tag{3}$$

where $C_i(t)$ is the state value of node i at the tth simulation iteration, and $f(\cdot)$ is the transform function that maps the expression level to the interval of $[0, 1]$. And in this paper, the sigmoid function is applied as the transform function,

$$f(x) = \frac{1}{1 + e^{-\gamma x}} \tag{4}$$

where $\gamma > 0$ is a parameter determining the steepness of the function in the area around zero. In our approach, we set $\gamma = 5$, which is a commonly used value in many FCMs learning algorithms [8]. In order to learn an appropriate weighted matrix, minimizing the total error between response sequences generated by the input and candidate FCM is an importance operation. Thus, the following equation is employed,

$$Data\_Error(W) = \frac{1}{N(T - 1)} \sum_{t=1}^{T-1} \sum_{n=1}^{N} (C_n(t) - \hat{C}_n(t))^2 \tag{5}$$

where T is the total number of time points in the response sequences, $C_n(t)$ is the value of node n at the tth iteration (time point t) in the response sequence generated by the input FCM, $\hat{C}_n(t)$ is the value of node n at tth iteration (time point t) in the response sequence generated by the candidate FCM.

The objective of FCM learning is to learn the weighted matrix. The total error between given response sequence and generated response sequence for all nodes is defined in Eq. (5). Thus, the error measure can be used as the core of fitness function,

$$f(W) = h(Data\_Error(W)) \tag{6}$$

where $h(\cdot)$ is an auxiliary function defined as follows,

$$h(x) = \frac{1}{1 + \alpha x} \tag{7}$$

where α is a predefined parameter. In this paper, α is set to 100. The auxiliary function $h(\cdot)$ is normalized to $(0, 1]$. Thus, the mathematical model of the FCMs learning problem is proposed as follows,

$$Maximize\ f(W) = h(Data\_Error(W)) \tag{8}$$

3   RCGA$_{\text{DEMATEL}}$-FCM

In RCGA$_{\text{DEMATEL}}$-FCM, the DEMATEL method is applied as a directed neighbor-hood search operator in RCGA, which can guide the searching process to the right direction by analyzing the causal and effect relationships between concepts in the FCM learning process. Subsection 3.1 describes the genetic operators used in RCGA$_{\text{DEMATEL}}$-FCM. The directed neighborhood search operator is presented in Subsect. 3.2. The implementation of RCGA$_{\text{DEMATEL}}$-FCM is given in Subsect. 3.3.

3.1   Genetic Operators

In RCGA$_{\text{DEMATEL}}$-FCM, the real-coded method [8] where a chromosome consists of a set of floating point numbers is applied. That is, each chromosome is a weighted matrix which consists of $N \times N$ genes, defined as follows,

$$W = \left[w_{11}, w_{12}, \ldots, w_{ij} \ldots, w_{N1}, w_{N2}, \ldots, w_{NN} \right] \tag{9}$$

where the values of w_{ij} are generated randomly in the range of $[-1, 1]$ at the first generation. In a population, the number of chromosomes is predefined by the parameter N_{pop}, and each chromosome is evaluated by the fitness function (see Eq. 6). After the population initialization, the genetic operators, such as the crossover, the mutation, and the selection strategy, are used to guide the learning process.

Crossover Operator. In the case of FCMs learning, arithmetical crossover [21] is considered as a suitable crossover operator. Suppose W_{p1} and W_{p2} be two parent chromosomes, and W_{c1} and W_{c2} be two child chromosomes. For each weight w_{ij} in both W_{p1} and W_{p2} conduct the following operations with the crossover probability p_c,

$$w_{ij}^{W_{c1}} = \tau \cdot w_{ij}^{W_{p1}} + (1 - \tau) \cdot w_{ij}^{W_{p2}} \tag{10}$$

$$w_{ij}^{W_{c2}} = (1 - \tau) \cdot w_{ij}^{W_{p1}} + \tau \cdot w_{ij}^{W_{p2}} \tag{11}$$

where τ is a random number in the range of $[0, 1]$.

Mutation Operator. The non-uniform mutation [21] is employed which can capture the abnormal situation efficiently. For each chromosome W^k in the population at the k-

th generation, create an offspring W^{k+1} through the non-uniform mutation with the mutation probability p_m as follows,

$$
w_{ij}^{k+1} = \begin{cases} w_{ij}^k + \left(w_{upper} - w_{ij}^k\right) \times \eta, \text{ when } \xi = 0 \\ w_{ij}^k - \left(w_{ij}^k - w_{lower}\right) \times \eta, \text{ when } \xi = 1 \end{cases} \tag{12}
$$

where the value of ξ is generated randomly, k is the number of generations, w_{upper} and w_{lower} are the boundaries of the weight value, and η is defined as,

$$
\eta = 1 - \varepsilon^{(1-k/\max\_generation)^b} \tag{13}
$$

where ε is a generated random number in the range of [0, 1], and b is a predefined parameter. In this paper, b is set to 5.

Selection Strategy. Stach *et al.* [8] first applied RCGA on FCM learning, in which the roulette wheel selection is used as the selection strategy. To make comparison in the experiments, it is also employed in this paper. In the roulette wheel selection, the probability of chromosome i being selected to be a member of the next generation, p_i, and is defined as,

$$
p_i = f_i \bigg/ \sum_{j=1}^{N_{pop}} f_j \tag{14}
$$

where f_i is the fitness of chromosome i.

3.2   Directed Neighborhood Search

In RCGA$_{\text{DEMATEL}}$-FCM, the directed neighborhood search operator is used to steer the search to the right direction in the objective space, which can expend the continuous solution space with many suboptimal solutions and make the search jump out local optima. There are two processes in this operator: *the Analysis Process* and *the Directed Search Process*, where the analysis process is used to analyze the influence degree of each concept in FCMs by the DEMATEL method and the directed search process is used to find the optimal weighted matrix based on the analysis process.

- *The Analysis Process*

At the later stage of RCGA, it tends to coverage to a local optimal weighted matrix, denoted as $W^{current\_optima}$. In general, $W^{current\_optima}$ has already contained almost all the causes and effects between concepts of the learning FCM model because of the small $Data\_Error(W^{current\_optima})$ at the later stage of RCGA. Then, DEMATEL is applied to analyze influence degree of each concept based on $W^{current\_optima}$ in the analysis process.

After a predefined number of generations, the learned FCM model contains a set of concepts with a learned weighted matrix $W^{current\_optima}$, as mentioned above. First, normalizing the learned matrix with Eq. (15),

$$X = \mu W^{current\_optima} \tag{15}$$

where μ is a normalized factor that defined as,

$$\mu = 1/max\left(\sum_{i=1}^{N} w_{ij}\right) \tag{16}$$

Thus, the total-relation matrix M can be calculated as,

$$M = X(1 - X)^{-1} \tag{17}$$

Then, the sum of each row (R_i) and the sum of each column (D_j) in M can be obtained,

$$R_i = \sum_{j=1}^{N} m_{ij} \tag{18}$$

$$D_j = \sum_{i=1}^{N} m_{ij} \tag{19}$$

Thus, the degree of influence for node i, denoted as H_i, is calculated as,

$$H_i = R_i - D_i, \ (i = 1, 2, \ldots, N) \tag{20}$$

- **The Directed Search Process**

With the degree of influence for each concept node obtained by the analysis process, we directionally fine-tune $W^{current\_optima}$ to obtain a set of matrices in the neighborhood of it in the directed search process and then optimize the optimal connection weighted matrix in these matrices.

In general, $H_i > 0$ represents that node i has a great effect on the other nodes in the learned FCM system and $H_i < 0$ indicates the contrary. Thus, we can fine-tune the values of w_{ij} (for $j = 1$ to N) in weighted matrix $W^{current\_optima}$ as follows,

$$w_{ij}^{neighbor} = w_{ij} + \lambda d \tag{21}$$

where $\lambda \in [0, 1]$ is the search step size, and d is the search direction, defined as,

$$d = |H_i|/H_i \tag{22}$$

That is, enhance the value of w_{ij} slightly when $H_i > 0$; otherwise, reduce the value slightly when $H_i < 0$. By altering the value of λ in the range of [0, 1], a set of weighted matrices, defined as $W^{neighbor}\_Set$, in the neighborhood of $W^{current\_optima}$ is obtained.

These weighted matrices make up the local search space which might contain several suboptimal solutions. Thus, we pick up the weighted matrix that has the maximum and positive increment. Based on the analysis process and the directed search process, the directed neighborhood search operator is conducted iteratively until the maximum number of generations reached. Algorithm 1 gives the details of this operator.

Algorithm 1: Directed Neighborhood Search(W)

```
Input:
     W: one chromosome (a N×N matrix);
Output:
     W*: the chromosome with the best fitness value;
Wneighbor: the new chromosome in the neighborhood of W;
Wneighbor_Set: the set of Wneighbor;
Nneibor: the number of Wneighbor;
N: the number of concept nodes;
```

$W^{neighbor}\_Set \leftarrow \emptyset$; $W^* \leftarrow W$; $best\_fitness \leftarrow f(W)$; /*See Eq. (6)*/
$X \leftarrow Nomalize\_Matrix(W)$; /*$X$ is calculated by Eq. (15)*/
$M \leftarrow X(1-X)^{-1}$;
for (each value m_{ij} in M) **do**
    $R_i \leftarrow \Sigma_{j=1}^{N} m_{ij}$; $D_j \leftarrow \Sigma_{i=1}^{N} m_{ij}$;
end for;
for $i = 1$ to N **do**
    $H_i \leftarrow R_i - D_i$;
end for;
for $n = 1$ to N_{neibor} **do**
    $\lambda \leftarrow U[0, 1]$;
    $W^{neighbor} \leftarrow \emptyset$;
    for (each weighted value w_{ij} in W) **do**
        $w_{ij}^{neighbor} \leftarrow w_{ij} + \lambda|H_i|/H_i$;
        $W^{neighbor} \leftarrow W^{neighbor} \cup w_{ij}^{neighbor}$;
    end for;
    $W^{neighbor}\_Set \leftarrow W^{neighbor}\_Set \cup W^{neighbor}$;
end for;
for (each matrix $W^{neighbor}$ in $W^{neighbor}\_Set$) **do**
    Evaluate the fitness function: $f(W^{neighbor})$;
    if ($f(W^{neighbor}) > best\_fitness$) **then**
        $best\_fitness \leftarrow f(W^{neighbor})$;
        $W^* \leftarrow W^{neighbor}$;
    end if;
end for;

U[a, b] means a value generated within [a, b] according to the uniform distribution.

3.3 Implementation of RCGA$_{DEMATEL}$-FCM

In RCGA$_{DEMATEL}$-FCM, after initializing the population and evaluating the fitness of each individual, the genetic operators, such as selection, crossover and mutation, are performed on the population. When the generation reaches to $\theta \times max\_generation$, the directed neighborhood search operator with the DEMATEL method is performed, which can expend the local search space and guide the searching process to the right direction. Since it tends to coverage at the later stage of RCGA, we predefine ε in the range of [0.5, 1). And the directed neighborhood search operator is only performed on the best weighted matrix in each generation. Then, choose the best individual after performing the directed neighborhood search. The process is conducted iteratively until the number of generation reaches to the predefined value. The framework of RCGA$_{\text{DEMATEL}}$-FCM is summarized in Algorithm 2.

Algorithm 2: RCGA$_{\text{DEMATEL}}$-FCM

Input:
    N_{pop}: the number of chromosome in a population;
    p_c: the probability of crossover;
    p_m: the probability of mutation:;
    max_generationtion: the maximum number of generations;
    θ: the predefined parameter in the searching process;
Output:
    W^*: the optimal weighted matrix;
W^x: the best chromosome in kth generation;
P_k: the parent population with N_{pop} chromosomes;
Q: the offspring population with N_{pop} chromosomes;

$k \leftarrow 0$;
$P_k \leftarrow$ Initialized the population with N_{pop} chromosomes;
while ($k < $ max_generation) **do**
    Evaluate P_k by Eq.(6) and record the current optimal chromosome W^x;
    $Q \leftarrow \emptyset$;
    while ($|Q| < N_{pop}$) **do**
        $[W_1, W_2, W_3] \leftarrow$ Roulette_Wheel_Selection(P_k);
        $[W_1', W_2'] \leftarrow$ Arithmetical_Crossover(W_1, W_2, p_c);
        $W_3' \leftarrow$ Non-uniform_Mutation(W_3, p_m);
        $Q \leftarrow Q \cup [W_1', W_2', \overline{W}_3']$;
    end while;
    Evaluate Q by Eq.(6) and record the current optimal chromosome W^x;
    $P_{k+1} \leftarrow Q$;
    if ($k > \theta \times$ max_generation) **then**
        $W^x \leftarrow$ Directed_Neighborhood_Search (W^x);
        $P_{k+1} \leftarrow Q[1: N_{pop}-1] \cup W^x$;
    end if;
    $k \leftarrow k+1$;
end while;
$W^* \leftarrow W^x$.

---

4 Experiments

In this section, experiments on both synthetic and real-life data with various scales are used to validate the performance of RCGA$_{\text{DEMATEL}}$-FCM. The crossover probability p_c, the mutation probability p_m, the predefined parameter θ in Algorithm 2 and the maximum number of generations are set to 0.9, 0.5, 0.75, and 3×10^5 respectively.

    Four performance measures, including *Data_Error* (defined in Eq. (5)), *Out_of_Sample_Error*, *Model_Error* and *SS_Mean*, are employed to evaluate the quality of obtained solutions. *Out_of_Sample_Error* is used to assess the generalization ability of the learned FCM. To calculate this criterion, P randomly chosen initial state vectors are assigned to both the input and the candidate FCMs [9]. Thus,

$$Out\_of\_Sample\_Error = \frac{1}{P(T-1)N}\sum_{p=1}^{P}\sum_{t=1}^{T-1}\sum_{n=1}^{N}\left|C_n^p(t) - \hat{C}_n^p(t)\right| \quad (23)$$

where $C_n^p(t)$ and $\hat{C}_n^p(t)$ respectively are the value of node n at the tth time point for data generated by input and learned FCMs started from pth initial state vector. *Model_Error* is applied to evaluate the candidate FCMs against the input FCMs directly,

$$Model\_Error = \frac{1}{N^2}\sum_{i=1}^{N}\sum_{j=1}^{N}\left|w_{ij} - \hat{w}_{ij}\right| \quad (24)$$

where w_{ij} and $\hat{w}_{ij}$ respectively are the value of the relationship between nodes i and j in the input and learned FCMs.

To evaluate the edge prediction ability of the proposed method, each weight from both candidate and input FCMs is transformed into a binary one to show the existence of links between concepts in the learned maps. In general, causal relationship with strength less than 0.05 is considered to be meaningless in practical problems [11]. Therefore, the abstract value of weight less than 0.05 is transformed to 0; otherwise, it is transformed to 1. Thus, the structural evaluation, *SS_Mean*, is calculated as,

$$SS\_Mean = \frac{2 \times Specificity \times Sensitivity}{Specificity + Sensitivity} \quad (25)$$

where

$$Specificity = \frac{N_{TP}}{N_{TP} + N_{FN}} \quad (26)$$

$$Sensitivity = \frac{N_{TN}}{N_{TN} + N_{FP}} \quad (27)$$

where N_{TP} is the number of correctly identified positives, N_{TN} is the number of correctly identified negatives, N_{FP} is the number of incorrectly identified positives, and N_{FN} is the number of incorrectly identified negatives [16].

4.1   Experiments on Synthetic Data

Experiments on synthetic data are conducted. The method of generating the test data is introduced in [11]. At first, a fraction of weights are chosen as the nonzero edges according to the desired density. Then, random values are assigned to these chosen edges in the range of [−1, 1], and the absolute value of each nonzero edge needs to be larger than 0.05. Thus, an FCM model is generated randomly. Second, initial values for all concepts are generated randomly in the range of [0, 1]. Then, the data response sequences are calculated by Eq. (3) according to the FCM model.

The experiments are conducted on FCMs with size 20, 40 and 100, and with density 20% and 40%. And the number of the time point for each node is 20. Tables 1 and 2 summarize the experimental results for the synthetic data. The total experimental results are averaged over 30 independent runs. $Out\_of\_Sample\_Error$ is calculated by both the input and candidate FCMs simulated from ten randomly chosen initial state vectors. The comparison between $RCGA_{DEMATEL}$-FCM and four other evolutionary-based methods, i.e., ACO with the decomposed method (ACO_{RD}) [12], BB-BC [13], DE [10], RCGA [8], and two Hebbian-based learning methods, i.e., DD-NHL [7], and NHL [6], are presented in Tables 1 and 2. All results of these compared methods are cited from existing references [14–16]. As can be seen, in general, $RCGA_{DEMATEL}$-FCM performs well, especially in terms of $Model\_Error$ and SS_Mean, both of which involve sufficient insights into the weighted matrices. In terms of $Data\_Error$, ACO_{RD} is better than the proposed algorithm in several cases, but with respect to $Model\_Error$ and SS_Mean, $RCGA_{DEMATEL}$-FCM outperforms ACO_{RD} and the five other methods in almost all cases. Since some of the compared algorithms did not provide this evaluation standard in the existing studies, we just compare $Out\_of\_Sample\_Error$ of the proposed method with that of ACO_{RD}, RCGA, DD-NHL, and NHL. In terms of $Out\_of\_Sample\_Error$, the proposed algorithm outperforms the other methods in all cases except two. These results demonstrate that the proposed method has a good performance in most cases.

Table 1. The comparison on synthetic data with density 20% (average ± standard deviation).

Nodes	Algorithms	Data_Error	Model_Error	SS_Mean	Out_of_Sample_Error
20	$RCGA_{DEMATEL}$-FCM	0.008 ± 0.001	0.362 ± 0.325	**0.35**	0.145 ± 0.131
	ACO_{RD}	**0.004** ± 0.003	**0.299** ± 0.033	0.24	**0.054** ± 0.040
	BB-BC	0.055 ± 0.014	0.435 ± 0.268	0.12	/
	DE	0.068 ± 0.011	0.423 ± 0.234	0.16	/
	RCGA	0.008 ± 0.009	0.426 ± 0.346	0.16	0.151 ± 0.149
	DD-NHL	0.203 ± 0.245	0.464 ± 0.316	0.14	0.201 ± 0.222
	NHL	0.201 ± 0.192	0.461 ± 0.348	0.13	0.199 ± 0.222
40	$RCGA_{DEMATEL}$-FCM	**0.019** ± 0.020	**0.375** ± 0.279	**0.34**	**0.162** ± 0.154
	ACO_{RD}	0.033 ± 0.008	0.388 ± 0.098	0.14	0.287 ± 0.165
	BB-BC	0.048 ± 0.045	0.410 ± 0.378	0.15	/
	DE	0.157 ± 0.032	0.552 ± 0.123	0.14	/
	RCGA	0.019 ± 0.022	0.453 ± 0.385	0.15	0.171 ± 0.187
	DD-NHL	0.194 ± 0.168	0.468 ± 0.388	0.12	0.198 ± 0.199
	NHL	0.205 ± 0.216	0.489 ± 0.388	0.15	0.211 ± 0.190
100	$RCGA_{DEMATEL}$-FCM	**0.052** ± 0.001	**0.395** ± 0.101	**0.31**	**0.317** ± 0.180
	ACO_{RD}	0.283 ± 0.008	0.424 ± 0.031	0.14	0.583 ± 0.286
	BB-BC	0.132 ± 0.015	0.419 ± 0.288	0.13	/
	DE	0.230 ± 0.167	0.553 ± 0.209	0.12	/
	RCGA	0.180 ± 0.051	0.530 ± 0.365	0.08	/
	DD-NHL \ NHL	/	/	/	/

Table 2. The comparison on synthetic data with density 40% (average ± standard deviation).

Nodes	Algorithms	Data_Error	Model_Error	SS_Mean	Out_of_Sample_Error
20	RCGA$_{DEMATEL}$-FCM	0.009 ± 0.009	**0.359** ± 0.305	**0.41**	0.143 ± 0.139
	ACO$_{RD}$	**0.003** ± 0.002	0.367 ± 0.011	0.16	**0.062** ± 0.052
	BB-BC	0.085 ± 0.009	0.434 ± 0.242	0.17	/
	DE	0.117 ± 0.012	0.493 ± 0.109	0.15	/
	RCGA	0.008 ± 0.008	0.413 ± 0.376	0.15	0.152 ± 0.149
	DD-NHL	0.203 ± 0.168	0.436 ± 0.348	0.13	0.203 ± 0.224
	NHL	0.187 ± 0.179	0.468 ± 0.322	0.10	0.201 ± 0.222
40	RCGA$_{DEMATEL}$-FCM	0.023 ± 0.022	**0.364** ± 0.294	**0.30**	**0.159** ± 0.162
	ACO$_{RD}$	**0.023** ± 0.008	0.416 ± 0.054	0.14	0.287 ± 0.201
	BB-BC	0.031 ± 0.010	0.447 ± 0.151	0.15	/
	DE	0.176 ± 0.064	0.581 ± 0.293	0.15	/
	RCGA	0.020 ± 0.022	0.436 ± 0.368	0.15	0.167 ± 0.189
	DD-NHL	0.187 ± 0.160	0.465 ± 0.384	0.12	0.206 ± 0.209
	NHL	0.205 ± 0.206	0.498 ± 0.389	0.12	0.213 ± 0.193
100	RCGA$_{DEMATEL}$-FCM	**0.072** ± 0.021	**0.376** ± 0.201	**0.37**	**0.219** ± 0.115
	ACO$_{RD}$	0.105 ± 0.032	0.434 ± 0.024	0.14	0.405 ± 0.332
	BB-BC	0.195 ± 0.039	0.453 ± 0.207	0.13	/
	DE	0.218 ± 0.163	0.601 ± 0.302	0.14	/
	RCGA	0.175 ± 0.120	0.548 ± 0.368	0.11	/
	DD-NHL \ NHL	/	/	/	/

"/" in Tables 1 and 2 means "it was not reported" in the existing studies.

4.2 Experiments on Real Life Data

In the following experiments, three real models suggested by Stach *et al.* [8, 9] that describe plant supervisory model with 9 concept nodes, deforestation model in the Brazilian Amazon with 12 concept nodes, and factors in the adoption of educational software in schools with 24 concept nodes are used.

The experimental results in terms of *Data_Error*, *Out_of_Sample_Error*, *Model_Error*, and *SS_Mean* of RCGA$_{DEMATEL}$-FCM are reported in Table 3. Since several compared methods used in Tables 1 and 2, such as ACO$_{RD}$, BB-BC, and DE, are not applied on these real life datasets in existing literatures, we compare the proposed method with four existing methods, i.e., RCGA [8], divide and conquer RCGA (D&C RCGA) [9], DD-NHL [7], and NHL [6]. All the results of the compared methods are cited form [15]. As can be seen, RCGA$_{DEMATEL}$-FCM outperforms all the other algorithms on these three models. Especially, the proposed algorithm achieves the smallest *Model_Error* and the largest *SS_Mean*, both of which involve sufficient insights into the FCM models. That is, the proposed algorithm can construct the real FCM models with higher precision without expert knowledge.

Table 3. Experimental results on real life data.

Algorithms	Data_Error	Out_of_Sample_Error	Model_Error	SS_Mean
Plant supervisory model (9 nodes)				
RCGA$_{DEMATEL}$-FCM	**0.004** ± 0.005	**0.102** ± 0.125	**0.208** ± 0.213	**0.44**
RCGA	0.005 ± 0.005	0.131 ± 0.141	0.395 ± 0.348	0.16
D&C RCGA	0.007 ± 0.005	0.136 ± 0.123	0.358 ± 0.325	0.16
DD-NHL	0.187 ± 0.184	0.189 ± 0.197	0.438 ± 0.316	0.13
NHL	0.188 ± 0.201	0.191 ± 0.201	0.419 ± 0.372	0.13
Deforestation model in Brazilian Amazon (12 nodes)				
RCGA$_{DEMATEL}$-FCM	0.005 ± 0.006	**0.113** ± 0.142	0.243 ± 0.235	0.41
RCGA	**0.005** ± 0.003	0.137 ± 0.153	\	\
D&C RCGA	0.114 ± 0.097	0.147 ± 0.141	\	\
DD-NHL	0.226 ± 0.241	0.221 ± 0.180	\	\
NHL	0.230 ± 0.241	0.231 ± 0.224	\	\
Adoption model of educational software (24 Nodes)				
RCGA$_{DEMATEL}$-FCM	**0.008** ± 0.002	**0.097** ± **0.056**	0.219 ± 0.185	0.43
RCGA	0.009 ± 0.006	0.154 ± 0.161	\	\
D&C RCGA	0.132 ± 0.137	0.183 ± 0.159	\	\
DD-NHL	0.213 ± 0.214	0.208 ± 0.210	\	\
NHL	0.220 ± 0.214	0.211 ± 0.203	\	\

"/" in Table 3 means "it was not reported" in the existing studies.

5   Conclusions

In this paper, a new FCM learning algorithm, RCGA$_{DEMATEL}$-FCM, is proposed for learning FCMs with varying sizes and densities. The experiments show that the proposed method has the ability to learn high quality FCMs from input data without expert knowledge. However, it still has some problems need to be overcome. The computational cost of the proposed method is a little bit high due to the matrix calculation in the DEMATEL method. Learning FCMs from data without expert knowledge is a difficult task due to the high complexity of systems. Thus, fully automated learning algorithms need to cope with a substantial challenge. The problems mentioned above and the application for large scale FCMs need to be concerned in the future work.

Acknowledgements. This work is partially supported by the Outstanding Young Scholar Program of National Natural Science Foundation of China (NSFC) under Grant 61522311, the Overseas, Hong Kong & Macao Scholars Collaborated Research Program of NSFC under Grant 61528205, and the Key Program of Fundamental Research Project of Natural Science of Shaanxi Province, China under Grant 2017JZ017.

References

1. Kosko, B.: Fuzzy cognitive maps. Int. J. Hum.-Comput. Stud. Int. J. Man-Mach. Stud. **24**, 65–75 (1986)

2. Froelich, W., Pedrycz, W.: Fuzzy cognitive maps in the modeling of granular time series. Knowl.-Based Syst. **115**, 110–122 (2017)
3. Pedrycz, W., Jastrzebska, A., Homenda, W.: Design of fuzzy cognitive maps for modeling time series. IEEE Trans. Fuzzy Syst. **24**(1), 120–130 (2016)
4. Papageorgiou, E.I., Poczeta, K., Laspidou, C.: Application of fuzzy cognitive maps to water demand prediction. In: IEEE International Conference on Fuzzy Systems, pp. 1–8 (2015)
5. Papageorgiou, E.I.: Learning algorithms for fuzzy cognitive maps - a review study. IEEE Trans. Syst. Man Cybern. **42**(2), 150–163 (2012)
6. Papageorgiou, E.I., Stylios, C.D., Groumpos, P.P.: Fuzzy cognitive map learning based on nonlinear Hebbian rule. In: Proceedings of Australian Conference on Artificial Intelligence, pp. 256–268 (2003)
7. Stach, W., Kurgan, L.A., Pedrycz, W.: Data-driven nonlinear Hebbian learning method for fuzzy cognitive maps. In: Proceedings of World Congress on Computational Intelligence, pp. 1975–1981 (2008)
8. Stach, W., Kurgan, L., Pedrycz, W., Reformat, M.: Genetic learning of fuzzy cognitive maps. Fuzzy Sets Syst. **153**(3), 371–401 (2005)
9. Stach, W., Kurgan, L., Pedrycz, W.: A divide and conquer method for learning large fuzzy cognitive maps. Fuzzy Sets Syst. **161**(19), 2515–2532 (2010)
10. Papageorgiou, E.I., Groumpos, P.P.: Optimization of fuzzy cognitive map model in clinical radiotherapy through the differential evolution algorithm. Biomed. Soft Comput. Hum. Sci. **9**(2), 25–31 (2004)
11. Chen, Y., Mazlack, L.J., Lu, L.J.: Learning fuzzy cognitive maps from data by ant colony optimization. In: Proceedings of Genetic and Evolutionary Computation Conference, 9–16 (2012)
12. Chen, Y., Mazlack, L.J., Lu, L.J.: Inferring fuzzy cognitive map models for gene regulatory networks from gene expression data. In: IEEE International Conference on Bioinformatics and Biomedicine, pp. 1–4 (2012)
13. Yesil, E., Dodurka, M.F.: Goal-oriented decision support using big bang-big crunch learning based fuzzy congnitive map: an ERP management case study. In: Proceedings of IEEE International Conference on Fuzzy Systems (2013)
14. Liu, J., Chi, Y., Zhu, C.: A dynamic multi-agent genetic algorithm for gene regulatory network reconstruction based on fuzzy cognitive maps. IEEE Trans. Fuzzy Syst. **24**(2), 419–431 (2016)
15. Chi, Y., Liu, J.: Learning of fuzzy cognitive maps with varying densities using a multi-objective evolutionary algorithm. IEEE Trans. Fuzzy Syst. **24**(1), 71–81 (2016)
16. Chi, Y., Liu, J.: Reconstruction gene regulatory network with a memetic-neural hybrid based on fuzzy cognitive maps. Nat. Comput. 1–12 (2016)
17. Zhu, Y., Zhang, W.: An integrated framework for learning fuzzy cognitive map using RCGA and NHL algorithm. In: Proceedings of the International Conference on Wireless Communications, Networking and Mobile Computing, pp. 10773–11195 (2008)
18. Ren, Z.: Learning fuzzy cognitive maps by a hybrid method using nonlinear Hebbian learning and extended great deluge. In: Proceedings of the 23rd Midwest Artificial Intelligence and Cognitive Science Conference (2012)
19. Gabus, A., Fontela, E.: DEMATEL: progress achieved. Futures **6**, 329–333 (1974)
20. Alizadeh, S., Ghazanfari, M., Fathian, M.: Using data mining for learning and clustering FCM. Int. J. Comput. Electr. Autom. Control Inf. Eng. **2**(6), 118–125 (2008)
21. Zhao, X., Gao, X., Hu, Z.: Evolutionary programming based on non-uniform mutation. Appl. Math. Comput. **192**(1), 1–11 (2007)

Dynamic and Adaptive Threshold for DNN Compression from Scratch

Chunhui Jiang$^{(\boxtimes)}$, Guiying Li, and Chao Qian

School of Computer Science and Technology,
USTC-Birmingham Joint Research Institute in Intelligent
Computation and Its Applications (UBRI), University of Science
and Technology of China, Hefei 230027, Anhui, People's Republic of China
{beethove,lgy147}@mail.ustc.edu.cn, chaoqian@ustc.edu.cn

Abstract. Despite their great success, deep neural networks (DNN) are hard to deploy on devices with limited hardware like mobile phones because of massive parameters. Many methods have been proposed for DNN compression, i.e., to reduce the parameters of DNN models. However, almost all of them are based on reference models, which were firstly trained. In this paper, we propose an approach to perform DNN training and compression simultaneously. More concretely, a dynamic and adaptive threshold (DAT) framework is utilized to prune a DNN gradually by changing the pruning threshold during training. Experiments show that DAT can not only reach comparable or better compression rate almost without loss of accuracy than state-of-the-art DNN compression methods, but also beat DNN sparse training methods by a large margin.

Keywords: Deep neural networks · Pruning · DNN compression

1 Introduction

In last few years, deep neural networks (DNNs) have made impressive performance on various artificial intelligence tasks like image classification [1,2], speech recognition [3] and natural language processing [4]. Thus DNNs are promising to apply to all kinds of intelligent devices. However, DNNs usually have massive parameters, which result in severe memory overhead and energy consumption [5]. For example, the number of parameters in two popular DNN models AlexNet [1] and VGG16 [6] are 61 million and 138 million, and the storage cost are 240 MB and 550 MB respectively, such a large memory usage prevents DNNs to deploy on mobile devices with limited hardware like smart phones. Therefore, reducing the parameters of DNNs without significant performance degradation is important for DNN coming into utility.

It was shown that there existed high redundancy in the overall parameters of a DNN [7], which means only a small part of parameters are needed to guarantee the performance in testing. Since then a lot of methods are proposed to compress DNNs, almost all of them operate on the reference models like tensor

© Springer International Publishing AG 2017
Y. Shi et al. (Eds.): SEAL 2017, LNCS 10593, pp. 858–869, 2017.
https://doi.org/10.1007/978-3-319-68759-9_70

decomposition, parameter sharing and network pruning, noting that reference models were firstly trained on the corresponding datasets. However, for a new dataset, it is very likely that there are no reference models which are trained on it, and the training of reference models themselves are time-consuming. For example, in [5], the training of AlexNet reference model took 75 h on NVIDIA Titan X, and the subsequent compression process took extra 173 h. So if the two previously separated steps, training of reference model and compression, can be combined as one, then significant time will be saved.

Network pruning is quite effective in compressing DNN models. The pruning thresholds play a key role in network pruning. The state-of-the-art pruning method, dynamic network surgery [8], computes pruning thresholds on reference models and keeps them fixed throughout the compression phase. With reference model, this fixed threshold scheme is effective because the weights distribution has little change during model compression. But it is not true for training, for example, either Xavier initialization [9] for LeNet-5 or Gaussian initialization for CIFAR10_CAFFE [10], is far away from compression model as shown in Fig. 1, which means their pruning thresholds are invalid in the training phase.

In this paper, we propose a dynamic and adaptive threshold framework (DAT) by which DNN training and compressing can be performed simultaneously. Dynamic threshold means we prune parameters gradually. Only a small part of weights is pruned at the beginning, but as the training goes on, more and more parameters are pruned. Compared to fixed threshold scheme which prunes huge number of weighs at the beginning, dynamic threshold is more reasonable

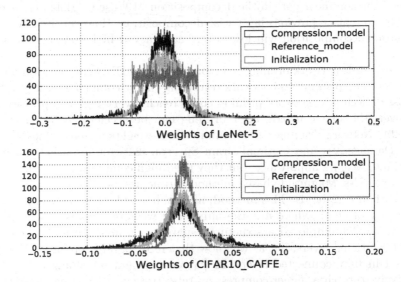

Fig. 1. Weights histogram of LeNet-5 (*top*) and CIFAR10_CAFFE (*bottom*). X axis is the range of weight values, and Y axis means the number of this value. Note that we only plot weights distribution of convolutional layers 2 (conv2) in above two models for demonstration, the similar pattern would be found in other layers.

because it is hard to judge the importance of initialized weights, and a good way is waiting for a few iterations as dynamic threshold does. Adaptive threshold means the thresholds change according to the weights distribution, noting that the weights distribution changes drastically over iteration in the training phase. In DAT framework dynamic threshold allows coarse-grained pruning and adaptive threshold allows fine-grained pruning. The experiments show that our proposed DAT framework is effective.

The rest of the paper is as follows. Section 2 presents related works. Preliminary and our proposed method are introduced in Sect. 3. In Sect. 4, we conduct comprehensive experiments and report the results. Conclusion and future work are made in Sect. 5.

2   Related Work

There have been many works aiming at DNN compression. [13] employed a fixed point implementation of DNN to replace float point scheme; [14] directly used binary weighs to alleviate the complexity of networks. The other works can be roughly divided into three categories: weight sharing, tensor decomposition and network pruning.

Weight sharing means grouping weights, within each group only one value or vector is needed like vector quantization [15] and HashedNets [16], which shares weights using hash buckets. Tensor decomposition is another way of DNN compression. [7,17] resort to low rank approximation of each layer matrix, [18] included the nonlinear part in the decomposition, [19] used a global error reconstruction to replace previous layer-wise decomposition. However, weight sharing and tensor decomposition will lose severe accuracy if high compression rate is needed.

By contrast, network pruning is a more promising DNN compression method, mainly because pruning and network retraining can be combined perfectly. Without loss of accuracy, network pruning could reach a very high compression rate. Moreover, the sparse matrix after pruning can be accelerated by extra hardware [20]. Network pruning set the unimportant weights to zero values, Optimal Brain Damage [21] and Optimal Brain Surgeon [22] computed hessian matrix to evaluate weights importance, but they need high computation overhead especially for DNNs. Magnitude-based methods prune weights whose absolute values are less than thresholds. This method, although simple, has the computational complexity of $\mathcal{O}(n)$, where n is the number of weights, thus is widely adopted by [5,8,23]. [23] employed a structured sparsity learning method to compress the convolutional layers, but as we know that most parameters of DNN are distributed in fully connected layers. In [5] pruning and retraining are repeated iteratively to reach a higher compression rate. However, the weight is discarded forever if be pruned, which constrain the compression and cause inefficient learning. This problem was solved by [8], which proposed dynamic network surgery and allowed the recovery of incorrect pruning. By this way, dynamic network surgery achieves state-of-the-art compression rate.

It should be emphasized that all methods of these three categories need reference models. Recently [12] studied l_1 and l_0 regularization of DNN systematically, and concluded that l_1 and l_0 regularization could lead to considerably sparse DNN. Note that our proposed DAT also works at the training stage, so we will compare DAT with regularization techniques in Sect. 4.

3 Dynamic and Adaptive Threshold (DAT)

In this section, we will first introduce dynamic network surgery (DNS) [8] in Preliminaries, then highlight the dynamic and adaptive threshold framework. Note that the DAT framework can also be combined with other pruning methods in addition to dynamic network surgery.

3.1 Preliminaries

Dynamic network surgery maintains a mask M_l for weight matrix W_l in layer l, where $1 \leq l \leq L$. M_l takes binary values in which 0 indicates being pruned and 1 indicates being kept, so W_l would keep dense throughout the compression. At the beginning of one iteration, M_l is updated as:

$$M_l^{(i,j)} = \begin{cases} 0, |W_l^{(i,j)}| < t_l \\ 1, |W_l^{(i,j)}| \geq t_l \end{cases} \tag{1}$$

and the change of $M_l^{(i,j)}$ from 0 to 1 means splicing, which is vital for DNS. t_l is a layer-wise threshold that is computed before model compression and keep fixed during the whole compression. After the update of $M_l^{(i,j)}$, weight matrix W_l is wrapped into $H_l = W_l \odot M_l$, noting that H_l is not dense because $\odot$ indicates element-wise product. It is H_l, not W_l which plays the role of "weights" in forward and backward propagation until the update of W_l:

$$W_l^{(i,j)} \leftarrow W_l^{(i,j)} - \alpha \frac{\partial Loss}{\partial (W_l^{(i,j)} M_l^{(i,j)})} \tag{2}$$

Note that Eq. 2 is not a standard gradient descent algorithm because the gradient is partial derivative of loss function to H_l but not W_l, on the other hand, Eq. 2 also updates the previously pruned entries in W_l, which makes the model compression dynamic.

3.2 Dynamic and Adaptive Threshold

Recall that our goal is to perform DNN training and compression simultaneously, now we elaborate how to achieve this goal by introducing a dynamic and adaptive threshold framework. The fixed threshold scheme computes t_l as:

$$t_l = \mu_l + c_l \sigma_l \tag{3}$$

where $\mu_l = \mathbb{E}(|\boldsymbol{W}_l|)$, $\sigma_l = \sqrt{Var(|\boldsymbol{W}_l|)}$ and c_l is a layer-wise hyper-parameter. Obviously this scheme is suitable to Gaussian-like distribution, which is true for reference models, but not true for initialization models. For example, Xavier initialization [9], which is used in standard LeNet-5 [11] training procedure of Caffe [10], initializes $\boldsymbol{W}_l$ by a uniform distribution $\boldsymbol{W}_l \sim U[-a, a]$, in this case, we have $\mu = \frac{a}{2}$, $\sigma = \frac{\sqrt{3}}{6}a$, so the choice of c need to be specially careful, $c \geq 2$ will cause $t = \mu + c\sigma > a$ and then all weights in this layer will be pruned!

The other problem of fixed threshold scheme is over pruning at the beginning. After initialization, the magnitude of weights distributes randomly, it is difficult to evaluate the importance of weights. If we prune a large part of weights this moment as fixed threshold scheme does, many important weights will be pruned and the performance of DNN models may suffer serious damage. We propose that these problems can be solved by making c_l **dynamic**. More concretely, c_l should be a function of iteration i. It is expected that c_l would range from $-c_{l,max}$ to $c_{l,max}$ as the iteration increases. We find the transformed $tanh$ function meeting our expectation perfectly, that is,

$$c_l(i) = c_{l,max} \cdot tanh(\frac{i - i_0}{\lambda}) \tag{4}$$

in which i_0 makes $c_l(i)$ equal to 0, and λ is a scaling factor. It should be noted that the threshold is low at the beginning, indicating only few weights are pruned. i_0 is an important demarcation point. When $i < i_0$, $c_l(i)$ takes negative values and the threshold t_l takes no more than μ_l, in this case, not too much weights are pruned. However, if $i \geq i_0$, t_l increases rapidly and approaches its extreme value, and most weights would be pruned. So in order to waiting for weights to exhibit their own importance, i_0 can not be too small. In this work, we empirically set i_0 to $i_{max}/4$. Note that there may exist other functions that are suitable for $c_l(i)$. However, in this work, we mainly want to demonstrate the effectiveness of a dynamic strategy, but not which strategy is best.

Considering the dramatic change of weight distribution during training, the fixed μ_l and σ_l computed from the initialization cannot cover the whole compression, which is different from compression with reference model, so μ_l and σ_l need to be **adaptive** instead of staying fixed. That is, μ_l and σ_l should also be the function of iteration i. Perhaps the easiest way to threshold adaption is employing

$$\mu_l(i) = \mathbb{E}(|\boldsymbol{W}_l(i)|) \tag{5}$$
$$\sigma_l(i) = \sqrt{Var(|\boldsymbol{W}_l(i)|)} \tag{6}$$

however, this strategy will cause drastic change of DNN structure, resulting in training inefficiency. So we adopt a smoother adaption method:

$$\mu_l(i) \leftarrow \mu_l(i) + \epsilon \cdot \Delta\mu_l(i) \tag{7}$$
$$\sigma_l(i) \leftarrow \sigma_l(i) + \epsilon \cdot \Delta\sigma_l(i) \tag{8}$$

in which $\Delta\mu_l(i)$ and $\Delta\sigma_l(i)$ are computed as:

Algorithm 1. Dynamic and Adaptive Threshold (DAT)

Input: $\{X, y\}$: training datum, i_{max}: maximum iterations
Output: $W, M = \{W_l, M_l : 1 \leq l \leq L\}$: weight and mask matrices of the compressed
    model
 1: Initialize: $W_l, \mu_l = \mathbb{E}(|W_l|), \sigma_l = \sqrt{Var(|W_l|)}, \forall 1 \leq l \leq L$
 2: **repeat**
 3:    **for** $l = 1$ to L **do**
 4:        Compute $\Delta\mu_l(i), \Delta\sigma_l(i)$ by Eq. 9, Eq. 10
 5:        Update $\mu_l(i), \sigma_l(i)$ by Eq. 7, Eq. 8
 6:        Compute $c_l(i)$ by Eq. 4
 7:        Compute threshold $t_l(i) = \mu_l(i) + c_l(i) \cdot \sigma_l(i)$
 8:    **end for**
 9:    Update M by Eq. 1 and forward propagation
10:    Back propagation and update W by Eq. 2
11:    $i = i + 1$
12: **until** convergence or $i \geq i_{max}$

$$\Delta\mu_l(i) = (\mathbb{E}(|W_l(i)|) - \mathbb{E}(|W_l(i-1)|)) \cdot e^{i/i_{max}} \qquad (9)$$

$$\Delta\sigma_l(i) = (\sqrt{Var(|W_l(i)|)} - \sqrt{Var(|W_l(i-1)|)}) \cdot e^{i/i_{max}} \qquad (10)$$

Now $\mu_l(i)$ and $\sigma_l(i)$ can still be updated by the change of weight distribution, but the step is controlled by ϵ, thus this strategy is smoother. The exponential term is designed to impose more importance to the update near maximum of iteration, because at that time $c_l(i)$ becomes almost saturated, and update of μ_l and σ_l should be more sensitive to the change of weights distribution. The whole algorithm procedure is summarized in Algorithm 1.

4 Experiments

In this section, comprehensive experiments are conducted on MNIST [11] and CIFAR-10 [26] to evaluate the performance of our proposed DAT framework. We claim that DAT is firstly a DNN compression method, so we compare DAT with state-of-the-art DNN compression methods, which include iterative network pruning (INP) [5] and dynamic network surgery (DNS) [8], noting that INP and DNS need reference models but DAT does not need. Then we compare DAT with DNN sparse training methods like l_1 and l_0 regularization [12].

4.1 Experimental Setting

Datasets and Reference Models. Both MNIST and CIFAR-10 have 50000 training images and 10000 testing images of 10 classes. MNIST is a handwritten digits database and CIFAR-10 is a natural images database. For MNIST, the classical LeNet-5 [11] is trained on it, and LeNet-5 has 4 learnable layers. For CIFAR-10, we choose CIFAR10_CAFFE which is defined in Caffe [10] and has 5 learnable layers. Both reference models are trained using standard protocols in

Caffe community. Finally, the LeNet-5 reference model achieves an accuracy rate of **99.09%** using 10000 iterations, and the CIFAR10_CAFFE reference model achieves **75.54%** accuracy rate using 5000 iterations.

Implementation Details. We conduct experiments using Caffe platform and the open source code from [8] on NVIDIA GTX TITAN X graphics card. Moreover, we follow the default setting of corresponding *.prototxt* files in Caffe unless otherwise specified. The random number seed is fixed when we initialize a model for fair comparison. We employ classification accuracy and compression rate as the evaluation metrics, in which compression rate is defined as total number of weights divided by number of weights after compression.

4.2 Demonstration of DAT's Effectiveness

We firstly demonstrate the effectiveness of our proposed DAT framework, including dynamic threshold scheme alone and the whole DAT scheme. Dynamic network surgery (DNS) [8] is taken as the comparative method. Although DNS is designed to work on reference models, in this subsection all methods are used for training from scratch for fair comparison. Because large scale pruning would inevitably result in loss in performance, more iterations are needed to ensure the recovery of accuracy. For example, the number of iterations is increased from 10000 to 16000 for training LeNet-5, and from 5000 to 8000 for training CIFAR10_CAFFE respectively. Note that drastic pruning will happen after i_0, so the learning rate from i_0 is increased for better compensating for the loss of accuracy, especially for LeNet-5 that originally adopts a monotone decreasing learning policy in Caffe. For each method, we explore the best c_{max} and then plot accuracy and compression rate curves over iterations in Fig. 2.

As is shown in Fig. 2, both dynamic threshold scheme alone and the whole DAT scheme can reach a rather high compression rate almost without loss of accuracy, which proves that our proposed method is highly effective in DNN compression. For both models, the dynamic only and DAT followed the same pattern in accuracy curves, they undergo a small drop after i_0, noting that for LeNet-5 $i_0 = 4000$ and for CIFAR10_CAFFE $i_0 = 2000$. Eventually the dynamic only and DAT reached the accuracy of 99.11% and 99.09% for LeNet-5, 75.30% and 75.33% for CIFAR10_CAFFE. These results are comparable to reference models (red dash line in Fig. 2), and they are much better than those of DNS, which are only 98.70% and 72.39%. This is also true for compression rate curve, i.e., the compression rates of the dynamic only and DAT are much higher than those of DNS. Different from accuracy curves, the dynamic only and DAT begin to rise in compression rate after i_0, and then exhibit different behaviours. DAT can reach a higher compression rate for both models, which is mainly due to the adaptive threshold scheme's adaptability to weight distribution.

In this subsection, it is shown that DAT can outperform DNS in both accuracy and compression rate, which demonstrate the effectiveness of our proposed dynamic and adaptive threshold framework clearly.

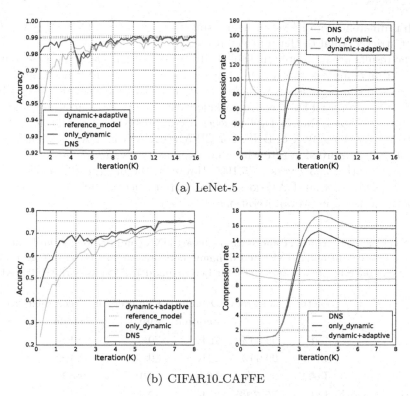

(a) LeNet-5

(b) CIFAR10_CAFFE

Fig. 2. Accuracy and compression rate comparison of different methods on LeNet-5 (a) and CIFAR10_CAFFE (b). Note that for each subfigure, accuracy curves (*left*) and compression rate curves (*right*) are plotted. (Color figure online)

4.3   Comparison with DNN Compression Methods

In this subsection, DAT is compared with state-of-the-art DNN compression methods. Under the condition of compression without accuracy loss, network pruning is a more efficient method than others like weight sharing and tensor decomposition, so we choose state-of-the-art DNN pruning methods, i.e., iterative network pruning (INP) [5] and dynamic network surgery (DNS) [8], as the compared methods. As for the evaluation metrics, overall iterations is used, in addition to accuracy and compression rate. For INP and DNS, overall iterations equals to the number of iterations in training phase plus that in compression phase, and for DAT, overall iterations is just the maximum number of iterations. The iterative number in INP is fixed to 3, which means the procedure of pruning and retraining are repeated 3 times.

Generally we keep the accuracy being comparable with that of reference model and then compare the compression rate of different methods, due to the tradeoff between accuracy and compression rate. For CIFAR10_CAFFE, this target is a little bit difficult because the range of accuracy is relatively large, which is different from LeNet-5. As a result, the accuracy of INP, DNS and DAT do not strictly equal to that of reference model, i.e. 75.54%.

The results are presented in Table 1. It is obvious that DAT and DNS outperform INP in compression rate by a large margin. Besides, INP need much more iterations to compress a DNN model, which is consistent with the results in [5] and [8]. Our proposed DAT is comparable with DNS in both accuracy and compression rate. For LeNet-5, DAT reaches a compression rate of 110×, which is slightly better than 108× of DNS. For CIFAR10_CAFFE, DAT is slightly worse than DNS in compression rate with 15.6× versus 16.0×, and is better than DNS in accuracy with 75.33% versus 75.19%. However, the biggest difference between DAT and DNS is that DAT does not need reference model, which results in dramatic decrease in overall iterations.

Table 1. Comparison of DAT and state-of-the-art DNN compression methods including iterative network pruning (INP) and dynamic network surgery (DNS). Note that the accuracy of reference model is 99.09% for LeNet-5 and 75.54% for CIFAR10_CAFFE.

	Method	Accuracy	Overall iterations	Compression rate	Need reference model?
LeNet-5	INP	99.09%	70 K	20×	YES
	DNS	99.09%	26 K	108×	YES
	DAT	99.09%	**16 K**	**110×**	**NO**
CIFAR10_CAFFE	INP	**75.78%**	23 K	8.8×	YES
	DNS	75.19%	13 K	**16.0×**	YES
	DAT	75.33%	**8 K**	15.6×	**NO**

4.4   Comparison with DNN Sparse Training Methods

Finally we compare DAT with two well-known DNN sparse training methods, i.e., l_1 and l_0 regularization. Note that most weights w satisfy $|w| < 1$, thus their l_1 regularization will be significantly larger than their l_2 regularization, so the weight decay factor should be much smaller. In experiments, the weight decay is set to 1/10 of the original value for LeNet-5 and 1/5 for CIFAR10_CAFFE [10]. The other problem of l_1 regularization is that l_1 encourages many weights near zero, but does not output exactly zero value weights! Therefore, for fair comparison, we add a pruning process after training while keeping the accuracy not decreasing. The l_0 regularization [12] directly set all weights to zero except the t largest-magnitude ones every n iterations. The main target of this subsection is the comparison between DAT and l_1, l_0 regularization, and for simplicity we use the same training iterations as the reference models, that is, 10000 for LeNet-5 and 5000 for CIFAR10_CAFFE.

The accuracy curve over iterations is plotted in Fig. 3. For LeNet-5, only DAT can meet the accuracy of reference model (the red dash line in Fig. 3), and

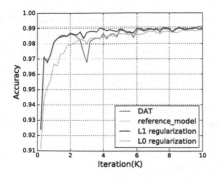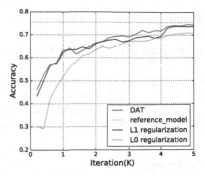

Fig. 3. Accuracy curves of different DNN sparse training methods on LeNet-5 (*left*) and CIFAR10_CAFFE (*right*). Note that the training iterations are 10000 for LeNet-5 and 5000 for CIFAR10_CAFFE. (Color figure online)

Table 2. Comparison of DAT with l_1 and l_0 regularization.

	LeNet-5		CIFAR10_CAFFE	
Method	Accuracy	Compression rate	Accuracy	Compression rate
l_1	99.0%	10×	73.55%	2.3×
l_0	98.88%	10×	70.92%	2.1×
DAT	**99.10%**	**63×**	**74.52%**	**10.8×**

for CIFAR10_CAFFE, no methods can reach the accuracy of reference model, mainly because of reduction of iterations. Besides, the accuracy of l_0 drop a lot for both models, compared with accuracy of DAT and reference model, which is mainly due to the fixed hard constraint t adopted by l_0 regularization. As for the compression rate, DAT reaches 63× and 10.8× for LeNet-5 and CIFAR10_CAFFE respectively as shown in Table 2. These results are surprising because the compression rate of DAT is several times better than the other two methods. Considering the accuracy of DAT is also higher, so we can draw the conclusion that DAT is quite an effective DNN sparse training method.

5   Conclusion

In this paper, we explore to compress DNN models without using reference models. A dynamic and adaptive threshold (DAT) framework is proposed to prune a DNN gradually by changing the pruning threshold during training, thus DNN training and compression can be performed simultaneously. Experiment results demonstrate that DAT can compress LeNet-5 and CIFAR10_CAFFE by a factor of 110× and 15.6× respectively, without the usage of reference models and almost without loss of accuracy. These compression rates are comparable or better than state-of-the-art DNN compression method. Also, DAT can beat DNN sparse training methods like l_1 and l_0 regularization by a large margin.

Although effective, our proposed method imports some hyper parameters and the searching of these hyper parameters is time-consuming. Therefore, in the future we plan to explore DNN compression from scratch with fewer parameters.

Acknowledgments. We want to thank the reviewers for their valuable comments. This work was supported by the NSFC (U1605251, U1613216), the Young Elite Scientists Sponsorship Program by CAST (2016QNRC001), the CCF-Tencent Open Research Fund and the Royal Society Grant on "Data Driven Metaheuristic Search".

References

1. Krizhevsky, A., Sutskever, I., Hinton, G.E.: Imagenet classification with deep convolutional neural networks. In: Advances in Neural Information Processing Systems, pp. 1097–1105 (2012)
2. He, K., Zhang, X., Ren, S., Sun, J.: Deep residual learning for image recognition. In: Proceedings of the IEEE Conference on Computer Vision and Pattern Recognition, pp. 770–778 (2016)
3. LeCun, Y., Bengio, Y., Hinton, G.: Deep learning. Nature **521**(7553), 436–444 (2015)
4. Collobert, R., Weston, J., Bottou, L., Karlen, M., Kavukcuoglu, K., Kuksa, P.: Natural language processing (almost) from scratch. J. Mach. Learn. Res. **12**, 2493–2537 (2011)
5. Han, S., Pool, J., Tran, J., Dally, W.: Learning both weights and connections for efficient neural network. In: Advances in Neural Information Processing Systems, pp. 1135–1143 (2015)
6. Simonyan, K., Zisserman, A.: Very deep convolutional networks for large-scale image recognition. arXiv preprint arXiv:1409.1556 (2014)
7. Denil, M., Shakibi, B., Dinh, L., deFreitas, N., et al.: Predicting parameters in deep learning. In: Advances in Neural Information Processing Systems, pp. 2148–2156 (2013)
8. Guo, Y., Yao, A., Chen, Y.: Dynamic network surgery for efficient DNNs. In: Advances in Neural Information Processing Systems, pp. 1379–1387 (2016)
9. Glorot, X., Bengio, Y.: Understanding the difficulty of training deep feedforward neural networks. In: AISTATS, vol. 9, pp. 249–256 (2010)
10. Jia, Y., Shelhamer, E., Donahue, J., Karayev, S., Long, J., Girshick, R., Guadarrama, S., Darrell, T.: Caffe: convolutional architecture for fast feature embedding. In: Proceedings of the 22nd ACM International Conference on Multimedia, pp. 675–678. ACM (2014)
11. LeCun, Y., Bottou, L., Bengio, Y., Haffner, P.: Gradient-based learning applied to document recognition. Proc. IEEE **86**(11), 2278–2324 (1998)
12. Collins, M.D., Kohli, P.: Memory bounded deep convolutional networks. arXiv preprint arXiv:1412.1442 (2014)
13. Lin, D.D., Talathi, S.S., Annapureddy, V.S.: Fixed point quantization of deep convolutional networks. arXiv (2015)
14. Courbariaux, M., Bengio, Y., David, J.P.: Binaryconnect: training deep neural networks with binary weights during propagations. In: Advances in Neural Information Processing Systems, pp. 3123–3131 (2015)
15. Gong, Y., Liu, L., Yang, M., Bourdev, L.: Compressing deep convolutional networks using vector quantization. arXiv preprint arXiv:1412.6115 (2014)

16. Chen, W., Wilson, J.T., Tyree, S., Weinberger, K.Q., Chen, Y.: Compressing neural networks with the hashing trick. In: ICML, pp. 2285–2294 (2015)
17. Denton, E.L., Zaremba, W., Bruna, J., LeCun, Y., Fergus, R.: Exploiting linear structure within convolutional networks for efficient evaluation. In: Advances in Neural Information Processing Systems, pp. 1269–1277 (2014)
18. Zhang, X., Zou, J., Ming, X., He, K., Sun, J.: Efficient and accurate approximations of nonlinear convolutional networks. In: Proceedings of the IEEE Conference on Computer Vision and Pattern Recognition, pp. 1984–1992 (2015)
19. Lin, S., Ji, R., Guo, X., Li, X., et al.: Towards convolutional neural networks compression via global error reconstruction. In: International Joint Conferences on Artificial Intelligence (2016)
20. Han, S., Liu, X., Mao, H., Pu, J., Pedram, A., Horowitz, M.A., Dally, W.J.: EIE: efficient inference engine on compressed deep neural network. In: Proceedings of the 43rd International Symposium on Computer Architecture, pp. 243–254. IEEE Press (2016)
21. LeCun, Y., Denker, J.S., Solla, S.A., Howard, R.E., Jackel, L.D.: Optimal brain damage. In: NIPs, vol. 2, pp. 598–605 (1989)
22. Hassibi, B., Stork, D.G., et al.: Second order derivatives for network pruning: optimal brain surgeon. In: Advances in Neural Information Processing Systems, p. 164 (1993)
23. Wen, W., Wu, C., Wang, Y., Chen, Y., Li, H.: Learning structured sparsity in deep neural networks. In: Advances in Neural Information Processing Systems, pp. 2074–2082 (2016)
24. Zaabab, A.H., Zhang, Q.J., Nakhla, M.S.: Device and circuit-level modeling using neural networks with faster training based on network sparsity. IEEE Trans. Microw. Theor. Tech. **45**(10), 1696–1704 (1997)
25. Ishikawa, M.: Structural learning with forgetting. Neural Networks **9**(3), 509–521 (1996)
26. Krizhevsky, A., Hinton, G.: Learning multiple layers of features from tiny images (2009)

Cooperative Design of Two Level Fuzzy Logic Controllers for Medium Access Control in Wireless Body Area Networks

Seyed Mohammad Nekooei[✉], Gang Chen, and Ramesh Rayudu

School of Engineering and Computer Science, Victorian University of Wellington, Wellington, New Zealand
{mohammad.nekooei,aaron.chen,ramesh.rayudu}@ecs.vuw.ac.nz

Abstract. Wireless Body Area Networks (WBANs) consists of various sensors which are attached on or even implanted in the body to improve health care and the quality of life. Soft computing techniques including fuzzy logic have been successfully applied to WBANs. However, most of the existing research works considered only single-level fuzzy logic controls (FLCs). In this paper, we propose a two-level control scheme at both the sensor level and the coordinator level to improve both the reliability and performance of Medium Access Controls (MAC) in WBANs. We also propose to use Cooperative PSO (CPSO) to automate the design of our two-level control scheme. With the goal of improving network reliability while keeping the communication delay at a low level, we have particularly experimented on four different collaborator selection methods for CPSO. Specifically, we show that network knowledge can help CPSO to select collaborators more effectively. Moreover, the FLCs designed by our approach is also shown to outperform some recently developed algorithms and the IEEE 802.15.4 standard.

Keywords: Fuzzy Logic Controllers · Wireless Body Area Networks · Media Access Control · Cooperative Co-Evolutionary Algorithms

1 Introduction

As an emerging technology, *Wireless Body Area Networks* (WBANs) deploy sensor nodes on the human body to monitor various biosignals such as blood pressure, heart beat rate and body temperature [4]. As shown in Fig. 1, each WBAN has a special node called the *coordinator* that exchanges information with the owner or an external medical health system to offer the chance to diagnose early symptoms of diseases. This coordinator is often supported by a more powerful device such as a smartphone.

It has been shown that reliability of the commonly used IEEE 802.15.4 standard for WBANs can be very limited in terms of *Packet Delivery Ratio (PDR)*, both for interference and non-interference scenarios [3,9]. To address this issue,

© Springer International Publishing AG 2017
Y. Shi et al. (Eds.): SEAL 2017, LNCS 10593, pp. 870–882, 2017.
https://doi.org/10.1007/978-3-319-68759-9_71

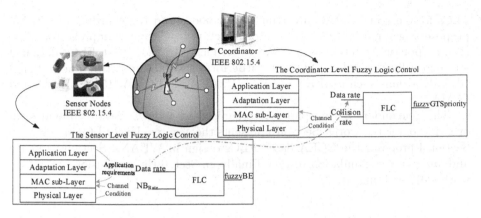

Fig. 1. Architecture of Cooperative Cross-Layer Fuzzy Medium Access Control (CoCLF-MAC) which includes the sensor-level fuzzy logic control and the coordinator-level fuzzy logic control

many researchers utilise *Fuzzy Logic Controllers* (FLCs) for *Medium Access Control* (MAC) at sensor level to improve the communication reliability and performance [8,9]. Different from these research works, we believe controllers should play a more important role for MAC. In particular, using FLCs at the coordinator level can also significantly improve reliability and performance of the network. Driven by this idea, in this research we aim to propose a *Cooperative Cross Layer Fuzzy Medium Access Control* (CoCLF-MAC), which uses FLCs both at the sensor level and the coordinator level to cooperatively improve the quality of the IEEE 802.15.4-based MAC in the context of WBANs.

Clearly, the effective design of FLCs is essential to our research. Meanwhile, designing two-level control schemes will significantly increase the complexity of the design process and potentially affect the effectiveness of the designed FLCs. Consequently, we propose to use Cooperative Co-Evolutionary Algorithms (CCEAs) in particular Cooperative PSO (CPSO) [2] for fully automated design of both sensor-level and coordinator-level FLCs through two separate sub-populations. CPSO has been chosen because of its proven effectiveness [2] and our familiarity. However, we do not rule out the possibility of using other CCEAs.

In order to use CPSO effectively, one major issue to be addressed in this paper is on the choice of collaborators from one sub-population while evaluating the candidate FLC design from the other sub-population of CPSO. For this purpose, we propose a new collaborator selection scheme based on our insight into efficient communication in WBANs and employ the network knowledge to judge the suitability of any potential collaborators. We found that our new collaborator selection method can clearly improve the effectiveness of the design process.

The contributions of this work can be summarised as follows: (1) From our knowledge, we are among the first to study CCEAs (i.e. CPSO) for designing

FLCs for cross layer MAC involving sensor nodes and the coordinator. (2) We propose a new method of collaborator selection in CPSO to improve the algorithm's practical usefulness. (3) We experimentally show that FLCs designed automatically through CPSO can outperform several competing and cutting-edge algorithms such as IEEE 802.15.4 [1], AGA [6], FCMA [15], CLFB [9] and D^2MAC [8].

The remainder of this paper is organised as follows: Sect. 2 provides an overview of related works. Section 3 presents the new two-level FLCs in WBANs. Section 4 proposes the CCEA-based FLCs design in WBANs. Section 5 reports and analyses the simulation results. Finally, in Sect. 6 the conclusion and future work will be discussed.

2   Literature Review

IEEE 802.15.4 is one of the widely used communication standards in WBANs [4]. To improve the reliability and performance of this standard in the context of WBANs, soft computing techniques, in particular fuzzy logic, have been popularly used in cross-layering MAC [8,9]. Existing studies have also clearly shown that fuzzy logic is particularly useful for cross-layer control of channel access due to its flexibility and simplicity [8,9]. We also proposed a *Cross-Layer Fuzzy logic based Backoff controller* (CLFB) [9] to control channel access in WBANs. Most of these research efforts have only considered using FLCs for the sensor level, neglecting the importance of utilising FLCs for the coordinator-level MAC.

In this paper, we address this issue by proposing CoCLF-MAC that cooperatively uses two FLCs, one at the sensor level and the other at the coordinator level. It has been shown that careful design of FLCs is essential for successful communications in WBANs [9]. Due to inherent interactions between sensor nodes and the coordinator, FLCs used by sensor nodes and the coordinator must cooperatively work together to achieve desirable results. Consequently, both FLCs need to be designed simultaneously.

Designing two FLCs jointly will obviously increase the design complexity. To address this issue, following the divide-and-conquer strategy, Potter and Jong [11] proposed the CCEA algorithm. In their algorithm, a problem is decomposed into several smaller sub-components and each sub-component can be evolved through a separate *Genetic Algorithm* (GA) sub-population. A few years later, Bergh and Engelbrecht [2] proposed *Cooperative Particle Swarm Optimiser* (CPSO) that can perform much better than the original PSO on several benchmark optimisation problems. This is achieved by using multiple swarms to optimise different components of the solution vector cooperatively. In this research, we decide to adopt a standard CPSO because of its proven effectiveness [2] and our familiarity.

Choosing suitable collaborators to evaluate candidate solutions in CCEAs and CPSO is difficult. Typically researchers prefer to choose the best fit solution from alternative sub-populations [2,11,13]. However, as a result of using this greedy method, CCEAs and CPSO could fall easily into local optima [2,13].

Therefore, some researchers have selected an alternative method which involves two candidate solutions, i.e. the best and a random candidate solution [7,13]. In this method, both selected collaborators are evaluated with the current candidate solution and the higher fitness determines the fitness of the current candidate solution [2,13]. Although these methods are commonly used by researchers, they are designed to tackle general optimisation problems. In this research we will exploit the unique characteristic of our design problem to find collaborators more effectively.

3 New Design of Fuzzy Logic Based Medium Access Control in WBANs

In this paper, we aim at proposing a two-level control scheme at both the sensor level and the coordinator level to improve IEEE 802.15.4 in the context of WBANs. As shown in Fig. 1, sensor-level FLC is used by sensors to adaptively adjust the backoff exponent, called *fuzzyBE*, to avoid collisions based on NB_{Rate} [9] and the application data rate. Being the moving average of the *Number of Backoffs (NB)* in IEEE 802.15.4, NB_{Rate} serves as a good indication of the channel condition. On the other hand, the application data rate is used to regulate the delay based on the channel access frequency [9]. All variables handled by our FLC are partitioned into four fuzzy levels. All the fuzzy rules for the sensor level are summarised in Table 1.

Based on the design of rule base in Table 1, it is clear to see that when NB_{Rate} is *Low*, short backoff delays are recommended. Accordingly, when NB_{Rate} is *High*, longer delay is produced. Furthermore, we suggest a longer delay for *High* data rate sensor nodes to reduce collisions and prevent blocking of low data rate sensor nodes.

Table 1. Fuzzy logic rule matrix for the sensor-level control

NB_{Rate}	Data rate			
	Low	Medium	Medium high	High
Low	$R^{(1)} : B1$	$R^{(2)} : B1$	$R^{(3)} : B1$	$R^{(4)} : B2$
Medium	$R^{(5)} : B2$	$R^{(6)} : B2$	$R^{(7)} : B2$	$R^{(8)} : B3$
Medium high	$R^{(9)} : B3$	$R^{(10)} : B3$	$R^{(11)} : B3$	$R^{(12)} : B4$
High	$R^{(13)} : B3$	$R^{(14)} : B4$	$R^{(15)} : B4$	$R^{(16)} : B4$

At the coordinator-level, our FLC is utilised to prioritise the requests for transmissions through *Guaranteed Time Slot* (GTS) based on both the channel collision rate and application data rate. Instead of serving each request according to the simple *First Come First Serve* (FCFS) order [1], the coordinator assigns communication bandwidth to sensor nodes by following their respective *fuzzyGTSpriority*. Collision rate, which is calculated by the coordinator, is a direct indication of the channel condition in the recent past. Similar to the sensor-level FLC, the coordinator-level FLC must adjust fuzzyGTSpriority based on data rate of each sensor node. For example, nodes with high data rate tend to access the channel more frequently and should be assigned higher priorities. This is important for reducing collisions and packet loss. All of the input and output variables for our FLC at this level are also fuzzified into four fuzzy levels. All the fuzzy rules are also summarised in Table 2.

According to Table 2, whenever collision rate is *High*, our FLC will consistently suggest the high priority to avoid collisions. As for *Low* date rate sensors, lower priority is consistently recommended to prevent unnecessary wastage of bandwidth.

Table 2. Fuzzy Logic rules for the coordinator-level control.

Collision rate	Data rate			
	Low	Medium	Medium high	High
Low	$R^{(1)} : P1$	$R^{(2)} : P1$	$R^{(3)} : P1$	$R^{(4)} : P1$
Medium	$R^{(5)} : P1$	$R^{(6)} : P2$	$R^{(7)} : P2$	$R^{(8)} : P3$
Medium high	$R^{(9)} : P2$	$R^{(10)} : P3$	$R^{(11)} : P3$	$R^{(12)} : P4$
High	$R^{(13)} : P3$	$R^{(14)} : P3$	$R^{(15)} : P4$	$R^{(16)} : P4$

Moreover, for simplicity and efficiency, we use the triangular shaped *Membership Function* (MF) for all input and output variables for both the sensor and coordinator level FLCs. Examples of such MFs are illustrated in Fig. 2.

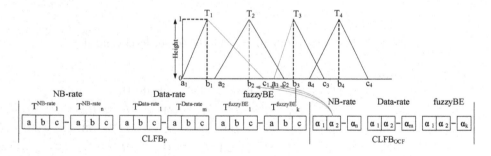

Fig. 2. Moderately restricted coding scheme (MRCS) in which T is the linguistic of each membership function. k is the number of overlapping control factors (OCFs) which are represented by α.

4   Evolutionary Design of FLCs in WBANs

In this section, we propose a direct method to automatically design FLCs for our two-level control scheme as shown in Fig. 1. As reported extensively in the literature [5,9], evolution computation techniques have been successfully applied to automate the design of various aspects of FLCs and are considered highly suitable for tackling our research problems. Specifically, we focus on designing the control parameters of all MFs through CPSO.

In this research, we take advantage of the modularity nature of our design problem. Particularly, we use two sub-populations in CPSO: the first sub-population contains individuals that encode FLCs to be used at the sensor level, and the second sub-population contains individuals that encode the FLCs to be used at the coordinator level.

In the context of WBANs, we can identify four important technical issues for CPSO-based design of FLCs:

1. **Coding scheme:** Each candidate solution in CPSO represents a separate FLC design and must follow a specific coding scheme which encodes all control parameters for each MF through a vector of real numbers. Previously, we have studied the influence of different coding schemes on the effectiveness and interpretability of the FLCs designed [9]. We experimentally showed that *Moderately Restricted Coding Scheme* (MRCS) [9], as illustrated in Fig. 2, can provide both good effectiveness and interpretability. Consequently, in this research, we utilise MRCS to encode candidate FLCs at both control levels.

2. **Fitness function:** Fitness function is an essential part of our design approach. Through properly designed fitness functions, we can obtain a desirable balance between reliability and performance in WBANs. Our main design goal is to optimise the reliability of WBANs (measured by PDR). On the other hand, the performance of the network has to remain competitive with respect to IEEE 802.15.4. In WBANs, throughput can be improved directly through increasing PDR. However, increasing PDR may lead to an increase in packet delay. We therefore decide to pursue PDR as the main objective and packet delay as a soft constraint, the violation of which will be penalised through the fitness function. Consequently, we have defined the fitness function as follows [9]:

$$F = \Delta PDR + \lambda \times \Delta Delay \tag{1}$$

where λ is a coefficient. We have studied the particular effect of λ and found that a proper value for λ to obtain a desirable trade-off between PDR and delay is 2.5 [9].

3. **Collaborator selecting method:** In CPSO, as each candidate FLC is part of the whole solution, while evaluating the fitness of any candidate FLC from one sub-population, we need to select a candidate FLC from the other sub-population as a collaborator. In this research, we will try to exploit our network knowledge to select collaborators more effectively.

As explained in Sect. 2, there are two straightforward ways to select collaborators from other sub-populations: (1) select the fittest candidate solution or gBest; and (2) select a random candidate solution. Besides the two, in this paper, we introduce a *Network inspired Collaborator Selection* (NiCS) scheme to select collaborators more effectively. Based on our experience of effective communication in WBANs, the criteria for collaborator selection have been summarised in Tables 3 and 4. These criteria define the support of MFs for both sensor-level and coordinator-level FLCs. The basic idea is to ensure that the support of partnering FLCs always falls into the right range which may help to promote a more effective collaboration.

Table 3. Collaborator selection criteria for the sensor-level FLC design

Input and output variable	Support of membership function			
	Low/B1	Medium/B2	Medium high/B3	High/B4
NB_{Rate}	$[0\ldots1)$	$(0\ldots3]$	$[1\ldots5]$	$[4\ldots6]$
Data rate	$[1\ldots50]$	$[10\ldots75]$	$[35\ldots100)$	$[50\ldots100]$
fuzzyBE	$[2\ldots5]$	$[3\ldots6]$	$[5\ldots7.5]$	$[6\ldots8]$

Table 4. Collaborator selection criteria for the coordinator-level FLC design

Input and output variable	Support of membership function			
	Low/P1	Medium/P2	Medium high/P3	High/P4
Collision rate	$[0\ldots30]$	$(0\ldots80]$	$[40\ldots100]$	$[70\ldots100]$
Data rate	$[1\ldots40]$	$[10\ldots60]$	$[35\ldots90]$	$[50\ldots100]$
fuzzyGTSpriority	$[0\ldots30]$	$(0\ldots70]$	$[30\ldots100)$	$[80\ldots100]$

According to Table 3, while CPSO is evolving FLCs at the coordinator level, we need to carefully select a FLC collaborator at the sensor level. For example, in view of rules $R^{(1)}$, $R^{(2)}$ and $R^{(3)}$ in Table 1, the support of B1 MF for fuzzyBE is set to $[2\ldots5]$ in Table 3. Consequently, sensor nodes do not need to wait before packet transmission as long as the channel is not busy. The rules in Table 1 also suggest that when the channel is highly congested, sensor nodes must apply backoff delay long enough to prevent collisions. Consequently, the support of B4 MF is in the range of $[6\ldots8]$.

As an another example, the support of Low MF for NB_{rate} in Table 3 is in the range of $[0\ldots1)$. This means that the channel is mostly free and highly likely a sensor node can send its packet within the current *Contention Window* (CW). On the other hand, High MF shows an extremely busy channel and its support falls in $[4\ldots6]$.

Similarly, selection criteria in Table 4 guide the selection of effective collaborators at the coordinator level to evolve FLCs in sensor level. For example, in view of the rules $R^{(1)}$, $R^{(2)}$ and $R^{(3)}$ in Table 2, the support of P1 MF shown in Table 4 implies that, as long as the channel is not busy, the coordinator does not need to assign communication bandwidth to the requested sensor nodes immediately. On the other hand, based on the rules $R^{(12)}$, $R^{(15)}$ and $R^{(16)}$ in Table 2, the support of P4 MF suggests that the coordinator needs to assign channel to the requested sensor nodes immediately to prevent collisions when the channel is highly congested. As another example, the support of Low MF for collision rate falls in $[0 \ldots 30]$, implying that the coordinator believes that the channel is fairly clear and will therefore assign the lowest priority to any requested sensor nodes.

---

define : NiCSpool is a pool of potential collaborators for each swarm, i.e. candidate FLCs for CLFB and CLFGA;
The jth swarm is denoted as $P_j, j \in [1..2]$;
for *each sub-population $j \in [1..2]$* **do**
> Copy potential collaborators into $NiCSpool_j$ based on criteria in Tables 3 and 4;
> **if** $NiCSpool_j > 0$ **then**
> > **if** $NiCSgBest == enable$ and $P_j.\hat{y} \in NiCSpool_j$ **then**
> > > $\quad |\quad P_j.\tilde{y} = P_j.\hat{y};$
> >
> > **else**
> > > $\quad |\quad$ randomly choose $P_j.\tilde{y}$ from $NiCSpool_j$;
> >
> > **end**
>
> **else**
> > **if** $NiCSgBest == enable$ **then**
> > > $\quad |\quad P_j.\tilde{y} = P_j.\hat{y};$
> >
> > **else**
> > > $\quad |\quad$ randomly choose $P_j.\tilde{y}$ from swarm jth;
> >
> > **end**
>
> **end**

end

Algorithm 1. The pseudocode of the NiCS algorithm. $P_j.\tilde{y}$ denotes the selected collaborator in the jth sub-population. The jth sub-population has a global best particle $P_j.\hat{y}$

As explained in Algorithm 1, if a candidate FLC meets these criteria, it could be considered as a potential collaborator. Otherwise, the collaborator can be chosen either randomly or as the fittest FLC candidate (gBest). In our new approach, we can select the candidate FLC from the pool of potential collaborators (NiCSpool) in two ways:

1. NiCS(gBest): if the fittest solution is within the potential collaborators, it is selected as the collaborator to evaluate the candidate solution; otherwise, the collaborator will be randomly selected from NiCSpool.

2. NiCS(random): randomly select a collaborator from the potential collaborators, regardless of whether the fittest selection is within NiCSpool.

In order to determine the fitness of each candidate solution, an evaluation method is needed. In this paper, we evaluate the candidate solution based on a common configuration of WBAN so as to improve the communication reliability and performance in this setting.

5   Simulation Implementation and Results

In this research, we have used OMNeT++ 4.4.1 as our network simulation tool. We built up the simulation scenarios based on the star topology with a single WBAN coordinator. To evaluate network conditions under different traffic loads, four different sensors, which are commonly used in many simulation studies [10], have been considered. A summary of different sensors and their communication features can be found in Table 5. We have used the log-normal shadowing model as the channel model. In comparison with the traditional Rayleigh and Ricean distributions, the log-normal shadowing model reproduces the small-scale fading in WBANs more accurately [12].

Table 5. Communication specifications of Sensor nodes used in the simulation.

Sensor node	ECG	Respiratory rate	Motion sensor	Blood pressure (BP)
Traffic generation distribution	Constant	Constant	Poisson	Constant
Data rate	156.25 Bps	15 Bps	64 Bps	512 Bps

To design two-level FLCs, the size of each sub-population in CPSO is set to 50. The maximum number of generations is set to 100. Under these settings, CPSO is close to convergence after 50 generations. Meanwhile, the fully connected topology is used for CPSO and $\omega = 0.7298$ and $c_1 = c_2 = 1.49618$ [14]. To have reliable results, CPSO under the same settings is repeated 30 times with different starting seeds.

5.1   Performance Measures

To quantitatively compare the reliability and performance of WBANs, we employ four well-known metrics which are *PDR*, *collision rate*, *throughput* and *Packet delay*. For a fair comparison with competing algorithms, each competing technology will run for 30 times independently. Again, the average results in reliability and performance will be used to compare with FLCs designed by our CPSO-based approach. In addition, the *Analysis of Variance* (ANOVA) test is performed to determine whether statistically significant differences in performance and reliability can be observed. Tukey's post-hoc analysis and t-test analysis are also utilised to realise the main source of difference.

5.2   Simulation Results

In this research, we explore four different collaborator selection methods, i.e. gBest, random, NiCS(gBest) and NiCS(random). As illustrated in Fig. 3, the results show that CPSO achieved consistently good results after 100 generations (5000 evaluations) with respect to all collaborator selection methods. Moreover, Fig. 3 shows that greedy methods for collaborator selection can be more effective than less greedy selection methods. For example, the gBest collaborator selection method is more effective than the random one. Furthermore, the simulation results confirm that our selection methods, i.e. NiCS(gBest) and NiCS(random), can enhance the effectiveness of the collaborator selection. For example, the NiCS(gBest) collaborator selection method is more effective than gBest during the first 10 generations in terms of both PDR and packet delay, statistically confirmed by ANOVA and Tukey's post-hoc analysis (p-value < 0.05). Similarly, NiCS(random) is also more effective than random collaborator selection method in our design problem. Generally, since CPSO with NiCS(gBest) achieved reasonably good results after 10 generations, whenever there is lack of computation power and time, NiCS(gBest) can be more desirable than other selection methods.

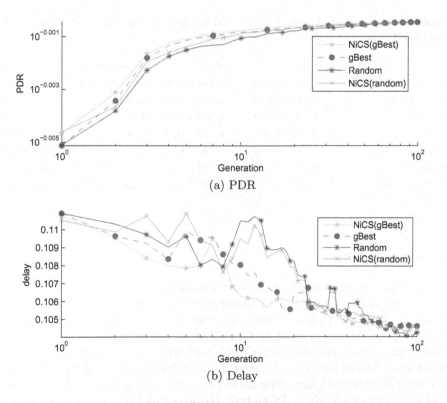

Fig. 3. CPSO convergence.

Comparison Between CPSO-Based FLC Design and Competing Algorithms. In order to demonstrate the effectiveness of CoCLF-MAC, we have compared it with several cutting-edge algorithms, i.e. IEEE 802.15.4 [1], CLFB [9], D^2MAC [8], AGA+ IEEE 802.15.4 [6], AGA+CLFB [6,9] and FCMA [15]. Among these algorithm, CLFB and D^2MAC use one-level control and the rest algorithms, i.e. IEEE 802.15.4, AGA+ IEEE 802.15.4, AGA+CLFB and FCMA, use two-level control. As presented in Table 6, CoCLF-MAC significantly outperforms IEEE 802.15.4, CLFB, D^2MAC, AGA+ IEEE 802.15.4, AGA+CLFB and FCMA in terms of both PDR and packet delay. The one-way ANOVAs give significant differences with p-value <0.0001. The corresponding Tukey's post-hoc analysis further confirms our conclusion. Specifically, while PDR achieved by CoCLF-MAC is significantly higher than IEEE 802.15.4, CLFB, D^2MAC, AGA+ IEEE 802.15.4, AGA+CLFB and FCMA, packet delay achieved by CoCLF-MAC is also significantly less than the rest algorithms.

Table 6 further reports the WBAN throughput upon using each algorithm. Statistical analysis confirms once again that CoCLF-MAC achieves significantly higher throughput than the rest algorithms. Moreover, it can also significantly reduce the collision rate in comparison to all competing algorithms.

Table 6. Comparison of CoCLF-MAC and competing algorithms, in terms of PDR and packet delay, throughput and Collision rate.

	PDR	Delay	Throughput	Collision rate
IEEE 802.15.4 [1]	0.831 ± 0.005	0.168 ± 0.007	9594.17 ± 32.93	0.322 ± 0.014
D^2MAC [8]	0.845 ± 0.004	0.271 ± 0.15	9601.40 ± 34.75	0.310 ± 0.014
CLFB [9]	0.828 ± 0.002	0.229 ± 0.003	9570.21 ± 16.03	0.331 ± 0.006
AGA+IEEE 802.15.4 [6]	0.903 ± 0.005	0.162 ± 0.121	10742.47 ± 72.76	0.162 ± 0.011
AGA+CLFB [6,9]	0.941 ± 0.002	0.149 ± 0.002	11061.79 ± 56.47	0.138 ± 0.007
FCMA [15]	$0.924 \pm 4.3 \times 10^{-4}$	0.151 ± 0.001	10906.71 ± 34.27	0.141 ± 0.003
CoCLF-MAC	$0.999 \pm 2.4 \times 10^{-5}$	0.104 ± 0.001	11976.03 ± 49.20	0.008 ± 0.005

6   Conclusion

In this paper, we proposed an EC-based approach to automatically design Fuzzy Logic Controllers (FLCs) for Cooperative Cross Layer Fuzzy MAC (CoCLF-MAC) in WBANs. Different form many works in the literature that utilised FLCs only at the sensor level, CoCLF-MAC explored and successfully demonstrated the importance of utilising FLCs both at th sensor level and the coordinator level. Meanwhile, we examined the usefulness of the well-know Cooperative PSO (CPSO) with four different collaborator selection methods. We showed that CPSO can successfully design both the sensor and coordinator control levels jointly to improve reliability and performance of WBANs. Moreover, automatically designed FLCs in our approach can achieve significantly better reliability and performance than cutting-edge algorithms such as IEEE 802.15.4, AGA+ IEEE 802.15.4, AGA+CLFB, FCMA, CLFB and D^2MAC. In the future, instead of training FLCs based on only one network setting, we will also try to evolve widely applicable FLCs by utilising multiple WBAN settings for training.

Acknowledgments. The author(s) wish to acknowledge the contribution of NeSI high-performance computing facilities to the results of this research. NZ's national facilities are provided by the NZ eScience Infrastructure and funded jointly by NeSI's collaborator institutions and through the Ministry of Business, Innovation & Employment's Research Infrastructure programme. URL https://www.nesi.org.nz.

References

1. IEEE Standard for local and metropolitan area networks–part 15.4: Low-Rate Wireless Personal Area Networks (LR-WPANs). IEEE Std 802.15.4-2011 (Revision of IEEE Std 802.15.4-2006), pp. 1–314. September 2011
2. van den Bergh, F., Engelbrecht, A.P.: A cooperative approach to particle swarm optimization. IEEE Trans. Evol. Comput. **8**(3), 225–239 (2004)
3. Cavalcanti, D., Schmitt, R., Soomro, A.: Performance analysis of 802.15.4 and 802.11e for body sensor network applications. In: Leonhardt, S., Falck, T., Mähönen, P. (eds.) BSN 2007. IFMBE Proceedings, vol. 13, pp. 9–14. Springer, Heidelberg (2007)
4. Cavallari, R., Martelli, F., Rosini, R., Buratti, C., Verdone, R.: A survey on wireless body area networks: technologies and design challenges. IEEE Commun. Surv. Tutor. **16**(3), 1635–1657 (2014)
5. Fleming, P., Purshouse, R.: Evolutionary algorithms in control systems engineering: a survey. Control Eng. Pract. **10**(11), 1223–1241 (2002)
6. Huang, Y.K., Pang, A.C., Hung, H.N.: An adaptive GTS allocation scheme for IEEE 802.15.4. IEEE Trans. Parallel Distrib. Syst. **19**(5), 641–651 (2008)
7. Li, X., Yao, X.: Tackling high dimensional nonseparable optimization problems by cooperatively coevolving particle swarms. In: 2009 IEEE Congress on Evolutionary Computation, pp. 1546–1553. May 2009
8. Mouzehkesh, N., Zia, T., Shafigh, S., Zheng, L.: D^2MAC: dynamic delayed medium access control (MAC) protocol with fuzzy technique for wireless body area networks. In: IEEE International Conference on Body Sensor Networks (BSN), pp. 1–6. May 2013
9. Nekooei, S.M., Chen, G., Rayudu, R.K.: Automatic design of fuzzy logic controllers for medium access control in wireless body area networks an evolutionary approach. Appl. Soft Comput. **56**, 245–261 (2017)
10. Otal, B., Alonso, L., Verikoukis, C.: Highly reliable energy-saving MAC for wireless body sensor networks in healthcare systems. IEEE J. Sel. Areas Commun. **27**(4), 553–565 (2009)
11. Potter, M.A., De Jong, K.A.: A cooperative coevolutionary approach to function optimization. In: Davidor, Y., Schwefel, H.-P., Männer, R. (eds.) PPSN 1994. LNCS, vol. 866, pp. 249–257. Springer, Heidelberg (1994). doi:10.1007/3-540-58484-6_269
12. Taparugssanagorn, A., Rabbachin, A., Hämäläinen, M., Saloranta, J., Iinatti, J., Member, S.: A review of channel modelling for wireless body area network in wireless medical communications. In: The 11th International Symposium on Wireless Personal Multimedia Communications. WPMC 2008 (2008)

13. Wiegand, R.P., Liles, W.C., Jong, K.A.D.: An empirical analysis of collaboration methods in cooperative coevolutionary algorithms. In: Proceedings of the 3rd Annual Conference on Genetic and Evolutionary Computation, GECCO 2001, pp. 1235–1242 (2001)
14. Xue, B., Zhang, M., Browne, W.: Particle swarm optimization for feature selection in classification: a multi-objective approach. IEEE Trans. Cybern. **43**(6), 1656–1671 (2013)
15. Zhou, J., Guo, A., Xu, J., Su, S.: An optimal fuzzy control medium access in wireless body area networks. Neurocomputing **142**, 107–114 (2014). SI Computational Intelligence Techniques for New Product Development

Statistical Analysis of Social Coding in GitHub Hypernetwork

Li Kuang, Feng Wang$^{(\boxtimes)}$, Heng Zhang, and Yuanxiang Li

State Key Lab of Software Engineering, Wuhan University, Wuhan 430072, China
fengwang@whu.edu.cn

Abstract. Social coding is a software development approach, which can facilitate hundreds of developers collaborating in one project simultaneously. Many researchers focus on the analysis of social network based on complex network models. However, the traditional complex network model cannot express the full information of collaboration. In this paper, in order to depict the properties of hypernetwork well and get a good simulation result, we investigate the time evolution of the GitHub dataset. We find that, (1) The hypernetworks show high level of self-organization; (2) From the neighbor connectivity of developers, some of the skilled developers wish to collaborate with skilled developers, whereas some skilled developers prefer to collaborate with freshman; (3) From the statistical properties of programming languages communities, the assortativity of *Java* community is obviously different from other communities, and the projects have a high probability of collaboration with those using the same programming languages.

1 Introduction

The complex networks are the useful mathematical representations of many real-world complex systems. However, as the emergence of new forms of social networks, such as the corporate elite networks [3], the actor collaboration network [18], and the scientific collaboration network [13], the traditional complex networks models cannot describe these social networks comprehensively. Therefore, researchers proposed many approaches to represent the social networks, such as simple unipartite graphs, bipartite graphs and tripartite graphs [11,16,18]. But these models fail to capture some elements of the original data, such as the homogeneity of nodes. Recently, the hypernetwork, proposed very early by Berge [1], has been widely used to analyze the evolution of social networks. Ghoshal *et al.* [6] studied the random hypergraphs and their applications. Zlatić *et al.* [23] defined and analyzed the topological quantities of hypernetworks for tagged social networks. Wang *et al.* [21] proposed a dynamical evolution model based on hyperedge growth and hyperdegree preferential attachment. Guang-Yong and Jian-Guo [9] proposed an evolving hypernetwork model that newly added hyperedge includes a new coming node and a number of nodes from a randomly selected local-world. Lately, Liu *et al.* [12] proposed two knowledge-generation dynamic evolving models with differences on evolving mechanisms.

© Springer International Publishing AG 2017
Y. Shi et al. (Eds.): SEAL 2017, LNCS 10593, pp. 883–895, 2017.
https://doi.org/10.1007/978-3-319-68759-9_72

In the hyperedge growth process, one model adopts the hyperdegree preferential attachment mechanism (HDPH), while the other models adopt the knowledge stock preferential attachment mechanism (KSPH). The knowledge stock stands for the amount of knowledge of each contributor, the knowledge accumulation process follows the Cobb-Douglas production function [4].

In this paper, we analyze the statistical properties of social coding networks via the evolution of hypernetworks. Social coding tools (such as GitHub) have brought some significant changes to the software development, because of its high level of transparency on knowledge sharing. GitHub, which has over 3.4 million users in 2014, is the leading code host in the world. Many researchers have discussed the way of collaboration in GitHub [2,15,20]. To get full information of the GitHub networks, we analyze the most two important properties, 'popularity' and 'similarity' of the hypernetwork.

The rest of the paper is organized as follows: Sect. 2 describes the collection of data and the construction of hypernetwork; Sect. 3 analyzes the statistical properties of social coding hypernetwork and the collaborations within the programming language community. Section 4 concludes our work.

2   Data Collection

We use the social collaboration data from the GHTorrent project[1]. It provides a scalable off-line mirror of GitHub's event streams and persistent data [7,8]. The structural data are stored in the MySQL database. In order to avoid the duplication of data, we use both *user* ID and *project* ID as a unique identity to extract the data. Thus, we ensure that each node represents a distinct developer and each hyperedge represents a distinct project. We can find the programming language and timestamp of each project. The dataset we obtained consists of 1028472 projects and 483438 developers registered during 2008 to 2012.

Based on the creation timestamps of the projects, we create 20 snapshots for the GH dataset for each season from 2008 to 2012. Therefore, we can investigate the dynamical evolution of the network. We define the hypergraph as $\mathcal{H}(t) = (V, E)$ for each snapshot at time t. Each vertex $v \in V$ represents a developer, and each hyperedge E_i represents a project, which includes all the developers collaborated in that project. For each snapshot at timestamp t, the hypergraph $\mathcal{H}(t)$ contains all the projects and developers emerged up to timestamp t. Here, the timestamp t can be non-integer. For example, the snapshot $\mathcal{H}(2009.5)$ contains all the projects created up to the date 2009.6.1. A simple hypernetwork model is shown as Fig. 1, the hyperedge set $E = \{E_1, E_2, E_3\}$, in which $E_1 = \{v_1, v_2, v_3\}$, $E_1 = \{v_5, v_6, v_7\}$, $E_1 = \{v_3, v_4, v_5\}$.

The growth processes of project number and developer number are illustrated in Fig. 2. We apply linear scale on x axis and log scale on y axis. The inset shows the average project numbers per developer. Both projects and developers show exponential growth with time evolution. The project numbers grow faster than

---

[1] http://ghtorrent.org/.

developers. We can observe that the number of projects is larger than the developer after half past 2011. The average project number per developer continually increases to 2.127 up to 2013. This phenomenon shows that the involvement of developers is increasing on the social coding. Developers are putting more times in the collaboration on the GitHub platform. The other reason is the GitHub allows developers to fork other projects to add their own modifications. The forked project is considered as unique project here. After few years of development, many successful projects are widely forked by developers.

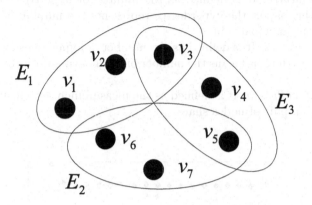

Fig. 1. Hypernetwork model.

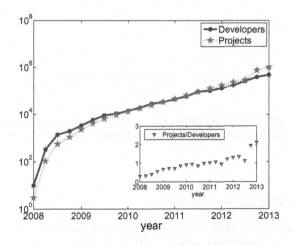

Fig. 2. Numbers of projects and developers from 2008 to 2012.

3   Statistical Properties of the Hypernetwork

Many properties have been analyzed during the evolution process of the hypernetwork, and 'popularity' and 'similarity' are the most important two properties for social coding network. Here in order to investigate the preferential attachment on 'popularity', we use the following definitions:

- *Assortativity*: It means that high degree nodes tend to connect with high degree nodes, and low degree nodes tend to connect with low degree nodes.
- *Node hyperdegree*: It is defined as the number of hyperedges attached to a node. In this paper, the hyperdegree represents the number of projects that a developer participates in.
- *Hyperedge degrees*: It is defined as the number of hyperedges overlapped with a hyperedge. Here, it means the number of neighboring projects that a project overlaps with.
- *Clustering coefficient*: It is defined as the measurement of how many common hyperedges a pair of nodes share.

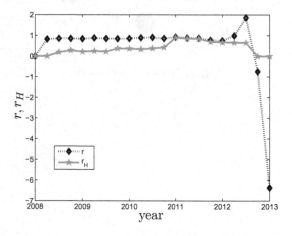

Fig. 3. Pearson coefficient (black diamond) and hyperdegree correlation coefficient (red star) of snapshot networks for each year from 2008 to 2012. (Color figure online)

3.1   Assortativity of Networks

In order to clarify the collaboration between hub developers, we apply the Pearson correlation coefficient r to measure the assortativity of networks [14]. It can be rewritten as:

$$r = \frac{K^{-1}\sum_i j_i k_i - \left[K^{-1}\sum_i \frac{1}{2}(j_i + k_i)\right]^2}{K^{-1}\sum_i \frac{1}{2}(j_i{}^2 + k_i{}^2) - \left[K^{-1}\sum_i \frac{1}{2}(j_i + k_i)^2\right]} \tag{1}$$

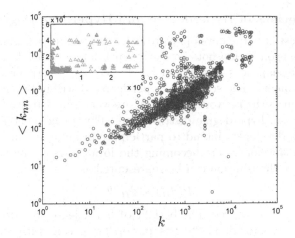

Fig. 4. Log-log plot of neighbour connectivity of networks in 2012. The inset shows linear plot of $< k_{nn} >$.

where j_i, k_i are the degrees of the nodes on both sides of the ith connected nodes, where $i = 1, \ldots, K$, and K is the total number of connections in a network. The positive or negative of r relates to assortative or disassortative mixing, respectively. As shown in Fig. 3, the Pearson coefficient is stable from year 2008 to 2012 with positive value around 0.8. After that, in the first half of the year 2012, it rises to 1.85. But in the second half of the year 2012, it drops dramatically to -6.37. We also analyze the hyperdegree correlations between developers by replacing the degree with hyperdegre in Pearson correlation coefficient. The hyperdegree correlation is represented by r_H. As shown in Fig. 3, the hyperdegree correlation r_H is similar with the Pearson coefficient r. The r_H of the networks keeps assortative mixing with positive value from year 2008 to 2012.

To investigate the causes of dramatic changes of correlation in 2012, we also measure the neighbour connectivity $< k_{nn} >$ of the snapshot network. Neighbour connectivity is the average degree of neighbours of a node with degree k. It is defined as:

$$< k_{nn} >= \sum_{k'} k' P(k' | k) \tag{2}$$

where $P(k' | k)$ is the conditional probability of an edge of a node with degree k connected to a node with degree k' [17]. The network is assortative mixing if the slope of the $< k_{nn} >$ curve is positive. It is disassortative mixing if the slope of the $< k_{nn} >$ curve is negative [14]. As shown in Fig. 4, the network of the year 2012 shows assortative mixing for $k < 1000$. However, for k in the interval $[10^3, 10^5]$, as shown in the inset of Fig. 4, the neighbour connectivity is scattered without any obvious pattern.

3.2   Distributions of Hyperdegree and Hyperedge Degree

In order to investigate the developer-project relationship, we count the hyperdegree distributions on 5 snapshots for each year from year 2008 to 2012. As shown in Fig. 5, all the snapshots show power-law hyperdegree distribution with similar power-law exponents. The scale-free hyperdegree distribution characterizes the self-organization of the network growth. Moreover, from 2010 to 2012, the snapshots show fat tail hyperdegree distributions. This phenomenon indicates that more and more developers intend to participate in large amount of projects on GitHub. These developers are becoming the loyal users of the GitHub society. The hyperdegree distribution can be represented as:

$$P(d_H) \sim d_H{}^{\gamma_H} \tag{3}$$

where d_H is the hyperdegree. The best fit of hyperdegree distribution (straight line) of the hypernetwork in 2012 is power-law fitting with exponent $\gamma_H = -2.875$.

The biggest difference of social coding network with other social networks is the hyperedge length (marked by m), which is defined as the number of nodes in a hyperedge. For example, the science collaboration networks have mean author per paper less than 9 [13]. However, the social coding network, such as GitHub, may have hundreds of developers collaborate in a single project without even knowing each other [15]. Therefore, we investigate the distribution of m on the 5 networks from year 2008 to 2012. As shown in Fig. 6, the hyperedge length follows power-law distribution, and the power-law exponent approximates to -2.555 on the network of year 2012 fitted by the straight line.

As Singh et al. [19] argued, the external cohesion (external contacts of a project) has an inverse U-shaped relationship with the success rate of projects. It means that moderate levels of external cohesion are the best for a project's success. Here, the external cohesion has same meaning with the hyperedge degree of a project. We analyze the hyperedge degree distribution of snapshot networks for each year from 2008 to 2012. As shown in Fig. 7, the 5 hyperedge degree distributions generally follow the power-law distribution with fat-tails. Because there are many projects have hundreds of developers, there are many projects with very large hyperedge degrees which can be seen in the curve of 2012 in Fig. 7.

3.3   Clustering Coefficient of Hypernetwork

In order to measure the clustering between nodes, we calculate the clustering coefficient of the hypernetwork. The clustering coefficient was proposed to measure the neighbourhood density of a node [22]. With the development of the hypernetwork, the definition of clustering coefficient has changed to focus on clustering between pairs of nodes. Based on the definition, several kinds of clustering coefficients have been proposed for hypernetwork. The most widely used one is HCC_{union} [10]:

$$HCC_{union}(u,v) = \frac{|M(u) \cap M(v)|}{|M(u) \cup M(v)|} \tag{4}$$

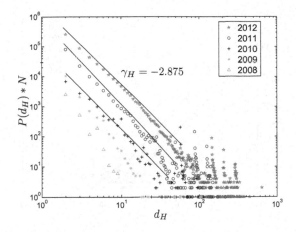

Fig. 5. Hyperdegree distribution of snapshot networks for each year from 2008 to 2012.

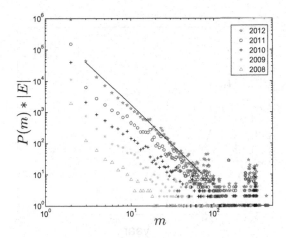

Fig. 6. Hyperedge length distribution of snapshot networks for each year from 2008 to 2012.

where $M(v)$ is the projects set that developer v participate in. Gallagher and Goldberg reviewed the definition of clustering coefficients in hypernetworks, and proposed several new definitions [5]. They compared all the definitions in the Protein interaction hypernetwork. Their results showed that HCC_{share} outperforms the others. HCC_{share} measures the amount of overlap amongst its adjacent hyperedges. It can be represented as:

$$HCC_{share}(u,v) = \frac{\sum_{E_i \in M(u)}(|E_i| - 1) - k(u)}{k(u)(|M(u)| - 1)} \tag{5}$$

where $k(u)$ is the node degree of u, E_i is the hyperedge, and $|E_i|$ means number of nodes in E_i. Here, we employ these two definitions, and get the corresponding

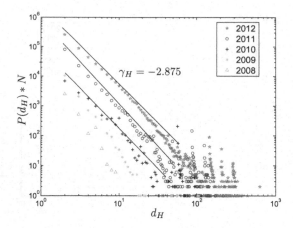

Fig. 7. Hyperedge degree distribution of snapshot networks for each year from 2008 to 2012.

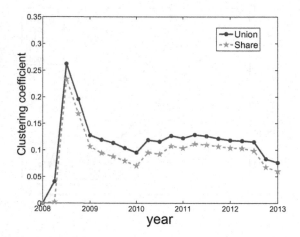

Fig. 8. Clustering coefficients of hypernetworks for each year from 2008 to 2012.

clustering coefficients for HCC_{union} and HCC_{share} on the hypernetwork of each season from 2008 to 2012. As shown in Fig. 8, we observe that these two coefficients obtain similar results. Therefore, we only consider the HCC_{union} in this paper. From Fig. 8, we find that the clustering coefficient increases sharply to 0.26 in the middle of 2008. After that, the clustering coefficient is stable around 0.1 with small variation. Until half past 2012, the clustering coefficient has an obvious decline to 0.083, and then continues to drop to 0.076. This phenomenon partly explains the dramatic drop of the Pearson coefficient at half past 2012. Many skilled developers (high degree nodes) choose to explore new collaboration parter (low degree nodes) rather than their acquaintances (high degree nodes).

3.4 Collaboration in Programming Language Communities

After the study of 'popularity' feature in GitHub, in this section we study how the 'similarity' affects the collaboration. The technology diversity influences the collaboration strategies of developer in GitHub. Here, we investigate the technology background from the perspective of the programming language of each project. There are about 100 programming languages which have been used in GitHub. As shown in Fig. 9, we make a statistical analysis on the number of programming languages used by projects in 2012. The percentages of top 8 languages are shown in the inset. Nearly half (46.0%) of the projects use the *JavaScript*, following by *Ruby* 24.5%, *Java* 20.2%, *PHP* 16.8%, *Python* 16.3%.

Table 1. Statistics of the five topical communities in 2012.

Dataset	Projects/developer	Hyperedge length	γ_H	Clustering	r
JavaScript	1.545	1.285	−3.17	0.061	0.794
Ruby	1.618	1.493	−2.929	0.090	0.739
Java	1.176	**1.980**	−3.246	0.083	**−3.81**
PHP	1.345	1.31	−3.266	0.058	0.915
Python	1.293	**2.22**	−2.696	0.073	0.798
All 2012	**2.13**	1.48	−2.875	0.076	**−6.37**

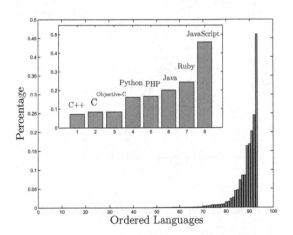

Fig. 9. Programming language statistics of hypernetwork in 2012.

We choose the top 5 languages to analyze the statistical properties on the community level. The language community is constructed by picking the projects with one language and persevering the connection between them. As shown in

Table 1, we compare the 5 language datasets with the whole dataset in 2012 on 5 properties, and the bias values are marked by bold style. The average numbers of projects per developer on 5 datasets are very close. However, all the 5 datasets have average projects less than the total dataset in 2012, because of the removal of projects with other languages on each developer. The average hyperedge length of *Python* and *Java* is higher than the remaining datasets, which means the *Python* and *Java* projects usually have more developers than the other projects. The power-law exponents of hyperdegree distribution γ_H for all the datasets are very close. From the above results, we can see that different language communities exhibit the same hyperdegree preferential attachment. The details of the hyperdegree distribution can be seen in Fig. 10. We observe that the tails of *Python* and *Java* are obviously larger than the other datasets. This phenomenon can be explained by the large size of projects and developers in *Python* and *Java* Communities. For the clustering coefficient, the language communities obtain similar results. It shows that the clustering between neighbours is consistent in the whole network. The most surprising result is that the Pearson coefficient of *Java* is extremely different from the other datasets. All the community datasets except *Java* show slight assortativity with positive r value. Only *Java* dataset shows strong disassortativity which is same as the whole 2012 dataset, which means the disassortativity of entire network can be caused by some certain groups of communities.

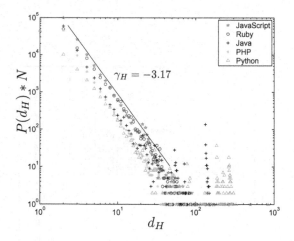

Fig. 10. Hyperdegree distribution of 5 language community hypernetworks in 2012.

In order to measure the inclination of collaboration between a pair of overlapping projects, we propose a metric $P_L(t)$, which is defined as the percentage of a pair of overlapped projects with the same language. It can be represented as:

Table 2. The percentage of a pair of overlapped projects with same language from 2008 to 2012

	2008	2009	2010	2011	2012
$P_L(t)$	86.9%	76.9%	77.8%	77.4%	70.4%

$$P_L(t) = \frac{\sum_{E_i \in E, E_j \in E, i \neq j} L(E_i, E_j)}{\sum_{E_i \in E, E_j \in E, i \neq j} C(E_i, E_j)}$$

$$\begin{cases} C(E_i, E_j) = 1 \text{ if } E_i \cap E_j \neq \emptyset \\ C(E_i, E_j) = 0 \text{ if } E_i \cap E_j = \emptyset \\ L(E_i, E_j) = 1 \text{ if } E_i \cap E_j \neq \emptyset \,\&\, l(E_i) = l(E_j) \\ L(E_i, E_j) = 0 \text{ if else} \end{cases} \quad (6)$$

where $C(E_i, E_j) = 1$, if hyperedge E_i overlap with E_j; else $C(E_i, E_j) = 0$, and $L(E_i, E_j) = 1$, if hyperedge E_i overlap with E_j and they have same programming language $l(E_i) = l(E_j)$; else $L(E_i, E_j) = 0$. We analyze the $P_L(t)$ on the five networks from 2008 to 2012. As shown in Table 2, the $P_L(t)$ are keeping at a high level with lower bound as 70.4% and upper bound as 86.9%. As mentioned above, there are about 100 languages in the whole GitHub society. Therefore, it means projects with the same language have a high probability of collaboration.

4 Conclusions

In this paper, we analyze 5 year data of GitHub, which is one of the largest open-source social coding community, from the evolution of hypernetwork. We firstly examine the statistical properties of the dataset, and find that the hypernetwork shows scale-free property on different dimensions, such as degree, hyperdegree, hyperedge length and hyperedge degree. It means the GitHub network has self-organized characteristics on collaboration. We also calculate the assortativity and clustering coefficients to investigate the collaboration strategy. In the community level, we test the statistical properties of community networks divided by the programming language. The real-world networks are complicated and dynamic. We can only capture one or two aspects of their properties. In the next step, we will focus on the investigation of some dynamic properties, such as the causes of suddenly drop of Pearson coefficient.

Acknowledgment. This work is supported by National Nature Science Foundation of China [Grant Nos. 61773296, 61672391].

References

1. Berge, C., Minieka, E.: Graphs and Hypergraphs, vol. 7. North-Holland Publishing Company, Amsterdam (1973)

2. Dabbish, L., Stuart, C., Tsay, J., Herbsleb, J.: Social coding in GitHub: transparency and collaboration in an open software repository. In: Proceedings of the ACM 2012 conference on Computer Supported Cooperative Work, pp. 1277–1286. ACM (2012)

3. Davis, G.F., Greve, H.R.: Corporate elite networks and governance changes in the 1980s. Am. J. Social. **103**(1), 1–37 (1997)

4. Douglas, P.H.: The Cobb-Douglas production function once again: its history, its testing, and some new empirical values. J. Polit. Econ. **84**(5), 903–915 (1976)

5. Gallagher, S.R., Goldberg, D.S.: Clustering coefficients in protein interaction hypernetworks. In: Proceedings of the International Conference on Bioinformatics, Computational Biology and Biomedical Informatics, p. 552. ACM (2013)

6. Ghoshal, G., Zlatić, V., Caldarelli, G., Newman, M.: Random hypergraphs and their applications. Phys. Rev. E **79**(6), 066118 (2009)

7. Gousios, G.: The GHTorrent dataset and tool suite. In: Proceedings of the 10th Working Conference on Mining Software Repositories, MSR 2013, pp. 233–236. IEEE Press, Piscataway (2013)

8. Gousios, G., Spinellis, D.: GHTorrent: GitHub's data from a firehose. In: 2012 9th IEEE Working Conference on Mining Software Repositories (MSR), pp. 12–21. IEEE (2012)

9. Guang-Yong, Y., Jian-Guo, L.: A local-world evolving hypernetwork model. Chin. Phys. B **23**(1), 018901 (2014)

10. Klamt, S., Haus, U.-U., Theis, F.: Hypergraphs and cellular networks. PLoS Comput. Biol. **5**(5), e1000385 (2009)

11. Lambiotte, R., Ausloos, M.: Collaborative tagging as a tripartite network. In: Alexandrov, V.N., van Albada, G.D., Sloot, P.M.A., Dongarra, J. (eds.) ICCS 2006. LNCS, vol. 3993, pp. 1114–1117. Springer, Heidelberg (2006). doi:10.1007/11758532_152

12. Liu, J.-G., Yang, G.-Y., Hu, Z.-L.: A knowledge generation model via the hypernetwork. PloS One **9**(3), e89746 (2014)

13. Newman, M.E.: The structure of scientific collaboration networks. Proc. Natl. Acad. Sci. **98**(2), 404–409 (2001)

14. Newman, M.E.: Assortative mixing in networks. Phys. Rev. Lett. **89**(20), 208701 (2002)

15. Onoue, S., Hata, H., Matsumoto, K.-I.: A study of the characteristics of developers' activities in GitHub. In: Software Engineering Conference (APSEC, 2013 20th Asia-Pacific), pp. 7–12. IEEE (2013)

16. Palla, G., Farkas, I.J., Pollner, P., Derényi, I., Vicsek, T.: Fundamental statistical features and self-similar properties of tagged networks. New J. Phys. **10**(12), 123026 (2008)

17. Pastor-Satorras, R., Vázquez, A., Vespignani, A.: Dynamical and correlation properties of the internet. Phys. Rev. Lett. **87**(25), 258701 (2001)

18. Ramasco, J.J., Dorogovtsev, S.N., Pastor-Satorras, R.: Self-organization of collaboration networks. Phys. Rev. E **70**(3), 036106 (2004)

19. Singh, P.V., Tan, Y., Mookerjee, V.S.: Network effects: the influence of structural capital on open source project success. MIS Q. **35**(4), 813–829 (2011)

20. Thung, F., Bissyandé, T.F., Lo, D., Jiang, L.: Network structure of social coding in GitHub. In: 2013 17th European Conference on Software Maintenance and Reengineering (CSMR), pp. 323–326. IEEE (2013)

21. Wang, J.-W., Rong, L.-L., Deng, Q.-H., Zhang, J.-Y.: Evolving hypernetwork model. Eur. Phys. J. B-Condens. Matter Complex Syst. **77**(4), 493–498 (2010)

22. Watts, D.J., Strogatz, S.H.: Collective dynamics of 'small-world' networks. Nature **393**(6684), 440–442 (1998)
23. Zlatić, V., Ghoshal, G., Caldarelli, G.: Hypergraph topological quantities for tagged social networks. Phys. Rev. E **80**(3), 036118 (2009)

Swarm Intelligence

Sparse Restricted Boltzmann Machine Based on Multiobjective Optimization

Yangyang Li[⊠], Xiaoyu Bai, Xiaoxu Liang, and Licheng Jiao

Key Laboratory of Intelligent Perception and Image Understanding of Ministry of Education, International Research Center for Intelligent Perception and Computation, Joint International Research Laboratory of Intelligent Perception and Computation, Xidian University, Xi'an 710071, Shaanxi Province, China
yyli@xidian.edu.cn

Abstract. This article proposes an efficient method for Restricted Boltzmann Machine (RBM) to learn sparse feature. Deep learning algorithms are used more and more often. The Deep Belief Network (DBN) model, which is composed of RBM, is considered as one of the most effective deep learning algorithms. RBM or auto-encoder (AE) is the basic model to build deep networks. However, RBM may produce redundant features without any constraints, then much improved RBM were proposed by added a regularization term to control sparsity of hidden units. Most of the proposed algorithms need a parameter to control the sparseness of the code. In this paper, we proposed a multiobjective optimization model to avoid user-defined constant that is a trade-off between the regularization term and the reconstruction error based on SR-RBM. We employ evolutionary algorithm to optimize the distortion function and the sparsity of hidden units simultaneously. Experimental results show that our novel approach can learn useful sparse feature without a user-define constant and it performs better than other feature learning models.

Keywords: Restricted Boltzmann machine · Sparsity · Quantum multiobjective optimization · Deep belief network

1 Introduction

In recent years, one of most important discovery in neuroscience [1–3] is the hierarchical structure of the mammal brain, it represented the raw information with multiple level of abstraction. So we could design architecture to represent information [4, 5] like the brain. Deep neural networks (DNNs) imitated the mammal brain's hierarchical structure for information representation, and it performs well in many applications [6–8]. The early successful neural networks (multilayer perceptron, MLP) is a feed-forward artificial neural network model, which maps multiple input datasets to a single output data set. Then convolutional neural networks (CNNs) which are suitable for 2-D data were proposed. Parameters sharing are employed to reduce the number of parameters and training time, and CNN works very well in practice for many tasks [9–11]. Hinton proposed Boltzmann machine (BM) [12], then Paul Smolensky proposed a modified paralleled Boltzmann machine could have exact inference with what is now

© Springer International Publishing AG 2017
Y. Shi et al. (Eds.): SEAL 2017, LNCS 10593, pp. 899–910, 2017.
https://doi.org/10.1007/978-3-319-68759-9_73

referred to as a restricted Boltzmann machine (RBM) [13]. RBM is an energy model which has two layers (visible layer and hidden layer). The visible layer is used to input training data, and the hidden layer is feature detector.

Since deep belief network (DBN) which stacked by RBM and trained in a layer-wised unsupervised learning manner appeared, it has become the main framework of deep learning. However, if there are no constraints on the hidden layers of RBM, the produced feature may be redundant or unstructured. To learn more useful representations, much improved models based on RBM or other feature extractor models like auto-encoder (AE) have been proposed [14–20]. Because the sparse representation model is consistent with the biological visual features, and can extract more abstract features from raw data. Scholars presented state-of-the-art results by added constraints on representations. Sparsity was first presented in [21], and sparsity was achieved with a sparsifying logistics module, which transforms the code vector into a sparse vector with positive components by a nonlinear front-end decoder [16]. Lee [17] proposed sparse RBM based on traditional RBM, which introduced a regularization term that penalizes a deviation of the expected activation of hidden units from given low-level. Ji [18] presented sparse-response RBM (SR-RBM) by introduced a user-defined coefficient to balance the trade-off between the regularization term and the Kullback-Leibler divergence. From the proposed variation of RBM, the sparsifying logistics module can be considered as a logistic function with adaptive bias, we need to define a weight parameter to control the sparsity term. In different yield, the optimal solutions are different. In order to obtain the optimum value, we must repeat the test many times, it is time-consuming. We could establish a multiobjective optimization model to overcome the shortcoming [22]. Multiobjective Optimization Problems (MOPs) have been in the rapid development and applied to a variety of applications [22–28]. Evolutionary algorithms are the most popular methods to solve multiobjective optimization problems.

In SR-RBM, Kullback-Leibler divergence between the distribution of the input data and the equilibrium distribution of RBM is a distortion function, and the sparsity-inducing term L1-norm of codes is used to achieve a small code rate [18]. Minimizing the distortion function amounts to learn enough information. However, achieving a small code rate leads to loss of information. Based on the two conflicting objectives, we employ a multiobjective optimization model to learn sparse useful feature. In order to obtain a satisfactory solution within a reasonable time, we need to design an efficient multiobjective optimization evolutionary algorithm (MOEA). In paper [29, 34], Adaptive Differential Evolution for Multiobjective Problems (ADEMO/D) incorporates concepts of multiobjective evolutionary algorithms based on decomposition was proposed. To increase the diversity of the population and convergence ability, we use self-adaptive quantum multiobjective differential evolution based on decomposition (SA-QDEMO/D) algorithm, because the quantum system is a complex nonlinear system and follows the superposition principle of states [30] and we use the quantum states to obviate time consuming. The proposed model optimizes two objectives simultaneously to obtain a set of Pareto optimal solutions, then a solution is selected according to a certain criterion. The main contribution is that we proposed a new idea to optimize the structure of deep neural networks or the feature learning model RBM and multiobjective optimization algorithm (SA-QDEMO/D) is used to optimize the parameters in SR-RBM to avoid the user-defined parameter, and compared to the other improved models, the novel approach learns more hierarchical representation and sparse features without a trade-off constant.

The remainder of this paper is organized as follows. Section 2, introduces the SR-RBM's structure and other related work of our new method. We explain the details of new approach learning procedure in Sect. 3. The experiments are shown in Sect. 4, and in Sect. 5 is the conclusion.

2 Background

2.1 Restricted Boltzmann Machine

RBM has two layers and can be seen as an undirected graph model, as showed in Fig. 1. The visible units v_i represent observable data, and hidden units h_i are utilized to detect features. The a and b respectively represent visible and hidden layer units' biases. The visible layer which is represented by vector v and the hidden layer which is represented by vector h are connected by a weight matrix W, there is no connection within the same layer.

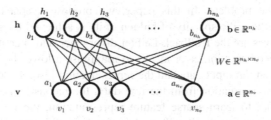

Fig. 1. Undirected graphical model of RBM.

In another way, RBM is a Markov random field which aims to represent visible units data with hidden units by maximizing the log-likelihood of training data as (1). The N is the number of samples.

$$L(\theta) = \frac{1}{N} \sum_{n=1}^{N} \log P_{\theta}(v^{(n)}) \tag{1}$$

Learning from rate distortion theory (RD) [31] which explores effective coding of the original data that is an encoding scheme using as few bits as possible while maintaining useful information of the original data according to a certain allowable distortion level. Based on the theory of RD, Ji proposed SR-RBM in [18], it tries to learn representation with a small code rate by constraining the hidden units with L1-norm of codes. The problem is described as follows

$$\min_{w,a,b} KL(P^0 \,||\, P_\theta^\infty) + \lambda \sum_{l=1}^{m} ||p(h^{(l)} \,||\, v^{(l)})||_1 \tag{2}$$

λ is a regularization parameter that controls the weight of the distortion with respect to the code rate and m represents size of training data. Since the RBM can be considered a Markov random field, the distortion function is the error in reconstructing the original data V by the decoded data from the activation probability of hidden units P.

3 Sparse RBM Based on Multiobjective Evolutionary Algorithm

In this paper, we propose a SR-RBM based on SAQDEMO/D method which employs a MOEA integrated with traditional RBM training technique to evolve RBM subject to distortion and sparsity function. Numerous proposed sparse RBM, like SR-RBM, it introduces a sparse penalty term on the hidden units and it needs a user-define constant to balance between distortion and the sparsity. Controlling the activation of hidden units at a low level improves generalization of RBM, but going too far will result high reconstruction error. In order to find a reasonable balance between distortion and sparseness of the codes without a user-defined constant, we employ a multiobjective model to solve the problem. In this paper, we propose a sparse RBM based on SAQDEMO/D method, the sparsity of hidden units is achieved by solving mops. The conflicting objectives are the Kullback-Leibler divergence and sparsity of hidden units. Minimizing the reconstruction error means to maximise a lower bound on the mutual information between the input data and the representation [36]. To learn useful feature and retain enough information from the raw data, the reconstruction error should be minimized. In order to learn sparse feature representation, the L1-norm of codes is minimized, without exception, it will lead to the loss of information. In our sparse RBM model, we optimize the two conflicting objectives at the same time to learn powerful sparse hierarchical feature representation from input data.

In our new model, the first objective function is to minimize the Kullback-Leibler divergence $KL(P^0 \,||\, P_\theta^\infty)$ in Eq. (2). $KL(P^0 \,||\, P_\theta^\infty)$ can be view as the distortion function. Minimizing the distortion function is to minimize the information loss between the input data and reconstructs the original data by the decoded data from the activation probability of hidden units. In principle, the objective function can be solved by applied the gradient descent algorithm. Because it requires so much time to approach equilibrium distribution, it is hard to compute the gradient of $KL(P^0 \,||\, P_\theta^\infty)$. Fortunately, the contrastive divergence (CD) algorithm is applied to approximate the gradient of $KL(P^0 \,||\, P_\theta^\infty)$ and CD is more effective. The second objective is to minimize the sparsity of hidden units, the sparsity-inducing term is the L1-norm of the activation probability of hidden units to achieve a small code rate [18].

Theoretically, the sparsity is represented by L0-norm, which is the number of nonzero hidden units [29]. But solving the L0-norm of codes is proved to NP-hard problem [37]. The L1-norm can produce sparse coefficients and be robust to irrelevant features [38, 39]. In this paper, we use L1-norm of codes to control the sparsity of hidden units.

The learning details of our new approach SRBM-SAQDEMO/D are summarized in Algorithm 1.

Algorithm 1

(1) Update the parameters using CD algorithm to approximate the gradient of $KL(P^0 \| P_\theta^\infty)$

$$w_{ij} := w_{ij} + \varepsilon(\langle v_i h_j \rangle_{P^0} - \langle v_i h_j \rangle_{P_\theta^1})$$

$$a_i := a_i + \varepsilon(\langle v_i \rangle_{P^0} - \langle v_i \rangle_{P_\theta^1})$$

$$b_j := b_j + \varepsilon(\langle h_j \rangle_{P^0} - \langle h_j \rangle_{P_\theta^1})$$

The ε is learning rate, $\langle . \rangle_{P_\theta^1}$ is the expectation over the reconstruction data from the original data, estimated one iteration of Gibbs sampling, because one-step Gibbs sampling will obtain a good enough approximation.

(2) Update the parameters using SAQDEMO/D algorithm.
(3) Repeat Steps 1 and 2 until converge.

Similar to SR-RBM training steps, we employ the CD learning algorithm to estimate the gradient of the Kullback-Leibler divergence at first. Next SAQDEMO/D is used to optimize the parameters to achieve sparseness subject to distortion function and sparsity-inducing term.

The self-adaptive quantum differential for multiobjective optimization problems is inspired by MOEA/D [32], SaDE [40], ADEMO/D [34]. The control parameters of the traditional DE are fixed, the computational cost is high by trial-and-error process. Then the self-adaptive differential evolution algorithm [40] was proposed. Our new approach incorporates concepts of MOEA/D and mechanisms of SaDE, and we add quantum principles into the new algorithm to exploit the power of quantum computation and accelerate convergence.

SAQDEMO/D is described as an MOEA/D platform, we employed Tchebycheff approach to converting an MOP into a number of scalar optimization problems. Let $\lambda^i (i = 1, 2, \ldots N)$ be a set of evenly distributed weight vector. The objective function of the ith subproblem is in the form [44].

$$g^{te}(\mathbf{x} \mid \lambda^j, z^*) = \max_{1 \leq j \leq m} \{\lambda_j^i | f_j(\mathbf{x}) - z_j^* |\} \tag{3}$$

The details are shown in Algorithm 2.

Algorithm 2.

1) Generate N uniformly spread weight vectors $\lambda^i (i=1,2,...N)$ using Tchebycheff approach
2) Compute the Euclidean distances between any two weight vector and select C closest weight vectors to be neighborhood, each weight vector $\lambda^i (i=1,2,...N)$
3) Initialize the population, evaluate each individual in the initial population
4) Initialize $Z = (z_1,...,z_m)^T$ by setting $z_j = \min_{1 \le i \le N} f_j(x^i)$
5) Set the counter G=0
6) Repeat:
   For each individual do
   Randomly select a mutation strategy
   F=normrnd(0.5, 0.3)
   Generate y by strategy $P_{k,G}$ using quantum gate with parameter F

   $$cr_k = normrnd(cr_k, 0.1)(0 \le cr_k \le 1)$$

   Produce y' by crossover using the cr_k

   For each j=1,...,m, If($z_j > f_j(y')$) then $z_j = f_j(y')$
       Update neighborhood:
       For each neighborhood index j
           If $g^{te}(y'| \lambda^j, z) < g^{te}(b^j | \lambda^j, z)$ then $b^j = y'$
   End for
   End for
7) G=G+1
8) Until G>max-generation

There are some parameters used in SAQDEMO/D as follows

- N: population size
- C: the number of neighbourhood weight vectors of every weigh vector
- cr: crossover rate
- F: scaling factor
- max-generation: the maximum number of generation
- Z: is the best value set found so far for every objective
- m: is dimension of the problem
- $B = \{b^1,...,b^N\}$ where b^j is the current solution to jth subproblem.

Because of network's structure and data set is huge, it may lead to high computational costs if we optimize for everyone. We select the stochastic data set Ds to be optimized. The objectives function are shown as (4)

$$\text{Minimize: } F(b) = \left(\sum KL(P^0||P_\theta^\infty), \sum_{v \in Ds} \|P(h|v)\|_1\right)^T \tag{4}$$

We only optimize the bias term instead of optimizing all the parameters to increase computational efficiency, and the bias directly control sparsity of hidden units. In our new model, the hidden units bias term b are the individuals of the population. In the initialization step, b which is initialized cannot be larger than current bias values during the evolutionary process.

After mutant, we need spatial transformation and need to select the candidate solution according to cr, the formula (5)

$$y'^j = \begin{cases} y^j, rand_j(0,1) < cr \\ b^j \end{cases} \tag{5}$$

where y'^j, y^j is the jth component of the new generated individual y', y, b^j is the current jth component.

In [34], there are three strategies used in the candidate pool for mops. We use the two strategies in our proposed model.

(1) "DE/rand/1/bin";
(2) "DE/rand/2/bin";

Strategies "DE/rand/1/bin" and "DE/rand/2/bin" are classical in DE, and their random individuals are always selected based on the scope [34].

In mops, the improvement in a Pareto optimal point in one objective often leads to a deterioration in other objective [32]. In practice, Mops is to find a set of Pareto front (PF) [33], including the optimal solutions. We are required to determine which solution in a Pareto set will be selected. MOPs researches have found some interesting regions, like knee areas [35]. Solutions in knee areas often demonstrate a better balance between the two objectives [22, 35] have the maximum marginal rates of return. Additionally, knee regions have proved to be a good choice in the study of mops and decision makers prefer solutions that lie in the knee areas in many applications [22, 29, 35]. In our method, we prefer a solution to lie in these knee areas with angle-based method [41]. We can find the knee area on the PF by finding the closest point on the PF to the knee point on smoothed Pareto front [22].

4 Experiments

In this section, we compare our model with RBM, SR-RBM to prove that our new model can learn powerful sparse features.

We test SRBM-SAQDEMO/D by the MNIST digit data set, the data set contains 60,000 training and 10,000 test images of handwritten digits (0–9) with size of 28*28 pixels [41]. The hidden units' number is 196, the number of visible units is 784. We compare our model with RBM, SR-RBM with different trade-off parameter. We set the trade-off parameter to be 0.02, 0.04, 0.06. In SAQDEMO/D, the population N = 50, the stochastic data set Ds = 100, the max-generation = 1000, the number of C closest weight vectors set is 20 according to experience. To verify the discriminative power of the representation learnt, their created representations are used to as input for the same linear classier. To reduce training time, we set size of training data set is 100, 500,

1000, 5000 respectively, and the test data set is set 20, 100, 200, 100. All the data set is sampled from the MNIST data set. The error rate (%) is shown in Table 1.

Table 1. Error rate on MNIST training.

Methods	Number of samples			
	100	500	1000	5000
RBM	29.54	16.78	12.36	11.01
SR-RBM (0.02)	28.18	15.67	12.26	8.11
SR-RBM (0.04)	27.35	14.32	11.21	7.48
SR-RBM (0.06)	28.11	15.23	12.11	8.01
Proposed model	**20.11**	**13.96**	**10.11**	**6.35**

In Table 1, the best results were highlighted in bold, the statistical results show that our proposed model can get the lowest error rates. More training examples, better results. In SR-RBM achieves best results with $\lambda = 0.04$, and the RBM shows the highest error rates. Providing more samples to the model produces a better result. SR-RBM and proposed model performs better when the number of hidden units increase. According to the statistics, the more hidden units, the worse RBM performs. Because there is no constraint in RBM, its representations will be more redundant when the number of hidden units increase.

We train the unsupervised feature extraction model and our proposed model with the same data set, we found that SR-RBM obtain the best performance with $\lambda = 0.04$, so we show the sparsity of the codes by different models, and SR-RBM with $\lambda = 0.04$, as Fig. 2. In DBNs, we regard the activation of probability of hidden units for input as its representation, the sparsities of hidden units can determine the performance of the model. From the output of hidden units Fig. 3, traditional RBM learn unstructured weight. Because there is a constraint in SR-RBM and our proposed mode, the sparsity of representation is better than traditional RBM. Our proposed model can learn sparse code with best performance which the hidden units are used to represent a small portion of the training data. From the visualization of bases Fig. 3, the bases of our proposed model is more regular and our proposed model can capture hierarchical features. We can find that our proposed model performs better than the other unsupervised feature extraction algorithms, our model can learn powerful hierarchical feature representations for raw data without a user-defined constant.

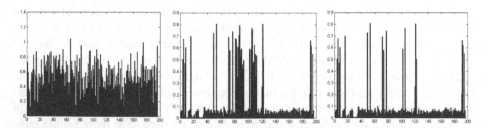

Fig. 2. Output of hidden units of RBM (left) and SR-RBM (mid) and our model (right).

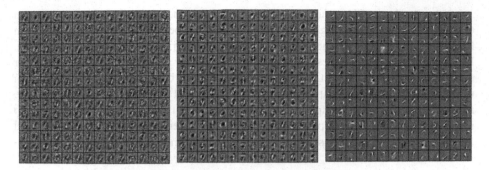

Fig. 3. Visualization of 196 bases of RBM (left) and SR-RBM (mid) and proposed model (right).

In order to prove our model, we test SRBM-SAQDEMO/D on CIFAR-10 dataset. The data set CIFAR-10 [43] consists of 32*32 color image including animals and vehicles. The CIFAR-10 dataset consists of 60000 color images in 10 classes, with 6000 images per class. There are 50000 training images and 10000 test images. The dataset is divided into five training batches and one test batch, each with 10000 images. The test batch contains exactly 1000 randomly-selected images from each class. The training batches contain the remaining images in random order, but some training batches may contain more images from one class than another. The training batches contain exactly 5000 images from each class.

The hidden units' number is 1000, the number of visible units is 3072, because CIFAR-10 is color image. The picture is 32*32*3, including three color pixels. Compared our model with RBM, SR-RBM with different trade-off parameter, we set the trade-off parameter λ to be 0.02, 0.04, 0.06. In SAQDEMO/D, the population $N = 50$, the stochastic data set Ds = 100, the max-generation = 100, the number of C closest weight vectors set is 20. To verify the discriminative power of the representation learnt, similar to previous experiments, their created representations are used to as input for the same linear classier, the training data set is set 100, 500, 1000, 5000 respectively, and the test data set is set 20, 100, 200, 100. All the data set is sampled from the CIFAR-10 data set. We test the dataset several times, for comparison, we choose the best results respectively. The error rate (%) is shown in Table 2.

Table 2. Error rate on CIFAR-10

Methods	Number of samples			
	100	500	1000	5000
RBM	87.34	86.71	82.36	61.01
SR-RBM (0.02)	86.12	85.56	81.36	54.11
SR-RBM (0.04)	84.32	84.12	80.21	53.36
SR-RBM (0.06)	85.15	85.10	82.51	53.82
Proposed model	**84.11**	**82.96**	**76.11**	**51.35**

Since the data set is natural image and images are more complex, the error rate on CIFAR-10 is higher than digit images. In Table 2, the best results were highlighted in bold, the statistical results show that our proposed model can get the lowest error rates. In SR-RBM achieves best results with $\lambda = 0.04$, and the RBM shows the highest error rates with a different data set. From the visualization of bases (see Fig. 4), RBM learn unstructured feature and feature of our proposed model is more regular. Because the natural picture is more complex, it is hard to capture the feature of picture in deep learning algorithm. Our proposed model performs better than the other unsupervised feature extraction algorithms and can learn powerful hierarchical feature representations for raw data.

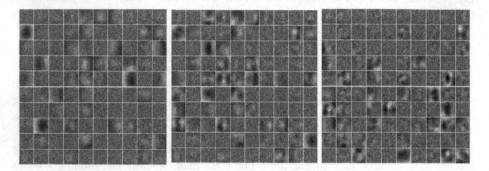

Fig. 4. Visualization of 196 bases of RBM (left) and SR-RBM (mid) and proposed model (right).

5 Conclusion

In this article, we proposed a sparse RBM based multiobjective optimization, the AQDEMO/D is used to optimize the hidden units bias term subject to distortion and sparsity. There have appeared many improved sparse features based on classic AE or RBM, this model achieved the small rate of code by introducing a sparsity-inducing term. We have to determine a constant which is a tradeoff between the sparsity term and reconstruction term, but selecting the constant by trial and error is time-consuming. In our proposed model, we overcome the disadvantage and propose a new idea for learning sparse feature. We employ a multiobjective optimization model to avoid a tradeoff parameter, and we convert the sparse feature learning problem into a multiobjective optimization problem with two conflicting objectives distortion function and sparsity of hidden units. In mops algorithm, we use the quantum states to obviate time consuming. The experiments is carried out on MNIST dataset and CIFAR-10 dataset, experimental results demonstrate proposed model is superior to both classical RBM and SR-RBM. There is a weakness in our model, the computational cost is high, especially in large scale data set. In future work, we hope some tricks are implemented to reduce the computational complexity, for example using Graphics process unit (GPU).

References

1. Felleman, D.J.: Distributed hierarchical processing in the primate cerebral cortex. Cereb. Cortex **1**(1), 1–47 (1991)
2. Lee, T.S.: Hierarchical Bayesian inference in the visual cortex. Opt. Soc. Am. A, Opt. Image Sci. Vis. **20**(7), 1434–1448 (2003)
3. Morris, G.: Anatomical funneling, sparse connectivity and redundancy reduction in the neural networks of the basal ganglia. Physiol.-Paris **97**(4–6), 581–589 (2003)
4. Kruger, N.: Deep hierarchies in the primate visual cortex: What can we learn for computer vision? IEEE Trans. Pattern Anal. Mach. Intell. **35**(8), 1847–1871 (2013)
5. Arel, I.: Deep machine learning—A new frontier in artificial intelligence research [research frontier]. IEEE Comput. Intell. Mag. **5**(4), 13–18 (2010)
6. Hou, W.: Blind image quality assessment via deep learning. IEEE Trans. Neural Netw. Learn. Syst. **26**(6), 1275–1286 (2015)
7. Silver, D.: Mastering the game of Go with deep neural networks and tree search. Nature **529**(7587), 484–489 (2015)
8. Xu, Y.: A regression approach to speech enhancement based on deep neural networks. IEEE/ACM Trans. Audio Speech Lang. Process. **23**(1), 7–19 (2015)
9. Krizhevsky, A., Sutskever, I.: ImageNet classification with deep convolutional neural networks. In: International Conference on Neural Information Processing Systems, vol. 25, pp. 1097–1105. Curran Associates Inc. (2012)
10. Karpathy, A., Toderici, G.: Large-scale video classification with convolutional neural networks. In: Proceedings of the IEEE conference Computer Vision and Pattern Recognition, pp. 1725–1732. IEEE (2014)
11. Sainath, T.N.: Deep convolutional neural networks for large-scale speech tasks. Neural Netw. **64**, 39–48 (2015)
12. Hinton, G.E., Sejnowski, T.J.: Learning and relearning in Boltzmann machines. In: Parallel distributed processing: explorations in the microstructure of cognition, vol. 1. MIT Press, pp. 45–76 (1986)
13. Fischer, A., Igel, C.: An introduction to restricted Boltzmann machines. In: Alvarez, L., Mejail, M., Gomez, L., Jacobo, J. (eds.) CIARP 2012. LNCS, vol. 7441, pp. 14–36. Springer, Heidelberg (2012). doi:10.1007/978-3-642-33275-3_2
14. Makhzani, A., Frey, B.: K-sparse autoencoders. Comput. Sci. (2013)
15. Rolfe, J.T.: Discriminative recurrent sparse auto-encoders. Comput. Sci. (2013)
16. Ranzato, M.: Sparse feature learning for deep belief networks. In: Proceedings of Advances in Neural Information Processing Systems, Vancouver, BC, Canada, pp. 1185–1192December (2007)
17. Lee, H.: Sparse deep belief net model for visual area V2. Adv. Neural. Inf. Process. Syst. **20**, 873–880 (2007)
18. Ji, N.-N.: A sparse-response deep belief network based on rate distortion theory. Pattern Recognit. **47**(9), 3179–3191 (2014)
19. Luo, H.: Sparse Group Restricted Boltzmann Machines. Statistics (2010)
20. Keyvanrad, M.A., Homayounpour, M.M.: Normal sparse deep belief network. In: International Joint Conference on Neural Networks, pp. 1–7 (2015)
21. Olshausen, B.A.: Emergence of simple-cell receptive field properties by learning a sparse code for natural images. Nature **381**(6583), 607–609 (1996)
22. Li, L.: An evolutionary multiobjective approach to sparse reconstruction. IEEE Trans. Evol. Comput. **8**(16), 827–845 (2014)

23. Chen, W.: Response surface and multiobjective optimization methodology for the design of compliant interconnects. IEEE Trans. Compon. Packag. Manuf. Technol. **4**(11), 1769–1777 (2014)
24. Garcia-Piquer, A.: Large-scale experimental evaluation of cluster representations for multiobjective evolutionary clustering. IEEE Trans. Evol. Comput. **18**(1), 36–53 (2014)
25. Svenson, J., Santner, T.: Multiobjective Optimization of Expensive-to-Evaluate Deterministic Computer Simulator Models. Elsevier Science Publishers B. V, Amsterdam (2016)
26. Asrari, A.: Pareto dominance-based multiobjective optimization method for distribution network reconfiguration. IEEE Trans. Smart Grid **7**(3), 1401–1410 (2016)
27. Csirmaz, L.: Using multiobjective optimization to map the entropy region. Comput. Optim. Appl. **1**, 1–23 (2016)
28. Branke, J.: Interactive evolutionary multiobjective optimization driven by robust ordinal regression. Bull. Pol. Acad. Sci. Tech. Sci. **58**(3), 347–358 (2016)
29. Gong, M.: A multiobjective sparse feature learning model for deep neural networks. IEEE Trans. Neural Netw. Learn. Syst. **26**(12), 3263–3277 (2015)
30. Li, Y.: Dynamic-context cooperative quantum-behaved particle swarm optimization based on multilevel thresholding applied to medical image segmentation. Inf. Sci. **294**, 408–422 (2015)
31. Cover, T.M.: Elements of Information Theory (Wiley Series in Telecommunications and Signal Processing). Wiley, Hoboken (2006)
32. Zhang, Q.: MOEA/D: a multiobjective evolutionary algorithm based on decomposition. IEEE Trans. Evol. Comput. **11**(6), 712–731 (2008)
33. Hillermeier, C.: Nonlinear Multiobjective Optimization. Birkhaüser Verlag, Basel (2001)
34. Venske, S.M.S., Gonçalves, R.A.: ADEMO/D: adaptive differential evolution for multiobjective problems. In: Brazilian Symposium on Neural Networks, pp. 226–231. IEEE (2012)
35. Rachmawati, L.: Multiobjective evolutionary algorithm with controllable focus on the knees of the Pareto front. IEEE Trans. Evol. Comput. **13**(4), 810–824 (2009)
36. Vincent, P.: Stacked denoising autoencoders: learning useful representations in a deep network with a local denoising criterion. J. Mach. Learn. Res. **11**(12), 3371–3408 (2010)
37. Davis, G.: Adaptive nonlinear approximations. Ph.D. dissertation, Department of Mathematics Courant Institute Mathematical Science, New York University, New York (1994)
38. Ng, A.Y.: Feature selection, L1 vs. L2 regularization, and rotational invariance. In: Proceedings of 21st International Conference Machine Learning, Banff, AB, Canada, pp. 379–387 (2004)
39. Lee, H., Battle, A.: Efficient sparse coding algorithms. In: Proceedings of Advances in Neural Information Processing Systems, Vancouver, BC, Canada, pp. 801–808 (2006)
40. Qin, A.K., Suganthan, P.N.: Self-adaptive differential evolution algorithm for numerical optimization. In: IEEE Congress on Evolutionary Computation, vol. 2, pp. 1785–1791 (2005)
41. Branke, J., Deb, K., Dierolf, H., Osswald, M.: Finding knees in multi-objective optimization. In: Yao, X., et al. (eds.) PPSN 2004. LNCS, vol. 3242, pp. 722–731. Springer, Heidelberg (2004). doi:10.1007/978-3-540-30217-9_73
42. The MNIST Database of Handwritten Digits. http://yann.lecun.com/exdb/mnist/
43. Learning Multiple Layers of Reatires from Tiny Images. Alex Krizhevsky (2009). http://www.cs.toronto.edu/~kriz/cifar.html/
44. Miettinen, K.: Nonlinear Multiobjective Optimization. Kluwer, Norwell (1999)

A Knee Point Driven Particle Swarm Optimization Algorithm for Sparse Reconstruction

Caitong Yue[1], Jing Liang[1(✉)], Boyang Qu[2], Hui Song[3], Guang Li[1], and Yuhong Han[4]

[1] School of Electrical Engineering, Zhengzhou University, Science Road. 100, Zhengzhou 450001, China
liangjing@zzu.edu.cn
[2] School of Electronic and Information Engineering, Zhongyuan University of Technology, Zhengzhou 450007, China
[3] Computer Science and Information Techonology, School of Science, RMIT University, Melbourne 3000, Australia
[4] MOE Key Lab of Specially Functional Materials and Institute of Optical Communication Materials, South China University of Technology, Wushan Road. 381, Guangzhou 510000, China

Abstract. Sparse reconstruction is a technique to reconstruct sparse signal from a small number of samples. In sparse reconstruction problems, the sparsity and measurement error should be minimized simultaneously, therefore they can be solved by multi-objective optimization algorithms. Most multi-objective optimizers aim to obtain the complete Pareto front. However only solutions in knee region of Pareto front are preferred in sparse reconstruction problems. It is a waste of time to obtain the whole Pareto front. In this paper, a knee point driven multi-objective particle swarm optimization algorithm (KnMOPSO) is proposed to solve sparse reconstruction problems. KnMOPSO aims to find the local part of Pareto front so that it can solve the sparse reconstruction problems fast and accurately. In KnMOPSO personal best particles and global best particle are selected with knee point selection scheme. In addition, solutions which are more likely to be knee points are preferred to others.

Keywords: Sparse reconstruction · Compressed sensing · Knee point · Multi-objective PSO

1 Introduction

Sparse reconstruction is originally generated from compressed sensing (CS) [1] and becomes a popular topic in recent years. It is widely used in signal processing, machine learning and computer vision [2–4]. Generally speaking, CS includes sparse representation, encoding measuring and sparse reconstruction. Sparse

© Springer International Publishing AG 2017
Y. Shi et al. (Eds.): SEAL 2017, LNCS 10593, pp. 911–919, 2017.
https://doi.org/10.1007/978-3-319-68759-9_74

reconstruction is a quite important component in CS. The sparse reconstruction problems can be modeled as:

$$\min_{x} \quad \|x\|_0 \quad s.t. \quad y = Ax \tag{1}$$

where $x = (x_1, x_2, \ldots x_n)^{\mathrm{T}}$ represents sparse signal (only a few components of the signal are non-zero and the rest are zero); A is $m \times n$ sensing matrix; $y = (y_1, y_2, \ldots y_m)$ is observation vector; $\|x\|_0$ represents the sparsity (the number of nonzero components) of x. The length of y is much smaller than x i.e. $m \ll n$. It is obvious that (1) is a constrained optimization problem. It is often converted into a single-objective optimization problem as:

$$\min_{x} \quad \|y - Ax\|_2^2 + \lambda \|x\|_0 \tag{2}$$

where $\|y - Ax\|_2^2$ is measurement error; λ is a positive weight balancing measurement error and sparsity. However, parameter λ is difficult to set, because it depends on specific characteristics of optimization problem. An effective way to deal with constrained problems is converting them into multi-objective optimization problems [5]. Thus, problem (1) is converted into multi-objective sparse reconstruction problem as:

$$\min_{x} \quad \left\{ \|x\|_0, \ \|y - Ax\|_2^2 \right\} \tag{3}$$

In (3), sparsity and measurement error are considered as two conflicting objectives. Li et al. [6] proposed a soft-thresholding evolutionary multi-objective algorithm (StEMO) to solve (3). In StEMO, soft-thresholding algorithm is embedded in NSGAII [7] to increase the convergence speed and improve the spread of solutions along the Pareto front (PF). StEMO tries to find the whole PF of sparse optimization problem. In 2012, Li [8] proposed a revised version of MOEA/D [9,10] to find the local part of trade-off solutions to sparse reconstruction problems. However, the range of sparsity should be provided. In fact, it has been proven in [6] that only solutions in knee region of Pareto front are preferred in multi-objective sparse reconstruction problems. In multi-objective optimization, knee point is one of the Pareto optimal solutions for which a tiny improvement in one objective will result in a severe degradation in at least another objective [11]. Knee region is the neighboring area of knee point in Pareto front, which is shown in Fig. 1. In this paper, a knee point driven multi-objective particle swarm optimization algorithm (KnMOPSO) is proposed to solve sparse reconstruction problems.

The contributions of this paper are as follows. Firstly, an angle-based knee point selection method is embedded in multi-objective particle swarm optimization. Secondly, maximal angle in angle-based knee point selection method is adopted as a second indicator in environmental selection. Thirdly, iterative half threshholding algorithm is employed in KnMOPSO as local search method. Fourthly, KnMOPSO is compared with five state-of-the-art sparse reconstruction algorithms on five test instances. In addition, KnMOPSO is applied to

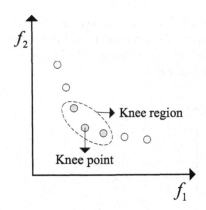

Fig. 1. The illustration of knee point and knee region.

reconstruct the signals in Sparco [12] which is a testing framework for sparse reconstruction.

The reminder of this paper is organized as follows. Section 2 introduces related works and motivation. Section 3 presents the details of the proposed algorithm; Experimental results are given in Sect. 4. The paper is concluded in Sect. 5.

2   Related Works and Motivation

Particle swarm optimizer (PSO) [13,14] searches optima by simulating the way bird flock foraging. It is first proposed to solve single-objective optimization problems. In PSO, the particles are led by global best particle (**gbest**) and personal best particle (**pbest**) to the optimal position. The position of ith particle is updated according to:

$$P_i(t) = P_i(t-1) + v_i(t) \tag{4}$$

where $P_i(t)$ is the position of ith particle at t^{th} generation; $v_i(t)$ represents the velocity of ith particle. The velocity of ith particle is updated according to:

$$v_i(t) = wv_i(t-1) + C_1r_1(\textbf{pbest}_i - \textbf{x}_i) + C_2r_2(\textbf{gbest} - \textbf{x}_i) \tag{5}$$

where w is inertia weight; C_1 and C_2 are parameters to control the trade-off between **pbest** and **gbest**; r_1 and r_2 are random numbers between 0 and 1.

As a population based evolutionary algorithm, PSO is suitable for multi-objective optimization. Most of the existing multi-objective PSO algorithms aim to derive the complete PF of the multi-objective optimization problem. Experimental results in [6] showed that knee region existed in multi-objective sparse optimization problems and the solutions in knee region were favored. Therefore we try to design a novel multi-objective PSO which can obtain knee region in sparse reconstruction problems. In the proposed algorithm, particles which are likely to be the knee point is selected as leaders. In addition, particles that are far away from knee region are removed in environmental selection. Therefore, the population converge to knee region fast and accurately. The expected evolutionary process is shown in Fig. 2.

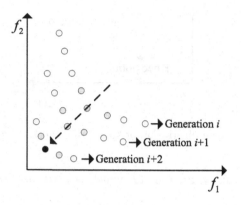

Fig. 2. The expected evolutionary process.

3   Details of Knee Point Driven Multi-objective Particle Swarm Optimization Algorithm

In this section, the proposed algorithm, knee point driven multi-objective PSO (KnMOPSO), is described in detail. Firstly, the general framework of KnMOPSO is presented. Secondly, knee point selection method is described in detail. Then, the local search strategy, iterative half thresholding algorithm, is introduced. Finally, the environmental selection scheme is described in detail.

The general framework of KnMOPSO is presented as follows. Firstly, randomly initialize the population P in the feasible region. Two external elitism archives, global best archive (GBA) and personal best archive (PBA), are established to store the history information. GBA is the global best archive of the swarm and the non-dominated history positions of the swarm are stored in GBA. PBA_i represents the personal best archive of the ith particle and the non-dominated history positions of the ith particle are stored in PBA_i. Then the knee points of these two archives are chosen as $gbest$ and $pbest_i$ respectively. The position and velocity of each particle are updated according to (4) and (5). To make sure the updated solution is sparse, iterative half thresholding is adopted as local search method. After the local search, PBA_i and GBA are updated. Particles in PBA_i and GBA are firstly sorted according to non-dominated relationship. If the number of non-dominated solutions is larger than predefined number, the extra particles are removed according to environmental selection scheme. Repeat the above processes until termination condition is satisfied. The procedure of KnMOPSO is shown in Algorithm 1.

Algorithm 1. KnMOPSO

1: Step 1: Initialize
2:   Randomly generate P in feasible region, $GBA = P$, $PBA_i = P_i$ ($1 \leq i \leq$ $populationsize$)
3: **repeat**
4:   Step 2: Select $gbest$ and $pbest_i$
5:     $gbest = $ knee point selection (GBA)
6:     $pbest_i = $ knee point selection (PBA_i)
7:   Step 3: Update $P_i(t)$ according to (4)
8:   Step 4: Local search
9:     $Pl_i(t) = $ iterative half threshholding $(P_i(t))$
10:   Step 5: Update PBA_i and GBA
11:   **for** $i = 1$; $i < populationsize$; $i + +$ **do**
12:     $PBA_i(t) = $ non-dominated selection$(PBA_i(t-1), Pl_i(t))$
13:     **if** size $(PBA_i(t)) >$ maximal number of PBA_i **then**
14:       Remove the extra particles from $PBA_i(t)$
15:     **end if**
16:   **end for**
17:   $GBA(t)=$non-dominated-selection$(PBA(t))$
18:   **if** size $(GBA(t)) >$ maximal number of GBA **then**
19:     Remove the extra particles from $GBA(t)$
20:   **end if**
21: **until** The termination condition is satisfied
22: **return** the knee point in GBA

The process of angle-based knee point selection method [15] is shown in Fig. 3. Four angles between the current particle and its neighbors are computed. Then the maximal angle is chosen as the angle of current particle. The angles of particles on the boundary is set to zero. The particle with the maximal angle is chosen as the knee point.

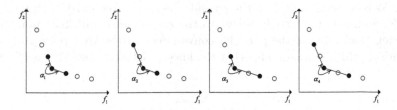

Fig. 3. Angle-based knee point selection method.

Iterative half thresholding algorithm [16] is a $L_{1/2}$ regulation method to solve sparse optimization problems. The $L_{1/2}$ regulation algorithm is able to find sparser solutions than L_1 regulation and it is verified to be a powerful method for sparse optimization problems. Iterative half thresholding algorithm is a fast solver to $L_{1/2}$ regulation and it has three main steps, which are gradient descent, regularization parameter optimization, and truncation of the small components in the signal. The truncation mechanism is as follow:

$$f_{q,1/2}(\boldsymbol{x}_i) = \begin{cases} \frac{2}{3}\left[1 + \cos(\frac{2}{3}\pi) - \frac{2}{3}\varphi_q(\boldsymbol{x}_i)\right] & \text{if } |\boldsymbol{x}_i| > \frac{\sqrt[3]{54}}{4}q^{\frac{2}{3}} \\ 0 & \text{otherwise} \end{cases} \tag{6}$$

where $\boldsymbol{x}_i$ is the ith dimension of the signal $\boldsymbol{x}$; $\varphi_q(\boldsymbol{x}_i) = \arccos(\frac{q}{8}(\frac{|\boldsymbol{x}_i|}{3})^{\frac{3}{2}})$; q is the regularization parameter.

Two selection indicators, dominated relationship and maximal angle in Fig. 3, are employed in the environmental selection. After local search, the population $Pl_i(t)$, and personal best archive at the previous generation, $PBA_i(t-1)$, are combined. Then, non-dominated solutions are selected in the combined population (line 12 of Algorithm 1). If the size of non-dominated solutions is larger than maximal number of PBA_i, all the non-dominated solutions are sorted in descending order according to maximal angles (introduced in Fig. 3). The particles with small angles are removed. GBA is updated in the same way with PBA_i.

4   Experimental Results

In order to verify the effectiveness of proposed algorithm, three different kinds of experiments are carried out. The parameters are set as follows. In (5), the inertia weight ω is set to 0.7298 and the constants, C_1 and C_2, are all set to 2.05 according to [17]. The population size is set to 50. The maximal number of GBA is equal to the population size and the maximal number of PBA_i is one fifth of the population size. The number of iterations in half thresholding algorithm is set to 10 according to [8].

Firstly, KnMOPSO is tested on a sparse signal with the length of 512, sparsity of 130, and 300 observations to show the evolutionary process of population. The distributions of population in the 2nd, 5th and 40th generation are shown in Fig. 4. As is shown in Fig. 4, in the second generation, the particles spread along the PF. Some of the particles move to the neighborhood of knee point in the 5th generation. Most of the particles convergence to the knee point in the 40th generation, which demonstrates that the knee point driven scheme is effective.

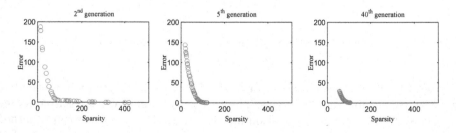

Fig. 4. The evolution of the population

Secondly, KnMOPSO is compared with MOEA/D-iHalfT [8], StEMO [6], MP [18], OMP [19] and Homotopy [20] on five sparse instances named I1–I5. The way to generate sparse instances refers to [21]. The information of I1–I5 is shown in Table 1. All the experiments are carried out 50 times. The mean values and standard deviations of measurement errors are shown in Table 2. It can be concluded that KnMOPSO achieves the smallest measurement errors on all test instances and it performs best on I1. OMP ranks second among all algorithms. MOEA/D-iHalfT performs relatively better on noiseless instances, I1 and I2, than instances with noise, like I3-I5. The measurement errors of StEMO are the largest on all test instances, because it aims to find the whole PF and tries to improve the diversity of PF.

Thirdly, KnMOPSO is employed to reconstruct sign spikes and gausspike signals in Sparco [12]. The original and reconstructed signals of sign spikes and

Table 1. Information of test instances

Instance name	Signal length	Number of observations	Sparsity	Variance of noise
I1	512	300	130	0
I2	512	260	130	0
I3	512	300	130	0.01
I4	512	260	130	0.01
I5	5120	2600	1300	0.01

Table 2. Measurement error

Algorithm name	I1	I2	I3	I4	I5
KnMOPSO	0.0050 ± 0.0059	0.0177 ± 0.0125	0.0189 ± 0.0057	0.0209 ± 0.0171	0.2911 ± 0.1635
MOEA/D-iHalfT	0.0646 ± 0.1508	0.0552 ± 0.1136	0.1837 ± 0.1134	0.1058 ± 0.0409	0.9105 ± 0.6552
StEMO	20.5647 ± 8.1449	29.5317 ± 10.5126	29.7182 ± 9.7391	29.9125 ± 9.3755	39.2327 ± 10.9593
MP	0.0862 ± 0.0122	0.1062 ± 0.0142	2.2139 ± 0.0124	2.4753 ± 0.0121	18.4469 ± 0.4541
OMP	0.0202 ± 0.0094	$0.0226 + 0.0084$	0.0312 ± 0.0003	0.0318 ± 0.0005	3.9406 ± 0.3393
Homotopy	13.7821 ± 2.7975	14.8489 ± 2.3467	15.1430 ± 3.1768	15.8337 ± 2.7786	51.5402 ± 1.0463

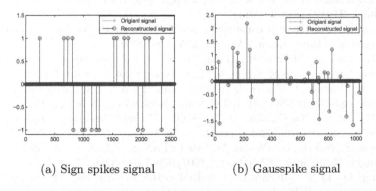

(a) Sign spikes signal   (b) Gausspike signal

Fig. 5. The comparison of original and reconstructed signals in Sparco

gausspike are shown in Fig. 5. As shown, the reconstructed signals are very close to original signals.

5 Conclusions

In this paper, a knee point driven multi-objective PSO is proposed aiming to obtain only the knee region of Pareto front in sparse reconstruction problem. Angle-based knee point selection method is employed in the proposed algorithm. Non-dominated relationship and knee point measurements act as two selection indicators in environmental selection. Experimental results show that the knee point driven scheme is able to drive the population to knee region. The proposed algorithm is compared with five sparse reconstruction algorithms on five test instances and KnMOPSO achieves the smallest error.

Acknowledgement. We acknowledge financial support by National Natural Science Foundation of China (61473266, 61673404, 61305080, and U1304602), China Post-doctoral Science Foundation (No. 2014M552013), Project supported by the Research Award Fund for Outstanding Young Teachers in Henan Provincial Institutions of Higher Education of China (2014GGJS-004) and Program for Science and Technology Innovation Talents in Universities of Henan Province in China (16HASTIT041).

References

1. Candès, E.J., Romberg, J., Tao, T.: Robust uncertainty principles: exact signal reconstruction from highly incomplete frequency information. IEEE Trans. Inf. Theory **52**, 489–509 (2006)
2. Lu, X., Li, X.: Group sparse reconstruction for image segmentation. Neurocomputing **136**, 41–48 (2014)
3. Shi, Y., Gao, Y., Liao, S., Zhang, D., Gao, Y., Shen, D.: A learning-based CT prostate segmentation method via joint transductive feature selection and regression. Neurocomputing **173**, 317–331 (2016)
4. Xu, Y., Zhang, D., Yang, J., Yang, J.Y.: A two-phase test sample sparse representation method for use with face recognition. IEEE Trans. Circ. Syst. Video Technol. **21**, 1255–1262 (2011)
5. Coello, C.A.C.: Treating constraints as objectives for single-objective evolutionary optimization. Eng. Optim.+A35 **32**, 275–308 (2000)
6. Li, L., Yao, X., Stolkin, R., Gong, M., He, S.: An evolutionary multiobjective approach to sparse reconstruction. IEEE Trans. Evol. Comput. **18**, 827–845 (2014)
7. Deb, K., Pratap, A., Agarwal, S., Meyarivan, T.: A fast and elitist multiobjective genetic algorithm: NSGA-II. IEEE Trans. Evol. Comput. **6**, 182–197 (2002)
8. Li, H., Su, X., Xu, Z., Zhang, Q.: MOEA/D with iterative thresholding algorithm for sparse optimization problems. In: Coello, C.A.C., Cutello, V., Deb, K., Forrest, S., Nicosia, G., Pavone, M. (eds.) PPSN 2012. LNCS, vol. 7492, pp. 93–101. Springer, Heidelberg (2012). doi:10.1007/978-3-642-32964-7_10
9. Zhang, Q., Li, H.: MOEA/D: a multiobjective evolutionary algorithm based on decomposition. IEEE Trans. Evol. Comput. **11**, 712–731 (2007)

10. Zhang, C., Tan, K.C., Gao, L., Wu, Q.: Multi-objective evolutionary algorithm based on decomposition for engineering optimization. J. Zhengzhou Univ. (Eng. Sci.) **36**, 38–46 (2015)
11. Zhang, X., Tian, Y., Jin, Y.: A knee point-driven evolutionary algorithm for many-objective optimization. IEEE Trans. Evol. Comput. **19**, 761–776 (2015)
12. Berg, E., Friedlander, M.P.: Sparco. (http://www.cs.ubc.ca/labs/scl/sparco/)
13. Kennedy, J.: Particle swarm optimization. In: Sammut, C., Webb, G.I. (eds.) Encyclopedia of Machine Learning, pp. 760–766. Springer, Heidelberg (2011). doi:10.1007/978-0-387-30164-8_630
14. Yan, X., Yan, J., Feng, Y.: Gradient and particle swarm optimization based hierarchical cluster algorithm in WSN. J. Zhengzhou Univ. (Eng. Sci.) **2**, 007 (2016)
15. Branke, J., Deb, K., Dierolf, H., Osswald, M.: Finding knees in multi-objective optimization. In: Yao, X., Burke, E.K., Lozano, J.A., Smith, J., Merelo-Guervós, J.J., Bullinaria, J.A., Rowe, J.E., Tiňo, P., Kabán, A., Schwefel, H.-P. (eds.) PPSN 2004. LNCS, vol. 3242, pp. 722–731. Springer, Heidelberg (2004). doi:10.1007/978-3-540-30217-9_73
16. Xu, Z., Chang, X., Xu, F., Zhang, H.: $L_{1/2}$ regularization: a thresholding representation theory and a fast solver. IEEE Trans. Neural Netw. Learn. Syst. **23**, 1013–1027 (2012)
17. Clerc, M., Kennedy, J.: The particle swarm-explosion, stability, and convergence in a multidimensional complex space. IEEE Trans. Evol. Comput. **6**, 58–73 (2002)
18. Mallat, S.G., Zhang, Z.: Matching pursuits with time-frequency dictionaries. IEEE Trans. Signal Process. **41**, 3397–3415 (1993)
19. Tropp, J., Gilbert, A.C.: Signal recovery from partial information via orthogonal matching pursuit. IEEE Trans. Inf. Theory **53**, 4655–4666 (2007)
20. Malioutov, D.M., Cetin, M., Willsky, A.S.: Homotopy continuation for sparse signal representation. In: 2005 IEEE International Conference on Proceedings of Acoustics, Speech, and Signal Processing (ICASSP 2005), pp. 733–736. IEEE (2005)
21. Li, H., Fan, Y., Zhang, Q., Xu, Z., Deng, J.: A multi-phase multiobjective approach based on decomposition for sparse reconstruction. In: IEEE Congress on Evolutionary Computation, pp. 601–608. IEEE (2016)

Multivariant Optimization Algorithm with Bimodal-Gauss

Baolei Li[1,2,3], Jing Liang[1(✉)], Caitong Yue[1], and Boyang Qu[3]

[1] School of Electrical Engineering, Zhengzhou University,
Science Road. 100, Zhengzhou 450001, China
liangjing@zzu.edu.cn
[2] Oil Equipment Intelligent Control Engineering Laboratory of Henan Province,
School of Physics and Electronic Engineering, Nanyang Normal University,
Nanyang 473061, China
[3] School of Electronic and Information Engineering,
Zhongyuan University of Technology, Zhengzhou 450007, China

Abstract. In multimodal problems, there is a trade-off between exploration and exploitation. Exploration contributes to move quickly toward the area where better solutions existed but is not beneficial for improving the quality of intermediate solution. Exploitation do well in refine the intermediate solution but increase the risk of being trapped into local optimum. Considering the trade-off and advantage of exploration and exploitation, a local search strategy based on bimodal-gauss was embedded into multivariant optimization algorithm by increasing the probability of locating global optima in solving multimodal optimization problems. The performances of the proposed method were compared with that of other multimodal optimization algorithms based on benchmark functions and the experimental results show the superiority of the proposed method. Convergence process of each subgroup was analyzed based on convergence curve.

Keywords: Multivariant optimization algorithm · Bimodal-gauss · Multimodal optimization · Swarm optimization · Exploration · Exploitation

1 Introduction

In swarm optimization algorithms, although genetic algorithm (GA) and particle swarm optimization (PSO) have been the proverbial techniques, they are limited for being inclined to be trapped into local optima or causing the premature convergence or failing in converging due to the confusion introduced by the presence of multiple optimal solutions in multimodal optimization problems.

To improve the probability of locating global optima in multimodal problems, many improved methods were proposed [1]. Liang proposed Comprehensive Learning Particle Swarm Algorithm (CLPSO) by using a novel learning strategy whereby all other particles' historical best information is used to update

© Springer International Publishing AG 2017
Y. Shi et al. (Eds.): SEAL 2017, LNCS 10593, pp. 920–928, 2017.
https://doi.org/10.1007/978-3-319-68759-9_75

a particle's velocity [2]. It has been shown that multiple cooperative evolution algorithms perform better than a single evolution algorithm (EA) in global optimization problems [3]. Then, a novel adaptive framework named as Population-based Algorithm Portfolios(PAP) is proposed through choosing the most appropriate one from the integrated EAs automatically [4]. Sampling by Gauss and Cauchy function at random has shown improvement in balancing exploration and exploitation [5]. Recently, a random drift particle swarm optimization with frequent coverage strategy, where not all but some randomly chosen dimensions were changed to generate new solutions, was proposed to solve high-dimension problems [6]. A novel diversity preservation scheme that directly promotes diversity at the level of search behaviors rather than merely trying to maintain diversity among candidate solutions was realize by negatively correlated search and achieved the best overall performance on 20 multimodal continuous optimization problems [7]. A history-based topological speciation (HTS) is proposed to make full use of search history. It relies exclusively on search history to capture the landscape topography and, therefore, does not require any additional fitness evaluations to be performed [8]. A guiding spark has been proved to improve the firework algorithm by means of historical information utilization [9]. The guiding spark increases the probability of moving forward the right direction. However, there are still rooms to improve the performance of swarm optimization algorithms in complex multimodal problems, including low dimension problems with countless local traps and high dimension problems whose local traps grow exponentially as the number of dimension increases [10,11]. The main reasons are as follows. Firstly, the located optima are rely likely on the initial distribution of individuals, because the local or global optima are too many to be covered [12]. Secondly, In a D dimensional orthogonal coordinate system, there exist 2^d directions. The probability of moving forward along the sole right direction is $\frac{1}{2^d}$ which is considerably small when d is large. Thirdly, the time complexity of finding the neighbors of each individual is significantly increased in some algorithms with multiple groups. The last but not least, the fitness landscapes of different problems have various characteristics, which make it difficult to set a suitable parameter for each problem.

As a result, an effective multimodal optimization algorithm should have the following characters, such as, giving consideration to both exploration and exploitation, having the ability of finding a promising direction, light complexity, having no parameter needed to set carefully [13]. Inspired by multivariant divisions of labor and strategies, the use of historical information, the Multivariant Optimization Algorithm (MOA) was proposed [14]. In MOA, Atoms search the solution space through alternating global-local search iterations where global exploration atoms explore the whole solution space to locate potential areas and then each potential area is allotted a group of atoms for local exploitation. Multivariant search groups are used to implement the global exploration and the local exploitation simultaneously, which helps to overcome the trade-off between global exploration ability and local exploitation ability.

However, the parameter (r), which determines the size of local potential areas, in MOA is troublesome. Large r is bad for accuracy of solution; small r increases the risk of premature convergence. To relieve MOA's sensibility to r, bimodal-gauss function was used to change r in this paper. The first modal tends to generate a small r, the second modal tends to generate a large r. The proposed method decreases the probability of premature convergence, due to large r, while guaranteeing the accuracy of solution by means of small r. The probability distribution of bimodal-gauss function, i.e., the mean and variance are adjusted according to the historical information.

In order to evaluate the performance of MOA with bimodal-gauss, contrast experiments based on benchmark functions are conducted. The results show that the proposed method improved the quality of solution.

2 Method

2.1 Multivariant Optimization Algorithm

In the MOA search process, global search atoms search the global space to locate potential areas and then local search atoms search each potential local area in detail to improve the results. After sufficient global-local search iterations multiple optimal solutions are located. For a multimodal problem which has d variables and m global optima. A global search atom $\mathbf{A}_g$ is generated according to

$$\mathbf{A}_g = [unifrnd(min_1, max_1), \cdots, unifrnd(min_d, max_d)] \tag{1}$$

where min_i and max_i are the lower and upper bounds for the ith variable, $unifrnd(min_i, max_i)$ returns a random number chosen from the continuous uniform distribution on the interval from min_i to max_i.

A local search atom $\mathbf{A}_l$ in the local area centering at the global atom $\mathbf{A}_g$ is generated according to

$$\mathbf{A}_l = \mathbf{A}_g + \frac{r}{\|h_1, \cdots, h_d\|}[h_1, \cdots, h_d] \tag{2}$$

where h_i is a continuous uniform distribution random value in [-1,1], r is the radius of local area.

2.2 The Efficiency of MOA

According to (1), the probability of generating a global atom at any point in the whole search space is the same. Thus, the probability of being generated in an area can by calculated by $\frac{S_a}{S_{tol}}$ where S_a is the hyper-volume of this area, S_{tol} is the total hyper-volume of the whole search space.

The probability of being generated in one of the attractive regions of global optima can be calculated by

$$P_g = \frac{\sum_1^m S_i}{S_{tol}} \tag{3}$$

where S_i is hyper-volume of the ith global optimum's attractive region.

In a local area of d-dimensional hyperspace, there are 2^d directions, and only one direction is toward the global or local optimum. For a local atom, the probability of drifting toward the global or local optimum can be calculated by

$$P_l = \frac{1}{2^d} \tag{4}$$

For a local atom, the probability of jumping out of the local optimum can be calculated by

$$P_j = \frac{S(B(\mathbf{A}_g))}{S(A(\mathbf{A}_g, r))} \tag{5}$$

where $S(A(\mathbf{A}_g, r))$ is hyper-volume of the local search area $A(\mathbf{A}_g, r)$ which is centered at $\mathbf{A}_g$ with a radius r. $S(B(\mathbf{A}_g))$ is hyper-volume of the area $B(\mathbf{A}_g)$ which is a part of $A(\mathbf{A}_g, r)$ but is not in the attractive region of the local optimum and any solutions in $B(\mathbf{A}_g)$ is better than $\mathbf{A}_g$. The value of r and size of $B(\mathbf{A}_g)$ have a great effect on the value of P_j. As a result, it is not easy to find a suitable value for r. The efficiency of MOA is depended on P_g and P_l.

2.3   MOA with Bimodal-Gauss

In MOA algorithm, an atom stands for a candidate solution of the optimization problem. The atoms are in two types: global search atoms and local search atoms. Global search atoms are generated uniformly at random in the resolution space and local search atoms are generated in the neighborhood of the global atoms recorded.

The proposed MOA algorithm searches the solution space by the steps illustrated in Table 1.

To improve P_l, one local atom is generated according to

$$\mathbf{A}_l = \mathbf{A}_g + \frac{\mu_1 \times rand}{\|\mathbf{A}_g - \bar{\mathbf{A}}_l\|}[\mathbf{A}_g - \bar{\mathbf{A}}_l] \tag{6}$$

where $\bar{\mathbf{A}}_l$ is the worst one in remembered local atoms found during the searching process. $rand$ is a uniform random number between 0 and 1. It can be seen that $\mathbf{A}_g$ moves in the direction which is obtained by learning from historical information.

To improve the quality of global atom in converged stage, one local atom is generated according to

$$\mathbf{A}_l = \frac{1}{n}\sum_{i=1}^{n}\mathbf{A}_l^i \tag{7}$$

where n is number of better atoms in each subgroup remembered during the searching process.

To improve P_j, the other local search atoms in the local area centering at the global atom $\mathbf{A}_g$ is generated according to the probability density

$$\mathbf{A}_l = \mathbf{A}_g + \frac{r}{\|h_1, \cdots, h_d\|}[h_1, \cdots, h_d]$$
$$P(r) = \frac{1}{\delta_1\sqrt{2\pi}}e^{-\frac{(r-\mu_1)^2}{2\delta_1^2}} + \frac{1}{\delta_2\sqrt{2\pi}}e^{-\frac{(r-\mu_2)^2}{2\delta_2^2}} \tag{8}$$

Table 1. Flow of proposed MOA

	Proposed MOA
Step1	Set the initial parameters of the MOA algorithm: the number of global atoms N, the number of each local-atom group and the maximum number of iterations
Step2	Generate and evaluate local search atoms. For each remembered global atoms, a group of local-atoms are generated in its neighborhood to refine the global atom or jump out of local trap
Step3	Update each local information. Compare the fitness value of each new atom with the atoms in the corresponding local area. If a new atom is better than the global atom, they should swap places. As well, the parameters of bimodal-gauss function should be updated. The redundant local atoms should be forgot to keep the size of the local-atom group
Step4	Generate and evaluate global search atoms. Firstly, generate a global atom, if it belongs to any domain of the remembered global atom, regenerate one to replace it, until the required number of global atom are generated. Secondly, evaluate each new global atom
Step5	Update the global information. Compare the fitness value of each new global atom with the remembered global atoms. If a new global atom is better than a remembered atom, the worst one in the remembered global atoms will be replaced by the new one. If the distance of two global atom is less than $\mu_1(0)$ the worse one will be abandoned
Step6	Check the termination criterion. If the iteration number reach its maximum, the algorithm will stop. Otherwise, return to Step 2

where r is a continuous bimodal-gauss distribution random value. The means and standard deviations of the two modes are (μ_1, δ_1) and (μ_2, δ_2), respectively.

For minimization problems, these parameters of bimodal-gauss function are adjusted according to the historical information which can be calculated by

$$
\begin{aligned}
&\mu_1(k+1) = \begin{cases} \mu_1(k), & if \quad \mathbf{A}_g(k+1) \neq \mathbf{A}_g(k) \\ (1+p\lambda)\mu_1(k), & if \quad \mathbf{A}_g(k+1) = \mathbf{A}_g(k) \end{cases} \\
&p = -p, \quad if \quad \mu_1 < \zeta \quad or \quad \mu_1 > \frac{1}{2d}\sum_{i=1}^{d}|max_i - min_i| \\
&\delta_1(k+1) = 0.5\mu_1(k+1) \\
&\mu_2(k+1) = \begin{cases} \frac{1}{3}\|\mathbf{A}_g^i(k) - \mathbf{A}_g^{i+1}(k)\|, i > N \\ \frac{1}{3}\|\mathbf{A}_g^i(k) - \mathbf{A}_g^1(k)\|, i = N \end{cases} \\
&\delta_2(k+1) = 0.5|\mu_2(k+1) - 2\mu_1(k+1)|
\end{aligned}
\tag{9}
$$

where N is number of global atoms, ζ is the required accuracy, the initial value of p is 1, $\mu_1(0) = 0.1\sqrt{\frac{1}{d}\sum_{i=1}^{d}|max_i - min_i|}$. From (9) we can obtain the figure of the designed bimodal-gaussfunction illustrated as Fig. 1.

It can be seen from Fig. 1 that the first mode has a high probability to generate small radius value; as a result, the accuracy of solution is guaranteed. What is more, the second mode is likely to generate large radius value, which is helpful to move quickly toward the optimum and to jump out of local trap.

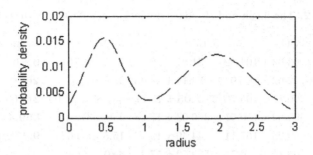

Fig. 1. Bimodal-gaussfunction

To improve the efficiency in high-dimension problems, the r generated by the first mode is used to generate a new solution through changing a randomly chosen dimension according

$$\mathbf{A}_l = \begin{cases} \mathbf{A}_l^i = \mathbf{A}_g^i + \frac{r}{\|h_i\|}h_i, & if \quad the \quad i^{th} \quad dimension \quad is \quad chosen \\ \mathbf{A}_l^i = \mathbf{A}_g^i, & else \end{cases} \tag{10}$$

3 Experiment

To compare the convergence accuracy of the proposed method with that of CLPSO and MOA, an experiment with 30 independent runs based on benchmark functions from [15,16] is carried out. The convergence is discussed based on the convergence curve. In this paper, CF1–CF6 in [15] is renamed as F1–F6 and CF1–CF6 in [16] is renamed as F7–F12, the dimension is 10, for each dimension $min_i = -5$ and $max_i = 5$. ζ is 0.01

3.1 Settings for Algorithms

In this experiment, $N = 4$ for F1–F6 and $N = 12$ for F7–F12, the number of each local group is suggested to be two times the dimension, so it is 20 in this paper. The maximum iteration number is 1000.

3.2 Simulation Results and Discussion

The results summarized in Table 2 are in the format: the mean $\pm$ the standard deviation of solutions' fitness values in 30 runs. The result of PSO, CLPSO and MOA were from [14].

Compare between PSO and CLPSO showed the power of comprehensive learning. Compare between CLPSO and MOA suggested that MOA improved the quality of located solutions except for F2 and F4. The reason may lie in that there are not subgroups in PSO or CLPSO. It is hard to give consideration to both exploration and exploitation for only one group of searchers. Multiple subgroups are assigned into different attractive basins in MOA, as a result, the

Table 2. The mean and standard deviation of solutions' fitness values

Function	PSO	CLPSO	MOA	Proposed MOA
F1	93.33 ± 104.82	31.81 ± 20.81	7.91 ± 1.761	$\mathbf{0 \pm 0}$
F2	122.02 ± 86.79	84.14 ± 23.63	58.1 ± 8.72	$\mathbf{26.91 \pm 35.44}$
F3	266.11 ± 105.75	$\mathbf{201.05 \pm 23.11}$	355.82 ± 53.05	212.63 ± 69.08
F4	392.62 ± 150.51	366.93 ± 17.68	436 ± 37.01	$\mathbf{359.41 \pm 41.74}$
F5	99.25 ± 167.11	44.49 ± 19	15.55 ± 2.02	$\mathbf{9.47 \pm 8.82}$
F6	802.11 ± 170.7	532.52 ± 57.3	$\mathbf{480 \pm 44.48}$	495.39 ± 67.74

confusion caused by multiple attractive basin are relieved. A subgroup in one basin has a high probability to converge into a local or global optimum, and the exploration in each iteration makes it is possible to jump out of local trap. We can conclude that multiple subgroups and multiple search strategies, including exploration and exploitation, can improve the probability of locating global optimum with high accuracy in complex multimodal problems.

Compare between MOA and the proposed MOA show the effectiveness of bimodal-gauss function. The proposed MOA performed better than MOA on all test functions except F6. The main new factor of the proposed MOA is that the radium of local search area is adaptive changing, the second mode of bimodal-gauss function guarantees that most of the search space is covered by search atoms so that the probability of locating any solution is larger than zero, what is more it's helpful to jump out of local trap. The first modal of bimodal-gauss function has two capacities, one is that large radium makes local atoms moves to the attractive pot quickly, the other is a small radium bring about fine movement toward the optimum. Above all, it is reasonable that the performance of MOA is enhanced by adjusting the size of local area based on bimodal-gauss function.

To analyze the convergence process of each subgroup, the mean fitness value over 30 runs were plot in Fig. 2, where each subgroup is described by one curve.

It is clear that some subgroups converge to different global optima gradually. However, the others' fitness values become large after descending, it's because that they move in to the basin where the other subgroup has entered, so it is absorbed and offered chance for comparative better global atoms in other basins. From Fig. 2, it can be seen that subgroup converge to the same basin and be absorbed frequently while some other basins where global optima exist have not exploited. How to solve this problem to increase the ability of locating more optima will be our next work. It is worth noticing that the fitness curve keeps on decreasing after about 200 generations. This phenomenon illustrated the process of being trapped and then escaping. It is reasonable because the small r decreases and increases in turn. The local atoms move toward a local optimum when the scope of exploitation area shrike. Meanwhile, the local atoms jump toward another local optimum when the scope of local exploitation area expands.

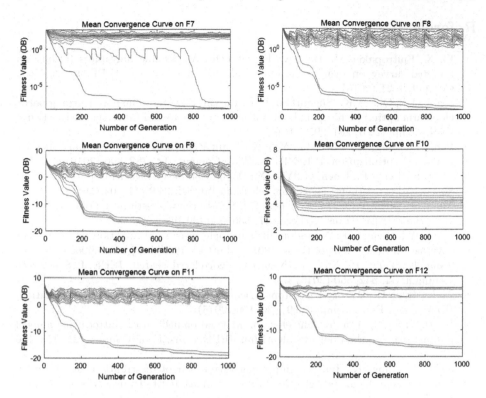

Fig. 2. Convergence curve of each subgroup

Given all that, we can come to the conclusion that the proposed MOA with bimodal-gauss function has the ability of locating the global optimum with higher probability and quality compared with CLPSO and MOA.

4 Conclusions

In this paper, the principle of MOA with bimodal-gauss and contrastive experiments are provide. The results suggest that the proposed method outperforms CLPSO and MOA in terms of quality of solution. The convergence process of each subgroup was analyzed based on convergence curve. The investigation of the basin scope to determine whether two subgroups should be merged or one should be divided into two, in order to increase the ability of locating more optima, theoretic analysis and intensive experiments based on CEC2015 benchmark functions will be our next work.

Acknowledgement. This work was supported by the National Natural Science Foundation of China (Nos. 61473266, 61305080), the key scientific and technological project of Henan province (No. 172102310334), the Science and Technology Foundation of Henan Educational Committee of China (No. 16A413012), the Special Project of Nanyang Normal University (No. ZX2016010).

References

1. Li, X., Epitropakis, M., Deb, K., Engelbrecht, A.: Seeking multiple solutions: an updated survey on niching methods and their applications. IEEE Trans. Evol. Comput. 1–21 (2016)
2. Liang, J.J., Qin, A.K., Suganthan, P.N., Baskar, S.: Comprehensive learning particle swarm optimizer for global optimization of multimodal functions. IEEE Trans. Evol. Comput. **10**, 281–295 (2006)
3. Peng, F., Tang, K., Chen, G., Yao, X.: Population-based algorithm portfolios for numerical optimization. IEEE Trans. Evol. Comput. **14**, 782–800 (2010)
4. Tang, K., Peng, F., Chen, G., Yao, X.: Population-based algorithm portfolios with automated constituent algorithms selection. Inf. Sci. **279**, 94–104 (2014)
5. Yang, Q., Chen, W.N., Li, Y., Chen, C.L.P.: Multimodal estimation of distribution algorithms. IEEE Trans. Cybern. **47**, 636–650 (2016)
6. Fang, W., Zhou, J.H.: A random drift particle swarm optimization with frequent coverage strategy. Control Decis. (2017). doi:10.13195/j.kzyjc.2016.0000
7. Tang, K., Yang, P., Yao, X.: Negatively correlated search. IEEE J. Sel. Areas Commun. **34**, 542–550 (2016)
8. Li, L., Tang, K.: History-based topological speciation for multimodal optimization. IEEE Trans. Evol. Comput. **19**, 136–150 (2015)
9. Li, J., Zheng, S., Tan, Y.: The effect of information utilization: introducing a novel guiding spark in the fireworks algorithm. IEEE Trans. Evol. Comput. **21**, 153–166 (2017)
10. Yang, P., Tang, K., Lu, X.: Improving estimation of distribution algorithm on multimodal problems by detecting promising areas. IEEE Trans. Cybern. **45**, 1438 (2015)
11. Yang, Q., Chen, W.N., Yu, Z., Gu, T., Li, Y., Zhang, H., et al.: Adaptive multimodal continuous ant colony optimization. IEEE Trans. Evol. Comput. **21**, 191–205 (2017)
12. Zhang, Y., Gong, Y.J., Zhang, H., Gu, T.L., Zhang, J.: Towards fast niching evolutionary algorithms: a locality sensitive hashing-based approach. IEEE Trans. Evol. Comput. **13**, 1–15 (2016)
13. Fieldsend, J.E.: Running up those hills: multi-modal search with the niching migratory multi-swarm optimiser. In: IEEE Congress on Evolutionary Computation-CEC 2014, pp. 2593–2600. IEEE (2014)
14. Li, B.L., Chen, J.H., Shi, X.L., et al.: On the convergence of multivariant optimization algorithm. Appl. Soft Comput. **48**, 230–239 (2016)
15. Liang, J.J., Suganthan, P.N., Deb, K.: Novel composition test functions for numerical global optimization. In: IEEE Congress on Swarm Intelligence Symposium-SIS2005, pp. 68–75. IEEE (2005)
16. Qu, B.Y., Suganthan, P.N.: Novel multimodal problems and differential evolution with ensemble of restricted tournament selection. In: IEEE Congress on Evolutionary Computation-CEC 2010, pp. 1–7. IEEE (2010)

Enhanced Comprehensive Learning Particle Swarm Optimization with Exemplar Evolution

Xiang Yu[1,2(✉)], Yunan Liu[1,2], Xiangsheng Feng[1,2],
and Genhua Chen[1,2]

[1] Provincial Key Laboratory for Water Information Cooperative Sensing
and Intelligent Processing, Nanchang Institute of Technology,
289 Tianxiang Road, Nanchang 330099, Jiangxi, China
xiang.yu@nit.edu.cn
[2] School of Information Engineering, Nanchang Institute of Technology,
289 Tianxiang Road, Nanchang 330099, Jiangxi, China

Abstract. Enhanced comprehensive learning particle swarm optimization (ECLPSO) is a metaheuristic recently proposed by us for global optimization. ECLPSO is balanced in exploration and exploitation; however, it still cannot satisfactorily address some complex multimodal problems. In this paper, we investigate further improving the exploration performance of ECLPSO through exemplar evolution (EE). EE encourages information exchange among different dimensions of the search space and performs mutation and selection on personal best positions that are exemplars guiding the flight of particles. EE is able to prevent the dimensions from getting stuck in stagnancy. Experimental results on various benchmark functions demonstrate that the EE strategy significantly improves the exploration performance of ECLPSO and helps ECLPSO to locate the global optimum region on all of the functions.

Keywords: Particle swarm optimization · Enhanced comprehensive learning · Exemplar evolution

1 Introduction

Particle swarm optimization (PSO) is a class of metaheuristics simulating the movements of organisms in a bird flock or fish school. PSO uses a swarm of particles, with each particle representing a candidate solution. All the particles "fly" in the search space. Each particle is accordingly associated with a position, a velocity, and a fitness indicating the particle's optimization performance. Each particle iteratively updates its position (or in other words the flight trajectory) in order to locate the global optimum. PSO is essentially a set of intelligent search strategies and PSO doesn't enforce any restriction on the optimization problem. As a result, PSO has been applied to solve a wide range of real-world optimization problems.

PSO needs to address two challenging issues, i.e. exploration and exploitation. Exploration refers to searching different regions of the search space so as to locate a small region where the global optimum resides in, while exploitation means concentrating the search around the located small region to find the global optimum. There are

© Springer International Publishing AG 2017
Y. Shi et al. (Eds.): SEAL 2017, LNCS 10593, pp. 929–938, 2017.
https://doi.org/10.1007/978-3-319-68759-9_76

many PSO variants that adopt different search strategies [1–5]. Comprehensive learning PSO (CLPSO) [1] is a state-of-the-art powerful PSO variant. In CLPSO, each particle learns from different exemplars on different dimensions of the search space. The exemplar can be the particle's historical position with the best fitness value discovered (i.e. personal best position) or some other particle's personal best position. CLPSO is good at preserving the particles' diversity and is thus excellent in exploration. However, CLPSO is weak in exploitation. We have recently proposed enhanced CLPSO (ECLPSO) [2] that significantly improves the exploitation performance of CLPSO.

Though ECLPSO is balanced in exploration and exploitation, the experimental results reported in [2] indicate that ECLPSO still cannot locate the global optimum region on some complex multimodal benchmark functions including the Rosenbrock's function, the Rotated Schwefel's function, and the Rotated Rastrigin's function. In this paper, we investigate further improving the exploration performance of ECLPSO through exemplar evolution (EE). EE encourages information exchange among different dimensions and performs mutation and selection on the personal best positions. EE is able to prevent the dimensions from getting stuck in stagnancy.

2 Background

2.1 Comprehensive Learning Particle Swarm Optimization

Let the search space be D-dimensional and there be N particles in the swarm. Each particle, denoted as i ($1 \leq i \leq N$), is associated with a D-dimensional velocity $V_i = (V_{i,1}, V_{i,2}, ..., V_{i,D})$ and a D-dimensional position $P_i = (P_{i,1}, P_{i,2}, ..., P_{i,D})$. CLPSO [1] relies on iterative learning to find the global optimum. In each iteration (or generation), V_i and P_i are updated on each dimension d ($1 \leq d \leq D$) as follows.

$$V_{i,d} = wV_{i,d} + cr_{i,d}(E_{i,d} - P_{i,d}) \tag{1}$$

$$P_{i,d} = P_{i,d} + V_{i,d} \tag{2}$$

where w is the inertia weight and linearly decreases from 0.9 to 0.4; c is the acceleration coefficient and $c = 1.5$; $r_{i,d}$ is a random number uniformly distributed in [0, 1]; and $E_{i,d}$ is the exemplar that guides the update of i's flight trajectory on dimension d.

The dimensional velocity $V_{i,d}$ is usually clamped to a positive value V_d^{max}, i.e.

$$V_{i,d} = \begin{cases} V_d^{max}, & \text{if } V_{i,d} > V_d^{max} \\ -V_d^{max}, & \text{else if } V_{i,d} < -V_d^{max} \\ V_{i,d}, & \text{otherwise} \end{cases} \tag{3}$$

Let P_d^{min} and P_d^{max} respectively be the lower and upper bounds of the search space on dimension d, V_d^{max} is often set as 20% of $P_d^{max} - P_d^{min}$.

In each generation, i remembers its personal best position $B_i = (B_{i,1}, B_{i,2}, ..., B_{i,D})$ that is associated with the best fitness value for i so far. The dimensional exemplar $E_{i,d}$ can be $B_{i,d}$ or $B_{j,d}$ with $j \neq i$, and the decision to learn whether from $B_{i,d}$ or $B_{j,d}$ depends on i's learning probability L_i. L_i is set according to Eq. (4) such that all the particles exhibit diverse learning capabilities.

$$L_i = 0.05 + 0.45 \frac{\exp(\frac{10(i-1)}{N-1}) - 1}{\exp(10) - 1} \tag{4}$$

CLPSO calculates i's fitness value only if i is feasible (i.e. within $[P_d^{\min}, P_d^{\max}]$ on each dimension d). CLPSO allows i to learn from the same vector of exemplars $E_i = (E_{i,1}, E_{i,2}, ..., E_{i,D})$ until i's fitness value ceases improving for a refreshing gap of g consecutive generations. g is suggested to be set as 7.

2.2 Enhanced Comprehensive Learning Particle Swarm Optimization

ECLPSO [2] enhances the exploitation performance of CLPSO by the employment of two strategies, i.e. perturbation based exploitation (PbE) and adaptive learning probabilities (ALPs).

The PbE strategy calculates the so-called normative interval $[B_d^{\min}, B_d^{\max}]$ for each dimension d in each generation, with $B_d^{\max}$ and $B_d^{\min}$ respectively being the maximum and minimum values of all the particles' personal best positions on dimension d. Once Eq. (5) becomes true, ECLPSO deems that the particles have located the small region where the global optimum resides on dimension d, then ECLPSO updates each particle i's dimensional velocity according to Eq. (6) instead of Eq. (1) for exploitation.

$$B_d^{\max} - B_d^{\min} \leq \alpha(P_d^{\max} - P_d^{\min}) \text{ and } B_d^{\max} - B_d^{\min} \leq \beta \tag{5}$$

$$V_{i,d} = w_2 V_{i,d} + c r_{i,d}(E_{i,d} + \eta(\frac{B_d^{\min} + B_d^{\max}}{2} - E_{i,d}) - P_{i,d}) \tag{6}$$

where α is the relative ratio and $\alpha = 0.01$; β is the absolute bound and $\beta = 2$; w_2 is the inertia weight used exclusively for exploitation and $w_2 = 0.5$; and η is the perturbation coefficient and η is randomly generated from a normal distribution with mean 1 and standard deviation 0.65. Note that η is also clamped to 10 times of its standard deviation on both sides of its mean.

The ALPs strategy adaptively adjusts each particle i's learning probability L_i in each generation to facilitate convergence. The ALPs strategy first sorts all the particles in the ascending order of the personal best fitness values. Then, the particles' learning probabilities are determined according to Eqs. (7) and (8).

$$L_i = 0.05 + L_{\max} \frac{\exp(\frac{10(K_i-1)}{N-1}) - 1}{\exp(10) - 1} \tag{7}$$

$$L_{\max} = 0.3 + 0.45 \log_{D+1}(M + 1) \tag{8}$$

where K_i is i's rank in the sorted sequence; M is the number of dimensions whose normative intervals have ever satisfied the exploitation activation condition specified in

Eq. (5) before or just in the present generation; and $L_{\max}$ is the maximum learning probability. M is also called the number of exploitation valid dimensions (EVDs).

3 Enhanced Comprehensive Learning Particle Swarm Optimization with Exemplar Evolution

It was noted in [3] that PSO might fail to find the global optimum or a near-optimum solution on some benchmark functions (particularly complex multimodal functions) because the particles are liable to get stuck in premature convergence on some dimensions of the search space simultaneously. To facilitate a stagnated dimension jumping out of the local optimum, it is beneficial to exchange useful information relevant to different dimensions [3]. In this paper, we propose an EE strategy that is expected to improve the exploration performance of ECLPSO. The EE strategy encourages information exchange among different dimensions and performs mutation and selection on the personal best positions. In each generation, the EE strategy works step by step as follows.

Step (1) For each particle i $(1 \leq i \leq N)$, let the mutated position of i's personal best position B_i be $Q_i = (Q_{i,1}, Q_{i,2}, \ldots, Q_{i,D})$, initialize Q_i to be the same as B_i on each dimension.

Step (2) Initialize the set of dimensions $\Omega = \{1, 2, \ldots, D\}$.

Step (3) If Ω is empty, go to step (6); otherwise, randomly select two dimensions d and h from Ω, and remove the two dimensions from Ω.

Step (4) Let δ be the mutation confirmation probability. Generate a random number s_1 uniformly distributed in [0, 1]. If $s_1 \leq \delta$, go on to step (5); otherwise, go back to step (3).

Step (5) For each particle i $(1 \leq i \leq N)$, perform mutation on $B_{i,d}$ according to Eq. (9).

$$Q_{i,d} = \begin{cases} s_3 B_{i,d} + (1 - s_3) B_{i,h}, & \text{if } s_2 \leq \lambda \\ B_{i,h}, & \text{otherwise} \end{cases} \tag{9}$$

where λ is the mutation tradeoff probability; s_2 is a random number uniformly distributed in [0, 1]; and s_3 is a random number uniformly distributed in [−1, 1]. If $Q_{i,d}$ trespasses $[P_d^{\min}, P_d^{\max}]$, then set $Q_{i,d}$ as a random value uniformly distributed between the trespassed boundary and $B_{i,d}$. After the mutation of all the particles on dimension d, go back to step (3).

Step (6) For each particle i $(1 \leq i \leq N)$, calculate the fitness value of its mutated position Q_i; if the fitness value of Q_i is better than that of B_i, replace B_i by Q_i.

The two probabilities δ and λ play important roles in the EE strategy. δ controls the number of dimensions to be mutated. Usually no more than half of the dimensions get stagnated [3]. δ is empirically set as 1. As can be seen from Eq. (9), λ controls whether to mutate $B_{i,d}$ as a linear combination of $B_{i,d}$ and $B_{i,h}$ or simply as the same value of $B_{i,h}$.

If the global optimum on dimension d and that on dimension h are same or close, then setting $Q_{i,d}$ as $B_{i,h}$ could directly lead to the discovery of the global optimum on dimension d if the particles have already located the global optimum region on dimension h; otherwise, setting $Q_{i,d}$ as $s_3 B_{i,d} + (1-s_3)B_{i,h}$ results in a random value in $[\min\{B_{i,d}, 2B_{i,h} - B_{i,d}\}, \max\{B_{i,d}, 2B_{i,h} - B_{i,d}\}]$, thereby helping dimension d to jump out of premature convergence. The empirical value chosen for λ is 0.5. Step (6) is a selection operation, as B_i is replaced by Q_i if the mutated position is associated with a better fitness value. Since personal best positions are used as exemplars guiding the flight of particles, once a stagnated dimension of a particle returns to normal, the particle can quickly disseminate its position information within the swarm [4, 5].

ECLPSO integrated with the EE strategy is called ECLPSO-EE for short. The flowchart of ECLPSO-EE is the same as ECLPSO [2] except that in step 18 ECLPSO-EE performs the EE strategy before increasing the generation counter. The time complexity of the EE strategy is $O(ND)$ basic operations plus $O(N)$ function evaluations (FEs). The time complexity of ECLPSO-EE is thus still the same as that of ECLPSO, i.e. $O(K(N\log N + ND))$ basic operations plus $O(KN)$ FEs, with K being the predefined number of generations.

4   Experimental Results and Discussions

14 benchmark functions used in [2] are also used for evaluating ECLPSO-EE. The 14 functions are respectively the sphere function f_1, the Schwefel's P2.22 function f_2, the Rosenbrock's function f_3, the noise function f_4, the Schwefel's function f_5, the Rastrigin's function f_6, the Ackley's function f_7, the Griewank's function f_8, two generalized penalized functions f_9 and f_{10}, the rotated Schwefel's function f_{11}, the rotated Rastrigin's function f_{12}, the rotated Ackley's function f_{13}, and the rotated Griewank's function f_{14}. The functions are unimodal, multimodal, or rotated. All the functions are 30-dimensional. f_5 and f_{11} have the global optimum at $\{420.96\}^{30}$, while all the other functions have the global optimum at $\{0\}^{30}$. ECLPSO-EE is compared with ECLPSO and CLPSO in order to understand how the proposed EE strategy improves the exploration performance. The swarm size is 40. All the metaheuristics use the same maximum number of FEs which is 200000 in each run on each function. Each metaheuristic is tested 25 times independently on each function. The algorithm parameters of CLPSO, ECLPSO, and ECLPSO-EE take the recommended empirical values stated in the previous sections. The following performance metrics are used for evaluating the metaheuristics on each function: (1) the mean, standard deviation (SD), best, median, and worst of the final solutions obtained from the 25 runs; and (2) the average number of EVDs of the 25 runs.

Table 1 lists the mean, SD, best, median, and worst final solution results of the 25 runs of all the metaheuristics on all the benchmark functions. Table 2 lists the EVDs results of ECLPSO-EE and ECLPSO on all the functions. To determine whether the solutions obtained by ECLPSO-EE are statistically different from those obtained by ECLPSO in terms of the mean and SD final solution results, two-tailed t-tests with degrees of freedom 48 and significance level 0.05 are carried out and the t-test results are listed in Table 3. Figure 1 illustrates the convergence characteristics of ECLPSO-EE and ECLPSO in terms of the global best fitness values of a median run on some selected functions including $f_1, f_2, f_3, f_4, f_{11}$, and f_{14}.

As can be seen from Table 1, ECLPSO-EE is very effective in exploration. ECLPSO-EE is able to find the global optimum on f_2, f_6, f_8, f_{12} and f_{14}, and a near optimum solution on all the other functions. In contrast, ECLPSO can find the global optimum only on f_6 and f_8, and CLPSO cannot derive the global optimum on any function. In addition, ECLPSO and CLPSO even cannot locate the global optimum region and get trapped in premature convergence on f_3, f_{11}, and f_{12}. The mean, SD, best, median, and worst final solution results of ECLPSO-EE are the best, followed by ECLPSO, and those of CLPSO are the worst. The t-test results listed in Table 3 show that the mean and SD final solution results of ECLPSO-EE are significantly different from those of ECLPSO on $f_2, f_3, f_4, f_{11}, f_{12}$, and f_{14}. All the observations verify that: (1) ECLPSO enhances the exploitation performance of CLPSO, however ECLPSO is still weak in exploration on some complex multimodal functions such as f_3, f_{11}, and f_{12}; (2) ECLPSO-EE, through employing the EE strategy, successfully improves the exploration performance and is able to locate the global optimum region on all the functions tested; and (3) the EE strategy also contributes to refining the final solution accuracy.

Table 1. Mean, SD, best, median, and worst final solution results of ECLPSO-EE, ECLPSO, and CLPSO on all the benchmark functions.

Benchmark function	ECLPSO-EE		ECLPSO	CLPSO
f_1	Mean	3.75E−120	1.00E−96	2.56E−14
	SD	1.51E−119	3.01E−96	8.77E−14
	Best	3.36E−123	2.11E−100	5.88E−16
	Median	3.13E−121	1.25E−97	4.49E−15
	Worst	7.63E−119	1.49E−95	4.45E−13
f_2	Mean	0	2.02E−31	3.12E−10
	SD	0	2.84E−31	1.96E−10
	Best	0	1.49E−32	1.32E−10
	Median	0	8.84E−32	2.61E−10
	Worst	0	1.11E−30	8.66E−10
f_3	Mean	1.28E−17	27.46	39.17
	SD	3.67E−17	15.03	21.31
	Best	1.93E−23	17.17	17.49
	Median	5.60E−19	24.71	28.03
	Worst	1.77E−16	76.75	81.22
f_4	Mean	7.20E−4	5.66E−3	4.91E−3
	SD	3.13E−4	1.03E−3	1.11E−3
	Best	2.54E−4	3.62E−3	3.98E−3
	Median	7.01E−4	5.65E−3	4.98E−3
	Worst	1.44E−3	7.64E−3	7.37E−3

(continued)

Table 1. (*continued*)

Benchmark function		ECLPSO-EE	ECLPSO	CLPSO
f_5	Mean	3.82E-4	3.82E-4	3.82E-4
	SD	0	0	2.42E-13
	Best	3.82E-4	3.82E-4	3.82E-4
	Median	3.82E-4	3.82E-4	3.82E-4
	Worst	3.82E-4	3.82E-4	3.82E-4
f_6	Mean	0	0	1.94E-6
	SD	0	0	1.74E-6
	Best	0	0	2.00E-7
	Median	0	0	1.26E-6
	Worst	0	0	6.90E-6
f_7	Mean	3.55E-15	3.55E-15	3.20E-8
	SD	0	0	5.28E-8
	Best	3.55E-15	3.55E-15	5.71E-9
	Median	3.55E-15	3.55E-15	2.03E-8
	Worst	3.55E-15	3.55E-15	2.78E-7
f_8	Mean	0	0	1.32E-9
	SD	0	0	2.70E-9
	Best	0	0	5.90E-12
	Median	0	0	1.67E-10
	Worst	0	0	1.06E-8
f_9	Mean	1.57E-32	1.57E-32	1.94E-16
	SD	8.38E-48	8.38E-48	1.97E-16
	Best	1.57E-32	1.57E-32	6.62E-18
	Median	1.57E-32	1.57E-32	1.47E-16
	Worst	1.57E-32	1.57E-32	7.55E-16
f_{10}	Mean	1.35E-32	1.35E-32	1.11E-13
	SD	5.59E-48	2.47E-34	1.60E-13
	Best	1.35E-32	1.35E-32	4.53E-15
	Median	1.35E-32	1.35E-32	4.48E-14
	Worst	1.35E-32	1.47E-32	7.22E-13
f_{11}	Mean	4.47E-4	1.16E3	1.28E3
	SD	7.77E-6	1.44E2	1.20E2
	Best	4.29E-4	8.53E2	9.48E2
	Median	4.47E-4	1.17E3	1.32E3
	Worst	4.61E-4	1.49E3	1.46E3
f_{12}	Mean	0	22.70	30.90
	SD	0	4.47	4.49
	Best	0	15.73	24.06
	Median	0	23.41	29.89
	Worst	0	29.59	41.21

(*continued*)

Table 1. (*continued*)

Benchmark function		ECLPSO-EE	ECLPSO	CLPSO
f_{13}	Mean	3.41E−15	3.55E−15	5.63E−8
	SD	7.11E−16	0	3.46E−8
	Best	0	3.55E−15	1.96E−−8
	Median	3.55E−15	3.55E−15	5.34E−8
	Worst	3.55E−15	3.55E−15	1.38E−7
f_{14}	Mean	0	2.22E−17	3.58E−5
	SD	0	4.53E−17	4.71E−5
	Best	0	0	9.19E−7
	Median	0	0	1.20E−5
	Worst	0	1.11E−16	1.63E−4

Though the EE strategy significantly improves the exploration performance, it doesn't benefit the exploitation process, as we can see from the EVDs results listed in Table 2. The EVDs results of ECLPSO-EE are respectively 0, 9, 8, and 29 on f_6, f_9, f_{10}, and f_{14}, while those of ECLPSO are all 30 on the 4 functions. The EVDs results of ECLPSO-EE and ECLPSO are all 30 on f_1, f_2, f_5, f_7, f_8, and f_{13}, while 0 on f_3, f_4, f_{11}, and f_{12}. It can be indicated from the observations that the EE strategy significantly improves the diversity of the personal best positions, hence the EE strategy benefits the exploration process but somewhat hinders the exploitation process.

Table 2. EVDs results of ECLPSO-EE and ECLPSO on all the benchmark functions.

	f_1	f_2	f_3	f_4	f_5	f_6	f_7
ECLPSO-EE	30	30	0	0	30	0	30
ECLPSO	30	30	0	0	30	30	30

	f_8	f_9	f_{10}	f_{11}	f_{12}	f_{13}	f_{14}
ECLPSO-EE	30	9	8	0	0	30	29
ECLPSO	30	30	30	0	0	30	30

Table 3. Two-tailed t-test values from the comparison of ECLPSO-EE and ECLPSO on all the benchmark functions.

	f_1	f_2	f_3	f_4	f_5	f_6	f_7
t-test	−1.67	−3.55[*]	−9.13[*]	−23.01[*]	0	0	0

	f_8	f_9	f_{10}	f_{11}	f_{12}	f_{13}	f_{14}
t-test	0	0	−1	−40.54[*]	−25.41[*]	−1	−2.45[*]

[*]The value is significant by a two-tailed t-test between ECLPSO-EE and ECLPSO.

As the convergence characteristics illustrated in Fig. 1 show, ECLPSO-EE converges much faster than ECLPSO on $f_1, f_2, f_3, f_4, f_{11}$, and f_{14}. The EE strategy helps the particles quickly locate the global optimum region. Based on the excellent experimental results of ECLPSO-EE on all the benchmark functions, ECLPSO-EE is thus recommended as a promising optimizer for global optimization.

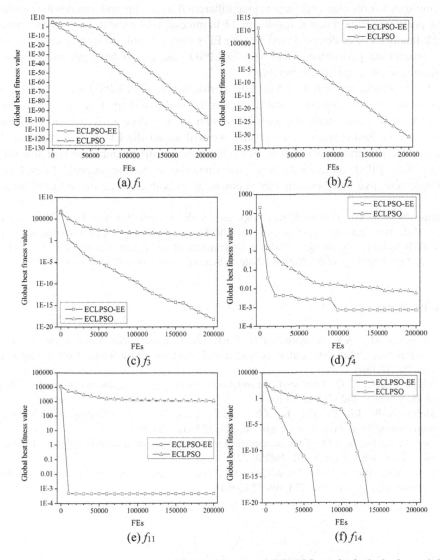

Fig. 1. Convergence characteristics of ECLPSO-EE and ECLPSO on $f_1, f_2, f_3, f_4, f_{11}$, and f_{14}.

5 Conclusions

ECLPSO is a state-of-the-art single-objective metaheuristic recently proposed by us. ECLPSO is balanced in exploration and exploitation, however it still cannot locate the global optimum region for some complex multimodal problems. In this paper, we have proposed further improving the exploration performance of ECLPSO through EE. EE encourages information exchange among different dimensions and mutates the personal best positions. Experimental results on 14 unimodal, multimodal, and rotated benchmark functions have demonstrated that the EE strategy is able to significantly improve the exploration performance and help ECLPSO find the global optimum or a near optimum solution on all the functions.

In the future, we will investigate the performance of ECLPSO with EE on more diverse benchmark functions and a number of real-world applications, particularly benchmark functions with the global optimum having different dimensional values. Based on the future performance results, we will adjust the EE strategy accordingly. Besides the EE strategy that improves the exploration performance, we will also study some strategy that can facilitate the exploitation process, for the purpose of developing a single-objective metaheuristic that is powerful on both exploration and exploitation.

Acknowledgements. This work was supported by the Jiangxi Province Key Laboratory for Water Information Cooperative Sensing and Intelligent Processing Open Foundation Project (2016WICSIP011), the Jiangxi Province Department of Education Science and Technology Project (GJJ151099), and the National Natural Science Foundation of China (61401187).

References

1. Liang, J.J., Qin, A.K., Suganthan, P.N., Baskar, S.: Comprehensive learning particle swarm optimizer for global optimization of multimodal functions. IEEE Trans. Evol. Comput. **10**, 281–295 (2006)
2. Yu, X., Zhang, X.-Q.: Enhanced comprehensive learning particle swarm optimization. Appl. Math. Comput. **242**, 265–276 (2014)
3. Meng, A.-B., Li, Z., Yin, H., Chen, S.-Z., Guo, Z.-Z.: Accelerating particle swarm optimization using crisscross search. Inf. Sci. **329**, 52–72 (2016)
4. Lim, W.H., Isa, N.A.M.: Two-layer particle swarm optimization with intelligent division of labor. Eng. Appl. Artif. Intell. **26**(10), 2327–2348 (2013)
5. Lim, W.H., Isa, N.A.M.: An adaptive two-layer particle swam optimization with elitist learning strategy. Inf. Sci. **273**, 49–72 (2014)

Recommending PSO Variants Using Meta-Learning Framework for Global Optimization

Xianghua Chu, Fulin Cai, Jiansheng Chen, and Li Li[✉]

College of Management, Shenzhen University, Shenzhen, Guangdong, China
lli318@163.com

Abstract. Since inception, particle swarm optimization (PSO) has raised a great interest across various disciplines, thus producing a large number of PSO variants with respective strengths. However, a variant may perform variously on diverse problems, which leads to the risk of the algorithm selection of PSOs for a specific problem without prior knowledge. Hence, it is worth investigating a link between problem characteristics and algorithm performance. To address this issue, we propose a recommendation system of PSO variants for global optimization problem using meta-learning framework. Benchmark functions in the learning instance repository are pictured by meta-features to obtain characteristics and solved by the candidate PSO heuristics to gather performance rankings. *k*-NN method is employed to develop meta-learning system for recommending the predicted rankings of candidate PSO-variants. Results show that the predicted rankings highly correlate to the ideal rankings and achieve high precision on best algorithm recommendation. Besides, problem surface characteristics play a key role in recommendation performance, followed by sample point characteristics. To sum up, the proposed framework can significantly reduce the risk of algorithm selection.

Keywords: Meta-learning · PSO variants · Global optimization and recommendation system

1 Introduction

Motivated by the swarm behavior of fish schooling and bird flocking, particle swarm optimization (PSO), a prestigious stochastic optimizer was proposed in 1995 [1, 2]. Since inception, researchers had proposed many interesting variants called PSO-variants to further improve the performance of PSO. Unfortunately, according to "No Free Lunch" theory, an almighty optimizer that works extremely well on every problem do not exist [3]. In fact, the performances of PSO variants significantly vary from problem to problem. Therefore, there is a practically inherent risk associated with the selection of an appropriate optimizer, as we do not have prior knowledge regarding which optimizer is appropriate for an unknown problem. However, it is feasible to use machine learning technique to bridge the gap between optimizer performance and problem characteristic, which is called meta-learning [4].

© Springer International Publishing AG 2017
Y. Shi et al. (Eds.): SEAL 2017, LNCS 10593, pp. 939–948, 2017.
https://doi.org/10.1007/978-3-319-68759-9_77

There are many researches show the promising results. Smith-Miles [6] and Kanda et al. [7] successfully implemented meta-learning concept to solve the algorithm selection problem for specific management optimization problem, such as quadratic assignment problem and traveling salesman problem. Bischl et al. [8] employed support vector regression and low-level features based on exploratory landscape analysis [9] to predict the expected number of function evaluations required to achieve target accuracy) of global optimizers for real-world black box optimization problem. Muñoz et al. [10] constructed a regression model to select the best parameters for the CMA-ES algorithm. In addition, a failure prediction model was developed using decision tree in [11]. As shown in [12], previous researches mostly focused on using regression model to selection the optimal one or using classification model to predict the successful one. However, the classification model is monolithic which means high computational budget. For a regression model, different problems get various magnitudes of difficulties to be modeled. Hence, predicting the rankings of candidate algorithms, it is hopefully to find out the truly best one by increasing the number of algorithms tried out [4].

In this study, we expand the meta-learning technique to a ranking based recommendation framework of PSO variants for global optimization problem, where six well-known PSO variants and the CEC2005 benchmark functions [13] are collected to build learning instance repository. A serious of meta-features with low computational cost characteristics and algorithm performance measurements are displayed. The meta-learning system using k nearest neighbor method is implemented to study the correlation between algorithm performances and problem features. Then, 10 representative tested functions are prepared to verify the performance of our framework. Finally, appropriate parameters of this implementation are identified. The performances which are far better than the default rankings are shown and the impacts of different types of meta-features are discussed.

This paper is organized as follows. In Sect. 2, we introduce the proposed PSO-variants framework for global optimization problem in details. In Sect. 3, we describe the experimental procedure based on k-NN method. The experimental settings and the main results are given. Finally, the conclusions are stated in Sect. 4.

2   The PSO-Heuristic Algorithms Recommendation Framework

In this section, our proposed framework is introduced, which is constructed upon Rice' model [5] as shown in Fig. 1. In priority, an instance repository is constructed by collecting the CEC2005 benchmark global optimization problems [13] and PSO-variants. After obtaining meta-feature and algorithm performance, the meta-learning system can be used to find out the link between them and offer predicted rankings of candidate algorithms. The details of algorithm performance and meta-feature are described in subsection.

2.1   Algorithm Performance

Particle swarm optimization (PSO) is a stochastic optimizer inspired by the swarm behaviors of bird flocking and fish schooling [2]. Until now, many different

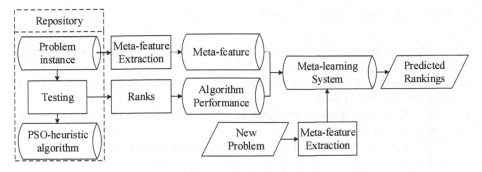

Fig. 1. A flowchart of proposed framework.

modifications have been proposed to improve the capability of the PSO. An inertia weight w is added by Shi and Eberhart [14] to balance the global and local search ability. By studying the convergence behavior of the PSO, a coefficient called constriction factor is introduced by [15], which can guarantee convergence of particles. [16] identifies that different neighborhood topologies have their own advantages in specific problems. Fewer neighborhoods may be more appropriate for complex problems, vice versa. Moreover, a unified PSO (UPSO) is developed by combining the global version and local version together [17]. To improve the performance of the original PSO on multimodal problem, a comprehensive learning strategy is proposed in [18], called comprehensive learning PSO (CLPSO), which ensures that each particle can learn from other particle's personal best position with probability on every dimension. A cooperative PSO (CPSO-H) [19] employs a global swarm to integrate the D-dimensional information providing by a one-dimensional swarm.

In summary, the PSO-variants mentioned above are uniquely designed for some specific tasks and it is worth to build an algorithm recommendation system by them. Please to note, the recommended rankings are made based on the ideal ranks, which shall better facilitate the recommendation process with scale-free and case-wise due to the mitigation of possibly high differences of the ranges of the object function values across the various benchmark function [20]. The average best function value (ABF) is employed from [21] to represent the algorithm performance which is used to derived the ideal ranks of candidate algorithms. After that, the ranks of adjacent algorithms would be tuned when the difference between them is not significant.

2.2 Meta-Feature

In this study, a total of 18 meta-features are provided and introductions are listed below. Some of them are widely used in meta-learning on classification and regression [22–24]. Meta-features are derived from N sample points. The meta-features involved can be categorized into two sets. The first set is used to summarize basic information of sample point characteristics, such as mean, median, standard deviation, skewness and kurtosis. The second set is to picture problem surface characteristics, such as gradient of problem surface, outlier ratio, ratio of local extrema, dispersion [25] and fitness distance correlation [26].

- The sample point characteristics (group1)

(1). $\bar{f}$: Mean of the object function value, which evaluates the general object function value of the problem space.
(2). $SD(f)$: Standard deviation of the object function value, which evaluates discrete degree of sample points.
(3). $\gamma_1(f)$: Skewness of the object function value, which measures the lack of symmetry of sample points.
(4). $\gamma_2(f)$: Kurtosis of the object function value, which measures the object function value.
(5). $Q1$: 25% quartile of the object function value, which represents the lower quartile of sample points.
(6). $Q2$: 50% quartile of the object function value, which represents the median quartile of sample points.
(7). $Q3$: 75% quartile of the object function value, which represents the upper quartile of sample points.
(8). ∇f: Altitude of search place, which evaluates the altitude of the search space by measuring the difference between the upper and lower bound of object function values of sample points.

$$\nabla f = lg(abs(max(f_i) - min(f_i))), \ i = 1, \ldots, N \tag{1}$$

- The problem surface characteristics (group2)

  The gradient value G_i of i th sample point is calculate as:

$$G_i = f(x_i) - f(x_i + step), \ i = 1, \ldots N. \tag{2}$$

where $x_i = (x_i^1, x_i^2, \ldots, x_i^D)$ is the position of point i; $f(x_i)$ refers to the object function value of the point i and the step is defined as 1% of the range of x_i.

(9). $\overline{|G|}$: Mean of Gradient of Problem surface, which evaluates how steep and rugged of the problem surface by observing its rate of change around the sampled points.
(10). $M(|G|)$: Median of Gradient of Problem surface.
(11). $SD(|G|)$: Standard deviation of Gradient of Problem surface, which evaluates the variation of the gradient on the surface.
(12). $|G|_{MAX}$: Max of Gradient of Problem surface, which illustrates the maximal degree of sudden change on the surface.
(13). Outlier ratio: Ratio of outliers of Problem surface, which evaluates percentage of extreme values among all through applying the Grubbs Test [27] that used to detect outliers in this study.
(14). Ratio of local minima: Ratio of local minima with 4 nearby points in Euclidian space, which distinguishes target surface between bumpy surface and flat surface.

(15). Ratio of local maxima: Ratio of local maxima with 4 nearby points in Euclidian space, which distinguishes target surface between bumpy surface and flat surface.

(16). Depth of local extrema (DLE): Averaged depth of local minima and maxima with 4 neighborhoods in Euclidian space, which describes how hard about particles jump out the local optima by looking into the average maximum object function value distance among neighborhoods.

(17). Dispersion (DISP): The pairwise Euclidian distance between the q best points, which identifies the global structure. In this study, q is equal to 20% of sampled point size.

(18). Fitness distance correlation (FDC): The relationship between the position and object function value, which identifies capability to identify deceptiveness in the search space.

3 Experiments

To evaluate and analyze the efficacy of the proposed framework, we adopt k-Nearest Neighbor (k-NN) as instance-based learning technique to build the meta-learning system. There are two stages of the experiments. In first, it is necessary to identify the best value of k and robustness of the framework. After the optimal k is confirmed, three groups of meta-feature sets (All meta-features, only group1 and only group2) are studied. It is important to note that the meta-learning framework is flexible and the k-NN is widely used in other studies, which present its efficiency and effectiveness [28, 29]. The distances between neighbors are defined as cosine similarity based on the meta-features. After that, the system output value is the recommended rankings of performance. The recommended rankings of algorithm a on the new problem i is calculated as

$$rr_{i,a} = \frac{\sum\limits_{j \in N(i)} similarity(i,j) ir_{j,a}}{\sum\limits_{j \in N(i)} similarity(i,j)} \tag{3}$$

where $rr_{i,a}$ and $ir_{i,a}$ are the recommended rank and the ideal rank of algorithm a on problem i; $N(i)$ represents the set of k-NN of problem i. After the predicted rankings rr_i is given, two most popular evaluation measurements in the meta-learning field are employed.

- The Spearman's rank correlation (SRC) coefficient [30], which is employed to represent the similarity between the recommended and the ideal rankings:

$$SRC_i = 1 - \frac{6 \sum_{a=1}^{na} (rr_{i,a} - ir_{i,a})^2}{na(na^2 - 1)} \tag{4}$$

where *na* denotes the number of candidate algorithms. In terms of this coefficient, a value of 1 represents total agreement and a value of -1 denotes total disagreement. The rankings are not related when it equals to 0.

– Hit ratio (*HR*): the percentage of precise matches between ideal best performer and recommended best one among all tested problems. This measurement represents the "precision" of the meta-learning system.

3.1 Experimental Setup

First of all is to construct a problem repository and CEC2005 benchmarks [13] are gathered. Next, six PSO-variants including PSO with inertia weight, Local version of PSO with inertia weight, Local version of PSO with constriction factor, CLPSO, CPSO-H and UPSO are collected to be candidate algorithms. All the parameters of candidate algorithms are set as suggestion in the original publication [14–19].

On the one hand, for all algorithms, each tested function is solved 30 times independently and the population size of algorithms are set as 40 [18]. The maximum number of FEs is set to 300 000. After the values of *ABF* are evaluated, the ranks of candidate PSO-variants for each global optimization problem are automatically derived. Some of the ranks would be tuned when the results of *t*-test at 0.05 level represent the differences between adjacent candidates are not significant. On the other hand, the sample points of each problem are gathered by Latin hypercube sampling (LHS) technique [31]. Then, the meta-features of problems are generated as description in Sect. 2.2. After this, the performances of problems correspond to its meta-features, which indicates the training data for *k*-NN is ready. In addition, in our preliminary study, the meta-feature extraction process of one problem takes less than 1 s, which indicates it is lower computation cost than a PSO-variant.

Finally, in order to validate the capability of the proposed framework, the recommendation process is evaluated by problems shown in Table 1 with various characteristics. To be fairness, the tested problems basically are not included in CEC2005 benchmarks. Moreover, all the tested problems are shifted. The average recommendation performance of each problem measured by *SRC* and *HR* is obtained by executing 30 independent runs. The meta-features of each run are calculated by resampling points. When gathering all the measurement values, they are averaged over 10 problems. Please note that, the experiments are studied on 30-dimension of six sampling sizes, i.e. 500, 2000, 4000, 6000, 8000 and 10000.

3.2 Experimental Results

In our first experiment, the meta-learning system is implemented with the number of neighbors (*k*) varied from 1 to 10, which aims to identify the performance of our framework and find out the most suitable *k*. Figure 2(a)–(b) show the *SRC* results for the meta-learning system recommendation, with the neighbor numbers for the six sampling sizes, respectively. The horizontal dotted line represents the mean *SRC* value for default rankings (the mean of the ideal rankings), called Baseline and serves as a reference for the quality of recommendation. As a whole, the performance curves of six

Table 1. Characteristics of the 10 tested functions

ID	Name	Range [X_{min}, X_{max}]^D	MM	Se	Sf	Rt	Ns	MS
f_1	Schwefel P2.2	$[-10,10]^D$	N	N	Y	N	N	N
f_2	Schwefel P2.21	$[-100,100]^D$	N	Y	Y	N	N	N
f_3	Rosenbroock	$[-100,100]^D$	N	N	Y	Y	N	N
f_4	Sphere	$[-100,100]^D$	N	Y	Y	N	N	N
f_5	Weierstrass	$[-0.5,0.5]^D$	Y	Y	N	N	N	N
f_6	Salomon	$[-100,100]^D$	Y	N	Y	N	N	N
f_7	Griewank	$[-600,600]^D$	Y	N	Y	Y	N	N
f_8	Weierstrass	$[-0.5,0.5]^D$	Y	N	N	Y	N	N
f_9	Mis-scaled Rastrigin 10	$[-5,5]^D$	Y	Y	Y	N	N	Y
f_{10}	Schwefel P1.2	$[-100,100]^D$	N	N	Y	Y	Y	N

Note: "MM" denotes multimodal, "Sf" denotes shifted operation, "Rt" denotes rotated operation, "Se" denotes separable, "Ns" denotes noisy, "Ms" denotes mis-scaled and "Y" means the function has the corresponding property, otherwise, it is "N".

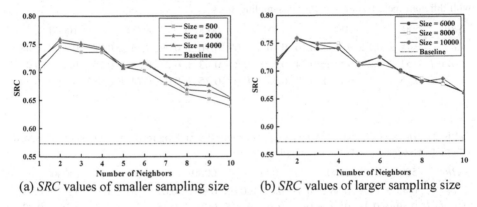

(a) *SRC* values of smaller sampling size   (b) *SRC* values of larger sampling size

Fig. 2. *SRC* values in relation to the number of neighbors and six sampling sizes.

sampling size have highly similar trends. Apparently, for all sampling sizes we tested, performances of the system are clearly better than the Baseline for $1 \leq k \leq 10$, which indicate the degree of superiority of the framework performance. In addition, we observe that the peak performances of every sample sizes are located at $k = 2$. When k is larger than 2, the slopes of performances steeply go poorer. Hence, the number of neighbor is set as 2 in the next experiment (2-NN). In addition, for small sampling size, the gaps between curves inch by inch reduce as the sampling size increases. When the sampling size is larger than 4000, the performance curves intertwine together.

The second experiment is to obtain further insights by investigating the impact of meta-feature. Meta-features are categorized into two groups as mentioned above, so three types meta-feature sets are studied including all meta-features (*All*), only group1 (*group1*) and only group2 (*group2*). The *SRC* and *HR* results for six sampling sizes are shown in Tables 2 and 3, which again show that our recommending rankings is great similar to ideal rankings with high precision (>80%). As we can see in Tables 2 and 3, the *SRC* value and *HR* value of *All* go better when the sampling size becomes larger. However, the degree of performance improvement goes less after the sampling size is 4000, which indicates that 4000 is an appropriate size for this framework and the meta-features generated by 4000 sampling points shall give a well picture of problem space. Then, for six sampling size in Tables 2 and 3, the performance of *group2* obviously makes a great contribution on the whole performance, due to the close proximity of the performance of *All* and *group2*. Hence, we can discover that the problem surface characteristics we gathered are core factors to influence results of recommendations and performances of PSO-variants. Nevertheless, in Table 3, there are notable gaps on the *HR* values between *All* and *group2*, which indicates that meta-features of *group1* still give an impact on advancing and stabilizing the hit ratio of learning system. In general, the results of two experiments demonstrate that the rankings predicted by our framework have great similarity to ideal rankings and show high precisions.

Table 2. *SRC* values (mean ± standard deviation) for the ranking recommendation of 2-NN with different meta-feature sets for six sampling sizes.

SRC	500	2000	4000	6000	8000	10000
All	0.75 ± 0.12	0.75 ± 0.10	0.76 ± 0.09	0.76 ± 0.09	0.76 ± 0.08	0.76 ± 0.08
group1	0.51 ± 0.26	0.51 ± 0.24	0.52 ± 0.23	0.52 ± 0.23	0.53 ± 0.23	0.54 ± 0.23
group2	0.75 ± 0.11	0.75 ± 0.09	0.75 ± 0.09	0.75 ± 0.08	0.74 ± 0.082	0.75 ± 0.09

Table 3. *HR* values (mean ± standard deviation) for the ranking recommendation of 2-NN with different meta-feature sets for six sampling sizes.

HR	500	2000	4000	6000	8000	10000
All	0.85 ± 0.11	0.88 ± 0.08	0.89 ± 0.08	0.90 ± 0.07	0.90 ± 0.07	0.90 ± 0.04
group1	0.69 ± 0.28	0.72 ± 0.24	0.74 ± 0.25	0.70 ± 0.25	0.71 ± 0.24	0.75 ± 0.22
group2	0.80 ± 0.08	0.83 ± 0.07	0.84 ± 0.05	0.83 ± 0.04	0.83 ± 0.06	0.83 ± 0.07

4   Conclusions

In this paper, we present an approach based on meta-learning framework to recommend PSO variants for global optimization problem, in which the relationship between problem characteristic and algorithm performance is captured and studied. In particular, the meta-learning system is induced by using k nearest neighbor (k-NN) method, which made recommendations according to the most similar problems. We also introduced new meta-features and provided an available meta-feature set, which is essential to the success of a meta-learning system. The problems included are described by the meta-features that can ensure the computational cost of our approach less than the trial and error approach.

Experimental results clearly demonstrate that the proposed framework make a promising recommendation of the rankings of the PSO variants for the global optimization problems. The values of *SRC* metric shows that our approach can provide better recommendations than the default rankings effectively and efficiently. In the second experiment, the meta-features are categorized into two groups and analyzed their impacts on recommendation results. It is clearly that problem surface characteristics play a key role in recommendation performance, followed by sample point characteristics.

In future work, other powerful learning mechanism is considerable to improve the accuracy of recommendation. Meanwhile, a large problem repository will be constructed and applied to make recommendation for real-world problem.

References

1. Eberhart, R., Kennedy, J.: A new optimizer using particle swarm theory. In: Sixth International Symposium on Micro Machine and Human Science, pp. 39–43 (1995)
2. Kennedy, J., Eberhart, R.: Particle swarm optimization. In: IEEE International Conference on Neural Networks, vol. 4, pp. 1942–1948 (1995)
3. Wolpert, D.H., Macready, W.G.: No free lunch theorems for optimization. IEEE Trans. Evol. Comput. **1**, 67–82 (1997)
4. Brazdil, P.: Metalearning: Applications to Data Mining. Cognitive Technologies (2009)
5. Rice, J.R.: The algorithm selection problem. Adv. Comput. **15**, 65–118 (1976)
6. Smith-Miles, K.A.: Towards insightful algorithm selection for optimisation using meta-learning concepts. In: IEEE International Joint Conference on Neural Networks, pp. 4118–4124 (2008)
7. Kanda, J., Carvalho, A.D., Hruschka, E., Soares, C., Brazdil, P.: Meta-learning to select the best meta-heuristic for the traveling salesman problem: a comparison of meta-features. Neurocomputing **205**, 393–406 (2016)
8. Bischl, B., Mersmann, O., Trautmann, H., Preu, M.: Algorithm selection based on exploratory landscape analysis and cost-sensitive learning. In: Conference on Genetic and Evolutionary Computation, pp. 313–320 (2012)
9. Mersmann, O., Bischl, B., Trautmann, H., Preuss, M., Weihs, C.: Exploratory landscape analysis. In: Proceedings of Genetic and Evolutionary Computation Conference, GECCO 2011, Dublin, Ireland, July, pp. 829–836 (2011)
10. Muñoz, M.A., Kirley, M., Halgamuge, S.K.: A meta-learning prediction model of algorithm performance for continuous optimization problems. In: Coello, C.A.C., Cutello, V., Deb, K., Forrest, S., Nicosia, G., Pavone, M. (eds.) PPSN 2012. LNCS, vol. 7491, pp. 226–235. Springer, Heidelberg (2012). doi:10.1007/978-3-642-32937-1_23
11. Malan, K.M., Engelbrecht, A.P.: Particle swarm optimisation failure prediction based on fitness landscape characteristics. In: IEEE Symposium on Swarm Intelligence, pp. 1–9 (2014)
12. Muñoz, M.A., Sun, Y., Kirley, M., Halgamuge, S.K.: Algorithm selection for black-box continuous optimization problems: a survey on methods and challenges. Inf. Sci. **317**, 224–245 (2015)
13. Suganthan, P.N., Hansen, N., Liang, J.J., Deb, K., Chen, Y.-P., Auger, A., Tiwari, S.: Problem definitions and evaluation criteria for the CEC 2005 special session on real-parameter optimization. KanGAL report (2005)

14. Shi, Y., Eberhart, R.: Modified particle swarm optimizer. In: IEEE World Congress on Computational Intelligence, pp. 69–73 (1998)
15. Clerc, M., Kennedy, J.: The particle swarm - explosion, stability, and convergence in a multidimensional complex space. IEEE Trans. Evol. Comput. **20**, 1671–1676 (2002)
16. Kennedy, J., Mendes, R.: Population structure and particle swarm performance. In: Proceedings of the 2002 Congress on Evolutionary Computation, pp. 1671–1676 (2002)
17. Parsopoulos, K.E., Vrahatis, M.N.: A unified particle swarm optimization scheme. In: International Conference of Computational Methods in Sciences and Engineering, pp. 221–226 (2004)
18. Liang, J.J., Qin, A.K., Suganthan, P.N., Baskar, S.: Comprehensive learning particle swarm optimizer for global optimization of multimodal functions. IEEE Trans. Evol. Comput. **10**, 281–295 (2006)
19. Frans, V.D.B., Engelbrecht, A.P.: A cooperative approach to particle swarm optimization. IEEE Trans. Evol. Comput. **8**, 225–239 (2004)
20. Liao, T., Molina, D., Tzle, T.: Performance evaluation of automatically tuned continuous optimizers on different benchmark sets. Appl. Soft Comput. **27**, 490–503 (2014)
21. Auger, A., Hansen, N.: Performance evaluation of an advanced local search evolutionary algorithm. In: The 2005 IEEE Congress on Evolutionary Computation, vol. 2, pp. 1777–1784 (2005)
22. Romero, C., Olmo, J.L., Ventura, S.: A meta-learning approach for recommending a subset of white-box classification algorithms for Moodle datasets. In: Educational Data Mining (2013)
23. Sun, Q., Pfahringer, B.: Pairwise meta-rules for better meta-learning-based algorithm ranking. Mach. Learn. **93**, 141–161 (2013)
24. Cui, C., Hu, M., Weir, J.D., Wu, T.: A recommendation system for meta-modeling: a meta-learning based approach. Expert Syst. Appl. **46**, 33–44 (2015)
25. Lunacek, M., Whitley, D.: The dispersion metric and the CMA evolution strategy. In: Proceedings of Genetic and Evolutionary Computation Conference, GECCO 2006, Seattle, Washington, USA, July, pp. 477–484 (2006)
26. Jones, T., Forrest, S.: Fitness distance correlation as a measure of problem difficulty for genetic algorithms. In: International Conference on Genetic Algorithms, pp. 184–192 (1995)
27. Grubbs, F.E.: Sample criteria for testing outlying observations. Ann. Math. Stat. **21**, 27–58 (1950)
28. Ferrari, D.G., Castro, L.N.D.: Clustering algorithm selection by meta-learning systems: a new distance-based problem characterization and ranking combination methods. Inf. Sci. **301**, 181–194 (2015)
29. Brazdil, P.B., Soares, C., Costa, J.P.D.: Ranking learning algorithms: using IBL and meta-learning on accuracy and time results. Mach. Learn. **50**, 251–277 (2003)
30. Neave, H.R., Worthington, P.L.: Distribution-free tests. Contemp. Sociol. **19**, 488 (1990)
31. Matala, A.: Sample Size Requierement for Monte Carlo–Simulations Using Latin Hypercube Sampling. Helsinki University of Technology, Espoo (2008)

Augmented Brain Storm Optimization with Mutation Strategies

Xianghua Chu, Jiansheng Chen, Fulin Cai, Chen Chen,
and Ben Niu(⊠)

Shenzhen University, Shenzhen, China
drniuben@163.com

Abstract. Brain storm optimization (BSO) is a recently proposed novel and promising swarm intelligence algorithm which models the human brainstorming problem-solving process. In BSO, the search areas are grouped into several clusters resulting in the diversity of population decrease in iterations. Hence, original BSO algorithm has suffered from low convergence speed and getting trapped into local optimum when solving global optimization problems since its inception. To address the issues, an augmented brain storm optimization with two mutation-based strategies (ABSO) is proposed in this study. First, a search technique based on non-uniform mutation is employed to accelerate the convergence speed of individuals locally. Second, a random mutation inspired by differential evolution is utilized to enhance the exploration capability globally. Finally, the performance of ABSO algorithm is tested on eighteen benchmark functions with various properties. Compared with the other algorithms, experimental results indicate that the proposed algorithm obviously enhance the performance of original BSO for global optimization in terms of solution accuracy and convergence speed.

Keywords: Global optimization · Brain storm optimization · Mutation-based strategies

1 Introduction

The traditional exact algorithms don't efficiently solve complex global optimization problems which have high-dimensional scale and complex problem spaces. Hence, many meta-heuristic optimization algorithms have attracted great interests from researchers across interdisciplinary. Specifically, Population-based algorithms could be categorized into two directions according to the learning mechanism [1]: One is evolutionary algorithms, which are based on the biological evolution process [2], such as genetic algorithm (GA) [3], evolutionary strategies (ES) [4], genetic programming (GP) [5], evolutionary programming (EP) [6], just name a few. The other one are swarm intelligence algorithms which are inspired by collective emergent behaviors in nature [7]. Many swarm intelligence algorithms have been proposed and widely accepted. For example, Ant colony optimization (ACO) takes inspiration from the foraging process of ants find optimum paths between nest and food sources through the cooperation among themselves [8, 9]. Particle swarm optimization (PSO) is inspired by

Y. Shi et al. (Eds.): SEAL 2017, LNCS 10593, pp. 949–959, 2017.
https://doi.org/10.1007/978-3-319-68759-9_78

simulating bird flocking behavior and information sharing to find food source [10]. Artificial bee colony algorithm (ABC) mimics the intelligent foraging behaviors of honey bee consisting of three collaborative groups of bees [11]. In swarm intelligence algorithms, the individuals tend to move towards the promising solutions through cooperation and information sharing in population.

Brain storm optimization (BSO) is a new swarm intelligence algorithm proposed by Shi [12] most recently. BSO is inspired by the collective problem-solving process of human behaviors, that is, brainstorming process [13, 14]: when people face a complex problem that an individual is difficult to solve, a group of people with diverse backgrounds will get together to brainstorm. As a consequence, the problem will be addressed with high probability. Shi successfully emulated this brainstorming process to design the BSO algorithm, of which the effectiveness has been demonstrated for global optimization problems [12]. While promising, BSO suffers from two shortcomings: First, BSO is underperforming on a diverse set of problems. Second, BSO is easy to get premature convergence. To address such issues, we propose a novel BSO algorithm with mutation-based strategies. A non-uniform mutation is employed to accelerate the convergence speed of individuals locally, while a random mutation inspired by differential evolution is utilized to enhance the exploration capability globally. The performance of ABSO algorithm is tested on eighteen benchmark functions with various properties.

The rest of this paper is organized as follows: the introduction of BSO algorithm is briefly reviewed in Sect. 2. Then Sect. 3 proposes the ABSO algorithm in details. The experimental setting compared with some other algorithms in Sect. 4. Section 5 demonstrates the effectiveness of the proposed algorithm. Finally, conclusions are summarized in Sect. 6.

2   The Introduction of BSO

In 2011, the Brain storm optimization (BSO) algorithm was proposed by Shi [12], which is easy to implement and understand. The procedure of original BSO algorithm is given in Algorithm 1. Generally, original BSO algorithm generates a new idea based on the current ideas through three strategies: clustering, creating (new individual generation) and selection [15]. Supposed that searching space is D-dimension with N ideas ($X_i = (X_i^1, X_i^2 \ldots X_i^D)$ represents the position of particle i), where $1 \leq i \leq N$, N denotes the population size and D represents the problem's dimension. During the iteration processes, original BSO firstly uses a k-mean clustering operator to group the solutions into several clusters, that is, this strategy divides all individuals into several clusters. Whereas in clustering operator, a probability value $P_{clustering}$ is employed to control the probability of a cluster center replaced by a randomly generated individual. Second, BSO creates N new ideas based on the current ideas. In other words, a new idea can be generated based on one or several ideas (or clusters), which is expected to move toward better and better solutions. In addition, the Gaussian random values are regarded as random values that are added to generate new ideas in the processes. The new ideas are generated according to following formula:

$$X^d_{new} = X^d_{old} + \xi * N(\mu, \sigma) \tag{1}$$

where X^d_{new} represents the dth dimension of the newly created ideas, and X^d_{old} is the dth dimension of the selected idea to generate new idea. $N(\mu, \sigma)$ denotes the Gaussian random function with mean μ and variance σ. ξ is a coefficient, which is used to trade-off the contribution of Gaussian random value. In addition, the ξ function is given by:

$$\xi = \log sig(\frac{0.5 * T - t}{k}) * rand() \tag{2}$$

where $logsig()$ represents a logarithmic sigmoid transfer function whose values within [0, 1]; the parameter T is the maximum number of iterations, and t means the current iteration number. K is a coefficient to change $logsig()$ function's slop, and then rand() is a random number in rang of [0, 1]. Finally, the new idea is evaluated, and replaces the old idea if the fitness values of the new idea better than the old idea.

Algorithm 1. The main procedure of the BSO algorithm

Initialization: randomly generate N ideas and evaluate the N ideas;
Do While termination criteria not met
   Clustering: cluster the N ideas into M clusters according to k-mean method;
   Creating: randomly select one idea or cluster and two ideas or clusters to create new ideas;
   Selecting: evaluate the new idea, and replace the old idea if the fitness values of the new idea better than the old idea;
End while

---

3   Mutation-Based Strategies for BSO

The original BSO algorithm is usually utilized to solve single-objective optimization problems, but it has two features to better solve multimodal optimization problems [12, 16]: One is the k-mean clustering operator that groups all individuals into several clusters, which is highly possible to maintain multi optimal solutions. The other one is the creating operator that generates a new idea by adding random noise to one or several ideas (or clusters), which is utilized to maintain the diversity of clusters and refine search areas [17]. However, BSO algorithm usually is not convergent quickly at first for complex multimodal problems. Hence, we draw into a search technique based on the non-uniform mutation-based method [18] to enhance the performance of original BSO algorithm for complex multimodal problems, which is good at searching the solution areas uniformly at early stage and very locally at later stage [19, 20]. The flowchart of non-uniform mutation-based method (mutation 1) is shown in Fig. 1. The non-uniform mutation-based method is utilized in this study better trade-off the exploration and exploitation ability of BSO algorithm. So it is very popular at multimodal functions. In this method, when the dth dimension of X^t_g is selected, a new solution generated by non-uniform mutation. The formulas are as follow:

$$X_{g,d}^{t'} = \begin{cases} X_{g,d}^{t} + \Delta(t, UB_d - X_{g,d}^{t}), & \text{if } random \geq 0.5 \\ X_{g,d}^{t} - \Delta(t, X_{g,d}^{t} - LB_d), & \text{if } random < 0.5 \end{cases} \tag{3}$$

where LB and UB are the lower and upper bounds of the variables X_g^t; t represents the current iteration; random is a random number within (0, 1). Function $\Delta(t, y)$ returns a value within $[0, y]$, which is defined as follow:

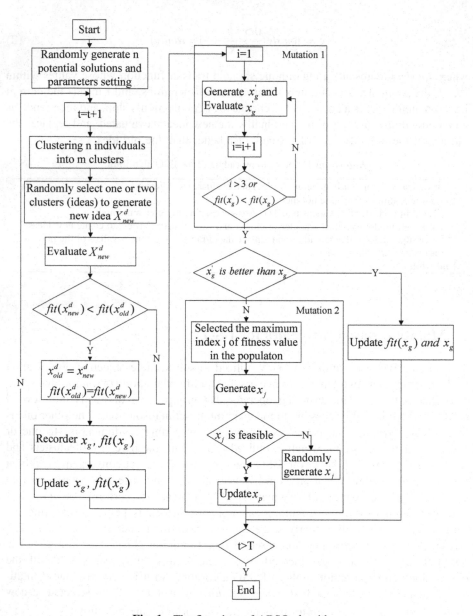

Fig. 1. The flowchart of ABSO algorithm

$$\Delta(t, y) = y \bullet (1 - R^{(1-\frac{t}{T})^b})$$ (4)

where R is a uniform random number in the range of [0, 1], T means that maximal number of iterations and b is a system control parameter determining the degree of dependency in the iteration number. The b is set to 1 in this study according to [19].

In addition, the original BSO is a kind of search space reduction algorithm [21], because all individuals are separated into several clusters. In other words, original BSO algorithm will trap into the local optimal solution due to all individuals will get into several clusters eventually, which means that the diversity of population will decrease quickly after iterations [22]. As a result, a random mutation (as shown in Fig. 1 (mutation 2)) method is inspired by DE algorithm [23], which helps individuals jump out the local search and improve the diversity of population. This thought mainly borrow ideas from the ABC [24]. In this method, for each target vector $X_{j,T}$, j represents that the position of maximum fitness value in the processes. And a mutation processes is calculated by:

$$X_{j,T} = X_{c_1^i,T} + \lambda \cdot (X_{c_2^i,T} - X_{c_3^i,T})$$ (5)

where the integers c_1^i, c_2^i, c_3^i are randomly generated from the within [1, N], which are also different from the index i. T is a current iteration; the scale factor λ is a constant factor, which is employed to trade-off the amplification of the differential variation. The larger λ means the high probability of escaping from the local optimum according to [25].

4 Experiment Settings

To comprehensively justify the performance of proposed ABSO, we have collected eighteen functions from [19, 26], used in the experimental tests. In this study, the functions are group into two categories: one includes 7 unimodal functions; the other includes 11 multimodal functions. During the calculation processes, these functions have two different attributes: shifted and rotated operator [26]. The purpose of shifting functions is employed to shift the optimal solution from its original position to a new position; and the rotated operator is utilized to increase the complexity of the function [19]. The details and properties of these functions are found in the Appendix.

The modified algorithm ABSO is tested on the benchmark functions compared with original BSO [12], Global PSO [10], local version of PSO (PSO_L) [27], OPSO [28], OLPSO [29]. For fair comparison and analyses, all the population size of test algorithms set to be 50 and the number of the dimension is 30, the number of runtimes is set as 30, and the maximum number of function evaluations (FEs) is set to be 300,000. Without loss of generality, all algorithms parameters setting are source from original references. Finally, the results of mean and standard deviation (SD) of the function values are recorded form the experiment.

5 Experimental Results

The experiment results for all algorithms are summarized in Table 1. Table 1 compares the mean values and the standard deviations of the all algorithms found in the search process. Surely, the best results are highlighted in **bold**. It is obvious that the performance of ABSO algorithm is better than other algorithms on most of the functions except $f_1, f_2, f_6, f_7, f_{13}$ from the Table 1. That is, the ABSO find a better fitness value than other algorithms by adding a local search technique and mutation method on multimodal functions. Meanwhile, the proposed strategies are also enhancing the performance of original BSO according to solution accuracy on unimodal functions f_1, $f_2, f_3, f_4, f_5, f_6, f_7$. Compared with PSO and PSO_L, ABSO also outperforms them except in f_1, f_2, f_6, f_7 and f_{13} functions. As for other algorithms, ABSO shows an obvious advantage that can find better fitness value for all the benchmark functions. So the proposed two operators make the ABSO algorithm accelerates converge to the better optimum and refine the solution areas. That is, ABSO can jump out the local optima and obtain very high improvement on solution accuracy and convergence rate on multimodal functions.

Table 1. Results of the 30-D functions

	Mean	SD	Mean	SD	Mean	SD
	f_1		f_2		f_3	
ABSO	4.84E−11	1.87E−10	0.005932	0.006117	**8.86E−01**	3.46E−01
BSO	2.27E−09	5.17E−09	0.231704	0.168281	1.84E+00	7.98E−01
PSO_L	1.25E−14	1.77E−14	1.03E−12	1.44E−12	1.25E+03	1.48E+03
OLPSO	0.013355	0.005785	0.028437	0.010229	1.22E+03	2.03E+02
OPSO	0.00037	0.001434	64.00787	13.06018	5.42E+04	1.34E+04
PSO	**1.57E−28**	1.31E−28	**6.00E−16**	8.11E−16	2.64E+00	2.81E+00
	f_4		f_5		f_6	
ABSO	**3.55E−02**	1.31E−02	**0.00E+00**	0.00E+00	340.337	519.8566
BSO	1.77E−01	5.55E−02	6.67E−01	7.24E−01	634.7337	389.5728
PSO_L	6.91E+00	2.70E+00	0.00E+00	0.00E+00	244.0463	693.2015
OLPSO	6.86E+00	5.82E−01	1.33E−01	3.52E−01	31.70031	31.65799
OPSO	6.05E+01	1.41E+00	2.93E+00	1.00E+01	17039.67	10824.23
PSO	3.84E−01	3.18E−01	6.67E−02	2.58E−01	**2.255197**	3.158424
	f_7		f_8		f_9	
ABSO	2.18E−07	2.18E−07	**4.57E−10**	3.36E−13	**6.21E−05**	2.41E−04
BSO	1.81E−06	1.74E−06	9.42E+00	1.82E+00	4.15E+01	7.01E+00
PSO_L	1.00E+06	2.72E+06	4.57E−10	0.00E+00	2.61E+01	5.01E+00
OLPSO	6.09E+03	7.76E+03	6.53E−05	3.49E−05	3.62E+00	1.66E+00
OPSO	4.74E+12	6.71E+12	4.57E−10	0.00E+00	4.43E+01	1.49E+01
PSO	**4.37E−11**	2.07E−11	4.46E+00	2.29E+00	2.04E+01	4.29E+00

(*continued*)

Table 1. (*continued*)

	Mean	SD	Mean	SD	Mean	SD
	f_{10}		f_{11}		f_{12}	
ABSO	**2.85E−03**	1.07E−02	**1.53E−01**	5.16E−02	**1.72E−06**	2.56E−06
BSO	5.68E+01	1.06E+01	2.53E−01	5.16E−02	8.93E+00	1.71E+00
PSO_L	2.43E+01	8.20E+00	3.93E−01	5.02E−02	2.07E−02	5.81E−02
OLPSO	3.94E+00	1.96E+00	1.25E+00	1.26E−01	9.10E−06	4.73E−06
OPSO	2.87E+01	3.86E+00	7.30E+00	1.04E+00	1.29E−01	2.12E−01
PSO	4.33E+00	2.53E+00	3.60E−01	7.37E−02	6.91E−03	2.68E−02
	f_{13}		f_{14}		f_{15}	
ABSO	8.28E−04	2.83E−03	**1.80E−01**	4.14E−02	**1.95E+03**	1.73E+03
BSO	7.98E−03	1.22E−02	2.67E−01	4.88E−02	5.14E+03	1.24E+03
PSO_L	**1.74E−11**	4.49E−11	3.62E−01	4.87E−02	2.80E+03	3.85E+02
OLPSO	2.66E−02	1.14E−02	1.22E+00	1.28E−01	2.67E+03	3.38E+02
OPSO	1.35E+00	5.21E+00	7.45E+00	1.41E+00	3.08E+03	1.12E+03
PSO	2.20E−03	4.55E−03	3.73E−01	5.94E−02	2.54E+03	3.44E+02
	f_{16}		f_{17}		f_{18}	
ABSO	**1.30E−05**	2.93E−05	**9.95E−01**	1.07E+00	**8.75E+00**	4.30E+00
BSO	4.32E−01	5.32E−01	7.55E+01	1.90E+01	4.66E+02	1.43E+02
PSO_L	7.80E−01	9.08E−01	4.32E+01	1.04E+01	4.38E+01	1.37E+01
OLPSO	2.13E−01	8.24E−02	8.50E+00	2.83E+00	1.75E+01	4.07E+00
OPSO	9.27E−01	1.54E+00	5.78E+01	1.31E+01	6.42E+01	1.48E+01
PSO	1.22E+00	8.25E−01	2.51E+01	6.48E+00	2.40E+01	6.27E+00

Finally, we plot the convergence processes according to the mean best fitness values over 30 runs for six functions; and Fig. 2 shows the convergence characteristics of all algorithms on six representative functions: unrotated unimodal function (f_4), unrotated unimodal function (f_5), unrotated multimodal function (f_{11}), and unrotated multimodal function (f_{12}), rotated multimodal function (f_{15}), rotated multimodal function (f_{16}). It is obvious that the ABSO converges faster than the other algorithms on two unimodal and four multimodal functions at the early process, and improve the global optimum at the end stage process. From the figures we can see that, ABSO could discovery a better optimum in a high speed at the beginning of searching processes. Finally, the curves further show that the proposed strategy obviously enhances the convergence speed of ABSO on the testing functions.

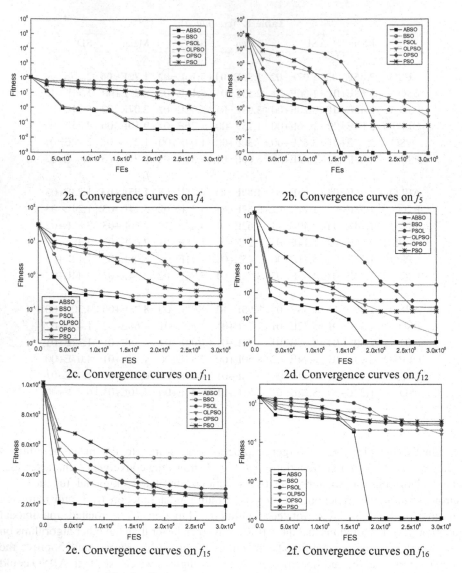

2a. Convergence curves on f_4

2b. Convergence curves on f_5

2c. Convergence curves on f_{11}

2d. Convergence curves on f_{12}

2e. Convergence curves on f_{15}

2f. Convergence curves on f_{16}

Fig. 2. Convergence curves of the 30-D functions

6 Conclusion

Though BSO has shown efficiency for global optimization, it exhibits defects including premature convergence and insufficient accuracy. In this paper, two special operators based on mutation are proposed to enhance the computational performance of BSO. Specifically, a non-uniform mutation is employed to accelerate the convergence speed of individuals locally, while a random mutation inspired by differential evolution is utilized to enhance the exploration capability globally. Experimental results demonstrate that the effectiveness and efficacy of the proposed ABSO on the global optimization problems, especially for multimodal functions.

Regarding the future work, we will apply the ABSO algorithm to more complex and large-scale testing problems to justify its performance. Moreover, the application of ABSO on real world problems is still our research direction.

Appendix: Benchmark Functions

The details of the benchmark functions are given in the below table, where 'D' denotes dimension, 'MM' denotes multimodal, 'Sf' denotes shifted operation, 'Rt' denotes rotated operation, 'Se' denotes separable. The value of the corresponding column is 'Y' if the function has the specific property, otherwise, it is 'N' (Table 2).

Table 2. Benchmark functions

#	Basic function	Search range	D	Optimal	MM	Se	Sf	Rt
f_1	Sphere	$[-100,100]^D$	30	0	N	Y	Y	N
f_2	Schwefel P2.2	$[-10,10]^D$	30	0	N	N	Y	N
f_3	Schwefel P1.2	$[-100,100]^D$	30	0	N	N	Y	N
f_4	Schwefel P2.21	$[-100,100]^D$	30	0	N	Y	Y	N
f_5	Step	$[-100,100]^D$	30	$[-0.5,0.5)$	N	Y	Y	N
f_6	Tablet	$[-100,100]^D$	30	0	N	N	Y	Y
f_7	Diff Power	$[-100,100]^D$	30	0	N	N	Y	Y
f_8	2D minima	$[-5,5]^D$	30	-2.9035	Y	Y	N	N
f_9	Rastrigin	$[-5,5]^D$	30	0	Y	Y	Y	N
f_{10}	Non-Rastrigin	$[-5,5]^D$	30	0	Y	Y	Y	N
f_{11}	Salomon	$[-100,100]^D$	30	0	Y	N	Y	N
f_{12}	Penalized 1	$[-50,50]^D$	30	-1	Y	N	Y	N
f_{13}	Penalized 2	$[-50,50]^D$	30	1	Y	N	Y	N
f_{14}	Salomon	$[-100,100]^D$	30	0	Y	N	Y	Y
f_{15}	Schwefel	$[-500,500]^D$	30	420.9687	Y	Y	N	Y
f_{16}	Ackley	$[-32,32]^D$	30	0	Y	N	Y	Y
f_{17}	Mis-scaled Rastrigin 10	$[-5,5]^D$	30	0	Y	Y	Y	N
f_{18}	Mis-scaled Rastrigin 100	$[-5,5]^D$	30	0	Y	Y	Y	N

References

1. El-Abd, M.: Brain storm optimization algorithm with re-initialized ideas and adaptive step size. In: IEEE Congress on Evolutionary Computation, pp. 2682–2686 (2016)
2. Bäck, T., Schwefel, H.P.: An overview of evolutionary algorithms for parameter optimization. In: IEEE Congress on Evolutionary Computation. vol. 1, pp. 1–23 (1993)
3. Austin, S.: An introduction to genetic algorithms. AI Expert 5, 49–53 (1990)
4. Rechenberg, I.: Evolutionstrategie: Optimierung technisher Systeme nach Prinzipien des Biologischen Evolution. Frommann-Holzboog Verland, Stuttgart (1973)
5. Koza, J.R.: Genetic Programming: on the Programming of Computers by Means of Natural Selection. MIT Press, Cambridge (1992)
6. Fogel, D.B., Fogel, L.J., Atmar, J.W.: Meta-evolutionary programming. In: Asilomar Conference. vol. 541, pp. 540–545 (1991)
7. Banks, A., Vincent, J., Anyakoha, C.: A review of particle swarm optimization. Part II: hybridisation, combinatorial, multicriteria and constrained optimization, and indicative applications. Nat. Comput. 7, 109–124 (2008)
8. Dorigo, M., Blum, C.: Ant colony optimization theory: a survey. Theor. Comput. Sci. 344, 243–278 (2005)
9. Marco, D., Montes, D.O.M.A., Sabrina, O., Thomas, S.: Ant colony optimization. IEEE Comput. Intell. Mag. 1, 28–39 (2009)
10. Kennedy, J., Eberhart, R.: Particle swarm optimization. In: Proceedings of IEEE International Conference on Neural Network. vol. 1944, pp. 1942–1948 (1995)
11. Karaboga, D.: An idea based on honey bee swarm for numerical optimization. Technical Report TR06 (2005)
12. Shi, Y.: Brain storm optimization algorithm. In: Tan, Y., Shi, Y., Chai, Y., Wang, G. (eds.) ICSI 2011. LNCS, vol. 6728, pp. 303–309. Springer, Heidelberg (2011). doi:10.1007/978-3-642-21515-5_36
13. Cheng, S., Qin, Q., Chen, J., Shi, Y.: Brain storm optimization algorithm: a review. Artif. Intell. Rev. 1–14, 445–458 (2016)
14. Shi, Y.: An optimization algorithm based on brainstorming process. Int. J. Swarm Intell. Res. 2, 35–62 (2011)
15. Cheng, S., Shi, Y., Qin, Q., Gao, S.: Solution clustering analysis in brain storm optimization algorithm. In: Swarm Intelligence (SIS), pp. 111–118 (2013)
16. Zhan, Z., Zhang, J., Shi, Y., Liu, H.: A modified brain storm optimization. In: IEEE Congress on Evolutionary Computation, pp. 1–8 (2012)
17. Guo, X., Wu, Y., Xie, L.: Modified brain storm optimization algorithm for multimodal optimization. In: Tan, Y., Shi, Y., Coello, C.A.C. (eds.) ICSI 2014. LNCS, vol. 8795, pp. 340–351. Springer, Cham (2014). doi:10.1007/978-3-319-11897-0_40
18. Michalewicz, Z.: Genetic Algorithms + Data Structures = Evolution Programs. Springer, Berlin (1996)
19. Hu, M., Wu, T., Weir, J.D.: An intelligent augmentation of particle swarm optimization with multiple adaptive methods. Inf. Sci. 213, 68–83 (2012)
20. Zhao, X.: Simulated annealing algorithm with adaptive neighborhood. Appl. Soft Comput. 11, 1827–1836 (2011)
21. Cheng, S., Shi, Y., Qin, Q.: Dynamical exploitation space reduction in particle swarm optimization for solving large scale problems. In: IEEE Congress on Evolutionary Computation, pp. 1–8 (2012)

22. Shi, C., Shi, Y., Qin, Q., Ting, T.O., Bai, R.: Maintaining population diversity in brain storm optimization algorithm. In: IEEE Congress on Evolutionary Computation, pp. 3230–3237 (2014)
23. Mallipeddi, R., Suganthan, P.N.: Differential evolution algorithm with ensemble of parameters and mutation and crossover strategies. In: Panigrahi, B.K., Das, S., Suganthan, P.N., Dash, S.S. (eds.) SEMCCO 2010. LNCS, vol. 6466, pp. 71–78. Springer, Heidelberg (2010). doi:10.1007/978-3-642-17563-3_9
24. Karaboga, D.: Artificial bee colony algorithm. Scholarpedia 5, 6915 (2010)
25. Gamperle, R., Muller, S.D., Koumoutsakos, A.: A parameter study for differential evolution. In: WSEAS NNA-FSFS-EC, pp. 293–298 (2002)
26. Chu, X., Hu, M., Wu, T., Weir, J.D., Lu, Q.: AHPS 2: an optimizer using adaptive heterogeneous particle swarms. Inf. Sci. **280**, 26–52 (2014)
27. Kennedy, J., Mendes, R.: Population structure and particle swarm performance. In: IEEE Congress on Evolutionary Computation, pp. 1671–1676 (2002)
28. Ho, S.Y., Lin, H.S., Liauh, W.H., Ho, S.J.: OPSO: orthogonal particle swarm optimization and its application to task assignment problems. IEEE Trans. Syst. Man Cybern. **38**, 288–298 (2008)
29. Zhan, Z.H., Zhang, J., Liu, O.: Orthogonal learning particle swarm optimization. IEEE Trans. Evol. Comput. 1763–1764 (2009)

A New Precedence-Based Ant Colony Optimization for Permutation Problems

Marco Baioletti[1], Alfredo Milani[1,2], and Valentino Santucci[1(✉)]

[1] Department of Mathematics and Computer Science,
University of Perugia, Perugia, Italy
{marco.baioletti,alfredo.milani,valentino.santucci}@unipg.it
[2] Department of Computer Science, Hong Kong Baptist University,
Kowloon Tong, Hong Kong

Abstract. In this paper we introduce ACOP, a novel ACO algorithm for solving permutation based optimization problems. The main novelty is in how ACOP ants construct a permutation by navigating the space of partial orders and considering precedence relations as solution components. Indeed, a permutation is built up by iteratively adding precedence relations to a partial order of items until it becomes a total order, thus the corresponding permutation is obtained. The pheromone model and the heuristic function assign desirability values to precedence relations. An ACOP implementation for the Linear Ordering Problem (LOP) is proposed. Experiments have been held on a large set of widely adopted LOP benchmark instances. The experimental results show that the approach is very competitive and it clearly outperforms previous ACO proposals for LOP.

Keywords: Ant Colony Optimization · Permutations Representation · Partial orders · Linear Ordering Problem

1 Introduction

Ant Colony Optimization (ACO) [7] is a popular meta-heuristic scheme for solving hard combinatorial optimization problems inspired by the foraging behavior of natural ant colonies. Since the seminal work of Dorigo in the early '90s [9], ACO has been extensively and successfully applied to permutation-based optimization problems, i.e., problems where a solution is a permutation of items. See for example the several ACO proposals for the traveling salesman problem [8,9], the quadratic assignment problem [10] or the permutation flowshop scheduling problem [17].

The typical ACO approach to permutation problems is to consider the items (to be ordered) as the solution components. Therefore, an artificial ant constructs a n-length permutation by starting from the empty sequence and iteratively adding up items until all the n items appear in the sequence exactly once.

© Springer International Publishing AG 2017
Y. Shi et al. (Eds.): SEAL 2017, LNCS 10593, pp. 960–971, 2017.
https://doi.org/10.1007/978-3-319-68759-9_79

Usually, the items are sequentially inserted from left to right, though simple variations, where the items can be inserted in arbitrary positions of the permutation, have been proposed [13].

To the best of our knowledge, this construction scheme is applied by all the ACO proposals for permutation problems available in literature. Basically, they all represent a permutation of n items directly as a n-length sequence without repetitions, thus, during the construction process, a partial solution is a sequence containing empty slots.

Though this representation is very natural, it is not always the most suited for the problem at hand. This is the case of the objective functions defined by means of non-local characteristics such as the precedence relations between the pairs of items contained in a permutation. Indeed, precedences are important in a variety of problems such as some scheduling problems [5,12] and, in particular, in the Linear Ordering Problem (LOP) [14] where the objective function is defined as the sum of the contributions associated to all the precedences encoded by a permutation. It is apparent that, in this case, adding a new item to a partial sequence induces a drastic change to the expected objective value of the permutation under construction.

In this paper, we propose the smoother approach of constructing a permutation by iteratively adding precedences to a, initially empty, partial order until a total order, i.e., a permutation, is formed. Starting from this idea, a new precedence-based ACO approach for permutation problems, namely ACOP, is introduced. The main novelty of ACOP is that a partial solution is a partial order, i.e., a collection of precedence relations (between items) which are transitively consistent. When this collection contains $\binom{n}{2}$ precedences, then a n-length permutation is mathematically guaranteed to be built.

ACOP has been implemented and applied to LOP. Experiments have been held on a large set of widely adopted benchmark instances where ACOP performances have been compared to state-of-the-art results. Moreover, a further experiment has been held to compare ACOP with, as far as we know, the only ACO approach to LOP available in literature, i.e., ACS-IM [6,16].

2   Ant Colony Optimization

2.1   ACO General Scheme

ACO algorithms [9,10,13] are inspired by the stigmergic foraging behavior of natural ant colonies. When a real ant discover a food source, it walks back to its nest by also leaving pheromone trails on the way, so other ants can sense the trails and reach the food themselves. Analogously, in ACO, artificial ants build up combinatorial solutions component-by-component using a probabilistic construction procedure biased by the artificial pheromone trails deposited on solution components by the best-performing ants of the previous iterations.

Let $f : S \rightarrow \mathbb{R}$ be the objective function to be optimized, where S is the set of solutions, then each $s \in S$ is composed by a certain number of components $c_1, c_2, \ldots, c_n$ taken from the set of possible components C. Clearly, S and C are problem dependent. For example, in the traveling salesman problem, C is the set of cities, while S contains all the permutations of C.

ACO aims to optimize f by iteratively probing S by means of N artificial ants. The ants indirectly communicate through a common data structure, called pheromone, which associates a real value τ_c to each solution component $c \in C$. The main scheme of ACO is depicted in Fig. 1, where, without loss of generality, maximization is assumed.

```
 1: function ACO(N, α, β, ρ, Δ_τ^{ib}, Δ_τ^{gb})
 2:     Initialize pheromone values τ_c for all c ∈ C
 3:     s^{gb} ← null
 4:     while termination condition is not met do
 5:         s^{ib} ← null
 6:         for i ← 1 to N do
 7:             s_i ← BuildSolution(α, β)
 8:             Evaluate f(s_i)
 9:             if f(s_i) > f(s^{ib}) then
10:                 s^{ib} ← s_i
11:             end if
12:             if f(s_i) > f(s^{gb}) then
13:                 s^{gb} ← s_i
14:             end if
15:         end for
16:         Optionally perform a local search on s^{ib} (and update s^{gb})
17:         EvaporatePheromone(ρ)
18:         DepositPheromone(s^{ib}, s^{gb}, Δ_τ^{ib}, Δ_τ^{gb})
19:     end while
20:     return s^{gb}
21: end function
```

Fig. 1. General scheme of ACO

Pheromone values are usually initialized to a constant value. Then, at every ACO iteration, each ant starts from an empty partial solution and builds up a complete solution by iteratively choosing components from C. In many problems, the set C_t of feasible components at construction step t is restricted by the choices done in the previous steps, thus, in general, $C_t \subseteq C$. The choice of a component c from C_t is influenced by its pheromone value $\tau_c \in \mathbb{R}^+$ and a problem dependent heuristic value $\eta_c \in \mathbb{R}^+$ which estimates the contribution of c to the solution quality. Formally, the probability of choosing $c \in C_t$ is

$$p(c) = \frac{\tau_c^\alpha \eta_c^\beta}{\sum_{k \in C_t} \tau_k^\alpha \eta_k^\beta}, \tag{1}$$

where the parameters $\alpha, \beta \in \mathbb{R}$ determine the influence of, respectively, pheromone and heuristic values.

The construction process terminates when N complete solutions (one per ant) have been generated. Each solution is evaluated using f and the pheromone is updated. First, for all $c \in C$, the pheromone value τ_c is evaporated as follows

$$\tau_c \leftarrow (1 - \rho)\tau_c, \tag{2}$$

where $\rho \in [0, 1]$ is the evaporation rate parameter. Then, a given amount of pheromone is deposited on the components belonging to the best solutions. Though various deposition strategies are possible [13], the most common ones consider the iteration and global best solutions, respectively, s^{ib} and s^{gb}. Formally, for all $c \in C$, the pheromone value τ_c is updated as

$$\tau_c \leftarrow \tau_c + I\left(c \in s^{ib}\right) \Delta_\tau^{ib} + I\left(c \in s^{gb}\right) \Delta_\tau^{gb}, \tag{3}$$

where: $I\left(c \in s\right)$ is 1 if component c belongs to solution s and 0 otherwise, while $\Delta_\tau^{ib}, \Delta_\tau^{gb} \in \mathbb{R}^+$ are the "awards" of pheromones for the components of, respectively, the iteration and global best solutions.

Finally, note that, before pheromone update, a local search refinement can be optionally applied to a selected set of solutions (usually, the iteration best).

2.2 Pheromone Models for Permutation Problems

While the typical permutation construction procedure of ACO schemes has been described in Sect. 1, here we provide a brief overview of the different pheromone models for permutation problems available in literature [5, 15].

One simple approach, denoted as PH_{abs} in [5], is to associate pheromone values to pairs composed by an item and an absolute position, in order to indicate the desirability to have a given item at a given position in the permutation.

Two other relevant approaches are PH_{suc} and PH_{rel} [5], which both assign pheromone values to ordered pairs of items. While PH_{suc} aims to encode the desirability of having the two items in consecutive positions of the permutation, PH_{rel} is less stringent and only indicates the desirability of the precedence relation between the two items independently of their distance in the permutation.

We highlight that, as far as we know, all the ACO proposals in literature using the pheromone model PH_{rel} build up the permutation as seen in Sect. 1, i.e., by iteratively adding items to a incumbent sequence till it becomes a complete permutation.

3 Permutations, Partial and Total Orders

Here, we provide a brief mathematical background useful to describe the representation of the (partial) solutions in ACOP. In particular: we introduce an encoding for generic partial orders of items, we show under which conditions the partial order is also a total order and how to obtain its corresponding permutation.

Let I be a finite set of items that, without loss of generality, can be taken as $I = \{1, \ldots, n\}$, then a strict partial order relation $\prec$ on I is a binary relation which satisfies the following properties:

- Irreflexivity: $a \not\prec a$, for all $a \in I$;
- Transitivity: if $a \prec b$ and $b \prec c$, then $a \prec c$, for $a, b, c \in I$;
- Anti-symmetry: if $a \prec b$, then $b \not\prec a$, for $a, b \in I$.

As any binary relation, a partial order $\prec$ on I can be represented as the set of pairs $P = \{(a, b) : a, b \in I \text{ and } a \prec b\}$, thus the pair $(a, b) \in P$ indicates the precedence $a \prec b$.

Conversely, given any finite set of precedences $P = \{(a_1, b_1), \ldots, (a_k, b_k)\}$, where $a_i, b_i \in I$ for $i = 1, \ldots, k$, such that the precedences in P do not violate any partial order property, it is possible to find the corresponding partial order $\prec_P$ on I generated by P, i.e., the smallest partial order which respects all the precedences in P. Operatively, $\prec_P$ is the transitive closure P^* of P, which is computed as follows. Let $P_0 = P$, then

$$P_{r+1} = P_r \cup \{(a, b) : \exists c \in I \text{ such that } (a, c), (c, b) \in P_r\}. \tag{4}$$

After a finite number s of steps, the sequence of sets $\langle P_r \rangle_r$ stabilizes (i.e., $P_s = P_{s+i}$ for any integer $i \geq 1$), because the maximum number of "compatible" precedences is finite and equal to $\binom{n}{2}$. Hence, $P^* = P_s$ and $a \prec_P b$ if and only if $(a, b) \in P^*$.

Importantly, the partial order $\prec_P$, represented by a given set of pairs P, can also be seen as the arcs set of the digraph $G_\prec$ whose nodes set is I and such that there is an arc $a \to b$ for each precedence $(a, b) \in P$. Therefore, a partial order P can be encoded by the $n \times n$ incidence matrix A of $G_\prec$, whose entries are

$$A_{ab} = \begin{cases} 1 & \text{if } a \prec b \\ -1 & \text{if } b \prec a \\ 0 & \text{otherwise.} \end{cases} \tag{5}$$

Furthermore, if $\prec$ also satisfies the property that for all $a, b \in I$, with $a \neq b$, either $a \prec b$ or $b \prec a$, then $\prec$ is a strict total order. For a total order, the matrix A does not contain any 0-entry, except in its main diagonal. Moreover, it contains $\binom{n}{2}$ 1-entries and the same number of -1s.

It is easy to see that there is a bijective correspondence between the set of total orders on I and the set $\mathcal{S}_n$ of the permutations of I. Indeed, given $\pi \in \mathcal{S}_n$, its corresponding total order $\prec_\pi$ is defined as all the precedences $a \prec_\pi b$ such that $a, b \in I$ and a appears before b in π. More formally, $a \prec_\pi b$ if and only if $\pi^{-1}(a) < \pi^{-1}(b)$, where π^{-1} is the inverse permutation of π. On the other hand, if $\prec$ is a total order, the corresponding permutation $\pi_\prec$ is recursively defined as: (i) $\pi_\prec(1) = a$ where $a \in I$ is the unique item such that $b \not\prec a$ for every $b \in I$, and (ii) $\pi_\prec(k) = a$ if $b \prec a$ only for all the $b \in \{\pi_\prec(1), \ldots, \pi_\prec(k-1)\}$.

Therefore, given a total order encoded by a matrix A (see Eq. (5)), the corresponding permutation π can be obtained by observing that $\pi(k) = a$ if and only if the a-th row of A has exactly $n - k$ 1s. Hence, by setting $\sigma(a)$ to n minus the number of 1-entries in the a-th row of A, for all $a = 1, \ldots, n$, and observing that σ is a permutation, then $\pi = \sigma^{-1}$.

As a further interpretation, note that a partial order $\prec$ individuates the set of permutations $Q_\prec \subseteq S_n$ such that $\pi \in Q_\prec$ if and only if π agrees with $\prec$, i.e., for all $a, b \in I$, if $a \prec b$ then $\pi^{-1}(a) < \pi^{-1}(b)$.

Finally, given a partial order $\prec$ and a new pair (c, d), with $c, d \in I$ and $c \neq d$, such that $d \not\prec c$, it is possible to extend $\prec$ with the precedence $c \prec d$ by simply computing the transitive closure of the set $P_\prec \cup \{(c, d)\}$.

4 ACOP: Ant Colony Optimization on Precedences

ACOP is a new Ant Colony Optimization algorithm for permutation based optimization problems which navigates the space of partial orders. Its aim is to optimize an objective function of the form $f : S_n \to \mathbb{R}$, where S_n contains all the permutations of a set I of n items.

The main structure of ACOP follows the same ACO general scheme depicted in Fig. 1. It handles a colony of N artificial ants and uses the pheromone model PH_{rel} previously described in Sect. 2.2, i.e., pheromone values are maintained in a $n \times n$ matrix where the entry $\tau_{a,b}$, with $a, b \in I$, is the amount of pheromone assigned to precedence $a \prec b$.

The original parts of ACOP are: (i) the (partial) solution representation, and (ii) the construction procedure performed by the artificial ants, i.e., the implementation of *BuildSolution* (see Fig. 1).

Indeed, every ant builds up a permutation by iteratively adding precedence relations to a partial order $\prec$, which is initially empty, until it becomes a total order. The pseudo-code of the procedure is depicted in Fig. 2.

```
 1: procedure BUILDSOLUTION(α, β)
 2:     A ← 0                                          ▷ All 0s in matrix A
 3:     np ← 0                                         ▷ Number of precedences in A
 4:     while np < (n choose 2) do
 5:         C = {(a, b) : A_{a,b} = 0 and a ≠ b}       ▷ Candidate set of precedences
 6:         (a, b) ← ChoosePrec(C, τ, η, α, β)         ▷ See equation (1)
 7:         Q ← {(a, b)}
 8:         while Q ≠ ∅ do            ▷ Insert (a, b) and compute the transitive closure
 9:             (a, b) ← remove an element from Q
10:             A_{a,b} ← 1
11:             A_{b,a} ← −1
12:             np ← np + 1
13:             Q ← Q ∪ {(a, c) : A_{a,c} = 0 and A_{b,c} = 1}
14:                   ∪ {(c, b) : A_{c,b} = 0 and A_{c,a} = 1}
15:         end while
16:     end while
17:     Return A
18: end procedure
```

Fig. 2. The permutation construction procedure of ACOP

The matrix A encodes the partial order $\prec$ that is initially empty, while the variable np is the number of 1s in A, i.e., the number of precedences of $\prec$. The loop of lines 4–16 iteratively adds 1-entries to A and terminates when A contains exactly $\binom{n}{2}$ 1-entries, i.e., when A encodes a total order which corresponds to a permutation. At each construction step, the ant chooses a precedence from C (line 5). This precedence can be safely added to $\prec$. The choice of line 6 is performed by considering pheromone and heuristic values as in the general ACO scheme provided in Eq. (1). The inner loop at lines 8–15 inserts the selected precedence in $\prec$, by removing some 0-entries from A and iteratively computing the transitive closure on A as described in Sect. 3. Finally, though, at the end of the procedure, the matrix A can be converted to a permutation (see Sect. 3), some objective functions can be directly computed on A, therefore *BuildSolution* returns the matrix A.

5   Application of ACOP to LOP

The Linear Ordering Problem (LOP) is a classical NP-Hard combinatorial optimization problem [14] and has received considerable attention because of its many applications in diverse research fields such as economy, graph theory, archeology and computational social choice.

LOP can be straightforwardly formulated as a matrix triangulation problem [14]. Given a $n \times n$ matrix H, LOP requires to find a permutation $\pi \in S_n$ of the row and column indices $\{1, \ldots, n\}$ that maximizes the objective function

$$f(\pi) = \sum_{i=1}^{n} \sum_{j=i+1}^{n} H_{\pi(i), \pi(j)} \tag{6}$$

The permutation structure of the LOP solutions allows to apply a variety of meta-heuristics and evolutionary algorithms specifically designed for the permutations search space. See for instance [1–4,11,18–20]. To the best of our knowledge, the only ACO approach to LOP has been proposed by Pintea et al. in [6,16].

An interesting observation is that the objective function of LOP can be directly computed on the permutation representation used by ACOP, i.e., on the matrix A returned by the function *BuildSolution* depicted in Fig. 2. Indeed, it is easy to see that Eq. (6) can rewritten as

$$f(A) = \sum_{a=1}^{n} \sum_{b=1}^{n} H_{a,b} \cdot \max\{A_{a,b}, 0\}. \tag{7}$$

Here, it is evident that the contribution of any single precedence relation (a, b) in the permutation to be evaluated is exactly $H_{a,b}$. Hence, a simple but effective choice for the heuristic function $\eta_{a,b}$ is to set $\eta_{a,b} = H_{a,b} + \epsilon$, where ϵ is a small positive quantity introduced to avoid null probabilities when $H_{a,b} = 0$.

Further details of the implementation of ACOP for LOP are as follows. Pheromone is deposited using a mix of the iteration-best and global-best strategies as depicted by Eq. (3). Inspired by [21], the pheromone values are constrained to the interval $[\tau_{min}, \tau_{max}]$, where $\tau_{max} = (\Delta_\tau^{ib} + \Delta_\tau^{gb})/\rho$ and $\tau_{min} = \tau_{max}/(2n^2 - n)$. All the pheromones are initialized to τ_{max}. $ChoosePrec$ (line 6 of Fig. 2) has been implemented as in [8], i.e., with probability q_0 the most probable precedence is chosen, otherwise a tournament is performed. Precedence probabilities are computed as in Eq. (1).

Finally, an enhanced variant of ACOP, called $ACOP^+$, has been devised. $ACOP^+$ performs a local search refinement on the iteration best solution at the end of every iteration. The local search has been implemented by iteratively applying the best item insertion move till no improvement is observed (see [14]). Moreover, in order to avoid stagnation, $ACOP^+$ reinitializes the pheromone values if no improvement to the global best solution has been observed during the last r iterations.

6   Experiments

The ACOP application to LOP has been experimentally investigated on the three widely known benchmark suites LOLIB, SGB and MB[1]. Therefore, a total of 105 LOP instances, with dimensionalities ranging from 44 to 250, has been considered.

The optima of these instances are known[2] and they have been used to compute two performance measures: the success rate (SR), and the average relative percentage deviation (ARPD). An algorithm is executed k times per instance, thus SR indicates the percentage of executions that reach the known optimum, while $ARPD = \frac{100}{k} \sum_{i=1}^{k} \frac{opt - run_i}{opt}$ is the average percentage deviation from the known optimum.

ACOP parameters have been experimentally tuned on a subset of 10 selected instances: the (lexicographically) first instances for every dimensionality available in the benchmarks. A set of settings have been individuated by some preliminary experiments, then a full factorial experimental design has been considered in order to choose the best setting. The involved parameters and their values are: $N \in \{20, 50, 100\}$, $\alpha, \beta \in \{1, 2\}$, $\rho \in \{0.05, 0.1, 0.2\}$, $q_0 \in \{0, 0.01, 0.1\}$, and $(\Delta_\tau^{ib}, \Delta_\tau^{gb}) \in \{(10, 0), (7.5, 2.5)\}$. Therefore, a total of 216 settings have been tested by performing 10 executions per instance with a termination criterion of 60 s. Then, the average rank of the ARPDs obtained in every instance are computed and the setting with the best average rank is chosen as the reference configuration of ACOP. This setting is $\left(N = 20, \alpha = 2, \beta = 2, \rho = 0.05, q_0 = 0.1, (\Delta_\tau^{ib}, \Delta_\tau^{gb}) = (7.5, 2.5)\right)$.

---

[1] The instances are available from http://www.optsicom.es/lolib.

[2] During the years and using a considerably large amount of computational time, they have been proved to be optima using exact methods [14].

The tuned setting has been used both for ACOP and ACOP⁺. The further parameter r of ACOP⁺ has been set to $r = 50$. Then, ACOP and ACOP⁺ have been executed 20 times on every instance. The termination criteria adopted are: 120 s for LOLIB instances, 300 s for SGB instances, and 600 s for the larger MB instances. All the experiments have been run on a homogeneous cluster of computers equipped with Intel Xeon X5650 processors clocking at 2.67 GHz. The SR, ARPD and the median time where the global best solution has been found are reported in Tables 1 (LOLIB) and 2 (SGB and MB).

Table 1. Experimental results on LOLIB instances

Instance		ACOP			ACOP⁺			Instance		ACOP			ACOP⁺		
Name	n	SR	ARPD	Time	SR	ARPD	Time	Name	n	SR	ARPD	Time	SR	ARPD	Time
N-t59b11xx	44	95	0.0004	0.437	100	0	0.133	N-t75d11xx	44	40	0.0009	4.145	100	0	0.089
N-t59d11xx	44	100	0	0.319	100	0	0.038	N-t75e11xx	44	100	0	0.854	100	0	0.046
N-t59f11xx	44	100	0	0.303	100	0	0.061	N-t75i11xx	44	100	0	1.463	100	0	0.227
N-t59i11xx	44	100	0	0.140	100	0	0.024	N-t75k11xx	44	100	0	0.330	100	0	0.024
N-t59n11xx	44	100	0	0.026	100	0	0.020	N-t75n11xx	44	100	0	0.138	100	0	0.022
N-t65b11xx	44	0	0.0163	1.003	100	0	0.115	N-t75u11xx	44	100	0	0.196	100	0	0.024
N-t65d11xx	44	100	0	0.467	100	0	0.056	N-be75eec	50	100	0	0.553	100	0	0.081
N-t65f11xx	44	100	0	0.195	100	0	0.023	N-be75np	50	0	0.0062	18.025	15	0.0002	0.172
N-t65i11xx	44	100	0	0.298	100	0	0.070	N-be75oi	50	75	0.0003	45.038	80	0.0002	0.090
N-t65l11xx	44	100	0	0.007	100	0	0.010	N-be75tot	50	90	0.0003	1.031	100	0	0.214
N-t65n11xx	44	100	0	0.191	100	0	0.051	N-tiw56n54	56	95	<0.0001	1.493	100	0	0.780
N-t65w11xx	44	100	0	0.345	100	0	0.023	N-tiw56n58	56	100	0	0.767	100	0	0.312
N-t69r11xx	44	100	0	0.067	100	0	0.024	N-tiw56n62	56	95	0.0011	1.780	95	0.0011	0.183
N-t70b11xx	44	100	0	0.295	100	0	0.028	N-tiw56n66	56	100	0	1.618	100	0	0.130
N-t70d11xx	44	10	0.0012	0.654	100	0	0.022	N-tiw56n67	56	60	0.0891	8.158	90	0.0218	0.364
N-t70d11xxb	44	100	0	0.675	100	0	0.047	N-tiw56n72	56	65	0.0008	28.039	100	0	0.259
N-t70f11xx	44	100	0	0.145	100	0	0.043	N-tiw56r54	56	60	0.0017	2.643	95	0.0009	0.637
N-t70i11xx	44	100	0	0.227	100	0	0.087	N-tiw56r58	56	100	0	1.509	100	0	0.186
N-t70k11xx	44	60	0.0041	0.907	100	0	0.039	N-tiw56r66	56	100	0	1.892	100	0	0.151
N-t70l11xx	44	100	0	0.033	100	0	0.043	N-tiw56r67	56	55	0.0002	1.610	100	0	0.089
N-t70n11xx	44	100	0	0.150	100	0	0.023	N-tiw56r72	56	95	<0.0001	1.503	100	0	0.101
N-t70u11xx	44	100	0	0.019	100	0	0.019	N-stabu70	60	0	0.0242	4.791	80	0.0052	1.670
N-t70w11xx	44	100	0	0.322	100	0	0.023	N-stabu74	60	35	0.0160	5.059	100	0	0.913
N-t70x11xx	44	100	0	0.464	100	0	0.023	N-stabu75	60	15	0.0418	4.303	95	0.0007	0.994
N-t74d11xx	44	45	0.0010	1.187	100	0	0.046	N-usa79	79	10	0.0306	25.779	30	0.0051	6.902
LOLIB Average										80	0.0047	3.432	96	0.0007	0.316

Tables 1 and 2 clearly show that both ACOP and ACOP⁺ obtained remarkable performances throughout all the instances of the benchmark suites considered. Regarding the success rates, ACOP obtained the optimum in at least one execution (SR > 0) on about the 57% of the instances, while ACOP⁺ reached the instance optimum on all the 105 instances. Moreover, in 63 cases, ACOP⁺ reached the optimum in all the executions performed (SR = 100). Most notably, also when the optimum is not reached, the very small ARPDs clearly show that both ACOP and ACOP⁺ have been able to obtain very high quality solutions. Indeed, the worst ARPD of ACOP, obtained in the N-sgb75.19 instance (see Table 2), is of only the 0.1057%, while for ACOP⁺ it is even smaller, i.e., 0.0218% in N-tiw56n57 (see Table 1). Furthermore, though the computational

Table 2. Experimental results on SGB (left) and MB (right) instances

Instance		ACOP			ACOP+			Instance		ACOP			ACOP+		
Name	n	SR	ARPD	Time	SR	ARPD	Time	Name	n	SR	ARPD	Time	SR	ARPD	Time
N-sgb75.01	75	0	0.0670	17.789	50	0.0063	2.983	N-r100a2	100	0	0.0155	29.261	65	0.0005	10.407
N-sgb75.02	75	0	0.0551	33.936	35	0.0002	6.568	N-r100b2	100	0	0.0224	31.812	5	0.0054	10.828
N-sgb75.03	75	0	0.0197	25.826	100	0	1.570	N-r100c2	100	0	0.0375	40.122	25	0.0053	13.498
N-sgb75.04	75	0	0.0225	28.953	100	0	1.509	N-r100d2	100	90	0.0003	24.370	100	0	6.515
N-sgb75.05	75	0	0.0413	41.994	100	0	1.252	N-r100e2	100	10	0.0015	27.703	75	0.0002	7.730
N-sgb75.06	75	0	0.0291	23.843	70	<0.0001	8.384	N-r150a0	150	70	0.0004	84.635	100	0	29.493
N-sgb75.07	75	0	0.0311	18.408	100	0	0.932	N-r150a1	150	0	0.0157	137.665	15	0.0005	58.211
N-sgb75.08	75	0	0.0341	28.849	100	0	2.774	N-r150b0	150	65	0.0002	74.576	100	0	8.287
N-sgb75.09	75	0	0.0166	69.700	50	0.0016	68.278	N-r150b1	150	0	0.0051	115.006	5	0.0019	36.030
N-sgb75.10	75	0	0.0413	54.677	100	0	2.720	N-r150c0	150	55	0.0007	84.107	100	0	13.054
N-sgb75.11	75	0	0.0841	28.972	50	0.0003	48.659	N-r150c1	150	5	0.0051	129.176	95	0.0001	47.817
N-sgb75.12	75	0	0.0272	14.141	100	0	2.418	N-r150d0	150	0	0.0044	102.742	90	<0.0001	31.073
N-sgb75.13	75	0	0.0125	28.362	30	0.0001	4.894	N-r150d1	150	0	0.0079	140.940	35	0.0011	72.893
N-sgb75.14	75	0	0.0258	46.338	60	0.0001	3.622	N-r150e0	150	100	0	71.879	100	0	7.742
N-sgb75.15	75	0	0.0850	34.499	90	0.0009	27.441	N-r150e1	150	5	0.0097	139.383	95	0.0001	50.005
N-sgb75.16	75	0	0.0379	16.061	100	0	3.171	N-r200a0	200	0	0.0016	340.860	100	0	70.777
N-sgb75.17	75	0	0.0545	44.567	100	0	1.640	N-r200a1	200	0	0.0042	403.498	95	<0.0001	140.697
N-sgb75.18	75	0	0.0435	54.402	70	0.0001	2.671	N-r200b0	200	0	0.0024	335.645	100	0	178.688
N-sgb75.19	75	0	0.1057	19.253	90	<0.0001	4.057	N-r200b1	200	0	0.0099	374.202	10	0.0009	221.687
N-sgb75.20	75	0	0.0415	14.087	70	<0.0001	2.573	N-r200c0	200	0	0.0029	305.989	45	0.0003	87.9785
N-sgb75.21	75	0	0.0453	18.634	75	<0.0001	6.069	N-r200c1	200	0	0.0036	349.472	100	0	89.4125
N-sgb75.22	75	0	0.0839	37.686	100	0	1.579	N-r200d0	200	0	0.0015	317.184	100	0	126.250
N-sgb75.23	75	0	0.0320	73.893	90	0.0005	4.519	N-r200d1	200	0	0.0160	459.413	5	0.0025	169.497
N-sgb75.24	75	0	0.0505	65.582	70	0.0001	6.877	N-r200e0	200	25	0.0004	276.738	100	0	55.321
N-sgb75.25	75	0	0.0613	40.212	80	0.0019	2.638	N-r200e1	200	20	0.0016	306.774	55	0.0004	140.123
								N-r250a0	250	15	0.0009	522.939	95	<0.0001	148.343
								N-r250b0	250	5	0.0006	528.481	75	<0.0001	369.338
								N-r250c0	250	10	0.0007	528.663	100	0	168.833
								N-r250d0	250	0	0.0034	557.957	95	<0.0001	318.197
								N-r250e0	250	0	0.0024	556.871	80	<0.0001	361.753
SGB Average		0	0.0460	35.227	79	0.0005	8.792	**MB Average**		16	0.0060	246.602	72	0.0006	101.683

Table 3. Experimental comparison with ACS-IM on non-normalized LOLIB instances

Instance	n	ACOP	ACOP+	ACS-IM	Instance	n	ACOP	ACOP+	ACS-IM
t59b11xx	44	0.0097	0	0.08	t75d11xx	44	0.0018	0	0.59
t59d11xx	44	0.0043	0	0.03	t75e11xx	44	0.0009	0	0.21
t59f11xx	44	0.0061	0	0.02	t75i11xx	44	0.0108	0	0.05
t59i11xx	44	0.0001	0	0.06	t75k11xx	44	0.0163	0	0.02
t59n11xx	44	0	0	0.19	t75n11xx	44	0	0	0.04
t65b11xx	44	0.0405	0	0.09	t75u11xx	44	0.0007	0	0.08
t65d11xx	44	0.0066	0	0.18	be75eec	50	0.0004	0	0.16
t65f11xx	44	0.0016	0	0.14	be75np	50	0.0089	**0.0002**	0.0004
t65i11xx	44	0.0102	0	0.19	be75oi	50	0.0023	0.0005	**0.004**
t65l11xx	44	0	0	0.03	be75tot	50	0.0037	**0.0001**	0.12
t65n11xx	44	0.0441	0	0.16	tiw56n54	56	0.0039	0	0.13
t65w11xx	44	0.0033	0	0.14	tiw56n58	56	0.0024	0	0.15
t69r11xx	44	0	0	0.41	tiw56n62	56	0.0068	0	0.08
t70b11xx	44	0.0043	0	0.03	tiw56n66	56	0.0057	0	0.13
t70d11xn	44	0.0095	0	0.05	tiw56n67	56	0.1623	0	0.45
t70d11xx	44	0.0005	0	0.13	tiw56n72	56	0.0106	**0.0002**	0.17
t70f11xx	44	0	0	0.16	tiw56r54	56	0.0057	**0.0003**	0.19
t70i11xx	44	0	0	0.15	tiw56r58	56	0.0085	0	0.16
t70k11xx	44	0.0084	0	0.05	tiw56r66	56	0.0086	0	0.09
t70l11xx	44	0	0	0.24	tiw56r67	56	0.0101	0	0.39
t70n11xx	44	0	0	0.1	tiw56r72	56	0.0630	0	0.11
t70u11xx	44	0.0015	0	0.07	stabu1	60	0.0665	**0.0015**	0.26
t70w11xx	44	0.0021	0	0.04	stabu2	60	0.0714	0	0.27
t70x11xx	44	0.0026	0	0.02	stabu3	60	0.0600	0	0.27
t74d11xx	44	0.0051	0	0.24					
Average							0.0141	**<0.0001**	0.1454

time to reach the best solution increases with the instance size n, the average times reported at the end of the tables show that the two algorithms are able to provide high quality solutions in a reasonable amount of time.

Finally, a comparison with the ACO algorithm for LOP proposed in [16], namely ACS-IM, has been performed. The results for ACS-IM have been directly taken from its original paper [16], while ACOP and ACOP$^+$ have been run for 20 executions on their same set of 49 instances (old non-normalized LOLIB instances[3]). The termination criterion has been set to 50 000 iteration as in [16]. The ARPD results are provided in Table 3.

The comparison reported in Table 3 clearly shows that ACOPs perform largely better than ACS-IM, thus promoting our proposal as the first prominent ACO approach to the linear ordering problem.

7 Conclusion and Future Work

ACOP, a new precedence-based ACO algorithm for permutation problems, has been proposed.

With respect to other proposals in literature, the main novelty of ACOP is to consider a permutation as a total order which is obtained through an incremental refinement of a, initially empty, partial order. The refinement process works by iteratively adding up a selected precedence relation together with the induced precedences. Also the pheromone model and the heuristic values are defined on the precedence relations.

This approach is particularly suited for those permutation problems where the precedence relations play an important role, for instance in the Linear Ordering Problem (LOP). An ACOP implementation for LOP is then proposed and experimentally validated on a wide set of popular LOP benchmark instances. ACOP is competitive with the state-of-the-art results and clearly outperform the previous ACO proposals for LOP.

Future research directions are: a thorough investigation of the pheromone update strategies in ACOP, the application to other permutation problems and the proposal of a ACO scheme for problems where the solutions are partial orders.

References

1. Baioletti, M., Milani, A., Santucci, V.: Algebraic particle swarm optimization for the permutations search space. In: Proceedings of IEEE Congress on Evolutionary Computation CEC 2017, pp. 1587–1594 (2017). doi:10.1109/CEC.2017.7969492
2. Baioletti, M., Milani, A., Santucci, V.: Linear ordering optimization with a combinatorial differential evolution. In: Proceedings of 2015 IEEE International Conference on Systems, Man, and Cybernetics, SMC 2015, pp. 2135–2140 (2015). doi:10.1109/SMC.2015.373

---

[3] Non-normalized LOLIB instances are available at https://www.iwr.uni-heidelberg.de/groups/comopt/software/LOLIB.

3. Baioletti, M., Milani, A., Santucci, V.: A discrete differential evolution algorithm for multi-objective permutation flowshop scheduling. Intelligenza Artificiale **10**(2), 81–95 (2016). doi:10.3233/IA-160097
4. Baioletti, M., Milani, A., Santucci, V.: An extension of algebraic differential evolution for the linear ordering problem with cumulative costs. In: Handl, J., Hart, E., Lewis, P.R., López-Ibáñez, M., Ochoa, G., Paechter, B. (eds.) PPSN 2016. LNCS, vol. 9921, pp. 123–133. Springer, Cham (2016). doi:10.1007/978-3-319-45823-6_12
5. Blum, C., Sampels, M.: Ant colony optimization for FOP shop scheduling: a case study on different pheromone representations. In: Proceedings of the 2002 Congress on Evolutionary Computation, CEC 2002, vol. 2, pp. 1558–1563 (2002)
6. Chira, C., Pintea, C.M., Crisan, G.C., Dumitrescu, D.: Solving the linear ordering problem using ant models. In: Proceedings of GECCO 2009, pp. 1803–1804 (2009)
7. Dorigo, M., Birattari, M., Stützle, T.: Ant colony optimization. IEEE Comput. Intell. Mag. **1**(4), 28–39 (2006)
8. Dorigo, M., Gambardella, L.M.: Ant colony system: a cooperative learning approach to the traveling salesman problem. IEEE Trans. Evol. Comput. **1**(1), 53–66 (1997)
9. Dorigo, M., Maniezzo, V., Colorni, A.: Ant system: optimization by a colony of cooperating agents. IEEE Trans. SMC, Part B **26**(1), 29–41 (1996)
10. Gambardella, L.M., Taillard, E.D., Dorigo, M.: Ant colonies for the quadratic assignment problem. J. Oper. Res. Soc. **50**(2), 167–176 (1999)
11. Gonçalves, J.F., Resende, M.G.C.: Biased random-key genetic algorithms for combinatorial optimization. J. Heuristics **17**(5), 487–525 (2011)
12. Li, K., Tang, X., Veeravalli, B., Li, K.: Scheduling precedence constrained stochastic tasks on heterogeneous cluster systems. IEEE Trans. Comput. **64**, 191–204 (2015)
13. López-Ibáñez, M., Stützle, T., Dorigo, M.: Ant colony optimization: a component-wise overview. Techreport, IRIDIA, Universite Libre de Bruxelles (2015)
14. Martí, R., Reinelt, G.: The Linear Ordering Problem: Exact and Heuristic Methods in Combinatorial Optimization. Springer Science & Business Media, Heidelberg (2011)
15. Montgomery, J., Randall, M., Hendtlass, T.: Solution bias in ant colony optimisation: lessons for selecting pheromone models. Comput. Oper. Res. **35** (2008)
16. Pintea, C.-M., Crisan, G.C., Chira, C., Dumitrescu, D.: A hybrid ant-based approach to the economic triangulation problem for input-output tables. In: Corchado, E., Wu, X., Oja, E., Herrero, Á., Baruque, B. (eds.) HAIS 2009. LNCS (LNAI), vol. 5572, pp. 376–383. Springer, Heidelberg (2009). doi:10.1007/978-3-642-02319-4_45
17. Rajendran, C., Ziegler, H.: Ant-colony algorithms for permutation flowshop scheduling to minimize makespan/total flowtime of jobs. Eur. J. Oper. Res. **155**(2), 426–438 (2004)
18. Santucci, V., Baioletti, M., Milani, A.: Algebraic differential evolution algorithm for the permutation flowshop scheduling problem with total flowtime criterion. IEEE Trans. Evol. Comput. **20**(5), 682–694 (2016). doi:10.1109/TEVC.2015.2507785
19. Santucci, V., Baioletti, M., Milani, A.: Solving permutation flowshop scheduling problems with a discrete differential evolution algorithm. AI Commun. **29**(2), 269–286 (2016). doi:10.3233/AIC-150695
20. Santucci, V., Baioletti, M., Milani, A.: A differential evolution algorithm for the permutation flowshop scheduling problem with total flow time criterion. In: Bartz-Beielstein, T., Branke, J., Filipič, B., Smith, J. (eds.) PPSN 2014. LNCS, vol. 8672, pp. 161–170. Springer, Cham (2014). doi:10.1007/978-3-319-10762-2_16
21. Stützle, T., Hoos, H.H.: Max-min ant system. Future Gen. Comput. Syst. **16**(8), 889–914 (2000)

A General Swarm Intelligence Model for Continuous Function Optimization

Satoru Iwasaki[1], Heng Xiao[1], Toshiharu Hatanaka[1(✉)], and Takeshi Uchitane[2]

[1] Department of Information and Physical Sciences, Osaka University, Suita, Japan
{satoru.iwasaki,heng.xiao,hatanaka}@ist.osaka-u.ac.jp
[2] Research Institute for Economics and Business Administration,
Kobe University, Kobe, Japan
uchitane@rieb.kobe-u.ac.jp

Abstract. We consider a general form of the swarm intelligence as a function optimization tool. This form is derived from a basis of mathematical swarming differential equation model, where several parameters are included in the model. These parameters are corresponding to a repulsion effect, an attractive effect and a gradient direction. We mainly consider a repulsion effect and unknown gradient estimation in this study. The nature of the proposed model by some typical numerical simulation results is described. Then, the numerous simulation results show that the behaviors of the swarm will change significantly, for example, aggregation and clustering by parameter setting. We are able to see basic behaviors of the swarm intelligence by the introduced model, the model could give us the insight to understand search behavior of swarm intelligence.

Keywords: Function optimization · Differential equation model · Swarm intelligence

1 Introduction

Swarm intelligence [1] is one of the nature mimicking algorithms for black box function optimization. Many instances of swarm intelligence are inspired by natural phenomena, such as fish school, social insects, and animal forecasting. By using swarm intelligence models, a plenty of algorithms were developed for complex function optimization problems including multi-objective optimization [2]. A particle swarm optimization (PSO) was proposed by Kennedy and Eberhart at 1995 [3]. Then, various swarm intelligence algorithms are developed, such as firefly algorithm (FA) [4], and cuckoo search [5]. In addition, there are many function optimization schemes stemming from some physical laws. For example, the charged system search (CSS) made use of Coulomb's law [6], while the gravitational search algorithm (GSA) made use of Newton's law of gravitation [7].

In general, a population-based optimization method has an attraction effect and a diffusion effect. By tuning these opposed interactions, the diversity for visiting wide regions of the search space as well as the ability to converge to the local minimum quickly is able to maintain in the search process. This is a well-known

© Springer International Publishing AG 2017
Y. Shi et al. (Eds.): SEAL 2017, LNCS 10593, pp. 972–980, 2017.
https://doi.org/10.1007/978-3-319-68759-9_80

problem of balancing between exploration and exploitation. On the other hand, as the swarm models are described by difference equations of a search agent or a particle, that is an individual of the swarm or population, each search method might have inherent dynamics according to its model. For example, PSO has second order dynamics which means that the present state is determined by the last two steps, and FA has first order dynamics which means that the present state is determined by the last step. In addition, there introduced some kind of interaction among agents and random effects, as shown in PSO each particle communicates each other via the local or global best and in FA a firefly is attracted by brighter ones with random walk. Thus, we consider that the swarm intelligence algorithms have an automated mechanism for balancing between exploration and exploitation. This mechanism is from interactions among agents. Here, from a context of function optimization, we consider that such interaction makes local and global gradient estimation of the objective function. Thus, a comprehensive view of swarm intelligence is summarized in the following two points, the first is to design a particle movement by dynamical system model, and the second is to estimate or to approximate an appropriate gradient by interaction among particles.

From this viewpoint, we consider a construction of optimization scheme by an ordinary differential equation model including a gradient estimation term. Uchitane proposed animal swarm based function optimization scheme [8] and showed its aggregation behavior in function optimization by using simulates perturbation.

Yang et al. attempted to analyze attraction and diffusion as effective mechanisms for exploitation and exploration in some nature-inspired algorithms such as FA and CSS [9]. For each algorithm in their paper, they implied that there are possibilities of controlling the exploitation and exploration by parameter tuning. In addition, Tan et al. studied adapting parameters of an evolutionary algorithm with a particular focus on a better balance of exploration and exploitation [10].

In this study, we consider a general form of swarm intelligence. Then in this paper, we introduce a simple model and examine it by numerous computer simulation. Note that randomness has also significant effects in swarm intelligence. In this paper, random effects are modeled as a simple random walk, however, the numerical simulation results could help us to understand search behavior of swarm intelligence for the function optimization.

2   Function Optimization

Let $f(x)$, $x \in R^D$ be a real valued function, where D is a dimension and x is a D dimensional vector. The function optimization is a problem to find x_0 that makes $f(x_0)$ be optimal, that is minimize or maximize.

A popular way to this problem is gradient methods such as the steepest descent method. However, it is still hard to obtain the best solution for unknown functions i.e. black box functions where a gradient and a landscape of function are unknown. A derivative–free optimization scheme is useful for unknown landscape function optimization, for example, Nelder-Mead method and simulated annealing are well known. Evolutionary computation and swarm intelligence are also derivative–free optimization method with multiple search agents and stochastic effects.

A particle swarm optimization (PSO) is described by the following model:

$$v_{t+1}^i = \omega v_t^i + r_1 c_1 (p_t^i - x_t^i) + r_2 c_2 (g_t - x_t^i), \tag{1}$$

$$x_{t+1}^i = x_t^i + v_{t+1}^i, \tag{2}$$

where, t indicates a iteration number and i denotes a particle index. Each particle x_t^i is a vector i.e. the position of the ith particle and v_t^i is also vector representing the velocity of the ith particle. The attractive coefficients c_1 and c_2 are constant values, and generally r_1 and r_2 are the uniform random numbers sampling from $[0, 1]$. The momentum term of each particle is represented by ω. Equation (1) describes dynamics of particles that depends on two memories p_t^i and g_t, where p_t^i is the personal best which is the best position found by the ith particle, and g_t is the global best which is the best position among personal best positions.

The other swarm intelligence models have a similar form to PSO model, but there is a difference in velocity update rule. These models are rather simple but have ability to achieve good performance in function optimization. However, the theoretical aspect of such heuristic approach is not enough in general. Especially, how to keep a balance between exploration and exploitation, and how to estimate a gradient by interaction among agents (particles) are important problems. In this study, we consider these points by exploring nature dynamics of swarm intelligence models. Then we show numerical simulation results using some typical benchmarks for the assumed dynamic model.

3   General Model

We assume that each search agent (particle) is driven by a dynamical system model that has an interaction with other agents, some kind of gradient estimate, random effect. Each agent performs according to the same dynamics, that means there are no leaders in the swarm. And we also assume that the model is able to be described by differential equations.

Here, we introduce the following general form of model:

$$v_{t+1}^i = \omega v_t^i - \sum_{j \in \Omega_i} h(x_t^i, x_t^j) - g^i(x_t^i), \tag{3}$$

$$x_{t+1}^i = x_t^i + v_{t+1}^i + \sigma \xi_t^i, \tag{4}$$

where $h(\cdot, \cdot)$ indicates an interaction between two agents and $g^i(\cdot)$ gradient estimates on the agents position. Ω_i denotes the set of the agents with which the ith agent interacts. ξ is a random number with zero mean.

The global best in PSO has a role to make interactions among particles. In this paper, we consider introducing an interactive term by function $h(x_t^i, x_t^j), (i, j = 1, 2, \ldots, n, j \neq i)$. Here, a repulsion effect that makes a particle move to an opposite direction each other is used as an interaction between every pair of particles in order to maintain diversity as follows:

$$h(x_t^i, x_t^j) = \alpha e^{-d\|x_t^i - x_t^j\|} \frac{x_t^i - x_t^j}{\|x_t^i - x_t^j\|}. \tag{5}$$

Here, α denotes the effectiveness of repulsion, and d is related to the range of repulsion effect can reach. Then, in this paper, we set $\Omega_i = \{j; j \neq i\}$, i.e., i^{th} agent interacts with the all other agents. We are able to define that Ω_i is a neighborhood of ith particle.

As shown in PSO, a particle estimates a gradient of the objective function at its position by the difference between the personal and global best and itself. In this model, we introduce a gradient estimate term by $g^i(\cdot)$, actually, a gradient estimate is performed by several ways. At first we can employ a simulates perturbation approach that is able to estimate gradient locally. In this paper, we employ the following finite-difference approximation,

$$g^i(x_t^i) = \gamma \frac{f(x_t^i + cs^i) - f(x_t^i - cs^i)}{2c} s^i, \tag{6}$$

where s^i denotes a random vector with 1 or -1 and c denotes a small positive number. An alternative executable approach is a gradient estimation by function approximation by using polynomial expression or kernel functions based on the particles positions. It may give rough estimate of a gradient and make an interaction among particles. We are also going to investigate this case and will show in another paper.

4   Numerical Examples

By using a general model of a swarm, we are carrying out numerous simulation experiments for various parameter settings. In this paper, for simplicity, we treat the case where the objective functions are 2-dimensional. Two typical benchmark functions, Sphere function and Double corn function are used. Sphere function is defined as follows;

$$f(x) = \|x\|^2, \tag{7}$$

and Double corn function is defined as follows;

$$f(x) = \sum_{k=1}^{2} \left(1 - \frac{2}{\|x - b_k\| + 1}\right). \tag{8}$$

Here, $b_1 = [0,0]^T$ and $b_2 = [3,3]^T$.

For simplicity, we deal with only $\sigma = \omega = 0$ in the following experiments. Note that there may be randomness derived from gradient estimation only. And even though there is no random walk effect, particles can show complex phenomenon coming from nonlinear dynamics.

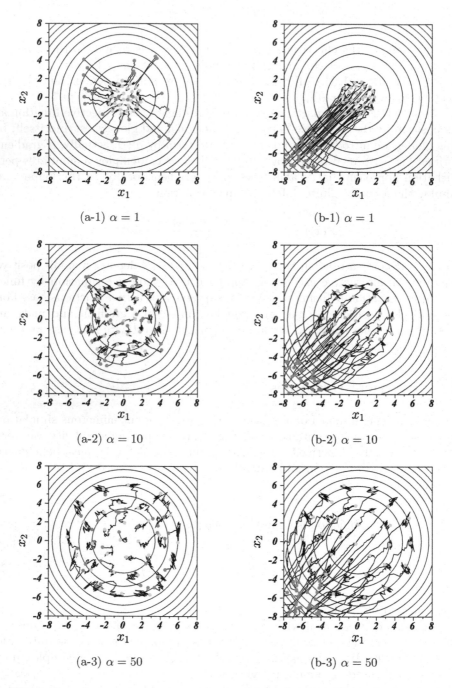

(a-1) $\alpha = 1$

(b-1) $\alpha = 1$

(a-2) $\alpha = 10$

(b-2) $\alpha = 10$

(a-3) $\alpha = 50$

(b-3) $\alpha = 50$

Fig. 1. Sample trajectories of particles for Sphere function (Color figure online)

4.1   Sphere Function

We set number of agents $n = 30$. The parameters in the Eq. (5) d and γ are 1 and 1, respectively. Figure 1 shows the typical examples of numerous numerical results for the Sphere function. Black lines describe trajectories of particles from initial positions (green dots) to final positions (red dots). Blue curves illustrate the contour lines of objective function.

As shown in Fig. 1, we can see that Fig. 1 shows that the final states form a pattern of concentric circles. Furthermore, as α increases, the diameters become larger, but the diameters do not depend on the initial positions. In particular, particles moves like a swarm in Fig. 1 (b-1). From this point of view, we expect to realize a swarm behavior only by using gradient estimate without direct aggregation interactions.

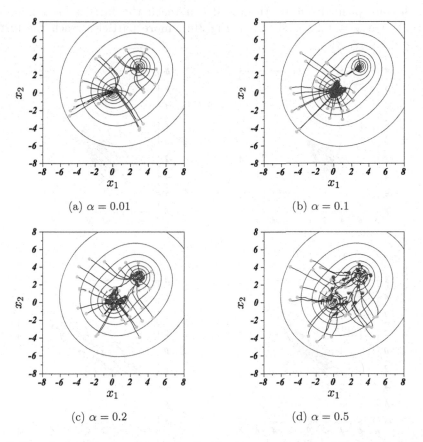

(a) $\alpha = 0.01$

(b) $\alpha = 0.1$

(c) $\alpha = 0.2$

(d) $\alpha = 0.5$

Fig. 2. Sample trajectories of particles for Double corn function. The initial positions are chosen from $[-5, 5]^2$.

4.2   Double Corn Function

We set $n = 30$, $d = 1$ and $\gamma = 5$. Figures 2 and 3 show the trajectories of particles for the Double corn function. Note that the α denotes the effectiveness of repulsion. Therefore, agents are almost influenced by the gradient estimation only when α is small, on the contrary, agents keep far distance each other when α is large.

When $\alpha = 0.01$, each particle falls in the nearby local minimum from the initial positions because they do not almost have the repulsion effects. When $\alpha = 0.1$, as shown in Fig. 3(b), almost all particles concentrate on the local minimum $(0,0)$, but some particles climb over the potential wall of objective function. The cause of this result is as follows. As some particles observe the swarm concentrating on the local minimum $(0,0)$ from the outside, they regard the swarm as a pseudo high potential area by the repulsion effects. Then, some particles are pushed out by them and can reach the further local minimum $(3,3)$. When $\alpha = 0.2$, as shown in Fig. 3(c), more particles reach the further

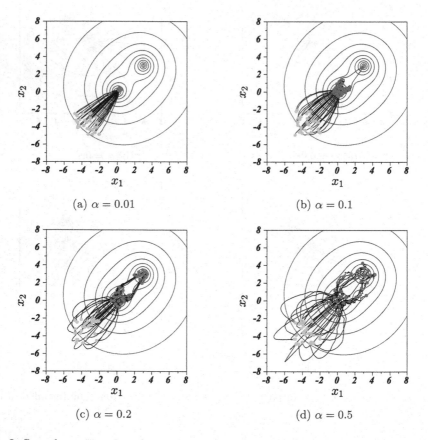

(a) $\alpha = 0.01$ (b) $\alpha = 0.1$

(c) $\alpha = 0.2$ (d) $\alpha = 0.5$

Fig. 3. Sample trajectories of particles for Double corn function. The initial positions are chosen from $[-5, -2]^2$.

local minimum $(3, 3)$ than $\alpha = 0.1$, and they make 2 clusters of the particles. Since the maximum number which each local minimum can hold decreases as α increase, the final states are almost same regardless of the initial states, see Figs. 2(c) and 3(c). When $\alpha = 0.5$, due to the pseudo potential which is made by the particles in either local minimum, some particles keep a balance between the middle of the local minima, see Figs. 2(d) and 3(d). Consequently, the boundary of the 2 clusters becomes unintelligible.

Figure 4 shows x_1 coordinate of particles at time steps $N = 4000$ for Double corn function and the initial positions are chosen from $[-5, -2]^2$.

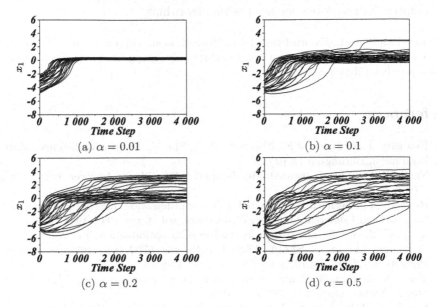

Fig. 4. x_1 coordinate of particles at time steps $N = 4000$ for Double corn function. The initial positions are chosen from $[-5, -2]^2$.

When $\alpha = 0.01$, all particles fall into the local minimum $(0, 0)$ within 1000 time steps. When $\alpha = 0.1$, all particles are trapped in the local minimum $(0, 0)$ within 2000 time steps, then 2 particles can reach another local minimum $(3, 3)$ within 3000 time steps. When $\alpha = 0.2$, some particles reach the local minimum $(3, 3)$ within about 1500 time steps, which means that the swarm searches wide range quickly. When $\alpha = 0.5$, some particles reach the local minimum $(3, 3)$ earlier than $\alpha = 0.2$, but it takes long time steps that all particles become stable states.

5 Conclusions

We have introduced the general swarming model formulation consisted by an interaction term, a gradient estimation function and a stochastic effect. In this paper, the interaction between two particles is a simple repulsion effect as shown in Eq. (5) for maintaining swarm diversity. However, as shown in Sect. 4, the particles could perform an aggregation behavior if parameters are suitably selected. In addition, by turning the repulsion effect, we could control a convergence speed shown by how the particles make clusters around a region of interest that are the local optima. We also control the diversity for traveling wide regions of search space. From this point of view, we expect to realize a swarm behavior only by using gradient estimate without direct aggregation interactions. We also expect that these researchers could be a theoretical basis for swarm intelligence and some kind of evolutionary computations for function optimization problems and be a motive for the development of novel algorithms.

Acknowledgement. Satoru Iwasaki and Heng Xiao are supported by JPSS program for Leading Graduate Schools, and a part of this study is supported by JPSS KAKENHI Grant number 15K00338.

References

1. Kennedy, J., Kennedy, J.F., Eberhart, R.C., Shi, Y.: Swarm Intelligence. Morgan Kaufmann, Burlington (2001)
2. Yang, X.-S.: Nature-inspired Metaheuristic Algorithms. Luniver Press, Frome (2010)
3. Kennedy, J., Eberhart, R.C.: Particle swarm optimization. In: Proceedings of IEEE International Conference on Neural Networks, vol. 4, pp. 1942–1948 (1995)
4. Yang, X.-S.: Firefly algorithms for multimodal optimization. In: Watanabe, O., Zeugmann, T. (eds.) SAGA 2009. LNCS, vol. 5792, pp. 169–178. Springer, Heidelberg (2009). doi:10.1007/978-3-642-04944-6_14
5. Yang, X.-S., Deb, S.: Engineering optimisation by cuckoo search. Int. J. Math. Model. Numer. Optim. 1, 330–343 (2010)
6. Kaveh, A., Talatahari, S.: A novel heuristic optimization method: charged system search. Acta Mechanica 213, 267–289 (2010)
7. Rashedi, E., Nezamabadi-pour, H., Saryazdi, S.: GSA: a gravitational search algorithm. Inf. Sci. 179, 2232–2248 (2009)
8. Uchitane, T., Yagi, A.: Optimization scheme based on differential equation model for animal swarming. Sci. Res. Publ. 2, 45–51 (2013)
9. Yang, X.-S., Deb, S., Thomas, H., Xingshi, H.: Attraction and diffusion in nature-inspired optimization algorithms. Neural Comput. Appl. 1–8 (2015). doi:10.1007/s00521-015-1925-9
10. Tan, K.C., Chaim, S.C., Mamun, A.A., Goh, C.K.: Balancing exploration and exploitation with adaptive variation for evolutionary multi-objective optimization. Eur. J. Oper. Res. 197, 701–713 (2009)

A Hybrid Particle Swarm Optimization for High-Dimensional Dynamic Optimization

Wenjian Luo$^{(\boxtimes)}$, Bin Yang, Chenyang Bu, and Xin Lin

Anhui Province Key Laboratory of Software Engineering in Computing
and Communication, School of Computer Science and Technology,
University of Science and Technology of China, Hefei 230027, Anhui, China
wjluo@ustc.edu.cn,
{byang151,bucy1991,iskcal}@mail.ustc.edu.cn

Abstract. High-Dimensional Dynamic Optimization Problems (HDDOPs) commonly exist in real-world applications. In evolutionary computation field, most of existing benchmark problems, which could simulate HDDOPs, are non-separable. Thus, we give a novel benchmark problem, called high-dimensional moving peaks benchmark to simulate separable, partially separable, and non-separable problems. Moreover, a hybrid Particle Swarm Optimization algorithm based on Grouping, Clustering and Memory strategies, i.e. GCM-PSO, is proposed to solve HDDOPs. In GCM-PSO, a differential grouping method is used to decompose a HDDOP into a number of sub-problems based on variable interactions firstly. Then each sub-problem is solved by a species-based particle swarm optimization, where the nearest better clustering is adopted as the clustering method. In addition, a memory strategy is also adopted in GCM-PSO. Experimental results show that GCM-PSO performs better than the compared algorithms in most cases.

Keywords: High-Dimensional Dynamic Optimization · Particle swarm optimization · Nearest better clustering · Problem decomposition

1 Introduction

Dynamic Optimization Problems (DOPs) are a special class of optimization problems whose objective function or constraints could change over time. For DOPs, an algorithm should not only be able to locate the global optima, but also be able to track the changes of optima. DOPs have drawn much attention in recent years due to the wide existence in real-world applications [1–3].

In evolutionary computation field, existing works about DOPs mainly focus on low-dimensional problems, while real-world dynamic optimization problems are often high-dimensional. High-dimensional optimization problems can be divided into three types [4, 5], i.e., separable problems, partially-separable problems and fully non-separable problems. In a separable problem, each pair of its decision variables does not interact, while variables in a fully non-separable problem interact with each other. For a partially separable problem, its decision variables can be divided into several independent sub-components, and variables in each sub-component are non-separable.

© Springer International Publishing AG 2017
Y. Shi et al. (Eds.): SEAL 2017, LNCS 10593, pp. 981–993, 2017.
https://doi.org/10.1007/978-3-319-68759-9_81

Thus, some high-dimensional problems can be easier to solve by decomposing the original problem into several independent sub-problems with lower dimensions, when the interactions between variables can be identified exactly [6–12]. However, existing problem-decomposition methods have not been used to solve dynamic optimization problems. Therefore, we propose a hybrid Particle Swarm Optimization algorithm based on Grouping, Clustering and Memory strategies, i.e. GCM-PSO for High-Dimensional Dynamic Optimization Problems (HDDOPs). The basic ideas of the hybrid algorithm are given as follows.

(1) First, we apply a problem decomposition method to detect interactions between decision variables. As a result, all variables are divided into several sub-components. Namely, variables from the same sub-component interact with each other, while variables from different sub-components do not. Here we adopt the commonly used differential grouping (DG) method proposed in [8].

(2) Second, in order to solve each sub-component, a species-based PSO is adopted. Here the Nearest Better Clustering method (NBC) in [13] is adopted to divide the swarm into species.

(3) Third, if an environmental change is detected, a memory strategy is applied to utilize the history information.

To the best of our knowledge, no benchmarks are specially designed for HDDOPs. Although some existing benchmarks for dynamic optimization, such as MPB [14] and GDBG [15, 16], can be extended to high-dimensional problems, they are fully non-separable problems. In order to simulate separable or partially separable HDDOPs, we give a High-Dimensional Moving Peaks Benchmark (HDMPB) based on the widely used MPB. The objective function of HDMPB consists of several independent MPBs, where each MPB is a non-separable sub-problem. Thus, HDMPB can be easily used to construct separable, partially separable and non-separable problems, respectively.

The rest of this paper is organized as follows. Section 2 introduces some related works, including PSO, NBC and DG. Section 3 describes the proposed benchmark. Section 4 details the proposed hybrid algorithm. The experimental results are provided and discussed in Sect. 5. Finally, Sect. 6 concludes this paper briefly.

2 Related Works

2.1 Particle Swarm Optimization

Particle Swarm Optimization (PSO) is modeled by simulating the behavior of social animals like birds [17–19]. The swarm of PSO is composed of some particles. Each particle which represents a solution has three components, i.e., velocity, current location and personal best location, and is connected to several other particles (called neighbors). The location of each particle is updated towards both its personal best location and neighborhood best. Among the different variants for updating the locations of particles, the constricted version [19] is widely used, and the form is given in formula (1)–(3).

$$v_{ij}(t+1) = \chi(v_{ij}(t) + c_1 r_1 (p_{ij}(t) - x_{ij}(t)) \\ + c_2 r_2 (\hat{p}_{ij}(t) - x_{ij}(t))) \tag{1}$$

$$x_{ij}(t+1) = x_{ij}(t) + v_{ij}(t+1) \tag{2}$$

$$\chi = \frac{2}{\left| 2 - \varphi - \sqrt{\varphi^2 - 4\varphi} \right|}, \text{ where } \varphi = c_1 + c_2, \ \varphi > 4 \tag{3}$$

where the parameter χ, known as the constriction factor, is used to ensure convergence; factors c_1 and c_2 are acceleration constants; r_1 and r_2 are random numbers uniformly distributed within $[0, 1]$; v_i and x_i are the velocity and location of the i-th particle; p_i and $\hat{p}_i$ denote the personal best location and neighborhood best particle's location of the i-th particle, respectively. The values of c_1, c_2 and χ are commonly set to 2.05, 2.05 and 0.729, respectively [19].

2.2 Nearest Better Clustering

NBC in [13] is based on the assumption that the distances between the best solutions of different basins are always much larger than the average distance between each solution and its nearest better one. The main steps of NBC are given as follows.

First, create an empty graph in which the number of nodes is equal to the size of the swarm.

Second, connect each solution with its nearest better solution by an edge, and the length of the corresponding edge is set as their distance. Calculate the average length of all the edges.

Finally, remove the edges longer than the product of the average length and a factor Φ. Each remained connected component is regarded as a species. The best solution in each species is the seed.

Algorithm 1 : NBC [13]

---

1. Calculate the distance among each pair of solutions;
2. Create an empty graph;
3. **For** each solution x_i **do**
4.   Find the nearest better solution x_j of x_i, connect nodes x_i and x_j in the graph by an edge with length of the distance between x_i and x_j;
5. **End**
6. Calculate the mean distance *meanDis* of the edges in the graph;
7. Remove edges which are longer than $\Phi * meanDis$;
8. Find out all the connected components in the graph, and each component forms a species;

2.3 Differential Grouping

Differential grouping proposed by Omidvar et al. [8] is an effective method to identify the interaction structure of decision variables. In [8], given a function denoted as

$f(X), X = (\ldots, x_i, \ldots, x_j, \ldots)$, the decision variables x_i and x_j are regarded as inter-acting variables, if the condition $|\Delta_1 - \Delta_2| > \epsilon$ is met. The values of Δ_1 and Δ_2 can be calculated as follows.

$$\Delta_1 = f(\ldots, x_i + \delta, \ldots, x_j, \ldots) - f(\ldots, x_i, \ldots, x_j, \ldots) \tag{4}$$

$$\Delta_2 = f(\ldots, x_i + \delta, \ldots, x_j + \delta, \ldots) - f(\ldots, x_i, \ldots, x_j + \delta, \ldots) \tag{5}$$

where ϵ is a small value which is set to 0.001 in this paper.

The basic idea of the differential grouping method is given as follows [8]. Firstly, identify the interactions between the first decision variable with other variables in a pairwise fashion by the method mentioned above. If any interactions are detected between the first variable and other variables, put them into a group as a sub-component. Otherwise, the first variable is seemed as a fully separable variable. After this process, the first sub-component is formed with the first variable and all variables interacted with it. Then the above process is repeated on the remaining variables until no variables left. It should be noted that all separable variables are placed in a single sub-component.

3   HDMPB

The proposed high-dimensional moving peaks benchmark (HDMPB) is based on the moving peaks benchmark (MPB) [14], which is widely used for simulating dynamic optimization problems. Although MPB can be extended to high dimensions, it is a fully non-separable problem. The proposed HDMPB, however, can simulate separable, partially separable and non-separable problems. The objective function of HDMPB consists of several independent MPBs, where each MPB is a non-separable sub-problem. Thus, the variables in different sub-problems (i.e., a sub-problem is an independent MPB) are not interactive. The form of HDMPB is given as follows.

$$\text{HDMPB}(x, t) = \sum_{k=1}^{K} \max_{i=1\ldots P}(H_{ki}(t) - W_{ki}(t)\sqrt{\sum_{j \in D_k} (x_j - X_{ij}(t))^2}) \tag{6}$$

where K denotes the number of sub-problems; D_k represents the set of variables with respect to the k-th sub-problem; H_{ki} and W_{ki} denote the height and width of the i-th peak in the k-th sub-problem, respectively; X_i represents the location of the i-th center point (i.e. the i-th peak for sub-problems); x_j is the location of the j-th dimension of x; and P is the number of center points, i.e. the number of peaks for each sub-problem.

The dynamics of the location, height and width of each peak are given as follows. As shown in formulas (7)–(8), the location of each peak shifts with a fixed length SL randomly, where r is a random vector. The height and width of a peak change according to formula (9)–(11), where *height_severity* and *width_severity* denote the change severity of height and width, respectively; and σ is a stochastic number fol-lowing normal distribution $N(0, 1)$.

$$v_i(t) = \frac{SL}{|(1-\lambda)r + \lambda v_i(t-1)|}((1-\lambda)r + \lambda v_i(t-1)) \tag{7}$$

$$X_i(t) = X_i(t-1) + v_i(t) \tag{8}$$

$$H_{ki}(t) = H_{ki}(t-1) + height\_severity * \sigma \tag{9}$$

$$W_{ki}(t) = W_{ki}(t-1) + width\_severity * \sigma \tag{10}$$

$$\sigma \sim N(0,1) \tag{11}$$

We use the form HDMPB-K-S to denote the tested problems, where K denotes the total number of sub-problems; and S denotes the number of variables involved in each sub-problem. For example, HDMPB-100-1 is a separable problem, and HDMPB-1-100 is a fully non-separable problem. For simplicity, the dimension of each sub-problem is equal. The tested problems, including fully separable problems, partially separable problems, and non-separable problems, are given as follows.

(1) HDMPB-100-1
(2) HDMPB-20-5
(3) HDMPB-10-10
(4) HDMPB-4-25
(5) HDMPB-2-50
(6) HDMPB-1-100

The settings of other parameters are listed in Table 1.

Table 1. Parameters for HDMPB.

Parameter	Value
D (dimension)	100
P (number of center points)	10
Change frequency	$1000 * D$
Height severity	7.0
Width severity	1.0
SL (shift length)	5, 10, 15, 20, 25, 30
λ (correlation coefficient)	0
Range of allele values	[0, 100]
Range of height	[30.0, 70.0]
Range of width	[1, 12]
Initial height for all peaks	50.0

4   Algorithm

The proposed GCM-PSO combines the problem decomposition method, the species-based PSO, and the adopted memory strategy. The pseudo code is given in Algorithm 2. The main steps are briefly described as follows. First, the interactions between decision variables are found out by the differential grouping method (Sect. 2.3) and all decision variables are divided into several independent sub-problems. Second, evolve the swarm for each sub-problem with a species-based PSO, where the nearest better clustering method (Sect. 2.2) is adopted to divide the swarm into species. Third, when a environmental change is detected, conduct the memory strategy to utilize the history information.

Algorithm 2 : GCM-PSO

1.   *memory* = ∅;
2.   Initialize the swarm *pop*;
3.   *groups* = Differential Grouping();
4.   **While** the stop condition is not achieved **do**
5.   **For** each group *j* in *groups* **do**
6.   *indices* = *groups*[*j*];
7.   *subPop* = *pop*[:, *indices*];
8.   *iteration* = 0;
9.   **While** *iteration* < *maxIteration* **do**
10.   Divide the *subPop* into species by NBC;
11.   **For** each species *s* **do**
12.   Remove redundant particles from *s* if the size is larger than P_{max};
13.   **For** each particle *p* in *s* **do**
14.   **If** *p* is the worst particle of *s* and the seed has not been improved for three successive generations **then**
15.   Mutate *p* around the seed of *s*;
16.   **Else if** *p* is the seed **then**
17.   Add a stochastic vector to *p*'s location;
18.   **Else**
19.   Update the particle *p* with (1) and (2);
20.   **End**
21.   **End**
22.   **End**
23.   Reinitialize the redundant particles removed above;
24.   *iteration* = *iteration* + 1;
25.   **End**
26.   **End**
27.   **If** the environmental change is detected **then**
28.   Re-evaluate the memory set and select the best particle M_{best} in the memory;
29.   Generate two random particles R_1, R_2. The distances between them and M_{best} are r_s;
30.   Replace the worst three particles of current swarm with R_1, R_2 and M_{best};
31.   Add at most five best seeds of the last generation into memory. If the memory is full, replace the nearest one;
32.   **End**
33.   **End**

In the following subsections, the problem decomposition method, the species-based PSO, and the adopted memory strategy are detailed, respectively.

4.1 Problem Decomposition

The differential grouping method [8] detailed in Sect. 2.3 is used to decompose the problems. Some modifications are introduced as follows.

In the original differential grouping, all the separable variables are put into a single sub-problem. However, if there are a lot of separable variables, the search space of this sub-problem is still too large. Therefore, similar to [6], if the number of separable variables is larger than S_{max}, divide the separable variables into several set of variables with the size of each set equal to S_{max}. It is noted that the last set may be less than S_{max}.

For non-separable variables, a threshold S_{min} is used. First, select all sub-problems whose dimensions are smaller than S_{min} into a list, and sort these sub-problems in descending order based on the number of the dimensions. Second, merge the last sub-problem into the first sub-problem and delete the last sub-problem from the list. Conduct the above process repeatedly until the dimension of the first sub-problem is larger than S_{min}. Then remove the first sub-problem from the list when its dimension is larger than S_{min} or it is the last one left. The above process would be repeated until the list is empty.

4.2 Species-Based PSO

The species-based PSO is adopted for each sub-problem, where NBC is used to identify the species. Some modifications are introduced as follows.

First, divide the swarm into species by the NBC method (Sect. 2.2). Note that in the original NBC, the parameter Φ is a fixed value. In this paper, the setting of Φ is given as follows.

$$\Phi = 1.2 + CurrentGen/MaxGen \tag{12}$$

where $CurrentGen$ and $MaxGen$ denote the current generation and the maximum generation in one environment, respectively. Namely, when a change is detected, the $CurrentGen$ is reset to 0.

Then, similar to [20], in order to prevent the particles from being too concentrated, a threshold factor P_{max} is adopted to limit the size of each species. Before evolving each species, perform the redundant checking first. That is to say, if the species size n is greater than P_{max}, the worst $n-P_{max}$ particles in the species will be reinitialized. The reinitialized particles would not participate in the evolution process until the next generation.

Finally, for each species, a global best PSO is used. Moreover, in order to enhance the exploitation ability, a neighborhood mutation strategy similar to [21] is adopted. The basic idea is given as follows: (1) each species seed is updated by adding a stochastic vector following the $N(0, 0.2)$ distribution to its current location; (2) if the seed has not been improved for three successive generations, the location of the worst particle in the species is updated by adding a stochastic vector following the $N(0, 1)$ distribution to the location of seed.

4.3 Memory

When a change is detected, the memory set would be re-evaluated. The best particle in the memory set is retrieved. Meanwhile, similar to [22], two random particles within the scope of $0.1 * r_s$ around the best memory particle are generated, where r_s is calculated according to formula (13) (from [20]). Then these three particles are used to replace the worst three particles of the current swarm. Next, add at most five best seeds into the memory set. If the memory set is full, the newly added particle will replace the nearest particle in the memory.

$$r_s = \frac{\sqrt{\sum_{i=1}^{dim}(ub_i - lb_i)^2}}{2\sqrt[dim]{p}} \tag{13}$$

where ub_i and lb_i denote the upper bound and lower bound of the i-th dimension, respectively; dim is the dimension of the sub-problem; and p represents the number of peaks of the sub-problems.

5 Experiments

5.1 Experimental Settings

For each problem, 30 independent runs are conducted and each run involves 60 environmental changes. The dimension (i.e., D) is 100. The function evaluation for each environment is set to $1000 * D$, namely 10^5.

The swarm size is 100 and the maximum size of each species P_{max} is dependent on the dimension. If the dimension is less than 20, P_{max} is set to 10, otherwise the value is 20. The parameters of differential grouping are set the same as in [8]. S_{min} and S_{max} are both set to 5. In addition, the size of memory is set to 50.

5.2 Performance Measurement

The mean error and standard deviation (STD) [15, 16] are used to measure the performance of different algorithms, which are calculated as follows.

$$mean = \frac{\sum_{i=1}^{runs}\sum_{j=1}^{changes}E_{ij}^{last}}{runs * changes} \tag{14}$$

$$STD = \sqrt{\frac{\sum_{i=1}^{runs}\sum_{j=1}^{changes}(E_{ij}^{last} - mean)^2}{runs * changes - 1}} \tag{15}$$

where E_{ij}^{last} denotes the best error of the j-th environment in i-th run; $runs$ and $changes$ represent the number of runs and changes, respectively.

5.3   Experimental Results

The proposed GCM-PSO is compared with GM-PSO (GCM-PSO without clustering), CM-PSO (GCM-PSO without grouping) and M-PSO (PSO with memory). It should be noted that the memory strategy used in the M-PSO and GM-PSO is similar to the memory strategy in GCM-PSO and CM-PSO. The only difference is that when updating memory, five best particles are selected rather than five best seeds because M-PSO and GM-PSO do not have species.

The experimental results on HDMPB with small change severity (i.e. small shift length) are shown in Table 2. The results show that GCM-PSO performs the best in all partially separable problems. For example, for the problem HDMPB-10-10 in Table 2, for the case the shift length (i.e., SL) is 5, the mean error of GCM-PSO is 30.90, much better than the values of CM-PSO, M-PSO and GM-PSO, which are 143.92, 185.63 and 116.95, respectively. Moreover, GCM-PSO tends to perform much better than the compared algorithms when the problem can be decomposed into more sub-problems. For example, in Table 3, for the case the shift length is 5 for the problem HDMPB-2-50 (consisting of two sub-problems), the mean error of GCM-PSO is 15.45, better than the value 22.20 of CM-PSO, the value 41.79 of M-PSO and the value 39.52 of GM-PSO. And for the case the shift length is 5 for the problem HDMPB-20-5 (consisting of 20 sub-problems), the mean error of GCM-PSO is 16.30, while the mean errors of CM-PSO, M-PSO and GM-PSO are 284.83, 355.89, and 185.31, respectively. Thus, GCM-PSO has more advantages over the compared algorithms when there are more sub-problems in HDMPB.

For the separable problem HDMPB-100-1, Table 2 shows that GCM-PSO performs the best when the values of shift length are 20, 25, 30, however, GM-PSO performs the best when the values of the shift length are 5, 10, 15. The reason may be explained as follows. By the modified differential grouping method, the HDMPB-100-1 is divided into 20 sub-problems. For each sub-problem, it consists of 5 independent 1D MPBs. Each MPB consists of 10 peaks. As a result, the 5D sub-problem may consist of 10^5 peaks. In such a complex environment, the local best PSO used in GM-PSO may have more advantages than the species-based PSO in GCM-PSO, because of its slow convergence speed.

For the non-separable problem case (i.e., HDMPB-1-100), Table 2 shows GCM-PSO performs worse than CM-PSO. The reason is that the differential grouping method wrongly identifies the problem as a partially separable problem and divides its variables into two sub-problems.

Considering that the maximum shift length value (i.e., 30) in the first experiment is still not very large in the $100 * D$ search space, another experiment is conducted by setting much larger values of shift length (i.e., 100, 200, 300, 400, 500, respectively), or applying a random change which means randomly re-initializing the position of each peak when the environment should be changed. The results are provided in Table 3. Table 3 shows that although these four algorithms tend to perform worse with the increasing of shift length, GCM-PSO still performs the best in all partially separable problems.

Table 2. Mean error and standard deviation values achieved by GCM-PSO, GM-PSO, CM-PSO and M-PSO on HDMPB for small change severity

Shift length		5	10	15	20	25	30
HDMPB-100-1	GCM-PSO	347.41 ± 64.47	332.72 ± 62.65	323.75 ± 60.51	**317.68 ± 58.96**	**316.45 ± 57.24**	**320.42 ± 57.07**
	GM-PSO	**309.16 ± 52.31**	**318.03 ± 53.42**	**322.36 ± 51.69**	324.84 ± 50.86	325.58 ± 51.46	327.04 ± 51.14
	CM-PSO	889.94 ± 133.03	834.83 ± 126.44	799.36 ± 122.52	760.32 ± 118.23	748.62 ± 114.46	738.27 ± 111.97
	M-PSO	976.85 ± 138.85	1043.3 ± 146.73	1081.20 ± 142.96	1108.30 ± 143.51	1113.10 ± 135.07	1089.40 ± 130.53
HDMPB-20-5	GCM-PSO	**16.30 ± 9.60**	**18.19 ± 9.81**	**20.21 ± 10.09**	**22.77 ± 9.94**	**25.25 ± 10.26**	**28.29 ± 10.79**
	GM-PSO	185.31 ± 38.16	198.08 ± 40.22	210.63 ± 42.48	216.82 ± 43.17	222.41 ± 43.04	225.87 ± 43.28
	CM-PSO	284.83 ± 54.01	285.80 ± 53.97	288.65 ± 54.05	289.22 ± 55.28	289.12 ± 55.51	295.80 ± 56.63
	M-PSO	355.89 ± 47.45	392.90 ± 53.17	426.45 ± 59.27	453.12 ± 63.11	468.69 ± 70.85	483.36 ± 71.99
HDMPB-10-10	GCM-PSO	**30.90 ± 21.35**	**32.30 ± 21.17**	**33.96 ± 22.83**	**34.86 ± 22.40**	**37.28 ± 22.52**	**38.38 ± 22.80**
	GM-PSO	116.95 ± 28.44	128.5 ± 29.16	137.63 ± 29.97	145.55 ± 29.86	153.83 ± 31.99	157.16 ± 30.99
	CM-PSO	143.92 ± 33.22	146.53 ± 32.93	149.66 ± 32.85	148.04 ± 33.51	151.09 ± 32.65	148.05 ± 33.63
	M-PSO	185.63 ± 32.17	211.02 ± 38.66	234.46 ± 43.84	248.64 ± 46.44	266.05 ± 52.65	277.64 ± 53.84
HDMPB-4-25	GCM-PSO	**25.31 ± 16.48**	**25.78 ± 16.27**	**26.22 ± 16.38**	**26.27 ± 16.14**	**26.41 ± 16.13**	**26.91 ± 16.30**
	GM-PSO	79.61 ± 23.17	86.47 ± 22.09	92.36 ± 22.17	97.66 ± 21.88	103.04 ± 22.72	107.07 ± 22.55
	CM-PSO	74.59 ± 26.76	73.22 ± 26.69	73.17 ± 26.61	72.66 ± 26.56	73.23 ± 25.27	73.80 ± 25.60
	M-PSO	92.56 ± 23.83	102.91 ± 24.79	113.24 ± 26.57	123.64 ± 28.81	132.39 ± 31.63	136.59 ± 31.68
HDMPB-2-50	GCM-PSO	**15.45 ± 11.47**	**16.11 ± 11.36**	**16.68 ± 11.37**	**14.81 ± 10.96**	**17.37 ± 11.46**	**17.33 ± 11.61**
	GM-PSO	39.52 ± 11.34	48.20 ± 13.93	53.36 ± 14.37	57.84 ± 14.97	61.96 ± 15.52	65.47 ± 15.62
	CM-PSO	22.20 ± 12.02	22.57 ± 11.92	23.95 ± 11.95	23.84 ± 11.65	23.73 ± 11.65	24.19 ± 11.94
	M-PSO	41.79 ± 13.27	49.74 ± 15.60	56.33 ± 17.40	62.07 ± 18.60	66.53 ± 19.71	71.11 ± 20.75
HDMPB-1-100	GCM-PSO	18.89 ± 12.13	18.60 ± 12.05	18.75 ± 12.07	19.31 ± 12.21	19.24 ± 12.49	17.62 ± 12.32
	GM-PSO	34.35 ± 15.68	39.17 ± 16.85	43.95 ± 17.58	48.40 ± 18.87	54.22 ± 20.38	59.31 ± 21.95
	CM-PSO	**7.30 ± 9.03**	**7.50 ± 8.96**	**7.65 ± 9.01**	**7.58 ± 8.96**	**8.00 ± 9.20**	**8.04 ± 9.22**
	M-PSO	25.17 ± 11.66	28.16 ± 12.17	31.34 ± 12.80	34.41 ± 13.43	36.97 ± 14.45	39.15 ± 15.48

Table 3. Mean error and standard deviation values achieved by GCM-PSO, GM-PSO, CM-PSO and M-PSO on HDMPB for large change severity

Shift length		100	200	300	400	500	Random
HDMPB-100-1	GCM-PSO	382.99 ± 65.15	427.03 ± 67.75	445.4 ± 70.92	455.4 ± 74.27	454.42 ± 74.22	461.39 ± 76.27
	GM-PSO	**349.61 ± 53.68**	**366.18 ± 51.65**	**381.04 ± 53.26**	**389.98 ± 55.06**	**395.74 ± 54.08**	**400.53 ± 55.16**
	CM-PSO	821.87 ± 124.03	932.59 ± 140.60	1005.4 ± 162.59	1053.9 ± 173.20	1048 ± 177.95	1064.5 ± 184.62
	M-PSO	1152.10 ± 121.75	1221.70 ± 130.77	1254.90 ± 136.13	1273.70 ± 138.51	1286 ± 139.65	1292.3 ± 139.59
HDMPB-20-5	GCM-PSO	**71.64 ± 20.61**	**91.22 ± 22.91**	**94.85 ± 23.49**	**94.97 ± 23.76**	**95.8 ± 23.59**	**95.38 ± 23.60**
	GM-PSO	243.51 ± 41.68	254.51 ± 45.72	262.47 ± 48.47	262.35 ± 47.02	261.91 ± 49.07	261.56 ± 48.97
	CM-PSO	284.24 ± 56.64	299.22 ± 59.86	319.39 ± 67.48	330.73 ± 70.81	333.21 ± 69.50	337.90 ± 73.39
	M-PSO	543.31 ± 69.13	596.29 ± 72.99	620.14 ± 79.96	638.94 ± 82.08	651.51 ± 89.11	660.28 ± 86.93
HDMPB-10-10	GCM-PSO	**69.84 ± 25.20**	**93.44 ± 28.39**	**97.51 ± 28.66**	**98.88 ± 30.01**	**99.1 ± 28.87**	**99.85 ± 28.95**
	GM-PSO	189.86 ± 34.23	205.21 ± 36.81	211.52 ± 38.16	215.33 ± 40.09	215.12 ± 39.90	217.02 ± 39.11
	CM-PSO	155.33 ± 37.73	165.62 ± 39.67	172.40 ± 42.31	172.82 ± 40.73	171.64 ± 41.99	173.09 ± 42.77
	M-PSO	353.65 ± 61.61	361.86 ± 59.84	365.02 ± 59.35	362.63 ± 58.61	360.37 ± 57.93	367.36 ± 61.66
HDMPB-4-25	GCM-PSO	**38.75 ± 15.91**	**52.84 ± 16.97**	**57.13 ± 20.90**	**58.19 ± 20.76**	**59.28 ± 20.41**	**59.60 ± 20.72**
	GM-PSO	145.90 ± 23.48	157.80 ± 29.01	158.05 ± 30.05	157.55 ± 29.24	158.94 ± 29.73	158.85 ± 30.70
	CM-PSO	77.06 ± 24.51	78.93 ± 21.55	76.24 ± 23.25	77.14 ± 23.79	76.83 ± 24.12	76.67 ± 24.43
	M-PSO	192.18 ± 36.85	209.15 ± 40.46	200.99 ± 39.74	196.93 ± 38.01	197.01 ± 38.28	195.15 ± 41.43
HDMPB-2-50	GCM-PSO	**24.01 ± 12.30**	**29.14 ± 15.23**	**32.1 ± 16.12**	**35.05 ± 16.57**	**35.66 ± 16.86**	**35.46 ± 16.57**
	GM-PSO	97.23 ± 21.82	110 ± 24.54	108.46 ± 22.10	107.34 ± 22.84	107.97 ± 24.32	107.87 ± 23.00
	CM-PSO	30.12 ± 13.54	35.88 ± 16.43	36.94 ± 16.36	39.99 ± 16.74	40.42 ± 16.88	40.32 ± 16.55
	M-PSO	107.35 ± 27.22	119.37 ± 28.14	116.17 ± 25.03	112.81 ± 24.31	111.57 ± 25.41	111.6 ± 23.86
HDMPB-1-100	GCM-PSO	19.35 ± 11.81	29.8 ± 14.87	36.75 ± 15.99	39.91 ± 17.04	38.95 ± 17.44	37.74 ± 17.41
	GM-PSO	108.37 ± 40.82	131.57 ± 43.03	130.27 ± 45.49	124.08 ± 40.16	124.1 ± 38.45	125.16 ± 39.67
	CM-PSO	**8.02 ± 8.56**	**11.57 ± 10.28**	**13.23 ± 11.25**	**15.55 ± 11.76**	**15.8 ± 11.60**	**16.55 ± 11.72**
	M-PSO	63.93 ± 23.93	71.31 ± 24.04	68.28 ± 24.78	64.26 ± 22.48	63.62 ± 21.37	64.70 ± 22.28

6 Conclusion

High-Dimensional Dynamic Optimization Problems (HDDOPs) commonly exist in real-world applications. However, to the best of our knowledge, there is not a specific benchmark designed for HDDOPs. Thus, we give a novel benchmark problem, called HDMPB, which can simulate separable or partially separable problems in addition to non-separable problems. The objective function of HDMPB is the sum of several independent MPBs, where each MPB is a non-separable sub-problem. Thus, the variables in different sub-problems (i.e., a sub-problem is an independent MBP) do not interact.

Moreover, we propose a hybrid particle swarm optimization algorithm (GCM-PSO) for HDDOPs. The main steps are given as follows. First, decompose HDDOPs into a number of sub-problems based on variable interactions by a differential grouping method. Then, evolve the swarm of each sub-problem with a species-based particle swarm optimization, where the nearest better clustering (NBC) is used to divide the swarm into species. In addition, a memory strategy is used to utilize historical information. To test the performance of the proposed algorithm, two experiments are conducted with small and large change severities, respectively. The experimental results show that GCM-PSO performs much better than the compared algorithms in all partially separable problems.

Acknowledgment. This work is partly supported by the National Natural Science Foundation of China (No. 61573327).

References

1. Cruz, C., González, J.R., Pelta, D.A.: Optimization in dynamic environments: a survey on problems, methods and measures. Soft. Comput. **15**(7), 1427–1448 (2011)
2. Nguyen, T.T., Yang, S., Branke, J.: Evolutionary dynamic optimization: a survey of the state of the art. Swarm and Evolutionary Computation. **6**, 1–24 (2012)
3. Bu, C., Luo, W., Yue, L.: Continuous dynamic constrained optimization with ensemble of locating and tracking feasible regions strategies. IEEE Trans. Evol. Comput. **21**(1), 14–33 (2016)
4. Tang, K., Yáo, X., Suganthan, P.N., MacNish, C., et al.: Benchmark functions for the CEC 2008 special session and competition on large scale global optimization. Nat. Inspir. Comput. Appl. Lab. USTC, China **24**, 153–177 (2007)
5. Li, X., Tang, K., Omidvar, M.N., Yang, Z., et al.: Benchmark functions for the CEC 2013 special session and competition on large-scale global optimization. Gene **7**(33), 8 (2013)
6. Hu, X.-M., He, F.-L., Chen, W.-N., Zhang, J.: Cooperation coevolution with fast interdependency identification for large scale optimization. Inf. Sci. **381**, 142–160 (2017)
7. Omidvar, M.N., Li, X., Yao, X.: Cooperative co-evolution with delta grouping for large scale non-separable function optimization. In: Proceedings of IEEE Congress on Evolutionary Computation (CEC), pp. 1–8. IEEE (2010)
8. Omidvar, M.N., Li, X., Mei, Y., Yao, X.: Cooperative co-evolution with differential grouping for large scale optimization. IEEE Trans. Evol. Comput. **18**(3), 378–393 (2014)

9. Yang, Z., Tang, K., Yao, X.: Large scale evolutionary optimization using cooperative coevolution. Inf. Sci. **178**(15), 2985–2999 (2008)
10. Yang, Z., Tang, K., Yao, X.: Multilevel cooperative coevolution for large scale optimization. In: Proceedings of IEEE Congress on Evolutionary Computation, pp. 1663–1670. IEEE (2008)
11. Mei, Y., Omidvar, M.N., Li, X., Yao, X.: A competitive divide-and-conquer algorithm for unconstrained large-scale black-box optimization. ACM Trans. Math. Softw. **42**(2), 13 (2016)
12. Omidvar, M.N., Yang, M., Mei, Y., Li, X., et al.: DG2: a faster and more accurate differential grouping for large-scale black-box optimization. IEEE Trans. Evol. Comput. (2017). http://ieeexplore.ieee.org/abstract/document/7911173/
13. Preuss, M.: Niching the CMA-ES via nearest-better clustering. In: Proceedings of 12th Annual Conference Companion on Genetic and Evolutionary Computation, pp. 1711–1718. ACM (2010)
14. Branke, J.: Memory enhanced evolutionary algorithms for changing optimization problems. In: Proceedings of IEEE Congress on Evolutionary Computation (CEC), pp. 1875–1882. IEEE (1999)
15. Li, C., Yang, S., Nguyen, T., Yu, E., et al.: Benchmark generator for CEC 2009 competition on dynamic optimization. Technical report, University of Leicester, University of Birmingham, Nanyang Technological University (2008)
16. Li, C., Yang, S., Pelta, D.A.: Benchmark generator for the IEEE WCCI-2012 competition on evolutionary computation for dynamic optimization problems. Brunel University, UK (2011)
17. Shi, Y., Eberhart, R.: A modified particle swarm optimizer. In: Proceedings of IEEE Congress on Evolutionary Computation (CEC), pp. 69–73. IEEE (1998)
18. Clerc, M., Kennedy, J.: The particle swarm-explosion, stability, and convergence in a multidimensional complex space. IEEE Trans. Evol. Comput. **6**(1), 58–73 (2002)
19. Shi, Y.: Particle swarm optimization: developments, applications and resources. In: Proceedings of IEEE Congress on Evolutionary Computation (CEC), pp. 81–86. IEEE (2001)
20. Parrott, D., Li, X.: Locating and tracking multiple dynamic optima by a particle swarm model using speciation. IEEE Trans. Evol. Comput. **10**(4), 440–458 (2006)
21. Das, S., Mandal, A., Mukherjee, R.: An adaptive differential evolution algorithm for global optimization in dynamic environments. IEEE Trans. Cybern. **44**(6), 966–978 (2014)
22. Luo, W., Sun, J., Bu, C., Liang, H.: Species-based particle swarm optimizer enhanced by memory for dynamic optimization. Appl. Soft Comput. **47**, 130–140 (2016)

Visualizing the Search Dynamics in a High-Dimensional Space for a Particle Swarm Optimizer

Qiqi Duan[1], Chang Shao[1(✉)], Xiaodong Li[1,2], and Yuhui Shi[1]

[1] Department of Computer Science and Engineering,
Southern University of Science and Technology, Shenzhen, China
{duanqq,shaoc}@mail.sustc.edu.cn,
xiaodong.li@rmit.edu.au, shiyh@sustc.edu.cn
[2] School of Science (Computer Science and Software Engineering),
RMIT University, Melbourne, Australia

Abstract. Visualization of an evolutionary algorithm may lead to better understanding of how it works. In this paper, three dimension reduction techniques (i.e. PCA, Sammon mapping, and recently developed t-SNE) are compared and analyzed empirically for visualizing the search dynamics of a particle swarm optimizer. Specifically, the search path of the global best position of a particle swarm optimizer over iterations is depicted in a low-dimensional space. Visualization results simulated on a variety of continuous functions show that (1) t-SNE could display the evolution of search path but its performance deteriorates as the dimension increases, and t-SNE tends to enlarge the search path generated during the later search stage; (2) the local search behavior (e.g. convergence to the optimum) can be identified by PCA with more stable performance than its two competitors, though for which it may be difficult to clearly depict the global search path; (3) Sammon mapping suffers easily from the overlapping problem. Furthermore, some important practical issues on how to appropriately interpret visualization results in the low-dimensional space are also highlighted.

Keywords: Visualization · Dimension reduction techniques · Particle swarm optimizer · PCA · Sammon mapping · T-SNE

1 Introduction

During the process of solving the high-dimensional continuous optimization problem, the individuals of an evolutionary algorithm generally produce a vast amount of data, though in most cases only small parts of them (e.g. the optimal value and position found during iterations) are utilized and stored. It is widely expected that the inherent properties of an evolutionary algorithm (e.g. how it works, when it fails) could be better understood via properly analyzing data generated during its optimization process. To fulfill this expectation, a variety of visualization techniques (e.g. [1, 2]) have been investigated. Visualization of the search dynamics may enhance the interpretability of evolutionary algorithms which are often considered as black-box stochastic optimizers.

© Springer International Publishing AG 2017
Y. Shi et al. (Eds.): SEAL 2017, LNCS 10593, pp. 994–1002, 2017.
https://doi.org/10.1007/978-3-319-68759-9_82

Considering the complex dynamic interactions between distributed individuals and unknown environments, however, it is not a trivial task to reasonably visualize the search dynamics of evolutionary algorithms in order to extract some useful insights.

In this paper, three visualization techniques, including principal component analysis (PCA) for linear mapping [3], non-linear Sammon mapping [4], and recently developed state-of-the-art t-distributed stochastic neighbor embedding (t-SNE) [5, 6], are compared and analyzed empirically for depicting the complex search dynamics for the particle swarm optimizer (PSO) with a global neighborhood topology [7]. More specifically, the evolution process of the global best position in the high dimensional space during the search process is projected in a 2-d space. Numerical experiments simulated on a variety of continuous functions are conducted to show some dramatic differences of these visualization results obtained by these three dimension reduction techniques. Furthermore, some important practical issues on how to appropriately interpret these visualization results are also discussed. The main contributions of this paper are *twofold*. First, we will provide a detailed comparative study for visualizing the search dynamics for PSO and identify advantages and disadvantages of three representative dimension reduction techniques. Second, we will point out that the structure mapped in the low-dimensional space, although regular, should be *carefully* interpreted.

The remaining of this paper is organized as following. Section 2 reviews visualization techniques commonly used for evolutionary algorithms, especially PSO. Three visualization techniques (i.e. PCA, Sammon mapping, and t-SNE) are described in details in Sect. 3. Section 4 provides experimental results and highlights some important practical issues. Finally, conclusions are given in Sect. 5.

2   Related Work

Many researchers have resorted to visualization techniques to better understand the search behaviors of an evolutionary algorithm. For example, Pohlheim [1] used multidimensional scaling to visualize the search path of the global best individual of a genetic algorithm (GA) through the optimization space. Similar works for visualizing GAs can also be found in [8–10]. However, most of them aimed at visualizing the search process for combinatorial optimization problems. Recently, Parsopoulos et al. [11] projected the particle swarm into the 2-d space spanned by two eigenvectors of the Hessian matrix of the objective function. However, this visualization strategy needs to calculate the Hessian matrix, which may limit its application scope. Based on a node-ring graph, Kelly and Jacob [12] designed a visualization system called evoVersion to depict the evolutionary history. However, the evoVersion system has not been extended to visualize the search process for continuous optimization.

Jornod et al. [2] provided an open-source tool based on Sammon mapping and Parallel Coordinates to visualize the particle swarm. Earlier similar works can be found in [13–16]. Kim et al. [17, 18] utilized Sammon mapping to reduce the dimension of the search trajectory for a GA and PSO, respectively. Considering the wide uses of Sammon mapping for visualizing evolutionary algorithms, we will select it as a comparative baseline and identify its one disadvantage (i.e. the *overlapping* problem), as will be mentioned in this paper later. Furthermore, a discrete particle swarm optimizer was visualized by Volke et al. [19] using a landscape metaphor. Kadluczka and Nelson [20] discussed some possible disadvantages of visualization techniques for combinational optimization problems. Halim et al. [21] designed a visualization system called Viz to depict the local search behavior for a combinatorial optimization problem. Different from the above work, we will identify some advantages and disadvantages of three visualization techniques for continuous optimization problems, which will be mentioned in this paper later.

Among them, perhaps the most commonly used visualization method is the convergence plot of fitness cost *versus* iterations [22, 23]. However, the convergence curve can only provide limited information about the complex search dynamics of the swarm. For example, the convergence plot showing an averaged lowest fitness cost does not necessarily depict the convergence behavior of the individuals, even on the simple convex function. Although the above works have explored several different scenarios to some extent, the visualization methodology is still in its fancy. For instance, it is difficult to say whether projection from a high to low dimensional space would still manage to retain the dynamic interactions between the individuals and the environment.

3   Comparing Three Visualization Techniques

Typically, evolutionary algorithms record at least two types of atomic data: the positions of some (if not all) individuals, and their corresponding cost values, but for different algorithms, extra valuable information derived from the above data (e.g. rankings of the population, distances among the individuals, and classifications of the swarm) may be added. For example, PSO with a global neighborhood topology records the personally-best positions and cost values as well as the global best, while the brain storm optimizer [24, 25] saves the positions and cost values of different cluster centers. From the viewpoint of algorithmic implementation, most of evolutionary algorithms discard the older data in favor of newer solutions, in order to effectively save memory. In this research, the global best positions of PSO changed over iterations are stored in order to support *offline* data analysis and visualization.

Here, three representative dimension reduction algorithms are selected to project the evolutionary history onto a 2-d space. The first is PCA [3], a widely used linear mapping approach, which gets an uncorrelated basis set via orthogonally transferring a set of samples. The second is Sammon mapping [4], which is a non-linear multidimensional scaling method where the importance of preserving relations between nearby points is emphasized. The third is the recently developed t-SNE [5, 6], one of the state-of-the-art dimension reduction techniques, which have obtained some significant success, especially in machine learning. Owing to the space limitation, readers are encouraged to refer to the corresponding references for more details. These three visualization techniques are chosen in this paper, in order to answer the question that whether the complex dynamic interactions between the individuals and the landscape could be retained when projecting data from a high to low dimensional space.

4   Experimental Results

In this section, comparative experiments have been conducted on 9 benchmark functions [26] and the CEC 2017 test suite [27]. The function dimension is set to 10, 30, 50, and 100, respectively. Owing to space limitation, only typical visualization results with regular structures are presented in this paper. For reproduction, the MATLAB source code is available upon request[1]. All parameter settings for both PSO and visualization techniques are given in the source code. Note that the figures plotted using the given source code may have some differences from the figures as shown below, owing to the inherent random nature of both PSO and visualization techniques except PCA. But the overall global pattern presented in the figures should be the same.

Figure 1(b–d) shows three different 2-d visualization results for search dynamics of the global best position on the 30-d Sphere function, which are obtained by PCA, Sammon mapping, and t-SNE, respectively. Note that a 3-d landscape surface of the Sphere function is also displayed in Fig. 1(a), in order to give some intuitions for the convex landscape. In Fig. 1(b–d), the colormap where the color changes from yellow to deep blue represents the progressive decrease of the fitness cost. As we can see from

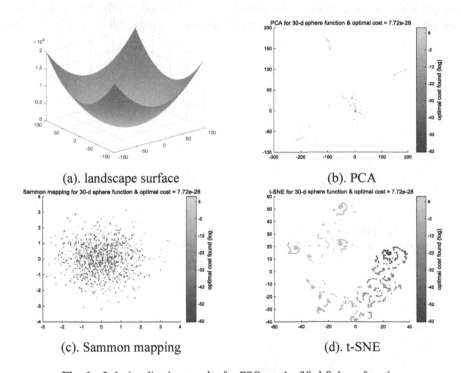

(a). landscape surface   (b). PCA

(c). Sammon mapping   (d). t-SNE

Fig. 1. 2-d visualization results for PSO on the 30-d Sphere function.

---

[1] Note that all the source code will be publicly available on Github.

Fig. 1(d), an *evolving* search path represented via color changes is generated by t-SNE, which can be considered as another form of the ancestry tree for the best solution proposed by Hart and Ross [28]. In the later search stage, all the individuals of the swarm crowd near the globally optimal position. However, t-SNE reduces the tendency to crowd together [5, 6], so that drawing the evolution of search path in the narrow region is made possible. However, the performance of t-SNE deteriorates seriously when the function dimension increases to 100. From Fig. 1(b), it can be observed that a deep-blue point approximately corresponds to the optimal position. Although the search path cannot be fully depicted, the *local* search behavior (i.e. the convergence behavior near the optima) can be identified by PCA. Different from t-SNE, PCA shows the *scalable* performance on the Sphere function from 30 dimension to 100 dimension. However, it is difficult for Sammon mapping to display both the *global* search dynamics and the *local* search behavior, since the resulting low-dimensional visualization solution generally shows considerable *overlaps* for high-dimensional functions [4], as shown in Fig. 1(c).

Similar conclusions can be also deduced on the 30-d Griewanks function with a multimodal fitness landscape, as shown in Fig. 2, except for Sammon mapping. Here Sammon mapping can show the *local* search behavior (i.e., convergence to the optima), though it appears to not depict the *global* search evolution clearly. For other dimensions (i.e. 10-d, 50-d, and 100-d), however, Sammon mapping still suffers from serious

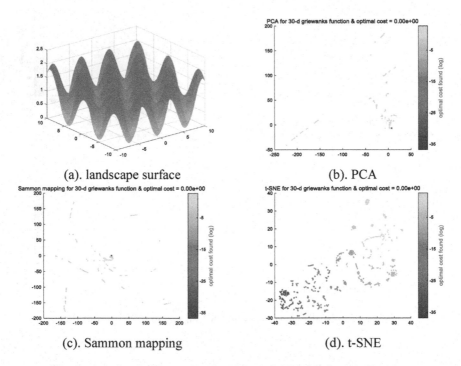

(a). landscape surface   (b). PCA

(c). Sammon mapping   (d). t-SNE

Fig. 2. 2-d visualization results for PSO on the 30-d Griewanks function.

overlaps as the same as Fig. 1(c). It is interesting that, in the early optimization stage, all the three can exhibit the exploration behavior of PSO represented by yellow points.

In Fig. 3, three dramatically different 2-d visualization results for PSO on the 30-d Rosenbrock function are shown and compared. Note that in the high-dimensional space, the Rosenbrock function is generally considered as a multi-modal function [26], despite a misleading convex shape as shown in Fig. 3(a) [29]. It is observed that t-SNE tends to have the ability to "zoom-in" the search path generated during the later search stage. The interpretation on the *evolving* search path is *a subjective matter* for the human observers, to some extent. Whether regular shapes generated in the low-dimensional space after mapping correspond to manifolds in the high-dimensional space or not needs to be further investigated. Here a preliminary analysis is shown in Fig. 4, based on the concepts of intra-cluster and inter-cluster distances. First, assume that the clustering structure shown in the 2-d space could preserve in the high-dimensional space. It is expected that the overall distance relationships in both the intra- and inter-cluster case could be also maintained.

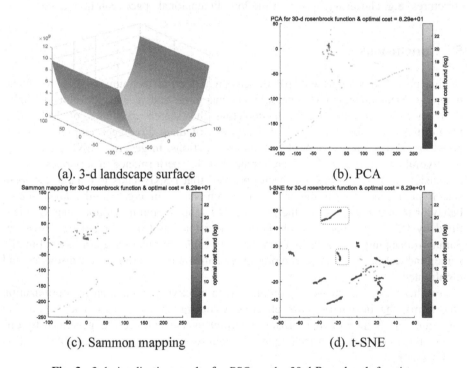

(a). 3-d landscape surface

(b). PCA

(c). Sammon mapping

(d). t-SNE

Fig. 3. 2-d visualization results for PSO on the 30-d Rosenbrock function.

The boxplots in Fig. 4 show the intra-cluster distances of the cluster one and two, which correspond to the points covered by red and green lines of Fig. 3(d) respectively, and the inter-cluster distances between the cluster one and two. As we can see from Fig. 4, the overall distance relationships in the 2-d space could be still maintained in the high-dimensional space, which may give some useful insights about the diversity of

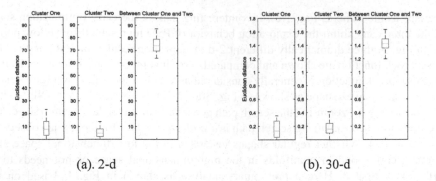

(a). 2-d   (b). 30-d

Fig. 4. Boxplots for intra-cluster and inter-cluster distances.

the individuals. However, finding and expressing the possible manifolds embedded in the high-dimensional landscape needs more sophisticated analysis tools. Overall, some structures, e.g. clustering, shown in the low-dimensional space, can be retained.

5 Conclusions

In this paper, three representative dimension reduction techniques, PCA for linear mapping, Sammon mapping for non-linear mapping, and recently developed t-SNE, were investigated extensively for depicting the search dynamics of PSO in a high-dimensional space. Merits and drawbacks of them have been empirically compared and shown on a variety of continuous functions. In general, t-SNE could show the evolution of the *global* search path but its performance deteriorates as the dimension increases. It has also been observed that t-SNE tends to enlarge the *local* search path generated during the later search stage. In contrast, the *local* search behavior (e.g. convergence of the individuals to the optimum position) may be identified by PCA with more scalable performance than its two counterparts. However, Sammon mapping suffers easily from the *overlapping* problem in most cases. Finally, some practical issues on these exploratory visualization techniques were discussed and highlighted.

Further works might include online and interactive visualization for optimization algorithms, the design of more effective visualization techniques, and so on. An ongoing work is how to appropriately interpret visualization results generated by different dimension reduction techniques, especially in the context of scalable function optimization.

References

1. Pohlheim, H.: Visualization of evolutionary algorithms - set of standard techniques and multidimensional visualization. In: Proceedings of 1st Annual Conference on Genetic and Evolutionary Computation, pp. 533–540. Morgan Kaufmann Publishers Inc. (1999)

2. Jornod, G., Di Mario, E., Navarro, I., et al.: SwarmViz: an open-source visualization tool for Particle Swarm Optimization. In: IEEE Congress on Evolutionary Computation, pp. 179–186. IEEE (2015)
3. Jolliffe, I.: Principal Component Analysis. Wiley, Hoboken (2002)
4. Sammon, J.W.: A nonlinear mapping for data structure analysis. IEEE Trans. Comput. **100** (5), 401–409 (1969)
5. Maaten, L., Hinton, G.: Visualizing data using t-SNE. J. Mach. Learn. Res. **9**(November), 2579–2605 (2008)
6. Maaten, L.: Accelerating t-SNE using tree-based algorithms. J. Mach. Learn. Res. **15**(1), 3221–3245 (2014)
7. Shi, Y., Eberhart, R.: A modified particle swarm optimizer. In: IEEE World Congress on Computational Intelligence, pp. 69–73. IEEE (1998)
8. Collins, T.D.: Applying software visualization technology to support the use of evolutionary algorithms. J. Vis. Lang. Comput. **14**(2), 123–150 (2003)
9. Lutton, E., Fekete, J.D.: Visual analytics and experimental analysis of evolutionary algorithms. INRIA (2011)
10. Lutton, E., Gilbert, H., Cancino, W., Bach, B., Parrend, P., Collet, P.: GridVis: visualisation of island-based parallel genetic algorithms. In: Esparcia-Alcázar, A.I., Mora, A.M. (eds.) EvoApplications 2014. LNCS, vol. 8602, pp. 702–713. Springer, Heidelberg (2014). doi:10. 1007/978-3-662-45523-4_57
11. Parsopoulos, K.E., Georgopoulos, V.C., Vrahatis, M.N.: A technique for the visualization of population-based algorithms. In: IEEE Congress on Evolutionary Computation, pp. 1694–1701. IEEE (2008)
12. Kelly, J., Jacob, C.: evoVersion: visualizing evolutionary histories. In: IEEE Congress on Evolutionary Computation, pp. 814–821. IEEE (2016)
13. Khemka, N., Jacob, C.: What hides in dimension X? A quest for visualizing particle swarms. In: Dorigo, M., Birattari, M., Blum, C., Clerc, M., Stützle, T., Winfield, Alan F.T. (eds.) ANTS 2008. LNCS, vol. 5217, pp. 191–202. Springer, Heidelberg (2008). doi:10.1007/978-3-540-87527-7_17
14. Khemka, N., Jacob, C.: VISPLORE: a toolkit to explore particle swarms by visual inspection. In: Proceedings of 11th Annual Conference on Genetic and Evolutionary Computation, pp. 41–48. ACM (2009)
15. Khemka, N., Jacob, C.: VISPLORE: exploring particle swarms by visual inspection. In: Sarker, R.A., Ray, T. (eds.) Agent-Based Evolutionary Search. Adaptation, Learning, and Optimization, vol. 5, pp. 255–284. Springer, Heidelberg (2010). doi:10.1007/978-3-642-13425-8_12
16. Franken, N.: Visual exploration of algorithm parameter space. In: IEEE Congress on Evolutionary Computation, pp. 389–398. IEEE (2009)
17. Kim, Y.-H., Moon, B.-R.: New usage of Sammon's mapping for genetic visualization. In: Cantú-Paz, E., et al. (eds.) GECCO 2003. LNCS, vol. 2723, pp. 1136–1147. Springer, Heidelberg (2003). doi:10.1007/3-540-45105-6_122
18. Kim, Y.H., Lee, K.H., Yoon, Y.: Visualizing the search process of particle swarm optimization. In: Proceedings of 11th Annual Conference on Genetic and Evolutionary Computation, pp. 49–56. ACM (2009)
19. Volke, S., Middendorf, M., Hlawitschka, M., et al.: dPSO-Vis: topology-based visualization of discrete particle swarm optimization. Comput. Graph. Forum **32**(3), 351–360 (2013). Blackwell Publishing Ltd.
20. Kadluczka, M., Nelson, P.C.: N-to-2-space mapping for visualization of search algorithm performance. In: IEEE International Conference on Tools with Artificial Intelligence, pp. 508–513. IEEE (2004)

21. Halim, S., Yap, R.H.C., Lau, H.C.: Viz: a visual analysis suite for explaining local search behavior. In: Proceedings of 19th Annual ACM Symposium on User Interface Software and Technology, pp. 57–66. ACM (2006)
22. Lotif, M.: Visualizing the population of meta-heuristics during the optimization process using self-organizing maps. In: IEEE Congress on Evolutionary Computation, pp. 313–319. IEEE (2014)
23. Wu, H.C., Sun, C.T., Lee, S.S.: Visualization of evolutionary computation processes from a population perspective. Intell. Data Anal. 8(6), 543–561 (2004)
24. Shi, Y.: Brain storm optimization algorithm. In: Tan, Y., Shi, Y., Chai, Y., Wang, G. (eds.) ICSI 2011. LNCS, vol. 6728, pp. 303–309. Springer, Heidelberg (2011). doi:10.1007/978-3-642-21515-5_36
25. Shi, Y.: An optimization algorithm based on brainstorming process. Emerg. Res. Swarm Intell. Algorithm Optim. 1–35 (2015)
26. Liang, J.J., Qin, A.K., Suganthan, P.N., et al.: Comprehensive learning particle swarm optimizer for global optimization of multimodal functions. IEEE Trans. Evol. Comput. 10 (3), 281–295 (2006)
27. Awad, N.H., Ali, M.Z., Liang, J.J., et al.: Problem definitions and evaluation criteria for the CEC 2017 special session and competition on single objective bound constrained real-parameter numerical optimization. Technical report, Nanyang Technological University, Singapore, November 2016
28. Hart, E., Ross, P.: GAVEL-a new tool for genetic algorithm visualization. IEEE Trans. Evol. Comput. 5(4), 335–348 (2001)
29. Wiles, J., Tonkes, B.: Visualisation of hierarchical cost surfaces for evolutionary computing. In: Proceedings of 2002 Congress on Evolutionary Computation, vol. 1, pp. 157–162. IEEE (2002)

Particle Swarm Optimization with Winning Score Assignment for Multi-objective Portfolio Optimization

Karoon Suksonghong[1] and Kittipong Boonlong[2(✉)]

[1] Faculty of Management and Tourism, Burapha University, Chonburi, Thailand
karoon@buu.ac.th
[2] Faculty of Engineering, Burapha University, Chonburi, Thailand
kittipong@buu.ac.th

Abstract. The successful implementation of particle swarm optimization (PSO) for solving portfolio optimization problems is widely documented. However, its execution is restricted within a single-objective optimization framework. The challenge of utilizing PSO based upon a multi-objective optimization framework is identifying the global best solution since a set of compromising solutions is obtained rather than a single best solution. The majority of the multi-objective PSO (MOPSO) proposed in the literature employs the Pareto dominance relation for updating solutions and repository. By using this method, unfortunately, performance of MOPSO deteriorates if the number of optimized objective increases because the chance that solutions do not dominate each other rises. To overcome this problem, the winning score assignment method is developed by taking into account the interacting relations between optimized objectives during fitness assignment process. The proposed method is integrated into the MOPSO and the resulting algorithm is named as the "winning score MOPSO" denoted by WMOPSO. The WMOPSO is experimented for solving portfolio optimization problems containing up to four optimized objectives. The performance of WMOPSO is benchmarked with its original version based upon four standard comparison criteria. Regardless of performance criteria, the comparison results reveal that WMOPSO outperforms MOPSO. In addition, its superiority is more pronounced for the many objective optimization problems.

Keywords: Winning score assignment · Particle swarm optimization · Portfolio selection · Many-objective optimization

1 Introduction

The most well-known multi-objective optimization problem (MOOP) in finance is portfolio optimization problem (POP). According to the mean-variance (MV) model [1], investors optimize their portfolio by minimizing the portfolio's risk and maximizing its expected return, simultaneously. This classical bi-objective POP can be simply resolved using either linear programming (LP) or quadratic programming (QP). Nevertheless, the successfulness of particle swarm optimization (PSO) for solving optimization problems

© Springer International Publishing AG 2017
Y. Shi et al. (Eds.): SEAL 2017, LNCS 10593, pp. 1003–1015, 2017.
https://doi.org/10.1007/978-3-319-68759-9_83

in the field of engineering and science attracts researchers to experiment PSO for solving POP. From the literature, Xu et al. [2] were the first study that implements PSO to solve the MV-POP. Thereafter, Cura [3] extended the previous application by incorporating the cardinality constraint that limits the number of asset held in the portfolio into the problem. Subsequently, short-sell constraint [4] and other practical constraints, namely, transaction cost, sector capitalize, and transaction lots [5] were considered for testing the application of PSO. These studies also conducted the performance comparison and reported that PSO outperformed the conventional genetic algorithm (GA).

It is worth noting that PSO implemented by studies mentioned above was executed within the single-objective optimization framework (SOOF) rather than multi-objective optimization framework (MOOF). In SOOF, portfolio's risk is set as minimized objective with respect to expected return and other practical constraints. Alternatively, all objectives are combined to form the aggregated objective function with the use of relative importance coefficients assigned to each optimized objectives. Although an optimal solution can be obtained by these approaches, several concerns were widely discussed in the literature. Firstly, prior knowledge about the preference for each objective and the given value of constraints which are subjective to decision maker is required. In many cases, these predetermined values unfavorably guided search mechanism of an algorithm to the wrong direction [6]. Secondly, since only one solution is obtained for each of optimization course, a series of separate runs with given values of preference coefficients and constraints is needed for generating the true Pareto solutions. This requires large computation time and makes solving a POP intractable in practice.

The main obstacle of utilizing PSO in MOOF is identifying the global best solutions. Unlike SOOF, there is no best solution for MOOP, instead a set of compromising solutions is obtained for each of algorithm run. Although, in the recent years, a number of multi-objective PSO (MOPSO) was developed [7–9], the majority of these proposed PSOs employed Pareto dominance relation for updating process and identifying the true Pareto solutions. Deb et al. [10] pointed out that, based on this selection scheme, chances that no solution can dominate the other are expectably high when the number of conflicting objectives of MOOP increases. Therefore, suitable techniques for screening out a large number of non-dominated solutions should be designed and equipped into MOPSO to enhance its capability for dealing with many-objective optimization problem [11].

In this paper, the winning score assignment method based on rank assignment scheme is proposed. An assignment mechanism, named as "winning score", is developed and integrated into several processes of the previously proposed MOPSO [9]. The winning score is designed by taking into account the interactions among optimized objectives. This significantly improves several processes resulting from the comprehensive selection criteria, such as, location updating, velocity adjusting, global best identifying, as well as diversity preserving. As a result, the proposed algorithm exhibits remarkable capabilities in dealing with many-objective optimization problem within the MOOF. Ultimately, the proposed algorithm is utilized for solving the real-world financial optimization problem with up to four optimized objectives. Moreover, its performance is benchmarked with the original MOPSO based upon the performance comparison criteria widely employed in the literature.

The paper is organized as follows. The proposed MOPSO with winning score assignment is discussed in Sect. 2. Section 3 explains the details of performance comparison criteria employed. The multi-objective portfolio optimization problems are formulated in Sect. 4. Section 5 demonstrates the numerical experiments and the results. Our conclusions are stated in Sect. 6.

2 MOPSO with Winning Score Assignment

For the multi-objective particle swarm optimization (MOPSO) [9], in each generation, population contains a number of solutions and repository which preserves the non-dominated solutions set. An individual i ($POP[i]$) from the population set will be updated by the linear combination with its personal best solution ($PBEST[i]$) and one selected solution ($REP[h]$) from repository. To maintain the diversity of solutions, mutation operator is performed on $POP[i]$ with the low probability. The mutated POP $[i]$ is compared to the current $PBEST[i]$ by the Pareto domination, then the dominating solution will be used to update $PBEST[i]$. However, if the solutions are not dominated each other, one from these two solutions will be randomly selected as the updated $PBEST[i]$. In the case that the mutated $POP[i]$ is not dominated by any solutions in the repository, it will be placed into the repository instead of solutions that it dominates. If the number of non-dominated solutions stored in the repository exceeds the fixed repository size, truncation process will be performed using variation of the adaptive grid [12] with 7 grids per objective dimension. This process is executed by dividing objective space into multiple regions. Then, a crowded region is searched and selected. Subsequently, one solution located in the picked crowded region is randomly removed. The Main procedure of MOPSO is illustrated in Fig. 1.

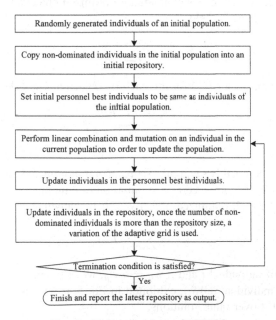

Fig. 1. Main procedure of MOPSO.

2.1   Winning Score Assignment Mechanism

The inspiration of winning score assignment can be described using decision making example of choosing a winner product to buy. Suppose that comparison criteria of 5 objectives between product A and B is considered. In the scenario that product A is better than B for the first four objectives, but it is worse than B for the fifth objective. By Pareto domination relation, product A does not dominate B. In reality, most people decide to buy product A, however, these is still a number of customer who choose product B. This example implies that the interacting relation such as, harmony, conflicts, and independency among the evaluated objectives exists [13]. Therefore, this interacting relation between objectives should be taken into account in the fitness assignment. Defining mathematically, given q_{ijk} is a competitive score where $q_{ijk} = 1$ if the objective k of the individual i is superior to that of the individual j while $q_{ijk} = -1$ if the objective k of i is inferior to that of individual j. Likewise, $q_{ijk} = 0$ if both individuals exhibit identical value of objective k. Let $\sup_{ij}$, $\inf_{ij}$, and eq_{ij} be the number of objectives of individual i which are superior to the corresponding objectives of individual j, the number of objectives of i which are inferior to that of j, and the number of objectives of i which are equal to that of j, respectively. For the objective k in an m-objective optimization problem, ρ_{ijk} for any individual pairs i and j is defined as

$$\rho_{ijk} = \begin{cases} \left(\sup_{ij} + \inf_{ij}\right)/2\sup_{ij}, & \text{when } i \text{ is superior to } j \\ \left(\sup_{ij} + \inf_{ij}\right)/2\sup_{ij}, & \text{when } i \text{ is inferior to } j \\ 1, & \text{when } i \text{ is equal } j \end{cases} \tag{1}$$

The deviation of ρ_{ijk} from the value of one depends on the ratio between the numbers of superior and inferior objectives resulting from solution comparison. This reflects the dependency and correlation among optimized objectives. Nevertheless, the following condition must be held.

$$\sum\nolimits_{k=1}^{m} \rho_{ijk} q_{ijk} = \sum\nolimits_{k=1}^{m} \rho_{jik} q_{jik} = 0 \tag{2}$$

Next, the winning factor (F_k) for the each of objective k is calculated by

$$F_k = \frac{\sum_{i=1}^{P-1}\sum_{i=1}^{P} \rho_{ijk}}{\sum_{k=1}^{m}\sum_{i=1}^{P-1}\sum_{i=1}^{P} \rho_{ijk}} \tag{3}$$

Thereafter, the competitive winning score of non-dominated solution i over solution j, denoted by w_{ij}, is computed as a summation of winning factor multiplying with competitive scores for all optimized objectives. It is mathematically expressed as:

$$w_{ij} = \sum\nolimits_{k=1}^{m} F_k q_{ijk} \tag{4}$$

For any pair of individual i and j, $w_{ij} = -w_{ji}$, $w_{ii} = 0$ and $-1 < w_{ij} < 1$. The winning score of the individual $i(WS_i)$, exhibited in Eq. 5, is a summation of competitive winning scores of it over other solutions.

$$WS_i = \sum_{j=1}^{P} w_{ij} \tag{5}$$

Concisely, Pseudo-code of the winning score assignment method is explained in Fig. 2. To validate our proposed winning score assignment method, it is necessary that solutions having high winning score are consistently situated close to the true Pareto front. In general, this condition can be proven by examining the significant negative relationship between winning score and distance from a solution to the true Pareto front in the objective space. Validation of the method is verified by considering a multi-objective minimization problem in which the ith objective denoted by f_i equals to the decision variable x_i where $x_i \in [0, 1]$. For this problem, only one true Pareto solution, whose all objectives have value of zero, can be obtained. In Fig. 3, each of 100 non-dominated solutions resulted from optimizing multi-objective minimization problems with three to ten objectives are plotted in the winning score (x)-distance to true Pareto solution (y) diagram. It is clearly noticeable from the scatter plots that the relationship between the winning score and distance to true Pareto solution is negative. In addition, the robustness of winning score assignment is further tested by conducting 4,950[1] comparisons between all pairs of 100 solutions for each problem. In each comparison, if a solution with higher winning score is positioned closer to the true Pareto solution than another one with lower winning score, the correctness counter is recorded. The results confirm that winning score can identify differences in levels of the

```
For k = 1 to the number of objectives
    For i = 1 to the number of non-dominated individuals minus 1
        For j = i+1 to the number of non-dominated individuals
            Evaluate ρ_ijk
        End for
    End for
End for
For k = 1 to the number of objectives
    Evaluate the winning factor (F_k) for objective k
End for
For i = 1 to the number of non-dominated individuals
    WS_i = 0
    For j = 1 to the number of non-dominated individuals
        Calculate w_ij
        WS_i = WS_i + w_ij
    End for
End for
```

Fig. 2. Pseudo code of the winning score assignment method.

---

[1] For 100 solution, all pair of solutions equal to $C(100, 2) = (100!)/(98!2!) = 4,950$.

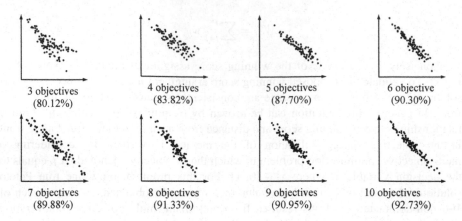

3 objectives
(80.12%)

4 objectives
(83.82%)

5 objectives
(87.70%)

6 objective
(90.30%)

7 objectives
(89.88%)

8 objectives
(91.33%)

9 objectives
(90.95%)

10 objectives
(92.73%)

Fig. 3. Plots of the non-dominated solutions of three to ten objectives minimization problems. The x-axis is winning score and the y-axis represents distance to the true optimal solution. The comparison correctness is reported in brackets as percentage form.

non-dominated solution with more than 80% accuracy. In addition, as stated earlier that the proposed method is intentionally designed for dealing with many-objective optimization problem, the accuracy are improving when the optimized objective increases. In contrast, conventional multi-objective optimizers assign equal ranks to all non-dominated solutions and use a diversity criterion which is totally not related to distance to true optimal solution for selecting a survivor solution. Besides, it can be said that the accuracy of selection is probably about 50%. Therefore, it is ensured that the winning score is remarkably reliable to represent the quality of a solution in a non-dominated solution set.

2.2   MOPSO with Winning Score Assignment

To enhance the capability of dealing with large objectives optimization problem, the proposed winning score assignment method is incorporated into three processes of the existing MOPSO [9]. The resulting algorithm is named as winning score MOPSO and denoted by "*WMOPSO*". Three processes that winning score assignment gets involve are selection of *REP*[h], updating of PBEST, and preserving solution diversity. To update *POP*[i], the current *POP*[i] interacts with solutions in depository. WMOPSO employs binary selection, whereby two non-dominated solutions is randomly selected from repository, and chooses solution with higher winning score to represent *REP*[h]. This improves selection criteria since the original MOPSO is always forced to randomly pick *REP*[h] because most of solutions in repository do not dominate each other. Secondly, the original MOPSO updates its *PBEST*[i] by comparing the updated *POP* [i] with the current *PBEST*[i]. There is always the case that these two solutions do not dominate one another. Therefore, algorithm has to inevitably choose one without any better comparison criterion to support. This may result in missing a good position in the search space. Similar concern arises in the case of diversity preservation method of the original MOPSO. As explained earlier, it is done by eliminating exceed solutions found in the crowded regions. However, solution to be removed is selected randomly. In contrast, WMOPSO adopting winning score as an additional selection criterion could alleviate aforementioned issues. Especially, winning score improve decision making on screening out solutions located in the crowded region since solution having lower winning score will be removed rather than simply random selection.

3 Performance Evaluation

In general, the non-dominated solutions obtained from a well-performed multi-objective optimizer should be located close to and uniformly distributed along the true Pareto front. To evaluate the performance of the proposed algorithm, four performance comparison criteria are employed and described as follows:

3.1 Solution Coverage

The solution set coverage was proposed by Zitzler et al. [14]. It is generally used for comparing between two non-dominated solution sets. It is mathematically defined as

$$C(\mathbf{A}, \mathbf{B}) = \frac{|\{b \in \mathbf{B};\ \exists a \in \mathbf{A} : a \prec b\}|}{|\mathbf{B}|} \tag{6}$$

where $C(\mathbf{A}, \mathbf{B})$ is coverage value resulting from comparing solution set $\mathbf{A}$ to $\mathbf{B}$ and its value is ranged from zero to one. $a \prec b$ means solution a covers, i.e. dominates or equals, b. Thus, $C(\mathbf{A}, \mathbf{B})$ having value of one implies that all solutions in $\mathbf{A}$ either dominate or equal to solutions in $\mathbf{B}$. On the other hand, $C(\mathbf{A}, \mathbf{B})$ that equals zero means that each of solutions in $\mathbf{A}$ neither dominate nor equal to any solutions in $\mathbf{B}$. From this notion, $C(\mathbf{A}, \mathbf{B}) > C(\mathbf{B}, \mathbf{A})$ indicates that solution set $\mathbf{A}$ is better than solution set $\mathbf{B}$.

3.2 Average Distance to True Pareto-Optimal Front (M_1)

The average distance to true Pareto-optimal solutions (M_1) [14] can be evaluated in the solution space or objective space. In this paper, the metric $M1$ is measured, in the objective space, by a distance of a solution i to the true Pareto front, di, which is the Euclidean distance of the solution i to its nearest solution j on the true Pareto front. The Euclidean distance is given by:

$$d_i = \sqrt{\sum_{k=1}^{m} \left(\frac{f_{ik} - f_{jk}}{f_{k,\max} - f_{k,\min}} \right)^2} \tag{7}$$

where f_{ik} and f_{jk} are the values of objective k for solutions i and j respectively, while $f_{k,\min}$ and $f_{k,\max}$ are the minimum and maximum values of objective k for the true Pareto solutions. Since the true Pareto front of the tested problems are not known, the artificial true Pareto front which is obtained from the merged non-dominated individuals from all runs of both algorithms is used in the evaluation of M_1. The distance, d_i, of a solution i is estimated as the Euclidean distance of the solution i to its nearest solution

j on the artificial true Pareto front. M_1 is the average of d_i for all individuals in a set of non-dominated solutions.

3.3   Error Ratio (*ER*)

Since the true Pareto solutions are unknown, M_1 is probably not sufficient for evaluating the performance of tested algorithms. To overcome this weakness, we further employed the error ratio [15] which indicates the ratio of solutions in a set that are not the members of the artificial true Pareto set. It can be expressed as

$$ER = \frac{\sum_{i=1}^{P} e_i}{P} \tag{8}$$

where P is number of members in a solution set. In case that solution i belongs to the artificial true Pareto set, e_i is recorded value of zero. In contrast, e_i exhibits value of one, if solution i is not a member of the artificial true Pareto set. Therefore, the smaller the ER value, the better the algorithm performance.

3.4   Spacing

Spacing criterion which is a diversity metric was proposed by Schott [16]. It is used to measure the uniformity of solution distribution in the objective space. The spacing is defined as the following equation.

$$\text{Spacing} = \sqrt{\frac{\sum_{i=1}^{P} (d_i - \overline{d_i})^2}{P - 1}} \tag{9}$$

where d_i is distance solution i to its nearest neighbor in objective space. The smaller the S value indicates that solutions are uniformly distributed and the gaps between solutions are consistently distanced.

4   Problem Formulation

According to Markowitz's mean-variance portfolio optimization problem (MV-POP), portfolio returns is maximize, while portfolio risk measured by portfolio variance is minimized. In the literature, empirical results revealed that the distribution of returns is not normal but skewed [17] and a rational investor prefers portfolio with high value of skewness [18]. Therefore, constructing portfolio by optimizing mean-variance-skewness (MVS) simultaneously would yield higher utility for investors. However, the most recent survey on POP [19] revealed that most of studies were restricted to MV-POP. The plausible reason is that solving MVS-POP in MOO framework is very difficult since it is a class of non-concave maximization problem whose true Pareto surface is non-smooth and discontinuous.

Suppose that the return, variance, and skewness of a portfolio are denoted by $R_p(\mathbf{x})$, $V_p(\mathbf{x})$, and $S_p(\mathbf{x})$, respectively. While, $\mathbf{x}$, representing a portfolio solution, is a $N \times 1$ vector of investment allocation proportion to N assets. Let vector $\mathbf{R}$ with size $N \times 1$ represents the returns of N assets. Besides, matrix Λ and Ω are the non-singular $N \times N$ variance-covariance matrix and $N \times N^2$ skewness-coskewness matrix, respectively. Therefore, the three optimized objectives of MVS-POP can be expressed by:

$$\text{Maximize: } R_p(\mathbf{x}) = \mathbf{x}^{\mathrm{T}}\mathbf{R} = \sum_{i=1}^{N} x_i R_i \tag{10}$$

$$\text{Minimize: } V_p(\mathbf{x}) = \mathbf{x}^{\mathrm{T}}\Lambda\mathbf{x} = \sum_{i=1}^{N} x_i x_j \sigma_{i,j} \tag{11}$$

$$\text{Maximize: } S_p(\mathbf{x}) = \mathbf{x}^{\mathrm{T}}\Omega(\mathbf{x} \otimes \mathbf{x}) = \sum_{i=1}^{N} \sum_{j=1}^{N} \sum_{k=1}^{N} x_i x_j x_k \gamma_{i,j,k} \tag{12}$$

where $\mathbf{x}^{\mathrm{T}}$ is the transpose of vector $\mathbf{x}$ and x_i is the proportion of investment allocated to asset i. R_i is the returns of asset i. $\sigma_{i,j}$ and $\gamma_{i,j,k}$ are covariance and co-skewness between assets, respectively. The sign $\otimes$ is the Kronecker product used for transforming the skewness tensor into a $N \times N^2$ matrix. Thus, the MVS-POP can be formulated within MOOF as follows:

$$\min F(\mathbf{x}) = \left[-R_p(\mathbf{x}), V_p(\mathbf{x}), -S_p(\mathbf{x}) \right]$$
$$\text{subject to: } \sum_{i=1}^{N} x_i = 1, \ x_i \geq 0 \tag{13}$$

The first constraint is considered to ensure that all investment is completely used. The second constraint implies that the short selling is not allowed. In practice, other constrains can be considered. Among other, the cardinality constraint attracts the most attentions from researchers and practitioners. It is used to limit the number of asset held in a portfolio. Empirically, investors prefer to hold a small number of assets in their portfolio in order for conveniently monitoring. In this study, cardinality constraint is incorporated into MVS-POP as the additional objective to be optimized. Thus, the cardinality MVS-POP, denoted by CMVS-POP, is formulated as:

$$\min F(\mathbf{x}) = \left[-R_p(\mathbf{x}), \ V_p(\mathbf{x}), \ -S_p(\mathbf{x}), \ \mathbb{K}_{x_i > 0}(\mathbf{x}) \right]$$
$$\text{subject to: } \sum_{i=1}^{N} x_i = 1, \ x_i \geq 0 \tag{14}$$

where $\mathbb{K}_{x_i > 0}(\mathbf{x})$ is the minimized objective that represents the number of assets having positive weight in a portfolio solution. This objective can be expressed mathematically as $\mathbb{K}_{x_i > 0}(\mathbf{x}) = \sum_{i=1}^{N} 1_{x_i > 0}$.

5 Simulation Experiment

The data set employed in this study is the real-world financial data extracted from *DataStream* which is publicly available. The monthly closing prices of the stocks listed in the Dow Jones Industrial Average index (DJIA) were collected. The sample period was arbitrary chosen from January 2004 to December 2011. It should be noted that DJIA is comprised of 30 large publicly owned companies based in the U.S. However, the stock of the VISA Inc. was dropped out from this study because it was firstly traded in March 19, 2008. Thus, 29 stocks were considered in our analysis. Next, using these series of stocks prices, the returns, covariance matrix, and co-skewness matrix were computed as expressed in Eqs. (10), (11), and (12), respectively.

To test the proposed algorithm, the WMOPSO was utilized for solving both MVS-POP and CMVS-POP having three and four objectives, respectively, to be optimized simultaneously. The WMOPSO was performed within the multi-objective optimization framework. In simulation runs, the population size and the repository size are both equal to 100. The number of iterations used in each of the 30 total runs is equal to 1000. Real-valued chromosome is employed and uniform mutation whose rate is exponentially decreased from one at beginning to zero at the end is utilized. To highlight the distinguish abilities of the proposed WMOPSO, its performance is benchmarked to that of the MOPSO based upon three comparison criteria.

Considering solution coverage criterion, the coverage values are illustrated using box plots and presented in Fig. 4. The box in the plot contains 50% of the data points from the 25th to 75th percentile. Observations outside the interquartile range were plotted on the whiskers of the box. As explained earlier, $C(\mathbf{A}, \mathbf{B}) > C(\mathbf{B}, \mathbf{A})$ implies that solution set $\mathbf{A}$ is better than solution set $\mathbf{B}$. It is revealed from the chart that, regardless of the optimized problem, WMOPSO obviously outperforms MOPSO since the coverage values of C(WMOPSO, MOPSO) are greater than those of C(MOPSO, WMOPSO) for both MVS and CMVS-POP. This suggests that solutions obtained from WMOPSO are more likely to dominate those from MOPSO. It is worth noting that when the optimized

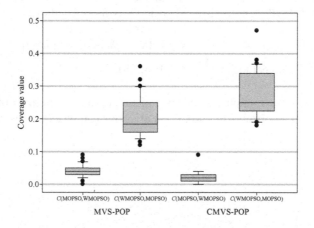

Fig. 4. Box plots of coverage results.

objective increases from three to four, the performance of MOPSO is deteriorated. Meanwhile, as articulated earlier that winning score assignment is deliberately developed for handling a many-objective optimization problem, WMOPSO performed even better for the case of CMVS-POP.

Considering solution optimality, the results of M_1 and ER criteria are reported, based on the best, worst, mean, and standard deviation (Std. Dev.) values, in Tables 1 and 2, respectively. Since M_1 and ER are both minimum criteria, it is clear from the results that solutions created by WMOPSO better achieve the optimality than those of MOPSO, regardless of statistics used. These evidences indicate that WMOPSO produces solutions that the majority are member of the true Pareto set and are located close to the true Pareto front. Analogous to coverage criterion, the superiority of WMOPSO is more pronounced for many-objective problem. Lastly, the results from spacing criterion reported in Table 3 reveal that solutions obtained from WMOPSO are better uniformly distributed in the objective space than those of MOPSO. This implies that, even though both algorithms employed the adaptive grid [12] in truncation of repository to achieve solution diversity, the proposed winning score seems to help marginally promote the uniformity of the solution.

Table 1. Results of M_1.

M_1	MVS-POP		CMVS-POP	
	MOPSO	WMOPSO	MOPSO	WMOPSO
Best	0.058226	0.025069	0.022230	0.006540
Worst	0.094086	0.051225	0.046817	0.024974
Mean	0.078784	0.038491	0.022230	0.006540
Std. dev.	0.009281	0.005924	0.036635	0.013038

Table 2. Results of error ratio (ER).

ER	MVS-POP		CMVS-POP	
	MOPSO	WMOPSO	MOPSO	WMOPSO
Best	0.500000	0.220000	0.420000	0.160000
Worst	0.810000	0.450000	0.840000	0.470000
Mean	0.682333	0.337333	0.671333	0.277667
Std. dev.	0.078814	0.051791	0.083325	0.067603

Table 3. Results of Spacing.

Spacing	MVS-POP		CMVS-POP	
	MOPSO	WMOPSO	MOPSO	WMOPSO
Best	0.037650	0.034310	0.037650	0.034310
Worst	0.101932	0.085970	0.101932	0.085970
Mean	0.075728	0.065306	0.075728	0.065306
Std. dev.	0.013534	0.012520	0.013534	0.012520

6 Conclusion

The winning score assignment method is proposed and integrated into the MOPSO. The proposed method help improving several selection schemes since the interaction between optimized objectives is considered during fitness assignment processes. The proposed algorithm, which is named as "winning score MOPSO" and denoted by "WMOPSO", is utilized for solving multi-objective portfolio optimization problem consisting of three and four optimized objectives. By benchmarking its performance with that of the original MOPSO based upon four standard performance comparison criteria, the results reveal that solutions obtained from WMOPSO are better than those of MOPSO since they exhibit the greater coverage value and the lower values of the distance to true Pareto front, the error ratio, and the spacing. This implies that WMOPSO improves not only the solution optimality but also the diversity of solutions. Lastly, it is ensured that WMOPSO is suitable for many-objective optimization problem since its superiority is more pronounced when optimized objective increases.

References

1. Markowitz, H.: Portfolio selection. J. Financ. **7**, 77–91 (1952)
2. Xu, F., Chen, W., Yang, L.: Improved particle swarm optimization for realistic portfolio selection. In: 8th ACIS International Conference on Software Engineering, Artificial Intelligence, Networking, and Parallel/Distributed Computing, pp. 185–190 (2007)
3. Cura, T.: Particle swarm optimization approach to portfolio optimization. Nonlinear Anal.: Real World Appl. **10**, 2396–2406 (2009)
4. Zhu, H., Wang, Y., Wang, K., Chen, Y.: Particle swarm optimization (PSO) for the constrained portfolio optimization problem. Expert Syst. Appl. **38**, 10161–10169 (2011)
5. Golmakani, H.R., Fazel, M.: Constrained portfolio selection using particle swarm optimization. Expert Syst. Appl. **38**, 8327–8335 (2011)
6. Messac, A., Puemi-Sukam, C., Melachrinoudis, E.: Aggregate objective functions and Pareto frontiers: required relationships and practical implications. Optim. Eng. **1**, 171–188 (2000)
7. Liu, D., Tan, K.C., Goh, C.K., Ho, W.K.: A multiobjective memetic algorithm based on particle swarm optimization. IEEE Trans. Syst. Man Cybern. B Cybern. **37**, 42–50 (2007)
8. Tripathi, P.K., Bandyopadhyay, S., Pal, S.: Multi-objective particle swarm optimization with time variant inertia and acceleration coefficients. Inf. Sci. **177**, 5033–5049 (2007)
9. Coello, C.A.C., Pulido, G.T., Lechuga, M.S.: Handling multiple objectives with particle swarm optimization. IEEE Tran. Evol. Comput. **8**, 256–279 (2004)
10. Deb, K., Thiele, L., Laumanns, M., Zitzler, E.: Scalable test problems for evolutionary multiobjective optimization. In: Abraham, A., Jain, L., Goldberg, R. (eds.) EMO. AIKP, pp. 105–145. Springer, Berlin Heidelberg (2005)
11. Purshouse, R.C., Fleming, P.J.: On the evolutionary optimization of many conflicting objectives. IEEE Tran. Evol. Comput. **11**, 770–784 (2007)
12. Knowles, J.D., Corne, D.W.: Approximating the nondominated front using the Pareto archived evolution strategy. Evol. Comput. **8**, 149–172 (2000)
13. Purshouse, R.C., Fleming, P.J.: Conflict, harmony, and independence: relationships in evolutionary multi-criterion optimisation. In: Fonseca, C.M., Fleming, P.J., Zitzler, E., Thiele, L., Deb, K. (eds.) EMO 2003. LNCS, vol. 2632, pp. 16–30. Springer, Heidelberg (2003). doi:10.1007/3-540-36970-8_2

14. Zitzler, E., Deb, K., Thiele, L.: Comparison of multiobjective evolutionary algorithms: empirical results. Evol. Comput. **8**, 173–195 (2000)
15. Van Veldhuizen, D.A.: Multiobjective evolutionary algorithms: classifications, analyses, and new innovations. DTIC Document (1999)
16. Schott, J.R.: Fault tolerant design using single and multicriteria genetic algorithm optimization. DTIC Document (1995)
17. Harvey, C.R., Liechty, J.C., Liechty, M.W., Müller, P.: Portfolio selection with higher moments. Quant. Fin. **10**, 469–485 (2010)
18. Samuelson, P.A.: The fundamental approximation theorem of portfolio analysis in terms of means, variances and higher moments. Rev. Econ. Stud. **37**, 537–542 (1970)
19. Metaxiotis, K., Liagkouras, K.: Multiobjective evolutionary algorithms for portfolio management: a comprehensive literature review. Expert Syst. Appl. **39**, 11685–11698 (2012)

Conservatism and Adventurism in Particle Swarm Optimization Algorithm

Guangzhi Xu[1,2], Rui Li[1,2], Xinchao Zhao[2(✉)], and Xingquan Zuo[3]

[1] Automation School, Beijing University of Posts and Telecommunications,
Beijing 100876, China
[2] School of Science, Beijing University of Posts and Telecommunications,
Beijing 100876, China
zhaoxc@bupt.edu.cn
[3] School of Computer Science, Beijing University of Posts and Telecommunications,
Beijing 100876, China

Abstract. Particle Swarm Optimization (PSO) is a widely used optimization algorithm in industrial and academic fields. In this paper, three improved PSO variants are proposed. The main ideas of them are that a coefficient v is added to control the velocity augment of particles to the new position on different dimension. The first one is under the guidance of conservatism which is an inspiration of Differential Evolution (DE), namely, particles preserve more information from their previous positions and move in a smaller search space. This algorithm shows that particles are possible to escape from the current neighborhood and for promising search area if they take more previous information. The second one is guided by adventurism for better exploration, which means a larger search space to particles. The third one can be considered as a compromise between conservatism and adventurism. This algorithm shows that a balanced cooperation with a little conservative in more adventures will make PSO more competitive. Experimental results show that the proposed strategies of all the three algorithms are effective based on CEC2015 benchmarks. All of them are better than the traditional PSOs and the third improved variant performs better than all the other competitors.

Keywords: Conservatism principle · Adventurism principle · Compromise principle · Particle swarm optimization

1 Introduction

Particle Swarm Optimization (PSO) [1,2] is one of the most important algorithms among intelligent optimization methods. It was proposed by Kennedy and Eberhat who were enlightened by foraging process of birds flock in 1995. The different particles of PSO share information and work cooperatively with each other and achieve the optimal solution of complicated problems after several iterations. PSO is simple and easy to implement when comparing with other intelligent optimization algorithms. The PSO algorithm has excellent global search capabilities,

© Springer International Publishing AG 2017
Y. Shi et al. (Eds.): SEAL 2017, LNCS 10593, pp. 1016–1025, 2017.
https://doi.org/10.1007/978-3-319-68759-9_84

however, its local search ability has some limitations. Many improved PSOs has been proposed in [4–7]. PSO also has been combined to other algorithms [8–11] to improve its performance. Differential evolution (DE) [3], especially DE/rand, usually possesses excellent population diversity and limited local search ability. Therefore, merging PSO and DE [12,13] is possible to potentially yield a balanced promising algorithm which has excellent local and global search capabilities and a fast converging speed. It is possible to offer the advantages of both algorithms while offsetting their disadvantages.

The first work in this paper is to propose a new hybrid optimization technique which synergistically couples the PSO and DE for solving the optimization problems. The proposed algorithm gathers diversity through the mutation operation of DE whereas the global search over the entire search space is accomplished by PSO updating operations. In this way it balances between exploration and exploitation to enjoy the best of both worlds. Experimental results indicate that the new hybrid algorithm has shown statistically and significantly better results on different test functions. After analyzing the reasons of the effect, we find that particles in this method preserve more information from their previous positions, so it is named as a conservatism principle.

The second work in this paper is to change this operation in a different thought, namely, adventurism. In this method, particles can move in a larger search spaces. It means a higher possible enhance a particles diversity to lead to befitting position. The experiment results show that this thought works very well. The third work in this paper is to compromise the above both algorithms. Compromise principle has been proved in this part and experimental results also shows its effect.

In Sect. 2, an overview of PSO algorithm is given. In Sect. 3, the conservatism principle and the reason on how to propose it is presented in details. In Sect. 4, adventurism principle and its work principle are explained. In Sect. 5, compromise principle is proposed. Comparing results and experimental analysis are listed in Sect. 6. Finally, the paper concludes in Sect. 7.

2   Overview of PSO Algorithms

The particle swarm optimization is a population-based, self-adaptive stochastic optimization technique. Like other evolutionary computation techniques, such as genetic algorithm and evolutionary programming, particle swarm optimization also initializes a population of individuals randomly. These individuals are known as particles and have positions and velocities. Each particle adjusts its velocity dynamically corresponding to its flying experiences and its neighbors. In the multidimensional search space each particle in the swarm is moved towards the optimal solution by adding the velocity with its position. The modified velocity of each particle can be updated using the following equations:

$$v_{ij}^{k+1} = w v_{ij}^k + c_1 r_1 (pbest_{ij}^k - x) + c_2 r_2 (gbest_{ij}^k - x) \tag{1}$$

$$x_{ij}^{k+1} = x_{ij}^k + v_{ij}^k \tag{2}$$

where x_{ij}^k is the current position of the i-th particle in j-th dimension at iteration k and v_{ij}^k is the velocity of the i-th particle in j-th dimension at iteration k. The updated position of each particle is calculated repeatedly until a pre-specified termination condition is met.

3   Conservatism Principle in PSO

In this section, an improved PSO variant, named conservatism principle (CCPSO), is proposed under the guidance of conservatism. In this algorithm, the particles will preserve more information from their previous position when the particles update their positions. Inspired by the mutation operation in DE, an operation named as conservatism principle has been proposed. In DE, mutation operation can be preserved information through crossover operation which described as follows. If a uniform random variable is larger than the crossover probability the information of previous position of the particle will be elaborated to the new individual.

$$u_{ij}^{k+1} = \begin{cases} v_{ij}^k & if \; r_{ij} < pc \\ x_{ij}^k & else \end{cases} \tag{3}$$

$r_{ij} \in [0, 1]$ is uniform random variable, v^k is the mutant/velocity vector and u^k is the trial vector. When the mutation operation executed on PSO, conservatism principle is proposed simultaneously as follows.

$$x_{ij}^{k+1} = \begin{cases} x_{ij}^k & if \; r_{ij} > pc \\ x_{ij}^k + v_{ij}^k & else \end{cases} \tag{4}$$

In this operation, one indicative parameter $s \in \{0, 1\}$ is introduced to control the update of particle position. Parameter pc is the crossover probability. Thus some dimensions of the previous position will remain unchanged for this objective in the next iteration. so, the position updating operation become

$$s_j = \begin{cases} 1 & if \; rand(0, 1) < pc \\ 0 & else \end{cases} \tag{5}$$

$$x_{ij}^{k+1} = x_{ij}^k + s_j \cdot v_{ij}^k \tag{6}$$

The variable $s \in \{0, 1\}$ is the control variable. When $s = 0$, $x_{ij}^{k+1} = x_{ij}^k$ this dimension of this particle will remain unchanged in this iteration. So some dimensions of this particle will be not changed in this iteration. Partial information of previous position can directly be preserved to the new position. Easy to prove that, formulas 5 and 6 is equivalent to formula 3 through formula 4.

Preliminarily comparing with PSO, Fig. 1 shows the effect of this method and more results of this comparison can be found in the Sect. 6 where f1 and f8 are CEC2015 benchmarks. The experimental results show that the conservatism principle can improve the performance of PSO. In the early stage, the curve of CCPSO drops slower than PSO which indicates that CCPSO has slow convergence. The possible reason is that the new position will also inherit some new genes from the newly generated temporary solution and others from the initial position even if the newly generated solution is worse than the initial one.

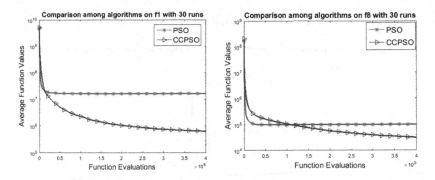

Fig. 1. PSO and CCPSO

4   Adventurism Principle in PSO

In evolutionary algorithms, larger search space usually means higher risk for divergence, so it is an adventure to make particles have larger search space. The adventure by the strategy of adventurism principle can be confirmed by experiment and analysis. In this improved variant, the position updating equation is modified as follows.

$$x_{ij}^{k+1} = x_{ij}^k + |s_j| \cdot v_{ij}^k \tag{7}$$

The random variable $s \sim N(0, 1)$, its distribution density function is as Fig. 2. So s has a probability of 68% in $[0, 1]$, s has a probability of 27% in $[1, 2]$, s has a probability of 5% when $s > 2$. That means particles can move to new position with different velocity value, from 0 to $2v$ with a probability of 95%, rather than a fixed value. So, the search space has become larger by this strategy according to the above analysis. An improved PSO variant, named Adventurism Principle PSO (CAPSO), is proposed if adventurism principle is applied to PSO.

Figure 3 shows a significant performance difference between PSO and CAPSO based on the preliminary experimental comparison. More experimental analysis can be found in Sect. 6. Adventurism principle can improve the performance of PSO because particles are possible to move to more exploring search spaces along the direction of the excellent flying velocity and within a reasonable size of space.

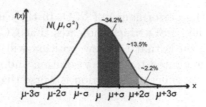

Fig. 2. Gaussian distribution of $x \sim N(\mu, \sigma)$

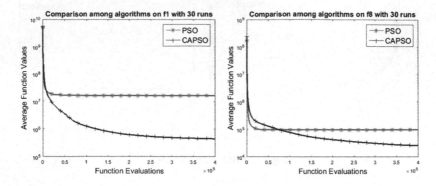

Fig. 3. PSO and CAPSO

5   Compromise Principle in PSO

Conservatism principle can improve the performance of PSO, however, the speed of convergence may be affected. Adventurism principle can also enhance the performance of PSO. As experiments revealed, algorithm with the adventurism principle strategy is much better than PSO with conservatism principle strategy in most cases, as shown in the Fig. 4 and in Sect. 6. Therefore, how to enlarge the search space of particles is an important enhancing direction for PSO algorithm. But too large search space which mismatches the inherent need of algorithm may decrease the quality of particles. So both strategies should cooperate each other to maximize their optimizing effects individually or simultaneously. It is natural to combine them cooperatively, Compromise Principle, and to utilize their advantages simultaneously.

Compromise principle is defined as follows.

$$l_j = \begin{cases} 0 & if \ s_j < -1 \\ 1 & else \end{cases} \tag{8}$$

$$x_{ij}^{k+1} = x_{ij}^k + |s_j| \cdot l_j \cdot v_{ij}^k \tag{9}$$

In the Eqs. (8 and 9), random variable $s \sim N(0,1)$, $l_j \in \{0,1\}$. If $s_j < -1$, $l_j = 0$, $x_{ij}^{k+1} = x_{ij}^k$. Currently, it is the conservatism principle with a probability about 15.7%. If $s_j > -1$, $l_j = 1$. Currently, it become the adventurism principle. Therefore, they cooperate harmoniously in Eqs. (8 and 9). PSO with

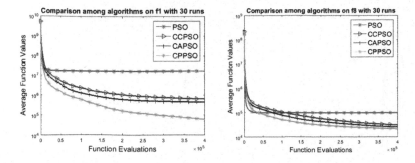

Fig. 4. PSO and CCPSO, CAPSO, CPPSO

compromise principle is denoted as CPPSO. The experiment shows that the strategy of compromise principle can improve the performance of PSO.

6 Experiment and Analysis

Ten benchmark functions (f1–f10) of IEEE CEC 2015 [12] competition benchmarks are used to verify the effectiveness of the algorithm in this paper. CLPSO [13] is also used to compare the proposed three improved PSO [2] variants to measure their effectiveness.

6.1 Experimental Setup

Several parameters are set as follows. The dimension of benchmark function is 30. Probability parameters $pc = 0.3$. All the algorithms are performed 30 runs independently on each benchmark; the final mean best results are recorded with 400 000 function evaluations. Population size is 50 for all algorithms [13].

6.2 Experimental Results and Analysis

The online performance comparison of five algorithms is shown as Fig. 5, in which the performance of all algorithms is clearly demonstrated.

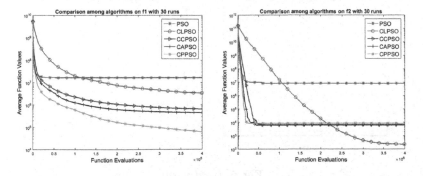

Fig. 5. Evolutionary performance comparison among five algorithms

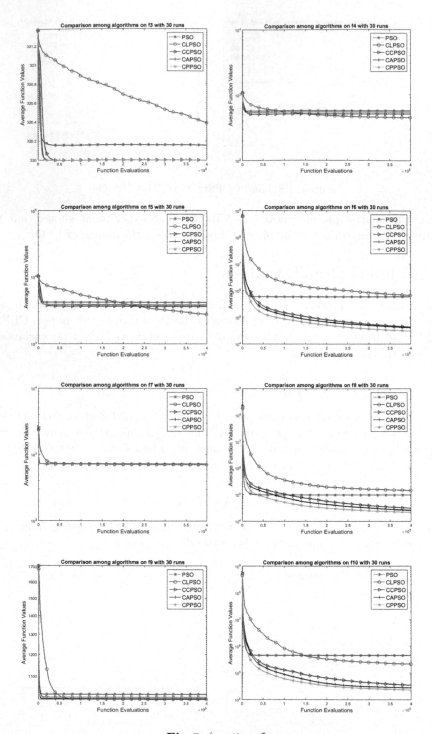

Fig. 5. (*continued*)

Table 1. Experimental comparison among algorithms

Functions	Algorithms	Min	Mean	Std	
f1	PSO	1.18E+06	1.65E+07	2.70E+07	−
	CLPSO	1.15E+06	3.42E+06	1.21E+06	−
	CCPSO	2.15E+04	6.51E+05	2.53E+06	−
	CAPSO	9.92E+03	4.50E+05	1.34E+06	−
	CPPSO	**1.80E+04**	**6.15E+04**	**5.11E+04**	
f2	PSO	4.42E+04	8.36E+06	1.50E+07	−
	CLPSO	2.01E+02	2.27E+02	3.80E+01	+
	CCPSO	2.23E+02	6.76E+03	6.08E+03	+
	CAPSO	2.02E+02	**6.20E+03**	5.60E+03	+
	CPPSO	**2.01E+02**	8.46E+03	**5.45E+03**	
f3	PSO	3.20E+02	3.20E+02	1.38E−01	−
	CLPSO	3.20E+02	3.20E+02	5.25E−02	−
	CCPSO	3.20E+02	3.20E+02	3.08E−06	+
	CAPSO	3.20E+02	3.20E+02	**4.17E−07**	−
	CPPSO	3.20E+02	3.20E+02	1.49E−06	
f4	PSO	4.81E+02	5.67E+02	4.35E+01	−
	CLPSO	**4.33E+02**	**4.47E+02**	**6.12E+00**	+
	CCPSO	4.55E+02	5.07E+02	3.06E+01	+
	CAPSO	4.84E+02	5.43E+02	3.96E+01	−
	CPPSO	4.62E+02	5.40E+02	4.04E+01	
f5	PSO	2.56E+03	4.17E+03	6.65E+02	−
	CLPSO	2.32E+03	**2.78E+03**	**3.02E+02**	+
	CCPSO	**2.12E+03**	3.64E+03	6.86E+02	+
	CAPSO	2.14E+03	3.84E+03	6.83E+02	+
	CPPSO	2.59E+03	3.88E+03	7.31E+02	
f6	PSO	7.09E+04	5.95E+05	9.47E+05	−
	CLPSO	1.71E+05	6.75E+05	3.16E+05	−
	CCPSO	5.32E+03	4.34E+04	2.66E+04	−
	CAPSO	7.70E+03	4.12E+04	3.99E+04	−
	CPPSO	**3.39E+03**	**3.06E+04**	**2.15E+04**	
f7	PSO	7.14E+02	7.25E+02	2.03E+01	−
	CLPSO	7.05E+02	**7.08E+02**	**1.45E+00**	+
	CCPSO	7.06E+02	7.09E+02	2.39E+00	+
	CAPSO	7.06E+02	7.10E+02	4.83E+00	+
	CPPSO	7.05E+02	7.11E+02	5.90E+00	
f8	PSO	1.75E+04	9.71E+04	6.26E+04	−
	CLPSO	3.01E+04	1.45E+05	7.77E+04	−
	CCPSO	5.02E+03	3.12E+04	2.73E+04	−
	CAPSO	2.43E+03	2.58E+04	2.85E+04	−
	CPPSO	**2.12E+03**	**2.18E+04**	**1.75E+04**	
f9	PSO	1.01E+03	1.02E+03	6.35E+01	−
	CLPSO	1.00E+03	**1.00E+03**	**1.68E−01**	+
	CCPSO	1.00E+03	1.01E+03	3.43E+01	−
	CAPSO	1.00E+03	1.01E+03	8.06E−01	+
	CPPSO	1.00E+03	1.01E+03	2.85E+01	
f10	PSO	3.14E+04	4.57E+05	6.87E+05	−
	CLPSO	5.34E+04	2.18E+05	1.33E+05	−
	CCPSO	**3.17E+03**	3.54E+04	2.94E+04	−
	CAPSO	5.72E+03	2.80E+04	**2.01E+04**	−
	CPPSO	3.67E+03	**2.33E+04**	3.53E+04	

The above figures indicate that the strategies and algorithms presented in this paper are effective. Especially for f1, f6, f8 and f10, all the three newly proposed algorithms are better than those of PSO and CLPSO. On other functions, all three new algorithms are better than those of PSO. The performance of three new algorithms is more consistent and robust. Those three curves have similar evolutionary behaviors and changing shapes, which shows that three algorithms have similar features. More detailed information can be found in the Table 1.

The minimum values, average values and standard deviation obtained by each run of each algorithm are statistically recorded in the Table 1 where The average function values are more important than the function error values in the experiments because the comparison performance difference is employed. Table 1 presents the statistical comparison results on CPPSO and its competitors based on the Wilcoxon rank-sum test with significance level being 0.05 on 10 functions. The p-values of CPPSO is marked as '+' for being better than each algorithm, marked as '−' for being worse than each algorithm, and marked as '=' for no statistical difference from each algorithm. The best minimum value for each item is indicated in bold. The performance of new algorithms are also compared with a classical PSO variant CLPSO [13].

Observed from Table 1, it can be seen that the new three PSO variants achieve a successful rate and the highest accuracy for the functions f1, f6 and f8. For function f1, CPPSO has a much smaller number of evaluations than others. For problem f6, CPPSO algorithm not only obtains the smallest average error, but also shows the smallest value of function evaluations. So, algorithm CPPSO is quite competitive when it is compared with other methods.

The average ranks among different algorithms can be found in the Table 2, in which the ranks in all functions of each algorithm are averaged and listed. The rank records the performance ranks of the comparative algorithms in dealing with each optimization function based on their obtained meanresults. This table shows that CPPSO has top rank among five PSO variants.

Table 2. Ranking of each algorithm

Algorithm	PSO	CLPSO	CCPSO	CAPSO	CPPSO
Rank	4.7	2.8	2.6	2.5	2.4

7   Conclusion

In this paper, three improved PSO variants are proposed. The first method is inspired by mutation operator of DE and the conservatism principle has been proposed. It shows that particles with more previous information perform better. The strategy of adventurism principle is proposed to consider a more adventurous method. The experiments and analysis demonstrate the feasibility and the effects of the ideas. However, both ideas have the naturally opposite inclination. So, how to balance them cooperatively is inherently required and compromise principle is proposed accordingly. The algorithmic analysis and experimental comparison indicate the effects and the potential of the strategies.

This research is supported by National Natural Science Foundation of China (61375066, 61374204). We will express our awfully thanks to the Swarm Intelligence Research Team of BeiYou University and to the reviewers for their helpful suggestions.

Acknowledgments. This research is supported by National Natural Science Foundation of China (61375066, 61374204, 11171040). A thousand thanks should be given to the reviewers for their constructive suggestions and comments, which improved the manuscript greatly.

References

1. Eberhart, R., Kennedy, J.: A new optimizer using particle swarm theory. In: International Symposium on MICRO Machine and Human Science, pp. 39–43. IEEE (2002)
2. Kennedy, J., Eberhart, R.: Particle swarm optimization. In: Proceedings of IEEE International Conference on Neural Networks, vol. 4, pp. 1942–1948. IEEE (2002)
3. Storn, R., Price, K.: Differential Evolution a Simple and Efficient Heuristic for Global Optimization over Continuous Spaces. Kluwer Academic Publishers, Dordrecht (1997)
4. Wang, G.G., Hossein Gandomi, A., Yang, X.S., et al.: A novel improved accelerated particle swarm optimization algorithm for global numerical optimization. Eng. Comput. **31**(7), 1198–1220 (2014)
5. Du, W.B., Gao, Y., Liu, C., et al.: Adequate is better: particle swarm optimization with limited-information. Appl. Math. Comput. **268**, 832–838 (2015)
6. Wang, H., Sun, H., Li, C., et al.: Diversity enhanced particle swarm optimization with neighborhood search. Inf. Sci. **223**, 119–135 (2013)
7. Zhang, L., Tang, Y., Hua, C., et al.: A new particle swarm optimization algorithm with adaptive inertia weight based on Bayesian techniques. Appl. Soft Comput. **28**, 138–149 (2015)
8. Mirjalili, S., Wang, G.G., Coelho, L.S.: Binary optimization using hybrid particle swarm optimization and gravitational search algorithm. Neural Comput. Appl. **25**(6), 1423–1435 (2014)
9. Mahi, M., Baykan, K., Kodaz, H.: A new hybrid method based on particle swarm optimization, ant colony optimization and 3-opt algorithms for traveling salesman problem. Appl. Soft Comput. **30**, 484–490 (2015)
10. Delice, Y., Aydoan, E.K., Zcan, U., et al.: A modified particle swarm optimization algorithm to mixed-model two-sided assembly line balancing. J. Intell. Manuf. **28**(1), 23–36 (2017)
11. Thangamani, C., Chidambaram, M.: A novel hybrid genetic algorithm with weighted crossover and modified particle swarm optimization. Artif. Intell. Syst. Mach. Learn. **9**(2), 25–30 (2017)
12. Liang, J.J., Qu, B.Y., Suganthan, P.N., et al.: Problem definitions and evaluation criteria for the CEC 2015 competition on learning-based real-parameter single objective optimization. Technical report 201411A, Computational Intelligence Laboratory, Zhengzhou University, Zhengzhou China, Nanyang Technological University, Singapore (2014)
13. Liang, J.J., Qin, A.K., Suganthan, P.N., Baskar, S.: Comprehensive learning particle swarm optimizer for global optimization of multimodal functions. IEEE Trans. Evol. Comput. **10**(3), 281–295 (2006)

A Competitive Social Spider Optimization with Learning Strategy for PID Controller Optimization

Zhaolin Lai[1], Xiang Feng[1,2($\boxtimes$)], and Huiqun Yu[1]

[1] Department of Computer Science, The East University of Science and Technology, Shanghai, China
xfeng@ecust.edu.cn
[2] Smart City Collaborative Innovation Center, The Shanghai Jiao Tong University, Shanghai, China

Abstract. Tuning the parameters of PID controller is a difficult problem, since it is hard to get the optimum parameters by the traditional methods, new methods are required. Nature-inspired algorithms perform powerfully and efficiently on global optimization problems. Social spider optimization (SSO) is one of the novel nature-inspired algorithms, and it exhibits good performance on avoiding premature convergence. However, the efficiency of SSO degrades when used in applications such as PID controller optimization whose objective function with highly correlated variables. In order to overcome this disadvantage, based on the SSO, a competitive social spider optimization (CSSO) is proposed in this paper. To enhance the performance of SSO, we regroup the spiders and the diversity of population is increased. Inspired by the competitive mating behavior of spiders, the competitive mating mechanism is introduced, and a learning strategy is used for the new born spider. The CSSO is applied to optimize the parameters of PID controller, and the simulation results show that the performance of CSSO is promising in PID controller optimization.

Keywords: Competition · Social Spider Optimization (SSO) · Learning strategy · PID controller

1 Introduction

The proportional-integral-derivative (PID) controller is widely used in the industry due to its simple structure and good performance [1,2]. However, it is hard to tune properly the parameters of PID controller because of the parameters are highly correlated. Besides, many industrial control systems are burdened with some problems (e.g. nonlinearities, high order and time delays) [3]. Since the classical tuning methods such as Ziegler-Nichols approach and gain and phase margin, can not get the optimal parameters of PID controller [4], the nature-inspired optimization algorithms are employed.

© Springer International Publishing AG 2017
Y. Shi et al. (Eds.): SEAL 2017, LNCS 10593, pp. 1026–1038, 2017.
https://doi.org/10.1007/978-3-319-68759-9_85

Recently, nature-inspired algorithms have become popularly in solving the complex problems of real world, this is because of their intelligence and effectiveness [5]. For instance, particle swarm optimization (PSO) algorithm [6] which simulates the flocking behavior of birds, artificial bee colony (ABC) [7] algorithm was inspired by the cooperative behavior of bee colonies, social spider optimization algorithm (SSO) [8] was based on the cooperative behavior of social spiders, and lightning search algorithm (LSA) [9] was presented according to the natural phenomenon of lightning.

Even though some nature-inspired algorithms have been applied in the applications for optimizing parameters of PID controller, most of the applications still use the outdated nature-inspired algorithms. As the new nature-inspired algorithms have a better search ability than the outdated ones, it will be meaningful employ the new ones in the problem of optimum PID controller. Based on the SSO algorithm, combined with the competition behavior of spiders [10], a competitive social spider optimization (CSSO) is proposed in this paper, and it is applied to optimize the parameters of PID controller.

The main contribution of this paper is that a CSSO algorithm is proposed based on the SSO algorithm for applying to optimize the parameters of PID controller. The CSSO is constructed by four main changes: (1) We regroup the spiders according to the biological principle. Not only the gender (male and female), but also the age (adult and juvenile) are considered. (2) For the two juvenile sub-swarms, two new different search methods are used, and it shows the diversity of search behavior. (3) The competition mechanism is introduced in the mating behavior, and the offspring will have a greater chance to be better compared with their parents. (4) The learning strategy is adopted for the new born spider, and it helps the population to avoid falling into local optimum.

The rest of this paper is organized as follows. Section 2 presents the description of the problem of optimum PID controller. Section 3 introduces main idea of SSO. Section 4 presents the proposed CSSO. Section 5 presents the experimental results and analysis. Finally, Sect. 6 draws the conclusion.

2   The Problem of Optimum PID Controller

The proportional integral derivative (PID) controllers have been widely used in many industrial applications for many years. The reason is that compared with most other advanced controllers, the PID controller structure is more simple, meanwhile, its principle is more easy to understand. The structure diagram of PID controller is shown in Fig. 1, and it controls system according to following formula:

$$u(t) = K_p[e(t) + K_i \int_0^t e(t)dt + K_d \frac{de(t)}{dt})] \tag{1}$$

where, $u(t)$ is the output of system, $e(t)$ is the signal deviation of system, K_p, K_i and K_d are proportional gain, integral gain and derivative gain, respectively.

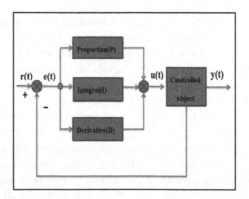

Fig. 1. The structure diagram of PID controller.

Generally, the index ITAE is used to evaluate the performance of the system during the process of control. The ITAE is computed as follows:

$$ITAE = \int_0^t t\,|e(t)|dt \tag{2}$$

Furthermore, overshoot is added to the objective function, then the index of optimal control system is obtained, which can be expressed as follows:

$$J = \int_0^t t\,|e(t)|dt + ct\,|e(t)|\,dt \tag{3}$$

Due to the performance of PID controller is determined by the parameters proportional gain (P), integral gain (I) and derivative gain (D), the problem of optimum PID controller, that is, search optimal combination for parameters P, I and D.

3   Social Spider Optimization Algorithm

The social spider optimization algorithm simulates the cooperative behaviors of spiders in the biological world. The colonies of spiders in the algorithm contain two categories: males and females, and the cooperative operators include: movement of spider, information transmitted by vibration in the communal web, mating among male and female spiders. The groups and the main operators of social spiders are shown in Fig. 2.

3.1   Movement of Spiders

The female spiders move either on the attraction or the repulsion direction for changing position. Such movement is a random behavior. In the algorithm, a random number $r_m(0 < r_m < 1)$ is generated, and a threshold PF is used to

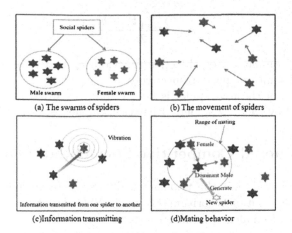

Fig. 2. The colonies of spiders and the cooperative operators.

decide which behavior should be selected. If r_m is greater than PF, then the repulsion movement is selected. Otherwise, attraction movement. The position changed of female spiders is computed as follows:

$$f_i^{t+1} = \begin{cases} f_i^t + \alpha \cdot Vc_i \cdot (s_c - f_i^t) + \beta \cdot Vb_i \cdot (s_b - f_i^t) + \delta \cdot (rd - \frac{1}{2}), if\ r_m < PF \\ f_i^t - \alpha \cdot Vc_i \cdot (s_c - f_i^t) - \beta \cdot Vb_i \cdot (s_b - f_i^t) + \delta \cdot (rd - \frac{1}{2}), otherwise \end{cases}$$
(4)

where, s_c is the individual closest to i and the weight of s_c is higher than i. s_b is the global best individual in the whole population. α, β, δ and rd are random number within the range [0, 1].

The movement of male spiders is according to their weight, the males' median weights w_{N_f+i} is considered as a threshold to choose which update operation. Therefore, the position changed of male spiders can be calculated as follows:

$$m_i^{t+1} = \begin{cases} m_i^t + \alpha \cdot Vf_i \cdot (s_f - m_i^t) + \delta \cdot (rd - \frac{1}{2}), if\ w_{N_f+i} > w_{N_f+m} \\ m_i^t - \alpha \cdot (\dfrac{\sum\limits_{k=1}^{N_m} m_k^t \cdot w_{N_f+h}}{\sum\limits_{k=1}^{N_m} w_{N_f+h}} - m_i^t), \qquad otherwise \end{cases}$$
(5)

where, s_f is the female spider closest to male spider i, and w_{N_f+i} is the weight of i th male spider.

3.2 Spiders Mating

The purpose of mating operator in the algorithm is to generate a new spider and replace the worst spider in the spider colony. Such operator is only performed among the dominant males and the female spiders within a range of mating r. The size of range of mating r is determined by the search space, and it can be calculated by following formula:

$$r = \frac{\sum_{i=1}^{n} b_i^h - b_i^l}{2 \cdot n} \qquad (6)$$

where, n is the dimension of objective function. b_i^h and b_i^l are the upper and lower bound of solution space, respectively.

If the weight of the new spider is better than the worst one, the worst one will be replaced by the new spider. Otherwise, the new spider will be discarded.

4   The Proposed Competitive Social Spider Optimization

It is widely accepted that the population diversity greatly contributes to the performance of evaluation algorithm [11]. In the SSO algorithm, it divides spiders into two swarms (females and males) in terms of gender. But in the biological world, there are adult and juvenile spiders in each gender, and they play different role according to the gender and the age. The behavior of mating only occurs between the adult male and the female spiders, and the spiders with the same gender compete to get the chance of mating. In view of this, we regroup the spiders, and then a serious of new mechanisms are introduced in order to improve the search performance of the proposed algorithm.

4.1   A New Regroup Mechanism for Spiders

In the social spider colony, it is obviously that there are only two colonies (females and males) according to the gender. Aviles [12] argues that spiders execute different tasks (e.g. web design, mating and predation) in terms of their gender. However, Keiser et al. [13] found that the task variation for spiders is associated with the body size, the age and the personality. Meanwhile, the juvenile collective behavior is effected by the adults [14]. Therefore, it is reasonable that we regroup the spiders. There are four sub-swarms altogether (see Fig. 3), and the behaviors of each sub-swarm are different.

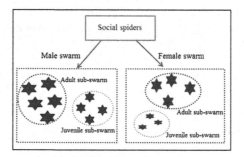

Fig. 3. The regrouping of spiders.

4.2 Movement for Juvenile Spiders

For the adult female sub-swarm and the adult male sub-swarm, the formulas of position changed are the same as the females and males in SSO. The position changed for adult female and male sub-swarm are according to formulas 11 and 12, respectively. As the highly influential individuals (keystone individuals) [15] have a large effect on the behavior of other individuals, the movement direction of juvenile male and female spiders depends on the best individual in the whole population and the best individual within the male and female swarm respectively.

As the best male or female individual need to transmits information to the juvenile male or female individual, and then there are two new kinds of vibrations. They are Vbf$_i$ and Vbm$_i$ which represent the information transmitted to individual i by the best female and the best male individual, respectively. These two types of vibration are calculated as follows:

$$\text{Vbf}_i = w_{bf} \cdot \exp(-d^2_{bf,i}) \tag{7}$$

$$\text{Vbm}_i = w_{bm} \cdot \exp(-d^2_{bm,i}) \tag{8}$$

where, w_{bf} is the weight of best female individual bf. $d_{bf,i}$ is the Euclidian distance between individual i and bf. w_{bm} is the weight of best male individual bm, and $d_{bm,i}$ is the Euclidian distance between individual i and bm.

During the process of search, a perturbation factor Pf^t is used to enhance the search ability for juvenile spiders, and the perturbation factor is calculated according to

$$Pf^t = e^{-(\varepsilon + \varepsilon \cdot \frac{t}{IterNum})} \tag{9}$$

where, $IterNum$ represents the total number of iterations. t is the t th iteration, and ε is a constant whose value equals to 3.

The position changed of juvenile female spiders is computed as follows:

$$u_i^{t+1} = u_i^t + \alpha \cdot Vb_i \cdot (s_g - u_i^t) + \beta \cdot Vb_i \cdot (s_{fb} - u_i^t) + Pf^t \tag{10}$$

where, s_g is the global best individual, and s_{fb} is the best individual within the female swarm.

The position changed of juvenile male spiders is computed as follows:

$$v_i^{t+1} = v_i^t + \alpha \cdot Vb_i \cdot (s_g - v_i^t) + \beta \cdot Vb_i \cdot (s_{mb} - v_i^t) + Pf^t \tag{11}$$

where, s_{mb} is the best individual within the male swarm.

4.3 Competitive Mating

According to the research of [14], in the spider colony, the behavior of intrasexual competition for mating opportunities, occurs not only between males, but also between females. During each iteration, adult spiders within the same gender are pairwise randomly selected for competitions. Specially, if the weights of the two spiders are the same, it will need to reselection. Therefore, the result of competition will generate a winner and a loser after each competition. The individual whose weight is better, will be the winner, and gets the chance of mating. The loser is the worse individual, and it will lose such chance in this competition. The mechanism of competitive mating is illustrated in Fig. 4.

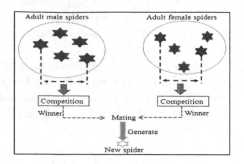

Fig. 4. The mechanism of competitive mating.

In each competition, the adult spiders within male or female swarm have the equal chance to be selected. Suppose that the number of adult male spiders is n_1, and the number of adult female spiders is n_2. We can get that the probability for any adult male to be selected is $\frac{1}{n_1}$, and the probability for female is $\frac{1}{n_2}$. The adult spider to win in one competition depends on its weight. For any adult spider i, whose weight is w_i, assume that its competitor is a, and the weight of a is w_a. If $\frac{w_i}{w_a} > 1$, then the probability for the adult spider i to be a winner is 1, otherwise, the probability is 0.

4.4   Learning Strategy for New Born Spider

After the mating, a new spider is generated, and its position is randomly initialized between the upper bound b_i^h and the lower bound b_i^l, and then we can calculate the position according to

$$new_i = b_i^l + rand(1, D) \cdot (b_i^h - b_i^l) \tag{12}$$

where, D is the dimension of objective function. $rand(1, D)$ generates a $1 \times D$ vector in which the value of each element is a random number within the range $[0, 1]$.

As the new spider borns from one male and one female spiders, it will learns from its father and mother spiders. In the real world, instead of all learning from the object, selected learning is an effective method makes the learner to be better. Therefore, in the learning strategy, the new spider learns one part from its parents. The main idea of learning strategy is shown in Fig. 5, which takes 10 dimensions as an example. In the figure, the selected learning vector V_1 whose

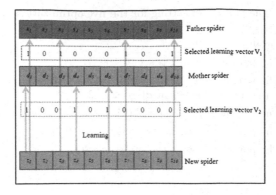

Fig. 5. The general idea of learning strategy which takes 10 dimensions as an example.

values of element are either 1 or 0, where 1 means the new spider learns from the corresponding element in father spider while 0 means not learns. Similar to V_1, the selected learning vector V_2 represents which part of mother spider should be learned for the new spider. In this paper, the two selected learning vectors V_1 and V_2 are randomly generated, and the length of the two vectors is equal to the dimension of objective function. If the value of element with the same index in V_1 and V_2 is 1, then the new spider will learn from the median value of parents in the corresponding index. Suppose that a vector V3 represents the result of logic AND operation by V_1 and V_2, then $V_3 = V_1 \wedge V_2$. Based on the learning strategy, the position of the new spider can be calculated after learning by the following formula.

$$
\begin{aligned}
new_i = new_i + (\neg V_3 \wedge V_1) \cdot (fa - new_i) \\
+ (\neg V_3 \wedge V_2) \cdot (mo - new_i) + V_3 \cdot \left(\tfrac{fa+mo}{2} - new_i\right)
\end{aligned}
\tag{13}
$$

where, fa is the father spider and mo is the mother spider. If the weight of the new spider is better than the worst spider in the whole population, the worst one will be replaced by the new spider. Otherwise, it indicates that the new spider is weak despite learning, and the new spider will be discarded.

5   Experiment and Analysis

In this section, the proposed CSSO is applied in optimization the parameters of PID controller. All the experiments were performed on the server with two quad-core CPU (2.4 GHz) and 24 G memory, and the platform is matlab R2009b in Red Hat Linux 7 operating system.

The performance of CSSO is compared with four other popular intelligence optimization algorithms, which are Artificial Bee Colony (ABC) algorithm, Particle Swarm Optimization (PSO), Social Spider Optimization (SSO), and Lightning Search Algorithm (LSA), respectively. In all comparisons, the maximum number of iteration is set to 500, and the population size is set to 100 for all

Table 1. The parameter setting for the five optimization algorithms

Algorithms	Parameter setting
ABC	The parameter *limit* is set to 100 [7]
PSO	The weight factor w is set to 0.9, and decreases linearly to 0.2; The learning coefficient $c1 = c2 = 2$ [6]
SSO	The threshold parameter PF is set to 0.7 [8]
LSA	The parameter *channeltime* is set to 10 [9]
CSSO	The parameter is set the same as SSO

the comparison algorithms. Besides, the parameter setting for each algorithm is listed in Table 1, and each algorithm is executed 40 independent runs.

As the nonparametric statistical technology has been widely used in computational intelligence recently [16], in this section, we use Friedman test to analyze the performance of each algorithm, and the value of rank was computed using software SPSS (the version is 17.0.0).

The process of optimization parameters P, I and D by the five algorithms is shown in Fig. 6. We can see from the figure that the curves of P and D are changed obviously except subfigure (b), in which the parameters are optimized by PSO. For the five algorithms, a phenomenon can be observed that the curve of P is similar to the curve of D, when P be changed, D also be changed. The direction of change (increase or decrease) for P and D are nearly the same. In addition, the curves of parameter I in all the subfigures are almost straight lines.

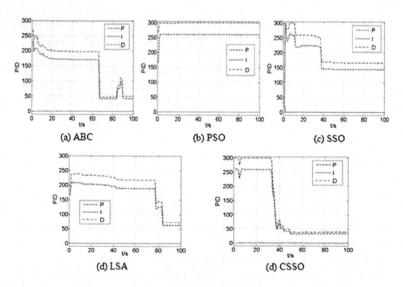

Fig. 6. Optimization parameters of PID controller by five different algorithms with 100 iterations.

Figure 7 shows the variation curves of evaluation index J for the five algorithms. It can be seen from the figure that the worst performance of algorithm is PSO, which can not search a better solution after 20 iterations. The CSSO performs the best performance among the five algorithms. The solution obtained by CSSO after 40 iterations is much better than previous, meanwhile, it is better than the solutions which searched by other four algorithms. For the SSO, it is better than ABC and PSO, but worse than LSA and CSSO according to the variation curves.

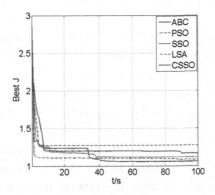

Fig. 7. The curve of performance index J for the optimization process with 100 iterations.

Table 2 summarizes the results on PID controller optimization for the five algorithms with 100, 200 and 500 iterations, respectively. The parameters P, I and D, the evaluation index J and the time consuming $Time(s)$ obtained by the five algorithms are listed in the table, where the best J are shown in bold. It can be seen from the table that the value of J obtained by CSSO, is the best among the five algorithms when iteration $= 100$, after the number of iteration is increased to 200, only the value of J obtained by SSO is changed, but the value still not better than 1.0580e+00 which is the result of CSSO at 100 and 200 iterations. With the number of iteration increasing to 500, the other four algorithms can search better solutions except for the PSO, and the best J is 1.0415e+00 obtained by CSSO. In terms of time consuming, the PSO spends the least time and the SSO spends the most time among the five algorithms. Figure 8 shows the ranks of optimization performance for the five algorithms by Friedman test, and the results are calculated according to the value of J in Table 2. As can be seen from the figure, the order of the optimization performance for the five algorithms is: CSSO, LSA, SSO, ABC, PSO.

1036   Z. Lai et al.

Table 2. The results on PID controller optimization

Algorithms	CSSO	ABC	PSO	SSO	LSA
Iteration = 100					
P	3.3540e+01	4.2645e+01	2.6006e+02	1.4338e+02	6.2532e+01
I	1.6623e−01	1.6486e−01	0	1.6401e−01	1.6272e−01
D	3.8687e+01	4.9554e+01	3.0000e+02	1.6540e+02	7.2803e+01
J	**1.0580e+00**	1.1651e+00	1.2744e+00	1.1155e+00	1.0827e+00
Time(s)	1.5729e+02	1.4319e+02	1.1307e+02	1.8436e+02	1.3294e+02
Iteration = 200					
P	3.3540e+01	4.2645e+01	2.6006e+02	1.4338e+02	6.2532e+01
I	1.6623e−01	1.6486e−01	0	1.6402e−01	1.6272e−01
D	3.8687e+01	4.9554e+01	3.0000e+02	1.6540e+02	7.2803e+01
J	**1.0580e+00**	1.1651e+00	1.2744e+00	1.0954e+00	1.0827e+00
Time(s)	3.8902e+02	3.5778e+02	2.5284e+02	4.5962e+02	2.9518e+02
Iteration = 500					
P	3.2841e+01	4.2052e+01	2.6006e+02	1.3517e+02	4.9955e+01
I	1.6702e−01	1.6486e−01	0	1.6402e−01	1.6354e−01
D	3.6214e+01	4.7205e+01	3.0000e+02	1.2352e+02	5.8233e+01
J	**1.0415e+00**	1.0947e+00	1.2744e+00	1.0826e+00	1.0651e+00
Time(s)	9.6318e+02	8.9471e+02	6.8329e+02	1.1047e+03	8.0615e+02

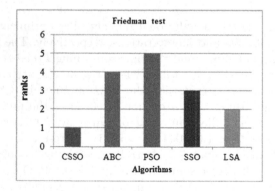

Fig. 8. The ranks of optimization performance for the five algorithms.

6   Conclusion

This paper presents a CSSO algorithm based on SSO for optimizing the parameters of PID controller. To enhance the performance of the SSO, the proposed method increases the diversity of population by regrouping the spiders according to the biological principle. In addition, because the spiders compete to mate in the nature, and then such mechanism is introduced for generate better off-spring. After a new spider is generated, a learning strategy is used to update the position of the new spider, and the population will have a greatly chance to avoid falling into local optimum. Through the simulation experiment, the results show that the performance of the proposed CSSO is promising in optimizing the parameters of PID controller.

Our future research will focus on two aspects. First, the convergence property of the CSSO will be analyzed theoretically. Second, the parallelism of CSSO will be implemented to speed up the computation.

Acknowledgement. This work was supported in part by the National Natural Science Foundation of China under Grant Nos. 61472139 and 61462073, the Information Development Special Funds of Shanghai Economic and Information Commission under Grant No. 201602008, the Open Funds of Shanghai Smart City Collaborative Innovation Center.

References

1. Yongzhong, L., Yan, D., Zhang, J., Levy, D.: A variant with a time varying pid controller of particle swarm optimizers. Inf. Sci. **297**, 21–49 (2015)
2. Wei, C., Söffker, D.: Optimization strategy for PID-controller design of AMB rotor systems. IEEE Trans. Control Syst. Technol. **24**(3), 788–803 (2016)
3. Visioli, A.: Tuning of PID controllers with fuzzy logic. IEE Proc. Control Theory Appl. **148**(1), 1–8 (2001)
4. Gaing, Z.L.: A particle swarm optimization approach for optimum design of PID controller in AVR system. IEEE Trans. Energy Convers. **19**(2), 384–391 (2004)
5. Feng, X., Zou, R., Yu, H.: A novel optimization algorithm inspired by the creative thinking process. Soft. Comput. **19**(10), 2955–2972 (2015)
6. Kennedy, J., Eberhart, R.: Particle swarm optimization. In: Proceedings of IEEE International Conference on Neural Networks, vol. 4, pp. 1942–1948 (2002)
7. Karaboga, D.: An idea based on honey bee swarm for numerical optimization. Technical report, Technical report-TR06, Erciyes University, Engineering Faculty, Computer Engineering Department (2005)
8. Cuevas, E., Cienfuegos, M., Zaldvar, D., Rez-Cisneros, M.: A swarm optimization algorithm inspired in the behavior of the social-spider. Expert Syst. Appl. Int. J. **40**(16), 6374–6384 (2016)
9. Shareef, H., Ibrahim, A.A., Mutlag, A.H.: Lightning search algorithm. Appl. Soft Comput. **36**, 315–333 (2015)
10. Clutton-Brock, T.: Sexual selection in males and females. Science **318**(5858), 1882–1885 (2007)
11. Črepinšek, M., Liu, S.H., Mernik, M.: Exploration and exploitation in evolutionary algorithms: a survey. ACM Comput. Surv. (CSUR) **45**(3), 35 (2013)
12. Aviles, L.: Sex-ratio bias and possible group selection in the social spider anelosimus eximius. Am. Nat. **128**(1), 1–12 (1986)
13. Keiser, C.N., Jones, D.K., Modlmeier, A.P., Pruitt, J.N.: Exploring the effects of individual traits and within-colony variation on task differentiation and collective behavior in a desert social spider. Behav. Ecol. Sociobiol. **68**(5), 839–850 (2014)

14. Modlmeier, A.P., Laskowski, K.L., Brittingham, H.A., Coleman, A., Knutson, K.A., Kuo, C., McGuirk, M., Zhao, K., Keiser, C.N., Pruitt, J.N.: Adult presence augments juvenile collective foraging in social spiders. Anim. Behav. **109**, 9–14 (2015)
15. Modlmeier, A.P., Keiser, C.N., Watters, J.V., Sih, A., Pruitt, J.N.: The keystone individual concept: an ecological and evolutionary overview. Anim. Behav. **89**, 53–62 (2014)
16. Derrac, J., García, S., Molina, D., Herrera, F.: A practical tutorial on the use of nonparametric statistical tests as a methodology for comparing evolutionary and swarm intelligence algorithms. Swarm Evol. Comput. **1**(1), 3–18 (2011)

Author Index

Adegboye, Adesola 727
Ahn, Chang Wook 373
AL-Dabbagh, Rawaa Dawoud 739
Al-Sahaf, Harith 499
Andreae, Peter 591

Bai, Xiaoyu 899
Baioletti, Marco 960
Bao, Lin 158
Boonlong, Kittipong 1003
Browne, Will N. 448
Bu, Chenyang 981

Cai, Fulin 939, 949
Cai, Shaowei 145
Cai, Xinye 39, 134, 694
Cao, Leilei 644
Cao, YingYing 27
Chan, Lipton 486
Chen, Aaron 170
Chen, Chen 949
Chen, Gang 473, 870
Chen, Genhua 929
Chen, Jiansheng 939, 949
Chen, Jianyong 236
Chen, Junfeng 347
Chen, Ke-Jia 3
Chen, Qi 422
Chen, Qunjian 462
Chen, Wei 27
Chen, Yi 97
Cheng, Ran 224
Cheng, Shi 27, 347
Cheung, Yiu-ming 260, 821
Chu, Xianghua 939, 949

Deng, Jingda 122
Derbel, Bilel 62
Diao, Yiya 631
Dissen, Håkon 297
Doi, Ken 321
Dong, Lihua 97
Du, Bingqi 272

Duan, Peiyong 671
Duan, Qiqi 994

Fan, Zheng-Jie 716
Fan, Zhun 39, 134, 694
Fang, Wei 833
Fang, Yi 134
Feng, Jiqiang 347
Feng, Liang 774
Feng, Xiang 1026
Feng, Xiangsheng 929
Foo, Yong Wee 486
Fu, Shen 248
Fu, Wenlong 556

Gao, Kaizhou 75, 671
Gao, Xiaoying 556
Ghandar, Adam 751
Goh, Cindy 486
Gong, Maoguo 797
Goodman, Erik D. 644
Gu, Fangqing 211, 260, 821

Han, Huang 515
Han, Yuhong 911
Hao, Zhi feng 656
Hartmann, Sven 170
Hatanaka, Toshiharu 972
He, Peng 97
He, Yaodong 397
Hongyue, Wu 515
Hou, Wenying 145
Huang, Han 248, 656
Huang, Zhixing 774

Imada, Ryo 321
Ishibuchi, Hisao 321
Iwasaki, Satoru 972

Jabur, Ahmed Jasim 739
Jiang, Chunhui 858
Jiao, Licheng 272, 899
Johnson, Colin 727

Kampouridis, Michael   727
Kenny, Angus   361
Kuang, Li   883

Lai, Zhaolin   1026
Lei, Xiujuan   347
Lensen, Andrew   543
Li, Baolei   920
Li, Bin   196, 617
Li, Changhe   631
Li, Gang   656
Li, Guang   911
Li, Guiying   858
Li, Hui   122, 644
Li, Junqing   671
Li, Li   939
Li, Lin   486
Li, Mengmeng   581
Li, Ming   684
Li, Miqing   224
Li, Rui   1016
Li, Wenji   134
Li, Xiaodong   75, 361, 994
Li, Xueqiang   248
Li, Yangyang   899
Li, Ying   774
Li, Yuanjie   145
Li, Yuanxiang   883
Li, Yun   27, 486
Li, Zhanjun   684
Liang, Jing   911, 920
Liang, Xiaoxu   899
Liefooghe, Arnaud   62
Lin, Jian   75
Lin, Qiuzhen   236
Lin, Xin   981
Liu, Bin   3
Liu, Hai-Lin   211, 260, 821
Liu, Jing   15, 385, 845
Liu, Lei   196
Liu, Lian   158
Liu, Qunfeng   27
Liu, Weiming   196
Liu, Yanan   75
Liu, Yi   448
Liu, Yunan   929
Liu, Ziquan   821
Lou, Yang   51, 397
Luo, Dike   75
Luo, Wenjian   981

Ma, Ailong   528, 786
Ma, Hui   170
Ma, Xiaoliang   462, 810
Ma, Yebin   631
Mei, Yi   435, 473
Milani, Alfredo   960
Mısır, Mustafa   39, 184, 694
Mo, Jiajie   134

Nekooei, Seyed Mohammad   870
Neshatian, Kourosh   605
Neumann, Frank   110
Nguyen, Hoai Bach   591
Nguyen, Su   435
Nie, Xin   158
Niu, Ben   949
Nojima, Yusuke   321

Ohnishi, Kei   373

Pang, Chengshan   196
Peng, Dezhong   224
Peng, Ye   334
Peng, Yiming   473
Picek, Stjepan   569
Polyakovskiy, Sergey   110

Qian, Chao   858
Qin, Xiaolei   797
Qin, Yuanlong   87
Qu, Boyang   911, 920

Rayudu, Ramesh   870
Ripon, Kazi Shah Nawaz   297

Sabar, Nasser R.   409, 706
Santucci, Valentino   960
Sato, Takanori   309
Sattar, Abdul   409, 706
Shang, Ronghua   272
Shang, Zhigang   581
Shao, Chang   994
Shao, Yan   684
Shi, Jialong   62
Shi, Yuhui   27, 347, 994
Shuling, Yang   515
Singh, Hemant Kumar   284
Solaas, Jostein   297
Song, Andy   409, 706

Song, Hui   911
Song, Mi   786
Su, Rong   671
Suksonghong, Karoon   1003
Sulaman, Muhammad   39, 694
Sun, Wenxue   694
Sun, Xiaoyan   158
Sun, Yifei   27
Sun, Yiwen   462, 810

Tong, Xin   617
Tran, Binh   569
Turky, Ayad   409, 706

Uchitane, Takeshi   972

Verel, Sébastien   62

Wagner, Markus   110
Wan, Yuting   528
Wang, Chen   170
Wang, Feng   883
Wang, Junchen   631
Wang, Kun   763
Wang, Mang   617
Wang, Shanfeng   797
Watanabe, Shinya   309
Wei, Hang   656
Wu, Junhua   110
Wu, Kai   15, 385
Wu, Yue   797

Xia, Chao   694
Xiao, Heng   972
Xiaobin, Wu   334
Xie, Zexiao   763
Xin, Du   334
Xu, Guangzhi   1016

Xu, Lihong   644
Xue, Bing   422, 448, 499, 543, 556, 569, 591

Yamada, Shinichi   605
Yang, Bin   981
Yang, Yanming   810
Yao, Xin   224, 284, 334
You, Yugen   134
Youcong, Ni   334
Yu, Huiqun   1026
Yu, Xiang   929
Yuan, Bo   87
Yuan, Yijing   272
Yue, Caitong   581, 911, 920
Yuen, Shiu Yin   51, 397
Yushan, Zhang   515

Zhang, Heng   883
Zhang, Liangpei   528, 786
Zhang, Ling   763
Zhang, Mengjie   422, 435, 473, 499, 543, 556
Zhang, Pengju   763
Zhang, Qingfu   62, 122
Zhang, Yazhen   833
Zhao, Xinchao   1016
Zhao, Yong   97
Zhen, Liangli   224
Zheng, Yu-Jun   716
Zhong, Jinghui   774
Zhong, Yanfei   528, 786
Zhou, Aimin   97
Zhou, Liqin   763
Zhou, Rongfang   97
Zhou, Xingang   631
Zhu, Lixia   158
Zhu, Qingling   236
Zhu, Zexuan   462, 810
Zou, Xumiao   845
Zuo, Xingquan   1016

Printed in the United States
By Bookmasters